Property

of

CHARLES B. HOEVEN
Alton, Iowa

PUBLIC PAPERS OF THE PRESIDENTS

OF THE UNITED STATES

PUBLIC PAPERS OF THE PRESIDENTS

OF THE UNITED STATES

Harry S. Truman

*Containing the Public Messages, Speeches, and
Statements of the President*

JANUARY 1 TO DECEMBER 31, 1951

1951

UNITED STATES GOVERNMENT PRINTING OFFICE

WASHINGTON : 1965

PUBLISHED BY THE
OFFICE OF THE FEDERAL REGISTER
NATIONAL ARCHIVES AND RECORDS SERVICE
GENERAL SERVICES ADMINISTRATION

FOREWORD

THE IMPORTANCE OF this series lies in the extraordinary character of the office of President of the United States.

A President's written and spoken words can command national and international attention if he has within him the power to attract and hold that attention. It is partly through the use of this power that leadership arises, events are molded, and administrations take their shape.

It is this power, quite as much as powers written into the Constitution, that gives to the papers of Presidents their peculiar and revealing importance.

Harry Truman

PREFACE

IN THIS VOLUME are gathered most of the public messages and statements of the 33d President of the United States that were released by the White House during 1951. Similar volumes are available covering 1945–1950, the administrations of Presidents Eisenhower and Kennedy, and the first year of President Johnson. Volumes covering the period January 1, 1952–January 20, 1953, and the year 1965 are under preparation.

This series was begun in 1957 in response to a recommendation of the National Historical Publications Commission. An extensive compilation of the messages and papers of the Presidents, covering the period 1789 to 1897, was assembled by James D. Richardson and published under congressional authority between 1896 and 1899. Since that time various private compilations were issued, but there was no uniform, systematic publication comparable to the *Congressional Record* or the *United States Supreme Court Reports*. Many Presidential papers could be found only in mimeographed White House releases or as reported in the press. The National Historical Publications Commission therefore recommended the establishment of an official series in which Presidential writings and utterances of a public nature could be made promptly available.

The Commission's recommendation was incorporated in regulations of the Administrative Committee of the Federal Register issued under section 6 of the Federal Register Act (44 U.S.C. 306). The Committee's regulations, establishing the series and providing for the coverage of prior years, are reprinted at page 678 as "Appendix D."

Preface

The text of this book is based on Presidential materials issued during 1951 as White House releases and on transcripts of news conferences. A list of White House releases from which final selections were made is published at page 657 as "Appendix A."

The full text of President Truman's news conferences is here published for the first time, since direct quotation of the President's replies usually was not authorized. Addresses and speeches have been printed as actually delivered.

Proclamations, Executive orders, and similar documents required by law to be published in the *Federal Register* and *Code of Federal Regulations* are not repeated. Instead, they are listed by number and subject under the heading "Appendix B" at page 669.

The President is required by statute to transmit numerous reports to Congress. Those transmitted during the period covered by this volume are listed at page 677 as "Appendix C."

The items published in this volume are presented in chronological order, rather than being grouped in classes. Most needs for a classified arrangement are met by the subject index. For example, a reader interested in veto messages will find them listed in the index under the heading "veto messages."

The dates shown at the end of item headings are White House release dates. In instances where the date of the document differs from the release date that fact is shown in brackets immediately following the heading. Other editorial devices, such as text notes, footnotes, and cross references, have been supplied where needed for purposes of clarity.

Remarks or addresses were delivered in Washington, D.C., unless otherwise indicated. Similarly, statements, messages, and letters were issued from the White House in Washington unless otherwise indicated.

Original source materials, where available, have been used to protect against substantive errors in transcription. In maintaining the integrity of the text, valuable assistance was furnished by Dr. Philip C. Brooks, Philip D. Lagerquist, and Jerry N. Hess of the Truman Library.

The planning and publication of this series is under the direction of David C. Eberhart of the Office of the Federal Register. The editor of the present volume was Warren R. Reid, assisted by Mildred B. Berry. Frank H. Mortimer of the Government Printing Office developed the typography and design.

WAYNE C. GROVER
Archivist of the United States

LAWSON B. KNOTT, JR.
Administrator of General Services
November 1965

CONTENTS

CONTENTS

LIST OF ITEMS

List of Items

List of Items

List of Items

List of Items

List of Items

List of Items

List of Items

List of Items

List of Items

List of Items

List of Items

List of Items

List of Items

List of Items

List of Items

List of Items

List of Items

List of Items

List of Items

List of Items

Harry S. Truman

1951

1 Statement by the President Upon Signing the Excess Profits Tax Act of 1950. *January 3, 1951*

THE Excess Profits Tax Act of 1950, which I have signed today, is the second step the Congress has taken since the start of aggression in Korea to help meet the rapidly rising costs of national defense. The Congress and its committees have acted with commendable speed in completing this complex piece of legislation and thereby have provided evidence for all to see that we are determined to finance the defense program without jeopardy to the stability of our economic system or the soundness of the Government's finances.

The 1950 tax legislation has increased Federal revenues very substantially. However, the task ahead of us will require more and much heavier taxes. I shall, in due course, submit to the Congress recommendations for substantial tax increases.

We shall have to canvass and recanvass every revenue possibility, including the new excess profits tax. In developing this tax in the few weeks at its disposal, the Congress may have been overly liberal in its concern over some corporations in special circumstances. Some of the provisions of this bill will probably give an undue advantage to some corporations, especially in relation to the tax burdens necessarily borne by others. Excessive exemptions and relief provisions create inequities and reduce the Government's revenues needlessly. For this reason, I am requesting the Secretary of the Treasury to keep excess profits tax under continuous review so that if it develops that some of its provisions need revision, the facts can be placed before the congressional committees without delay.

NOTE: The Excess Profits Tax Act of 1950 is Public Law 909, 81st Congress (64 Stat. 1137).

2 The President's News Conference of *January 4, 1951*

THE PRESIDENT. Please be seated.

I have no special announcements to make this morning. I will try to answer questions, however.

[1.] Q. Mr. President, do you have any comment on the change in the Rules Committee of the House?

THE PRESIDENT. No. The House makes its own rules, and we will try and operate with the rules, as usual, hoping to get the program through in the usual manner.

[2.] Q. Mr. President, Senator Taft, in that connection, said yesterday that in delaying your State of the Union Message 1 week you hold up the work of the Congress 2 weeks?

THE PRESIDENT. I don't see how that message could have been delayed 1 week when Congress only started yesterday. If you look up the record, you will find that the message on the state of the Union is being delivered as promptly as it ever is in any year. It takes the Congress, anyhow, another 2 weeks to organize.

[3.] Q. Mr. President, do you have any comment on the military situation as it is now developing in Korea?

THE PRESIDENT. No. I have no comment. [*Pause*]

What's the matter with these press conferences? The last time I had it, I urged you to get up——

Q. We're making notes, Mr. President.

Q. We're writing it down——

[4.] Q. Mr. President, this is a question I asked you a few weeks ago, and I will ask it again. At what point do you have to consult Congress on its constitutional right to declare war?

THE PRESIDENT. I will take care of that, May,[1] when the time comes. It isn't here yet.

Q. You know that a resolution by Mr. Coudert of New York [2]——

THE PRESIDENT. I read something about it in the paper. I have not received any official notice of it.

Q. Mr. President, I didn't get your answer to her first question, I was getting her question——

THE PRESIDENT. I said the proper action would be taken on that when the time came, but the time is not here yet. I hope it will never come.

[5.] Q. Mr. President, General Eisenhower is shortly to leave for Europe on a rather important assignment, perhaps the most important assignment this country has to offer anyone at this time.[3] Can you comment on that today?

THE PRESIDENT. The General is coming to see me, and after we have had a conference, I will comment on it.

Q. When do you plan to see him, sir?

THE PRESIDENT. I think the date is Saturday morning. I'm not sure. I think that's it.

[6.] Q. Mr. President, I am rather puzzled by Mrs. Craig's question. Has there

been some change in the procedure——

THE PRESIDENT. Not at all. There has been no change whatever. That was just a confusing question, Bob,[4] that's all it was.

Q. It confused me a little.

THE PRESIDENT. The answer was not confused.

Q. No, sir.

Q. Sir, do you consider that my question was confusing?

THE PRESIDENT. Yes. Intended for that purpose, May, I think.

Q. No, sir, it is being discussed at the Capitol a good deal, that we are at war and that Congress has not declared war.

THE PRESIDENT. I have no comment to make on that, May.

Q. Yes, sir.

Q. Well, Mr. President, the Nation is not formally at war, isn't that so?

THE PRESIDENT. No—that is correct. We are carrying out an obligation for the United Nations.

Q. I beg your pardon, sir?

THE PRESIDENT. Carrying out an obligation for the United Nations, one which was assumed when we signed the charter.

[7.] Q. Mr. President, are we going to ask the United Nations for permission to bomb China?

THE PRESIDENT. I have that—do *not* have that under consideration.

Q. Do *not*—all right, sir.

THE PRESIDENT. That might require the action that May is talking about.

[8.] Q. Mr. President, since this is 1951, how do you view the prospects of this Nation staying out of war in 1951?

THE PRESIDENT. I can't comment on that now. I sincerely hope, of course, personally, that we will not get into war. That has been my fight for 5 years. But I can't now comment on your question very well.

---

[1] Mrs. May Craig of the Portland (Maine) Press Herald.

[2] On January 3, 1951, Representative Frederic R. Coudert, Jr., of New York, introduced a joint resolution (H.J. Res. 9) requiring congressional authorization for sending military forces abroad. The resolution was referred to the Committee on Armed Services.

[3] On December 19, 1950, the President had designated General of the Army Dwight D. Eisenhower as Supreme Allied Commander, Europe (see 1950 volume, this series, Items 308 and 310).

[4] Robert G. Nixon of International News Service.

[9.] Q. Mr. President, now that we have an ambassador in Spain, is there any contemplation of including Spain in the NATO program and the international army?

THE PRESIDENT. It has not been under consideration.

Q. Has not been?

THE PRESIDENT. It has not been under consideration. At least, not by me.

[10.] Q. Mr. President, may I clear up a point?

THE PRESIDENT. Sure.

Q. You said you were—that the Government did not have under consideration asking the United Nations for permission to bomb China. Is that correct, sir?

THE PRESIDENT. That's correct—that's correct.

Q. Well, Mr. President, is it correct to assume that we would not bomb China without checking it with the United Nations?

THE PRESIDENT. That is correct.

[11.] Q. Mr. President, can we further infer that you still have hopes of diplomatic negotiations that will——

THE PRESIDENT. We are always hopeful for negotiations to settle the difficulty.

[12.] Q. Mr. President, do you intend to renominate the RFC Board?

THE PRESIDENT. I have it under consideration.

[13.] Q. Mr. President, you said that you were hopeful of negotiations. Does that mean that you are in favor of a 4-power conference?

THE PRESIDENT. That matter was answered yesterday by the Secretary of State just as it is—if you will read that—that statement of his was approved by me.[5]

[14.] Q. Mr. President, nobody has asked you a question about price controls

yet this morning. Is anything—any action in view by the Government in the near future on controls?

THE PRESIDENT. We are working on that all the time, and just as fast as we can get around to it. It is a tremendous job to set up a price control organization, and they are working on it constantly, and I think it will go into effect as fast as it is physically possible to get it done.

Q. Will that include the so-called essentials of living?

THE PRESIDENT. That would require an amendment to the law.

Q. Would you elaborate on that just a little bit, sir? I didn't understand what would require an amendment to the law.

THE PRESIDENT. Control of the price of farm products.

Q. Mr. President, does this program that you speak of, then, mean that we would put everything under price control and wage control if the law permits?

THE PRESIDENT. That is correct. As soon as it is possible to get it done.

Q. Just to bottle it up correctly, Mr. President, they are working now on a plan to put price control and wage controls wherever it can be done within the law? You would have to have a change in the law to deal with foods?

THE PRESIDENT. That's correct.

Q. Would you recommend, Mr. President, that the Congress make such a change in the law?

THE PRESIDENT. I will let you know about that in the State of the Union Message.[6]

Q. Mr. President, you are referring to the farm parity problem?

THE PRESIDENT. Yes.

[15.] Q. Mr. President, would you clear up—I wasn't clear——

THE PRESIDENT. I beg your pardon?

---

[5] For the statement by Secretary of State Dean Acheson at his press conference on January 3, 1951, concerning the proposed foreign ministers meeting, see the Department of State Bulletin (vol. 24, p. 90).

[6] Item 4, this volume.

Q. ——I wasn't clear on what you hoped to be settled by diplomatic negotiations. Is that the situation in Korea?

THE PRESIDENT. All the troubles in the world.

Q. I beg your pardon, sir?

THE PRESIDENT. All the troubles in the world. That is what the United Nations was set up for.

[16.] Q. Mr. President, I am afraid some of us didn't quite get clear your reply on price controls and wage controls?

THE PRESIDENT. I said that the price and wage controls would be put into effect as soon as it is physically possible to get it done where they are necessary.

Q. "Should" be or "will" be?

THE PRESIDENT. Will be——

Q. Thank you.

THE PRESIDENT. ——that's the word—*will*.

[17.] Q. Mr. President, on Mr. Collingwood's[7] question on the Big Four—[*inaudible*]—that is apart from the United Nations?

THE PRESIDENT. The Big Four now works under the direction of the United Nations because the United Nations Charter takes the place of all those things, and the United Nations is the forum in which we have to make world peace if it can be made. It is all right for the Big Four to negotiate on things that specifically affect the Big Four, and that is what that program is for.

Q. That wouldn't—the Big Four takes care of all those things in the United Nations?

THE PRESIDENT. That's correct. I think negotiation is the proper way to settle all these things. That is the reason we set up the United Nations.

Q. Mr. President, I don't want to labor the point——

THE PRESIDENT. All right.

Q. ——but the—I think we have addressed ourselves in a note to Russia that we want to explore all the problems—that are causing tension—in the Big Four?[8]

THE PRESIDENT. That's right, causing tension between the United States and Russia, if you want to be specific about it——

Q. Yes, sir.

THE PRESIDENT. ——that's correct—that's correct.

Q. Now we will take that up with the Big Four. Now I wonder what the differentiation is—in your mind—between that and the United Nations—I mean, is there some—[*inaudible*]

THE PRESIDENT. No, it is not. That is under the—when we settle those differences, the United Nations will be in complete operation.

Q. I see, sir.

[18.] Q. Mr. President, do you believe that you need the approval of Congress to send additional troops to Europe? That seems to be——

THE PRESIDENT. No, I do not.

[19.] Q. Mr. President, a lot of us—a lot of people are concerned about delays. They are wondering why it takes this long, since the bill was passed last September,[9] to set up these price control and wage controls; and they are wondering why the military appropriations bill to Congress was delayed last November; and they are wondering why the message is delayed. Can you tell the American people why?

THE PRESIDENT. Yes, I will tell them why. Not here. You can answer that question yourself, if you will think just a little bit about it.

----

[7] Charles Collingwood of the Columbia Broadcasting System.

[8] For the text of the U.S. note of December 22, 1950, see Department of State Bulletin (vol. 24, p. 11).

[9] The Defense Production Act of 1950, approved September 8, 1950 (64 Stat. 798).

[20.] Q. Mr. President, when the phrase "Big Four" is used, that refers to the level of the foreign ministers, or——

THE PRESIDENT. That's correct. That refers to the foreign ministers of Russia, France, Great Britain, and the United States.

Q. Not to the heads of states?

THE PRESIDENT. Not to the heads of state.

[21.] Q. Mr. President, I am afraid I am still a little confused about this price and wage control. I understood you to say at one point that you are taking steps to put everything under price and wage control just as soon as it can be done. Then I understood you to say later that price and wage controls would be put into effect as soon as possible where they are necessary?

THE PRESIDENT. That is correct. I think eventually it is going to be necessary for a complete across-the-board proposition, but that will require some legislation, as I told you a while ago.

Q. That is rationing——

THE PRESIDENT. How's that?

Q. ——rationing, or you mean price and wage control?

THE PRESIDENT. Well, we will cross that bridge when we get to it.

[22.] Q. Mr. President, this is a local question.

THE PRESIDENT. Fine.

Q. Have you received a letter from the Maine congressional delegation suggesting that surplus potatoes should be turned into industrial alcohol rather than destroyed?

THE PRESIDENT. No, I haven't received any such letter.

Q. I think it has been sent to you. Would you comment on that, sir?

THE PRESIDENT. No comment.

[23.] Q. Mr. President, last night at a dinner, Senator Taft said that he liked to talk to women reporters because he could tell them that he would like to kick President Truman's teeth in. Is there any place, Mr. President, where you would like to kick him? [*Laughter*]

THE PRESIDENT. Oh, no! No comment on that. [*More laughter*]

[24.] Q. Mr. President, how do you feel about the leadership which the Senate selected—Senator McFarland of Arizona——

THE PRESIDENT. I am very fond of Senator McFarland. I wrote him a letter of congratulations yesterday.

Q. ——and Senator Johnson?

THE PRESIDENT. And Senator Johnson of Texas in the same category. They are both friends of mine and always have been.

[25.] Q. Mr. President, do you think satisfactory progress is being made in the control of inflation?

THE PRESIDENT. I think we are making the best progress that it is possible to make. I don't know whether it is satisfactory or not, that depends entirely on the viewpoint.

[26.] Q. May I ask a frivolous question?

THE PRESIDENT. Sure. [*Laughter*]

Q. Do you have any comment on the London tailors who seem to be quite horrified about your manner of dress?

THE PRESIDENT. I don't think it's any of their business! [*Laughter*]

Q. Couldn't hear the question, Mr. President.

THE PRESIDENT. He wanted to know if I had any comment on the London—horrification of the London tailors over the way I dress, and I said it is none of their business.

Q. It's the neckties—it was the neckties.

THE PRESIDENT. What's the matter with the neckties?

Q. They didn't say—but they said they were awful.

THE PRESIDENT. Oh, did they? There are a lot of awful ones in the United States then.

[27.] Q. Mr. President, to go back once more to the price control——

THE PRESIDENT. All right, Smitty,[10] go ahead.

Q. ——you said controls eventually would be necessary for complete across-the-board wage and price control and it would require additional legislation. You envision food in

---

[10] Merriman Smith of the United Press Associations.

that eventuality?

THE PRESIDENT. Yes, of course. That is one of the fundamental causes of the rise in the cost of living.

Reporter: Thank you, Mr. President.

NOTE: President Truman's two hundred and forty-ninth news conference was held in the Indian Treaty Room (Room 474) in the Executive Office Building at 10:30 a.m. on Thursday, January 4, 1951.

3 Statement by the President on the Establishment of the United Defense Fund. *January 5, 1951*

THE FORMATION of the United Defense Fund is highly gratifying to me and, I am sure, to everyone concerned with the national defense effort.

It is good to know that, through this fund, many of our voluntary health and welfare agencies and the Nation's Community Chests have joined forces to raise, through the Chests and other united community efforts, the money that will provide special services to our Armed Forces personnel and to communities in areas affected by the defense effort.

The United Defense Fund is heartening evidence that, while we as a nation are mobilizing our resources of men, money, and goods to defend democracy, we are not neglecting to fortify the inner defenses of the human heart and spirit.

I salute this united effort for its fine example of teamwork. This attitude reflects the attitude of the whole Nation which now, as perhaps never before, must have unity of purpose, of will, and of deed.

4 Annual Message to the Congress on the State of the Union. *January 8, 1951*

[As delivered in person before a joint session]

Mr. President, Mr. Speaker, Members of the Congress:

This 82d Congress faces as grave a task as any Congress in the history of our Republic. The actions you take will be watched by the whole world. These actions will measure the ability of a free people, acting through their chosen representatives and their free institutions, to meet a deadly challenge to their way of life.

We can meet this challenge foolishly or wisely. We can meet it timidly or bravely, shamefully or honorably.

I know that the 82d Congress will meet

this challenge in a way worthy of our great heritage. I know that your debates will be earnest, responsible, constructive, and to the point. I know that from these debates there will come the great decisions needed to carry us forward.

At this critical time, I am glad to say that our country is in a healthy condition. Our democratic institutions are sound and strong. We have more men and women at work than ever before. We are able to produce more than ever before—in fact, far more than any country ever produced in the history of the world.

6

I am confident that we can succeed in the great task that lies before us.

We will succeed, but we must all do our part. We must all act together as citizens of this great Republic.

As we meet here today, American soldiers are fighting a bitter campaign in Korea. We pay tribute to their courage, devotion, and gallantry.

Our men are fighting, alongside their United Nations allies, because they know, as we do, that the aggression in Korea is part of the attempt of the Russian Communist dictatorship to take over the world, step by step.

Our men are fighting a long way from home, but they are fighting for our lives and our liberties. They are fighting to protect our right to meet here today—our right to govern ourselves as a free nation.

The threat of world conquest by Soviet Russia endangers our liberty and endangers the kind of world in which the free spirit of man can survive. This threat is aimed at all peoples who strive to win or defend their own freedom and national independence.

Indeed, the state of our Nation is in great part the state of our friends and allies throughout the world. The gun that points at them points at us, also. The threat is a total threat and the danger is a common danger.

All free nations are exposed and all are in peril. Their only security lies in banding together. No one nation can find protection in a selfish search for a safe haven from the storm.

The free nations do not have any aggressive purpose. We want only peace in the world—peace for all countries. No threat to the security of any nation is concealed in our plans and programs.

We had hoped that the Soviet Union, with its security assured by the Charter of the United Nations, would be willing to live and let live. But I am sorry to say that has not been the case.

The imperialism of the czars has been replaced by the even more ambitious, more crafty, and more menacing imperialism of the rulers of the Soviet Union.

This new imperialism has powerful military forces. It is keeping millions of men under arms. It has a large air force and a strong submarine force. It has complete control of the men and equipment of its satellites. It has kept its subject peoples and its economy in a state of perpetual mobilization.

The present rulers of the Soviet Union have shown that they are willing to use this power to destroy the free nations and win domination over the whole world.

The Soviet imperialists have two ways of going about their destructive work. They use the method of subversion and internal revolution, and they use the method of external aggression. In preparation for either of these methods of attack, they stir up class strife and disorder. They encourage sabotage. They put out poisonous propaganda. They deliberately try to prevent economic improvement.

If their efforts are successful, they foment a revolution, as they did in Czechoslovakia and China, and as they tried, unsuccessfully, to do in Greece. If their methods of subversion are blocked, and if they think they can get away with outright warfare, they resort to external aggression. This is what they did when they loosed the armies of their puppet states against the Republic of Korea, in an evil war by proxy.

We of the free world must be ready to meet both of these methods of Soviet action. We must not neglect one or the other.

The free world has power and resources to meet these two forms of aggression—resources that are far greater than those of the Soviet dictatorship. We have skilled and vigorous peoples, great industrial strength, and abundant sources of raw materials. And above all, we cherish liberty. Our common ideals are a great part of our strength. These ideals are the driving force of human progress.

The free nations believe in the dignity and the worth of man.

We believe in independence for all nations.

We believe that free and independent nations can band together into a world order based on law. We have laid the cornerstone of such a peaceful world in the United Nations.

We believe that such a world order can and should spread the benefits of modern science and industry, better health and education, more food and rising standards of living—throughout the world.

These ideals give our cause a power and vitality that Russian communism can never command.

The free nations, however, are bound together by more than ideals. They are a real community bound together also by the ties of self-interest and self-preservation. If they should fall apart, the results would be fatal to human freedom.

Our own national security is deeply involved with that of the other free nations. While they need our support, we equally need theirs. Our national safety would be gravely prejudiced if the Soviet Union were to succeed in harnessing to its war machine the resources and the manpower of the free nations on the borders of its empire.

If Western Europe were to fall to Soviet Russia, it would double the Soviet supply of coal and triple the Soviet supply of steel. If the free countries of Asia and Africa should fall to Soviet Russia, we would lose the sources of many of our most vital raw materials, including uranium, which is the

basis of our atomic power. And Soviet command of the manpower of the free nations of Europe and Asia would confront us with military forces which we could never hope to equal.

In such a situation, the Soviet Union could impose its demands on the world, without resort to conflict, simply through the preponderance of its economic and military power. The Soviet Union does not have to attack the United States to secure domination of the world. It can achieve its ends by isolating us and swallowing up all our allies. Therefore, even if we were craven enough—I do not believe we could be—but, I say, even if we were craven enough to abandon our ideals, it would be disastrous for us to withdraw from the community of free nations.

We are the most powerful single member of this community, and we have a special responsibility. We must take the leadership in meeting the challenge to freedom and in helping to protect the rights of independent nations.

This country has a practical, realistic program of action for meeting this challenge.

First, we shall have to extend economic assistance, where it can be effective. The best way to stop subversion by the Kremlin is to strike at the roots of social injustice and economic disorder. People who have jobs, homes, and hopes for the future will defend themselves against the underground agents of the Kremlin. Our programs of economic aid have done much to turn back communism.

In Europe the Marshall plan has had an electrifying result. As European recovery progressed, the strikes led by the Kremlin's agents in Italy and France failed. All over Western Europe the Communist Party took worse and worse beatings at the polls.

The countries which have received Marshall plan aid have been able, through hard work, to expand their productive strength—in many cases, to levels higher than ever before in their history. Without this strength they would be completely incapable of defending themselves today. They are now ready to use this strength in helping to build a strong combined defense against aggression.

We shall need to continue some economic aid to European countries. This aid should now be specifically related to the building of their defenses.

In other parts of the world our economic assistance will need to be more broadly directed toward economic development. In the Near East, in Africa, in Asia, we must do what we can to help people who are striving to advance from misery, poverty, and hunger. We must also continue to help the economic growth of our good neighbors in this hemisphere. These actions will bring greater strength for the free world. They will give many people a real stake in the future and reason to defend their freedom. They will mean increased production of goods they need and materials we need.

Second, we shall need to continue our military assistance to countries which want to defend themselves.

The heart of our common defense effort is the North Atlantic community. The defense of Europe is the basis for the defense of the whole free world—ourselves included. Next to the United States, Europe is the largest workshop in the world. It is also a homeland of the great religious beliefs shared by many of our citizens—beliefs which are now threatened by the tide of atheistic communism.

Strategically, economically, and morally, the defense of Europe is a part of our own defense. That is why we have joined with the countries of Europe in the North Atlantic Treaty, pledging ourselves to work with them.

There has been much discussion recently over whether the European countries are willing to defend themselves. Their actions are answering this question.

Our North Atlantic Treaty partners have strict systems of universal military training. Several have recently increased the term of service. All have taken measures to improve the quality of training. Forces are being trained and expanded as rapidly as the necessary arms and equipment can be supplied from their factories and ours. Our North Atlantic Treaty partners, together, are building armies bigger than our own.

None of the North Atlantic Treaty countries, including our own country, has done enough yet. But real progress is being made. Together, we have worked out defense plans. The military leaders of our own country took part in working out these plans, and are agreed that they are sound and within our capabilities.

To put these plans into action, we sent to Europe last week one of our greatest military commanders, General Dwight D. Eisenhower.

General Eisenhower went to Europe to assume command of the united forces of the North Atlantic Treaty countries, including our own forces in Germany.

The people of Europe have confidence in General Eisenhower. They know his ability to put together a fighting force of allies. His mission is vital to our security. We should all stand behind him, and give him every bit of help we can.

Part of our job will be to reinforce the military strength of our European partners by sending them weapons and equipment as our military production expands.

Our program of military assistance extends to the nations in the Near East and the Far East which are trying to defend their freedom. Soviet communism is trying to make these nations into colonies, and to use

9

their people as cannon fodder in new wars of conquest. We want their people to be free men and to enjoy peace.

Our country has always stood for freedom for the peoples of Asia. Long, long ago it stood for the freedom of the peoples of Asia. Our history shows this. We have demonstrated it in the Philippines. We have demonstrated it in our relations with Indonesia, India, and with China. We hope to join in restoring the people of Japan to membership in the community of free nations.

It is in the Far East that we have taken up arms, under the United Nations, to preserve the principle of independence for free nations. We are fighting to keep the forces of Communist aggression from making a slave state out of Korea.

Korea has tremendous significance for the world. It means that free nations, acting through the United Nations, are fighting together against aggression.

We will understand the importance of this best if we look back into history. If the democracies had stood up against the invasion of Manchuria in 1931, or the attack on Ethiopia in 1935, or the seizure of Austria in 1938, if they had stood together against aggression on those occasions as the United Nations has done in Korea, the whole history of our time would have been different.

The principles for which we are fighting in Korea are right and just. They are the foundations of collective security and of the future of free nations. Korea is not only a country undergoing the torment of aggression; it is also a symbol. It stands for right and justice in the world against oppression and slavery. The free world must always stand for these principles—and we will stand with the free world.

As the third part of our program, we will continue to work for peaceful settlements in international disputes. We will support the United Nations and remain loyal to the great principles of international cooperation laid down in its charter.

We are willing, as we have always been, to negotiate honorable settlements with the Soviet Union. But we will not engage in appeasement.

The Soviet rulers have made it clear that we must have strength as well as right on our side. If we build our strength—and we are building it—the Soviet rulers may face the facts and lay aside their plans to take over the world.

That is what we hope will happen, and that is what we are trying to bring about. That is the only realistic road to peace.

These are the main elements of the course our Nation must follow as a member of the community of free nations. These are the things we must do to preserve our security and help create a peaceful world. But they will be successful only if we increase the strength of our own country.

Here at home we have some very big jobs to do. We are building much stronger military forces—and we are building them fast. We are preparing for full wartime mobilization, if that should be necessary. And we are continuing to build a strong and growing economy, able to maintain whatever effort may be required for as long as necessary.

We are building our own Army, Navy, and Air Force to an active strength of nearly 3½ million men and women. We are stepping up the training of the reserve forces, and establishing more training facilities, so that we can rapidly increase our active forces far more on short notice.

We are going to produce all the weapons and equipment that such an armed force will need. Furthermore, we will make weapons for our allies, and weapons for our own reserve supplies. On top of this, we will build the capacity to turn out on short notice arms and supplies that may be needed for a full-scale war.

Fortunately, we have a good start on this because of our enormous plant capacity and because of the equipment on hand from the last war. For example, many combat ships are being returned to active duty from the "mothball fleet" and many others can be put into service on very short notice. We have large reserves of arms and ammunition and thousands of workers skilled in arms production.

In many cases, however, our stocks of weapons are low. In other cases, those on hand are not the most modern. We have made remarkable technical advances. We have developed new types of jet planes and powerful new tanks. We are concentrating on producing the newest types of weapons and producing them as fast as we can.

This production drive is more selective than the one we had during World War II, but it is just as urgent and intense. It is a big program and it is a costly one.

Let me give you two concrete examples. Our present program calls for expanding the aircraft industry so that it will have the capacity to produce 50,000 modern military planes a year. We are preparing the capacity to produce 35,000 tanks a year. We are not now ordering that many planes or that many tanks, and we hope that we never have to, but we mean to be able to turn them out if we need them.

The planes we are producing now are much bigger, much better, and much more expensive than the planes we had during the last war.

We used to think that the B–17 was a huge plane, and the blockbuster it carried a huge load. But the B–36 can carry five of these blockbusters in its belly, and it can carry them five times as far. Of course, the B–36 is much more complicated to build than the B–17, and far more expensive. One B–17 costs $275,000, while now one B–36 costs $3½ million.

I ask you to remember that what we are doing is to provide the best and most modern military equipment in the world for our fighting forces.

This kind of defense production program has two parts.

The first part is to get our defense production going as fast as possible. We have to convert plants and channel materials to defense production. This means heavy cuts in civilian uses of copper, aluminum, rubber, and other essential materials. It means shortages in various consumer goods.

The second part is to increase our capacity to produce and to keep our economy strong for the long pull. We do not know how long Communist aggression will threaten the world.

Only by increasing our output can we carry the burden of preparedness for an indefinite period in the future. This means that we will have to build more powerplants and more steel mills, grow more cotton, mine more copper, and expand our capacity in many other ways.

The Congress will need to consider legislation, at this session, affecting all the aspects of our mobilization job. The main subjects on which legislation will be needed are:

First, appropriations for our military buildup.

Second, extension and revision of the Selective Service Act.

Third, military and economic aid to help build up the strength of the free world.

Fourth, revision and extension of the authority to expand production and to stabilize prices, wages, and rents.

Fifth, improvement of our agricultural laws to help obtain the kinds of farm products we need for the defense effort.

Sixth, improvement of our labor laws to help provide stable labor-management relations and to make sure that we have steady production in this emergency.

Seventh, housing and training of defense workers and the full use of all our manpower resources.

Eighth, means for increasing the supply of doctors, nurses, and other trained medical personnel critically needed for the defense effort.

Ninth, aid to the States to meet the most urgent needs of our elementary and secondary schools. Some of our plans will have to be deferred for the time being. But we should do all we can to make sure our children are being trained as good and useful citizens in the critical times ahead.

Tenth, a major increase in taxes to meet the cost of the defense effort.

The Economic Report and the Budget Message will discuss these subjects further. In addition, I shall send to the Congress special messages containing detailed recommendations on legislation needed at this session.

In the months ahead the Government must give priority to activities that are urgent—like military procurement and atomic energy and power development. It must practice rigid economy in its non-defense activities. Many of the things we would normally do must be curtailed or postponed.

But in a long-term defense effort like this one, we cannot neglect the measures needed to maintain a strong economy and a healthy democratic society.

The Congress, therefore, should give continued attention to the measures which our country will need for the long pull. And it should act upon such legislation as promptly as circumstances permit.

To take just one example—we need to continue and complete the work of rounding out our system of social insurance. We still need to improve our protection against unemployment and old age. We still need to provide insurance against the loss of earn-ings through sickness, and against the high costs of modern medical care.

And above all, we must remember that the fundamentals of our strength rest upon the freedoms of our people. We must continue our efforts to achieve the full realization of our democratic ideals. We must uphold the freedom of speech and the freedom of conscience in our land. We must assure equal rights and equal opportunities to all our citizens.

As we go forward this year in the defense of freedom, let us keep clearly before us the nature of our present effort.

We are building up our strength, in concert with other free nations, to meet the danger of aggression that has been turned loose on the world. The strength of the free nations is the world's best hope of peace.

I ask the Congress for unity in these crucial days.

Make no mistake about my meaning. I do not ask, or expect, unanimity. I do not ask for an end to debate. Only by debate can we arrive at decisions which are wise, and which reflect the desires of the American people. We do not have a dictatorship in this country, and we never will have one in this country.

When I request unity, what I am really asking for is a sense of responsibility on the part of every Member of this Congress. Let us debate the issues, but let every man among us weigh his words and his deeds. There is a sharp difference between harmful criticism and constructive criticism. If we are truly responsible as individuals, I am sure that we will be unified as a government.

Let us keep our eyes on the issues and work for the things we all believe in.

Let each of us put our country ahead of our party, and ahead of our own personal interests.

I had the honor to be a Member of the Senate during World War II, and I know from experience that unity of purpose and of effort is possible in the Congress without any lessening of the vitality of our two-party system.

Let us all stand together as Americans. Let us stand together with all men everywhere who believe in human liberty.

Peace is precious to us. It is the way of life we strive for with all the strength and wisdom we possess. But more precious than peace are freedom and justice. We will

fight, if fight we must, to keep our freedom and to prevent justice from being destroyed.

These are the things that give meaning to our lives, and which we acknowledge to be greater than ourselves.

This is our cause—peace, freedom, justice.

We will pursue this cause with determination and humility, asking divine guidance that in all we do we may follow the will of God.

NOTE: The President spoke at 1 p.m. His address was broadcast nationally.

---

5   Special Message to the Congress on the Need for More Equal Apportionment of Congressional Districts.   *January* 9, 1951

To the Congress of the United States:

In compliance with the provisions of Section 22 of the Act of June 18, 1929, as amended (2 U.S.C. 2a), relating to the decennial censuses and the apportionment of Representatives in Congress, I transmit herewith a statement prepared by the Director of the Census, Department of Commerce, giving the whole number of persons in each State as ascertained under the 17th decennial census of population, and the number of Representatives to which each State is entitled under an apportionment of the existing number of Representatives. All Indians are included in the tabulation of total population, since all Indians are now subject to Federal taxation.

Under the law, each State will be entitled commencing in the 83d Congress, to the number of Representatives shown in the statement. In a House of 435 members, the number fixed by law, the population changes reflected by the census will require a change in the number of Representatives for sixteen States. Seven States will gain, and nine States will lose seats.

In accordance with the statute, it will be the duty of the Clerk of the House of Rep-

resentatives, within fifteen calendar days after the receipt of the statement I am now transmitting, to certify to the executive of each State the number of Representatives to which such State is entitled. The statute then prescribes the ways in which any changes in the number of Representatives shall be handled until the States shall have redistricted in accordance with the changes in population.

These procedures of existing law are of great value to the operation of our Government. They provide an established method of carrying out, almost automatically, the constitutional plan for apportioning Representatives among the States on the basis of population.

However, certain problems have arisen with respect to the creation of appropriate districts within the States, which merit the consideration of the Congress.

Over the years, widespread discrepancies have grown up between the populations of the various Congressional districts. While some variation is inevitable, the extreme differences that now exist can and should be corrected. For example, there is one State in which, according to the 1950 census, the smallest district has a population of under 175,000 and the largest district has a population exceeding 900,000. In many States, there are differences of two or three hundred thousand people between the smallest and largest existing districts in the State. While about half of the Congressional districts throughout the country are between 300,000 and 400,000 in population, there are some fifty districts with a population of 250,000 or less, and, at the other extreme, some fifty districts with a population of 450,000 or over. Furthermore, as population has increased, several States have added Congressmen-at-large instead of redistricting as they should.

Such defects in our system of Congressional districts obstruct the effective operation of the democratic principles on which our whole Government rests. It is fundamental to the whole structure of the Constitution that all citizens have equal representation, so far as practicable, in the House of Representatives. This basic principle is not carried out unless Congressional districts are drawn up to reflect population changes.

The present statute clearly contemplates that the States will redistrict after an apportionment. Redistricting is the task of the State legislatures and must, of course, continue to be so. However, it is also a matter of national concern, and the Congress has a Constitutional obligation in this field which cannot be overlooked. Article I, Section 4, of the Constitution provides that the times, places and manner of holding elections for Representatives shall be prescribed in each State by the legislature thereof, but Congress may by law make or alter such regulations.

For many years the Congress exercised this power. From 1842 through 1911 the apportionment statutes enacted by the Congress as the result of each succeeding census required each State having more than one Representative to divide itself into single-member districts, thus holding down the number of Congressmen-at-large. This requirement is not included in the legislation which now governs the subject. Furthermore, prior to 1929, many of the apportionment statutes enacted by the Congress called upon the States to follow certain standards in establishing Congressional districts. They usually provided, as for example in the 1911 Act (37 Stat. 13), that in each State entitled under the apportionment to more than one Representative, the Representatives should be elected by "districts composed of contiguous and compact territory, and containing as nearly as practicable an equal number of inhabitants." These standards provided a guide for the States which was, in most cases, followed.

It seems to me desirable that the Congress at this time should give its attention to this important problem and enact legislation, supplemental to the permanent legislation on this subject, which would provide the States with standards for establishing Congressional districts and indicate the Congressional interest in compliance with such standards.

Such legislation might reaffirm the basic policy of our Government to have single-member districts. It might also repeat the old and accepted standard that Congressional districts be composed of contiguous and compact territory and contain as nearly as practicable the same number of individuals. To give more definitiveness to such standards, it might be advisable for the Congress to consider establishing limits for the permitted deviations in population between districts. It would be possible, for example, for the statute to specify that no district in any State should deviate upwards or downwards from the average population of all Congressional districts within that State by more than a specified percentage. In terms of the present census, assuming an average district of about 350,000 persons, a percentage permitting a range of about 50,000 above and below that figure would probably allow for the practical difficulties which State legislatures face in drawing up district boundaries.

The Congress should not be satisfied merely with enacting such standards. It should assume responsibility for seeing that the standards are in fact complied with. This might be done by providing for adequate reports from the States on the action they have taken in redistricting and by providing for continued Congressional attention to the results. I believe that the enactment

of the standards by itself will have a tremendous influence and that most States will seek earnestly to comply. If there are occasions in which flagrant refusal to comply is made manifest, the Congress has the power under the Constitution to take the matter in its own hands.

In any case, it is important that the proper redistricting be done promptly. Redistricting should be completed not later than the spring of 1952 so that the Congressional elections of that year may give fair representation to all citizens of our country.

HARRY S. TRUMAN

NOTE: The following table accompanied the President's message:

DEPARTMENT OF COMMERCE
Bureau of the Census
Washington 25

Population of the United States by States, 1950 and Apportionment of Representatives in Congress, 1950 and 1940

			Apportionment of 435 Representatives according to 1950 population		
				Change from present number of Representatives	
State	Population, 1950	Present number of Representatives	Number	Increase	Decrease
(1)	(2)	(3)	(4)	(5)	(6)
United States............	150, 697, 361	435	435	14	14
Alabama..............................	3, 061, 743	9	9	....	....
Arizona...............................	749, 587	2	2	....	....
Arkansas..............................	1, 909, 511	7	6	....	1
California.............................	10, 586, 223	23	30	7	....
Colorado..............................	1, 325, 089	4	4	....	....
Connecticut...........................	2, 007, 280	6	6	....	....
Delaware..............................	318, 085	1	1	....	....
Dist. of Columbia.....................	802, 178	....	....	....	....
Florida...............................	2, 771, 305	6	8	2	....
Georgia...............................	3, 444, 578	10	10	....	....
Idaho.................................	588, 637	2	2	....	....
Illinois...............................	8, 712, 176	26	25	....	1
Indiana...............................	3, 934, 224	11	11	....	....
Iowa..................................	2, 621, 073	8	8	....	....
Kansas................................	1, 905, 299	6	6	....	....

15

Population of the United States by States, 1950 and Apportionment of Representatives in Congress, 1950 and 1940—Continued

State	Population, 1950	Present number of Representatives	Apportionment of 435 Representatives according to 1950 population		
				Change from present number of Representatives	
			Number	Increase	Decrease
(1)	*(2)*	*(3)*	*(4)*	*(5)*	*(6)*
Kentucky...........................	2,944,806	9	8	....	1
Louisiana..........................	2,683,516	8	8	....	....
Maine.............................	913,774	3	3	....	....
Maryland..........................	2,343,001	6	7	1	....
Massachusetts.....................	4,690,514	14	14	....	....
Michigan..........................	6,371,766	17	18	1	....
Minnesota.........................	2,982,483	9	9	....	....
Mississippi........................	2,178,914	7	6	....	1
Missouri..........................	3,954,653	13	11	....	2
Montana..........................	591,024	2	2	....	....
Nebraska..........................	1,325,510	4	4	....	....
Nevada...........................	160,083	1	1	....	....
New Hampshire....................	533,242	2	2	....	....
New Jersey........................	4,835,329	14	14	....	....
New Mexico.......................	681,187	2	2	....	....
New York..........................	14,830,192	45	43	....	2
North Carolina....................	4,061,929	12	12	....	....
North Dakota......................	619,636	2	2	....	....
Ohio..............................	7,946,627	23	23	....	....
Oklahoma.........................	2,233,351	8	6	....	2
Oregon...........................	1,521,341	4	4	....	....
Pennsylvania......................	10,498,012	33	30	....	3
Rhode Island......................	791,896	2	2	....	....
South Carolina....................	2,117,027	6	6	....	....
South Dakota......................	652,740	2	2	....	....
Tennessee.........................	3,291,718	10	9	....	1
Texas.............................	7,711,194	21	22	1	....
Utah..............................	688,862	2	2	....	....
Vermont...........................	377,747	1	1	....	....
Virginia...........................	3,318,680	9	10	1	....
Washington........................	2,378,963	6	7	1	....
West Virginia......................	2,005,552	6	6	....	....
Wisconsin.........................	3,434,575	10	10	....	....
Wyoming..........................	290,529	1	1	....	....

6 Remarks at the Woodrow Wilson Foundation Award Ceremonies. *January* 10, 1951

Mr. Chairman, Mrs. McAdoo, and all these distinguished guests:

I am grateful for the honor that the Woodrow Wilson Foundation has conferred upon me. In the words of the citation, the award is conferred "for courageous reaction to armed aggression on June 25, 1950." The courageous reaction to the Communist aggression in Korea is the reaction of all the American people—and I think of all the free countries in the world. By giving wholehearted support to the United Nations in its effort to put down lawless aggression, and to uphold the rule of law, our people are living up to the responsibilities which Woodrow Wilson foresaw 30 years ago or more.

Woodrow Wilson labored for what at one time seemed a hopeless cause. He sought to establish an effective world organization. He urged us to lead the world in the search for a just and lasting peace. Although he could not live to see it, the seeds Wilson planted are now bearing fruit.

The American people today recognize the truths that Wilson proclaimed, and by the vigorous support of the United Nations our country has taken the lead in mobilizing the strength of free men against the forces of tyranny and despotism.

While I am honored to accept this award, I do so not in my name but in the name of the people of the United States. It is their award, it is they who have made this decision, that while peace is precious to us, freedom and justice are more precious.

I myself, as an individual, feel entirely unworthy of the honor which you have conferred upon me. As President of the United States I highly appreciate the honor which has been conferred upon me by the Woodrow Wilson Foundation.

I was in a field in July 1912, driving a binder and binding wheat, and there was a little telegraph station about a quarter of a mile from one corner of that field which, being 160 acres, was half a mile long on each side—2 miles altogether—and when I had driven around it each time, I would go to the telegraph station to see how the convention in Baltimore was coming along. And from that minute on I was a fan of Woodrow Wilson, who I think is one of the five or six great Presidents that this country has produced. And to receive an honor like this from a foundation dedicated to him is about the highest honor that any man can achieve.

I thank you very much for giving it to me.

NOTE: The President spoke in his office at the White House at 12:15 p.m. His opening words referred to Dr. Harry D. Gideonse, president of Brooklyn College and of the Woodrow Wilson Foundation, and to Mrs. Eleanor Wilson McAdoo, daughter of President Wilson.

Mr. Truman was the first President to receive the Wilson award, a bronze medallion designed by Jan Mestrovic.

7 The President's News Conference of *January* 11, 1951

THE PRESIDENT. Please be seated.

I have a couple of announcements I want to make to you before we start.

[1.] The Economic Message will go up to the Congress tomorrow, and it will be ready for your use some time late this

evening, I think.[1] And if you will get in
touch with Mr. Short [2] on that, you can taunt
him all you like.

[2.] There has been a great deal of conversation about the Fair Deal, lots of comment on it since the message.[3] I want to get
it straight, and I am having a mimeographed
statement prepared for you, which is a quotation from the message, which I think you
ought to read very carefully.

[*Reading, not literally*] "We stand behind the Fair Deal and the Democratic platform as much today as ever.

"We do, however, recognize that in an
emergency like the present, first things come
first, and our defense programs must have
top priority.

"There is no reason for anyone to be in
doubt about this. I said it as plainly as I
could in my State of the Union Message. Let
me refresh your memory by reading a few
paragraphs in that message:

" 'In the months ahead, the Government
must give priority to activities that are urgent—like military procurement, atomic
energy, and power development. It must
practice rigid economy in its nondefense
activities. Many of the things we would ordinarily do must be curtailed or postponed.

" 'But in a long-term defense effort like
this one, we cannot neglect the measures
needed to maintain a strong economy and a
healthy democratic society.

" 'The Congress, therefore, should give
continued attention to the measures which
our country will need for the long pull. And
it should act upon such legislation as
promptly as circumstances permit.' "

I just want to put you clear on that, because there has been a lot of speculation
about whether I am going back on the
Democratic platform or not. I am not.

Now you can ask your questions, if you
like.

[3.] Q. Mr. President, the Chicago
Daily News has a story from Tokyo, saying
there is evidence of Washington stripping
General MacArthur [4] of authority to speak
freely on the Korean war. It says that they
have taken away from General MacArthur
all authority to issue decisions on current
ground or military operations in Korea?

THE PRESIDENT. It is not true.

Q. It is not true?

THE PRESIDENT. It is not true. If you will
call up the Defense Department, they will
confirm what I am telling you.

[4.] Q. Mr. President, in connection
with the statement which you read us concerning the Fair Deal, I think a lot of the
speculation arose because in your message
this year, unlike your message last year, you
did not specifically ask for repeal of the Taft-
Hartley Act, for example, but asked for
improvements——

THE PRESIDENT. Asked for labor legislation
that would clarify the situation so that we
could get along better than we had been
getting along in the past. If that requires
the repeal of the Taft-Hartley Act, why
that's it.

Q. And if it doesn't?

THE PRESIDENT. That is up to the Congress
to make the decision.

[5.] Q. Mr. President, Senator Connally
made a speech on the floor today and said,
"As for the future, I am confident that the
executive branch will consult Congress on
troop commitments to the integrated European defense forces now being mobilized."
Is that an accurate reflection of your position?

THE PRESIDENT. Let me read something

---

[1] See Item 11.
[2] Joseph Short, Secretary to the President.
[3] The State of the Union Message, Item 4.

[4] General of the Army Douglas MacArthur, USA,
Commander in Chief, United Nations Command in
Korea.

here, May.[5] I didn't intend to say anything about that unless you asked the question, and I thought maybe you would.   [*Laughter*]

[*Reading*] "Under the President's constitutional powers as Commander in Chief of the Armed Forces he has the authority to send troops anywhere in the world. That power has been recognized repeatedly by the Congress and the courts.

"This Government will continue to live up to its obligations under the United Nations, and its other treaty obligations, and we will continue to send troops wherever it is necessary to uphold these obligations."

Now, Dean Acheson in his testimony before the Foreign Relations Committee made it perfectly plain that the Atlantic Treaty did not require that troops be sent, but that each country itself should make up its own mind as to what was necessary for the defense of the Atlantic Treaty countries.

That is a matter of record in the Foreign Relations Committee, and that is what Senator Connally was referring to.

Q. Mr. President, could I ask you to read that a little more slowly, so that we can quote it?

THE PRESIDENT. Well—how much of it? You want both those paragraphs read again?

Q. The first one again.

THE PRESIDENT. [*Reading*] "Under the President's constitutional powers as Commander in Chief of the Armed Forces, he has the authority to send troops anywhere in the world. That power has been recognized repeatedly by the Congress and the courts."

And I can give you the page, and the number of the citation, if you want it. I haven't got it with me just now, but you will find decisions by at least three Chief Justices on that very subject.

Q. Well, Mr. President, Senator Connally

[5] Mrs. May Craig of the Portland (Maine) Press Herald.

did not dispute your right to do so, he defended it; but he said that he understood you would consult with Congress before you would do it, and continuing: "It is my understanding that administration leaders plan to do so."

THE PRESIDENT. We always do that, May. We never make any moves in foreign affairs or on any domestic affairs, or any other affairs, that we do not very considerably consult with the committees that are interested in it. We have always done that, and there has been no change in that policy, and won't be. And any Senator who wants to talk to the President can always get a date to do it.

Q. Mr. President, have you made any commitments, verbal or written, to the Atlantic Pact countries, on how many divisions we will send to Europe?

THE PRESIDENT. No. Can't make a commitment like that because we don't know how many we are going to have.

Q. Well, Mr. President, just to make it explicit, you make no distinction, then, in the exercise of your constitutional powers to send troops, say, for reinforcement of our garrison in Germany, or later, perhaps, in sending troops for a North Atlantic army. Do you feel you have as much of a right to do one as the other?

THE PRESIDENT. I do. But, of course, in the latter case, the Congress would be consulted before we do it, as we always do.

Q. I just wondered, in the people who want to make a date, would that include Senator Taft?

THE PRESIDENT. What's that?

Q. You said any Senator who wanted to consult with you on foreign policy——

THE PRESIDENT. Or any other subject.

Q.——will that—would that include Senator Taft?

THE PRESIDENT. Why certainly. I made that perfectly plain last week.

Q. Mr. President, please let me get this

straight. You said that you had the authority by court and Constitution to send them anywhere in the world. Did those opinions given by the courts say that you had to consult Congress?

THE PRESIDENT. No, it did not——

Q. Well, Mr. President——

THE PRESIDENT. ——and I do not have to unless I want to. But of course I am polite, and I usually always consult them. [*Laughter*]

Q. Mr. President, you wouldn't be bound—necessarily bound by any opinion——

THE PRESIDENT. Well——

Q. ——consulting is one thing——

THE PRESIDENT. ——the opinions are all in favor of the President's exercise of the Presidential power when in his judgment it is necessary.

Q. I didn't mean that——

THE PRESIDENT. The opinions don't have any bearing on what the President intended, because they are all on his side.

Q. No, I don't have reference to policy opinions—congressional opinions—I mean you said that you would consult, and I said that wouldn't necessarily mean that you would be bound by——

THE PRESIDENT. No, no. That's correct.

Q. Mr. President, things have been going sort of fast here—[*laughter*]—then you will consult Congress before we send any troops to Western Europe, is that correct?

THE PRESIDENT. No, I didn't say that. I said in case of necessity for the defense of the Atlantic Charter countries—*treaty* countries—of course I would consult the Congress. It may be necessary to use troops in Germany in an emergency. You can't tell.

Q. Mr. President, could you be more explicit about the form that consultation would take? Would it be with the Senate Foreign Relations Committee? Would the whole Congress——

THE PRESIDENT. No—it would be with the Senate Foreign Relations and Armed Services Committees, which we always consult on every subject that has to do with foreign relations and with defense. I want to make that perfectly plain.

Q. Mr. President, maybe it's my "tin" ear, but I didn't get this straight yet. In this particular case, with the debate raging in Congress over whether you do or do not have the authority to send troops to Europe—and Mr. Hoover said not another man or another dollar should be sent—the debate has been quite general. Do I understand that you will ask Congress for permission——

THE PRESIDENT. No.

Q. ——before sending troops——

THE PRESIDENT. No, you do not want to take that view of the thing. I said that—in case of necessity and it became necessary, for the defense of the Atlantic Treaty countries, that Congress would be consulted before troops were sent. I don't ask their permission, I just consult them.

Q. Well, Mr. President, do you—when you say "if it became necessary for the defense of the Atlantic Treaty countries," you seem to be presuming hostilities, and things of that sort, taking place at that time, or would that include increasing forces in Germany or France now?

THE PRESIDENT. Yes—well, the latter.

Q. The latter?

THE PRESIDENT. The latter.

Q. In other words, Mr. President, no further United States troops—no troops aside from the occupation forces in Germany itself—would be sent to, say, England, France, Belgium, or Holland without consultation with the Congress?

THE PRESIDENT. Of course the Armed Services and Foreign Relations Committees would be consulted and told about it.

Q. Mr. President——

Q. Mr. President, just one thing——

THE PRESIDENT. Let Doris Fleeson⁶ finish, Tony,⁷ you have got a front seat.

What is it?

Doris Fleeson: Not one of the Republican triumvirate of Senators Wherry, Millikin, and Taft is a member of either the Foreign Relations or the Armed Services. In what way would it be possible for you to bring them into the consultation, or do you feel that the Foreign Relations Committee and Armed Services Committee would cover it for the minority party?

THE PRESIDENT. They have a perfect right to sit with those committees whenever they feel like it; and as I said before, the front door of the White House is always open.

Q. Well—but Mr. President, to go back to Senator Taft, he is not a member of the committees——

THE PRESIDENT. That's not my fault——

Q. ——and he is not——

THE PRESIDENT. ——that's not my fault. He controls the Republican side of the House. If he is not a member of the committee it is because he doesn't want to be.

[6.] Q. If I may get back to the question of General MacArthur, has he sent any recommendations to the White House, or to the Pentagon, for withdrawal of United Nations forces from Korea?

THE PRESIDENT. He has not. He is taking orders.

[7.] Q. Mr. President, this business of—this discussion about consulting Congress, does it envision, as far as your plans are concerned, any new move in the way of conciliation?

THE PRESIDENT. No. It has always been done.

Q. The same procedure?

THE PRESIDENT. Same procedure that has been followed ever since I have been here,

and I came here January 3d, 1935, officially—spent 10 years in the Senate, and spent the other 6 up here.

Q. You have the committees in——

THE PRESIDENT. All the time.

Q. ——and tell them your plans?

THE PRESIDENT. We always do that. It's nothing new at all.

Q. Mr. President, there is one thought I was not getting on the question of consultation. You don't need their permission, but as a matter of courtesy you would consult them?

THE PRESIDENT. Certainly. You must always bear in mind, in the background, that it is necessary for the Congress to appropriate the money for the Government to be carried on.

[8.] Q. Mr. President, you are not going to invite Senator Taft to come to see you?

THE PRESIDENT. As I told you time and again, the door has always been open. I don't have to make special invitations to Senators. They ask to come to see me, and I let them.

[9.] Q. Mr. President, on this question of troops to Europe, which may have been confused by tossing it back and forth on a number of technicalities, is it the administration's—the Government's—excuse me—present intention to increase our forces in Europe to give to General Eisenhower something with which he can build a defense?

THE PRESIDENT. Why certainly.

Q. It's our——

THE PRESIDENT. Certainly.

Q. Thank you.

THE PRESIDENT. What's the use of going to all this trouble if we are not going to make use of what we are doing?

Q. That's the point. It doesn't require congressional approval, but you would consult——

---

⁶ Doris Fleeson of the Bell Syndicate.
⁷ Ernest B. Vaccaro of the Associated Press.

THE PRESIDENT. Why certainly—that's right, that's right. I'll keep telling it over and over and over—just keep on asking! [*Laughter*]

Q. Well, Mr. President, to belabor this thing to the end—[*more laughter*]——

THE PRESIDENT. Go ahead.

Q. ——have you consulted with those committees about sending these troops to Europe under General Eisenhower?

THE PRESIDENT. No, I have not. General Marshall has. Dean Acheson has. They have been consulted. General Marshall and Dean Acheson represent me when they are down before these committees.

Q. Mr. President, what will be the effect, sir, of an attempt on the part of Congress to restrict, through the appropriations bill, the use of forces——

THE PRESIDENT. That is up to the Congress, if they want to go to the country with that—and I'll go with them. And I licked them once.

Q. As I understand it, sir, the decision already has been made to send our forces to Europe——

THE PRESIDENT. Those that are necessary, yes.

Q. Now just—what will you consult these committees about, if the decision has been made?

THE PRESIDENT. Well, we will have to wait and see what General Eisenhower's report is before we make any definite plans.

Q. About size, and so forth?

THE PRESIDENT. That's right.

[10.] Q. Mr. President, a week ago, I believe it was, you said that prices and—I hope this—I am not intruding on this talk—Atlantic Pact thing—but you said a week ago that price and wage controls were on the way. What is the picture on that?

THE PRESIDENT. Just the same as it was. Price and wage controls are on the way, and as soon as it is possible it will be put into effect. Mr. Wilson[8] will confirm that, if you want to ask him about it.

Q. May I clear up a point? Last week you told us, if I remember right, that it would take legislation to control the prices of farm products, and you asked us to look and wait and see in the State of the Union Message as to whether you would recommend that?

THE PRESIDENT. I did. I did recommend that.

Q. I am not clear in my own mind as to whether it is the administration's aim to change the provisions on parity or not?

THE PRESIDENT. No, no. It doesn't have anything to do with parity. This is the consumers prices that I am referring to, of things to eat.

Q. In other words, sir, there is no intention to change the law so that a ceiling can be set below parity?

THE PRESIDENT. No, the farmers and labor and industry must all be on a par. They must all be treated exactly alike. That is what the intention of Mr. Wilson's setup is, to see that everybody is fairly treated—and that includes the consumer who is being gouged a little right now.

[11.] Q. Mr. President, has Governor Dewey of New York been approached for any job in the Government?

THE PRESIDENT. No.

[12.] Q. Mr. President, some people are assuming that civil rights has been put aside for a while?

THE PRESIDENT. No.

[13.] Q. Mr. President, on the subject of price controls, we all know, of course, that ever since last June prices have gone up and up and up, and they are continuing to rise. I believe Mr. Valentine[9] said yesterday af-

---

[8] Charles E. Wilson, Director, Office of Defense Mobilization.
[9] Dr. Alan Valentine, Administrator, Economic Stabilization Agency.

ternoon that they had abandoned the idea of going over for a 30-day voluntary freeze on prices now. Well, that means that more time, apparently, is going by before price controls are put on, and prices may go up more. When this thing does jell, does the administration intend to roll any of these prices—price rises back?

THE PRESIDENT. We will cross that bridge when we get to it. I don't know whether you had any experience in World War II on price controls and wage adjustments. I did. And that was part of my job on that committee. And it is one of the most difficult things in Government, to do just what we are trying to do now. We are trying to do it in an orderly manner, and trying to profit by the mistakes which we made in World War II.

[14.] Q. Mr. President, do you intend to use subsidies like you did in World War II?

THE PRESIDENT. I will answer that question when it becomes necessary. I can't answer it now.

[15.] Q. Mr. President, how much of a tax increase are we going to need in 1951?

THE PRESIDENT. I will send the tax message down just as soon as I can get it ready.[10] If you will carefully read Mr. Snyder's [11] interview yesterday, he covered it thoroughly.

[16.] Q. Mr. President, do you plan to send a special message to Congress dealing with the need for control of food prices?

THE PRESIDENT. No, I do not.

Q. Mr. President, I wonder if you could go a little more into detail on how that food price control system would work, if you don't control parity prices?

THE PRESIDENT. Parity has nothing to do with price and wage controls at all. It is an entirely different question. All we are after—you will find that the farmer has not

---

[10] See Item 28.
[11] John W. Snyder, Secretary of the Treasury.

profited by these increased food prices at all. I had the Secretary of Agriculture make a survey, and the wholesale prices of farm products are very little above what they were in June.

Q. Mr. President, I think that question might be directed, if I may interpolate, to the fact that the present law says that prices cannot be set below parity. I believe the question I would like to have an answer to, if possible, too, is whether or not that provision of the law might have to be weighed, or changed?

THE PRESIDENT. Well, whatever is necessary to be done to meet the situation will be done.

[17.] Q. Mr. President, how soon after General Eisenhower's return will it be possible to send troops to Europe?

THE PRESIDENT. I can't answer the question.

[18.] Q. Mr. President, what do you think of the idea of paying Chinese "commies" to prevent the use of——

THE PRESIDENT. What do you mean?

Q. Well, there is—one of our correspondents recently returned from Korea thought it might be a good idea to pay so much to the "commies" who came over to our ranks for surrendering a machinegun. [*Laughter*]

THE PRESIDENT. You are talking about bribery now, and I don't have anything to do with that. I don't believe in it. That's what ruined the Chiang Kai-shek government, just that sort of procedure.

Q. [*From the back of the room*] Thank you, Mr. President. [*Laughter*]

Merriman Smith (United Press Associations): Thank you, Mr. President. [*More laughter*]

NOTE: President Truman's two hundred and fiftieth news conference was held in the Indian Treaty Room (Room 474) in the Executive Office Building at 4 p.m. on Thursday, January 11, 1951.

8   Remarks at a Buffet Supper for Democratic Members of Congress.   *January 11, 1951*

THANK YOU very much. I would like to know what chance a country man from Missouri has after *that* and *that* [*Pointing to Vice President Barkley and Speaker Sam Rayburn*].

I heard the Vice President say that he and Sam considered themselves statesmen when they came into the Congress in 1913. I have an old definition for a statesman, a very old one: A statesman is a dead politician.

I have no desire yet to be in that class. I don't want to see my friend the Vice President, or my friend the Speaker in that class, either. But they are living statesmen. They have done a job for their country that is unequaled in its history. As President of the United States, I am one of the luckiest of the Presidents to have a Vice President and a Speaker such as Mr. Barkley and Mr. Rayburn. There have been Vice Presidents and Vice Presidents, and there have been Speakers and Speakers, but I don't think there has ever been a team as close together, and as anxious to do the country the best job possible, as is now presiding over the Senate, and presiding over the House of Representatives.

I have just received an engraving of a picture presented to Henry Clay in 1821, and they were presenting that picture to Henry Clay on account of the fact that he had succeeded in having a resolution passed in the House of Representatives, authorizing the then President of the United States to recognize the provinces of South America, when in his judgment they had become independent republics. Just a short time before that, Mr. Clay had been responsible for the Missouri Compromise which made Missouri a State along with Maine on a com-

promise basis—Maine got in first, Missouri almost never did. But in 1850 Mr. Clay agreed to another compromise, which in the middle fifties he changed into the Kansas-Nebraska bill, and brought on the War Between the States.

In going over these various things, and the people who have occupied these positions, you will remember that Andrew Jackson had about as much trouble as any President that was ever in office. He had a Vice President from South Carolina, and his name was Calhoun. And when Jackson was on his deathbed, someone asked him what were the two things he had left undone that he wished he had done while he was President; and he said one was that he should have hanged John C. Calhoun, and shot Henry Clay. Well, now, there is no such parallel here.

But you know, the Presidents of the United States who have apparently had the most trouble, and who have been most viciously attacked in the public prints, are those whom we class as the great Presidents. There never was any man as bitterly attacked as George Washington. You should go down to the Library of Congress sometime, and get out the papers from New York and New Orleans, and other places around all over the country, and read the things that were said about George Washington. They were terrific and terrible. The same thing was said about Jefferson. Of course, nobody has been as bitterly attacked as old Jackson was, and he didn't care—and neither do I.

And one of the most misrepresented Presidents in the public prints was Abraham Lincoln. He went to Gettysburg one time, and made about a four-paragraph speech. And there was a gentleman there who spoke for

2 hours, and I'll bet there is hardly a man here who can name that gentleman who was the main speaker at the celebration.

On that day, when Lincoln made that famous speech, old Horace Greeley, and Dana and Medill in Chicago, said Lincoln had disgraced the country by the terrible speech he made on that day. There isn't a man here who has not at one time or another memorized that Gettysburg address. I'll bet you can't say a word of what the other gentleman said, and I'll bet you can't name him—Edward Everett.

Well, another man who was viciously mistreated while he was President was Grover Cleveland. You should read some of the things they said about Grover while he was President of the United States.

And they hounded Wilson to his grave.

But those men made the impression on the country that has made the country great. I don't think I can make any such impression, but I want to say to you that I have the responsibility which belongs to the President of the United States. I am exercising that responsibility to the best of my ability, and I expect to do the very best I can for the United States of America, and for the world. That's all I can do.

In order to accomplish the purpose which I think Almighty God intended this country to carry out, we must, as the Government of the United States—and you are just as much a part of it as I am, and you are elected for that purpose—we must work together, not only for the welfare of the United States itself, but for the welfare of the whole world.

Since Mr. Rayburn and Mr. Barkley have deemed it wise to go back into history, I am going back a little further than they did and draw analogies to the situation we face now.

All of you remember what happened to Xerxes when he attempted to pulverize the Greek Republics. You all remember what a terrible time the Roman Republic had when Hannibal was winning victories for 21 years in Italy. I don't know whether you remember it, but if it had not been for Charles Martel there would have been no Christian Europe. He prevented the downfall of Christian Europe at Tours. Then along about 500 years after that, there was a certain Mongol—and we are troubled with Mongols right now—who got as far west as Vienna; but he was stopped at Vienna and never got any further. The Christian world survived.

We are faced now with those people who believe in the individual, and who believe in a moral code based on the Sermon on the Mount—which is the best exposition of what a man ought to be that has ever been enunciated; and on the other side we are faced with those people who do not believe in a moral code, who only make commitments to break them. They are—I can't say they are immoral, because that has a definite meaning in our language—but they are unmoral. They believe in the material things and not the spiritual.

Now this country, and the free countries of Europe and Asia, must band together to make an effort to put morals above materials. That's all I am striving for.

I want peace in the world. But I don't want peace at any price. I want peace with freedom and justice.

I don't think there is a citizen in this country of ours who does not believe that, if he has been raised right—had the right sort of mother, and most of us have.

I hope—I sincerely hope—that this great organization, the Congress of the United States, will remember that honor and justice are greater for the welfare of your children and mine—and I hope my grandchildren—than fat and ease.

NOTE: The President spoke at 8:55 p.m. at the Shoreham Hotel in Washington.

9 Remarks to Members of the National Advisory Committee on the Selection of Physicians, Dentists, and Allied Specialists. *January 12, 1951*

Dr. Rusk, ladies and gentlemen:

I appreciate that introduction, and I hope I can deserve it.

I am vitally interested in what you are trying to do. I have always been interested in physical and mental health. I think it is vitally important that any man in public life or in private life should be physically fit. If he is physically fit he is much more likely to be mentally fit.

I have always thought it was a terrible reflection on the richest and greatest republic that the sun has ever shone upon, that 34 percent of its young men were found unfit for military service in World War II. I have always hoped that we could overcome that shortcoming. I believe we can. I don't think there is any reason why we cannot do it. What you gentlemen have been doing for the military services I think can be done for the civil population, too.

I am not only interested in physical health, I believe there is as much in preventing things from happening to your body as there is in curing it after it happens. I have spent a lot of time in an attempt to stop accidental killings in this country, in industry and on the road. I think we demonstrated over a 4-year period that the efforts we put forth have saved in the neighborhood of 10,000 to 12,000 lives a year, and immense numbers of people who would otherwise have been crippled.

I hope that you will continue your efforts for a health program for this great Nation of ours that will be practical and that will work.

Right now we are short—very short—of doctors and nurses, both in the armed services and in the country at large. I am urging the Congress to take some notice of that situation and try to help us produce more doctors and nurses in the immediate future, for the welfare of this Nation as a whole.

I hope you will continue your good work. I hope that the results of your meeting are concrete—and Dr. Rusk tells me they are— and that when we finally wind up we will not only be the greatest nation in the world but the healthiest nation in the world.

Thank you very much.

NOTE: The President spoke at 11:45 a.m. in the Indian Treaty Room (Room 474) in the Executive Office Building. In his opening words he referred to Dr. Howard Rusk, Chairman of the National Advisory Committee on the Selection of Physicians, Dentists, and Allied Specialists. The Committee was established by Executive Order 10166 of October 4, 1950 (3 CFR, 1949–1953 Comp., p. 346).

10 Statement by the President Upon Signing the Federal Civil Defense Act of 1950. *January 12, 1951*

THE Federal Civil Defense Act of 1950, which I have signed today, is designed to protect life and property in the United States in case of enemy assault. It affords the basic framework for preparations to minimize the effects of an attack on our civilian popula- tion, and to deal with the immediate emergency conditions which such an attack would create.

I congratulate the Congress for its speedy and thorough consideration of this legislation. I shall soon transmit to the Congress a request for an initial appropriation of funds to carry on the Federal responsibilities under the new act.

The act will permit the Federal Government to provide matching grants of funds to the States for constructing air raid shelters. The act also allows certain measures to be taken by the Federal Government directly, such as the procurement and stockpiling of necessary medical and other materials and supplies and the provision of suitable warning systems.

Each of these fields of action pose complex problems that cannot be solved overnight. We have carefully developed plans to meet those major problems.

The master plan for meeting attacks by an aggressor against our cities and their people was published last September. It was the result of several years of study and work on the part of many people, both in and out of government, in this country and abroad.

This master plan, entitled "United States Civil Defense," is now serving as a blueprint for American States and cities in their preparations to safeguard American lives and homes.

The Federal Government can and will provide the necessary coordination and guidance for the civil defense program. I have named Millard F. Caldwell, former Governor of Florida, to head the Federal Civil Defense Administration.

It is the expressed policy and intent of Congress, however, that the responsibility for civil defense should be vested primarily in the States and their political subdivisions. I, therefore, call upon all citizens to lend their support to civil defense in their own communities.

Much has been done, but much remains to be done. It will require the best efforts of all of us to get ready, and to stay ready, to defend our homes. No true American would want to give less than his best to that cause, and no one who knows the American people could ask for more.

NOTE: The Federal Civil Defense Act of 1950 is Public Law 920, 81st Congress (64 Stat. 1245).

"United States Civil Defense," a report by the National Security Resources Board, was published by the Government Printing Office (1950, 162 pp.). It was also issued as House Document 705 (81st Cong., 2d sess.). For the President's message to Congress transmitting the report, see 1950 volume, this series, Item 251.

See also Item 131.

11   Annual Message to the Congress: The President's Economic Report. *January 12, 1951*

To the Congress of the United States:

We face enormously greater economic problems, as I transmit this fifth annual Economic Report, than at any time since the end of World War II. Although our economic strength is now greater than ever before, very large new burdens of long duration are now being imposed upon it.

The United States is pledged and determined, along with other free peoples, to check aggression and to advance freedom. Arrayed against the free world are large and menacing forces. The great manpower under the control of Soviet communism is being driven with fanatic zeal to build up military and industrial strength. We invite disaster if we underestimate the forces working against us.

The economic strength of the free peoples of the world is, however, superior to that of their enemies. If the free nations mobilize and direct their strength properly, they can support whatever military effort may be necessary to avert a general war or to win such a war if it comes. The resources are on our side. The only question is whether they will be used with speed and determination. The answer will depend upon unity of purpose and of action—unity among the free nations, unity here in the United States.

Unity is imperative on the economic front. On this front, under the American system, everybody is involved—every businessman, worker and farmer; every banker and scientist and housewife; every man and woman. We can win our way through to ultimate triumph if we all pull together. Decisive action, essential to our safety, should not be halted by controversy now.

It is in this spirit that I transmit this Economic Report to the Congress.

THE NATURE OF THE TASK

We must understand the nature of our defense effort here at home. Our job has three parts.

In the first place, we must achieve a large and very rapid increase in our armed strength, while helping to strengthen our allies. This means more trained men in uniform, and more planes, tanks, ships, and other military supplies. Second, we must achieve, as rapidly as possible, an expansion of our *capacity* for producing military supplies. This must be substantially greater than would be required to achieve our present targets for armed strength; it must be large enough to enable us to swing rapidly into full-scale war production if necessity should require. And third, we must maintain and expand our basic economic strength—important both to military production and to our civilian economy—so that we can continue to grow stronger rather than weaker if it should prove necessary to continue a defense effort of great size for a number of years.

The first part of this task—the primary military build-up—imposes the major immediate burden on the economy.

For the fiscal years 1951 and 1952 combined, new obligational authority enacted or anticipated for our primary national security programs—for our military forces, for economic and military aid to other free nations, for atomic energy and stockpiling, and for related purposes—will probably total more than 140 billion dollars. Actual expenditures on these programs in the fiscal year 1950, the last full year before the Korean outbreak, totaled about 18 billion dollars. At the present time, they are running at an annual rate of somewhat more than 20 billion dollars. By the end of this calendar year, they should attain an annual rate between 45 and 55 billion dollars, or from 25 to 35 billion dollars above the present rate. The actions we are taking should enable us, within twelve months, to expand this rate of expenditure very rapidly if necessity should require.

Current expenditures for these purposes now represent about 7 percent of our total national output. By the end of this year, this proportion may rise to as much as 18 percent. This compares with the roughly 45 percent of our total output that we were devoting to defense during the peak year of World War II. While the present program is thus very substantially short of the requirements imposed by full-scale war, it nonetheless requires a major diversion of effort. Furthermore, there will be a much more severe drain on some particular supply lines. By the end of the year, our expanding defense programs, including stockpiling, may be absorbing up to a third or more of the total supply of some of our basic commodities, such as copper, aluminum, and natural rubber. While direct defense requirements for steel may not total more than 10 percent of total output, the needed expansion of our essential industrial capacity will require a much greater diversion of steel from ordinary civilian uses.

In terms of manpower, our present defense targets will require an increase of nearly one million men and women in the armed forces within a few months, and probably not less than four million more in defense production by the end of the year. This means that an additional 8 percent of our labor force, and possibly much more, will be required by direct defense needs by the end of the year.

These manpower needs will call both for increasing our labor force by reducing unemployment and drawing in women and older workers, and for lengthening hours of work in essential industries. These manpower requirements can be met. There will be manpower shortages, but they can be solved.

The second part of the job is to build up our *capacity* for producing military supplies—our military production base. For example, our present aircraft program calls for capacity to produce 50,000 planes a year. Our present program for tanks calls for the capacity to produce 35,000 tanks a year. We are not now placing orders for that many planes or tanks, but we are getting ready to produce them if we need them.

There are many cases where our immediate production needs will require the diversion of plants now devoted to civilian production, but we cannot be satisfied with this solution alone. We must increasingly create new capacity to meet defense production targets. This will give us more economic strength, which means more power in reserve for any contingency. The job is made easier because we still have substantial reserve plant and equipment, as a result of the industrial reserve policy instituted at the close of World War II. It is a great program, but we can meet it.

The third part of the job is to increase our basic industrial strength—to build up

our facilities for the production of steel, aluminum, power, and other basic commodities and services. This ability should be brought to a level where it can carry the present defense burden without the necessity for irksome controls extending over a long period. This will also increase our ability to meet any requirements for a greater military effort.

In the case of steel, for example, we must raise the capacity of the industry from its present level of about 103 million ingot tons a year by enough to support our defense effort and to sustain our civilian economy. The Council of Economic Advisers estimates that this will require an increase in capacity to about 120 million ingot tons in the next three or four years. This estimate is not necessarily final. But it suggests the kind of growth we are working for in our economy in the years immediately ahead.

To increase our steel supply, we must also increase our supplies of iron ore. Output of the high-grade Lake Superior ore fields can be maintained at present levels for only a few years longer. Thereafter, we shall have to rely more and more on lower-grade domestic ores and on imported supplies. Expansion of domestic plants for treating low-grade ores, and of ore production facilities in Labrador and Venezuela, together with related transportation facilities, is essential.

Electric power is another field in which we must expand capacity promptly. At the present time, electric power is in short supply in the Pacific Northwest, in the Tennessee Valley area, and in some other regions. The supply is expected to become increasingly short throughout the country, as demands will increase faster than the expansion of capacity now planned. Reserves will fall more and more below safe and desirable margins. Already the reserve margin has practically disappeared, in areas where the power shortage is most acute. Yet, expansion of capacity now planned in atomic energy, chemicals, and aluminum and other metals related to the defense effort, will impose an additional load of 4 to 4½ million kilowatts on our power facilities.

In the face of this situation, we should plan to increase our generating capacity by well over 20 million kilowatts during the next three years. The major share of this expansion must come from private utility enterprises. The large public hydroelectric projects take more time, but I am recommending the development of additional public power capacity in the Pacific Northwest, in the Tennessee Valley area, at Niagara Falls, along the St. Lawrence River as a part of the seaway and power project, and elsewhere, to contribute needed additions to the power supply as quickly as they can be built.

These are but two examples of the need to build up our productive capacity. If we were now engaged in full-scale war, we could not afford to devote manpower and materials to these longer-range programs. But to fail to do so under present circumstances would be short-sighted and potentially costly. Action now is essential, to make us stronger year by year in all of the components which enter into any military strength that we may need in future.

THE POWER OF THE AMERICAN ECONOMY TO
PERFORM THE TASK

There is no question that our economy can sustain the great exertions outlined above, and still remain strong and grow stronger. The past performance and present condition of the American economy make this plain.

In the ten years since this Nation decided that fascist aggression had to be stopped, the growth of our economic power has been prodigious. Comparing 1950 with 1940, our total output, in actual units of goods and services, is more than 50 percent higher. Farm production is up 25 percent. The total labor supply has increased by 9 million, and civilian employment by 13 million. In addition, we have more and better tools and equipment. Steel capacity is up more than 20 percent; oil refining capacity up 40 percent; electric power capacity up 70 percent. On our farms, there are two or three times as many tractors, trucks, and power-driven machines. Farm use of electric power has gone up three or four times.

It is sometimes thought that most of this economic growth occurred during World War II. True, under the dire necessity of wartime, we expanded with very great speed. But during the past five years, we have added greatly to the productive strength attained before V-J Day. More than 90 billion dollars (in 1950 prices) have been invested by private enterprise in plant and equipment. Total manufacturing capacity has increased by between 25 and 30 percent. Steel capacity is 12 percent higher; that of our chemical and machinery industries, 60 to 70 percent higher. Civilian employment late in 1950 was 8 million above the peak year of World War II, and output per man-hour for the economy as a whole has advanced by about 10 percent.

There has been very recent demonstration of our economic power, and of our capacity for further growth. In the first half of 1950, the upsurge of business recovery from the mild recession of 1949 was swift and comprehensive. This demonstrated the soundness of our economic structure. In the second half of the year, the pace of economic expansion became more rapid. Every part of the economy responded to the challenge of international developments. During these six months, private investment in construction, equipment, and additions to inventory reached the record annual rate of 53 billion dollars. Taking the year as a whole, industrial production was 14 percent higher than in 1949, and by June had exceeded the 1948 peak. The total output of goods and services during the year 1950 was 7 percent higher, in real terms, than during the previous year. It is now running at an annual rate more than 10 percent above the average for 1949. Civilian employment increased by about 1.3 million from 1949 to 1950, and there were more people in civilian jobs at the peak of 1950 employment than ever before.

Our economic history shows that we have risen to our greatest heights in the face of our greatest dangers. From the beginning of World War II to the time of our peak effort, we stepped up farm output by 20 percent, and industrial production by nearly 90 percent. Our total national output rose by more than 60 percent. If it had been necessary, we could have done much more.

We may not be able to add to our production so rapidly in the years immediately ahead. We had more unused resources of manpower, plant, and materials in 1940 than we have now. There are now some relative shortages of raw materials. On the other hand, as long as we avert a total war, we can devote a larger part of our total resources to building up our economy than we did after Pearl Harbor.

The accompanying Annual Review by the Council of Economic Advisers estimates, after careful examination of our economic resources, that we can and should achieve an annual rate of total output more than 7 percent above the current level by the end of this year. The estimates made by the Council at the start of 1950, concerning how much the economy could grow in real terms during the year, were realized. I believe that this progress will continue. We must plan and work together, to increase the total productive strength of our economy by at least 25 percent within the next five years.

We have not reached, and cannot foresee reaching, any final ceiling on our productive power. Throughout the years we have grown, despite ups and downs, and we will continue to grow. We have a growing population. We have business initiative and daring. We have workers of great skill and energy. We have the ability to make practical use of new scientific discoveries and inventions. We have, despite some shortages, bountiful natural resources. Above all, we have faith, justified by accomplishment, in our economic system.

This great vitality of our economy provides the answer to the question of whether we can sustain the burden of our defense program. In relative terms, this burden at present is much less than it was in World War II. At the peak of World War II, we were devoting about 45 percent of our national output to defense. By the end of this year, we will be devoting about 18 percent to defense. During World War II, even when defense production was at its highest, we maintained a strong economy. Civilians made sacrifices, but they did not suffer.

Our total output today has reached approximately the 1944 peak. More important, we are now maintaining this rate of production with much shorter hours and less strain upon facilities. Our productive potential is not as fully mobilized as at the height of World War II. If we approached the same degree of economic mobilization, our total output would be very much greater, and so would our output of defense items. Our contemplated defense program, even if it were doubled, would still be clearly within our capabilities.

THE INFLATIONARY DANGER

While it is clear that we have the productive ability to meet even far greater defense demands on our economy, we must not be misled into thinking that we can make the change to a defense economy easily. It will require effort, restraint, and sacrifice by all of us.

The character of our economy must now be changed rapidly to meet the new challenge. Those types of production which support the expanding defense effort must be greatly enlarged. The part of our total national output going into defense should rise from 7 percent to nearly 18 percent, during the year 1951. By the end of the year, the expanding defense program may be absorbing one-third or more of some basic materials.

In some respects, it will be harder to convert to defense production than it was in 1940. Then, there were idle plants and men and materials which could be channeled into the defense effort. Since our economy has recently been running full blast, the defense program will have to pull men and materials, as well as plants, away from existing peacetime uses. This will pull millions of people away from normal peacetime production.

Although we can increase production, we cannot do it quickly enough to expand the defense program, and at the same time still have as much left over for other purposes. We must put heavy restraints upon nonessential business activity. During the past few years, nearly 70 percent of our growing national output has gone into consumption. This has led to higher standards of living, which is the ultimate purpose of a peacetime economy. But the total supply of consumer goods cannot be increased this year, and many types of goods must be sharply curtailed. Yet the population will continue to grow; new families will continue to be formed; and more incomes for practically all groups will be generated by more production, more employment, and longer hours. The excess of consumer demand over available goods will rise by many bil-

lions of dollars.

This will cause intense and mounting inflationary pressures, which must be counteracted.

During 1950, even before the defense expansion gathered speed, inflation started to march. Wholesale prices rose almost 15½ percent, and passed the previous all-time peak in the second half of the year. Particular price increases were even more spectacular, with chemicals rising by 21½ percent, and textiles by 24 percent. The average price of goods to consumers rose over 6 percent; and there was over a 4½ percent rise to a new all-time peak in the six months from June to December.

Incomes also started to rise sharply. During the year, real weekly earnings in manufacturing, after adjusting for changes in prices, rose by 10 percent. Corporate profits before taxes rose by about 6 billion dollars above the previous record year. Most types of income, particularly in the second half of the year, rose faster than production.

If inflation continues to gain cumulative force, it will multiply the cost of the defense program. It will undermine production, destroy confidence, generate friction and economic strife, impair the value of the dollar, dissipate the value of savings, and impose an intolerable burden upon fixed income groups. This must not happen.

To fight inflation, demand must be held down until supplies can catch up. This is why we must have a stringent stabilization program. It will mean sacrifices by everybody. But under the conditions now facing us, restraints will serve the interest of all.

PRINCIPLES FOR ACTION

As we prepare ourselves for the stern task which confronts us, we must keep in mind five basic principles. These are: (1) all of us must plan; (2) all of us must serve; (3) sacrifices must be shared fairly; (4) we must develop all our resources wisely; (5) we must work with our allies in the common cause.

All of us must plan

A defense emergency requires far more planning than is customary or desirable in normal peacetime. The military build-up is a planned effort. The mobilization of industrial support for this military build-up is a planned effort. The industrial cutbacks and civilian restraints, necessary to achieve military and economic mobilization, are planned efforts. The major decisions as to how much goods and services must be left over for consumers, to maintain a strong base for the whole undertaking, also require planning. In a defense emergency, all of these problems are interrelated.

In these critical times, it is recognized that Government must assume leadership in this planning. It has the prime responsibility for national security. It has access to the basic information. The most important operation toward this end is the broad programming of various major requirements; the balancing of these requirements against supply; and the development of policies to satisfy needs according to priority of purpose.

But the Government cannot develop these basic plans alone. The necessary experience and know-how are to be found throughout our whole economic system. Through constant consultation, these talents should be drawn into the whole planning effort. After the basic economic plans are outlined, most of them will have to be carried out by businessmen, workers, and farmers. They will be able to carry out these plans better, if they have had a chance to participate in creating them from the start.

These basic economic plans set general targets or goals. The details must be filled in by people all over the country. It may become necessary for the Government to indicate that longer hours of work are de-

sirable. But working arrangements are made between employers and employees. The Government may indicate that more steel is needed. But steel production is in private hands. The Government may indicate that more cotton will be needed. But cotton is grown by farmers.

Businessmen always plan; and now they must plan how they can best help to make their country stronger. Labor organizations always plan; and now they must plan their contribution to the defense effort. Farmers also plan; and they, too, must now plan to play their full role in the national security effort. Government plans can aid, but cannot substitute for, this individual and group planning. To neglect this, would be to undermine one of the greatest sources of our economic strength.

All of us must serve

In a defense emergency, all those on the home front should serve, to the limit of their ability, in the kind of work for which they are best fitted.

Businessmen should serve, by employing their financial resources and managerial skills to produce the greatest possible amount of the goods which the Nation needs. In the period ahead, businessmen will have responsibility for a much larger part of the investment program than during World War II, when a very high percentage of investment in new capacity was made by the Government. Our ability to reach production goals will depend in large measure upon how effectively businessmen do their job.

Farmers should serve, by increasing their output. They have less manpower than before World War II, but far more machinery and fertilizer, and far better scientific methods. They can also serve, by making shifts in output which are responsive to the needs of the defense economy.

Workers should serve, by helping to improve productivity. They should seek out jobs which are essential to the defense effort. They should cooperate by working longer hours wherever it will help the defense effort. More people should seek work than in normal times.

Millions of others, in addition to businessmen, industrial workers, and farmers, are now called upon to do their jobs more efficiently, and to readjust their efforts to the needs of national defense.

For all to serve in full measure, it must be in a common cause and not primarily for personal gain. This does not mean that we should undermine the incentives which lead to more production. But the rewards for increased production cannot be as great under a defense program as they are in normal peacetime. This is because most of the increased production must go into national defense, and consequently cannot be used to improve incomes or lift standards of living.

Each group and individual will be more willing to put forth greater effort, if it appears clearly that everybody is doing the same. Businessmen, workers, and farmers will be willing to work harder, to the extent that they feel that they are working harder to serve their country, and not just to benefit somebody else. There should be a sense of equality of service in the defense program. Public policies must help to assure this.

Service by all is even more important than sacrifice, because it is work, and more work, that increases production.

Sacrifices must be shared fairly

No matter how efficiently we do our jobs, all of us must make sacrifices.

Businessmen must make sacrifices. They must pay much higher taxes. While profits should not be taxed to the extent which would jeopardize production or destroy incentives, businessmen cannot expect to retain profits on the scale which would be expected during normal peacetime prosperity. They must also accept restraints and controls upon many of their business practices—including price policy and the use of materials and manpower—which are not customary in peacetime. They must be willing to withdraw from enterprises which are nonessential and wasteful during a national emergency.

Workers must make sacrifices. They must seek the jobs which need doing, in the locations where these jobs must be done, instead of the jobs which may be most pleasant in the locations which are most convenient. They must accept restraints and controls upon wages, designed to prevent the wage increases which would be attainable if more goods were being produced for wage earners to buy. While the right to bargain collectively will be preserved, workers—along with management—must find ways to settle disputes without stopping essential production.

Farmers must make sacrifices. They should receive their fair share of available national income. But they cannot expect to avoid their fair share of the cost of national defense. Over the past two decades, farm standards of living have risen substantially, and they needed to rise, because farmers had lagged far behind others in sharing the national income. But that rate of progress cannot be continued in these perilous times.

All economic groups must pay much higher taxes.

American families must make sacrifices. They can expect very sharp curtailments in the supply of durable equipment which brings convenience and entertainment to the home. They will have to make their household goods last longer, their automobiles and appliances, their linen and clothes. They must save a larger portion of their incomes. Many of them must postpone buying a new house.

These sacrifices will not prevent us from maintaining a strong and growing economy, capable of supporting the current defense program or any greater program that we may need to undertake. On the contrary, these sacrifices will make for a stronger nation by curbing inflation. They will make us stronger, not only by augmenting our military strength, but also by enabling us to increase the productive facilities which can lighten the economic burden in the long run.

It is essential that the sacrifices which are necessary in these critical times be shared fairly by all groups. Businessmen will be more cooperative in sacrificing peacetime profit objectives and paying more taxes, if it is clear that this is not being done just so farmers and workers can have more income. Farmers will be more cooperative in sacrificing peacetime farm income objectives, if it is clear that this is not being done just so workers can get more wages and businessmen can get more profits. Workers will be more cooperative in sacrificing peacetime wage objectives, if it is clear that this is not being done just to provide more profits for business or more farm income. Professional people, civil servants, office workers, and those living on fixed incomes, will be willing to accept their share of necessary sacrifices, to the extent that it is clear that this is not being done just to provide for other people more profits or wages or farm income. All will be willing to make far more sacrifices for national defense and to keep our economy strong, if the burden is shared on a fair and equitable basis.

We must develop all our resources wisely

The rapid expansion of the defense program must be the first objective in all that we do. But military strength does not depend upon guns and armed forces alone. These forces must be equipped by our industry, fed by our farms, and supported by all the people. There must be a continuing balance between the build-up of military strength and the build-up of economic strength.

In a total war, this balance would be very different from what it should be now. In a total war, we would have total military mobilization, accomplished by considerable depletion of other kinds of strength. In the current situation, we must place considerable stress upon economic strength, or run the danger of being weak at some future time if total military strength should then be required.

With these purposes in mind, we must apportion materials and manpower carefully among military needs, stockpiling, and industrial needs. We must divide industrial supply carefully, so as to expand in some areas while contracting in others. We must divide total civilian supply carefully between industry and consumers, so that we do not weaken manpower while improving tools.

The handling of our natural resources is a vital aspect of this problem. Many projects must be cancelled or deferred, but those necessary for defense and essential civilian needs must go forward. If we allow our agricultural and range lands and our forests to deteriorate, and if we misuse critically needed minerals and supplies of water, we shall become weaker each year instead of stronger. If we do not expand the use of some of these resources—as, for example, through carefully selected power developments—we cannot expect to reach the full potential of our industrial strength. We can cut down enough on the private and public use of materials and manpower for nonessentials to accomplish these essential projects.

Our human resources are our main economic strength. When we finally win in the contest between freedom and slavery, it will not be primarily because of our superior technology. It will be primarily because we value human beings, and because the free man can outproduce the oppressed man.

No danger could be greater than to concentrate so blindly upon building up our military strength that we neglected and impoverished the ultimate sources of that strength. Three examples will illustrate this principle.

First, we cannot afford in the immediate future to devote as large a part of our resources to the improvement of health services and facilities as we had planned to do in normal peacetime. But we cannot maintain a sound base for whatever military mobilization may be needed in the months or years ahead, if we let sickness and inadequate health standards continue to take their heavy toll. We must devote somewhat more of our resources toward improving the health of the general public. Whether the children of today will be the soldiers or civilians of tomorrow, they must grow to a strong and healthy maturity.

Second, we cannot in the immediate future find the materials and manpower to build as many new schools and provide as many new teachers as we had planned to do in prosperous peacetime. But whether the youth of today is to become a soldier or a civilian citizen tomorrow, he must receive the general education for citizenship and the technical training which a modern army, a modern factory, and a modern farm all require.

Third, we cannot expect in the immediate future to achieve all of the expansion of social security which we had planned for in prosperous peacetime. But some of the hazards which social security is designed to guard against are increased by the mobilization effort. Increased protection against these hazards will make the mobilization effort more effective. In addition, the expansion of some contributory social security programs

can be an important factor in meeting the stabilization problems we will face during this period, because their immediate effect would be anti-inflationary.

In these three matters, we should give vigorous attention to meeting human needs in such a way as to increase our economic and military strength.

A strong America must be strong throughout.

We must work with our allies in the common cause

To meet the present danger, we must help to strengthen our allies, and they must help to strengthen us.

The effort must be made by the community of free nations, working together, and contributing their common strength in accordance with their ability to do so. As the single most powerful member of the community of free nations, our country has the special responsibility of leadership. We must help other free nations to do their share effectively.

In two world wars, this country has been spared the ravages of war on its own soil. Partly as a consequence, the United States has grown stronger, while some of the other free nations have become relatively weaker. Under these circumstances, it would be wrong for us to shrink from bearing a larger part of the burden now. We are able to bear it. We must bear it.

Since the Korean outbreak we have sharply shifted the emphasis in our economic assistance programs toward supporting the defense programs of the free countries associated with us, and we have greatly enlarged our military assistance program.

There is no water-tight distinction between military assistance and economic assistance. Our friends abroad need both. For their military efforts to be strong, their economies must be strong. When we contribute to their military strength, we leave more of their own resources free to improve their economic strength. When we contribute to their economic strength, we leave more of their own resources free to build up their military strength. The relationship between the two types of assistance should be determined realistically on grounds of efficiency, and not by arbitrary labels.

The programs of economic assistance thus far undertaken have added greatly to the strength of other nations friendly to us— nations believing in freedom and justice. This gain could be dissipated, if the military build-up which they must now undertake should weaken their economies.

The close connection between a nation's economy and its military efforts makes it impossible for peoples to be allies on one front and strangers on other fronts. When we join together for military purposes, we must also cooperate for economic purposes. When we consider jointly the distribution of armed forces, we must consider cooperatively the use of strategic economic assets.

In this whole process of cooperation, the strongest must do the most, but all must do their part. While our resources are great, they are not unlimited. As we make a portion of our resources available for use by others, we expect them to use this aid well and efficiently in the common purpose. In addition, our aid will enable them in many cases to increase their production, for their use and ours, of materials which we do not have, or do not have in sufficient quantity.

GOVERNMENT ECONOMIC POLICIES

The actions of the Government are being redirected to meet the overriding demands of national security. The Budget I shall transmit next week provides only for urgent needs for Government activities and services in this defense period. Many Government programs are being sharply curtailed. The

departments and agencies of Government are moving rapidly ahead with their part in the defense effort, and deferring wherever possible any work which is not immediately necessary.

The same principle should guide the Congress in enacting legislation at this time. We must all put first things first.

Certain immediate tasks will confront the Congress at this session, as it enacts the legislation necessary to carry us forward. I mentioned these briefly in my Message on the State of the Union earlier this week. Some of them are discussed more fully in this Economic Report, and in the Budget Message to follow. In a number of cases, however, details are still being worked out, and I shall transmit recommendations in later special messages.

The first priority, of course, attaches to the support of our own military services and of our combined efforts, with other free countries, to build up the strength of the free world. In both cases, we are concen· trating on the urgent task of preparing stronger defenses against aggression. At the same time, we are building a foundation for continuous growth in the ability of free men, in our country and elsewhere, to advance the cause of freedom.

Toward these ends, the economic policies of the Government should now be directed.

Expansion of production

Industrial production. Under the Defense Production Act, enacted last September, we have taken the first essential steps to give priority to defense requirements out of current industrial production. In the field of priorities and allocations, where Government action has already been vigorous, steps have already been taken (a) to insure that defense requirements for production materials and facilities are met on schedule; (b) to distribute the remaining available supply

37

of critical materials and products equitably among other users after defense requirements have been satisfied; (c) to provide materials for needed expansion of productive capacities; and (d) to promote conservation of scarce materials and the development of substitutes. The commodities affected have included aluminum, cobalt, cadmium, copper, nickel, rubber, steel, tin, zinc, and other basic materials. Selective rather than general curtailment is now being put into effect, and a comprehensive materials control plan is being prepared for use when necessary. Priorities and allocations powers will have to be renewed by the Congress this year, if our production control program is to be continued. It is, of course, essential that this be done.

In placing orders, the Defense Department and the other agencies concerned are adjusting contracting and subcontracting policies to broaden the supply base and to bring in more small producers. Procurement is being related more closely to geographic availability of manpower, materials, and equipment resources. Procurement cost-price policies are being centered upon efficiency problems. Greater uniformity of standards is being developed for all procurement activities.

In planning and carrying out the military procurement program, the Department of Defense is giving major emphasis to obtaining productive capacity broad enough to support a much larger military procurement program than the one now under way. Thus, the Department is spreading orders among as many contractors as practicable, and tooling-up plants with reserve capacity, so that military procurement can be further enlarged on short notice if necessary.

In addition, we have begun the work of obtaining increased plant capacity in key industries, among them steel and aluminum. Two main types of assistance are now being furnished by the Government to help private industry expand: accelerated amortization under the new tax laws, and long-term Government loans under the Defense Production Act. These aids will help to secure much of the needed expansion.

Under the authorization of the Defense Production Act, Government agencies have received requests for direct loans totaling more than 830 million dollars, and are processing requests for accelerated amortization involving outlays for plant expansions totaling nearly 4 billion dollars. Of those on which approval has already been recommended, 66 from the steel industry alone represent capital outlays of more than 1¼ billion dollars.

Our loan program for expansion of productive capacity and supplies will soon require more funds than have so far been made available. The program will of course need to be continued in operation beyond June 30, 1951, the current expiration date. In addition, our present aid programs will need to be backed up by legislative authority for direct government construction of industrial facilities, in those special cases where private enterprise cannot undertake the job even with the government assistance available.

These and other aspects of our economic mobilization laws are now under review by the Director of Defense Mobilization. After he has completed his investigations, detailed recommendations will be made to the Congress for appropriate revision of the Defense Production Act and other related statutes.

In addition to our efforts to expand industrial capacity, steps are being taken to increase production of essential raw materials, both here and abroad. Through financial aids for exploration and development and long-term expansion loans, authorized under the Defense Production Act, and through our stockpiling and foreign economic aid programs, we are stepping up the production and procurement of critical materials, both at home and abroad.

Iron ore constitutes one of our most serious potential shortages. As the Annual Economic Review points out, we should be receiving large shipments from the new Venezuela and Labrador developments by 1954 or 1955. This is urgently needed to meet the expected decline in ore production from the Lake Superior region. But to avoid extremely high-cost transportation, and hence high-cost steel operations, we should start at once on the St. Lawrence Seaway and Power Project, so that imported iron ore can be shipped efficiently by water to the great steel producing centers of the Middle West.

The St. Lawrence project is vital also to bring in a new source of power for industry in the Northeast. We must have more power, in this and other areas, if we are not to place sharp limits on our industrial capacity.

Agricultural production. Our farms are no less involved in the production effort than our factories and mines. The demand for farm products has increased greatly since the Korean outbreak. Military needs for cotton and wool have risen sharply. Military food requirements are also rising, as more men come into military service. There has been an exceptionally high civilian demand for meats and many other foods, and this is expected to continue.

In the face of these rising demands, we now have low supplies of cotton and wool. Our food supplies, while entirely adequate for the time being, will clearly have to be increased. The Government is moving now to help meet the need for increased production, especially of cotton, corn, wheat, wool, and livestock. Acreage allotments and marketing quotas have been set aside. Price supports at 90 percent of parity have been announced for cotton and wheat for the 1951 crop year. Every effort is being made to bring the new cotton crop to a level 60 percent above that of last year.

Our farms are now more mechanized than ever before. To get out the increased crops, they will need a steady supply of farm machinery and spare parts. Fertilizers will be equally necessary to meet expanding production goals. Our farmers are using much more fertilizer than before the war, and will need still more to get the yields that we are after. Many of the things the farmers need will be in short supply. Farm and industry requirements will have to be balanced very carefully. But we will do our best to see to it that the essential farm needs are met.

Manpower. We cannot produce in industry or agriculture without the trained workers to do the job. As the defense production job speeds up, we will have to be increasingly careful about the distribution and use of the skilled labor we have available. We will have to train more and more new workers who are not now in the labor force. Major emphasis should be upon training and recruitment of unmarried women and married women without young children. Support should be extended to nursery schools as an aid to mothers who want jobs.

Additional shifts and longer hours in some defense industries are being encouraged. Industry hiring standards are being reviewed, to provide suitable jobs for more workers. Arrangements are under study to protect the pension and seniority rights of workers who shift to defense jobs. Health, education, rehabilitation, and training programs are being reshaped to concentrate upon problems of defense workers. Existing housing, community facilities, and service programs are being modified, and construction is being shifted to defense areas.

We are already setting up voluntary labor-management committees to work with the United States Employment Service in the principal defense areas. These committees will help to shift workers into essential industries, and will gain cooperation in installing the most efficient hiring practices and promoting the best use of skilled workers on the job. To provide better protection of workers who leave their communities to take defense jobs in other States, the unemployment insurance system should be improved.

It is now quite clear that, just as in World War II, we will need special legislation to provide housing and community facilities and services for defense workers in areas where adequate quarters are not now available.

We will need to encourage private construction of rental housing in these areas. We will need publicly financed construction of housing and related facilities where private enterprise is unable to handle the job. We will need additional aid to community facilities and services in defense production centers. The Housing and Home Finance Administrator has submitted recommendations for legislation to accomplish these purposes. I hope that prompt action will be taken by the Congress.

Health services and education

It is clear that we cannot neglect the education and health of our people, without the most serious results for a long-run defense effort. Obviously, we will not now have available the resources to build or staff as many schools and clinics and hospitals in as many places as we hoped to do in normal times. But the quality of essential services must be maintained and improved, as fast as can be managed. This is imperative for the success of the defense job.

It is not enough to train people as workers—or as soldiers. They have to be healthy enough to get a job and do it effectively. Right now, sickness is keeping about a million workers off the job every day. Right now, failure to meet health standards is making about a quarter of our young men unavailable for military service. During World War II, about six million men were rejected by the armed services for physical or mental disabilities.

We cannot afford this waste of manpower, our most vital resource. As a first step, we must obtain more doctors, more dentists, and more nurses. The growing needs of the armed forces, piled on top of civilian needs, threaten the most dangerous shortages unless prompt action is taken by the Congress.

At the same time, we must expand our local public health services. They are essential to our civil defenses, and to the maintenance of safe health standards in our growing production centers.

As we move into a period when we will have an urgent need for all our trained men and women, we must face the fact that nothing can make up for faulty basic education in our primary and secondary schools. This is as true for the men in military service, as for the factory worker or the farm hand.

Our public school system faces the greatest crisis in its history. More than ever before, we need positive action by the Federal Government to help the States meet their educational tasks. We simply cannot afford to let overcrowding, or lack of equipment or staff impair the basic education of our young people.

Under legislation passed last year, the Federal Government is stepping up its aid to school districts overburdened as a result of Federal activities. But special aid of this type to particular school districts will not come anywhere near meeting the general crisis which exists. Therefore, it is vital that the Congress act now to give the States general aid for school maintenance and operation.

Economic stabilization

The Government has been moving ahead in several ways to stabilize the cost of living and hold down inflation.

Taxation. We should make it the first principle of economic and fiscal policy in these times to maintain a balanced budget, and to finance the cost of national defense on a "pay-as-we-go" basis.

The Congress is to be commended upon the successful completion of two vitally important pieces of tax legislation since the middle of the calendar year 1950. But it was commonly acknowledged that these were only the first steps. We must now, as rapidly as possible, take the next step, and it must be a very big step, in view of the size of the new defense funds which have necessarily been appropriated and the required additions to these funds which will be set forth more fully in the Budget Message. Legislation should be enacted, at this session of the Congress, to increase taxes by very much more than they were increased by the last two major tax bills which the Congress enacted.

These new taxes are required to finance the defense effort; and to help keep total spending within the capacity of current production, so that inflation does not reduce the purchasing power of the defense budget, reduce the real value of people's savings, generate speculative buying and hoarding, and impede essential production. The real economic cost of this defense effort is that we must work harder, reduce consumption, and forego improvements in farm, business, and household equipment. This cost cannot be put off into the future. It must be paid by the people now, one way or another, and it should be paid through taxation, in the manner consciously determined by the Congress and not by the uncontrolled and inequitable incidence of inflation.

The new tax increases, now required, must press harder upon every source of available revenue. Corporations should pay much higher taxes. Individuals should pay much higher taxes. Excise taxes should be higher and more extensive. Many loopholes in the tax laws should be closed. In the near future, after further consultation with legislative leaders, new tax proposals will be transmitted to the Congress.

Taxation must be supplemented by greatly increased saving. Every dollar saved means a dollar less of inflationary price pressure. The alternative to saving is not buying more goods now, because more goods are not now available. The saving will give a nest egg with which to buy the goods at a later time when they again become plentiful. The alternatives to more saving are either more taxes or inflation.

Savings help most in the defense effort, and do the most to hold down inflation, when they are invested in Government bonds. The Treasury will continue its policy of reducing the amount of debt held by banks and placing the maximum proportion of Government securities in the hands of the public, particularly individuals. The savings bond program supports this goal and encourages saving.

Credit controls. Controls over business and consumer credit also help hold down inflation.

Regulations W and X, issued by the Federal Reserve Board, have established higher down payments and shorter repayment periods for those who buy durable goods and new one- and two-family houses on credit. Multifamily housing is now being brought under Regulation X. As the detailed requirements for the defense program and other vital purposes become clearer, it may be necessary to make further changes in these regulations. These regulations are well suited to help deal with moderate reductions in supply. If circumstances force acute reductions, more direct measures will be needed to assure equitable distribution. In the meantime, the authority to control housing credit through Regulation X should be enlarged by the Congress to include credit for the purchase of existing homes exempt under the present law.

The Federal Reserve Board has also taken steps to restrain excessive bank lending, by raising bank reserve requirements and allowing short-term interest rates to rise.

Price and wage controls. We must use direct controls, as well as these tax and credit measures, in order to deal with the problem of inflation.

In the case of prices and wages, considerable work has been done. In addition to the mandatory order affecting automobile prices, substantial progress has already been made through negotiations towards securing effective price stabilization in such basic materials as steel, copper, lead, zinc, and certain basic industrial chemicals. Negotiations to secure effective price stabilization are under way with producers of other basic products. A number of regulations for mandatory action are in preparation.

We must achieve general stability as rapidly as possible, and hold it for the duration of the present emergency. This will require the broad extension of price and wage controls to hold down the upward spiral. The staffs to apply broader controls are now being rapidly gathered.

In the case of prices, the general policy must be to hold the price line with utmost vigor, as the instances are rare indeed where further price increases are needed, either to stimulate production or to provide adequate profit incentives. In these rare cases, some price adjustments subsequent to stabilization may become necessary to stimulate vital production.

It is my confident belief that price adjustments, after stabilization, will not be only in an upward direction. In many industrial lines, extensive additional production, made possible in many instances by military orders added to civilian orders, will result in lower costs, which can be passed on both to civilian buyers and to the Defense Department.

To prevent excessive speculation in farm products, and wide fluctuations in their prices, the Department of Agriculture should be granted authority to control speculative trading and to strengthen its regulation of commodity exchanges.

Price and wage stabilization must both be undertaken, because of the economic connection between prices and wages. It follows from this that neither price action nor wage action can be decided upon in isolation. The decisions must be reconciled. They must be subject to central direction. But it does not follow that prices and wages are precisely similar, or can be treated identically. Prices are only one factor in the incomes of business, which may rise or fall independently of prices. But wages are the very livelihood of millions of families. This makes wage stabilization the more difficult part of the task. But it must be undertaken if prices are to be stabilized.

A more rapid rise of total wages available for spending than of the production of goods which workers can buy will not make more goods available, but rather will add to inflationary pressures. Since the amount of goods available for consumers cannot be increased in the near future, and many types of goods must be severely contracted, the objective should be to limit correspondingly total spending of wages. Strong tax and savings programs are required, but stabilization of wage rates is also necessary. This is particularly necessary because, even with no wage rate increases, there will be an expanding volume of total wages. Hundreds of thousands of new workers will be employed, and hours of work will be longer. Moreover, there are a few kinds of situations where adjustments in wage rates will be necessary and desirable. But this should be done only upon a clear showing of necessity in exceptional circumstances. The predominant general rule should be to achieve stable wage rates until the flow of consumer goods can be increased.

It would be impossible to achieve lasting wage stabilization without holding the line on the cost of living. This makes it all the more important to stabilize the price level. Unless this line is held, it will not be practical to avoid some "cost of living adjustments" in wages in some cases. However, there are many groups which could not be protected in this way. And to extend such adjustments without limitation, even in all those cases where it could be done, would add to the process of wages chasing prices and prices chasing wages. The only way out of this dilemma is to stabilize the cost of living, and to do it quickly.

Wage stabilization also involves the problem of incentives. Without incentives, it would be harder to sustain longer hours of work in defense industries, and to spur on workers toward their participation in efforts to improve productivity. As we look forward to years of constantly increasing effort to strengthen our economy, this problem of incentives cannot be overlooked. Yet the peacetime increases in wages, which normally provide incentives, would under current conditions add to inflationary forces. Consideration should be given to the suggestion that, where some wage adjustments become necessary over the long pull to provide incentives, the increased potential spending power should be diverted from the actual spending stream until inflationary pressures

become less serious. Various constructive proposals may be developed to obtain this deferred effect. Wage adjustments related to increased social security contributions would be one method. Other effective savings programs should also be considered.

I firmly believe that effective wage stabilization must draw heavily upon the experience and viewpoint of workers and employers with practical experience. That is the principle underlying the Wage Stabilization Board. The Board is to be commended for its policy of consultation with representatives of labor, management, and the public. I earnestly trust that a sound and fair wage stabilization policy will quickly result. Such a policy will provide the best foundation for effective wage stabilization in detail. The principles which I have outlined can be the starting point for a wage stabilization policy which will receive the cooperation of those who would be affected and which will serve the best interests of the Nation in this emergency.

In the interest of economic stabilization all groups should consider what they receive before taxation. Of course, heavier taxes will make it harder for everybody. But for any group to seek to adjust its income upward, to counteract the higher taxes which the defense program is making necessary, would tend to relieve that group from its share in the cost of achieving national security.

I am sure that every group will be willing to accept the necessary sacrifices in this emergency, if the whole stabilization program is fair and equitable. Effective price and wage controls, much higher taxes on business profits, along with many other restrictions which will affect the whole population, are all aspects of a comprehensive stabilization program in which everyone will do his part.

It is already plain that the present rent

control law has been made obsolete, in the light of the necessary curtailment in the rate of housing construction and the current inflationary pressures. Since rents are such a key element in the cost of living, I recommend that the Congress extend and strengthen the rent control law.

International economic programs

Our program of military and economic aid for the strengthening of the community of free nations, including our programs for underdeveloped areas, are of vital importance. They are closely related to other aspects of our foreign economic policy. The defense program increases the importance of strategic raw materials, and we are already working with other free nations to increase the supply of these materials, and to distribute them fairly. We should take cooperative action with the free nations, to make sure that critical materials are used to strengthen the common defense of freedom, and are not diverted to other purposes. In a short time, I shall send to the Congress detailed recommendations on our international economic programs.

Use of export controls and allocations will enable the United States to carry out more effectively its part of international allocations agreements, and to distribute more efficiently other commodities in short supply.

The power to control exports, now scheduled to expire June 30th, should be extended.

International trade policies should be adjusted to joint requirements. While the defense effort will require a wide increase in trade controls, a large part of the world's trade will continue to be conducted in normal channels. The common defense objective can be furthered by the reduction of tariffs, quotas, and other trade barriers. To this end, the Trade Agreements Act should be extended, our customs laws and procedures should be simplified, and the import tax on copper should again be waived.

SUMMARY OF ECONOMIC DEVELOPMENTS IN 1950

By June 1950, the economy had almost fully recovered from the mild recession of the previous year. Employment and production were high, and prices were rising. The anticipated expansion of our defense program, following the Korean outbreak, led to still further increases in employment and production. It created strong inflationary pressures.

In this situation, many economic indicators reached record highs, and most of them are still rising. Higher employment, longer hours of work, and overtime payments raised wages and salaries and swelled the already high demand of consumers. On all fronts, strong demand raised prices, and in some shortage areas the price advance was rapid. Increased volume at higher prices boosted business profits. The obvious need for greater productive capacity stimulated business investment. Rising living costs and high business profits led to increasingly successful efforts to obtain wage increases.

The record levels of employment, production, and business investment have demonstrated the vigor of our economy. But the spiraling rise in prices, wages, and profits is a warning that inflation endangers our economic prospects and our defense efforts.

Civilian employment averaged almost 60.0 million persons in 1950, compared with 58.7 million in 1949. The gain in nonagricultural employment was about 1.8 million, but farm jobs declined by about 500 thousand. Employment increased steadily throughout the year, except for a small seasonal drop in the fall months. At the end of the year, employment was at an all-time record for December.

44

Unemployment, after reaching a peak of 4.7 million persons in February, dropped markedly through most of the year. It reached a low of 1.9 million in October, and then rose slightly in the last two months of the year. At the end of 1950, only 3.6 percent of the labor force was unemployed. This is near a practical minimum for a peacetime economy, but is not irreducible under present conditions.

Production of goods and services as a whole in 1950 was 7 percent greater than in 1949. This was a record for any postwar year, and apparently was close to the record reached in World War II. In the fourth quarter of 1950, total production was 10 percent higher than for the year 1949.

The physical production of goods alone (not including services) was 11 percent greater than in 1949, despite a 2 percent drop in agricultural output. Industrial production increased 14 percent. Gains were especially marked in the case of durable goods. More steel was produced in 1950 than in any previous year. The automobile industry operated at a record rate during most of the year. Electric power rose 13 percent over 1949. Construction, measured in physical terms, reached an all-time high, and averaged 17 percent above 1949.

Prices moved upward throughout 1950, the pace of the advance increasing sharply after the Korean developments at midyear. Wholesale prices in December were at an all-time high, 10.9 percent above the June level and 15.4 percent above December 1949. The price increases were not limited to a few commodities, nor to a few groups. For a few weeks after the Korean outbreak, farm and food prices rose sharply. The rise in industrial prices, while at first less spectacular, was steady and persistent. At times, the violent gyrations in prices of imported raw materials have been in the spotlight. But now the rise in wholesale prices has been quite general, affecting all major categories of goods.

Consumers' prices rose over 6 percent during 1950, the major part of the rise occurring in the latter half of the year. They ended the year at a record level. Rising living costs absorbed a considerable part of the gains in consumer incomes.

Wages and salaries and other labor income rose continuously in 1950, reflecting wage rate increases, longer hours of work, and increased employment. By the fourth quarter, they had reached a record high of 155.9 billion dollars, 16 percent above the level a year earlier. Weekly earnings in all manufacturing industries rose from $54.43 in November 1949 to $62.06 in November 1950, a gain of 14 percent.

Wage increases were widespread and substantial in the second half of the year, being accelerated by a continued rise in the cost of living and by expectations of wage and price controls.

Profits of American business, before taxes, exceeded all records in 1950, reaching 40.2 billion dollars, or 46 percent above the level of 1949. They attained a peak annual rate of 48.0 billion dollars in the fourth quarter. The previous peak rate was 35.3 billion in the third quarter of 1948. The higher profits reflected increased output, greater sales, and higher prices.

Corporate profits after taxes, and net incomes of unincorporated business, also made new records. The net income of farm proprietors rose in the latter half of the year. By the fourth quarter, it was 9.4 percent above the fourth quarter of 1949, although 25 percent below the postwar peak in the second quarter of 1948.

Money and credit expanded with the growth of the Nation's output and the rise in prices. Many components of business and consumer debt reached new highs.

The housing boom stepped up the growth

in residential mortgage debt, from an 11 percent increase during 1949 to 17 percent during 1950. Consumer installment credit increased 22 percent in the first nine months of 1950, compared to a rise of 15 percent in the same period of 1949. Government policies helped restrain the rate of consumer credit expansion during the last quarter of the year.

Total privately-held bank deposits and currency increased by 6.4 billion dollars, reaching 176 billion by the end of the year.

Personal income, at an annual rate of 233 billion dollars in the final quarter of 1950, was 14 percent greater than a year earlier, and more than 8 percent above the second quarter of 1950. Although the annual rate of personal taxes increased by over 2 billion dollars from the first half to the second half of the year, personal income after taxes rose by 11 billion. The rise in prices partly offset this increase, but there was a gain of about 2 percent in consumer purchasing power.

Consumption expenditures in the second half of the year far surpassed those of any previous period, nearing an annual rate of 200 billion dollars. The increase was especially marked in the purchase of durable goods. A substantial part of the increased consumer expenditures was a reflection of higher prices.

Personal net saving dropped from a rate of 6.5 percent of disposable income in the first half of the year to a rate of 3.1 percent in the third quarter, reflecting the first wave of post-Korean buying. Then it rose to 6.4 percent in the final quarter.

Private domestic investment in construction, equipment, and additions to inventory rose very sharply, increasing 19 percent from the first half of 1950 to the second half, and increasing 67 percent from the second half of 1949 to the second half of 1950. In the second half of 1950, this investment reached an all-time record of 53 billion dollars at a seasonally adjusted annual rate. The increase during 1950 was most marked in the case of producers' durable equipment.

The investment trend was already upward before the Korean attack led to an expansion of the defense program, and to a rapid further rise in investment. Private and Government surveys indicate that business plans to spend more for plant and equipment in 1951 than in 1950.

The resumption of inventory accumulation during the first half of 1950 was a factor contributing to business recovery. Economic developments made it difficult for business to build up inventories immediately after midyear; the strong demand forced some reduction in the third quarter. But in the fourth quarter, inventory accumulation was marked.

The use of capital funds by nonfinancial corporations was almost 24 billion dollars above 1949. Three-fifths of these funds were obtained internally from retained earnings and depreciation allowances.

Construction put in place in 1950 was 23 percent higher than for the year 1949, and greater than in any previous year. The sharpest increase was in housing. A peak of 149,000 new dwelling units was started in May, and approximately that level was maintained through August. In the fourth quarter, starts fell sharply, partly as a result of credit restrictions.

International developments greatly stimulated domestic demand and production, but the pressure of foreign purchases lessened. Exports in 1950 were nearly 1.9 billion dollars less than in 1949. The surplus of exports over imports fell from 6.2 billion dollars in 1949 to an annual rate of 3.0 billion in the first half of 1950. An increase in our imports, after we decided to speed up the rebuilding of our defenses, brought this annual rate down to the probably transitory level of 600 million in the second half.

Both the volume and prices of imports increased substantially. In 1950 our export surplus was less than our foreign aid, but this aid declined substantially from the 1949 level.

Government transactions showed a close balance between receipts and expenditures for the year as a whole. Cash receipts increased while expenditures fell in the second half of 1950. After a cash deficit of 4.2 billion dollars (annual rate) in the first half, there was a surplus of 2.9 billion in the second half. But the effect upon business operations of the anticipated increase in the military program more than offset any counterinflationary impact of the cash surplus.

An increase of 1.1 billion dollars in Federal cash receipts from calendar year 1949 to calendar year 1950 was due to higher economic activity, to increased employment tax rates, and to higher withholding tax rates on individuals in the closing months of the year. Collections from corporate income taxes will increase substantially this year, reflecting high profits in 1950 and increased tax rates.

HARRY S. TRUMAN

NOTE: The message and the complete report (241 pp.) are published in "The Economic Report of the President, Transmitted to the Congress January 1951" (Government Printing Office, 1951). As printed above, an illustrative diagram has been deleted.

12 The President's News Conference on the Budget. *January* 13, 1951

THE PRESIDENT. [1.] I want to call your attention particularly to this memo sheet, which sets out as nearly as possible what the budget totals are, and how they are allocated; and there is a statement on the second sheet which explains the situation as well as it can be explained.

The budget this year is larger by a great many billions of dollars, on account of the fact of the defense program that we are trying to implement both here and abroad. The expenditures for local government have been decreased about $1,100 million—as you will see on this sheet—and we are making further efforts to eliminate what we consider unnecessary expenditures. But when a person goes to work and makes wild statements about how many billions of dollars you can take out of the budget, you can be morally certain that he knows nothing about the figures in the budget. [*Laughter*]

If you remember last year, we published a small summary of the budget, and explained exactly where the funds came from, and

where they went. We will have that same booklet out in about 2 weeks, for your information and guidance.

I don't mind people being honestly against what I may believe to be the right thing, but I would like for them, when they discuss the thing, to at least know half as much about it as I do.

Now, if you want to ask any questions, I will be glad to try to answer them.

[2.] Q. Mr. President, on page M26 (p. 76),[1] about the middle of the page, third paragraph down, you say, "In addition, the Department of Defense is constructing additional plants and facilities to produce military items not ordinarily produced by private firms for the civilian market." I am wondering if you would elaborate on that, to indicate what type of materials and what

[1] Page references in parentheses, throughout this news conference, indicate where the subjects referred to may be found in the Budget Message as printed herein (Item 13); all other references correspond to the page numbers in the Budget as published in House Document 17 (82d Cong., 1st sess.).

type of plants that refers to?

THE PRESIDENT. That refers principally to the expansion of plants that will have to produce this defense supply. The Defense itself, under the general defense appropriation, has authority to create whatever production is necessary to meet the emergency. That is what that means.

[3.] Q. Mr. President, before we get started on this, on M7 (p. 63) that chart recommended new obligational authority for 1952. Will you not explain just what that is?

Director Lawton: It is the appropriations and other authorities to incur obligations and to enter into contracts, to issue orders that are provided in this budget, and in the legislation proposed under the budget for each agency of Government. It is the authority for the military to order airplanes. It is the authority for the Internal Revenue Bureau to hire personnel to collect taxes— that kind of authority. The difference between that and expenditures is the difference between placing an order and getting delivery on that material later on, at whatever period it comes off the line and payment is made out of the Treasury for that material. It is the difference between ordering a thing and receiving and paying for it—which may, in the case of some types of equipment, be as much as 18 months to 2 years.

THE PRESIDENT. It is that same old argument between the anticipated budget and the cash budget.

Q. Let's not get into that.

THE PRESIDENT. I thought maybe I could get you on that. [*Laughter*]

Q. I would like to know how you figure this—I do not understand how you make a commitment for, say, fiscal year 1953 as well as 1954?

Director Lawton: You are making commitments in 1952 for some goods that may be delivered in 1953 or 1954, and paid for.

Q. And paid for?

Director Lawton: When delivered.

Q. How do you figure it, because I cannot understand why you have got interest the same amount?

Director Lawton: Interest is a purely cash appropriation. It is an indefinite appropriation of as much as may be necessary. There is no fixed amount set beforehand. It is set by basic law, that you pay whatever interest is due on bonds, and it is a cash expenditure again—interest upon cash. You don't have to get an advance appropriation for interest.

Secretary Snyder: That estimate is on conditions as they are right now.

Director Lawton: That's right.

Q. What I am trying to figure is, we are making expenditures of 71.6 in fiscal 1952. Those are actual cash expenditures?

Director Lawton: Cash out of the Treasury, yes, sir.

Q. Now, during 1952 we will commit ourselves for $94 billion more, is that correct?

Director Lawton: Not more. You will commit yourself for $94 billion, out of which will be paid out—represented by the $71 billion. The 71 billion represents commitments made in prior years and in the current year. And there are tables in the budget that will show the distinction between the amount of cash out of current appropriations and out of prior year appropriations.

Q. Commit some 70 billion more?

Secretary Snyder: Not necessarily.

THE PRESIDENT. That is an estimate.

Q. How much do we commit?

Director Lawton: The carryover will be nearly 60 billion.

Q. Is that where you get your 140 in the Economic Message?

Director Lawton: The 140 in the Economic Message are the items shown in here for the 1951 and 1952 obligations, and if you take that memo tablet, it is just about the total of the major national security programs that is shown in the first two columns.

Q. This is the total of new appropriations in the 1952 fiscal year; that is, the $94 billion?

Director Lawton: 94 billion is the total new obligational authority, whether it comes from appropriations or borrowing authority, such as the Export-Import Bank provisions in here, or anything else—anything that can authorize the Government to make commitments.

Q. Are there many in the new 1952 bill?

Director Lawton: Many that the Congress will have to be obligated in the 1952 bill.

Q. Is that carryover from the 1951 to 1952?

Director Lawton: No, at the end of 1952.

Q. At the end of 1952.

Director Lawton: It says in 1951 and 1952 some 1951 funds will still carry over some expenditures into 1952—longtime procurement.

Q. What is the total of that carryover?

Director Lawton: About 60.

Q. Paid in subsequent years?

Director Lawton: In subsequent years.

Q. Ten billion, nine in supplementals in sight for the remainder of this fiscal year, as I gather?

Director Lawton: That's right.

THE PRESIDENT. That's correct.

Q. That carryover, then, that reduces actual expenditures below what is given here?

Director Lawton: No, sir.

THE PRESIDENT. No, that is in addition.

Director Lawton: That is in addition, yes.

Q. Where is that 60 billion shown?

Director Lawton: It is a sum that you would have to get from taking the obligational authority, shown in the table in the budget, and deducting from it the expenditures in the 2 years.

THE PRESIDENT. That is a good exercise in arithmetic for you.

Q. How much?

Q. What shows the 60 billions?

THE PRESIDENT. It doesn't show it as a separate figure. You have got to take the authorizations and figure out how much are going to be paid for in 1951 and 1952. Then, what is left of it will go into this 60 billion.

Director Lawton: Just as an example, the obligational authority in 1951 is $87½ billion, present and proposed. You will spend in 1951, 47, which leaves a 40 billion carryover to start with.

Q. I get it.

Q. How much of the 71.6 for spending will require congressional action by appropriations for obligations?

THE PRESIDENT. All of it will. All the authority either has or will be authorized by the Congress.

Q. Yes, sir.

THE PRESIDENT. Can't spend money without an authorization.

Secretary Snyder: He meant this year.

Q. How much more will Congress have to——

THE PRESIDENT. Maybe I didn't understand your question. Ask that again.

Q. I know some part of that 71.6 is covered by past congressional action, but I wonder how much of it is dependent upon future congressional action?

Director Lawton: I would think that approximately half of it, at least, will be out of 1952 appropriations.

Q. Half has to be authorized?

THE PRESIDENT. Yes.

Director Lawton: At least. I can give you that exact figure, if you will call later on. It is in here—in the tables.

Q. Mr. President, since this carryover at the end of fiscal 1952 will be approximately 60 billion, can we figure, then, that the budget in 1953 and 1954 will be substantially higher, cashwise, than this 71 billion?

THE PRESIDENT. I imagine that they will be. That is cash now. I don't know that it is in the authorization because we can't tell how the developments will work out. That is anybody's guess.

[4.] Q. Mr. President, I found in this budget last night, but I cannot locate it now, what appeared to me to be a third deficiency appropriation of $10 billion. Is that correct?

THE PRESIDENT. That is correct. It is in there.

[5.] Q. Mr. President, on page M17 (p. 70), under stockpiling, you indicate that you will ask for an additional supplemental appropriation of $820 million for the current fiscal year?

THE PRESIDENT. That is for 1952—1952.

Q. Oh! Then on page 266, under Strategic and Critical Materials, you talk about asking for a supplemental of about a billion dollars. The question is, are those references to the same request, or are they separate requests?

THE PRESIDENT. I will have to look and see. The billion, so I am informed by the Budget Director, are supplementals that went into this last session, and the 800 goes to the 1952.

Q. Well, now, is that——

THE PRESIDENT. Give this fellow a chance, he has been trying to get up for 10 minutes.

[6.] Q. On page M49 (p. 94), it says, "No other loans will be made under this program," referring to the loans to educational institutions, "until the outlook for college enrollment shows a clear need for such housing." Yet I think there is 36 million in the budget for 1952 for that purpose. Will you explain that difference?

THE PRESIDENT. You will have to ask that question again.

Q. In your message on page M49 (p. 94), at the top, in regard to those loans for educational institutions for housing, it says, "No other loans will be made under this program until the outlook for college enrollment shows a clear need for such housing."

THE PRESIDENT. That means just what it says.

Q. 36 million for this purpose?

Mr. Staats: It will be necessary to have funds under this program for defense programs, but it is limited strictly to that.

Q. That is what it is for?

THE PRESIDENT. Strictly for defense.

[7.] Q. Is the third deficiency included in the expenditures for fiscal 1951?

THE PRESIDENT. Those amounts that are going to be spent in 1951 are included.

Q. What I am trying to do, sir, is locate that 10 billion third deficiency in these tables on defense spending.

Director Lawton: That is new obligational authority. There will be very little of it that will be spent. They will be—the orders will be placed before the end of this fiscal year, but very few if any deliveries will be made out of that fund.

Q. What will the actual amount of the appropriation be?

Director Lawton: The appropriation will be 10 for that purpose.

Q. We have now about 43—which I believe is correct—for defense purposes, now appropriated for this fiscal year?

Director Lawton: For the military.

Q. Yes. I am talking about defense—43 billion now appropriated for defense purposes?——

Director Lawton: Yes—yes.

Q. ——for this fiscal year? Then there will be a third deficiency, making that——

Director Lawton: It will be up in the—54.181—that is the figure in this table.

THE PRESIDENT. 54.181—it's on that memo sheet.

Director Lawton: It is included in that. That is the difference between the present appropriations and what we have shown here as the amount that will be appropriated during the fiscal year.

[8.] Q. Revenue estimates—personal income——

Secretary Snyder: May I answer that? The revenue figure that is used in the Budget Message is calculated on the basis of an annual average income to the individual of $245 billion per annum.

Q. What is it now?

Secretary Snyder: The November figure—that is the latest official figure we had—was running a little over $232 billion per annum.

Q. Mr. Secretary, is that a calendar or fiscal year estimate?

Secretary Snyder: That is the estimate that the Department of Commerce puts out every month, you know, but it is for the calendar year, yes.

Q. Mr. Snyder, what was the estimate for the budget in the calendar year?

Secretary Snyder: 221, I believe it was.

THE PRESIDENT. 221 is correct.

[9.] Q. Mr. President, you spoke of taxes several times in the message. Can you say whether it is the idea that the new taxes should take effect at the start of this fiscal year?

THE PRESIDENT. Well, that is a matter for the Congress to decide. I hope that they will take a position as soon as they possibly can.

Q. Could that possibly mean that you might recommend starting as of the first of the calendar year?

THE PRESIDENT. I shall recommend that they start as quickly as the Congress will agree to have it done. I hope it will be the first of the year.

[10.] Q. Mr. President, referring to receipts, on the very first page (p. 61), it shows estimated receipts for 1951 about 44 billion, and that estimated receipts for 1952

are 55 billion. That shows an increase of about 11 billion. Now, the new taxes that we have had since then were approximately $5 billion on personal income, and an estimated 3 billions on excess profits, which would make 8 billion. I presume that this is because of inflation and expansion in the——

Secretary Snyder: No, increased income.

THE PRESIDENT. Increased income, not inflation.

Q. I was about to add that. The Secretary didn't give me a chance.

THE PRESIDENT. The receipts go up automatically every year after income.

Secretary Snyder: With the rate of increase and the anticipated defense burden of spending that comes from.

Q. Getting back to the receipts, where it says 40 billion, the increase would be 7 billion, is that right?

Secretary Snyder: It is a conservative estimate, we think.

Q. Mr. President——

THE PRESIDENT. [11.] Give Joe Fox [2] a chance. What is it, Joe?

Q. On M11 (p. 66), Mr. President, is it correct to assume that the new tax figure will be 16.5?

THE PRESIDENT. What's that, Joe?

Q. On M11—I say is it correct——

THE PRESIDENT. I know what you are talking about. I will answer that question in my tax message, Joe. [*Laughter*]

[12.] Q. Mr. President, you said a minute ago that you hoped that taxes would take effect the first of the year. Did you mean retroactively to the first—1951?

THE PRESIDENT. The excess profits tax was a retroactive tax—December 1st or first of the year, if I remember correctly. It is a precedent that can be followed.

---

[2] Joseph A. Fox of the Washington Evening Star.

Q. I would like to know, do you want the tax to take effect on January 1st?

THE PRESIDENT. Yes, I would like to have it take effect on January 1st. That is perfectly plain.

Q. Does that apply to the individual plan?

THE PRESIDENT. That applies to anything that is made, I hope.

[13.] Q. Mr. President, is there anything in here for added interest on bonds that aren't used that are not turned in, to encourage people not to sell their bonds?

Secretary Snyder: Well that—number one—Congress will have to act on that, and issue an order for the extension period. That is what you are referring to, on maturing bonds—the E-bonds that begin to mature in May. This year, there will be, I believe, 1,100 million of E-bonds that will mature in the calendar year 1951. If we should decide to ask for an automatic extension of these bonds, we will have to go to Congress to get that authority. There is no figure in here to cover that interest that will be involved there. It is "bottomed" on maintaining the outstanding date, so if they are on those bonds it will be on some others, don't you see? So it actually is covered in here on the basis of our present indebtedness.

Q. Has that decision been made?

Secretary Snyder: Not yet.

[14.] Q. Mr. President, I would like to ask you a question that I think the so called economy bloc in Congress will ask you. On page M6 (p. 62), you say, about this budget, "It reflects reductions in other expenditures, in order to divert a maximum of resources to the overriding requirements of national security." I assume you mean nondefense spending? Now, in this little pamphlet here, in the middle of the page, total major fixed and other charges for 1952, it shows a reduction of 3.21 billion—total 1.82. Is that what you claim you are reducing?

THE PRESIDENT. Turn back to the first page, and you will see right in the middle of the page exactly what I am claiming. It is 1,082 million—that is correct.

Q. That is what I wanted to be sure of, that being the difference between the 20 billion and the 21.66, is that it?

Q. Where does that go?

Q. Where is that figure?

THE PRESIDENT. In the center of this sheet.

Secretary Snyder: You have to learn arithmetic. Subtract the right figure from the left, and there it is.

THE PRESIDENT. Right in the center of this mimeographed page it's a little bit different—you will find a figure over in the right-hand corner of 19,084 million. Next to that, you will find 20 billion, 166. If you subtract that figure from that figure, you will get the figure I gave you.

[15.] Q. On page M41 (p. 88), right in the middle of the page, "To avoid the unnecessary accumulation and loss of perishable agricultural commodities, legislation is needed to permit direct payments to producers, in lieu of market price supports to Government purchases." Is that the Brannan farm plan?

THE PRESIDENT. That is the Brannan plan. That states it very clearly. It took you a long time to dig that one out! [*Laughter*]

[16.] Q. I would like to ask if—it isn't in this budget—you said you were going to cut back on nonessentials. It seems to me that you have got everything in here that you have asked for before, perhaps?

THE PRESIDENT. 11½ billion is set out there as having been cut out of this budget, in asking for appropriations for the things that are not directly considered necessary for defense.

Q. Can you pinpoint those?

THE PRESIDENT. Yes, I will pinpoint them for you—133 items. If you will ask the Budget, I will make a list of them. Forty percent of the items in the budget have been cut back—*forty-two percent.*

Secretary Snyder: Forty-two percent and 135 items, isn't that it?

THE PRESIDENT. Forty-two percent and 135 items. And you can have a list of those items from the Budget.

Q. That totals a billion, .08?

THE PRESIDENT. That's right.

Q. Can you give us an example right now?

THE PRESIDENT. I can't think right off. I will give you a list, and then you will have it, then there won't be any inaccuracies in the total. I can't memorize all those things, because I had to pass on every single item individually. A stack of papers that high— [*indicating*]—I will let you go through them, if you like. [*Laughter*]

[17.] Q. I would like to get back to Joe Fox's question, on page M6 (p. 62).

THE PRESIDENT. Yes, I know where it is.

Q. "I shall shortly recommend an increase in tax revenues, in the conviction that we must attain a balanced budget to provide a sound financial basis for what may be an extended period of very high defense expenditures." Now isn't it inescapable that you have to ask for 16 billion plus?

THE PRESIDENT. Not necessarily. It may be for 20 plus before we get through.

Q. You mean you may ask for 20 plus?

THE PRESIDENT. I am going to ask whatever it takes. I can't set that figure until the Treasury finds out exactly what it will be, then I will ask for it.

Q. Down 16, but it may be more?

THE PRESIDENT. According to this budget, it would.

Q. I would like to know what the administration's policy is?

THE PRESIDENT. I am going to tell you in the message. I am not going to tell you this morning.

Q. That has not been decided?

THE PRESIDENT. No, the figure has not been decided. But I have made it perfectly plain that I don't see any sense in increasing the Federal national debt when we have got a prosperous country such as we have now, and we ought to pay as we go. I have always thought that. I thought that in World War II.

Q. You have insisted on a pay-as-we-go policy, paying for this program out of current revenues?

THE PRESIDENT. That is as far as we can, yes.

Q. Whatever it is, the policy still stands to pay for the whole program out of current revenue?

THE PRESIDENT. That is my policy—always has been.

Q. That might result in an increase in taxation of 60 percent?

THE PRESIDENT. I can't give you the figure, but I will give it to you very carefully when I write this message.

Q. Assuming everything going up in proportion, that would be what it would be.

THE PRESIDENT. Well, you make your figure from the figures that are before you.

Q. In view of the uncertainty as to military programs, and the rate of military procurement, it is possible that if procurement does not move as rapidly as is planned, the request might be less that 60?

THE PRESIDENT. That is correct. That is the reason I cannot give you the exact figure now, but I am going to try to give you as nearly an accurate figure as I can.

Q. Can you give us a range?

THE PRESIDENT. No, I won't. You make your own range. You have got the figures there before you.

[18.] Q. Mr. President, at your press conference the other day, you said you might ask for legislation on food prices. You didn't say the Brannan plan. Now, is it the Brannan plan?

THE PRESIDENT. It has no connection with that at all—it has no connection with that at all. This is the consumer food price that I am talking about.

Q. Doesn't the Brannan plan include keeping prices low to consumers?

THE PRESIDENT. Yes, it does, but that has nothing to do with price control matters. That is a matter that will require legislation. It was purposely examined by this last Congress.

Q. That is different from food subsidies?

THE PRESIDENT. Yes—entirely different.

Q. Is your food subsidy in here?

THE PRESIDENT. No, it is not.

[19.] Q. Do you expect to revise these figures, including the military figure, before you send up those facts?

THE PRESIDENT. No, I do not. No, I do not.

Q. 16.5?

THE PRESIDENT. No, I do not intend to do any revising. This budget is going up just as it is, but we have got to examine the whole situation as thoroughly and completely as we can, and then go up there with an intelligent message, and try to get action on it. That is the object.

[20.] Q. Mr. President, would you comment on the statement of such Senators as George and Millikin, that tax increases of the magnitude you propose would wreck the economy?

THE PRESIDENT. I don't agree with them, that's all the comment I will make. I think this economy can stand what we are doing here. I wouldn't make the statements I do if I didn't believe that. And I have every assurance from the people on whom I rely for information, that that is the case.

[21.] Q. Mr. President, do you plan to submit a special message on taxes outlining your recommendations?

THE PRESIDENT. Yes.

Q. Can you say approximately when that will go up?

THE PRESIDENT. As soon as we can get it ready. I hope within the next 30 days.

[22.] Q. Mr. President, does the fact that the budget contains no inclusion of expenditures for farm subsidies and food subsidies mean that we won't have food subsidies in order to keep down the cost of living?

THE PRESIDENT. Not necessarily—not necessarily.

[23.] Q. Mr. President, I would like to ask Mr. Lawton, if I may, about those 135 items. Do you have them mimeographed and available in printed form?

Director Lawton: No. They are in the tables here, but we haven't got it mimeographed yet. We can identify the particular items.

THE PRESIDENT. We will try and have them all put together and mimeographed for you at a later date, but we can't do it between now and Monday.

[24.] Q. Mr. President, getting back to the balanced budget, you are arriving at your 20 billion figure by anticipating 1952 estimated deficits?

THE PRESIDENT. This budget is based on an anticipated deficit of 16.1 or 2, I forget what the figure is.

Q. A deficit of 16.5 for 1952? Is that where you arrive at your 20 billion figure?

THE PRESIDENT. No, I said it might be anywhere between 16 and 20. I am not going on record on that. I will give you that in the message. You can ask all those questions you want all the way around, and I will answer them in exactly the same way.

Q. Mr. President, depending on how that third supplemental appropriation breakdown is expended in 1951 and 1952, isn't it possible that the deficit for fiscal 1952 will be larger than 16.5 billion?

THE PRESIDENT. I don't think so. These estimates have been very carefully made.

Director Lawton: If you will look at page A15, it indicates how much of 1952 expenditures are out of 1952 authorizations, and how much out of prior years—the same for 1951. It's the total at the bottom.

Q. I don't have that here.

Secretary Snyder: It's in the green book.

Director Lawton: Page A15.

THE PRESIDENT. It's in the green book. The last total on the table.

[25.] Q. Mr. President, in view of the fact that on page 65 you do not show any new appropriations for the ECA, does that indicate that that will be wound up for 1950 current fiscal, June 30th?

THE PRESIDENT. No, they will not. Those appropriations are shown as a defense item—international affairs. You will find it under international affairs.

Q. Has there been any decision whether ECA will be continued beyond June 30th?

THE PRESIDENT. It will have to be continued beyond June 30 positively. We had hoped to wind it up on June 30, but conditions are entirely different now from what they were at the time we were trying to wind it up. 1952—what I am talking about is the date in this budget. It is supposed to be wound up at the end of fiscal 1952.

Q. There has been some question as to whether or not it might be wound up on June 30 this year?

THE PRESIDENT. Never was any question on that; 1952 is when it was intended to be wound up. I think I set that date myself.

[26.] Q. Mr. President, on page M53 (p. 97), Social Security, Welfare, and Health, I don't find health insurance in there. Has that been dropped for the time being?

THE PRESIDENT. No, it has not. It's on page M56 (p. 100).

Q. That is the old national health insurance program?

THE PRESIDENT. Yes. You will find it on page M56. Better watch out, you may get a speech out of me on that. [*Laughter*]

[27.] Q. Mr. President, do I understand that regardless of any future authorization or obligations, $70 billion is all that the Government expects in the next fiscal year, regardless of any future authorization?

THE PRESIDENT. No, no.

Q. What could happen to increase that figure?

THE PRESIDENT. It is based on this budget. Can't tell what emergency may come along.

Q. Short of any emergency, sir?

THE PRESIDENT. It is based on the budget here, as nearly as we can figure it out. That is what the budget is for—the best guesses we can make.

[28.] Q. Mr. President, I got a little confused about which June 30th you were talking about on ECA?

THE PRESIDENT. June 30, 1952.

Q. ECA would be continued beyond June 30, 1951?

THE PRESIDENT. Yes.

[29.] Q. Mr. President, while we are on the New Deal, let's get it all straight.

THE PRESIDENT. Yes.

Q. Fair Deal—I mean Fair Deal.

THE PRESIDENT. What is it?

Q. On page M30 (p. 80), "I again recommend that the Congress enact legislation to establish a Federal Fair Employment Practice Commission to prevent discrimination in industry." Are you going to do any more about it than what is down in here?

THE PRESIDENT. Of course I am. I wouldn't put it in there if I wasn't going to do something about it. I don't talk through my hat.

[30.] Q. Mr. President, in trying to pin down the 6 billion to pay taxes, if you have a $60 billion carryover into 1952, and you carry military expenses continuing it at the rate into the year of 40 billion, you could have a budget approaching $100 billion for military—mainly for military—a 1953 budget of around $100 billion.

THE PRESIDENT. We will see what that looks like when we get to that point. Then we will talk about it at that time.

[31.] Q. You said that that would be pay-as-you-go?

THE PRESIDENT. I am hoping that that will be a pay-as-you-go. That is what I am working for.

Q. Didn't you estimate a $55 billion cost in your Economic Report?

Director Lawton: That was the spending rate.

THE PRESIDENT. The Budget Director said it was the spending rate as of the end of the year, 1951—calendar 1951.

[32.] Q. Mr. President, under the heading Proposals, I believe you are repeating the $300 million aid to education. That was not enacted in the last Congress?

THE PRESIDENT. That is correct—that is correct.

[33.] Q. Then on page M31 (p. 80), revision of unemployment insurance, is that also a repetition of your message request of a year ago—or 2 years ago, I have forgotten which—for extension of unemployment insurance—expansion of it?

THE PRESIDENT. Yes. Yes, expansion of it. It is practically the same request as was made 2 years ago, and last year.

The Budget Director calls the attention to the fact that it is all set out in my message of last April.[3]

Q. The April message?

THE PRESIDENT. Yes. That part which

has not been enacted is what we are talking about here.

Q. Will there be specific messages on these items of new legislation?

THE PRESIDENT. Well, we are always writing letters and telephoning. I don't know whether you would call it a special message or not. There will be some special messages, but not on every item in the request, because some of them will be taken care of without that.

[34.] Q. Mr. President, may I ask one question about that third supplemental—10 billion. Do we know exactly how much, if any, of that will be expended in 1951, how much is included in the $47 billion expenditure figure for fiscal 1951?

Director Lawton: Very little of it.

[35.] Q. Mr. President, running through your method in the explanation of the various functions, there is new emphasis on our contributions towards defense. Does that mean that these various functions are going to take on a new turn, or is that simply more or less the things that they have been doing?

THE PRESIDENT. No, it means just exactly what it says.

It is very difficult to decide just exactly what is entirely defense and what is not. I imagine that there are some people who would class the White House as unnecessary to the defense effort, and you can go right down through all the rest of the agencies. Those agencies that are set out here, and are justified as making a contribution to the defense effort, are doing just that, or we wouldn't say so. Tax collection is another one. Do you think tax collection is essential to the national defense? You can take a dozen different things. And, of course, those things have to be collected, or you wouldn't have any national defense, if you want to go around and justify it. But that

---

[3] The President's special message to the Congress on the unemployment insurance system (see 1950 volume, this series, Item 84).

is what we are referring to in that part of the message.

[36.]   Q. Mr. President, I would like to ask this question of Director Lawton. On pages M60–M61 (pp. 102, 103), the Budget recently did estimate what the cost of gratuitous insurance as against National Service Life Insurance would have been over the past 10 years—between 1940 and 1949—had it been put into effect during the past war. I was wondering if there had been any estimates made on what the cost to the Federal Government would be on a current basis, if this recommended legislation is enacted?

Director Lawton: We have not made it on an annual basis. We made the estimate, which was given to the committee considering it, which was about 800 million in savings. The General Accounting Office made an independent estimate and they came out with 788 million; and the committee estimate, I believe, is somewhat higher. That was over the 10-year period. It depends on the number of people that would be in the Armed Forces, and the number of casualties.

[37.]   Q. How much of that is defense and how much is nondefense?

Director Lawton: 12 billion, 4 includes the—all of the extensions of military and economic aid, of course, and the expansion of defense production.

Q. Can you break that down between those items and the nondefense items?

Director Lawton: They are all indicated in each of these headings which ones they are.

Q. What page is that?

Director Lawton: In each of the individual sections—in each table—proposed legislation is separately set forth.

[38.]   Q. Mr. President, on page M51 (p. 96)—this is rather a small item—the budget includes expenditures of $106 million for the fiscal year for buildings and current operating expenses. Is that schools? I wonder if Mr. Lawton could tell us how much of that 106 is capital outlay for buildings, and how much is operating expenses?

Director Lawton: I cannot give you that figure. I don't have it right here.

[39.]   Q. May I ask a question about this military budget? You said you were not setting out the details of the $60 billion at the present time. Will that only come to light when the defense people from the Pentagon go up before the Appropriations Committee, or will you send a special message?

THE PRESIDENT. When they have those figures in detailed arrangement, so they can furnish them to me—there is some delay on that—they will be available just as quickly as they can be.

Q. They will be available?

THE PRESIDENT. Supplemental budget, so the Budget Director tells me.

Secretary Snyder: You are talking about for 1952 now?

Q. I am talking about funds for 1952 for the military—the complete military budget.

Secretary Snyder: He is not talking about the supplementals. He is talking about the 1952 estimates here. They will be apparent when they go up with the appropriations.

Director Lawton: Same detail as would be set up in this budget for later submission.

Q. Could you give us a rough estimate of the portion of the military budget that will go for hardware, equipment such as airplanes, and so forth?

THE PRESIDENT. The Budget Director says he cannot answer that question until he gets the details from the Pentagon.

[40.]   Q. Mr. President, can you give an idea as to the rough timing of the tax message? When is it going up?

THE PRESIDENT. I hope it will be sometime within the next 30 days. It may take longer than that. Depends altogether on how fast the experts work.

Q. Sir, this is the last chance you will have of getting a retroactive tax?

THE PRESIDENT. I understand that very well.

Q. The Ways and Means Committee is going to start hearings on the 6th of February.

THE PRESIDENT. Sixth of February, yes.

Q. Yes, sir.

THE PRESIDENT. I hope so. I will tell you what the Secretary of the Treasury was saying to me. They are working on a renegotiation act this week. They will continue work on it next week, and as soon as he gets it ready then they are going to start hearings on the tax bill, and the Secretary says we are going to try to have the tax message ready, so we won't be delayed.

[41.] Q. Mr. President, in connection with your interest in the pay-as-you-go policy, have you had any advice as to how high a budget the Federal Government could sustain and still expect to pay for it?

THE PRESIDENT. No, I have not. No, I have not.

[42.] Q. On the 10 billion, 9 figure for international security is there any breakdown, Mr. President, on that figure as to how much would be for European military aid?

Director Lawton: The bulk of it would be.

Q. What page are you talking about?

Q. Page M7 (p. 63), the table there of the new obligatory authority for the 1952 fiscal year, it's the second figure following the 60 billion.

THE PRESIDENT. The Budget Director informs me that it has not yet been broken down between military and economic, but it will be. It depends on how much material we will have to supply, and how much they can supply themselves. And that will have to be worked out as we go along.

General Eisenhower can give us some idea, when he gets back.

[43.] Q. Mr. President, if you were writing this budget, what would you call this, a $94 billion or a $71 billion budget?

THE PRESIDENT. I would call it a $71 billion budget, which I have just done. This is my budget. I signed it. What is in that is what I am saying.

[44.] Q. Mr. President, on page M52 (p. 96)——

THE PRESIDENT. M52? All right.

Q. Two questions I would like to ask there. One is in reference to the coverage on social security. Does that statement regarding the millions of people still uncovered mean that you will plan a special message asking for extension of H.R. 6000? [4]

THE PRESIDENT. The message of last April covers that situation, and it is still what I want.

Q. And the next sentence, which says, "Pension and insurance plans for special groups should supplement social security benefits, as industry pensions already do, for several million workers." Would you define what you mean by "special groups"?

THE PRESIDENT. The Railroad Retirement Act is one special group in particular, and there are all sorts of pension plans in the employ of both State and Federal Governments. That is principally what is referred to.

[45.] Q. Mr. President, did you ask for a specific amount in this budget to pay for the Brannan plan?

THE PRESIDENT. No.

Q. Have you any idea what it might cost?

THE PRESIDENT. No.

[46.] Q. Mr. President, on page M57 (p. 99), I find a very interesting observation,

---

[4] H.R. 6000, as enacted, is the Social Security Act Amendments of 1950, Public Law 734 (64 Stat. 477).

speaking of veterans, "Before many years, nearly all the population may be veterans, or the dependents of veterans," and the subsequent paragraph—if I read it right—means that someday we are going to be, if we keep on increasing military forces, we are all going to be taking in each other's wash.

THE PRESIDENT. That is correct. If you will just sit down and analyze the situation, the present rate of increase will be 49 million people, veterans or dependents, inside the next 3 or 4 years.

[47.] Q. Mr. President, on this sheet, you have opposite Federal National Mortgage Association, for 1952, a minus sign. Does that mean that the Federal National Mortgage Association does not start taking in money——

Director Lawton: Liquidation.

THE PRESIDENT. The sale of mortgages.

[48.] Q. Mr. President, in my reference to the statement about pension and insurance plans for special groups, which supplements social security benefits, as industry pensions already do have several million workers, are you referring to the fact that the General Motors plan and the Ford plan increases the social security billing in part to take care of the cost?

THE PRESIDENT. A great many of the big industries, Standard Oil Co. of New Jersey, Standard Oil Co. of Indiana, all had pension plans.

Q. You think that Government pensions and railroad worker pensions should likewise be increased, is that the idea?

THE PRESIDENT. No, no. The idea is that the Government approach to the thing should be equal for everybody. Then if they have an additional pension, that is just their good luck.

Q. You are not referring, then, to persons who are not covered by pensions in any way, shape, or form, you are referring to those who are covered, but who have not had an adjustment in the rate, through collective bargaining or some other way in the last——

THE PRESIDENT. No, that has no connection with it whatever. What I am trying to do is to get everybody fairly and equitably covered under the Social Security Act. Then, if they happen to have these pensions, they are just that much better off for it.

Q. I don't follow that.

THE PRESIDENT. We don't want to take their pensions away from them, because most of them made contributions to these pensions and they are entitled to them; but the idea that I have in mind is to cover them all under social security. Then if they have pensions on top of that, why that is their good luck.

Q. Oh, I see.

[49.] Q. Mr. President, are you considering a national sales tax?

THE PRESIDENT. Every sort of tax that will be necessary to raise revenue undoubtedly will be considered by the experts. I am not considering any kind of special tax myself personally.

[50.] Q. Mr. President, on page M7 (p. 63), that basic table there, I notice the agricultural budget expenditure went down from 2 billion, 784 to 986 million, and they are going up to 1 billion, 429. Would you explain why that is?

THE PRESIDENT. We sold $680 million worth of cotton, that is what makes the difference.

[51.] Q. Mr. President, I would like to ask a question about M59 (p. 102), on the GI bill. You give a warning there, that the reenactment of the GI bill the way it was in World War II would mean a perpetuating of some of the difficulties and the features of that bill. Are you planning to recommend any legislation to cover—set up any standby legislation—that is, a standby bill, in the event we should get into a general war, or would you wait?

THE PRESIDENT. What we have in mind is a GI bill of rights, in the case you refer to, without some of the difficulties we had to contend with in the other that we have had experience with. There were several things in that bill that turned out to be rackets, and some of them are being investigated now for fraud. There is no use going ahead with something that you have had experience with which you know won't work, and I want to see an equitable bill of rights for those people who serve under the present emergency.

Q. People in Korea now are not covered?

THE PRESIDENT. Yes—they are not covered. They ought to be—they ought to be. They are fighting just as hard as anybody did— and harder, I think.

[52.] Q. One more question, please. On page M61 (p. 103), what do you attribute the value of some 212—no—yes—212 billion—million—in veterans life insurance dividends by fiscal '51 and fiscal '52?

Director Lawton: That is the lag in the payment of these dividends which have been worked on this year. It's the distribution between the 2 years of the actual cash outgo for this current year's dividend.

Q. It is not an increase?

Q. Same dividends are being paid?

Director Lawton: This year's dividend is going to be at the tail end of the year, and it will be somewhat distributed this year— some of the actual checks will go out in July or August. When they begin on June 30th, it draws down from one fiscal year to the other in the actual issuance of checks.

[53.] Q. Mr. President, there is a statement on page 740 in the big book, regarding postal rates, in which you want to reduce the deficit from $521 million to 160. Is there any—through legislation—is there any way that you can indicate some of the ways in which that rate increase will be handled at the present time?

THE PRESIDENT. Yes, the Postmaster General is working on a program right now that will meet that very situation, and as soon as he has it ready I will give you the figure. The 160 million refers to the Government's use of the postal service. That is the reason it runs to below 160 million because the Government has to pay its share as well as anybody else. That also includes airmail subsidies.

[54.] Q. Mr. President, you mentioned the fact that those who contributed to old-age insurance were entitled to get the money, was that what you said?

THE PRESIDENT. Yes, that is correct.

Q. Are you aware that if they get as much as $50 on the outside—they may never get a nickel on what they have contributed?

THE PRESIDENT. No, I was not aware of it—I am not aware of it.

Q. There is considerable complaint about that in the congressional mail. And it is said that that might keep older people out of the war labor market.

THE PRESIDENT. I don't think so, May.[5] They are as patriotic as we are. I hadn't heard that complaint, to tell you the truth.

Q. It was only as much as $15, but now if they earn $50 a month, they would not get all the insurance to which they have contributed.

THE PRESIDENT. Well, I will have to take a look at that.

Q. Will you do that?

THE PRESIDENT. Yes.

Q. It's in the mail.

THE PRESIDENT. May, are you anticipating having that held against you? [*Laughter*]

Q. No.

[55.] Q. Mr. President, on page M27 (p. 78), toward the bottom, "I am recommending a further extension of rent control authority, with provision for recontrol when

---

[5] Mrs. May Craig of the Portland (Maine) Press Herald.

necessary to protect tenants in defense areas against exorbitant rent increases." My city and State happen to be among those that have been decontrolled by action of the State general assembly, and I wonder if you could elaborate for me on how you believe this "where necessary" should operate, and how would that be determined?

THE PRESIDENT. Particularly in defense areas, where increased population in defense areas will soon be. That is particularly what it refers to, and where the rent groups will immediately go to work.

Q. May I ask about Norfolk, for example, where I suppose there will be again a pretty hefty increase in rents? You would determine when rent controls should be reimposed in Norfolk under the legislation you have in mind?

THE PRESIDENT. Well, we will have—I think the Housing Expediter would be the man to make the decision, after a survey.

Q. The authority, then, would be vested in the Housing Expediter to recontrol?

THE PRESIDENT. It should be. It should be.

Q. To protect tenants in defense areas, not tenants in other areas?

THE PRESIDENT. I would like to see them all protected, but I was using that as a horrible example.

Reporter: Thank you, Mr. President.

NOTE: President Truman's two hundred and fifty-first news conference was held in the State Department Auditorium at 10 o'clock on Saturday morning, January 13, 1951. The President was assisted in presenting information on the budget by Secretary of the Treasury John W. Snyder and by Frederick J. Lawton, Director of the Bureau of the Budget, and Elmer B. Staats, Assistant Director.

---

13   Annual Budget Message to the Congress: Fiscal Year 1952. *January* 15, 1951

To the Congress of the United States:

I transmit herewith my recommendations for the Budget of the United States Government for the fiscal year ending June 30, 1952.

This is a Budget for our national security in a period of grave danger.

It calls for expenditures of 71.6 billion dollars in the fiscal year 1952—a total 78 percent above expenditures for the year which ended last June 30. That increase is one measure of the vast new responsibilities thrust upon the American people by the communist assaults upon freedom in Asia

and the threats to freedom in other parts of the world.

The new emphasis on military preparedness reflects the necessities of the world situation today. It reflects no shift of purpose. Our purpose remains to secure and strengthen peace. We are determined to seek peace by every honorable means—mindful of our responsibility to ourselves, to our friends and allies, and to humanity everywhere to spare the world the tragedy of another world war. We are likewise determined to spare ourselves and the world

BUDGET TOTALS

[Fiscal years.   In billions]

	1950 actual	1951 estimated	1952 estimated
Receipts (excluding proposed new tax legislation)...............	$37.0	$44.5	$55.1
Expenditures...	40.1	47.2	71.6
Deficit...	—3.1	—2.7	—16.5

the even deeper tragedy of the surrender of justice and freedom.

Another system—powerful in resources, hostile in intent, and ruthless in method—is seeking the destruction of all the values we would preserve. That system is under the mastery of men unrestrained by considerations of responsibility to their people and guided by twisted dogma. They can be restrained only if defensive strength is arrayed against them. Our best hope now is to build our strength to the point necessary to bring them to caution, if not to wisdom. We are compelled to make the creation of strength a paramount aim.

In our drive to build up our defenses, we and the countries associated with us have a twofold goal—first, military forces strong enough to provide a powerful deterrent to those who may be contemplating new aggression; second, readiness for immediate mobilization of all our power if that becomes necessary.

This Budget reflects our determination.

First, it incorporates our expenditures for military purposes—to build swiftly an active force of highly trained men, equipped with the most modern weapons, and supported by ready reserves of men, supplies, and equipment.

Second, it includes our expenditures to help other threatened nations rebuild their strength and to participate with them in a program of mutual aid and common defense.

Third, it embodies our Government programs for the expansion of productive capacity and the concentration of needed capacity on defense requirements—at the expense where necessary of normal civilian purposes.

Fourth, it contains expenditures for programs which will maintain and develop our national strength over the long run, keeping in mind that the present emergency may be of long duration and we must therefore be prepared for crises in the more distant as well as in the immediate future.

Fifth, it reflects reductions in other expenditures, in order to divert a maximum of resources to the overriding requirements of national security.

As a sixth budgetary measure, I shall shortly recommend an increase in tax revenues in the conviction that we must attain a balanced budget to provide a sound financial basis for what may be an extended period of very high defense expenditures.

CONTENTS OF THE BUDGET

The accompanying comparative table shows projected expenditures for the major programs or functions of the Government for the fiscal year 1952, revised estimates for the current year, and actual expenditures for the year which ended last June 30. Estimated appropriations and other new obligational authority for 1952 are also shown. Differences between obligational authority and expenditures are accounted for by the fact that obligational authority granted in one fiscal year may be spent in part in subsequent fiscal years.

The table covers expenditures from general and special funds of the Treasury, plus net expenditures of wholly owned Government corporations. The estimates include requirements under proposed as well as existing legislation. Expenditures from trust funds are excluded from this table, but operations of the major trust funds are discussed in subsequent sections of the Budget Message.

The requirements of national security are reflected in every major function of the Budget. The entire Government is being redirected to meet the compelling demands of national security, and each functional category includes activities which support,

BUDGET EXPENDITURES AND AUTHORIZATIONS BY MAJOR FUNCTIONS

[Fiscal years. In millions]

	Expenditures			Recommended new obliga- tional authority for 1952[1]
Function	*1950 actual*	*1951 estimated*	*1952 estimated*	
Military services.....................................	$12, 303	$20, 994	$41, 421	$60, 971
International security and foreign relations........	4, 803	4, 726	7, 461	10, 956
Finance, commerce, and industry................	227	368	1, 524	1, 568
Labor...	263	212	215	225
Transportation and communication..............	1, 752	1, 970	1, 685	1, 414
Natural resources.............................	1, 554	2, 117	2, 519	2, 111
Agriculture and agricultural resources............	2, 784	986	1, 429	1, 483
Housing and community development............	261	409	[2] — 102	1, 018
Education and general research..................	114	143	483	468
Social security, welfare, and health..............	2, 213	2, 520	2, 625	2, 552
Veterans' services and benefits....................	6, 627	5, 746	4, 911	4, 426
General government...........................	1, 108	1, 252	1, 351	1, 140
Interest......................................	5, 817	5, 722	5, 897	5, 897
Reserve for contingencies........................	....	45	175	200
Adjustment to daily Treasury statement...........	+330	....	....	....
Total...................................	40, 156	47, 210	71, 594	94, 429

[1] This column excludes 4,075 million dollars of recommended appropriations to liquidate prior year contract authorizations.

[2] Excess of receipts over expenditures.

directly or indirectly, the defense effort.

The two largest categories—military services and international security and foreign relations—are devoted in their entirety to the broad objectives of national security. The military services category includes the costs of the Armed Forces and certain additional programs closely related to the military, particularly the stockpiling of strategic and critical materials and the activities of the National Advisory Committee for Aeronautics. Under the international security and foreign relations heading are the costs of weapons provided to our North Atlantic Treaty allies and to other free nations, as well as expenditures for economic assistance and for the expanded international information program.

The military and international categories account for expenditures of 41.4 and 7.5 billion dollars, respectively, in the fiscal year 1952. Together they total 48.9 billions, or nearly 69 percent of the total Budget.

This total is an increase of 90 percent over the 25.7 billion dollars estimated as expenditures for these purposes during the current year—accounted for almost wholly by the great expansion of the military procurement program.

Our military requirements are of several kinds. We must maintain and supply our forces fighting in Korea. We must provide modern equipment for the expansion of our Army, Navy, and Air Force to the present combined goal of nearly three and a half million men. We must provide equipment for training purposes and for the civilian components not on active duty. We must provide military items to our allies as an essential part of our own defense. We must build a production base and matériel reserves against the contingency of full-scale war.

These demands do not press evenly on all sectors of defense production. In some areas, large supplies of military items remain from

63

the recent war and reduce the need for new large-scale production. Our reserve naval fleet, for example, is an asset which reduces sharply the need for mass construction of new warships. In some cases, the record-breaking military production of the war years has left us with reserves of productive capacity. In other cases present capacity is far from adequate. The economic mobilization program will therefore be selective in character—in some areas, an all-out drive, with extensive conversion of civilian capacity; in other areas, a comparatively small expansion of present production rates.

At the same time that we sharply increase our own military production, Canada and the Western European nations with whom we are allied under the North Atlantic Treaty will be making comparable efforts. Nations outside the North Atlantic organization, including our neighbors in Latin America, are also making important contributions to the common security. Our international programs recognize that this Nation's own security is directly related to the security and defensive strength of our allies and that equipment and materials supplied to help arm their forces or to support their military production are, in fact, additions to our own defensive strength.

Figures shown in this Budget for both the military and the international security programs may be subject to substantial adjustment as the defense program progresses. Detailed estimates of new obligational authority for these categories are not included in the Budget at this time, in order to permit more thorough programing of specific requirements. Actual expenditures will depend on how rapidly we are able to produce the military items for which funds are made available.

A defense program of the size now being undertaken must be supported by a strong and expanding economic base. Five major categories of Federal programs contribute directly to this economic base. These are: (1) finance, commerce, and industry; (2) labor; (3) transportation and communication; (4) natural resources; and (5) agriculture and agricultural resources. Together these categories make up 7.4 billion dollars of expenditures in the fiscal year 1952, or 10 percent of the Budget.

This total compares to 5.7 billion dollars estimated as expenditures for these purposes in the current fiscal year. The increase reflects primarily our programs to expand private production facilities through Federal action, to administer economic controls, and to add capacity for atomic energy activities.

Four other categories of Budget expenditures include programs which contribute to national strength through protecting and improving the health, education, and well-being of the individuals and families who make up the Nation. These classifications are: (1) housing and community development; (2) education and general research; (3) social security, welfare, and health; and (4) veterans' services and benefits.

These four categories account for a total of 7.9 billion dollars, or 11 percent of Budget expenditures in the fiscal year 1952. This represents a reduction of nearly a billion dollars from the current year's anticipated expenditures. If it were not for the major new programs of civil defense and defense housing, community facilities, and services, the total reduction would be even greater

The general operations of Government—including the legislative and judicial branches and such general activities of the executive branch as tax collection, civil-service retirement payments, and central supply, records, and buildings services—amount to 1.4 billion dollars, or 2 percent of the 1952 Budget. Apart from the expected costs of dispersal of Government agencies, this group of expenditures is also scheduled to decline from the 1951 level.

Interest payments will amount to an estimated 5.9 billion dollars in the fiscal year 1952, or 8 percent of the total Budget.

In order that our resources can be diverted to meet the demands of national security, strict economy in nondefense spending is required. Such a policy is incorporated in this Budget. For example, the only major new public works projects included in the Budget are those directly necessary to the defense effort. Construction on many public works projects now under way has been substantially curtailed. Many other activities are being contracted. Expenditures for the maintenance of Government property have been held to a minimum consistent with protection of Government investments. Cost increases, such as the rise that has already taken place in the prices of what the Government buys, are in many instances being absorbed by the agencies through compensating economies. Increases have been allowed where increasing workloads must be met or where further accumulation of backlogs of work cannot be tolerated, but only to the extent that the work cannot be taken care of through increased efficiency or reductions in service standards.

MANAGEMENT OF THE GOVERNMENT'S
PROGRAM

Direction of the Nation's security program in this critical period will require the highest degree of administrative effectiveness in the Federal Government. Concerted efforts are being made to strengthen the organization and management of the executive branch for the extraordinarily difficult tasks that lie ahead. During the coming period, we must be able to make quickly such changes in the assignment of governmental functions as are needed to carry out national security programs. Under the Defense Production Act, I have by Executive order created the Office of Defense Mobilization, the Defense Production Administration, the Economic Stabilization Agency, and other emergency agencies with extensive delegation of authority. However, authority under that act covers only a part of the range of defense functions. During World Wars I and II the President was given emergency reorganization powers. These powers were extensively used to keep Government organization continuously in line with mobilization needs. Such authority for temporary changes is needed in the current emergency and should be one of the early measures considered by the Congress.

In addition to concentrating on the organization and management of the defense program, I shall continue to emphasize throughout the Government the management improvement program, instituted in 1949 to achieve greater efficiency in all Federal activities.

The last Congress took many important legislative actions aimed at improving governmental administration. Other actions are, however, still required. Some of these measures I shall incorporate in reorganization plans to be submitted to the Congress under the Reorganization Act of 1949. Others require legislation, including such important matters as improvements in the civil-service system and in the administration of the postal service.

The actions in the field of organization and management which we have taken in the past years have increased the ability of the Government to deal with a major defense effort. We must continue to make progress in this field.

PAYING THE COSTS OF DEFENSE

When the American people resolved to undertake the defense program now under way, they accepted also the necessity for the increases in their taxes that the new level of expenditures requires. National security in the present world can be attained only with direct and heavy cost to each one of us.

High taxes are indispensable to our successful mobilization. They are required to preserve confidence in the integrity of the Government's finances, to distribute the heavy financial costs of defense fairly among all the people, to reduce excessive demand for raw materials and industrial products required for national defense, and to choke off inflationary pressures. We cannot as a Nation buy a defense establishment of the size that is now being constructed and still as individuals expect to spend our money to the same degree as before for normal peacetime purposes. Unless positive action is taken on the tax front, our defense effort will be in continuous jeopardy.

The tax legislation passed last year substantially increased our revenues. The Revenue Act of 1950, approved within 3 months after the invasion of the Republic of Korea, increased income taxes on individuals and corporations and closed some loopholes in the income tax laws. The corporation excess profits tax, passed in the final week of the Eighty-first Congress, also increased our revenues while at the same time placing the higher levies upon those businesses which can best afford to pay increased taxes.

In spite of these new tax measures, a deficit of 16.5 billion dollars is estimated for the fiscal year 1952 if no further tax legislation is enacted. At this time, sound public finance and fiscal policy require that we balance the Budget. I shall shortly transmit to the Congress recommendations for new revenue legislation.

Even a balanced budget will not of itself serve to keep our economy stable during a period of rapidly rising defense expenditures. The full amount of inflationary pressure is not measured by the budget deficit alone, since this reflects only payments actually made. The Department of Defense alone will have been granted for the fiscal years 1951 and 1952 an estimated 112 billion dollars of obligational authority for its military functions, and additional amounts will have been made available for foreign military-aid programs. Bidding for manpower and materials, which pushes prices upward, begins as soon as procurement contracts to be paid from these authorizations are signed, even though expenditures may not take place for a year or more. Other positive stabilization measures, including allocations, and credit, price and wage controls, are essential to offset the inflationary pressures which are not reflected in the single figure of the budget deficit.

The following table provides a breakdown of anticipated budget receipts during the fiscal year 1952, based on existing legislation, compared with actual receipts during the fiscal year 1950 and revised estimated receipts for the current year.

Under existing legislation, including the recently enacted tax measures, budget receipts for the fiscal year 1952 are estimated at 55.1 billion dollars. This is 10.6 billion dollars higher than the estimate for the current year. Receipts from direct taxes on corporations show the greatest increase, 6.4 billion dollars over corresponding receipts for the current fiscal year. The combined effects of the Revenue Act of 1950, the Excess Profits Tax Act, and peak levels of corporate profits are reflected in this estimate. Direct taxes on individuals increase 4.4 billion dollars as

BUDGET RECEIPTS

[Fiscal years.   In millions]

Source	1950 actual	1951 estimated	1952 estimated
Direct taxes on individuals:			
Individual income taxes....................................	$17, 409	$21, 599	$26, 025
Estate and gift taxes.......................................	706	710	755
Direct taxes on corporations:			
Income and excess profits taxes............................	10, 854	13, 560	20, 000
Excises..	7, 597	8, 240	8, 222
Customs...	423	600	620
Employment taxes:			
Federal Insurance Contributions Act........................	2, 106	2, 960	3, 823
Federal Unemployment Tax Act.............................	226	239	263
Railroad Retirement Tax Act...............................	551	565	613
Railroad Unemployment Insurance Act......................	9	10	10
Miscellaneous receipts......................................	1, 430	1, 325	1, 333
Deduct:			
Appropriation to social security trust fund....................	−2, 106	−2, 960	−3, 823
Refunds of receipts..	−2, 160	−2, 336	−2, 703
Budget receipts...	37, 045	44, 512	55, 138

NOTE.—Includes only receipts under existing legislation.

a result of the high levels of income anticipated and a full year of operation under the Revenue Act of 1950.   Although the collections from certain excise taxes will decline as production of some manufactured goods is affected by shortages of materials, receipts from other excises and all other major sources will increase.

BORROWING AND PUBLIC DEBT

At the beginning of the current fiscal year the public debt stood at 257.4 billion dollars. The debt will rise to approximately 260 billion dollars by June 30, 1951, as a reflection of the financing of the budget deficit for the current fiscal year.   The amount of the increase in debt beyond June 30, 1951, depends upon the extent to which the projected deficit for the fiscal year 1952 is reduced through the enactment of additional tax legislation.

PROGRAMS

The following sections outline in more detail the character and extent of the programs

which are to be financed from this Budget. Further detailed descriptions of the programs of the Government, as well as certain special analyses covering public works, grants to State and local governments, investment and operating expenditures, and Federal credit programs, are included elsewhere in the Budget.

MILITARY SERVICES

The free nations of the world will continue to seek settlement of international disagreements peaceably and honorably within the framework of the United Nations—but they will rebuild their defenses rapidly.   The communist attacks in Korea have served notice upon us all that the Soviet rulers are willing to risk the peace of the world to carry out their ambitions.

In response to the grave common peril, the free world is now moving forward, with increasing speed, determination, and unity, to build powerful defenses.   This mutual effort is required both to deter further communist aggression and to insure that we shall emerge victorious if war is thrust upon us.

This Nation, as the strongest member of the free world, must provide the leadership in this great undertaking by developing its own military forces and, at the same time, assisting the other free nations on a large scale, in order to quickly achieve adequate mutual defenses.

The recommended program for building our own military strength is discussed in this section. The program for assisting other free nations in developing their strength is discussed under international security and foreign relations.

Department of Defense.—One year ago, I proposed a military program for the fiscal year 1951 based on active forces totaling about 1.5 million men and women, in a state of relative readiness, and backed by a moderate rate of military production and a substantial level of research and development.

The communist attacks in Korea and the imminent possibility of further attacks elsewhere have already caused us to quadruple the budget for the Department of Defense. To the initial enactment of 13.3 billion dollars in new obligational authority for the fiscal year 1951, including nearly a billion dollars of prior year authorizations made available, the Congress has in the past 6 months added 28.7 billion dollars. In this Budget I am tentatively including an additional 10 billion dollars of obligational authority. This will make a total of 52 billion dollars for the fiscal year 1951.

Because of the extensive planning involved, I am not submitting detailed 1952 estimates for the Department of Defense at this time. The Budget includes, however, an over-all estimate of 60 billion dollars, which is expected to be the approximate total of new obligational authority requested this spring for the fiscal year 1952.

The expenditure estimates for the military functions of the Department of Defense are also tentative. At the present time expenditures of 20 billion dollars are estimated for the fiscal year 1951 and 40 billion dollars for 1952.

The increased funds for fiscal years 1951 and 1952 will serve four major interrelated purposes. First, they will support the current increase in the strength of our active forces; second, they will finance the military production program designed to produce rapidly the modern equipment needed to supply our forces; third, they will provide reserves of equipment for still larger United States forces should these become necessary; and, fourth, they will help us to develop the production capacity of the country to the point where we could move rapidly to full mobilization should the need arise.

Six months ago our active military forces numbered less than one and a half million men and women. They have already been increased by about a million and this Budget includes funds to reach and maintain our present goal of nearly a million more.

We also have now available for rapid mobilization more than two million men and women in the National Guard and the Reserves of the Army, Navy, and Air Force. The Budget provides funds to increase the strength and degree of readiness of these Reserve organizations.

While the exact size and disposition of our active forces by units and geographic location must be kept secret in times like the present, in general we are increasing rapidly the number of active units. In the Army, we have called to active duty several National Guard divisions and reactivated certain regular divisions. We shall soon have a force more than twice as strong as our pre-Korea Army. In the Navy, by continuing to reactivate ships from the "mothball" fleet, we shall soon raise the active fleet

MILITARY SERVICES

[Fiscal years.   In millions]

	Expenditures			Recommended new obligational authority for 1952 [1]
Program or agency	1950 actual	1951 estimated	1952 estimated	
Department of Defense—military functions........	$11,889	$20,000	$40,000	$60,000
Activities supporting military services:				
Stockpiling of strategic and critical materials....	438	900	1,300	820
Selective Service System:				
Present program...........................	9	37	....	....
Proposed legislation........................	....	....	45	50
National Advisory Committee for Aeronautics...	54	62	78	68
Reconstruction Finance Corporation (net receipts).	—107	—40	—43	....
Other..	20	35	41	33
Total.....................................	12,303	20,994	41,421	60,971

[1] This column excludes 2,702 million dollars of recommended appropriations to liquidate prior year contract authority.

to a strength more than 50 percent above that of a year ago. This Budget provides for maintaining two full Marine divisions plus additional separate units. In the Air Force, we are expanding the structure from 48 to 84 air wings; these will be rapidly brought up to full strength in trained men, and additional wings will be added.

The expansion of the active forces is reflected in the Budget not only in larger total amounts for pay and allowances, but also in increased funds for housing, training, and maintaining such forces.

We are now establishing training centers, bases, and camps for the enlarged forces. Furthermore, in order to prepare for the possibility of further mobilization, we shall be opening facilities with sufficient capacity to handle larger active forces than our immediate goals require. This Budget will provide, therefore, for a considerable increase in military public works expenditures—primarily to expand and improve troop training centers and air bases.

By far the largest part of the funds requested for the military services will be used to procure modern equipment. We have

large stocks of some types of equipment, such as rifles and naval ships, which need only to be taken from storage and, in some cases, modernized. But in many other types, such as planes, tanks, electronic equipment, recoilless weapons, and rockets, we need to put into rapid production new models incorporating basic improvements that have been made since the end of World War II. This means a major production effort in order to obtain the best and most modern equipment for our enlarged active forces and for large reserve stocks.

This effort will require prompt and accurate planning and scheduling of military procurement and production in order to anticipate and forestall potential bottlenecks in materials, manpower, or facilities. For example, schedules must be laid out for producing the many complicated components of modern military airplanes, such as jet engines and electronic fire-control equipment, so that the components can be brought together as smoothly and efficiently as possible into finished aircraft. Some delays and frictions will inevitably occur in a production program as large and urgent as that upon

69

which we are now embarked. But the experience and teamwork of military and civilian officials, of private businessmen and workers, will produce results very rapidly.

At the same time that the output of military equipment is stepped up, a base is being developed for moving to full-scale mobilization if the need should arise. For this reason, military orders are being spread among suppliers, instead of being concentrated in a few large firms. Production lines will be set up and manufacturers will be made familiar with our production needs over and above the immediate necessities of our present procurement plans. In this way, military production can be increased still further on short notice if that becomes necessary.

For example, we expect to develop an aircraft industry that will be capable of turning out 50,000 planes in a year, even though we will not be actually procuring that many. These planes, on the average, will be approximately 50 percent heavier than those used in World War II. Similarly, we shall organize to produce 35,000 tanks in a year, although we are not ordering that many now. This means, of course, planning for the readiness of basic materials, manpower, and components, as well as final assembly lines.

The process of putting military equipment into production will not stop or retard our research and development work. On the contrary, we shall increase our efforts to maintain superiority in all kinds of weapons and equipment. Expenditures for the military research and development program will amount to nearly a billion dollars in the current fiscal year. The developmental work and the production program will be planned so that our troops will be supplied with the best weapons in the world.

Stockpiling.—If full mobilization becomes necessary, larger quantities of scarce materials such as copper, chromium, cobalt, and nickel will be required immediately. Many of these scarce materials are not produced in the United States, and others cannot be produced at a rate sufficient to meet all-out military needs. We are consequently acquiring and storing large reserve stocks of these materials.

This program will be expanded and developed in accordance with our total defense needs. The controls which have been established over the use of certain of these materials will assist us in meeting our stockpile requirements. We are also participating in the development of international controls. In addition, vigorous steps are being taken, by ourselves and our allies, to expand the production of strategic and critical materials both at home and abroad.

A total of 2.9 billion dollars of new obligational authority has been made available for the stockpile program during the current fiscal year and I am requesting an additional 820 million dollars of obligational authority for fiscal year 1952. Expenditures for fiscal year 1951 are estimated at 900 million dollars and for fiscal year 1952 at 1.3 billion dollars. These estimates must be considered tentative since the stockpiling program is constantly changing in response to new developments in both requirements and supply.

Selective service.—To provide the personnel needed for the expansion and maintenance of our military strength it will be necessary to rely heavily upon continued inductions through the Selective Service System. I shall therefore shortly request the Congress to enact the necessary legislation.

National Advisory Committee for Aeronautics.—The basic and applied research of the National Advisory Committee for Aeronautics is an essential part of our total military research program for maintaining and increasing our lead in the design of military aircraft. The spending authority recommended for this agency will provide for substantial expansion during fiscal year 1952.

INTERNATIONAL SECURITY AND FOREIGN
RELATIONS

The combined strength of the free world, in people, in industrial capacity, and in natural resources, greatly exceeds that of the Soviet Union and its satellites. This great strength must be mobilized and organized. Most of all, it must be united in purpose. The Soviet rulers are doing their best to split apart the free nations. If the free world let that happen, we would be handing the Soviet Union a victory without a struggle.

The Soviet rulers since the last war have been devoting a very large percentage of their resources to building military forces greatly in excess of any justifiable defense requirements. If these forces should be unleashed and succeed in conquering Western Europe, the Soviet rulers would more than double the industrial power now in their hands. If the communist forces should seize other major areas of the world, the Soviet rulers would control vastly increased reservoirs of manpower and raw materials. In either case they would win new strategic bases for further aggression. The key to United States security is to join in building the free world's defenses.

In the joint effort, the citizens of other free countries, like our own citizens, will be making personal sacrifices. Each free nation must make the largest contribution it can to the mutual defense. This Nation has greater industrial strength than the rest of the free world combined, and must therefore provide assistance on a large scale to other nations working with us in the joint defense drive. This assistance will permit the other free nations to accelerate the efforts they are already making with their own resources and their own energies.

I estimate that expenditures of 7.5 billion dollars will be required for all of our international programs in the fiscal year 1952. This total will be 2.7 billion dollars more than the expenditure for international programs in each of the fiscal years 1951 and 1950. In 1952, the great preponderance of total expenditures for military and economic aid will go directly for the rapid buildup of mutual defense forces. More than one-half of total expenditures will be for procurement of military equipment to be shipped from this country to our allies. I shall request appropriations of 9.7 billion dollars for these mutual security programs, in addition to an increase of 1 billion dollars now requested

INTERNATIONAL SECURITY AND FOREIGN RELATIONS

[Fiscal years. In millions]

| Program or agency | Expenditures | | | Recommended new obligational authority for 1952 [1] |
	1950 actual	1951 estimated	1952 estimated	
Military and economic assistance (present programs, and proposed legislation)......................	$4,572	$4,466	$7,112	[2] $10,664
Conduct of foreign affairs:				
Overseas information and education............	34	57	166	115
Participation in international organizations......	55	53	35	32
Other State Department activities...............	142	150	148	145
Total...........................	4,803	4,726	7,461	[2] 10,956

[1] This column excludes 47 million dollars of recommended appropriations to liquidate prior year contract authority.

[2] Includes 1 billion dollars in new lending authority for the Export-Import Bank

in the lending ceiling of the Export-Import Bank. Actual expenditures by the Bank in the fiscal year 1952 will, of course, be only a fraction of the increase in lending authority.

The complete request for appropriations will be presented to the Congress as soon as remaining details of the program are worked out.

In general, our assistance programs will continue to take two forms—provision of military equipment and provision of economic assistance. But the balance between these two forms of aid will shift very sharply, and will differ according to the strategic, political, and economic situation in each free world area requiring assistance.

Military and economic assistance to Europe.—The heart of our foreign policy in Europe is the North Atlantic Treaty, which was ratified by the Senate on July 21, 1949. Like all international undertakings which endure, this treaty is founded upon mutual interest. Americans know that the survival of this Nation would be gravely imperiled if the free peoples and industrial power of Western Europe were to fall under communist subjugation. Correspondingly, the majority of Europeans are fully aware of the interdependence of their security and ours. Over the coming months, the nations of Western Europe will be calling up increasing numbers of their young men for military service. They will be diverting their resources to production of military weapons. They will be imposing additional controls on their civilian economies, particularly on civilian consumption. They will be joining with us, through the joint staff organizations which already exist, in standardizing equipment and training and in strategic and tactical planning. They are placing major elements of their forces under the unified command of the Supreme Headquarters of the Allied Powers in Europe.

The North Atlantic Treaty Organization is now a going concern. It is backed by an impressive reservoir of skilled people and industrial power. It includes not only the military potential of this country and Canada, but also the combined strength of the nine European members of the North Atlantic Treaty—Great Britain, France, Italy, Belgium, Holland, Luxembourg, Norway, Denmark, and Portugal. These nine nations alone number altogether 175 million people, or almost as many as the Soviet Union. Iceland is also a full participant. Greece and Turkey, which within the past few years have proved their steadfastness under the threat of aggression, are closely associated with the mutual effort.

The power of all these nations, pursuing a common course under the United Nations, is being directed to the creation of highly trained and well equipped forces-in-being, and a much larger mobilization base. The combined European and American forces will serve as a powerful deterrent to communist aggression in Europe. There is genuine hope, moreover, that arrangements can soon be completed for German participation in the common defense.

In order to reach the required level of combined strength in the shortest possible time, it will be necessary for the United States to give our European partners considerable assistance. The bulk of this assistance will be in the form of military equipment and supplies. We and our allies are determined that the mutual defense forces shall be equipped with modern and effective weapons. Although the European countries are undertaking to convert a substantial portion of their industries to arms production, they cannot by themselves produce rapidly enough all the complex and expensive weapons needed to arm their forces. Our tremendously productive economy must turn out many of the weapons needed to arm the European forces.

To achieve the rapid increase in European defenses that is necessary, our program of economic aid to Europe must, with a few exceptions—notably the aid program in Austria—be directed to support of the European military build-up, rather than to promoting further general economic expansion. The progress made to date under the recovery program is standing us and the entire free world in good stead in the present situation. In most European countries industry is now producing at well above prewar peaks, and this enlarged industrial strength can in substantial part be converted to military production. Moreover, the improved lot of the ordinary citizen, made possible in part by the European recovery program, has resulted in a higher degree of political cohesion and a firmer resolve to defend democracy and free institutions against aggression.

Western Europe's requirements for economic aid to support her program for building defensive forces arise directly from the disparity between her requirements for essential imports from the dollar area and her ability to earn dollars. In order to move ahead rapidly with defense plans, European countries will require materials and equipment of certain types which they can obtain only from the United States. These supplies include items essential directly in their armament factories, materials for essential consumer goods, foodstuffs, and materials for their most vital export industries. But because these countries will be diverting to rearmament a large proportion of the resources which would otherwise be engaged in producing for export, they cannot for the time being obtain, without help from us, all the dollars needed to pay for these essential dollar imports.

Much remains to be done in the mutual effort to achieve rapid strengthening of European defenses. In general, the commit-

ments made by the European countries to the North Atlantic Treaty Organization have not been large enough up to this time. But these countries share the deep new sense of urgency which recent events have given us, and these difficulties will be rapidly overcome. It must be clearly understood that the military and economic aid which I am recommending to assist European nations to rearm will be conditioned upon their carrying out their full responsibilities for building the defensive strength of the North Atlantic Treaty community. The entire free world is in grave peril. This peril can only be surmounted by arduous joint efforts, in which each nation carries out to the full its allotted responsibilities.

Assistance to other areas of the free world.—The heightened communist pressures in Asia, the Near East, and other non-European areas require that we accelerate our existing programs of military assistance, which now provide military equipment to certain countries which can use it effectively and are faced by internal and external communist pressures. However, in comparison with our assistance to Europe, which will be predominantly in the form of military equipment, our total program of assistance to the non-European areas of the free world must place proportionately more emphasis upon building security through helping the people and governments of these areas to solve pressing economic problems.

To varying degrees, in different parts of the non-European free world, the crucial problem in resistance to communism is the attitudes and aspirations of the people. In some of these areas, millions of people live in desperate conditions of poverty, insecurity, ill health, and illiteracy. To them communism may appear as a possible escape from unendurable conditions of life. These people must be given real faith in their future within the free world through concrete evidence that their age-old problems have been recognized and that effective steps are being taken to solve them.

In many of these countries the governments are increasingly aware of the real problem presented by the low living standards of their people and are taking such steps as they can to deal with this problem. But many of these governments do not yet have adequate numbers of trained administrators and technical and professional personnel, and lack the capital funds necessary to carry out critical developmental projects. The United States cannot close the gap between reality and aspirations with generalized economic aid, especially in the present period of extreme pressure on our economy. What we can do is to work with these people and their governments to help them solve their problems. By making available to them knowledge and skills to supplement their own, together with modest amounts of loan capital and assistance grants, we can help these governments to bring tangible benefits to their people, and achieve an increase in the unity and resource strength of the free world.

In certain other non-European areas many of the countries have more experienced governments and a better start toward economic development. In these instances, economic and technical assistance can make an important contribution by breaking economic bottlenecks. Often the necessary projects in these areas are suitable for financing through loans.

We do not propose to assist countries where the governments are not sincerely trying to improve the economic conditions of their people. Our economic and technical assistance will be granted only where it is asked for by national governments which adopt in good faith the policies necessary to make the aid effective, and to make full use of their own resources.

Our total program of economic assistance to non-European areas of the free world will make a major contribution to increasing productivity in agricultural, industrial, and extractive industries. Part of the increased output must go directly to improving living standards and public services. Another part, including raw materials and particularly strategic materials needed for the mutual defense of the free world, can be traded with the more industrialized nations for capital goods needed for further economic development.

In Asia, we are now supplying military equipment to certain nations faced by communist threats against their independence. We are also providing economic assistance to help meet urgent problems in various parts of Southeast Asia, including Indonesia, Indo-China, Burma, Thailand, and Formosa, and a developmental program in the Philippines is being inaugurated. Both military and economic aid may have to be extended to additional Asian countries, and certain present programs will have to be accelerated. In addition, we are continuing our economic assistance to Japan, which is progressing steadily toward self-support.

In the crucial Near East, we are providing military assistance, loan capital, and technical assistance. We are continuing our support of the United Nations effort to reintegrate the refugees from Palestine. Our assistance to the Near East nations is essential to build up their strength against communist pressures.

In Africa, developmental and technical assistance programs are being carried out in the overseas territories of the Western European countries, in large part through the use of European recovery program counterpart funds. These programs, by improving living standards, will help to curb the growth of communist pressures and will bring about expanded output of vitally needed strategic materials.

In the Western Hemisphere we are joined with our Latin-American neighbors in a mutual effort to strengthen our combined defenses and to build increased economic strength. The balanced economic development of Latin America has been, and continues to be, an essential objective of American foreign policy. This policy is being supported by the public lending agencies which are providing capital for essential projects for which private financing is not available. The activities of the Institute of Inter-American Affairs in the field of technical cooperation are a demonstration of the practical value of the Point IV concept. It is essential that our lending and technical assistance activities be continued, with a special concentration of effort on projects to develop further the economic base of the Latin-American countries and to facilitate and expand the production of strategic materials vital to the free world in this emergency period.

In many of these areas, extremely important contributions to the total effort are being made by American private capital and non-profit institutions.

The technical assistance program, administered in part by United Nations agencies, is gaining momentum in many areas, and through small expenditures is making an important contribution to productivity.

A steady outflow of loan capital for critical projects is being maintained by the International Bank for Reconstruction and Development and the Export-Import Bank. The increased need for undertakings to expand output of defense materials adds to the importance of the functions of the Export-Import Bank at this time. The Bank now has only about 500 million dollars of uncommitted lending authority. I recommend that the lending authority of the Bank be increased at this time by 1 billion dollars.

Our total program of assistance to non-European areas of the free world is making a major contribution to the ability of these areas to withstand internal and external communist pressures. The recommendations to be sent to the Congress will in part represent a continuation of these going programs, modified to take account of physical limitations of supply in this country, the increased dollar earnings of some of the areas, and the general sharpening of communist pressures.

Conduct of foreign affairs.—Effective conduct of our foreign relations takes on increasing importance in the critical world situation. The role of the diplomatic forces of the Government is of highest importance in organizing and making effective the mutual defense program. The need for a continuous flow of political and economic intelligence and the heightened tempo of activity in all aspects of international relations places a heavy burden upon the existing facilities of the Government.

This Government in cooperation with others is now organizing international machinery for dealing with world shortages of materials. In order to insure that scarce materials are used in the manner which will best serve the common defense, application of controls over international movements of certain commodities will be required. A substantial proportion of world trade will continue, however, through normal markets. In order to carry forward our long run policy of developing among the free nations workable trade patterns and a greater volume of world trade, I urge the Congress to extend the Reciprocal Trade Agreements Act.

Through the international information and education program, we are carrying to the rest of the world the truth about our own objectives, and exposing the evil objectives of the communist conspiracy. During the fiscal year 1951, I requested, and Congress approved, a considerable expansion in this activity, including construction of additional overseas radio broadcast facilities in the United States and abroad. I intend to request from the Congress an additional appropriation of 100 million dollars for this purpose during the current fiscal year. The expanded program will result in expenditures of 57 million dollars in fiscal year 1951 and 166 million dollars in fiscal year 1952.

In order that our political, economic, and military efforts may have their maximum effect, our purposes and objectives must be made clear to all. We must promote understanding and unity among the free peoples of the world and instill hope in the hearts and minds of those who have already fallen victim to aggression. Truth is on the side of the free nations of the world. We must make full use of this advantage.

FINANCE, COMMERCE, AND INDUSTRY

In the modern world, more than ever, military strength depends on economic strength. Since World War II, the Government's programs have been directed toward achieving a strong and growing economy. The strength of our economy is now one of our greatest assets in deterring communist imperialism and in enabling us to meet military emergencies.

In the last 6 months, we have moved rapidly both to meet immediate defense requirements and to expand our capacity to produce airplanes, tanks, and other defense necessities. This has meant action by private initiative and by Government along a broad economic front. We are reopening all our reserve synthetic rubber plants. A substantial increase in steel and aluminum capacity is already well under way, and we will soon take measures to increase production of other key materials. Freight car production is being sharply increased. Expansion of both private and public power capacity is being

accelerated. Mineral resources are being explored and developed both at home and abroad.

The broad authority provided under the Defense Production Act has been a major factor both in increasing the output of defense equipment and materials and in guarding against inflation and disruption of our economy. While expenditures under this authority help to finance defense-supporting programs in other functional categories, they are all shown under the finance, commerce, and industry category of the Budget. They comprise over 90 percent of the 1.5 billion dollars in expenditures estimated for this category in the fiscal year 1952.

Major provisions of the Defense Production Act expire next June 30. It is already clear that they should be not only extended but broadened in several important respects. After the Director of Defense Mobilization completes his review of the legislation that is needed, I shall transmit specific recommendations to the Congress.

Expansion of production.—The most immediate and direct stimulants to defense production are the procurement contracts of the armed services. The Department of Defense is spreading contracts among as many contractors as practicable in order to develop the broad industrial base necessary for rapid mobilization. Where necessary, financial assistance is provided through advance payments and through Federal guarantees of private loans to defense contractors and subcontractors. In addition, the Department of Defense is constructing additional plants and facilities to produce military items not ordinarily produced by private firms for the civilian market.

Rapid expansion in output of defense equipment and supplies also depends on an adequate supply of raw materials and components. To encourage private businessmen to expand capacity in these areas, the

FINANCE, COMMERCE, AND INDUSTRY

[Fiscal years.　In millions]

Program or agency	Expenditures			Recommended new obligational authority for 1952
	1950 actual	1951 estimated	1952 estimated	
Defense production and economic stabilization:				
Expansion of production (net):				
Present programs............................	....	$260	$400	....
Proposed legislation........................	....	....	700	$1,200
Allocations, price and wage controls:				
Present programs............................	....	36	3	
Proposed legislation........................	....	....	273	
Rent control:				
Present program............................	$22	13	1	330
Proposed legislation........................	....	....	23	
Export control:				
Present program............................	4	3	(1)	
Proposed legislation........................	....	....	4	
Business loans and guarantees:				
Reconstruction Finance Corporation (net expenditures)......................................	166	26	90	....
Business promotion and regulation:				
Department of Commerce......................	26	19	17	17
Antimonopoly programs......................	8	8	8	8
Other.......................................	6	6	6	6
Promotion and regulation of financial institutions:				
Reconstruction Finance Corporation (net receipts).	—12	—10	—8	....
Other (mainly Securities and Exchange Commission).....................................	7	7	7	7
Total.................................	227	368	1,524	1,568

¹ Less than one-half million dollars.

tax laws now permit the portion of new investment attributable to defense requirements to be written off in 5 years for income tax purposes. Where the need is greater than private lenders can finance or the risk more than they can properly take, the Government is making direct loans or participating with private lenders. In other cases, the Government is entering into long-term procurement contracts, or is purchasing and installing Government-owned equipment in defense plants. Even with these liberal incentives, however, private enterprise cannot be expected to construct certain urgently needed, specialized productive facilities. For this reason, new legislation should include additional authority to construct Government-owned plants and facilities.

Production and distribution controls.—In order to build our defenses rapidly and efficiently, we must resort to direct governmental allocation to assure the proper use of our industrial facilities and materials. This means reimposing many of the production and distribution controls which were so successfully employed in the recent war years. Already steps have been taken to prevent excessive inventories, to cut back the amounts of critical materials going into nondefense uses, and to limit the production of certain nondefense goods using critical materials.

These controls must be augmented to keep

77

pace with our rising production program. When the full impact of defense procurement is felt this spring and in the fiscal year 1952, even more comprehensive controls over the use of materials will become essential.

Price and wage controls.—While expansion in productive capacity will eventually mean a larger total output, its immediate effect is to add to inflationary pressures by absorbing manpower and materials which otherwise could be used to produce consumer goods. Vigorous use of credit controls and increased taxes, together with voluntary restraint by business and labor, have made it possible until recently to avoid direct controls over prices or wages.

At the present time, we are beginning to impose price and wage controls. Extension of such controls now appears inescapable. To administer such controls, as well as to promote effective voluntary cooperation, price and wage specialists are being recruited and offices are being opened in various cities as rapidly as they can be manned.

Rent control.—The developments in our defense program clearly require a further extension of rent control. Excessive rent increases will inevitably occur in many decontrolled communities where military installations are reopened or defense production expanded. The Congress has already recognized the changed situation by providing a temporary extension of controls beyond December 31, 1950, for all cases where communities have not taken affirmative decontrol action. I am recommending a further extension of rent control authority with provision for recontrol where necessary to protect tenants in defense areas against exorbitant rent increases.

Export controls.—Continuation of export controls is necessary to prevent undue drain from our economy of materials necessary for defense and essential civilian consumption and to make sure that the supplies made

available for export make the maximum contribution to our international security objectives. These controls also help to prevent inflationary price increases. I recommend that export control authority be extended beyond the present expiration date of June 30, 1951.

Business loans and guarantees.—As part of the realinement of credit programs last summer, the Reconstruction Finance Corporation sharply curtailed nondefense loans involving substantial amounts of materials and other resources important for defense requirements. Within these limits, loans to small business production have been emphasized.

Under this policy, new loan authorizations this year have been reduced to less than half the level for the same period last year. Net expenditures for the fiscal year 1952 are estimated to decline by 76 million dollars from the fiscal year 1950. Estimated net expenditures for the fiscal year 1951 are even lower, but this reflects repayment last September of the 92-million-dollar Kaiser Steel Company loan.

The Corporation will continue to make loans for defense purposes, wherever borrowers are unable to obtain adequate credit elsewhere on reasonable terms but can meet the usual credit standards under the Corporation's statutory authority. Only if borrowers cannot qualify for loans under these standards are they eligible for loans from Defense Production Act funds.

LABOR

A sustained defense program calls for a highly productive and mobile working force—well-trained, with skills fully utilized, and with good working conditions and labor relations. Mobilizing our strength requires changes in the numbers, location, and use of workers. We must make the most effective use of the technical ability, energy, and resourcefulness which have always characterized America at work.

Already, as defense production begins to rise, shortages of skilled workers such as machinists, tool and die makers, and draftsmen are occurring. Although there are still more than 2 million unemployed, in most of the 150 major labor market areas the number of idle workers has been decreasing, and in more than a third of the areas unemployment has practically disappeared.

In the next few months, nearly a million more men and women will be called into the Armed Forces. At the same time, more workers will be needed for defense industries. This means that hundreds of thousands of new workers—primarily women, but also older men and physically handicapped persons—must join the working force and that many people already employed must move to more essential activities.

To assure full utilization of manpower, we must quickly train new workers. We must increase our efforts to avoid losses of production caused by accidents, disputes, or poor working conditions. Production will be scheduled, materials allocated, and new plants located with careful consideration of labor supply. Where migration cannot be avoided, the Federal Government will assist localities to the extent necessary in getting adequate housing and other community facilities and services.

Although the Federal Government can assist in many ways, solving our manpower problems calls primarily for initiative and cooperation by management and labor. Agreements on seniority and welfare provisions will be needed to facilitate transfers of workers to essential activities. Training, upgrading, and other improvements in manpower utilization must be accomplished in the plant and the community. Labor-management committees are being set up in major labor market areas to promote all possible voluntary adjustments.

Because existing Federal labor programs are being redirected, most expenditures for defense activities in the manpower field will be made under regular appropriations. For additional defense activities which may become necessary, Defense Production Act funds will be used. Total expenditures under regular appropriations for the fiscal year 1952 are estimated at 215 million dollars. Three-fourths of this total is for grants-in-aid to pay all costs of administering the Federal-State system of public employment offices and unemployment insurance.

Placement and unemployment insurance activities.—The State employment services

LABOR

[Fiscal years. In millions]

Program or agency	Expenditures			Recommended new obligational authority for 1952
	1950 actual	1951 estimated	1952 estimated	
Placement and unemployment insurance activities:				
Department of Labor..........................	$214	$165	$165	$174
Railroad Retirement Board....................	13	7	10	10
Labor standards and training:				
Department of Labor..........................	11	14	14	14
Department of the Interior: Mine safety.........	4	4	4	4
Labor relations................................	13	13	13	13
Labor information, statistics, and general administration.....................................	8	9	9	9
Total..................................	263	212	215	225

will have greatly increased responsibilities for recruitment, transfer, and placement of workers for defense industry and for our basic civilian economy. To minimize labor pirating and unnecessary migration, I urge that employers hire through their local employment services to the greatest extent possible. The employment services will try to place local workers, including women, older workers, minority groups, and the physically handicapped, before recruiting from other areas. I also urge industry to use each individual's skill to the utmost and to adopt hiring specifications which do not exaggerate the strength and skills required.

In contrast to the expansion in employment service activities, the work of handling unemployment insurance claims will decrease because of high employment stimulated by defense production.

Labor standards and training.—In recent years, Federal programs of on-the-job training have emphasized the promotion of better apprenticeship standards. At the end of the fiscal year 1950, registered training programs employed 215,000 apprentices. A drive to increase the number of apprentices in key defense industries such as machine tools, metal working, and aircraft manufacture is now being launched. Further, a program to encourage on-the-job training of production workers and supervisors is being started with funds allocated to the Department of Labor.

World War II experience indicates that unless we intensify our preventive efforts, accidents will increase during a period of defense build-up, because of new kinds of production and new workers. To prevent loss of workers and loss of production, Defense Production Act funds will be used to help States plan special industrial safety campaigns and to train industrial supervisors and State safety inspectors.

To produce enough for defense, we must use wisely all our available labor resources. Even less than in other times can we now afford to discriminate in employment against the millions of workers in our labor force who are members of minority groups. Following the Federal experience with a Committee on Fair Employment Practice in World War II, eight States and a number of cities have established successful regulatory commissions to deal with employment practices. I again recommend that the Congress enact legislation to establish a Federal Fair Employment Practice Commission to prevent discrimination in interstate industries.

Labor relations.—Prompt handling of disputes in the sensitive field of labor relations is imperative if we are to avoid interruptions in defense production. A 25-percent increase is being recommended in the Federal Mediation and Conciliation Service's mediation staff to enable it to act in any dispute affecting defense production.

Trust accounts and unemployment insurance legislation.—The receipts from payroll taxes on employers and the benefit payments for unemployment insurance go into and come out of the State and railroad accounts of the unemployment trust fund and are not included in Budget totals. For the fiscal years 1949 and 1950, unemployment insurance benefit payments exceeded the tax collections because of the temporary rise in unemployment. This year and next, the reserves in the trust fund will build up as unemployment continues to drop.

In this high employment period, we should take steps to bring the self-supporting unemployment insurance system up to date. After the Congress enacts improved Federal standards, time will be required for the States to bring their laws into conformity. Recommendations are now before the Congress to raise benefits, which now average less than a third of previously earned weekly wages, and to extend coverage, which has not kept

UNEMPLOYMENT TRUST FUND

[Fiscal years. In millions]

Item	1950 actual	1951 estimated	1952 estimated
Receipts:			
Deposits by States and railroad unemployment taxes...........	$1, 113	$1, 215	$1, 296
Interest...	167	175	183
Payments:			
State and railroad unemployment withdrawals................	−2, 013	−962	−715
Net accumulation..	−733	428	764
Balance in fund at close of year..............................	7, 425	7, 853	8, 617

up with that of other social insurance programs. The revision of unemployment insurance should also repeal last year's amendment which places a premium on court litigation as a means of determining claims for benefits.

TRANSPORTATION AND COMMUNICATION

Our transportation and communication systems, already handling a high level of traffic, must be prepared for the even greater loads that would result from the full impact of mobilization.

New freight cars, ore boats, and other equipment recently ordered by the carriers will increase their capacity for meeting these larger needs. Equally important, however, will be the steps that must be taken to obtain the maximum utilization of existing capacity. Such action depends principally upon the cooperative efforts of carriers and shippers, but the Federal Government will provide leadership for these efforts and, where necessary, will impose controls to assure that all appropriate conservation measures are put into effect.

The Government must also continue to carry out its responsibilities for regulating the economic and safety aspects of transport and communication, for providing basic facilities and services, and for furnishing necessary financial aid. Federal programs have contributed to the growth of well-developed transport and communication systems; they must now assist these systems to adjust to the new demands placed upon them.

To carry out its many responsibilities in these fields, the Government will spend an estimated 1.7 billion dollars in the fiscal year 1952, or 285 million dollars less than in the fiscal year 1951. This expenditure decline depends, however, upon legislation which I am recommending to increase postal rates and thereby reduce the postal deficit.

Merchant marine.—Recent experience demonstrates again the large shipping demands imposed by an overseas military operation. To transport and supply our troops in Korea, more than 150 vessels of the Maritime Administration reserve fleet have been placed in operation to augment the merchant ships already operating in the Pacific and those which could be transferred from other areas. Our ability to meet rapidly this emergency need can be credited largely to the Government's long-range programs for supporting an active merchant marine and for preserving the surplus vessels of World War II.

Substantial assistance to our active merchant fleet is now provided through direct subsidies, tax benefits, long-term construction loans at low interest rates, and various other aids. Most important among these measures are the construction and operating subsidies, designed to offset lower foreign

TRANSPORTATION AND COMMUNICATION

[Fiscal years.   In millions]

Program or agency	Expenditures			Recommended new obligational authority for 1952[1]
	1950 actual	1951 estimated	1952 estimated	
Promotion of merchant marine:				
Maritime Administration and other..............	$100	$190	$354	$57
Provision of navigation aids and facilities:				
Panama Canal and Panama Canal Company......	8	18	8	....
Corps of Engineers:				
Present programs..........................	190	193	202	221
Proposed legislation: St. Lawrence project.....	....	....	15	20
Coast Guard................................	149	189	200	197
Promotion of aviation:				
Civil Aeronautics Administration...............	159	182	199	166
Provision of highways:				
Bureau of Public Roads.......................	472	466	468	[2] 524
Alaska roads (Interior), and other..............	25	30	28	17
Regulation of transportation....................	16	15	15	16
Other services to transportation:				
Reconstruction Finance Corporation.............	−11	−3	−5	....
Coast and Geodetic Survey....................	12	11	12	12
Alaska Railroad.............................	32	40	22	17
Postal service (deficit):				
Present programs...........................	593	632	521	521
Proposed legislation: Postal rate increase........	....	....	−361	−361
Regulation of communication...................	7	7	7	7
Total.....................................	1, 752	1, 970	1, 685	1, 414

[1] This column excludes 748 million dollars of recommended appropriations to liquidate prior year contract authorizations.

[2] Includes 500 million dollars in obligational authority already provided by Federal-Aid Highway Act of 1950.

costs on essential trade routes. In fundamental scope and concept, this subsidy program continues to provide the most workable means for assuring an adequate base of vessels and shipyards, labor and management, for possible future expansion.

We are, however, supplementing this program with certain emergency measures, directed toward specific mobilization needs. Funds appropriated a few days ago will permit an immediate start on the construction of new and faster cargo ships better able to avoid attack by modern submarines. The desirable level of construction in future years is now under study. As a further measure,

the Secretary of Commerce is establishing a National Shipping Authority within the Maritime Administration to handle existing functions related to shipping operations and to serve as the nucleus for future expansion of operations if circumstances require. Among other functions, this Authority will be prepared to provide marine war-risk insurance for private operators, should the need arise.

Navigation aids and facilities.—The defense program has attached a new and special urgency to the construction of the St. Lawrence seaway and power project. Besides the large amounts of additional electric power which the project would make available, it would also provide economical and safe access, through the seaway, to the large deposits of iron ore in Labrador and Quebec. As expanding requirements for steel bring us closer to the depletion of our high-grade domestic ore reserves, the importance of these nearby deposits will correspondingly increase. Construction of the St. Lawrence project should be started at the earliest possible date, and I urge the Congress to authorize this program without delay.

The river and harbor program of the Corps of Engineers includes three other new power development projects, with estimated expenditures of 28 million dollars in the fiscal year 1952. These projects are discussed below under natural resources. Except for these and other projects involving power generation, construction and maintenance in this program have been substantially curtailed.

In addition to its normal functions of promoting the safety of life at sea and enforcing the maritime laws, the Coast Guard has recently been assigned responsibility for protecting our ports against sabotage. In the fiscal year 1952, the port security program will account for 23 million dollars of the total Coast Guard expenditures of 200 million dollars.

Aviation.—Facilities and services provided by the Civil Aeronautics Administration are essential for the safe operation of both civil and military aircraft. The present program for modernizing the Federal airways system has been expressly designed to meet the common needs of both groups, and the new facilities now being installed will permit the efficient handling of increased military traffic in the present emergency.

Some adjustments in aviation programs are being made in order to meet special military needs. Air navigation services in the Pacific have been expanded because of the airlift to Korea. The air traffic control system, normally concerned only with safety in flight, is now taking on the new function of identifying and controlling civil aircraft movements as a part of our air defense.

In keeping with the general public works policy of this Budget, construction of new facilities in the fiscal year 1952 will be limited to those projects which are most closely related to national security, or to civilian needs of an urgent nature. The same standards will be applied to grants for State and local airport construction.

In addition to the nearly 200 million dollars that will be spent in 1952 for aviation facilities and services, the Government will spend a substantial amount in subsidies to the airlines through mail payments. Federal financial assistance has been a major factor in the industry's rapid growth, and should be continued to the extent necessary for the sound development of civil aviation. The method of paying this subsidy should be changed, however, in order to provide the public with full information as to its cost. At present, the airline subsidy is merged with compensation for the cost of handling mail and included in postal expenditures. These two elements should be separated, and the subsidy portion paid by the Civil Aeronautics Board from funds appropriated specifically for that purpose. I again urge the Congress to enact legislation providing for this separation.

Highways.—Partly as a result of reduced construction and maintenance during World War II, our highway system is not yet fully prepared to handle the current peak levels of motor traffic. While long-range improvement is needed in all classes of roads, we must concentrate in the present emergency upon overcoming those road deficiencies which are most serious from the standpoint of national defense or essential civilian traffic.

The impact of defense traffic will be especially heavy upon the National System of Interstate Highways, a limited network of roads selected because of their special importance to both peacetime and defense needs. Substantial relocation and reconstruction are required in order to provide the width, strength, and other characteristics needed to handle anticipated traffic. In reviewing State and local requests for Federal aid, the Bureau of Public Roads will give primary emphasis to projects on this system, and to the principal urban roads which connect with it.

Construction will be started in the fiscal year 1951 on a small number of access roads immediately required to serve defense installations. As additional factories and military camps are activated for the defense program, the need for new or improved access roads will correspondingly increase. So far as possible, these and other emergency needs should be met by diversion of funds from roads of less urgency.

Postal service.—On the basis of existing postal rates, the postal deficit for the fiscal year 1952 is estimated at 521 million dollars. This actually represents a higher level than that shown for 1951, since the 1951 estimate of 632 million dollars includes a nonrecurring expenditure of 152 million dollars, for retroactive adjustment of railway mail rates. No allowance is made in these estimates for possible future increases in mail transportation rates which may result from regulatory proceedings now pending before the Interstate Commerce Commission and the Civil Aeronautics Board.

The Postmaster General is taking many steps to reduce the cost of postal operations. Significant economies have already been realized through recent reductions in service. Experiments in the mechanized sorting of mail are being conducted. A streamlined money-order system will be established by July 1951. These and other similar measures will permit reductions in postal expenditures, some of which will be realized in the fiscal year 1952. At best, however, the total potential savings from improved efficiency are relatively small in relation to the present size of the postal deficit.

Since the end of the war, the productivity of postal employees per man-hour worked has increased by over 10 percent, and the steps now being taken will permit further gains in the future. Despite this improved productivity, however, the average cost per postal transaction has increased by nearly 60 percent during the same period, mainly as a result of employee pay raises and transportation rate increases. In the absence of adequate postal rate increases, the average revenue per transaction has increased by less than 10 percent. The resulting deficit of over one-half billion dollars would be unsound at any time, but it is especially untimely in a period when the Federal Budget must sustain extremely heavy defense expenditures. I therefore repeat, most emphatically, my many previous recommendations for rate legislation which will bring postal revenues into line with present costs, reducing the deficit to the cost of handling Government mail and other costs which are not properly chargeable to the general users of the postal service.

NATURAL RESOURCES

The economic and military strength of this country is dependent upon the availability and wise use of our basic natural resources. These resources, while extensive, are not unlimited. Our land, forest, water, mineral, power, atomic, and other resources made a vital contribution toward winning World War II and are now called upon to support the present military expansion. The Federal Government has a large responsibility for assuring the use of these resources to maximum advantage.

Our natural resources programs are being modified in order to make the greatest immediate contribution to our national security. In some cases, it is necessary to postpone desirable long-range developments in order to accomplish urgent immediate objectives. Maintenance and rehabilitation on all programs are limited to those expenditures necessary to prevent deterioration of the vitally important resources which are basic to our continued economic expansion. The resource programs of the various agencies emphasize the development of Alaska for economic security and national defense.

Expenditures for natural resources are estimated at 2.5 billion dollars for fiscal year 1952, half of which will be spent on the atomic energy program. Other large expenditures are those for flood control and reclamation, including hydroelectric power generation, and for the Tennessee Valley Authority program.

Estimated expenditures for the fiscal year 1952 exceed those for 1951 by over 400 million dollars. This net expansion reflects increases of 459 million dollars for atomic energy and 65 million dollars for the Tennessee Valley Authority, a combined decrease of 141 million dollars for the flood control and reclamation programs, and small changes for other programs.

Atomic energy.—At the same time that we are actively pursuing industrial and other peacetime applications of atomic energy, present world developments demand intensification of the national security aspects of the program. The very substantial increases appropriated for the atomic energy program in fiscal year 1951 will provide for enlargement of production capacity for atomic materials and weapons. A portion of the funds recommended for 1952 provides for certain construction projects under this expansion program.

The Budget recommends increases also for the procurement and processing of raw materials, the production in existing plants of fissionable materials and weapons, and the investigation and development of new and improved weapons. The 1952 funds also allow for continuing development of new designs of nuclear reactors, including those for the production of fissionable material, the generation of power, and the propulsion of ships and aircraft. The Atomic Energy Commission will continue its vigorous program in basic and applied research in the physical sciences and in biology and medicine.

Land and water resources.—A year ago I appointed a Water Resources Policy Commission to recommend policies to guide Federal participation in the development, conservation, and use of water resources. This Commission has now submitted the first volume of its report and will submit two additional volumes. The Commission's report will be reviewed to determine what administrative actions and legislative recommendations may be needed to improve the Government's water and related land-use programs.

Although long-range improvement of our river basins is essential for the continued economic strength of the country, in the fiscal year 1952 we must emphasize those aspects of the programs which primarily support the national defense. Immediately after the first attack in Korea, all Government agencies were directed to review their programs and to adjust them to meet urgent needs. Many of the river basin projects contribute to defense as well as civilian industrial requirements through providing low-cost electric power in shortage areas. These projects are being pushed forward. Other projects, though desirable from a long-range standpoint, are being curtailed or deferred. As a result of these actions, combined expenditures required in the fiscal

NATURAL RESOURCES

[Fiscal years. In millions]

Program or agency	Expenditures			Recommended new obligational authority for 1952[1]
	1950 actual	1951 estimated	1952 estimated	
Atomic energy:				
Atomic Energy Commission.....................	$550	$818	$1,277	$870
Land and water resources:				
Corps of Engineers: Flood control..............	438	469	412	404
Department of the Interior:				
Bureau of Reclamation.......................	298	349	259	257
Hells Canyon project (proposed legislation)..	....	....	6	8
Power transmission (Bonneville, Southwestern, and Southeastern Power Administrations)...	36	54	65	63
Indian land resources.......................	26	41	25	22
Bureau of Land Management and other (Interior).................................	10	9	9	10
Tennessee Valley Authority (net)..............	19	171	236	249
International Boundary and Water Commission, and other................................	4	7	14	17
Forest resources:				
Forest Service and other Agriculture............	75	86	93	92
Department of the Interior....................	3	2	4	5
Mineral resources:				
Bureau of Mines and other (Interior)...........	34	29	33	36
General resources surveys:				
Geological Survey............................	16	18	22	23
Fish and wildlife resources:				
Fish and Wildlife Service and other............	23	28	31	30
Recreational use of resources:				
National Park Service........................	22	36	33	25
Total....................................	1,554	2,117	2,519	2,111

[1] This column excludes 370 million dollars of recommended appropriations to liquidate prior year contract authorizations.

year 1952 for continuation of projects of the Bureau of Reclamation and the Corps of Engineers now under way—involving dams, power facilities, canals, channels, and levees—are estimated to decrease by nearly 150 million dollars from the 1951 level.

Following a careful review of power requirements for the defense program, seven new projects, all of which will provide substantial power benefits, are included in this budget. These new projects, together with the installation of additional power units in projects already under way and the related

facilities required to transmit the power, are estimated to cost in total 1.5 billion dollars and to provide 3.9 million kilowatts of installed capacity. The projects are Hells Canyon, The Dalles and Ice Harbor in the Columbia Basin, Old Hickory on the Cumberland River, a steam plant in the Tennessee Valley, Gavins Point on the Missouri River, and the St. Lawrence seaway and power project. These seven are the only new projects recommended for the river-basin programs. Four of them are in the river and harbor program, and funds for them are included in the transportation category.

The new projects together with projects completed or under way by the Bureau of Reclamation, Corps of Engineers, and Tennessee Valley Authority will provide ultimate capacity of 20 million kilowatts. Funds recommended in 1952 for the Bonneville, Southwestern, and Southeastern Power Administrations, Bureau of Reclamation, and Tennessee Valley Authority will provide properly scheduled facilities to transmit power to principal load centers.

I am also including funds in this Budget to plan for the urgently needed redevelopment of Niagara power facilities made possible by the recent treaty with Canada.

Following the Flood Control Act of 1950, I directed the Federal agencies concerned to work together on preparation of a comprehensive plan for development of the resources of the Arkansas, White, and Red River Basins and the New England-New York area. The Budget for 1952 provides funds to continue the surveys.

Mineral and other resource programs.— During and since World War II, the Bureau of Mines and the Geological Survey have concentrated upon research on the adequacy of mineral resources, the discovery of new resources, and means for improved development, conservation, and use of existing reserves. All of these activities have a clear defense significance and budget increases are recommended to accelerate them.

Funds for the management, protection, and development of other resources are at somewhat lower levels than would be desirable for good conservation practice. Increases are recommended for supervision and sale of timber resources and construction of access roads to increase the cut of timber, and for range improvement and fish and wildlife development to add to the supply of food and other essential products. Because of their importance to planning for defense

projects, increases are also recommended for topographic mapping and water resources investigations. Programs for the management and development of national park areas and resources of Indian lands, and for other services to Indians have been held to the 1951 level or below.

To insure effective use of their lands, the Indians are in need of credit facilities. I recommend legislation which would augment the loan fund authorized in 1934 in an amount sufficient to meet the demands for credit over the next 5 to 10 years. Such legislation is preferable to a piecemeal approach of providing credit for selected tribes through individual bills.

AGRICULTURE AND AGRICULTURAL RESOURCES

During the period of concentration upon defense expansion, our Federal agricultural programs must serve one central purpose— the maintenance of our capacity to produce abundant quantities of food and fiber to meet our own needs and critical needs of friendly countries. Government farm programs now in effect make up, in general, the kinds of activities needed for the defense period. Some of these programs are being redirected to provide a greater contribution to the defense effort, as for example the production of fibers required for clothing and equipment for the Armed Forces.

American agriculture today is in a strong financial condition. The high postwar demand for agricultural products has maintained farm production and income at high levels. Gross farm income in the calendar year 1950, although below the peak level of 1948, was approximately three times as high as in 1940, and will show a further increase in 1951.

With this outlook for agricultural prices and farm income, total Federal expenditures for agriculture and agricultural resources are expected to decline from 2.8 billion dollars

AGRICULTURE AND AGRICULTURAL RESOURCES

[Fiscal years.   In millions]

Program or agency	Expenditures			Recommended new obligational authority for 1952
	1950 actual	1951 estimated	1952 estimated	
Stabilization of farm prices and farm income:				
Commodity Credit Corporation—price support, supply, and purchase programs (net)..........	$1, 606	¹ —$296	$238	$427
Removal of surplus agricultural commodities.....	96	92	75	² 73
International Wheat Agreement (Commodity Credit Corporation)........................	76	117	115	77
Sugar Act....................................	60	61	70	72
Federal crop insurance and other................	7	8	6	8
Financing farm ownership and operation..........	146	157	141	163
Financing rural electrification and rural telephones..	294	312	269	118
Agricultural land and water resources:				
Conservation and use (including administrative expense accounts).........................	275	309	304	310
Soil Conservation Service and flood control......	61	65	63	64
Research, and other agricultural services..........	163	161	148	171
Total.....................................	2, 784	986	1, 429	1, 483

¹ Excess of receipts over expenditures.

² Excludes $77 million of this permanent appropriation recommended to be made available for reimbursement to the Commodity Credit Corporation for the 1950 costs of the International Wheat Agreement.

in the fiscal year 1950 to 1 billion dollars in 1951 and to 1.4 billion dollars in 1952. Most of the change in agricultural expenditures from 1950 to 1952 is due to decreased expenditures for agricultural price supports.

Stabilization of farm prices and farm income.—Expenditures of the Commodity Credit Corporation for price-support purposes have declined greatly since mid-1950 because of the rise in farm prices and the short cotton crop. During the fiscal year 1951, it is now estimated that the Corporation will realize net receipts of 296 million dollars compared with net outlays in 1950 of 1.6 billion dollars. Receipts from sales of nearly 3.5 million bales of cotton acquired from the 1948 crop will alone more than offset other expenditures for price support.

Present estimates of production, consumption, and exports of 1951 crops indicate that

net expenditures for price support will be 238 million dollars in the fiscal year 1952. While commodity inventories are currently proving to be valuable in meeting increasing needs for foods and fibers, losses have occurred in the disposal of a number of perishable commodities, and further losses are expected to occur in 1952. To avoid the unnecessary accumulation and loss on perishable agricultural commodities, legislation is needed to permit direct payments to producers in lieu of market price supports through Government purchases. This would allow excess perishable commodities to move into consumption and would make our price support provisions more compatible with our international trade policy. To help the Commodity Credit Corporation dispose of its existing surpluses, it should be authorized to pay transportation and repackaging costs on surplus commodities distributed to public and private welfare organizations.

In addition to Commodity Credit Corporation price support expenditures, a permanent appropriation, equal to 30 percent of customs duties, is available for removal from the market of surplus agricultural commodities, mainly perishables. With increasing demands for farm commodities, the total amount of this fund will not be necessary for this purpose in the fiscal year 1952. Accordingly, I recommend that 77 million dollars of the permanent appropriation be used to reimburse the Commodity Credit Corporation for costs of the International Wheat Agreement in the fiscal year 1950.

Under the International Wheat Agreement, the United States guarantees the export of a certain quantity of wheat at the maximum price of $1.80 per bushel during the 4 years of the Agreement. The loss arising from the difference between this agreed-upon price and the higher domestic price of wheat is met from Corporation funds, with reimbursement later from appropriated funds. Because of an increase in export quotas and higher domestic wheat prices, expenditures for the Wheat Agreement are estimated to rise to 117 million dollars in the fiscal year 1951 and 115 million in 1952.

Expenditures under the Sugar Act of 1948 will increase in the fiscal year 1952 because of the larger volume of domestic sugar production in 1950 and 1951, and the provision in the law for mandatory payments to sugar producers.

Financing farm ownership and operation.—The loan programs supervised by the Farm Credit Administration will, in the defense period, facilitate farm operations and encourage farm ownership. These loan programs are largely financed by borrowing in the open market, and only the supervisory expenses of the Farm Credit Administration and changes in net investment of Government capital in the supervised banks and other corporations are included in Budget totals.

The loan activities of the Farmers' Home Administration, which also assist farm operations, are financed by funds borrowed from the Treasury. These activities are expected to remain at approximately the same level in the fiscal year 1952, with a decrease in farm ownership loans offset in part by some expansion in production and subsistence loans to meet the needs of reclamation settlers and low-income farmers for essential operating credit not available from other credit sources. The disaster loan program is expected to decline in 1952 below the abnormal levels required in 1950 and 1951.

Financing rural electrification and rural telephones.—By June 30, 1950, approximately 86 percent of all farms were electrified, compared with 48 percent in 1945. Last year, a new program to extend and improve rural telephone systems was begun. Although under normal conditions it would be desirable to continue the rapid progress on rural electrification and the provision of adequate rural telephones, shortages of metals, particularly aluminum and copper, and of electronic equipment, make it necessary to proceed more slowly with both the electrification and telephone programs. I recommend that the Rural Electrification Administration new loan authorization be reduced from the 297 million dollars available in 1951 to 109 million dollars in 1952. Expenditures will decline by a smaller amount because of the backlog of loans committed but not yet advanced. The reduction in new loan authorization will permit improvement and expansion of existing distribution capacity where essential, but will require some curtailment of loans for new facilities.

Conservation.—Efforts to promote conservation and development of agricultural land and water resources are aided by the Department of Agriculture through the technical advice and assistance of the Soil Conservation Service, the flood control program, and the conservation payments program. Although some phases of these programs may in future years need to be expanded to maintain and improve our soil resources, the higher priority which must now be given to defense programs requires in the 1952 Budget a policy of no expansion of present conservation programs. I, therefore, recommend that funds for flood control and the Soil Conservation Service be held at the present level and that the advance authorization for the conservation and use program in the 1952 crop year, which will largely determine expenditures in the fiscal year 1953, be continued at the 1951 crop-year level of 285 million dollars.

Research and other agricultural services.— An appropriation of 171 million dollars is recommended for the continuing basic services for agriculture, including research on crop varieties, livestock and poultry, and the production and marketing of farm products; control and eradication of insects and plant and animal diseases; meat inspection; payments to States for experiment stations and cooperative extension work; and general overhead expenses of the Department of Agriculture. This amount also includes 33 million dollars to reimburse the Commodity Credit Corporation for 1950 expenses of the program to eradicate foot-and-mouth disease in Mexico. Although there are many worthwhile research and service programs which it would be desirable to expand under more normal conditions, I recommend at this time that they be held at or below their 1951 level. Finally, I recommend legislation to enable

the Commodity Exchange Authority to control speculative trading and to strengthen its regulation of commodity exchanges.

HOUSING AND COMMUNITY DEVELOPMENT

In the years since World War II, we have made a good start toward achieving adequate housing and community facilities for our people. In the last 12 months over 1,350,000 new housing units were produced, a third above the previous record level. About half of this new housing was financed with mortgages insured or guaranteed by Federal agencies. Under the comprehensive legislation enacted by the Eighty-first Congress, the Federal Government has begun to aid in clearing slums and redeveloping our cities; to assist local housing authorities in providing adequate housing for low-income groups; to promote better farm housing; and to conduct or sponsor the basic research needed to realize the full potentialities of the construction industry.

Continuance of the high level of housing construction achieved in 1950, while entirely desirable in normal times, would use materials and manpower now needed to meet defense requirements. Accordingly, to help the defense program go ahead full speed and to reduce inflationary pressures on construction costs, it has been necessary to take measures to reduce residential construction this year by more than a third, to a level of about 850,000 units annually.

To meet defense needs, four major revisions have been made in our housing and community development programs. First, comprehensive limitations have been imposed on all types of credit to finance new housing construction, as well as on all Government-guaranteed credit to finance purchase of existing homes. Second, in both existing and proposed new programs, we are giving top priority to military and defense-related housing and community facilities.

HOUSING AND COMMUNITY DEVELOPMENT

[Fiscal years.   In millions]

	Net expenditures or net receipts (—)			Recommended new obligational authority for 1952 [1]
Program or agency	1950 actual	1951 estimated	1952 estimated	
Defense housing, community facilities and services (proposed legislation)......................	....	....	$100	$150
Civil defense:				
Federal Civil Defense Administration............	....	$10	265	450
Reconstruction Finance Corporation.............	....	5	65	....
Aids to private housing (present programs):				
Housing and Home Finance Agency:				
Federal National Mortgage Association.......	$579	189	—530	....
Federal Housing Administration [2]............	—30	—6	—5	....
Home Owners' Loan Corporation............	—242	—80	(3)	....
Other..................................	5	7	—11	....
Veterans Administration: Direct loans..........	....	73	—5	....
Department of Agriculture: Farm housing.......	12	28	23	23
Reconstruction Finance Corporation.............	—25	—40	—20	....
Other housing and community development programs:				
Housing and Home Finance Agency:				
Public housing programs...................	—37	158	—138	28
Loans to educational institutions...........	....	1	36	....
Slum clearance and urban redevelopment.....	(3)	10	65	[4] 350
Advance planning loans and other..........	4	32	15	5
Reconstruction Finance Corporation...........	—6	14	24	....
Other (mainly Interior).....................	1	8	14	12
Total.................................	261	409	—102	1,018

[1] This column excludes 5 million dollars of recommended appropriations to liquidate prior year contract authorizations.
[2] Excludes net receipts of Mutual Mortgage Insurance Fund, now shown under trust accounts.
[3] Less than one-half million dollars.
[4] Represents obligational authority already provided by Housing Act of 1949.

Third, subject only to defense priorities, we are giving special emphasis to housing for lower-income groups in accordance with the general objectives of national housing policy. Fourth, we are rapidly organizing under newly enacted legislation to meet the civil defense requirements of the Nation.

Most of the existing Federal programs are financed by authorizations already made by the Congress in basic statutes. Partly because of the sharp curtailments in programs, only a small part of those authorizations will be spent in the fiscal year 1952. Moreover,

sales of mortgages purchased by the Government in earlier years and collections on loans will cause a substantial excess of receipts over new expenditures for several going programs. Therefore, despite increased expenditures for civil defense and for the proposed new defense-supporting legislation, the housing and community development category as a whole in the fiscal year 1952 will realize estimated net receipts of 102 million dollars.

Defense housing, community facilities and services.—As the defense effort accelerates, additional housing and community facilities and services in many key areas will undoubtedly be required to take care of the influx of defense workers and military personnel. We shall continue to place primary reliance on the initiative of private builders and local communities to provide the new construction and services required. To reinforce and supplement this initiative, I am recommending several basic changes in legislation to meet specific defense needs for housing, community facilities and services.

The expansion in the defense program makes more urgent the provision of an adequate supply of rental housing. Military installations and defense plants will find it difficult to meet their expanding manpower requirements if adequate housing is not available at reasonable rents. For this reason, despite the cutbacks in total construction, it is essential to increase new private rental housing in defense areas. The legislation which I am proposing will provide more liberal insurance for loans financing construction of a limited number of rental units in these areas. In addition, it will extend the temporary program for insurance of military housing loans beyond the present expiration date of June 30, 1951, and will include similar insurance for mortgages to finance rental housing near installations of the Atomic Energy Commission.

The adaptability of prefabricated housing to defense housing requirements makes it imperative that present producers of proven efficiency be able to obtain adequate financing for their operations—especially for the distribution of such housing. The proposed legislation will help meet the special financing problems of this industry.

In some areas where the most rapid expansion in military or defense-related activities will occur, local communities and private builders cannot be expected—even with these new aids—to meet all the emergency requirements for housing and community essentials. This problem will be particularly acute where large installations are located in small communities or isolated areas. To prevent delays in recruitment and to assure a reasonably stable labor supply in such areas, the Federal Government should have authority, as in World War II, to construct housing units and to make loans and grants for community facilities and services. This authority should be limited to meeting defense needs and even then should be available only when these needs could not otherwise be met. Accordingly the proposed legislation would authorize direct Federal construction of defense housing and provision of Federal funds for community facilities and services. For these purposes, as well as for the necessary extension and expansion of defense-related private housing aids, the Budget includes estimated appropriations of 150 million dollars.

Civil defense.—With modern methods of warfare our Nation could be subjected to a sudden, devastating enemy attack. The military services have responsibility for warding off attack, but effective civil defense can sharply reduce the injuries, loss of life, and destruction of homes and factories that otherwise might occur.

Under legislation just enacted, the Federal Civil Defense Administration will provide equal matching grants to States for the construction of shelters and other protective facilities in critical target areas. These grants account for the larger part of the expenditures projected for this program in the fiscal year 1952. The Administration will also begin building a national reserve of supplies and equipment. In addition, the Reconstruction Finance Corporation will make loans to public authorities for public works which can serve both as shelters and for other community purposes, when the Administrator certifies that there is a civil defense necessity for such projects.

Aids to private housing.—The record levels of private housing construction in recent years have been stimulated in large part by widespread and generous Federal credit aids—mainly Federal insurance or guarantees of private mortgage loans and Federal purchases to support the market for these mortgages. By reducing the liberality of these aids, it has been possible to cut back housing construction in recent months without imposing direct controls.

Federal National Mortgage Association.— Changes in law and administrative policy governing the Federal National Mortgage Association have sharply curtailed new purchases of mortgages (except those covered by earlier commitments) and have helped to stimulate an increasing volume of sales of mortgages previously purchased. As the large backlog of old commitments is gradually drawn down, the net expenditures of this program will continue to decline. In the fiscal year 1952 net receipts of 530 million dollars are expected, primarily from the accelerated sales program. By that time, we plan to return this secondary mortgage market largely to a stand-by status and to place a substantial part of the unused mortgage purchase authority in reserve for possible future emergency requirements.

Federal Housing Administration.—The higher down payments and other limitations placed on housing credit have caused a sharp decline in applications for mortgage insurance under existing Federal Housing Administration programs. Nevertheless, in 1952, roughly one-half the total new housing produced, as well as purchases of nearly 200,000 existing homes, will probably be financed with the aid of Federal mortgage insurance. From the standpoint of the Federal Budget, these programs will continue to show net receipts, since the estimated premium income will exceed administrative expenses and probable losses.

Home Owners' Loan Corporation.—The Home Owners' Loan Corporation will be liquidated before the close of the current fiscal year. All of the Federal investment of more than 3.7 billion dollars made during the depression years of the 1930's will be repaid in full and in addition the earned surplus of 14 million dollars will be paid to the Treasury. These payments will successfully complete one of the largest emergency financing operations of the depression years.

Direct veterans loans.—Under the Housing Act of 1950, the Administrator of Veterans' Affairs was given temporary authority to make a maximum of 150 million dollars in direct housing loans to veterans in areas where, even with the support of the secondary market, adequate financing is not obtainable. Experience to date indicates only a limited need for such loans, which private lenders should be able to provide. Accordingly, I do not recommend the extension of this program beyond the current fiscal year.

Farm housing.—As part of the general limitation of new housing construction, new loans for farm housing in the fiscal year 1952 will be held to less than a third of the 75 million dollars authorized in the basic statute.

Public housing programs.—In the fiscal year 1952, construction of an estimated 75,000 new units will be started under the low-rent public housing program, well below the annual level of 135,000 units authorized by the Housing Act of 1949. These units will serve two major purposes. They will not only help meet the long-neglected housing needs of low-income families, but will also make an important contribution to defense housing requirements. To make sure that the full defense potentialities are realized, the Public Housing Administration, to the maximum extent feasible, will give preference to projects serving defense areas and will require local housing authorities to give military personnel and defense workers preference as tenants.

During the current year, the initial construction is being financed largely through temporary Federal loans. In 1952 and later years, however, both the initial construction and the permanent capital investment in the local projects will be largely financed by obligations issued by the local housing authorities to private investors on the security of the annual Federal contributions. In the fiscal year 1952, collections and private refinancing of earlier loans will cause substantial net receipts. Federal expenditures for annual contributions to help pay rentals of low-income tenants will increase moderately, but in the case of projects occupied by defense workers the income of the occupants will be sufficient to make Federal contributions unnecessary to help pay their rents.

Loans to educational institutions.—Soon after the aggression in Korea last summer, authorizations under this program were suspended to permit reappraisal of college housing needs. On the basis of this reappraisal, a maximum of 40 million dollars out of the 300 million dollars authorized by the Housing Act of 1950 has been provided, to be used only for college housing directly contributing to defense. No other loans will be made under this program until the outlook for college enrollment shows a clear need for such housing.

Slum clearance and urban redevelopment.—The long-range program for clearance of slums and redevelopment of the major urban areas, for both private and public use, is still in its early stages. Commitments for planning advances have been issued to 70 cities.

Because of the great importance of encouraging orderly development of our cities—and the small amounts of manpower

and other resources involved in the early years—steady progress should continue in the planning stage of this program. Local authorities also may acquire sites, but will not demolish existing buildings or otherwise redevelop areas unless the redevelopment is consistent with defense requirements. Under this basic policy, net expenditures of 65 million dollars are anticipated for the fiscal year 1952—primarily for planning advances and temporary loans for acquisition of sites. This contrasts with the additional 350 million dollars in authority which becomes available in 1952 under the basic statute.

Advance planning loans.—Advances to State and local governments for public works planning have been suspended except when the projects involve defense-related or essential civilian requirements. While in a normal peacetime economy this program makes a major contribution to economic stability, it does not now appear advisable to extend it beyond the present expiration next October.

EDUCATION AND GENERAL RESEARCH

The challenge of communist imperialism requires the full potential of all our people—their initiative, their knowledge, their skills, and their ideals. These qualities have given this Nation world leadership in science and industry. Education and research are vital to the maintenance of this leadership.

The highly developed technology of the Nation requires an educated people equipped to operate this productive system efficiently. Likewise, it requires continuing basic research and the practical application of new knowledge and new techniques. Yet we start our defense effort with an educational system which fails to provide adequate educational opportunities for all our people, and with a lack of balance in the Nation's research activities.

The Federal Government took a major step last year toward achieving a better balance in research through the creation of the National Science Foundation, but urgently needed general legislation in the field of education was not enacted. This Budget includes provision for grants to the States for the operating expenses of elementary and secondary schools to assist in improving educational opportunities for our children. This proposal accounts for more than half of the total estimate of 483 million dollars of expenditures for education and general research in the fiscal year 1952, and for most of the estimated increase over 1951.

In addition to programs included in this total, many Federal agencies carry on specialized education and research activities which are included under other categories, such as veterans' services and benefits, military services, and agriculture.

Promotion of education.—Strong elementary and secondary educational systems throughout the country are vital to national strength and to the improvement of individual opportunity. Although educational opportunities are excellent in some parts of the country, children and youth in too many of our communities still do not receive adequate education. Inequalities exist primarily because of differences in the financial resources of the States and localities.

The Nation as a whole suffers from these inequalities. The results are demonstrated most sharply in times like the present. The military services even find it necessary to teach some inductees reading and writing before they can begin combat training. From the standpoint of national security alone, as well as the enlargement of opportunities for the individual, the Nation needs to see that every youth acquires the fundamental education and training which are essential to effective service, whether in the Armed

EDUCATION AND GENERAL RESEARCH

[Fiscal years.　In millions]

	Expenditures			Recommended new obligational authority for 1952 [1]
Program or agency	1950 actual	1951 estimated	1952 estimated	
Promotion of education: Office of Education:				
General aid for operating expenses, elementary and secondary schools (proposed legislation)...	....	....	$290	$300
Vocational education.........................	$27	$27	27	27
Education of children on Federal property and in emergency areas.............................	....	39	106	78
Other programs...............................	14	8	8	9
Educational aid to special groups.................	5	7	8	5
Library and museum services.....................	9	11	12	12
General purpose research:				
National Science Foundation.....................	....	([2])	3	10
National Bureau of Standards...................	9	12	11	8
Seventeenth decennial census (Commerce).......	42	32	10	9
Other (mainly Census Bureau).................	8	7	8	10
Total.....................................	114	143	483	468

[1] This column excludes 29 million dollars of recommended appropriations to liquidate prior year contract authorizations.

[2] Less than one-half million dollars.

Forces, in industry, or on the farm. I therefore urge the Congress to authorize Federal financial assistance to help the States provide a level of elementary and secondary education that will meet the minimum needs of the Nation. The Budget includes a tentative appropriation estimate of 300 million dollars for this purpose.

To help meet one particular educational problem, laws were enacted last year to make a single agency—the Federal Security Agency—responsible for giving financial assistance to schools or, if necessary, establishing schools for the education of children living on Federal property or in areas especially affected by Federal activities. Previously a variety of arrangements existed, and some of these children were denied free public education. The Budget includes expenditures of 106 million dollars in the fiscal year 1952 for buildings and current operating expenses under these new laws.

In view of the present necessity to provide training for defense production, a part of the appropriations for the general purpose of vocational education and training should be used for the training of workers for defense and essential civilian production. This Budget provides for the designation of 10 million dollars of the proposed vocational education appropriation for the fiscal year 1952 for this purpose.

Last year I recommended a program of aid to college students to help equalize educational opportunities. The proposal is omitted from the Budget pending reconsideration of the kind of program that will best fit into Selective Service policies and general manpower requirements.

Science Foundation.—The National Science Foundation, established by law last year, is now organized and planning its program. The limited funds available to it in the current fiscal year will not permit the Foundation to proceed beyond initial preparations.

An appropriation request for the fiscal year 1952 will be submitted this spring to enable the Foundation to initiate the important work of formulating a national policy for basic research, stimulating such research, and training scientific personnel.

SOCIAL SECURITY, WELFARE, AND HEALTH

Last year the Congress enacted important improvements in our social security program. Coverage under old-age and survivors insurance was extended to some 10 million additional workers. Eligibility requirements were relaxed for older people, so that many more will qualify for retirement annuities in the near future. The level of benefits was raised substantially and the taxable wage base was increased moderately, to make the benefits and the taxes more commensurate with earnings.

In taking this step, the Congress clearly decided that social insurance, rather than public assistance, is to be the primary vehicle for providing social security in this country. This accords fully with our American tradition of self-reliance. In the future, the great majority of American families will obtain, through their own and their employers' contributions, a considerable degree of insurance protection against poverty arising from the old age or death of the wage earner.

In spite of these far-reaching improvements, however, the Nation's social insurance program still does not measure up to the full needs or aspirations of the American people; nor has it by any means achieved the scope of protection that our economy can afford and should give. Millions of people, including self-employed farmers, many domestic and agricultural workers, many public employees, and members of the Armed Forces, still are not under social insurance. Our aim should be to establish for all employed people a minimum protection that each person takes with him wherever he works.

Pension and insurance plans for special groups should supplement social security benefits, as industry pensions already do for several million workers. Moreover, we need to fill important gaps in our social insurance system by providing protection on a prepaid basis against the costs of medical care and the loss of family income in cases of disability. These measures will help to provide that material security which is essential to a vigorous democracy and a highly productive labor force.

All Federal programs of social security, welfare, and health are estimated to require expenditures of 2.6 billion dollars in the fiscal year 1952, an increase of 105 million dollars over the current year. Three-fourths of the expenditures are for public assistance, for accident compensation payments, and for the

transfer of railroad payroll tax receipts to the railroad retirement trust account. The amounts of these expenditures are all determined by statutory requirements. The remaining one-fourth provides for all the public health activities of the Government, for aid to various special groups, and for the Federal Bureau of Investigation and other crime control and correction services.

Public assistance.—The same legislation which extended coverage of old-age and survivors insurance also made changes in the Federal-State public assistance program. It authorized Federal grants for assistance to totally and permanently disabled persons, extended the aid for dependent children to include a relative who takes care of such children, and provided for Federal sharing of payments made by the States to hospitals

SOCIAL SECURITY, WELFARE, AND HEALTH

[Fiscal years. In millions]

Program or agency	Expenditures			Recommended new obligational authority for 1952 [1]
	1950 actual	1951 estimated	1952 estimated	
Public assistance: Federal Security Agency.........	$1,125	$1,282	$1,302	$1,302
Aid to special groups:				
Vocational rehabilitation (Federal Security Agency).....................................	26	22	24	24
School lunch (Agriculture)......................	83	83	83	83
Indian welfare and other (Interior).............	29	41	43	44
Other (Federal Security Agency)................	1	1	1	1
Retirement and dependents' insurance:				
Railroad Retirement Board.....................	583	598	646	646
Federal Security Agency and other..............	9	7	7	7
Promotion of public health: Federal Security Agency and other:				
Present programs............................	242	349	350	268
Proposed legislation:				
Aid to medical education....................	....	....	25	30
Local health services.......................	....	....	5	5
Crime control and correction: Department of Justice and other.................................	91	107	106	109
Accident compensation: Department of Labor.......	24	30	33	33
Total....................................	2,213	2,520	2,625	2,552

[1] This column excludes 141 million dollars of recommended appropriations to liquidate prior year contract authorizations.

and doctors furnishing medical care for persons receiving public assistance.

With many more persons eligible now or in the near future for old-age and survivors insurance benefits, and with the increased employment opportunities of the defense economy, public assistance should conform more nearly to its intended purpose of filling gaps in social insurance. Thus, increases in expenditures resulting from the new public assistance legislation are expected to be largely offset by decreases resulting from a reduction in the number of children and old people on the public assistance rolls. The estimated expenditures of 1.3 billion dollars for public assistance in the fiscal year 1952 exceeds by 20 million dollars the amount for the current year.

Aid to special groups.—The present Federal-State program for rehabilitation of the disabled will return 65,000 persons to productive work this year. This program should be expanded. Bringing these people into the ranks of the gainfully employed, besides improving their economic self-reliance, adds to our national productive capacity.

Railroad Retirement Board.—Expenditures shown for the Railroad Retirement Board represent principally a bookkeeping transfer of payroll taxes, collected from railroad workers and companies, to the railroad retirement trust account, where they are added to the reserve against future benefit payments. The estimate for the fiscal year 1952 also includes a 33-million-dollar payment by the United States to the trust account for the cost of military service credits for railroad workers. Increased railroad payrolls expected in 1952 are responsible for a rise of 48 million dollars in the estimate. I again recommend that these taxes be transferred to the fund as they are collected, rather than in advance of collection, in order to correct the present indefensible practice

whereby the Federal Government pays interest on money that it advances to the fund.

Promotion of public health.—If we are to meet successfully the challenge that confronts this Nation, we can less than ever afford to waste the good health of our people. But the present emergency makes even more difficult the maintenance of good health.

Our chronic shortage of doctors, dentists, and nurses will be aggravated as more of them are called into the Armed Forces. Therefore, we need, more than ever, prompt enactment of legislation that will help to increase enrollment in medical and related schools, by assisting them to meet their costs of instruction and to construct additional facilities where needed. Scholarships should be provided to attract larger enrollments in nursing schools and grants should be made to States for vocational training of practical nurses. Estimated Budget expenditures in the fiscal year 1952 include 25 million dollars for this proposed program.

Many communities that will be faced with added health burdens arising from defense needs do not have adequately staffed local health departments—indeed, some communities have none at all. To help overcome this deficiency, I urge the Congress to enact legislation which will make possible more adequate Federal grants to the States for the strengthening of their local health services. The Budget includes 5 million dollars as the estimated first-year cost of this proposed legislation.

More than one-half of all Federal expenditures for the promotion of public health—estimated at 350 million dollars for the existing programs in the fiscal year 1952—consists of grants to State and local governments. These grants are available for a variety of public health programs, including general health services, hospital construction, maternal and child health, and control of certain specific diseases such as venereal disease, tuberculosis, cancer, mental illness, and heart disease.

Federal expenditures for hospital construction grants are estimated at 136 million dollars, about 4 million dollars less than in the current year. Federal expenditures for other existing programs of grants to States are estimated at 72 million dollars, a slight increase over 1951, due entirely to the expanded grants for maternal and child welfare services provided by the recent amendments to the Social Security Act. The principal direct Federal programs are the research and hospital activities of the Public Health Service.

Trust funds.—The three major retirement systems administered by the Government are the old-age and survivors insurance, railroad retirement, and Federal employee retirement and disability programs. Benefit disbursements are made directly from trust accounts and are not included in Budget expenditures. Receipts of the trust funds are mainly employer and employee payroll contributions. In the case of the railroad retirement system, these receipts are included in total Budget receipts and are transferred to the trust account as a Budget expenditure. The Government contributes as an employer to the Federal employee retirement funds and, for those Federal workers who are not covered by these special programs, to the old-age and survivors insurance system. These contributions appear as Budget expenditures. Payroll contributions received from other employers and from workers for old-age and survivors insurance are transferred directly to the trust fund and are not included in total Budget receipts. Accumulated assets in the three major trust funds now total 20 billion dollars; the money is invested in Government securities and the interest earned is added to the principal of each trust fund.

Receipts and expenditures under the proposed medical care insurance program would be handled through a trust account, paralleling the procedures for old-age and survivors insurance. A period of preparation will be required to set up the health insurance system. I am proposing that in the meantime a small payroll tax of one-fourth of 1 percent each on employees and employers be levied to provide for initial expenses.

VETERANS' SERVICES AND BENEFITS

In the fiscal year 1952 expenditures for veterans' services and benefits will be under 5 billion dollars for the first time in 6 years. This results from a further decline in requirements for the readjustment of veterans of World War II.

During the coming years, because we shall need to maintain larger Armed Forces, virtually all our able-bodied young men may be required to serve their country in its military forces. Before many years, nearly all the population may be veterans or the dependents of veterans.

This means a profound change in the social and economic import of Government programs which affect veterans. It requires a clear recognition that many of the needs of our veterans and their dependents can be met best through the general programs serving the whole population. Therefore, in legislation directed particularly to the problems of servicemen and their dependents, we should provide only for those special and unique needs which arise directly from military service. We should meet their other needs through general programs of the Government.

Readjustment benefits.—A decline of nearly 800 million dollars in expenditures for veterans' readjustment, to 1.6 billion dollars estimated for the fiscal year 1952, will result almost entirely from reduced enrollments for education and training.

SOCIAL SECURITY, WELFARE, AND HEALTH

(Major trust funds)

[Fiscal years.   In millions]

Fund and item	1950 actual	1951 estimated	1952 estimated
Federal old-age and survivors insurance trust fund:			
Receipts:			
Transfer of employment taxes............................	$2, 106	$2, 960	$3, 823
Interest and other.......................................	257	299	313
Transfers from Budget accounts...........................	4	4	4
Payments of benefits and administrative expenses..............	−783	−1, 674	−2, 177
Net accumulation.......................................	1, 584	1, 589	1, 963
Balance in fund at close of year............................	12, 885	14, 474	16, 437
Railroad retirement fund:			
Receipts:			
Transfers from Budget accounts...........................	583	598	646
Interest on investments..................................	62	70	75
Payments of benefits, salaries, and expenses..................	−304	−329	−350
Net accumulation.......................................	341	339	371
Balance in fund at close of year............................	2, 064	2, 403	2, 774
Federal employees' retirement funds:			
Receipts:			
Employee contributions..................................	359	327	311
Transfers from Budget accounts and other..................	305	305	325
Interest...	144	161	175
Payments of annuities and refunds, and expenses..............	−268	−287	−312
Net accumulation.......................................	540	506	499
Balance in fund at close of year............................	3, 860	4, 366	4, 865
Medical care insurance trust fund (proposed legislation):			
Receipts from payroll contributions..........................	....	....	275
Payment for initial expenses................................	....	....	−35
Net accumulation..	....	....	240
Balance in fund at close of year............................	....	....	240

Under the Servicemen's Readjustment Act, eligible veterans are required to initiate their courses of training by July 25, 1951. Accordingly, with the program drawing to a close, the enrollment in institutional, on-the-job, and farm-training courses in the fiscal year 1952 is expected to average about 1 million, a decline of some 600,000 from 1951. By the end of the fiscal year 1952 more than 7,500,000 veterans will have received education and training under this program at a cost of 13.9 billion dollars.

Other expenditures for readjustment benefits cover guarantees of veterans' loans, un-

VETERANS' SERVICES AND BENEFITS

[Fiscal years. In millions]

Program or agency	Expenditures			Recommended new obligational authority for 1952 [1]
	1950 actual	1951 estimated	1952 estimated	
Readjustment benefits:				
Education and training.......................	$2,596	$2,159	$1,414	$1,117
Loan guarantees............................	61	105	110	
Unemployment and self-employment allowances..	141	18	10	94
Other......................................	76	79	45	24
Compensation and pensions.....................	2,223	2,198	2,223	2,223
Insurance....................................	480	95	74	73
Hospitals and medical care:				
Current expenses............................	605	601	650	659
Hospital construction........................	159	212	155	....
Other services and administration (mainly Veterans Administration).............................	286	279	230	236
Total....................................	6,627	5,746	4,911	4,426

[1] This column excludes 28 million dollars of recommended appropriations to liquidate prior year contract authorizations.

employment allowances, tuition and supplies for the training of disabled veterans, and Government grants to certain seriously disabled veterans. Government expenditures for the loan guarantees in the fiscal year 1952 are estimated at 110 million dollars, largely for a gratuity of 1 year's interest on the guaranteed portion of each loan. By the end of the fiscal year 1952 over 3 million veterans will have borrowed 18 billion dollars in Government-guaranteed loans for homes, farms, and businesses.

The Eighty-first Congress enacted legislation to meet the special rehabilitation needs of disabled veterans injured in Korea. By renewing the program of vocational rehabilitation which was in effect during and after World War II for disabled veterans, and by providing medical treatment, hospital services, and monthly compensation, the Government is assisting our disabled veterans to return to a self-reliant and productive role as civilians.

Broader problems of policy arise when we consider the readjustment needs of nondis-

abled veterans. In preparing to meet their needs, we naturally think first of the combat veterans of the Korean fighting, but we must remember that during the coming years the lives of nearly all our young men also may be interrupted for service to their country. When the time comes that these future veterans can be discharged, we must be sure that they will be able to readjust rapidly to normal civilian pursuits.

The provision of education benefits, vocational training, loan guarantees, and unemployment allowances to World War II veterans represented a new and more positive approach to the veterans' readjustment problem than the pensions and bonuses previously provided. There is ample evidence that the "GI bill" has benefited the Nation as well as millions of veterans, despite abuses which impaired the readjustment of some veterans and added to the cost of the whole program.

Any future program should not only avoid past mistakes but should also be fitted to our changed economic and military outlook.

The readjustment needs of the men in the Armed Forces now and in the future are likely to be quite different from the needs of World War II veterans. The requirements of future veterans will depend on how long our young men serve, what they do while in military service, and their ages and family responsibilities at time of discharge. The need for special programs for veterans will depend also on how many of our young men serve, the job opportunities open to them afterward, and the types of services available to them under governmental programs for the population as a whole. When all these factors are considered, it is clear that an extension of the "GI bill," without material changes, would perpetuate provisions not suited to changed conditions. It could result in excessive expenditure of public funds and still fail to accomplish the objective of helping the veteran to readjust.

The full assessment of these complicated problems requires careful study in order that we may adopt the best policies for future Government programs affecting veterans. In that assessment, we need to take careful account of our own national experience over the last 6 years and the requirements imposed by our changed military and economic needs.

Compensation and pensions.—It is estimated that payments for compensation and pensions will total more than 2.2 billion dollars in the fiscal year 1952, and will be made to an average of 3,168,000 individuals and families. This is an increase over the current year of 113,000 in the average number of cases, and of 25 million dollars in expenditures. Of the compensation cases, which result from service-connected disabilities or deaths, 82 percent relate to military service during or after World War II. Of the pension recipients, 7 percent are veterans or the dependents of veterans of World War II.

The total of 2.2 billion dollars for 1952 includes 1.5 billion dollars in compensation payments, covering an average of 345,000 families of deceased veterans and 2,010,000 veterans with service-connected disabilities. Also included is 80 million dollars for subsistence allowances to service-disabled veterans in the vocational rehabilitation program, a decrease of 56 million dollars below the 1951 level. Pension payments will be made in an estimated 812,000 non-service-connected cases. The total of 605 million dollars for these pension payments is 75 million dollars higher than in the current year.

Insurance.—Government liabilities for life insurance programs for servicemen and veterans are mainly for the costs of administration and for payments on account of deaths traceable to the extra hazards of military service.

In view of the Korean hostilities and the current enlargement of the Armed Forces, there is pressing need for new legislation to assure financial protection to the families of servicemen. The present national service life insurance program does not meet this need. Because it is optional, the protection is not carried by some servicemen and is held in less than adequate amounts by others. The system is complex and costly and absorbs excessive manpower, especially when the Armed Forces are large and manpower scarce.

It would be more equitable, and over the last decade it would have been more economical, to provide a free and automatic $10,000 indemnity to the survivors of all who die while in military service, and to establish a special new system of voluntary insurance open only to veterans whose insurability at standard rates has been impaired by military service. I recommend that this Congress now enact such legislation and extend its benefits to the dependents of those servicemen who have died while on active duty since June 27, 1950, if they did not have a like amount of servicemen's insurance protection.

Hospitals and medical care.—Expenses for hospital and medical care are estimated at 650 million dollars in the fiscal year 1952, 49 million more than in the current year. The average number of patients in hospitals and homes is estimated at 138,000, an increase of 5,000 over the current year. Approximately two-thirds of present patients are being treated for non-service-connected disabilities.

The presently approved construction program of 766 million dollars, to provide 36,500 new hospital and domiciliary beds, will be four-fifths completed by the end of the fiscal year 1952. Obligational authority already available is more than adequate to complete the program.

Trust funds.—About 6.5 million life insurance policies are now outstanding under two trust funds operated for servicemen and veterans. One is for the Government life insurance program established for servicemen in World War I; the other is for national service life insurance, its World War II counterpart.

Expenditures from these trust funds are expected to exceed receipts by 265 million dollars, because dividends estimated at 546 million dollars will be paid to policyholders in the fiscal year 1952. During the fiscal years 1950 and 1951 dividends which had accumulated over an extended period were paid from these funds, so that the trust fund expenditures in those two years exceeded receipts by 2 billion dollars. At the end of the fiscal year 1952, the Government securities and cash held by the funds will still exceed 6.4 billion dollars.

GENERAL GOVERNMENT

Expenditures for general government in the fiscal year 1952 are estimated at 1.4 billion dollars, an increase of 99 million dollars over the current year. This total includes 164 million dollars for the dispersal of governmental facilities.

Dispersal of Government facilities.—The acceleration of the defense effort requires

VETERANS' LIFE INSURANCE FUNDS

(*Trust funds*)

[Fiscal years.　In millions]

Item	1950 actual	1951 estimated	1952 estimated
Receipts:			
Transfers from general and special accounts....................	$475	$90	$68
Interest on investments......................................	249	210	204
Premiums and other...	440	490	514
Total...	1, 164	790	786
Expenditures:			
Dividends to policyholders..................................	2, 687	334	546
Benefits and other..	414	478	505
Total...	3, 101	812	1, 051
Net withdrawal...	— 1, 937	— 22	— 265
Balance in funds at close of year............................	6, 692	6, 670	6, 405

103

GENERAL GOVERNMENT

[Fiscal years. In millions]

	Expenditures			Recommended new obligational authority for 1952 [1]
Program or agency	1950 actual	1951 estimated	1952 estimated	
Dispersal of Government facilities (proposed legislation)..	....	$6	$164	....
Federal financial management:				
Bureau of Internal Revenue.....................	$227	248	254	$256
Customs collection, debt management, and other (mainly Treasury)..........................	129	139	134	139
General Accounting Office.....................	35	33	31	32
Other central services:				
Central property and records management (mainly General Services Administration)............	118	139	164	145
Civil Service Commission.....................	16	18	20	20
Legal services (Justice).......................	8	9	10	11
Government Printing Office....................	9	10	11	19
Government payment toward civilian employees' general retirement system.....................	302	305	320	320
Legislative functions............................	40	43	48	39
Judicial functions..............................	24	31	25	25
Executive direction and management.............	7	12	8	7
Other general government:				
Immigration control (Justice)..................	31	33	36	37
Public building construction (General Services Administration)............................	9	38	9	....
Weather Bureau..............................	24	25	26	27
Claims and relief acts (Treasury)...............	71	96	50	....
Other..................	58	67	41	63
Total....................................	1, 108	1, 252	1, 351	1, 140

[1] This column excludes 5 million dollars of recommended appropriations to liquidate prior year contract authorizations.

additional Government buildings to accommodate the increased number of Federal employees in the District of Columbia. From the viewpoint of security, the new buildings should not be located in the central area of the District of Columbia but should be located within commuting distance and sufficiently removed from each other to assure continuity of operations in the event of air attack. Long-range planning goals for the Capital area also call for dispersal of Government buildings. I therefore urge the Congress to provide the necessary authority and funds to begin promptly

a program for the dispersal of Government offices now located in the District of Columbia.

As distinct from dispersal, functions will be decentralized to locations outside the vicinity of the District of Columbia only in those instances where the functions involved can be permanently located at further distances without significant loss of efficiency.

Federal financial management.—New tax legislation has created additional problems of tax collection. The increase in the estimate for the Bureau of Internal Revenue will permit continued strengthening of audit and enforcement activities to try to insure that every person pays his full and fair share of taxes.

Present customs law imposes unnecessary difficulties upon the Nation's importers and hampers the conduct of international trade. I therefore urge the Congress to enact legislation to simplify customs procedures along the lines of recommendations previously transmitted.

Central property and records management.—When the General Services Administration was established in 1949, the Federal Government inaugurated a Government-wide effort to improve real and personal property management, including procurement, warehousing, traffic, utilities, and records management. In the last few months, special emphasis has been given to measures to eliminate every nonessential requirement for supplies and equipment; to set inventory ceilings at minimum levels in each agency and make any excess stocks available to other agencies; to screen thoroughly all surplus property declarations before making sales to the public; and to reduce the volume of records so as to release scarce office space and equipment.

Payments on Federal real estate.—As an outcome of conferences with State and local government officials, a proposal will shortly be transmitted to the Congress for a general plan to reduce the effects of Federal real estate acquisitions on State and local government finances. Payments to State and local governments would not generally begin until the second year after enactment of this measure.

Civilian employees retirement.—The Budget includes 320 million dollars for the annual Government contribution to enable the civil-service retirement and disability fund to cover its currently accruing obligations. Federal employees covered by the system are required by law to contribute 6 percent of their salaries toward future benefits. The Government contribution, designed to cover the remaining cost of benefits, amounts to approximately 2.6 percent of the payrolls of covered employees plus interest on the Government's liability to the fund for deficiencies in previous contributions.

INTEREST

The interest payments made by the Federal Government arise primarily from the huge additions made to the Federal debt in World War II. All interest payments are financed by permanent indefinite appropriations and therefore do not require annual Congressional action.

Interest on the public debt.—Interest payments on the public debt are estimated at 5.8 billion dollars for the fiscal year 1952, continuing the gradual increase of recent years. This increase is the product of a great num-

INTEREST

[Fiscal years.   In millions]

| Item | Expenditures | | | Obligational authority (permanent indefinite) |
	1950 actual	1951 estimated	1952 estimated	
Interest on the public debt.....................	[1] $5,720	$5,625	$5,800	$5,800
Interest on refunds...........................	93	90	92	92
Interest on uninvested trust funds...............	4	7	5	5
Total...................................	5,817	5,722	5,897	5,897

[1] Includes 225 million dollars in nonrecurring payments resulting from a shift in reporting methods.

ber of factors, relating not only to the amount of Federal securities outstanding, but also to the composition of the debt by type of security and the interest rate structure of the debt.

About one-third of the increase in interest for the fiscal year 1952 is accounted for by the continued expansion of special issues to Government trust funds at rates of interest higher than the average on the public debt as a whole.

Second, the current increase in public debt is also reflected in higher interest expenditures.

A third important factor is the accrual of interest on savings bonds. These accruals are continuing to increase as the large volume of World War II savings bonds gets closer to maturity. Interest on savings bonds alone accounts for a little more than one-fourth of the total interest on the public debt. Most of this interest is received by individuals and is a reflection of the widespread distribution of the public debt at the present time.

Interest on refunds.—On most refunds of receipts interest is paid because the Federal Government has had temporary use of the funds. Most of the refunds result from overpayment of taxes. The interest rate paid on tax refunds, like that collected on tax deficiencies, is considerably higher than the average rate paid on the public debt.

I have presented a Budget to meet our country's needs in a period of danger.

We are building the military and economic strength which alone has meaning to the men who control world communism. This is the only realistic road to a world peace based on justice and individual freedom.

For the third time in this century we as Americans must subordinate our peacetime goals to what is required for the survival of the Nation. Our national objectives in the coming months demand unity of purpose among us and a spirit of dedication on the part of everyone. Our young men will devote more years to military service. All of us will work longer and harder than we have worked before. We will pay much heavier taxes. We must defer, in many cases, new governmental programs to enrich our national life and contribute to our individual and family welfare. But in return we will get something precious— strength to meet and overcome the barbaric threat of communism in whatever manner it confronts us.

We in this Nation have always, in time of national emergency, risen with unity and vigor to the defense of our free institutions and way of life. We are responding now. We go forward with faith and confidence to meet and win the tests ahead.

HARRY S. TRUMAN.

NOTE: The message and the budget document (1032 pp.) are published in House Document 17 (82d Cong., 1st sess.).

14 Special Message to the Congress on the Transfer or Sale of Surplus Military Property. *January 15, 1951*

To the Congress of the United States:

On January sixth, I approved H.R. 9893, 81st Congress, an Act "To authorize certain construction at military and naval installations, and for other purposes".

The installations which will be provided

under this Act are urgently needed by the military services. I approved H.R. 9893 for that reason. However, one provision of this legislation, section 407, will have unfortunate results, which may not have been foreseen by the Congress. I recommend that this section be repealed as soon as possible.

Section 407 reads as follows:

"Notwithstanding any other provision of law, the Departments of the Army, Navy, and Air Force may not grant or transfer to another Government department or agency other than a military department or to any other party any land or buildings of a permanent nature, or any interests in such property, except equipment no longer serviceable and except easements, leases, or permits deemed to be in the public interest, which shall have been acquired, constructed, or installed pursuant to the provisions of this or any previous Act except as authorized by an Act of Congress enacted subsequent to the date of enactment of this Act."

This section, if permitted to stand, may seriously impede our mobilization effort by causing unnecessary and unwarranted delay in the transfer for other governmental uses of property excess to the needs of the military departments. The Atomic Energy Commission, for example, is not a military department. In time of emergency, transfers of Army, Navy, or Air Force property to enable that Commission to carry out its responsibilities should not have to be handled by separate enactments of the Congress.

By the same token, the military departments should not be delayed, as this section would delay them, in effecting exchanges of property with private owners. To illustrate, section 407 would prevent the Air Force from extending a runway at an air base by exchanging a portion of the air base lands for private lands contiguous to it needed for the runway extension. I am sure no such restriction was intended by the Congress.

There are contained in the Federal Property and Services Act of 1949, provisions which were enacted for the specific purpose of making possible the most efficient utilization of excess military property, including fixtures. In my judgment, section 407 repeals these provisions by implication. Furthermore, this section would appear to circumvent the provisions of that same Act which charge the Administrator of General Services with the duties and responsibilities to promote maximum utilization of excess property among government agencies. I cannot believe that it was the intent of the Congress to bring about this effect, or that the Congress will wish section 407 to stand in the way of immediate administrative action for transfer of property vital to the conduct of programs assigned to defense agencies other than the military departments.

Finally, it seems to me unwise at a time when the Congress will be fully concerned with matters of greatest national importance, to go through the process of reviewing in detail, transaction by transaction, the sale or disposition to the general public of such few pieces of property as may be determined to be surplus to the needs of the government as a whole. It seems to me inevitable that there would be delay in handling such matters with a resulting expensive administrative burden upon agencies of the Department of Defense for maintaining and protecting such property until Congressional action has been completed.

For these reasons, therefore, I urge the Congress to repeal section 407 of this Act at its earliest opportunity.

HARRY S. TRUMAN

NOTE: As enacted, H.R. 9893 is Public Law 910, 81st Congress (64 Stat. 1221). On September 28, 1951, section 407 of the law was repealed by Public Law 155, 82d Congress (65 Stat. 366).

15 Memorandum Establishing a National Manpower Mobilization Policy. *January 17, 1951*

To the Heads of Executive Departments and Agencies:

There is hereby promulgated, effective immediately, the attached National Manpower Mobilization Policy which I have approved on the recommendation of the National Security Council, the Secretary of the Treasury, the Secretary of Labor and the Director of the Office of Defense Mobilization.

This policy shall be adhered to by all departments and agencies with respect to programs under their control, subject to such amendments and supplements as may from time to time be issued by the Director of the Office of Defense Mobilization pursuant to authorities vested in him.

HARRY S. TRUMAN

NATIONAL MANPOWER MOBILIZATION POLICY

Aims of manpower mobilization

1. The primary aim of manpower mobilization is to safeguard our national security through the maximum development and use of our human resources. In particular, this involves:

a. Providing manpower for the Armed Forces in sufficient numbers and with the mental, physical, and occupational qualifications necessary for national defense.

b. Providing manpower for producing the materials and services necessary to the Armed Forces, to meet commitments of aid to other nations and to support the civilian economy.

c. Constantly increasing our mobilization potential through training and educational programs to expand our supply of persons with highly developed skills essential to civilian and military activities. Providing manpower for protection of the civilian health and welfare.

2. The most efficient use of the Nation's manpower will be of vital importance in any prolonged effort to keep the strength of the United States at a high level and will be of the utmost importance in the event of full mobilization. Consequently, it is important that manpower measures taken now be consistent with and contribute to the most advantageous use of our manpower should full mobilization become necessary.

3. We must rely heavily on science and technology. The most effective use must be made of our supply of individuals having the special skills required to develop and produce the necessary equipment and to use and maintain it in the Armed Forces. Malutilization of such individuals represents a direct and unnecessary reduction of our defense potential.

4. While recognizing the very high priority of the Armed Forces' requirements for certain numbers and classes of manpower, the needs of mobilization also require a vigorous civilian economy. The manpower necessary to defense production, to civil defense, to agriculture, and to the production of essential civilian goods and services and to sustain our commitments of aid to other nations, must be considered as integral parts of a balanced mobilization program.

5. To assure the most effective use of our manpower to meet these needs, it is essential that we establish principles and adopt a series of policies which will lead to the most effective use of our manpower resources. Wherever statutory authorization is necessary to put these into effect, it will be sought from the Congress.

Principles of manpower mobilization

6. In achieving these objectives, the national manpower mobilization program will be based upon the following principles:

a. Each individual will be expected to serve in the capacity in which he can contribute most to the total mobilization program.

b. Employers, both private and governmental, will assure full utilization of those abilities and skills of each individual which will contribute most to the total mobilization program through such measures as minimum manning, training, and assignment of duties in accordance with needs, skills, and potentialities.

c. The Government will develop and administer manpower programs designed to enlist to the fullest possible extent the support and resourcefulness of individuals in the achievement of the mobilization program.

Basic manpower mobilization policies

7. The following basic manpower mobilization policies are necessary to give effect to the principles stated above, but do not prejudice or limit extension of manpower policies as further needs of mobilization evolve.

a. The size of the Armed Forces will be determined by the President. He will be provided with the Department of Defense requirements to meet strategic plans; with full information on the prospective supplies of manpower, and on the manpower requirements for defense production, agriculture, civil defense, and other essential purposes.

b. The greatest care must be exercised to assure that the supply of persons possessing critical skills will be distributed among military and civilian activities in a manner which will contribute most to the mobilization program. When the total need for workers with critical skills for civilian and military assignments is expected to exceed the supply that can be made available, the requirements for persons with such skills will be reviewed and distribution of the supply will be measured by the relative urgency of the need for critical skills as between the Armed Forces and the civilian economy.

c. Policies in respect to recruitment of individuals from civilian life and call-up of members of the unorganized reserves will have as their objective the use of persons possessing irreplaceable skills where they can make their maximum contribution to the total mobilization program.

d. Policies governing occupational deferment of persons subject to induction under the Selective Service Act will provide for: (1) the occupational deferment of persons possessing critical skills if they are currently using such skills in essential activities, except to the extent the military services require persons with those skills; (2) deferment of a sufficient number of individuals in educational and training institutions to provide an adequate continuing supply of professional and highly skilled manpower.

e. Recruitment, placement, distribution, training, and utilization of the civilian labor force (including Government employees) will be based primarily upon voluntary measures for manpower mobilization. This policy will be carried out through such measures as: (1) providing appropriate employment information to guide workers to jobs in which they can make their maximum contribution; (2) developing recruitment and rehabilitation activities needed to expand the labor force; (3) training persons to meet civilian manpower requirements and providing appropriate placement services; (4) providing assistance to employers in promoting maximum utilization of the labor force including women, physically handicapped, older workers, and minority groups; (5) providing adequate housing and community services; and (6) assisting workers to arrange for their transfer to essential jobs in other areas.

f. Governmental manpower controls will be used when and to the extent needed to assure successful execution of the mobilization program. Such controls will apply to employers, to workers, or to both. They will include (1) restricting indiscriminate labor turnover through control of separations (2) giving effect to manpower allocations by placing employment ceilings on employers with respect to the total number of workers, the number of men or the number in particular skills; (3) controlling of employer hiring, and (4) enforcing adherence to utilization standards, including full use of women, handicapped workers, and minority groups.

g. All manpower programs will be geared to the needs and problems of specific geographical areas.

h. As mutually desirable to the United States and friendly nations, workers will be brought into the U.S. for, or their services utilized within the borders of their own country on, work of value to the mobilization program. Full use of domestic manpower resources will be made before bringing in foreign workers.

i. Production will be scheduled, materials allocated, and procurement distributed with careful consideration of available manpower. Whenever feasible from an economic and security standpoint, production facilities, contracts, and significant subcontracts will be located at the sources of labor supply in preference to moving the labor supply.

j. The full understanding and assistance of labor organizations, employer associa-

tions, professional societies, civic and community groups, and State and local governments will be sought in carrying out these functions.

k. Each department will, itself, implement the policy and be responsible for its supervision.

16 The President's News Conference of January 18, 1951

THE PRESIDENT. Please be seated.

I have no special announcements for you this morning, but I will try to answer questions if I can.

[1.] Q. Mr. President, do you wish to comment on your meeting with Dr. Bennett and Mr. Rockefeller [1] yesterday, I believe on the point 4 program?

THE PRESIDENT. Had a very satisfactory meeting with them, and they are making great progress.

[2.] Q. Mr. President, did you know in advance and approve of the plan of the State Department in sending Mr. Webb to Byrnes' inauguration? [2]

THE PRESIDENT. Yes.

Q. And do you have any comment on that speech?

THE PRESIDENT. None. No comment.

[3.] Q. Mr. President, what can you say about price and wage controls and when they will be imposed?

THE PRESIDENT. I think they have been stated as they will be carried out—Mr. Wil-

son,[3] I think, made a statement in Philadelphia last night on it, which is in line. They will carry it out just as fast as they can. As I have told you time and again here, it takes time.

Q. There was some suggestion here that you went beyond what Mr. Wilson said last night; that is, that these controls would be put into effect within a few days, Mr. President?

THE PRESIDENT. I didn't say that. I said as soon as it was practicable.

Q. Well, I don't want to pursue the thing too far, but could you comment on— [*laughter*]—the fact that an unnamed official——

THE PRESIDENT. No comment.

Q. Would you say——

THE PRESIDENT. I said no comment.

[4.] Q. Mr. President, there is a story in one of the morning papers that Eric Johnston is going to join Mr. Wilson as his chief economic adviser?

THE PRESIDENT. I haven't talked to Mr. Wilson about it, but I imagine he will talk to me, if he decides to do that.[4]

[5.] Q. Mr. President, could you tell us

---

[1] Henry G. Bennett, Technical Cooperation Administrator, and Nelson A. Rockefeller, Chairman of the International Development Advisory Board.

[2] Under Secretary of State James E. Webb attended the inauguration of former Secretary of State James F. Byrnes as Governor of South Carolina in Columbia, S.C., on January 16, 1951. Governor Byrnes' inaugural address was printed in the Congressional Record (vol. 97, p. A358).

[3] Charles E. Wilson, Director, Office of Defense Mobilization.

[4] Eric A. Johnston took office as Administrator of the Economic Stabilization Agency on January 24, 1951.

what you and Senator Anderson and the farmers of the Southwest talked about the other day about importing 400,000 Mexican nationals to work on the farms?

THE PRESIDENT. I don't think that matter was taken up with me.

Q. Could you tell us what you did talk about?

THE PRESIDENT. No. I don't remember.

[6.] Q. Do you have any comment on the action of the Chinese Communists in the rejection of the cease-fire?

THE PRESIDENT. Dean Acheson commented on that completely yesterday, with my entire approval. He covered it thoroughly and completely, after consultation with the President. Be sure and make that plain.[5]

[7.] Q. Mr. President, as the poor people have to pay the bulk of the new taxes anyway, is not a sales tax, or Federal sales tax, the easiest to pay?

THE PRESIDENT. I can't answer that. I am having my experts work on it now, and as soon as I get the opinion of the experts, then I will make up my mind on it.

Q. Mr. President, we understand you are having your experts work on the possibility of a sales tax?

THE PRESIDENT. No, I am not. I am having them work on the possibility of taxes necessary to raise the revenue to meet the expenses.

[8.] Q. Mr. President, now that the Chinese Communists have rejected the cease-fire proposal, will we try to get the United Nations to brand Communist China as an aggressor?

THE PRESIDENT. Of course.

Q. And vigorously?

THE PRESIDENT. Yes, of course—with everything we can bring to bear.[6]

[9.] Q. Mr. President, a report is published this morning to the effect that this Government is considering a diversionary action by Chiang Kai-shek's forces from Formosa to the mainland——

THE PRESIDENT. I can't answer you on that——

Q. ——can you comment on that?

THE PRESIDENT. ——and I can't comment on it.

[10.] Q. Mr. President, Senator Fulbright has now introduced a bill which would abolish the RFC Board and substitute a single governor. It has been stated that he discussed that with you some weeks ago. Could you give us your personal comment on that idea, sir?

THE PRESIDENT. The only thing I can say to you is that we have been considering the situation with regard to the RFC, and I hope in a short time to come up with a suggestion.

Q. You haven't decided definitely yet——

THE PRESIDENT. No.

Q. ——at this time?

THE PRESIDENT. I can't, until I get all the facts, and I don't think all the facts have been exposed as yet.

Q. And you are not definitely committed right now to the idea of reappointing the same five directors?

THE PRESIDENT. The same five directors will continue to serve under the old appointments, but if it is necessary to reappoint them, I will do it.

[11.] Q. Mr. President, is it true that you are considering creation of a new FEPC for the war industries?

THE PRESIDENT. The Budget Message answers that.[7]

---

[5] For Secretary of State Acheson's statement, released to the press on January 17, see the Department of State Bulletin (vol. 24, p. 164).

[6] For a statement by the President on Ambassador Austin's resolution declaring the Chinese Communists aggressors in Korea, see Item 22 [1].

[7] See Item 13 (p. 80).

Q. Mr. President, can that be created—this is a question of mechanics—can that be created under the powers that you have, or must you have legislation?

THE PRESIDENT. When the time comes to do it, we will find out the best way to do it, and do it legally. It will not be done illegally! [*Laughter*]

[12.] Q. Mr. President, this question may be too early, but have you yet decided whether you will address the meeting of the Council of Foreign Ministers of the American Republics?

THE PRESIDENT. It has been suggested by the Secretary of State that I address them, and I have the matter under consideration.[8]

[13.] Q. This is a local question—I didn't mean to——

THE PRESIDENT. That's all right.

Q. ——ask it—you have in the past expressed your approval of the Passamaquoddy tidal power project. The Maine delegation yesterday introduced a bill for funds for a major survey. Could you say whether you would favor a major survey?

THE PRESIDENT. I have always favored it. I am for the Bay of Fundy project, May. I don't want to confine it to the Passamaquoddy project. I am for the Bay of Fundy project, which is the whole project and includes Canada.

Q. International?

THE PRESIDENT. Yes.

[14.] Q. Mr. President, have you asked Dr. Steelman[9] to try again for a settlement of the wage dispute——

THE PRESIDENT. No, I didn't ask him in the first place to take any hand in it. He was requested by the railroad unions to take a hand in that, and he accommodated them. They reached an agreement and signed it.

[15.] Q. Mr. President, the Democratic

leadership of the Senate is preparing a resolution, in which it will say that if it is necessary, it will be desirable to send troops to Europe at this time. Was that move taken with your consent?

THE PRESIDENT. I know nothing about it. If the Democratic majority in the Senate takes an action like that, I shall appreciate it very highly.[10]

Q. Would you abide by the—or is that beside the point—by the outcome of the vote?

THE PRESIDENT. What's that?

Q. Would you abide by the outcome of the vote, or have you——

THE PRESIDENT. I shall do whatever is necessary to meet the situation as it comes up.

Q. Mr. President, I would like to get that clear. You would like to see the Senate approve——

THE PRESIDENT. I would appreciate it very highly.

Q. If they would affirmatively approve the sending of troops——

THE PRESIDENT. Why certainly—certainly. Of course I would appreciate it, but I will do whatever is necessary to meet the situation when it comes up.

Q. Mr. President, you don't intend to request that as an administration——

THE PRESIDENT. No. I am making no request. I think I was told that it was the Democratic majority in the Senate that was working on it, and I am happy that they are.

Q. That is the resolution which would express approval of your——

THE PRESIDENT. That is correct.

Q. ——existing authority?

THE PRESIDENT. That is right—which is constitutional, by the way. [*Laughter*]

You know, it's a peculiar situation, some-

---

[8] See Item 59.

[9] John R. Steelman, The Assistant to the President.

[10] See Item 71.

times, that arises here. Last week, I made it perfectly plain exactly what I would like to do with the legislative branch of the Government, and the statement that I made about consultation was not quoted in a single paper in the United States. At the—at the same time, 2 or 3 weeks ago, there was a question came up here about atomic energy and its use for national defense. It was rather badly garbled and created an argument that was entirely unnecessary.

Now, I will appreciate it most highly, in this emergency, if you will state the facts as I state them to you. That's all I ask. I don't care what you say on the editorial page, but I wish you would state the facts on the news pages just as they are.

And I am not scolding you, I am just stating a fact.

Q. Mr. President, what *was* that statement that was not used last week?

THE PRESIDENT. Oh, I will have somebody read it to you. I didn't bring it with me, but I made a clear and complete statement about consulting the legislative branch, and it wasn't quoted anywhere. I will send it to you.[11]

Q. I would sure like to see it.

THE PRESIDENT. I will give it to you.

---

[11] Later in the day the White House issued the following release:

"The question and answer from last week's press and radio conference to which the President referred today was as follows:

"QUESTION: Well, Mr. President, Senator Connally did not dispute your right to do so, he defended it; but he said that he understood you would consult with Congress before you would do it, and continuing: 'It is my understanding that administration leaders plan to do so.'

"ANSWER: We always do that. We never make any moves in foreign affairs or on any domestic affairs, or any other affairs, that we do not very considerably consult with the committees that are interested in it. We have always done that, and there has been no change in that policy, and won't be. And any Senator who wants to talk to the President can always get a date to do it."

Q. I know that *I* reported it fully out of here.

THE PRESIDENT. I will send it to you. You may have. I am not blaming you. It is sometimes the rewrite man that scratches things out.

Q. Mr. President, *I* said that you would consult members of the Senate Foreign Relations and Armed Services Committees.

THE PRESIDENT. That is correct.

Q. Mr. President, I am sure we all reported that.

THE PRESIDENT. Well, you probably did, I say, but sometimes your rewrite man doesn't do exactly what you want.

Q. Mr. President, you used the word "quote," as I understand it. My office called the White House to check if that particular section could be quoted, and was told no. We used it without quotation.

THE PRESIDENT. I will send you all a copy of it, so that you will understand just what I am talking about.

[16.] Q. Mr. President, are you going to have the House Ways and Means Committee members down to talk over taxes before they start their hearings?

THE PRESIDENT. Whenever I have the tax message ready, I will have them down and discuss it with them, as I always do.

Q. Any idea when that tax message is going up, Mr. President?

THE PRESIDENT. As quickly as I can get it ready. I can't set a date on it. The hearings are going to start the first part of February. I hope to have the message ready before the hearings start.

Q. Before the hearings?

THE PRESIDENT. Yes.[12]

[17.] Q. Mr. President, Eddie Folliard says, in an article in Look, that you do not choose to run——

THE PRESIDENT. I don't think I used those

---

[12] For the tax message, see Item 28.

words. Those are Coolidge's words. [*Laughter*] I don't think Eddie used those.

Q. —— the idea that you would prefer to run for the Senate or the House——

THE PRESIDENT. I have no comment on it. The article speaks for itself, and it was a very nice article, I will say that for Eddie.[13] [*Laughter*]

[18.] Q. Mr. President, are there any prospects you will be able to get away to Key West?

THE PRESIDENT. No prospects at the present time, I am sorry. I understand, though, that we haven't missed anything. It has been colder down there than it has been up here.

[19.] Q. Mr. President, if you will excuse me for saying so, I was at the last press conference. I don't recollect a thing you said that I didn't see in some papers.

THE PRESIDENT. I will send you a copy of this quote about which I am talking. It is a very interesting quote.

Q. The point we mean, Mr. President, is we didn't have permission under press conference rules to quote you directly——

THE PRESIDENT. You don't have to alibi to me. I like all of you, and I think you are making a sincere effort to report things as they are. I am not blaming you at all for things that don't come out in the papers.

Q. I mean, we don't have authority to take it out and put it in quotation marks.

THE PRESIDENT. Of course you don't. That's true. You won't get it, either.

[20.] Q. Mr. President, Senator Holland has introduced a resolution to abolish the poll tax by constitutional amendment. I wonder if you had any comments on that, or on any of the other so-called compromise resolutions that Congressman Brooks Hays has discussed in the past?

THE PRESIDENT. No, I can't comment on it because I haven't read it carefully and I am not familiar with it; therefore I can't comment on it.

[21.] Q. How about comment on the atomic bomb?

THE PRESIDENT. I will invite you to read the New Yorker, which gave an exact and complete transcript of what was said and what was meant.[14] It was all explained in the New Yorker. I am giving the New Yorker a kick, because they wrote a good article—just as I gave Eddie a kick over there awhile ago.

Q. You mean kick or plug, sir?

THE PRESIDENT. A kick upstairs, Smitty.[15] I always consider that I am pushing them upstairs when I compliment them, and I think that is what I intend to do.

Q. Thank you, Mr. President.

NOTE: President Truman's two hundred and fifty-second news conference was held in the Indian Treaty Room (Room 474) in the Executive Office Building at 10:30 a.m. on Thursday, January 18, 1951.

---

[14] John Hersey, "The Wayward Press; President Truman's press conference, November 30th," New Yorker, December 16, 1950. For the text of the press conference to which the article referred, see 1950 volume, this series, Item 295.

[15] Merriman Smith of the United Press Associations.

---

[13] Edward T. Folliard, "Truman Does Not Choose to Run," Look magazine, January 30, 1951, p. 31.

17 Letter to the Chairman, Committee on Religion and Welfare in the Armed Forces, on the Conclusion of the Committee's Work. *January 19, 1951*

Dear Mr. Weil:

The members of the President's Committee on Religion and Welfare in the Armed Forces deserve the thanks of the entire Nation for the work they have accomplished in the approximately two years during which they have been active. I, personally, have been extremely gratified at the splendid way in which the Committee and its staff have carried out their responsibilities.

The work the Committee has done has always been highly valuable. This work takes on increased significance as we face an uncertain future. I am sure that in the future, the Committee's reports and recommendations will provide a storehouse of wisdom from which we will frequently draw guidance on matters affecting the well-being of our military personnel. I regret that the Congress did not see fit to provide the funds which would have enabled your Committee to continue its constructive and important work.

Please extend my good wishes and gratitude to every member of the Committee and its staff for a job well done.

Very sincerely yours,

HARRY S. TRUMAN

[The Honorable Frank L. Weil, Chairman, The President's Committee on Religion and Welfare in the Armed Forces, Room 1045, Tempo R Building, 4th and Jefferson Drive, S.W., Washington 25, D.C.]

NOTE: The President's Committee on Religion and Welfare in the Armed Forces was established by Executive Order 10013 of October 27, 1948 (3 CFR, 1943–1948 Comp., p. 835).

The President's letter was included in a White House release announcing that the Committee would conclude its activities on February 28, 1951. The release noted that the President had received the members of the Committee at the White House and personally thanked them for their services. It also included the names of the members and the text of Chairman Weil's letter to the President, summarizing the accomplishments of the Committee.

See also Item 100.

18 Remarks at a Dinner of the Society of Business Magazine Editors. *January 19, 1951*

IT SEEMS that this occasion would not be complete if a politician didn't get a chance to say a few words.

I am glad to congratulate Paul Wooton, because when I first came here to Washington in 1935, Paul Wooton was our neighbor—and he was a real neighbor. You never forget kind treatment when you move into a strange place. Just to show you the difference in the attitudes of people when a strange man comes to town, my daughter at that time was about 10 years old—I hope you won't spread that around—and Paul Wooton lived in the apartment below us.

And he was as kind to Margaret as anybody could be. And when anybody is kind to Margaret, I never forget it. And neither do I forget it when they are not!

Paul Wooton has done a great service to the city of Washington. He has had so many honors that I don't know whether I can name them all or not. Joe Short, in coming over here with me, said that Paul was president of the Press Club 2 years before he was, and he taught Joe Short how to introduce distinguished people. He was instrumental in bringing this organization to the White House—as I said—at least once a year

since I have been President, and twice when
he could get in. This silver quill presented
to Paul is because of his work with this
organization, and I think he has earned it.

I have always been pleased when this organization called on me. We have always
had a good time. They have always given
me some information that I couldn't use—
and a great deal that I could, for which I
was highly appreciative.

Now, we are faced with two things right
now. We are faced with aggression, and
we are faced with inflation. I want this
organization to help the Government of the
United States to meet both, and you can
make a great contribution if you do that—
and I know you will, as your president has
said.

We are faced with inflation because of
conditions in the world. I don't think there
is any man here who would want to see the
thing for which we are fighting lost because
we are not able to control ourselves. I think
we can control ourselves. I think we can
meet this situation. I think that every man
who has studied the position and the condition of the United States is in favor of
trying to meet this program that the Government is now putting out with everything
that it has.

I don't care whether he is in business, or
whether he is in politics, or whether he
works with his hands for a living, I think
every patriotic American—and I don't know
any unpatriotic one at this minute—is
anxious to see our success in meeting our
home situation. And I think they are just
as anxious to see us meet the situation with
which we are faced, because fate has made
us the leaders of the world. We shirked it
in 1920. We cannot shirk it now, because
it is ours. We must meet it, and it will take
everything we have, with all the brains we
can mobilize to meet it.

I don't pretend that I know everything.

I surround myself with men who understand the various branches of government,
who understand the world situation; and by
pooling all those brains and all the others
that we can mobilize we will be able to meet
the situation.

It is a struggle between people who believe
in spiritual values, and people who believe
in nothing but materialism. We are fighting
for freedom, for the right to worship as we
please, in any church we choose to attend,
the right to read what we please, and the
right to speak what we please, and the right
to elect public officials of our own choosing—
and then to give them hell after they are
elected!

Dictators don't believe that. There is no
difference between dictators, if you study
your history. There has not been any difference in any police state that ever existed in
the history of the world. They are all alike.
They are all for the enslavement of the individual for the benefit of the state.

We believe that the state exists for the
benefit of the individual, and that is what
we are fighting for.

There isn't any difference between Hitler
and Mussolini, in the Tarquins of ancient
Rome, in the Kings of Sparta, in Charles I
of England, and Louis XIV—and Stalin.
They are all just alike. Alexander I of
Russia was just as much a dictator as any
other that ever existed. They believed in
the enslavement of the common people.

This Republic of ours has been founded
on a different program. I think the greatest
part of the Constitution of the United States
is the Bill of Rights, and I believe that we
should give everything we have to see that
that Bill of Rights is maintained for the
benefit of the individual.

This is not the first time in the history of
the world that the moral forces have been
faced with the materialist forces. If you go
down through history, you will find that the

fight has been to maintain the right to worship as we please, talk as we please, and act as we please, so long as we don't interfere with the rights of others. This has been the struggle down through all the ages.

I am just as sure as I stand here that we are going to win that struggle, because there have been times in the history of the world when we have been much closer to losing it than we are now.

There has never been a nation in the history of the world placed on a stronger foundation than ours. There has never been a nation in the history of the world as unselfish, and with the ideals that believe in the welfare of every individual in the world as well, as our own. There has never been a nation in the world which in time of victory has helped the vanquished to recover as we have. I don't think you will find a situation like that anywhere in the history of the world.

We have our troubles. Somebody sent me a cartoon from Punch a day or two ago, in which the cartoonist was depicting an argument in the senate of the Carthaginians, and one able senator of the Carthaginians was saying that Hannibal should not be allowed to use elephants simply because the senate should control the use of those elephants.

That has been going on ever since we have had senates and senators, and I have served 10 years in the Senate, and I know just exactly how they feel, and I know just exactly what the difficulty is.

And we are going to meet it. There is not a Senator in the Senate who is not just as anxious as I am to see the United States Government continue as a free government in the world.

And actually, no matter what they say for publication, when the time comes for action, they will be right there—I am just as sure

of that as I stand here.

But it is an interesting thing to study the history of these things. When Louis XIV was trying to be the master of all Europe, there were men in the Parliament of Great Britain who decided that the best thing to do would be not to try to defend their forts in Belgium and on the Continent, but to withdraw to the island of Great Britain and wait for Louis XIV to come and get them. Thank God they did not do that—they did not do that. They met the situation, and freedom prevailed in the world.

And we are going to meet it, and freedom is going to prevail in the world.

But, in order to do that, we must have the cooperation of the people who make up this great Nation of ours. And I am appealing to you gentlemen to put out the facts. Honest criticism is necessary. I don't object to that. There is nothing new you can say about me, anyhow. But honest criticism is helpful. Nobody objects to that. But when it comes to the fundamental things, I know that every one of you will be in there pitching.

I wish I could have been here and had dinner with you, but you know, in these times, I have so many documents to read and so many papers to sign—up to now I have had to sign my name 600 times a day, and now I think it runs about 800—I don't have a chance, and I can't do the things that I am supposed to do and attend functions of this kind for pleasure.

I came over here merely because Paul Wooton was our good neighbor, and because I wanted to say to you that I hope you will cooperate to the fullest extent possible to meet this situation with which we are faced.

Thank you very much.

NOTE: The President spoke at 9:10 p.m. at the Statler Hotel in Washington. He presented the Society's first annual award for service to the business press to Paul Wooton, Washington correspondent for the New Orleans Times-Picayune.

19 Letter to William S. Paley on the Creation of the President's
Materials Policy Commission. *January* 22, 1951

[Released January 22, 1951. Dated January 19, 1951]

Dear Mr. Paley:

I am very pleased that you have agreed to serve as the Chairman of the President's Materials Policy Commission.

As you and I have discussed, this Commission within the Executive Office of the President is to study the broader and longer range aspects of the nation's materials problem as distinct from the immediate defense needs. I hope the Commission can report to me within the next six to nine months.

This is one of the crucial problems facing the nation. By wise planning and determined action we can meet our essential needs for military security, civilian welfare, and the continued economic growth of the United States. We cannot allow shortages of materials to jeopardize our national security nor to become a bottleneck to our economic expansion. The task of the Commission, therefore, will be to make an objective inquiry into all major aspects of the problem of assuring an adequate supply of production materials for our long-range needs and to make recommendations which will assist me in formulating a comprehensive policy on such materials.

I believe the Commission should study, together with any other aspects deemed by it to be pertinent, such questions relating to production materials as:

(1) The long-range requirements outlook.

(2) The long-range supply outlook.

(3) The prospect and estimated extent of shortages.

(4) The consistency and adequacy of ex-

isting Government policies, plans and programs.

(5) The consistency and adequacy of private industry practices.

In analyzing these items consideration should be given to the needs and resources of the nations with which the United States is cooperating closely on military security and economic matters.

In formulating final recommendations, your Commission should take into account all possible methods of bringing supplies and requirements of essential materials into balance.

The Commission will enjoy the cooperation of all agencies of Government whose functions and interests relate to your assignment. And of course you will want to solicit the cooperation of private industry. Although the Commission will organize its own regular staff and secretariat, it may call upon other agencies for any special staff assistance which may be needed. The direct expenses of the Commission and its immediate staff will be defrayed from the appropriation Emergencies (National Defense) 1951.

Very sincerely yours,

HARRY S. TRUMAN

[Mr. William S. Paley, President, Columbia Broadcasting System, New York, New York.]

NOTE: The President's letter was made public as part of a White House release announcing the establishment of the Commission and listing the following as members: William S. Paley, Chairman, George Rufus Brown, Eric Hodgins, Arthur H. Bunker, and Edward S. Mason.

20 Statement Upon Issuing Order Establishing the
President's Commission on Internal Security
and Individual Rights. *January 23,* 1951

I HAVE today established a Commission on Internal Security and Individual Rights. The Commission will be composed of nine members. Fleet Admiral Chester W. Nimitz will serve as Chairman.

The Commission will consider in all its aspects the question of how this Nation can best deal with the problem of protecting its internal security and at the same time maintaining the freedoms of its citizens. It will consider the harm that comes from the wrong kind of action as well as the good that comes from the right kind of action.

The Commission will make a thorough examination of the laws, practices, and procedures concerning the protection of our Nation against treason, espionage, sabotage, and other subversive activities, and of the operation of and any need for changes in such laws, practices, and procedures. The Commission will also consider the methods used by public or private groups for the purpose of protecting us against such activities. It will consider these matters from the standpoint of protecting both the internal security of our country and the rights of individuals, and will seek the wisest balance that can be struck between security and freedom. The Commission will report its conclusions and recommendations for legislative, administrative, or other action it deems appropriate.

I consider the task of this Commission to be of extraordinary importance. The world is in the midst of a struggle between freedom and tyranny. The United States is one of the leaders of the free world—not just because we are powerful in material things, but because we have preserved and expanded the freedom of our people. We have built our society in the faith and in the practice of freedom—freedom of worship, freedom of speech, freedom of association and political belief.

We in this country have always been ready to protect our freedom—to protect it against external or internal enemies and to protect it against unwarranted restrictions by government. From time to time in our history, we have faced the need to protect our freedom from these different kinds of encroachment. Each of these occasions has presented our Nation with new and often conflicting considerations. To reconcile these considerations, and to find the proper national policy, is always difficult, and is especially so at times, like the present, when our freedom is severely threatened abroad and at home.

Today, we are particularly concerned by the threat to our Government and our national life arising from the activities of the forces of Communist imperialism. In addition to the vigorous action we are taking abroad to meet this threat, we must be sure that our laws and procedures at home are adequate to protect our system of government against unconstitutional attacks and to preserve our national security against treason, espionage, sabotage, and other subversive acts designed to weaken or overthrow our Government. At the same time, we are concerned lest the measures taken to protect us from these dangers infringe the liberties guaranteed by our Constitution and stifle the atmosphere of freedom in which we have so long expressed our thoughts and carried on our daily affairs.

These are problems of momentous importance for our country and its future, and for the future of our leadership in the world.

They should be approached in a serious and fairminded way by all our citizens. We must not let our differences about how to solve these problems degenerate into partisan controversies. We must continue to protect our security within the framework of our historic liberties, without thought of partisan advantage or political gain.

To keep these great problems from falling into the arena of partisanship, I am appointing this Commission of distinguished citizens on a nonpartisan basis. I believe the people of this country will receive from them an authoritative judgment on these problems, based on the facts and formulated in the national interest, with no question of political advantage.

The Commission will undoubtedly wish to focus its primary attention on Federal laws and procedures. But I do not believe the Commission should limit itself to reviewing Government actions. Instead, I hope it will consider afresh, in all its present-day ramifications, the recurrent question of how a free people protect their society from subversive attack without at the same time destroying their own liberties.

This question is, of course, far broader than the activities of the Federal Government. It concerns State and local governments as well, private groups of all kinds, and citizens in their daily work and in their homes. I hope that the report of this Commission will provide guidelines of sufficiently wide application to be helpful in protecting both internal security and individual rights in every part of our national life.

The field of study for this Commission is very complex and far-reaching. Much study will be necessary before a report can be drafted. I am giving instructions that the Commission shall have complete freedom to conduct its study as it sees fit. I am asking the Commission to make such interim reports as it may deem desirable, and I hope

the Commission will find it possible to complete its work in a year.

One of the important matters for the Commission to consider is the operation of the Government employee loyalty and security programs. I wish to make it clear, however, that this Commission is not being established as an appeals tribunal for individual cases. The Commission will be expected to report on the effectiveness and fairness of the Government's loyalty and security programs. In doing this, the Commission may wish to inspect individual case files—and it will be authorized to do so to whatever extent it may determine to be necessary.

In connection with loyalty and security procedures, and also in considering the operation of such statutes as the Internal Security Act of 1950, the Commission will necessarily be reviewing information of very high security classifications. I am directing the Commission therefore, to take appropriate measures to safeguard the security of any classified or confidential information it may wish to examine.

I intend to do everything I can to enable this Commission to make a thorough and careful study.

We in the United States have a special responsibility for leadership in these critical times, when free men the world over are strongly resisting the challenge of the Communist drive for world domination. We must guard our freedom well—guard it from armed assault, guard it from subversive infiltration, guard it from internal suppression and the deadly imposition of conformity. For the kind of freedom we have enjoyed in this country has been the shining goal for millions in other lands—and the results of freedom in this country have been the shattering reply to the false claims of Communist imperialism.

If we are to continue growing in strength

here at home—if we are to continue leading the world toward peace with freedom and justice—we must both protect the security of our Nation and safeguard the freedom of our people.

I know the Commission on Internal Security and Individual Rights will under-

take its work in full recognition of the immense importance and worldwide significance of its task.

NOTE: The Commission was established by Executive Order 10207, "Establishing the President's Commission on Internal Security and Individual Rights" (3 CFR, 1949–1953 Comp., p. 389).

See also Items 22 [2], 35, 104, 278.

21 Remarks at a Dinner in Honor of Joshua Evans.
January 24, 1951

I AM HERE because, as I said about Paul Wooton the other night, Mr. Evans—and I never call him anything but Mr. Evans; you see he was my banker—was kind to me when I needed it.

You know, there used to be an old humorist in the eighties by the name of Josh Billings, and he had one saying that I never forgot. He said, "Always be kind to your poor relations, some of them may suddenly become rich some day, and it will be hard to explain."

I will say that to Paul Wooton and Mr. Evans, that they were kind to a poor Senator when he came to town. They didn't look into the future. Mr. Evans used to be willing to float a little slow paper once in a while and I never forgot it. And I am here tonight to pay tribute to him, because he was my friend when I needed it. I never forget those things, as I don't forget other things—as I told you the other night.

I want to express appreciation to this orchestra for rendering the things that I think most of, and I want to pay a compliment to that young Mr. Graham who sang here a while ago. He has a lovely voice, and I want to give him the same advice that I gave my daughter. He is 17 years old. You finish that education and get yourself a degree from a standard college—I don't care which one it is—because nobody can take that away from you. Then, if you feel

that you want a musical career, go and get it. That is what my baby did. I wouldn't let her start in the musical profession until she had finished her education at George Washington University, and she not only spent 4 years getting herself a degree, she got me one for nothing!

I enjoy a meeting like this. I don't very often get a chance to come to dinners of this kind just for friendship's sake. The dinner is usually a formal affair, with the President as a drawing card and principal speaker. And sometimes he has nothing to say—but he has to say it anyway.

I never had any fear of bankers. I almost became one. I spent some of my teenage years, until I was 22 years old, working in a bank at home. I started in at $35 a month, which was an immense salary in those days, and wound up drawing $125 a month and being responsible for a million dollars a day in a cage—and I am still out of jail, they haven't caught up with me yet.

I almost became a musician, too. The editor of the Star here—he and I were discussing our careers that might have been as musicians. I didn't finish my career as a musician, and I understand that the president of the bank here also wanted to be a musician just as I did. But we branched off into other fields, and maybe we will profit by the experience we had in those various fields, because I think I am ready for my daughter to become a professional musician, and this young man here, I think, will have a wonderful voice in the days to come.

I have no yen to get into banking. I have had a great many wonderful friends— Thornton Cooke, that you spoke of—Jo Zach Miller, who is executive vice president of the biggest bank in Kansas City, and numerous other great bankers have been friends of mine. They never were willing to lend me money, because I wasn't worth it, but then they sometimes helped me politically, and bankers have great influence politically, just as doctors do. I have been wondering how I am going to get that doctors' situation in hand so they will come back and still be political friends of mine. We will manage it someway.

I want to thank every one of you for the friendly meeting we have had, and to thank Josh Evans for retiring so that I could have a pleasant evening.

I hope he doesn't retire. There is still too much left in him to retire. No man with the physical condition which the doctors say he has—and my doctor says the same thing, he says if he took care of just me he wouldn't

have anything to do—and I think that is the same situation with you, Dr. Bloedorn, if your only patient is Josh Evans, you will be broke all the time.

I hope he will continue in the public service, in which he has always been interested. It wouldn't surprise me to see him come back here and start a bank in competition with Riggs and Hamilton National, and make a success of it in the next 10 years. You see, I got acquainted with other bankers who became my friends, and I appreciate that, too, owing to the fact that Mr. Evans was willing to float a little loose paper for me.

It has been a pleasant evening. I have enjoyed it immensely, and I hope you, Mr. Evans, have a most happy career from now on.

NOTE: The President spoke at 11:05 p.m. at the Mayflower Hotel in Washington. In his opening remarks he referred to Joshua Evans, Washington banker and civic leader, and Paul Wooton, Washington correspondent for the New Orleans Times-Picayune (see Item 18). Later the President referred to Thornton Cooke, an officer in the Columbia National Bank in Kansas City, Mo., Jo Zach Miller III, an officer of the Commerce Trust Co. in Kansas City, and Dr. Walter A. Bloedorn, Washington physician.

22 The President's News Conference of January 25, 1951

THE PRESIDENT. Please be seated.

I have two or three announcements here that I would like to make, before we start off. You will find a mimeographed copy of this first one outside, when we get through.

[1.] [*Reading*] "Ambassador Austin [1] has fully and forcefully presented the views of this Government on our attitude toward aggression by the Chinese Communists.

---

[1] Ambassador Warren R. Austin, U.S. Representative to the United Nations.

These views have the solid support of the Executive, the Congress, and the people of the United States.

"Each member of the United Nations must make its own decision on this issue. For my part, I believe in calling an aggressor an aggressor. The question of what can and should be done about the aggression in Korea, of course, must be discussed with all other friendly nations.

"Obviously this is no time for rash or unwise action. This is a time for clear thinking and firmness.

"Let me stress again that the American resolution contains—as all our proposals have contained—a method for bringing about a cease-fire, and opening the way for peaceful settlement of outstanding issues."

[2.] And I want to announce the appointments on the Commission of which Admiral Nimitz is the Chairman.[2]

The Reverend Karl Morgan Block, Episcopal Bishop of California——

Q. Mr. President, we have no way of checking that—is that C for Carl?

THE PRESIDENT. K — K-a-r-l — Morgan B-l-o-c-k.

Q. And where is he from, sir?

THE PRESIDENT. Episcopal Bishop of California. You will have to learn to write shorthand. [*Laughter*]

Senator John A. Danaher of Connecticut and Washington.

Harvey Firestone, Jr.[3]

William E. Leahy, lawyer here in Washington who is head of the Selective Service—he is head, I believe, still, of the Selective Service.[4]

Q. Where is Firestone from, Mr. President?

THE PRESIDENT. I don't know. I suppose Ohio.

Joseph Short (Secretary to the President): Akron, Ohio.

THE PRESIDENT. I imagine so.

Q. Could we have the spelling of Leahy's name, Mr. President?

THE PRESIDENT. L-e-a-h-y—William E.

Charles H. Silver, vice president of the American Woolen Co. of New York.

Q. What was that last name again, Mr. President?

THE PRESIDENT. Charles H. Silver.

Q. American Woolen Mills?

THE PRESIDENT. Vice president of the American Woolen *Company*—not the American Woolen Mills, it's Company. American Woolen Company.

Anna Lord Strauss.

Q. How do you spell Lord?

THE PRESIDENT. L-o-r-d. [*Laughter*] I will have to get Bill Hassett[5] to tell you his sightseeing story in New York.

Q. How many S's in Strauss, please, sir?

THE PRESIDENT. S-t-r-a-u-s-s—two s's. She is former president of the League of Women Voters.

The Reverend Emmet M. Walsh, Coadjutor Bishop of Youngstown, Ohio.

Q. For us Presbyterians, could you repeat that again, sir? [*Laughter*]

THE PRESIDENT. Rev. Emmet M. Walsh, Coadjutor Bishop of Youngstown, Ohio. I don't believe he's a Presbyterian though. [*More laughter*]

Russell C. Leffingwell, former Assistant Secretary of the Treasury and a former partner of Morgan and Co.

Q. And what was the last name, sir?

THE PRESIDENT. L-e-f-f-i-n-g-w-e-l-l. [*Laughter*]

Q. Former Assistant Secretary of the Treasury?

THE PRESIDENT. Former Assistant Secretary of the Treasury and a former Morgan partner.

[3.] General Eisenhower will return Wednesday from his tour of the countries belonging to the North Atlantic Treaty Organization. That same day he will report to me, to a special meeting of the Cabinet, and to a standing group of the NATO. On Thursday and Friday he will make further reports to the Congress. His radio report to the Nation is scheduled for Friday night.

---

[2] The President's Commission on Internal Security and Individual Rights (see Item 20).

[3] Chairman and chief executive of the Firestone Tire and Rubber Co.

[4] Director of Selective Service for the District of Columbia.

[5] William D. Hassett, Secretary to the President.

The schedule will be mimeographed and handed out to you as soon as it is ready.

Q. Is that Wednesday or Thursday?

THE PRESIDENT. Wednesday.

Q. No, the 2 days for the report?

Mr. Short: The report is due on Wednesday.

THE PRESIDENT. Thursday and Friday—he will report to me on Wednesday, and the Cabinet—and then he will report to the——

Mr. Short: This will all be available, Mr. President.

THE PRESIDENT. This will all be available at the door, Joe says, so you won't have to worry about it.

[4.] Q. Mr. President, on that list of the Nimitz Commission, there is to be a vice chairman——

THE PRESIDENT. Mrs. Strauss is to be the vice chairman.

Q. Mrs. Strauss?

THE PRESIDENT. Yes. Anna Lord Strauss. I guess she is Mrs. — I don't know.

Mr. Short: Miss.

THE PRESIDENT. Miss, Joe says. I am mistaken. It is Miss Anna Lord Strauss. I beg her pardon.

[5.] "The Federal Budget in Brief" will be ready tomorrow.[6]

Now you can start in with your questions, if you have any.

Q. Would you explain that Budget?

THE PRESIDENT. It is a little book about that thick—[*indicating*]. You can analyze the budget and you can't make a mistake if you read it carefully, and it covers the whole thing from cover to cover. It is a big book, too, but it is a little book.

[6.] Q. Mr. President, in connection with the appointment of this commission, would you comment on the criticism made

today by Senator Ferguson,[7] who states that you have given this Commission as one of its jobs the task of preparing suggestions for legislation, that you are giving them access to all the personnel files and others, which he says you denied to congressional committees who have the constitutional duty of——

THE PRESIDENT. I think Senator Ferguson is slightly mistaken in his statement, and I don't care to comment on the rest of it.

Q. Could you tell us the mistake, sir?

THE PRESIDENT. No. You make it out yourself.

Q. Senator Ferguson further charges, I believe, that this is a political device?

THE PRESIDENT. Well, Senator Ferguson is trying to make something political out of it, but I am not.

Q. Mr. President, does the Commission have the authority to use acts of Congress, such as the acts of congressional committees that may impinge on an individual's freedom?

THE PRESIDENT. I will—I think you had better read the Executive order on it. I think that is covered in the Executive order, if I am not mistaken.[8]

[7.] Q. Mr. President, is it true you will not appoint a successor to District Commissioner Guy Mason for some time?

THE PRESIDENT. I will appoint the Commissioner as soon as I am ready, and I will let you know right away.[9]

[8.] Q. Mr. President, Senator Burnet

---

[6] "The Federal Budget in Brief, Fiscal Year 1952" (Government Printing Office: 1951, 241 pp.).

[7] For the statement made on the floor of the Senate by Senator Homer Ferguson of Michigan, see the Congressional Record, vol. 97, p. 680.

[8] Executive Order 10207, "Establishing the President's Commission on Internal Security and Individual Rights" (3 CFR, 1949–1953 Comp., p. 389).

[9] The term of District of Columbia Commissioner Guy Mason expired February 3, 1951. He served until March 9, 1951, and was succeeded by F. Joseph Donohue on March 12.

Maybank, the chairman of the Banking and Currency Committee, said this week that failure of the Government to impose price controls sooner had brought the country to the brink of disaster. Have you got any comment?

THE PRESIDENT. I don't think the country is anywhere near disaster.

[9.] Q. May I ask one more question? Can you deny reports that cotton is liable to be included in price controls?

THE PRESIDENT. What is it you are trying to get me to deny? I never deny anything. [*Laughter*]

Q. In the last war, cotton was not included under price controls. What I want to know is if you can deny the report that all-out controls will include cotton?

THE PRESIDENT. I will deny nothing. [*Laughter*]

I think that the thing you are trying to drive at is that the price control laws are going to require some legislative amendments to make them complete. And as soon as Mr. Wilson [10] is ready with those amendments, he will go down and ask for them.

Q. Mr. President, you mean by that statement, sir, that a request for changes in the Defense Production Act will be made by Mr. Wilson, and not by yourself in a special message?

THE PRESIDENT. It will be made by Mr. Wilson, with my approval.

Q. Thank you, sir.

[*Pause*]

THE PRESIDENT. You are running out of soap?

Q. No, we are running out of lead, sir.

[10.] Q. Mr. President, there is a report up on the Hill that they are trying to introduce a bill taking away your tax-free expense account. Are you afraid of that?

THE PRESIDENT. I have no comment on that. I haven't seen the bill, and I know nothing about it. I didn't ask for that in the first place, if you will remember.

Q. Would you be in favor of taking away Congress's tax-free expense accounts?

THE PRESIDENT. I don't think we should get into an argument over that. I spent a year and a half trying to get the Congress to pay itself higher salaries. If they want to "ball" themselves up, that's all right, that's their business, but they can't do that to me while I am in office. [11]

[11.] Q. Mr. President, have you any comment on Senator McCarran's subcommittee to work on un-American activities in the Senate?

THE PRESIDENT. The Senate committee has a right to work on anything that the Senate itself authorizes them to do. I have no comment in that particular case.

Q. Some of the people thought up on the Hill, that the creation of this committee shows some effort to bypass that?

THE PRESIDENT. Had nothing to do—had nothing to do with it whatever.

[12.] Q. Could you say anything about the subjects which you intend to discuss with the French Prime Minister?

THE PRESIDENT. With whom?

Q. The French Prime Minister, Pleven?

THE PRESIDENT. No. I can't comment on that now.

[13.] Q. Mr. President, will you ask for the Brannan plan any time soon now, in an effort to keep food prices down?

THE PRESIDENT. It is in the Budget Message, May. [12] It has already been asked for.

---

[10] Charles E. Wilson, Director, Office of Defense Mobilization.

[11] The Revenue Act of 1951, approved October 20, 1951 (65 Stat. 569), removed the tax exemption provision relating to the expense allowances of the President, the Vice President, the Speaker, and Members of Congress, effective in January 1953.

[12] Mrs. May Craig of the Portland (Maine) Press Herald.

Q. I thought perhaps you had seen the bill——

THE PRESIDENT. No, that is up to Congress to write its own bill—which it usually does.

Q. Is it on your "must" legislation?

THE PRESIDENT. Yes, it has always been. That ought to take care of potatoes, too, May, I think. [*Laughter*]

Q. No. [*More laughter*]

[14.] Q. Mr. President, I have gone over the Executive order since my last question, sir, and I don't see any reference to the Congress at all. I wonder if it was your intention, in setting up this Commission, that they should examine the activities of congressional committees?

THE PRESIDENT. No. No, I don't intend to. I don't intend to investigate investigating committees. I am only trying to meet it on the basis of a program which will be fair to all concerned.

Q. They could not examine investigating——

THE PRESIDENT. They might examine the hearings of an investigating committee, but they are not investigating an investigating committee.

Q. Mr. President, about that preceding question on the loyalty files, you made some files available to the Tydings subcommittee. Is it your intention to make files available to the commission on the same basis?

THE PRESIDENT. On exactly the same basis.

Q. Well, Mr. President, what is the basis? As I remember it, the Tydings committee had to examine the files at the White House, is that right?

THE PRESIDENT. That's right.

Q. Is that the basis you speak of?

THE PRESIDENT. That is it exactly.

Q. Mr. President, in other words, this new commission when they want to look into a file in which there is some security, they will have to come here to the White House?

THE PRESIDENT. They will ask me about it, and I will give them permission to see it.

Q. Mr. President, did you make the files available in the Anna Rosenberg case to the Senate committee?

THE PRESIDENT. I don't remember whether I did or not. I would have——

Q. We understood that you did.

THE PRESIDENT. I *would* have, if they had asked for it. I can't remember whether I did or not.

Q. Whether there is a distinction between one or the other?

THE PRESIDENT. I don't think there is any.

Q. They sent the full files in the Rosenberg case and did not in the other committees?

THE PRESIDENT. Oh, yes they did. They had all the full files they asked for in the Tydings investigation, and in several other instances they have had the same privilege. But they have had to ask me for them, and I have to authorize them to see them. That is the formality they have to go through.[13]

Q. This committee has the same—they come to you, and you give them the permission——

THE PRESIDENT. That's right.

Q. ——in individual cases?

THE PRESIDENT. That's right.

Reporter: Well, thank you, Mr. President.

THE PRESIDENT. You are welcome.

NOTE: President Truman's two hundred and fifty-third news conference was held in the Indian Treaty Room (Room 474) in the Executive Office Building at 4 p.m. on Thursday, January 25, 1951.

---

[13] In November and December 1950, the Senate Committee on Armed Services, with Senator Millard E. Tydings of Maryland as chairman, held hearings on the nomination of Anna M. Rosenberg to be Assistant Secretary of Defense. With the President's permission, the FBI file on Mrs. Rosenberg was made available to a subcommittee of the Tydings committee. The nomination was confirmed by the Senate on December 21, 1950.

For availability of investigating agency files in other cases, see 1950 volume, this series, Item 79 and note.

23 Memorandum Urging Agency Cooperation in Enforcing
Price and Wage Stabilization Orders. *January* 27, 1951
[Released January 27, 1951. Dated January 26, 1951]

To the heads of executive departments and agencies:

IT IS imperative that the economic stabilization orders issued today receive the fullest possible support by business and industry and by the people of the nation. The initial success of these orders in accomplishing their purposes for the good of all will require sacrifice and a high degree of self-restraint. The Federal Government must be prepared to do everything in its power to insure equitable and just administration of these orders and to obtain full compliance with them.

Until such time as the Economic Stabilization Agency can recruit and train the staff it will need, all departments and agencies should make whatever contribution they can to assure the success of our efforts to stabilize prices and wages. It is understood that essential work now programmed may have to be postponed temporarily. Therefore, as President of the United States and pursuant to the authority vested in me by the Constitution and statutes, including section 403 of the Defense Production Act of 1950, I call upon each agency to make its resources in staff, and knowledge and experience available to the Economic Stabilization Agency, including the Office of Price Stabilization and the Wage Stabilization Board, to the extent requested by the Director of Defense Mobilization.

Specifically, each agency shall provide such cooperation and assistance, consonant with law, as it can, of the following types:

1. Assignment of personnel in Washington, D.C., and in regional and field offices on a reimbursable loan basis for temporary periods as agreed upon in individual cases, including

(a) Personnel qualified in investigation, intelligence, and enforcement duties and functions, and the supervision and administration thereof, except that, in view of the responsibility of the Federal Bureau of Investigation in the field of internal security, no agents shall be assigned without the consent of the Attorney General.

(b) Personnel qualified in the study and analysis of costs, prices, wages, working conditions, and other economic and social data relating thereto.

2. Furnishing any available reports, information, or other data concerning costs of production, distribution and transportation, prices and price trends, profits, and wages and wage trends.

3. Providing such other services, information, and facilities as may be appropriate.

In many cases rapid implementation of this program will require early notification of field offices and establishments, by you, of arrangements whereby these offices and establishments can be most effective in providing assistance.

HARRY S. TRUMAN

NOTE: On January 26, 1951, the Office of Price Stabilization, Economic Stabilization Agency, issued a General Ceiling Price Regulation (16 F.R. 808) freezing prices on most commodities and services at the highest levels charged between December 19, 1950, and January 25, 1951. At the same time, as required by the Defense Production Act of 1950, wages and other compensation were frozen at the rates paid on January 25, by order of the Wage Stabilization Board, Economic Stabilization Agency (16 F.R. 816).

24 Remarks at a Special Ceremony for Sam Rayburn. *January* 30, 1951

THE PRESIDENT. *Mr. Speaker, Mr. Vice President, Mr. Chief Justice:*

I have a very pleasant duty to perform this morning: to congratulate the Speaker of the House of Representatives on having served longer as Speaker of the House than any other man in the history of this Republic.

And in order to show him that I feel very kindly to him—if he has to be shown that—I had a gavel made of wood from the White House that was used in 1817 to rebuild the White House after the British burned it.

But this is to Sam Rayburn who has served as Speaker of the House of Representatives longer than any man in the history of the Republic, with honor and devotion to his country, date January 30, 1951, and it is signed by the President.

Mr. Speaker!

The Speaker: Mr. President, to me this is a great occasion, for many reasons: to be here in your presence and with you, and to receive this presentation, evidence of your friendship and your trust. I appreciate every colleague of mine and every friend from the Hill, including the newspapermen and photographers and television people, whom sometimes I have a little trouble with. To everyone, from the depths of a grateful heart, I thank you.

This is a great day to me. It means much to me. It means much to my family, and to my friends back in Texas who have so long trusted me by voting for me and making me their Representative.

Here again, Mr. President, again I thank you most sincerely.

[*At this point, at the invitation of the President, the Vice President spoke, followed by Chief Justice Fred M. Vinson, House Minority Leader Joseph W. Martin, Jr., and House Majority Leader John W. McCormack. The President then resumed speaking.*]

This has been a great day for me. Way back in the early days I tried to get out of the way and let Sam Rayburn be nominated for Vice President. I didn't have any luck, and now I am privileged to present him with this memento of a long term of service. I have had no greater pleasure in any time I can remember.

NOTE: The President spoke at 10 a.m. in his office at the White House. His opening words referred to Sam Rayburn, Speaker of the House of Representatives, Vice President Alben W. Barkley, and Chief Justice Fred M. Vinson.

Mr. Rayburn had just broken the record for service as Speaker previously held by Henry Clay of Kentucky, who served 3,056½ days in that office.

The full transcript of the ceremony is published in the *Congressional Record*, February 5, 1951 (vol. 97, p. 991).

25 Joint Statement Following Discussions With Prime Minister Pleven of France. *January* 30, 1951

SINCE Prime Minister Pleven arrived in Washington on January 29 three meetings between the President and the Prime Minister have been held. Those who participated as advisers were:

United States: Dean Acheson, Secretary of State, John W. Snyder, Secretary of the

Treasury, General George C. Marshall, Secretary of Defense, Charles E. Wilson, Director of Defense Mobilization, William Foster, Administrator, Economic Cooperation Administration, General Omar Bradley, Chairman of the Joint Chiefs of Staff, W. Averell Harriman, Special Assistant to the President,

Philip C. Jessup, Ambassador at Large, David K. E. Bruce, U.S. Ambassador to France, Willard Thorp, Assistant Secretary of State for Economic Affairs, Dean Rusk, Assistant Secretary of State for Far Eastern Affairs, Thomas D. Cabot, Director Designate of International Security Affairs, Department of State, Donald R. Heath, U.S. Minister to the Associated States of Indo-China, Charles E. Bohlen, U.S. Minister to France, James C. H. Bonbright, Deputy Assistant Secretary of State for European Affairs, Henry A. Byroade, Director, Bureau of German Affairs, Department of State.

France: Henri Bonnet, French Ambassador to the United States, General of the Armies Alphonse Pierre Juin, French Resident General in Morocco, Ambassador Alexandre Parodi, Secretary General, Ministry of Foreign Affairs, Ambassador Herve Alphand, French Deputy to the North Atlantic Council, Guillaume Guindey, Director of the Ministry of Finance, Raoul de Vitry, French Representative to the Central Committee on Raw Materials, Tezenas de Montcel, Inspector General representing the Ministry of the Associated States, Jean Daridan, Minister Counselor, French Embassy, Pierre Paul Schweitzer, Financial Counselor, French Embassy, Gontran de Juniac, Counselor, French Embassy, Colonel Allard, Chief of Staff to General de Lattre de Tassigny, M. de Marranches, Aide to General Juin.

At the conclusion of their conferences, the President and the Prime Minister issued the following joint statement:

The President and the Prime Minister exchanged views on the broad subject of international affairs and they touched upon all the questions that are of common interest to France and the United States. Once again they found that there exists a fundamental identity of views between the two countries.

The President and the Prime Minister reaffirmed their belief that the principle of collective security, embodied in the Charter of the United Nations, is the chief bulwark of world peace and of the independence and survival of free societies in the world. They agreed that, in conformity with this principle, aggression must not be rewarded or the menace of aggression appeased. It is in this spirit that the President and the Prime Minister examined the means to assure coordinated action and turned to the more detailed questions as set forth below.

I. Far Eastern Problems

The President and the Prime Minister found themselves in complete agreement as to the necessity of resisting aggression and assisting the free nations of the Far East in their efforts to maintain their security and assure their independence.

The situation in Korea was discussed and they concurred that every effort must be exerted to bring about an honorable solution there. Until that end can be accomplished resistance by United Nations forces to aggression must continue. Both France and the United States will support action directed toward deterring aggression and toward preventing the spread of hostilities beyond Korea.

With regard to Indo-China, the Prime Minister described the heavy responsibilities borne by France in that area and the great cost, both in lives and money, she has paid in resisting the communist onslaught in order to maintain the security and independence of the Associated States, Viet Nam, Cambodia, and Laos. The Prime Minister declared that France was determined to do its utmost to continue this effort. The President informed the Prime Minister that United States aid for the French Union forces and for the National Armies of the Associated States will continue, and that the increased quantities of material to be delivered under the program authorized for the current fiscal year will be expedited.

The President and the Prime Minister agreed that continuous contact should be maintained between the interested nations on these problems.

II. Problems of Europe

The President and the Prime Minister both recognized the vital importance of Europe to the defense of the entire free world. The Prime Minister described the French efforts to achieve European unity. He stressed in this regard the French desire to see disappear the divisions and rivalries that oppose a harmonious development of the European economy and the establishment of a strongly organized Europe. The Prime Minister stated that the policy of the French Government was to favor the creation of a broad European market open to competition by all through the abolition of cartels and discriminatory practices.

The President and the Prime Minister were in fundamental agreement that the cause of peace in Europe and the world would be furthered by a progressively closer integration in every aspect of a democratic Germany into a vigorous Western European community.

The Prime Minister brought the President up to date on the recent developments relating to the Schuman Plan Treaty. He expressed appreciation for the interest and the comprehension which this plan found in the United States. The President hoped that the treaty would be concluded in satisfactory form at the earliest possible moment. The Prime Minister also mentioned that new steps are anticipated in the same direction, particularly in the field of agriculture.

The Prime Minister also referred to the conference to be convened in Paris on February 6th, to consider the formation of a European Army based on European political institutions and within the framework of the North Atlantic Treaty Organization. The President welcomed the conference and expressed his hope for its success. He informed the Prime Minister that the United States would be glad to accept the invitation to send an observer, and that Ambassador David Bruce would be designated.

III. Atlantic Defense Plans

The President and the Prime Minister exchanged views with regard to the progress made by both countries in their defense programs. The President described to the Prime Minister the great efforts now being made by the United States. Mr. Pleven outlined the steps taken by France in this field and added that the French Government would neglect no opportunity to intensify its rearmament and particularly to accelerate as much as possible the execution of existing programs.

The President and the Prime Minister reaffirmed their conviction that German participation in the common defense effort as envisaged last month at Brussels would strengthen the security of Europe without altering in any way the purely defensive character of the North Atlantic Treaty Organization.

IV. Economic Problems

The President and the Prime Minister also reviewed certain q u e s t i o n s concerning United States assistance to France in the economic field. They clarified procedures so that United States assistance will make its most effective contribution to the French defense effort.

They agreed that the solution of the raw materials problems ought to be the aim, not only of national action, but also of international action undertaken with the utmost speed and vigor. The objectives of such action are to give the necessary priority to defense requirements and to meet essential civilian needs through the stimulation of production, the equitable distribution of available supplies, the avoidance of waste in nonessential uses and of unnecessary accumulation of stocks. The two governments, together with that of the United Kingdom, are presently proposing the formation of International Commodity Groups which will take up immediate problems of material shortages of common concern to the countries of the free world.

They recognized the importance of dealing with the problem of inflation and rising prices, which adversely affect the common defense effort. They agreed that not only should vigorous national action be taken but that wherever international measures may effectively contribute to this objective they would give their full support.

The President and the Prime Minister wish to state that the supreme objective of the foreign policies of the United States and France is the establishment and maintenance of durable peace based on law and justice.

The measures which they have discussed and undertaken in common with other free nations for the development of adequate defense under the North Atlantic Treaty and for the development of European unity are directed solely to that end.

Moreover, the two governments have never neglected in the past and will never neglect in the future any genuine opportunity to settle international problems by negotiation.

The discussions between the President and the Prime Minister have shown again that no menace or maneuver will succeed in shaking the fundamental unity which exists between the United States and France.

26 Letter to the Director, Bureau of the Budget, on the Establishment of a Federal History Program.
January 31, 1951

[Released January 31, 1951. Dated January 29, 1951]

My dear Mr. Lawton:

During this period of national emergency, the Federal Government has found that the historical records maintained during the previous periods of emergency have been of great value. The histories of a number of the temporary agencies of World War II have been especially helpful in current mobilization planning.

I believe that we should analyze the development of our present activities while the problems are fresh in the minds of the participants. Such analyses will help us to solve the problems we shall face in the future.

For these reasons, I should like you to es-

tablish a Federal history program for all the agencies engaged in emergency activities. The active direction of the program should be undertaken by the Bureau of the Budget, although the preparation of the studies themselves should be carried out by the individual agencies.

In order to be of greatest value, these studies should not give a detailed review of accomplishments, but should concentrate upon the objective analysis of the problems confronted, how they were met, and the reasons underlying policy and administrative decisions. Failures as well as successes should, of course, be included. Historians should have full access to source materials and they should draw upon both written and unwritten sources of information. Agency heads should see that the historians have ready contact with key officials and are enabled to follow decisions on policy and administration as they are made.

I am confident that this program will be useful in improving operations. The studies that result can help orient new officials and give all officials a broader understanding of agency problems and policies. These studies will also assist in the preparation of reports to the Congress. Agency historians, however, should not be diverted into current operations.

It is important to start this program quickly, in order to profit from the lessons we are already learning. I hope that you will report to me from time to time on the progress of the agencies in carrying forward the historical program.

Very sincerely yours,

HARRY S. TRUMAN

[The Honorable Frederick J. Lawton, Director, Bureau of the Budget, Washington, D.C.]

27 Remarks at the Democratic National Congressional Committee Dinner. *January 31, 1951*

IT IS a very great privilege for me to be invited here tonight. I appreciate it most highly. I want to say that your chairman of the committee, who carried on the campaign for the organization, did a remarkable job, and I will say also that Bill Boyle was extremely cooperative with them. I think I know something about it.

You know, I wear a lot of hats. First, I am President and chief executive of the greatest Republic in the world, and I wish I could fill that job as it ought to be filled.

Then I am the head of the Democratic Party, as long as I am President. And your chairman, Bill Boyle, and Clint Anderson over in the Senate, are the organization which makes it possible for Democrats to come into the Congress.

Then I have another duty. I am the social chief of state. I have to entertain all the visiting firemen, give them dinners, listen to their wants, just the same as I have to listen to the wants of Congressmen and Senators, and have to say no sometimes and make them like it—which is really a job.

And, I have got another job, which is Commander in Chief of the Armed Forces of the United States.

And never a day goes by that in all four of those classifications I don't have to act. And there's a sign on my desk which says, "The Buck Stops Here."

But, to tell you the truth, I enjoy the associations that I have. Sometimes I have to make terrible decisions. I try to make those decisions after prayerful consideration, and always hope that those decisions, in the long run, will be the correct ones.

If they are not, I am not ashamed to say that we will change that decision and see if we can't find the right answer. That is as important in a public official as it is to try to do the job correctly. If he is human, he will make mistakes. If a man doesn't make mistakes, he doesn't do a thing, anyway. The man who does things is bound to make a few mistakes.

Yesterday I had a most pleasant duty to perform. I helped the Speaker of the House celebrate his "coming-of-age" as the longest-termed Speaker that the House of Representatives ever had.[1] Don't let him tell you that he is 87 years old, because he's not. I know he is just as young as any of you.

It was a pleasure to present him with a gavel from wood that was put into the reconstruction of the White House in 1817, after the British burned it. We had to take all that out of the White House, and we have now an inside of the White House that is—unless they drop an atomic bomb on it—going to stand there for the next thousand years, I hope—and I am sure it will, for it will be the symbol of liberty that it will stand for.

Now, last night I was invited to a dinner with the Texas delegation. Sam Rayburn gave the dinner. And I don't think I ever saw so large a number of good-looking wives of Congressmen and Senators as were at that dinner. And you should have seen Sam strut his stuff!

He had two Kentuckians and a Missourian there, to help him celebrate. And the two Kentuckians had served in the Congress—one of the Kentuckians had served in the Senate. And they were reminiscing how they came to the House of Representatives—that is, the two Kentuckians and the Speaker—and it seems that one of those "amateur" Congressmen long ago is now the Chief Justice of the United States, and the third one is sitting right there—the Speaker.

What I am trying to bring home to you gentlemen who have just come into this great organization—the greatest legislative body in the world today and in the history of the world—is that you never can tell what is going to happen to you.

And I want to tell you gentlemen who are veterans here that you had better be nice to these young fellows, because you never can tell what will happen to them. I told a bunch

of bankers the other night[2] that Josh Billings had a saying that I think is apropos of the treatment of new Members of Congress. He said that it is always well to be nice to your poor relations, because they might suddenly become rich some day, and it would be hard to explain, if you hadn't been nice to them.

So you had better be nice to these young Congressmen. One of them may be Speaker some day, one of them may be Chief Justice of the Supreme Court—maybe Vice President.

I was an "amateur" Senator once. And I was, at the bankers dinner, bringing home the fact that there had been a couple of Senators and two or three people outside the Senate who had been extremely nice to the junior Senator from Missouri when he didn't know anybody, and he was standing by that pillar that you were talking about, Sam. And well, I don't know, the junior Senator from Missouri didn't become suddenly rich, but he became suddenly very popular after the election of 1948.

I hope that all you young men who are coming in now will remember that it is work that counts. You may believe, sometimes, that you are not accomplishing much. You may think that you are only one out of 435. I remember I thought I was one out of 96, and a mighty small one out of that 96. But hard work and application to the job for which you came here, and the fact that you belong to the great party of the United States, will someday reward you. You can't help but come to it, because there are so few people who like to work. Nearly everybody wants somebody else to do the job. I am speaking from experience, because I worked like a dog in the Senate, and look at the trouble it got *me* into!

You don't have to take that advice—and

---

[1] Item 24.

[2] Item 21.

I would advise you not to, if you are going to try to get these four jobs that I hold— I would divide any one of them up, if I could, but I can't pass those jobs around.

There is one thing about this job, it has no future to it.

Every young man wants something to look forward to.

Again, I can't say to you how much I appreciate the privilege of being here tonight, and finding out what an orator John McCormack is, and what a great adviser Sam Rayburn is, and what a great chairman I have in the Democratic Committee.

I tell you—I have learned a lot of things here tonight! I didn't know George Allen ever did any work, but I find out he has been working. I hope that when the next occa-

sion for this meeting comes about, that there will be so many new Democrats in the House of Representatives that this room won't hold them.

NOTE: The President spoke at 9:55 p.m. in the Caucus Room of the Congressional Hotel in Washington. In the course of his remarks he referred to William M. Boyle, Jr., chairman of the Democratic National Committee; Senator Clinton P. Anderson of New Mexico; Sam Rayburn, Speaker of the House of Representatives; the "two Kentuckians," Alben W. Barkley, Vice President of the United States, and Fred M. Vinson, Chief Justice of the United States; Congressman John McCormack of Massachusetts, majority floor leader in the House; and George E. Allen, former member of the Board of Directors of the Reconstruction Finance Corporation and treasurer of the Democratic National Congressional Committee.

The dinner was given by the Democratic National Congressional Committee for 19 new Democratic members of the House of Representatives.

28   Special Message to the Congress Recommending a "Pay as We Go" Tax Program.   *February 2, 1951*

To the Congress of the United States:

In the January messages to the Congress, I stated my intention of making further recommendations on a number of important matters. One of the most urgent of these is the need for increased taxation.

The budget for the fiscal year ending June 30, 1952, which was transmitted to the Congress, included estimated expenditures of 71.6 billion dollars, and estimated receipts under present tax laws of 55.1 billion dollars.

It is my firm conviction that we should pay for these expenditures as we go. A balanced budget now is just as important a mobilization measure as larger armed forces, allocations of basic materials, and controls over prices and wages.

This is true for three main reasons.

First, we should pay as we go because that is the way to keep the Government's finances on a sound footing.

We are now strengthening our national security, in order to increase our ability to meet whatever situation may arise in the future. Our Government financial policies, like every other part of our national effort, must be designed to leave us stronger, not weaker, as the years go by. If in this period we pay for our necessary expenditures as we go along, rather than adding to the public debt, we will obviously be better prepared to meet our future needs whatever they may be.

There is a question as to how high we can push taxes without having serious effects upon the productive growth of our economy. But I am sure that we could increase Federal revenues by considerably more than enough to cover the expenditures now anticipated without reaching those limits. During recent years we have taxed ourselves at high levels—and during those years our economy has bounded forward: incomes have risen rapidly, new plants and industries have sprung up, and the standard of living of our people has increased steadily. The growth in the strength of our economy that has occurred under these tax rates gives us confidence that we can safely pay the estimated expenditures for the next fiscal year out of taxes.

Second, we should pay for defense as we go because that is the way to distribute the cost of defense fairly.

We cannot escape paying the real cost of defense now—the cost in materials and days of work that are devoted to defense purposes. Whatever we do about taxes, the amount of goods available for consumers to buy is only going to be what is left over after defense needs are met.

We could try to escape the financial cost of defense by borrowing—but that would only transfer the financial problem to our children, and would increase the danger of inflation with its grossly unfair distribution of the burden.

The sensible and honest thing to do now is to tax ourselves enough, as we go along, to pay the financial costs of defense out of our current income.

Our Federal tax system can spread the cost of defense fairly among our people. There are many ways in which the fairness of the present tax system can and should be improved, but on the whole we have a good system. It recognizes differences in incomes and in family obligations. It protects incentives for initiative and effort. It takes account of the special needs of new undertakings and the expansion of existing businesses.

I am convinced, after studying the matter thoroughly, that the people of our country—and I am thinking primarily of the average family of modest income—will all be better off if everybody pays his fair share of the financial costs of defense in taxes now. If we don't do that, we will only be putting off the evil day, and making matters worse for ourselves in the future.

Third, we should pay as we go to help prevent inflation.

If we do not tax ourselves enough to pay for defense expenditures, the Government will be spending more than it takes in, and the extra money it spends will add to total purchasing power and inflationary pressures.

Inflationary pressures will be strong, of course, even with the budget balanced. Military production results in wage payments, and buying of materials, long before the goods are produced and paid for by the Government. Businessmen who build new plants spend money well in advance of producing any goods for the Government or consumers to buy. Furthermore, consumers have accumulated large amounts of cash and other liquid assets which they are free to spend if they so choose.

Thus, inflationary pressures will be strong even after taxes are increased enough to balance the budget. We will still need direct controls over prices and wages. But it may not be possible to make those controls effective unless we tax ourselves enough. Certainly, those controls will be far more effective if we pay for expenditures through taxes as we go along.

During World War II, taxes were not high enough, and the Government was forced to borrow too much. As a result, when controls were taken off after the war, prices skyrocketed and we paid in inflation for our failure to tax enough. The value of people's savings was cut down by the higher prices they had to pay.

We must not let that happen now. We must have both an adequate tax program and proper controls on prices and wages if we are to prevent inflation and preserve the value of savings and fixed incomes.

For these reasons, the case for a pay as we go tax program is conclusive at the present time, and I urge the Congress to continue to keep that goal before it.

I believe that the wisest and most practical approach to this goal is to enact the tax program we need this year in two parts rather than enacting the full tax program all at once.

Government expenditures will be increasing very rapidly during the next few months. We will have to act fast if our revenues are to keep pace with rising expenditures.

I recommend that as rapidly as possible the Congress enact revenue legislation to yield additional taxes of at least 10 billion dollars annually, and later in the year enact the remaining amounts needed to keep us on a pay as we go basis.

If we follow this course, our revenues will keep pace with increasing expenditures, and we shall have some months in which to observe economic developments and to consider the several serious questions that will need to be resolved before all parts of this year's tax program are enacted.

For example, we will have better information on exactly how much we shall need to balance the budget. As I explained in the Budget Message, our estimates of military expenditures are still tentative. In particular, the amount we spend for military equipment will depend on how fast the production lines are geared up and the equipment is actually turned out. If our military production program can be got under way faster— as we hope it can—expenditures will, of course, be larger than the budget estimates.

Moreover, the Congress has not yet had an opportunity to act on the budget. I believe the Congress will find that the budget is sound, and provides only for the essential needs of our Nation in this time of world

crisis. Nevertheless, the appropriations actually enacted by the Congress will, of course, control the actual expenditures.

Furthermore, the economic developments of the months ahead—the impact of the defense effort and of tighter controls on prices and wages and profits—should be considered before the balance of our tax program for the coming fiscal year is completed.

These uncertainties, however, do not affect our obvious need for much larger taxes—and our need for the bulk of them very soon. I am therefore transmitting, for the consideration of the Congress at this time, my recommendations as to the best way to raise at least 10 billion dollars now.

I know the Congress will want to consider these problems very carefully, and to review my recommendations in the light of their own independent analysis. The Secretary of the Treasury is prepared to discuss these matters in detail with the committees of Congress.

I believe we should meet our immediate objective by increasing existing taxes. The present Federal tax structure, while marred by imperfections, contains the most equitable types of taxes we have been able to devise. Under these taxes, our economy has demonstrated a surge in productive power to increasingly higher levels.

I recommend an immediate increase in personal income taxes to bring in 4 billion dollars in additional revenue.

The personal income tax is the mainstay of our Federal tax system. It should be the major source of the additional revenue we need.

This is true because it is the personal income tax that allows us the greatest opportunity to be fair. It is the personal income tax above all else which takes account of differences in ability to pay—both differences in income and differences in family obligations. It allows an exemption of $600 per person, and deductions for charitable contributions, extraordinary medical expenses, and other expenses as provided by law. Under present law, a single person earning a net income of $3,000 a year pays a tax of about 16 percent of his income, or $488, while a married person with two dependents and earning the same net income pays a 4 percent tax, or $120. The average rate of tax reaches 50 percent at about the $45,000 income level for a single person and the $90,000 income level for a family of four.

In increasing the yield of the personal income tax, everyone should realize that the higher taxes cannot be limited to the upper income groups. To obtain revenue commensurate with our defense expenditures, all taxpayers must contribute, because the bulk of the income in this country is received by persons whose incomes are between $2,000 and $10,000 a year. We should tax the upper income groups—and tax them heavily—but it will also be necessary to tax people with moderate incomes.

I do not believe that the personal exemption of $600 should be lowered at the present time. Although the exemption was $500 during World War II, the present $600 exemption is less generous, in terms of present costs of living, than was $500 six or eight years ago.

I recommend, second, an increase in corporation income taxes to yield an additional 3 billion dollars.

The corporation income tax is the major supplement to the personal income tax in our present Federal tax system. Basic corporation tax rates now begin at 25 percent on corporation profits less than $25,000, and increase to 47 percent for larger corporations. Those corporations covered by the excess profits tax pay more—up to a maximum set by law of 62 percent of net profits.

In the light of high and rising corporate profits, the increase in corporation taxes I propose will leave corporations generally able to maintain the dividend and reinvestment policies of recent years.

The first tax returns under the new excess profits tax law will be received later this spring. We shall then be in a position to consider what changes in the excess profits tax law are desirable to obtain more revenue from that source. I believe, therefore, we should defer this matter until later this year.

I recommend, third, increases in selective excise taxes to yield 3 billion dollars. Under present circumstances, these increases should be concentrated upon less essential consumer goods, and upon goods which use materials that will be in short supply.

In addition to the tax increases recommended above, I recommend that the Congress carry further the program it started last year to close loopholes in the present tax laws.

The revenue to be gained by closing these loopholes is not large in comparison with our needs. But in terms of fairness, and willingness of people to pay their share of taxes, closing these loopholes is worth a very great deal.

Those required to bear higher taxes for defense are entitled to the assurance that others will not be permitted to avoid them. The last Congress closed several important loopholes. But a number remain.

I have previously called attention to the gross under-taxation of the oil and mining industries, to the broad loopholes in the estate and gift taxes, and to the undue preferential treatment granted to capital gains in comparison with ordinary income. I urge the Congress to examine these provisions of the law very carefully, together with those relating to life insurance companies and to holders of securities now exempt from income taxes, and to review the tax status of organizations now exempt under present law. I do not believe any of us, in good conscience, can take action to increase taxes on the man, with a wife and two children, who earns $60 a week—an increase I am now recommending—without at the same time taking action to reduce the glaring inequities in present law—some of which permit a man with one hundred times as much income to avoid paying any taxes at all.

In addition to the changes in the law that are needed to close loopholes, we shall continue to improve our enforcement efforts to make sure that the taxes which are due under present laws are actually paid.

The tax program I am proposing will require higher rates in some cases than those paid during the last year. I believe our people understand that if we had paid higher taxes then we would be better off today. I believe our people are ready and willing to pay the taxes needed to cover essential Government expenditures in this time of danger.

I am convinced that the average citizen in our country will be best served by fair tax laws which will balance the budget. He will be better off now, because he will pay his share of the cost of defense now, once and for all. He will be better off in the future, because his savings and his future income will not be dissipated by inflation.

The American people understand that the cost of freedom is high at a time when aggression has been loosed on the world. I urge the Congress to act rapidly so that we can pay that cost as we go.

HARRY S. TRUMAN

NOTE: For a statement by the President upon signing the Revenue Act of 1951, see Item 264.

29 Letter to the Chairman, Board of Governors, Federal Reserve System, on the Treasury Defense Financing Program. *February 2, 1951*

Dear Tom:

I want the members of the Federal Reserve Board and the members of the Federal Open Market Committee to know how deeply I appreciate their expression of full cooperation given to me yesterday in our meeting.

As I expressed to you, I am deeply concerned over the international situation and its implications upon our economic stability.

Your assurance that you would fully support the Treasury Defense financing program, both as to refunding and new issues, is of vital importance to me. As I under- stand it, I have your assurance that the market on government securities will be stabilized and maintained at present levels in order to assure the successful financing requirements and to establish in the minds of the people confidence concerning government credit.

I wish you would convey to all the members of your group my warm appreciation of their cooperative attitude.

Sincerely yours,

HARRY S. TRUMAN

[The Honorable Thomas B. McCabe, Chairman, Board of Governors, Federal Reserve System]

30   Address in Philadelphia at the Dedication of the Chapel
of the Four Chaplains.   *February 3*, 1951

Dr. Poling, associate chaplains, and ladies and gentlemen:

This chapel commemorates something more than an act of bravery or courage. It commemorates a great act of faith in God.

The four chaplains whose memory this shrine was built to commemorate were not required to give their lives as they did. They gave their lives without being asked. When their ship was sinking, they handed out all the life preservers that were available and then took off their own and gave them away in order that four other men might be saved.

Those four chaplains actually carried out the moral code which we are all supposed to live by. They obeyed the divine commandment that men should love one another. They really lived up to the moral standard that declares: "Greater love hath no man than this, that a man lay down his life for his friends."

They were not afraid of death because they knew that the word of God is stronger than death. Their belief, their faith, in His word enabled them to conquer death.

This is an old faith in our country. It is shared by all our churches and all our denominations. These four men represented the Protestant, the Catholic, and the Jewish beliefs. Each of these beliefs teaches that obedience to God and love for one's fellow man are the greatest and strongest things in the world.

We must never forget that this country was founded by men who came to these shores to worship God as they pleased. Catholics, Jews, and Protestants, all came here for this great purpose.

They did not come here to do as they pleased—but to worship God as they pleased, and that is a most important distinction.

The unity of our country comes from this fact. The unity of our country is a unity under God. It is a unity in freedom, for the service of God is perfect freedom.

If we remember our faith in God, if we live by it as our forefathers did, we need have no fear for the future.

Today, many people have become full of fear. If we reaffirm our common faith we can overcome these fears.

This does not mean that we can always be sure what the future will bring. We cannot always know what the outcome of events will be. President Lincoln once said, "The Almighty has His own purposes."

But we need not be afraid of the outcome if we go on trying to do the right thing as God gives us to see the right.

That is what we are trying to do in the world today. We are trying to establish world peace, so that all men can live together in brotherhood and in freedom. And to do that, we are working with other nations to create the rule of law in the world.

And what does this rule of law mean? Let me give you an example. In the early days of our western frontier, law and order were not yet established. Disputes were settled in favor of the man who was quickest on the draw. Outlaws terrorized whole communities.

Men who wanted to see law and order prevail had to combine against the outlaws. They had to arm themselves. At times they had to fight. And after they had put down lawless violence, the courts took over and justice was established. And then it was possible for all citizens to get on with the important work of building up their own communities, paving the streets and building schools, and giving all the people a chance at the right kind of life.

That is just what we are trying to do today in the international field. If we can put a stop to international aggression, order can be established and the people of the world can go ahead full speed with the constructive tasks of peace.

We are not trying to do this job by ourselves. We could not do it by ourselves if we tried. We are acting as one member of a whole community of nations dedicated to the concept of the rule of law in the world. As in all other communities, the members of this community of nations have many different ideas and interests and do not all speak with one voice. Some are cautious and some are impatient.

We cannot always have our own way in this community. But we have a tremendous responsibility to lead and not to hang back.

Fate has made this country a leader in the world. We shirked our responsibility in the 1920's. We cannot shirk it now. We must assume that responsibility now, and it will take everything we have—all the brains and all the resources that we can mobilize.

Leadership carries with it heavy responsibilities. Good leaders do not threaten to quit if things go wrong. They expect cooperation, of course, and they expect everyone to do his share, but they do not stop to measure sacrifices with a teaspoon while the fight is on.

We cannot lead the forces of freedom from behind.

The job we face is a hard one. Perhaps it will be harder in the few years immediately ahead than it will be in the years thereafter. If we can get over the present crisis successfully—if we can restrain aggression before it bursts into another world war, then things will be easier in the future. And I think we can do this. We can't be sure, of course, but there is good reason to hope for success.

In recent months the United Nations has been faced with a serious challenge. But it is meeting that challenge courageously, and it is still man's best hope of establishing the rule of law in the world.

General Eisenhower has brought home the report that the people of Europe, in spite of their difficulties and their many problems, want to preserve their freedom. He has told us of the effort they are making. They are working very hard, and if we all work together, we can be successful.

When things look difficult, there are always a lot of people who want to quit. We had people like that in the Revolutionary War, and we have had them in every war and every crisis of our history. Thomas Paine called them summer soldiers and sunshine patriots. If we had listened to them, we would never have been a free and independent nation. We would never have had a strong and prosperous country. We would not be strong enough now to stand up against Communist aggression and tyranny.

The sacrifices that are being made today by the men and women of this country are not being made in vain. Our men are in Korea because we are trying to prevent a worldwide war. The men who have died in Korea have died to save us from the terrible slaughter and destruction which another world war would surely bring.

Their sacrifices are being made in the spirit of the four chaplains in whose memory this chapel is dedicated. They are being made in defense of the great religious faiths which make this chapel a place of worship. These sacrifices are being made for the greatest things in this life, and for the things beyond this life.

I have faith that the great principles for which our men are fighting will prevail.

NOTE: The President spoke at 3:10 p.m. at the chapel in the Russell H. Conwell Memorial Church, Broad and Berks Streets, Philadelphia, Pa. In his opening words he referred to Dr. Daniel A. Poling, chaplain of the sanctuary and father of one of the four World War II heroes.

The chapel was dedicated on the eighth anniversary of the torpedoing of the American troopship *Dorchester* off the coast of Greenland. The four chaplains were Lt. John P. Washington, Catholic, Lt. Alexander D. Goode, Jewish, and Lts. George L. Fox and Clark V. Poling, Protestant.

31 Remarks to a Group of Methodist Ministers.
February 7, 1951

THAT is a wonderful letter, and I am pleased to have it. And he is just right about the necessity for the mobilization of the moral forces in the world against the unmoral forces. That is all we are trying to do.

There are forces in the world now that do not believe in our ethical and moral code. Their policy up to date has been to make agreements only to break them at their convenience, especially if it entails any hardship on their part. And I have been working with everything that I have to mobilize all the moral forces we have in the world for the welfare of the world as a whole.

The United States Government has no ambitions as a colonial power or as an exploiter of people or other races. Our only ambition is to see that the people in the world have the things that are necessary to make life worthwhile, and that they have and live by the moral code in which we believe.

That is the fundamental principle of the foreign policy of the United States. That has been the foreign policy of the United States. That has been the foreign policy of the United States since 1939, and I hope it will be a continuing policy of the United States as long as we are in business as a nation, because in 1920 I think the Almighty intended us to take leadership in the world to meet the very situation with which we are faced now. We didn't accept that invitation, and the Second World War was the result. Since the end of World War II we have

been trying to assume our responsibility as a world power, and as a leader of the moral forces in the world which we believe are right and just. I hope we will continue to assume that leadership and do what we can to maintain peace in the world. The operations through which we are going now are being made in an endeavor to prevent a third world war, and God help us, because I hope we will never have another world war, with the terrible destructive weapons which we have now.

How much better to spend these immense sums of money for human welfare instead of immense sums of money to create engines of destruction, although under the conditions with which we are now faced we have got to have those engines of destruction, in order to maintain our own place in the world. And I hope you will all understand that and appreciate it.

I appreciate your coming in here, and I am glad to have the opportunity, in this short time, to explain to you my viewpoint on the conditions with which we are faced in the world at the present time.

I hope you will all consider that carefully, and pray over it. We pray here.

It has been a pleasure to have you.

NOTE: The President spoke at 11:45 a.m. in his office at the White House. The text of the letter to which he referred follows:

My dear President Truman:

I deeply regret that it was impossible for me to accompany the Methodist Ministers from Illinois on this year's Washington Institute. We greatly appreciate your graciousness in making possible this visit to you in these troublous times which keep you so very busy.

We are aware in a small way of the heavy weight of responsibility which falls upon your mind and heart. We, as ministers of the gospel of Christ, believe the only way such responsibilities can be successfully carried is through a mind saturated with prayer. We believe you to be a praying man.

We want you to know that whether our party affiliations differ or not from yours, you are our President and this is our much loved country. We are praying that Divine guidance may be given you in your momentous decisions. We believe all up-

right Americans should pray for you and your counselors that moral and Christian standards shall be maintained in all our relations with the leaders of other nations.

Mr. President, we are also praying for the leadership of other nations, Christian or non-Christian, that the spirit of the living God may atmosphere their minds to meet fairly all high moral and Christian approaches made to them.

The Lord be with you, and with thy spirit.

Very sincerely,

J. RALPH MAGEE,
Bishop, Chicago Area, The Methodist Church.

32 Remarks at a Luncheon Given in His Honor by the Secretary of the Interior. *February 7, 1951*

I WANT to drink a toast to the Secretary of the Interior and his great committee.

I appreciate your asking me to come over here today. It is a pleasure. I very seldom get a chance to have a meeting like this with the Members of the Congress, because I just don't have any space. I am always glad to see any of you when you come down, but you know how difficult it is to get an appointment for the simple reason that I begin at 9 o'clock in the morning, and every 15 minutes from then until 1 o'clock I meet somebody who thinks he has business with the President—and I guess most of them do—and then from 3 o'clock until 5 or 6 the same thing goes on.

I want you to introduce a measure to inaugurate longer hours and shorter pay—I would like very much to have a 24-hour day, and at least a 10-day week, if you can arrange it, so that there will be time enough for me to get the job done that I have to do.

You are all interested in public works, and in the continuation of those things that are necessary to keep the country running, in spite of the emergency with which we are faced. My friend here is in favor of making the Republican River navigable. That is on account of its name, and not because it has any merit otherwise.

And every single one of you has a very important project of the same sort in your district or your State. I have several in Missouri, but since I am not a Senator from Missouri and can't do anything about it, and since I am not a Congressman from Missouri and not on a committee like this, there is nothing I can do about it. And I can't make any special recommendations, because if I do I will be accused of increasing the unnecessary expenditures of the Government, and in all likelihood will be cut off from special appropriations for Missouri, which is all right; and in return for that I will try to reciprocate with every State in the Union.

I hope we can have meetings like this often. I have found that when you are acquainted with people, no matter whether they are on your side from a partisan standpoint or not, you find that there is not a great deal of difference. Most every Member of the two bodies that constitute the Congress is just as interested in the welfare of the country as the rest of us.

It is a lucky thing that I had 10 years' experience in the Senate, and in that way became personally acquainted with most of you. Those that I do not know are those who have come in since 1944—since April 12, 1945, to put it accurately—and I am sorry that I am not better acquainted with those who came later. I think, if they would consult me, I could give them a little advice on whom to see—how to get things through the Senate, at least.

Were I allowed to do that, my first suggestion would be—if they are interested in things in which this committee is interested—to see this Senator right here. Anything you want to get done in reclamation and public works, you had better see Carl Hayden, for he knows everybody in the Budget, he knows every Senator on this committee, and he knows every Representative on the same committee in the House. And don't try to beat him in anything, because

he can outmaneuver you in spite of everything you can do, and there are a half-a-dozen people around this table that can do the same thing.

So, if you will just advise these new fellows, if they really want to get things done in the Congress—and this doesn't mean that the President wants to see them—but if they really want to get things done in the Congress, they had better consult *me*.

NOTE: The President spoke at 2:15 p.m. in the dining room at the Department of the Interior Building. The luncheon honoring the President was attended by Members of the Senate Committee on Public Works and other Members of the Congress. In the course of his remarks, the President referred to Senator Carl Hayden of Arizona, a member of the Senate Appropriations Committee.

33   The President's News Conference of *February 8*, 1951

THE PRESIDENT. Please be seated. I have had some of you gentlemen suggest that I sit down—[*laughter*]—that maybe I could do a better job sitting down. I feel better on my feet, but I will sit down if that is what you want, if you can get along better.

[1.] I wanted to read you a statement about the railroad situation before I start.[1]

[1] On February 2, 1951, the White House released a statement by Joseph Short, Secretary to the President, in response to inquiries regarding the railroad strike which climaxed a 2-year dispute over wages and working conditions. In 1950, the release noted, railroad unions had rejected the recommendations of an emergency mediation board, and the Government took control of the railroads in August of that year (see 1950 volume, this series, Item 221). The leaders of the unions stated that the employees would remain at work during Government operation. Union representatives then met in the White House with representatives of railroad management, and both groups signed an agreement on December 21, 1950. Work stoppages continued, however, and the February statement described the union representatives as "now attempting to escape responsibility for this agreement," on the grounds that their union committees had not ratified it.

[*Reading*] "I have been gravely concerned about the interference with essential military and civilian railroad transportation. It is bad enough in other times; it is intolerable in an emergency.

"On the other hand, I have been proud of the vast majority of railroad workers who have stuck to their jobs in spite of their grievances. Consideration is also due the strikers who returned to work when advised of the dangers of the tieup.

"However, there are still some ill-advised or irresponsible men who are disregarding the emergency needs of their country.

"It is essential that precautions be taken against recurrences of such threats to our national security.

"Accordingly, I have directed the Secretary of the Army to take appropriate action immediately."

And that announcement will come out sometime later today, which will explain the whole situation.

Q. Mr. President, would you mind reading that last sentence a little slowly for us? I have directed——

THE PRESIDENT. "Accordingly, I have directed the Secretary of the Army to take appropriate action immediately."

Q. Mr. President, how about the sentence before that, please, sir?

THE PRESIDENT. Well, all right.

Q. Is that mimeographed?

THE PRESIDENT. Yes, it is mimeographed, and it will be available for you at the door. "It is essential that precautions be taken against recurrences of such threats to our national security." That is the sentence you asked for?

Q. Thank you.

Q. Mr. President, does that mean the Army is going to take over the railroads?

THE PRESIDENT. That will be explained in the order which will come out later in the day.

Q. They are running it now?

THE PRESIDENT. The Army is operating the railroads now. But I have directed the Army to issue an order, which will explain fully what is to be done.

Q. It will be out later in the day?

THE PRESIDENT. This statement is all I care——

Q. Could you give us a hint, Mr. President?

THE PRESIDENT. No, you had better wait. You had better wait until it comes out.

Q. Mr. President, will that order come from the White House or the Pentagon?

THE PRESIDENT. It is—the Secretary of the Army is issuing the order at my direction. I am not shirking my responsibility.

Q. What time will that be out?

THE PRESIDENT. Later in the day. I can't tell you the exact hour. I hope by noon.

Q. Mr. President, I take it that this order will more effectively prevent any such walkouts in the future?

THE PRESIDENT. Well, you wait and read the order; it will explain itself.[2]

Q. Mr. President, could you tell us, sir, about any progress being made, or not being made, toward a settlement of the basic controversy in this walkout?

THE PRESIDENT. Well, they are still talking with each other. As you know, an agreement was signed and they acted like a bunch of Russians. They went back on their signatures.

[2.] Q. Mr. President, I would like to ask three questions if I may. The day before yesterday the White House sent to the Capitol for 10 copies of the Fulbright report on the RFC.[3] I would like to ask first, sir, have you found in that report any basis for criticism on your part of the activities of either Mr. Dawson[4] or your RFC directors?

THE PRESIDENT. No, I haven't.

Q. And second, do you feel that Mr. Dawson should ask for a public hearing before the committee, in view of what has been said about him?

THE PRESIDENT. Well, let me see, I brought that along with me, because I thought maybe you might ask that question. [*Laughter*] You know, I spent 10 years in the Senate,

[2] Department of the Army General Order 2, February 8, 1951, ordered the dismissal with loss of seniority rights for all employees of the Army-operated railroads who failed to continue work, unless physically unable to do so. It also provided wage increases for operating employees pending settlement of the dispute, and back pay at the increased rate. In the event no settlement was reached within a reasonable time, the order stated, the Army would recommend enactment by the Congress of appropriate legislation to assure normal rail service and a settlement.

[3] "Study of Reconstruction Finance Corporation: Favoritism and Influence," interim report of the Committee on Banking and Currency (Senate Report 76, 82d Cong., 1st sess., February 5, 1951). Senator J. W. Fulbright of Arkansas, chairman of the Subcommittee on Reconstruction Finance Corporation, submitted the report.

[4] Donald S. Dawson, Administrative Assistant to the President, formerly personnel director of the RFC.

and I wrote a lot of reports—[*more laughter*]—but I am happy to say I never wrote one like this.

They make a recommendation to begin with, that the Federal Loan Administrator period was the one in which the RFC functioned best. The Federal Loan Administrators were, to begin with, Jesse Jones and Fred Vinson, and then John Snyder.[5]

And as soon as the war was over, everybody wanted to return to the situations as they existed previous to 1940. So the RFC was set up with its board of directors, as any other great financial institution is operated. Then there were some difficulties, in fact I had almost as much difficulty getting people to act as directors of the RFC as I have had with all these emergency agencies which we have been trying to set up.

And then along in the fall of 1949, I sent down a reorganization plan which transferred the RFC to the Department of Commerce, and set up the Secretary of Commerce in the same sort of situation as was the Federal Loan Administrator. And that reorganization plan was rejected at the behest of this committee that has written this asinine report. And now they are recommending just such a setup as I sent them back in 1949.

And what puzzles me—and I am going to ask some of these gentlemen to come up and explain it to me, because I don't think I am fundamentally dumb in most things, especially where it affects administration in Government—one sentence here is most important.

[*Reading*] "In presenting this report"—I still don't understand what they mean—"the subcommittee wishes to distinguish between

improper influence as such and the improper use of the Corporation's authority in response to influences which in themselves may be perfectly proper. This report deals primarily with the latter. The subcommittee expresses no opinion as to the propriety of the activities of other individuals named in the report, and it makes no charges against those individuals."

Well now, when I made a report to the Congress, I made specific charges if I thought they were necessary.

Then it says [*reading*]: "The subcommittee believes no one will be injured unfairly by its report. However, it will accord the opportunity for a public hearing to those who feel that unfair injury has been given."

Well now, I went through and read the report. I couldn't find where there was any fault with any loans that had been made. They charged some attorneys here in town had been too active in presenting cases before the RFC, and I found an immense number of letters on most of those loans from Senators and Representatives—a big pile of them here—most interesting.[6] But nothing is said in this report about undue influence, outside the President.

The objective of this report seems to have been a reflection on the President himself. And I am sorry for that, because I have never in my life brought pressure on the RFC or

---

[5] Jesse H. Jones was Secretary of Commerce, as well as Federal Loan Administrator, until his resignation in 1945. At the time of the news conference, Fred M. Vinson was Chief Justice of the United States and John W. Snyder was Secretary of the Treasury.

[6] In a statement made public by the White House on February 23, 1951, Joseph Short, Press Secretary to the President, pointed out that earlier the President had requested and received from the RFC copies of numerous letters written by Senators and Congressmen to the RFC in connection with loans. The material was considered by the President in connection with his plan for reorganization of the RFC. The statement continued: "Since the President knows of no evidence of illegal influence on the RFC by any member of the executive branch or the legislative branch, he sees no useful purpose in making public the Congressional correspondence. If, however, the subcommittee feels otherwise the material will be sent to the subcommittee of the Senate Banking and Currency Committee at its request."

any other agency of the Government to do anything except in the public interest. And all these RFC loans are supposed to be made in the public interest. And it is my opinion that they have been made in the public interest.

There may have been mistakes. There is no organization in Government, or in private business, or anywhere else, that can get through life without making mistakes. A man who makes no mistakes is a man who never does anything.

But as far as this report is concerned, I can't find out what the committee is driving at. I am going to have them come up, as soon as the chairman gets back to town— he left town when he found out I wanted to see him [7]—[*laughter*]—and maybe I can find out exactly what they are driving at. If I can, I, as President of the United States, will try to straighten out any difficulties with which the committee thinks they are faced.

Q. Mr. President, my recollection of the Truman committee [8] was that those reports were submitted to the agency concerned some days ahead, for their criticism or correction?

THE PRESIDENT. That's right, and for their right to be heard, if there was anything that was not properly stated.

Q. Was that done——

THE PRESIDENT. It was not done.

Q. ——in connection with this report?

THE PRESIDENT. It was not done.

Q. Mr. President, will you tell us whether you will renominate the five members of the RFC Board, or——

THE PRESIDENT. I have that matter under consideration, and when I get ready to make the announcement I will let you know.

Q. Are you considering also a possible

change in the organization of the RFC— going back——

THE PRESIDENT. I shall expect to send down a reorganization plan substantially the same as I sent down in 1949.

Q. Mr. President, is this one of the matters that you intend to discuss with Chairman Maybank? [9]

THE PRESIDENT. That is one of the matters, yes. There are several others that I want to discuss with him.

Q. Could you tell us anything about the other matters?

THE PRESIDENT. No, no. I don't want to discuss them publicly. I want to discuss them with the chairman first. I always give them that courtesy.

Q. Mr. President, this reorganization plan, the plan you will submit again, do you mean by that, sir, that you again will recommend that the RFC be put in the Commerce Department?

THE PRESIDENT. Well, I haven't come to a definite conclusion on that, but I am working on a reorganization plan. You see, a number of the Senators on this committee came down to see me some time ago, and talked about a reorganization plan for the RFC, and I told them that I would go to work on one. We are working on it. We can't do these things in 2 days. It takes a little while.

Q. Mr. President, is there a possibility you might recommend it be put under Treasury, not Commerce?

THE PRESIDENT. There is a possibility, but Commerce is where it belongs because it is a business proposition.[10]

[3.] Q. Mr. President, out of Tokyo and through the General MacArthur censorship,

---

[7] Subcommittee Chairman J. William Fulbright was in Miami Beach, Fla.

[8] The Special Committee to Investigate the National Defense Program, chaired by Mr. Truman while in the Senate.

[9] Senator Burnet R. Maybank of South Carolina, chairman of the Committee on Banking and Currency.

[10] For the special message to the Congress transmitting the reorganization plan relating to the RFC, see Item 39.

the heads of the UP and AP bureaus wrote stories saying, without any qualification, that General MacArthur had recommended to you that Chiang Kai-shek's troops be released for use in Korea and on the mainland. Would you give us any comment on that, sir?

THE PRESIDENT. Such a communication has not reached me.

Q. Does General MacArthur usually advise in the field of foreign policy decisions, or——

THE PRESIDENT. I have no comment. The President is responsible for foreign policy, however. I thought you knew that, if you would read the Constitution.

[4.] Q. Mr. President, as a result of your meeting with the Cotton State Senators, do you now feel that raw cotton should be free from price controls?

THE PRESIDENT. That matter is under consideration by the proper authorities. I had a very pleasant meeting with those Senators, and the matter was referred for consideration to the Secretary of Agriculture and to the Production Control Administration.

[5.] Q. Could you discuss, sir, food prices generally, with specific reference to the executive branch's attitude toward the parity formula?

THE PRESIDENT. I have no comment.

[6.] Q. Mr. President, about this time of year we always ask you this question. A number of Members of Congress on both sides of the aisle have been saying that they are going to squeeze water out of the budget?

THE PRESIDENT. They are welcome to try. You know, they tried to squeeze water out of the budget the year before, and instead of squeezing it out they put about a billion-and-a-half on to it, and then asked me to do the cutting, after the budget came to me. I am not going to do it this year for them. We will see how much water they can squeeze out of it. It is a good budget—a

tight budget. I dare them to do anything to it.

[7.] Q. Senator Williams introduced a resolution calling upon you for the removal of the collector of internal revenue for the third district of New York. Have you any comment?

THE PRESIDENT. I cannot understand what it is I am called upon to do?

Q. Remove the collector of internal revenue in the third New York collection district?

THE PRESIDENT. I know nothing about it. I can't comment on it, because I don't know both sides of the question, and I don't usually make moves of that sort unless I know the facts.[11]

[8.] Q. Mr. President, have you any comment on the clemency order by Mr. McCloy on the Nazi war criminals? [12]

THE PRESIDENT. No comment.

[9.] Q. Mr. President, can you give us any more details on your meeting yesterday with Mr. Hoover on the Indian famine situation?

THE PRESIDENT. Mr. Hoover made all the announcement that is necessary.[13]

[10.] Q. Do you have any comment on the House action yesterday on reciprocal trade with the limiting amendments?

THE PRESIDENT. No, I have no comment on that, because legislation is not for my consideration until it reaches me. You never

---

[11] Senate Resolution 63, submitted by Senator John J. Williams of Delaware, called for the removal from office of James W. Johnson, because of lack of administrative ability. It was referred to the Committee on Finance.

[12] On January 31, 1951, John J. McCloy, U.S. High Commissioner for Germany, and Gen. Thomas T. Handy, U.S. Commander in Chief, European Command, announced their decisions in a review of 101 war crimes sentences.

[13] Former President Herbert Hoover spoke to members of the press after his meeting with President Truman and administration officials to discuss the possibility of U.S. aid to India to relieve the famine caused by crop failures.

can tell what it is going to be until I get it. I will comment on it when it reaches me.

[11.]   Q. Mr. President, do you feel that you have a full understanding with the Federal Reserve Board over interest rates?

THE PRESIDENT. I have always felt that I had a full understanding with the Federal Reserve Board. I made that very plain in the letter which I wrote to them.[14]

Q. Mr. President, have you any comment on the memorandum prepared by Mr. Eccles [15] afterwards——

THE PRESIDENT. No comment——

Q. ——implying a disagreement?

THE PRESIDENT. No comment.

Q. Mr. President, I was writing sort of fast and getting writer's cramp——

THE PRESIDENT. Well, Tony,[16] we'll back up. [*Laughter*]

[12.]   Q. I wonder if we could appeal to Mr. Romagna [17] on that first reference to the RFC report, the first question and your answer about Mr. Dawson?

[*The President gave this permission but while the reporter was looking for the notes, questions continued to be asked, as follows:*]

[13.]   Q. Could you comment on the possible effect on the Federal budget if Government interest rates were to be——

THE PRESIDENT. Well, anybody that understands figures knows what that would do to the budget. All you have got to do is figure it. You are a budget expert, you ought to know. [*Laughter*]

Q. Thank you very much. I didn't know that.

---

[14] See Item 29.

[15] Marriner S. Eccles, member of the Board of Governors of the Federal Reserve System. On February 4, the Washington Sunday Star carried an article entitled "Eccles Astonished by Truman Stand on Interest Rate Policy—Disputes Assumption that Board Supports Treasury Position." The article is reprinted in the Congressional Record, vol. 97, p. 1005.

[16] Ernest B. Vaccaro of the Associated Press.

[17] Jack Romagna, White House Official Reporter.

THE PRESIDENT. I have always thought you were one.

Q. Mr. President, is it your understanding that the majority of the Federal Reserve Board agree with you?

THE PRESIDENT. Yes.

Q. I didn't get the question?

THE PRESIDENT. He said did I understand that a majority of the Federal Reserve Board agreed with me, and I said yes I did understand that. In fact, I thought all of them did, because I was not present at their private meeting behind closed doors. All I know is what they said to me in the meeting with me.

[*At the President's direction, the question and answer referred to heretofore was read back*]

[14.]   Q. Mr. President, now that that has been read back, you didn't answer—do you think Mr. Dawson ought to ask for a public hearing?

THE PRESIDENT. I do not. They ought to have asked Mr. Dawson to come down and be heard before they made this asinine report. That would have been fair. It is up to them. I have got confidence in Mr. Dawson. That is up to the committee, not me.

[15.]   Q. Mr. President, as long as we are going back—[*Laughter*]—is the railroad recommendation going to be like the one you sent up once before?

THE PRESIDENT. It will speak for itself, when it comes out. You will have to wait a little while.

Q. I thought—later you said that the railroad unions were like Russians?

THE PRESIDENT. As to agreement.

Q. You said they signed an agreement, then backed out on it. You didn't say which side was acting like Russians?

THE PRESIDENT. Which side ran out on the agreement? That's all you need to do. Smitty,[18] use your head! [*Laughter*]

---

[18] Merriman Smith of the United Press Associations.

Q. Mr. President, in accepting the agreement, whatever action you direct the Army to take, the railroads are going to be operated——

THE PRESIDENT. That's the idea, exactly. The railroads are going to run no matter what it takes to run them.

Q. You will ask the Army to use its own railroad personnel?

THE PRESIDENT. Now wait until you read the order. I appreciate that you would like to know, but I am not going to give it to you until it comes out.

Merriman Smith (United Press Associations): Mr. President, have you got anything else to say? [*Much laughter*]

THE PRESIDENT. No, I haven't.

NOTE: President Truman's two hundred and fifty-fourth news conference was held in the Indian Treaty Room (Room 474) in the Executive Office Building at 10:30 a.m. on Thursday, February 8, 1951.

34   Special Message to the Congress on the Famine in India. *February* 12, 1951

To the Congress of the United States:

I recommend that the Congress provide assistance to the Republic of India to meet the food crisis which now confronts the people of that country.

The people of India are in desperate need of emergency assistance from this country in meeting their food problems.

A series of natural disasters—earthquakes, floods, droughts, and plagues of locusts—greatly reduced the 1950 grain crop in India. The result has been to impair the ability of India to feed the population in its major cities and in many rural areas.

The average Indian food consumption is little more than half of our own. Grain constitutes more than three-quarters of the Indian diet. India has a large and effective rationing system, through which a large portion of the Indian population receives some or all of its necessary food grain supplies.

One hundred and twenty-five million people are covered by the rationing system. Some 45,000,000 depend almost entirely upon their government ration for their food grain supplies. Already the Government of India has found it necessary to cut the standard grain ration from 12 ounces to 9 ounces a day and take other drastic measures to meet the growing distress. Grain reserves have reached a dangerously low point.

Total grain requirements for ration distribution this year are estimated by the Government of India at about 9,000,000 long tons or 336,000,000 bushels. To maintain the rationing system, even at a level below last year's, the Government of India finds that it will have to import close to 6,000,000 tons in 1951. India is procuring almost 4,000,000 tons of this total through the use of its own foreign exchange resources. This grain is to be purchased in Australia, Argentina, Burma and other countries. It includes about 1½ million tons of grain which India is procuring for cash from this country and Canada in accordance with its quotas under the International Wheat Agreement.

Procurement of the remaining 2,000,000 tons—about 75,000,000 bushels—which India estimates it will need, presents a serious problem. This grain will have to come in large measure, if not entirely, from this country. The Government of India has requested the United States to make this amount available, with shipment to begin as soon as possible. India finds that it does not now have funds available to pay for this amount, and yet, if action is not taken, there may be a real danger of famine in India.

We cannot turn a deaf ear to India's appeal. Our friendship for the people of India and our traditional concern for human suffering impel us to take every reasonable step we can to alleviate mass hunger and distress. Furthermore, the needs of the people of India have a special claim upon our sympathies at this time.

India is the largest of the new nations of Asia which have attained independence since the end of World War II. Following the voluntary withdrawal of the British in 1947, the Indian people adopted a constitution and began their existence under it, as a sovereign democratic republic, on January 26, 1950, little more than a year ago. India's constitution, which is similar to our own, provides for universal suffrage and for the protection of its citizens in a way akin to our own Bill of Rights. The people of India are striving earnestly to establish representative government and democratic institutions as a unified and independent nation.

Like any nation which has just achieved independence, India is confronted with great difficulties—difficulties which have been aggravated by the crisis in Asia caused by the aggressive forces of communist imperialism. The present food crisis, if permitted to continue, would magnify these difficulties and threaten the stability of India.

It is important to the free world that the democratic institutions which are emerging in India be maintained and strengthened. With a population of almost 350,000,000 people, India has substantial mineral resources and important industries. Its continued stability is essential to the future of free institutions in Asia.

I recognize that there are important political differences between our Government and the Government of India with regard to the course of action which would most effectively curb aggression and establish peace in Asia. However, these differences should not blind us to the needs of the Indian people. These differences must not deflect us from our tradition of friendly aid to alleviate human suffering.

It is not our objective in foreign affairs to dominate other nations. Our objective is to strengthen the free nations through cooperation—free and voluntary cooperation based on a common devotion to freedom. Our actions have demonstrated our adherence to this objective throughout the world. It is natural that the Indian people should turn to us for aid in meeting the threat of famine that now confronts them. We should meet their appeal in the spirit which guides our relations with all free nations.

I am confident that the American people and their representatives in Congress will respond to this urgent call for help. Already, numerous voices from all over the country have urged the Government to send food; and a number of members of both parties in the Congress are strongly supporting this popular demand.

I have had the executive departments concerned make a careful study of our ability to meet the Indian request. We do not have an oversupply of food grains. Our current carryover of grain stocks is not excessive for a critical period like the present. Nevertheless, from a supply standpoint it is possible for us to make available up to 2,000,000 tons of grain without reaching the danger point. Inland transportation and other facilities to bring the grain to shipside will present some difficulties in light of other heavy demands. To provide sufficient ocean transportation to get the grain to India in time, it will be necessary to take some ships from our reserve fleet and recondition them. These ships, on their return voyages, can also help to relieve the shortage of shipping which now impedes the flow of scarce materials to this country.

The Indian Government finds that it is not now able to pay cash for the additional 2,000,000 tons. It is, however, prepared to pay, and will pay, the very substantial ocean freight charges. India has limited foreign exchange reserves, and will have a somewhat unfavorable balance of payments this year. It is planning to use the major portion of its reserves, beyond the necessary cover for its currency, on a long range economic development program. It is, of course, of major importance that India develop its resources and provide a better economic base for its citizens, many of whom live in dire poverty. Unless India can undertake such a program, its economic troubles will increase, the standard of living of its people will continue to decline, and there will be no end to its history of recurrent famine.

In view of these factors, and the pressing need for immediate assistance, it seems desirable to make a substantial portion of the requested grain available promptly on a grant basis, with India paying for the cost of transportation. This initial grant will avert the imminent danger and provide time to explore in greater detail the need for the balance of the Indian request and to determine the best way of supplying the amounts needed.

I therefore recommend that the Congress, at this time, authorize the full amount requested by the Indian Government, but that it appropriate funds now only for the first million tons, deferring the appropriation of funds for the balance until the situation has been further clarified.

If the Congress adopts this program, I propose that a mission be sent to India under the Economic Cooperation Administration to observe the distribution of the grain and to assist in carrying out the program. This mission would make an on-the-spot appraisal of the full extent of the Indian needs. It would examine other supply possibilities and the terms upon which additional grain should be supplied from the United States.

As in the case of other foreign aid programs, we would expect our representatives in India to be given every opportunity to observe the distribution of the grain and to be sure that the aid we are supplying is distributed fairly. We would also expect that the Indian people be kept informed through full and continuous publicity as to the source of the grain. Similarly, we would expect the Government of India to deposit in a special account local currency equivalent to the proceeds from the sale in India of the grain we supply on a grant basis. This account would be used for the development and improvement of the Indian economy.

As the Congress is aware, this is the practice we have followed in those countries which have received aid under the programs of the Economic Cooperation Administration. In the case of India, such counterpart funds would offer a splendid opportunity for the improvement of Indian agriculture, the development of important natural resources and industries, and other projects of benefit to the people of India. We would also expect the Government of India to do all it can to expand supplies and otherwise to lessen the danger from crop shortages in the future.

The purpose of this program is to meet the current emergency in India, and to stimulate measures to forestall such crises in the future. It does not constitute a precedent for continuing to provide food to India on a grant basis or for providing similar aid for other countries.

I strongly urge that the Congress take immediate steps to put this program into effect. It is within our means. Human lives depend upon our taking prompt action. Shipments must begin by April if this food is to reach India in time to meet the present emergency.

In this critical time in the affairs of the world, it is vital that the democratic nations show their concern for the well-being of men everywhere and their desire for a better life for mankind. But words alone are not sufficient. We must implement our words by deeds. We must counter the false promises of Communist imperialism with constructive action for human betterment. In this way, and in this way only, can we make human liberty secure against the forces which threaten it throughout the world today.

HARRY S. TRUMAN

NOTE: See Item 124.

35 Remarks at the Swearing In of the President's Commission on Internal Security and Individual Rights. *February* 12, 1951

ADMIRAL, I want to congratulate you on assembling a commission such as this, with yourself as chairman. I am highly appreciative of the willingness of all of you to act in this capacity. The scope of the Commission's task is carried in the statement of January 23d,[1] which sets out what we hope to accomplish.

The Government's loyalty program, I think, has worked well. The Commission will probably find ways in which it can be improved, and should try to find ways in which that loyalty program can be improved.

It must be kept in mind fundamentally, however, that the Bill of Rights, in my opinion, Judge, is still the principal part of the Constitution of the United States so far as the individual in this country is concerned. And we must find a balance where we can be sure that the employees of the Government are loyal to the Government, and are really interested in the welfare of the United States of America, and at the same time see that the rights of individuals are amply protected so that there will be no one who feels that he has been persecuted because he will have to answer questions before this commission.

You have the authority to administer oaths and they must answer the questions that you ask. They must give you a fair and straightforward statement when you ask for it.

[1] Item 20.

You have access to the loyalty files of the FBI, just as the loyalty boards have had directly. You will not have to come to me for that authorization, because it is already implied, and the Attorney General and the chief of the FBI understand that. So that you will have access to whatever papers are necessary to find out the facts, and by obtaining them in that way, nobody can say that the files have been rifled, as we were charged with doing when we furnished files to the Tydings committee. We were charged here in the White House that the files had been picked and rifled so that they couldn't use them. There wasn't a word of truth to that.

I have the utmost confidence in the manner in which this commission is set up. I have very great confidence in your chairman, and always have had. I am anxious that this job be done in the manner that will stop witch hunting and give us the facts.

I have always been of the opinion—and maybe I shouldn't express an opinion to this commission before it starts—that the rank and file of the employees of the Government of the United States are as fine people as you can find anywhere in the world. I believe that just as sincerely as I sit here. But when you have some 2,200,000 people, it is natural that there will be some special instances where mistakes are made in their employment. If that were not the case, it would not be necessary to have courts.

And so with that, I am here to tell you that you have the complete and earnest cooperation of the President—and that is pretty good backing, so they tell me—and of all the other officials of the Government.

NOTE: The President spoke at 11:30 a.m. in the Cabinet Room at the White House. His opening word "Admiral" referred to Fleet Admiral Chester W. Nimitz, Chairman of the Commission. Later in his remarks he referred to Judge Bolitha J. Laws, Chief Judge of the United States District Court for the District of Columbia. Admiral Nimitz' remarks in response to the President were also released.

See also Items 20, 22[2], 104, 278.

36 Remarks to a Group of Trainees from NATO Countries.
February 13, 1951

I WOULD LIKE to say to you young men that this we appreciate. I think this is the best public relations between nations that can possibly be carried on. I understand that we have exchanges in the other countries, doing over there just what you have been doing here. When we get better acquainted, we learn to understand each other, and at your age is the time to get a perfect understanding of what people are like and what they are trying to do.

Our only ambition in the world is for peace, and a lasting peace. We have no designs on any nation, either for territory, conquest, or otherwise. We want to see everybody happy. If we can accomplish that, we will have lasting peace. And I hope you young gentlemen will go back and work for just that.

Thank you, gentlemen.

NOTE: The President spoke at 3:10 p.m. in his office at the White House to eight cadets from North Atlantic Treaty Organization countries who were about to receive training in the armed forces of the United Nations.

37 The President's News Conference of
February 15, 1951

THE PRESIDENT. [1.] Please be seated. I have one short announcement to make, and that is that on Saturday I am going over to inspect the Aberdeen, Md., Proving Grounds. This will be placed on the bulletin board, and anybody that feels like he would like to fire a bazooka or get fired at by one, will be welcome to go. That's all I have.

Q. What time are you leaving, Mr. President?

THE PRESIDENT. Nine o'clock.

Q. In the morning?

THE PRESIDENT. Yes.

Q. By train?

THE PRESIDENT. By train.

Q. What time will you come back?

THE PRESIDENT. When we get through. I don't know what time that will be.

Q. Mr. President, does this possibly indicate you might visit some other Armed Forces installations around the country?

THE PRESIDENT. Well, I haven't any under consideration right now.

[2.] Q. Mr. President, there have been some reports on the air lately that you are no longer in favor of the Federal-State accord on the St. Lawrence——

THE PRESIDENT. That is not true.

Q. ——on letting the States handle it?

THE PRESIDENT. If you will read the messages I sent down, you will find that that is not true.

Q. I remember in 1945 you said you were in favor of it.

THE PRESIDENT. Why certainly—there is no misunderstanding between the State of New York and the President.

[3.] Q. Mr. President, the term of Governor Stainback of Hawaii was supposed to end last August. Do you intend to appoint a new Governor before the Hawaiian legislature——

THE PRESIDENT. No, I do not.

Q. You do not?

THE PRESIDENT. No.

[4.] Q. Mr. President, you received a letter from the Federal Reserve Board on the maintenance of Government credit terms to the percentage——

THE PRESIDENT. I haven't seen it.

Q. You have not received the letter?

THE PRESIDENT. I haven't seen the letter.

Q. So you can't comment?

THE PRESIDENT. I can't comment on it.

[5.] Q. Mr. President, Justice Douglas made an address out in Tucson yesterday, rather critical of Asiatic policy—saying that the Asiatic world was in a form of revolution akin to the French Revolution and the American Revolution. Is there anything you might care to say about that?

THE PRESIDENT. No comment.

[6]. Q. Mr. President, you recently wrote Federal Reserve Board Chairman Mc-Cabe that you understand that you have the assurance that the market on Government securities will be stabilized and maintained at present levels.[1] Is it still your understanding that you have that assurance, sir?

THE PRESIDENT. That letter has said exactly what I meant, and still says what I mean.

[*Pause*]

What's the matter with everybody? [*Laughter*]

Q. We're writing.

Q. Have to write.

Q. That's important.

THE PRESIDENT. Too bad—you didn't used to do that when I made you stand up. [*More laughter*]

[7.] Q. Mr. President, Mr. DiSalle [2] said today—I think Mr. DiSalle asked Police Commissioner Murphy [3] of New York to take the enforcement job of price administration?

THE PRESIDENT. I think that would be a good appointment, if we can get him to do it. Mr. Murphy looks exactly like Grover Cleveland, and he is a fighter, too.

[8.] Q. Mr. President, it has been some time since you have made any comment on the progress on the fighting in Korea. Would you care to do that today?

THE PRESIDENT. I have no comment. I think there is more in the papers about that than any comment I could make.

Q. Mr. President, do you care to discuss where we go from here in Korea?

THE PRESIDENT. What about? Where is it you want to go?

Q. Well, the 38th parallel—or not?

THE PRESIDENT. I have no comment on that. That is a military matter, and the President of the United States has never interfered with military maneuvers in the field, and he doesn't expect to interfere in it now.

Q. Any comment on the senatorial strategists who want to go into Pingyang, then call it off?

THE PRESIDENT. No, I haven't. No comment. We have got a lot of strategists up there.

---

[1] See Item 29.

[2] Michael V. DiSalle, Director of Price Stabilization.

[3] Police Commissioner Thomas F. Murphy of New York City.

[9.] Mr. Short: [4] Mr. President, I think that quote from McCabe was an inaccurate quote.

THE PRESIDENT. What one was that?

Mr. Short: The quote from the McCabe letter that was read over there.

THE PRESIDENT. I don't think that was an accurate quote. Joe says he doesn't believe that that quote that was read over there from a letter I wrote to McCabe was an accurate one. Jack,[5] let's find it and read it back.

Q. Mr. President, I read the quote as saying that: "As I understand, I have your assurance that the market on Government securities would be stabilized and maintained at present levels"—and it goes on— "in order to assure the successful financing requirements, and to establish in the minds of the people confidence concerning Government credit."

THE PRESIDENT. I think I expressed appreciation at their cooperation, if I remember correctly.

Q. That is not the full quote. That was a paragraph from the letter.

THE PRESIDENT. I think you had better quote the full letter, because I say that letter still stands. I will see that you get the full letter.

Mr. Short: If you will come to my office, I will make the full letter available.

Q. Mr. President, it was in reply to your letter to Chairman McCabe that he responded the following day. Is that letter not a reply to this?

THE PRESIDENT. I haven't seen the letter.

[10.] Q. Mr. President, you were asked about crossing the 38th parallel, and you replied that that was a military matter. Is it——

THE PRESIDENT. That is a strategic matter.

It is a strategic matter, and it is in the hands of the Commanding General of the Far East.

Q. The point I was going to make is that there has been a lot of discussion about the political aspects of crossing the 38th parallel——

THE PRESIDENT. Oh, yes, and there will be a lot more discussion on that subject, too, but I don't intend to comment on it today.

Q. Mr. President, do you mean that the United Nations' permission of last October to cross the 38th parallel still holds good?

THE PRESIDENT. It is still in effect.

Q. Mr. President, just so we don't get into a "rowdy-dowdy," the way we did on that atomic bomb thing, do you mean by that, sir, that this—you don't mean discussing it whether we need more authority, or whether this is still——

THE PRESIDENT. No, I think the Commanding General of the Far East Command has all the authority necessary to carry on the military operations. And that is his job.

Q. I see.

[11.] Q. Mr. President, I have been reading a lot in the papers—society columns— about various trip plans you have—— [*Laughter*]

THE PRESIDENT. As you know, Tony,[6] I told you the other day that I thought that was a trial balloon sent up by the pressroom of the White House. [*Laughter*]

Q. But these people don't operate out of our pressroom.

THE PRESIDENT. I know, but then they are friends of nearly everybody in the pressroom, and you attend cocktail parties and places, and that is where all these rumors start. [*More laughter*]

Q. They have left me out of all of them.

THE PRESIDENT. They have me too, Tony.

[4] Joseph Short, Secretary to the President.
[5] Jack Romagna, White House Official Reporter.

[6] Ernest B. Vaccaro of the Associated Press.

All I know is what I see in the papers.

Q. Well, Mr. President, aside from trial balloons, are you going anywhere?

THE PRESIDENT. Well, I am going out to Aberdeen Saturday.

Q. After Aberdeen, sir?

THE PRESIDENT. I can't answer that today.

Q. What about Guantanamo, Mr. President? That is a——

THE PRESIDENT. That's a lovely place. That's a lovely place.

Q. Will you go there, sir?

THE PRESIDENT. I would like to go there, but I doubt very much whether I will have the opportunity.

[12.] Q. Mr. President, have you received any recommendations from Hiram Bingham [7] on tightening up requirements for——

THE PRESIDENT. No, I have not. I have not.

Q. Do you have any comment on his reported request that Federal agencies be enabled to discharge personnel, or reject a person for employment, if there is some reasonable doubt of their loyalty?

THE PRESIDENT. That is a matter that the Nimitz commission [8] is going into completely, and I don't care to comment on it now.

[13.] Q. Mr. President, do you feel the Ways and Means Committee's action on the delay of the $10 billion tax bill is endangering the anti-inflation program?

THE PRESIDENT. Yes, I am very sorry that they decided to delay. The objective in sending down the message I did on the tax program [9] was as quickly as possible to obtain a tax measure that would help stop inflation; and then the deliberations could be carried on when it becomes necessary for

further taxes, which will amount to about $16½ billion altogether.

Q. You are still sticking to it?

THE PRESIDENT. The message speaks for me.

Q. Thank you.

THE PRESIDENT. I still believe what the message said.

[14.] Q. Mr. President, the price of food continues to go up. Is there anything that you have in mind at present—rollbacks to take care of that——

THE PRESIDENT. The Stabilization people are working on that now, and I have done everything I can at the present time.

Q. I wonder, sir, if you were going to make a specific request of Congress for legislation to change provisions in the Defense Production Act, on the setting of farm prices on priorities?

THE PRESIDENT. If Mr. Wilson [10] and his Defense Production people feel that that legislation is necessary, I shall ask for it.

Q. But you haven't any plan in view at the moment?

THE PRESIDENT. Not now. I have the—the Defense Production organization is working on the situation, in a sincere effort to prevent a spiral of prices in food—and other things as well.

[15.] Q. Mr. President, do you think that commercial banks should, at this time, have a normal loan policy; that is, to go on making loans as they would in normal times, in spite of efforts to control prices?

THE PRESIDENT. I am not an expert on that, and I can't answer that question.

[16.] Q. Mr. President, do you plan any further action, if a settlement is not reached in the rail dispute soon?

THE PRESIDENT. I beg your pardon?

Q. Do you plan to appoint a new mediator to return the rail dispute negotiations to the

---

[7] Hiram Bingham, Chairman, Loyalty Review Board, U.S. Civil Service Commission.

[8] The President's Commission on Internal Security and Individual Rights.

[9] Item 28.

[10] Charles E. Wilson, Director, Office of Defense Mobilization.

White House, if a settlement is not reached soon?

THE PRESIDENT. They are still in conference, and I have no comment to make on that.

[17.] Q. Mr. President, have you any comment on General Marshall's testimony today? [11]

---

[11] Secretary of Defense George C. Marshall spoke before the Senate Foreign Relations and Armed Services Committees on the question of assigning U.S. ground forces to duty in Europe (see Department of State Bulletin, vol. 24, p. 328, or "Hearings Before the Committee on Foreign Relations and the Committee on Armed Services, United States Senate, Eighty-Second Congress, First Session, on S. Con. Res. 8").

THE PRESIDENT. General Marshall's testimony is in line with what I believe, and that is the reason he made the statement. We have been working on that policy right along, and he set it out very simply and clearly.

Q. Mr. President, have we overlooked anything?

THE PRESIDENT. I don't believe you have. I can't think of anything!

Reporter: Thank you, Mr. President.

NOTE: President Truman's two hundred and fifty-fifth news conference was held in the Indian Treaty Room (Room 474) in the Executive Office Building at 4 p.m. on Thursday, February 15, 1951.

---

38 Remarks in the Enlisted Men's Mess Hall, Aberdeen, Md., Proving Ground. *February* 17, 1951

THANK YOU very much. I can't tell you how very much I appreciate the privilege of another visit to Aberdeen Proving Ground. This is my third visit. The last one, I think, was somewhere in the neighborhood of 1943, when I was here with a number of Senators and Congressmen to witness the same sort of demonstration with the new weapons at that time that we have been witnessing today.

I want to compliment the Commanding General of this post on the presentation which he made to us this morning on the technical side. I am very sure that we have a number of newspapermen with us today who had a liberal education on projectory, and the gun at one end and the target at the other. And I am sure that most of them have learned all about mathematics, when we saw that wonderful machine that agrees with Einstein—somebody told me that it would arrive at the same result in a very short time that Einstein would in a lifetime. That is one of the great things that came out of the war.

I was visiting Detroit one time, and interviewing Henry Ford on the war effort at that time. This was back in late 1942 or early 1943, when we were trying to get tractors and ordnance, and the automobile companies were transferring their production lines from automobiles to wartime implements.

Knowing that Henry Ford was a pacifist, I asked him what he thought about the conditions with which we were faced. He said that he thought we had to meet the conditions, but he was very certain that things would come out of the tremendous effort which ourselves and our allies had put forth that would be of great benefit to civilization. And that has been absolutely true.

One of the things that has come out of that effort, in this country particularly, has been peace terms between the Army, Navy, and Air Force. If nothing else had been accomplished in that war but that, it would have been one of the worthwhile products of that terrible struggle.

I notice here that unification works completely. I was told that the Army, Navy, and Air Force were cooperating in the experiments which are going on at this station. Talking about the Air Force, I served myself in the Army cafeteria back here, in the style I was accustomed to in 1917 and 1918.

It has been a very satisfactory visit to me, and I hope it has been an education to all those who came along with me. I hope it will be my privilege at some later date to visit installations of a similar nature which have to do with naval experiments and air experiments as specialties. I am very much interested in field artillery and small weapons. And for your information, I was at Fort Sill in 1917 and 1918, and in 6 months they gave me a university education on ballistics and projectories. So to some extent— I say, to some extent—I could understand what those highly educated gentlemen were talking about this morning when they gave us those lectures.

I hope you will all go home with a feeling that we are putting forth all these efforts for peace, and not with any idea of destroying any other nation or any other government.

I have just had the privilege of meeting five Korean veterans, who are here in front of me. All of them have spent various lengths of time in Korea, all of them have been hurt, all of them have recovered, and all of them are making good soldiers here on this post. That is something to be proud of.

I was just saying to the Commanding General of this post that there is nothing that appeals to me more than a man in uniform who is proud of that uniform and who wears it as if he is proud of it.

And there is nothing in the world more disgusting to me than to see a slouchy man in uniform. That is the only thing I ever fuss about in Washington—and I don't have to do that very often, I am happy to say.

You men here, at least today—in this weather, no matter how bad it is—are wearing your uniforms as if you were proud of them, and that makes me proud to be your Commander in Chief.

NOTE: The President spoke at 1:45 p.m. In his remarks he referred to Maj. Gen. Edward E. MacMorland, Commanding General of the Aberdeen Proving Ground, Aberdeen, Md.

---

39   Special Message to the Congress Transmitting Reorganization Plan 1 Relating to the Reconstruction Finance Corporation. *February* 19, 1951

To the Congress of the United States:

I transmit herewith Reorganization Plan No. 1 of 1951, prepared in accordance with the Reorganization Act of 1949.

The reorganization plan provides strengthened administration of the Reconstruction Finance Corporation by placing in a single Administrator of the Reconstruction Finance Corporation the functions of the present Board of Directors, except those that are specifically set forth and assigned to a new Loan Policy Board and to a board of

review. The Administrator is thus made the executive head of the Corporation with major responsibility and authority over the administration of the Government programs carried out by the Corporation.

At the same time that this plan provides strengthened administration for the Corporation, it also provides certain additional safeguards with respect to loan policy and to specific loan applications. Under the reorganization plan, the Loan Policy Board promulgates general policies which shall govern the granting and denial of applications for financial assistance by the Corporation. The reorganization plan likewise includes new provisions for ensuring that all loan applications are handled in accordance with established policy.

In addition to providing strengthened administration of the Corporation and additional safeguards with respect to loan policy and the approval of specific loan applications, the reorganization plan provides the basis, by virtue of the composition of the Loan Policy Board, for better coordination of the Corporation's loan policies with other policies, programs and activities of the Government. The reorganization plan provides that this Board shall have five members, all ex officio. These are the Administrator of the Corporation, the Deputy Administrator, the Secretary of the Treasury, the Secretary of Commerce, and one additional member to be designated from time to time by the President from among officials of the Government who are required to be appointed by the President and confirmed by the Senate. The participation of these officials will facilitate the development of loan policies consistent with the requirements of other broad programs of the Government.

Especially important is the participation of the Secretary of Commerce who, as head of Department of Commerce, administers most of the Government programs for non-financial aids to business. Giving him a voice on the Loan Policy Board will aid in bringing under common policies the financial aids to business administered by the Corporation and the non-financial aids carried on in the Department of Commerce. Government aid to small and independent business should be particularly benefited by the participation of the Secretary of Commerce.

Specifically, the provision in the reorganization plan for a financial assistance pro-

cedure governing the processing of applications in excess of $100,000 to any borrower strengthens and gives statutory prescription to an administrative arrangement already existing in the Corporation. In handling such loans under the reorganization plan, applications will be referred for analysis and recommendation to a board of review composed of not less than five employees of the Corporation. Whenever the Administrator approves or denies an application for financial assistance on which a board of review has recommended otherwise, he must set forth, in a memorandum to be placed in the files of the Corporation the reasons for his action. This procedure is provided in order to assure that all applications for loans involving large sums are fully analyzed by the technical staff of the Corporation and that the recommendations of the staff are fully available to the Administrator when acting finally upon such applications.

The reorganization plan continues the Reconstruction Finance Corporation as a separate corporate entity in the executive branch of the Government. Those functions which are currently performed by the Corporation or any of its agencies or officers pursuant to a delegation or assignment of functions made by the President will be subject to termination or modification of any such delegation by the President.

After investigation I have found and hereby declare that each reorganization included in Reorganization Plan No. 1 of 1951 is necessary to accomplish one or more of the purposes set forth in section 2(a) of the Reorganization Act of 1949. I also have found and hereby declare that by reason of these reorganizations, it is necessary to include in the reorganization plan provisions for the appointment and compensation of the Administrator and Deputy Administrator of the Reconstruction Finance Corporation.

The rates of compensation fixed for these officers are, respectively, those which I have found to prevail in respect of comparable officers of the executive branch of the Government.

The taking effect of the reorganization included in Reorganization Plan No. 1 of 1951 may not in itself result in substantial immediate savings. However, the important objective of achieving the maximum effectiveness in the administration of the Government's lending programs to aid business will be advanced. Increased effectiveness will in turn produce indirect savings. An itemization of these savings is not practicable.

The reorganization plan is especially important at this time of national emergency. It will strengthen the administration of the Reconstruction Finance Corporation and at the same time provide additional safeguards with respect to loan policy and the approval of individual loans. It will make possible the more effective coordination of the Government's general loan policies. I strongly urge the approval of the reorganization plan as a means of achieving these objectives.

HARRY S. TRUMAN

NOTE: Reorganization Plan 1 of 1951 is published in the U.S. Statutes at Large (65 Stat. 773) and in the 1949–1953 Compilation of Title 3 of the Code of Federal Regulations (p. 1018). It became effective May 1, 1951.

40 Remarks to the Voice of Democracy Contest Winners.
February 20, 1951

IT IS a pleasure to greet you. It seems that the young ladies win their prizes at an earlier date than the young men—18 against 17, if I am not mistaken.

But you are to be congratulated on what you have done. It is a contribution to the welfare of the country, and highly appreciated by me.

I think this is the fourth time, if I am not mistaken, that you are having a meeting on this very same subject and for this very same reason, and I hope you will continue

in your careers and keep on putting out this information for which you won these prizes.

NOTE: The President spoke at 11:35 a.m. in his office at the White House, where he received the four high school students who had written winning broadcast scripts on the subject "I Speak for Democracy": Robert A. Burnett of St. Louis, Mo., Marcia Anne Harmon of Del Rosa, Calif., Norita Newbrough of Baton Rouge, La., and Ricardo Romulo of Washington, D.C., son of Gen. Carlos P. Romulo, Secretary of Foreign Affairs of the Philippine Republic.

The contest was sponsored by the U.S. Junior Chamber of Commerce, the National Association of Broadcasters, and the Radio-Television Manufacturers Association.

41 Remarks at a Masonic Breakfast.
February 21, 1951

Mr. Chairman, Frank, and distinguished guests from all over the country, and the Supreme Court and legislative branch of the Government, and the Secretaries of the executive branch:

This seems to have been a rather fixed-up proposition, to inform the President what his Cabinet and the Court and the legislative branch think of him. I am glad to know it. It is very satisfactory. I appreciate it most highly, but what I had expected to discuss with you this morning is a continuation of what these able and distinguished gentlemen have brought to your attention.

We have an emergency. I declared an emergency back in the latter part of 1950, because it was really on us—and it is on us now. And it is difficult—very difficult—for people to realize, as things go along as usual, that the Government is faced with the most tremendous emergency that any government has ever been faced with in the history of the country. And I say that because I know the history of the country very well. I know that we are going through some of the same things that were gone through in 1860, and 1916, and 1941.

We have made every effort possible to avoid a great many of those mistakes. We have not been able to avoid them all, but we are profiting by experience, and I think that I am very, very fortunate in having experienced men in every key position who understand the situation and who are honestly working it out on the basis it should be worked out.

It was necessary for me to appoint a production manager, an administrator for the Defense Production authority. He has had his difficulties, because it is very difficult to get people to understand that now is not the time to get all the traffic will bear, now is not the time to "get," because the Government is in a position where it has to have certain materials to meet the thing that General Marshall is working on: to keep the peace.

That is all this is for. It is an effort to prevent a third world war. And we are gradually approaching a position in the world where that can be prevented, if we have the support and cooperation of all the segments of the population. And that means industry, labor, the farmer, and you gentlemen—and all the white-collar people who do the inside work to make these other things operate.

Now it is necessary, I think, in this country, as well as around the world, to try to mobilize the moral forces of the world against the unmoral forces. We need to mobilize the moral forces in this country of ours to prevent selfishness of certain groups from an endeavor to take advantage of this situation.

Everybody, I don't care who he is or what his condition or his position is—from the President of the United States to the laborer who digs in the trench—must make some sacrifice in order that the whole country may be mobilized to meet the serious situation with which we are faced.

Now, for 5 years I have been endeavoring to mobilize the moral forces of the world, those forces which believe in the Sermon on the Mount, those forces which believe in a God, those forces which believe in the welfare of the individual, who believe that the Government is formed for the welfare of the individual and not that the individual is formed to be a slave to the Government.

That is what we are faced with. That is what we are trying to implant in the world.

I am here to say to you that if we could have expended the tremendous sums of money which were necessary to meet Hitler and Mussolini in the development of the resources of this world, there would have been no necessity for the slaughter of all the young men of that generation in Europe. Not at all.

It is a tremendous outlook that we have for the future of the world as a whole, if we can develop the undeveloped parts of the world to meet the pressure of populations in countries like China and India and central Europe.

It can be done. It is not impossible. But we have to understand that we are faced with an unmoral force which does not keep its agreements, which does not believe in the things for which this Government stands and for which the other free governments in the world do stand.

Now, it is your duty—you come from every section of the United States—to see if you can't revive that moral force in our own population that causes a man to give some sacrifice for the welfare of the rest of the human race.

That is your business. You are taught that. That is a part of your creed. All I am asking you to do is to help the President of the United States to mobilize the moral forces in the world to meet the unmoral forces in the world.

It can be done, and we are doing it—with some handicaps, I will admit. We have our troubles. Mr. Wilson has had his troubles, and he will have some more before we get through. But Mr. Wilson and the President of the United States will work

those troubles out. This Government is going forward, not backward.

We are not in the midst of any political campaign at the present time. In all probability we will be in the midst of one next year, and we will meet that situation as we have met it before.

But that is not the object now. The object now is to meet the emergency with which we are faced, and to meet it on a basis so that everybody will make his proper contribution, and nobody will come out with any special privilege.

Now, if you gentlemen will give me a lift on that, this breakfast will have been worthwhile.

Thank you very much.

NOTE: The President spoke at 9:10 a.m. at the Statler Hotel in Washington. In his opening remarks, he referred to Frank S. Land, founder and Secretary General of the Order of DeMolay. He later referred to Charles E. Wilson, Director of the Office of Defense Mobilization.

42 Statement by the President on the Highway Safety Conference. *February* 22, 1951

BECAUSE traffic accidents still result in appalling loss of life, personal injury, and economic wastage, the President's Highway Safety Conference is to be reconvened in Washington the week of June 10. Meanwhile, Maj. Gen. Philip B. Fleming, as General Chairman of the Conference, is to initiate whatever other action may be needed to promote greater highway safety.

The Conference will be asked to reappraise current safety activities, determine the areas in which more effective action is required, and provide organized assistance to State and community officials and military authorities in stepping up the program to save lives on American streets and highways.

It is essential that each citizen, as driver

or pedestrian, cooperate in the safety program, for most accidents are caused by individual carelessness and disregard of regulations.

Traffic accidents constitute serious proportions in these critical times. Preliminary figures for 1950 indicate that the number of deaths approached 35,000, personal injuries were suffered by 1,200,000, and the economic losses are estimated at $2¼ billion. The figures for last year are the highest since 1941—the alltime high year. This is the price the American public has paid for carelessness, ignorance, disregard of the law, and inefficient driving.

The toll can be reduced. A practical program of action was developed at the first national conference, which I called in 1946, and it has demonstrated encouraging results. For the Nation as a whole, the number of traffic deaths has been cut from 11.3 per 100 million vehicle miles of travel in 1945 to less than 7 in 1950. The program has reduced accidents wherever it has been applied.

However, it has not offset the huge increase in motor vehicle usage. Today 48 million automobiles, trucks, and buses operate over our street and highway network, compared with a 1941 prewar peak of 34.5

million. Safety activities must be enlarged and intensified to match this greatly increased exposure to accident. The States and cities soon will complete a new annual inventory of traffic activities which, upon analysis, will direct efforts to those points where action must be taken.

NOTE: On the same day the White House made public a statement entitled "Summary of Highway Safety Needs." The statement emphasized the need for better enforcement, particularly in rural areas, and for better administration of traffic courts.

For the President's remarks to the Highway Safety Conference, see Item 121.

43 Remarks at the White House Photographers' Association Award Ceremonies. *February* 24, 1951

I AM most happy to again hand out these first prizes for these historic pictures.

You know I have, I guess, about as great a collection as anybody of pictures and cartoons, particularly the pictures that win these

prizes, and it gives me a great deal of pleasure to again hand this cup to the winner.

NOTE: The President spoke at 8:35 p.m. at the Library of Congress in Washington, where he opened the Association's eighth annual exhibit.

44 Memorandum Requesting a Study of the Problems of Debt Management and Credit Controls. *February* 26, 1951

Memorandum for the Secretary of the Treasury, the Chairman of the Board of Governors of the Federal Reserve System, the Director of Defense Mobilization, the Chairman of Council of Economic Advisers:

I have been much concerned with the problem of reconciling two objectives: first, the need to maintain stability in the Government security market and full confidence in the public credit of the United States, and second, the need to restrain private credit expansion at this time. How to reconcile these two objectives is an important facet of the complex problem of controlling inflation during a defense emergency which requires the full use of our economic resources.

It would be relatively simple to restrain private credit if that were our only objective, or to maintain stability in the Government security market if that were our only objective. But in the current situation, both objectives must be achieved within the framework of a complete and consistent economic program.

We must maintain a stable market for the very large financing operations of the Government. At the same time, we must maintain flexible methods of dealing with private credit in order to fight inflation. We must impose restraints upon nonessential private lending and investment. At the same time, we must maintain the lending and credit facilities which are necessary to expand the industrial base for a constant buildup of our total economic strength. Instead of fighting inflation by the traditional method of directing controls toward reducing the overall level of employment and productive activity, a defense emergency imposes the harder task of fighting inflation while striving to expand both employment and production above what would be regarded as maximum levels in normal peacetime.

What we do about private credit expansion and about the Government securities market is, of course, only a part of the problem that confronts us. A successful program for achieving production growth and economic stability in these critical times must be based upon much broader considerations.

We must make a unified, consistent, and comprehensive attack upon our economic problems all along the line. Our program must include, in proper proportion, production expansion policy, manpower policy, tax policy, credit policy, debt management and monetary policy, and a wide range of direct and indirect controls over materials, prices, and wages. All of these policies are necessary; each of them must be used in harmony with the rest; none must be used in ways that nullify others.

We have been striving in this emergency to develop such a unified program in the public interest. Much progress has already been made, both on the production front and on the anti-inflation front. Many peacetime activities of Government, including the activities of lending and financing agencies, have been pruned down. Cutbacks of civilian supplies and allocations of essential materials have been successfully undertaken. Important expansion programs for basic materials and productive capacity needed in the defense effort have been gotten underway. Price and wage controls have been initiated. Restraints on consumer and real estate credit have been applied. Large tax increases have been enacted and additional tax proposals are now pending. In all these fields further action is being planned and will be taken as needed.

One outstanding problem which has thus far not been solved to our complete satisfaction is that of reconciling the policies concerning public debt management and private credit control. Considering the difficulty of this problem, we should not be discouraged because an ideal solution has not yet been found. The essence of this problem is to reconcile two important objectives, neither of which can be sacrificed.

On the one hand, we must maintain stability in the Government security market and confidence in the public credit of the United States. This is important at all times. It is imperative now. We shall have to refinance the billions of dollars of Government securities which will come due later this year. We shall have to borrow billions of dollars to finance the defense effort during the second half of this calendar year, even assuming the early enactment of large additional taxes, because of the seasonal nature of tax receipts which concentrate collections in the first half of the year and because of the inevitable lag between the imposition of new taxes and their collection by the Treasury. Such huge financial operations can be carried out successfully only if there is full confidence in the public credit of the United States based upon a stable securities market.

On the other hand, we must curb the expansion of private loans, not only by the banking system but also by financial institutions of all types, which would add to inflationary pressures. This type of inflationary pressure must be stopped to the greatest extent consistent with the defense effort and the achievement of its production goals.

The maintenance of stability in the Government securities market necessarily limits substantially the extent to which changes in the interest rate can be used in an attempt to curb private credit expansion. Because of this fact, much of the discussion of this problem has centered around the question of which is to be sacrificed—stability in the Government securities market or control of private credit expansion. I am firmly convinced that this is an erroneous statement of the problem. We need not sacrifice either.

Changing the interest rate is only one of several methods to be considered for curbing credit expansion. Through careful consideration of a much wider range of methods, I believe we can achieve a sound reconciliation in the national interest between maintaining stability and confidence in public credit operations and restraining expansion of inflationary private credit.

We have effective agencies for considering this problem and arriving at a proper solution.

Over the years, a number of important steps have been taken towards developing effective machinery for consistent and comprehensive national economic policies. One of the earliest steps in this century was the establishment of the Federal Reserve System before World War I. At that time, under far simpler conditions than those now confronting us, the Federal Reserve System was regarded as the main and central organ for economic stabilization. After World War II, in a much more complex economic situation and a much more complex framework of governmental activities affecting the economy, the Council of Economic Advisers was established by the Congress under the Employment Act of 1946 to advise the President and help prepare reports to the Congress concerning how all major economic policies might be combined to promote our economic strength and health. Still more recently, in the current defense emergency, the Office of Defense Mobilization has been established to coordinate and

direct operations in the mobilization effort. In addition, some of the established departments, such as the Treasury Department, have always performed economic functions which go beyond specialized problems and affect the whole economy.

Consequently, I am requesting the Secretary of the Treasury, the Chairman of the Federal Reserve Board, the Director of Defense Mobilization, and the Chairman of the Council of Economic Advisers to study ways and means to provide the necessary restraint on private credit expansion and at the same time to make it possible to maintain stability in the market for Government securities. While this study is underway, I hope that no attempt will be made to change the interest rate pattern, so that stability in the Government security market will be maintained.

Among other things, I ask that you consider specifically the desirability of measures: (1) to limit private lending through voluntary actions by private groups, through Government-sponsored voluntary actions such as was done in a narrow field by the Capital Issues Committee of World War I, and through direct Government controls; and (2) to provide the Federal Reserve System with powers to impose additional reserve requirements on banks.

Under the first heading, I am sure that you are aware of the efforts that are already underway by the American Bankers Association, the Investment Bankers Association, and the life insurance association. I want you to consider the desirability of this or other kinds of private voluntary action in bringing about restraint on the part of lenders and borrowers.

I should like you to consider also the establishment of a committee similar to the Capital Issues Committee of World War I, but operating in a broader area. The objectives of such a committee would be to prevail upon borrowers to reduce their spending and to curtail their borrowing and to prevail upon lenders to limit their lending. The activities of this committee could be correlated with those of the defense agencies under Mr. Wilson with the objective of curtailing unnecessary uses of essential materials.

Furthermore, I should like you to consider the necessity and feasibility of using the powers provided in the Emergency Banking Act of 1933 to curtail lending by member banks of the Federal Reserve System. These powers are vested in the Secretary of the Treasury subject to my approval. The Secretary could by regulation delegate the administration of this program to the 12 Federal Reserve banks, each to act in its own Federal Reserve district under some flexible procedure. The program could be extended to institutions other than member banks, if desired, by using the powers provided by the Trading with the Enemy Act.

Under the second heading, you will recall the recommendation I made to the Congress a number of times in recent years to provide additional authority for the Federal Reserve System to establish bank reserve requirements. I should like you to consider the desirability of making that or another recommendation with the same general purpose at the present time.

You are all aware of the importance of this problem and the need for an early resolution. I should like your study to proceed as rapidly as possible in order that I may receive your recommendations at a very early date. I am asking the Director of Defense Mobilization to arrange for calling this group together at mutually convenient times.

At the same time that we are working to solve this problem of maintaining the stability of the Government securities market

and restraining private credit expansion, we shall, of course, continue vigorously to review Government lending and loan guarantee operations. Since the middle of last year, we have taken a series of steps to curtail such operations and limit them to amounts needed in this defense period. I am directing the agencies concerned to report to me by March 15 on the nature and extent of their current lending and loan guarantee activities so that these operations may again be reviewed as part of our overall anti-inflationary program.

NOTE: The President read the memorandum at a meeting held in his office at the White House at 11 a.m. An accompanying White House release listed the following as present at the meeting: Thomas B. McCabe, Chairman, Board of Governors, Federal Reserve System; Charles E. Wilson, Director, Office of Defense Mobilization; Edward H. Foley, Under Secretary of the Treasury; Charles S. Murphy, Special Counsel to the President; Leon H. Keyserling, Chairman, John D. Clark, and Roy Blough, of the Council of Economic Advisers; William McChesney Martin, Jr., Assistant Secretary of the Treasury; Allan Sproul, Vice Chairman, Federal Open Market Committee; and Harry A. McDonald, Chairman, Securities and Exchange Commission.

On May 31, 1951, the White House made public the report requested by the President. Transmitted by letter dated May 17 and signed by the Director of Defense Mobilization, the report (8 pp., mimeographed) contained the following conclusions:

"The measures thus far adopted make up the beginning of an effective program of credit restraint. There is, however, no assurance that these measures will prove sufficient to deal with the inflationary situation that may be anticipated as the national security program expands. Additional measures are needed to contribute to the anti-inflationary program and at the same time maintain stability in the market for Government securities.

"In general, the additional measures which should be taken are: the extension and reinforcement of the Voluntary Credit Restraint Program, whose work this Committee wholeheartedly endorses; the enactment of legislation to permit continuation and some broadening of selective credit controls; an emergency increase in the authority of the Board of Governors to require, in case of need, supplementary reserves for all insured banks. With a view to the possibility that all other anti-inflationary measures fail, or that needed powers may not be obtained in time, plans should be readied for the imposition of mandatory limits on total credits extended by banks and other financial institutions (excepting essential loans) if, in an extraordinary emergency, such controls should become necessary."

For a statement by the President in response to a joint announcement by the Treasury Department and the Federal Reserve System that they had reached accord on debt-management and monetary policies, see Item 52.

45   Special Message to the Congress on Increasing the Postal Rates. *February 27, 1951*

To the Congress of the United States:

For the last several years, the United States postal service has been incurring very large deficits. The rapidly rising costs of delivering the mail have been substantially larger than the postage revenues received. The deficits have had to be made up by general tax revenues—or, to put it bluntly, the general taxpayer has been giving large subsidies to certain users of the postal system.

In the fiscal year 1952, the postal revenues are expected to be about 1,840 million dollars. Postal expenditures, at present cost levels, are expected to be about 2,361 million dollars, leaving a deficit of about 521 million dollars. This deficit may be larger if the Interstate Commerce Commission and the Civil Aeronautics Board raise transportation rates for carrying mail, as they have been requested to do by the railroads and airlines, or if other cost increases occur.

A postal deficit of more than one-half billion dollars is obviously unsound, especially at a time when every effort must be made to reduce the size of the Federal budget. The taxpayers of this country are faced with an unavoidably large burden in financing our defense program. It is unreasonable and unfair that they should also have to pay for postal costs which should be borne by those who receive the direct benefit of postal service.

At present, all major types of postal service, except first-class mail, are operated at a loss. Losses are especially heavy for second-

class mail (newspapers and magazines) and third-class mail (mainly circulars and advertising matter). Together, these two classes of mail account for over $300 million of the anticipated deficit.

The large deficits being incurred in postal operations result primarily from post-war cost increases. The largest part of postal expenses is accounted for by the salaries of postal workers and the costs of transporting mail. These personnel and transportation costs are about 96 percent of all postal expenses.

During the past five years, these costs have risen sharply. The salary increases for postal employees enacted in 1945, 1948, and 1949 have added approximately 800 million dollars to annual costs. The cost of transporting mail by rail and by air has risen, since July 1, 1945, by about 175 million dollars on an annual basis. Including increased rentals and equipment and supply costs, the annual cost of operating the postal system is now more than one billion dollars higher than it was in 1945—more than a 100 percent increase in five years.

These increased costs obviously could not have been avoided. Postal employees should receive fair salaries. The railroads and air lines are entitled to fair compensation for carrying the mail.

To some extent, the effect of higher salary and transportation rates has been offset by increased output per man-hour worked. Since the end of World War II, the productivity of postal employees per man-hour has increased by more than 10 percent—which compares favorably with the record of private industry over the same period.

The Post Office is constantly working to improve the efficiency of postal operations. The Post Office Department has been considerably reorganized. Simplified accounting methods are being instituted. A streamlined money order system will shortly be established. Some services have been cut down or eliminated. Research on new and better methods for sorting and handling mail is going forward all the time.

But the plain fact is that no possible increase in efficiency could absorb the extremely large cost increases that have taken place. In spite of the increase in productivity per man-hour since 1945, the average cost of each postal transaction has increased by nearly 60 percent. During the same period, the average revenue from each transaction has increased by only 5½ percent.

Under these circumstances, it is clearly necessary to increase postal rates in order to reduce the postal deficit.

Accordingly, I recommend, as I have recommended a number of times over the past several years, that the Congress increase postal rates sufficiently to wipe out the bulk of the present postal deficit, which should not be borne by the general taxpayer.

The deficit should not be eliminated completely. Some postal costs are incurred to carry mail sent on official business by the Legislative, Executive and Judicial Branches of Government. The airline subsidies—the amounts paid to the airlines over and above the cost of carrying air mail—are also charged to the Post Office. These, and a few over special expenses, amounting in all to about 160 million dollars, are incurred for general purposes of the Federal Government, and it is only reasonable that we should pay for them as we pay for other

Federal expenditures, through Federal taxes.

The bulk of the deficit, however—estimated in fiscal year 1952 at 361 million dollars—is incurred in the course of providing postal service to users other than the Federal Government. There is no good reason for taxing our people to pay these costs. Postal rates should be raised enough to cover them.

Increasing postal rates presents many complex problems of detail, since our system of postal rates has been built rather haphazardly over the years. In the light of current conditions, it contains many deeply-ingrained inequities and special privileges. The Committees of Congress who are responsible for determining most postal rates will, of course, want to consider carefully the specific rates for each class of mail and type of service. The Postmaster General is prepared to present a number of suggestions for raising postal rates to more reasonable levels. I wish to emphasize here a few of the major considerations which seem to me important in raising rates.

1. First-class mail (ordinary letters and cards) in total more than pays its way at the present time. Postal and post cards, however, do not. Consequently, the only major change in first-class mail rates I believe to be warranted at this time is in the rate on such cards. These cards were authorized by the Congress in 1872 at a rate of one cent each. The same low rate prevails today. This year more than four billion postal cards will be handled through the mails—over 90 percent of them used for commercial and advertising purposes. The cost of handling each card is 2.8 cents, while the revenue is one cent. I believe this rate should be raised to two cents, which would bring in, on the present volume, about 47 million dollars of additional revenue.

2. Major changes are needed in postal rates for second-class mail (newspapers and

magazines). In the fiscal year 1952, more than six billion individually-addressed newspapers and magazines are expected to be carried, at a cost of about 242 million dollars. But the postage paid will be only about 42 million dollars. Thus the newspaper and magazine publishers will have 200 million dollars—or 80 percent—of their postal costs paid for them by the general public.

Newspapers and magazines are now carried for 1½ cents a pound, without regard to distance, for the reading matter they contain, and a graduated rate for the advertising matter in them, rising from 1½ cents a pound, for distances up to 150 miles, to 7 cents a pound, for distances over 1,800 miles. These rates were intentionally set low, when they were established, in order to encourage the spread of information and education among our citizens. This is still a desirable objective, but clearly does not warrant a subsidy as extreme as that which now exists.

For example, the popular, digest-type magazines, which carry no advertising, are sent by mail throughout the country at the rate of 1½ cents per pound. Since on the average, three copies of this type of magazine weigh one pound, the postage works out to about one-half cent per copy transported anywhere in the United States. (It costs more to handle a copy of such a magazine than it does to handle an ordinary letter, for which a person pays 3 cents—six times as much postage.) It seems ridiculous for the taxpayers to be paying postage bills for magazines like these, which can well afford to pay their own way. Increasing the postage on such magazines obviously would not detract measurably from the purpose of spreading information and education among our citizens.

The large-circulation magazines which carry many pages of advertising pay a somewhat higher rate of postage, but one which is still only a small fraction of what it costs the postal service to handle these magazines. This means that, in plain fact, under present postal rates, the general taxpayers are generously subsidizing the advertisers, who are able to send their advertising into the homes of our people at less than cost. There seems to me no excuse whatever for the general taxpayers to subsidize advertisers. Surely advertising was not part of the public information and education which the Congress intended to subsidize 70 years ago when it established second-class mail!

These excessive subsidies for newspapers and magazines are not only wrong, they are seriously inequitable. Books, which are surely as important as newspapers and magazines in disseminating information, and mail-order catalogues, which carry advertising generally similar to that in newspapers and magazines, are classified as fourth-class mail. Under the recommended rates, there will be little, if any, subsidy in carrying these publications—a startling discrimination in comparison to the situation on second-class mail.

Newspapers and magazine publishers have substantially increased their subscription and advertising rates in recent years—in many cases doubling or tripling these rates. Second-class postage rates, on the other hand, are close to the average level of 1879, when this class of mail was first established. Publishers who charge prices geared to present-day costs cannot reasonably expect to pay postage at rate levels 70 years old.

For these reasons I believe it is imperative now to increase second-class mail rates. If these rates are doubled—which is the least that should be done—this would bring in only about 40 million dollars, and the general taxpayers would still be subsidizing second-class mail to the extent of more than 60 percent of its postal costs.

As a matter of long-term policy, second-class mail should be brought gradually toward self-sufficiency in postal revenues. The immediate recommendations for rate increases which the Postmaster General will make should be regarded as only the first step. Further changes should include adjustments in the basic structure, as well as in the level, of second-class rates. Accordingly, I am asking the Postmaster General to review the second-class rate structure thoroughly, looking toward later consideration by the Congress.

3. More than 10 billion pieces of third-class mail (mostly circulars and advertising matter) are anticipated in fiscal year 1952. The costs of carrying this mail are now estimated to be about 271 million dollars. Third-class postal revenues, however, are expected to be about 148 million dollars, leaving an estimated deficit of about 123 million dollars.

The circulars and advertising matter which make up most of third-class mail are usually mailed in bulk at one cent for each piece. It costs nearly as much, of course, to handle a piece of this mail as it does to handle a first-class letter which has a three-cent rate. I believe the minimum rate should be increased from one to two cents, which would increase revenue by about 66 million dollars, and cut the deficit on this class of mail by more than half.

4. The postal rates on fourth-class mail (parcel post) can be changed either by action of the Congress, or by action of the Interstate Commerce Commission approving changes proposed by the Postmaster General. Last year the Congress instructed the Postmaster General to seek the consent of the Commission for rate increases sufficient to make this class of mail pay its way. This he has done, and increases are now being considered by the Commission which would bring in an additional 105 million dollars in revenue, enough to cover the fourth-class deficit.

5. In addition to carrying the four classes of mail, the post office provides certain special services. The major services for which fees are charged—registry, insurance, C.O.D. mail, and special delivery—are being operated at a loss, estimated at about 29 million dollars in fiscal year 1952.

I believe that the fees for these services should be increased by enough to eliminate the deficit in this portion of the postal operation. Furthermore, I believe the Postmaster General should be given authority to revise these fees from time to time in order to keep them in line with costs. Such authority was included in a bill passed by the House of Representatives last year.

These various suggestions, together with certain less important changes, will, if enacted by the Congress, wipe out the bulk of the postal deficit. Some deficit will remain, above the amount that is properly chargeable to the general taxpayers. The amount of this remaining deficit is not certain now, in view of the possibility of higher transportation rates and other cost increases. Consequently, I am not now recommending all the rate increases that should be enacted to put the Post Office on a self-sufficient basis. However, as soon as the outlook on future costs is more clear, the Postmaster General will submit to the Congress such further recommendations for rate increases as may then be necessary to reduce the deficit to a proper level.

I strongly urge the Congress to correct the present unsound condition of the postal revenues. This is a time of emergency, when we must raise taxes on everyone to meet the heavy costs of stronger military defenses. Now, more than ever, it is wrong to ask the taxpayer to bear costs which should be borne by users of the mail service—users many of whom have enjoyed large special privileges in the form of low, subsidized postal rates.

The Federal budget I submitted to the

Congress in January was based on the assumption that the postal deficit would be reduced from over 500 million dollars to about 160 million dollars—the amount which is properly chargeable to the general taxpayer. My tax recommendations were likewise based on this assumption. To the extent that postal rates are not raised enough to meet that objective, even higher taxes will be needed to balance the budget.

HARRY S. TRUMAN

NOTE: On October 30, 1951, the President signed S. 1046, an act to readjust postal rates (Public Law 233, 82d Cong., 65 Stat. 672).

46   Remarks to a Group From the 82d Airborne Division. *February 27, 1951*

MR. SECRETARY, it is a pleasure to see all these fine young men from, I understand, every State and Territory in the Union. I have been interested in your organization for a long time. Back in 1943 or 1944, I made an inspection of Fort Bragg as chairman of the Senate committee who was looking after things. I went up with the airborne people and wanted to jump out, and I almost got arrested by the major general because he said he would be court-martialed if I jumped out, so I didn't get to jump. I still have that anticipation and I hope some day to do it.

It is a pleasure to me, as I said before, to see you young men who are so thoroughly and completely interested in the welfare of the Nation. I know you will go back and put in everything you have so that if it ever becomes necessary for us to face a complete emergency you will be ready to make your contribution just the same as the rest of us will have to make ours.

I hope you have an enjoyable visit here. I understand that your principal interest up here is to see how the Congress works. Now, if you can find that out—and I served 10 years with the Congress—you will be a great bunch of young men.

NOTE: The President spoke at 12:15 p.m. in the Rose Garden at the White House. His opening words "Mr. Secretary" referred to Secretary of the Army Frank Pace, Jr. The group of 52 paratroopers was stationed at Fort Bragg, N.C.

47   Radio and Television Remarks Opening the Red Cross Campaign. *February 27, 1951*

[Broadcast from the White House at 10:55 p.m.]

THANK YOU, Mr. Harriman.

We have heard tonight about the work of the Red Cross, and about how much it needs the help of every one of us.

I enrolled in the Red Cross earlier today— in fact, Mr. Harriman just enrolled me—and I hope that every American citizen will enroll in the Red Cross in the weeks ahead and give to the limit for its great work.

The Red Cross expresses our basic national ideal of giving a helping hand to others. Clara Barton, who founded the Red Cross in this country, made it her business to give aid to the wounded and the suffering in our Civil War. She did not have much to start with, only the feeling that it was her duty to help those who were in pain or distress. She went to the battlefields on her own. No one asked her to go— nobody made her go—but she went to help others because she knew that was the thing to do.

The simple faith of Clara Barton laid the foundation of one of the greatest humanitarian organizations in our history. The American people responded to her example. They shared her faith and still share it, and by following her example they have made the American Red Cross the great institution that it is today.

The Red Cross is a voluntary organization. Nobody is compelled to work in it or to give to it, and yet it bears a heavy national responsibility to meet the needs of our people in time of distress.

In the last few months the responsibilities of the American Red Cross have been greatly increased. The national emergency has imposed new burdens upon it. The Red Cross is mobilizing its resources to give aid to our fighting men abroad and to increase our preparedness at home.

The American Red Cross has the responsibility of collecting whole blood to save the lives of our soldiers in Korea.

The American Red Cross has the responsibility of serving the men in our Armed Forces and their families, as it has served them in every period of mobilization or conflict since it was founded.

Today the American Red Cross has a very important part in our plans for civil defense, in addition to its usual duties in connection with disasters such as floods and fires. The American Red Cross has to be prepared to meet any eventuality in the case of armed attack on this country.

These responsibilities must be met. They can be met only if all of us support the Red Cross—only if we give our blood—or enroll in one of its many services—or donate what we can to pay its expenses.

The Red Cross is a voluntary organization, as I said before. It is our organization, yours and mine. It belongs to all the American people. It gives us a chance to show how free men can work together in a spirit of good will for the benefit of all.

Voluntary action by people who believe in a common cause is still the greatest force in the world. It is far more effective than any form of tyranny or despotism.

If we, as a nation, get together in that spirit of freedom, I am sure that we can overcome the crisis that faces the free world—and I believe that we can bring the world nearer to the peace which all men desire.

NOTE: The President was introduced by E. Roland Harriman, President of the American National Red Cross.

48 Statement by the President on the 39th Anniversary of the Founding of the Girl Scouts. *February 28, 1951*

DURING the years since 1912, when girl scouting was founded, your organization's program of service to home, community, and country has become an integral part of the lives of millions of young people. On March 12, when you celebrate your 39th anniversary, every member can be proud of being part of a movement that is a growing force for freedom and for good citizenship in our Nation. I extend my warmest greetings to all Girl Scouts on this occasion.

There are today more than a million and a half girls in the United States taking part in the Girl Scout program and pledged to do their duty to God and country. In your troops you are learning skills that will enable you to take care of yourselves and to be of service to others; you are building strong bonds of friendship with children of other lands; you are learning how to work together for the good of all. The promptness with which you and your leaders have volunteered for civil defense is evidence of your willingness to serve community and country. Our Nation's civil defense program needs the support of everyone. It is gratifying to know that you are prepared to serve in time of emergency.

The gratitude of every citizen is due to the thousands of adult volunteer workers who make the Girl Scout program possible. I send them my best wishes for continued success and progress.

49   The President's News Conference of *March* 1, 1951

THE PRESIDENT. [1.] Please sit down. I had a very satisfactory telephone call this morning. The 15 nonoperating unions, representing a million workers, reached an agreement at the bargaining table.

I congratulate them, and I congratulate the carriers also, for having reached that agreement. And that agreement was reached without any threats of strikes, or any strike, and I think everybody is happy over it.[1]

Now I am ready for questions.

[2.] Q. Mr. President, did you receive a telephone call this morning from the Labor Policy Committee?

THE PRESIDENT. I received a telephone call from Mr. Steelman[2] about this settlement I am telling you about. I had no telephone call from the Labor Policy Committee. I am not expecting one.

Q. Mr. President, it seems that labor's principal objection to the defense organization is the tenure in office of Mr. Charles Wilson.[3] Do you plan any change?

THE PRESIDENT. No, I do not. I didn't know about that.

Q. What was that, Mr. President?

THE PRESIDENT. I said I didn't know about that statement he just made.

Q. Well, Mr. President, I wonder if you would tell us what you plan to do about labor's boycott of the defense mobilization program?

THE PRESIDENT. No comment.

Q. Do you think it is a rather serious situation?

THE PRESIDENT. No comment.

Q. Will it delay you, or in any way change your traveling plans?

THE PRESIDENT. Not at all—so you can pack your grips and get ready to go on Friday.

Q. Mr. President, does the presence of the Secretary of Labor[4] here this morning mean anything?

THE PRESIDENT. He happened to be at the White House for a conference and I brought him over.

Q. Mr. President, what do you plan to work out if the Wage Stabilization Board's labor members refuse to go back?

THE PRESIDENT. No comment. No comment. When I take the action, you will all know about it.

---

[1] For an earlier statement on the railroad situation, see Item 33 [1].

[2] Dr. John R. Steelman, The Assistant to the President.

[3] Charles E. Wilson, Director, Office of Defense Mobilization. On February 28 the United Labor Policy Committee had withdrawn union representatives from all mobilization agencies.

[4] Secretary of Labor Maurice J. Tobin.

[3.] Q. Well, Mr. President, that question kind of—I was a little slow on my feet—could you tell us——

THE PRESIDENT. You never are, May,[5] but go ahead. [*Laughter*]

Q. ——could you tell us what the Secretary of Labor's conference was about?

THE PRESIDENT. No——

Q. You said he was in for a conference?

THE PRESIDENT. ——no.

[4.] Q. Mr. President, in the light of events, have you changed your evaluation of the Fulbright plan report?[6]

THE PRESIDENT. No comment.

[5.] Q. Mr. President, I notice that General Romulo and the Philippine Ambassador[7] called on you yesterday. Do you care to make any comment?

THE PRESIDENT. I had a very pleasant conference with General Romulo and the Ambassador. And the general informed me that, as soon as he has finished his work in the United Nations, he was going to the Philippines and going to try to help implement the Bell report.[8]

[6.] Q. One of the labor men, general chairman of the Katy Railroad[9] Locomotive Firemen and Enginemen, said yesterday that labor men still felt that they could not get your ear, and they felt that if Franklin Roosevelt had been in the White House that the matter would have been taken care of

months ago. Would you care to comment on that?

THE PRESIDENT. Well, my only comment on that is—is that the situation is one of collective bargaining, and the President ought not to interfere with collective bargaining.

[7.] Q. Mr. President, we have word from Moscow this morning that the Russians have accepted a preliminary meeting of Big Four representatives. Do you have any comment on their action?

THE PRESIDENT. Of course I haven't, because I don't know about it yet. Maybe it will come to me during the day.

[8.] Q. Mr. President, have you any opinion on the Kefauver crime report?[10]

THE PRESIDENT. No, I haven't.

[9.] Q. Mr. President, who is this collective bargaining between, that you refer to?

THE PRESIDENT. Between the railroad operators and the unions, that's all.

Q. Just the railroads?

THE PRESIDENT. That's right.

Q. You weren't referring to the other——

THE PRESIDENT. Not at all—not at all. The only reason they ever came to the White House was at their own request. I didn't ask them there.

[10.] Q. Mr. President, do you feel that the mobilization agency can operate without the active support of organized labor?

THE PRESIDENT. I have no comment.

Q. Mr. President, do you have any comment on the contention by the labor group that labor is not properly represented in the mobilization——

THE PRESIDENT. No comment. You might just as well quit. You had better ask ques-

---

[5] Mrs. May Craig of the Portland (Maine) Press Herald.

[6] "Study of Reconstruction Finance Corporation: Favoritism and Influence," interim report of the Committee on Banking and Currency, February 5, 1951 (Senate Report 76, 82d Cong.).

[7] Gen. Carlos P. Romulo, Foreign Secretary of the Philippines and Philippine Delegate to the United Nations, and His Excellency Joaquin M. Elizalde, Philippine Ambassador to the United States.

[8] "Report to the President of the United States by the Economic Survey Mission to the Philippines" (Department of State Publication 4010; Government Printing Office, 1950).

[9] The Missouri-Kansas-Texas Railroad.

[10] "Second Interim Report of the Special Committee to Investigate Organized Crime in Interstate Commerce" (Senate Report 141, 82d Cong., 1st sess.; Government Printing Office, 1951; 35 pp.). Senator Estes Kefauver of Tennessee was chairman of the committee.

tions about something I can answer. [*Laughter*]

[11.] Q. I will try then. Do you still feel, Mr. President, that there is no point in Mr. Donald Dawson [11] testifying before the Fulbright committee?

THE PRESIDENT. No comment.

Q. May I ask you this question, sir. Have you read any of the seven, eight, or nine hundred letters written to the RFC by Members of Congress? [12]

THE PRESIDENT. Oh, yes. I have read a lot of them.

Q. Could you tell us about any of them?

THE PRESIDENT. No, sir—and I won't.

Q. Another question, sir, on that subject. Has the job status of Mrs. Merl Young [13] been changed in the White House?

THE PRESIDENT. No comment. I hate to treat you this way. I would like to give you a lot of headlines. [*Laughter*]

[12.] Q. Mr. President, the Vice Chairman of the National Resources Board has resigned. Is Symington going to resign? [14]

THE PRESIDENT. Not that I know of. He hasn't said so to me.

[13.] Q. Mr. President, would you be able to tell us whether the 22d amendment would have any effect on your future plans?

THE PRESIDENT. Well, sir, I think I commented on that, through Mr. Short, that the amendment did not affect President Truman.

And that's all the comment I have to make.

[14.] Q. Mr. President, does Mr. Charles E. Wilson still have your full confidence?

THE PRESIDENT. He certainly has.

[15.] Q. Mr. President, in view of this labor development, do you plan to make any public appeal in regard to this situation, or could you say—could you tell us of any steps you might have in view?

THE PRESIDENT. No, I can't comment on that at the present time.

Q. Do you regard it as a very serious development in our——

THE PRESIDENT. No, I don't.

[16.] Q. Mr. President, maybe you can tell us this?

THE PRESIDENT. All right, go ahead. What is this, foreign relations? [*Laughter*]

Q. No, sir.

THE PRESIDENT. He's an expert on foreign relations.

Q. I am sort of curious whether Mr. Tobin's conference this morning had anything to do with the possibility of changing your manpower setup?

THE PRESIDENT. No, it did not.

Q. Well, Mr. President, I wonder if you would go a little further—do you feel confident that labor, by and large, will continue to meet the Nation's needs in producing these weapons and other things necessary in the mobilization effort?

THE PRESIDENT. Well, let me tell you something. Sometime back, I declared a national emergency, and that national emergency affects every segment of the economy. And the program that we are trying to implement is one that will not ruin the most prosperous Nation in the world, but will be worked out in such a manner that that prosperity can continue. And if that prosperity can continue, it affects labor, farmers, industry, white-collar people, and everybody in the Nation.

---

[11] Donald S. Dawson, Administrative Assistant to the President, formerly personnel director of the RFC.

[12] See Item 33 [2].

[13] Mrs. E. Merl Young, a secretarial assistant in the office of the personal secretary to the President.

[14] Earlier in the day, the White House had released an exchange of correspondence between the President and Robert J. Smith in which the President accepted Mr. Smith's resignation as Vice Chairman of the National Security Resources Board, to become effective on March 15, 1951. W. Stuart Symington was Chairman of the Board. On April 17, Mr. Symington was appointed Administrator of the Reconstruction Finance Corporation (see Item 82).

[17.] Q. Mr. President, I would like to get into foreign relations, if I may?

THE PRESIDENT. Sure, go ahead.

Q. In a statement on the powers of the President, which was sent to the Capitol from the executive departments, it says that the use of congressional power to declare war has fallen into abeyance because wars are no longer declared in advance. How would you fill the gap between the constitutional declaration of war by Congress and the Executive actions?

THE PRESIDENT. Well now, I would advise you to read the history of 1941—December 7. I think that will answer your question.

Q. Well, couldn't you tell me how you propose to do it?

THE PRESIDENT. No, I cannot, because I am not faced with any such condition.

Q. Well, may I ask you one other question——

THE PRESIDENT. Sure.

Q. ——in relation to the same document? It says that debates over the prerogatives and powers of Congress and the President are essentially sterile, if not dangerous, to the success of the foreign policy?

THE PRESIDENT. That is correct.

Q. Do you mean that Congress ought not even to debate foreign policy?

THE PRESIDENT. Oh, no. I don't mind their talking about anything they want to. This is a free country. They can make any number of speeches they want, on any subject they want to, but that does not mean that it helps the relations with the rest of the world.

Q. Do you think then, that congressional participation in the declaration of war is completely out?

THE PRESIDENT. No, I didn't say that.

Q. Well, I am trying to get——

THE PRESIDENT. I know what you are trying to get, you are trying to get a concrete

answer from me, and you are not going to get it. [*Laughter*]

[18.] Q. Mr. President, any comment on the Japanese treaty? [15]

THE PRESIDENT. No, I have no comment on that.

[19.] Q. Mr. President, have you any comment on the disclosures made so far in the investigation campaign against Senator Tydings? [16]

THE PRESIDENT. No, I have no comment. I think they speak for themselves.

[20.] Q. Mr. President, the demands of labor were set forth at this policy meeting. They were put forward as recommendations by Mr. Johnston. [17] Would the President approve those modifications as an order, were they so put to him?

THE PRESIDENT. No. I think Mr. Johnston wrote that letter in an endeavor to get things straightened out. And I think he made a sincere effort to get it done.

Q. Mr. President, do you anticipate or expect labor to return to the mobilization effort?

THE PRESIDENT. I will tell you about that in a couple of weeks, Smitty. [18]

Q. Mr. President, what do you think of labor's charge that the whole mobilization

---

[15] On February 27, 1951, a White House release announced that John Foster Dulles had given the President an oral report of the activities of the Japanese Peace Mission in Japan, the Philippines, Australia, and New Zealand. Mr. Dulles reported that exploratory conversations with leaders of these countries had promoted closer agreement as to a peace settlement. The release further stated that the President expressed his gratification and asked the Mission to continue its work.

[16] The Subcommittee on Privileges and Elections of the Senate Committee on Rules and Administration was holding hearings on the Maryland senatorial election of 1950, in which John Marshall Butler defeated the incumbent Millard E. Tydings.

[17] Eric A. Johnston, Administrator, Economic Stabilization Agency.

[18] Merriman Smith of the United Press Associations.

program is being run by big business? That seems to be their——

THE PRESIDENT. I don't think there is any necessity for my commenting on that.

Q. Mr. President, do you consider the walkout of the labor delegation in the nature of a strike against the Government?

THE PRESIDENT. Oh, no. Just a disagreement.

Q. Mr. President, you said that you would tell us about that in a couple of weeks. Are you thinking in terms of any specific statement?

THE PRESIDENT. No. You will be down in Key West, Smitty. I will talk to you then.

[21.] Q. Do you think the price control measures taken so far by Mr. DiSalle [19] really will do anything to prevent soaring prices?

THE PRESIDENT. Of course I do.

Q. How?

THE PRESIDENT. Well, read the report of the Department of Agriculture which just came out. That will help you.

[22.] Q. Mr. President, does that "couple of weeks" suggest you are going to sit on this thing about that long before you act?

THE PRESIDENT. It might be 1 week, it might be 2 weeks, it might be 3 weeks— 3 months. You can't tell. You had better wait and see how developments come out.

Q. I didn't understand that question, what was that?

THE PRESIDENT. He wanted to know

whether my "couple of weeks" statement meant any specific time. I was just trying to say it did not.

Q. Well, Mr. President the way he phrased the question was whether you were going to sit on the problem for that——

THE PRESIDENT. I never sit on any problem. [*Laughter*]

[23.] Q. Mr. President, this is along the same line. Would you not go along with this statement, that labor should have more power in policymaking in this emergency than in the last war?

THE PRESIDENT. I won't go along on any statement that I don't make myself.

Q. Mr. President, would you care to make a statement on what labor should do at this point?

THE PRESIDENT. No. I would not.

Q. I think we might as well give up, Mr. President——

Q. Have we overlooked anything? [*Laughter*]

THE PRESIDENT. Tony [20] says we ought to give up. No, I have no further comments, Smitty.

Q. Thank you, Mr. President.

THE PRESIDENT. I will answer any questions you have got on your mind! [*More laughter*]

NOTE: President Truman's two hundred and fifty-sixth news conference was held in the Indian Treaty Room (Room 474) in the Executive Office Building at 10:35 a.m. on Thursday, March 1, 1951.

---

[19] Michael V. DiSalle, Director of Price Stabilization.

[20] Ernest B. Vaccaro of the Associated Press.

---

50   Remarks to the Winners of the 10th Annual Science Talent Search. *March 1, 1951*

IT IS a pleasure to me to welcome you here. I hope you will all go through with what you have started, and wind up just as Mr. Davis has said your predecessors have, be-

cause the power and welfare of this country is wrapped up in scientific research.

I just had the Atomic Energy Commission in to see me a few days ago, and it is remarkable what they are doing toward making that splintering of the atom eventually work for the peacetime welfare of the world.

You young ladies and gentlemen can make a great contribution to all those things that are associated with scientific research.

I was over at Aberdeen the other day, looking at tanks and weapons and guided missiles and all the other things which you hear about. And when I got through I didn't then have any feeling of mystery about why the Chinese have not been able to push us out of Korea, because we have better equipment and better weapons.

But the weapons we want are not those for destruction, but weapons for the welfare of the world and the improvement of all mankind so that we won't have to spend tremendous sums for destruction, but use those tremendous sums for the improvement of the welfare of all the races in the world.

If you will turn around there and look at that globe behind you, you will find that there are many, many places that need development and that can be developed to make this world a much better place in which to live.

[*At this point the President walked over to the globe which was presented to him by General Eisenhower in 1945 at the Potsdam conference. He then resumed speaking.*]

For instance, in the great river systems down here—[*indicating the continent of South America*]—they have more water than Niagara—a fall that is greater than Niagara. And then there are these lakes up here—[*indicating*]—whose waters now run out into the Amazon River, and they are going to be diverted for the cultivation of this part of the coast along in here, and give Bolivia a seaport.

And over here, on this plateau, there are 65,000 square miles of blackland, just like Illinois, Iowa, and the lower Missouri, six to eight thousand feet above sea level, that will produce anything that can be raised in a temperate zone, although it is almost directly on the Equator. They can raise enough food on that—they don't have any cattle grazing there—to support 100 million people.

And in this place over here—[*indicating the continent of Africa*]—it can support another 100 million people with developments which have not been carried out. If they could be done in this valley—[*indicating*]—it will support 25 million people as it did when Babylon and Nineveh were great cities, if irrigation projects were installed.

And all the oil resources of this section here—[*indicating*]—are greater than any other place in the world. And this country right here—[*indicating*]—can produce food enough for a hundred million people. Think what that will mean, when the resources up in here—[*indicating*]—have been developed. Alexander the Great was along in this river—[*indicating*]—and there are traces of him in Afghanistan. And if the resources of that section were properly developed, 300 million people could be supported.

Now, that is part of your job, to see whether we can get that done or not. And that is the reason I am glad to see you, and hope you will remember what I have told you about that globe when you go back to school, and see what kind of contribution you can make to carrying out the peace and welfare of the world. That is what we are after.

Thank you very much.

NOTE: The President spoke at 12:05 p.m. in his office at the White House. In his remarks he referred to Watson Davis, Director of Science Service, who conducted the talent search for Westinghouse Electric Corporation. The group was composed of 40 young men and women, all winners of Westinghouse Science Scholarships.

51 Remarks on the Floor of the Senate at a Gavel Presentation Ceremony for Vice President Barkley. *March 1, 1951*

MR. PRESIDENT, I wish it were a fact that I was returning permanently to the scene of my former "crimes and misdemeanors," which have got me into more trouble than any man in the world has ever gotten into.

But I am here for a specific purpose today. On March 4, which is Sunday, your Presiding Officer, the President of the Senate, the Vice President of the United States, and the former Leader of the Majority, will have been here longer than any other man in the history of the Senate. He will have served 38 years in the Congress of the United States.

To commemorate that event, I had the White House carpenters make this gavel of wood that was put into the White House in 1817, after the fire, and removed in 1949 in the reconstruction.

And I have had this inscription put on the outside of the box. It says, "This box and gavel were made from wood used in rebuilding the White House about 1817, and removed in 1949."

And then I had this inscription put on the gavel. And I will leave it to the gentlemen of the Senate as to whether it is the truth or not. "To the Vice President of the United States, Alben W. Barkley, to commemorate 38 years of continuous service in the Congress of the United States." And I signed it as President, and dated it the White House, March 4, 1951.

Now, the President of the Senate and the Vice President of the United States has a record, when it comes to speechmaking, of no terminal facilities. In his position as Presiding Officer of the Senate, he never has the power or the right to exercise those "no terminal facilities."

Yet I am sure this morning that the Senate, by unanimous consent, is going to give him a chance to reply to me for presenting him with this gavel.

Mr. Vice President, I hope you will use this for the welfare of the Government of the United States.

NOTE: The President spoke at 12:35 p.m.

52 Statement by the President in Response to a Joint Announcement by the Treasury Department and the Federal Reserve System. *March 3, 1951*

I AM INFORMED that the Secretary of the Treasury and the Chairman of the Board of Governors of the Federal Reserve System are today making the following joint announcement:

"The Treasury and the Federal Reserve System have reached full accord with respect to debt-management and monetary policies to be pursued in furthering their common purpose to assure the successful financing of the Government's requirements and, at the same time, to minimize monetization of the public debt."

I am highly gratified at this agreement, which represents a very important step forward in the solution of the problems outlined in my memorandum of February 26th to the Secretary of the Treasury, the Director of the Office of Defense Mobilization, the Chairman of the Board of Governors of the

Federal Reserve System, and the Chairman of the Council of Economic Advisers.

Consideration of other aspects of the problems outlined in the memorandum of February 26th will continue to go forward as originally planned.

NOTE: The statement was released at Key West, Fla. For the President's memorandum of February 26, see Item 44.

53   Letters Relating to the International Development Advisory Board's Report on Foreign Economic Policy. *March* 11, 1951

[Released March 11, 1951. Dated March 9, 1951]

To the Chairman of the International Development Advisory Board:

Dear Mr. Rockefeller:

I am impressed by the report of the Advisory Board on International Development. It demonstrates, clearly and forcefully, the reasons why a lasting peace can be attained only by a wise combination of strong military defenses and an effective campaign of international economic development.

A broad program of economic development is necessary, as I pointed out in my Inaugural Address, to carry out this country's international objectives of peace and freedom. Since that Address, international problems have become critical and we are now engaged in a tremendous mobilization program. More than ever, greater production, particularly in the underdeveloped areas, is essential to the stability and freedom of those areas and to the peace of the whole world. Recent events in economically underdeveloped areas have demonstrated that men will defend the cause of freedom when they know from experience that it is the true way to economic and social progress. Economic stagnation is the advance guard of Soviet conquest.

The Point IV concept, properly carried out, is essential to the successful defense of the free world. In the words of your report, "strengthening the economies of the under-developed regions and an improvement in their living levels must be considered a vital part of our own defense mobilization."

Moreover, economic development is the spearhead of the forces of freedom. The building of military strength is not enough to win the peace we seek. We must press the attack in the battle of raising the living standards and fulfilling the hopes of mankind for a better future.

The task, as you have pointed out, is one that the United States cannot undertake alone. We depend, in many respects, on the other free nations, and they on us. International partnership is necessary to build an expanding world economy in which all can have a fair share.

It is a great satisfaction to me that a nonpartisan group, such as your Board, representing labor, education, business, agriculture and other aspects of our national life, should reach unanimous agreement on matters of such concern to the future of our country. I am sure that your report will do a great deal to put the problem of international economic development in its proper perspective.

In the near future, I shall send recommendations to the Congress concerning the legislation required for foreign defense and economic assistance for 1952. I know that your report will be of great help in enabling the Congress and the Executive Branch to develop the kind of program which is needed to carry out our national objectives.

I am sending your report immediately to the Chairmen and the ranking minority members of the Senate Foreign Relations Committee and the House Foreign Affairs Committee and I hope that you will be able to give them further information on this important subject, if they so desire. I am also directing the Government agencies concerned to give your report their immediate consideration.

Please accept my deepest personal appreciation for the task which your Board has accomplished and the leadership which you have contributed to it. You, your Board, and your staff can take great pride in the contribution which you have made toward a solution of some of the critical problems which this Nation faces.

Sincerely yours,

HARRY S. TRUMAN

[Mr. Nelson Rockefeller, Room 5600, 30 Rockefeller Plaza, New York, N.Y.]

To Senators Tom Connally, chairman, Arthur H. Vandenberg, and Alexander Wiley of the Senate Foreign Relations Committee; and Representatives John Kee, chairman, James P. Richards, and Charles A. Eaton of the House Foreign Affairs Committee:

My dear —————:

You will recall that on November twenty-fourth I appointed the members of the International Development Advisory Board established by the Congress under Section 409 of the Act for International Development. I nominated Mr. Nelson Rockefeller as the Chairman of the Board.

At that time I requested the Board to undertake as its first task a consideration of the proposals of the Gordon Gray Report concerning our policy toward the underdeveloped areas. The International Development Advisory Board has now completed that task and has submitted a report to me, a copy of which I am enclosing herewith.

I am sure you will find, as I have, that this is a most thoughtful and stimulating report. In this report, the group of distinguished citizens who make up the Board has done us all a great service by analyzing the ways and means of making the economic part of our foreign policy more effective in building the strength of the free world. I know this report will be most helpful in completing the legislative recommendations on foreign aid I shall shortly submit to the Congress. I am sure that you and the members of your Committee will find it valuable in your consideration of the economic aspects of our foreign policy. I have asked Mr. Rockefeller to supply you with any further information and background about the work of his Board that you may desire.

Sincerely yours,

HARRY S. TRUMAN

NOTE: The letters were part of a White House release made public at Key West, Fla. The release stated that the report was also transmitted to the Vice President, the Speaker of the House of Representatives, members of the Cabinet, the Budget Director, the Economic Cooperation Administrator, the Defense Mobilization Director, and the Defense Production Administrator. It included the text of a brief transmittal letter to Cabinet members and agency officials.

The report, entitled "Partners in Progress" (Government Printing Office: 1951, 120 pp.), was prepared in response to the President's letter of November 24, 1950 (see 1950 volume, this series, Item 289).

The White House also made public a brief summary of the report.

54 Letter to Senator Flanders on Disarmament. *March* 14, 1951

Dear Senator Flanders:

I appreciate very much the letter of February 26, 1951, signed by you and a number of other Senators and Representatives, in which you urge that we follow up the plea for peace through disarmament, made in my address before the United Nations General Assembly last October.

This expression of your views will give added strength to the efforts of the free nations to establish a just and lasting peace in the world. While we must continue to build up vigorously our military strength as long as world conditions make such a course essential, we must, at the same time, keep on working toward the control and reduction of armaments and armed forces. We must work toward the time when material and human resources, rather than being used for armaments, can be used to advance the well-being of mankind. That is and must remain our goal.

We have been working toward this end in the United Nations. As you know, the Charter of the United Nations gives to the General Assembly and the Security Council responsibility to work out principles and plans for disarmament by the member nations.

At the time the Charter was adopted, it was hoped that this great objective of the United Nations would be carried out speedily and without international friction.

This has not proved to be the case. The laborious effort of five years has been thwarted by the constant opposition of one of the great powers.

To keep the record straight, I think it would be well to review briefly the history of these events.

At its first meeting in January 1946, the General Assembly established a United Nations Atomic Energy Commission and gave it the task of developing a plan for the control of atomic energy, under effective safeguards, to insure its use for peaceful purposes only, and to bring about the complete prohibition of atomic weapons.

This Commission labored long and diligently. It came up with a comprehensive plan which the General Assembly approved, in November 1948, by an overwhelming majority.

However, the Soviet Union refused to approve the plan adopted by the General Assembly. As a consequence, the plan could not be put into effect, since no agreement for the control of atomic weapons can be effective if any one of the great nations refuses to cooperate.

Meanwhile, the United Nations had set up a second Commission to consider the control and reduction of the ordinary weapons and instrumentalities of war. This was the Commission for Conventional Armaments. In general, it had the task of developing a plan to regulate armed forces and armaments other than those falling within the atomic category. As one of its first projects, this Commission worked out a plan for taking a census or inventory of the non-atomic armaments and of the armed forces of all principal nations, subject to supervision and verification by a body of international inspectors. The purpose of this plan was to obtain the verified information necessary for the development of an intelligent system of armament reduction and control.

This plan made sense and was swiftly accepted by the majority of the United Nations in December 1949. But here again a majority was not enough. The Soviet Union, one of the major military powers, refused to accept this proposal. And, as in the case of the plan for controlling atomic energy, this refusal made it impossible to put the program into operation.

At the same time that the Soviet Union has been following a course of obstruction in the United Nations toward all concrete disarmament proposals, it has been building up its own armaments as a central feature of its expansionist foreign policy.

At the end of World War II, the United States hastily demobilized and reduced the size of its armed forces. So did other free nations. But the Soviet Union continued to maintain armed forces at a high level—far higher than necessary for purely defensive purposes. Furthermore, it encouraged a ruthless program of rearmament on the part of the nations which have fallen under its control and influence.

The great disparity between the armaments of the Soviet Union and its satellites on the one hand, and the free nations on the other, is one of the basic reasons for the defensive alliances and defense programs which are now being jointly pursued by the nations of the free world. Since the Soviet Union has failed to cooperate in any genuine plan for the international limitation of armament, we have been compelled to look to our defenses.

It is essential to our national security that we build up our defenses as quickly and vigorously as possible. We do not know what further aggressive plans may be in the making by the adversaries of the free world. But by rearming, the free world may attain benefits above and beyond preparedness against attack. Our defense program, if carried through, will have the effect of discouraging aggression, and may eventually lead to a change in the tactics of the Soviet Union and of its current satellites, which would ease the present international tension. That is our great hope.

Our present armament program, there-fore, has a double purpose. It is above all an effort to prevent a world conflict, while at the same time it is an effort to prepare our defenses to meet such a conflict if it is forced upon us. What we are striving for is peace and international order.

In the field of disarmament, the free nations have been unable to make any progress while their own military forces have been inferior to those of the Soviet Union. But paradoxical as it may seem, when the free nations have built up their forces, they may be able to convince potential aggressors that the control and reduction of armaments is a desirable policy.

In the face of the plans of the free world for increased defense forces, Soviet propaganda is beginning to take notice of the belief of the free nations that Soviet armed strength is excessive. We can expect great propaganda efforts by the Soviet system to deflect the free nations from their defense plans. We must not be deflected. But as we continue to increase our defenses, we must press, by every possible means, for a real change in the attitude of the Soviet Union.

My address on October 24 suggested a new procedural approach to the question, in the hope that it might offer a way out of the existing deadlock. I suggested the possibility of combining the work of the United Nations Atomic Energy Commission and the Commission on Conventional Armaments in a new and consolidated disarmaments commission.

The General Assembly, on December 13, 1950, established a committee of Twelve to study the proposal. This committee is directed to work on the "ways and means whereby the work of the Atomic Energy Commission and the Commission on Conventional Armaments may be coordinated and on the advisability of their functions being merged and placed under a new and consolidated disarmament commission." This committee has had two meetings, the second of which was held on March 2. The United States Representatives at the United Nations have been actively pushing the work of this committee. We hope that it will be able to make recommendations which will revitalize the efforts of the United Nations for international disarmament.

Before we can enter into any concrete program to reduce armaments we must be sure that the principles which I outlined in my address of October 24 are adhered to. A program of disarmament must include all kinds of weapons, must have unanimous agreement of all the nations having substantial armaments and armed forces, and must be so thoroughly and continuously policed as to be fool-proof. These are the principles on which we stand and which we continue to offer to other nations as the basis for any plan for armaments reduction and control.

Such a program is difficult to achieve even when there is a reasonable degree of trust and confidence between nations. It is almost impossible unless there is free and open interchange of information across national borders.

As you indicated in your letter, increased freedom of communication is, therefore, a necessary step in an effective program of disarmament.

The need for authentic information has been pointed up by recent Soviet assertions concerning the size of its own armed forces in relation to those of the free nations. The United States would welcome a thorough exploration of this subject. On March 2, 1951, our Deputy Representative on the United Nations Commission on Conventional Armaments reasserted the position of this country and invited a census, under United Nations auspices, of armed forces of the member nations.

Continuing emphasis on disarmament is a necessary and vital part of our foreign policy. We must always be seeking for new approaches to this problem and we must take advantage of every opportunity that presents itself to work toward genuine disarmament proposals.

I am very happy indeed that this major element in our foreign policy has your support and that of your colleagues in both Houses of Congress. I want to have your continued counsel and advice in these matters. I hope that when I return to Washington I will have an early opportunity to discuss these questions further with you and your colleagues as you suggested in your letter.

Sincerely yours,

HARRY S. TRUMAN

[The Honorable Ralph E. Flanders, United States Senate, Washington, D.C.]

NOTE: The letter of February 26 urged that the President's plea for peace through disarmament, made before the United Nations Assembly on October 24 (see 1950 volume, this series, Item 271), be followed up by definite proposals to be made by our representative on the United Nations Council.

The Congressmen suggested "That the first step proposed be the lifting of the iron curtain and the resumption of at least that degree of freedom of communication between all the peoples of the earth which existed between the nations of Western Europe and the American continents prior to the second World War; that the proposal be for complete disarmament of all nations under the direction and surveillance of the United Nations; that a United Nations Commission be set up to effect disarmament in an orderly, complete and rapid way; that a United Nations Police Force be established in accordance with the original intention of the Charter which shall be superior in size and armament to any forces available to the member nations for the maintenance of civil order; and finally, that the proposal be permanently in effect and repeatedly offered until it is accepted."

The letter was signed by Senators Ralph E. Flanders, Lester C. Hunt, H. Alexander Smith, Walter F. George, Estes Kefauver, Margaret Chase Smith, Robert C. Hendrickson, Charles W. Tobey, Lister Hill, Mike Monroney, Edward J. Thye, A. Willis Robertson, and John C. Stennis, and by the following members of the House of Representatives:

Brooks Hays, Laurie Battle, and A. S. J. Carnahan. In addition, the following members of the House authorized the affixing of their signatures to the letter: James C. Auchincloss, Frances P. Bolton,

Walter H. Judd, Christian A. Herter, Robert Hale, and John W. Heselton.

The letter of February 26 and the President's reply were released at Key West, Fla.

55 Letter to Department and Agency Heads on the Report of the Water Resources Policy Commission. *March* 14, 1951

My dear —————:

The final volume of the report and recommendations of the Water Resources Policy Commission, which I appointed in January 1950, has now been published. Copies of this report have been made available to you. The Commission has clearly done a very thorough job, and its report and recommendations should be extremely helpful to all of us.

It is my intention, after careful review of the report and recommendations, to take such administrative actions and to submit to the Congress such legislative recommendations as seem appropriate from time to time. With this purpose in mind, I have asked the Director of the Bureau of the Budget to take charge of the staff work incident to this review. The Director will communicate with you in a short time regarding the arrangements for undertaking this task, including the designation of particular individuals to represent your Department and to work with him on this matter.

The Commission was appointed because a need had developed over the past several years for careful reexamination of our national water resources policies and related land use problems. The report thus concerns basic policies underlying the Federal Government's responsibilities in this field, rather than recommendations for or against specific projects. Since the Commission was appointed the United States has embarked upon an expanded defense program which in some areas will place even greater demands

upon these land and water resources especially in connection with hydro-electric power. This defense work should go forward as fast as practicable, but it must proceed with due regard for the long-range objective of conserving and developing our water resources for all their values, for the benefit of all the people. The report should prove a valuable guide in helping to keep this long-range objective in mind.

In many public statements, I have stressed the fact that accomplishment of this objective requires the combined efforts of Federal, State and local governments, as well as private interests, and I have emphasized the importance of carrying out the Federal Government's share of this task in a manner which will reflect the fullest participation and collaboration of the people of the areas most directly affected. I know that you have borne these considerations in mind in your administration of the programs in your charge, but I hope that in your study of the report you will pay particular attention to these problems—including the problem of striking an appropriate balance in achieving both a local voice in these matters and responsible administration of those functions which are properly the role of the Federal Government.

Sincerely yours,

HARRY S. TRUMAN

NOTE: This is the text of identical letters sent to the Secretaries of Defense, Interior, Agriculture, and Commerce; the Chairman, Federal Power Commission; and the Administrator, Federal Security Administration.

The report of the President's Water Resources Policy Commission was printed in three volumes: "A Water Policy for the American People," "Ten Rivers in America's Future," and "Water Resources Law" (445, 801, and 777 pp.; Government Printing Office: 1950).

The President's letter was released in Key West, Fla.

For the President's letter to the Chairman of the Commission requesting a study of national water resources, see 1950 volume, this series, Item 1. See also Item 306 of that volume.

56 The President's News Conference at Key West. *March 15, 1951*

THE PRESIDENT [*to the photographers*]. I think you fellows have had enough now. Get out of here, and let me go to work! [*Laughter*]

[1.] I have these two statements which— copies will be handed to you. One of them is on the Reorganization Act that was turned down by the House.

[*Reading*] "I am sorry to hear that the House has not seen fit to approve the proposed Reorganization Act of 1951. If enacted, the bill would have provided a more expeditious means of making organizational changes needed for the best administration of the defense program. The bill had the full support of the Citizens' Committee for the Hoover Report and had been passed by the Senate. While the defeat of the bill eliminates a sound and desirable method for enabling the President to proceed with the cooperation of the Congress in obtaining organizational changes, I shall nevertheless continue to work for the improvement of the organization of the executive branch through the methods which remain available."

I still hope that the House will pass the Senate bill.

[2.] Then, I am establishing a National Advisory Board on Mobilization Policy, which will consist of labor, industry, agriculture, and public members.[1] The Chair-

man will be Mr. Wilson.[2] It will serve as an advisory board to the President.

Now I will try to answer questions, if I can.

[3.] Q. Mr. President, on that first statement, does that affect housing, or is that Defense Department?

THE PRESIDENT. It was defense reorganization entirely. The Executive order explains itself—I mean the reorganization plan explains itself. All you have to do is read it.

[4.] Q. Do you anticipate that labor, having "walked out" on the defense program, will send representatives to sit on this new mobilization advisory board?

THE PRESIDENT. I don't think labor walked out. I think labor is as interested in the national defense program as is any other segment of the economy of the United States. I am not worried about that part of it at all, as I have told you before.

Q. You believe they will cooperate?

THE PRESIDENT. There isn't any doubt about it.

Q. Have you had any positive indications, Mr. President——

THE PRESIDENT. I haven't asked anybody— I haven't asked for any positive statements on the subject. *I* am making the order. We will see what will happen. I am satisfied that it will work. I wouldn't make it if I didn't think so.

Now, anything else?

---

[1] Executive Order 10224, establishing the National Advisory Board on Mobilization Policy, was signed by the President on March 15, 1951 (3 CFR, 1949–1953 Comp., p. 736).

[2] Charles E. Wilson, Director, Office of Defense Mobilization.

Q. Yes, sir—well, this doesn't take the place of that wage board, Mr. President?

THE PRESIDENT. No, no—this is the same as the old advisory board that was with the President all during the Second World War. The former Governor of North Carolina was the Chairman of that board—former Under Secretary of the Treasury—and I finally made him Ambassador to Great Britain——

Q. Max Gardner.

THE PRESIDENT. ——Max Gardner. And he died before he could get to London.

Q. This is patterned after World War II, sir?

THE PRESIDENT. Yes.

Q. That was called the mobilization board, too?

THE PRESIDENT. Yes. It was an advisory board to the President—met once or twice a month. I used to meet with them at least once a month to discuss everything under the sun, just as I do with you gentlemen— and ladies.

What's on *your* mind?

[5.] Q. I've got a question—I was trying to frame it. [*Laughter*] You are ahead of me.

THE PRESIDENT. Go ahead and ask it.

Q. This, sir. Since you have been in Key West, Mr. DiSalle[3] has issued an order on restaurants which in general, the OPS says, will let prices go up on the menu. Mr. Johnston[4] has modified the 10 percent formula to deal with the escalator clauses in the cost of living, and modified his formula to permit that modification to apply to white-collar workers in the industries. Could you say on the overall anti-inflation policy, is the administration trying to roll back—is the administration trying to hold the line where it is, or is the administration trying to brake

or slow down the advance in the cost of living?

THE PRESIDENT. The administration is trying to meet the situation in the best manner possible, and we shall continue to try to do just that. That is all the answer I have.

[6.] Q. Mr. President, yesterday I asked Joe[5] if you had seen the popularity poll in the Miami Herald—the Gallup poll on popularity. I wonder if you had any comment on it?

THE PRESIDENT. I commented on that in 1948. The comment is just the same—the comment is just the same. [*Laughter*]

Q. I have forgotten what it was, sir? Could you name it?

THE PRESIDENT. Well, I would advise you to go and study history.

Q. Mr. President, I think we all remember the overall—we remember the attitude you had toward the polls, but none of us has a 1948 newspaper morgue here in Key West.

THE PRESIDENT. Neither have I. So we are even with you. Your home offices must have them. [*Laughter*]

[7.] Q. Mr. President, I would like to ask you a question. I had a man on my radio program on Saturday night who caused considerable consternation by saying positively that he had heard that Mrs. E. Merl Young[6]—he had heard a few minutes before that Mrs. E. Merl Young had been fired?

THE PRESIDENT. No comment.

Q. No comment?

THE PRESIDENT. No comment. Is that what you came down here to ask me? [*Laughter*]

Q. No, I came down to see you, and you are looking very well.

THE PRESIDENT. That's wonderful—I appreciate that very much. [*More laughter*]

[8.] Q. Mr. President, going back to the

---

[3] Michael V. DiSalle, Director of Price Stabilization.

[4] Eric Johnston, Administrator, Economic Stabilization Agency.

[5] Joseph Short, Secretary to the President.

[6] Mrs. E. Merl Young was a secretarial assistant in the office of the personal secretary to the President.

statement on reorganization, you said you would do the best you can with other means available. What would they be, war powers?

THE PRESIDENT. Well, the Reorganization Act itself is still in effect, but this was a special program devoted entirely to defense, in an effort to reduce the expense of the defense program.

[9.] Q. Mr. President, do you see any change in Russia's attitude, sir, as a result of our increasing defense buildup?

THE PRESIDENT. I can't answer that question.

[10.] Q. Mr. President, how do you feel?

THE PRESIDENT. I feel all right. [*Laughter*] I always feel all right.

Q. I would like to ask a question on that point, sir. Have you lost weight since you have been down here?

THE PRESIDENT. I am exactly the same weight I was when I came down here. It is awfully hard to lose down here. [*Laughter*]

Q. What is that weight?

THE PRESIDENT. It varies between 175 and 178.

Mr. Short [*to the President*]: You are not going to make a liar out of me? [*Laughter*]

THE PRESIDENT. No, Joe, you told the truth.

Q. You said 176.

THE PRESIDENT. I said 175 to 178. I think I weighed 176 this morning.

Q. That's what Joe said.

THE PRESIDENT. That's right. I try to tell Joe every day what I weigh, and what I have for breakfast, which hand I wipe my mouth with, so that you fellows will be right up to date on everything that goes on. [*More laughter*]

[11.] Q. Well, Mr. President, do you have any new comment on the RFC inquiry?

THE PRESIDENT. No comment. I am glad the House has passed the Reorganization Plan.[7]

[12.] Q. Mr. President, are you going to be at this party at the Casa Marina tomorrow night?

THE PRESIDENT. I can't tell you what the situation will be at that time. I would like very much to come. I don't know whether I will be able to.

[13.] Q. Mr. President, will the United Nations forces be allowed to advance beyond the 38th parallel?

THE PRESIDENT. That is a tactical matter for the field commander. A commander in chief 7,000 miles away does not interfere with field operations. We are working to free the Republic of Korea and set it up as the United Nations wants it. That doesn't have anything to do with the 38th parallel.

[14.] Q. Mr. President, what do you think of that UP poll that pictured Truman-Douglas [8] running one/two for 1952?

THE PRESIDENT. Well, I expressed my opinion on polls, and the same on that—it's the same on that.

Q. Mr. President, would you tell us one thing that we are all wondering? Are these stories true that you are going to run for the Senate in 1952? Are they inspired, or what?

THE PRESIDENT. No comment, Bert.[9] No comment. You can still speculate and draw your own conclusions. You wouldn't have any fun if you didn't have something like that to talk about. [*Laughter*]

Q. I would rather write about facts.

THE PRESIDENT. Well, I hope you will continue to do just that. You won't have any quarrel with me if you do. [*Laughter*]

[7] For the President's message to Congress transmitting Reorganization Plan 1, relating to the Reconstruction Finance Corporation, see Item 39. On March 14, H. Res. 142, opposing the plan, failed of passage.

[8] Senator Paul H. Douglas, Democrat, of Illinois.

[9] Bert Andrews of the New York Herald Tribune.

[15.] Q. Mr. President, would you like to say anything——

THE PRESIDENT. Hi, Bob.[10]

Q. ——how are you, sir?—at this time about the move in Congress lately to place some restraints upon your constitutional powers—that you will send troops to Europe——

THE PRESIDENT. Bob, do you think that the Constitution can be amended by a Senate and House resolution?

Q. No sir, I don't.

THE PRESIDENT. All right.

Q. I thought maybe——

THE PRESIDENT. I don't either.

Q. ——you might go further along the line of the whole—the impact of that whole movement in Congress on people abroad——

THE PRESIDENT. Oh, no. I don't have anything to do with the actions of the Congress. They are a free, elective body. They are elected to carry out all the legislative provisions of the Constitution of the United States. I am elected to carry out the Executive powers in that same Constitution, and we usually get along all right in the end.

Q. You will go ahead, sir, with the——

THE PRESIDENT. We are going to do whatever is necessary to meet the present emergency under the Constitution of the United States. That is what I am sworn to uphold and defend, and I propose to do just that.

Q. Sir, do you see any harm in any such restrictions, that is, limiting 4 million on the——

THE PRESIDENT. You want to get me into a discussion of a legislative matter which is not before me, and I don't intend to do that.

Q. Well, your spokesmen have opposed any such limitations on the Hill, haven't they?

THE PRESIDENT. I don't know that I have any special spokesman. There are lots of

Democrats and Republicans down there who are doing everything they can to support the foreign policy of the United States.

Q. Doing what to it, sir?

THE PRESIDENT. To support it. A number of Democratic and Republican Senators and Congressmen who are doing everything they possibly can to support the foreign policy of the United States.

Q. Excuse me—support?

THE PRESIDENT. It is a bipartisan foreign policy.

Q. Support the policy——

THE PRESIDENT. Support the bipartisan foreign policy of the United States.

Q. That would include, also, your fixing the limits on the number of divisions that General Eisenhower——

THE PRESIDENT. I won't go into that.

[16.] Q. Mr. President, yesterday, in the disarmament letter,[11] there were no specific proposals for what we might do to disarm the world and set up a basis for peace.

THE PRESIDENT. I think you will find as far back as 1945 specific proposals on the whole subject. Our plan and program has been before the United Nations ever since the Second World War ended, and there has not been any change in those plans and proposals.

Q. You are referring specifically to the atomic weapons?

THE PRESIDENT. The disarmament program and the control of atomic energy and everything else has been thoroughly and completely covered. Our stand has never been any different—it isn't any different now from what it was then.

Q. That was reiterated——

THE PRESIDENT. Time and again. Time and again.

[17.] Q. Mr. President, can you comment, sir, on the possibility of Mr. Donald

---

[10] Robert G. Nixon of International News Service.

[11] Item 54.

Dawson [12] appearing or not appearing before the RFC subcommittee?

THE PRESIDENT. No comment.

Q. Has he been to Key West?

THE PRESIDENT. No, he hasn't. That doesn't mean that he won't be coming if he wants to. All the rest of us are here.

Q. He canceled a speaking engagement in Washington the other day, saying that he was coming down here.

THE PRESIDENT. That's all right—I haven't been in touch with him.

[18.] Q. Mr. President, there is one question I would like to ask. Are you going to run for reelection?

THE PRESIDENT. Now, Tony,[13] that is a question that we will leave up in the air so that Bert and these other fellows can have something to speculate on for the rest of the year. [*Laughter*]

Bert Andrews: I only write facts.

THE PRESIDENT. That's right—and he can speculate, too. [*Laughter*]

I have no comment on that question.

[19.] Q. One more question?

THE PRESIDENT. Shoot.

Q. Why did you change from that wonderful shirt that you had, to this modest one?

THE PRESIDENT. Because it was dirty and needed washing. [*Much laughter*]

Q. We saw the pictures of you in it.

THE PRESIDENT. That is a very quiet grey and white shirt. It didn't show up very well in the pictures, but as I said, it's in the laundry now, that's the only reason I don't have it on.

[20.] Q. They are saying you plan to visit Paris next year. Do you plan to make such a visit?

THE PRESIDENT. I have no plans for next year.

[21.] Q. Mr. President, we have received an exchange of letters on Mr. McCabe.[14] Have you anything more to say on it?

THE PRESIDENT. No, I think those letters speak for themselves. Mr. McCabe has been trying to quit for 2 years. We didn't want him to quit while this controversy was on between the Treasury and the Federal Reserve Board.

[22.] Q. Mr. President, General MacArthur submitted a statement this morning saying we need sizable forces to stabilize the defense line in Korea anywhere along the peninsula, and if he got sizable forces he could drive the Communists back across the Yalu River and hold them there.

THE PRESIDENT. I haven't seen that statement. It has not reached me officially, so I can't comment on it.

Q. Mr. President, is there any outlook for peace in Korea this year?

THE PRESIDENT. I can't answer the question.

Q. What was the question?

THE PRESIDENT. He wanted to know if there was any outlook for peace in Korea, and I told him I couldn't answer the question.

Q. I wish you could.

THE PRESIDENT. I wish I could, too. I would if I could.

[23.] Q. Mr. President, do you like Key West as much this year as ever?

THE PRESIDENT. Oh, yes—always like it. Very pleasant place to be, except that I had to wear an overcoat yesterday.

Q. Mr. President——

---

[12] Donald S. Dawson, Administrative Assistant to the President, formerly personnel director of the RFC.

[13] Ernest B. Vaccaro of the Associated Press.

[14] On March 15, the White House made public the President's letter accepting the resignation of Thomas B. McCabe as Chairman, Board of Governors, Federal Reserve System, effective March 31. The release also included Mr. McCabe's letter of resignation, dated March 9, and a second letter to the President from Mr. McCabe on March 14 in which he recommended William McChesney Martin, Jr., Assistant Secretary of the Treasury, as his successor.

THE PRESIDENT. It has been one of the most pleasant visits we have had down here. We had one bad day. What was that, Tony?

[24.] Q. Well, I just wondered if you had any comment on statements like those of Senator Knowland,[15] who suggests you ought to come home and clean house?

THE PRESIDENT. No comment.

Q. What was the question?

THE PRESIDENT. He wanted to know if I had any comment on Senator Knowland's statement that I ought to come home and clean house. My house is always clean. [*Laughter*]

Q. Would that be your answer, Mr. President, seriously, to a lot of cartoons and editorials that have said some of these things indicate a lack of moral and ethical responsibility among some of the people around you?

THE PRESIDENT. That is not true. Pointblank. Categorically. It is just *not* true.

Q. Well, Mr. President, you still stand on the statement, then, that nothing illegal has been shown in any of these letters, or——

THE PRESIDENT. I was only commenting on that letter—on the congressional letters which I have read.[16] I have not gone to the bottom of them. I have made no FBI investigation or anything of that kind. But the letters I have read were just simply requests that certain loans be considered and granted. Nothing illegal in that. I never wrote any letter of that sort in my life while I was in the Senate, and I was there for 10 years.

Q. Do you consider the letter Senator Murray [17] wrote regarding an RFC hotel loan, where his son profited as the attorney—do you consider——

THE PRESIDENT. I have no comment to make on that.

Q. Mr. President, since somebody else started it, do you have any comment on Mr. Dawson staying "for free" at the Saxony Hotel?

THE PRESIDENT. No comment. I can only refer you to my own actions under similar circumstances.

Q. Mr. President, nobody questions *your* actions. I think you know that.

THE PRESIDENT. I hope not.

Q. What did you do, then, under similar circumstances?

THE PRESIDENT. I never wrote letters to Government departments urging that they do anything. The only two Government agencies before which I ever appeared during the 10 years I was in the Senate were the Interstate Commerce Commission and the Securities and Exchange Commission, when I was trying to get railroad securities on the open market so anybody could buy them, on bids. And I succeeded in getting that done; that was in the public interest.

Q. Mr. President, I am not trying to belabor this thing, but when you said it is not true, pointblank, categorically not true, you mean that your people are——

THE PRESIDENT. Tony is trying to find out whether my people are honorable or not—that are around me. They are. [*Laughter*]

Q. That is what I wanted to be sure of.

Q. All of them, Mr. President?

THE PRESIDENT. Yes. I wouldn't have them if they weren't.

Q. Sir, I have worn out two pencils.

THE PRESIDENT. Poor Tony. I can't lend you one. I left mine in the house. [*Laughter*]

Q. Mr. President, you have, however, written letters to Government agencies as a Senator—giving references, etc., or suggesting promotions for people?

[15] Senator William F. Knowland, Republican, of California.

[16] See Items 33 [2] and 49 [11].

[17] Senator James E. Murray, Democrat, of Montana.

THE PRESIDENT. I can't remember any.

Q. Clark Clifford?

THE PRESIDENT. I can't remember. Clark Clifford worked for me.[18]

Q. Well, Mr. President——

THE PRESIDENT. Clark Clifford did not come to Washington until I was President of the United States.

Q. He was a Navy officer?

THE PRESIDENT. Yes. I didn't ask for anybody to promote him to the Army, Navy, etc., during the war.

Q. Mr. President, by your saying that when Senator you did not write such letters, I assume you are referring to the letters that have been written by Members of Congress?

THE PRESIDENT [*indicating*]. Three or four hundred.

Q. Well now, is the implication there that you do not——

THE PRESIDENT. There is no implication, and you needn't try to put any implications——

Q. No, sir—no, I wouldn't consider you said so.

THE PRESIDENT. I didn't say so.

Q. I was trying to follow through on your——

THE PRESIDENT. That's all right.

[25.] Q. Mr. President, I would like to ask you an easy question, sir?

THE PRESIDENT. Shoot.

Q. Almost coming up is the anniversary of your taking the oath. Would you like to comment on how hard the first 6 years are?

THE PRESIDENT. No, I don't think there is anything to be said.

You know, I will make this comment, though, that all a President of the United States can do is to endeavor to make the Government—the executive branch—run in

the public interest. I have striven very hard to accomplish that purpose. And the administration of no President can be evaluated during his term, or within 25 or 30 years after that term. Thomas Jefferson has just now come into his own as a President. Same thing is true of Jackson, and Lincoln, and Grover Cleveland. The same thing will be true of Wilson and Franklin Roosevelt. It takes an objective survey of what has happened and what was trying to be accomplished to decide whether a President has been a success or not. And you can't decide that now or here, and neither can I.

Q. Why don't you put that on the record so we can get it from Jack [19] and use it with direct quotes or without the quotes?

THE PRESIDENT. You are perfectly welcome to use it. I will have Jack give it to you because that is a statement of fact, as you all know, if you study history.

Q. You have been refreshing yourself, I believe, on some of this from that book "Lincoln and the Press."

THE PRESIDENT. Well, yes, but it wasn't anything new to me, because I had seen nearly everything that was in that book before it was published. Not the manuscript, you understand but historically speaking.

If you really want to find the man who was about the most abused man in the history of the country in the press, go down to the Library of Congress and read some of the newspaper comments on George Washington. You will find a lot of things that you didn't know about, that are not in history.

Q. Well, Mr. President, I would like to ask you one more question. Why don't you put all of this on the record, give us the Q and A of the whole press conference, and let us get a transcript of it?

---

[18] Clark M. Clifford was Special Counsel to the President until his resignation January 31, 1950 (see 1950 volume, this series, Item 24).

[19] Jack Romagna, White House Official Reporter.

THE PRESIDENT. Well, I don't think that is necessary, Bert. I don't mind those two answers before——

Q. Consider it a separate press conference——

THE PRESIDENT. I don't mind these last two or three questions being on the transcript order, but I don't think there is any use putting the whole press conference on the record.

Q. I was just trying to make it easy on the people that are writing.

THE PRESIDENT. I know. Tony here is having a hard time making his pencil notes.

Q. You have given us some very good answers.

Q. I would like to second Bert's motion, were you to go along with him.

THE PRESIDENT. No, no. When Jack gets the transcript, I will discuss the matter with Joe.

Q. Will you do that?

Joe Short: I don't think the transcript will be ready today or——

THE PRESIDENT. Well, whenever it is ready.

Joe Short: It won't be ready for some time.

THE PRESIDENT. Well, I am just telling you exactly what I think and what I am trying to accomplish. All I am working for is the welfare of the United States, and I think nearly every other Government employee with whom I am working is trying to do the same thing, under a severe handicap.

Q. Perhaps we can put that in quotes?

THE PRESIDENT. Character assassination is a terrible thing.

Q. You said that George Washington was the most abused man by the press. Do you consider that the press abuses you? [*Laughter*]

THE PRESIDENT. Oh no, the press doesn't abuse me. The press is very kind to me. [*More laughter*] I have no quarrel with the press. Never have.

But you ought to read those things, you will—they are just as interesting as can be. You should see what was said about Washington and Jefferson, and John Quincy Adams, and Andrew Jackson. And I believe the man who got the worst treatment besides George Washington in the press was Grover Cleveland. Nobody was as roundly abused as Cleveland in his first term.

Q. You are not saying that you have got some bad treatment from the press?

THE PRESIDENT. No, I didn't say that—I didn't say that.

Q. We can draw that inference.

THE PRESIDENT. Any inference you want to draw, that is your conclusion, not mine.

[26.] Q. Mr. President, we have been talking in a historical vein. I remember it was back in the second Roosevelt term, and the President said that he thought his administration would be remembered—it struck me at the time—for its social security program.

THE PRESIDENT. That's right.

Q. I am just wondering now, what you think of your administration, if there is anything it will be remembered for?

THE PRESIDENT. I hope it will be remembered for its sincere effort for world peace. And if we accomplish that, if we get through this era without a third world war, I think that probably is what it will be remembered for.

Q. Could we put that in direct quotes, Mr. President?

THE PRESIDENT. Well, I will let you argue that with Joe.

Q. If we get through this era without a third world war, is that what it will be remembered for?

THE PRESIDENT. For world peace—establishment of world peace. And I think that the establishment of world peace, and the implementation of the so-called point 4 program will be the things that will be most remembered, if they are successfully concluded. We can't tell what is going to happen, and I am not making any prophecies.

Q. Starting off, sir, with your address closing the United Nations——

THE PRESIDENT. Opening the United Nations and closing it, and also the San Francisco statement on the Asiatic policy, and the United Nations statement after that on world policy. I think that is the meat of the whole epoch of this present administration.

And that doesn't mean that I am responsible for that. That means that the whole

Government—legislative, executive, and judicial—have been putting forth the same sort of an effort for world peace. You see, there have been two generations of the young men of Europe slaughtered, and it is a difficult gap to fill. I hope it won't happen again.

Bert Andrews (New York Herald Tribune): Mr. President, I think I will impersonate Mr. Smith, and say "Thank you very much."

THE PRESIDENT. It's nice to be with you.

NOTE: President Truman's two hundred and fifty-seventh news conference was held on the lawn of the Little White House in Key West, Fla., at 3:30 p.m. on Thursday, March 15, 1951.

57 Telegram to General Marshall on the Strength of the U.S. Armed Forces. *March* 21, 1951

[Released March 21, 1951. Dated March 20, 1951]

I APPRECIATE your report that, as of March 21, 1951, the strength of the United States Armed Forces will be double what it was nine months ago, when communist forces invaded the Republic of Korea. I wish to commend you and all your associates in the Army, the Navy, and the Air Force for the strenuous efforts which have made such growth possible. This tremendous gain in our strength has been made necessary by the lawless aggression of communist forces in Korea, and by the menace of still further communist attacks against other free nations. The armed forces we are building, and the supplies for them which our factories, farms, and mines are turning out, are for the protection and preservation of our freedoms. The speed with which we have been able to strengthen our defenses should be a source of inspiration and encouragement to men everywhere who love freedom. It is evi-

dence of our determination, in company with other free nations, to establish and maintain world peace.

I am confident that, under your wise leadership, the Department of Defense will continue to build the strength we need, fully supported by the Congress and by the American people.

HARRY S. TRUMAN

[General George C. Marshall, Secretary of Defense]

NOTE: The text of the telegram from General Marshall follows:
Mr. President:
As of tomorrow, 21 March 1951, the strength of our Armed Forces will be exactly double what it was on 25 June 1950. This doubling of our strength has been accomplished less than nine months after the communist aggression against the Republic of Korea. For your information, the strength we have already attained—a total strength in excess of 2,900,000—was not attained in World War II until more than 21 months after our build-up started in June 1940, following the fall of France, and more than 3 months after Pearl Harbor.

GEORGE C. MARSHALL

58 Statement by the President on the Forthcoming Visit of the President of France. *March* 23, 1951

PRESIDENT Vincent Auriol of France, Mme. Auriol, their son Paul, French Foreign Minister Robert Schuman, and members of their official party are already on the high seas on their way to this country as official guests of the U.S. Government.

This Government is looking forward with great pleasure to this visit and I shall be very happy to welcome our distinguished guests.

France and the United States have a long history of inspiring friendship. And the ties between the two countries, as partners in the struggle to achieve peace in the world, have never been closer.

I wish our visitors a very pleasant voyage. I am honored and delighted to have them come.

59 Address Opening the Meeting of the Foreign Ministers of the American Republics. *March* 26, 1951

Mr. Secretary, Your Excellencies, ladies and gentlemen:

It is an honor to open this meeting of the Ministers of Foreign Affairs of the American Republics. I am happy to extend to you a wholehearted welcome to our country and to our Capital City. On behalf of the United States, I hope that this will be a most satisfactory and successful meeting.

This is the fourth meeting of the Ministers of Foreign Affairs of the American Republics. This meeting, like the earlier ones, is held at a time of international danger. When the first meeting was held, in 1939, war had just broken out in Europe. As that conflict spread to nation after nation, and threatened to extend to all parts of the world, the Foreign Ministers of the American Republics held two more meetings in 1940 and in 1942 to plan a common course of action against the common danger.

As a result of our concerted efforts, our countries did not become a theater of war. The nations of this hemisphere succeeded in protecting the American Continents from invasion. And, as a result of our common efforts, the people of the Americas were able to contribute power and resources which

turned the tide against aggression and brought victory to the forces of freedom.

Today, we meet again to consider our common defense. We meet again to work out ways and means by which our united strength may be employed in the struggle for freedom throughout the world.

The American Republics all owe their national beginnings to the same set of ideals— the same concepts of human and international freedom. We have all followed and we will continue to follow two basic principles. First, we believe that international affairs should be based upon cooperation among free and independent nations, and not upon coercion or force. Second, we believe that the aim and purpose of government is to promote the welfare of all the people—not just the privileged few.

These principles have long been the basis of relations among the American Republics. The same principles are now embodied in the Charter of the United Nations where they have become the foundation of a new society of nations. The statesmen of the American Republics have shown their continuing devotion to these principles by the great and constructive work they have done in creating and strengthening the United Nations.

Today, these principles are under relentless attack from a center of power which denies the whole concept of human freedom—whether it be spiritual freedom, or economic freedom, or political freedom.

Communist imperialism attacks and undermines national independence and international cooperation. In their place, it substitutes the rule of force. Communist imperialism also seeks to destroy the system of government that serves the welfare of the people. Instead, it sets up a system under which the people exist only to serve the purposes of the government. As a result the Soviet system is one of unbridled power, imposing slavery at home and aggression abroad.

The aggressive expansion of the Soviet power threatens the whole world. In Europe we see it trying to engulf the nations from which we have drawn our cultural beginnings. If Soviet subversion and Soviet armed force were to overthrow these nations, the consequences for all of us in the Western Hemisphere would be disastrous. We would lose those cultural and religious ties which mean so much to us. The international trade on which we are so dependent would be violently disrupted. Worst of all, we would be confronted by a hostile power on the shores of the Atlantic, capable of using the great economic resources of our conquered friends to strike across the ocean at our own independence.

We must not and will not let that happen. We in the Western Hemisphere must help the free men of Europe who are resisting Soviet expansion.

In the Far East, Communist imperialism presents us with another threat. There we see many new nations emerging, as our own countries once did, from colonial status to full independence. For these new nations, we of the Western Hemisphere have the greatest feeling of fellowship. But Communist imperialism has fallen upon these new nations with its weapons of internal subversion and external attack. It seeks to overpower them before they are strong enough to stand alone.

If Soviet communism were to be successful in this venture, it would be a terrible blow to the bright promise of the principles of freedom and peace which we uphold. The great manpower of Asia would become one of the instruments of the aggressive expansion of the Soviet system toward our own hemisphere.

Both to the east, therefore, and to the west, we are confronted by great perils. Our future progress, our very survival, lie in the defense of the world order of free nations of which we are a part. Our very existence depends upon the success of those principles which our countries stand for, and which we have supported in the United Nations. There is no safety for any of us in abandoning these principles. There will be no security in the world without the United Nations. Powerful and productive as the Western Hemisphere is, we cannot make it safe by building a wall around it.

Instead of withdrawing into our hemisphere in a hopeless attempt to find security through retreat, we must concert our defenses and combine our strength in order to support men in Europe and Asia who are battling for freedom. That is the only course that can lead to security or peace or freedom for us or for men anywhere in the world.

Recognition of this fact lies behind the aid the United States has given to the rebuilding of Europe. It lies behind the struggle the free nations are now waging in the hills of Korea. The resistance of the United Nations to aggression in Korea—a resistance that has the firm approval of all the nations represented here—is of momentous importance. It has shown that the free nations are determined to defend their ideals of national independence and human welfare.

The issue in Korea is the survival of the principles on which we have built our countries. The principal of national independence and self-government is at stake there, as well as the principle that government shall be for the welfare of the people. If justice and order do not prevail in Korea, they will be in danger everywhere in the world.

Heroic sacrifices are being made in Korea to check the forces of aggression and to protect us against the terrible destruction and vastly greater sacrifices of a world conflict. By standing firm in Korea and by preparing to meet aggression elsewhere we are doing our best to prevent a third world war.

This meeting in Washington, therefore, must consider not only what should be done to improve the defense of this hemisphere, but also what measures we can best undertake to support and strengthen the United Nations in its effort to establish world peace.

We meet here as a region which has already, in the solemn treaty of Rio de Janeiro, announced its intention to defend itself through cooperative action. We are pledged to resist the common foe.

We must now plan as a primary task for the strengthening and the coordinated use of our defense forces in this hemisphere. We must also consider how we may best use our strength to support the cause of freedom against aggression throughout the world.

The success of our defense program depends upon our economic strength. In these troubled times, defense production must have prior claim upon our economic resources. We shall have to increase the production of strategic materials. We shall have to divert manufacturing capacity to defense purposes.

These necessities will create many difficult practical problems for our countries to solve.

There will be shortages of basic materials and other commodities. There will be limitations on certain kinds of capital expansion.

The first step in solving these problems is to face them in a spirit of cooperation. We must recognize that we are engaged, as good neighbors, in a common enterprise that is vital to our survival as free and democratic nations. We must establish the principle of sharing our burdens fairly. We must act together to meet essential civilian needs, and at the same time we must act together to be sure that scarce supplies are limited to essential uses. We must try to prevent wild and speculative price movements in our international trade, whether in raw materials or manufactured products.

Our defense needs are not, of course, limited to the things that go into the making of weapons. We need to build up our economic strength in a much broader way. It is essential to our security that we constantly enlarge our economic capacity. Our defense needs include, in many cases and in many areas, more food, better education, and better health services. They include, in certain cases, the building of roads, dams or power plants.

We must remember that the real strength of the free nations lies in the will and determination of their peoples. The free nations stand for economic progress and social advancement. They grow in strength by going forward along the road of greater economic opportunity for all.

Over the last 10 years our countries have made great economic progress. In most of the countries represented here, national income is at least twice what it was in 1939.

An important factor in our advance is the program of technical cooperation which we have joined together to carry out. Joint projects for spreading technical knowledge have already made notable achievements in improving the health, education, and living standards of our people. We intend to press on with this kind of activity.

The American Republics are full of breathtaking possibilities for future economic development. These possibilities can be made realities only if we work and plan together for a long time ahead. I like to think, for example, of the possibility of developing the vast areas of wilderness, such as the eastern slopes of the Andes, and turning them into new and fertile farmland. And I like to think of a project about which I talked to the President of Chile, which contemplates the diversion of water from those high mountain lakes between Bolivia and Peru for making a garden on the coast of South America to the west for Chile and Peru, and in return giving Bolivia a seaport on the Pacific. I had a very pleasant conversation with the President of Chile on that subject. And I like to think of the development of the Paraná, Paraguay, and Uruguay Rivers. Think what wonderful possibilities are in those great waterways for development.

And those are only samples, for all over the continent of South America there are greater resources undeveloped than were ever in these United States of America. And I know that we can develop them for the welfare of the whole world as well as for ourselves.

I like to think of the possibilities of industrial development in your countries. I remember with pride the part which this country played, even during the troubled times of the last war, in helping to create a steel industry in Brazil. I think with satisfaction of the progress that has been made by Chile and other countries in setting up factories and hydroelectric projects in recent years.

Our countries do not have unlimited resources to devote to the creative developments such as these. We cannot do as much, in the midst of a defense emergency, as we could in normal times. But we must do all we can.

It is the genius of our democratic type of society that we are constantly creative and constantly advancing. We hold out to all people the prospect of bettering their condition, not in the dim future, not after some terrible and bloody upheaval, but steadily through the years, in the simple activities of our daily life.

In our countries we do not measure our prosperity by the power of the state. We do not measure the progress of our society in terms of military might. We do not measure our advancement in terms of the profits or the luxuries of the few. Our yardstick is the welfare of the many. We think in terms of the average man—how he lives, what he can buy, and the freedom he enjoys. These are the standards by which we measure our development.

And, by these standards, we are marching steadily forward. And we shall continue that march!

Our vision of progress is not limited to our own countries. We extend it to all the peoples of the world.

We know that people are very much alike in their basic aspirations wherever they may be or whatever language they may speak. We recognize that the people of Russia, the people of the Soviet satellite states, are very much like us in what they want for themselves and for their children. We hope that some day they will find it possible to turn their leaders from their present path of tyranny and aggression.

Our goal is self-development, not imperialism.

Our goal is peace, not war.

Our goal, not only for ourselves but for all peoples, is a better world—materially, morally, and spiritually.

NOTE: The President spoke at 4 p.m. in Constitution Hall. His opening words referred to Secretary of State Dean Acheson and to the 20 Foreign Ministers of the Latin American countries represented at the meeting.

The Fourth Meeting of Consultation of Ministers of Foreign Affairs of American States was held in Washington from March 26 through April 7, 1951.

60 Statement by the President Upon Signing Bill Extending the Interest-Bearing Life of Matured Savings Bonds. *March 26, 1951*

IT GIVES ME real pleasure to approve the enrolled enactment of H.R. 2268. This legislation will be a great convenience to Series E Savings Bond holders who desire to retain their investments in E bonds. Under its authority, the owners of maturing Series E bonds may, if they desire, simply keep the bonds and continue to earn interest on their face amounts for up to 10 more years.

Americans by nature are thrifty, and Series E bonds are popular among a great many of our citizens as a medium for savings. The privileges extended under the new legislation make them even more attractive.

Those bonds offer to even the smallest savers the opportunity of providing for their own future security and at the same time becoming direct shareholders in their Government. A sizable portion of the present public debt is held by E bond owners.

With our Nation again facing tremendous mobilization demands, a vigorous program of personal saving becomes one of the most effective weapons against inflation. Therefore, the retention of maturing Series E bonds, and of course additional purchases of all types of savings bonds, will contribute effectively to the defense program.

I wish to take this opportunity to congratulate the Congress for its speedy action on this important legislation.

NOTE: As enacted, H.R. 2268 is Public Law 12, 82d Congress (65 Stat. 26).

61 Remarks to Members of the Associated Church Press. *March 28, 1951*

WELL, I am glad to greet you again. I think you have been here a couple of times before. I was hoping that the sun would shine on this proposed rose garden—which it will be a little later on in the season—but it seems to have gone back on us this morning.

I have one subject on which I am somewhat "hipped," but a good subject cannot be reiterated too many times, and that is the endeavor of those countries who believe in the freedom of the individual to mobilize the moral forces of the world for the welfare of mankind against the unmoral forces in the world.

I have been very emphatic on this subject on occasion after occasion—I guess people, after a while, will get tired of my continually talking on this one subject, but it is the most important thing we are faced with in the world today. And your audience, your readers, are the ones who can do most toward causing that mobilization.

In this time of crisis with which we are faced now, petty things should be forgotten, denominational quarrels should be overlooked. Everybody is headed for the same place, and they are headed on the same train, and under the same engineer.

What we want to do is to see that those

forces in the world that believe in honor and ethics, and uprightness and the keeping of agreements, are in control of the world when we are finished. And that is for the welfare of the people—all the people, not for the welfare of governments.

Our Government is a government of the people, for the people, and by the people, and we are trying to make it work as best we can. And we are making it work. What we want to do is to convince the people behind the Iron Curtain that we do not, under any circumstances, want to control or tell them what to do. All we want is for them—for their own welfare and benefit— to do the things that are necessary for the welfare of their own people, and to do it in

their own way. Raise the curtain, and let us see how they do it. Maybe they can teach us something. I know we can teach them something, if they will come and look at us. But they won't come and make the effort to implement the mobilization of the moral forces of the world—all of them—against the unmoral forces.

Then we will have peace in the world. And that's all we are striving for. That's all in the world we are striving for.

I thank you very much. I appreciate your coming. I hope you enjoy your visit, and I hope you don't catch cold standing out here in this shower.

NOTE: The President spoke at 11:50 a.m. in the Rose Garden at the White House.

62 The President's Toast at a State Dinner for President Auriol of France. *March 28, 1951*

I HAVE a pleasant duty to perform in presenting you with this decoration. We know that you deserve it, and we hope you will wear it with pleasure.

[*Reading citation*] "The President of the United States of America, authorized by Act of Congress July 20, 1942, has awarded the Legion of Merit, Degree of Chief-Commander, to His Excellency Vincent Auriol, President of the French Republic and Commander in Chief of her armed forces, for exceptionally meritorious conduct in the performance of outstanding service.

"His Excellency Vincent Auriol, President of the French Republic, and Commander in Chief of her armed forces since January 1947, has displayed unswerving friendship to the United States and to the ideals held

by all democratic nations, and has done much to assure the success of these ideals. His constant aim in stimulating the historical bonds of close friendship between France and the United States, and his strong backing of a mutual, progressive and liberal foreign policy, have presented the rest of the world with the guiding example of continuing cooperation between the Republic of France and the United States of America." Signed by the President, and dated at the White House.

I drink a toast to His Excellency the President of France, to the first official visit that any President of France has ever paid to the United States.

NOTE: The President proposed the toast at 10 p.m. at the Carlton Hotel in Washington. The text of President Auriol's response was not released.

63   The President's News Conference of
      March 29, 1951

THE PRESIDENT. Please be seated.

[1.]   Tony,[1] I've got two or three memos here, so you had better get yourself two or three sharp pencils.

Q. Okay, sir. [*Laughter*]

THE PRESIDENT. I was sure that you would be asking me some questions on this subject, and I thought I might as well tell you about it, and then it may bring some questions to mind that you otherwise wouldn't ask!

[*Reading, not literally*] "Every war has left a trail of crime in its wake, and the last war did that, too. I have been deeply concerned about it, and we have been taking positive steps to combat it.

"As early as 1946, the Attorney General convened a national conference for the prevention and control of juvenile delinquency. This was an effort to eliminate crime at its roots, and the program is having good results.

"In the meantime, we have been studying quietly but consistently the problems of adult crime, particularly organized crime which spills over State boundaries.

"About a year ago I directed the Attorney General to call a conference of Federal, State, and municipal enforcement officials. This conference produced some proposals for cooperative attack on crime which are already being used, and produced other proposals which are being carefully studied.

"At my direction, the Attorney General has also during the last 18 months—this is a special order of my own—convened special grand juries in Miami, Los Angeles, Kansas City, Newark, Philadelphia, and Scranton to seek out offenders against the Federal tax, narcotics, white slave, and other laws. In the regular course of its work, the Justice

---
[1] Ernest B. Vaccaro of the Associated Press.

Department filed over 36,000 criminal cases in the last fiscal year. Many notorious gangsters have been and are being prosecuted under these Federal statutes.

"In addition the Treasury and Justice Departments have, under my orders, given unstinted cooperation to the present Senate Committee to Investigate Organized Crime in Interstate Commerce. The committee deserves great credit for focusing public attention on the need for ever greater efforts to stamp out crime.

"The eradication of crime is a job for everyone. The Federal Government cannot evade its responsibilities any more than the States and the municipal governments can. And, above all, the individual citizens cannot evade their responsibility for their patronage without which gaming—gambling, vice, and narcotics peddling—could not exist.

"The respective responsibilities of the Federal Government and the State governments are clear. The Constitution specifies that police powers within the States are for the States themselves to enforce. The Constitution clearly gives the Federal Government power to regulate interstate traffic.

"It has always been and always will continue to be the policy of this administration to back up the States in their inherent police powers by every appropriate measure. We supported legislation to prohibit the interstate shipment of slot machines in violation of State laws, and to prohibit the use of interstate communications facilities to transmit gambling information. We already have laws to back up the States in their enforcement of local narcotics and alcohol laws. The postal laws forbid the use of the mails for transmitting lottery, obscene, and fraudulent material. There are many more measures which need not be cataloged here.

"On the other hand, I do not want anyone to be deceived that Federal action by itself can solve the problems of crime. The primary responsibility rests with State and local authorities, and with individual citizens who must obey the laws enacted by their representatives in government.

"It is vitally important that this Nation remain strong morally, as well as economically and militarily.

"I say again, the eradication of crime is a job for every citizen in the country."

[2.] Now I have a statement on wheat for India, which I think you will be interested in. This one is ready, and the other one will be ready very shortly.

[*Reading, not literally*] "India has an urgent need for grain to prevent suffering and starvation. This I pointed out in my message of February 12th to the Congress. My views have not changed. We can, at some sacrifice, spare the grain. We should do so—first, to save human lives, and secondly to strengthen freedom and democracy in an important area of Asia. Moreover, we should provide the first million tons promptly as a grant. We can then explore in greater detail the situation with respect to the remaining million tons.

"India must have 6 million tons of grain in order to meet the famine conditions caused by severe drought. India has made arrangements to buy 4 million tons through ordinary sources including United States suppliers. To pay for the additional 2 million tons of grain will place too great a strain on the financial resources of India and would prevent the carrying out of its essential development program. In addition, with the provision of grain to India as a grant, the Indian Government will deposit the local currency coming from the distribution of the grain to the Indian people into a special account which can be used for agricultural development projects in India agreed to by us. These projects will help alleviate the recurrence of such conditions as the present.

"The House Foreign Affairs Committee carefully investigated this matter, and on March 5th favorably reported a bill to provide the grain to India. This bill has bipartisan support. It reflects the desire of the American people to help the Indian people in their present emergency.

"Prompt action is vital. The monsoon season occurs in India during the summer. Many roads are then made impassable and grain shipments to remote areas are greatly impaired. Each day's delay after April 1st in starting shipments will leave a serious gap in India's food supply later this summer and cause great suffering. I hope, therefore, that the Congress will enact the necessary legislation as soon as possible after the Easter recess."

Now you may ask questions, if you like.

[3.] Q. Mr. President, do people who say pretty flatly that you are going to run again in 1952 know what they are talking about?

THE PRESIDENT. I don't think anybody knows what he is talking about when he talks about my reelection. And we will attend to that when the time comes.

Q. Mr. President, the Democratic National Committee issued a speech today by Michael Galvin, Under Secretary of Labor, who predicts that you will be reelected with 56 percent of the vote next year?

THE PRESIDENT. That's a nice prediction, but I haven't seen the speech and I can't comment on it.

Q. It was not cleared by the White House?

THE PRESIDENT. It was not. [*Laughter*]

Q. You said you don't think anyone knows whether or not——

THE PRESIDENT. *I* do.

Q. ——anyone but you?

THE PRESIDENT. That's right.

Q. Then you *have* made up your mind one way or the other?

THE PRESIDENT. I didn't say that. [*Laughter*]

Q. How could you know?

THE PRESIDENT. Well, I know what I am going to do. I will tell you about it, in due time. [*Laughter*] I don't know why you have to know so far in advance, because the Democratic and Republican committees don't meet until July. They finally make the decision, you know. The President, of course, will have something to say about the Democratic Convention, as he did last year.

Q. Same thing, Mr. President?

THE PRESIDENT. Well, I will answer that when the time comes. [*More laughter*]

[4.] Q. Mr. President, in connection with your crime statement, I wonder if you would care to comment on the testimony of former Mayor O'Dwyer, that he appointed to office friends and relatives of gangsters? [2]

THE PRESIDENT. I have no comment.

Q. Sir, may I ask, also, is there any change contemplated in his status as Ambassador?

THE PRESIDENT. No.

Q. What did he ask?

THE PRESIDENT. He wanted to know if there was any change contemplated in his status as an ambassador, and I said no.

Q. Mr. President, did you watch any of the hearings on television?

THE PRESIDENT. No. I've got other things to do besides watch television. I never look at it unless my daughter is on it. [*Laughter*]

[5.] Q. Mr. President, would you tell us a little bit about what you and Sean Mac-Bride [3] discussed?

THE PRESIDENT. I think he made a clear report of what the discussion was about when he went out of the office. I have nothing to add to it.

[6.] Q. Mr. President, would you comment on the controversy which has been raised, not only in this country but in England and other allied countries, concerning General MacArthur's latest statement? [4]

THE PRESIDENT. No comment. I have no comment.

Q. Mr. President, I have a question along that line, too. Could you say whether any new instructions have been transmitted to General MacArthur in the last few weeks concerning the crossing of the 38th parallel?

THE PRESIDENT. Instructions are as they always have been, and they refer strictly to the tactical situation. General Marshall [5] answered that very clearly yesterday in his press conference.

Q. Yes, sir. Now, one other along that same line. There have been some reports in the last couple of days that a new statement of policy is under preparation by this country and the other allied powers, seeking an end to the Korean fight. Did you see it?

THE PRESIDENT. I have no comment on that.

[7.] Q. Mr. President, there seems to be—we would like to have official clarification of the seemingly conflicting statements between Wilson [6] and General Marshall?

THE PRESIDENT. Well, I think I can clarify it for you. I talked to both of them before

---

[2] William O'Dwyer, United States Ambassador to Mexico and former mayor of New York City, appeared before the Special Committee to Investigate Organized Crime in Interstate Commerce, United States Senate, on March 19 and 20, 1951.

[3] Minister for External Affairs for Ireland. A White House release of March 23, 1951, stated that Mr. MacBride on that day paid a courtesy call on

the President in the course of his unofficial visit to the United States. They had, the release noted, "a friendly discussion concerning the present state of relations between the United States and Ireland."

[4] See note to Item 77.

[5] Gen. George C. Marshall, Secretary of Defense.

[6] Charles E. Wilson, Director, Office of Defense Mobilization, at a news conference on March 27, had emphasized the nation's military strength. General Marshall, on the other hand, stressed the need for public and Congressional support for a long-term defense effort.

they issued their statements. I knew what they were going to say. General Marshall, of course, is worried about the apparent letdown in the minds of the people that there is an emergency in existence now. The emergency is just as great now as it ever has been. And it is just as necessary that we carry out a program in full at this minute. In fact, it is more necessary than it ever has been since the emergency has been in existence.

Mr. Wilson has been interested in production, getting his production lines in working order, to meet the emergency with which we are faced. He has been very successful in that production program. He has had some difficulties with some of the other programs, but we are working on them and I think eventually the whole thing will be brought together so we will have a successful conclusion to the program which we have outlined. I don't think there is anything contradictory in those two statements at all.

[8.] Q. Mr. President, about one of the things in Mr. Wilson's program that has not been going so well—referring to the situation regarding labor's participation, it has been a month or more since labor's representation was ended. I wonder if you would care to comment on the progress——

THE PRESIDENT. Progress is being made toward a settlement of that situation, and we will eventually get it settled.

Q. This labor quarrel has been going on, Mr. President, I think, for about 6 weeks, and 5 or 6 weeks ago you stated that you had complete confidence in Mr. Wilson. Since then, definite demands that you dispense with the services of Mr. Wilson have been made by certain leaders of unions——

THE PRESIDENT. Those demands have not been made to me.

Q. If they were made to you, what would be your reply, sir?

THE PRESIDENT. I would give them the same reply that I gave 6 weeks ago.

Did you—[*indicating*]—want to ask a question?

[9.] Q. Mr. President, could you give us a personal impression about President Auriol, the human angle of your personal contact with him?

THE PRESIDENT. It has been very, very cordial. I like him very much. And I think we understand each other, just as all the rest of my wonderful guests have made a wonderful impression on me. The President of France and his family are wonderful people, and he has ideas for the continuation of the cooperation between France and the United States. I think you will find a statement to that effect was issued after our conference this morning.[7]

[10.] Q. Mr. President, there has been a step-up of shipments of war materials, such as oil and scrap, etc., into China through Hong Kong. I wonder whether you have had—that has come to your attention, and whether you have any comment?

THE PRESIDENT. It has, and we are looking into it.

Q. Are you going to do anything about it?

---

[7] "The President of the French Republic outlined to the President of the United States conditions in France, the progress of the French rearmament program and the present situation in Indochina where French forces and the forces of the Associated States (of Indochina) are successfully opposing Communist aggression.

"The remarks of the President of the French Republic included a statement that the French people were determined to defend themselves against foreign aggression and that, in this spirit, they are giving all out support to the North Atlantic Treaty Organization. He emphasized that all these efforts were directed toward the maintenance and strengthening of peace.

"The President of the United States stated that he was encouraged by President Auriol's remarks and expressed his confidence that peace could and would be maintained and that the democratic peoples would preserve unshakable unity in pursuit of their great objective: peace for all the world." Department of State Bulletin, vol. 24, p. 563.

THE PRESIDENT. I don't know.

[11.] Q. Mr. President, one of the press associations early in the week carried a—I recall it was an informed story—that you had suggested to Mr. Donald Dawson that he should appear before the Fulbright committee.[8] Would you comment on that, sir?

THE PRESIDENT. I don't comment on informed stories about which I know nothing.

Q. Don't you think, sir, that there is an obligation on the part of someone to give an explanation about the Dawson matter to the public, who pays his salary?

THE PRESIDENT. That is a matter for the committee to decide itself. I am not running the committee.

Q. Do you mean, Mr. President, that if you were, you would subpoena him?

THE PRESIDENT. I didn't say that. I don't think it would be necessary to subpoena anybody from the White House, if it was necessary for him to testify.

[12.] Q. Mr. President, has there been any change in the declared policy of the United States and United Nations last June to liberate, unify, and stabilize all of Korea?

THE PRESIDENT. Never been any change in that policy, May.[9]

[13.] Q. Mr. President, who would be the authority to judge whether it was necessary for him to testify? Would that be a White House responsibility, or the committee's?

THE PRESIDENT. That bridge will be crossed when we get to it.

[14.] Q. Mr. President, in regard to May's question, that might imply that we still would go all the way to the Yalu River?

THE PRESIDENT. I am making no implications of that kind.

Q. I mean your answer, I was afraid——

THE PRESIDENT. Well, thank you for that, but there is no implication of that kind at all.

Q. Thank you, sir.

[*Pause*]

THE PRESIDENT. Have you run dry, or something? [*Laughter*]

Q. Mrs. Craig: Well, no, sir. I did emphasize the word *all*.

[15.] Q. Mr. President, I wonder—I want to ask you if you would tell us when you anticipate getting out the directive with respect to deferment of college students?

THE PRESIDENT. We are working on it now. We will get it out as promptly as we can get it ready.[10]

[16.] What was that you said, May?

Q. Yes, sir—excuse me for interrupting——

THE PRESIDENT. That's all right.

Q. ——but I did in my question say *all* of Korea.

THE PRESIDENT. I heard you—I heard you.

Q. Do you think that goes all the way to the Yalu?

THE PRESIDENT. It has no bearing on military operations in the field, May, whatever, and it is a military matter you are asking me about now, not a policy matter.

What was your question?

[17.] Q. Are you going to submit next week your message on revising the Defense Production Act?

THE PRESIDENT. I don't know whether I will have it ready by that time or not. As soon as I can get it ready, I shall submit it.[11]

Q. Will you be able to tell us whether you are going to recommend any modifications of parity?

THE PRESIDENT. I am not ready to discuss the measures yet, because they have not

---

[8] See Item 33 [2].

[9] Mrs. May Craig of the Portland (Maine) Press Herald.

[10] On March 31, 1951, the White House made public Executive Order 10230 of that date, amending the Selective Service regulations (3 CFR, 1949–1953 Comp., p. 740).

[11] See Item 91.

been thoroughly thrashed out. I will give you the complete information on it when I get ready.

[18.]   Q. Mr. President, you don't intend to fire Mr. Dawson, do you?

THE PRESIDENT. No, I do not. He is sitting right there. He is not fired yet.

[19.]   What did you say, Tony?

Ernest B. Vaccaro (Associated Press): I was writing! [*Laughter*]

THE PRESIDENT. I am going to get you an automatic pencil, Tony, that works electrically.

[20.]   Q. Mr. President, do you have under consideration a speaking tour, either during the spring or summer?

THE PRESIDENT. No. I have got too much to do to be thinking about anything but the work of the President at the present time. That doesn't mean, Tony, that we may not take a tour if I feel it is necessary. Eventually we have, if you remember.

Q. Where does that leave me? [*Laughter*]

THE PRESIDENT. That leaves you up in the air.

Q. What would make it necessary? When might you take that tour, Mr. President?

THE PRESIDENT. I am making no—I am not entering into a discussion. I said I have got too much to do, right here now, to even think about it.

[21.]   Q. Mr. President, on this discussion about the 38th parallel and the various points of geography in Korea, do I understand it correctly that the part of the peninsula that is occupied by our armies in there fighting, is dependent upon the situation of conflict and not upon any arbitrary line of geography?

THE PRESIDENT. That is correct. General Marshall answered that very carefully yesterday. That covers the situation. But I want it to be distinctly understood that we are for a free Korea, with a free government, when we get through.

[22.]   Q. Mr. President, would you discuss the UMT and draft bill legislation in the House——

THE PRESIDENT. No, I can't discuss pending measures in either branch of the Legislature. That is their business to discuss it. I will discuss it when it comes before me for consideration.

[23.]   Q. Mr. President, I am afraid I am still a little bit hazy——

THE PRESIDENT. That's too bad—I'll try to clear it up.

Q. ——on this 38th parallel. You say as a tactical matter General MacArthur still has the authority he has always had to cross the 38th parallel if he needs to?

THE PRESIDENT. That is correct.

Q. That doesn't necessarily imply that our troops will go all the way to the Yalu?

THE PRESIDENT. It depends altogether on the military situation, and I can't anticipate that military situation because there isn't even a general in the field who can anticipate how military maneuvers are going to come out. If you will study your history you will find that some of them were good guessers and some of them weren't.

[24.]   Q. Mr. President, about the cost of living, do you think that the price level can be rolled back to the pre-Korea level?

THE PRESIDENT. I can't answer that question. I wish they could be, but I don't know whether they are going to be able to do it or not. It is a gigantic job, and one that is almost impossible unless you have the complete and wholehearted cooperation of every branch of the economy. And that is what we are trying to get now, get a new approach to it and make it work. It has to be made to work. And eventually we will make it work.

[25.]   Q. Mr. President, in your references to General Marshall's statements yesterday, are you referring specifically to his statement that any general advance over the 38th parallel would be a political matter?

THE PRESIDENT. I am referring to General Marshall's statement as a whole on that subject. I want to make that just as clear as I can.

Smitty—are you going to stay here all day, or do I have to dismiss this class? [*Much laughter*]

Merriman Smith (United Press Associations): Well—thank you, Mr. President. [*More laughter*]

NOTE: President Truman's two hundred and fifty-eighth news conference was held in the Indian Treaty Room (Room 474) in the Executive Office Building at 4 p.m. on Thursday, March 29, 1951.

64   Letter to the Members of the Philippine War Damage Commission in Response to Their Final Report. *March* 29, 1951

Dear ——————:

As the Philippine War Damage Commission terminates its work, I wish to commend you and the other members of the Commission on the outstanding manner in which you have discharged your responsibilities. It is particularly noteworthy, and something all too rare in government annals, that the Commission, in advance of the time prescribed by Congress, has been able to complete the tremendous task of considering 1,248,901 claims and paying out more than $388 million at an administrative cost well below that provided by law.

The program which your Commission undertook following the passage of the act of Congress of April 30, 1946 represented something new in the history of the United States because this Government had never before assumed the responsibility of restoration of private property destroyed in time of war. The program was one, however, that the American people, who were themselves still mourning the loss of some 300,000 of their own sons and daughters and who then, as now, were confronted with staggering postwar problems, never questioned. In recognition of the loyalty and friendship of the people of the Philippines, all were agreed that we should assist them in getting a firm start on the road back toward the reestablish-

ment of a normal economy. Your Commission has played a vital role in helping the people of the Philippines in this task. Your program has strengthened the Philippine economy, it has helped restore many important buildings and facilities throughout the Islands, and it has enabled thousands of people to reestablish themselves in business, in agriculture, and in other pursuits.

The Philippine and American people have been closely associated for more than fifty years and it is my earnest hope that the two nations will continue that close association and cooperation in meeting the great problems which confront all freedom-loving people today. I believe that the work of the Commission has contributed materially to the realization of that hope.

In accepting your resignation on completion of a task well done, I wish to express my personal appreciation for your outstanding services as a member of the Philippine War Damage Commission, and to commend the Philippine and American members of your staff for their splendid contribution.

Very sincerely yours,

HARRY S. TRUMAN

NOTE: This is the text of identical letters sent to each of the three members of the Commission: Frank A. Waring, Chairman; Francisco A. Delgado, and John A. O'Donnell.

The Commissioners' letter to the President, dated March 26, and transmitting the report, was released with the President's reply. The report, "Rehabilitation of the Philippines: Final and Ninth Semi- annual Report of the United States Philippine War Damage Commission, Manila, Philippines, March 31, 1951," was printed by the Government Printing Office (1951, 96 pp.).

65 The President's Toast at a Dinner in His Honor Given by President Auriol at the French Embassy. *March* 30, 1951

Mr. President, Madame Auriol:

I am deeply touched by the statements of the President of the great French Republic. He has made it perfectly plain to you, as he has already made it plain to me, that France is forever our friend, that France will do its part in our obligation under the Atlantic Treaty to maintain the peace of the world.

One hundred and sixty years ago or more France took a chance on a young nation being born. France did not lose by that chance. In the last two generations we have shown our friendship for your great Republic, which stands for liberty, equality, and fraternity—which is what we stand for, too, liberty, equality, and fraternity. Mr. President, I am just as sure as I stand here that the United States of America will never forget its friendship for France.

I don't know whether any of you have ever understood exactly what the First World War and the Second World War meant to France. France lost about a million seven hundred thousand men killed in action in the First World War. If we had lost in that same proportion, it would have been about 5½ millions. France had about 2 million men wounded and disabled. Had it been in the same proportion for the United States, it would have been 6½ millions.

In this last number two war, France had more than 800,000 killed and 187,000, I think, if I am not mistaken, murdered after it was all over—after hostilities ceased in France.

If we had had the whole Mississippi Valley destroyed, every city from New Orleans to Minneapolis and a hundred miles on each side, we would have been probably—comparatively speaking—in the condition that France was in after the First World War and after the Second World War.

We can't appreciate it, because that did not happen to us; and we can't appreciate what happened to Britain, we can't appreciate what happened to Holland, Belgium, and Norway, and all those countries of central Europe that have been devastated and the people taken to slave labor camps because they believed in liberty.

Now, our objective, our whole objective, is peace in the world. That is what we are trying to attain. And to attain peace in the world, we want to raise that Iron Curtain and make France, Britain, Belgium, Holland, and Norway, and those countries who stayed with us through the fight, free and equal with the rest of mankind in the world, so that they will not suffer from fear of being overrun once more in another generation.

That is all we are working for. That is the objective of the Marshall plan. That is the objective of the Atlantic Pact, that is the objective of the Western Hemisphere pact, the ministers of which are now meeting here in Washington to continue to implement the policy which we are trying to pursue.

Mr. President, it gives me a great deal of pleasure to toast His Excellency the President of France, Madame Auriol, and the great Republic of France.

NOTE: The President spoke at 10:15 p.m. at the French Embassy in Washington, in response to a toast of President Vincent Auriol of France.

The text of President Auriol's toast was not released.

66 Statement by the President on the Third Anniversary of the European Recovery Program. *April 2, 1951*

ON THIS third anniversary, it gives me great pleasure to congratulate you who have carried out so well the aims of the European recovery program.

When General Marshall first made his proposal, the shadow of economic collapse, with its attendant evils of unemployment, of hunger and political unrest, hung over the countries of Western Europe. The great question in 1947 was whether free institutions could survive.

Today, thanks primarily to their own efforts, the people of Western Europe, together with our help, have rebuilt the economies of their countries and have developed a new spirit of confidence in themselves and in their free institutions. To my mind, this spirit, this rising confidence in the hearts of the people, is one of the greatest sources of strength in the free world.

By working together, economic recovery has been substantially achieved. However, with the present threat to world peace, new tasks have been imposed upon us. The free nations are now combining to convert their resources into military strength to preserve the peace and defend our freedoms.

The splendid organization which has been developed under the Economic Cooperation Administration can make an important contribution in helping develop this strength. Accordingly, I intend to recommend to the Congress that ECA be maintained on a continuing basis to help carry out the programs essential to the security of the free world.

There is much to be done in Europe, in Asia, and in other parts of the world to help the free countries build their military, economic, and spiritual defenses against aggression from without and subversion from within. One of our essential objectives is to develop, in cooperation with other free nations, an expanding world economy, the benefits of which can be shared by us all.

On this anniversary, I extend to all of you my sincere thanks for what you have done. I am confident that in its new tasks the ECA will continue to make a vital contribution in helping to build the strength of the free world upon which security and freedom rest.

NOTE: The statement was read for the President by W. Averell Harriman, Special Assistant to the President, at a meeting held for employees of the Economic Cooperation Administration at the Statler Hotel in Washington. For the statement by the President upon signing the Foreign Assisance Act on April 3, 1948, see the 1948 volume, this series, Item 64.

67 The President's Toast at a Dinner for the Foreign Ministers of the Pan American Union. *April 2, 1951*

Your Excellencies the Foreign Ministers of our sister Republics, and Ambassadors who represent you here, Mr. Vice President, Mr. Chief Justice, Mr. Speaker:

The is a most happy occasion for me. I hope that you have enjoyed your visit here as much as we have enjoyed having you.

From what I can hear from the Secretary of State, you have made great progress as a result of this most important meeting of the foreign ministers of the 21 Republics of the Western Hemisphere.

The President of France, I think, made a very great address to your organization, in which he emphasized the necessity for complete cooperation, not only in this hemisphere but among all the free countries of the world, if we do not expect to be completely overwhelmed by a theory of government in which none of us believes.

It gives me great pleasure tonight to have had you as guests of the President of the United States. It also gives me very great pleasure to offer a toast—not in the Russian style. Were we to do it in the Russian style we would drink 21 toasts. In this instance I shall offer a toast to the 20 Presidents of the sister Republics of the Western Hemisphere.

NOTE: The President proposed the toast at a stag dinner at the Carlton Hotel in Washington. In his opening words he referred to the foreign ministers and ambassadors of the 21 nations comprising the Pan American Union, Alben W. Barkley, Vice President of the United States, Fred M. Vinson, Chief Justice of the United States, and Sam Rayburn, Speaker of the House of Representatives. Later the President referred to Dean Acheson, Secretary of State, and to President Vincent Auriol of France, who had addressed a meeting of the foreign ministers in Washington on March 31.

Foreign Minister Manuel C. Gallagher of Peru responded with an address and a toast.

68 Address at the Cornerstone Laying of the New York Avenue Presbyterian Church. *April 3, 1951*

Dr. Docherty, ladies and gentlemen:

Speaking of that foundation, Doctor, it's too bad you didn't have to listen to the laying of the foundation of the White House. It's on the same sort of soil as your church is located. If you remember, they had to put a foundation under the Washington Monument because they didn't start it right, for the very same reason that you had to put this foundation under your church. And I think we are told in the Scriptures that if we build our house on a rock, it will stand, even if we have to manufacture that rock.

It is a great privilege for me to be able to take part in this service. The New York Avenue Presbyterian Church has played an important part in the history of Washington. For almost 150 years a Presbyterian congregation has worshiped on or near this spot. During all that period, this church has preached the Christian message to this busy Capital City.

As you have remarked, Doctor, several of our Presidents worshiped here, and of course among them the most famous, Lincoln.

This new building demonstrates that you are still going forward in the same spirit which moved those early worshipers who first came to the swamps and woodland of this National Capital a century and a half ago. May you long continue in that same missionary spirit.

The essential mission of the church is to teach the moral law. We look to our churches, above all other agencies, to teach us the highest moral standards of right and wrong. We rely on the churches particularly to instill into our young people those moral ideals which are the basis of our free institutions.

This great Republic is founded on a firm foundation based on those very principles— the Constitution of the United States.

Religion is not an easy thing. It is not simply a comfort to those in trouble or a means of escaping from present difficulties, as some people today would have us believe.

Religion is not a negative thing. It is not merely a series of prohibitions against certain actions because they are wicked.

Our religion includes these elements. But it also includes much more. It is a positive force that impels us to affirmative action. We are under divine orders—not only to refrain from doing evil, but also to do good and to make this world a better place in which to live.

Every one of us should measure the actions of his daily life against this moral code which our religion gives us. Every one of us, according to the strength and wisdom God gives to him, should try his best every day to live up to these religious teachings.

More than this, religion should establish moral standards for the conduct of our whole Nation, at home and abroad. We should judge our achievements, as a nation, in the scales of right and wrong.

The democracy we cherish and our free institutions depend upon the observance of the moral code—in private life and also in public life. Selfishness and greed can tear this Nation apart, just as they have torn apart other great nations in the past. Our only defense against them is to follow those moral principles which have been handed down to us by our forefathers and which are enshrined today in churches such as this one.

We talk a lot these days about freedom— freedom for the individual and freedom among nations. Freedom for the human soul is, indeed, the most important principle of our civilization. We must always remember, however, that the freedom we are talking about is freedom based upon moral principles. Without a firm moral foundation, freedom degenerates quickly into selfishness and license. Unless men exercise their freedom in a just and honest way, within moral restraints, a free society can degenerate into anarchy. Then there will be freedom only for the rapacious and those who are stronger and more unscrupulous than the rank and file of the people.

If we neglect these truths, our whole society suffers.

This is readily apparent in the case of some of the evils that continually confront us. For example, when organized crime and vice run loose and are accepted and patronized by the people, they threaten our free institutions and debase our national life. These evils are clearly moral issues and our religious beliefs command us to fight against them.

It is not so readily apparent that moral issues are involved in some of the other evils we have been fighting against in this country. But it is nevertheless true that the evils of the sweatshop and the slum, the evils of needless disease and poverty, and the evils of social injustice are, at the bottom, moral issues. Such conditions arise because men have neglected the moral law. They arise because men do not actually live up to the religious principles they profess to believe in.

When we move to correct these evils, through our personal conduct, through community action, or through the Government, we are responding to the divine command— to the Golden Rule—which requires us to do unto others as we would be done by.

Of course, this is a struggle that is never finally won. There are many injustices in our country that need correction today, and need them badly. We must continue to weigh our national life in the scales of justice, and keep on striving to improve it.

In the world at large, as well as in our domestic affairs, we must apply moral standards to our national conduct. At the present time our Nation is engaged in a great effort to maintain justice and peace in the world. An essential feature of this effort is our program to build up the defenses of our country.

There has never been a greater cause. There has never been a cause which had a stronger moral claim on all of us.

We are defending the religious principles upon which our Nation and our whole way of life are founded. We are defending the right to worship God—each as he sees fit according to his own conscience. We are defending the right to follow the precepts and the example which God has set for us. We are defending the right of people to gather together, all across our land, in churches such as this one.

For the danger that threatens us in the world today is utterly and totally opposed to all these things. The international Communist movement is based on a fierce and terrible fanaticism. It denies the existence of God and, wherever it can, it stamps out the worship of God.

Our religious faith gives us the answer to the false beliefs of communism. Our faith shows us the way to create a society where man can find his greatest happiness under God. Surely, we can follow that faith with the same devotion and determination the Communists give to their godless creed.

That is what we must do. Our religion must live in our hearts, not as a set of dull rules learned by rote, but as a burning faith. Only such a faith—only a living allegiance to such a faith—can carry this country through the trials which are ahead of it.

This is a matter that comes home to every one of us. We have many different jobs to do and different parts to play in our country's defense of its freedom and its beliefs.

If each of us, wherever he may be—in a factory or a mine, on a farm or in an office, or in the home—if each of us does his best to help, we need have no fear of the outcome.

We should continue to ask ourselves whether we are responding to this cause with the moral conviction and the faith which it demands.

Every day our newspapers tell us about the fighting in Korea. Our men there are making heroic sacrifices. They are fighting and suffering in an effort to prevent the tide of aggression from sweeping across the world. They are fighting to prevent the much greater sacrifice and suffering which

all of us would endure if another world war comes.

Although we read about these sacrifices in our newspapers every day, we have a tendency to think of the defense effort only in selfish terms—in terms of avoiding personal inconvenience or making some personal gain. Our young men are offering their lives for us in the hills of Korea—and yet too many of us are chiefly concerned over whether or not we can buy a television set next week, or make the profit we expect to make this year, or how we can turn the situation to our own selfish advantage.

This is a failure to understand the moral principles upon which our Nation is founded. This is a faltering in our allegiance to the moral faith we have inherited from our fathers.

If we truly believe in God, we ought to ask ourselves what He may be thinking of our present attitude and our present conduct. Considering all the advantages that God has given us as a nation and all the mercies that He has shown to us from our very beginnings, we ought to ask ourselves whether we today are worthy of all that He has done for us. We ought to ask ourselves whether we, as a people, are doing our part; whether we are carrying out our moral obligations.

I do not think that anyone can study the history of this Nation of ours—study it deeply and earnestly—without becoming convinced that divine providence has played a great part in it. I have the feeling that God has created us and brought us to our present position of power and strength for some great purpose. And up to now we have been shirking it. Now we are assuming it, and now we must carry it through.

It is not given to us to know fully what that purpose is. But I think we may be sure of one thing. That is, that our country is intended to do all it can, in cooperation with other nations, to help create peace and preserve peace in this world. It is given to us to defend the spiritual values—the moral code—against the vast forces of evil that seek to destroy them.

This is a hard task. It is not one that we have asked for. At times, we would like to lay it down. And, as we go on with it, we shall see that it is full of uncertainties and sacrifices.

But we need not be afraid, if we have faith.

There is a lesson for us in the passage from the Bible which has just been read here. That part of the Book of Ezra describes the rebuilding of the temple in Jerusalem after the long captivity in Babylon. You remember how the writer describes the people shouting with a great shout when the foundation of the new temple was laid. And then the author goes on to tell us that some of those in the crowd, particularly the old men, did not shout. They wept when they saw the foundation stones set in place.

These were the men who remembered all the sacrifices—all the suffering of all the people—what their people had undergone during the captivity. They knew that these sacrifices had not been made in vain. They realized that, in spite of all their troubles, and in the face of overwhelming odds, their faith had prevailed. And so they were too deeply moved to shout; they wept for joy.

They gave thanks to God "because He is good, for his mercy endureth forever."

If we hold true to our faith, as they did, I am sure that we will be able to offer, on some future day, the same heartfelt prayer of thanksgiving and joy. We too will be able to give God the glory for the victory of freedom and justice and peace for which we are striving today.

We, too, shall say: "He is good, for His mercy endureth forever."

[*After concluding his address the President presented to the church the silver trowel he had used in laying the cornerstone, as follows.*]

Doctor, it is a great pleasure for me to present to you this trowel, which I myself had specially made for this occasion. I hope this trowel will stand in your church as a symbol of a trowel to spread religion and truth through the congregation and throughout the world.

[*The President then received a copy of the New Testament from Peter John Marshall, son of the late pastor of the church who was also chaplain of the United States Senate at the time of his death. He then resumed speaking.*]

Well, thank you very much for this Testament. I appreciate very much having it. And all I can say to you is, I hope you will grow up to be as good a man as your father.

NOTE: The President spoke at 3:15 p.m. In his opening words he referred to Dr. George M. Docherty, pastor of the New York Avenue Presbyterian Church in Washington.

69 Statement by the President on the Second Anniversary of the Signing of the North Atlantic Treaty. *April 3*, 1951

ON THE second birthday of the North Atlantic Treaty it is appropriate that we take stock of our progress.

The most encouraging fact which stands out today is that Europe is stronger and in a better position to defend itself than it was a year ago.

This stems from the determination of the free peoples of Europe to help themselves. Their determination as well as their strength has been increased by the assistance which we have been able to give them. Even more important, our joint efforts have acquired greater effectiveness through the establishment of General Eisenhower's unified command. For the first time in history there exists in peace an integrated international force whose object is to maintain peace through strength. Six years ago General Eisenhower led such a force to victory, but we devoutly pray that our present course of action will succeed and maintain peace without war.

The armed forces of the North Atlantic Treaty countries will grow more rapidly in the future as stepped-up training and production programs begin to bear fruit. An enormous military production program is underway in the United States, and our allies, despite limited facilities and resources, have already more than doubled their rate of military production.

Just as important as the forces which we are building together is the spirit of cooperation and joint effort which has been greatly strengthened. This is a solid achievement which will bring rewards of happiness and prosperity to our peoples long after the passing of the present emergency.

The events of the past 2 years have proved beyond question the wisdom of the course we adopted in signing the North Atlantic Treaty. Developments since the war have made it more clear than ever before that no nation can find safety behind its own frontiers—that the only security lies in collective security.

While we have reason to take pride in our accomplishments, we cannot forget that the road ahead is still long and hard. The people of the United States and the people of Europe must accept heavy burdens, with both determination and patience. I am confident that we will march forward together, with speed and vigor. Above all, I feel certain that we will not relax the great effort which is now underway.

NOTE: For the President's address on the occasion of the signing of the North Atlantic Treaty on April 4, 1949, see the 1949 volume, this series, Item 68.

The text of the treaty is printed in the U.S. Statutes at Large (63 Stat. 2241), and in the Department of State Bulletin (vol. 20, p. 339).

70   The President's News Conference of *April 5, 1951*

THE PRESIDENT. Please be seated.

[1.] I am very happy this morning to greet the visitors from Latin America. We are glad to have them as guests this morning. I appreciate their coming here.

I have a couple of releases which will be handed to you after this press conference is over.

One is on the adoption of Senate Resolution 99,[1] and the other one is in regard to the request for funds for the Voice of America.[2]

Both of those statements will be available to you after the press conference is over. Any questions in regard to those two things

will be answered in those two releases.

Now I am ready for any questions you want——

Q. I just have a very simple question. What is Resolution 99?

THE PRESIDENT. It's the resolution that has to do with the sending of troops to Europe.

Q. Will you entertain any questions, sir, about that?

THE PRESIDENT. I will listen to them, of course. I will answer them if I feel like it.

Q. I just wonder if the Senate's action will alter your policy in any way regarding sending troops to Europe?

THE PRESIDENT. The only thing under consideration in that resolution is the sending of four divisions, which was approved.

[1] See Item 71.
[2] See Item 72.

Q. Mr. President, how do you feel about the section in which they say that it is essential that you not send more without their approval?

THE PRESIDENT. Well, the situation will develop as we go along. The Senate and the House have always been consulted in any major policy, and that situation will develop in the usual manner. Every part of our foreign policy has been carried out after careful consideration and consultation with both Houses of the Congress from the beginning, since I have been President on April 12, 1945. The policy had been carried out by President Roosevelt, and I continued the policy.

[2.] Q. Mr. President, it has been reported that you will soon submit a complete subsidy program for minerals and farm products in Congress——

THE PRESIDENT. It has not been put up to me yet, so I am not in a position to answer your question. I don't know anything about it.

[3.] Q. Mr. President, do you think that the world crisis is deteriorating, particularly in the Far East, recently?

THE PRESIDENT. I think the crisis under which we issued the Executive order creating the situation with which we are faced, is just as it was in the beginning.[3] And it is necessary for us to carry out our defense program—even more necessary now than it was then—because we are nearing a situation which will accomplish the purpose for which we started out.

[4.] Q. Mr. President, Sam Rayburn, after telling us in the White House yesterday that he discussed the world—that *you* had discussed the world situation with him, took the floor of the House to say that large

---

[3] Proclamation 2914 of December 16, 1950, "Proclaiming the Existence of a National Emergency" (3 CFR, 1949–1953 Comp., p. 99).

numbers of troops were massing in Manchuria, and not all of them by any means were Chinese——

THE PRESIDENT. I have no comment on Speaker Rayburn's statement, but the Speaker is a truthful man.

Q. Mr. President, on your "no comment," he also said that he thought we may be at the beginning of world war III.

THE PRESIDENT. I have no further comment to make on Speaker Rayburn's comment.

Q. I wonder if your statement covered the whole of the——

THE PRESIDENT. No further comment.

Q. Mr. President, aside from your statement, do you think there is a danger of a major world war greater today than at any time, say, since the end of World War II?

THE PRESIDENT. It is just as great as it ever has been. We were faced with that in the Berlin airlift. We were faced with it in Greece and Turkey. We were faced with it in Iran, when the troops of the Allies and Russia moved out of Iran. We were faced with it in Korea as an actual fact on June 25th. That situation has been a dangerous one for the last 5 years—last 4 years, I will say.

Q. Mr. President, do you agree with Senator Connally's belief that there won't be a third world war this year?

THE PRESIDENT. I hope there never will be a third world war. That is what we are trying to prevent. That is the reason for all this preparation.

[5.] Q. Mr. President, these gentlemen seem to think you know whether there is going to be a war or not. Do you know who is going to win the Derby? [*Laughter*]

THE PRESIDENT. Well, I think I have a better chance to get concrete information on that than I have on the other—[*laughter*]—

although I have more information than anybody else in this country on that subject. I
can't give you a tip on the Derby, however.

[6.] Q. Mr. President, are you going to
send a message soon on extending the controls section of the Defense Production Act?

THE PRESIDENT. Yes, that is in the course
of preparation now.[4]

Q. Have you decided whether you will
ask modification of the parity provision in
the act?

THE PRESIDENT. I can't tell you what the
recommendation will contain until I have
finished writing it, but as soon as it is ready
I will see that all of you have a copy of it.

[7.] Q. Mr. President, is Jonathan
Daniels still welcome at the White House?

THE PRESIDENT. Why, of course.

Q. Well, Mr. President, this is—[pause]—
he said——

THE PRESIDENT. What's the matter, May?[5]
[Laughter]

Q. Well, I don't know—[more laugh-
ter]—this is strictly a feminine question.

THE PRESIDENT. All right—go ahead.

Q. Did you say, or do you think that congressional wives think their husbands know
better how to run the country? I mean, he
said in there that you felt that if Congressmen did not think they knew better than you
did how to run the country, at least their
wives did?

THE PRESIDENT. Well, I haven't read the
article. I probably won't read it. The only
comment that has been made on it was made
by Mr. Short, and I back him up in that
comment.[6]

Q. I wonder if it was laudable for wives
to think their husbands know best?

THE PRESIDENT. Of course it is. [More
laughter]

[8.] Q. Mr. President, along the same
line, who are those four or five people that
Hersey said you are going to punch in the
nose?

THE PRESIDENT. I have no comment to
make on that. As I said awhile ago, I
haven't read the article and I know nothing
about the——

Q. This is the Hersey piece.[7]

THE PRESIDENT. Yes, I know—and I don't
intend to read it—I am not interested in it.
People have a right to say what they please
about me if they want to. I have no
objection.

[9.] Q. Mr. President, will your meeting
with the United Labor Policy Committee
this afternoon be confined to the mobilization advisory board, or will you spread it
out to cover other things?

THE PRESIDENT. I can't answer a question
like that because the meeting has not taken
place yet. After it is over, I will tell you
what took place.

[10.] Q. Mr. President, will Mr.
Churchill visit you?

THE PRESIDENT. Why, of course. He
wouldn't think of coming to this country
without coming to see me, and I wouldn't
think of going to Great Britain without
going to see him, either.

[11.] Q. Well, that reminds me also——

THE PRESIDENT. All right, May.

Q. Austine Cassini[8] said this morning

---

[4] See Items 91, 176, 199.

[5] Mrs. May Craig of the Portland (Maine) Press
Herald.

[6] "What Truman Would Do to Congress," by
Jonathan Daniels, a former aide to Presidents
Roosevelt and Truman. The article appeared in the
April 14th edition of Colliers' magazine.

[7] The article by John Hersey, entitled "The Wayward Press; President Truman's Press Conference,
November 30th" appeared in the New Yorker magazine on December 16, 1950. For the press conference to which the article referred, see 1950 volume,
this series, Item 295.

[8] Writer and columnist.

that you and Mrs. Truman were going to Paris with Miss Margaret and that you would probably stop in on the King and Queen of England on your way back?

THE PRESIDENT. May, no such plans have been made, because my presence is needed right here in this country. The fact that I went to Key West gave a lot of people spasms and jitters, so I couldn't think about going outside the country!

[12.] Q. Mr. President, this massing of troops in Manchuria, are you——

THE PRESIDENT. I can't comment on that, and I don't intend to answer any further questions on it at all.

[13.] Q. Mr. President, I want to ask you one thing. Provided that you did have some people in mind that you would like to punch their noses, after you step out, would you be punching in 1952 or 1956?

THE PRESIDENT. Tony,[9] let's wait until developments take place. Your question will answer itself. [*Laughter*]

[14.] Q. Do you think the tax increase of $10 billion is enough to drain off enough buying power?

THE PRESIDENT. Mr. Snyder spoke for the administration when he appeared before the committee. You will get your answer from

---

[9] Ernest B. Vaccaro of the Associated Press.

Mr. Snyder's statement to the committee.[10]

[15.] Q. Mr. President, has General MacArthur been authorized to bomb bases in Manchuria?

THE PRESIDENT. That is a question that cannot be answered because it is a military strategy question, and it is not a question that I can answer.

Q. I wonder if we could have that question——

THE PRESIDENT. He asked me if General MacArthur had been authorized to bomb bases in Manchuria, and I said that is a military strategy question that I cannot answer.

Tony, how do you decipher all those things? I see you are messing it all up. You write a little in one place, and then you go down and write in between.

Q. It isn't easy! [*Laughter*]

Q. Have you got anything else on your mind, Mr. President?

THE PRESIDENT. No, I haven't.

Reporter: Thank you, Mr. President.

NOTE: President Truman's two hundred and fifty-ninth news conference was held in the Indian Treaty Room (Room 474) in the Executive Office Building at 10:30 a.m. on Thursday, April 5, 1951.

---

[10] On April 2 Secretary of the Treasury John W. Snyder, testifying before the House Committee on Ways and Means, stated that the administration was going to reduce its request for additional taxes to $10 billion.

---

71   Statement by the President on Senate Resolution 99.
April 5, 1951

THE ADOPTION by the Senate of Senate Resolution 99 is further evidence that the country stands firm in its support of the North Atlantic Treaty. It reaffirms the basic principle of our foreign policy—that the security of the United States is intimately bound up with the security of other free nations.

The clear endorsement of the appointment of General Eisenhower and the plans to assign troops to his command shows that there has never been any real question but that this country would do its part in helping to create an integrated European defense force.

Our main task now is to get on with the

job of building our own strength and help to build the strength of the free world—a job which we all agree should continue to be carried out through collaboration by the executive and the legislative branches of the Government.

NOTE: Senate Resolution 99 is published in the Congressional Record (vol. 97, p. 3282) and in the State Department Bulletin (vol. 24, p. 637).

72 Statement by the President on the Voice of America. *April 5, 1951*

THERE IS now pending before the Congress a request for funds to build a worldwide network of radio broadcasting facilities. These facilities are needed to help us win the battle for the minds and hearts of men. They would help us hold our own in the vital communications field in the event of war.

I understand that some Members of Congress advocate sharply reducing funds needed for these facilities. I find it hard to believe that this report could be true since it would constitute a complete reversal of the House Appropriation Subcommittee's action last summer when the entire broadcasting facilities plan was put before the committee.

In approving the first segment of the total plan at that time, the committee stated that: "The committee is firmly convinced of the absolute and immediate necessity of these appropriations which are so closely connected with our national defense and security." These facilities would help us hold our own in the vital communications field in the event of war.

While it had been expected to request funds for the worldwide network of radio facilites over a period of 3 fiscal years, I directed the State Department that it should request funds for the entire project immediately in order that it might be completed as soon as possible in the interest of national security.

The completion of this radio facilities expansion program is necessary to insure the delivery by radio of our campaign of truth to the people behind the Iron Curtain. The facilites program has been developed since the initiation of Soviet radio jamming which seriously interfered with American and other free world broadcasts. The program was worked out with leading electronics scientists in universities and private industries as well as in Government.

NOTE: For the appropriation for the Voice of America see the Departments of State, Justice, Commerce, and the Judiciary Appropriation Act, 1952, approved October 22, 1951 (65 Stat. 575).

73 Letter to the President of the Red Cross on the Progress of the Fund Campaign. *April 6, 1951*

[Released April 6, 1951.   Dated April 5, 1951]

Dear Mr. Harriman:

I have been watching with the deepest interest the progress of the 1951 Red Cross Fund Campaign. I want to congratulate the millions of Americans who have already responded to this great cause. I want also to compliment you and the great band of other active Red Cross workers for your efforts.

But above all, I want everyone—particularly those who have not yet made their ·contribution—to know how vital the success of this campaign is to the welfare of our armed services and to our people.

Never in its glorious history has the Red Cross had such urgent tasks. It is serving our fighting men on the battlefields and at the training centers. It is training volunteers for civil defense for the welfare of the people at home if ever attacked. It is gathering blood to save military and civilian lives. These and other tasks have grown steadily as a consequence of the nation's need to mobilize for defense. If our countrymen are informed of these needs, I am sure they will subscribe and oversubscribe the campaign goal.

I urge my fellow Americans to give generously and promptly to the 1951 Red Cross Fund Campaign.

Very sincerely yours,

HARRY S. TRUMAN

[Mr. E. Roland Harriman, President, The American National Red Cross, National Headquarters, Washington 13, D.C.]

NOTE: Mr. Harriman's letter, dated March 30, was released with the President's reply. The letter stated that the Red Cross fund campaign was falling short of its goal and that a substantial increase in the original fund estimates would be needed because of the additional responsibilities placed upon the Red Cross by the Korean conflict.

74 Letter to the Economic Stabilization Administrator on the Problem of Wage Stabilization in the Transportation Industry. *April 6*, 1951

My dear Mr. Johnston:

On March 1, 1951 a collective bargaining agreement was signed between the carriers represented by the Eastern, Western, and Southeastern Carrier's Conference Committees and the non-operating employees represented by the Fifteen Cooperating Railway Labor Organizations.

At present, there is no functioning administrative machinery by which this agreement can be reviewed and either approved or rejected in whole or in part in the light of wage stabilization rules and regulations.

As you know, the settlement of labor disputes in the transportation industry is covered by the Railway Labor Act of 1926. Traditionally, the Government has provided separate machinery to deal with the distinctive problems of the transportation industry. During World War II, the established machinery for settlement of labor disputes in transportation was altered somewhat by the creation of a National Railway Labor Panel which under certain circumstances investigated disputes and reported thereon to the President. (E.O. 9172, May 22, 1942). Subsequent to the National War Labor Board's assumption of wage stabilization responsibilities, the National Railway Labor Panel was assigned certain responsibilities relating to the application of wage stabilization policies to the transportation industry subject to the Railway Labor Act of 1926. (E.O. 9299, February 4, 1943). Such recommendations became final unless and except to the extent the Economic Stabilization Director otherwise directed.

As experience demonstrates, there are many advantages in combining the wage stabilization functions and the labor dispute settlement function within the same agency. I wish that you would examine ways and means by which the officials now responsible for the settlement of labor disputes in the in transportation was altered somewhat by ter the wage stabilization program in that industry, subject to your direction and control in conformity with the Defense Production Act of 1950. In exploring this matter you will want to work with officials of the National Mediation Board.

I ask that you submit to me your views and recommendations on the general matter. Considerable care will have to be taken in devising sound and workable procedures and organizational relationships. The task is to facilitate administration of the wage stabilization program and use to the best advantage the existing resources of the National Mediation Board.

In the meantime, it is essential that some interim machinery be established whereby the agreement in the "non-operating" case be reviewed and recommendations for action be submitted to you. Accordingly, I am asking that you immediately establish an emergency panel to consider the "non-operating" case on its merits and to submit recommendations to you promptly regarding its disposition. Such recommendations

could be made effective upon the approval of the Administrator. This emergency panel might also be directed by you to consider other wage cases in the transportation industry pending the establishment of more permanent machinery.

Sincerely yours,

HARRY S. TRUMAN

[Honorable Eric Johnston, Economic Stabilization Administrator, Washington, D.C.]

NOTE: On April 9 the Administrator established a Temporary Emergency Railroad Wage Panel. The panel conducted open hearings on April 13 on the problems posed by the March 1, 1951, agreement referred to in the President's letter. The panel's report led to the issuance by the Administrator of Wage Adjustment Order 1 (April 24, 1951; 16 F.R. 3559).

With respect to the President's statement as to the need for permanent stabilization machinery, the National Advisory Board on Mobilization Policy recommended on April 17 that the Wage Stabilization Board be reconstituted. On April 21, 1951, the President signed Executive Order 10233 "Amending Executive Order 10161 with Respect to Wage Stabilization and Settlement of Labor Disputes" (3 CFR, 1949–1953 Comp., p. 743).

---

75   Statement by the President on Making Public the Report of the Commission on Migratory Labor.   *April 7*, 1951

I HAVE today received the report of the Commission on Migratory Labor which I appointed in June 1950. I asked this Commission to investigate the whole range of problems associated with the use of migratory labor to meet agricultural labor needs.

This report makes an impressive contribution to a subject which should be of serious concern to all of us. It will be useful to Government officials and the general public alike.

The report contains a careful and painstaking collection of the basic facts about social, economic, health, and educational conditions among migratory workers. It analyzes in detail the forces which have caused increasing use of migrants, particularly foreign

workers, in agriculture. It deals systematically with basic public policy issues.

The report suggests that primary reliance must be placed on the use—and better use—of our domestic farm labor force. The report makes a number of suggestions and recommendations for Federal and State legislative and administrative action.

The report represents diligent and careful work on the part of the Commission and deserves the careful consideration of all of us—of the Congress, the executive agencies, and the general public.

I want to thank the members of this Commission for their efforts. Their contribution will assist greatly in developing fair and practical solutions to what is admittedly a complicated problem.

NOTE: The President's Commission on Migratory Labor was established on June 3, 1950, by Executive Order 10129 (3 CFR, 1949–1953 Comp., p. 317).

For the White House statement announcing the establishment of the Commission, see 1950 volume, this series, Item 153.

The report of the Commission is entitled "Migratory Labor in American Agriculture" (Government Printing Office, 1951, 188 pp.).

76 The President's Toast at a Dinner in His Honor Given by the Foreign Ministers of the Latin American Republics. *April 7*, 1951

THANK YOU very much. I can't begin to express to you my appreciation for your courtesy and kindness in honoring me tonight at this wonderful dinner. I don't think I have ever seen a Statler Hotel dining room set up in a more beautiful and perfect manner than it has been set up for this occasion this evening.

I want to pay tribute to the orchestra. They played those Viennese waltzes, and one of my daughter's songs, "Cielito Lindo," which she sings at nearly every concert. Tonight she is in Corpus Christi, Tex., and will sing a program there on Monday afternoon. I also enjoyed that tango immensely.

Now, Your Excellencies, it is difficult for me to express the full measure of my gratitude for the tribute to me. And I take it that this tribute is to the country and to the President of the United States, and not to me as an individual. You will have to remember that the President of a great country—and all your countries—represents the people, and that you honor him not as an individual—as a private individual—but as the head of a state. And I appreciate that. I thank you in all sincerity on behalf of the people of the United States.

I say to you that our Nation is profoundly appreciative of the honor and the great privilege of having you as distinguished guests on this great and historic occasion.

I thank you, Doctor, for your moving tribute to the spirit of my country. There

is little I can say to amplify Dr. Tello's eloquent statement of what our Americas stand for. As your spokesman, the doctor is my spokesman, too, in expressing the spirit of the Americas, that "permanent, moral reservoir of the human race, always available to all the free peoples of the earth."

Tonight, I think that all the free peoples of the world will feel that they can draw even greater strength from this Western Hemisphere reservoir. The work which you have completed today in your Fourth Meeting of Consultation, exemplifies the ability of free nations to recognize the grave threat to their common security, and to take measures to meet it.

International communism, by subversion, threats, and aggression, seeks to crush and undermine and finally destroy the independence of the Americas, and to impose an alien rule on our lands. We can't let that happen here.

In recognition of that evil intent, we have come together. And today, in the signing of the final act of your meeting, you have proclaimed that the American Republics and their peoples will act in concert to mobilize the moral and spiritual, military and economic strength for the defense of this hemisphere. Further, you have affirmed our common determination to aid freedom-loving peoples everywhere who work for the defeat of Communist tyranny.

That is proof of the vitality of free men

and their institutions. All of us must carry out the programs of emergency cooperation which you have so promptly and wisely advised. It should be carried forward in the same way they were conceived, in an atmosphere of good will and equality.

And, with God's help, we shall and we will persevere until we attain victory in a world where free men can enjoy the fruits of their labor, and live together as good neighbors.

And good neighbors we are. And good neighbors we will continue, from now henceforth; and we hope that we can set an example for the rest of the world, and make all the world good neighbors, with not a single enemy in it.

May I offer a toast to all the American Republics, and to the heads of all those American Republics, and those of you who are gathered here tonight.

NOTE: The President proposed the toast at a dinner at the Statler Hotel in Washington on the evening of the final day of the Fourth Meeting of Consultation of Ministers of Foreign Affairs of American States. Dr. Manuel Tello, Acting Foreign Minister of Mexico, delivered the principal address of the evening.

Excerpts from Document 145, the Final Act of the Fourth Meeting, are published in the Department of State Bulletin (vol. 24, p. 606).

77 Statement and Order by the President on Relieving General MacArthur of His Commands. *April 11, 1951*

[1.] *Statement by the President:*

With deep regret I have concluded that General of the Army Douglas MacArthur is unable to give his wholehearted support to the policies of the United States Government and of the United Nations in matters pertaining to his official duties. In view of the specific responsibilities imposed upon me by the Constitution of the United States and the added responsibility which has been entrusted to me by the United Nations, I have decided that I must make a change of command in the Far East. I have, therefore, relieved General MacArthur of his commands and have designated Lt. Gen. Matthew B. Ridgway as his successor.

Full and vigorous debate on matters of national policy is a vital element in the constitutional system of our free democracy. It is fundamental, however, that military commanders must be governed by the policies and directives issued to them in the manner provided by our laws and Constitution. In time of crisis, this consideration is particularly compelling.

General MacArthur's place in history as one of our greatest commanders is fully established. The Nation owes him a debt of gratitude for the distinguished and exceptional service which he has rendered his country in posts of great responsibility. For that reason I repeat my regret at the necessity for the action I feel compelled to take in his case.

[2.] *Order by the President to General MacArthur:*

I deeply regret that it becomes my duty as President and Commander in Chief of the United States military forces to replace you as Supreme Commander, Allied Powers; Commander in Chief, United Nations Command; Commander in Chief, Far East; and Commanding General, U.S. Army, Far East.

You will turn over your commands, effective at once, to Lt. Gen. Matthew B. Ridgway. You are authorized to have issued such orders as are necessary to complete desired travel to such place as you select.

My reasons for your replacement will be made public concurrently with the delivery to you of the foregoing order, and are contained in the next following message. (See attached Statement by the President.)

NOTE: On April 11 the White House released the text of an order from Secretary of Defense George C. Marshall to Lt. Gen. Matthew B. Ridgway informing him that the President was appointing him to succeed Gen. Douglas MacArthur. He also notified General Ridgway that Lt. Gen. James A. Van Fleet would take his place as commander of the 8th Army in Korea.

On the same day the White House also made public the following:

1. A message, dated December 6, 1950, from the Joint Chiefs of Staff to General MacArthur. The message transmitted the text of a Presidential memorandum, dated December 5, directing that no speech, press release, or other public statement concerning foreign or military policy should be released until cleared by the State Department or the Department of Defense, and further directing that advance copies of speeches or press releases be submitted to the White House.

2. A message, dated March 20, 1951, from the Joint Chiefs of Staff to General MacArthur, informing him that the President was about to announce

that the United Nations was prepared to discuss conditions of settlement in Korea.

3. A statement by General MacArthur, published in the New York Times of March 24, 1951, pointing out the weaknesses of Red China "even under inhibitions which now restrict activity of the United Nations forces and the corresponding military advantages which accrue to Red China." The statement also contained two paragraphs which are noted in Item 108 [2] below.

4. A message, dated March 24, 1951, from the Joint Chiefs of Staff to General MacArthur informing him that the President had directed that his attention be called to the memorandum of December 6, 1950 (1 above), and further informing him that "in view of the information given you 20 March 1951 (2 above) any further statements by you must be coordinated as prescribed in the order of 6 December."

5. A letter to Representative Joseph W. Martin, Jr., House Minority Leader, dated March 20, 1951, which Representative Martin published in the Congressional Record of April 5 (vol. 97, p. 3380), and which spoke of "meeting force with maximum counter force" in the Korean conflict.

78   Radio Report to the American People on Korea and on U.S. Policy in the Far East.   *April* 11, 1951

[Broadcast from the White House at 10:30 p.m.]

My fellow Americans:

I want to talk to you plainly tonight about what we are doing in Korea and about our policy in the Far East.

In the simplest terms, what we are doing in Korea is this: We are trying to prevent a third world war.

I think most people in this country recognized that fact last June. And they warmly supported the decision of the Government to help the Republic of Korea against the Communist aggressors. Now, many persons, even some who applauded our decision to defend Korea, have forgotten the basic reason for our action.

It is right for us to be in Korea now. It was right last June. It is right today.

I want to remind you why this is true.

The Communists in the Kremlin are en-

gaged in a monstrous conspiracy to stamp out freedom all over the world. If they were to succeed, the United States would be numbered among their principal victims. It must be clear to everyone that the United States cannot—and will not—sit idly by and await foreign conquest. The only question is: What is the best time to meet the threat and how is the best way to meet it?

The best time to meet the threat is in the beginning. It is easier to put out a fire in the beginning when it is small than after it has become a roaring blaze. And the best way to meet the threat of aggression is for the peace-loving nations to act together. If they don't act together, they are likely to be picked off, one by one.

If they had followed the right policies in the 1930's—if the free countries had acted together to crush the aggression of the dictators, and if they had acted in the beginning when the aggression was small—there probably would have been no World War II.

If history has taught us anything, it is that aggression anywhere in the world is a threat to the peace everywhere in the world. When that aggression is supported by the cruel and selfish rulers of a powerful nation who are bent on conquest, it becomes a clear and present danger to the security and independence of every free nation.

This is a lesson that most people in this country have learned thoroughly. This is the basic reason why we joined in creating the United Nations. And, since the end of World War II, we have been putting that lesson into practice—we have been working with other free nations to check the aggressive designs of the Soviet Union before they can result in a third world war.

That is what we did in Greece, when that nation was threatened by the aggression of international communism.

The attack against Greece could have led to general war. But this country came to the aid of Greece. The United Nations supported Greek resistance. With our help, the determination and efforts of the Greek people defeated the attack on the spot.

Another big Communist threat to peace was the Berlin blockade. That too could have led to war. But again it was settled because free men would not back down in an emergency.

The aggression against Korea is the boldest and most dangerous move the Communists have yet made.

The attack on Korea was part of a greater plan for conquering all of Asia.

I would like to read to you from a secret intelligence report which came to us after the attack on Korea. It is a report of a speech a Communist army officer in North Korea gave to a group of spies and saboteurs

last May, 1 month before South Korea was invaded. The report shows in great detail how this invasion was part of a carefully prepared plot. Here, in part, is what the Communist officer, who had been trained in Moscow, told his men: "Our forces," he said, "are scheduled to attack South Korean forces about the middle of June. . . . The coming attack on South Korea marks the first step toward the liberation of Asia."

Notice that he used the word "liberation." This is Communist doubletalk meaning "conquest."

I have another secret intelligence report here. This one tells what another Communist officer in the Far East told his men several months before the invasion of Korea. Here is what he said: "In order to successfully undertake the long-awaited world revolution, we must first unify Asia. . . . Java, Indochina, Malaya, India, Tibet, Thailand, Philippines, and Japan are our ultimate targets. . . . The United States is the only obstacle on our road for the liberation of all the countries in southeast Asia. In other words, we must unify the people of Asia and crush the United States." Again, "liberation" in "commie" language means conquest.

That is what the Communist leaders are telling their people, and that is what they have been trying to do.

They want to control all Asia from the Kremlin.

This plan of conquest is in flat contradiction to what we believe. We believe that Korea belong to the Koreans, we believe that India belongs to the Indians, we believe that all the nations of Asia should be free to work out their affairs in their own way. This is the basis of peace in the Far East, and it is the basis of peace everywhere else.

The whole Communist imperialism is back of the attack on peace in the Far East. It was the Soviet Union that trained and equipped the North Koreans for aggression.

The Chinese Communists massed 44 well-trained and well-equipped divisions on the Korean frontier. These were the troops they threw into battle when the North Korean Communists were beaten.

The question we have had to face is whether the Communist plan of conquest can be stopped without a general war. Our Government and other countries associated with us in the United Nations believe that the best chance of stopping it without a general war is to meet the attack in Korea and defeat it there.

That is what we have been doing. It is a difficult and bitter task.

But so far it has been successful.

So far, we have prevented world war III.

So far, by fighting a limited war in Korea, we have prevented aggression from succeeding, and bringing on a general war. And the ability of the whole free world to resist Communist aggression has been greatly improved.

We have taught the enemy a lesson. He has found that aggression is not cheap or easy. Moreover, men all over the world who want to remain free have been given new courage and new hope. They know now that the champions of freedom can stand up and fight, and that they will stand up and fight.

Our resolute stand in Korea is helping the forces of freedom now fighting in Indochina and other countries in that part of the world. It has already slowed down the timetable of conquest.

In Korea itself there are signs that the enemy is building up his ground forces for a new mass offensive. We also know that there have been large increases in the enemy's available air forces.

If a new attack comes, I feel confident it will be turned back. The United Nations fighting forces are tough and able and well equipped. They are fighting for a just cause. They are proving to all the world that the principle of collective security will work. We are proud of all these forces for the magnificent job they have done against heavy odds. We pray that their efforts may succeed, for upon their success may hinge the peace of the world.

The Communist side must now choose its course of action. The Communist rulers may press the attack against us. They may take further action which will spread the conflict. They have that choice, and with it the awful responsibility for what may follow. The Communists also have the choice of a peaceful settlement which could lead to a general relaxation of the tensions in the Far East. The decision is theirs, because the forces of the United Nations will strive to limit the conflict if possible.

We do not want to see the conflict in Korea extended. We are trying to prevent a world war—not to start one. And the best way to do that is to make it plain that we and the other free countries will continue to resist the attack.

But you may ask why can't we take other steps to punish the aggressor. Why don't we bomb Manchuria and China itself? Why don't we assist the Chinese Nationalist troops to land on the mainland of China?

If we were to do these things we would be running a very grave risk of starting a general war. If that were to happen, we would have brought about the exact situation we are trying to prevent.

If we were to do these things, we would become entangled in a vast conflict on the continent of Asia and our task would become immeasurably more difficult all over the world.

What would suit the ambitions of the Kremlin better than for our military forces to be committed to a full-scale war with Red China?

It may well be that, in spite of our best

efforts, the Communists may spread the war. But it would be wrong—tragically wrong—for us to take the initiative in extending the war.

The dangers are great. Make no mistake about it. Behind the North Koreans and Chinese Communists in the front lines stand additional millions of Chinese soldiers. And behind the Chinese stand the tanks, the planes, the submarines, the soldiers, and the scheming rulers of the Soviet Union.

Our aim is to avoid the spread of the conflict.

The course we have been following is the one best calculated to avoid an all-out war. It is the course consistent with our obligation to do all we can to maintain international peace and security. Our experience in Greece and Berlin shows that it is the most effective course of action we can follow.

First of all, it is clear that our efforts in Korea can blunt the will of the Chinese Communists to continue the struggle. The United Nations forces have put up a tremendous fight in Korea and have inflicted very heavy casualties on the enemy. Our forces are stronger now than they have been before. These are plain facts which may discourage the Chinese Communists from continuing their attack.

Second, the free world as a whole is growing in military strength every day. In the United States, in Western Europe, and throughout the world, free men are alert to the Soviet threat and are building their defenses. This may discourage the Communist rulers from continuing the war in Korea—and from undertaking new acts of aggression elsewhere.

If the Communist authorities realize that they cannot defeat us in Korea, if they realize it would be foolhardy to widen the hostilities beyond Korea, then they may recognize the folly of continuing their aggression. A peaceful settlement may then be possible.

The door is always open.

Then we may achieve a settlement in Korea which will not compromise the principles and purposes of the United Nations.

I have thought long and hard about this question of extending the war in Asia. I have discussed it many times with the ablest military advisers in the country. I believe with all my heart that the course we are following is the best course.

I believe that we must try to limit the war to Korea for these vital reasons: to make sure that the precious lives of our fighting men are not wasted; to see that the security of our country and the free world is not needlessly jeopardized; and to prevent a third world war.

A number of events have made it evident that General MacArthur did not agree with that policy. I have therefore considered it essential to relieve General MacArthur so that there would be no doubt or confusion as to the real purpose and aim of our policy.

It was with the deepest personal regret that I found myself compelled to take this action. General MacArthur is one of our greatest military commanders. But the cause of world peace is much more important than any individual.

The change in commands in the Far East means no change whatever in the policy of the United States. We will carry on the fight in Korea with vigor and determination in an effort to bring the war to a speedy and successful conclusion. The new commander, Lt. Gen. Matthew Ridgway, has already demonstrated that he has the great qualities of military leadership needed for this task.

We are ready, at any time, to negotiate for a restoration of peace in the area. But we will not engage in appeasement. We are only interested in real peace.

Real peace can be achieved through a settlement based on the following factors:

One: The fighting must stop.

Two: Concrete steps must be taken to insure that the fighting will not break out again.

Three: There must be an end to the aggression.

A settlement founded upon these elements would open the way for the unification of Korea and the withdrawal of all foreign forces.

In the meantime, I want to be clear about our military objective. We are fighting to resist an outrageous aggression in Korea. We are trying to keep the Korean conflict from spreading to other areas. But at the same time we must conduct our military activities so as to insure the security of our forces. This is essential if they are to continue the fight until the enemy abandons its ruthless attempt to destroy the Republic of Korea.

That is our military objective—to repel attack and to restore peace.

In the hard fighting in Korea, we are proving that collective action among nations is not only a high principle but a workable means of resisting aggression. Defeat of aggression in Korea may be the turning point in the world's search for a practical way of achieving peace and security.

The struggle of the United Nations in Korea is a struggle for peace.

Free nations have united their strength in an effort to prevent a third world war.

That war can come if the Communist rulers want it to come. But this Nation and its allies will not be responsible for its coming.

We do not want to widen the conflict. We will use every effort to prevent that disaster. And in so doing, we know that we are following the great principles of peace, freedom, and justice.

79   Statement by the President on the Invitation to General MacArthur To Address a Joint Session of Congress.   *April 13, 1951*

I AM happy to learn from Speaker Rayburn that Congress is planning to invite General MacArthur to address the Members of both Houses. I regard it as fitting that Congress bestow this honor on one of our great military men.

80   Address at the Jefferson-Jackson Day Dinner.   *April 14, 1951*

Mr. Chairman, Mr. Vice President, Mr. Speaker, fellow Americans:

It gives a man a feeling of great humility, and a feeling of great inadequacy, when he hears the wonderful statements which have been made here tonight about his responsibilities and his ability. I hope I can fulfill the things that are necessary to meet those responsibilities.

This is a meeting of Democrats. More important than that, it is a meeting of Americans. It is a meeting of Americans who put the welfare of their country first.

This is a time when all Americans should put their country first. This is no time for business as usual—or for politics as usual.

There are some people, I am sorry to say, who are playing petty politics, right now, with the future of the country and the peace of the world at stake. These people seem to think that it is more important to win the next election than it is to prevent another world war.

I don't want any Democrat to have any such ideas. I want every Democrat to put patriotism above politics.

My friends, our country is in deadly danger. We face a powerful and ruthless enemy. The only way we can prevail over that enemy is for every man and woman in this country to put national interest above personal interest.

What we are trying to do is to establish peace in the world. And the only way you can have peace in the world is to bring about international law and order.

The men we are honoring here tonight—Thomas Jefferson and Andrew Jackson—knew that.

In their day the United States was small and weak.

Nevertheless, Jefferson and Jackson stood up for international law and order. They worked for peace, but they would not stoop to appeasement. They knew that the United States could not be safe unless it was willing to fight for what was right.

When Jefferson was President, our merchant ships were attacked by the Barbary pirates who ruled the north coast of Africa. Those pirates lived by robbery and human slavery. They were collecting huge sums of money in tribute from European nations. Then the Barbary pirates began to demand that the United States pay them millions of dollars for leaving our ships alone. They were arrogant, they were brutal, and they got away with it until someone finally stood up against them.

Jefferson decided to put a stop to the whole thing. He knew that there were times when a country has to fight against international crime. He sent the United States Navy to Africa. He sent the Marines ashore

at Tripoli. He carried the battle to the enemy nearly 5,000 miles away from the United States.

We smashed the power of those bandits, and we won the praise and gratitude of the world. The Pope at that time, Pius VII, declared, "The American commander, with a small force and in a short space of time, has done more for the cause of Christianity than the most powerful nations of Christendom have done for ages."

Now, Jefferson did not believe this Nation could submit to pirates, and neither do we. There is no room for piracy in a free world.

Now, as then, there are times when our country has to fight for law and order.

Today, however, the danger we face is not just a gang of pirates in one part of the world. It is a danger that threatens every nation on earth, every religious faith, every home, and every person in this land. It is the danger that arises from the plans of the Kremlin to conquer the civilized world.

The rulers of the Kremlin have abandoned any serious attempt to improve the lives of the peoples they control. They are taking the men and women and the resources under their control and welding them into a mighty machine for war and conquest. They think they can divide the democratic nations and overthrow them one by one.

If they can do that, they will succeed in isolating and surrounding the United States. Then we should either have to fight a terrible war, against great odds—or yield to the demands of the Kremlin.

Either alternative would be a desperate one.

We must meet this threat just as firmly as Jefferson met the threat of the Barbary pirates.

There is no higher purpose to which we can dedicate ourselves as Democrats and Americans.

228

For 5 years we have been checking and countering the threats of Communist expansion—all around the world. We have been helping to strengthen free nations to stand up and resist this pressure. Our policy thwarted the Soviet master plan of expansion. So the Communist leaders resorted to open aggression.

This called for a showdown.

The free world gave its answer.

We went to the defense of Korea.

When we did that, nearly everyone in the United States approved. Nearly everyone but the Communists—everyone but the Communists—agreed that it was the only thing to do. But now, there are people who say we should not have done it. There are people who say we should get out of Korea.

These people are making a terrible mistake. They think that we could stop the fight if we got out of Korea. That is not true.

If we got out of Korea, the Communist leaders would strike somewhere else. They would strike at Japan, or the Middle East, or in Europe. And sooner or later they would go on to strike at South America and at our own country.

We do not have a choice between fighting in Korea and not fighting at all. Our choice lies between fighting in Korea or fighting somewhere else—somewhere more difficult— and probably somewhat closer to home.

Our struggle against aggression in Korea has had profound effects.

First, it is preventing our Communist enemy from carrying out his plans. By fighting in Korea, we have kept the rulers of the Kremlin from conquering other countries on their list.

Second, it has given the free world warning, and what is vastly more important, time to begin building up its own defenses. We fight for time. Our struggle has made it clear, not only here, but abroad, that the free world must prepare to defend itself.

Third, our firm stand in Korea has placed a great strain on the whole system of dictatorship. Dictators cannot survive continued reverses. Cracks are already beginning to appear in the structure of international communism.

I do not want to hear anyone say that our effort in Korea has been wasted. Our men there have been fighting for you and for me—for every one of us; for our homes, our futures, and the future of our children—just as surely as if they were fighting on our own soil.

They are fighting in Korea to save us from having to fight on our own soil.

My friends, they are fighting to prevent the sacrifices and suffering of a third world war.

It is important to remember that our purpose in Korea is to stop the world war that would result if Communist aggression were to go unchecked. Our purpose is to restore peace.

If the Communist leaders have learned the lesson that aggression will not be tolerated by the free nations of the world, it should be possible to reach a peaceful settlement in Korea. But it must be settled on a basis that will protect the objectives for which the United Nations are fighting.

To reach such a settlement the Soviet and Chinese Communist leaders must abandon their aggression.

On that point there can be no compromise.

We will not engage in appeasement.

We will make no deals that would reward aggression.

Let there be no mistake in the Kremlin. We want peace—in Korea and in the rest of the world. But we will not give in to aggression.

We know that appeasement does not lead

to peace. Appeasement leads to war. Our efforts to prevent war must be founded upon the preservation of freedom and justice.

That is why we are supporting the United Nations.

That is why we are aiding the free countries to build their economic strength.

That is why we are building up our own military defenses, and helping other free nations to build theirs.

These are basic elements of our foreign policy.

Our foreign policy is a world policy, a policy for world peace—peace not only in the Western Hemisphere, but peace in Europe, peace in Asia, peace and prosperity all around the world.

It is a foreign policy which is above party. In recent years our foreign policy has been shaped and supported by many leaders in both political parties working together. Our foreign policy is truly bipartisan. It is arrived at by give-and-take, and improved by criticism and discussion.

That is the way it ought to be, and the way we are going to try to keep it. We welcome fair and honest debate.

But in recent months we have heard too much political hokum attacking the bipartisan foreign policy.

The people who are making these attacks cannot agree on any foreign policy of their own. They are just against the foreign policy this country is following. They are not trying to help this country find its way in these troubled times. They are just trying to confuse us. Why? Why do they try to confuse us? I ask you again, why? Because they think if the country is confused and confused enough, they may be able to win the next election. I will tell them right now, as I told them once before, they won't be!

Let me give you a few examples of the

thinking of these confusers. And the confusers are not altogether confined to politics, either.

They say they want a powerful defense system, second to none—but they are against universal military training.

They say they want other free nations to resist aggression—but they don't want us to send any troops to help our friends and allies.

They want us to get out of Korea—but they urge us to wage an aggressive war against China. Now, beat that one, if you can!

They say it will provoke Russia to attack if we send troops to Europe—but they are sure Russia won't be provoked if we carry the war to China. It has been categorically stated that Russia will not come in if we bomb Manchuria. The statement was made to me about the Chinese not coming into Korea, and it was made on good authority, too, and I believed it.

They say they want to crush communism—and yet they want us to draw back into our shell and let the rest of the world be overrun by the Reds.

They say they are worried because the Russians outnumber us—but they are not interested in keeping allies who can help us.

The long and short of it is that they want defenses without spending the money, they want us to wage war without an army, they want us to have victory without taking any risks, and they want us to try to run the whole world and to run it without any friends.

You know, it is rather peculiar that these confusers never blame the enemy for anything. The only place they can think of to place the blame is on the President of the United States. I will tell you this: we are not diverted by these political attacks. Every President in the history of this country that has ever done anything has had the same experience, and if I paid any attention to these foolish things which I have been going through here, I would never be able to get my job done. It runs off me like water off a duck!

We have a big job to do here at home. Our job is to get our defense program carried out quickly and efficiently.

We have made tremendous strides in building our defenses in the last few months. We have more than doubled the size of our Armed Forces since last June 25, the newest types of planes and tanks are coming off the assembly lines, and we are building an industrial system which can turn out more military supplies than ever before in our history. And that was the greatest turnout in the history of the world.

With our European partners, we are building a strong combined defense force for the North Atlantic area, under the leadership of a great American, Gen. Dwight D. Eisenhower.

At a time like this, when we as a nation are having to build up our Armed Forces and turn out all the material they need, we cannot—as individuals—do all the things we would normally do here at home. We can't build all the new houses we would like to build. We can't buy all the new gadgets and conveniences we would like. All of us will have to wait a while or do without many things we want.

But I know all Americans will gladly sacrifice some of the material comforts of life to defend the freedoms which give us our inner strength and security.

The Democratic Party has pioneered in the great advances our Nation has made in providing a better life for all our people. The Democratic Party has led the way to better homes, better education, better health, and higher incomes. The Democratic Party

has led the way to new respect for the dignity and worth of the individual. These achievements have come about because of our basic belief—the belief that every individual—and every group—in our Nation should have a fair deal.

A fair deal has been our pledge to the American people.

It is still our pledge.

In a time of national emergency like the present, when we all face danger together, it is more important than ever before that everyone have a fair deal.

A fair deal for everyone today means that we all share—and share alike—the responsibilities and the sacrifices of our defense program.

On the battlefields of Korea our men fight together for a common purpose. Black and white, rich and poor, share common hardships and often a common fate. The laborer's son, the farmer's son, and the businessman's son are fighting shoulder-to-shoulder in Korea.

We must have that same united approach to the common cause here at home.

It is as clear now as it was in Jefferson's day that we can enjoy the benefits of freedom only if we assume the responsibilities that go with it.

At this critical time in world history, men and women everywhere look to our Nation for leadership. They know that hope for a better life, human freedom, decency, justice, religion—all these things—depend upon the vigor with which we lead the free world in its fight for survival.

We shall not fail them.

We have known danger many times before, and we have never yielded. The ideals of Jefferson and Jackson have carried us through crises in the past.

They have given us a better and a fuller life.

I am confident that these same ideals will lead us to our goal of a free and peaceful world.

NOTE: The President spoke at 10:30 p.m. at the National Guard Armory in Washington. In his opening words he referred to John L. Sullivan, former Secretary of the Navy and chairman of the dinner, Alben W. Barkley, Vice President of the United States, and Sam Rayburn, Speaker of the House of Representatives. The address was carried on a nationwide radio and television broadcast.

81   Letter to Committee Chairmen on the Need for Assistance to Yugoslavia. *April 16, 1951*

My dear Mr. Chairman:

As you know, the United States has provided emergency food assistance to Yugoslavia during the past months to meet the threat to the security of that country caused by the recent drought: initially, under the provisions of the Mutual Defense Assistance Act, the Economic Cooperation Act, and through loans made by the Export-Import Bank; and then under the provisions of the Yugoslav Emergency Relief Assistance Act.

The drought which gave rise to the need for assistance, however, not only caused a shortage in the availability of food for consumption in Yugoslavia, but also has made it impossible for Yugoslavia to export the agricultural products with which Yugoslavia normally obtains the resources to pay for imports of critically needed raw materials. The consequent shortage of raw materials, which includes those basic to the needs of the Yugoslav armed forces, is so acute as to jeopardize the combat effectiveness of the Yugoslav armed forces and to weaken the ability of Yugoslavia to defend itself against aggression. This development seriously affects the security of the North Atlantic area.

As I explained to you in my letter of November 24, 1950 and for the reasons stated therein, I have found that Yugoslavia is a nation whose strategic location makes it of direct importance to the defense of the North Atlantic area, and that an immediate increase in its ability to defend itself over that which exists if no assistance is supplied will contribute to the preservation of the peace and security of the North Atlantic area.

I have determined, therefore, after consultation with the Governments of the other nations which are parties to the North Atlantic Treaty, that in order effectively to carry out the purposes of the Mutual Defense Assistance Act of 1949, as amended, it is essential as an immediate measure to use not to exceed $29 million of the funds appropriated for the purposes of Title I of that Act to provide raw materials and similar supplies for Yugoslavia in amounts and kinds equivalent to certain consumption needs for supporting its armed forces. I am, under the authority of that Act, approving the procurement and shipment of such materials and supplies.

This letter constitutes the notification required by Section 408(c) of the Mutual Defense Assistance Act, as amended.

Sincerely yours,

HARRY S. TRUMAN

NOTE: This is the text of identical letters addressed to the Honorable Richard B. Russell, Chairman of the Senate Armed Services Committee, the Honorable Tom Connally, Chairman of the Senate Foreign Relations Committee, the Honorable Carl Vinson, Chairman of the House Armed Services Committee, and the Honorable John Kee, Chairman of the House Foreign Affairs Committee.

For the President's letter of November 24, 1950, see 1950 volume, this series, Item 290.

82 Letter to Stuart Symington on His Appointment as Administrator
of the Reconstruction Finance Corporation. *April 17, 1951*

Dear Stuart:

The Senate action last week assures that the provisions of Reorganization Plan No. 1 of 1951 regarding the Reconstruction Finance Corporation will become effective April thirtieth. I am writing at this time to ask you to accept the position of Administrator in order that I may promptly submit your name to the Senate.

I hope you will accept, because your broad experience in private business and government is needed to provide the effective and efficient administration necessary to handle the important responsibilities of the RFC.

Because of the current importance of mobilization activities affecting the procurement and production of critical and strategic materials, special attention must be given this field.

Your experience with the Surplus Property Administration, the Air Force, and the National Security Resources Board with respect to government procurement and disposal programs gives you special qualification for this phase of the work.

Today, the RFC both purchases and smelts all the tin in this country, and operates all synthetic rubber activities. It is my desire that insofar as possible rubber purchases and operations also be consolidated under the RFC.

Finally, I want to continue the policy of making the RFC program an effective part of our efforts to assist the growth and development of small business in this country.

What I have outlined above is challenging, and presents an opportunity to you for rendering further public service.

Sincerely yours,

HARRY S. TRUMAN

[Honorable Stuart Symington, Chairman, National Security Resources Board, Washington, D.C.]

NOTE: Mr. Symington's letter of acceptance was released with the President's letter.

See also Item 39.

83 Statement by the President on the Point Four Program.
April 18, 1951

DR. HENRY G. BENNETT, administrator of the point 4 program, has given me an informal report of the progress of the program to date. I am pleased with what he has told me.

The point 4 program is more necessary today than ever. The threat of Communist aggression compels the free world to build strong military defenses. But communism cannot be stopped by arms alone. One of its most dangerous weapons is its false appeal to people who are burdened with hunger, disease, poverty, and ignorance.

The point 4 program is part of the defense of the free world. It is the best answer to the false promises of communism. It offers the plain people of the world a way to do what they want most to do—improve their conditions of life by their own efforts.

The point 4 program is being welcomed in that spirit by the free countries of Asia, Africa, the Middle East, and Latin America. Point 4 general agreements have been signed with 22 governments. About 360 American technicians are at work on point 4 projects in 28 countries. More than 240 technicians from 34 countries are being trained in the United States.

But this is only the beginning. Dr. Bennett tells me that, with relatively small appropriations, point 4 can help some 50 countries with a population of almost a billion people double their food production in 5 to 10 years. Comparable advances can be made by these countries in public health and education, as well as in other aspects of economic development.

84 Statement by the President on the Security of the Far East. *April 18, 1951*

THE UNITED STATES is moving steadily forward in concert with other countries of the Pacific in its determination to make ever stronger the position of the free world in the Pacific Ocean area.

In connection with the reestablishment of peace with Japan, we are discussing with the Japanese Government the implementation of its expressed desire for a post-treaty security arrangement pursuant to which United States Armed Forces might on a provisional basis remain in and about Japan.

The United States maintains, and expects to continue to maintain, its Armed Forces in the Ryukyus, particularly at Okinawa.

In the Philippines the United States is accorded certain military operating rights and facilities pursuant to an agreement with the Government of the Philippines and the whole world knows that the United States recognizes that an armed attack on the Philippines would be looked upon by the United States as dangerous to its own peace and safety and that it would act accordingly.

The Governments of Australia and New Zealand, in connection with the reestablishment of peace with Japan, have suggested an arrangement between them and the United States, pursuant to Articles 51 and 52 of the United Nations Charter which would make clear that in the event of an armed attack upon any one of them in the Pacific, each of the three would act to meet the common danger in accordance with its constitutional processes; and which would establish consultation to strengthen security on the basis of continuous and effective self-help and mutual aid.

The possibilities of such an arrangement were fully explored by Mr. Dulles at Canberra, Australia, and Wellington, New Zealand, and have since been informally discussed with the appropriate subcommittee of the Senate Foreign Relations Committee and the Foreign Affairs Committee of the House.

I have now asked the Secretary of State, the Secretary of Defense, and Mr. Dulles, as my special representative in relation to the Japanese peace settlement and related matters, to pursue this matter further concurrently with the prosecution of the other negotiations necessary to bring the Japanese peace settlement to an early and satisfactory conclusion.

The series of arrangements and dispositions outlined above, will strengthen the fabric of peace in the whole Pacific Ocean area, where security is strongly influenced by sea and air power. They constitute natural initial steps in the consolidation of peace in that area and also will contribute to the building of universal peace as sought by the United Nations and under which great goal the efforts of our Nation are now being largely dedicated.

NOTE: The White House issued releases on February 27, April 11, May 3, and June 15, 1951, announcing that John Foster Dulles, Consultant to the Secretary of State, had reported to the President on his discussions in Japan, Australia, New Zealand, the Philippines, France, and the United Kingdom preparatory to the conclusion of a peace treaty with Japan.

Mr. Dulles pointed out that although there had been initial differences of opinion on important matters, these had all been cleared away, and a draft treaty had been prepared. The President expressed gratification at the progress which had been made and the enlargement of the area of agreement in relation to the prompt conclusion of a fair and just Japanese Peace Treaty.

85 The President's News Conference of *April* 18, 1951

THE PRESIDENT. Please be seated.

[1.] I understand there are some visiting editors and some people from ASNE here today. On account of the fact that I found it impossible to appear at their meeting, if they will meet me over here in the side room, I will be glad to shake hands with them.[1]

[2.] I want to say something before we start that will save you a lot of misery. My position on the Far Eastern situation is well known. General MacArthur is coming here tomorrow to state his position, and therefore for that reason there is no use your asking me any questions that pertain to those two subjects. So now we're ready to go forward with the press conference.

Q. Mr. President, may we quote that?

THE PRESIDENT. Why do you have to quote that? I am just making a statement as to how the press conference is to be operated. There is no sense in your quoting it. No!

[3.] May,[2] I got a card today with your picture on it and a whole lot of things about you.

Q. Nice, wasn't it?

THE PRESIDENT. I thought it was.

Q. Thank you.

[4.] Q. Mr. President, are you going to act this week to set up this new Wage Stabilization Board?

THE PRESIDENT. I am working on it now. I was very happy at the way my advisory commission is working out. It is accomplishing just the thing that I set it up to do, and I think before we get through we'll have the thing in operating order so we can go right ahead with the program.[3]

[5.] Q. Mr. President, can you set a date when you will send up recommendations for changes in the defense program act?

THE PRESIDENT. We are working on it now. It takes a little time to get ready. I hope in the next 10 days, but I can't guarantee that.[4]

[6.] Q. Mr. President, does your answer on the Wage Board mean that you have accepted the advice the Board gave you yesterday?

THE PRESIDENT. Yes, it does. That is what I set it up for. When you get a majority of three to one, it is about time to operate.

Q. Mr. President, do you expect to designate the members?

THE PRESIDENT. We will have to work the thing out as we go along. We're making steps forward. I am making no positive statements on anything. We will cross that bridge when we get to it.

[7.] Q. Mr. President, does the administration plan any definite action to end the textile strike in the South?

THE PRESIDENT. It has not been put up to the administration.

---

[1] President Truman had been scheduled to address the annual meeting of the American Society of Newspaper Editors on Thursday, April 19, but he had canceled it in order not to interfere in any way with General MacArthur's appearance before the Congress at 12:30 p.m. that day. For the same reason the regular Thursday news conference was held on Wednesday.

[2] Mrs. May Craig of the Portland (Maine) Press Herald.

[3] See Item 74.

[4] See Item 91.

[8.] Q. Mr. President, I wonder whether you will clarify a phrase or two in the statement on the contemplated Pacific understanding.[5] You say here the three powers, the United States, New Zealand, and Australia, would act to meet the common danger in accordance with its constitutional processes. Would that mean that an attack on one would be considered an attack on all?

THE PRESIDENT. It would be similiar to the guarantees that are in the Atlantic Pact. They will be modeled on that treaty. That is what is intended to be conveyed there.

[9.] Q. Mr. President, does the administration approve of Government agencies subsidizing technical schools and paying prospective employees to attend?

THE PRESIDENT. I haven't gone into that. I think it has been the custom ever since the Government has been in existence, and so I can't answer your question without looking up the facts. I don't know what you are aiming at.

Q. Specifically, sir, in Dayton, Ohio, the Air Force has subsidized two business schools and is paying 120 employees $42 a week apiece to learn typewriting, and they plan to establish similar courses in Washington *and* subsidize *them*; but Mr. Ramspeck, Civil Service Commission, has objected.

THE PRESIDENT. Well, now, that is a matter I think you ought to take up with the Air Force. I don't know anything about it. It is news to me.

Q. But, Mr. President——

THE PRESIDENT. I have no statement to make on it. You are not going to get me on record on anything. [*Laughter*] You talk to Harry Byrd[6] about that. He will tell you more about it!

[10.] Q. Mr. President, do you intend to see General MacArthur or ask him to report to you?

THE PRESIDENT. That comes under the statement that I made at the beginning of this.

Q. Mr. President, at the risk of also coming under that heading, Congressman Armstrong came back here the other day after a trip to the Far East, and he said that General Ridgway felt the same as General MacArthur did about the use of Chinese Nationalist troops. Do you know if that is a fact or not?

THE PRESIDENT. No, I don't. There is one way for him to find out!

Q. Mr. President, without discussing present-day generals, could you draw on your knowledge of history and tell us about the careers of Horatio Gates and Winfield Scott?

THE PRESIDENT. Well, I think that is a matter you amateur historians ought to look up. It is very interesting.

[11.] Q. Mr. President, did Mr. Magnuson[7] go to Japan as your personal representative?

THE PRESIDENT. He did not; he went on his own hook. [*Laughter*] He was going in behalf of his Committee, I think. His trip was entirely a legitimate one for the Congressman.

What was the question back there?

[12.] Q. Mr. President, do you have any afterthoughts about the American Foreign Ministers Conference—developing phases or other aspects of it?

THE PRESIDENT. I was very happy over the results of the Pan American Foreign Ministers Conference.[8] I think I issued a statement on that subject; I am not sure.

[13.] Q. Mr. President, could you add a personal comment to the statement issued by the State Department commenting on

---

[5] See Item 84.

[6] Senator Harry F. Byrd of Virginia.

[7] Senator Warren G. Magnuson of Washington, member of the Senate Interstate and Foreign Commerce Committee.

[8] See Items 67 and 76.

the signatories to the Schuman plan?

THE PRESIDENT. I am very happy, as the State Department expressed my views. They submitted that statement to me before it was issued and I am in complete accord with it.[9]

[14.] Q. Mr. President, would you comment on something that Mr. Short [10] said— no plans for the White House to invite MacArthur——

THE PRESIDENT. I think Mr. Short answered that question, and he would not have made it if he hadn't had the permission of the President. Mr. Short has learned

a lot of things now. He makes no tactical errors like that.

[15.] Q. Well, Mr. President, if I might go back to your refusal to allow us to say anything about the statement, it puts us in a jam because people think we didn't ask you questions.

THE PRESIDENT. What statement?

Q. Your original statement.

THE PRESIDENT. He wanted to quote it verbatim here. There is nothing in the world to prevent you from putting up an alibi and your paraphrasing the thing.

Q. Well, I wanted to make sure, because you said——

THE PRESIDENT. That's all right.

Q. ——it was for the press conference only.

THE PRESIDENT. Well, I said I didn't want this quoted verbatim. Now, you can paraphrase it; if you want to make an alibi that you couldn't get any answers out of me that will be all right! [*Laughter*]

Q. Mr. President, have we overlooked anything?

THE PRESIDENT. I don't think so!

Reporter: Thank you, sir.

---

[9] The statement, released by the State Department on April 18, is as follows:

"According to press reports, the ministers of six countries meeting in Paris to complete negotiation on political provisions of the Schuman plan have agreed on the major issues and this morning have formally signed the text.

"The department wishes to state that the ability of the ministers to reach a decision on the variety of complex and delicate issues with which they were confronted provides striking evidence of the constructive spirit and continuing good will which have characterized the Schuman plan negotiations from the very first. The early ratification of the plan by the parliaments of the six countries would go far toward convincing the world that Western Europe has the courage and the ability to develop the solidarity which is essential for the survival of the free world."

[10] Joseph H. Short, Secretary to the President.

NOTE: President Truman's two hundred and sixtieth news conference was held in the Indian Treaty Room (Room 474) in the Executive Office Building at 4:30 p.m. on Wednesday, April 18, 1951.

86 Statement by the President on the Death of Senator Vandenberg. *April 19, 1951*

ARTHUR VANDENBERG was a patriot who always subordinated partisan advantage and personal interest to the welfare of the Nation.

In his passing the Senate has lost a pillar of strength in whom integrity was implicit in every decision he made and in every vote he cast during a long tenure. The Nation mourns a leader who had wisdom, fortitude, and courage. A grateful country will hold

his memory in lasting remembrance.

The senior Senator from Michigan never gave hasty judgments. He formed his opinions only after deliberate study of every aspect of every problem that came before him. His courage was fortified by a good conscience. So he had no fear of the consequences to his personal fortunes when the time came for him to differ from men of great power and influence within his own party on the paramount issue of foreign policy.

Of course we know that his independence cost him dearly in everything save honor. But to him his country's welfare, the security of the Nation and a just and enduring peace in a world of free men were above and beyond all other considerations. He even risked health and life in the cause of peace. When the heat of controversy has subsided and the present conflict of principle and policy has been resolved, I believe that the verdict of history, rendered through the perspective of time, will be for Senator Vandenberg.

87   Statement by the President on the Occasion of the Transfer of a Statue of Simón Bolívar to the Avenue of the Americas in New York City. *April* 19, 1951

ON THIS DAY, April 19, the 130th anniversary of Venezuela's demand for independence, it is fitting for us to recall that the life and work of the Liberator, Simón Bolívar, are still highly significant to all free peoples of the world. His precepts have a direct bearing on the problems of our greatest concern at this present time. Bolívar, who believed in freedom and in union to defend it, said: "It is essential that our society be a society of sister nations, divided at present in the exercise of their sovereignties by the course of human events; but united, strong, and powerful in ability to aid one another against foreign aggression."

I am happy to join in paying homage to the great Liberator.

NOTE: The President's statement was read at 2 p.m. by Robert Moses, Park Commissioner of New York City, at the dedication ceremonies in Central Park.

The statue was moved to the entrance of the park from its former location in the park near West 83rd Street where it was first dedicated in 1921. The new site was to be known henceforth as Plaza Bolivar.

88   Remarks to a Group of British Publishers and Editors. *April* 20, 1951

WELL, it is a pleasure to be able to receive you gentlemen this morning. I first of all want to say to you how greatly we suffered from the loss of Mr. Bevin. I became personally acquainted with him at Potsdam. He was there as a part of the English delegation and he came later as Foreign Secretary. He has been over here I think on three different occasions in which I had very close association with him and became one of his admirers. I think we suffered a great loss when he had to give up, although I am certain his working policies will be carried on by his successors.

I think one of the ways in which our understandings can be clarified and we can go ahead with the necessary things we have to do as partners in the United Nations and in the world is a complete understanding of each other. I understand you have 50 men stationed in this part of the world, and we have an equal number or more in Great Britain furnishing us the same information. One great thing about our association, we speak the same language, or substantially. Our western twang is not thoroughly understood and sometimes we are stumped by some of British speech. But we have the same ideals in mind as to government and welfare of the people, and I hope that that understanding will continue to be clarified and we of necessity will continue to carry out our mutual obligations under the Atlantic Treaty and the United Nations.

I think our only hope for world peace is the working out of the United Nations Charter so it is a practical thing and a living thing. It took Great Britain a long, long time to get what they finally came up with as their Constitution. It took us 80 years. We go through many woes and travail before we finally get this thing to work, but those of us who know what we are after should never give up, and I know the British are famous for their bulldog stubbornness. I hope you come back.

NOTE: The President spoke at 12 noon in his office at the White House. In the course of his remarks he referred to Ernest Bevin, former Secretary of State for Foreign Affairs of the United Kingdom, who died in London on April 14, 1951.

89 Letter to the Chairman, Science Advisory Committee.
April 20, 1951

My dear Dr. Buckley:

For some time, I have been considering the best means whereby scientists of the country could be assisted and encouraged in their participation in the mobilization program. At the same time, I have been increasingly mindful of the many demands which the Federal programs are placing upon scientific resources, and of the reliance which the Government properly places upon the successful prosecution of scientific research and development activities.

The Federal Government has a considerable number of agencies engaged in research and development activities of significance for both peacetime purposes and national defense. There are currently in existence a number of arrangements for coordinating segments of the work of these agencies. I have been concerned, however, that our existing arrangements do not provide adequate liaison among the agencies principally concerned with our national research and development effort, nor between them and the Office of Defense Mobilization. Such liaison is obviously essential to securing the full contribution of scientists to our defense planning.

I have therefore determined to establish a Science Advisory Committee of the Office of Defense Mobilization, to be available to the Defense Mobilization Director and to me,

a. To provide independent advice on scientific matters especially as regards the objectives and interrelations of the several Federal agencies engaged in research of defense significance, including relevant foreign relations and intelligence matters.

b. To advise on progress being made in dealing with current scientific research problems of defense significance and also concerning defense research matters which need greater attention or emphasis.

c. To advise concerning plans and methods for the implementation of scientific effort for defense.

d. For transmitting the views of the scientific community of the country on research and development matters of national defense significance.

I am therefore appointing you as Chairman, and am asking the following to serve as members of the Committee: Dr. Detlev W. Bronk, as President of the National Academy of Sciences, Dr. William Webster, as Chairman of the Research and Development Board, Dr. Alan Waterman, as Director of the National Science Foundation, Dr.

Hugh Dryden of the Interdepartmental Committee on Scientific Research and Development, Dr. James B. Conant, Dr. Lee DuBridge, Dr. James R. Killian, Dr. Robert F. Loeb, Dr. J. Robert Oppenheimer, Dr. Charles A. Thomas.

I have discussed the creation of this Committee and its functions with Mr. Charles E. Wilson, as much of its work will be related to his responsibilities as Defense Mobilization Director. We are in agreement that the Committee should be established within the Office of Defense Mobilization. In this way, it will be in a direct position to participate in the mobilization program directed by Mr. Wilson as it affects scientific research and development. It will likewise be in a position to advise both Mr. Wilson and me concerning the interrelationship of the mobilization program and the achievement of our long-range objectives of con-

tinued progress in scientific research and development.

I am forwarding copies of this letter to the heads of the Government agencies primarily concerned with research and development activities with the request that they extend you their full cooperation. Likewise, I expect that you will freely call on private scientific groups and individuals for assistance. I shall welcome the recommendations of the Committee and shall call upon it for advice from time to time.

Sincerely yours,

HARRY S. TRUMAN

[Dr. Oliver E. Buckley, President, Bell Telephone Laboratories, 463 West Street, New York 14, N.Y.]

NOTE: A White House release of April 20, announcing the membership of the Science Advisory Committee, contained a summary of the letter to Dr. Buckley, dated April 19.

90 The President's News Conference of April 26, 1951

THE PRESIDENT. Please be seated.

[1.] Before you start off, I think maybe I'd better remind you of a statement that I made in a speech on April 11th.[1] I want to quote one paragraph, and it covers the Far Eastern situation pretty well. This is a quotation, and the speech is available to you. I am sure all of you have it.

[*Reading*]: "The Communist side must now choose its course of action. The Communist rulers may press the attack against us. They may take further action which will spread the conflict. They have that choice, and with it the awful responsibility for what may follow. The Communists also have the choice of a peaceful settlement which could lead to a general relaxation of tensions in the Far East. The decision is

theirs, because the forces of the United Nations will strive to limit the conflict if possible."

I think that statement sums up the policy of the United States. And since the Senate committees are going into the thing in detail, I think the best approach to this whole situation is to let the Senate committees get the facts and come to a conclusion.

Now I am ready for questions.

[2.] Q. Mr. President, did you promise the Federal judgeship in the Eastern District of Texas to Galloway Calhoun?

THE PRESIDENT. I did not. I never promise judgeships to anybody. I try to pick the best man for those places, and I don't do it on a promise basis politically or otherwise.

Q. Yes, sir. Thank you.

[3.] Q. Do you care to express an opin-

---
[1] See Item 78.

ion whether the congressional hearings should be opened or closed?

THE PRESIDENT. That is the business of the Senate and not mine.

[4.] Q. Mr. President, General MacArthur's spokesman said the General did not have the faintest idea of why he has been relieved. Would you care to comment on it?

THE PRESIDENT. Everybody else knows why! [*Laughter*]

Q. Mr. President, is General MacArthur subject to assignment, is he off duty forever, or what is his status, exactly?

THE PRESIDENT. May,[2] may I quote the law to you—that was passed at my suggestion—to create permanent, lifetime jobs for the five-star generals and admirals who have been at the top in the winning of World War II. They are on exactly the same status as General Pershing was after the First World War.

Q. Then your telling General MacArthur he could travel wherever he pleased at the time of his replacement didn't mean that he was not subject to recall by you for duty?

THE PRESIDENT. That is correct. I've recalled General Eisenhower, I've recalled Admiral Nimitz, and——

Q. Do you have anything in mind for General MacArthur?

THE PRESIDENT. Not at the present time, May. Of course I knew what you were after all the time. [*Laughter*] I could have told you in the first place, if you had asked the question straight out, instead of going all around. I would have answered it just the same.

Q. Well, it gave me some interesting information.

THE PRESIDENT. I didn't think you knew the law.

Q. Yes, I did.

THE PRESIDENT. What is it, Eddie?[3]

[5.] Q. Mr. President, do I take it that this new offensive is the occasion for that statement you read to us at the outset, or is it something that's about to come on Capitol Hill? I would like to know what the occasion——

THE PRESIDENT. Well, it had reference particularly to the hearings in the Senate.

Q. Mr. President, may we at this time attach particular importance to the last two words of the statement you just read, "if possible"?

THE PRESIDENT. What do you mean? I don't understand the connection——

Q. There have been reports recently that General Ridgway has been informed that if necessary he may bomb in Manchuria, that United Nations countries have been informed of that decision?

THE PRESIDENT. I have no comment to make on that statement at all.

Q. May I ask you one more question?

THE PRESIDENT. Yes, surely—as many as you want.

[6.] Q. Are you in a position to confirm the report in the New York Times of the conversation results of your Wake Island conference with General MacArthur?[4]

THE PRESIDENT. I have no comment to make on that, either.

Q. Mr. President, I have a question on that also.

THE PRESIDENT. Go ahead.

Q. A number of reporters have asked for the record on that Wake Island meeting, and

---

[2] Mrs. May Craig of the Portland (Maine) Press Herald.

[3] Edward T. Folliard of the Washington Post.
[4] On April 21 the New York Times printed a summary of the Wake Island conversations based on what the writer described as "documented sources on the meeting." Among other things the article stated that General MacArthur had expressed doubt that Red China would intervene in Korea and was so confident of victory that he offered what he regarded as his best troops for service in Europe. The article was written by Anthony H. Leviero.

See also Item 95 [6].

had been told that they could not get it as the record was with you and could only be given out with your consent. And then Mr. Leviero, who is a very fine reporter, asked for it and got it. I was hoping that in the future if there was anything to be given out—scoops like that—we could all have a chance at it. [*Laughter*]

THE PRESIDENT. I remember a certain turmoil that was created by an interview I had with Arthur Krock. And some of your people wept and cried, and I finally made a statement that I would talk to anybody I pleased any time I pleased. I didn't talk to Mr. Leviero, however.

Q. Mr. President, you say you did or did not?

THE PRESIDENT. Did *not!*

[7.] Q. You said after that you quoted from your speech of April 11th, and you said you believed the best thing was to let the Senate committees get the facts.

THE PRESIDENT. That's right.

Q. Did you mean to imply by that, that the Joint Chiefs of Staff should declassify some of the documents in their hands?

THE PRESIDENT. We will cross that bridge when we get to it.

Q. Mr. President, I am a little concerned about that date, April 11th. Where was it you spoke then?

THE PRESIDENT. Over the radio in the White House!

[8.] Q. Mr. President, could you give us any comment on the situation in Korea as it has developed in the last few days? [5]

THE PRESIDENT. I have no comment. I am not in the field, and of course I can't comment on the situation.

---

[5] On April 24 a new offensive by Chinese Communist troops broke through the lines of the United Nations forces and carried the Communists south of the 38th parallel. The advance had moved as far south as Munsan, 20 miles northwest of Seoul, by April 26.

[9.] Q. Mr. President, will Mr. Dawson [6] comply with the new request for him to testify?

THE PRESIDENT. I will answer that question when it comes up to me. It isn't up to me as yet.

[10.] Q. Mr. President, will you favor decentralizing Government agencies, now that the dispersal plan has been discarded?

THE PRESIDENT. It is my understanding that the Senate Committee on Public Works went very carefully into the situation and voted almost unanimously. There was only one vote in the Committee against the reporting of the bill which was before the Congress. That was a good bill, and one that was in the public interest. Senator Holland made a good fight to get it over. I think eventually something along the lines as reported by the Public Works Committee will be put into effect for the welfare of the country, as it should be.

[11.] Q. Mr. President, would you have any objection to the publication of that Wake Island document now?

THE PRESIDENT. I am not in a position to answer that question, Smitty.[7]

[12.] Q. Mr. President, have you talked with Paul Hoffman about his becoming Secretary of State?

THE PRESIDENT. No, I haven't. He isn't going to become Secretary of State—I can say that to you. I have a Secretary of State with whom I am very well satisfied.

[13.] Q. Mr. President, Governor Scott of North Carolina came up here a couple of days ago, trying to line up a Democratic presidential candidate for a speech down in North Carolina next year. Do you think he would be able to come?

THE PRESIDENT. Well, I think that any

---

[6] Donald S. Dawson, Administrative Assistant to the President.

[7] Merriman Smith of the United Press Associations.

Democratic candidate would be glad to speak in North Carolina.

[*Long pause*]

What is the matter, boys and ladies? Are you out of questions?

[14.] Q. Mr. President, General Whitney,[8] who is General MacArthur's aide, said yesterday that all of the top level military commanders in Korea were in agreement with General MacArthur's policies. Can you say anything about that.

THE PRESIDENT. I have no way of knowing whether that is true or not, so I cannot comment on it. When I came back from Wake Island, at the request of General MacArthur I made Whitney a major general.

Q. Mr. President, what is General Whitney's status now?

THE PRESIDENT. He seems to be the press secretary and secretary for General MacArthur. All I know is what I see in the newspapers. [*Laughter*]

Q. As to the military?

THE PRESIDENT. I know nothing about that at the present time. I think the best thing for you to do would be to take it up with the Secretary of Defense. He probably would tell you straight from the shoulder just what his status is.

Q. Mr. President, apart from his appearances before Congress, are there any restrictions on General MacArthur's utterances on foreign or military policy?

THE PRESIDENT. Oh no. He is in the United States now, and he can say what he pleases and go where he pleases and do whatever he likes. I have no strings on him. I do have strings on him, but I don't intend to pull them.

Q. Mr. President, is General Whitney allowed to say anything he wants to——

THE PRESIDENT. It seems to be the case.

Q. Do you have any strings on General Whitney?

THE PRESIDENT. Yes, but I am not going to pull them. I am glad to have him talk. He's telling a lot of things that ought to be said.

[15.] Q. Mr. President, are you sending an economic message to Congress today?

THE PRESIDENT. Yes, at noon.[9]

Q. Can you tell us anything about it?

THE PRESIDENT. I think the best plan would be for you to read the message when it goes down to Congress. It will be there at 12 o'clock, and then be open for publication. I don't like to give out a message before the Congress has a chance to hear it read.

[16.] Q. Mr. President, could I ask you this one thing about Wake Island?

THE PRESIDENT. Ask anything you like, May.

Q. Thank you. Tony's story said it was documented. I thought that during the time you were alone with General MacArthur there was no record. I don't know where I got that impression.

THE PRESIDENT. I think probably your impression is correct.

Q. How could it be documented?

THE PRESIDENT. I might have documented it myself, you can't tell, May. I say I might have. That doesn't give you anything at all, does it?

Q. No, sir. [*Laughter*]

Q. At that Wake Island conference, sir, did General MacArthur apologize to you?

THE PRESIDENT. I can't answer questions like that, Smitty; you know it.

I think a great deal of information will come out at the Senate hearings that will interest you. And I don't want to comment on that because that is up to the Senate committees. I wish you would read history.

---

[8] Maj. Gen. Courtney Whitney.

[9] See Item 91.

It is most interesting. There was a Senate committee called "The Committee on the Conduct of the War." After the Battle of Gettysburg they got General Meade down before that Committee, and abused him like a pickpocket. It is a most interesting document. There are several other instances of the same sort. History seems to repeat itself as we go along through the world. This is not anything new or original, what's happened in the last few weeks. If you will study history, you will find a most easy and simple answer to everything in which you are interested.

Q. Could you tell us where to look, Mr. President? [*Laughter*]

THE PRESIDENT. Well, I will tell you one place that you can look that will be most interesting, Sandburg's "Life of Lincoln"—there are only six volumes of it, about that thick—[*indicating*]. And then "Lincoln Finds a General," which recently came out. And if you will read the memoirs of General Grant, you'll find something most interesting in that. And I could cite you two or three other instances. I think if you will read President Polk's diary, you will find something most interesting about Winfield Scott that will amuse you very much. You might also read Washington's diary on his troubles with the Conway cabal and Charles Lee. They are most interesting.

Q. Mr. President, could you give us about a three-paragraph summary? [*Laughter*]

THE PRESIDENT. No, I'm going to make you do a little work on your own. [*More laughter*] You will have to do a little work on your own. I think the Library of Congress would fix you up, if you asked them. They have a Legislative Reference Service there that will give you anything you want. They abused General Meade like a pickpocket—you read that.

Q. I think you said, Mr. President, that history repeats itself. Now do you infer, sir, that General MacArthur is about to be——

THE PRESIDENT. I make no inferences—I ask you to read history and draw your own inferences. I'm making none for you. I'm just referring you to some very interesting things that have happened in the past.

Q. Mr. President, General Scott ran for President after he was fired.

THE PRESIDENT. Yes he did. So did General McClellan, if I remember correctly.

Q. Do you care to comment on that?

THE PRESIDENT. No, I have no comment at all. [*Laughter*]

Q. Thank you, Mr. President.

NOTE: President Truman's two hundred and sixty-first news conference was held in the Indian Treaty Room (Room 474) in the Executive Office Building at 10:30 a.m. on Thursday, April 26, 1951.

---

91 Special Message to the Congress Recommending Extension and Broadening of the Defense Production Act. *April 26, 1951*

To the Congress of the United States:

I recommend that the Congress extend for two years the Defense Production Act of 1950, which is now scheduled to expire on June 30, 1951. I also recommend that the Act be strengthened in certain respects.

The Defense Production Act was enacted in September, 1950—two months after the communist attack on free Korea had made clear the peril in which all free nations stand. It was a legislative expression of the national resolve to meet the worldwide communist threat with a vast increase in our military and economic strength.

The Act provides the basic authority for our defense mobilization program. It contains specific provisions for expanding production and for maintaining economic stability—the two essentials of the defense program.

Since last summer, we have made a strong beginning in getting defense production started, and we have laid the basis for an effective program to stabilize prices and the cost of living.

We have doubled the number of men in our active Armed Forces since last June. We have nearly doubled the rate of production of military planes during the past year. Monthly deliveries of military equipment and supplies have doubled since last June. In Europe, we have joined our associates in the North Atlantic Treaty in establishing a unified defense force, to be made up of units from the Treaty countries, under the command of General Eisenhower. The Mutual Defense Assistance Program has been stepped up substantially, and other free nations, particularly in Europe, are rapidly enlarging their defense establishments, as we are.

Since last summer, we have taken initial actions in the fields of taxes, credit controls, price and wage controls, and other measures necessary to stop inflation and keep it stopped.

No one should deceive himself, however, by assuming that we can now relax our strenuous efforts. Quite the opposite is true. What we have done so far consists essentially of laying a solid basis for future effort.

The major impact of the military build-up on our economy is still to come. Our planned expansion of defense production will not reach its peak for at least a year—and the inflationary pressures brought on by the defense effort likewise have not yet reached their peak.

The blunt fact is that the hardest part of the job still lies ahead. Nothing could be more foolhardy than to slacken the intensity of our defense mobilization effort just because we have gotten off to a good start.

When the Congress passed the Defense Production Act and when it passed the military appropriations acts, it clearly intended that we should proceed with all speed to strengthen ourselves and join in strengthening the forces of freedom throughout the world. I have heard no voice raised in favor of turning back before the job is finished.

The full range of powers included in the Defense Production Act will be needed—and needed badly—until we are "over the hump" in our defense mobilization program. We hope that will be about two years from now—always assuming that world war is avoided. All our plans must recognize, of course, that while we hope we can influence the actions of aggressors, we cannot control them—we hope we can prevent general war, but there is no way we can be sure.

For at least the next two years we shall be driving urgently forward in our defense mobilization program. Therefore, it is of the greatest importance that the Defense Production Act be extended for that period.

Defense Production

Titles I, II, and III of the Act relate to production.

Since June, 1950, the Government has placed orders for planes, tanks, guns, and other military equipment, facilities, and supplies in the amount of over 26 billion dollars. As yet, only a small part of these orders have been filled and the goods delivered. Furthermore, over 58 billion dollars more in orders have yet to be placed before the end of June, 1952.

This is a tough production program because we must build our strength as rapidly as we can. The world situation could explode at any time, and we must make every day count.

Consequently, the Government is using

extensively the powers granted in the Defense Production Act to divert materials and plants from less important to more important uses. Under these powers, important metals, chemicals, and other materials—including such basic materials as steel, copper, and aluminum—are being controlled and channeled to the places they are most needed.

For the next year, at least, it is obvious that controls over materials will have to become tighter and tighter, as more and more of them will be diverted to essential production. Consequently, the allocations and priorities systems authorized in the Defense Production Act will be even more necessary than they are now.

There is much more to our production program, however, than simply diverting scarce materials and converting existing plants to defense production. As a Nation, we are expanding our ability to produce minerals and fuels; we are building new factories and transportation facilities—we are enlarging the economic capacity of the country, so that, in time, we shall be able to support a high level of military strength, resume our progress in raising living standards, and be stronger for meeting any new military demands.

For example, the capacity of the steel industry, which was 100 million tons a year last June, will be expanded, within two years, to at least 117 million tons a year. The aluminum industry had a capacity last June of 750,000 tons a year; by 1953 it should rise to 1,300,000 tons. The electric power capacity of the nation—67,500,000 kilowatts at the beginning of this year—is being rapidly increased; we need to add at least 22,000,000 more kilowatts in the next three years.

The Defense Production Act carries powers under which the Government is helping to build new plants and finance additional output. The Government is making or guaranteeing loans to private business-

men. It is buying some critical materials and equipment—particularly imported materials—and reselling them to private businessmen. It is also supporting the development of new domestic and foreign sources of supply for vital materials. These powers will have to be used to an increasing extent as our defense production expands.

In addition to these production aids under the Defense Production Act, under the Revenue Act of 1950 the Government is allowing businessmen, in certain cases, to write off part of the cost of new plants and equipment needed in the defense effort more rapidly than the usual depreciation periods under the tax laws. Some 5 billion dollars worth of new plant construction is being encouraged in this way.

Even with the existing production aids, it may not be possible to obtain the supplies and equipment needed unless the Government is given one power to help expand defense production which it does not now have. That is the general power, which was used extensively and successfully in World War II, to build defense plants. At the present time, with some exceptions, whether or not defense plants are built depends finally upon the decision of private businessmen. Certainly if private businessmen can and will build all the necessary facilities, without excessive cost to the taxpayers, that is preferable. But first and foremost, the Government must have the authority to obtain essential production.

To help expand defense production, the Government also needs the power to give special financial aid to high cost producers in order to obtain essential production from them without increasing price ceilings. Such "differential" subsidies were used very successfully in World War II, and saved American consumers and taxpayers many millions of dollars, because it was much cheaper to subsidize some high cost producers than to raise prices on the entire production of the commodities affected.

In summary, to accomplish our defense production goals, the Defense Production Act should be extended and strengthened, and adequate funds to carry out its provisions should be authorized.

Economic Stabilization

Titles IV, V, and VI of the Defense Production Act relate to stabilization.

It will be a tough job to accomplish the production goals of our defense effort. It will, in many respects, be even harder to prevent our defense effort from resulting in skyrocketing prices—with increased defense costs, disruption of production, and hardship for millions of families.

For the next two or three years, the economy will be running at forced draft. Industrial production and employment will be reaching new records. People will be working longer hours, many at overtime pay. Farmers will be producing and selling more crops. All of this will mean higher incomes—more money available for people to spend. At the same time, much of our manpower and plant capacity will be diverted to building defense plants and producing military goods—leaving that much less civilian goods for people to buy.

More money to spend than there are goods to buy—that creates the so-called "inflationary gap." Without an effective stabilization program, the excess spending power could be translated into higher and higher prices.

If we are successful in preventing another world war, at the end of two or three years we should be able to close the inflationary gap by producing enough civilian goods to match the buying power of businesses and consumers. This can be done when our expenditures for military purposes and for new plants will have leveled off—and the vastly increased productive power of the country can be devoted in greater proportion to civilian goods.

But in the meantime, until we are "over the hump," we face an extremely difficult problem in stopping inflation.

Fortunately, we are now in a relatively good position to prepare for the tough period ahead. After the Korean invasion, and again after the Chinese intervention, there were speculative buying rushes by businessmen and consumers which, coupled with the expansion of defense orders, resulted in prices surging upward. The wholesale price index rose 16 percent from June 27, 1950, to February 6, 1951. The index of consumer prices rose 8 percent from June 15, 1950, to February 15, 1951.

Now, however, tax, credit, and price and wage control actions have taken hold. Production has increased substantially, and the buying wave has—at least for the time being—died down. Consequently, the upward rush of prices has been checked. The wholesale price index rose only 0.5 percent between February 6 and April 17, 1951. The latest consumer's price index figures, those of March 15, show a rise of only 0.4 percent in the month following February 15—the first full month of price control. We have made a good beginning and we must now go on to achieve more complete stabilization.

We are now having something of a "breathing spell." But it will not last. This fall and winter the economy will be hit by the full impact of military production. Supplies of civilian goods will be reduced while larger production, employment and military spending will be putting still greater buying power in the hands of the public.

Inflationary pressures, which are serious now, will be critical then. We must therefore use the present period to get prepared for the hard problems which lie ahead. The present "breathing spell" is a fortunate occurrence—it gives us a chance to get hold of the price structure and build a set of controls which will hold firm. This opportunity will not come again. We must not waste it. The Executive agencies will do their utmost with the powers they have and the Congress will need to enact additional legislation.

In taking action now, our simple, central goal must be to bring the rise in prices and the cost of living to a halt—and hold the line. It will take strong and determined measures to do that.

1. Most important of all, we must increase taxes quickly and adequately—paying for Government expenditures as we go, through a fair tax program. This will spread the cost of defense equitably and help stop the inflationary spiral.

2. We must increase personal savings—dollars saved now are subtracted from the buying power pushing prices upward, and will be available later when more consumer goods will be produced.

3. We must reduce borrowing and buying on credit for non-defense purposes—by consumers and businessmen—since borrowed money adds to the pressure on prices.

4. We must have fair ceilings on prices, including the prices of farm products, and on rents, in order to stabilize the cost of living during the defense period, to hold down the cost of the defense program to the taxpayers, and to prevent profiteering.

5. We must stabilize wages and salaries at fair levels, to restrain excessive consumer demand and to prevent rising business costs from forcing price increases.

This is an anti-inflation program that will work. It includes measures to absorb excess purchasing power, and measures to stop prices and costs from jumping upward. This program will work if all these measures are employed to support and reinforce one another. We must fight inflation on every front and with every possible weapon if we are to succeed.

Taxes

A large Federal deficit would be a powerful inflationary force, because the Government would be pouring more money into the economy than it was taking from it. The effects would be multiplied in a period of rising expenditures, when Government orders and the private borrowing and spending which they stimulate exceed the actual budget expenditure figures.

An effective stabilization program requires that we hold Federal expenditures to the minimum necessary for national security and a strong Nation. The January budget reflects such a policy, and I know the Congress will apply the same standard in reviewing it.

An effective stabilization program also requires that taxes be high enough at least to balance the budget.

The Federal Government will show a surplus for the current fiscal year, ending on June 30. This is a good record. But, unfortunately it does not mean we are on a pay-as-we-go basis. During the present quarter and from here on out, until taxes are raised, we will be operating at a deficit. The latest figures show that to balance the budget as defense outlays continue to rise will require the Congress to enact during this year at least the 10 billion dollars in additional taxes I have recommended.

The people of our country are going to have to pay for the defense program sometime; the sensible thing to do is for us to pay for it as we go, through fair taxes.

Savings

This is also the sensible time to put every possible dollar into savings. Every additional dollar saved helps hold down the cost of living, and puts aside money that will be available later on, when consumer goods are again plentiful.

During World War II, the American people invested unprecedented amounts in savings bonds, thus withdrawing billions of dollars which otherwise would have pushed prices upward during the war; after the war those savings helped many a family. It is vital again now to encourage savings— through payroll savings plans and other regular methods of savings bond purchase, and through encouraging people to hold on to their savings bonds as they come due, and thereby earn more interest.

The most effective way of all to assure adequate saving is to provide convincing assurance to savers that inflation will not cut down the value of their savings. This is one of the many reasons why we need to increase taxes and to extend and strengthen present economic stabilization legislation.

Credit Controls

Credit controls, like taxation and savings, attack inflation at the source, by reducing purchasing power which would otherwise be directly used to bid up the prices of goods.

A good deal has been done since last June to curtail the expansion of consumer and real estate credit. Higher down payments and quicker payment of balances are being required of buyers of new houses, automobiles, household appliances, and other durable goods. These credit controls are already showing good results—for example, the amount of credit outstanding to buyers of automobiles, which had risen steadily since 1945, has declined every month since last October and total installment credit dropped by about half a billion dollars in the first three months of this year. The provisions in the Defense Production Act authorizing such credit controls need to be extended; furthermore, we need the authority to control credit terms on the sale of existing houses, as well as new ones.

We are in a less favorable situation regarding bank credit to businessmen. Bank loans have risen, week after week, almost without interruption. Many of these loans are necessary—for example, loans to businessmen to expand defense production. But it is very important to cut down on unnecessary loans. Non-essential business investments should be deferred because they compete for scarce materials and manpower.

Several steps have been taken to dampen bank credit expansion. The discount rates of the Federal Reserve banks have been raised. The Federal Reserve Board has increased the reserve requirements of member banks almost to the legal maximum. The Treasury has offered long-term nonmarketable bonds in exchange for long-term marketable bonds, in order to cut down the supply of securities that might be used for credit expansion. In addition, the Federal Reserve Board has recently requested all banks and other lenders to cut down on their non-essential lending. Government lending agencies are already applying strict standards in screening and limiting their loans.

It is not yet clear whether further actions will be needed, but we should obviously be prepared to take them. The Government has certain emergency powers it can use to place direct controls over bank lending, if that proves to be necessary. In addition, I believe that the Federal Reserve Board should be given authority by the Congress to impose additional requirements for bank reserves. I expect to transmit specific recommendations on this subject to the Congress in the near future.

Furthermore, I recommend that the Congress authorize the control of margins for speculation on commodity futures markets. Whenever the speculative fever hits these markets, we should be able to dampen it promptly with reasonable requirements for minimum margins. This is the same kind of authority which the Federal Reserve Board now exercises in respect to the stock markets.

Price and Wage Controls

Price and wage controls do not cure the basic cause of inflation—the inflationary gap between the supply of goods and the volume of buying power.

The cure can come about only by closing the gap—through tax, saving, and credit programs which reduce the demand for goods, on the one hand, and production programs which increase the supply, on the other. But until the inflationary gap is closed through these measures, price and wage controls are indispensable in checking the price rises which otherwise would result. At the present time, it is clear that these controls must be maintained and strengthened.

On January 26, a general ceiling price regulation was issued, freezing most prices at the highest level they had reached in the previous four weeks. At the same time, a similar regulation stopped, for the time being, further wage increases.

Both the price and wage freezes of January were intended as emergency measures to hold down price and wage increases temporarily, until more workable regulations could be developed and the staff assembled to put them into effect. These January regulations were a necessary step. But, inevitably, they froze all sorts of distortions and inequities into the price and wage structure.

They left some sellers operating at a loss, and others making excessive profits. They caught many retailers in an unfavorable position as against their wholesalers; many wholesalers as against manufacturers; many manufacturers as against raw materials producers. They caught many workers in the process of negotiating for wage adjustments which other workers had already obtained. Many of these kinks in the price-wage

structure have to be ironed out in order to achieve a situation which is fair and reasonable enough to hold firm against the new inflationary pressures we expect. Necessarily, there will continue to be some differences in the impact of price and wage regulations as among individuals or firms; these will be minimized, but they are inevitable if we are to have real stabilization.

In the case of prices, the Office of Price Stabilization has been moving ahead with the adjustment process since the January freeze. Adjustments have been completed for many products and industries, but not for all. Roll-backs from January prices have been required on a number of raw materials and finished products. More roll-backs are planned. In other cases, some price increases will have to be allowed where sellers are caught unfairly between high costs and low prices. But these increases must be held to the minimum that will result in adequate production and reasonable returns. The upward spiraling of prices which is involved in translating cost increases into price increases must be prevented.

The Office of Price Stabilization expects to complete this adjustment process in the near future, and to have then a firm structure of price control with prices on the average very close to the January level. This adjusted price structure is the line we propose to hold against the new inflationary pressures which we foresee.

The Office of Price Stabilization will move as rapidly as is administratively feasible to apply a general standard of not permitting price increases in any industry when the level of profits for that industry is more than 85% of its average profits for the best three of four years 1946–1949.

This standard is roughly the same as that used in the excess profits tax law, and is fair and reasonable during a time of national emergency. Corporate profits are now running at the all-time record rate of 48 billion dollars a year—more than 14 billion dollars higher than in 1948, and about 20 billion dollars higher than in 1949. There is clearly room for cost absorption in profits such as these.

In addition, the Office of Price Stabilization has been directed to work out specific dollars and cents ceilings on individual commodities wherever possible. This is of vital importance both as a means of checking unwarranted price increases and in order that the buying public may know the legal price and help enforce it.

In the case of wages, unfortunately, the process of changing over from the wage freeze to a fair longer-run wage stabilization program was interrupted by the split-up of the Wage Stabilization Board in February. In the absence of a Board, only slow progress has been made toward establishing fair and workable wage stabilization policies.

Within the last week, however, I have issued an Executive Order re-establishing the Wage Stabilization Board. The further development of fair wage stabilization policies for the longer run should now go rapidly forward. In formulating such policies, many factors will have to be weighed, including changes in the cost of living, substandards of living, and cases of hardship or inequity. At the same time, it is obvious that workers will have to forego substantial increases in wages which would be permissible if the danger of inflation were not so great—just as businessmen and farmers will have to forego substantial increases in income for the same reason.

The Defense Production Act has special provisions regarding ceilings on farm products. It prohibits setting price ceilings on agricultural commodities below either the parity price or the highest price attained in the May 24–June 24, 1950, period, whichever is higher. This provision has led to con-

siderable misunderstanding; it has often been said to prevent price ceilings on farm products. This is, of course, not so. Prices of several of the major farm products, including meats, cotton, and wool, are above the legal minimums and consequently are subject to price ceilings. For example, a dollars-and-cents ceiling has been placed on cotton at the producer level.

Prices paid to farmers for some farm commodities, however, are below parity. These prices cannot be controlled, under the present law, until they rise to the parity level. This has led to some proposals to change the law to permit price ceilings to be placed on farm products below parity levels. I do not believe such proposals are justified under present circumstances. The parity principle, which is the basis for our agricultural laws, is the best guide we now have available to judge what is a fair return to farmers.

I do believe, however, that for price control purposes, the parity price for each commodity prevailing at the start of its normal marketing season should be applied throughout the balance of the marketing season, just as is the case in most of our agricultural price support programs. I recommend that the Defense Production Act be amended to provide for this. Under this amendment, the parity price will continue to be a minimum standard for each price ceiling. The amendment will, however, substantially improve the administration of price control on food products and will forestall the inflationary effects of frequent changes in the computation of the parity price of individual farm commodities.

The current outlook is for stable food prices, at least for some months to come. However, if we find that we cannot hold the line on food prices with the powers recommended here, we shall need to consider legislation authorizing the use of other devices, including limited food subsidies to prevent necessary farm price increases from being reflected in rises in the cost of living. Such subsidies were very successful in World War II, and saved consumers and taxpayers far more than they cost. The stabilization agencies are keeping close watch on the areas where need for these subsidies may develop, and the Congress will be kept informed.

Price controls will be successful only if buyers and sellers are well informed about what the law and regulations require. The Office of Price Stabilization is now doing its best to inform them. But there is need also for tough and aggressive enforcement action against the small minority who would willfully violate the law. The Defense Production Act needs to be strengthened in a number of respects to tighten up the Government's enforcement powers. For example, the courts should be given authority to impose higher civil penalties for violations than the law now permits.

Rent Control

A serious deficiency in the present stabilization structure is the absence of an effective rent control law. For millions of families with low or moderate income, rent accounts for as much as 15 percent or more of the total family budget. If costs of living are to be stabilized, it is obvious that increases in rents must be stopped and the line held, just as with other prices.

There is still in effect a rent control law, due to expire on June 30. We are fortunate that this law is still on the books. But it is entirely inadequate to help meet the inflationary pressures which will confront us in the coming months.

The present law was enacted before the Korean outbreak as a last step in the liquidation of the rent controls left over from the war. About 6.7 million housing units are still under Federal control, compared to 16 million housing units under control at the peak of the World War II rent control program. In addition, one State and one municipality have control measures of their own.

Before the Korean outbreak, it was contemplated that Federal control would be removed from these last remaining units by June 30, 1951, at the latest. Since Korea, however, reactivation of military camps and other installations in various parts of the country has placed great pressures on nearby housing accommodations and in a number of instances has brought a shocking increase in rents. This has become a heavy and totally unjustified burden on many men in service. In some communities where rents have been decontrolled, servicemen's rents have risen as much as 100%. In some defense areas, also, expansion of production facilities by private industry and by the military services or the Atomic Energy Commission has begun to send rents soaring. Over the nation as a whole, the volume of new housing—which was helping to relieve the housing shortage and the pressure on rent levels—has had to be sharply curtailed.

All of these circumstances call for new rent legislation. The Government should have power to establish rent controls in any community where they are needed to stabilize the situation, stop profiteering, and hold down living costs. Of course, if State and local action results in holding rents to reasonable levels, the Federal Government would not act.

In addition to the control of rents on residential housing, an effective stabilization program in this period requires that the Government be able to control business rents. Rents are an important part of the cost of doing business at wholesale and retail levels. With the high levels of business activity, sales and warehouse space has been at a premium for many months. Business rents are rising in many cities and further sharp increases are threatened in the coming months. Unless controls are authorized, many businesses, particularly small firms, will face rent and hence cost increases, which will either drive them out of business or require a break in price ceilings.

The keystone of our stabilization program is to share fairly the necessary burdens imposed by the defense effort. We can do this best by holding the cost of living stable, by preventing profiteering by anyone, and by paying for our military needs through higher taxes. A rounded stabilization program, such as I have outlined, can accomplish these ends.

Summary of Proposed Changes in the Defense Production Act

In this message, I have discussed the more important of the amendments which I believe should be made in the Defense Production Act at this time. Others will be presented to the Congressional Committees by appropriate officials of the Executive Branch.

In summary, the more important amendments to the Act which I now recommend would:

1. Extend the life of the Act for two years, until June 30, 1953.

2. Authorize the Government to build and operate defense plants, where necessary, to produce essential materials and equipment.

3. Permit the use of differential subsidies to obtain essential production from high-cost sources of supply without increasing price ceilings.

4. Provide for controls over credit on existing housing, and regulation of speculative trading on commodity exchanges.

5. Allow the parity price for each farm commodity as of the beginning of its marketing season to be used for price control purposes throughout the marketing season.

6. Provide stronger means to enforce price control regulations.

7. Authorize effective control over both residential and commercial rents, wherever needed to stabilize the cost of living and the cost of doing business.

If, as we proceed with the defense mobilization program, it becomes evident that we need further legislative action to assure that our goals are met, I shall make further recommendations to the Congress.

While the Congress is considering these proposals and enacting those which it deems desirable, the Executive Branch will continue to use vigorously the range of powers it has now. In the course of its forthcoming deliberations, the Congress will have available to it for consideration all of the experience and information which the Executive agencies can provide.

We are engaged in a historic effort to hold together all of the free peoples of the world in the face of the greatest danger ever confronting them. As a leader in that effort, we must demonstrate to the whole world that the founding fathers were wise in their faith that our Government of divided powers would never suffer disunity or frustrate necessary action in time of peril. The Executive Branch and the Congress are both responsive to the American people—and the needs of the people are now both clear and imperative.

HARRY S. TRUMAN

NOTE: For the statement by the President upon signing the Defense Production Act Amendments, see Item 176.

92   Letter to the Speaker Transmitting the Budget for the Military Functions of the Department of Defense.   *April* 30, 1951

Sir:

I transmit herewith for the consideration of the Congress my budget recommendations for the military functions of the Department of Defense for the fiscal year ending June 30, 1952.

My recommendations for appropriations amount to $57,604,254,390, including $1,-424,839,700 to liquidate prior authorizations. The balance, $56,179,414,690, represents new obligational authority. In addition, I am submitting an estimate of $4,500,000,000, which represents the funds needed in 1952 for a large military public works program to be recommended soon for authorization. This makes a total of $60,679,414,690, compared to the $60,000,000,000 tentative estimate contained in the January Budget for fiscal year 1952, and to the $47,590,608,844 which has been enacted or recommended for the current fiscal year.

These recommendations for appropriations do not materially alter the estimates of expenditures made in January for fiscal years 1951 and 1952. The revised estimate of expenditure for 1951 is 19.4 billion dollars, compared to 20 billion dollars carried in the January Budget. For fiscal year 1952, expenditures are estimated at 39.5 billion dollars compared to 40 billion dollars carried in the January Budget.

The major expansion in our defense expenditures is one part of our total program to enable us and the other free nations to save the world from another and more frightful global war. It is also a program to enable us, if general war should be thrust upon us, to halt the enemy's forces and strike back decisively at the center of the enemy's power.

We are now meeting the savage thrust of communist aggression in Korea. Our fight-ing men and those of our allies are today locked in battle with the armed forces of Soviet satellites. Our men are being supplied with the best in modern military equipment, supplies, and ammunition.

They are inflicting terrible punishment on the communist armies. They have checked the plans of the Kremlin to extend communist control to other parts of Asia. They have won time for the free nations to prepare their defenses against the world-wide Soviet plan of world domination.

The aggression in Korea is only part of the Kremlin strategy to achieve world domination. The Soviet Union is prepared to use armed force elsewhere in the world, and is using many other methods than military force to gain its ends.

The struggle which the Kremlin has initiated is global in scope, and involves almost every aspect of human endeavor. All the free nations, wherever they may be, are affected by the aggressive designs of the despots in the Kremlin. And they are affected not only by the military power these men control, but also by their attacks upon the economic, social and moral life of free men.

To meet this threat the free world must strengthen its military defenses and its economic and social foundations. The free nations must carry the attack to the enemy in the realm of the minds and convictions of men.

This budget estimate represents, therefore, but one of the parts of our national security program. Other parts have already been sent to the Congress, or will shortly be submitted. Last week I submitted proposals for needed legislation to enable our economy to carry out our defense production plans.

Some time ago, I forwarded recommendations for the expansion of our campaign of truth. I expect shortly to submit an integrated program to help other free nations build up their military and economic strength, in combination with ours.

All these elements are essential to enable us to win the kind of struggle that the Kremlin has brought about. Together, they constitute approximately three-fourths of the total Federal budget.

In money terms, by far the largest part of this total security program is the cost of building up our own military strength. The funds I am today recommending will carry forward the rapid build-up in military strength upon which our Nation embarked, when the aggression in Korea showed that the Soviet rulers were willing to push the world to the brink of a general war to get what they want.

We are building our military strength in the way best calculated to meet the military threat that confronts us.

The major element in this threat is the military strength and military production of the Soviet Union. The armed forces of the Soviet Union today far exceed any reasonable defense requirements. Its economy is harnessed to war production.

If the Soviet Union chooses to unleash a general war, the free world must be in a position to stop the attack and strike back decisively and at once at the seats of Soviet power. We believe that the best path to peace is through building combined defenses for the free world sufficiently powerful to insure disaster for the aggressors if they launch a new world war.

Our military program must be aimed at this central problem.

We want to keep the conflict in Korea from spreading, if possible, because we are trying to stop aggression without starting a third world war. Furthermore, we need time to prepare our defenses to meet a general war if it is thrust upon us.

Supplies and equipment are now flowing to Korea in abundant quantity. More supplies for Korea are in the pipeline. We will continue to send to Korea the arms that are needed by our forces to repel aggression in that area.

The major emphasis of this budget estimate is upon building up our Armed Forces and our productive capacity toward the level of preparedness necessary in the event of all-out war. In addition to maintaining our forces on active duty, funds are provided for a war reserve of supplies and equipment and for the creation of a mobilization base—including reserve forces, military installations, and industrial capacity—to enable us to mobilize quickly, if necessary, for an all-out war effort. At the same time, the level of preparedness which this budget is designed to create is one which is well within our ability to maintain for many years, if necessary.

This budget is based on our estimate at this time of the military build-up required to meet our security objectives. But our planning must remain flexible. In the event of a change in the international situation, the present program may have to be substantially modified.

The funds I am recommending today will finance the following elements of our armed strength.

In the last ten months, we have more than doubled the active strength of our Armed Forces. During the fiscal year 1952 we will reach our present goal of about 3.5 million men and women. These forces will steadily increase in combat readiness as those now in training status are assigned to combat units.

For the Army, these funds will equip and maintain 18 divisions plus separate combat and supporting units. The Navy, under these recommendations, will maintain an active fleet of 1,161 ships. The Marine Corps will maintain 2⅓ divisions and other supporting units. The Air Force will continue to build toward 95 air wings.

In addition to these forces on active duty, about 2 million men and women will be in the Military Reserve and ROTC programs and the National Guard establishments. The value of the reserve forces has been proved again in recent months, as 520,000 reserves have been called to active duty. We shall continue to emphasize the training of more reserve forces.

Most of the funds in this military budget will be spent for military equipment and supplies, and for constructing bases, camps, and other facilities. Of the total of 60.7 billion dollars of new obligational authority, about 43 billion dollars is for procurement and construction. About 34.7 billion dollars will be used to purchase heavy equipment such as ships, planes, tanks, artillery, trucks, ammunition, guided missiles, and electronics. Planes alone total 14.5 billion dollars of this.

This equipment will be of the most up-to-date kinds, and will substantially complete the program of modernizing the combat equipment of the Armed Forces.

We shall, at the same time, continue to step up the research and development program. The funds in this budget will support a program about 20 percent larger than in the current fiscal year and about two-and-one-half times as large as in fiscal year 1950.

This military program will have an increasing impact on our economy, especially as equipment orders are translated into actual production.

The present plans for our military and other security programs—including mutual security assistance to friendly countries and the stockpiling program—are estimated to require about 20 percent of the total national output by the end of fiscal year 1952. This is substantially less than the 45 percent of total output which was going to security purposes at the peak of World War II. But it will involve a rapid and substantial shift of resources. It will give us serious production problems and will require forceful action against inflation.

In my message of April 26 recommending the extension and strengthening of the Defense Production Act I urged renewal of the authority under which we are now regulating the flow of scarce materials, so as to assure the performance of defense contracts. I also outlined the tax increases and other measures which must be taken in order to offset these inflationary pressures. These recommendations are vital to our security program. The national defense will be seriously hampered if they are not enacted.

The necessity which is now thrust upon the Government to draw heavily upon manpower, materials, and industrial facilities, for national defense, requires efficient scheduling of procurement, production, and facilities expansion. Both the civilian and military agencies of Government are concerned with these matters, and both are moving to improve their effectiveness as the defense program grows.

This military budget is essential to our national security. The outbreak of aggression, the threat of general war that overhangs the world, make it imperative to increase our defenses rapidly and efficiently.

Our arms must be up to date and adapted to the many facets of the struggle we face. There is no one weapon—no Maginot Line—

that can make us secure. We must work together with other free nations. We must be prepared to use all the great resources of our economy to produce whatever may be necessary for our protection and for the preservation of freedom throughout the world.

If we all work together, as our people have always worked together in time of national danger, we shall succeed.

HARRY S. TRUMAN

[Honorable Sam Rayburn, Speaker of the House of Representatives]

NOTE: On October 18, 1951, the President signed the Department of Defense Appropriation Act, 1952 (65 Stat. 423).

93 Remarks to Key Officials on the Budget for the Military Functions of the Department of Defense. *May* 3, 1951

[Released May 3, 1951. Delivered April 27, 1951]

FOR THE LAST several weeks many of you gentlemen have been involved in an intensive effort to develop the military budget for 1952. That budget represents one of the most significant programing jobs that this administration is going to place before the Congress this year. It is the major reason for our asking the Congress and the country to go along with many emergency actions.

I am most anxious that each one of you share the personal concern which I have about this military program and about the importance of carrying it through in an orderly and effective way. I have stated many times that in this limited mobilization situation inflation is a major enemy. The way we administer this program can do a lot to help spread inflation or to help restrict it and to turn the inflationary spiral. It is because the administration of this military program is of such major importance in our stabilization effort and in our worldwide program that I have called you together.

Passage of this budget will place tremendous procurement and spending authority in the hands of the Department of Defense and the three services. The schedules call for $34.7 billion in hard goods from 1952 appropriations in addition to $27 billion already available—a total of $61.7 billion for equipment for our own forces. To this will have to be added the military construction program and the equipment needs of our allies. Again, I repeat that this is going to place a particularly heavy management job on the entire executive branch to see that we buy wisely—buy what we need—put what we buy to good use—and do the whole job in a way that does not weaken our basic economy.

The fiscal controls which we normally use to keep many of our operations under scrutiny aren't sufficiently precise to meet our needs during this period of intensive mobilization activity. We have all recognized that the accomplishment of this military program is going to have a major impact on the economy. Broad adjustments in the economy have to be made to handle it and that is the basic job of the Office of Defense Mobilization, the Defense Production Administration, and the rest of our emergency agencies. But these agencies cannot help by working on a dollar basis—they have to work with the specifics of materials, facilities, and end items.

The services must establish effective supporting control systems to manage both the personnel and the production and procurement areas included in this dollar budget program. Again, you all recognize this.

257

But one of the main reasons for my assembling this group is to emphasize the importance of giving this matter immediate attention and starting, in a systematic way, a regular process of watching and knowing how well we are doing our procurement and production job, particularly on the critical military items, and what effect it is having in the economy generally.

Specifically, before this money becomes available for expenditure, we must have accomplished the following two actions:

a. Creation by the Department of Defense of a system to control the requirements for and check on utilization of civilian and military personnel. I want the Budget Bureau to review this system and help in its establishment. We must prevent any hoarding of manpower in this program.

b. Detailed programing in the Department of Defense of the dollars for procurement and production based on procedures which insure the production of important long-lead-time military items and hold down on the procurement of short-term easy-to-get items in order to build up our production facilities on a balanced basis.

Mr. Wilson is going to be responsible for seeing that this facilities expansion and production job is done—and that the Defense Production Administration and other mobilization agencies play an active and appropriate part in this process. In this respect, it is recognized that the Department of Defense has the primary responsibility to organize its programs and procedures. But in order that these large programs can be integrated into the economy in an orderly manner, and effective stabilization be accomplished, the mobilization agencies must participate actively in the programing and scheduling job.

I'm going to be even more specific. I understand that there is agreement among the Office of Defense Mobilization, the Defense Production Administration, the Defense Department, and the Bureau of the Budget that the following steps are feasible and should be accomplished before this money becomes available for expenditure:

a. Establishment of specific, realistic production schedules covering items comprising at least 70–75 percent of the dollars for hard goods items.

If we are going to keep a healthy mobilization base and avoid severe, unnecessary jolts on the economy we must be sure that we don't move ahead too far on the relatively easy items and that the timing of our procurement is related to real requirements.

The dollars that have been provided for these hard goods items are based on objectives which are going to be very difficult to reach. We don't want to be blocking ourselves on production matters by bidding up prices or by needless competition among ourselves. We are going to be in this a long time. The military—in their own best interest—must manage this job better than they did in World War II and better than they are set up to do it now—because it is a long-range job—it isn't a quick up and quick down affair.

The Department of Defense has to have the machinery to establish for itself the priorities in its program—this means that the Joint Chiefs have to be ready to give their advice on what is most essential, and the Munitions Board and the mobilization agencies have to know where and what the program is at all times. It is a problem of getting our resources behind the most important items and programs. For example, if there are insufficient electronic items for all scheduled production, who gets what is available?

To try to do the military job and accomplish the necessary supporting production, the mobilization agencies are instituting the controlled materials plan. We want to make this plan work. I know from World War II experience that a controlled materials plan cannot work unless firm production schedules have been established. This is an additional reason for doing this job now.

b. Establishment of definite policies under which instructions can be given to the procurement officers, so that the whole range of soft goods and unscheduled items—for which there is more than 5 billion in this budget—can be bought in an orderly manner.

I want to stop the business of buying huge amounts of items common to the economy by some procurement officer down the line merely because he feels he has a directive to obtain everything he needs for 2 years in the next 2 months.

Also, I want to be sure that we set up proper inventory control systems so that inventories can be checked before we buy and so that we know what we have when we need to use it. Again, each one of you has a big stake in this matter of trying to demonstrate that the Government can carry out the kind of program envisioned in this budget without taking numerous, unwise actions.

c. Establish a control of the major special procurement programs, such as facilities, tools, lumber, petroleum, wool, and cotton goods, on as firm a basis as possible.

I know that much good work has been done on these programs. They are particularly sensitive, however, and need constant attention and improvement.

If, during the next 2–3 months, the Department of Defense and the mobilization agencies can work together to firm up the procurement and production program in the three areas I've outlined we will have made the first step toward getting set to manage this dollar program well.

All of us should recognize the differences between the present situation regarding procurement and production and that which prevailed during World War II. Now we are not aiming at a full war economy—we are trying to maintain a high readiness status for a long period—we are trying to develop greater economic strength both here and abroad—we have to plan our present job to do all these things and still meet the military goals—which are high.

I want again to stress the importance of doing this job well. It will require the close working cooperation of the Defense Department and the mobilization agencies. From a dollar standpoint this is nearly three-fourths of our governmental effort. I am going to try to follow closely how we are set up to perform this major job. I'm going to ask Mr. Wilson, Mr. Lovett, and Mr. Lawton to give me a report 2 weeks from today as to the steps that have been put in motion to make the reviews I've listed—and to set up a system which will let us keep the procurement and production job under close control.

Both the Defense Department and the mobilization agencies—the Office of Defense Mobilization, Defense Production Administration, National Production Authority, etc.—could profit from these reviews in that together you are getting a better understanding of the job ahead of you and steps that need to be taken to accomplish it. I am sure that you in the Defense Production Administration and the National Production Authority will find that you have a big job ahead of you to make possible the realization of our military production goals.

Another reason for undertaking this kind of a review and scheduling operation on an urgent basis is that we will have to use such a system to prepare our 1953 budgets and to review the progress of this program in October and November. In other words, you should establish a system now so that the production schedules are always available to be reviewed and to furnish the guide for financial requirements. You should not look upon this as a one-time operation which will not have further utility.

NOTE: The President's remarks of April 27 were made public on May 3 as part of a White House release which stated that the President had met with key defense, mobilization, production, stabilization, and budget officials as one of a series of steps he had taken to see that the defense mobilization program was carried out rapidly, efficiently, and with full teamwork among the agencies concerned.

The following were listed as present: Robert A. Lovett, Deputy Secretary of Defense, Lyle S. Garlock, Assistant Comptroller for Budget, Department of Defense, Frank Pace, Jr., Secretary of the Army, Karl R. Bendetsen, Assistant Secretary of the Army, Francis P. Matthews, Secretary of the Navy, Dan A. Kimball, Under Secretary of the Navy, Thomas K. Finletter, Secretary of the Air Force, Eugene M. Zuckert, Assistant Secretary of the Air Force, Gen. Omar N. Bradley, Chairman, Joint Chiefs of Staff, Gen. J. Lawton Collins, Chief of Staff, Army, Adm. Forrest P. Sherman, Chief of Naval Operations, Gen. Hoyt S. Vandenberg, Chief of Staff, Air Force, John D. Small, Chairman, Munitions Board, Charles E. Wilson, Director of Defense Mobilization, William H. Harrison, Defense Production Administrator, Edwin T. Gibson, Deputy Administrator for Staff Services, Defense Production Administration, Manly Fleischmann, Administrator, National Production Authority, Frederick J. Lawton, Director, Bureau of the Budget, Elmer B. Staats, Assistant Director, Bureau of the Budget, William F. Schaub, Deputy Chief of the Division of Estimates, Bureau of the Budget, and George E. Ramsey, Chief of the National Security Branch of the Division of Estimates, Bureau of the Budget.

94 Remarks to a Group of Foreign Journalists. *May 3, 1951*

IT IS a very great pleasure for me this morning to have the privilege of meeting you gentlemen. I hope you are having a pleasant visit in this country of ours, and that you will find out some things for yourselves that when you go back you can say will be true.

That is what we are interested in, in this around-the-world effort of ours to get peace. If we can get the truth to the people, the peace will come automatically. That is one of the hardest things to do.

I have heard some of the greatest publications on the Continent—in Great Britain, Asia, Africa—mentioned this morning when you were introduced to me, and I am happy that you are here. If there is anything we can do to contribute to your enjoyment, or to furnish you with any information that you are interested in, I hope all the people meeting you and seeing that you see things will work with you. If they don't, maybe if you will tell me about it, they will.

NOTE: The President spoke at 12:10 p.m. in the Rose Garden at the White House.

95 The President's News Conference of *May 3, 1951*

THE PRESIDENT. Please be seated.

I have no special announcements to make today. I will listen to questions and try to answer them.

[1.] Q. Mr. President, the Prime Minister of Israel[1] arrived here today, to see you tomorrow and launch a half-billion-dollar

bond drive for his country. Would you comment on his trip?

THE PRESIDENT. He is going to have lunch with me tomorrow.

Q. Could you say anything about——

THE PRESIDENT. That's all the comment I have to make. I will carry on the conversations with *him,* and not in the press.

---

[1] Prime Minister David Ben-Gurion of Israel.

[2.] Q. Mr. President, as you probably know, on the Hill today, General Mac-Arthur said that——

THE PRESIDENT. No, I *don't* know—only what I have seen in the papers——

Q. I beg your pardon.

THE PRESIDENT. ——but go ahead.

Q. I will revise my question. General MacArthur said on the Hill today that on January 12 the Joint Chiefs of Staff approved completely his war plans, and he assumed that either you or General Marshall must have overridden the Chiefs on that?

THE PRESIDENT. Don't you think you had better wait until the evidence is all in, before you come to a conclusion on such things as that? There are plenty of things that will come up on this line on which you ought to wait until you have all the facts, before you come to a conclusion. I can't answer the question.

Q. Mr. President, in that connection, in the light of recent developments and utterances, would you agree that "old soldiers just fade away"?

THE PRESIDENT. What do you think? [*Laughter*]

[3.] Q. Mr. President, in view of the report of the Senate Crime Investigating Committee Tuesday, do you think Ambassador O'Dwyer[2] is properly qualified to be an Ambassador of the United States?

THE PRESIDENT. I still have confidence in Ambassador O'Dwyer.

Q. Do you think the average American thinks he is properly qualified?

THE PRESIDENT. I don't know what the average American thinks, but I don't think that a man can be tried in public and convicted without knowing all the evidence.

Q. Have you any other comment on the work of the committee?

----

[2] William O'Dwyer, U.S. Ambassador to Mexico and former Mayor of New York City.

THE PRESIDENT. No comment. What committee are you talking about?

Q. The crime committee.

THE PRESIDENT. Oh—oh—I didn't think about that! Too many of them—that's right.

[4.] Q. Mr. President, speaking of the other committee, General MacArthur said that he considers invalid your reasons for dismissing him. He said he not only carried out every directive but that it can be said he was not in opposition to policy which he was not aware of, and that he does not know what the policy is?

THE PRESIDENT. Did you hear my answer to the gentleman over here? That's the same answer.

[5.] Q. Mr. President, coming back to the Kefauver Committee, sir, do you care to comment on their findings that Costello had considerable influence in the Democratic organization in New York?

THE PRESIDENT. The what?

Q. That Frank Costello exerted considerable influence in the Democratic organizations in New York?

THE PRESIDENT. I can't answer that because I don't know.

[*Pause*]

What's the matter with you boys? [*Laughter*]

[6.] Q. Mr. President, in other words, getting back to General MacArthur—in other words, you are confident when the entire case is in, that the country will feel that you were justified in the action taken?

THE PRESIDENT. Well, when the facts are all known, there will be but one answer, and I have given that answer already.

Q. Well sir, I meant by that—by my question—that with the hero's welcome that he got and everything, that a lot of people are still in doubt.

THE PRESIDENT. Well, I say, if you will just

wait until all the evidence is in, you can then draw your own conclusions, and I think they will be the correct ones.

Q. Mr. President, in the publication of the Wake Island conference,[3] there was no reference to the time when you and MacArthur met alone. Have you any intention of issuing any kind of memorandum on what went on between the two of you?

THE PRESIDENT. I do not. There was nobody present there but the general and myself. It was a purely personal conference, and there was no record kept of it whatever, although I know what took place there. I do not intend to comment on it.

Q. You made no memorandum of it?

THE PRESIDENT. No.

[7.] Q. Mr. President, some of the Congressmen on the Hill are reporting around about that Mr. Ed Flynn of New York[4] came to the White House opposed to the St. Lawrence Seaway, and after he talked with you he went away in favor of it. And that after that Mr. Buckley,[5] the Chairman of the Public Works Committee, said he couldn't go against his good friend Mr. Flynn and that perhaps there had been other conversations at the White House lately, with various members of the House Public Works Committee, regarding deals on the St. Lawrence Seaway? Would you say that there have been?

THE PRESIDENT. Well now, you are making a lot of implications that are founded absolutely on false premises.

There is not a word of truth in anything you have asked me. When this St. Lawrence Seaway came up, I called the Committee itself in toto—every member of it—down, and had it thoroughly and completely explained to them by everybody who knew what the implications of the St. Lawrence Seaway are. After that conference the Committee was in favor of the St. Lawrence Seaway and that included the Chairman. Ed Flynn never said a word to me about the St. Lawrence Seaway. In fact, I think he may be against it. I have never talked to him about it.

Q. I see, sir. Then there have been no deals made to ——

THE PRESIDENT. Not that I know of. I don't make deals on legislation. I put the legislation up to the Congress, and then it is up to the Congress to act on it. There couldn't be any deals made on that piece of legislation.

[8.] Q. Mr. President, did you approve the price control order on meat?

THE PRESIDENT. I did.

Q. I didn't know whether it had come up to you direct?

THE PRESIDENT. It was put up to me and I approved it.

[9.] Q. Mr. President, in that part of the Wake Island conference that was attended by other people, were you aware personally that there was a woman in the other room taking down what——

THE PRESIDENT. No, I was not.

Q. Mr. President, General MacArthur has expressed an opinion on the question of whether or not Russia might intervene?

THE PRESIDENT. He is entitled to that opinion—he is entitled to any opinion he chooses.

Q. You have the benefit of the information gathered by the Central Intelligence Agency——

THE PRESIDENT. ——which he didn't have because he wouldn't let the Central Intelligence Agency work in Japan until just recently.

---

[3] On May 2 the Senate Armed Services and Foreign Relations Committees released the administration's documents on the Wake Island conference preliminary to their hearings, beginning May 3, on the dismissal of General MacArthur.

See also Item 90 [6].

[4] Edward J. Flynn, Democratic national committeeman from New York State.

[5] Representative Charles A. Buckley of New York.

Q. And you were surrounded by men who have had experience in Moscow. I wonder if you had any opinion about what Russia might or might not do?

THE PRESIDENT. No, I have no opinion to express. My opinions have been in action.

Q. Why wouldn't he let the CIA work there?

THE PRESIDENT. I don't know. You will have to ask him. He'll answer you, I expect.

Q. Mr. President, today there were—even though he wouldn't let the CIA work there, I think that he said that the CIA last November had given the opinion that the Chinese Communists wouldn't come in?

THE PRESIDENT. I didn't know that. The CIA usually reports to me. If they made any such report to him, they didn't make it to me.

Q. Isn't it true, sir, that they made a report to you on November 21?

THE PRESIDENT. They make a report to me every day, so they must have made a report to me on November 21, but I don't know what was in it. That has been quite a while ago.

Q. It was my idea that it was quite contrary to what he said today.

THE PRESIDENT. If it's a secret document, I don't know how you found out about it.

Q. Mr. President, when was the CIA——

THE PRESIDENT. I don't remember the exact date. If you will talk to Gen. Bedell Smith,[6] he can tell you.

Q. I am not sure he will, Mr. President.

THE PRESIDENT. What?

Q. I am not sure he will.

THE PRESIDENT. He's the right kind of an intelligence man, isn't he! [*Laughter*]

Q. Not unless you were to call him up and say that he could.

THE PRESIDENT. Well, I won't do that, but I am telling you the truth and the facts.

---

[6] Gen. Walter Bedell Smith, Director of the Central Intelligence Agency.

Q. There was a report——

THE PRESIDENT. I don't need to be checked up on it, but go ahead.

Q. There was a report made to you by CIA in advance of the November 24, 25, 26 intervention by the Chinese, pointing out the danger of Chinese intervention, is that not correct, sir?

THE PRESIDENT. I don't know. I will have to look it up. I say I get those reports every day and they are that thick [*Indicating*]. I read them every day, too, but I can't tell you the exact date or what was in any special report, without going back and looking it up.

Q. I don't mean——

THE PRESIDENT. I understand.

Q. ——the date, I mean in advance of the actual Chinese——

THE PRESIDENT. I can't answer that, without looking it up.

Q. I don't want to belabor this——

THE PRESIDENT. All right. Go ahead.

Q. ——but were you surprised, from your knowledge of CIA and the other reports that came to you, when the Chinese Communists did come in, sir?

THE PRESIDENT. I think everybody was not exactly surprised; they were sorry to see it happen.

Q. Well, General MacArthur seems to have been surprised.

THE PRESIDENT. He was very much surprised. [*Laughter*]

Q. Mr. President, who persuaded General MacArthur to let the CIA operate?

THE PRESIDENT. General Smith—General Smith.

Q. I didn't catch the question, sir?

THE PRESIDENT. He wanted to know who persuaded General MacArthur to let CIA intelligence get into his office, and I said General Smith did that. He made a trip over there for the purpose.

Q. Mr. President, could you tell us what the opinion of the Joint Chiefs of Staff and the CIA was, prior to the Chinese intervention, on whether they would or would not come in?

THE PRESIDENT. That is a matter of record and will probably be answered in the Committee by the Chiefs of Staff themselves. That is the best place to get it.

Q. Mr. President, I am not clear on something there. Do I understand that for a time General MacArthur would not let the Central Intelligence Agency work under his command or in his office?

THE PRESIDENT. That is correct.

Q. And there came a time when General Smith persuaded him to let the CIA in?

THE PRESIDENT. That is correct.

Q. Sir, could you say was that this year, or——

THE PRESIDENT. I don't remember the date. It can be looked up. I will have Joe Short [7] look it up and give it to you.

Q. After the Chinese intervention?

THE PRESIDENT. I can't answer that, because I don't know.

Q. Mr. President, would you care to express an opinion as to whether you believe it was unwise for General MacArthur not to have let the CIA come in?

THE PRESIDENT. I am expressing no opinion at the present time. I will give you my opinion when the time is right for it.

Q. Well, Mr. President, General Smith made one trip to Tokyo in January. Has he made more than one trip, or is that the one?

THE PRESIDENT. I think he made only one trip. I don't know the date. I can't confirm that date.

Q. Mr. President, by what authority or how could a general refuse to let the Central Intelligence Agency come in?

THE PRESIDENT. That is for you to guess at. I can't tell you.

Q. Mr. President, I recall that at Wake Island, when the conference broke up,

around noon I think, and the statement was issued that—on the basis of the statement that we received, there was an air of optimism about closing out the conflict in Korea. Could you say whether General MacArthur persuaded those present at the conference that the Chinese would not come in, and that——

THE PRESIDENT. I don't know what effect it had on the other members of the conference, but he persuaded me that they would not come in.

Q. Well, could you say where the order originated which permitted the United Nations forces, then, to go up to the Yalu River?

THE PRESIDENT. That is a matter of tactics in the field, and is the responsibility of the field commander. I never interfere with field commanders in any of their maneuvers.

[10.] Q. Mr. President, you said in the early part of the conference that you had complete confidence in Ambassador O'Dwyer. I take it it would naturally follow, then, that you have no intention of recalling him?

THE PRESIDENT. You are correct.

Q. Thank you.

[*Pause*]

THE PRESIDENT. What's the matter? [*Laughter*]

Q. Will you accept his resignation, sir, if he were to——

THE PRESIDENT. Now, Duke,[8] what do you want to ask a loaded question like that for? [*Laughter*] You know I am not going to answer that. I don't look for any such procedure. He's a fighter, just like I am.

[11.] Q. Mr. President, on Wake Island there was something said about you and General MacArthur being in agreement on the matter of Formosa. Since then, there seems to be quite a divergence of opinion on——

---

[7] Joseph H. Short, Secretary to the President.

[8] Duke Shoop of the Kansas City Star.

THE PRESIDENT. No comment—I can't answer that question.

Q. Mr. President, General MacArthur said today, "I do not believe that it will be within the capacity of the Soviet to mass any great additional increment of force to launch any predatory attack from the Asiatic continent." Has that opinion been expressed before?

THE PRESIDENT. Not that I know of. All I have seen about opinions like that have been in the press, and I like to have them from the source before I comment on them.

Q. Is there anything else that you would like to tell us, Mr. President?

THE PRESIDENT. Not a thing.

Reporter: Thank you, Mr. President.

THE PRESIDENT. Thank you very much.

NOTE: President Truman's two hundred and sixty-second news conference was held in the Indian Treaty Room (Room 474) in the Executive Office Building at 4 p.m. on Thursday, May 3, 1951.

96   Address at a Dinner of the Civil Defense Conference.
May 7, 1951

Governor Caldwell, distinguished guests, and fellow Americans:

This conference is being held to consider one of the most important tasks facing our country.

The lives of many millions of our fellow citizens may depend on the development of a strong civil defense.

The threat of atomic warfare is one which we must face, no matter how much we dislike it. We can never afford to forget that the terrible destruction of cities, and of civilization as we know it, is a real possibility.

There are two things our country must do to face this awesome and terrible possibility.

One of them is to look to our civil defense. So long as there is any chance at all that the atomic bombs may fall on our cities, we cannot gamble on being caught unprepared. Let's not fool ourselves—there is such a chance. We must prepare for it.

The other thing we must do is to try to prevent atomic war from coming. That is what I have been working for ever since I became President. That is what our foreign policy is all about.

The foreign policy of the United States is based on an effort to attain world peace. Every action we have taken has had this aim in view.

We are right in the midst of a big debate on foreign policy. A lot of people are looking at this debate as if it were just a political fight. But the stakes are a lot more important than the outcome of an election. The thing that is at stake in this debate may be atomic war.

Our foreign policy is not a political issue. It is a matter of life and death. It is a matter of the future of mankind.

These two things—civil defense and foreign policy—are what I will talk to you about tonight. As you see, they are closely tied together. And they are both concerned with a form of warfare which is more destructive than anything the world has ever known before in its history.

Our civil defense problem starts with a few basic facts.

Because there was an atomic explosion in the Soviet Union in 1949, we must act on the assumption that they do have atomic bombs.

They have planes that could drop atomic bombs upon our cities.

No matter how good our air defense may be, or how big an air force we build, a determined air attack by the Soviet Union could drop bombs upon this country. Our air force experts say planes would get through, however good our defenses may be.

The purpose of atomic attacks would be to strike a death blow at our cities, to burn out our centers of production, and to create panic among our people.

There is no complete protection against an atomic bomb attack. But there is a lot we can do to reduce the number of deaths and injuries and to check panic.

We must organize ourselves—in every city, factory, office, and home. Civil defense is a responsibility which begins with the individual. It begins with you—it begins with you. It is shared with the city, the State, and the Nation.

We have two immediate jobs. One is to teach all our people how to protect themselves in the event of an enemy attack. The other is to organize and train millions of volunteers as active members of the United States Civil Defense Corps. That is what you are here for.

The question we are putting up to you men and women at this conference is: How can we do these jobs as quickly and as efficiently as it is possible? We need your help in getting our fellow citizens to realize that this is a very serious business. So long as we face the threat of an atomic attack on the United States, we have got to build a strong civil defense organization.

But even with such an organization, our losses in an atomic war, if we should have one—and God forbid—those losses would be terrible. Whole cities would be casualties. Cleveland or Chicago, Seattle or New York, Los Angeles or Washington, or any of our other great cities might be destroyed. And they could be destroyed.

Even with such losses, frightful as they would be, I think this country would survive and would win an atomic war. But even if

we win, an atomic war would be a disaster.

The best defense against the atomic bomb is to prevent the outbreak of another world war and to achieve a real peace. We must bend all our energy to the job of keeping our free way of life, and to keep it without another war.

We can have peace only if we have justice and fair dealing among nations. The United Nations is the best means we have for deciding what is right and what is wrong between nations. It is a great attempt to make the moral judgment of mankind effective in international affairs. Nothing is more important if mankind is to overcome the barbaric doctrine that might makes right.

Our best chance to keep the peace and to stay free is for nations that believe in freedom to stick together and to build their strength together. That is what we call collective security.

We have been trying since the last war was over and even before it was over to build a system of collective security among those countries who really believe in the principles of the United Nations.

I think we have made a lot of progress. I know that some people have become impatient with our efforts to establish collective security, because we have not yet succeeded in attaining world peace. But we are on the right road.

There are cynics who scorn the United Nations, who are indifferent to the need for cooperation among the free peoples. They do not understand that our best hope for peace is to bind together the nations that are striving for peace and to increase their strength to stop aggression.

The United Nations is being severely tested today because of the Korean conflict. The fighting there is requiring great sacrifices. In a time of crisis there is a tendency to look for some easy way out regardless of the consequences. But we must not be misled. We must not lose sight of the world picture and the critical importance of the United Nations if we are to reach a permanent solution.

Communist aggression in Korea is a part of the worldwide strategy of the Kremlin to destroy freedom. It has shown men all over the world that Communist imperialism may strike anywhere, anytime.

The defense of Korea is part of the worldwide effort of all the free nations to maintain freedom. It has shown free men that if they stand together, and pool their strength, Communist aggression cannot succeed.

The firm stand of the United Nations in Korea has checked the advance of the Communist imperialism throughout Asia. It is using up the military resources of the Chinese Communists to such an extent that they are not able to carry out the designs of Communist imperialism against the independence of other Asian countries. And the people of those countries who have been resisting Communist aggression have now been given new hope and new courage.

The Communist assault in Indochina has been checked by the free people of Indochina with the help of the French. In Malaya the British are holding firm against Communist guerrilla attacks. In the Philippines, in Burma, and in other places in Asia, Communist-led guerrillas are being blocked.

The fight against aggression in Korea has also dealt a heavy blow to the Kremlin conspiracy outside of Asia. It has brought new hope and courage to free men in Europe, and in the Middle East, who face the Soviet menace across their frontiers. The fight against Communist aggression in the Far East is the fight against Communist aggression in the West and in the whole world as well.

The struggle in Korea is a long and a hard one. But it can be won—and our policy is designed to win it.

The Chinese rulers are losing large numbers of their soldiers. As these losses increase, it will become clearer and clearer to them that aggression does not pay. They can have peace when they give up their aggression and stop the fighting.

Meanwhile, the strength of all the free nations is growing. The Soviet plan of world conquest is becoming more and more impossible to achieve. If we stick to our guns, and continue to punish the aggressors, we can end the aggression in Korea and restore peace.

We have been urged to take measures which would spread the fighting in the Far East. We have been told that this would bring the Korean conflict to a speedy conclusion; that it would save the lives of our troops. In my judgment that just isn't true. I believe we have a better chance of stopping aggression in Korea, at a smaller cost in the lives of our troops and those of our allies, by following our present course.

Let me tell you that I have studied this question for a long time. It is not a question that can be decided in the light of Korea alone. It does not affect just the Far East alone. It is not a local question. It affects Korea and Japan, and the security of our troops in those places. But it also reaches Europe, and the future of the North Atlantic Treaty, and the security of free people there and everywhere else in the world. It is a decision that affects the future of the United Nations and the future of the whole world.

I have refused to extend the area of the conflict in the Far East, under the circumstances which now prevail, and I am going to tell you exactly why.

I have refused first on military grounds. The best military advice I have been able to obtain—the best collective military advice in this country—is that this course of action would not lead to a quick and easy solution of the Korean conflict.

On the contrary, it could very well lead to a much bigger and much longer war. Such a war would not reduce our casualties in the Far East. It would increase them enormously.

Such a war would expose our troops to devastating air and submarine attacks. It would seriously endanger Japan and the Philippines. And it would unite the Chinese people behind their Communist rulers.

Furthermore, a deep involvement on our part in a war in China, whatever the outcome there, would have critical military consequences in Europe. There is nothing that would give the Kremlin greater satisfaction than to see our resources committed to an all-out struggle in Asia, leaving Europe exposed to the Soviet armies.

These are the military dangers.

But there are other dangers. The Kremlin is trying, and has been trying for a long time, to drive a wedge between us and the other free nations. It wants to see us isolated. It wants to see us distrusted. It wants to see us feared and hated by our allies.

Our allies agree with us in the course we are following. They do not believe that we should take the initiative to widen the conflict in the Far East. If the United States were to widen the conflict, we might well have to go it alone.

If we go it alone in Asia, we may destroy the unity of the free nations against aggression. Our European allies are nearer to Russia than we are. They are in far greater danger. If we act without regard to the danger that faces them, they may act without regard to the dangers that we face. Going it alone brought the world to the disaster of World War II. We cannot go it alone in Asia and go it in company in Europe. The whole idea of going it alone is the opposite

of everything we have stood for since World War II. Going it alone in Asia might wreck the United Nations, the North Atlantic Treaty, and the whole system of collective security we are helping to set up.

That would be a tremendous victory for the Soviet Union.

We do not intend to fall into that trap. I do not propose to strip this country of its allies in the face of Soviet danger.

The path of collective security is our only sure defense against the dangers that threaten us. It is the path to peace in Korea; it is the path to peace in the world.

We are determined to do our utmost to limit the war in Korea. We will not take any action which might place upon us the responsibility of initiating a general war—a third world war. But if the aggressor takes further action which threatens the security of the United Nations forces in Korea, we will meet and counter that action.

I repeat, I am convinced that the course we are now following in Korea is accomplishing the most for peace—and at the least cost in American lives. All of us wish that no Americans had to fight or die. But by fighting on a limited scale now, we may be able to prevent a third world war later on.

Remember this, if we do have another world war, it will be an atomic war. We could expect many atomic bombs to be dropped on American cities, and a single one of them could cause many more times the casualties than we have suffered in all the fighting in Korea. I do not want to be responsible for bringing that about.

Some people do not understand how the free world can ever win this long struggle without fighting a third world war. These people overlook the inner weaknesses of the Soviet dictatorship. They forget that the free world is stronger—stronger in its determination, stronger in its staying power, stronger in its human resources—than any system of slavery under a totalitarian dictatorship.

The Kremlin's system of terror, which appears to be its main strength, is one of its greatest weaknesses. Dictatorships are based on fear. They cannot give their people happiness and peace. They have nothing to offer except aggression and slavery.

As the aggressive tactics of the Kremlin are checked by the collective defenses of a free world, the futility of the whole Communist program is becoming more and more apparent to the people under Soviet control.

We can already see this process at work. In China the failure of the Korean adventure is weakening the hold of the Communist government. Wholesale arrests and executions are taking place. In the same way the pressure of the police state is increasing in the other satellite countries.

Yugoslavia has thrown off the Kremlin yoke. Every day refugees flee across the border from the Iron Curtain countries into the free countries of Europe.

There are growing signs of internal tension and unrest behind the Iron Curtain.

We must remember that the peoples under the Soviet rule of terror are not only our friends but our allies. They are victims of a terrible tyranny. We do not hate them. We have had friendly relations with them in the past, and we can have such friendship again.

As the free nations build their strength and unity, this fact will compel a change in the Soviet drive for power and conquest. The Soviet rulers are faced with the growing strength of the free world, the increasing cost of aggression, and the increasing difficulty of driving their people to greater and greater hardships. They will be forced by these pressures from within and without to give up aggression. It will then be possible to make progress with a program for international control and the reduction of armaments and for the peaceful settlement of disputes.

Our programs of economic aid and technical assistance, and our campaign of truth, not only strengthen the free peoples, they weaken the dictatorships. They remind the victims of tyranny that a better world lies outside their prison. They build up the hope of freedom everywhere.

Everything we can do to strengthen the free world; every dollar we spend for assistance to other nations; every effort we make to resist aggression in Korea, and around the world, brings closer the day of genuine peace.

We are not engaged in a struggle without end. We are engaged in a struggle which has the definite goal of peace. Peace under law is the victory we seek.

To achieve this goal we must work together, steadfastly and patiently. We must not be led astray. The real issue is whether we stand alone, or whether we stand and work with the other free peoples of the world.

I am confident that the American people will not yield either to impatience or defeatism. I am sure that our courage and wisdom are equal to the great task we are now undergoing. And I believe that with all our resources, our human energies, and our commonsense, we shall be successful in the great objective of defending freedom and bringing peace to the world.

NOTE: The President spoke at 10:30 p.m. at the Statler Hotel in Washington. In his opening words he referred to Millard Caldwell, Civil Defense Administrator and former Governor of Florida. The address was carried on a nationwide broadcast.

97 Special Message to the Senate on the Convention on Wage and Hour Statistics Adopted by the International Labor Conference. *May 9, 1951*

To the Senate of the United States:

On January 17, 1949 I transmitted to the Senate a convention (No. 63) concerning the statistics of wages and hours of work in the principal mining and manufacturing industries, including building and construction, and in agriculture, adopted by the International Labor Conference at its twenty-fourth session, Geneva, June 2–22, 1938. In my message transmitting the convention I requested that the Senate give its advice and consent to ratification thereof, subject to an understanding that the convention shall apply only to the continental United States.

As a result of a reappraisal of the situation in regard to the territorial application of the convention, I now request that the Senate give its advice and consent to ratification sub-ject only to the understanding that the convention shall not apply to the Canal Zone until such time as extended thereto by proclamation of the President of the United States of America.

For the information of the Senate I transmit herewith the report of the Secretary of State with respect to this matter, together with a copy of a letter from the Secretary of Labor to the Secretary of State.

HARRY S. TRUMAN

NOTE: The report of the Secretary of State and the letter from the Secretary of Labor are printed in Executive H (82d Cong., 1st sess.). The convention and related documents are printed in Executive G (81st Cong., 1st sess.).

For the President's special message to the Senate transmitting the convention on January 17, 1949, see 1949 volume, this series, Item 13.

98 Remarks at a Conference of the Industry Advisory Councils of the Department of the Interior. *May 9, 1951*

THANK YOU very much. My first visit to this auditorium, Mr. Secretary, was on a "Meet-the-Press" program, when I was a United States Senator, making some investigations in the Second World War. It was not a very satisfactory meeting for me. I hope this one will be more satisfactory to you. It came out all right, though. They got me into more trouble than any man has ever gotten into in the history of the world!

―――――

Mr. Secretary, and gentlemen of the Conference:

I am glad to meet with you gentlemen here today.

I know that you are all ready to do everything you can to help out in this time of emergency―and I want to emphasize that statement: The country never has been in a greater emergency―and I know you will do a good job. You have a fine man to work with in Oscar Chapman. He is thoroughly familiar with the natural resources you gentlemen are here to advise us about, and we could not have a better man in charge of the mobilization of those resources for the defense effort.

Now, I want to say to you that every man that I have asked to help in this project has been a man of ability and patriotism, and don't let anybody tell you anything else.

I appreciate very much the fact that you are willing to come and help us with our mobilization problems. It shows that when our country has a big job to do, people are ready to pitch in and help. And let me tell you now, our country does have a big job to do—just about the biggest and the hardest job in history.

One of the worst difficulties we have to overcome is the feeling that we can relax because we are not in an all-out war. That is a terrible mistake. We cannot afford to relax. We have three enemies to overcome, one abroad and two at home.

Aggression is the first one. We are shooting that one out in Korea, as we did in Greece and Berlin and other places.

Number two is inflation. That is a home product we are taxing and by controls curing inflation—we hope.

Number three is the worst of all, and that is relaxation. You can't cure the tendency to relax every time there is a lull in the hostilities. The Secretary of the Treasury was talking to me at the Cabinet meeting recently, in which he said that every time it looks as if we are winning, either the fight against inflation or the fight against aggression, you can see the country relax as the crisis and securities and things of that kind go up and down. You must meet this situation head on. And the thing that you gentlemen can do is to overcome the worst of our three enemies: relaxation.

Our mobilization problem is different in some ways from what it was in World War II, but it is just as urgent and just as important to our national survival.

Today, the danger is worldwide, but the actual fighting is limited to a small area, where we are trying to keep it. We are trying to keep the conflict limited and to bring it to a victorious end just as rapidly as possible.

But peace in Korea will not put an end to the global danger of Soviet aggression. We must build up enough military strength— enough military strength actually in existence—to convince the Kremlin that it ought not to start a world war.

We must prepare ourselves to mobilize quickly for war in case the Kremlin is reckless enough, in spite of everything, to plunge the world into a general conflict.

Our defense experts—both military and civilian—have developed a definite, concrete plan to do these two things. This plan provides for bigger, active Armed Forces, and lays the foundation for complete mobilization if that should become necessary. We must carry out that plan as rapidly as we possibly can. We want to reach our goals just as fast as the men can be trained, the plants built, and the equipment and supplies turned out.

During the next couple of years, while we are building up this military strength, we shall be diverting materials, converting plants, and disrupting normal life for businessmen and consumers. It will not be as drastic a shakeup as if we were in a global war, but whatever the situation calls for must be done. Our continued existence as a nation may depend on how well we carry out this program.

In the next year or two, the military production program is going to require extensive use of production controls and a good strong anti-inflation program. So far, we have only begun to feel the effect of military demands on our supplies of raw materials, manpower, and plant capacity. But we are going to feel this effect severely in the months to come. The largest part of the problem is still ahead of us. Now, I want to emphasize that: The largest part of the problem is still ahead of us.

Since last June about $26 billion worth of orders have been placed for military equipment and construction. Only a small part of that has been delivered as yet. Moreover, we still have about $58 billion worth of orders to place, in the next 14 months, under our present military plans. You can easily see, therefore, that the demands of military production on materials and manpower will be going up month by month for a long time. That is why it is urgently necessary that the Congress continue for 2 years more the production controls authorized by the Defense Production Act.

It is also urgently necessary for the Congress to extend the authority for inflation controls—controls on prices, wages and credit, and rents. And by that I mean adequate authority to do the job—authority not crippled by a lot of special exemptions for special groups. This is absolutely vital for the future of this great Nation of ours.

Most of you are businessmen who understand the terrible effects that the inflationary spiral could have on our economy if it is not kept in check. Now you have got a leading businessman in control of that very thing. You know how extremely important it is to hit inflation and hit it hard. To do that we will have to use price and wage controls for the next 2 or 3 years at least.

There are some people who think we can now abandon price and wage controls and still stop inflation. They say that heavy taxes and other so-called indirect controls can do the whole job from here on. But as bigger and bigger military orders hit our economy, that will be clearly impossible.

Of course, heavy taxes are needed, and I'm doing my best to get the Congress to enact enough taxes to keep the budget in balance. I would be delighted if each one of you would urge your Congressman and Senators to raise taxes.

I am serious about this; I think you ought to be asking the Congress for higher taxes. But when you do that, be sure to urge them to extend price and wage controls, too. It all goes together, if we are going to meet this situation.

The plain fact is that when you expand

production, as we are doing now in this country, people have more money to spend. And when that expanded production goes into military goods, there aren't enough civilian goods for people to spend the extra money on. This creates an inflationary gap. That is what is going to happen over the next year or two. There is no escaping it. It is going to get worse before it gets better. And those who are spreading the foolish notion that we can get through this period without price and wage controls are doing the country an immense amount of harm.

We hope that this period will not be long and that the time will come in 2 or 3 years when we can begin to take controls off. We are moving as rapidly as we can to expand the productive capacity of the country. Assuming that the Kremlin does not bring on a world war, we hope that our productive capacity will soon be great enough so that we can carry the defense program and still produce an ample supply of civilian goods. When that time comes, we should be able to do without controls.

If we are to bring that about, you gentlemen here must help us. You are particularly concerned with producing various types of raw materials and minerals, fuel and power. Increased capacity to produce these vital materials is basic not only to our defense, but to the kind of economy we want to have in the future.

I see no limit to the economic future of this country. I have said that time and again and have been called a dreamer and a visionary for doing it, but it is coming about.

In the first half of this year, we are producing goods and services at an estimated annual rate of about $307 billion. This is about the same, allowing for price changes, as the annual rate achieved in 1944—the peak production year of World War II. The present rate is almost $40 billion higher than what we did in 1948. But we have not yet reached the ceiling. We have the resources and the technology to grow by about 5 percent a year over the next few years. In about 3 years this would lift our output to about $350 billion, measured in present prices. And we can go far beyond that.

That is the sort of picture I ask you gentlemen to keep before you during this emergency period. The world is in a dangerous condition, but we know what we must do about it. It will take patience and determination. It will take good solid American patriotism—the kind that puts the national interest ahead of the selfish interest.

The people of the United States, together with the people of the other free countries, can win a victory in the struggle with Soviet communism. I'm just as sure of that as I'm sure I am standing here.

What it will take is hard work by everybody in the country, willingness by everybody to carry his fair share of the load.

That is what we are asking of you gentlemen here. And I am very sure that you are going to do your part.

Thank you very much.

NOTE: The President spoke at 10:20 a.m. at the Department of Interior Auditorium in Washington. In his opening remarks he referred to Oscar L. Chapman, Secretary of the Interior.

The industry advisory councils were appointed by the Secretary of the Interior. They represented the petroleum, gas, minerals, bituminous coal, coke, mining machinery, electric utility, and canned fish industries.

99   Remarks at a Ceremony in Observance of National Music Week.   *May 9, 1951*

I APPRECIATE most highly your thoughtfulness in presenting me with this wonderful piano as the culmination of the celebration of National Music Week. My fondness for music, I'm happy to say, is in line with the other Presidents you have named.

I have always been very, very fond of music. Since I was 12 or 13 years old, I have heard all the great pianists from that time until now, and I have heard all the great singers from that time until now.

I had a smattering of piano education from the time I was about 7 until I was 14 or 15 or 16, and decided that I would have to go to work and earn a living. There are some people in the country who think maybe the country would have been better off if I had gone ahead and become a professional musician. I can't say that I agree with them. I am prejudiced, however.

I have heard Paderewski; in fact, he gave me a lesson on how to play his Minuet in G once. And I have heard De Pachmann, and Josef Lhevinne, who I think was the greatest of them all.

I have heard De Pachmann play the famous Mozart Sonata, the 9th, which he always played. And I have heard the great Myra Hess, and Augusta Cotlow, and also these modern ones—Iturbi and Rubinstein—I wasn't old enough to hear the first Rubinstein; and nearly all the modern pianists. In fact, I found a very talented young man in the Army at Potsdam, Eugene List—he doesn't spell it like the great composer of the last century.

I am still very much interested in music and what it does for people. My daughter has some interest in music. My wife had, too, when she was younger and has now. My sister has. My mother was very fond of music, and my father used to sing in the church choir. So I come by my love of music honestly.

I am sorry to say that I do not pretend to be a proficient pianist or a musician that could contribute anything to the real music of the age. I am very fond of light opera, and some of the parts of heavy opera. I can't say that I can go to a "high hat" opera for social purposes and enjoy it all. But there is usually one aria or one song in nearly every great opera that is worth listening to—most of the rest of opera music is boring. I don't want you to say that out loud, it may hurt the Metropolitan Opera! [*Laughter*]

I am very fond of Gilbert and Sullivan. There used to be a musical show when I was a young man called "The Girl From Utah"—with Julia Sanderson, Donald Brian, and Joseph Cawthorn—and there were the operas of Gilbert and Sullivan. And there was Fay Templeton and Emma Trentini in "The Firefly." Those were all great, great shows.

[*At this point it was brought to the President's attention that Otto Harbach, the composer of "The Firefly," was among those present. The President then resumed speaking.*]

"The Merry Widow" and other light operas that came along about that time were all highly appreciated by the people. Now they are to some extent coming back. We can get them all on records, of course, and I have several of all those old musical shows, and a great many records of the great pianists playing those wonderful things of Mendels-

sohn and Beethoven, Mozart and Bach and Chopin.

I hope I will always have an appreciation of music, and that you will continue what you are doing to educate our people to love good music. I have no objection to the noise they call music these days, any more than I have to the "daubs" they call art these days, but I would like to see you continue to get people interested in good music. Whenever we have a banquet here, this gentleman, Major Santelmann, usually plays the music, and he knows what I like and he plays it for me, and I think everybody there enjoys it and that it contributes to the musical education of a great many of the people for whom you have played; and other bands as well—whenever I have had a chance to listen to them.

I want to thank you all for the courtesy which you have shown me, and I appreciate it.

Thank you very much.

NOTE: The President spoke at 12:15 p.m. in the Fish Room at the White House. In the course of his remarks he referred to Maj. William F. Santelmann, leader of the United States Marine Band.

The piano was constructed as a joint and cooperative work of all the members of the Piano Manufacturers Association. The materials that went into its production came from many of the member states of the United Nations.

The presentation was made by Otto J. Mallery, president of the National Recreation Association, sponsor of National Music Week.

---

100   Statement by the President in Response to Report of the Committee on Religion and Welfare in the Armed Forces. *May 10, 1951*

THE REPORT of the President's Committee on Religion and Welfare in the Armed Forces is the first complete appraisal of these important programs since World War II. I am confident it will provide an

invaluable guide for our expanding Armed Forces in the days to come and serve as a basis for allocating adequate funds for these essential services.

It is clear from the report that our Armed

Forces are making good progress in the efforts to build strong unit and individual morale through the provision of worthwhile opportunities for service men and women to use their free time in constructive ways. However, the Committee has specifically pointed out a number of ways in which improvement can be effected.

I regret that the Congress has not seen fit to provide funds for the continuance of the work of the President's Committee on Religion and Welfare in the Armed Forces. The Committee has produced impartial appraisals on many important aspects of life in the Armed Forces, and it has helped to promote and secure constructive activities for service men and women through its work in civilian communities located near installations of the Armed Forces.

NOTE: The report, describing the Committee's study of the Armed Forces special services and recreation programs, was entitled "Free Time in the Armed Forces" (Government Printing Office, 1951, 79 pp.). The report was the third in a series evaluating aspects of morale in the Armed Forces, the other two dealing with the military chaplaincy (see 1950 volume, this series, Item 297) and the Armed Forces information and education program. An earlier report, "Community Responsibility to Our Peacetime Servicemen and Women," was made public by the President on April 8, 1949 (1949 volume, this series, Item 73).

For the President's letter to the Chairman on the conclusion of the Committee's work, see Item 17.

---

101   The President's News Conference of *May 10, 1951*

THE PRESIDENT. Good morning everybody. Please be seated.

I don't have any announcements for you this morning, but I will try to answer questions if I can.

[1.] Q. Mr. President, the Veterans Administration tells me that they are absolutely right in denying hospitalization to this non-service-connected Korean combat veteran in Arizona. And they say that because we are not at war in Korea they cannot hospitalize those veterans. Would you care to comment on that?

THE PRESIDENT. No comment. I think the Veterans Bureau answered that. It is a matter that is up to Congress. They are simply obeying the law.[1]

I want to say further that these Korean veterans ought to be treated in exactly the same way as all the other war veterans have been treated. And they will be; but it requires a change in the law to do it.

[2.] Q. Mr. President, sometime ago you answered this question with some finality, but in the hullabaloo over this MacArthur thing it has been revived, the reports that Mr. Acheson will get out in 2 weeks, in 2 months, or 3 months, or something like that. I wonder if you still——

THE PRESIDENT. That is a rumor that has no foundation in fact.

What is it, Tony?[2]

[3.] Q. I was just asking—there was a story out yesterday that you were going to recall Ambassador O'Dwyer from Mexico?

THE PRESIDENT. That is news to me. I hadn't heard about it. That is a rumor that has no foundation in fact, too, Tony. [*Laughter*]

[*Pause*]

Well, well, well! What's the matter this morning? I guess one of the things that's the matter with you is because all your questions have been answered, either Mon-

---

[1] See Item 102.

[2] Ernest B. Vaccaro of the Associated Press.

day night [3] or by General Marshall.[4] I think that is probably what's the trouble. [*More laughter*]

[4.] Q. Would you care to give us a general comment, sir, on the way that the MacArthur hearings have been developing?

THE PRESIDENT. I am very satisfied with General Marshall's testimony. I think he has made a great witness, and I know this: he has told the exact truth, word for word.

[5.] Q. Mr. Truman, I had one.

THE PRESIDENT. Shoot, May.[5]

Q. General Marshall said, and Secretary Acheson also said in his speech to the Chamber of Commerce,[6] our purpose was not to drive the Communist forces out of Korea militarily. He said, quote, a political rather than a military objective of the United Nations. How can we unify them politically if we don't get them out militarily?

THE PRESIDENT. Well, May, if you can answer that question you will be a genius. [*Laughter*] I will let you answer it. That

is a good question for you to answer, May. The comment speaks for itself. I have no comment on it.

[6.] Q. Mr. President, when you nominated Mon Wallgren to head the National Security Resources Board, there was a great deal of comment about the fact that he might not be capable of filling the position, which would make him a czar in wartime. The NSRB does not seem to be heard of anymore. It is a group operating—it is only a planning agency——

THE PRESIDENT. That is all it was ever supposed to be—a planning agency. It was never intended to be anything else. It is a part of the staff of the President of the United States, and it will continue to be just what it always has been.

Q. And you are not going to appoint a new——

THE PRESIDENT. Yes, I am going to appoint a new Chairman, because it is part of the staff of the President. There will be a new Chairman appointed.

[7.] Q. Mr. President, along that same line, Mr. Gorrie's [7] designation, I think, is temporary?

THE PRESIDENT. Temporary. He is Acting Chairman. He is acting in the position of Acting Chairman, just as John Steelman was for a long time.

[8.] Q. Would you care to comment on the fight over beef price ceilings?

THE PRESIDENT. Well, I will tell you what I would like for you to do. Go back and read a little history in 1946. This is just the same old fight. Whenever you tread on the toes of anybody, he has to scream. I think it will work out as it should. If we are going to have controls, we have got to put them into effect as far as we can. That order was put up to me, and I approved.

Q. Mr. President, will you back up Mr.

---

[3] See Item 96.

[4] In early May 1951 Secretary of Defense George C. Marshall testified at Senate committee hearings during the investigation of the military situation in the Far East and the facts surrounding the relief of General of the Army Douglas MacArthur from his assignments in that area.

In his testimony Secretary Marshall stated, "From the very beginning of the Korean conflict, down to the present moment, there has been no disagreement between the President, the Secretary of Defense, and the Joint Chiefs of Staff that I am aware of.

"There have been, however, and continue to be basic differences of judgment between General MacArthur, on the one hand, and the President, the Secretary of Defense, and the Joint Chiefs of Staff, on the other hand."

His complete testimony is printed in "Hearings Before the Committee on Armed Services and the Committee on Foreign Relations, United States Senate, on the Military Situation in the Far East, Part 1" (Government Printing Office, 1951, Parts 1–5, 3691 pp.).

[5] Mrs. May Craig of the Portland (Maine) Press Herald.

[6] The text of the address by Secretary of State Dean Acheson before the U.S. Chamber of Commerce in Washington on April 30 is printed in the Department of State Bulletin (vol. 24, p. 766).

[7] Jack Gorrie, Acting Chairman of the National Security Resources Board.

DiSalle [8] on the beefsteak——

THE PRESIDENT. I have already backed him up.

Q. You are not going to let him down on that?

THE PRESIDENT. I okayed the order to begin with. What about that, May? Are you getting steak any cheaper now?

Q. Not yet. [*Laughter*]   Not yet.

[9.] Q. Mr. President, are you considering a diplomatic promotion for Mrs. Perle Mesta [9] as an Ambassador?

THE PRESIDENT. I haven't thought about it. If I decide to give her a promotion, why I will do it.

—————
[8] Michael V. DiSalle, Director of Price Stabilization.
[9] U.S. Minister to Luxembourg.

Q. Do you think she will ask for one?

THE PRESIDENT. I don't think so. You don't ask for things like that. They come to you unsolicited. I have made many an Ambassador since I have been President, and none of them ever asked me for the job. Those who have asked me for the job usually don't get them! [*Laughter*]

Reporter: Mr. President, if you don't have anything else to tell us, can we say "Thank you"?

THE PRESIDENT. Yes indeed, Bob,[10] it's all right. Thank you all very much.

NOTE: President Truman's two hundred and sixty-third news conference was held in the Indian Treaty Room (Room 474) in the Executive Office Building at 10:30 a.m. on Thursday, May 10, 1951.

[10] Robert G. Nixon of International News Service.

102   Letter to the President of the Senate and the Speaker of the House Recommending Legislation Extending Benefits to Veterans of the Korean Action. *May 10, 1951*

Dear Mr. ————:

Attached is a draft of legislation which would extend certain benefits to persons who shall have served in the Armed Forces on or after June 27, 1950.

I believe the desirability of such legislation will be readily apparent to the Congress. Unless and until such legislation is enacted, certain individuals already separated from the military service, and whose needs are acute, will be denied medical and hospital care.

In view of this situation, I hope the Congress will take favorable action on this legislation at the earliest possible date.

Sincerely yours,

HARRY S. TRUMAN

NOTE: This is the text of identical letters addressed to the Honorable Alben W. Barkley, President of the Senate, and to the Honorable Sam Rayburn, Speaker of the House of Representatives.

On May 11, 1951, the President signed a joint resolution which extended the same medical and hospital benefits enjoyed by veterans of World War II to any person who had served in the U.S. Armed Forces on or after June 27, 1950 (65 Stat. 40).

103   Letter to the Chairman, Board of Foreign Scholarships, on the Fulbright Program. *May 11, 1951*
[Released May 11, 1951. Dated May 10, 1951]

Dear Dr. Johnson:

I have read with interest the resolution adopted by the Board of Foreign Scholar-

ships on April 7, 1951, and I would like to take this opportunity to thank the members of the Board for their outstanding public service.

The program on which they have been working (created by Public Law 584, 79th Congress, and commonly known as the Fulbright Act) provides for the international exchange of students, professors, research scholars and teachers.

This program is vitally important in widening the knowledge and technical ability of the peoples of the twelve participating countries. Even more important, it is helping us all to understand each other better than ever before. And it is proving effective in combatting communist lies and distortions about social, economic and political conditions and objectives in our respective countries.

The Board of Foreign Scholarships, as well as the Department of State and the binational educational foundations and commissions overseas, is to be commended for the significant success already achieved and for the considerable prestige which is accruing to this program abroad.

I am pleased to accept the resolution of the Board of Foreign Scholarships, to approve the principles it embodies and to reaffirm

my unqualified support for the purpose which this program represents.

Very sincerely yours,

HARRY S. TRUMAN

[Walter Johnson, Ph.D., Chairman, Board of Foreign Scholarships, 5625 Kenwood Avenue, Chicago 37, Illinois]

NOTE: In the resolution the Board of Foreign Scholarships expressed "(1) its commendation for the excellent administration of the Fulbright Act by the Department of State, (2) its deep thanks for the thorough and highly valuable staff work performed by the Department for the Board of Foreign Scholarships, and (3) its confidence that in the continued administration of this program by the Department of State the exchange of persons under the Fulbright Act will make a lasting and significant contribution to the aims and objectives of American foreign policy."

The White House release making public the resolution and the President's letter pointed out that from the time Public Law 584 was enacted on August 1, 1946 (60 Stat. 754), the United States had signed executive agreements with 20 countries to provide for the exchange of students, professors, research scholars, and teachers. As a result, 1,907 Americans had received awards to study, teach, lecture, or conduct research in foreign countries, and 1,731 nationals of other countries had received awards for similar projects in the United States. In addition 646 foreign students had received scholarships for study in American schools in their home country, and it was expected that 3,310 persons would be beneficiaries under the program for the current year.

---

104   Letter to the Chairman, Committee on the Judiciary, on the Commission on Internal Security and Individual Rights. *May 12, 1951*

Dear Senator McCarran:

I am writing to request that the Senate Committee on the Judiciary give further consideration to H.R. 2829, to exempt the members and certain employees of the Commission on Internal Security and Individual Rights from the operation of certain conflict-of-interest statutes.

It has become apparent that this Commission, as it is presently constituted, cannot effectively perform its functions unless such

legislation as this is passed. Enclosed are copies of two letters I have received from the Commission which indicate why this is the case.

As one of these letters indicates, the members of the Commission are submitting their resignations to me. I have decided to hold my action upon these resignations in abeyance while I make this request for action by your Committee.

There are many precedents for legislation exempting individuals from the operations of these conflict-of-interest statutes, particularly where outstanding citizens are called upon to render part-time service to the Government. In recent years, it has been made clear that exemptions of this character in some cases are indispensable to the successful operation of the Government. In a time of national emergency like the present, it becomes more essential than ever to allow the Government to avail itself of the services and advice of patriotic and public spirited citizens who might be technically barred from service because of these statutes.

For example, it would be extremely difficult, if not impossible, to operate the Selective Service System, and our entire Defense Mobilization effort, if an exemption from these statutes were not made for many of the men who serve in carrying out these programs.

It would be little short of disastrous to adopt a general policy under which no exemptions from these statutes would be allowed. I would agree, of course, that the exemptions should be made carefully, and only when they serve an important public purpose and where there is likely to be no real conflict of interest.

In my judgment, the Commission on Internal Security and Individual Rights is one of the cases where an exemption is clearly justified. I have sought by this means to obtain the best possible advice concerning some of the basic questions affecting the survival of our democracy. I sought to obtain this advice from a group of distinguished citizens—representative of the best elements of our national life. I believe that the character of this Commission is above reproach, and that there can be no reasonable ground for any fear that its members would use their offices to further any personal interest, even if it were possible for them to do so.

The purpose of this Commission is to make recommendations concerning the problems involved in providing for the internal security of the United States and at the same time protecting the rights and freedoms of individuals. Surely there can be no quarrel with these purposes. Surely there can be no denying their importance.

One of the problems which the Commission was established to study is the operation of the Government's Employee Loyalty Program. I am convinced that the present program is basically sound, and I am certain that with rare exceptions the employees of the Federal Government are completely loyal to the United States. I believe that they constitute one of the finest and most loyal groups among our citizenry.

Nevertheless, it has been widely charged that there are disloyal employees in the Government service. Therefore, a study such as would be made by this Commission is of the utmost importance both as a protection to the national security and as a protection to the good names of the thousands upon thousands of loyal employees in the Government service.

It seems to me that the Congress would be as anxious as I am to make sure that there are no communists or other subversives in the Government employ. While this was not the only purpose for which this Commission was created, surely it is one of the most important.

I earnestly hope that the Congress will pass this legislation to make it possible for the Commission to go ahead speedily with its work which means so much to the Nation's safety and welfare.

Sincerely yours,

HARRY S. TRUMAN

[Honorable Pat McCarran, Chairman, Senate Committee on the Judiciary, Washington, D.C.]

NOTE: H.R. 2829, exempting the Commission from the conflict of interest laws, was passed by the House of Representatives on March 19, 1951. On April 30 the Senate Judiciary Committee voted 6–3 against a motion to report the bill favorably. Senator Mc-Carran stated that no personal issue was involved and that the Committee had unqualified confidence in the members of the Commission. The only issue, he said, was whether the laws should be complied with in full.

Two letters to the President from Fleet Adm. Chester W. Nimitz, Chairman of the Commission, were also made public on May 12. The first, dated April 4, 1951, pointed out the difficulty of obtaining qualified legal personnel who would not be affected by the conflict of interest laws. It stated that the

Commission had deferred formal action on matters coming within the scope of its authority, pending action by the Senate Committee on the Judiciary.

The second letter from Admiral Nimitz, dated May 8, 1951, reviewed the precedents for holding that an exemption for the Commission was justified, including the exemption which had been accorded to the Hoover Commission in 1947. Resignations of all members of the Commission were attached to the letter.

See also Items 20, 22[2], 35, 278.

---

105   Veto of Bill Relating to Land Acquisition and Disposal Actions by the Army, Navy, Air Force, and Federal Civil Defense Administration.   *May 15, 1951*

To the House of Representatives:

I return herewith, without my approval, H.R. 3096, a bill "Relating to the acquisition and disposition of land and interests in land by the Army, Navy, Air Force, and Federal Civil Defense Administration."

This bill would impose certain restrictions on the real estate transactions of the military departments and of Federal Civil Defense Administration. In general, it would require those agencies to come into agreement with the Committees on Armed Services of the Senate and House of Representatives with respect to the acquisition or disposal of real property, including leases involving an annual rental in excess of $10,000, and including transfers of real property between the military departments or to other Federal agencies, or to States, with certain minor exceptions. A recital of compliance with the Act in an instrument of conveyance, including a lease, or a recital that the conveyance or lease is not affected by the Act would be conclusive evidence of the fact so recited. The bill would also repeal Section 407 of Public Law 910, 81st Congress, which requires the authority of an Act of Congress enacted subsequent thereto in order for a military department generally to dispose of real property. It would also repeal a proviso

contained in the Act of April 4, 1944 requiring the Secretary of the Navy to come into agreement with Congressional Committees prior to the acquisition or disposition by the Department of the Navy of any land acquired for naval use.

On January 15, 1951, I sent a message to the Congress urging that it repeal Section 407 at its earliest opportunity. In that message I stated that that Section, if permitted to stand, may seriously impede our mobilization effort by causing unnecessary and unwarranted delays in the transfer for other governmental uses of property excess to the needs of the military departments.

While H.R. 3096 would effect the repeal of Section 407 of Public Law 910, it would subject to the decision of Congressional Committees, not only those transactions that are covered by Section 407 of Public Law 910, but also transactions involving all phases of the real estate transactions of the Department of Defense and of the Federal Civil Defense Administration, with exceptions applicable for the most part to minor and relatively unimportant transactions.

While the Congress or its members have a special interest in a number of real estate transactions by the Executive Branch of the Government, full information with respect to those transactions has in the past and will in the future be made readily available to the interested Committees of the Congress. However, a legal requirement for the submission of countless real estate transactions to the scrutiny of the Congressional Committees in an effort to furnish them with information on the relatively few transactions as to which those Committees have a special interest, would result in the imposition of a severe and unnecessary administrative burden on the Department of Defense. It would not only result in the diversion of personnel from other vital tasks to the preparation of the innumerable reports that would be required but would also result in continuing delays that might well prove to be a serious impediment to the defense procurement program. The delays that would be effected are not only the delays involved in the physical preparation of the reports required, their presentation to the Congressional Committees, and the review of those reports by the Committees or their staff, but much greater and more serious delays resulting from the inability of the Department of Defense to plan its operations in the future until the Congressional Committees have acted. The transactions that would be required to be submitted to the Committees are not isolated transactions unrelated to other transactions in the future but have a definite relationship to future as well as other current transactions and affect the whole planning program. The uncertainties and delays inherent in the securing of Congressional approval can only operate to the detriment of such a planning program.

One of the effects of the bill would be to force to a substantial degree the centralization in Washington of real estate operations that could otherwise be more efficiently handled in the field. A very substantial portion of the transactions by the Department of Defense originate in the field since the real es-

tate operations of the Department of the Army, the most active department in this field, are on a highly decentralized basis. The requirement that would be contained in H.R. 3096 would have the effect of destroying that decentralization and cancelling the savings in time and money that have resulted in the past. Moreover, it would destroy the flexibility that now exists with respect to those operations that permits rapid changes and revisions of plans. Under the procedure contemplated by H.R. 3096, changes and variations in plans would have to run the whole gamut from field office to Congressional Committee and back again. Thus the delay will be significantly greater than would be apparent on the surface. The acquisition of general purpose space in many cities throughout the United States is handled by the General Services Administration rather than by the military departments. In those cases the military departments submit their needs to the General Services Administration which acquires or leases space on behalf of the military department concerned. In those cases no report can be made to the Congressional Committees until it has been determined from the General Services Administration the form in which it proposes to make the space available. A delay thereafter might have the unfortunate effect of causing the Government to lose the opportunity to acquire the space sought.

It may well be expected that the delays that would be encountered under the present bill would be greater than that experienced by the Department of the Navy under the Act of April 4, 1944. That is true because the number of significant transactions would be much greater under this bill than under the 1944 Act. The requirement of review by Congressional Committees in the matter of acquisition and disposal of real property would to a large degree duplicate existing machinery in the agencies directly involved, as well as those in the General Services Administration. It would hinder the orderly management of Federal property as contemplated by the Federal Property and Administrative Services Act of 1949 which was recently enacted by the Congress. Moreover, the requirement of a review of the transfer of property between the military departments of the Department of Defense is, in effect, a contradiction of the principle of increased interservice utilization of property by the military departments, which is an essential feature of unification.

Moreover, the enactment of this legislation would seem to be particularly inopportune at this time in view of the current international situation and the increasing demands for expeditious action in connection with the defense procurement program. I cannot help but feel that the Congress would not knowingly place unnecessary obstacles, such as that inherent in H.R. 3096, to the expeditious consummation of that defense procurement program.

Finally, I am concerned by what appears to me to be a gradual trend on the part of the legislative branch to participate to an even greater extent in the actual execution and administration of the laws. Under our system of Government it is contemplated that the Congress will enact the laws and will leave their administration and execution to the executive branch. The delays discussed above, which would inhere in the enactment of H.R. 3096, testify to the wisdom of that constitutional policy. It would seem particularly inappropriate to depart from that policy in the field of military procurement during a period of national emergency when expeditious action may be vital to the survival of our nation.

For these reasons, I am returning this bill without my approval but with the assurance that the agencies covered by the bill will cooperate with the appropriate Congressional Committees in furnishing the information they desire in a manner that will not interfere with the orderly operation of their real estate transactions.

I again recommend that Section 407 of Public Law 910, 81st Congress, be repealed for the reasons set forth in my Message of January 15, 1951.

HARRY S. TRUMAN

---

106 Statement by the President Upon Signing Bill To Facilitate the Financing of Defense Contracts. *May 15, 1951*

I HAVE today approved S. 998, "To facilitate the financing of the defense contracts by banks and other financing institutions, to amend the Assignment of Claims Act of 1940, and for other purposes."

I have signed this bill because it is important to encourage private financial institutions to make loans for defense production. It is particularly important that small business be given this kind of financial aid in order to increase its participation in the defense program as promptly as possible.

This bill will facilitate the financing of defense contracts, but there is reason to believe that the provisions relating to tax claims and social security contributions provide a broader basis for exemptions than is necessary or sound. It may well be that interests of the United States with respect to taxes and those of persons covered by the Social Security Act with respect to contributions withheld from their pay are subordinated unnecessarily to the interests of private lending institutions.

I do not believe that it was the intent of Congress to bring about such a result or that the complete exemptions which may be mandatory under the bill are needed to accomplish its central purpose. Therefore, I am asking the Secretary of the Treasury to review the effects of this legislation most carefully, and if he finds it necessary, to present to the Congress appropriate recommendations for its amendment.

NOTE: As enacted, S. 998 is Public Law 30, 82d Congress (65 Stat. 41).

107   Address at the National Conference on Citizenship. *May 17, 1951*

Madam Chairman, Mr. Attorney General, distinguished guests, and ladies and gentlemen:

It is a very great pleasure for me to be here this morning, and I am glad to join in welcoming this conference to Washington. I am strongly in favor of what you are doing here to help the people of this country to become better citizens. The citizen's job is an important one. It is the most important job in this great Republic.

The job of being an American citizen, a citizen of the United States of America, keeps growing more difficult and more important every day. In some countries the important decisions are made by the rulers, and the citizens have to do what they are told. In our country the citizens make the basic decisions, and the officials of the Government have to do what the people tell them—sometimes.

We must make the right decisions. You, as citizens, must make the right decisions. Never was there a time when the right decisions are so necessary as they are at this time.

As the problems before our country become more complicated and more dangerous, our citizens must give greater attention to their job of making the basic decisions. It is your country, as well as mine. It is your responsibility, as well as mine. If you do not assume that responsibility—and you are part of that responsibility—there is nobody to blame but yourselves when things go entirely wrong. There is less margin for error than there used to be making these decisions. Wrong decisions in this day and age may wreck the country—wreck it for all time.

There is a great deal of serious business before the Government of this country now. This business concerns our national defense and our national survival. Important decisions have to be made by the Congress, the President, and the country, and they must be made soon. These decisions ought to be above petty politics, because the welfare of the country depends upon them.

Citizens should understand the facts. You know, the hardest thing in the world to find is a real fact. And the easiest thing to do is to garble and confuse the facts. I repeat, that the easiest thing to do in the world today is to garble and confuse the facts. We have a great deal of that going on right now.

I hope, when you leave this conference, you will take home with you an understanding of the major problems we face, and a sense of urgency about the decisions your Government has to make. If this understanding can be spread among all the citizen groups you represent, I believe these decisions will be made promptly, and I believe they will be made right.

If citizens know the facts, and let their elected representatives know that they want the national interest put above every political interest and every special interest, then there won't be any question about keeping our Nation strong and secure. This is one of the most important things that this conference can do.

We must face up to the major problems, face up to them and solve them—solve them in the interest of all the people and not in the interest of just a favored few.

I would like to outline for you a few of the major problems we have to face.

There is a lot of discussion nowadays about military strategy. That's all right. Military strategy is important, and everybody ought to be concerned about it. And I want to say to you that our Defense Department is headed by the ablest group of men that this or any other country ever had for planning and carrying out its defense policy.

But, there are a lot of other problems that are equally important. We have the hard problems of defense production, the problem of taxes, the problem of stabilization—these are just examples of a few of the problems that we have. Unless we face these problems, we won't be able to have any military strategy at all. And no matter how able our Defense Department men may be, there won't be anything to plan for.

The danger we face is very serious, the most dangerous we have ever faced in all our time. Our country faces the danger of war from an aggressive and imperialist foreign power. Meeting this danger is all-important. And to meet that danger, we should all stand together.

I think that some people fail to realize that this threat is very real. They think there is still time to play petty politics.

That is a terribly dangerous attitude. We must all get together behind the program adequate to meet the perils we face. We must get together now—without waiting and without playing petty politics.

The defense program comes first, that is our first and greatest problem. Our defense program and defense production must come ahead of everything else. If we let our defense program get snarled up, or delayed, or slashed, we would be courting disaster.

The suggestion was made by one Senator the other day, that we ought to cut down the goal for our Armed Forces by half a million men. And this same Senator wants to go for an all-out war in China all by ourselves. At a time like this, such a cut would be foolish—not only foolish it would be most dangerous.

Slashing the size of our Armed Forces would not be economy; it would be an invitation to war.

Let me drive that home. What we are attempting to do now, in the next year and a half, we anticipate may cost about $60 billion—an expenditure over a year and a half which may ward off world war III. One week of all-out war would cost from 10 to 20 times that.

Which is the sanest expenditure?

Do I have to drive that home to you, to say which you think is the sanest expenditure?

Now, in addition to that defense program of ours, we must work with our allies. We must have friends in this troubled world. Yet some Senators, and some other people, would have us go it alone. In this world of ours in this day, we can't go it alone.

There is a free world, and there is a slave world. We belong to the free world, and we are the head of the free world. We have got to accept that responsibility and carry out that responsibility.

Our defense program has two parts. One part is building up our own Armed Forces and our national strength. The other is helping our allies build up their strength so they can do their share in preventing war and stopping aggression. Both these parts of our defense program are essential to our security.

Unless we help our allies, we might have to face the real danger alone. Unless our allies are strong, the Kremlin might take them over, and the danger of war would increase. Without allies, our defense would be more difficult, and more costly—more costly in dollars, and what is much more important, most costly in lives. There is no economy in slashing our foreign aid program. Penny-pinching now may mean throwing away the lives of our soldiers later on.

One of the reasons we are in this condition is because we did not accept our responsibility immediately after the war was over. In 1945 a universal service law was asked for by the President of the United States. That universal service law passed in 1945 or early in 1946 would have saved billions of dollars now. The people who prevented the enactment of a universal service law in 1945 are trying by every means at their command to prevent it now. We must not let them prevent it, because it is essential to the safety of the world—to our own safety.

We must build our economy for defense. We have the most amazing prosperous economy in the history of the world; and we have got to keep it that way.

Our defense program includes not only increasing our Armed Forces, making planes, tanks, and guns for them and for our allies. It also includes having and keeping a strong economy here at home. We must be able to turn out greater and greater quantities of goods for our armed services, in case we have to meet an all-out attack. We have to have the economic strength to carry our defense program for a long time to come. If we are to be in this position, we need more factories, more electric power, and a higher production of basic materials. We need a sound and efficient civil economy to support our defense production. This means housing for defense workers, and adequate public services to keep the defense production functioning efficiently.

When we talk about cutting nondefense expenditures, we must be sure we don't cut the strength and the support of our defense effort. People who are trying to do this are not helping our country. On the contrary, they are injuring it. If these "pull-backs" have their way, they will ruin our economy, and our country at the same time.

We must have a stabilized economy. Next to our defense program, the most important thing is economic stabilization. Economic stabilization means preventing inflation. This includes price control, wage control, and rent control.

All these controls expire on June 30th, just 6 weeks from now. The Congress is now considering whether these controls should be extended for another 2 years. Of course, they have to be extended. If they are not, our whole economy will be in great danger, and every family in the country will suffer—the inflationary pressures will increase.

Pressures on prices have eased off a little lately, but these pressures will come back stronger than ever in the next few months.

The more defense money we spend, the higher prices will tend to go. It is a dangerous situation we are faced with. Already the defense expenditures for the Army have increased the price of those things which the Army has to buy by more than $530 million. The increased cost of the Navy expenditures for the same purpose would have bought four of the largest air carriers—the most expensive battleships in the world.

By June 30 we will have spent about $19 billion on defense since the attack in Korea a year ago. In the year beginning July 1st our defense spending will probably increase to about $40 billion. If we do not control inflation, that $40 billion will only buy half as much as it would even now. After we have built our defenses up enough to meet the present danger, we hope we won't have to spend at such a high rate, and prices will be easier to hold.

Now, everybody says prices must be held down. Everybody says prices must be held down, but you must hold down everybody's prices but mine—everybody else must take a cut, but be careful don't touch mine. But right now it will take everything we can do to hold these prices down, and if we can hold them down until we get over the hump of our defense program, we will be past the danger point. If we can't, the cost of living will go through the roof. And that will mean ruin for our defense program, and ruin for our strength as a Nation.

Now, if we are going to control prices, the Congress has got to say, and say it in no uncertain terms, that it wants prices controlled. Every special interest in the country is in Washington, or on its way, to lobby for a little exception for itself. And most of them can make out a pretty good case for themselves. There are enough special interest fellows appearing before the Senate Finance Committee to run the hearings well into June.

The public interest fellows are not being heard because they don't know what's happening. Now, you public interest people better get here and look after your interests!

It will be nice to give these private interest fellows some exceptions, but we can't have such a lot of exceptions and still have effective price control. If we handed out all the exceptions that are asked for, price control would be just like a sieve, and the tide of inflation would pour through it.

I don't think some of these special interest fellows understand what would happen if we had all-out inflation, but when they come down here and ask for special interest, that is what they are asking for: all-out inflation.

Now, you consumers can make a strong demand for price control.

We are not going to be able to hold the cost of living against the tremendous inflationary pressures ahead, unless we have a good, strong price control law, and a good strong rent control law. If you want that kind of law—if you, the consumers of this country, want Congress to provide a strong price control system, you had better see, and you had better write to your Congressman.

Now, you see things in the paper, write to your President—I get 40,000 letters a day, as a result of this or that, or a special occasion, but I am saying to you—I am saying to you right now, you had better let your Congressman know where you stand. You had better see him and tell him about it while you are here. Tell him you want a price control law that will work which doesn't injure anybody. Price control, or any other control, we want an equitable control that will be fair to everybody, the producer, the middleman and the consumer. That is what we are working for.

The special interests and the lobbies will wreck this stabilization program, as sure as you're born, unless the main body of our citizens of this country get busy and do something about it. And that is what I am urging you to do.

We must pay-as-we-go, with a fair tax program. Now this is something that touches the most touchy nerve in the country: the pocketbook nerve.

Another thing that ought to be of special concern to every citizen in this country is our tax program. We have to have more taxes, if we are to pay for our defense program and hold down inflation. Nobody likes to pay more taxes, but we have got to do it because more taxes are essential to the safety and welfare of this country. So far, we have been doing fairly well in paying for our defense program as we go along. But our defense expenditures are going to increase rapidly. We can't keep on paying as we go unless we get the tax money wherewith to do it.

Taxes are not so hard to take if everybody pays his fair share, in accordance with his ability to pay. But, if we let the special groups come in and riddle the tax program with special exemptions, we won't have a good tax program, or a fair tax program. We won't be able to balance the budget, and we won't be able to stop inflation.

I hope you will all realize, and will take home as one of the messages of this conference, that higher taxes are necessary to our defense program and to our survival as a Nation.

Now, I don't think people ought to have any trouble agreeing on the national interest. I think everybody—every citizen—is a patriot, and that he believes that the national interest comes first, and that at a time like this, when some of our young men are fighting and dying to stop Communist aggression, and when so many of our boys face a period of military service to prepare for whatever may lie ahead, it ought to be easy for this country to get together in unity of spirit and action.

It ought to be the easiest thing in the world to agree upon a good defense program, and a good foreign aid program, and a sound program to hold down the cost of living. But it is not easy. It is one of the most difficult things which any President has ever faced. I am going to face it, and with your help I am going to put it over. Now, we must get the facts to the people, and that is hard to do.

One of the main reasons, I think, is that most of our citizens—those who do the fighting, and pay the bills, and keep the country going—are just too occupied to make their voices heard. If they had all the facts, and their representatives in Washington knew how they felt, I don't think we would have so much trouble with these great problems.

That is why the work of this Conference means so much in the present crisis of the world. The future depends on the opinions and the decisions of the American people.

If you can develop ways of keeping our citizens better informed, of helping them to understand the increasing duties of their citizenship, I have no doubt that this country will make the right decisions, and that those decisions will lead the world to a just and lasting peace. And that is what we all want.

NOTE: The President spoke at 11:50 a.m. at the Statler Hotel in Washington. In his opening words he referred to Corma Mowrey, president of the National Education Association, and Attorney General J. Howard McGrath.

The sixth annual meeting of the National Conference on Citizenship was sponsored by the Department of Justice and the National Education Association.

108 The President's News Conference of *May* 17, 1951

THE PRESIDENT. I have no announcements to make. I will try to answer questions, however.

[1.] Q. Mr. President, what do you think of the House action in overriding your veto of the real estate bill? [1]

THE PRESIDENT. Didn't know about it. Hasn't got to me yet.

Q. The vote was 312 to 68.

THE PRESIDENT. I will have to investigate it, and see on what basis they did it, before I can comment on it.

[2.] Q. Mr. President, there has been a persistent story among Democratic Senators

[1] The veto was later sustained by the Senate. See Item 105.

up on the Hill, that far from having thought up the idea of dismissing General MacArthur, as some Republicans charge, Secretary Acheson actually at first opposed it when it was mentioned. Would you comment on that?

THE PRESIDENT. Yes. Secretary Acheson, at the conference which I called on the subject, the first time, advised caution. After the whole thing was thoroughly discussed between the Secretary of Defense, Mr. Acheson, General Bradley, and Mr. Harriman, they all came to the conclusion that the action had to be taken. I had made up my mind before I had consulted them, but I wanted to hear what they had to say.

Q. Mr. President, you had your mind made up at the time of the Martin letter? [2]

THE PRESIDENT. My mind was made up at the time of the ultimatum to the Chinese Communist commander.

Q. Even before the Martin letter?

THE PRESIDENT. Yes.

Q. I am sorry, sir, did you say that——

THE PRESIDENT. I said my mind was made up when the ultimatum was sent by General MacArthur to the Chinese commander.

Q. Mr. President, that meeting you speak of, was that April, I think——

THE PRESIDENT. Yes—April 6th.

Q. That meeting was where——

THE PRESIDENT. On Friday—Friday morning.

Q. ——where Secretary Acheson first advised caution?

THE PRESIDENT. Yes.

Q. Mr. President, your mind was made up as to what, sir, to——

THE PRESIDENT. That I needed a new general in the Far East.

Q. Mr. President, could you say why that ultimatum brought you to that decision?

THE PRESIDENT. I think that was pretty thoroughly explained by General Marshall in his testimony. He stated the facts.

Q. Mr. President, just—do you recall that date?

THE PRESIDENT. April 6th.

Q. I mean of the ultimatum?

Q. March 24th.

THE PRESIDENT. ——March 24th, yes. It was March 20. March 20, wasn't it?

Q. It was March 24th.

THE PRESIDENT. It was before the Martin letter.

Mr. Short: We will look it up, sir.

THE PRESIDENT. Joe says he will look it up, the exact date.[3]

Q. Mr. President, just to get that straight, do you mean, sir, that even if General MacArthur had not written the letter to Mr. Martin, that you would have placed a new general in command in the Far East?

THE PRESIDENT. That is just what I mean. That Martin letter just added fuel to the

---

[2] The letter, dated March 20, 1951, was sent by Gen. Douglas MacArthur to Representative Joseph W. Martin, Jr., of Massachusetts. It stated, in part, that "if we lose the war to communism in Asia the fall of Europe is inevitable, win it and Europe most probably would avoid war and yet preserve freedom. As you point out, we must win. There is no substitute for victory." The full text of the letter is printed in the Congressional Record (vol. 97, p. 3380).

[3] General MacArthur's statement on Korea, dated March 24, 1951, said in part, "The enemy therefore must by now be painfully aware that a decision of the United Nations to depart from its tolerant effort to contain the war to the area of Korea through expansion of our military operations to his coastal areas and interior bases would doom Red China to the risk of imminent military collapse.

"These basic facts being established, there should be no insuperable difficulty arriving at decisions on the Korean problem if the issues are resolved on their own merits without being burdened by extraneous matters not directly related to Korea, such as Formosa and China's seat in the United Nations."

The text of the statement was released by the White House on April 11, 1951, at the same time that General MacArthur was relieved of his Far East command. See also Item 77.

With respect to the use of the word "ultimatum" in connection with the March 24 statement, see *Memoirs by Harry S. Truman*, volume 2, page 442.

fire, which had been going on for about a year. I made a 14,400 mile trip on my own steam, in order to talk to him and try to get an understanding. And I thought I had it; as I told you gentlemen when I came back here.

[3.] Q. Mr. President, this is rather a local question. What are the prospects for funds for channelization of the Rio Grande? I think you discussed this with the New Mexico and Texas Senators——

THE PRESIDENT. They are not very good right at this minute.

Q. Mr. President, has the Bureau of the Budget given you a recommendation on that project?

THE PRESIDENT. The Bureau of the Budget has the thing under advisement, as has the Secretary of the Interior; and they are going to discuss the matter further with me.

[4.] Q. Mr. President, I would like to get one more piece on this—in the case of the MacArthur letter to Martin, is that what determined the timing of your action?

THE PRESIDENT. No.

Q. Could you tell us, sir, whether you had taken any action between the ultimatum statement and the Martin letter?

THE PRESIDENT. I had been carefully studying the situation over, and reviewing the facts for the past year. I hadn't discussed it with anybody.

Q. Mr. President, if I may pursue that just once more——

THE PRESIDENT. Yes, go ahead.

Q. ——in your statement explaining why General MacArthur was relieved,[4] you said that General MacArthur did not—was unable to give wholehearted support to the—let's see—Government's policy?

THE PRESIDENT. That is correct.

Q. Then, I take it that this ultimatum indicated to you that he was unable to give

wholehearted support?

THE PRESIDENT. That is correct—that is absolutely correct.

Q. Mr. President, I understood you to say that you had been studying this for a year. Had you been considering relieving him about 12 months ago?

THE PRESIDENT. Yes. On several occasions, particularly one—in that—the incident of the Veterans of Foreign Wars, in August.[5]

I didn't want to relieve him. I sent a message to Congress as soon as World War II ceased, and asked the Congress to make all five-star generals and five-star admirals, admirals of the fleet and generals of the army for life, on full pay and emoluments with a secretary and an orderly, for the rest of their lives. And naturally, I didn't want to do anything that would in any way injure the standing of those admirals and generals, for I think the country is exceedingly grateful, and still is grateful, for the war effort which those generals put forth in World War II; and that includes General Mac-Arthur. My ideas on that haven't changed a bit. This is a different situation and a different program.

What is it?

Q. Mr. President, General MacArthur indicated in his testimony that at your private conference at Wake Island you agreed to drop the subject of Formosa. Would you give us a little more light on that?

THE PRESIDENT. No, I can't. No further comment on that.

Q. Mr. President, the Senate Committee today sustained the right of General Bradley to treat as confidential his conversations with you in the April 6th meeting, a position which you had taken.

THE PRESIDENT. They did exactly right, and I am happy that they did.

Q. Now, of course, there are certain

---

[4] See Item 77.

[5] See 1950 volume, this series, Item 226.

charges and assertions being made that this adds a lot of mystery to what happened on April 6th.

THE PRESIDENT. Who is making those charges? The Republicans that are trying to overthrow the foreign policy of the United States? I don't think anybody who understands the Government of the United States is making any such charges.

Q. Quite apart, sir, from any right to demand from you information on what happened on April 6th, would you care to say anything voluntarily about what happened on April 6th?

THE PRESIDENT. All the information in connection with the thing is taken by the actions and the decisions which I make. The conversations with my advisers and my private staff before decisions are made is my business and mine alone.

Q. Mr. President, could you clear up the point of whether Acheson changed his mind or withdrew his cautionary note after this April 6th meeting, or was that later?

THE PRESIDENT. He made the cautionary suggestion at the April the 6th meeting. When all the facts were on the table, there was no objection on Acheson's part at all.

Q. At the same meeting? He didn't change his mind then?

THE PRESIDENT. No, because there were three or four meetings.

Q. That was the point I wanted to clear up, that he didn't change his mind at that meeting?

THE PRESIDENT. I didn't ask anybody to declare himself at that meeting. I stated the case and advised them to have a meeting on Saturday afternoon; and they had one Saturday afternoon, and one on Sunday. And I had another meeting with them on Monday. It was not hurriedly done. It was very carefully considered.

Q. Mr. President, General Marshall——

THE PRESIDENT. Yes.

Q. ——that could be—you did hurry it up because there was a leak. Would you explain that?

THE PRESIDENT. The thing that was hurried up was the message, not the act.

Q. No. I understand that.

THE PRESIDENT. Well, I don't want you to get it mixed up. It was reported that there had been a leak. Therefore, the message was sent directly to the General.

Q. Mr. President, could you tell us the reasons that Secretary Acheson advanced for advising caution?

THE PRESIDENT. Political. Purely. Said it would stir up the fuss that it did. And he was right. [*Laughter*]

[5.] Q. Sir, may I ask you a question not on MacArthur? Are you going to continue letting the head of the National Petroleum Council be an industry man, or are you going to require that he be a governmental employee?

THE PRESIDENT. My theory is that the Council ought to remain just as it has.

[6.] Q. Mr. President, can you tell us anything about the Nimitz commission? As I understand it, you refused to accept the resignations of the members of that commission, pending some word from Capitol Hill, or some——

THE PRESIDENT. Well, I think the letter that I sent to the Chairman of the Judiciary Committee with the supporting documents covers the whole thing.[6] I haven't anything further to say on it.

Q. No word from down there?

THE PRESIDENT. I haven't heard from them yet.

[7.] Q. Mr. President, if I can ask you a little matter about the 35th Division——

THE PRESIDENT. Sure.

Q. ——reunion in Topeka. Are you going this year?

THE PRESIDENT. I hope to be able to go, but

---

[6] See Item 104.

I won't know how conditions here will be; and I won't know until just shortly before the meeting takes place, which is on June the 9th, I think.

[8.] Q. Mr. President, would you care to say in your own words, sir, what this ultimatum issued by General MacArthur to the Chinese general did to the plan of the 14 nations involved to seek a peace?

THE PRESIDENT. I can't comment on that now.

[9.] Q. The other question is, have you got a successor in mind for Senator Pope, whose retirement you announced? [7]

THE PRESIDENT. I am trying to find one. I haven't one in mind right now. As soon as I find him, I will tell you who he is.

[10.] Q. Mr. President, Mon Wallgren [8] said this week that he is getting quite anxious to get home. I wonder if you have any place in mind for him?

THE PRESIDENT. I have that under consideration. He has not resigned as yet, but he has told me that he thinks he will probably want to enter politics in the great State of Washington next year, and he wants to come home and get himself ready.

[11.] Q. Sir, you are a careful student of American history, would you care to comment on some historical precedents for this keeping of Presidential conversations confidential?

THE PRESIDENT. Well, nearly every President has had the same experience. You can just pick up the life of any President you choose, and you will find experiences just like this in the lives of nearly every one of them.

Q. Could you name any?

THE PRESIDENT. Well, I don't recall any specific instances. Grover Cleveland had the same trouble, so did Abraham Lincoln. And Andrew Jackson was quite active in that line. Andrew Johnson, I think, had the worst experience of any of them, but if you go on down the line you will find that nearly every President has had the same experience. It is nothing new.

[12.] Q. Mr. President, Senator Maybank said yesterday he doubted whether they can renew the price control law by June 30th. Do you think Congress should go home without doing that?

THE PRESIDENT. Read the speech I made this morning at the Statler Hotel.[9] That will answer your question.

[13.] Q. Mr. President, could I put my question another way?

THE PRESIDENT. Go ahead.

Q. Maybe it won't be so involved. I meant that you regarded that this action of General MacArthur was one that exceeded his authority?

THE PRESIDENT. I certainly do, because a thing of that kind should have been submitted to the Joint Chiefs of Staff before it was done.

Q. Well, Mr. President, it has been said that it was a little more than that, that there was bad faith on the part of General MacArthur and snatched your ideas, if I may put it that way?

THE PRESIDENT. My suggestion to you is to read General Marshall's testimony [10] ——

Q. Yes, I did.

THE PRESIDENT. ——on the subject.

Q. I did.

THE PRESIDENT. That covers it thoroughly.

Q. That is your view, too?

THE PRESIDENT. That covers it thoroughly.

Q. That is your view, too?

THE PRESIDENT. I didn't say that. I didn't

---

[7] James P. Pope, member of the Board of Directors of the Tennessee Valley Authority.

[8] Mon C. Wallgren, Chairman, Federal Power Commission, and former Governor of the State of Washington.

[9] See Item 107.

[10] See Item 101 [3].

say that. I said it covers it thoroughly.

[14.] Q. Mr. President, one thing I want to clearup. If Mon Wallgren goes into politics in the great State of Washington, would he run for Governor or Senator?

THE PRESIDENT. Well now, you will have to ask Mon. They are both open. He can run for either one.

Q. I know, and he has done both.

THE PRESIDENT. He has done both, that's right.

Merriman Smith (United Press Associations): Thank you, Mr. President.

THE PRESIDENT. It's all right, Smitty.

NOTE: President Truman's two hundred and sixty-fourth news conference was held in the Indian Treaty Room (Room 474) in the Executive Office Building at 4 p.m. on Thursday, May 17, 1951.

109   Remarks at the Armed Forces Day Dinner. *May 18, 1951*

Mr. Chairman, General Marshall, distinguished guests—the armed forces of Japan and Korea, and our gallant allies who are alongside our armed forces in Korea:

I want to impress upon you, on this second anniversary of Armed Forces Day, that we are in the midst of one of the greatest crises this country has ever faced.

You fighting men, and you fighting allies in Korea and Japan, are holding the line, while we endeavor at this end to attain a peaceful settlement of the situation in the world.

For 5½ long years we have been striving to attain a peace in the world that would be lasting.

We did not institute aggression in Korea. We did not institute aggression in Greece. We did not institute aggression in Berlin.

We do not want war. We want peace.

The United Nations was organized for the purpose of enforcing the peace in the world.

When the North Koreans and Chinese began their aggressive attacks and marched into South Korea, a republic which had been set up by the United Nations and under their aegis, it was necessary that the peace-loving nations of the world enforce that peace, and stop the aggression.

And that is exactly what we are trying to do.

When we sit here tonight, in our evening clothes, partaking of food on white table-cloths, and enjoying ourselves in other ways, bear in mind that there are men fighting and dying in an endeavor to reach that peace for which we have been striving since World War II ceased.

Remember that these men are baring their breasts for liberty and unity in the world.

It is necessary that the people of the United States, the greatest and most powerful free nation in the world—and I say that not in a bragging way, but because it happens to be the truth—the people of the United States have assumed the responsibility which no other nation in the history of the world has assumed.

We are the leaders of the free peoples of the world. It is necessary that we display that leadership, and we must display it here at home by a unity so that those young men on the battlefields of Korea shall not die in vain, so that those young men in Korea may accomplish the purpose for which they are fighting.

It is necessary that you here at home remember that this is a world crisis, that this crisis must be met through the leadership of the United States of America, and it is up to you people here at home to see that that is accomplished.

In order to accomplish that purpose, you must quit your bickering here at home, you must quit playing petty politics, you must remember that there are certain things that have to be done here at home, if we are going to accomplish the purpose.

We are fighting for time. The young men in Korea and Japan are fighting for time—for us.

There is always an emphasis on the casualties in Korea. Of course, when there is fighting, there are casualties.

But, did it ever occur to you that if this necessity with which we are faced is not met, that the casualties in Korea will be one small drop in the bucket from one of those horrible bombs of which we talk so much.

Think—think—think what a responsibility your President faces in a situation of this kind. If you would think, and think clearly on this subject, you would get behind me and help me to win this peace.

And that is what I am asking you to do.

And that is what our armed forces are in the field to do.

It is up to you.

We have the greatest defense organization in the history of the world. There has never been a defense organization headed by so many distinguished men, who know what they are doing, from experience. There has never been a government of the United States as united as the executive branch of this Government of ours is now.

It is up to the other branches of the Government to see that we will accomplish the purpose which God intended us to accomplish, and that is to lead the world to peace.

I hope every one of you will go home and get down on your knees and pray for guidance to do the right thing, that these young men who are now fighting on the battlefields of Korea shall not die in vain.

It is up to you.

NOTE: The President spoke at 10:22 p.m. at the Statler Hotel in Washington. In his opening words he referred to Charles E. Wilson, Director of the Office of Defense Mobilization, who presided at the dinner, and Secretary of Defense George C. Marshall.

The President's remarks were broadcast directly to the armed forces in Korea by shortwave radio.

The dinner was sponsored by the Military Order of World Wars, the Navy League, and the Air Force Association.

---

110   Letter to the Chairman, Democratic National Committee, on the Midwest Conference and the Western States Conference of the Democratic Party. *May 21, 1951*

Dear Bill:

I want to extend my warm greetings to all of the good Democrats who have gathered from 24 states for the meetings of the Midwest Conference and the Western States Conference.

The Democratic Party today has the responsibility of helping to guide this great nation through one of the most dangerous crises of history.

In order to do this, the leaders of our Party must understand the tremendous problems our country faces, and the things we have to do to keep our nation safe and strong. And then the leaders of our Party must get these facts to the people. They must work with the members of the Government and with other public spirited citizens to get the facts of our present international situation and our foreign policy and our defense policy to the people.

In spite of the confusers, in spite of the men of little faith, our country is meeting this crisis firmly and strongly. Our country has never been engaged in a more important struggle than the present conflict in Korea. It has never been embarked on a better or more important effort than our present policy of uniting the free nations and strengthening them to put a stop to the forces of aggression and the danger of another world war.

Our aim is peace—a just and lasting peace. That is what I have been working for ever since I became President.

Our policies are designed to bring about peace. The Soviet rulers can, of course, plunge the world into war, in spite of all we are trying to do. But our policy of unifying and strengthening the free world offers the best hope of avoiding war. No other policy offers as much. If we try to find security by going it alone in the world, or by withdrawing and isolating ourselves from the rest of the world, we would be headed for disaster. We might very well bring about the world conflict we are trying to prevent.

This is not a political matter. It is a matter of life and death for our country and our way of life.

I want the officials of this Administration to tell the delegates at this conference exactly what is going on in Washington, and what our citizens must do to bring our country through this crisis successfully. And I know that these Washington officials want to have the views of the delegates. All of us in the Government need the thinking and judgment of those outside.

I am asking, personally, for a full report on all the discussions.

I wish that I could discuss these things at the Denver meeting but it is impossible for me to leave Washington at this time. However, please tell the folks from the West and Midwest that I hope to get a chance to see some of them in person before too long. When I get the chance I'll have plenty to tell them.

Very sincerely yours,

HARRY S. TRUMAN

[The Honorable William Boyle, Brown Palace Hotel, Denver, Colorado.]

NOTE: The Western States Conference and the Midwest Conference met in Denver, Colo., on May 23 and 24, and the Democratic National Committee met there on May 25.

111 Letter to Senator Maybank on the Limitation on Public Housing in the Appropriations Bill. *May 22, 1951*

Dear Mr. Chairman:

I am deeply concerned about the crippling limitation on the public housing program which the House included in H.R. 3880, the Independent Offices Appropriation Bill. This will have an adverse effect on our defense effort. It seems to me of great importance that your subcommittee consider the consequences very carefully and I earnestly hope the limitation can be removed before the Congress completes action on this bill.

As passed by the House, the bill contains an arbitrary limit of 5,000 public housing units which can be started in the next fiscal year and an equally arbitrary limit of 50,000 units for each year thereafter.

To all intents and purposes this means repealing the public housing provisions of the Housing Act of 1949. That was one of the best laws to be passed by any recent

Congress. We need it now as much as ever. It would be tragic to have it set aside in this fashion.

Since the Korean outbreak, the public housing program has been directed mainly toward meeting lower-income housing needs in our defense areas. These areas have been given priority in the approval of new projects. All new projects are required to give preference to essential lower-income defense workers. Many of our increasingly crowded defense centers need every spare unit of public housing they can get, to help attract and house these workers. Yet under the House bill, construction of new projects will be virtually halted.

Families of men now in military service and veterans of World War II who meet the income limitation also have preference for public housing. Their needs also are ignored by the provisions of this bill.

Last summer, when it became necessary to curtail total home construction in the interest of the defense effort, plans for building low-rent public housing were cut back proportionately. In the January budget, funds were requested for only 75,000 new units in fiscal 1952. This contrasts with the 135,000 units per year authorized by the Housing Act of 1949 and is well in line with the 40 percent over-all reduction which we have been seeking in the pre-Korean volume of new starts.

In reducing the volume of housing starts, our aim has been to spread the remaining supply equitably among all income groups.

We certainly do not want to make the lower-income families, those hardest pressed for decent housing, bear by far the heaviest share of the cuts in new housing supply. Yet, that is exactly what this bill will do. This is not only unwise and unjust—it is clearly in conflict with the National Housing Policy set forth by the Congress.

A great many communities have made plans and committed funds to start construction of public housing units in the next fiscal year. Sites have already been purchased for nearly 63,000 of these units. If the limitations of the House bill are allowed to stand, virtually none of them could be built next year. The Housing and Home Finance Administrator has a complete report on the status of Municipal programs and the expected effect of the House limitation, city by city. He will be glad to make this available to you.

I feel sure that when all these facts are taken into account, the Congress will agree that the public housing limitations in the Independent Offices Appropriation Bill should be removed and the funds requested in the budget restored for the next fiscal year.

Very sincerely yours,

HARRY S. TRUMAN

[Honorable Burnet R. Maybank, Chairman, Independent Offices Subcommittee, Appropriations Committee, United States Senate]

NOTE: On August 31, 1951, the President approved the Independent Offices Appropriation Act, 1952 (65 Stat. 268). The act raised the construction restriction for fiscal year 1952 to 50,000 dwelling units and eliminated restrictions for future years.

112 Letter to Judge Learned Hand on His Retirement From Active Service. *May 23, 1951*

Dear Judge Hand:

Your impending retirement fills me with regret, which I know is shared by the American people. It is hard to accept the fact that,

after forty-two years of most distinguished service to our Nation, your activities are now to be narrowed.

It is always difficult for me to express a

sentiment of deep regret; what makes my present task so overwhelming is the compulsion I feel to attempt, on behalf of the American people, to give in words some inkling of the place you have held and will always hold in the life and spirit of our country.

Your profession has long since recognized the magnitude of your contribution to the law. There has never been any question about your preeminent place among American jurists—indeed among the nations of the world. In your writings, in your day to day work for almost half a century, you have added purpose and hope to man's quest for justice through the process of law.

As judge and philosopher, you have expressed the spirit of America and the highest in civilization which man has achieved. America, and the American people, are the richer because of the vigor and fullness of your contribution to our way of life.

We are compensated in part by the fact that you are casting off only a part of the burdens which you have borne for us these many years, and by our knowledge that you will continue actively to influence our life and society for years to come. May you enjoy many happy years of retirement, secure in the knowledge that no man, whatever his walk of life, has ever been more deserving of the admiration and the gratitude of his country, and, indeed, of the entire free world.

Very sincerely yours,

HARRY S. TRUMAN

[Honorable Learned Hand, United States Circuit Judge for the Second Circuit, New York, N.Y.]

NOTE: Judge Hand served as Judge of the United States District Court for the Southern District of New York from 1909 to 1924, and as Judge of the United States Circuit Court, Second Circuit, from December 20, 1924, to June 1, 1951. His letter, dated May 15, announcing his retirement, was released with the President's reply.

113   The President's News Conference of May 24, 1951

THE PRESIDENT. Please be seated.

[1.] I want to read you a reminder, then you can ask me questions.

[*Reading, not literally*] "I just want to remind everyone that next Wednesday is Memorial Day, and that we all have a duty on that day to pray for permanent peace as well as to honor the heroes of past wars.

"In the proclamation which I issued on May 23, 1950, pursuant to a joint resolution of the Congress, I proclaimed each succeeding Memorial Day as a day of prayer for permanent peace, and suggested 11 o'clock in the morning, eastern daylight saving time, as an appropriate time for each American according to his own religious faith, to beg divine aid in bringing enduring peace to a troubled world.

"I called then, and I call again upon the press, radio, television, and other media of public information to participate in this observance.

"This proclamation was first issued before the Communist aggression which made it necessary for the free nations to turn back the invaders in Korea. With our men, and the men of the other free nations, fighting this Memorial Day in Korea, it is more important than ever that we join—every one of us—in praying for the peace which is our objective."

You will have copies of this available when you go out, and I hope you will see that it gets proper circulation.

I am ready for questions now.

[2.] Q. Mr. President, some of the Democrats out in Denver [1] have indicated that they would follow your preference in the selection of a convention city. Do you have any preference as between Chicago and Philadelphia?

THE PRESIDENT. No. That is a matter that the committee has to pass on. Either city is good. I have been in both places and had a good time. Nominated a winning ticket in both places! [*Laughter*]

Q. Philadelphia seemed to work better than anywhere else, didn't it, Mr. President?

THE PRESIDENT. Well, Philadelphia was a little more controversial, but it came out all right.[2]

Q. I meant for yourself, sir?

THE PRESIDENT. Well, I am not sure about that. That depends on your viewpoint. [*Laughter*]

[3.] Q. Mr. President, your Secretary of Agriculture said that he hoped you would run in 1952. Do you share in that hope?

THE PRESIDENT. That is mighty nice of him, and I appreciate what he has to say. [*More laughter*]

Q. Mr. President, along that line, a few weeks ago, you said that you made up your mind, but that you were the only one that knew what your decision was?

THE PRESIDENT. That is still good.

Q. I wonder if the ruckus kicked up over General MacArthur has changed your mind——

Voices: Louder—louder. Can't hear— can't hear back here!

THE PRESIDENT. He wanted to know if the ruckus kicked up over a great general from the Far East had changed my mind as to my

ideas on the Presidency for the next 4 years. It has no effect on it whatever.

Q. What was your answer?

Q. The season is still on?

THE PRESIDENT. The season is still on. I said it has no effect on it. The season is still on. [*Laughter*]

Q. Would you care to elaborate on that line, sir?

Q. You said before that you had made up your mind?

THE PRESIDENT. Yes. That is correct. But that doesn't close the gate to anybody else. You see, the Democratic Party is a little different from other parties. Anybody in the world who wants to, can run for the nomination for President in the Democratic Convention, and a lot of people do, always.

Q. Mr. President, has Mrs. Truman made up her mind as to whether you are going to run?

THE PRESIDENT. Mrs. Truman has never been very enthusiastic about my holding public office, but she has had to put up with it for 30 years. And I don't blame her at all. She and I understand each other.

Q. Mr. President, also with reference to Denver, Bill Boyle read a letter out there saying that you hoped to see some people before very long.[3] Would you define that "before very long" for us?

THE PRESIDENT. Well, I think I told you— all you people that are interested in that sort of thing, that I would give you plenty of notice so that you could get your suitcases packed in plenty of time. Now, when the time comes around, I will make the announcement—if it does come around—so that you will have plenty of time to get ready to go with me, and I know all of you will want to go. [*Laughter*]

[4.] Q. Mr. President, Ambassador

---

[1] The Western States Conference and the Midwest Conference of the Democratic Party met in Denver on May 23 and 24, and the Democratic National Committee met there on May 25. See also Item 110.

[2] The 1948 convention of the Democratic Party was held in Philadelphia.

[3] See Item 110.

Cowen of the Philippines is in town.[4] Do you expect to see him on Philippine matters some time soon?

THE PRESIDENT. I didn't understand the question?

Q. Ambassador Cowen of the Philippines is in town for consultations. Do you care to make any comment on his visit?

THE PRESIDENT. Well, I will see him. Whenever an Ambassador wants to see me, I always see him. I saw him when he first came back.

[5.] Q. Mr. President, if you should pack your bags and hit the road, would it be to resell the country on your foreign policy, or with some political overtones in view?

THE PRESIDENT. Well, of course, that matter would have to take care of itself at the time, but the objective would be to tell the truth about domestic and foreign policy, just as I did in 1948. When the people have the facts, you can't fool them.

Q. If you or Mrs. Truman should decide that you might not want to run in 1952, have you any preferences?

THE PRESIDENT. Well now, that is a hypothetical question, and not one that I can answer at this press conference.

Q. There has been some talk in the background about the Democrats having an eye on another general whom the Republicans are also planning on?

THE PRESIDENT. Well, I have heard something about that. There was something like that going on in 1948, if I am not mistaken. [*Laughter*]

[6.] Q. Mr. President, will you make public soon the report of Mr. Wilson[5] on the economic outlook, which is supposed to be out sometime early in the week?

THE PRESIDENT. I don't know anything

about any such report. I get a report from the Economic Advisers—who are there for that purpose—every week, and those reports are always available for——

Q. Mr. President, this is one that goes back to your memorandum, following the so-called differences between the Treasury and the Federal Reserve?[6]

THE PRESIDENT. That report has been under consideration. I have no comment to make on it as yet, because I have not analyzed it as completely as I want to.

[7.] Q. Mr. President, back to your opening statement about the peace, there are rumors of peace feelers supposed to be coming from the Communist side. Would you say that the prospects for peace are better now?

THE PRESIDENT. I think the Secretary of State answered that question very fully yesterday.[7]

[8.] Q. Mr. President, have you any thoughts on the situation in Iran? For example, do you favor arbitration?

THE PRESIDENT. I want to answer you again as I did the other gentleman over here, that the Secretary of State answered that very fully yesterday.[8] If you will read his com-

---

[4] Myron M. Cowen, U.S. Ambassador to the Philippines.

[5] Charles E. Wilson, Director of the Office of Defense Mobilization and Chairman of the National Advisory Board on Mobilization Policy.

[6] See Item 44.

[7] At his press conference on May 23, Secretary of State Dean Acheson stated that the policy of the United States toward China had not changed, and that the United States Government still hoped to be able to negotiate a Korean peace settlement with the Communist regime in Peiping.

[8] At his news conference on May 23, Secretary Acheson stated, "We believe very earnestly that the controversy between the British Government and the Iranian Government is a controversey which can be and should be settled by negotiation between those parties, and we indicated some of the principles which we thought were important in controlling the general conduct of those negotiations. . . . The United States is the friend of, and is deeply concerned in the welfare and strength of both parties to the controversy." The text of his remarks on the subject is printed in the Department of State Bulletin (vol. 24, p. 891).

ments from his press conference, you will have the answer.

[9.] Q. Mr. President, do you consider this your second term?

THE PRESIDENT. Well, if you would read a little history, you will find that the first term of any President is the term to which he is elected.

Q. Well, that is a hypothetical situation. If you were a candidate in the next term, you would be running—it would be your second term?

THE PRESIDENT. Yes, but that wouldn't make any difference, for the simple reason that I am exempted from that amendment, anyway—specifically.

Q. I was speaking only of tradition, not of the——

THE PRESIDENT. Well, let's cross that bridge when the time comes to do it.

Q. Would you care to express your views on the tenure of the Presidency?

THE PRESIDENT. No. I will do that at a later date.

[10.] Q. Mr. President, this is a local question. In New York there have been two long-standing vacancies on the U.S. District Court.

THE PRESIDENT. That is correct.

Q. The New York Lawyers Association has asked if you will appoint Lloyd Paul Stryker and Mr. Dimock.[9] Is there any comment on that?

THE PRESIDENT. I have them under consideration.

Q. You have them under consideration?

THE PRESIDENT. Yes, I have them under consideration along with several others. And as soon as I come to a conclusion on it, I will announce it in plenty of time.

I am very careful about the appointment of judges to the Federal Courts. It is, I think, one of the most important things that the President of the United States does, because that is where the people come in contact with the Government under law. That is one of the greatest things that our Government stands for, is Government under law. And I am exceedingly careful about the appointment of Federal judges, and that is the reason I have hesitated about making these appointments. These gentlemen that have been recommended by the Bar Association are good men, but I think others are under consideration also.

[11.] Q. Mr. President, is there anything you can tell us now about a new Ambassador to Ireland?

THE PRESIDENT. No, I can't tell you a thing about it because I don't know anything about it.

[12.] Q. Mr. President, nobody seems to have rasied the MacArthur controversy this morning. [*Laughter*] Would you care to comment on Senator Wiley's [10] proposal that you testify before the——

THE PRESIDENT. Last week I made my position very clear on that controversy, and I have no further comment to make to that.

[13.] Q. Mr. President, General Van Fleet [11] said today the 8th Army is "attacking all along the entire front, and there is no limitation on its objective." I just wonder if that is any change at all in——

THE PRESIDENT. Not at all. The commanders in the field have absolute control of the tactics and strategy, and they always have.

[14.] Q. Mr. President, do you feel that

---

[9] Lloyd P. Stryker and Edward J. Dimock, New York attorneys. Mr. Dimock was appointed to the United States District Court for the Southern District of New York on June 11, 1951.

[10] Senator Alexander Wiley of Wisconsin, ranking Republican on the Senate Committee on Foreign Relations which was holding joint hearings with the Senate Armed Services Committee on the removal of General MacArthur from his command in the Far East.

[11] Gen. James A. Van Fleet, new commander of the 8th Army in Korea.

Congress has made as much speed as it perhaps should have in the passage of the more vital legislation that is before it?

THE PRESIDENT. Well now, that is a very, very delicate question you have asked me. [*Laughter*] And I am not ready as yet to enter into a controversy with the Congress.

You can never tell what the record of a Congress will be until that Congress has adjourned for the period for which it has been meeting. Now, I never want to comment on the record of the Congress, because if you will remember very carefully, the same question was asked me about the 81st Congress, and I told you then that the record of the Congress is not the record until it is made. Now this session is not over yet, by any means, and there is still another session of the 82d Congress that takes place on the 3d of January 1952, and therefore I don't want to make any comments on the situation.

I have been very much worried about the necessity for the extension of the emergency matters that will expire the 30th day of June. It is absolutely essential that the Defense Production Act with its amendments be in operation by that time.[12] The Congress has been exceedingly busy on hearings of one sort and another, and there is just too much work for any one man to do in every field down there, I know, because I spent 10 years down there. And so I will wait to make the comment on your question when we have the results.

Q. That is what I had in mind, Mr. President, sir, these matters that are expiring on June 30th, and need renewal.

THE PRESIDENT. I am very much worried about them, but I do think they will certainly get around to take care of that situation before the time expires.

[15.] Q. Mr. President, since you spent 10 years in the Senate, what do you think

of this "In Tuesday Out Thursday Club"?

THE PRESIDENT. What is that?

Q. What do you think about the Congressmen who go home on a weekend and come back on a Tuesday—who go home on a Thursday——

THE PRESIDENT. I have no comment on that. That is a matter that the Congress itself must take care of. That is out of my bailiwick. You see, I am the Executive, and the legislative branch of the Government has to tend to its own business.

[16.] Q. Mr. President, once more, have you decided whether you are going to Topeka for the 35th Division [13]——

THE PRESIDENT. No, I haven't. I would like very much to go. I have never missed one, and I had hoped conditions would be so that I could go. I have had about as much pressure on that from my friends as I have had on any other one thing. I can't tell you now whether I will go or not. It depends on the situation here, of course.

Q. What was the date of that, Mr. President?

THE PRESIDENT. Ninth of June.

[17.] I do have a comment that I want to make to you, that I want to have an understanding with you on. Some of my good friends who write columns, and whom I read with pleasure, have been saying lately that I had a "cocky" attitude. Now, I don't like that word, because I think it is "confident" that they want to say. And if you remember, after the election in 1948, I was exceedingly careful not to appear cocky, or as if I wanted to press somebody down. I am not in that mood now.

I think, however, that the program and policies that the Executive has been endeavoring to put into effect are right, and I think that the people of the United States and of the world believe that they are right. And

[12] See Item 176.

[13] Reunion of the 35th Division Association.

I am confident that those policies will go into effect legislatively and otherwise because they are right. And I don't want to assume any cocky attitude toward anybody, no matter who he is. I just want to make that plain—because I don't feel that way, and never have.

Q. Your program for peace, sir?

THE PRESIDENT. Yes, the whole program is based on world peace; and both the domestic and the foreign policy are policies which we hope will cause world peace and prevent a third world war, which would in effect, I believe, destroy freedom and everything else in the world. We would probably go back to the Dark Ages if we have another world war. I don't want to have it. That's all I have worked for for 6 years, is peace in the world.

Q. Would there be any objection to our quoting you directly on that?

THE PRESIDENT. Well, I have no objection. Talk it over with Joe Short,[14] and if he works it out with you, it will be all right.

Q. If such a decision is made, may we have copies of it?

THE PRESIDENT. Yes, you may—you may.

Mr. Short: The decision won't be made in time for you to dictate.

THE PRESIDENT. I have no objection to that because that is the way I feel, and I want you to understand it. Nothing in my life amounts to anything but world peace. That is all I am working for.

Q. Would it be possible for us to get one sentence in the last part of it for quotation now?

THE PRESIDENT. Talk to Joe. He is my

[14] Joseph H. Short, Secretary to the President.

Press Secretary.

Mr. Short: I think we had better wait until this is over.[15]

Q. Haven't we got enough energy and intelligence in this country to keep from slipping back into the Dark Ages, even if we would have to fight another war?

THE PRESIDENT. I hope that is true, but you know what happens to governments and what happens to people. And if a third world war should come, we will not be in the position that we have been in the other two. We will be a battlefront. We can look forward to destruction here, just as the other countries in the Second World War. And you never can tell what will happen to people when that takes place.

I think we have enough intelligence and energy to meet any situation with which we are confronted, but I am not willing to take a chance on it. That is the reason I don't want a third world war.

[18.] Q. Mr. President, have you received, or do you expect a report from Senator Magnuson on his trip to the Far East?

THE PRESIDENT. I have no doubt the Senator will come to see me and tell me about his trip.

Reporter: Thank you, Mr. President.

THE PRESIDENT. You are entirely welcome.

NOTE: President Truman's two hundred and sixty-fifth news conference was held in the Indian Treaty Room (Room 474) in the Executive Office Building at 10:30 a.m. on Thursday, May 24, 1951.

[15] On the same day the White House made public a transcript of the President's statement Item [17.] beginning with the words, "I do have a comment" and concluding with, "That is the reason I don't want a third world war."

114   Special Message to the Congress on the Mutual Security Program. *May 24, 1951*

To the Congress of the United States:

Three weeks ago I transmitted to the Congress a request for 60 billion dollars for the United States defense establishment during the fiscal year ending June 30, 1952.

I am now recommending for the fiscal year ending June 30, 1952, a Mutual Security Program as follows:

(1) Military assistance to other free nations in the amount of 6.25 billion dollars.

(2) Economic assistance to other free nations in the amount of 2.25 billion dollars, primarily to support expanded defense efforts abroad.

These amounts compare with 5.3 billion dollars appropriated for military assistance, and 3.0 billion dollars for economic assistance, in the current fiscal year.

The program for our own Armed Forces and this Mutual Security Program interlock. The one builds upon the other. The purpose of each is the security of the United States—the security of American lives and homes against attack and the security of our rights and liberties as law-abiding members of the world community.

Our country has greater economic strength and larger potential military power than any other nation on earth. But we do not and we should not stand alone. We cannot maintain our civilization, if the rest of the world is split up, subjugated, and organized against us by the Kremlin.

This is a very real and terrible danger. But it can be overcome. To do so, we must work with the rest of the free world: we must join other free nations in common defense plans; we must concert our economic strength with theirs for the common good; and we must help other free countries to build the military and economic power needed to make impossible the communist dreams of world conquest.

This is hard common sense and sound economy. The dollars spent under the Mutual Security Program will build more strength in support of our security than we could build at home with the same expenditure of funds.

This Mutual Security Program brings together our various foreign aid programs, including the arms aid of the Mutual Defense Assistance Program, economic assistance for Europe—now being directed primarily to support of rearmament—and our economic aid to underdeveloped areas under the Point IV concept. Every one of these programs has proved its worth.

In preparing the present recommendations, each of these separate programs has been revised in the light of the emergency situation that exists in the world and the extraordinary demands that are being placed on our Nation. The amounts, the geographical areas, and the purposes of the aid have all been chosen in order to bring about the greatest possible increase in the security of the United States and the whole free world.

Under this program, the United States will send tanks, guns, and planes to a number of free countries, in Europe and other parts of the world, which are building up armed forces against the threat of communist attack. We will also send economic help to a number of countries—economic help ranging from machinery and materials with which to make weapons, to seeds, medicine, and technical assistance with which to conquer communism's allies of starvation and sickness.

This program was designed with three major characteristics of the Soviet threat in mind:

First, the Soviet threat is world-wide. In Europe, in Asia, in our own hemisphere, the strategy of the Kremlin concentrates on trying to pick off the free countries one by one, so that their resources and people can be organized against the rest of the free world. That is why the Mutual Security Program includes essential help to free countries all around the world which are exposed to the danger of internal or external communist pressures.

Second, the Soviet threat is total, it affects every form of human endeavor. Communist attack may come in the form of armies marching across frontiers; or it may come in the form of internal subversion. Economic warfare, psychological warfare, political infiltration, sabotage, the marching of armies—these are interchangeable aggressive weapons which the Soviet rulers use singly or together according to shifting calculations of greatest advantage. That is why the free world must concentrate upon building not only military strength, but also economic, political, and moral strength. That is why the Mutual Security Program includes economic as well as military assistance.

Third, the Soviet threat is of indefinite duration. The free world must take into account both the possibility that the Soviet rulers may soon start all-out armed aggression, and the possibility that they may carry on their aggressive tactics for many years by measures short of all-out war.

That is why the task of the free world now is not only to build defenses urgently in the immediate future, but also to prepare for the long pull. We of the free countries must make preparations now so that when our armed forces have been built up we will be able to maintain them for years, if necessary, and at the same time grow in underlying economic strength more soundly and more rapidly than the Soviet dictatorship.

The free nations have the resources and the will to overcome all these aspects of the Soviet threat. Together, our potential strength is enormous. The free nations have 75 per cent of the world's industrial capacity and most of the world's raw materials.

Most important of all, free men, all around the world, have the determination to stop communist aggression and to achieve peace. The communist aggression in Korea dispelled any lingering doubts that the Kremlin is willing to threaten the peace of the world.

The job before the free nations is to organize their potential resources and together to convert them into actual military and economic strength. Our associates in the free world are now making vigorous efforts to this end. The Mutual Security Program will provide them with resources required to supplement and make effective their efforts. It is not a program under which we will carry the rest of the free world on our backs. It could not succeed if that were the case. The program is founded on the principle of mutual effort and the knowledge that we can help effectively only those who help themselves.

The proposed aid is related to the resources available to each recipient country, its economic stability, and the burdens it has assumed. Our aid will be provided only for essential needs that the country cannot meet by its own efforts. The need for aid will be continuously reviewed in the light of each country's performance and of economic and political changes.

The bulk of the assistance under the Mutual Security Program will be military equipment. Most of this will go to our partners in the North Atlantic Treaty, but in addition substantial quantities will be supplied to nations in Asia and the Middle East. Military equipment to supplement their own will be provided to countries when they have organized forces which require this equipment in order to become effective fighting units. With our assistance, the free world as a whole will be able to strengthen its military defenses rapidly. Without such aid, the necessary buildup would be dangerously delayed if not impossible.

In addition to supplying military equipment, this program will provide economic aid for a number of countries. In most countries in Europe, and in some countries in other parts of the world, this economic aid will enable the recipients to carry on larger defense programs than would otherwise be possible. In a few cases, some further economic help is necessary to continue progress toward recovery. In Asia and other underdeveloped areas, this program will enable the people to make headway against conditions of poverty and stagnation which are principal assets of Soviet infiltration.

The condition of the people in the underdeveloped areas would be a matter of humanitarian concern even if our national security were not involved. Major improvement in these conditions is necessarily a long-term process, in which the countries' own efforts, private investment, and public developmental loans should play the largest part. Carefully selected projects of technical assistance and initial development on a grant basis, however, can speed up this process and provide tangible benefits even in the short run.

The underdeveloped countries in Asia, South America, and Africa, produce strategic materials which are essential to the defense and economic health of the free world. Production of these materials must be increased. Loans and developmental help are needed. The development of the resources of those countries helps them by raising their standard of living and increasing their resistance

to communist subversion, and helps the whole free world by increasing the supply of raw materials essential to defense and to an expanding world economy.

To enable the underdeveloped areas to expand their production of strategic materials, they must be assured of being able to obtain the essential supplies and equipment they need from our country. Indeed, our entire security program will be successful only if the materials available to the free world are distributed in the way that will best contribute to the build-up of total free world strength. The Mutual Security Program, like the program for our own Armed Forces, has been examined from the standpoint of the availability of supplies, materials and equipment that are required to carry it out. We believe these resources can and must be made available out of the expanding production of the free world.

In each area, the United States aid which I propose will be a small part of the total resources available for military and economic purposes—but that small proportion is crucial. In all these areas of the world, larger amounts of United States assistance could be put to good use and would pay real dividends. But I have limited the assistance I am recommending to what is absolutely necessary, under the emergency conditions we are in today, to help these countries build essential military and economic strength.

I propose that the total funds required under the Mutual Security Program be divided as follows:

MUTUAL SECURITY PROGRAM, 1952

[in millions of dollars]

	Economic	Military
Europe	1,650	5,240
Middle East and Northern Africa	125	415
Asia	375	555
Latin America	22	40
Administrative Expenses	78	.....
Total	2,250	6,250

The military aid for Greece and Turkey is included in the amount for the Middle East. The amount of the economic aid for Europe includes the economic aid for Greece and Turkey. For convenience, the estimated requirement for administrative expenses for the entire program—approximately 78 million dollars is shown as a single figure under economic aid.

The amounts requested for economic aid include 13 million dollars to be furnished the United Nations and the Organization of American States for their technical assistance programs.

The economic, as well as the military aid recommended, is grant assistance to be provided through appropriated funds. Loans by the Export-Import Bank will also continue to play an important role in our efforts to assist the economic progress of friendly countries. In order that full use may be made of the opportunities for loans, especially to develop strategic materials, I recommend that the lending authority of the Export-Import Bank be increased by one billion dollars. Not all of the increased lending authority, of course, will be used in the coming year.

With this program of assistance to the total free world effort, we will move forward rapidly toward a situation giving reasonable assurance against aggression.

Moreover, the Mutual Security Program is designed to taper off as soon as our safety will permit. The creation of effective military forces in being, coupled with increased productivity, will make it possible, within a few years, for most areas of the free world to maintain their defenses and sustain their economies without further grant assistance from this country.

The creation of this strength will provide a defensive shield against aggression for all the free world. Ever since the war, the free nations have been going forward to develop their resources and improve the lot of their people. Ever since the war, the free nations have been working together to create a world community in which each nation, respecting world law, can play its distinctive and honorable role.

The only kind of war we seek is the good old fight against man's ancient enemies—poverty, disease, hunger, and illiteracy. This is an effort which makes use of the great elements of our strength—our economic power, our science, our organizing ability, our political principles, our enthusiasm as free men with faith in the future. This is an effort to build, not to destroy; to grow in freedom and justice and mutual respect; to replace the force of arms with the force of peaceful change.

We have no doubt about the outcome of this free world effort. But we must be strong and we must have strong partners if we are to discourage new acts of violence by the power-hungry, and to win the opportunity to carry on our work of peaceful progress.

For the time-being, therefore, the emphasis in our cooperation with the other free nations must be on building our defensive shield against aggression. This shield threatens no one. It will never be used for aggression. But it will be used instantly for defense.

The strengthening of the free world along these lines is the best hope of producing changes in the policies of the Soviet Union without a world war. Military defense forces will put a stop to the Kremlin's hope of easy conquest. Growing prosperity in the free countries will frustrate Soviet political warfare. In these circumstances, the Soviet rulers will face growing internal pressures. The peoples under Soviet control will grow more and more restive under the burden of an aggressive and futile policy of hostility toward the whole world. The rulers of the Soviet Union will be forced by these pressures to abandon their policy of aggression.

It is too early to predict how or when this policy will change. But this program of mutual security will help to bring about such a change. It is certain that the united vigor and cooperative action of the free world can produce such results if we act in time. No system based on slavery and terror can long withstand the tremendous human energies that are released by the advance of freedom.

EUROPE

For the security of the United States, for the survival of freedom in the world, free Europe is a critical area that must be defended.

The people of Europe free from Soviet control number 300 million. They operate a great industrial plant, second only to our own. They occupy a uniquely strategic location. They are at once the most tempting prize for Soviet ambitions and our strongest allies in the world struggle for freedom.

The loss of Europe to the Soviet Union would not only be tragic in itself; it would also result in a tremendous shift of world power. It would compel us to convert the United States into an isolated garrison state.

That is why, three years ago, when the countries of Europe were trembling on the brink of economic collapse, the United States launched its program of aid for European recovery.

That is why, two years ago, the United States and Canada joined ten Western European countries—Iceland, Great Britain, Norway, Denmark, the Netherlands, Belgium, Luxembourg, France, Portugal, and Italy—in the North Atlantic Treaty, declaring that an attack on one would be considered an attack on all.

The North Atlantic Treaty reflects the basic fact of international life that the freedom of Western Europe and the freedom of North America are inseparable.

Under that Treaty, defense plans have been developed by the military leaders of the North Atlantic Treaty countries. Under General Eisenhower's central command, a unified army, navy, and air force is being organized for the defense of Western Europe, composed of national forces assigned by individual nations.

The key element in the defense of free Europe is the ability to hold on the ground. Western Europe lacks the insulation of wide oceans. Major preparations must therefore be made to hold its lands—by well-armed manpower on the ground, by the great striking force of airpower, and by a seapower which commands its surrounding waters and important lines of communication.

The European countries themselves are providing the great majority of the forces needed. The United States also has Army, Navy, and Air Force units in Europe, which add to the power of the combined defense forces, and more units will move there, both from this country and from Canada.

Our European partners in the North Atlantic Treaty now have over 2 million men under arms, plus large numbers of trained reserves. The bulk of Western Europe's armed forces are pledged to General Eisenhower's command. Moreover, some of these countries—notably France and Britain—have sizeable forces fighting in Malaya, Indo-China, and Korea, and have other important overseas defense commitments. The combat power of Western European forces is rising steadily as equipment becomes available and periods of military service are lengthened.

Rearmament will cause a severe drain on the Western European countries. Through their own efforts, national and collective, and with the vital assistance of the Marshall

Plan, Western Europe has made a remarkable record of economic recovery since 1947. Production and trade have been restored and financial conditions have been greatly improved. In the free countries of Europe, communism has been checked and thrown back. The original goals of the Marshall Plan have been largely achieved.

But the western European countries are by no means yet free from the after effects of the most destructive war in history.

They are living on a very narrow economic margin. Whereas our standard of living is nearly 50 per cent higher than it was before World War II, theirs has only recently reached their pre-war levels, which were much lower than ours.

The European countries cannot move rapidly into sufficient large-scale military production to provide all the equipment required for the essential expansion of their forces. Over the next few years, they do expect to increase their production of military equipment. In the coming fiscal year, it will be more than double the pre-Korean rate. But the most they can do will not be enough to equip their armed forces on the time schedule necessary for the common defense.

The United States, with its huge and flexible industrial capacity and greater margin for diverting resources to military production, can and should continue to supply military equipment to our allies in Western Europe. In this way, many divisions, air squadrons, and naval vessels can be brought to active duty in the next year or two which otherwise could not be.

In the immediately coming years, the crucial need is to produce the initial equipment for a very rapid buildup of forces. The expanding European productive capacity will contribute increasingly to this buildup. With this capacity, Europe should be able to meet the smaller continuing maintenance

and replacement requirements without substantial outside aid.

The military aid for Europe I am recommending amounts to 5.3 billion dollars. I also recommend economic assistance for this area for the coming year in the amount of 1.65 billion dollars.

Because of the degree of economic recovery which has been attained, the total economic assistance I am requesting for European countries next year—despite the large new burdens of European rearmament—is substantially reduced from the amount we have provided in the current fiscal year.

However, in the free countries of Europe which are rearming, the proposed increases in military production and the building of armed forces will require large diversions of manpower and other economic resources away from production of goods for consumption, for investment, and for export. To carry these greatly enlarged military burdens, our partners in Europe will be taking measures to increase taxes and mobilize their resources through economic controls. Despite determined efforts in this direction they will need some continuing economic assistance.

Some aid is also proposed for Western Germany, which by its support of occupation forces is assisting the defense effort and which may later make more direct contributions to the common defense. In Austria and Trieste, which cannot directly contribute to the rearmament effort, but whose economies are handicapped by special difficulties, economic aid must also be continued to maintain political stability. Certain economic assistance for Yugoslavia is proposed to help meet its minimum requirements in maintaining strength against the threat of Soviet imperialism.

This economic aid is critical—that is, it is the essential condition of an increase in European military effort. It should make possible European production many times larger than the amount of the support given.

MIDDLE EAST

The countries of the Middle East are, for the most part, less developed industrially than those of Europe. They are, nevertheless, of great importance to the security of the entire free world. This region is a vital link of land, sea, and air communications between Europe, Asia, and Africa. In the free nations of the Middle East, lie half of the oil reserves of the world.

No part of the world is more directly exposed to Soviet pressure. The Kremlin has lost no opportunity to stir these troubled waters, as the post-war record amply demonstrates. Civil war in Greece; pressure for Turkish concessions on the Dardanelles; sponsorship of the rebellious Tudeh party in Iran; furthering of factional strife in the Arab States and Israel—all reflect a concerted design for the extension of Soviet domination to this vital area.

There is no simple formula for increasing stability and security in the Middle East. With the help of American military and economic assistance, Soviet pressure has already been firmly resisted in Turkey and the Soviet-inspired guerrilla war has been decisively defeated in Greece. But the pressure against the Middle East is unremitting. It can be overcome only by a continued build-up of armed defenses and the fostering of economic development. Only through such measures can these peoples advance toward stability and improved living conditions, and be assured that their aims can best be achieved through strengthening their associations in the free world.

To these ends, I am recommending 415 million dollars in military aid, for Greece, Turkey, and Iran; a portion of this aid will be available for other Middle Eastern nations if necessary. I am also recommending 125 million dollars in economic aid for Middle Eastern countries, exclusive of Greece and Turkey for whom economic aid is provided as part of the program for Europe. This amount also includes programs of technical assistance to Libya, Liberia, and Ethiopia, three independent states of Africa whose economic problems are similar to those of the Middle Eastern countries.

Continuing military aid for Greece and Turkey will make possible the further strengthening of these countries' large and well trained armed forces, which have already displayed their valiant resolution in the fight for freedom in Korea. In Iran, continuing military aid is required to help build internal security and defense, together with economic aid to help sustain the Iranian economy and give impetus to the much needed longer-term process of economic development for the benefit of the Iranian people.

In the Arab States and Israel, the fundamental requirement is a regional approach to the basic problems of economic development. This is urgently needed to reduce existing tensions, especially through the orderly settlement of homeless refugees. The program for the Arab States will expand needed food production through the development of land and water resources. The program for Israel will help that country to maintain her economy during an especially trying period of her national development. At the same time, the program of assistance to the Arab refugees from Palestine, which will necessarily extend beyond the coming fiscal year, has the three-fold purpose of assisting the settlement of refugees, of strengthening those States wherein they settle, and assisting both Israel and the Arab States by removing this threat to the peace of the area.

The program I am now proposing is a balanced program for strengthening the security of the Middle East. It will make a solid contribution to our hopes for peace.

ASIA AND THE PACIFIC

In Asia, in a vast area stretching from Afghanistan to Korea, free countries are struggling to meet communist aggression in all its many forms. Some of these countries are battling the communist armies of Soviet satellites; some are engaged in bitter civil strife against communist-led guerrillas; all of them face the immediate danger of communist subversion.

Soviet intentions with regard to these countries are unmistakably clear. Using the weapons of subversion, false propaganda and civil war, the Kremlin has already reduced China to the status of a satellite. The Soviet rulers have turned their satellite armies loose on the Republic of Korea. Communist rebellion is raging in Indo-China. In Burma, the Philippines, and other places, communist-inspired groups are stirring up internal disorder. In all countries, they are trying to exploit deep-seated economic difficulties—poverty, illiteracy and disease.

This campaign threatens to absorb the manpower and the vital resources of the East into the Soviet design of world conquest. It threatens to deprive the free nations of some of their most vitally needed raw materials. It threatens to turn more of the peaceful millions of the East into armies to be used as pawns at the disposal of the Kremlin.

Aside from immediate considerations of security, the continued independence of these nations is vital to the future of the free world. Many of these nations are new to self government. They have dedicated themselves to the ideals of national independence, of human liberty, and social progress. Their hundreds of millions of citizens are eager for justice and liberty and a stake in the future.

These countries demonstrate the power and vitality of the ideals of our own American Revolution; they mark the sweeping advance across the world of the concepts of freedom and brotherhood. To lose these countries to the rulers of the Kremlin would be more than a blow to our military security and our economic life. It would be a terrible defeat for the ideals of freedom—with grave spiritual consequences for men everywhere who share our faith in freedom.

All these considerations make it essential for the United States to help the free countries of Asia in their struggle to make good their independence and bring economic and social progress to their people. Where the governments of these countries are striving to establish free and stable political institutions, to build up their military defenses, and to raise the standard of living above the level of bare subsistence, we can and should give them assistance. We cannot replace their own strong efforts, but we can supplement them.

This Mutual Security Program is intended to do that. On the military side, it will supply certain of the Asian countries with items of military equipment and the training they need for their defense forces. On the economic side, it will provide a number of the Asian countries with the most urgently needed commodities, machinery, and tools, and with technical advice in such fields as agriculture, industry, health, and governmental administration.

The assistance I am recommending for Asian countries, 555 million dollars in military aid and 375 million dollars in economic aid, is so planned as to meet the most pressing needs in the various countries, and is intended to provide the crucial margin of resources which will enable them to move forward.

Military assistance under this program will go to the Chinese armies on Formosa, to help keep that island out of the hands of Communist China. It will go to Indo-China, where over 100,000 French troops are fighting side-by-side with the forces of Viet Nam, Laos, and Cambodia against communist-led forces. It will go to the Philippines and to Thailand, to help build forces strong enough to insure internal security and discourage outside attack. Some of these military assistance funds will also be available for allocation to other countries in the area if a critical need arises.

The military aid under this program will supplement other military efforts against communism in Asia. The countries we will be aiding, and a number of others, are supporting military forces with their own funds. France is supplying the largest part of the military supplies needed in Indo-China, and Britain is supplying her forces which are fighting guerrillas in the Malay States. The substantial military aid we are giving to the forces of the Republic of Korea is included in the budget for our military services.

The struggle for security and peace in Asia is far more than a military matter. In many of the Asian countries, including all the countries which need military aid, economic assistance is also required.

These countries urgently need help in their efforts to overcome the desperate conditions of poverty, illiteracy, and disease which are the heart of the Asian problem. It is a terrible fact that poverty is increasing rather than diminishing in much of Asia. Millions of people exist at bare subsistence levels.

The Asian countries are doing what they can on their own to meet this problem. An encouraging proposal affecting a number of these countries is the Colombo Plan for technical assistance and economic development worked out under the auspices of the British Commonwealth. In addition, some aid to Asian countries will be furnished through the programs of the United Nations.

These sources of aid alone will not, however, suffice to reverse the downward trend in living standards. Aid from the United States is also necessary.

Sizeable programs of technical assistance and capital development are now being carried on by the Economic Cooperation Administration in some of these countries under the Point IV concept. A portion of the funds I am now recommending will provide for continuing these programs and extending them to other countries. These funds will be used to send out technical experts and equipment needed to improve health, agriculture, transportation, and communications services and assist in the development of natural resources.

In addition, the funds I am now recommending will provide necessary economic support for defense programs in Indo-China, Formosa, and the Philippines.

Finally, the economic aid funds I am requesting for Asia include 112.5 million dollars for the United Nations Korean Reconstruction Agency. Together with 50 million dollars which are likely to remain unexpended from funds available for Korean aid for the present fiscal year, these funds will be made available to the Agency at such time as conditions in Korea permit the reconstruction program to be undertaken.

In preparing these recommendations for economic aid, projects which should be financed by loans have been excluded. The investment of private capital and public loans from the International Bank for Reconstruction and Development and the

Export-Import Bank will play an important part in the economic progress of Asia, as in other parts of the world.

In the administration of this program, loans, grants and technical assistance will be meshed together with the plans and efforts of each of the recipient countries for the development of its own resources. Only in this manner can the various kinds of outside aid available to an Asian country be used most effectively and without duplication or overlapping.

These economic programs will have as their goal the creation of conditions eliminating the need for further grant aid for economic development. Such programs look toward the creation of sound government finances and public services, and toward more stable economic and political foundations for raising living standards and creating broader opportunities. It will take time to reach these goals but they must be steadily pursued. Our aid will provide a dynamic force in that direction and will thus contribute strongly to freedom and peace in Asia.

LATIN AMERICA

The United States and the other American Republics agreed in 1947, in the Treaty of Rio de Janeiro, that an armed attack upon one of them is to be regarded as an armed attack on all, and to act together for the common defense.

Our good neighbors to the south are more than willing to share in defending the hemisphere. But there are real limits on their ability to do so without some aid from us. They produce little modern military equipment.

During World War II, defense tasks in Latin America required the use of over 75,000 United States troops as well as considerable United States naval forces. The armed forces of the Latin American states did not at that time have the equipment or training to carry out those defense tasks by themselves.

It makes good sense that, in planning the defense of this hemisphere, the United States should aid the Latin American countries to prepare for and take over certain hemisphere defense tasks that are of interest to us all; tasks they are willing to do and well able to handle, with a little help in equipping and training their forces. Consequently, I am recommending 40 million dollars in military assistance to these countries.

In addition, I recommend 22 million dollars in economic aid to carry forward the excellent technical assistance work that is now underway in the other American states in developing agriculture, natural resources, and health, education and other types of basic services. This type of assistance has already proved its worth in the Latin American area. It is helping to raise living standards, hasten economic development, and strengthen both peoples and governments in warding off the danger of communist subversion.

This grant assistance is helping to lay the foundation for an expanding volume of capital development, through public and private loans and investments, in the other American Republics. The United States is already providing major economic help to Latin American countries through loans by the Export-Import Bank. Fortunately, the relative geographic security and the economic position of the American Republics make possible large amounts of private loans and investments—the normal and desirable means of fostering economic development.

ADMINISTRATION OF THE PROGRAM

The proposed organization for administering the Mutual Security Program is based on the experience we have had so far, under the arrangements established by the Congress in legislation authorizing previous military and economic aid programs.

The administration of military aid will be handled, as at present, by the Department of Defense, which will be able to insure full coordination between United States production of equipment for our own forces and equipment for our allies. The Department of Defense is responsible for evaluating the equipment deficiencies of the forces of our allies, under mutually agreed strategic concepts, and is charged with procurement, inspection and transportation of military equipment provided by this country.

Administration of economic assistance for Western Europe and most of the countries in the Middle East, Africa, and South and Southeast Asia will be carried on by the Economic Cooperation Administration. This agency has already proved its effectiveness in aiding countries to achieve economic recovery and is now administering economic assistance in support of our mutual defense and security objectives in Europe and Southeast Asia. The economic aid programs for Latin America and certain other countries in which the economic aid is limited almost wholly to technical assistance are now administered by the Technical Cooperation Administration of the State Department. Consideration is now being given to the question of whether or not it would be desirable to transfer the administration of these programs to the Economic Cooperation Administration during the period that that agency is administering other foreign economic aid programs.

These agencies will work very closely with the Export-Import Bank and the International Bank for Reconstruction and Development in achieving a proper integration between loan and grant programs.

In order to insure coordinated policy guidance in administering military and economic aid programs, a key coordinating committee has been established composed of senior representatives of the executive agencies concerned. This International Security Affairs Committee has developed out of the experience of an executive committee that had previously been coordinating operations under the Mutual Defense Assistance Act. The chairman of the new committee, the Director of International Security Affairs, is a senior official of the Department of State confirmed by the Senate, and occupies a position authorized by the Congress under the Mutual Defense Assistance Act.

I recommend this Mutual Security Program to the Congress as another vital step along the road to real security and lasting peace. Peace through collective strength is a difficult course. It is not without danger. There can be no absolute assurance of success. But there are far greater dangers in any other course.

We cannot win peace through appeasement. We cannot gain security in isolation. We will not surrender.

Let it never be forgotten, however, that we are ready as we have always been, to follow the road of peaceful settlement of disputes, of control and reduction of armaments, of cooperation in applying man's talents to the building of a just and prosperous world society.

If the rulers of the Soviet Union did not drown their words of peace with the drums of war, if their professions of peaceful intent were matched by deeds, the century in which we live could become the brightest man has known upon this earth. For our part, if peace could be made sure, the American people would be glad to invest a part of the resources we must now allocate to defense to a large scale program of world-wide economic development.

The benefits of such a program would be immense; the cost a small part of what we must now pay to build our defenses at home and abroad. With such a program, we could, in cooperation with other peoples, inaugurate the most hopeful and fruitful period of peaceful development the world has ever seen.

This was our vision six years ago, when the war came to a close. Let us never forget it. And let us never give up our hopes and our efforts to make it a reality.

HARRY S. TRUMAN

NOTE: For the statement by the President upon signing the Mutual Security Act, see Item 250.

115 Remarks to Members of the Conference of United States Attorneys. *May 24, 1951*

Mr. Attorney General and members of his staff:

I am very happy to welcome you here this morning, as I usually do when you come to Washington. I think on the last trip I went down to the auditorium and made a long-winded speech to you. I won't inflict one on you this morning, because I know you have had a good one already and probably will have some more before you get through.

I am interested, though, in what you are doing and what the Attorney General is trying to do in the way of law enforcement.

I might remark that you are standing in a very famous rose garden. Great events have taken place here in this garden. I give a large number of Medals of Honor to our Armed Forces men here in this garden. I have given medals to nearly all the great generals of our allies—to the French and the British, the Belgians, Italians—nearly every one of our great allies has had some leading military man here who has received a medal here in this garden.

I remember particularly giving one to General Wainwright after he came back right out of a Japanese prison, and he told me that he thought I would be having him court-martialed because he had to surrender Bataan rather than my giving him a Medal of Honor. I don't think I ever gave one that was appreciated more.

Some remarkable things happened to these young men—most fantastic and unbelievable things that they do. I remember one in particular, a great big captain who had been a sergeant when the event for which he got his medal took place. He was about 6 foot 2, and weighed 200 pounds, and I had to stand on tiptoe to get the medal around his neck. He had captured 196 or some fantastic number of Germans—did it all by himself by going into a village and throwing hand-grenades into windows and houses, and when he ran out of grenades he threw rocks, and the Germans came out and surrendered to him. I said to him, "Young man, I don't want you to throw any rocks at me." And he said, "Mr. President, I wouldn't do that." He was much more scared when I was giving him that medal than he was throwing those grenades.

Then I had another young man who was a naval hospital steward. He told me that he was a conscientious objector, and he had a fantastic citation. On Okinawa he had carried out wounded men—he himself was wounded, and he wouldn't let them take him off, and he was wounded again before the rest of the wounded were removed, when finally they had to carry him off.

I said, "Young man, how does it come that you were on the battlefront and a conscientious objector?" He said, "Well, I just decided that I could serve the Lord there as well as anywhere else, if I didn't have to kill anybody." That was a real honest, conscientious young man, trying to do the best he could for his country yet still sticking to his beliefs.

I had another young man with both legs off up to here, and in a wheelchair. He had a fantastic citation, one that was almost unbelievable. When I gave him the medal I said, "Young man, you have made a great sacrifice for your country." "Well," he said, "Mr. President, I just have one life to give for my country, and it still can have it if it wants it."

Now that is what makes up the backbone of this country. That is a cross section of the United States, where you good people come from.

Now, it is your business to see that the laws of the United States of America are properly and rigidly enforced, for the welfare of the country. As I have told you once before, I don't want you to persecute anybody. It is your business to see that when men who are brought to the courts where you have to act as United States attorneys— it is your business to see that they have a fair trial, as well as to see that they are punished for their misdeeds.

We have had crime investigations by Senate committees, with which we cooperated entirely and fully. I called the Attorney General and the head of the collection agency over here—Internal Revenue Department— and all the other agencies that have to do with law enforcement, and told them to give the committees all the cooperation they could. When the committees have found certain things that exist that ought not to exist in this country, most of them are things that should be remedied by the State governments. Some of them are things that affect the United States and interstate business.

And it is your business to see that those things that affect the laws of the Federal Government are taken care of, that every man who has been breaking those laws is punished.

But I want to reiterate again that justice is what we are after. We are not out to persecute anybody. We are out to see that the good people are not harmed by criminals. But we must also see that no innocent man gets punished for something that he did not do.

Now, I am most happy to have you here. I appreciate your willingness to come and call on me. I know you are going to have a constructive—and have had a constructive— meeting, and that when you go back you will be feeling more like doing your job than you did when you came here.

Have a good time while you are here. Washington is a wonderful place to visit, but it is an awful place to live in.

Thank you very much.

NOTE: The President spoke at 12:35 p.m. in the Rose Garden at the White House. In his opening words he referred to Attorney General J. Howard McGrath.

116   Remarks at the Dedication of the Carter Barron Amphitheater. *May 25, 1951*

Mr. Secretary, ladies and gentlemen:

I don't know when I have been in a more impressive and well worthwhile ceremony.

The entertainment which Carter had been having here in Washington, and which was given here for him tonight, was magnificent—the singers beyond compare, the dancers wonderful; Eugene List, I met him at Potsdam, and had him sent to Paris for that A Flat, Opus 42 Chopin Waltz. The two pieces he played tonight were played especially because he thinks I like them—and I do.

It is a pleasure to me to be able to make a small contribution to the memory of Carter Barron and for the dedication of this wonderful amphitheater. This amphitheater is the result of the efforts of Carter Barron. I knew him very well. He was just what Walter Pidgeon said he was, he was the ideal southern gentleman.

I spent many hours with Carter, talking about this great Capital of the United States—literally and really the capital of the world. He and I talked about the improvement of this wonderful city. We talked of the necessity for expanding its plan, and for making it just what it ought to be: the most beautiful city in the world, and also the most useful.

We discussed many a time an auditorium that would seat 40,000 people and a stadium that would seat 100,000 people, and this amphitheater, for the purpose for which it was constructed, and for which it is being used.

Those are grand plans. I knew a city planner in Chicago one time, named V. H. Burnham, and he had a motto which said, "Make no little plans. Great plans can always be amended to meet the situation. Little plans can never be expanded into great plans."

I hope that Washington City and the Government which is responsible for this great Capital, will bear that in mind. I am doing everything I can to make this the great city it ought to be.

I was very fond of Carter, and it is fitting that the first play given in this theater should be called, "The Faith of Our Fathers." We ought to think deeply about that phrase "faith of our fathers." We ought to ask ourselves what the faith of our fathers really was, and what it means to us today.

The faith of our fathers is expressed in the Declaration of Independence and in the Bill of Rights. It is set forth in perfectly simple terms: "We hold these truths to be self-evident, that all men are created equal, and that they are endowed by their Creator with certain unalienable Rights."

This faith is the basis of free government. This faith is the basis of the Declaration of Independence, and the Constitution of the United States, the greatest document of government that was ever written in the history of man.

Many times in our history this faith has appeared to weaken, and our Government has appeared to have turned toward backward reaction. After that has happened, however, men have gone back to the faith of our Declaration of Independence and our Bill of Rights, and they have found there the strength and the courage to make our country stronger and better.

There are now many other nations that share our faith in free government. Since 1776 this faith has swept around the world. It now includes the free nations of Europe, and South and Central America, the Near East and Africa, and in recent years it has created many new and independent free nations in Asia.

This faith is the only hope for peace and freedom in the world.

Faith and free government have always been opposed by dictatorships. Today it is being threatened by a new and terrible tyranny. Hitler and Mussolini never had anything to match the terrible secret police of the Kremlin. The situation in Russia is almost fantastic. Nobody there can go to bed without the fear that the secret police may come in the night and take them away, never to be seen again. The Soviet is extending this slave system to the countries they now control.

In Eastern Germany—and I have this on the authority of no less a person than the Bishop of Eastern Berlin, who paid me a visit not very long ago—in Eastern Germany, thousands of persons have been kidnapped by the secret police. They just disappear, and are never heard of again. They kidnap the children between the ages of 10 and 16, and carry them off to Moscow. And those children never come home.

This is the kind of danger we are facing. This is what we are up against. It is our business, and our duty, to keep this thing from spreading. If we are to preserve freedom in the world, we must act together with the other nations that share our faith. We must try to create world peace under law. We must have a worldwide organization of nations that will put a stop to war and settle disputes peacefully.

This has been the constant aim of our foreign policy. This is what we are fighting for in Korea. We are fighting in Korea to preserve the United Nations, and to give it strength and power to enforce its mandates. We are fighting in Korea to prevent a third world war. That is the greatest cause in the world.

Our men and boys are fighting in Korea, struggling and dying to save us from the horrors of a third world war. They are fighting to make a world organization that will prevent war in the future.

It is up to us to see that they do not fight and die in vain.

It is up to us to stop petty bickering, to support them by our words, by our deeds, and by our prayers.

If we can stop that petty political bickering, stop the misrepresentations, and the character assassinations in this country, I am sure that our faith will succeed, we will be living the faith of our fathers, and victory will be ours.

We must believe in the faith of our fathers. We must believe in freedom and justice and fairness. We must believe in human rights and civil rights for every man, be he yellow, red, black, or white. We must act in accordance with that belief, and if we do act in accordance with the faith of our fathers, there will be no question about the outcome, we will attain world concord and world peace.

NOTE: The President spoke at 9:40 p.m. at the Carter Barron Amphitheater in Rock Creek Park in Washington. In his opening words he referred to Secretary of the Interior Oscar L. Chapman, who presided at the ceremonies.

Mr. Barron was a motion picture executive and civic leader in Washington until the time of his death on November 16, 1950.

Eugene List, a pianist, had played for Stalin, Churchill, and the President at the Potsdam Conference in 1945.

Walter Pidgeon, motion picture entertainer, read a eulogy of Mr. Barron by James Russell Wiggins, magazine editor of the Washington Post.

---

117 Statement by the President on the Foreign Aid Rider in the Third Supplemental Appropriation Act. *June 2, 1951*

I HAVE today approved H.R. 3587, the Third Supplemental Appropriation Act for the fiscal year 1951. This act provides urgently needed funds for carrying on important activities of the Government.

Unfortunately, the act also contains a legislative "rider"—that is, a piece of legislation quite unrelated to the major purpose of the act, which is to appropriate funds. This rider—section 1302—makes broad and sweeping changes in our procedures for restricting trade between the free world and the Soviet Union and its satellites. It is thus a major piece of legislation affecting our foreign policy, but it was never considered by the House Foreign Affairs Committee or the Senate Foreign Relations Committee.

This rider is seriously defective. However, I have signed this act because the appropriations it carries are so urgently needed, and because section 1302 does authorize exceptions from its provisions in the interest of national security. Unless the power to make exceptions is broadly used, this rider will result in weakening, rather than strengthening, the security of the United States and the collective security of the free world. I strongly urge the Congress to replace this hasty rider with more workable legislation at the earliest possible moment.

Briefly, section 1302 provides, first, that no economic or financial assistance (other than military assistance) may be given to any country which exports to the Soviet Union and its satellites arms, armament, or military materiel. Second, such aid may not be granted if a country exports any article or commodity which "may be used in the manufacture of arms, armaments, or military materiel." And, third, aid must be withheld if a country exports to the Soviet bloc any article or commodity the shipment of which to the Soviet bloc from the United States is prohibited.

The section further provides that in order for any country to be eligible for economic assistance from the United States, it shall certify monthly that it has not shipped any of these items to the Soviet bloc since the 15th day after the enactment of the act. The National Security Council is authorized to grant exceptions to these provisions in the security interests of the United States. Such exceptions are to be reported to six committees of the Congress.

I am sure that the Congress intended, in enacting this section, to strengthen the security of the United States and the rest of the free world by preventing the Soviet bloc from acquiring goods, through trade, which will enlarge Soviet military strength in relation to that of the free world.

With that purpose, everyone agrees. The United States and other free nations have been pursuing this objective for a long time, and much greater progress has been made than has generally been realized.

Section 1302 is of little practical importance insofar as it applies to the shipment of arms, ammunition, implements of war, and atomic energy materials. Long before the Korean conflict, shipments of these items to the Soviet bloc were prohibited by the United States, by the Western European countries, and by most of the other free nations of the world. Prohibitions on the shipment of these items are effective and complete.

The difficulties with section 1302 arise out of its application to ordinary items of trade and commerce. As to these items it is not well designed to achieve its ostensible purpose. In fact, in several important respects it will make it more difficult to achieve that purpose.

First, the section fails to recognize that trade is a two-way street.

Today, the free nations get from the Soviet bloc substantial amounts of such commodities as coal, grain, timber, manganese, chrome, asbestos, and iron and steel products which are of major importance to the common defense of the free world. Principal exports to the Soviet bloc consist of such things as textiles and textile fibers, machinery and equipment of some kinds, various foods and raw materials, and a diversified list of miscellaneous commodities. It is obvious that many of these items "may be used in the manufacture of arms, armaments, or military materiel," in the words of section 1302. But that is not sufficient reason for prohibiting their export to the Soviet bloc, if the free world receives in return goods of greater value.

Some free nations, as a result of trade patterns of many years' standing, are more dependent on imports from the Soviet bloc than others. Those free nations most dependent upon the Soviet bloc for imports contributing substantially to their food supply and defense effort naturally have great difficulty in reducing exports to the Soviet bloc. They are in a much more difficult situation than are countries like the United States, which are not so dependent upon imports from the Soviet bloc.

The problem of trade between the Soviet bloc and the free world is thus a matter of evaluating, in terms of relative importance, what the free world gets from the bloc for what it must give in return. The oversimplified approach of section 1302 is clearly wrong.

Second, section 1302 attempts to achieve by coercion what must be achieved by cooperation. No one nation can successfully force its own system of controls upon every other nation. Our experience so far shows that effective controls can be accomplished by cooperation.

The United States strictly controls its own exports to the Soviet bloc. The shipment of many items is embargoed. All exports of any kind from the United States to any country in the Soviet bloc require licenses. Their type and quantity are carefully scrutinized to make sure that they will not be of strategic value to the Soviet bloc. In addition to the controls that apply generally to exports to countries in the Soviet bloc, shipment of all commodities to China is forbidden and United States ships are not allowed to call at Chinese ports.

The United States has also been a leader in urging other free nations to join in international control of exports to the Soviet bloc.

Of necessity, publicity concerning control methods and results has been restricted. Much progress has been made, however. The countries of Western Europe which are cooperating with us in the common defense program have taken action to prohibit or control exports of strategic goods to the Soviet bloc. These nations, together with Canada and the United States, substantially control most of the industrial products of the free world.

When aggression broke out in Korea, approximately 145 categories of articles had already been embargoed to the Soviet bloc from these Western European countries as well as from the United States and Canada. Many of these categories include dozens of individual articles. The quantities which could be shipped in numerous other categories were limited.

Through continuing cooperative efforts since that time, further restrictions have been worked out. At present, about 90 percent of the items which the United States regards as being of primary strategic significance are subject to virtual embargo by the Western European countries.

In addition to these steps, the United Nations on May 18, 1951, by a vote of 47 to 0, agreed to a complete embargo on the shipment of strategic materials to Communist China. The United States will continue to work in the United Nations for increasingly effective international action to deny materials of value to the Chinese aggressors.

We have come a long way in our efforts to achieve international controls over exports to the Soviet bloc, and these controls are becoming increasingly effective.

A third major defect with section 1302 is that if we cut off our aid to a friendly country, we might hurt ourselves more than we hurt the Soviet Union.

The indiscriminate approach of section

1302 for cutting off economic aid to other countries ignores the vital interest which the United States has in the contribution that aid makes to the security of the whole free world. Cutting off this aid could strike a death blow at the tremendous defense effort in which the free nations are now engaged.

The success of our defense effort depends upon the ability of the free world to maintain and expand its economic strength. Our programs for economic and financial assistance are directed to that end. In some countries, they are directed toward helping other nations build the industrial facilities required to produce weapons for defense. In certain underdeveloped countries they are directed to assuring the basic economic stability which is essential if those countries are to resist both internal and external threats to their independence. In other countries they are aimed at expanding the capacity of the free world to produce vitally needed strategic materials—for example, copper, steel, aluminum, and uranium. The security of the United States, as well as the other free nations, is deeply involved in the success of these efforts. The defense structure we are striving to create—both here at home and in Europe under General Eisenhower—will rot and topple unless it rests on a sound economic foundation.

In addition to these major defects, section 1302 also contains certain technical provisions which are unfortunate. For example, the provision for certification is complicated and difficult to apply and does not add to our ability to carry out the ostensible purpose of the section.

Because of the defects I have described, section 1302 will make it more difficult for this country to make further progress in its effort to bring about effective international controls over trade with the Soviet bloc.

The National Security Council has been guiding the work of the executive agencies in this effort. The Council has been carrying on a continuous scrutiny of the trade of every country in the free world with the Soviet bloc. Information on the quantities and types of commodities shipped to and received from the Soviet bloc by every free country has been examined. The trade controls exercised by these countries have been considered.

Against this background, the Council has decided the actions that the United States should take. In doing so, the Council has viewed the United States security in its broadest terms. It has taken into account the security value of imports received from the bloc, the contribution of each country to the collective security of the free world and the importance of United States aid in facilitating their defense efforts.

For the most part there are very few articles left of any real strategic importance that are moving to the Soviet bloc in any significant quantity. There are still a number of trade situations with which we are not yet satisfied. Control of trade at certain transshipment points is difficult of solution. As would be expected, not all friendly nations agree with us precisely as to which articles are of the most strategic value to the Soviet bloc. We are constantly endeavoring, however, to correct all of these weak spots—and progress is constantly being made.

We will continue these endeavors and will make every possible effort to administer section 1302 to accomplish the purposes which the Congress intended without impairing the security interests of the United States. In order to do this, I think it likely that the National Security Council will find it necessary to make exceptions on a broad scale until the Congress has an opportunity to give this matter further consideration.

I am sure that the Congress and the Executive have the same general objective in mind in prohibiting trade that is injurious to the security interests of the United States and in finding the most practical and effective method of doing so.

Because of the compelling objections to section 1302 in its present form, I urge the Congress to enact improved legislation to replace it at an early date. Such improved legislation should be based, I believe, on the following principal considerations:

1. The purpose of the legislation should not be blindly to cut off as much trade as possible, but to cut off trade only when such action will add to the security of the United States and the rest of the free world.

2. The legislation should take account of the offsetting value of what we receive from the Soviet bloc as compared with what we send to them; it should take account of the differing importance of different commodities and not treat all commodities alike; and it should take account of the value to us of

the increased strength for freedom which our economic aid brings about.

3. The legislation should provide for simple, effective and straightforward administration.

Legislation of this type would be helpful to the Nation's security. I strongly urge that the Congress enact such legislation to replace section 1302.

NOTE: As enacted, H.R. 3587 is Public Law 45, 82d Congress (65 Stat. 52).

On June 15, 1951, the President suspended operation of the amendment for a period of 90 days on the advice of the National Security Council.

Provisos in section 1302 of the act authorized the granting of exceptions following a determination and report by the National Security Council. On June 15 the White House made public the Council's determination and report on the granting of an interim general exception under section 1302, together with determinations and reports relating to the trade of Austria and Norway with members of the Soviet bloc. Subsequent National Security Council actions under section 1302 were also made public by the White House. They are listed in Appendix A under the following dates: August 3, 31, September 12, 14, 20, 24, October 1, 4, November 5.

118   The President's News Conference of June 7, 1951

THE PRESIDENT. Please be seated.

[1.] I have got a statement here I want to read to you, which I think will obviate some questions, and then we will go on with the questions.

[*Reading*] "Since the threat of Communist aggression made it necessary for us to step up our defense efforts, we have been working to control inflation. We have known that uncontrolled inflation would weaken our defense effort, and impose terrible hardship upon millions of families. By applying a combination of measures, we have had considerable success in bringing inflationary forces under control.

"The Congress enacted two tax bills, which have so far kept our defense spend-

ing on a pay-as-you-go basis.

"The Government has tightened up on inflationary consumer credit and installment buying, and is moving to restrain inflationary bank credit.

"The Government has put price and wage controls into effect.

"These Government actions—together with voluntary action by consumers and businessmen—have stopped the upward rush of prices. Since early February, when the general ceiling price regulation went into effect, wholesale prices have increased less than 1 percent. During the last month they have actually declined. Consumer prices have leveled off, and food prices have come down a little.

"The recent price wars between department stores in certain cities are a good indication that our anti-inflation program is working. Without this program the scare buying, speculation, and excessive accumulation of inventories would almost certainly still be going on.

"Most of the legislation which has made it possible to hold inflation in check will expire at the end of this month. It is extremely important that the Defense Production Act be extended and strengthened if we are to keep the heavy pressures of the next few months from becoming an unmanageable torrent of inflation.

"The present situation is only a breathing spell. Inflationary pressures will grow rapidly later this year, and still more next year. That is true because our economy, now operating at a peak, with full employment, is going to feel the shock of greatly increasing defense expenditures.

"The annual rate of expenditures for national security is steadily going up. Before the middle of next year, it is scheduled to be twice as high as it is now. This represents an increase of well over $30 billion at an annual rate. The budgetary surplus of recent months will be replaced by a growing deficit, due to this rapid increase of defense expenditures. This is why it is necessary for us to increase taxes and to continue and strengthen our other control measures.

"If controls are not extended, this $30 billion increase in defense spending would, it is estimated, stimulate at least another $30 billion of spending by businessmen and consumers. This would not result in more goods being produced. It would only result in more money being spent for the same goods, thus driving prices and wages up in a terrific spiral.

"The American people are wondering whether the programs which have started to protect them from inflation are going to be continued and strengthened to meet this growing danger. Some of the special interest groups have come out for killing all wage and price controls."

They make no bones about it.

[*Continuing reading*] "This critical issue is now before the Congress.

"We must meet this issue head on.

"The control of inflation is not a partisan issue; it is a national need. Everybody—every Member of Congress, every person in the executive branch, and every citizen—must work together to bring about the control of inflation." [1]

Mimeographed copies of those will be handed to you as you go out.

[2.] Q. Mr. President, since the conference the other morning with former Governor Turner and Mr. Flynn of Kansas City, [2] there are rumors afloat that there is talk of a compromise on the meat price—beef price rollback——

THE PRESIDENT. I know nothing about it.

Q. There is a 10 percent rollback that went into effect——

[1] On June 8, 1951, the White House released the text of a letter to the President, dated June 5, from the Council of Economic Advisers. The letter was in response to the President's request that the Council set forth an up-to-the-minute appraisal of the economic situation and give their opinion of the so-called "softening" of the economy.

The Council stated that inflationary pressures in the months and year ahead would be stronger than any since the initial Korean outbreak, and advised that an even stronger anti-inflationary program would be needed. The Council recommended tax increases, restraints upon inflationary credit, enlarged savings, reasonable restraints upon profits, wages, and other forms of income, and continuation and improvement of the production aids contained in the Defense Production Act. The letter concluded that the United States need not have inflation, but that inflation was likely "if we relax our efforts, or fail to strengthen the weak links in the chain of effective controls."

For the statement by the President upon signing the Defense Production Act Amendments, see Item 176.

[2] Former Governor Roy J. Turner of Oklahoma and Michael J. Flynn of Kansas City, Mo.

THE PRESIDENT. I can't answer—I can't answer your question, because the conference was held after I had introduced the conferees to Mr. Wilson and Mr. DiSalle and Mr. Johnston,[3] and I don't think any concrete conclusions have been reached. All these gentlemen wanted to do was put the facts before the control board—which they did. I don't know anything about any compromise, or anything else in connection with it. And I have no connection with it whatever.

Q. You couldn't say whether there is anything that might have——

THE PRESIDENT. No.

Q. It's in the hands of Mr.——

THE PRESIDENT. It's in the hands of Mr. Wilson and his control board.

Q. Well, Mr. President, may we phrase that another way? So far as you are concerned, the rollbacks will go into effect as scheduled?

THE PRESIDENT. No, there's nothing to phrase, because I don't know whether they will or not. Those people have it under consideration. When they get ready to announce it, why you can get the information from them. Mike DiSalle will tell you what he intends to do without wasting any words. No pressure has been put on him to do anything, by the President or anybody else. All these people want to do is to place the facts before the people in charge of the controls. They started out their statement by saying that they want to cooperate in every way, and they had no kick on what had been done.

[3.] Q. Mr. President, do you wish to comment on the visit of the President of Ecuador, Galo Plaza,[4] coming later this month?

---

[3] Charles E. Wilson, Director, Office of Defense Mobilization, and Chairman, Defense Mobilization Board, Michael V. DiSalle, Director of Price Stabilization, and Eric Johnston, Administrator, Economic Stabilization Agency.

[4] See Items 129, 130, 134, 136.

THE PRESIDENT. Well, he is paying the customary visit of a President of a South American Republic, and we are very glad to have him come.

[4.] Q. Mr. President, I wonder if I could clear up a little confusion in my mind here? One 10 percent rollback has gone into effect, sir. One again is scheduled for August 1st and one for October 1st.

THE PRESIDENT. That is correct.

Q. Is there any chance they will not go into effect now?

THE PRESIDENT. I can't answer the question. You will have to wait and get the answer from Mike DiSalle, after he has digested the information which has been furnished him. No interference has been made with any of the rollbacks so far as that is concerned.

Q. I wonder if I could ask you a further point? In Chicago yesterday, the regional head of the OPS said that the meat producers are holding back stock for market in an effort to force Congress to eliminate meat controls. Would you care to comment——

THE PRESIDENT. I don't think that is correct. The feed lots couldn't—they can't hold them back. When the cattle are ready to go, they have to leave the feed lots. I wish you could have heard the conversation that took place the other day on how to create a pound of beef. It is quite interesting.

Q. Mr. President, do you think that this talk of meat prices is exaggerated?

THE PRESIDENT. Very much so. I don't think there is any intention on the part of the feeders to do anything that will prevent people from getting meat.

[5.] Q. Mr. President, on the inflation, I have often been asked as to how it prevents inflation by the curtailment of house buying of individuals through increase in debentures, and limitation of mortgage credit, at the same time the encouragement of spending on behalf of Government housing?

THE PRESIDENT. I don't think you phrased that exactly right. The idea was to put a ceiling on the sale of mortgages for construction, because that inflated the credit of the country; and the Government housing that is contemplated is generally in defense areas, where housing is short and where nobody will build for commercial purposes.

Q. But isn't it true that——

THE PRESIDENT. For instance, in Alaska the men and the officers and everybody else who are living in tents and shacks, where it sometimes goes 60 below zero, nobody will go up there and build commercial housing. That is one of our principal defense points in the perimeter around the United States.

Q. What I had particularly in mind was the increase in the number of units in the bill passed by the House, which went to the Senate.[5]

THE PRESIDENT. The bill passed by the House was a ridiculous one—strictly ridiculous. The Senate put the 50,000 back that were asked for, so that we can save something. If you will analyze the thing, it, I think, authorized 135,000 units. I requested the Congress to authorize construction of 50,000 units which were badly needed for the purpose that I am telling you about, and the House cut it to 5,000. There is no use for all that—might as well wipe it out.

Q. I didn't know that was defense housing, I thought that was——

THE PRESIDENT. Principally defense housing. It is not all defense housing, but it is principally defense housing.

[6.] Q. Mr. President, I don't know whether you received this letter, but five Federal judges in Chicago have sent you a letter—they sent copies to their Senators— pointing out that three vacancies have existed out there—Federal judgeship vacancies—for almost a year, and they asked you to fill the

vacancies to help break up the logjam. Do you have any comment?

THE PRESIDENT. It was just mighty nice of them. I appreciate it. But I have had it under consideration for a year, and it is still under consideration. I don't like people giving letters to the press. I would like to have that letter from the five judges sent me individually, then I could answer it.

[7.] Q. Mr. President, I have got a couple of political questions.

THE PRESIDENT. Fire away. [*Laughter*] That's my field.

Q. Tony Vaccaro [6] had a piece back awhile ago about Bill Boyle [7] urging you not to take this trip. I wonder if——

THE PRESIDENT. Well now, Mr. Boyle and I discussed the matter after he came back from Denver. The matter is still under consideration. There are arguments on both sides of the question. I had no intention of going out until we find out whether our program is coming through the Congress or not, and I can't come to that conclusion until Congress adjourns.

Q. Sort of later in the summer?

THE PRESIDENT. You are as good a prophet as I am. I can't tell you when they will adjourn.

What was the other question?

[8.] Q. The other question I had, on the border of politics, is the recommendation of Senator Douglas that in the event you do not run next year, that both parties—"for the sake of national unity," I think was the phrase—would nominate General Eisenhower?

THE PRESIDENT. With Senator Douglas as Vice President? [*Laughter*]

[9.] Q. Mr. President, about a week ago the Government manpower committee that works with Mr. Wilson recommended that

---

[5] See Item 111.

[6] Ernest B. Vaccaro of the Associated Press.

[7] William M. Boyle, Jr., Chairman of the Democratic National Committee.

going on a 40-hour week must not be set aside during this defense mobilization. Do you share that view?

THE PRESIDENT. I think if you will read the Executive order I signed this morning you will find out what my views are.[8]

Q. Well, may we have that pleasure, sir?

THE PRESIDENT. You will find it, I think, in the Federal Register—I think tomorrow.

[10.] Q. Mr. President, is Mr. Harriman going to be appointed head of the National Security Resources Board?

THE PRESIDENT. I have it under consideration.

[11.] Mr. President, do you see any improvement in the Iranian oil situation?[9]

THE PRESIDENT. I can't comment on that. I have no comment on it at all. I hope there is improvement. I hope the thing will be settled to the satisfaction of both parties, and in an equitable manner for both parties. That is all I can hope. I have expressed my views, I think, in two messages on it.

[12.] Q. Mr. President, you recently characterized the 80th Congress as a "do-nothing" Congress. How do you characterize this one?

THE PRESIDENT. Well now, you can't characterize a Congress until it finishes its work. Another thing, the session isn't over yet, and it still has another session on the 3d of January. I will comment on it when they adjourn in July of next year.

[13.] Q. Mr. President, I wonder, now that Secretary of State Acheson has testified for some days before the Senate committee, if you can give any comment on his testi-

mony, whether you think he has done a good job?[10]

THE PRESIDENT. Why certainly, he has done an excellent job. He has told the truth, and the truth needs to be told these days, as it is very seldom done politically—particularly by the opposition.

Does that answer your question, Tony? [*Laughter*]

Q. A little faster than I had anticipated! [*More laughter*]

[14.] Q. Mr. President, there was a report in the afternoon papers that you might review, or an administrative officer of the Government might delay, an act of Congress which suggested that no economic help be given to nations which were trading with the Iron Curtain countries. Do you care to comment?

THE PRESIDENT. You are talking about the Kem amendment, I think?[11]

Q. Yes sir.

THE PRESIDENT. I think I commented on that in a paper which has been released to the press. Everything that needs to be said on that was said in that comment I made.

[15.] Q. Mr. President, I have another question, sir. You mentioned the price war in the prepared statement. Do you consider that unfavorable, or favorable?

THE PRESIDENT. I think it is very favorable. I think all these people loaded up with inventories in the scare buying, and they have

---

[8] Executive Order 10251 "Suspension of the Eight-Hour Law as to Laborers and Mechanics Employed by the Department of Defense on Public Work Essential to the National Defense" (3 CFR, 1949–1953 Comp., p. 757).

[9] U.K.-Iranian dispute over the nationalization of the oil industry in Iran. See Items 140 [4, 19], 150, 155, 200 [2].

[10] From June 1–9, 1951, Secretary of State Dean Acheson testified at Senate committee hearings on the dismissal of General MacArthur from his command in the Far East. His testimony is printed in "Hearings Before the Committee on Armed Services and the Committee on Foreign Relations, United States Senate, on the Military Situation in the Far East, Part 3" (Government Printing Office, 1951, Parts 1–5, 3691 pp.).

[11] Foreign aid amendment to the Third Supplemental Appropriation Act, introduced in the Senate by Senator James P. Kem of Missouri, among others. See also Item 117.

come to see that these inventories were fool- ishly acquired, and now they are trying to get rid of them. That is all it amounts to. It is just a merchandise program—move- ment of merchandise program, let's put it.

[16.] Q. Mr. President, you have done this several times, but just to bring it up to date, do you have any intention of Mr. Acheson leaving the Cabinet at this time?

THE PRESIDENT. Yes, serious objection. He is *not* going to leave. [*Laughter*]

Q. What was that question, Mr. Presi- dent?

THE PRESIDENT. You asked your question backwards, and I answered it backwards. [*More laughter*]

What was your question back there?

Q. Couldn't hear the last question, sir.

THE PRESIDENT. Ask your question again, so that they can hear.

Q. I just wanted to bring it up to date— you have no intention of letting Mr. Ache- son leave?

THE PRESIDENT. That is not the way you asked it, but I would say none whatever.

Q. That is what I meant to ask.

Q. Anything else, Mr. President?

THE PRESIDENT. Not a thing.

Q. Hold it!

[17.] Joseph H. Short, Secretary to the President [*addressing the President*]: Do you want to talk to them any more about that Executive order—overtime for mechanics and labor employed by the Defense Depart- ment?

THE PRESIDENT. Let the order speak for it- self—let the order speak for itself.

He just wanted me to elaborate on the Executive order, but you read it. It will tell you all about it.

Q. Thank you, Mr. President.

THE PRESIDENT. It's all right.

NOTE: President Truman's two hundred and sixty- sixth news conference was held in the Indian Treaty Room (Room 474) in the Executive Office Building at 4 p.m. on Thursday, June 7, 1951.

119　Letter to the Director, Bureau of the Budget, on the Utilization of Manpower in the Federal Government. *June 9, 1951*

[Released June 9, 1951. Dated June 8, 1951]

My dear Mr. Lawton:

The present emergency has caused great demands on the manpower resources of our country, with shortages of manpower in cer- tain special areas already being felt. It is extremely important that all possible steps be taken to eliminate these shortages and to assure the availability of manpower for all essential mobilization activities. Adequate solution to our manpower problems will re- quire the exercise of energy, imagination and ingenuity on the part of every employer and employee.

The Federal Government, as the largest single employer in the country, should set the example in accomplishing this objective.

Therefore, I expect the head of each execu- tive department and agency to take all neces- sary actions to conserve manpower and gen- erally to bring about maximum effectiveness and economy in the utilization of personnel. This manpower conservation program should be given top priority throughout the executive branch.

In order to assist the departments and agencies in achieving the results I desire, I want you, together with the Chairman of the Civil Service Commission, to issue instruc- tions on steps which can be taken to conserve manpower, and to advise and consult with the departments and agencies on specific problems which they may have in carrying out this program. I am also asking that the Bureau of the Budget and the Civil Service Commission request reports from all departments and agencies and conduct regular inspections and surveys so that reports can be made to me on progress in conserving manpower, including recommendations for further actions which may be necessary.

This program to achieve conservation and utilization of manpower in the Federal Government is endorsed by the Manpower Policy Committee of the Office of Defense Mobilization, and is in line with its over-all program for conserving manpower throughout the country.

I am sending a similar letter to the Chairman of the Civil Service Commission.

Sincerely yours,

HARRY S. TRUMAN

[Honorable Frederick J. Lawton, Director of the Bureau of the Budget, Washington 25, D.C.]

120 Letter to Senator Hayden on the Effect of Certain House Amendments on Hydroelectric Power Policy. *June 11, 1951*

Dear Carl:

I am writing to express my deep concern over certain drastic limitations on the use of our Nation's power resources which appear in H.R. 3790, the Interior Department appropriation bill for the fiscal year beginning July 1, 1951, in the form in which that bill passed the House of Representatives and is now before your subcommittee.

These limitations are contained in amendments to the bill added on the House floor. Two kinds of amendments were made. First, in a number of cases, the House cut out funds to build badly needed transmission lines which could carry the power produced at Government dams to the areas where it is to be used. Second, a legislative "rider"—the so-called Keating Amendment—was tacked on to the bill. This rider would go much beyond these appropriation cuts and result in an entirely new policy for disposing of the power produced by Federal projects.

Taken together, these amendments would seriously restrict the operation of Federal hydroelectric power projects for the national defense and in the public interest. They would, moreover, reverse basic power policies which have been approved many times by the Congress in order to promote balanced economic growth throughout the country.

For many years, we have been developing hydroelectric power as an integral part of the Government's task of harnessing our rivers for navigation, flood control, reclamation, and other beneficial public uses. In many areas, such low-cost power, added to other power supplies, has brought rapid economic growth.

Today, the need for more power is immediate and pressing. The expansion of our power resources has become one of the most essential basic tasks in our mobilization effort. Government and industry alike recognize that more power is vitally needed to strengthen the national defense. We must move as fast as we can, within current limitations on materials, to increase all available supplies of power, public and private, so that we can meet the growing demands of defense industry and agriculture in all parts of the country. Federal public works which will produce sizable amounts of power have been given the highest priority among the limited numbers of public works now being built by the Government.

It is absolutely imperative that we move forward with these Federal power projects, as well as with the expansion of private facilities now planned or underway. But it is not enough to produce the power. When taxpayers' funds are invested to produce power, the benefits of that power ought to be made widely available to people who need it, at the lowest possible rates consistent with sound business principles.

To achieve this end, the Congress has provided by law that public bodies (such as municipalities and public utility districts) and cooperatives (such as rural electrification cooperatives) should receive power from Federal projects as preference customers—since these organizations are obviously interested in low rates, rather than in high profits. To the same end, the Congress has authorized the Federal power agencies to build transmission lines where necessary to carry power to "load centers"—convenient places for marketing power at wholesale to preference and other customers.

Without the authority to build transmission lines, the Government would be unable to carry out the mandate of Congress to see that Federally-produced power is sold at low rates. Private power companies have always been willing to buy Federal power at the "bus-bar"—that is, at the dam site—and resell it at rates yielding them high profits. To keep power rates down, the Government has built many transmission lines to load centers and, in most instances, has served preference customers directly over its own transmission facilities. In addition, where private companies have been willing to carry Federal power from load centers to preference and other customers for a satisfactorily low charge, the Government has made so-called "wheeling" agreements for this transmission service.

Both of these methods can and do work

successfully. But if they are to work successfully, the Government must have the authority and funds to plan and construct needed transmission lines. Without this, the Government—or, more accurately, the consumers of power from Federal projects—would be at the mercy of the private power companies. That is exactly what would be achieved by the amendments made to H.R. 3790 on the House floor.

Funds were included in the January Budget for transmission lines only in cases where they are urgently needed to carry out the mandate of Congress in marketing power from Federal projects. These funds were substantially approved by the House Appropriations Committee. And yet they were slashed—on the House floor—and if these slashes stand, consumers in the southeastern states, in the southwestern states, in California, in the Missouri Basin, in the Pacific Northwest, will have to pay higher prices—or not get the power they need.

Furthermore, the Keating amendment, barring Federal transmission lines in "areas" where wheeling agreements are in effect, would throw away the authority needed to ensure widespread benefits from Federal power at low cost.

Wheeling agreements, in general, do not guarantee the delivery of power to preference customers—they simply make the surplus carrying capacity of the private power company's lines available to the Government. At any time the private company makes use of its lines for other purposes, preference customers may be dropped from service. Obviously, therefore, the Government needs continuing authority to build transmission lines in case the wheeling agreement does not bring the results it was intended to achieve.

Furthermore, most of the present wheeling agreements do not take care of the additional power that will be produced from dams now being constructed. When that power is ready for marketing, if the Government does not have the authority to build transmission lines, there is no assurance whatever that it will be possible to reach satisfactory wheeling agreements for the new power. Indeed, past experience indicates the contrary. A number of the present wheeling agreements were successfully negotiated only after the Congress had actually appropriated funds for the construction of specific transmission lines in the areas affected.

For these reasons, it is clear that the amendments made on the House floor would disregard past experience and the will of Congress repeatedly expressed after careful deliberation. These amendments would be a long step in the direction of making the taxpayers' investment in power facilities serve the profits of the private power companies.

In some cases, these cuts, in addition to playing into the hands of the private utilities, will result in the waste of Government funds already spent. For example, the House eliminated funds to complete work on the Western Missouri Project—a group of important transmission facilities being built by the Southwestern Power Administration. This project is already sixty percent completed, at a cost so far of nearly $3 million. This money will be entirely wasted—and the real need for these facilities ignored—if construction is now stopped for lack of further funds.

This bill, as it passed the House, makes such a sweeping attack on Government transmission lines that it would actually limit the supply of critically-needed power. The Government builds transmission lines in many cases to interconnect its power projects, because that is the way to operate most efficiently and get the most power produced for the money invested. And yet funds needed for such purposes were left out of the House bill.

For example, funds were left out of the bill for the badly needed interconnection between the Government's power projects in the Pacific Northwest and in California. That interconnection will mean more power in the Northwest and more power in California, because it will make it possible to send power which is not needed in one area to the other at times when it is needed there. Such an interconnection is simply a matter of common sense—it is a good, fast way to increase the Nation's power supply.

I earnestly hope that the unfortunate amendments incorporated in H.R. 3790 will not be allowed to stand and that the funds requested by the Interior Department at the hearings of your subcommittee will be restored to the bill. I am sure that many of those who voted for the amendments in the House were misled as to their effects. I am confident that once the facts are known the Congress will wish to provide, in this time of emergency, for the full use of our hydroelectric power projects for the national defense and in the public interest.

Very sincerely yours,

HARRY S. TRUMAN

[Honorable Carl Hayden, The United States Senate, Washington, D.C.]

NOTE: On August 31, 1951, the President approved H.R. 3790, the Interior Department Appropriation Act, 1952 (65 Stat. 248).

121   Remarks at the Highway Safety Conference.
       June 13, 1951

Mr. Chairman, ladies and gentlemen:

I am most happy to welcome you to this conference. Most of you have set aside your regular duties to work with us to make our highway system safe. That is the spirit of public service that our country needs—and needs badly at this time.

I am glad to know that we have with us a number of distinguished guests who are here as official representatives of other countries. We welcome them most heartily. We hope that they will benefit from this meeting, and we know that we will benefit by having them here with us.

As we meet here today, the United States and the other free nations of the world face a great danger. That fact makes the work of this conference more important than ever.

In these troubled times we are working as hard as we can to make our country stronger. Our purpose is to prevent another world war by building our defenses and by strengthening the free peoples who are allied with us.

This need for a strong America makes your work doubly urgent. Highway accidents strike directly at our national strength. A highway accident does just as much damage to the defense effort, as a deliberate act of sabotage by a hostile agent.

The defense effort depends upon the efficient movement of goods and people over public highways and roadways. Highway transportation, like railway transportation, is indispensable to production on our farms and our factories, and to every phase of the Nation's work. Traffic accidents slow down production and weaken our whole economy. Traffic accidents are a sheer economic waste.

Every year highway accidents cost us nearly $3 billion—$3 billion it costs us in highway accidents! This is the cost of wrecked vehicles, hospital and medical expenses, and time lost from work. This is a terrible price to pay for carelessness and inefficiency.

We are supposed to be the most efficient nation on earth, and also we are supposed to be the most careless. But here we have a combination—of carelessness and inefficiency—as to what causes most highway accidents.

It has been 5 years since I called the first highway safety conference here in Washington. Much has been accomplished since that time. That conference drafted a comprehensive action program. Since then, organizations have been set up in many communities and many States to put that program into effect. However, we still have a long way to go.

When we met in 1946, deaths from traffic accidents were averaging about 11 per 100 million miles of travel. That figure has been cut down to about 7 at the present time; a reduction of more than a third. That is very gratifying, but it is not enough.

Another encouraging sign is the report of the Federal agencies that operate fleets of motor vehicles. In 1949 they had a traffic fatality rate of 7 per 100 million vehicle miles of travel. Last year this had been brought down to 3.5 per 100 million miles. That is a reduction of more than a half.

Many individual States and communities are making good safety records, too, and I congratulate them. Last year the accident rate in some States was less than half as high as it was in others. Among cities the same wide range is found. What we need to do now is to find a way to bring the accident rate in every State and city down to the level of the best record—and even lower. That is possible! Let us do it!

That is a very urgent task. Because the sad fact is that, in spite of the progress we have made in reducing the rate of accidents, the total number of accidents is going up. This is because there has been a tremendous increase in highway travel.

At the time of that 1946 conference there were 30 million vehicles on the road. Today the number is 50 million, an increase of 66 percent. Mileage of travel has skyrocketed in the same proportion.

Our safety efforts, helpful as they have been, have not kept pace with this increase in travel. Last year 35,000 persons were killed, and more than a million were injured in traffic accidents. Tens of thousands of those who were hurt were disabled for life.

We have been attempting to stop an act of aggression in Korea for the last year. The total casualties for the whole operation have been less than 80,000, and that includes everything: sickness, and death in jeeps by accidents, killed on the front, captured on the front, and wounded. It has been less than 80,000, and that means every kind of death and injury that could take place in that operation. That is on the mind and tongue of every citizen. But right here at home we kill and permanently injure a million and 35,000 people, and there is no outcry by the sabotage press, no misstatement by the columnists or the congressional demagogues. And I wonder why? I wonder why? Now, that is an opportunity for every one of those fellows to pick on the administration, and they ought to make use of it.

These 35,000 deaths in 1950 represented an 11 percent increase over 1949. Unless the upward trend is reversed—and soon reversed—this year will set another tragic record.

We must prevent this from happening. We must not have a traffic death record. This is a challenge to every State, and to every community, and to the Federal Government.

It is a challenge to us, first, to improve our highway system.

For nearly 20 years, highway improvement programs have lagged far behind our needs. This has been because of the depression and war, and also because of the tremendous increase in the number of vehicles. Much of our main road mileage is worn out and obsolete, and the replacement program has not kept pace with the increased use.

Since World War II the program has been expanded, but now there are new difficulties arising, particularly in the matter of construction materials.

Some highway projects may have to be deferred. But good roads are essential, and we must not make the mistake of thinking that highways are expendable in an emergency period.

In reducing the accident rate, safe roads by themselves are not enough, we must have safe drivers. And that is the most important thing in the whole safety drive campaign, to have safe drivers.

One of the best things we can do to produce safe drivers is the training of our high school boys and girls. One third of the eligible boys and girls now receive some kind of instruction in safe driving. About half of these are getting training behind the wheel. These youngsters with driver training have only half as many accidents as those who have not had such training. These excellent records promise a great deal for the future. Every boy and girl in high school deserves the opportunity to get that training.

To do our task, we must have the continuous and intelligent support of the American people.

Each citizen has a personal responsibility to support the highway safety program, and what is more important, to be a good driver himself.

This will take self-discipline, but it can be done. It's a simple matter of good citizenship.

Perhaps we can understand the scope of our problem better if we remember that sometime in this year 1951, the number of traffic deaths since 1900 will pass the million mark. One million men, women, and children have been killed on our streets and highways since the turn of the century— since the turn of the century.

Nearly as many Americans have been killed in automobile accidents as have been killed in all the wars of our history, beginning 175 years ago with the War for Independence.

Those who have died in the service of their country rest in honored glory. They gave their lives for the purposes to which this Nation is dedicated. But there is no noble purpose in death by traffic accidents. The slaughter going on every day on our roads and streets is unnecessary and inexcusable.

I hope that during this Conference you will renew your determination to reduce this slaughter, and that you will go home and get others to join you in vigorous support of the highway safety program.

If you do, and if your fellow Americans everywhere join you, thousands upon thousands of lives will be spared in future years. You will perform a great service for your country, and much suffering and sorrow will be avoided.

Now, I want to say something in particular about the permanent chairman of this conference. Unfortunately, General Fleming cannot be with us today, but Mrs. Fleming is here in his place.

A little more than 5 years ago, on May 7, 1946, General Philip Fleming was awarded the Army Distinguished Service Medal for "outstanding service to the Government." He had successfully directed a tremendous construction program during the war. This included a wide variety of buildings and facilities for the Army and Navy, in the United States, Puerto Rico, Virgin Islands, Alaska, and Central America. I know what I'm talking about with respect to this medal, for I gave it to the general myself.

Since that date General Fleming has rendered equally distinguished service in several high Government posts. And as general chairman of the President's Highway Safety Conference during its entire existence, he has worked unsparingly to build and strengthen the highway safety movement.

These nationwide conferences, like the one which we are having now, and the ones which have preceded it, bear the lasting imprint of General Fleming's personality—his capacity for wise and friendly leadership in a great humanitarian cause.

It is eminently fitting that we should recognize this unique service here today. For that purpose, I have something here to present to the general, a gift from the Highway Safety Conference, and I am going to ask Mrs. Fleming to receive it for him.

Let me read the inscription: "Philip Bracken Fleming. In appreciation of his immeasurable service, and unfailing guidance in the cause of highway safety"—the President's Highway Safety Conference presents this. And I present it for the conference in the name of the President of the United States.

It gives me great pleasure, Mrs. Fleming, to make the award for the conference, and I hope the general will soon be fully recovered and working in the public service, as he has always worked ever since I have known him.

Thank you very much.

NOTE: The President spoke at 11 a.m. at Constitution Hall in Washington. The President's Highway Safety Conference was held during the period June 13–15, 1951.

122   Remarks to the Delegates to the 21st National 4-H Club Camp.   *June 14, 1951*

Mr. Secretary, Mrs. Warren, members of this great organization, the 4-H Clubs of America:

I am more than happy to welcome you again to the White House. I was very much afraid that we were going to be rained out, but the weather cleared up just especially for you. Some of my people around the house thought it wouldn't be possible to use the Rose Garden, for the simple reason that they were afraid it would be too wet, but I believe it has dried off so it's all right, and the weather is with us.

I want to congratulate you on what you have been doing and congratulate you on improving the life and ways of the farm. When I was on the farm—and I hope to go back to the farm someday; some people are in a hurry for me to go back, but I'm in no hurry—but when I do go back, I want to find things still further improved. And I think you are going to contribute to that improvement.

As I started to say, when I was running the farm, where my brother is now and my two nephews, we had to have from 5 to 15 people all the time to help operate that farm.

Now, these two young men—my nephews—operate it by themselves. I tell them they have never done a day's work in their lives, for they ride for everything. They go out and get a wagonload of corn in an hour and a half, that used to take me 2 days. They can go out and plant a field in a third of the time that it took me to plant it.

That is the mechanized farm age that has reduced the drudgery, and reduced the number of men that are necessary to produce the food that keeps this country and the world going.

We must continue to improve the production of food, for food is the fundamental basis of a high standard of living.

If we have plenty to eat and plenty to wear—and those things come from the farm—you can usually be in a pretty happy frame of mind. Whereas if you are hungry, or you don't have the clothing necessary to make a proper appearance, you are in a bad way.

I hope you will continue just what you are doing now, to contribute to that improvement of the welfare of the people who produce the food and clothing for the United States and a large part of the world.

It is certainly a pleasure to have had you here.

[*At this point the President was presented a gold key. He then resumed speaking.*]

I certainly appreciate the presentation of this key. I had an honorary Phi Beta Kappa key presented to me by the University of Missouri, and I don't think a bit more of that than I do of this; and I thank you for it.

NOTE: The President spoke at 12:05 p.m. in the Rose Garden at the White House. In his opening words he referred to Charles F. Brannan, Secretary of Agriculture, and Mrs. Gertrude L. Warren who was in charge of matters relating to 4-H Club work at the Department of Agriculture.

The gold key was presented to the President by Marjorie Nold of Savannah, Mo., and Richard Golob of Sunnyside, Wash.

123 Radio and Television Report to the American People on the Need for Extending Inflation Controls. *June* 14, 1951

[Broadcast from the White House at 10:30 p.m.]

My fellow Americans:

I am going to talk to you tonight about a real, practical, down-to-earth problem that affects the daily life of every American citizen. It affects your savings, your pocketbook, and your standard of living.

This is the problem of inflation and high prices. We have to keep prices down. This is hard to do. It is going to get a lot tougher as time goes on. The problem is going to be with us for 2 more years at least. It is important for us to face these facts, and do what has to be done to keep inflation under control.

Right at this time the Congress is considering a bill to extend and improve the laws under which we are controlling prices, wages, credit, and rents. This is a bill to extend and amend the Defense Production Act.

Some of you may not realize that our present powers to control high prices are due to expire in about 2 weeks—on the 30th of this month. That leaves just 16 days—14 working days—for the Congress to pass a new law. I repeat—if the Congress does not pass a new law, price controls will expire on June 30th.

Last April I sent to the Congress recommendations for improving and continuing our laws for controlling inflation. For the last 6 weeks committees of the Senate and the House of Representatives have been busy holding hearings on that problem. Now, both committees are hard at work deciding what kind of a bill to recommend. And very soon both the House and the Senate will start to debate and then vote on the measure.

This will be one of the most crucial debates that the Congress has had in a long time. The way the issue is decided will have a direct, personal effect on every American—and it will affect the whole future of our defense effort and our chance to have peace in the world.

There are millions of families in this country living on low or fixed incomes. A lot of people live on salaries or pensions. And above all we must remember the families of the men in our Armed Forces. These people simply cannot keep up with the cost of living if we let inflation controls go out the window. They know this and they are worried about what is going to happen. I am getting hundreds of letters from them.

Here is one from Mrs. David Green, of Brooklyn, N.Y. Mrs. Green writes:

"Dear President Truman:

"I am a homemaker. My husband earns a fixed salary. During the past year my standard of living has declined, as prices went up.

"I know that I am expressing the sentiments of millions of homemakers when I write you to continue the struggle against inflation.

". . . Please continue this struggle for a high American standard of living."

Here is another letter, from Mr. J. A. Pels, of Cincinnati, Ohio. Mr. Pels writes:

"Dear Sir:

"I am writing this in reference to controls . . . I am in my 79th year. I am retired. I have a fixed income. . . .

"When controls were taken off the last time, the Wise Men"—by that I think he means the "know-it-alls"—"stated that everything would be cheaper. On the contrary, the prices jumped up so that it hurt. A $2.00 shirt cost $5.00. . . .

"God help the many thousands who are in

the same position I am in. . . .

"Please, Mr. President, I beg of you to keep the controls, all of them, in force for the sake of us who need this protection."

Now I want Mr. Pels and Mrs. Green and all the others who have written me to know that I am doing everything I can to keep controls in force.

The other day I called in a group of Senators and Congressmen—leaders of both parties in the committees that are working on the defense production bill. I told them how important it is for the country that we get a good bill passed. I think they all agreed. But some of them told me they were under a lot of pressure from the special interests to do away with controls, and that the consumers were not making themselves heard.

Well, I told them that I represented the consumers and that I was speaking for them. And I am speaking for you and working as hard as I can to convince the Members of Congress that we must have a strong anti-inflation law. But I can't do the whole job by myself.

This is something the whole country should support.

It's up to all of us.

It's up to us, not as Democrats or Republicans but as Americans concerned about our welfare and our country's welfare. This fight we have to make is not a partisan fight. Inflation is not partisan. It strikes all the people in all parties. This is a fight for everyone to join—a fight for the very life of this Nation.

We all know what inflation can do to people. It can take their savings away from them. It can take the food right out of their mouths. It can cause widespread suffering and despair to us and to our families.

In addition to what inflation can do to us in our everyday lives, it can also wreck our program of national defense.

The other day General Marshall told the Congress that the price increases have added about $7 billion to the cost of the military equipment we have bought since the Korean outbreak. This means inflation has cost us $7 billion for arms alone in 1 year—that is, now we pay $7 billion more than we would have paid last June—and we still have most of our military equipment to buy.

Think what this means in terms of taxes we must pay. Think what this will mean in the future if we let inflation run wild after June 30th.

We've got to have a good, strong inflation-control law on the books if we are going to get through this emergency successfully.

Some people have the idea that if the fighting stopped in Korea we could cut down our defense effort enough to do away with the danger of inflation. That is not true.

We would need controls even if the fighting in Korea stopped tomorrow. The threat of Communist aggression is worldwide, and must be met with worldwide defenses. We are carrying on a tremendous mobilization program which is absolutely necessary to prevent Soviet rulers from starting a third world war.

Government spending for defense will increase very fast in the next few months. And the more money the Government spends on defense the greater the danger of rising prices. Controls are absolutely necessary, for at least the next 2 years, no matter what happens in Korea.

Everybody should understand that the price rises we have had so far are only curtain raisers to what will come along if the Congress fails to pass a strong price control law.

Up until now there have been no real shortages of civilian goods to push prices up. Price increases so far have been due mostly to the wave of buying by businessmen and consumers who were afraid of shortages and wanted to get in under the wire.

This buying wave pushed prices up so rapidly that in January the Government had to put on a general freeze of prices and wages. This was a rough, emergency step, but it did check the price rise. As price controls took hold, people gained confidence and the buying wave subsided.

Since February we have been building up our price and wage control organization and improving our emergency controls. Most prices have held steady. A few have gone up slightly, but many have gone down. Many retailers, caught with overloaded shelves, have been starting bargain sales to get rid of the merchandise they acquired in the buying rush last winter.

Prices look steadier now than at any time since last September. This makes some people think the worst is over. But that just isn't so.

The full force of inflationary pressure is still to come.

Military production is just now getting underway on a big scale. The output of civilian goods is just now beginning to be seriously cut back.

In the next few months, as shortages of civilian goods develop, the danger of inflation will become more and more serious. It will take the hardest, toughest kind of controls to keep prices from going through the roof. Unless we have a good strong law, we won't have a chance.

Some people are telling the Congress now that we can get along without price, or wage, or rent controls. They call them "direct" controls and say they are bad and should be wiped out.

That's the way the National Association of Manufacturers is talking these days. That's what its representatives told congressional committees working on the defense production bill. These lobbyists say that we can curb inflation without price control

simply by tighter credit controls and higher taxes. But, strange to say, when it comes to taxes, these same people are going around urging another committee of Congress to go easy on raising taxes on corporate profits.

These people who say we should throw out price controls and rent controls are all wrong. They are just as wrong now as they were back in 1946. They told us then that if we would just put an end to price controls, everything would be rosy and prices would stay right in line. Do you remember that? The National Association of Manufacturers put full-page advertisements in the papers all over the country, saying if we would just take off price controls there would be plenty of things to buy at reasonable prices. The National Association of Manufacturers had its way in 1946. The Congress failed to pass a good price control law. And then we had the biggest wave of price increases in modern history.

Do you think the National Association of Manufacturers has learned anything from that? They haven't learned a thing—not a thing! Here they are again giving us the same old song and dance: take off price controls and everything will be just dandy.

These people were wrong before and they are wrong now.

In fact, the danger of price increases today is much worse than it was in 1946, and the situation is much different. Whatever difference of opinion there may have been about the need for price controls then, there is no possible doubt that price controls are needed now. Now we are in a great mobilization effort. Requiring 20 percent of our national production is defense. Now our men are fighting in Korea. This is no time to yield to selfish interests who scorn equality of sacrifice.

Fortunately, most businessmen—especially small businessmen—do not agree with the National Association of Manufacturers.

Most of them know that their future prosperity and the prosperity of the country depend upon good, strong price controls at this time.

Small businessmen, like working people and consumers, know what this country is up against. They know we must have controls that bite down hard if we are to succeed.

Your Government is getting ready to meet the inflationary wave that is coming this fall.

The Office of Price Stabilization has put controls on the prices of most commodities. It is now working out dollar and cents ceilings to be posted in retail stores. Posters are going up at every meat counter showing the legal price for beef. The OPS will soon have a lot more food prices posted in grocery stores; and more and more goods of other kinds are going to be tagged with the legal price.

All along the line we are working to tighten up our control system and to get it in shape to meet the big test that is coming. That's what Charlie Wilson and Eric Johnston and Mike DiSalle and others are doing. And I am keeping after them to keep on improving their operations.

We are getting results now—good results. You can buy work shoes in Philadelphia now for the same or less than you had to pay last January, when the price freeze was ordered. You can buy cotton house dresses in Los Angeles for less than they cost 5 months ago. You can buy those little jars of baby food in Boston or Chicago for less than they cost last winter.

This is not perfect—a lot of these prices were high to start with—but it is real progress.

All of this will be wasted if we don't get the right kind of control law from Congress. If we get no law, or if we get the wrong kind of law, we will not be able to keep the prices from running wild.

I suppose a lot of people think it's a sure

thing that Congress will agree to the right kind of law. But we just can't take that for granted. After the representatives of the administration testified in favor of a good, strong law, the congressional committees heard some 124 witnesses, representing all sorts of private organizations. And do you know how many of them came out for the bill? Twenty—just twenty. All the rest were against the whole anti-inflation program, or they opposed very important parts of it, or they were trying to get special exemptions for themselves.

At a time like this, when men are fighting and dying for our country, and for the peace of the world, it is wrong for any of us to place private interests above the national interest.

Price controls put some burdens on all of us. We may have to forgo profits or wage increases or keep some extra records that we wouldn't ordinarily keep. But the burdens are small compared to the benefits for all of us. A strong control law will be good for the workers, good for businessmen, good for farmers, and good for consumers.

In that connection I should like to say a word to the farmers and ranchers who grow beef cattle. You know I am a friend of agriculture. I have worked long and hard to hold farm prices up when the farmer was getting hurt. I was for fair prices for the farmer then, and I am for fair prices for the farmer now.

Recently, as you know, Mike DiSalle put out an order that will bring down beef prices to the consumer. That order was put out with my approval. That order will bring beef cattle prices down from about 150 percent of parity to about 125 percent of parity. I think that's fair enough in a time of national emergency. I think most farmers and ranchers would agree that is a fair price.

But certain lobbyists claiming to represent cattle growers have put on a terrific hullabaloo down here in Washington. These lobbyists are saying that the cattle growers and the cattle feeders of this country won't be satisfied with a fair profit. And these lobbyists say if they can't get what they want the cattle growers and feeders will go on strike against the Government and the people of this country. These lobbyists are actually threatening us—all of us—that if they don't get big profits at the consumer's expense we won't get any meat. They say the cattle will be held off the market and the American people will be starved out until the Government gives in. The Government is not going to give in.

Now, I don't believe for a minute that most of the cattle growers or cattle feeders in this country feel that way or would conspire to do that sort of thing against the public interest.

I don't believe these lobbyists here in Washington really speak for the cattle producers of the country. In fact, I am very sure that they don't. I do not believe our cattlemen would keep meat away from our soldiers and defense workers. I don't believe they would cut off the supply of leather to make shoes for our Armed Forces in the field.

I think they are just as patriotic as the rest of us and want to do what's fair and right.

Many of them have told me that they realize that beef prices have been too high. They are willing to accept some reduction if they can be sure that the burden will be fairly distributed and the benefits will be passed on to the consumer. That is what's bothering most of the cattle feeders.

If the Congress makes it clear that price controls are going to stay in effect, then the growers and feeders will ship their beef cattle to market in the normal way. Once they are convinced that the controls are going to stay on, and that the controls are fair, I am sure the cattlemen will go along. I just do not believe—no matter what some people

who claim to speak for the cattlemen are saying—I just do not believe that the cattle growers and feeders of this country are going to strike against their country and their fellow citizens.

The situation we face is far too serious for that.

This is a time of national danger. The welfare of all of us is at stake. If inflation gets away from us, and wrecks our savings and ruins our economy, it would be the easiest victory the Kremlin could ask for. Communist Russia would win the whole world to totalitarianism without firing a shot.

That is what the Communists have been hoping for. They have been hoping for years for the collapse of the American economy.

For years we have been proving the Communists to be wrong. We have prevented depressions. We have proved over and over again—to the Kremlin's confusion and dismay—that instead of collapsing, our economy is growing stronger and stronger.

We must keep right on proving that.

And the way to do it is to have an anti-inflation program, including price controls, wage controls, rent controls, credit controls—controls that really hold down prices and the cost of living. When some of us have to take a cut in profits, or pass up a wage increase we might otherwise get, let us remember that we are making a contribution to the peace of the world. The men who are fighting in Korea would tell us it's a very small contribution after all. And they are right. They are not here to speak for themselves, but we know what we ought to do to back them up.

The people of this country, acting together, are stronger than any special interest. If we work together as a team, if everyone does his part, we can beat inflation, we can secure the defenses of this Nation and keep down the cost of living for the average family.

Nothing is more important to the longrun strength of our economy and to our work for world peace.

Peace in this world is what every thinking man and woman is praying for. It is what

I am working and praying for.

It is up to the Congress to pass a strong anti-inflation law so this country can do its full part in the fight for world peace.

124 Statement by the President Upon Signing the India Emergency Food Aid Act. *June 15, 1951*

I AM delighted to be able to sign this act of Congress which will make it possible for the United States to send to the people of India up to 2 million tons of food grains.

This act is an expression of the spontaneous, heartfelt desire of the American people to help the Indian people in their time of need. We are deeply grateful to divine providence that we can provide that help.

India suffered a series of terrible natural disasters last year—earthquakes, floods, droughts, and locust plagues—which seriously cut down India's food production and threatened millions of the Indian people with famine.

India has bought all the food she can with the funds she has. The United States alone is already sending India about 1,500,000 tons of food grains, much of it at reduced cost. This food is flowing toward Indian ports at the rate of 250,000 tons a month.

Under this act we shall be able to supply India on special and easy credit terms the additional food which India needs but for which India does not now have funds available.

These shipments of food from the United States will supply nearly two-thirds of all the food which India is buying abroad to meet its emergency. These shipments will save untold millions of our fellow human beings in India from great suffering.

I note with particular satisfaction two provisions of the act. The first of these is designed to strengthen Indian-American un-

derstanding and friendship by permitting the use of $5 million of the interest to be paid by India on the loan to bring a greater number of Indian students, professors, and technicians to the United States for study and to send more Americans to India.

The other provision authorizes free ocean transportation for relief supplies to India given by individuals and private organizations. This kind of help to stricken humanity is a tradition of the American people—whether to the sufferers of the great Russian famine and the victims of the Japanese earthquake in the early twenties or to the starving in Rumania in the late forties.

In India today American voluntary help is providing highly nutritional foods, vitamins, and medicines to the needy in the famine-threatened areas. The American Red Cross is forwarding supplies for community services in cooperation with and at the request of the Indian Red Cross. CROP—the Christian Rural Overseas Program—a union of Protestant and Catholic relief agencies—is collecting gifts in kind primarily for hospitals, orphanages, and welfare centers. CARE, a federation of many voluntary organizations, is delivering packages including foods, hand plows, and tools to further food production.

This collective effort of the United States Government and American voluntary agencies shows our humanitarian concern for all distressed people. In view of the great need in India I urge that we continue and expand the voluntary aid being given by the American people through the voluntary agencies.

In signing this act, I extend the heartfelt best wishes of the American people to the people of India and express our admiration for the courage and fortitude with which the Indian Government and people are moving ahead to solve the problems thrust upon them by natural disasters.

NOTE: The India Emergency Food Aid Act of 1951 is Public Law 48, 82d Congress (65 Stat. 69).

On June 19 the President issued Proclamation 2931, "Activation and Operation of Vessels for Transportation of Supplies Under Section 5 of the India Emergency Food Aid Act of 1951" (3 CFR, 1949–1953 Comp., p. 116).

125   Statement by the President on the Ratification of the Charter of the Organization of American States.   *June 16, 1951*

IT HAS BEEN very gratifying to me to sign the instrument of ratification of the Charter of the Organization of American States. This charter, drawn up and signed for the 21 American Republics by their representatives at the Bogotá Conference in 1948, provides the constitutional basis for Western Hemisphere unity, through consultation and joint action, within the framework of the United Nations.

In the present period of world tension, that unity assumes an even greater importance. Fortunately, the organization which the countries of this hemisphere have developed since 1890 has now been given a permanent structure, in this charter, at a time when inter-American cooperation is increasingly important. The unity of the Western Hemisphere which found its full wartime expression in the Act of Chapultepec in 1945, was reaffirmed and implemented by the Rio Treaty in 1947. It was demonstrated more recently by the achievements of the Consultative Meeting of Foreign Ministers held in Washington a little over 2 months ago.

The moral, material, and military strength of the Western Hemisphere is rooted in this unity in the cause of freedom. The destinies of our 21 nations are closely linked together for the security and for the well-being of our respective peoples. We are bound together by a common past and by common beliefs; we must move forward together working always in close cooperation.

The benefits of over a century of friendly association of the nations of the Western Hemisphere are today providing an example for free sovereign peoples over the world. If there ever was a time for such an example, it is now. The foundations of inter-American unity, which are mutual respect and dignity among countries of sovereign equality, are just as vital to the maintenance of world peace. This is the true meaning and significance of the policy of the good neighbor.

NOTE: The Charter of the Organization of American States was favorably considered by the Senate on August 28, 1950, and was ratified by the President on June 15, 1951. It entered into force on December 13, 1951, and was proclaimed by the President on December 27, 1951. The text of the Charter is printed in the United States Treaties and Other International Agreements (2 UST 2394).

126 Statement by the President Upon Signing the Trade Agreements Extension Act. *June 16, 1951*

I HAVE today signed H.R. 1612, the "Trade Agreements Extension Act of 1951." The act extends until June 12, 1953, the authority of the President to enter into reciprocal trade agreements with other countries and, in connection with these agreements, to make certain changes in United States tariff rates.

By extending this authority by an overwhelming majority, the Congress has reaffirmed its continued adherence to a program which has been a cornerstone of United States foreign policy for 17 years. Under this authority the trade agreements program will be administered with the same spirit and the same objectives that have animated it from the beginning. Through our trade agreements with other nations, and in particular through the multilateral trade agreement known as the General Agreement on Tariffs and Trade, the United States will continue its efforts with other countries to expand trade by the reduction or elimination of barriers, and thus to build up the strength of the free world.

In signing the Trade Agreements Extension Act, however, I must point out that some of the new procedural provisions are cumbersome and superfluous. Although these provisions are intended to insure that American producers will not suffer serious injury from the operation of the program, they do not materially add to the safeguards which already exist under present administrative procedures.

I am very much concerned at the fact that some of these new provisions single out particular types of products for special consideration. One of the basic principles of the trade agreements program, repeatedly enunciated in the Congress, is that the Congress should confine its legislative mandate in this field to general principles. The dangers of reverting to product-by-product legislation in the field of tariffs are obvious.

NOTE: As enacted, H.R. 1612 is Public Law 50, 82d Congress (65 Stat. 72).

127 Letter in Response to Report of the National Historical Publications Commission. *June 16, 1951*

Dear Mr. Larson:

I have read with great interest the preliminary report of the National Historical Publications Commission which you sent me on May twenty-fourth. I am highly pleased at the Commission's proposals for the publication of some of the vital records of American history which are not now generally available. I particularly hope that the Commission's interest in the papers of James Madison will bring results and that definite plans for their publication can be completed this year, the 200th anniversary of Madison's birth. I would also like to see plans made soon for the publication of Benjamin Franklin's papers. Franklin did as much as any man in our history to shape the kind of country we live in today, and yet some of his most interesting and valuable writings exist, I am told, only in manuscript.

Since I first asked the Commission, a year ago, to see what could be done to make more of the basic source materials of our history available to the general public, we have found it necessary to take up arms again in the defense of freedom. This seems to me to make the work of the National Historical Publications Commission more important than ever. The lives of men like Madison and Franklin—as well as many others discussed in the Commission's report—are full of meaning today. Madison and Franklin fought for human rights and they helped create the first government in modern times devoted solely to the well-being of its citizens. The period of danger we are in may last for many years. I am convinced that the better we understand the history of our democracy, the better we shall appreciate our rights as free men and the more determined we shall be to keep our ideals alive. Publications such as the Commission recommends will greatly help to further this understanding.

As I have said before, the editing and publishing of the papers of national leaders should be carried out principally by private means. I agree with the Commission that most of this work can be done at universities, historical societies, and other non-Federal institutions throughout the country. The Federal Government should, however, assist in every appropriate way. The facilities of the Library of Congress, the National Archives and other Federal agencies will, of course, be made freely available for this work. Perhaps the Federal Government might also assist by sharing the printing expenses of some of the materials which have been collected and edited elsewhere, but the publication of which is blocked by high costs.

I hope that the Commission's report will be widely distributed among historians and other scholars and freely discussed by them so that we may have the benefit of their views. I shall await with interest further reports of the Commission's activities.

Sincerely yours,

HARRY S. TRUMAN

[Honorable Jess Larson, Administrator, General Services Administration, Washington 25, D.C.]

NOTE: Mr. Larson's letter of May 24, transmitting the report of the National Historical Publications Commission, was released with the President's reply.

The Commission (established in 1934 (48 Stat. 1123), and reconstituted by the Federal Records Act of 1950 (64 Stat. 583)) was directed by Congress to cooperate with and encourage other agencies, both governmental and nongovernmental, in collecting, preserving, and publishing papers important for an understanding and appreciation of the history of the United States. The Commission was transferred to the General Services Administration in 1949.

On May 17, 1950, when President Truman accepted the first volume of "The Papers of Thomas Jefferson" in a ceremony at the Library of Congress, he expressed the hope that the volume would "inspire educational institutions, learned societies, and civic-minded groups to plan the publication of the works of other great national figures." He announced at that time that he was requesting the National Historical Publications Commission to report to him on what could be done to make available the public and private writings of other prominent Americans (see 1950 volume, this series, Item 136).

In its preliminary report to the President, entitled "A National Program for the Publication of the Papers of American Leaders" (1951, 47 pp.), the Commission listed 66 persons whose papers were recommended to historians for publication. Included in the group were Benjamin Franklin, John Adams, John Quincy Adams, Alexander Hamilton, and James Madison.

In April 1954 the Commission submitted a further report to the President entitled "A National Program for the Publication of Historical Documents" (Government Printing Office, 1954, 106 pp.). See also Public Papers of the Presidents, John F. Kennedy 1963, Item 26.

---

128 Directive Establishing the Psychological Strategy Board. *June* 20, 1951

Directive to: The Secretary of State, The Secretary of Defense, The Director of Central Intelligence:

It is the purpose of this directive to authorize and provide for the more effective planning, coordination and conduct, within the framework of approved national policies, of psychological operations.

There is hereby established a Psychological Strategy Board responsible, within the purposes and terms of this directive, for the formulation and promulgation, as guidance to the departments and agencies responsible for psychological operations, of over-all national psychological objectives, policies and programs, and for the coordination and evaluation of the national psychological effort.

The Board will report to the National Security Council on the Board's activities and on its evaluation of the national psychological operations, including implementation of approved objectives, policies, and programs by the departments and agencies concerned.

The Board shall be composed of:

a. The Undersecretary of State, the Deputy Secretary of Defense, and the Director of Central Intelligence, or, in their absence, their appropriate designees;

b. An appropriate representative of the head of each such other department or agency of the Government as may, from time to time, be determined by the Board.

The Board shall designate one of its members as Chairman.

A representative of the Joint Chiefs of Staff shall sit with the Board as its principal military adviser in order that the Board may ensure that its objectives, policies and programs shall be related to approved plans for military operations.

There is established under the Board a Director who shall be designated by the President and who shall receive compensation of $16,000 per year.

The Director, within the limits of funds and personnel made available by the Board for this purpose, shall organize and direct a staff to assist in carrying out his responsibilities. The Director shall determine the organization and qualifications of the staff, which may include individuals employed for this purpose, including part-time experts, and/or individuals detailed from the participating departments and agencies for assignment to full-time duty or on an ad hoc task force basis. Personnel detailed for assignment to duty under the terms of this directive shall be under the control of the Director, subject only to necessary personnel procedures within their respective departments and agencies.

The participating departments and agencies shall afford to the Director and the staff such assistance and access to information as may be specifically requested by the Director in carrying out his assigned duties.

The heads of the departments and agencies concerned shall examine into present arrangements within their departments and agencies for the conduct, direction and coordination of psychological operations with a view toward readjusting or strengthening them if necessary to carry out the purposes of this directive.

In performing its functions, the board shall utilize to the maximum extent the facilities and resources of the participating departments and agencies.

HARRY S. TRUMAN

129 Remarks of Welcome to the President of Ecuador at the Washington National Airport. *June* 20, 1951

Mr. President:

It is a great pleasure to welcome you to the United States. We shall do all in our power to make your stay among us pleasant and interesting.

I am pleased to extend this welcome to

you as President of the United States. We share with you a common devotion to the democratic way of life. Your visit is a symbol of the longstanding friendship that has always existed between our two countries.

It is a source of gratification that Ecuador and the United States are working together with the other free nations to assure the security and peace of the world. Our countries are inspired by a high regard for individual freedom and human welfare.

We are honored by your visit and most heartily extend our best wishes to you personally for the prosperity and well-being of the people of your great country.

Mr. President, you are most welcome.

NOTE: The President spoke at 3:10 p.m. His Excellency Galo Plaza, President of Ecuador, was received with a 21-gun salute and full military honors.

130 Toasts of the President and the President of Ecuador. *June* 20, 1951

My friends:

We are exceedingly lucky tonight in having a guest who is the President of one of our great friends in South America, the President of the Republic of Ecuador.

This is a situation which I don't think will happen again in a generation: The President of Ecuador was born in New York City. He was educated in Maryland, and at the University of California, and the Georgetown School of Foreign Service. He speaks much better American English than I do. He tells me that he studied English because English has no grammar and you can say what you please and anybody can understand what you are saying. I agree with him on that.

He comes from a most remarkable country, one in which I have always been interested, and one which I hope to see before I have to pass out of this world of tears. It has a historical background that is most remarkable. You read of the great empire that was in Ecuador, in Peru, and Bolivia, when Pizarro landed on the west coast of South America—a kindly, lovable people, who had a government that was in the interest of the people.

And that is what this President is working for in Ecuador, just the same as we are working for the same thing here in the United States.

Just recently, one of the most remarkable adventures happened since Leif Ericson came to Vinland in the year 900, and it started at Guayaquil, with the complete cooperation of the Government of Ecuador, and landed in the Pacific islands after a 4,000 mile trip in a raft made of balsa logs from Ecuador. I hope that all of you will take time to read that book called "Kon-Tiki." It is almost out of this world—almost unbelievable; but with the help of the Government of the Republic of Ecuador, these six boys built this raft and made the trip.

Now, Ecuador was one of our greatest friends in World War II. The President assures me that Ecuador will continue to be our friend. And we appreciate that most highly, for we want every Republic south of us to be friends to us.

We have neighbors on the north, and we have neighbors on the south. Those neighbors are not afraid of us. They are friendly to us. They know that we have no designs on their sovereignty or on their resources.

I fear very much that that is not the case with Romania or Bulgaria or Hungary or

Czechoslovakia or Poland. The free countries of Western Europe do not feel towards their powerful neighbor as our neighbors feel towards us—and that is one of the happiest things in the history of the world.

The President of Ecuador also tells me that he spells protocol with a *k,* and that he doesn't give a damn about it. That is another thing on which we completely agree.

Mr. President, it certainly is a pleasure to have you here as our guest. I hope you will enjoy your visit. You need no introduction to America. You know it as well as I do. You speak our language better than I do.

My friends, to His Excellency, the President of Ecuador.

NOTE: The President proposed the toast at a State Dinner held at the Carlton Hotel in Washington. President Galo Plaza's response follows:

Mr. President, Mr. Barkley, ladies and gentlemen:

Indeed, it is a very great honor for the President of a small country to be received by the head of the State that leads the free world today. And it is particularly interesting from my own point of view, because I am not only the representative of my country, but I am also the spokesman for all of Latin America. And maybe I am in a very particular position to be an exceptional spokesman: the fact that I was born in the United States, the fact that I went to school here, and on the other hand, I am Latin American for many, many generations back. On my mother's side were founders of the city of Quito 400 years ago. My father came from a family that was expelled from Colombia because they fought for liberty.

So you can see that, being a Latin—a 100 percent Latin—but on the other hand, having grown up in the United States, having learned to love your way of life, to admire it and want it for my own people, I can maybe explain things, say things, understand things, and be a messenger for my people before you, and on the other hand, explain to my people in Latin America what the United States means, and what the United States wants.

Indeed, maybe it is the first time in history that a great nation, being the leaders of the world, has no intention of conquering land or subjugating people. It has never happened before.

You have only one great ideal, you want for the rest of the world what your people already have.

And this is my mission in Latin America, understanding you as I do, loving the United States as I do, convincing my people of what the United States is, and why we should be with you.

I consider this the prime objective of my visit here, thanks to the very kind invitation of the President of the United States.

On the other hand, he has mentioned certain secrets. I have told him about spelling protocol with a *k,* and not knowing too much grammar, and therefore considering English just the language that I could learn because you can say things in so many ways, take a shortcut and still make sense, while Spanish is a very grammatical language. I have been allergic to grammar all my life, so English was right down my alley.

On the other hand, there is still another detail that the President did not mention. We haven't been in each other's way because we are both left-handed, we have been eating here with the left hand all the time, which is also very significant.

Mr. President, it is a great honor for me to be here. I want to toast you, sir: to your great country, and to your devoted wife and talented daughter—we miss them here tonight.

131   Letter to the Speaker Proposing an Accelerated Civil Defense Program.   *June 21, 1951*

Sir:

I have the honor to transmit herewith for the consideration of the Congress the Budget for the fiscal year 1952 in the amount of $535,000,000 for the Federal Civil Defense Administration.

For the first time in our history, this country faces the threat of a sudden devastating attack at any time on our major cities.

We must act on the assumption that the Soviet Union has atomic bombs and that they have the planes that can drop those bombs on our cities. Our Air Force experts tell us that in any determined air attack enemy planes could drop bombs on our cities, no matter how good our defenses may be.

There is no complete protection against an atomic air attack, but there is a great deal that can be done to reduce the number of deaths and injuries that might result. The lives of many millions of people may depend on the development of a strong Civil Defense Program to meet such an attack.

Every city, factory, office and home must be organized for Civil Defense. As long as there is a chance of any kind that atomic bombs may fall on our cities, we cannot gamble. We cannot be caught unprepared.

The development of the Nation's preparedness is out of balance if, at the same time our armed forces are being strengthened, measures are not taken providing the means to minimize civilian casualties, to deal with emergency conditions, and to restore vital facilities in the period immediately following attack. The Civil Defense Program will not only protect the civilian population, but will also help to maintain the industrial productivity necessary to support our military forces.

Because of the importance of Civil Defense in the protection of our people, property and production on the home front, I recommend immediate action on this appropriation in the interest of national security.

The program proposed in these estimates is not all that will be required to give this Nation a fully effective civil defense. However, it covers the minimum amount necessary to help the States organize and teach our people how to protect themselves against atomic attack; and to assist the States to make a start in procuring sirens, fire, rescue, communication, and other types of equipment required to warn the public of an attack and to fight the effects of such an attack. It also covers a Federal reserve supply of critical medical, emergency welfare and public works items because such a reserve is more economical and will permit with safety a lower inventory level than if each city were to procure its own reserve.

The estimate of appropriation to match State contributions for protective shelters is a substantial start on a program to protect the public in congested areas. The standards and criteria for evaluating existing structures have been developed and surveys are being carried out in cities to determine (1) the existing buildings usable as shelters, (2) the existing buildings which can be modified for use as shelters, and (3) the amount of new construction required. Work on the modification of existing structures will be given first priority and can be started as soon as funds are made available.

The details of these proposed appropriations are set forth in the attached letter from the Director of the Bureau of the Budget with whose comments and observations thereon I concur.

> Respectfully yours,
>
> HARRY S. TRUMAN

[The Honorable Sam Rayburn, Speaker of the House of Representatives]

NOTE: On November 1, 1951, the President signed the First Supplemental Appropriation Act, 1952 (65 Stat. 736), which provided an appropriation of $74,945,000 for the Civil Defense Administration.

132 The President's News Conference of *June* 21, 1951

THE PRESIDENT. That clock is 7 minutes fast! [*Laughter*]

I have no announcements to make. If you want to ask me some questions, I will try to answer them.

[1.] Q. Mr. President, do you plan to do anything about the United Airline pilots strike?

THE PRESIDENT. Not at present.

[2.] Q. Mr. President, have you any

comment on General MacArthur saying that you silenced pertinent witnesses——

THE PRESIDENT. No comment.

Q. Mr. President, may I ask another question?

Q. What was the answer?

THE PRESIDENT. No comment.

Q. Mr. President, as a President who has had some experience, what do you think of General MacArthur's whistlestop speeches?

THE PRESIDENT. I have no comment on that, either. [*Laughter*]

[3.] Q. Mr. President, there are reports—new reports—of a projected peace proposal by the United Nations in the Korean struggle. The reports say that such a proposal will be made this weekend.

THE PRESIDENT. It has not been taken up with me. I can't comment on it. I think a thing of that kind would come to me before any action was taken on it.

[4.] Q. Would you tell us, Mr. President, something about your talk last night with the President of Ecuador, and your impressions of him?

THE PRESIDENT. I think very highly of the President of Ecuador. We had very pleasant conversations, and I enjoyed the visit with him very much. I think he is a good man who is anxious to do the right thing.

[5.] Q. Mr. President, do you think it will be possible for you—the executive branch of the Government—to control prices and hold back inflation under the control bill as it is taking shape now in the Senate and House banking committees?

THE PRESIDENT. I don't know what shape that bill will be in until it comes to me for signature. I will comment on it completely and thoroughly at that time. You can't tell what a bill will contain until it has gone through conference, and been passed by both Houses. You can't comment on a bill in the committee.[1]

Q. The Senate gave us a rather broad hint.

THE PRESIDENT. I can't answer the hint. I want to see the bill.

[6.] Q. Mr. President, in your talks with the Ecuadoran President, did you come to any mutual understanding on economic or military matters, or other matters?

THE PRESIDENT. We have not talked on business matters at all. This is purely social. He will see me Friday to talk business matters which he came to see me about. We will probably issue a communique on it.[2]

[7.] Q. Mr. President, was Jonathan Daniels acting on anything more than reportorial instinct when he said that you would be a candidate again?

THE PRESIDENT. I think you state the case exactly. [*Laughter*]

Q. Mr. President, do you think Mr. McCardle[3] stated the case, or Mr. Daniels?

THE PRESIDENT. I don't understand what you are talking about.

Q. You said that you thought somebody had stated the case exactly.

THE PRESIDENT. Well, I thought *this* reporter stated the case correctly. [*Laughter*]

Q. *This* reporter? Thank you.

THE PRESIDENT. You mixed me up a little bit.

Q. I meant to, sir.

THE PRESIDENT. I was sure of that! [*More laughter*]

[8.] Q. Mr. President, in connection with the visit of the President of Ecuador, do you have a feeling that inter-American relations generally are on a good plane?

THE PRESIDENT. Yes, I do.

Q. You signed the charter recently—the OAS?[4]

THE PRESIDENT. I think the inter-American

---

[1] See Items 140 [2], 176.

[2] See Item 134.

[3] Carl W. McCardle of the Philadelphia Evening Bulletin.

[4] See Item 125.

relationship is on a better plane than it has ever been in history, and I hope to keep it that way, as far as I am concerned.

[9.] Q. Mr. President, I wonder if you would mind telling us what you will see the Joint Chiefs of Staff about this afternoon?

THE PRESIDENT. Just seeing the Joint Chiefs of Staff.

[10.] Q. Mr. President, on the floor of the Senate this week, Senator McCarthy said that General Marshall was masterminding a great conspiracy here, of which you were unaware. Would you care to comment on that?

THE PRESIDENT. No comment. I don't know how the Senator can read my mind.

Q. We didn't get that reply, Mr. President.

THE PRESIDENT. I said I didn't see how anybody can read my mind. I said the Senator—I don't see how anybody can read my mind. It is very difficult, as Mr. Lawrence [5] over here found out. [*Laughter*]

[11.] Q. Mr. President, do you see any possibility of improvement in the Iranian oil situation?

THE PRESIDENT. I didn't hear that question, will you please repeat it?

Q. Do you see any possibility of improvement in the Iranian oil situation?

THE PRESIDENT. I think the Secretary of State commented on that yesterday fully.[6]

[12.] Q. Mr. President, are you ready yet to fill those judgeship vacancies in Illinois—northern Illinois?

THE PRESIDENT. No, I am not. Whenever I am ready, I will let you know.

[13.] Q. Mr. President, have you anything to say about the cuts which now have been written into the appropriation bill?

THE PRESIDENT. No comment, for the simple reason that the bill has not come to me for consideration as yet, at which time I will make the necessary comment.

Q. Pretty definite pattern there——

THE PRESIDENT. You can't tell what a bill will be until it has passed both Houses.

[14.] Q. Mr. President, would you care to comment on the arrest of 21 more Communists in New York——

THE PRESIDENT. Will you please repeat the question, I didn't hear?

Q. Would you care to comment on the arrest yesterday of 21 more Communists under the Smith Act?

THE PRESIDENT. I still couldn't hear the question. Will you talk into that microphone, so we can all hear? I'm sorry.

Q. Would you care to comment on the arrest yesterday of 21 more Communists under the Smith Act?

THE PRESIDENT. No comment. [*Laughter*]

[15.] Q. Mr. President, in relation to the appropriation bill—putting it a little this way—do you, as the Chief Executive, believe the Government can operate efficiently with 10 percent less employees?

THE PRESIDENT. I will answer that when the bill comes before me in its final form.

[16.] Q. Mr. President, the CIO released today a statement by Phil Murray,[7] urging you to issue an order for a national emergency FEPC at the earliest possible moment. Do you plan to do that?

THE PRESIDENT. The request has not reached me yet.

---

[5] William H. Lawrence of the New York Times.

[6] Speaking at his news conference on June 20, Secretary of State Dean Acheson described the Iranian oil situation as critical, and appealed to Iran to reconsider her rejection of the Anglo-Iranian Oil Company's offer of 10 million pounds as a first step toward settlement of the nationalization dispute.

Mr. Acheson said that the United States had hoped that the British financial offer would provide a basis for fruitful negotiations that not only would be agreeable to the British company but also would recognize the desire of the Iranians for the nationalization of their oil resources.

---

[7] Philip Murray, president of the Congress of Industrial Organizations.

Q. If it should reach you, are you likely——

THE PRESIDENT. I will not—no comment on that.

[17.] Q. Mr. President, were you wearing a straw hat from Ecuador yesterday? Someone said that the President had given you——

THE PRESIDENT. I was wearing a straw hat from Ecuador that I have had for about 3 years. It is still in good shape. [*Laughter*]

Q. Who gave it to you, do you recall?

THE PRESIDENT. It was sent to me from Ecuador by somebody who went down there on a visit, from some official who wanted to be kind to the President. But it is a good hat. [*Laughter*]

[18.] Q. Mr. President, are you going whistlestopping this summer or fall?

THE PRESIDENT. Going what?

Q. Whistlestopping?

THE PRESIDENT. Well, I can't answer that question until I find out what the Congress is going to do, as we still have an immense amount of legislation that has to be passed. I have to stay here until it is passed.

Q. You mean that you will wait for Congress to act, not necessarily pitching the trip on what Congress actually does?

THE PRESIDENT. No, no, I can't do anything until Congress gets through its action.

Q. Do you have any more fashion notes for us, Mr. President?

THE PRESIDENT. None at all. [*Laughter*]

Reporter: Thank you, sir.

NOTE: President Truman's two hundred and sixty-seventh news conference was held in the Indian Treaty Room (Room 474) in the Executive Office Building at 10:37 a.m. on Thursday, June 21, 1951.

133   Remarks to a Group of Newsboy Bond Salesmen. *June 21, 1951*

THE SECRETARY of the Treasury tells me that you have been very cooperative and very helpful in selling bonds. I want to thank you for it.

You are doing something that is good for your country, something that is good for yourselves, and something that is good for those to whom you succeed in selling bonds, for bonds are a favor to them.

I hope you will continue to cooperate with the Secretary of the Treasury in this effort of ours to keep down inflation.

No man is in a bad fix when his savings are invested in Government bonds. It is the safest investment in the world, and always has been.

I want to thank you very much. I am sorry that the weather had to give you a sweat bath out here in our Rose Garden today, but since we have been fenced in, we don't get much breeze up here. I don't see that it is going to hurt any of you very much, though, because I imagine you get up a sweat every day in your business.

Thank you all very much.

NOTE: The President spoke at 3:05 p.m. in the Rose Garden at the White House. In his opening words he referred to Secretary of the Treasury John W. Snyder.

The boys represented newsboys throughout the country who distributed savings bond pledge cards to their customers during the month of May.

The group was attending the National Carrier Congress then meeting in Washington.

134 Joint Statement Following Discussions With the President of Ecuador. *June 22, 1951*

THE PRESIDENT of the Republic of Ecuador and the President of the United States of America have met in Washington, D.C., and have reaffirmed their determination to continue their support of the efforts of the United Nations to reestablish peace in the world. They will remain steadfastly united in the present emergency. The two nations solemnly declare their attachment to the principles set forth in the Charters of the United Nations and of the Organization of American States and in other international agreements to maintain peace and security. They intend to defend themselves against aggression, to settle their disputes by peaceful means, improve the living standards of their peoples, promote their cultural and economic progress, and ensure respect for the fundamental freedoms of man and the principles of social justice that are the bases of their democratic systems.

President Plaza expressed the desire of his Government to cooperate closely with the United States and other free nations in the adoption of measures for increasing the production and processing of basic and strategic materials for the defense emergency. At the same time, he also emphasized the need to strengthen the economy of his country, and the two Presidents discussed ways in which the United States might be of assistance.

In recognition of the importance of Ecuadoran plans for fuller economic development, it has been agreed to make joint studies of the economic potentialities of Ecuador and the most effective means for furthering the fuller use of Ecuadoran resources to accelerate its economic and social progress.

President Plaza expressed his recognition of the value of the Point IV technical cooperation now in progress in the fields of agriculture, health, sanitation, education, transportation, and related fields and his gratification that the United States is prepared sympathetically to consider further requests for technical assistance from the Government of Ecuador.

In the cultural field, it has also been agreed to enter upon the negotiation at an early date of a cultural convention between Ecuador and the United States to improve and broaden the cultural relations between the two countries. Such a convention would encourage and further stimulate the present cultural exchange between Ecuador and the United States.

135 Address at the Dedication of the National Institutes of Health Clinical Center. *June 22, 1951*

Mr. Ewing, distinguished guests, ladies and gentlemen:

We are here today to lay the cornerstone of a building which will be devoted to the service of mankind. The men and women who work in this clinical research center will be striving to save human lives and to prevent human suffering.

This is a noble purpose.

As a people, we have constantly sought better health and longer lives for our citizens. We have done so not merely because human strength and human intelligence are great national assets. Far more important, we believe that there is something sacred about every human soul that God has put on this earth.

We believe in the rights of the individual. We acknowledge his supremacy over the state. This is the great mark of distinction between our democracy and the totalitarian dictatorships. In the totalitarian countries little value is placed on human life. People are herded into slave labor camps by the millions, and are allowed to die like flies from starvation, disease, or hardship.

In our country the Government exists to serve the people. Our Government is one of the instruments through which the people achieve freedom, happiness, and the good things of life.

This is true in the field of health as in other parts of our national life. Advances in medical knowledge and medical care in our country have come about through the combined efforts of private individuals and institutions and local, State, and Federal agencies.

This clinical research center will advance the work that is being done by all of us to achieve better health. I am especially glad to participate in these ceremonies, because I believe so strongly in the importance of medical progress. And I know what amazing advances can be made, because I know what has happened in my own lifetime.

At the turn of the century the average American could expect to live only 49 years. The two biggest killers, pneumonia and tuberculosis, exacted a frightful toll. Diphtheria and typhoid ran wild. We were losing 130 of every thousand babies before they were a year old. Our maternal death rate was very high—more than six mothers died in childbirth for every thousand babies born. In World War I, 141 American soldiers out of every 10,000 were cut down by disease—more than were killed by the enemy bullets.

Today, many of these scourges have been almost completely eliminated. The death rate from tuberculosis, pneumonia, and other infectious diseases is at the lowest point in medical history. We have reduced infant mortality by more than two-thirds. Our maternal death rate is now less than 1 mother per 1,000 births. The death rate from disease in our Armed Forces in World War II was only about 6 in every 10,000, as compared with 141 in 10,000 in the First World War.

Most remarkable of all, we have extended the average life 18 years in this short half century. The average American baby born this year can expect to live 67 years—until the year 2018. And I was 67 last month—too bad!

Medical science has won victory after victory over the deadliest diseases of a generation ago. During the first half of the 20th century, it is safe to say that we successfully conquered the infectious diseases. Now, in the second half of the century, we are facing an even greater challenge—the battle against chronic diseases.

Over 1 million Americans died last year from cancer, heart trouble, diabetes, and other chronic illnesses. As the life span of our people has grown longer, the mortality from these illnesses has risen. Last year the death rate from heart disease was the highest ever recorded for any single human ailment, and it was 20 percent higher than 10 years ago. Fifteen percent more people died of cancer last year than they did 10 years ago.

The most heart-rending of the chronic afflictions, and perhaps the most serious, is mental illness. Over 600,000 hospital beds—about 50 percent of the hospital beds in this country—are occupied by the mentally ill.

All these chronic illnesses take a tremendous human toll. It is estimated that more than 25 million Americans suffer to some degree from chronic diseases.

Modern medicine must find ways of detecting these diseases in their early stages and of stopping their destructive force. That will be the major work of this clinical research center. There could be no more useful expenditure of the taxpayers' funds.

The center will be operated by the Public Health Service of the Federal Security Agency. It will be the home of one of the greatest groups of scientists ever gathered together for basic and applied medical research.

Basic research has been at the core of the great advances in medicine during the last half-century, and the scientists of the Public Health Service have been in the forefront of this research.

Scientists of the Public Health Service were the first to discover that pellagra was caused by a dietary deficiency, and they devised the means for its prevention and cure. They found the cause of Rocky Mountain spotted fever and how to vaccinate against it. They developed the use of fluorides for the protection of teeth, opening the way to the major reduction of dental decay.

Public health research workers right here at Bethesda developed a vaccine against typhus. Their vaccine has kept our forces in Korea free from typhus, while the North Korean and Chinese Communists have suffered seriously from that disease.

The fine record of the Public Health Service research workers promises well for the future. This magnificent building will give them many new opportunities to forge ahead in the field of medical discovery. I am particularly glad that one of the wings of the building has been especially designed for work with radioactive materials—to put to peaceful and constructive use our increasing knowledge of atomic energy. I am just as sure as I stand here that we are going to discover uses for this great force that we have released that will be for the welfare of mankind, instead of for its destruction. And

that is what I am looking forward to.

This clinical research center will not be an isolated enterprise. Research scientists from medical schools, private hospitals, and other private institutions will come here to share in the work. And the Federal Government will continue to make grants-in-aid for medical research in other places. In 1950 the Public Health Service made more than 1,500 research grants totaling about $14 million. These grants went to universities, hospitals, and medical schools in every part of the United States.

In the last few years Government assistance to medical research has been greatly expanded. At one time there was a great hue and cry by the viewers-with-alarm that Federal assistance would threaten freedom of research. That is a very, very familiar statement that goes on all the time. That wasn't true, of course. The fact is that the presidents of some of our leading universities have gone on record to the effect that Federal assistance has broadened both the scope and the freedom of medical research. Their experience with these research grants is proof that Government aid does not mean Government control.

Today there is a growing awareness that medical research needs support from the Federal Government, from State and local governments, and from industry, endowment funds, and private contributions. It will take support from all these sources to give us the rapid progress we need.

At the same time that we are moving forward with medical research, we must drive ahead to translate the new knowledge gained by research into better medical care for more people. Here we have run into difficult problems, but we are making progress.

We have made great strides in the field of public health. The Federal, State, and local governments have formed an effective partnership. In 1950, $231 million was spent for State and local public health services. Forty-five million dollars of this was provided by the Federal Government, $96 million by State governments, and $90 million by local governments.

These funds were used by public health doctors and nurses who are in the front lines of the fight against disease—X-raying to find tuberculosis, inoculating against diphtheria and typhoid, treating venereal disease, guarding the purity of water and milk supplies, organizing health services for civil defense, and performing a host of other services to protect the health of the American family.

Yet, our present local public health system is woefully inadequate to meet its responsibilities. Thirty-two million Americans live in areas which are not served by full-time public health workers.

I am happy that the United States Senate at its present session has passed legislation to help strengthen and expand the Nation's local public health units in our cities and counties. I hope that the Congress will complete action quickly on this legislation. Stronger local public health units are essential to better health in this great country.

We are now making good progress in meeting our needs for hospitals and health centers. The projects already approved under the national hospital program, started in 1946, will give us 65,000 additional hospital beds and 240 new health centers, with the Federal Government contributing about one-third of the cost. These hospitals are being built where they are needed most. Most of them are small hospitals of 50 beds or less, and most of them are located in towns of 10,000 people or less.

Hospital and research centers are worthless, however, without trained medical personnel to staff them. In recent years the education of students in the medical, dental, nursing, and allied professions has not kept pace with the increase in population. These shortages are crippling hospital services all over the country. Less than a month ago, every Washington newspaper carried front page stories on the closing of many hospital beds in this area because of a critical health personnel shortage.

These shortages are being aggravated by the needs of our Armed Forces. Our military medical men are doing a magnificent job in saving lives on the Korean front, but we have had to dip deeply into our medical strength over here to accomplish this.

In order to supply more doctors and nurses, we will have to strengthen and expand our schools. In spite of the best efforts of the medical schools, they have had to turn away thousands of applicants each year. The income of the medical schools has not risen to meet the rising costs of medical education. They are today in the most precarious financial condition in their history. President Hoover, as honorary chairman of the National Fund for Medical Education, pointed out recently that the financial condition of our medical schools is so acute that few can continue even their present programs without large-scale financial aid.

Legislation to remedy this situation is now before the Congress. This legislation will provide emergency Federal aid for 5 years to tide the schools over the present crisis. The overwhelming majority of the medical school deans support this legislation. It is not intended to replace private sources of support. On the contrary, I am sure it will broaden this support in the same way in which both public and private sources, joined together, have broadened the base and scope of medical research. I hope that the Congress will act on this legislation soon.

Finally, we have the problem of meeting the cost of medical care. The research discoveries which will be made at this clinical center and elsewhere must not be confined to a chosen few, simply because the rest of us cannot afford to use them.

At the present time most people find it very difficult to pay for medical care. I have been very glad to see the growth of the many private health insurance plans over the last several years. But the plain fact is that they do not meet the problem. They are not reaching the overwhelming majority of low and middle income families.

Less than 4 million Americans have reasonably complete medical care insurance, and 75 million have no health insurance at all. Skyrocketing medical costs are pushing millions of Americans into the medically indigent class.

Since 1945 I have been proposing to meet this problem by national health insurance. This proposal has generated a great deal of controversy. I still believe it is sound, and that the Nation would be greatly strengthened by its adoption.

I want to make it clear, however, that I am not clinging to any particular plan. What I want is a good workable plan that will enable all Americans to pay for the medical care they need. And I will say here and now that if the people who have been blocking health insurance for 5 years will come up with a better proposal—or even one that is almost as good—I'll go along with them. I want to get the job done, and I am not concerned in the slightest with pride of authorship.

But I am concerned with results. Medical care is for the people and not just for the doctors—and the rich. Our objective must be to make the best modern medical care available to more and more people. I intend to keep right on working for that as long as I am President of the United States, and also after I get through being the President of the United States.

I have been speaking of the medical needs of our own country. We should never forget, however, the extremely fortunate position we are in compared to the rest of the world.

Throughout the world almost half the people—more than 1 billion men, women, and children—are victims of preventable disease. Millions of them are weakened by malaria. Millions die each year from tuberculosis. Three babies out of every ten die in infancy.

In many parts of the world the average life expectancy is under 30 years. That was our expectancy in 1890. This means that the average farmer or industrial worker in these countries has but a few years of limited productivity before death.

Obviously, people with such handicaps face immense difficulty in striving for economic and social progress. It is urgently necessary that we help them to learn and put into effect modern medical knowledge and public health methods. This is one of the most important parts of the work we must do under the point 4 program.

We know what can be done. In Western Europe, when World War II ended, disease was rampant and epidemics threatened wide areas. Experts said that 20 years' effort in public health had been lost as a result of the war.

Now in 3 years, with our help, the tide was turned. By 1948, death rates in Western Europe were the lowest ever recorded. Tuberculosis, which had spread to an alarming extent, was reduced to a lower level than ever before. Malaria was nearly wiped out as far east as Greece. Typhus and smallpox were gone. The public health work in Europe was more completely successful than the efforts made in any other field of postwar rehabilitation.

Of course, this was done in Europe, where there was a large group of medically trained specialists. We cannot expect such quick results in the underdeveloped areas of the world. They are desperately short of doctors and nurses and health facilities of all kinds. In parts of Iran, for example, there is only one doctor for each 80,000 people. It will take time to remedy these conditions. But progress is being made.

More health technicians are being trained. Last year, thousands of professional health workers came to the United States for training—they came from the Philippines, Latin America, and many other areas all around the world.

We are also sending our specialists abroad. For example, last year, a team of our public health officers flew to Indochina and helped the people there plan a campaign against malaria and other serious diseases. Another team spent 10 weeks in Iran, showing village physicians and government medical officers how to vaccinate and use DDT.

This public health work is the key to improving conditions in the underdeveloped areas. No funds we can spend will bring richer rewards in human progress and in strength for peace. This is recognized by other countries as well as our own, and splendid work is being done in this field by the World Health Organization.

The United States was one of the founding members of the World Health Organization. It is a source of deep satisfaction to me that Surgeon General Scheele of the Public Health Service was elected to the presidency of its annual assembly in Geneva just a month ago.

As we lay the cornerstone of this clinical center, I see in this structure a symbol of what is finest in our way of life.

The work that is done here in Bethesda will bring life and health to all mankind. This center is a specific and exciting expression of man's humanity to man. It will save the lives and alleviate the suffering of our own children and grandchildren. But, more than that, it will serve men of all religions, all races, and all nations—everywhere in the world.

May it serve for many generations as a monument to our desire for human health and happiness in a world at peace.

NOTE: The President spoke at 3:35 p.m. at the site of the National Institutes of Health in Bethesda, Md. His opening words referred to Oscar R. Ewing, Administrator of the Federal Security Agency. The address was broadcast.

136   Toasts of the President and the President of Ecuador. *June 22, 1951*

Mr. President, Señora Plaza, ladies and gentlemen:

I can't tell you how very much I appreciate the kind remarks which you have just made. Your visit here has been most helpful to the cause of understanding democracy in the Western Hemisphere, and in all the world for that matter.

The Vice President reported to me, sir, that you had made the best speech that the Congress has listened to in many a day—and I made them an address last January!

We are most happy that you are here. We hope you have had a pleasant visit. We know that you have created a better understanding between the Government of the United States and the Government of Ecuador, if that needed to be done.

Our ambition and interest is world peace. And that, I know, is your ambition and interest.

I am extremely sorry that Mrs. Truman and my daughter have not been here to meet Señora Plaza and your lovely daughters.

Margaret is in Paris. Mrs. Truman had to be in Independence with her mother who is not very well—she is 89 years old—and her daughter has to be with her as much as possible.

I hope, Mr. President, that you will have a most pleasant visit all over these United States. I know you will have a cordial welcome wherever you go. They can't do anything else but give you a cordial welcome, because they are interested—all the citizens of this country—in the welfare of the whole hemisphere, and I am sure the whole world. It is a pleasure to me to be your host and the representative of the 150 million citizens of the United States of America.

I hope that the time will come when it will be possible for me—whether I am President or not—to visit that wonderful city of Quito. I studied that book carefully and sincerely when you gave it to me, and it made me want to be in Quito all the more. I have always wanted to go there, because it is one of the most wonderful capitals of the world, from a historical standpoint and from its situation—the only capital in the world that is right under the equator. It has a very high elevation. And it has a wonderful people. And in the book which you gave me, it has marvelous architecture.

I wonder if you would join me in a toast to His Excellency, the President of Ecuador, and his wonderful First Lady, Señora Plaza.

NOTE: The President's toast was in response to a toast proposed by President Galo Plaza at a state dinner which he gave for President Truman in the Congressional Room of the Statler Hotel in Washington. The toast proposed by President Plaza follows:

Mr. President, Mrs. Barkley, ladies and gentlemen:
I am about to leave Washington tomorrow, and I have no words that can appropriately describe my feelings, after the cordial reception that I have received from my friends, from the Government, and from everyone here in Washington. I will never forget this visit to your great city.

This morning the President of the United States gave me the greatest surprise of all. I called on him, and he put on my chest the Medal of Merit.

I did not know that I was going to receive this great honor. It came as an absolute surprise. And I have just told him that it couldn't have been better if he had given me a battleship instead.

This morning, when I visited him, I gave the President a book, with pictures and descriptions of our city of Quito. The book is written in both Spanish and English, and it has descriptions of our old colonial city and our old churches built during colonial times 250 and 300 years ago.

The book was given to the President for a reason. I want to invite him tonight to come to Quito and visit me, and I wanted him to be well-read on the city.

In times like these I think it is appropriate to repeat what I have been saying at different opportunities: all the countries of the free world—and the countries of Latin America in particular, and speaking for my own country—we realize our responsibilities, and we are willing to help to the limit of our possibilities.

At the beginning of the last war, a few hours after the attack on Pearl Harbor, Ecuador offered the United States the use of the Galapagos Islands and points on the coast of Ecuador, without any strings attached to them, just a contribution—a small contribution—but our contribution, the very minute an emergency appeared.

And I want to make it clear that if such an emergency came about again, my country would be willing to put at the disposal of the United States and the United Nations the same facilities as before, or any others that we may have that might prove worthwhile to the cause of the free world.

As I said before, my gratitude has no limits for this opportunity, thanks to the invitation of the President of the United States to come here. It is one more proof of the greatness of this country. I am not the head of a great country. There is no great result of any nature that can be derived from my visit. But the United States—the Government of the United States, the people of the United States—are not measuring the size of what I have done; it is the quality of what I have done. It is what I stand for, whether it be done in a country of 300 million or a small country like mine. That is very important. That is one more proof of what the Christian philosophy of this country stands for.

I may say, at this time, that the problems of today, the importance of what happens in the United States to the rest of the world has kept us all posted and informed on your problems, your politics, your achievements.

And, we follow very closely the outstanding performance of the President of the United States. We admire him. He has a tremendous job. He not only has to fight the enemies of his country—the enemies of his philosophy of life—but he has another great enemy to face, an enemy from among his own people—and in including his people, I am speaking of all the people in the free world—that great enemy is lack of understanding.

We all feel the same way. We all want to defend what we have, but we cannot agree on the way of going about it. And therefore the decisions of the head of the most powerful nation in the world many times has to be carried out in spite of great misunderstanding.

I am sure that in the future, when these trying times are seen with the necessary perspective that only time can bring about, that the figure, the personality, of your President will at last be seen in all its value.

I want you, ladies and gentlemen, to join me in drinking to the health of the President of the United States.

137 Letter to the President of the Senate and to the Speaker of the House Transmitting Report of the National Advisory Board on Mobilization Policy. *June 23, 1951*

[Released June 23, 1951. Dated June 22, 1951]

My dear Mr. ————:

I have received the attached report from the National Advisory Board on Mobilization Policy, which I am forwarding for the information of the Congress.

This is an especially timely report, because two pieces of defense legislation—the tax bill and the Defense Production Act amendments—are about to be considered by the Congress. The Board naturally did not concern itself with the details of this legislation. But I should like to call the attention of the Congress to the main conclusion stated by the Board. The Board unanimously concluded that during the past year "the dangers confronting our national safety and economic stability have in no sense diminished, and that consequently the Congress should as rapidly as possible complete consideration of and take action upon pending legislation relating to the national emergency." The Board unanimously concluded also that "such action as the Congress may take should be for a long enough period of time—which means at least a year—so that the planning and execution of the mobilization program may not be fatally harassed by prolonged nation-wide uncertainty concerning national policy."

I most heartily endorse these conclusions. We do need rapid action by the Congress,

and legislation of at least a year's duration— I have recommended two years—in order to carry forward our defense mobilization effort successfully.

I should like to add one point which did not come within the Board's considerations. I have been considerably distressed by some provisions in the defense production bills reported by the Senate and House Banking and Currency Committees. These provisions take the easy way—to relax controls and hope for the best—which is extremely dangerous. All of us should realize that we are in a hard, tough fight with inflation in this country—just as we are in a hard, tough fight with aggression in Korea. A relaxed, soft attitude is an invitation to disaster.

I recommend most strongly that the defense production bills be strengthened by the Congress, so that we can build the defense of our country without undermining the standard of living of our people or weakening the American dollar.

Very sincerely yours,

HARRY S. TRUMAN

NOTE: This is the text of identical letters addressed to the Honorable Alben W. Barkley, President of the Senate, and to the Honorable Sam Rayburn, Speaker of the House of Representatives.

The National Advisory Board on Mobilization Policy was established by Executive Order 10224 of March 15, 1951 (3 CFR, 1949–1953 Comp., p. 736).

The Board was composed of Charles E. Wilson, Director of Defense Mobilization, who served as Chairman, and 16 other members representing business, labor, and agriculture.

The Board's report, released on June 22, stressed the fact that recent events, both military and economic, had brought to the fore the issue of whether the United States should continue in full force or relax the mobilization efforts begun as a result of the Korean conflict. The report stated that the members of the Board unanimously agreed that the dangers confronting the national safety and economic stability had not diminished and that Congress should take immediate action on pending legislation relating to the national emergency.

The report cautioned against creating too large a military establishment. With regard to industrial mobilization it recommended an increase in productive output of 5 to 7 percent a year. Anticipating inflationary pressures as a result of rapid increase in production, the report recommended price and wage controls, a sound tax policy, control of interest rates and business credit, and a vigorous and effective savings campaign.

The full text of the Board's report is printed in House Document 183 (82d Cong., 1st sess.).

---

138   Address in Tullahoma, Tenn., at the Dedication of the Arnold Engineering Development Center. *June 25, 1951*

Governor Browning, General Carroll, Mr. Evins, Senator Kefauver, distinguished Members of the House of Representatives, honorable mayors, Mrs. Arnold, ladies and gentlemen:

Congressman Evins, you forgot to introduce my mayor when you were introducing the mayors. There is a mayor in Tennessee here who was a second lieutenant in my Battery D in France during the First World War, and his name is Bill Kleeman, up here in Fayetteville. I just want you to know that.

I am glad to be here in Tennessee to dedicate this great aviation development center. The great industrial progress of Tennessee, and of the whole South, makes it possible to build this key defense installation in this area. I am sure that the presence of this center here will contribute further to the growth and prosperity of this region.

Governor, I want to thank you most sincerely for the remarks that you had to make before I started. I think they were just exactly what they should have been; and as a Tennessee orator always does, it was done exactly right.

It is most appropriate that this center for pioneering in the science of flight should bear the name of General Henry H. Arnold.

"Hap" Arnold was a great pioneer in the development of our Air Force. He was one of the first three officers in our Armed Forces to learn to fly a plane. He won his first flying trophy in a Wright biplane that had a 40-horsepower engine turning two propellers by a chain and sprocket method—the same kind of power transmission as a bicycle has.

General Arnold lived to command a mighty Air Force of 80,000 planes. Instead of 40 horsepower, some of the planes in that Air Force had 10,000 horsepower. And the power transmission system of some of those planes was more like a skyrocket than a bicycle.

General Arnold had a lot to do with those improvements. He knew that you can't have a first-class air force with a second-class aircraft. He would have been delighted with this air research center, which will do so much to make further improvements possible.

I am happy to dedicate this center to his memory and to name it the "Arnold Engineering and Development Center" in the presence of his family and friends.

The scientists who work here will explore what lies on the other side of the speed of sound. This is part of our effort to make our air power the best in the world—and to keep it the best in the world. This applies to the planes of the Air Force, the Navy, and the Marines. It applies to our guided missiles and all the future developments that science may bring.

The purpose of our Air Force is to help keep the peace of the world. This is our fundamental objective. A large and powerful air force is one of the essential weapons we must have to prevent aggression—or to crush aggression if it happens.

We need many other weapons as well—military, economic, and psychological weapons—if we are to prevent a third world war. And we must keep finding new and better methods in each of these fields, just as we must keep developing faster and more powerful planes.

We must use every possible means of securing and maintaining the peace. Our whole policy is based on world peace. That has been our policy all along. It is still our policy, and it hasn't changed one bit.

Since World War II we have done our best to build an international organization to keep the peace of the world. We have done that in the interest of the United States, because the only sure way to keep our own country safe and secure is to have world peace. The United Nations is the most far-reaching attempt that man has ever made to protect himself against the scourge of war.

But the rulers of the Soviet Union had a different idea. They did not want to cooperate in keeping the peace. The people of Russia—the common everyday people of Russia—want peace just as much as anyone else, but their rulers in the Kremlin saw that the nations of the world had been weakened and demoralized by the agonies of the war. They saw a chance to move in and impose their own system of slavery on other nations.

We tried to settle postwar problems with the Soviet Union on a decent and honorable basis. But they broke one agreement after another. We offered to place the means of atomic warfare under effective international control. That was an offer to save mankind forever from the horror of an atomic war. But the Soviet Union refused to accept it—refused to accept the most unselfish offer for peace any nation in the history of the world ever made. We had a monopoly on that weapon, and we offered to surrender it to the world, for peace. The Russians wouldn't accept that.

Our actions showed that we were for peace. Even though our efforts were rejected by the Soviet rulers, our actions won for us the confidence and trust of other free nations. In spite of all the false and lying propaganda of the Kremlin, it was clear to all the world that we wanted peace.

At the same time, we made it clear to all the world that we would not engage in appeasement. When the Soviet Union began its campaign of undermining and destroying other free nations, we did not sit idly by.

We came to the aid of Greece and Turkey when they stood in danger of being taken over by Communist aggression in 1947. As a result, these countries today are free and strong and independent.

We came to the aid of the peoples of France and Italy in their struggle against the political onslaught of communism. In each of these countries, communism has been defeated in two free elections since 1947. There is no longer any danger that they will vote themselves into the hands of the Soviet Union.

We came to the aid of the brave people of Berlin when the Kremlin tried to take them over. We and our allies kept Berlin alive by the airlift and it is still free today.

We came to the aid of China when it was threatened by Communist civil war. We put billions of dollars worth of arms and supplies into China to aid the Chinese Nationalist Government. We gave them more help than we gave Greece or Turkey or Berlin or Italy. The Government of Greece took our aid and fought for freedom. But many of the generals of Nationalist China took our aid and surrendered it and themselves to the Communists.

We can investigate the situation in China from now until doomsday, but the facts will always remain the same: China was taken over by the Communists because of the failure of the Nationalist Government to mobilize the strength of China to maintain its freedom.

After all, our aid can be effective only when people help themselves. We are continuing to give aid to the Chinese Nationalists on Formosa, and that aid will be effective if they are now willing to do their part.

On June 25, 1950, one year ago today, the Communist rulers resorted to an outright war. They sent Communist armies on a mission of conquest against a small and peaceful country.

That act struck at the very life of the United Nations. It struck at all our hopes for peace.

There was only one thing to do in that situation—and we did it. If we had given in—if we had let the Republic of Korea go under—no nation in the world would have felt safe. The whole idea of a world organization for peace would have melted away. The spirit of resistance would have been broken and the free nations would have been open to conquest one by one.

We did not let that happen. We remembered Japan and Manchuria, Italy and Ethiopia, and Hitler and the Saar Basin. For the first time in history a world organization of nations took collective military action to halt aggression. And, acting together, we halted it.

A year ago today, Korea looked like an easy conquest to the Soviet rulers in Moscow

and their agents in the Far East. But they were wrong. Today, after more than a million Communist casualties—after the destruction of one Communist army after another—the forces of aggression have been thrown back on their heels. They are back behind the line where they started.

Things have not turned out the way the Communists expected.

The United Nations has not been shattered. Instead, it is stronger today than it was a year ago.

The free nations are not demoralized. Instead, they are stronger and more confident today than they were a year ago.

The cause of world peace has not been defeated. On the contrary, the cause of world peace is stronger than it was a year ago.

We have been fighting this conflict in Korea to prevent a third world war. So far we have succeeded. We have blocked aggression. And we have kept the conflict from spreading.

Men from the United States and from many other free countries have fought together in Korea. They have fought bravely, heroically, often against overwhelming odds. Many have given their lives.

No men ever did more for their country or for peace and freedom in the world than those men who have fought in Korea.

The attack on Korea has stimulated the free nations to build up their defenses in dead earnest. Korea convinced the free nations that they had to have armies and equipment ready to defend themselves.

The United States is leading the way, with defense expenditures of $40 billion. Other nations are devoting a large share of their national effort to our mutual defense.

Never before in history have we taken such measures to keep the peace. Never have the odds against an aggressor been made so clear before the attack was launched.

The Kaiser and Hitler, when they started

their great wars of aggression, believed that the United States would not come in. They counted on being able to divide the free nations and pick them off one at a time. There could be no excuse for making that mistake today.

We have the United Nations—which expresses the conscience and the collective will of the free world.

We have the Organization of American States—which is building the strength of this hemisphere.

We have the North Atlantic Treaty—which commits all the nations of the Atlantic community to fight together against aggression.

We have unified land, sea, and air forces in Europe, under the command of General Eisenhower.

We are strengthening the free nations of the Far East and setting up collective security arrangements in the Pacific.

We are building up our defenses and the defenses of other free nations, rapidly and effectively.

Most important of all, we have shown that we will fight to resist aggression. The free nations are fighting—and winning—in Korea.

Never before has an aggressor been confronted with such a series of positive measures to keep the peace. Never before in history have there been such deterrents to the outbreak of a world war.

Of course, we cannot promise that there will not be a world war. The Kremlin has it in its power to bring about such a war if it desires. It has a powerful military machine, and its rulers are absolute tyrants.

We cannot be sure what the Soviet rulers will do.

But we can put ourselves in a position to say to them: attack—and you will have the united resources of the free nations thrown against you; attack—and you will be con-

fronted by a war you cannot possibly win.

If we could have said that to the Kaiser or to Hitler or to Tojo the history of the world would have been very different.

It hasn't been easy to bring the free nations together into this united effort to resist aggression. It hasn't been easy to work out these alliances, and to build up our defenses, and to hold the line against great odds and discouragement in Korea. It hasn't been easy—but it is a record of tremendous progress in man's age-old struggle for peace and security.

We have made great progress, but we are not yet out of danger.

The Kremlin is still trying to divide the free nations. The thing that the Kremlin fears most is the unity of the free world.

The rulers of the Soviet Union have been trying to split up the nations of the North Atlantic Treaty. They have been trying to sow distrust between us and the other free countries. Their great objective is to strip us of our allies and to force us to "go it alone."

If they could do that, they could go ahead with their plan of taking over the world, nation by nation.

Unfortunately, it isn't only the Kremlin that has been trying to separate us from our allies. There are some people in this country, too, who have been trying to get us to "go it alone." There are people here who have been sowing distrust of our allies and magnifying our differences with them. Some of these people are sincere but misguided. Others are deliberately putting petty politics ahead of their country's safety.

Now, I have no objection to honest political debate. That's the way things get decided in this country.

But some of the people who are trying to get us to "go it alone" aren't engaging in honest political debate. They know they couldn't win that way. So they have launched a campaign to destroy the trust and confidence of the people in their Government.

They are trying to set the people against the Government by spreading fear and slander and outright lies. They have attacked the integrity of the Joint Chiefs of Staff. They have maliciously attacked General Bradley, who is one of the greatest soldiers this country ever produced. They have tried to besmirch the loyalty of General Marshall, who directed our strategy in winning the greatest war in history. They have deliberately tried to destroy Dean Acheson, one of the greatest Secretaries of State in the history of this country.

Now let me tell you something. All the members of the Cabinet have done most important things for this country in the defense effort, but Dean Acheson's job has been to bring entire nations to our side—to fight on our side if there is a showdown. And that is exactly what he has done. And he has been successful at it. He has done a lot more for this country than all his slanderers put together.

That political smear campaign is doing this country no good. It's playing right into the hands of the Russians. I have said that right along: it's playing right into the hands of the Russians.

Lies, slander, mudslinging are the weapons of the totalitarians. No man of morals or ethics will use them.

It's time that smear campaign was stopped.

As far as I am concerned, there ought to be no Democrats and no Republicans in the field of foreign policy. We are all Americans, all citizens of this same great Republic. We have had a bipartisan foreign policy in this country since before Pearl Harbor. I would like to keep it that way. I know a great many Republicans who want to keep it that way, too.

And I say to them—this is the time, now,

to show the real loyalty of the Republican Party to the great ideals on which this country is founded. Now is the time to put a stop to the sordid efforts to make political gains by stirring up fear and distrust about our foreign policy. Now is the time to say to the dividers and the confusers: No political party ever got anywhere in the long run by playing fast and loose with the security of the Nation in time of great peril.

Partisan efforts to label our foreign policy as "appeasement"—to tag it as a policy of "fear" or "timidity"—point to only one thing: They point to our "going it alone" down the road to world war III.

Is it a policy of fear to bring the free nations of the world together in a great unified movement to maintain peace? Is it a policy of timidity to come to the aid of the Greeks and the Turks and the other free peoples who are fighting back against the Communist threat? Is it a policy of appeasement to fight armed aggression and hurl it back in Korea?

Of course it is not. Anybody with any commonsense knows it is not.

And look at the alternatives these critics have to present. Here is what they say. Take a chance on spreading the conflict in Korea. Take a chance on tying up all our resources in a vast war in Asia. Take a chance on losing our allies in Europe. Take a chance the Soviet Union won't fight in the Far East. Take a chance we won't have a third world war.

They want us to play Russian roulette with the foreign policy of the United States— with all the chambers of the pistols loaded.

That's the kind of wisdom and thinking that has been coming out of the dividers and confusers in the last few months.

This is not a policy. This is not the way to defend this country and the cause of world peace in these dangerous times. No President who has any sense of responsibility for the welfare of this great country is going to meet the grave issues of war and peace on such a foolish basis as that.

I am glad that we have had the recent hearings in the Senate on our foreign policy. These hearings have been thorough and they have been conducted fairly. The way that committee has conducted them has been as a breath of fresh air in the United States Senate. They have done a great deal to explain to our people the situation the world is in, and the way we are meeting it. They have demonstrated, again, that we are on the right course.

But the important problem right now is not the past; it is the future. The world will not stand still while we examine the whole course of our foreign policy since 1941.

We are right in the middle of a great effort to build up our defenses and to check aggression. We can't go on with this effort unless the Congress enacts certain basic legislation.

Every group in the country has a vital part to play in our great effort for peace. The part of the Congress is to give the country the legislation we need to go forward. Without that, none of the rest of us can do our job.

We must have effective laws to curb inflation and to boost defense production.

We must have the appropriations needed to build up our defense forces.

We must have legislation to enable us to continue our policy of military and economic aid to our allies.

To make our Nation safe, we must have strong allies. We cannot have them unless we help the other free countries to defend themselves. Time is too short, and the danger too pressing to wait for these war-weakened countries to build up their own defenses without help from us. This aid is vital to our plans for defense, to our national security, to our hopes for peace.

Let me show you just how essential it is. We all know that our Air Force is very important. But did you ever stop to think how much its effectiveness depends on our allies?

The Air Force has to have bases overseas to be in the right place to give full protection to our own country, as well as to our allies. This is a clear example of how joining with other free nations for mutual defense helps us also.

Our allies cannot maintain and defend the necessary bases unless we give them aid. Giving aid to our allies is just as necessary as building airplanes if we are to have world peace.

Our military buildup, our development of weapons, our economic strength at home, our foreign aid programs, our efforts in the United Nations are all parts of a whole. They are all essential to our program for peace.

There is no one weapon—no single service—no particular military or diplomatic device—that can save us by itself. All our efforts are needed.

We now have a program that is using all these elements of our national policy for the great purpose of peace. We are improving it as we go along. And we are getting good results.

We must get on with the job.

We must build up our strength, but we must always keep the door open to the peaceful settlement of differences.

We are ready to join in a peaceful settlement in Korea now, just as we have always been. But it must be a real settlement which fully ends the aggression and restores peace and security to the area and to the gallant people of Korea.

In Korea and in the rest of the world we must be ready to take any steps which truly advance us toward world peace. But we must avoid like the plague rash actions which would take unnecessary risks of world war or weak actions which would reward aggression.

We must be firm and consistent and level-headed. If we get discouraged or impatient, we can lose everything we are working for. If we carry on with faith and courage, we can succeed.

And if we succeed, we will have marked one of the most important turning points in the history of man. We will have established a firm peace for the whole world to last for years to come.

That is a goal to challenge the best that is in us. Let us move toward it resolutely with faith in God and with confidence in ourselves.

NOTE: The President spoke at 12 noon. In his opening words he referred to Governor Gordon Browning of Tennessee; Maj. Gen. Franklin O. Carroll, Director, Research and Development, Air Material Command; Representative Joseph L. Evins and Senator Estes Kefauver, both of Tennessee; and Mrs. Arnold, widow of General of the Air Force Henry H. (Hap) Arnold, in whose honor the center was named.

The address was broadcast.

139 Remarks to Members of the Student Citizenship Seminar. *June 27,* 1951

IT IS a pleasure to have you. I understand you are in Washington studying the Government and its operation. I hope you will find out all about it. I have been trying to find out all about it for 60 years—and I still have a lot to learn.

It is an interesting thing, though, to have the young people of the country interested enough in the Government to come here and give it the once-over, trying to get the information that will be helpful in the next generation, when you have to take over the reins of the Government.

Find out how it is operated, and be in a position to operate it when the time comes for you to do it—and the time will come, and will come all too suddenly. It will be upon you before you know it.

But I am more than happy that you are interested in the Government of the United States. You also want to become interested in your local government, and city government, and county government, and State government. They all hook in together. They all have a bearing on your welfare and your future. You ought to know just as much about all of those branches of government as you possibly can learn.

I hope you have had a successful tour here, and that you will continue to have a good time. I won't keep you standing in this sun any longer.

NOTE: The President spoke at 12:55 p.m. in the Rose Garden at the White House. The Student Citizenship Seminar, held under the auspices of the YMCA and YWCA, was attended by more than 100 students from colleges and universities all over the country.

140 The President's News Conference of *June 28,* 1951

THE PRESIDENT. Please be seated.

[1.] I have an announcement to make, that Francis P. Matthews will be Ambas-sador to Ireland and Dan Kimball will be Secretary of the Navy.

[2.] And I have a very important statement that I would like for you to listen to very carefully. It will be available in mimeographed form as soon as the conference is over.

[*Reading, not literally*] "I am very much worried by the course of events in the Congress on extension of the Defense Production Act.

"The way things are going, there is a real possibility that the Congress won't get any bill passed in time to keep the whole act from expiring day after tomorrow. That would take off all the controls on prices and wages—and our production controls and credit controls and rent controls as well. Everything would go.

"This is a terribly dangerous possibility. I remember vividly what happened to prices when we had a gap in our control powers back in the summer of 1946. Food prices alone rose 14 percent in 1 month.

"But there is another possibility just as dangerous—that the Congress will act before the deadline Saturday by passing a bill so crippled and confused with special interest amendments that it would be worse than useless in the fight against inflation.[1]

"If either of these things happen, the consumers in this country will take a beating, and our whole defense effort—our whole stake in the free world's security—would be placed in serious jeopardy.

"I hope—I earnestly hope that neither of these things will come to pass. I hope the Congress will either send me a good law by Saturday, or at least extend the present law past the June 30 deadline, until they can get a good new law in shape.

"One way or the other, it is absolutely vital that we have no break in our anti-inflation program. We must keep our program going. We simply have to do this. We must get the right kind of authority from Congress to do the job.

[1] See Item 176.

"I hope we are going to get it."

You will have that available as soon as the conference is over.

Now, if you want to ask me any questions, I will try to answer them.

Q. Mr. President, do you consider the bill in its present shape in the Senate a good bill?

THE PRESIDENT. No. Period. [*Laughter*]

Q. Mr. President, do you feel that the Senate has surrendered to these selfish interests——

THE PRESIDENT. Well now, you'll have to draw your own conclusions. I make no comments on Senators or Members of the House.

[3.] Q. Mr. President, can you shed any light for us on the status of the suggestion by Soviet Russia that the Korean conflict reach a truce stage?[2]

THE PRESIDENT. I think you will find that the statement made by the State Department this morning covers that question. They submitted it and I approved it.[3]

[2] On June 23 Jacob A. Malik, Soviet delegate to the United Nations, made a radio broadcast as part of the United Nations series "Price of Peace." At the conclusion of his talk, Mr. Malik said:

"The Soviet peoples further believe that the most acute problem of the present day—the problem of armed conflict in Korea—could also be settled.

"This would require the readiness of the parties to enter on the path of a peaceful settlement of the Korean question. The Soviet peoples believe that as a first step discussions should be started between the belligerents for a cease-fire and an armistice providing for the mutual withdrawal of forces from the 38th parallel.

"Can such a step be taken? I think it can, provided there is a sincere desire to put an end to the bloody fighting in Korea." (Department of State Bulletin, vol. 25, p. 45.)

[3] The statement, released by the State Department on June 28, follows:

"The United States has sought in New York and in Moscow a clarification on certain aspects of the statement made by Jacob A. Malik, the Soviet representative at the United Nations, on June 23.

"Deputy Foreign Minister Gromyko received the United States Ambassador in Moscow on June 27. In discussing Mr. Malik's statement, Mr. Gromyko

Q. Mr. President, do you think that the Russian overtures are a sign that the stand taken by your administration in the Mac-Arthur controversy was justified?

THE PRESIDENT. Yes.

Q. Didn't hear that, Mr. President.

THE PRESIDENT. Yes.

Q. I didn't hear the question.

THE PRESIDENT. He wanted to know if I thought that the stand taken in the Mac-Arthur controversy by the administration was the right one, and I said yes. I thought so when I took it, and I think so now.

Q. Mr. President, if I may raise this question, I didn't understand it that way. I thought the question was: do you think that the Russian overtures are a sign that the stand taken by the administration is the right one?

THE PRESIDENT. Yes to that, too. I don't see any difference in the meaning.

[4.] Q. Mr. President, the letter released a little bit ago from the Premier of Iran,

asking for your support of the Iranian Government—do you support the Iranian Government——

THE PRESIDENT. I have the matter under consideration. I appreciate very much the Iranian Premier writing me as he did. The matter is under consideration. I can make no comment on the—as to action, at this time. I hope the matter will be settled. It is a serious situation, and there is plenty of opportunity for its settlement.[4]

[5.] Q. Mr. President, on this Soviet peace gesture by Malik the other day, do you think that the clarifications which Admiral Kirk[5] received from Gromyko yesterday are sufficient so that we can now go ahead a bit and explore the matter some more?

THE PRESIDENT. I hope so.

[6.] Q. Mr. President, on this Iranian crisis, if you were asked to mediate—or if you have been asked to mediate—will the United States agree to mediate?

THE PRESIDENT. We have not been asked to mediate, and I can't make an answer to something that has not been done. That is a hypothetical question.

[7.] Q. Mr. President, when does the change in the Navy Department take effect?

THE PRESIDENT. As soon as it can be worked out. I imagine it will be 30 days or so before. It won't take effect today.

[8.] Q. Mr. President, how is that investigation of the China lobby coming along?

THE PRESIDENT. I can't answer the ques-

---

indicated that it would be for the military representatives of the Unified Command and of the Korean Republic Command, on the one hand, and the military representatives of the North Korean Command and of the Chinese volunteer units, on the other, to negotiate the armistice envisaged in Mr. Malik's statement. The armistice, Mr. Gromyko pointed out, would include a cease-fire and would be limited to strictly military questions without involving any political or territorial matters; the military representatives would discuss questions of assurances against the resumption of hostilities.

"Beyond the conclusion of an armistice, the Soviet Government had no specific steps in mind looking toward the peaceful settlement to which Mr. Malik referred. Mr. Gromyko indicated, however, that it would be up to the parties in Korea to decide what subsequent special arrangements would have to be made for a political and territorial settlement. He said that the Soviet Government was not aware of the views of the Chinese Communist regime on Mr. Malik's statement.

"The implications of Mr. Gromyko's observations are being studied. The Department of State is consulting with the representatives of other countries having armed forces in Korea under the Unified Command." (Department of State Bulletin, vol. 25, p. 45.)

---

[4] On June 28 the White House made public a letter to the President from Prime Minister Mohammed Mosadeq of Iran. The letter stated in part, "The Imperial Iranian Government has been duty-bound to put into force the law enacted by the two Houses of Parliament concerning the nationalization of the oil industry all over Iran and the modus operandi of that law in the quickest possible time." The Iranian Government nationalized the oil industry on June 21.

[5] Adm. Alan G. Kirk, U.S. Ambassador to the Soviet Union.

tion. The Congress is doing the investigating, not I.

Q. Mr. President, on that, you asked the executive departments to make available to the Congress——

THE PRESIDENT. That's right. All the information that we had.

Q. Have you had any report on that?

THE PRESIDENT. I have not.

[9.] Q. Mr. President, is Paul Fitzpatrick [6] under consideration for an ambassador?

THE PRESIDENT. Not that I know of.

Q. There have been reports in the New York State press to that effect.

THE PRESIDENT. Well, Paul Fitzpatrick is a fine gentleman, but he has never talked to me about being an ambassador anywhere.

Q. What was the question, Mr. President?

THE PRESIDENT. He wanted to know if I had Paul Fitzpatrick under consideration for an ambassadorship.

[10.] Q. Mr. President, do you plan to do anything about the United Airlines [7]——

THE PRESIDENT. The matter is being worked on every day. I can make no comment on the condition of things now. I sincerely hope it will be settled.

[11.] Q. Mr. President, what is the next step to be taken in furthering a possible truce in Korea?

THE PRESIDENT. Well now, I can't make a public answer to a question like that. We are working on it all the time. You can't transact business of that kind in public.

Q. Well, can you say, sir, whether this Government is making any further approach towards settlement of the——

THE PRESIDENT. This Government has been trying to get the matter settled ever

since it started on June 25, 1950, and it is still trying to get it settled.

[12.] Q. Mr. President, the American Bar Association and the New York City Bar Association have opposed the confirmation of Frieda Hennock [8]——

THE PRESIDENT. That isn't—as I have said, that isn't unusual. I have had plenty of good judges opposed by the Bar Association. It doesn't mean a thing in my young life. [*Laughter*]

Q. You don't plan to withdraw the nomination?

THE PRESIDENT. Not at all. I am always glad to have the Bar Association endorse them if they want to give it, but I never appoint a man because he has been endorsed by the Bar Association.

[13.] Q. Mr. President, do you now feel that—as a result of the week's developments—that the Malik peace suggestion was seriously——

THE PRESIDENT. I think the State Department release this morning covers that. I have no further comment to make on it.

Q. Mr. President——

Q. ——Mr. President, if I—excuse me——

THE PRESIDENT. What? [*Laughter*]

Q. It won't take a second——

[14.] THE PRESIDENT. Go ahead, Eddie.[9]

Q. I will yield to you in a minute there. [*More laughter*]

Mr. President, if there should be a truce in Korea as many expect, and there should be suggestions that we slow down in our arms expansion program here and abroad, what would be your reaction?

THE PRESIDENT. That would be one of the

---

[6] Chairman, New York Democratic State Committee.

[7] On June 20, 900 pilots and copilots employed by United Airlines went on strike.

Frieda B. Hennock, member of the Federal Communications Commission, had been nominated to be United States District Judge, Southern District of New York. Her nomination was not confirmed by the Senate and she remained in her post on the Commission until July 1, 1955. See also Item 283.

[9] Edward T. Folliard of the Washington Post.

most disastrous things that could happen to the country.

What did you want to ask me, Smitty? [10]

Q. I have to write this answer down first. [*Laughter*]

THE PRESIDENT. All right. There should be no slowdown.

[15.] Q. Mr. President, getting down to local politics, is there a possibility that you may make a tour through the Southern States before the convention?

THE PRESIDENT. Well, I have made one trip down there. I don't know whether I will be invited to come again or not. I am always open for invitations.

[16.] Q. Mr. President, aside from the State Department's statement, how do you feel about prospects for peace in Korea, as a result of the developments of the past week?

THE PRESIDENT. Well, I haven't yet made up my mind on it, Smitty, because the thing has not been worked to a conclusion. I hope it will work out. Everybody wants peace, and so do I.

[17.] Q. Mr. President, Governor Stevenson, a few days ago, invited you to the Illinois State Fair——

THE PRESIDENT. That's right.

Q. Are you going?

THE PRESIDENT. I can't tell you. I gave him the same answer. I didn't—too far in advance for me to tell whether I can go or not. Of course I would like to go to the Illinois State Fair—and the Missouri State Fair, and the Texas State Fair, and two or three others—but I can't go to all of them.

[18.] Q. Mr. President, in connection again with the Malik speech the other day, there have already been suggestions up on the Hill that any settlement near the 38th parallel would amount to appeasement.

Would you care to comment on that?

THE PRESIDENT. No, I can't comment on that at this time.

[19.] Q. Mr. President, may I ask for enlargement of your comment on the Iranian move? You said, I believe, there will be plenty of opportunity for settlement——

THE PRESIDENT. I said there *is* plenty of opportunity for settlement. I didn't say there *will* be.

Q. What structures did you have in mind, sir? The World Court—the United Nations——

THE PRESIDENT. The company and the Government of Iran should get together—and the Government of Great Britain—and make an equitable settlement.

Q. Bilateral action?

THE PRESIDENT. It would be—the company and the two governments. And I hope they will do that. But I can't get into the thing. It is not in my territory. It is not in my sector. [*Laughter*]

Q. Mr. President, that doesn't mean that you are not using the—that you would not use every effort possible to bring about——

THE PRESIDENT. Of course we have been doing that right along. We have been using every effort possible to bring about a settlement, and we will continue to do just that.[11]

Q. You are speaking of Iran, not Korea?

THE PRESIDENT. Well, I am speaking of Iran. It will apply to either one.

You aren't hot, are you, Tony? [12] [*Laughter*]

Reporter: Thank you, Mr. President.

THE PRESIDENT. It's all right, Smitty.

NOTE: President Truman's two hundred and sixty-eighth news conference was held in the Indian Treaty Room (Room 474) in the Executive Office Building at 4 p.m. on Thursday, June 28, 1951.

---

[10] Merriman Smith of the United Press Associations.

[11] See Items 140 [4], 150, 155.

[12] Ernest B. Vaccaro of the Associated Press.

141   Statement by the President on Transferring the Trust Territory
of the Pacific Islands and American Samoa to Civilian
Administration. *June 29, 1951*

I HAVE today signed Executive orders transferring administrative responsibility for the Trust Territory of the Pacific Islands and for American Samoa from the Secretary of the Navy to the Secretary of the Interior, effective July 1, 1951.

The establishment of civilian administration in these island areas is a historic event. It conforms with a long-established American tradition of conducting the affairs of civil populations under civilian authority. It is one further step in the extension of additional civil rights to the island Territories under our jurisdiction. A similar transfer of responsibility from the Secretary of the Navy to the Secretary of the Interior was carried out on Guam on August 1, 1950, simultaneously with the enactment of organic legislation for that Territory.

For 50 years American Samoa has been served well and faithfully by the United States Navy, which, as the administering authority, had as its primary concern the well-being of the Samoan people. Since the end of the Second World War, the United States Navy has exercised similar functions in the Trust Territory of the Pacific Islands. The concern of the Department of the Navy for the well-being of the peoples of these areas was an expression of the interest of the people and Government of the United States in the people and culture of these Pacific islands. That interest will continue and will grow under civilian administration. The experience of the Department of the Interior in promoting the political, economic, and social advancement of our Territories will serve as assurance to the people of the United States and of the islands concerned that sound policies looking toward their welfare will be carried forward without interruption in American Samoa and in the Trust Territory of the Pacific Islands.

It is a matter of particular satisfaction to me that this transfer of responsibility has been worked out in a planned, orderly manner, in which the Department of the Navy and the Department of the Interior have collaborated through administrative agreements. These agreements, embodied in memorandums which were approved by the President, will assure the people of the islands concerned of the continuation of their essential services, and will assure the people of the United States of the greatest possible economy and most efficient administration.

NOTE: The President referred to Executive Orders 10264 and 10265 (3 CFR, 1949–1953 Comp., pp. 765, 766).

142   Letter to the Chairman, Council of Economic Advisers, in
Response to Report "The New England Economy."
July 2, 1951

Dear Mr. Keyserling:

Thank you for transmitting to me the report on the New England economy submitted to the Council of Economic Advisers.

Studies of regional economic problems can be a valuable aid in development of national economic policies and I hope that this study of New England's long-run problems will contribute to future planning for the economic growth and progress of the nation.

Very sincerely yours,

HARRY S. TRUMAN

[Honorable Leon H. Keyserling, Chairman, Council of Economic Advisers, Washington 25, D.C.]

NOTE: The 205-page report, entitled "The New England Economy," was printed by the Government Printing Office.

143   Letter to the President of the Senate on the Continued Need for Effective Price, Wage, and Production Controls.
July 4, 1951

[Released July 4, 1951.   Dated July 3, 1951]

My dear Mr. Vice President:

I am forwarding to you for your information copies of the second Quarterly Report to the President by the Director of Defense Mobilization. This report is being distributed to the press today for release to the morning papers of Thursday, July 5, 1951.

This report is a stimulating document. Mr. Wilson has reported our progress to date on our mobilization program. He has underscored the successes that have been achieved, but he has not overlooked the delays and difficulties which have beset some parts of the program.

Above all, his report makes it crystal clear that in these last three months we have still been in the early stages of our defense effort—still tooling up, still getting organized. The heaviest burdens, the hardest part of the job lie ahead. The full impact of our program will begin to be felt in the next year. The efforts we have made so far will only begin to pay off in big-scale military production and expanded productive capacity during the coming year. The great production job that lies ahead of us will remain to be done whether or not we are able to stop the fighting in Korea.

Everything that Mr. Wilson says in this report emphasizes the tremendous importance of obtaining good, strong control legislation to see us through this crucial period, while we are building our defensive strength. We need strong production con-

trols, price and wage controls, credit controls and rent controls—we need them all and we must be prepared to use them all, if we are to keep our economy on an even keel, protect our living standards, and meet the defense goals which this report describes.

The Congress has now extended until July 31 the Defense Production Act and our present rent control law. Both these laws would otherwise have expired June 30, with nothing on the statute books to keep our program going. The Senate has passed a new bill, to take the place of these present laws and the House of Representatives is scheduled to debate this new measure shortly. It is a matter of great urgency that the Congress complete action on this new bill well before July 31. And it is absolutely vital that the new bill be a strong one, which will give this Government the powers it must have to do the job Mr. Wilson has outlined in his report.

It is my earnest hope that in the days ahead, the Congress will review with care the consequences of enacting a weak measure and will come forward with the strong legislation we need so badly. Otherwise, the consumers in this country may be plundered by renewed inflation and our whole mobilization program threatened with disaster.

Very sincerely yours,

HARRY S. TRUMAN

[Honorable Alben W. Barkley, Vice President of the United States, Washington, D.C.]

NOTE: The White House release states that "a similar letter" was sent to the Honorable Sam Rayburn, Speaker of the House of Representatives.

The second quarterly report to the President by the Director of Defense Mobilization, entitled "Meet-ing Defense Goals: A Must for Everyone," was published by the Government Printing Office (1951, 48 pp.).

See also Items 176 and 199.

144 Address at the Ceremonies Commemorating the 175th Anniversary of the Declaration of Independence. *July 4, 1951*

[Broadcast from the Washington Monument grounds at 9:30 p.m.]

Mr. Chairman, distinguished guests, ladies and gentlemen:

This is a very special occasion. Here in Washington tonight, up in Philadelphia, and throughout our whole country, we are celebrating an anniversary of great importance. On this day 175 years ago the representatives of the American people declared the independence of the United States.

Our forefathers in Philadelphia not only established a new nation—they established a nation based on a new idea. They said that all men were created equal. They based the whole idea of government on this God-given equality of men. They said that the people had the right to govern themselves. They said the purpose of government was to protect the unalienable rights of man to life, liberty, and the pursuit of happiness.

These were sensational proposals. In 1776 a nation based on such new and radical ideas did not appear to have much chance of success. In those days power centered in Europe. Monarchy was the prevailing form of government. The divine right of kings was still widely accepted.

The new Nation was small, remote, poor, and, in 1776, apparently friendless. Europe did not for a moment believe this new kind of government would work, and, to tell the truth, fully a third of our own people did not believe it would work, either.

We can hardly imagine the courage and the faith it took to issue the Declaration of Independence in those circumstances.

Today we can see that the members of the Continental Congress were right. Less than two centuries later the nation born that day, instead of being small, stretches across a whole continent. Instead of being poor, the United States is wealthier than any other nation in the world. Instead of being friendless, we have strong and steadfast allies.

The transformation during these 175 years seems to be complete; but it is not. Some things have not changed at all since 1776.

For one thing, freedom is still expensive. It still costs money. It still costs blood. It still calls for courage and endurance, not only in soldiers, but in every man and woman who is free and who is determined to remain free. Freedom must be fought for today, just as our fathers had to fight for freedom when the Nation was born.

For another thing, the ideas on which our Government is founded—the ideas of equality, of God-given rights, of self-government—are still revolutionary. Since 1776 they have spread around the world. In France in 1789, in Latin America in the early 1800's, in many parts of Europe in the mid-19th century, these ideas produced new governments and new nations. Now in the 20th century, these ideas have stirred the peoples in many countries of the Middle East and Asia to create free governments, dedicated to the welfare of the people. The ideas of the American Revolution are still on the march.

There is another way in which our situation today is much like that of the Americans in 1776. Now, once more, we are engaged in launching a new idea—one that has been talked about for centuries, but never successfully put into effect. In those earlier days we were launching a new kind of national government. This time we are creating a new kind of international organization. We have joined in setting up the United Nations to prevent war and to safeguard peace and freedom.

We believe in the United Nations. We believe it is based on the right ideas, as our own country is. We believe it can grow to be strong, and accomplish its high purposes.

But the United Nations faces stern, determined opposition. This is an old story. The Declaration of Independence was also met by determined opposition. A spokesman for the British King called the Declaration "absurd," "visionary," and "subversive." The ideas of freedom and equality and self-government were first fiercely opposed in every country by the vested interests and the reactionaries. Today, the idea of an international organization to keep the peace is being attacked and undermined and fought by reactionary forces everywhere—and particularly by the forces of Soviet communism.

The United Nations will not succeed without a struggle, just as the Declaration of Independence did not succeed without a struggle. But the American people are not afraid. We have taken our stand beside other free men, because we have known for 175 years that free men must stand together. We have joined in the defense of freedom without hesitation and without fear, because we have known for 175 years that freedom must be defended.

This determined stand has cost us much

in the past year. I do not intend to dwell upon the money cost on the Fourth of July, the day on which we dedicated "our fortunes" as well as "our lives and our sacred honor" to the cause of freedom. I am much more deeply concerned that our stand has cost the lives of brave men. I report it with sorrow, but with boundless pride in what they have done—for the men who have fallen in the service of the United States during the past year have died for the same cause as those who fell at Bunker Hill and Gettysburg, in the Argonne forest and on the Normandy beaches. They died in order that "government of the people, by the people, for the people, shall not perish from the earth." They have died in order that other men might have peace.

On this day, sacred to those who established freedom in the United States, we should all pay tribute to the men who are fighting now to preserve our freedom. The troops under the command of General Ridgway, including not only our own but those of 16 other free nations, constitute, I believe, the most magnificent army on the face of the globe today. We are all familiar with the splendor of their heroic deeds.

I should like to say something to that army, something that I think is felt by free men in every country in the world: Men of the armed forces in Korea, you will go down in history as the first army to fight under the flag of a world organization in the defense of human freedom. You have fought well, and without reproach. You have enslaved no free man, you have destroyed no free nation, you are guiltless of any country's blood. Victory may be in your hands, but you are winning a greater thing than military victory, for you are vindicating the idea of freedom under international law. This is an achievement that serves all mankind, for it has brought all men closer to their goal of peace. It is an achievement that may well prove to be a turning point in world history.

Our aims in Korea are just as clear and just as simple as the things for which we fought in the American Revolution. We did not fight that war to drive the British out of the North American Continent. We did not fight it to destroy the military power of England, or to wipe out the British Empire. We fought it for the simple, limited aim of securing the right to be free, the right to govern ourselves. We fought it to secure respect for the principles of the Declaration of Independence.

It is much the same with Korea. We are not fighting there to conquer China, or to destroy the Soviet Empire. We are fighting for a simple aim—as important to us today as the goal of independence was in 1776— the aim of securing the right of nations to be free and to live in peace.

The Charter of the United Nations says that its purpose is to "maintain international peace and security" and "to take effective collective measures . . . for the suppression of acts of aggression."

We are fighting to uphold this purpose of the United Nations. That is what we have been doing in Korea.

We have made it clear that those words mean what they say. We have taken collective measures to suppress aggression, and we are suppressing it.

We have shown the world that the United Nations Charter is not just a scrap of paper— but something very real, and very powerful. To establish this is worth all the sacrifices and all the effort we have been making, because this is the way to peace.

Our constant aim in Korea has been peace, under the principles of the United Nations. Time and again, since the aggression started, we have proposed that the fighting be stopped, and that peace be restored in accordance with those principles.

Now, at last, the Communist leaders have offered to confer about an armistice. It may be that they have decided to give up their aggression in Korea. If that is true, the road to a peaceful settlement of the Korean conflict is open.

But we cannot yet be sure that the Communist rulers have any such intention. It is still too early to say what they have in mind. I do not wish to speculate on the outcome of any meetings General Ridgway may have with the commanders on the other side. I hope these meetings will be successful. If they are not, it will be because the Communists do not really want peace. Meanwhile, let us keep our heads, and be vigilant and ready for whatever may come.

We must remember that Korea is only part of a wider conflict. The attack on freedom is worldwide. And it is not simply an attack by fire and sword. It is an attack that uses all the weapons that a dictatorship can command: subversion, threats, violence, torture, imprisonment, lies, and deceit.

We cannot ignore the danger of military outbreaks in other parts of the world. The greatest threat to world peace, the tremendous armed power of the Soviet Union, will still remain, even if the Korean fighting stops. The threat of Soviet aggression still hangs heavy over many a country—including our own. We must continue, therefore, to build up our military forces at a rapid rate. And we must continue to help build up the defenses of other free nations.

And we must continue the struggle to overcome the constant efforts of the Soviet rulers to dominate the world by lies and threats and subversion.

The Soviet rulers are trying to destroy the very idea of freedom, in every part of the world. They are trying to take from us the confidence and friendship of other nations. They hate us not because we are Americans, but because we are free—because we are the greatest example of the power of freedom.

The Soviet rulers are engaged in a relentless effort, therefore, to persuade other nations that we do not, in fact, stand for freedom. They are trying to convince the people of Europe that we intend to exploit them. They are telling the people of Asia—who are for the most part ill informed about our purposes—that we mean to fasten new chains upon them. They are trying to make the rest of the world believe that we want to control them for our own profit—that the ideas of our Declaration of Independence are a sham and a fraud.

This shrewd, this unscrupulous, this evil propaganda attack—we cannot overcome with military weapons. You cannot transfix a lie with a bayonet, or blast deceit with machinegun fire. The only weapons against such enemies are truth and fair dealing.

The way to meet this attack is to show that it is false—to live up to our ideals—to prove that we mean them.

The world looks to us. This country is the living proof that personal liberty is consistent with strong and stable government. This country proves that men can be free.

As a result, the freedom of the American citizen means a great deal more than his individual safety and happiness. It means that men everywhere can have the freedom they hope for.

Anyone who undertakes to abridge the right of any American to life, liberty, or the pursuit of happiness commits three great wrongs. He wrongs the individual first, but in addition, he wrongs his country and he betrays the hopes of mankind.

It is for this reason that persecution of minorities, which is wrong anywhere, is worse in America. It is for this reason that vilifying men because they express unpopular opinions is less to be tolerated here than in any other country. It is for this reason that holding men in bondage—personal, political, or economic—is a graver scandal here than elsewhere. It is for this reason that "to promote the general welfare" is more urgently required of the American Government than any other.

We have made great strides in broadening freedom here at home. We have made real progress in eliminating oppression and injustice and in creating security and opportunities for all. I am proud of our record in doing these things.

Today, more than ever before, it is important that we continue to make progress in expanding our freedoms and improving the opportunities of our citizens. To do so is to strengthen the hopes and determination of free men everywhere.

Moreover, it is doubly important today that we set an example of sober and wise and consistent self-government. We face a long period of world tension, and great international danger. We have the hard task of increasing production and controlling inflation in order to support the strong Armed Forces we must have for years to come.

One of our most difficult tasks, because it is new to our people, is that of organizing civil defense. Because we have been spared the rough schooling which the people of Europe have had, too many Americans are still skeptical and tardy.

All these tasks challenge the ability of free people to govern themselves with both reason and resolution. There are people who say our democratic form of government cannot do these things. They say we cannot stick to a hard, tough policy of self-denial and self-control long enough to win the struggle. They say we are no match for the steady, ruthless way the Soviet rulers seek their goals.

These people, and they are not all Communists by any means, say that we can't take it, over the long pull. They say we will either lose our heads and rush into a world war, or that we will relax and give up our efforts to maintain peace. They say that the demagogues and the special interests will tear us apart from within. These people do not believe that free men and self-government can survive in the struggle against Communist dictatorship.

I think these prophets of doom are wrong. I think the whole history of our country proves they are wrong. I believe the last few months show that we will not be stampeded into war, or broken up by distrust and fear.

But we are going through a period that will test to the utmost our self-control, our patriotism, and our faith in our institutions. The very idea of self-government is being put to the test in the world today as it has never been tested before.

If we do not succeed in this country— if we do not succeed in building up our Armed Forces, in controlling inflation, and in strengthening our friends and allies—then the cause of self-government, the cause of human freedom, is lost. If we with all that we have in our favor do not succeed, no other free government can survive—anywhere in the world—and the whole great experiment that began in 1776 will be over and done with.

I believe we will succeed.

The principles of the Declaration of Independence are the right principles. They are sound enough to guide us through this crisis as they have guided us through other crises of the past. Freedom can overcome tyranny in the 20th century as surely as it overcame the tyrants of the 18th century.

There is a text inscribed on the Liberty Bell, the bell that rang out a hundred and seventy-five years ago to announce the signing of the Declaration of Independence. When the Pennsylvania Provincial Assembly ordered that bell for the statehouse in Philadelphia, they directed that it should bear certain words, "well-shaped in large letters." You remember what those words were: "Proclaim Liberty throughout all the land unto all the inhabitants thereof."

We should write these words again today. We should write them in everything we do in this country—"well-shaped in large letters"—by every deed and act, so that the whole world can read them. We have written them in the deeds of our soldiers in Korea—for the men of Asia and all the world to see. Let us write them in all that we do, at home and abroad, to the end that men everywhere may read them and take hope and courage for the victory of freedom.

145 The President's News Conference of July 5, 1951

THE PRESIDENT. Please be seated.

[1.] I understand that we have with us this morning some visiting editors from some of the NATO countries—France, the Netherlands, Belgium, Denmark, Great Britain, Norway, and Luxembourg. We are glad to have them with us, and I will be glad to meet them after the press conference is finished.

I have nothing further to tell you, unless you want to ask some questions. [*Pause*] [*Laughter*]

Shall we adjourn the conference? [*More laughter*]

[2.] Q. Mr. President, the House begins consideration of the economic control bill today. Have you any fresh word to say about it—your hopes——

THE PRESIDENT. Yes, I have. I sincerely hope they will give us a workable controls bill along the lines of the message which I sent them on the subject.[1]

[3.]   Q. Mr. President, Princess Elizabeth, the heir to the British throne, and her husband the Duke of Edinburgh are going to visit Canada in the next few months. There is some speculation in this country whether they will have an invitation to come here. Would you say anything about it?

THE PRESIDENT. I have no knowledge of their plans. Of course, they would be welcome to come here, but I will have to find out what their plans are, before we can take formal notice of the fact.

[4.]   Q. Mr. President, do you intend to send another message to Congress on the controls bill?

THE PRESIDENT. No, I do not. I have talked enough about it. I made some remarks about it last night, if you remember. I have written letters and done everything I can possibly do. I am going to keep on putting forth an effort to get a controls bill that will work.

[5.]   Q. Mr. President, some weeks ago we had the pleasure of having Miss Truman with us. Did she make any statement to you about her impressions of our country?

THE PRESIDENT. I didn't understand—I am sorry—I can't hear from back there.

Mr. Short [2]: I wonder if you could come to one of the microphones there?

THE PRESIDENT. Come to the microphone.

Q. Mr. President, I am coming from Luxembourg. Some weeks ago we had the pleasure to have Miss Truman with us. Didn't she make any statement to you about the impressions of our country?

THE PRESIDENT. Oh, yes. She had a most cordial reception, and enjoyed the visit immensely. They were just as kind to her as they could be.

[6.]   Q. Mr. President, there still seem to be lacking three Federal judges in the Northern District of Illinois——

THE PRESIDENT. They won't lack for long. [*Laughter*] You will know about them pretty soon.

What was your question?

[7.]   Q. Mr. President, do you have any comment to make on the conviction of that AP reporter in Czechoslovakia—Oatis?

THE PRESIDENT. The State Department issued a statement on the subject, which was submitted to me for approval, and I am in agreement with that statement.[3]

[8.]   Q. Mr. President, do you feel now that you have compromised—[*inaudible*]— with Governor Turner of Oklahoma—[*inaudible*]—that came up here to save your control program?

Voices: Can't hear—can't hear.

THE PRESIDENT. Ask that question again— I think, if I understood you, you wanted to know if I had compromised with the beef people. I never had any idea——

Q. Not a compromise——

THE PRESIDENT. ——I never had any idea of compromising with them. I merely wanted to hear their side of the story. I wanted to get it down where they would have a fair hearing. I didn't enter into the thing only to see that they got a fair hearing. I approved the beef rollback, if you remember—which doesn't make me very popular with the cattlemen.

[9.]   Q. Mr. President, may I put in

---

[3] William N. Oatis, Associated Press representative in Prague, was arrested on April 23, 1951. On July 4 he was found guilty of espionage and sentenced to 10 years' imprisonment, with 5 years off for good behavior. The Department of State release of July 4 called his trial a "ludicrous travesty of justice in which the victim was required to speak his prefabricated 'confession' as a part of a public spectacle exhibiting all the usual Communist trial techniques" (see Department of State Bulletin, vol. 25, p. 92). In 1953 Mr. Oatis was pardoned by the Czechoslovakian Government.

---

[1] Item 91.
[2] Joseph H. Short, Secretary to the President.

and ask about a plug for Philadelphia? The Fourth of July, yesterday—I mean, a newspaper which shall be nameless— [*laughter*]—yesterday had a project which I—under the theme "United We Stand," in which we had a flag flown in by each—I mean, a star from each State, with a message from each Governor, and a bar from each of the Original Thirteen Colonies, and then a—the flag was raised by a halyard, made up from strands of the Army, Navy, and Air Force—this is a pretty long question—I wonder if you—[*laughter interrupting*]——

THE PRESIDENT. Go ahead.

Q. ——I wonder if you think it is a pretty good idea? [*More laughter*]

THE PRESIDENT. Yes. If you will remember, when the matter was under discussion back some months ago, I requested the Chief Justice of the United States to act as chairman for the celebration of the 175th anniversary of the signing of the Declaration of Independence, which was yesterday. Then a commission was appointed, which consisted of the leaders on both sides of the House—in the House and in the Senate; and the result of that Commission's work, and the work of the Chief Justice, was the show put on at Philadelphia—which was a good one, the one that was put on here, and nearly every community in the United States— similar celebrations took place.[4] I am very much pleased with the results.

Q. Mr. President, Merriman Smith is not going to like this, even in absentia— [*laughter*]—but when the time comes, we think we would like to have Harold Oliver of the AP say "Thank you, Mr. President." I don't think the time has arrived yet.

THE PRESIDENT. That is up to you—I will answer questions as long as I can.

Harold Oliver: Mr. President, at the risk of usurping authority, I will say "Thank you, sir". [*Laughter*]

THE PRESIDENT. I guess that will do it.

NOTE: President Truman's two hundred and sixty-ninth news conference was held in the Indian Treaty Room (Room 474) in the Executive Office Building at 10:30 a.m. on Thursday, July 5, 1951.

[4] On July 3 the White House made public the report to the President by the Commission for the Commemoration of the 175th Anniversary of the Signing of the Declaration of Independence. The report stated, in part, that the program for the anniversary had as its principal aim the rededication by all Americans to the great basic principles of the Declaration. It noted that in response to the Commission's plea for national observance of these principles, more than 10,000 communities, including 73 metropolitan cities, had arranged special programs of rededication to be held on the Fourth of July.

146 Remarks Upon Presenting Congressional Medals of Honor to Capt. Raymond Harvey, Capt. Lewis L. Millett, M. Sgt. Stanley T. Adams, and Corp. Einar H. Ingman, USA.
July 5, 1951

IT IS a privilege to perform this ceremony. Due to conditions over which I have had no control, it has been my duty to award more Medals of Honor than all the rest of the Presidents put together.

It is a proud moment when we can hear citations read such as these you have just listened to. It is also a proud moment for me to hang the medals around the necks of these young men.

They are the backbone of the Government of the United States. Always, when the emergency calls for it, they come forward and deliver what is necessary to win.

That is the reason we will win the cold war. That is the reason we will maintain the peace in the world. That is the reason this Republic of ours will continue to endure—because we have innumerable young men just like these four, who stand out for the welfare of this country, always.

I have told them many a time that I would much rather have that Congressional Medal of Honor than to be President of the United States. I don't think very many of

them believe me, but it is true.

I congratulate you young men again on a great job well done.

NOTE: The President spoke at 12:15 p.m. in the Rose Garden at the White House. The citations, describing the actions in Korea for which the medals were awarded, are printed in the Congressional Record (vol. 97, p. 7696).

147 Message to the President of the Presidium of the Supreme Soviet, U.S.S.R., Transmitting a Resolution Expressing American Friendship. *July 7,* 1951

I HAVE the honor of transmitting to you a resolution adopted by the Congress of the United States with a request that its contents be made known by your government to the people of the Soviet Union.

This resolution expresses the friendship and goodwill of the American people for all the peoples of the earth and it also re-emphasizes the profound desire of the American Government to do everything in its power to bring about a just and lasting peace.

As Chief Executive of the United States, I give this resolution my sincere approval. I add to it a message of my own to the Soviet people in the earnest hope that these expressions may help form a better understanding of the aims and purposes of the United States.

The unhappy results of the last few years demonstrate that formal diplomatic negotiations among nations will be largely barren while barriers exist to the friendly exchange of ideas and information among peoples. The best hope for a peaceful world lies in the yearning for peace and brotherhood which lies deep in the heart of every human being. But peoples who are denied the normal means of communication will not be able to attain that mutual understanding which must form the basis for trust and friendship. We shall never be able to re-

move suspicion and fear as potential causes of war until communication is permitted to flow, free and open, across international boundaries.

The peoples of both our countries know from personal experience the horror and misery of war. They abhor the thought of future conflict which they know would be waged by means of the most hideous weapons in the history of mankind. As leaders of their respective governments, it is our sacred duty to pursue every honorable means which will bring to fruition their common longing for peace. Peace is safest in the hands of the people and we can best achieve the goal by doing all we can to place it there.

I believe that if we can acquaint the Soviet people with the peace aims of the American people and government, there will be no war.

I feel sure that you will wish to have carried to the Soviet people the text of this resolution adopted by the American Congress.

HARRY S. TRUMAN

[His Excellency Nikolai Mikhailovich Shvernik, Chairman of the Presidium of the Supreme Soviet of the Union of Soviet Socialist Republics]

NOTE: Senate Concurrent Resolution 11, agreed to June 26, 1951, is published in the U.S. Statutes at Large (65 Stat. B69).

See also Items 188 [6] and 197.

148   Remarks to Members of the 25th Infantry Division Association. *July 7, 1951*

IT IS a pleasure to be with you this morning. You can understand exactly what I think of the 25th Division when I made your Commanding General the Chief of Staff of the Army—and he is a good one.

You naturally ought to be exceedingly proud—and I know you are—of the record of your great fighting organization.

Your record in the South Pacific, and the present record in Korea, is beyond compare. And I want to say to you that it gives me pleasure, and I feel highly honored that General Collins would ask me to appear before his organization, just to congratulate you on your career, on your patriotism, and on the good that you have done this great United States of America.

Thank you very much.

NOTE: The President spoke at 11:30 a.m. at the Statler Hotel in Washington. In his remarks the President referred to Gen. J. Lawton Collins, Chief of Staff, United States Army.

149   Letter to the President of the Senate Recommending Legislation To Terminate the State of War With Germany. *July 9, 1951*

Dear Mr. Vice President:

The progress which has been made in the recovery of Europe and in the strengthening of democratic institutions there makes it appropriate at this time to end the status of Germany as an enemy country. Bit by bit in recent years we have carried out a policy, agreed upon with our allies, of building up a freely elected German government, and returning to the German people an increasing degree of control over their affairs. This policy has been most successful. As a legal matter, however, we are still in a state of war with Germany. It therefore becomes desirable, in pursuance of our policy, to bring this state of war to an end.

Six years ago, when the wartime allies achieved complete victory over Germany, the country was destitute and there was no effective German government. Allied control was the only way to manage the prostrate country. We went forward with a clearly stated policy which anticipated that after a period of Allied occupation and reconstruction we would be able, together with our allies, to conclude a treaty of peace with a newly-established German government—a government truly representative of the German people, willing to assume its responsibilities as a member of the world community and anxious to work with its free neighbors in maintaining the peace and fostering the prosperity of Europe.

We have never deviated from this policy. Neither have our British and French allies. Unfortunately for all of us, however, and especially for the people of Germany, Soviet Russia has actively prevented the growth of a representative democratic government in a unified Germany, and has thus made impossible for the time being the arrangement of a final peace settlement. The Soviet effort has been, instead, to cut the eastern third of Germany away from the rest of the country and to develop it as a province of the new Soviet Empire.

As it became plain that we could not expect Soviet cooperation in rebuilding all of Germany as a self-respecting, democratic and peaceful nation, we were forced to change our approach. The ultimate fulfillment of our German policy had been delayed, but we were determined to do all we could to advance that policy in the part of Germany under our control. We were joined in our efforts by the British and French governments. Together with them, we gave the German people under our jurisdiction the chance to create their own government. Now, approximately two-thirds of the area of prewar Germany and three-fourths of the German people are free of Soviet control, within the present borders of the German Federal Republic. The Government of the Federal Republic rests on a democratic constitution worked out by representatives of the people themselves and approved by the Western Occupying Powers. Since its birth in September 1949, this German government has shown steadily increasing responsibility and readiness to take its place in the community of free nations and to do its share toward building peaceful and cooperative relationships with its neighbors of the West.

On their side, the occupying powers have shown faith in the German people and in the government of the Federal Republic by a continuing process of relaxing occupation controls on the one hand and increasing the scope of the Federal Republic government's responsibility on the other. This process has been accompanied by a changing attitude on both sides. The relationship of conqueror and conquered is being replaced by the relationship of equality which we expect to find among free men everywhere.

Last September, the governments of Great Britain, France, and the United States took another step in harmony with their developing policy when they joined in the following statement regarding continuation of a state of war with Germany:

"In the spirit of the new relationship which they wish to establish with the Federal Republic, the three governments have de-cided, as soon as action can be taken in all three countries in accordance with their respective constitutional requirements, to take the necessary steps in their domestic legislation to terminate the state of war with Germany.

"This action will not affect the rights and status of the Three Powers in Germany, which rest upon other bases. It will, however, create a firmer foundation for the developing structure of peaceful and friendly relationships and will remove disabilities to which German nationals are subject. It is hoped that other nations will find it possible to take similar action in accordance with their own constitutional practices."

In this statement, our Government and the governments of the other Western occupying powers clearly recognized the desirability of bringing the existing technical state of war to a close, and pledged themselves to take action in collaboration with one another to that end. Since this declaration was issued, discussions have been held with the other friendly countries who are also in a technical state of war with Germany, and most of them have indicated their willingness to take similar action in the near future—thus lifting Germany from its present enemy status.

Ending the state of war with Germany will have many tangible benefits. Germans who wish to travel or do business here will receive the status accorded to nationals of other friendly governments. They will no longer be classed as enemies. While Germans have been permitted to have commercial relations with this country since the Presidential proclamation of December 31, 1946, declaring hostilities at an end, German citizens are still subject to certain disabilities, particularly with respect to suits in United States courts. General disabilities of this kind will be eliminated by the termination of the present state of war.

The termination of the state of war with Germany will not affect the status of the occupation. The rights of the occupying powers do not rest upon the existence of a state of war, as such, and will not be affected by its legal termination. The rights of the occupying powers result from the conquest of Germany, accompanied by the disintegration and disappearance of its former government, and the Allied assumption of supreme authority. We are not surrendering these rights by terminating the state of war. We do intend, however, in agreement with our allies, to grant the Federal Republic increasing authority over its own affairs, and eventually to see Germany restored as a fully sovereign nation.

Similarly, the termination of the state of war will not affect in any way the rights or privileges, such as the right to reparations, which the United States and its citizens have acquired with respect to Germany as a result of the war.

Furthermore, it is not intended that the termination of the state of war shall in any way change or alter the program, which Congress has authorized, of seizing, under the Trading With the Enemy Act, German property in this country on or before December 31, 1946, and using the proceeds to pay just and legitimate claims arising from the war in accordance with the War Claims Act of 1948. The vesting of German property under this program does not extend to property acquired since the resumption of trade with Germany on January 1, 1947, following the cessation of hostilities. It is limited to German property and rights located here before or during the period of hostilities.

Most of this Germany property has already been identified and vested. This government does not intend to embark on any new program in this field. However, some of the property already subject to vesting is believed to be cloaked or hidden and not yet discovered, and some is still under examination or subject to legal proceedings. Most of the property remaining unvested is involved in problems of conflicting jurisdiction between this and other governments, which are in the process of settlement by negotiation under authority of legislation which was enacted in September of last year.

Should the vesting power lapse immediately, this government would find it difficult to wind up this program in an orderly way, or to carry out its commitments for the equitable settlement of intergovernmental differences relating to enemy property.

Completion of the vesting of wartime enemy property, even after the conclusion of peace, is commonly accepted practice in connection with the settlement of claims between the nations which were at war. Our peace treaties with Bulgaria, Hungary, Rumania and Italy all authorize the continued vesting and retention of such property.

In the absence of treaty provisions, however, there may be legal obstacles to the continued vesting of German property, after the termination of the state of war, unless there are changes in our existing statutes. According to the terms of the Trading With the Enemy Act, many of its powers expire at the "end of the war," a phrase which the Act defines to mean the date of proclaiming the exchange of ratifications of a treaty of peace, or an earlier date fixed by Presidential proclamation. There is some doubt that the vesting powers of the Trading With the Enemy Act can be exercised after the termination of the state of war, unless expressly provided for in new legislation.

This doubt should be eliminated, and it should be made clear that the Congress intends the vesting of German property for the purpose of paying war claims to continue.

In these circumstances, I believe that the

best method for terminating the state of war with Germany would be by the enactment of appropriate legislation in advance of the issuance of a Presidential proclamation.

Such action will give the German people a new demonstration of our desire to help bring them back to membership among the nations of the free world. It will represent another and logical step on the road which leads towards the eventual restoration of German independence.

I will appreciate it if you will lay this matter before the Congress for its considera-tion. For the convenience of the Congress, I am attaching a draft of a joint resolution that would be appropriate to achieve these objectives.

Very sincerely yours,

HARRY S. TRUMAN

NOTE: The White House release states that "a similar letter" was sent to the Honorable Sam Rayburn, Speaker of the House of Representatives. The text of the draft resolution was also made public.

On October 19, 1951, the President signed a bill which terminated the state of war between the United States and Germany (65 Stat. 451). See also Item 273.

150   Message to the Prime Minister of Iran Following the Breakdown of Oil Discussions With Great Britain.
July 9, 1951

[Released July 9, 1951. Dated July 8, 1951]

My dear Mr. Prime Minister:

I am most grateful to Your Excellency for giving me in your recent letter a full and frank account of the developments in the unhappy dispute which has arisen between your government and the British oil interests in Iran. This matter is so full of dangers to the welfare of your own country, of Great Britain and of all the free world, that I have been giving the most earnest thought to the problems involved. I had hoped that the common interests of the two countries di-rectly involved and the common ground which has been developed in your discussions would open the way to a solution of the troublesome and complicated problems which have arisen. You know of our sympathetic interest in this country in Iran's desire to control its natural resources. From this point of view we were happy to see that the British Government has on its part accepted the principle of nationalization.

Since British skill and operating knowl-edge can contribute so much to the Iranian oil industry I had hoped—and still hope—that ways could be found to recognize the principle of nationalization and British in-terests to the benefit of both. For these reasons I have watched with concern the breakdown of your discussions and the drift toward a collapse of oil operations with all the attendant losses to Iran and the world. Surely this is a disaster which statesmanship can find a way to avoid.

Recently I have come to believe that the complexity of the problems involved in a broad settlement and the shortness of the time available before the refinery must shut down—if the present situation continues—require a simple and practicable modus vivendi under which operations can continue and under which the interests of neither side will be prejudiced. Various suggestions to this end have failed. The time available is running out.

In this situation a new and important development has occurred. The Interna-tional Court of Justice, which your Govern-ment, the British Government and our own all joined with other nations to establish as the guardian of impartial justice and equity has made a suggestion for a modus vivendi.

Technical considerations aside, I lay great stress on the action of the Court. I know how sincerely your Government and the British Government believe in the positions which you both have taken in your discussions. However, I am sure you believe even more profoundly in the idea of a world controlled by law and justice which has been the hope of the world since the San Francisco Conference. Apart from questions of jurisdiction no one will doubt the impartiality of the World Court, its eminence and the respect due to it by all nations who signed the United Nations treaty.

Therefore, I earnestly commend to you a most careful consideration of its suggestion. I suggest that its utterance be thought of not as a decision which is or is not binding depending on technical legal considerations, but as a suggestion of an impartial body, dedicated to justice and equity and to a peaceful world based upon these great conceptions. A study of its suggestion by your Government and by the British Government will, I am sure, develop methods of implementing it which will carry out its wise and impartial purpose—maintaining the operation of the oil industry and preserving the positions of both Governments. Surely no government loses any element of its sovereignty or the support of its people by treating with all possible consideration and respect the utterance of this great court. Our own government and people believe this profoundly. Should you take such a position I am sure that the stature of Iran would be greatly enhanced in the eyes of the world.

I have a very sincere desire, Mr. Prime Minister, to be as helpful to you as possible in this circumstance. I have discussed this matter at length with Mr. W. Averell Harriman who as you know is one of my closest advisers and one of our most eminent citizens. Should you be willing to receive him I should be happy to have him go to Tehran as my personal representative to talk over with you this immediate and pressing situation.

May I take this opportunity to assure Your Excellency of my highest consideration and to convey to you my confidence in the future well-being and prosperity of Iran.

HARRY S. TRUMAN

NOTE: Prime Minister Mohammed Mosadeq's reply, dated and released July 11, 1951, follows:

Dear Mr. President:

I have the honor to acknowledge receipt of your friendly message of 8th July handed to me by His Excellency the Ambassador of the United States in Teheran just after the government of Iran had taken its decision with regard to the findings of the International Court of Justice at The Hague. I deem it my duty to thank you once again, Mr. President, for the care you have always taken in the welfare of this country.

As I mentioned in my previous letter, the government and people of Iran recognize the government and the people of the United States as the staunch supporters of right and justice and appreciate therefore, with complete sincerity, the interest you are taking in the solution of the economic difficulties of Iran in general and in the oil question in particular.

I am extremely glad to note your reference, Mr. President, to the sympathy and interest of the American Nation in the realization of Iran's national aspirations and the acceptance of the principle of nationalization of the oil industry; for Iran has had and is having no aim other than the acceptance of this principle by virtue of the laws ratified by the two Houses of Parliament, and has always been ready, within the terms of these laws to take any measures for the removal of the present disputes. It is, therefore, a matter of great regret that, insofar as Iran can judge, no proposal or suggestion has been made, up to the present, by the former oil company denoting their acceptance of the principle of nationalization of the oil industry in accordance with the laws ratified by the Parliament—laws which the government is duty bound to put into force. On the contrary, in their note of 29th June, the representatives of the former oil company made proposals which were against the provisions of these laws and which resulted in the termination of the discussions.

Provided, of course, that our indisputable national rights are respected in accordance with the laws concerning the nationalization of the oil industry, the government and the people of Iran are ready to enter into immediate discussions with the aim to remove all the disputes so that there may be no stoppage in the production and exploitation of oil— a situation which the government of Iran has always been anxious to avoid and which, as you have mentioned, Mr. President, is causing losses to all concerned.

With reference to your desire, Mr. President, to help our country I must state without hesitation that the Iranian nation and government fully appreciate this high intent in all sincerity and candor, more so when they find that you have shown your readiness, Mr. President, to send to Teheran as your Special Representative Mr. Averell Harriman, one of the most distinguished American citizens, for consultations.

In the light of our knowledge of Mr. Harriman's personality and his vast experiences, and considering the fact that he will act as your representative, the Iranian government welcomes this gesture and hopes to take full advantage of consultations with a man of such high standing. In the meanwhile it would also give him the opportunity to become directly acquainted with our views and to obtain first hand knowledge of our living conditions and requirements.

May I avail myself of this opportunity to offer you, Mr. President, the expressions of my best and most sincere regards.

MOHAMMED MOSADEQ

See also Items 140 [4, 19], 155.

151 Remarks Upon Accepting a Piece of the Rock of Corregidor as a Gift From the People of the Philippines. *July 10, 1951*

Mr. Ambassador, Colonel, Major:

It gives me great pleasure to accept this token from the Philippine people for the people of the United States of America.

It is the symbol of our friendship and partnership in war and in peace, and it will be a continuing symbol of our friendship from now on.

I shall send it to the Smithsonian Institution here in Washington, where almost all the American people can have a look at it. Sometime or other everybody in the United States goes to the Smithsonian Institution, and I want this token of friendship from the Philippine people to be in a position where

every American can see it when they come to Washington.

I am very thankful for this presentation, and I appreciate it most highly, Mr. Ambassador, Colonel, and Major. It is very kind of you.

NOTE: The President spoke at at 12:10 p.m. in his office at the White House. His opening words referred to Joaquin M. Elizalde, Philippine Ambassador to the United States, and to Col. Harry Peck and Maj. Manuel Acosta who took part in the action of Corregidor and Bataan during World War II.

The presentation took place during Philippine Achievement Week, which marked the progress of the Philippine Republic during its 5 years of independence.

152 Letter to Committee Chairmen on the Need for a Pay Increase for Federal Employees. *July 12, 1951*

[Released July 12, 1951. Dated July 11, 1951]

"Dear ————:

The House and Senate Post Office and Civil Service Committees now have under consideration legislation to adjust the compensation of Federal employees. I am writing you to urge that favorable action be taken on this legislation at this session of the Congress.

As a matter of public policy, the Federal Government should maintain fair and equitable compensation and working conditions for its own employees. Aside from equitable considerations, the present emergency demands prompt and adequate adjustment of federal compensation levels as a practical matter so that the government may continue to attract and retain skilled employees of the highest competence.

There are many factors which must be considered in establishing scales of compensation for federal employees. One of the most important is the relationships in the pay rates for the various grades of positions. Federal pay scales in the higher grades tend to be too low in relation to the lower grades for the type of executive responsibilities required. Steps were taken to correct this situation by enactment of the Classification Act of 1949. I consider it vital, as a matter of sound business practice that these gains be retained. Therefore, I urge most strongly that any increase enacted be on an across-the-board percentage basis rather than on a uniform dollar or sliding scale basis, so that disproportionately lower adjustments for the middle and upper grades may be avoided.

Detailed studies by the Civil Service Commission and the Bureau of the Budget indicate that a 7 percent across-the-board increase would constitute a fair and reasonable adjustment in Classification Act compensation scales at the present time.

Employees in the postal service should receive the same general rate of increase as Classification Act employees. Two additional changes appear to be desirable with respect to pay schedules in the postal service. First, I recommend legislation which would permit the Postmaster General to employ substitute postal workers initially at Grade 3 instead of Grade 1 to bring the pay of these

workers in line with prevailing rates of pay. Second, certain inequities existing in the pay rates for the supervisory grades should be eliminated.

Under the present laws, many of our Federal employees not covered by the Classification Act or included in the postal service are paid in accordance with scales prevailing in the communities in which they are employed, and their pay levels have already generally been adjusted to pay levels for private employment. No legislative adjustment is required for this group.

I know that your committee is fully cognizant of the fine work being done by our Civil Service employees. I wish to take this opportunity, however, to say as I have said before, that the nation is fortunate in having a loyal, hard-working, conscientious Civil Service, without which it would be impossible to accomplish the tremendous tasks of the present emergency. I am sure that you will want to join with me in taking this step toward seeing that the Civil Service is maintained at a high level of competence and effectiveness.

Very sincerely yours,

HARRY S. TRUMAN

NOTE: This is the text of identical letters addressed to the Honorable Olin D. Johnston, Chairman of the Senate Post Office and Civil Service Committee, and to the Honorable Tom Murray, Chairman of the House Post Office and Civil Service Committee.

On October 24, 1951, the President approved two bills increasing the salaries of civil service and postal workers (Public Laws 201 and 204, 82d Cong., 65 Stat. 612, 622).

153 The President's News Conference of *July* 12, 1951

THE PRESIDENT. Please be seated.

[1.] The Secretary of the Treasury called me just before I left the office over there, and said he wanted me to be sure to remind you

that there is going to be a defense bond drive this fall. He announced it in Rochester, N.Y., and it will begin Labor Day, September 3d—there will be a national broadcast of the opening program, in which I will in all probability take part.[1]

Defense is everybody's job, and buying defense bonds is a highly effective way to help do the job. Volunteering for work in the bond drive is another way of paying for the defense program. The Treasury will see that the time and the talent of every volunteer worker is put to use.

And I guess we will call on all of you to work on it.

Anybody that has any questions now, I will try to answer them.

[2.] Q. Mr. President, do you consider that the disclosure within the House Armed Services Committee that only 87 B-36's are ready to fight is a breach of security?

THE PRESIDENT. The information given to the Committee was confidential information, and I think it goes without saying that that sort of information is not for release. The Defense Department, I think, made a statement on the subject.

[3.] Q. Mr. President, I have a couple of questions. When the armistice becomes effective in Korea, will the fleet remain to protect Formosa?

THE PRESIDENT. I will answer that question when the operation takes place.

[4.] Q. The other question is, can you tell us anything specific that is being done to help obtain the release of William Oatis?[2]

THE PRESIDENT. Everything that is possible is being done, just as was done in the case of Vogeler,[3] and as has been done in the case of the Archbishop.[4] And the same proce-

dure is being followed. We are doing everything we can.

Q. You don't want to mention anything specific——

THE PRESIDENT. No, no.

[5.] Q. Mr. President, have you done anything, or will you do anything soon, regarding the appointment of those three badly-needed Federal judges in Illinois?[5]

THE PRESIDENT. Yes. Whenever I get ready to make the appointments, I will let you know about it.

[6.] Q. Mr. President, when you appointed General Eisenhower to the present job,[6] was there any understanding between you as to a specific period of time this job would last?

THE PRESIDENT. No, there was not.

[7.] Q. Could I ask one more question? Could you say approximately when you expect to announce, sir, your decision whether you will be in politics in 1952? [*Laughter*]

THE PRESIDENT. Well, I will give you plenty of notice on that. I will make that announcement in my own time.

Did you have something?

[8.] Q. Yes. Mr. President, Harold Stassen made this statement about your appointment of Governor Youngdahl[7] for a local judgeship. He said it was a brazen attempt to grab the governorship of Minnesota in 1952 for Senator Hubert Humphrey

---

[1] Item 213.

[2] See Item 145 [7].

[3] Robert A. Vogeler, an American citizen, was arrested in Hungary on November 18, 1949, and was sentenced to 15 years' imprisonment on charges of espionage and sabotage. He was released on April 28, 1951, after long negotiation between the U.S. and Hungarian Governments.

[4] In June 1951, Archbishop Josef Grösz, successor to the imprisoned Cardinal Mindszenty as head of

the Roman Catholic Church in Hungary, was tried with eight other Hungarian citizens on charges of conspiracy and violation of currency regulations. Attempts were made at his trial to implicate employees of the American Legation at Budapest.

[5] See Item 132 [12].

[6] The President designated General of the Army Dwight D. Eisenhower as Supreme Allied Commander, Europe, on December 18, 1950 (see 1950 volume, this series, Items 308, 310).

[7] Luther W. Youngdahl, Republican Governor of Minnesota, nominated by the President to become a Federal judge in the district court of the District of Columbia.

or one of his henchmen. Any comment?

THE PRESIDENT. No comment.

[9.] Q. Mr. President, have you any comment to make on Mr. Harriman's mission?

THE PRESIDENT. Well, Mr. Harriman is leaving tomorrow for Iran, and I hope that his mission will be successful. I am going to talk with him about it in the morning.[8] He is with the Secretary of State now.

[10.] Q. Mr. President, I understand that a labor leader has asked you to appoint a Negro to fill the vacancy created by Mr. Niles,[9] and I wonder if you have any comment on that?

THE PRESIDENT. I shall not do that. Mr. Niles in all probability will come back to his job—I hope.

[11.] Q. Mr. President, Princess Elizabeth and Prince Philip are to visit Canada at the end of September. Would you invite them to the United States?

THE PRESIDENT. Yes.

Q. You would?

THE PRESIDENT. Have done it.

Q. Have you received a reply, Mr. President?

THE PRESIDENT. No. Just done today. [*Laughter*]

[12.] Q. Mr. President, would you care to speculate politically on what you know of General Eisenhower—would you say he was a Democrat or a Republican?

THE PRESIDENT. Well now, that would be pure speculation. I don't know. I never discussed the matter with him at all. The best way to find out about that is to ask the General himself. I am sure he would give you an answer. [*Laughter*]

Q. Mr. President, I have a question in that connection. You once told us that you took General Eisenhower at his word, and that you did not expect him to ever run for President?

THE PRESIDENT. No, no—I didn't put the word *ever* in there. I said I had taken him at his word when he told me in January of 1948 that he would not run in 1948 for President. That is as far as I went on that.

Q. Do you still have that view, Mr. President?

[13.] Q. Mr. President, getting back to your announcement of the defense bond drive, the present control legislation that Congress is working on does not seem to be indicated as much of a weapon against inflation, and I was wondering if the administration plans to do anything to safeguard the buyers of defense bonds against inflation?

THE PRESIDENT. Well now, I can't answer questions about that controls bill until it gets to me. It is not legislation as yet. It is still being made up. When it comes to me, then I will answer your question.

Q. I was trying to direct my question more to the defense bonds——

THE PRESIDENT. I can answer your question when I see what sort of bill they give me.

What was your question?

[14.] Q. Do you have any assurance about General Eisenhower beyond 1948?

THE PRESIDENT. I had no discussion with him on the subject at all.

[15.] Q. Mr. President, do you care to express any opinion at this time on the progress of the truce talks in Kaesong? [10]

THE PRESIDENT. I wish you would ask that question again?

Q. Do you care to express any opinion at this time on the progress of the truce talks in Kaesong?

THE PRESIDENT. No. I have no comment on that.

---

[8] See Item 155.

[9] David K. Niles resigned as Administrative Assistant to the President, effective May 31, 1951.

[10] On July 8 U.N. representatives met with Communist officers at Kaesong, on the 38th parallel, to arrange for discussions of a truce in Korea. The discussions began on July 10.

[16.] Q. Mr. President, have you any comment on the cable from the American labor delegation at the Milan conference? [11]

THE PRESIDENT. I didn't know about it. What did it say?

Q. I was under the impression that the cable had been sent by the delegation from the CIO and the Mine Workers and the A.F. of L., asking you to take immediate action on the Hungarian deportation——

THE PRESIDENT. I haven't seen it. No such cable has reached me.

Mr. Short.[12] Mr. President, it was received and referred to Dr. Steelman.[13]

THE PRESIDENT. Joe says it was received and referred to Dr. Steelman. I haven't seen it.[14]

[17.] Q. Mr. President, when are you going to reappoint that renegotiation board on defense contracts?

THE PRESIDENT. Well, that is a matter that is up to the Defense Department, and we have been discussing it; and as soon as it is necessary for such a board to be in operation, why it will be appointed.

Q. Thank you.

[18.] Q. Mr. President, would you care to say anything about the initialing today of the Pacific Security Pact?

THE PRESIDENT. There was—the only thing that was done with the Pacific Security Pact—that was discussed by the Secretary of State and myself, and was approved by me for negotiation. We hope it will be signed in San Francisco at the same time the Japanese treaty is signed.[15]

---

[11] The 2d congress of the International Confederation of Free Trade Unions.

[12] Joseph Short, Secretary to the President.

[13] John R. Steelman, The Assistant to the President.

[14] For the President's statement on the mass deportations in Hungary, see Item 173.

[15] A draft tripartite security treaty was initialed by the United States, Australia, and New Zealand on July 12. The ANZUS Treaty was signed September 1, 1951, ratified by the President April 15, 1952, and entered into force April 29, 1952.

[19.] Q. Mr. President, will Mr. Harriman be authorized to discuss the Iranian oil crisis with the British as well as the Iranians?

THE PRESIDENT. Yes. Of course he will. You can't be a negotiator unless you can talk to both sides.

Q. Does that——

THE PRESIDENT. He is my Special Representative for the purpose of trying to get this thing settled, and I hope he is successful at it. He is very good at that business.

Q. Does that mean he will afterwards go to London?

THE PRESIDENT. It is possible. If that is necessary, he will, of course.

[20.] Q. Mr. President, this is my first conference. My impression of you is that you look a lot younger than I thought you would. [*Laughter*]

THE PRESIDENT. Well, sir—if you will—[*laughter interrupting*]—that's a mighty good way for you to start out at a press conference! [*More laughter*]

Q. Could you tell me if you feel like you are in better physical condition now than you were when you first became President?

THE PRESIDENT. Oh yes, I am in better physical condition than I have ever been in my life. I always have been in good physical condition. I don't know that there's any way to compare it. I am still young enough to make a good race—foot race, I mean. [*Laughter*]

Q. That wouldn't be an announcement, would it?

THE PRESIDENT. No, no. I have taken you boys on walks with me on several occasions, and most of them came in with their tongues hanging out. I haven't been bothered with you since. [*More laughter*]

[21.] Q. Mr. President, although you don't want to talk about the controls bill, you have expressed yourself in the past as fearing that we would get an unworkable controls bill.

THE PRESIDENT. That is correct.

Q. If that bill that comes out of Congress is not as good as you would like to have it, would you feel that this was an instance of that letdown and relaxation which you have also warned against?

THE PRESIDENT. Well now, that would require comment on a bill that is not yet—that has not yet been written, and I don't think it is well to comment on legislation when it is in the formative stage. If you will just be a little patient and wait until the bill gets to me, I will make all the comment on it necessary, on whether it is good or bad.

Q. Mr. President, a couple of weeks ago you made a comment to one of our great radio audiences, that you hoped that many of them would write in asking for—asking Congress to support your controls bill. The Post Office—and Congress—says they have not written in——

THE PRESIDENT. Well, that is——

Q. ——the people have not written in. Do you plan to make another appeal?

THE PRESIDENT. No. I think I have made all the appeals that it is necessary for me to make.

Q. You have gone as far as you——

THE PRESIDENT. I have done everything I know to do, to inform the people of the United States just what they are up against, and what they may be up against if there is no control.

Q. It's up to them from now on?

THE PRESIDENT. It is a matter that the Congress will have to work on, they will have to take the responsibility.

Mr. Short. You didn't ask any radio audience to write in to Congress, sir.

THE PRESIDENT. Joe says I never asked any radio audience to write in to Congress. I don't remember that I had—although I

might be mistaken. I don't think I ever asked anybody to write to his Congressman. I don't believe in that. I think that is propaganda. If a man is wholeheartedly inspired to write his Congressman on something in which he is interested, that's all right. I never did—when I was in the Senate, I never paid the slightest attention to propaganda messages, and I used to get them by the thousands.

Q. Mr. President, do you agree with Congressman Rabaut that this is a "horse-meat Congress"? [16]

THE PRESIDENT. A what?

Q. A "horse-meat Congress"? [*Laughter*]

THE PRESIDENT. Well, I can't answer that until I get the controls bill.

[22.] Q. Mr. President, the State Department published a version of the Japanese peace treaty today. Would you comment on that?

THE PRESIDENT. No. I think the treaty speaks for itself. I approved it. I approved that draft—I approved that draft that the State Department published.[17]

I hope the Japanese treaty can be promptly signed, I might say that.

[23.] Q. Mr. President, if you do decide to make that race—other than the foot race—do you plan to make a swing down South? [*Laughter*]

THE PRESIDENT. Well now, I will have to

---

[16] On July 9 Representative Louis C. Rabaut of Michigan, addressing the House, said, "This Eighty-second Congress stands at the threshold of immortality. We have an opportunity that few Congresses have to insure our place in history. If we deny to the Government the authority to roll back prices and maintain firm economic controls, we are sure to be remembered. We will be remembered by the American people as 'the horse-meat Congress'—the Congress that put the old gray mare on the family dinner table" (Congressional Record, vol. 97, p. 7810).

[17] The draft peace treaty and two declarations by Japan are printed in the Department of State Bulletin (vol. 25, p. 132).

answer that question when the announcement that goes with it is made, and I am
not ready to make it yet.

Q. I see. You see, I am from the South.

Q. What was your answer, we didn't
hear?

THE PRESIDENT. I said I would have to
answer that question when the announcement is made that goes with it, and I wasn't
ready to make that announcement yet.

Q. Mr. President, you said *when* the announcement is made, didn't you?

THE PRESIDENT. No—I said *if*. *If* is the
word.

Q. Mr. President, I heard different.

THE PRESIDENT. You can use *when* if you
want to, I don't care—doesn't make any difference. When I get ready to make the
announcement, that is what it will amount
to, anyway, one way or the other—*if* or
when.

Q. Is that *it*, Mr. President?

THE PRESIDENT. That's all I have, unless
somebody has another question he wants to
put.

Reporter: Thank you, Mr. President.

NOTE: President Truman's two hundred and seven-
tieth news conference was held in the Indian Treaty
Room (Room 474) in the Executive Office Building
at 4 p.m. on Thursday, July 12, 1951.

---

154   Special Message to the Congress on the Employment of Agricultural Workers from Mexico. *July* 13, 1951

To the Congress of the United States:

I have approved S. 984, an Act relating to
the recruitment and employment of agricultural workers from Mexico.

If promptly followed up by other needed
measures, this Act can be a first step toward
a comprehensive program to bring badly
needed improvements in the living and
working conditions of migratory farm workers, both foreign and domestic. At the same
time, this Act can help to assure an adequate
supply of labor to meet the needs of American agriculture. On the other hand, if enactment of this legislation becomes an excuse
for delay on these other measures, it will
hamper our efforts to meet more basic problems—including the pressing problem of
illegal immigration.

For that reason, I could not have given my
approval to this Act had I not been assured
by Congressional leaders that supplementary
legislation and appropriations would receive
prompt consideration at this session.

For many years, the Mexican Government,

by agreement with the United States, has
allowed its citizens to come into this country
on contracts with agricultural employers to
assist in harvesting vital crops—principally
cotton, sugar beets, citrus fruits, and vege-
tables—and mostly in the southwestern part
of the United States.

During and since the last war, the recurrent shortages of farm labor in the United
States have made the addition of contract
workers from Mexico a vital factor in bringing in the crops. Last year, for example,
70,000 Mexican workers were legally admitted to this country for contract work
during the harvesting season.

However, both this Government and the
Mexican Government have become increasingly concerned about violations of the contract terms under which Mexican citizens
are employed in this country. We must
make sure that contract wages will in fact
be paid, that transportation within this
country and adequate reception centers for
Mexican workers will in fact be provided.

It is necessary, therefore, that this Government be able to stand behind all contracts and guarantee performance in the future, if any more Mexican citizens are to be legally recruited for work in the United States. Until this can be done, Mexico has taken steps to terminate the agreement under which her citizens were brought to this country in the past and will make a new agreement only if these guarantees are given.

It is the purpose of S. 984 to give this Government the authority needed to make a mutually satisfactory new agreement with Mexico, which would include these guarantees. Under the terms of this Act, the United States Government, subject to a fixed reimbursement by the employer, will be able to recruit and transport Mexican workers to reception centers in this country, to house and care for these workers until they are employed, to help them make arrangements with American employers, and to guarantee performance by employers of the terms of their employment contracts.

With this authority, it should be possible to reach a new agreement with Mexico. This Act will thus take care of one immediate problem, the harvesting of crops this year. It will also undoubtedly improve the situation of Mexican workers brought into this country for contract work. A government-to-government guarantee of wages and work standards for these workers will be a real step forward.

But this is very limited progress, which hardly touches our basic farm labor problems. The really crucial point, which this Act scarcely faces, is the steady stream of illegal immigrants from Mexico, the so-called "wetbacks", who cross the Rio Grande or the western stretches of our long border, in search of employment. These people are coming into our country in phenomenal numbers—and at an increasing rate. Last year 500,000 illegal immigrants were apprehended and returned to Mexico. In 1949, less than 300,000 were returned.

There are many thousands of these people who have escaped detection and remain in this country today. Thousands more will find their way here before the year is out. Since these unfortunate people are here illegally, they are subject to deportation if caught by our immigration authorities. They have to hide and yet must work to live. They are thus in no position to bargain with those who might choose to exploit them.

And many of them are exploited, I regret to say, and are left in abject poverty. They live always under the threat of exposure and deportation. They are unable, therefore, to protest or to protect themselves.

The presence of these illegal workers has a seriously depressing effect on wages and working conditions in farm areas throughout the southwest. The standards of living and job opportunities of American farm workers are under constant downward pressure. Thousands of our own citizens, particularly those of Latin descent, are displaced from employment or forced to work under substandard conditions because of the competition of these illegal immigrants.

Everyone suffers from the presence of these illegal immigrants in the community. They themselves are hurt, first of all. Our own workers—as well as the legal contract workers from Mexico—are hurt by the lowering of working and living standards. And the farmers are hurt, too. Instead of a well trained, reliable supply of workers, they are increasingly dependent on a rapidly-shifting, ill-trained domestic labor force, supplemented legally or illegally from foreign sources. They face a crisis in their labor supply at every season. They are forced, year after year, to makeshift last minute measures to save their crops.

The President's Commission on Migratory Labor, in its recent report on the situation throughout the Nation,[1] put the issue this way:

"Shall we continue indefinitely to have low work standards and conditions of employment in agriculture thus depending on the underprivileged and the unfortunate at home and abroad to supply and replenish our seasonal and migratory work force? Or shall we do in agriculture what we already have done in other sectors of our economy—create honest-to-goodness jobs which will offer a decent living so that domestic workers, without being forced by dire necessity, will be willing to stay in agriculture and become a dependable labor supply? Just as farm employers want able and willing workers when needed, so do workers want reliable jobs which yield a fair living. Neither is being satisfied."

S. 984 does not face up to that basic issue.

The Act does, it is true, provide that Mexican workers may not legally be brought in unless the Secretary of Labor certifies a real shortage of domestic workers. The Act also provides that employment of Mexican contract labor must not adversely affect wages or working conditions of domestic workers. But these safeguards have little meaning so long as illegal immigration continues—so long as illegal workers are in fact used by American employers to take the place of other workers.

If we are to begin to meet the basic problem, we must do two things right away. First, we must put a stop to the employment of illegal immigrants. Second, we must improve the use of our domestic labor force. These steps will require more sanctions than our laws now provide and more administrative machinery and services than are now

available. Therefore, I recommend that the Congress take the following action:

First, legislation should be enacted providing punishment for the offense of harboring or concealing aliens who have entered this country illegally. While we have a law on the books purporting to make this an offense, that law is not enforceable, because no penalty was adequately provided. This should be remedied at once. In addition, to help discourage the smuggling of aliens, the existing provisions of law punishing transportation of illegal immigrants must be strengthened. While such legislation will be very useful in bringing illegal immigration from Mexico under control, it will also be a valuable addition to our general immigration laws.

Second, legislation should be enacted to clearly establish the authority of personnel of the Immigration and Naturalization Service to inspect places of employment, without a warrant, where they have reason to believe that illegal immigrants are working or quartered. Immigration inspectors are able to cope with known illegal immigrants by obtaining warrants for their arrest. But where there are places of employment, consisting of many acres of land on which many workers are employed and quartered, inspection is necessary to find out whether illegal immigrants are among those workers. The inspections would involve no more, and probably a good deal less, than inspections of mines or factories by public authorities to assure compliance with accident prevention laws. Of course, a farmer's dwelling should be safe from search without a warrant. But there is no reason why other premises which serve as places of employment should not be open for inspection to aid in the enforcement of our immigration laws.

Third, a supplemental appropriation should be made available immediately to the Immigration and Naturalization Service to

---

[1] The report of the President's Commission on Migratory Labor is entitled "Migratory Labor in American Agriculture" (Government Printing Office, 1951, 188 pp.).

expand its personnel in the southwest so that all types of enforcement work can be stepped up—including apprehension, investigation, and deportation of illegal entrants. I shall shortly send a budget estimate for this purpose to the Congress.

It is absolutely impossible, without the expenditure of very large amounts of manpower and money, to seal off our long land borders to all illegal immigration. But these three actions by the Congress will give us the tools we need to find and deport illegal immigrants once here and to discourage those of our own citizens who are aiding and abetting their movement into the country.

In this connection, I am glad to report that the Government of Mexico is contemplating more stringent measures on its own account to help curtail illegal crossings of our border.

As a fourth measure for immediate Congressional action, I shall shortly forward to the Congress a supplemental budget estimate for the Farm Placement Service of the Labor Department.

It is not enough to take strong action against the stream of illegal immigrants. If we are to make real progress toward solving our basic farm labor problem, we must improve the utilization of our own citizens in the farm labor force, and reduce to a minimum our dependence on foreign sources. As a first step, we need at once to strengthen the machinery of the Department of Labor for surveying labor market needs and recruiting workers to fill these needs. This will be essential if we are to do an effective job under S. 984, in deciding how many contract workers to bring across the border and where they ought to be employed. It will be essential if we are to make this importation of foreign workers truly supplemental to our own resources of farm labor and give the fullest opportunity to

those of our citizens who seek employment on the farm.

The additional funds for the Farm Placement Service will be used to expand labor-market studies which will be undertaken in cooperation with the Department of Agriculture. These funds will also permit an expansion of the field staff in rural areas, where large-scale employment of farm labor is required. The aim in these areas will be to find out exactly what workers are needed and find the right workers to do the job.

Finally, these funds will be used to expand the Government's operations in the manner required under S. 984, including transportation and reception of Mexican workers, inspection of contract operations and handling of complaints.

Unless all of these activities of the Farm Placement Service can be built up quickly and effectively, orderly operations under S. 984 will be impossible and we will lose the chance to make full use of our domestic supply of farm workers or to determine on a realistic basis our need for workers from abroad.

These four measures, supplementing the provisions of S. 984, will give us a real program with which to tackle the basic problems of farm labor in the southwest. They will help us also to make a start in other areas where agriculture is dependent on large-scale use of migratory workers.

There is one provision of S. 984 which could interfere quite seriously with our efforts to maintain labor standards in this country. This is the provision which so defines agricultural employment as to allow the Secretary of Labor to bring in Mexican workers for employment in food processing trades as well as on the farm. It is essential that we keep the importation of Mexican workers from reducing the job opportunities or working conditions of our own citizens employed in these trades. To that end, I believe the Congress should repeal this pro-vision. In the meantime, it will be necessary for the Secretary of Labor to use his discretion with great care and to authorize the employment of Mexican workers in these trades only in case of some genuine, unmistakable emergency.

The measures which I am now recommending to the Congress will not take care of all our problems by any means. The President's Commission on Migratory Labor, a group of distinguished citizens, recently completed an extensive investigation of migratory labor problems throughout the country. The Commission's report was submitted two months ago and is being intensively studied within the Executive Branch. It is a very useful and constructive document and it emphasizes, among other things, that the migratory workers in this country will need specially adapted programs to improve housing conditions and health, education, and social security. They will need these things if they are to develop

into the kind of labor force so badly needed in agriculture today—a labor force which really meets the long-run requirements of large-scale "industrialized" farm production.

From time to time, therefore, as the report of this Commission is studied and appraised, I intend to send further recommendations to the Congress, looking toward more improvements in the working conditions and living standards of our migrant workers. Meanwhile, it is my earnest hope that the Congress will lose no time in acting on the recommendations outlined in this message.

HARRY S. TRUMAN

NOTE: As enacted, S. 984 is Public Law 78, 82d Congress (65 Stat. 119).

On August 16 the President approved H.J. Res. 311, making interim appropriations to the Department of Labor to begin the task of bringing Mexican farm workers into the United States under the terms of Public Law 78. For the statement by the President upon signing the bill see Item 192.

On March 20, 1952, the President approved S. 1851, an act giving immigration officers additional authority to prevent Mexican farm workers from entering or remaining in the United States illegally (Public Law 283, 82d Cong.; 66 Stat. 26).

155 Remarks to W. Averell Harriman Before His Departure on a Mission to Iran. *July 13, 1951*

THE PRESIDENT. I want to express to you my appreciation for your willingness to undertake this trip to Iran. It is a very important job that you have undertaken, and one which I think you can handle with satisfaction and success.

All of us want to wish you a pleasant trip, and I hope that you will express to the Iranian Government that our interest is the

interest of world peace, and the welfare of Iran and the rest of the world.

We have no selfish interest in the matter whatever.

NOTE: The President spoke at 11:55 a.m. in the Rose Garden at the White House. Brief remarks by Secretary of State Dean Acheson, Secretary of Defense George C. Marshall, and Mr. Harriman were also released.

See also Item 150.

156 Letter to the Executive Secretary, National Security Council, Requesting a Study of the Employee Security Program. *July 14, 1951*

Dear Mr. Lay:

I have become seriously concerned by a number of reports I have heard recently concerning the administration of the provisions of existing law which authorize the heads of the various departments and agencies to discharge Government employees, or to refuse Government employment to applicants, on the ground that they are poor security risks.

If these provisions of law are to achieve their purpose of protecting the security of the Government without unduly infringing on the rights of individuals, they must be administered with the utmost wisdom and courage. We must never forget that the fundamental purpose of our Government is to protect the rights of individual citizens and one of the highest obligations of the Government is to see that those rights are protected in its own operations.

The present situation does not make for good administration. There are no uniform standards or procedures to be followed in the different departments and agencies concerned. Neither is there any provision for review at a central point as there is in the case of the Government Employee Loyalty Program. This is a problem that falls within the scope of the work which I have asked to have undertaken by the Commission on Internal Security and Individual Rights. However, the work of that Commission has been delayed because of the failure of the Senate Committee on the Judiciary to report legislation which would exempt the members and staff of the Commission from the conflict-of-interest statutes.

I believe that the present problems involved in the administration of the Government Employees Security Program are so acute that they should be given at least preliminary consideration without waiting further for the Commission on Internal Security and Individual Rights. Consequently, I should like the National Security Council, utilizing its Interdepartmental Committee on Internal Security, and with the participation of the Civil Service Commission, to make an investigation of the way this program is being administered, and to advise me what changes are believed to be required. In particular, I should like consideration given to whether provision should be made for uniform standards and procedures and for central review of the decisions made in the various departments and agencies.

When the Commission on Internal Security and Individual Rights is able to resume its work, it would, of course, have the benefit of the work done pursuant to this request.

I am asking each of the departments and agencies concerned to cooperate fully in this study.

Sincerely yours,

HARRY S. TRUMAN

[Mr. James S. Lay, Jr., Executive Secretary of the National Security Council]

NOTE: The report by the Interdepartmental Committee on Internal Security on the Government Employee Security Program, dated April 29, 1952 (45 pp., mimeographed), was submitted to the President by the National Security Council.

157 Message to the President of France on Bastille Day. *July 14, 1951*

ON THE OCCASION of your national holiday, I wish to extend to you, Mr. President, and to the French people the heartiest best wishes and congratulations of the American people. I recall with particular pleasure your visit to Washington last April and the opportunity which it gave us all to further friendship of our two countries.

During the past year the French and American peoples have made heavy sacrifices for liberty. They have successfully resisted aggression. Their strength, together with that of other freedom-loving peoples, has grown steadily. The continuation of these joint efforts will assure peace because it will discourage aggression.

I wish also to congratulate you on the progress, thanks in considerable part to French initiative, in the development of a closer community relationship among the free nations of Europe and the North Atlantic community in both the economic and defense fields. These combined efforts will, I am certain, promote the stability, prosperity and strength not only of Europe, but of the entire free world.

HARRY S. TRUMAN

[His Excellency, Vincent Auriol, President of the French Republic, Paris, France]

158 Remarks in Grandview, Mo., After Viewing the Flood Disaster Area. *July 17, 1951*

WE HAVE just made an investigation of the flood situation from St. Louis to Salina, Kans., and from Salina to Miami, Okla. And it is one of the worst disasters, I think, that the country has ever suffered from water. I am informed by General Pick that it is the worst.

I have had the Chief of Engineers, a representative of the Department of Agriculture, a representative of the Federal Housing Administrator, and the Production Director of the war production setup with me today, and they are expecting to work together to see if we can meet this situation as promptly as possible in every manner that is necessary to alleviate suffering, and to put the community back on its feet again.

NOTE: The President spoke at 5:45 p.m. at the airport in Grandview after viewing the disaster area from the air. His remarks were broadcast.

Accompanying the President on the inspection trip were Charles E. Wilson, Director, Office of Defense Mobilization; Maj. Gen. Lewis A. Pick, Chief of Engineers, United States Army; Donald E. Smith, Director of the Kansas City Commodity Stabilization Office, Department of Agriculture; and Chester W. Anderson, Regional Engineer of the Federal Housing Administration.

See also Items 162, 163.

159 Letter to the President of the Senate on a Pending Bill To Increase Public Assistance Payments. *July 18, 1951*

Dear Mr. Vice President:

I understand that the Senate Committee on Finance has reported to the Senate an amendment to H.R. 2416, a tax bill already passed by the House. This amendment is intended to increase by about three dollars per month the Federal share of State public assistance payments to needy individuals who

395

are aged, blind, or disabled. A similar increase of about two dollars per month would be provided for dependent children. This amendment would add about $140 million per year to Federal expenditures for public assistance.

It seems to me that any legislation to increase public assistance payments should take account of the relationship between those payments and the amounts paid under our old age and survivors insurance system.

In considering increases in public assistance payments, it is vitally important that we all keep clearly in mind the basic purpose of public assistance. Its purpose is and has always been to supplement our social insurance system. Our aim has been to expand coverage of social insurance and gradually reduce the need for supplementary public assistance programs. It is essential that a proper relationship be maintained between insurance benefits and assistance payments. At the very least, average benefits from insurance should be as high as average payments under public assistance. Today, the average payment in both programs is about forty-three dollars per month. An increase in public assistance alone would, therefore, result in an average insurance benefit lower than the average assistance payment.

This would be a highly undesirable result for the future of both programs. As the Senate Committee on Finance pointed out in its report on the Social Security Act Amendments of 1950:

"Your committee's impelling concern . . . has been to take immediate effective steps to cut down the need for further expansion of public assistance . . . Unless the insurance system is expanded and improved so that it in fact offers a basic security to retired persons and to survivors, there will be continual and irresistible pressure for putting

more and more Federal funds into less constructive assistance programs. We consider the assistance methods to have serious disadvantages to the long-run approach to the Nation's social security problem."

The logic of this report certainly applies in the case of the present amendment. The relationship between the insurance and assistance programs established by the Social Security Act Amendments of 1950 should not now be upset to the detriment of insurance.

If public assistance payments are now to be increased, then old age and survivors insurance benefits should also be increased to at least an equal degree.

Fortunately, it is now possible to increase these insurance benefits without changing the actuarial status of the old age and survivors insurance system as calculated when the Social Security Act Amendments were adopted last year. This is true because the increases in wages which have since taken place will mean a greater increase in the income of the insurance fund than in the liabilities which that fund will be called upon to bear.

As for the increase in public assistance payments provided by the amendment now before the Senate, I believe that consideration should be given to including a provision which would make it entirely clear that the additional funds are actually to be passed along without delay, to the people who receive State aid.

Although practically all the States would receive additional Federal funds under the formula provided in this amendment, the amendment itself provides no assurance that these increases would be passed on promptly to individuals. When the Federal share in the public assistance program was increased in October 1948, the short-run effect was to substitute some Federal funds for State and local funds going into current programs. An immediate result was to make the average increase in payments to individuals less, in many cases, than had been intended by the Congress. If new increases are now to be authorized, we should take care to avoid a repetition of this experience.

Sincerely yours,

HARRY S. TRUMAN

[Honorable Alben W. Barkley, Vice President of the United States, Washington, D.C.]

NOTE: The Senate passed H.R. 2416 with amendments on July 19, and on July 26 the bill was referred to the House Ways and Means Committee for consideration of the changes made by the Senate. The bill was not reported out by the Committee.

160 Remarks to a Group Representing the French Provincial Press. *July 18, 1951*

THANK YOU, Mr. Ambassador. It is a pleasure, indeed, to welcome you here this morning. From what I can understand, this delegation represents the country press of France, as we would say. The Ambassador says the provinces. We are most happy to have the papers that circulate among the citizens outside of Paris, let me say, to come over here and find out just exactly how friendly we feel to that great republic of yours.

I also want to thank you most sincerely, from the bottom of my heart, for the most cordial reception which you gave to my daughter on her tourist trip to France. She has been at home now for about 3 days, and I haven't had a chance to get a word in edgeways because she spends her time telling me about her various adventures in France and other places.

Especially was she highly pleased with the cordiality of the reception which the great

President of France gave her. She was highly pleased at her opportunity to see those wonderfully historic buildings which are not only in Paris but she got to Chartres and several other places which she had been invited to see on her trip.

I hope you have a most pleasant visit here, and if you have any daughters who need entertaining in the United States, just let me know.

It certainly is a pleasure to welcome you here today. I hope you have a most pleasant visit to this country, and that you will enjoy yourselves here as much as my daughter did in France.

NOTE: The President spoke at 12:50 p.m. in the Rose Garden at the White House. In his opening words he referred to Henri Bonnet, French Ambassador to the United States.

The press release of the President's remarks refers to the group as the "French Provincial Press Study Group" and states that their visit was sponsored by the Economic Cooperation Administration.

161 Message to the Congress Transmitting the First Annual Report of the Civil Service Commission Under the Classification Act of 1949. *July 19, 1951*

To the Congress of the United States:

Pursuant to the provisions of Section 1102 of the Classification Act of 1949, I am transmitting herewith the first annual report of the Civil Service Commission under the Act,

and submitting my recommendations based upon the report of the Commission.

The Civil Service Commission makes the following recommendations:

(a) To exempt certain trades, crafts, and

laboring positions from the Classification Act and to base their pay rates on the prevailing rates in local communities.

(b) To authorize the Commission, under certain conditions, to permit initial appointments at a pay step above the minimum rate of the grade.

(c) To authorize the President to increase the number of positions in Grades GS–16, GS–17, and GS–18.

(d) To assure that downward reclassification of a position will not reduce the salary of an incumbent employee.

With regard to the first two of the above-listed recommendations of the Civil Service Commission, it is my opinion that they are sound in theory and worthy of careful consideration. Since the time of the initial formulation of the recommendations, however, the economic control program enacted by the Congress has developed to the point where new considerations are imposed. Accordingly, these recommendations have been under study by the Wage Stabilization Board to determine the inflationary impact, if any, which may be involved. It is recommended, therefore, that action on these proposals be held in abeyance until the completion of these studies, whereupon specific legislative measures will be recommended to the Congress.

The question of increasing the number of authorized positions in Grades GS–16, GS–17, and GS–18 is the subject of a general review now being conducted by the Civil Service Commission and the Bureau of the Budget pursuant to my directive of April 12, 1951. It is contemplated that this review will result in the formulation of a legislative proposal which will combine existing authorities for such grades into a single statute and which will provide at the same time for an orderly, systematic and economical control over the numbers of such grades.

The fourth listed recommendation of the Civil Service Commission has my concurrence.

With reference to the general level of compensation under the schedules of the Classification Act of 1949, I have recommended to the Civil Service Committees of the Senate and the House of Representatives early and favorable action on pending measures to increase such schedules by approximately 7 percent. I desire to emphasize the great importance to the defense program of the early enactment of this legislation.

The report of the Civil Service Commission transmitted herewith reflects a year of constructive development in the field of public personnel administration. The Congress and the Civil Service Commission are to be congratulated upon this substantial progress.

HARRY S. TRUMAN

NOTE: The 23-page report is printed in House Document 195 (82d Cong., 1st sess.).

162 Letter to the President, American National Red Cross, on the Flood Disaster Areas in the Middle West. *July* 19, 1951

Dear Mr. Harriman:

Early yesterday I returned from a survey flight over the flood-stricken areas of Kansas, Missouri and Oklahoma. I was appalled at what I saw. The extent and the violence of the destruction to homes, farms and industries was tragic.

But at the same time there was a heartening thing to be seen. This was the magnificent way in which help was forthcoming.

I speak of the relief work carried out by the various branches of the military, by the Federal, State and municipal governments, and by the Red Cross. There were many others.

The act under which the $25,000,000 authorized by Congress will be expended specifies that the responsibilities of the Red Cross shall not be limited or in any way affected.

In addition to all that the constituted authorities can do to help restore normal life in the communities, there is a vital job to be done by the Red Cross. That job is with people, with those whose lives have been so dislocated by their flood losses that, without help, they cannot get back on their feet. Human welfare is the most important job. It is a job that cannot wait. It was for that reason the people through the Congress, in 1905, officially entrusted the responsibility for such work to the American National Red Cross.

The real work of the Red Cross in the flood area is just beginning. Its heaviest task is still ahead. Months from now, long after the memory of these floods is slipping from the minds of people in other sections, the Red Cross will still be on the job assisting the victims. The money the Red Cross provides for rebuilding a house or for refurnishing it, or for helping a family to find the means to help itself, will be given outright, not lent. This assistance will be given only on the basis of the needs of the families involved.

This job of the Red Cross is going to take a lot of money—more than the Red Cross can provide from its present resources.

For that reason I call upon all Americans now to contribute as generously as they can, at least $5,000,000, through their local Red Cross chapters to aid our flood-stricken fellow citizens in Kansas, Missouri, Oklahoma and Illinois.

Sincerely yours,

HARRY S. TRUMAN

[The Honorable E. Roland Harriman, President, American National Red Cross, Washington, D.C.]

NOTE: See also Items 158 and 163.

---

163   Letter to the Director, Office of Defense Mobilization, on Federal Activities in the Flood Disaster Areas. *July* 19, 1951

Dear Mr. Wilson:

I am deeply concerned with the seriousness of the flood damage throughout the Middle West. Approximately two million acres of farm land in an area extending one thousand miles in length have been inundated. A critical national transportation bottleneck has been created, and industrial activities of great significance to the defense effort have been brought to a standstill. The total personal, industrial, and agricultural damage is presently estimated at well over a billion dollars.

Our first concern must be for the people in that area, who have been subjected to untold hardship and tragic losses. To alleviate their suffering the Congress has acted expeditiously in providing emergency funds. As you know, I have designated the Administrator of the Housing and Home Finance Agency to take leadership in coordinating the activities of the Federal Government under the provisions of the Disaster Relief Act. Under his supervision, action is being taken to provide immediate relief and assistance to supplement the efforts of State and local governments.

This disaster has had serious effects upon the economy of the Nation and on the mobilization program. The economic life of the stricken area must be restored without delay. Agricultural, industrial, transportation and other facilities damaged or destroyed by the flood must be put back into operation.

In addition to the immediate assistance now being provided under the Disaster Relief Act, I am requesting you to direct and coordinate the activities of the Federal Departments and agencies toward the restoration of the general economy of the area. In employing the available powers and resources of the Federal Government you should give consideration, among other things, to the allocation of materials and facilities including transportation, to the extension of financial assistance and to the adjustment of stabilization measures. In carrying out this task you and the Admin-

istrator of the Housing and Home Finance Agency will, of course, work closely together and will have the full cooperation of those departments and agencies which can be of aid.

I am sending copies of this letter to the Secretaries of the Treasury, Defense, the Interior, Agriculture, Commerce, and Labor, the Administrator of the Reconstruction Finance Corporation, and the Administrator of the Housing and Home Finance Agency.

Very sincerely yours,

HARRY S. TRUMAN

[Honorable Charles E. Wilson, Director, Office of Defense Mobilization, Washington 25, D.C.]

NOTE: See also Items 158 and 162.

164 Letter to Mrs. C. Irving Guyer on the Need for Controlling Inflation. *July* 19, 1951

Dear Mrs. Guyer:

Thank you for your thoughtful letter about the need for price controls. It means a great deal to me to get letters like yours. And I have been getting many of them— letters from places like Houston, Texas and Oakland, California and Cincinnati, Ohio; good, heartening letters from big cities and small towns and rural R.F.D.'s all across America.

These letters prove what I believe so strongly, that millions and millions of Americans—housewives like yourself and workers and businessmen and farmers—know the facts about inflation and understand them very well. They know the lobbyists are working hard here in Washington to get the Congress to pass weak control laws, which will keep us from putting up a successful fight against inflation. And they know how badly off we'll be if the lobbyists win.

I don't think you can fool most Americans once they have the facts. And I'm convinced

that more and more Americans are learning the facts about inflation. And the more of our fellow citizens who do know the facts, the easier it will become to ward off the lobbyists' attacks and get the kind of legislation that the people of this country need and are entitled to.

You asked me in your letter to speak for you and all the other housewives, who aren't represented here in Washington by any lobby organization. Of course I will do that. It's what I have been doing. It's what I'm here to do. I have been speaking for you and working for you as hard as I can to make clear what the issues are in this fight against inflation and to convince the Congress that we must get a strong new control law on the books.

Let me say this to you. If we can't beat off the lobbies this time, we will just make a new start and try again. I want you to remember always, that though the special interests may have a triumph now and then, the people's interest is sure to carry in the end. Once the people know the facts and understand where their interests really lie, they are an irresistible force. Nothing can stop them.

That is our whole history as Americans.

I would like to ask you to remember one thing more. In Springfield, Massachusetts the cattle ranchers of the West may seem very far away. It must be hard, sometimes, not to identify them all with their self-styled "spokesmen" in Washington. It is just as hard, sometimes, for people out West not to identify all Eastern businessmen—even small businessmen like your husband—with the "spokesmen" of the "big interests" in New York, or the paid propagandists of the National Association of Manufacturers.

But these are both mistakes—mistakes none of us can afford. Most of the cattlemen and most of the businessmen are good patriotic Americans, who want to safeguard their own interests, like anybody else, but not at the country's expense.

I am sure you know this. I am sure you realize how little the big paid lobbyists in Washington may really represent the members of their own organizations, much less anybody else. But these "spokesmen" have been filling the air with so many violent accusations against whole groups of Ameri-

cans, that I fear sometimes lest many of us may forget how much we have in common—how much our welfare as individuals is bound up with our common welfare as American citizens, working together.

If we all remember that and keep it constantly in mind—in spite of all the shouting by the "spokesmen" and the "special pleaders," we can win the battle for price controls and the bigger battle that lies behind it—the battle for peace and security in the world.

Sincerely yours,

HARRY S. TRUMAN

[Mrs. C. Irving Guyer, 58 Rockland Street, Springfield, Massachusetts]

NOTE: The President wrote in reply to Mrs. Guyer's letter of July 10, also released, in which she described her efforts as "a fairly representative middle class housewife," with five children and a "small businessman" husband, to "keep our heads above the rising tide of inflation."

Mrs. Guyer wrote: "I understand that right now Washington is crowded with lobbyists, lobbyists representing the cattle interests, the real estate interests, the farm interests etc., all fighting to weaken price control legislation or to eliminate it entirely. Nowhere have I heard of any lobbying being done for a very large and pretty important group of Americans who will certainly be seriously affected by any further inflation—the housewives.

"Since I cannot afford a trip to Washington to lobby for the housewives personally, I am writing to ask you, Mr. President, to speak for us."

165   The President's News Conference of *July* 19, 1951

THE PRESIDENT. Please be seated.

I have no announcements to make this morning. I will try to answer questions.

[1.] Q. Mr. President, does this Government have any evidence that Russia has achieved an atomic explosion since the first announcement in 1949? [1]

---

[1] For the President's statement of September 23, 1949, announcing the first atomic explosion in the U.S.S.R., see 1949 volume, this series, Item 216.

THE PRESIDENT. No.

[2.] Q. Mr. President, some time ago, Mon Wallgren announced that he was going to retire as head of the Federal Power Commission. He has not retired, and I wonder if he is staying at your urging?

THE PRESIDENT. He had some business that had to be wound up in which he was familiar with all the evidence, and he is waiting until that business is wound up, before he leaves.

Q. Mr. President, in connection with that related subject, the Federal Power Commission last week decided in the Phillips Petroleum case in a fashion which seems to overrule the Truman veto of the Kerr bill.[2] I wondered if that had come to your attention?

THE PRESIDENT. No, it has not. I don't think it has any connection whatever.

Q. Mr. President, were you aware of the decision?

THE PRESIDENT. Yes, I am aware of the decision.

Q. Can't hear, sir—can't hear.

THE PRESIDENT. He wanted to know if I was aware of the decision of the Federal Power Commission. I told him, yes, I am aware of it. The Federal Power Commission had all the evidence and decided the thing on the evidence, as far as I know. That is what it is for.

[3.] Q. Mr. President, the State Department recently said that you would shortly issue a proclamation required under an amendment to the reciprocal trade acts, barring some Russian and Chinese furs. Is that proclamation imminent?

THE PRESIDENT. I haven't seen it.[3]

[4.] Q. Mr. President——

THE PRESIDENT. Yes, Duke?[4]

Q. ——there seems to be some slight con-

fusion out your home county way, about who is going to spend the $25 million?[5]

THE PRESIDENT. Well, I will take care of that when we get around to it, Duke. I haven't yet heard from the Governor of Missouri that he needs any of it, and I can't operate until I do hear. As soon as I get the thing lined up, why you will be informed exactly how it is going to be handled.

Q. Can't ask him any more?

THE PRESIDENT. It will be under my control, you will be sure of that. Why, if it is necessary—we will have to wait and see what developments are. We don't know yet what is required. That is what that survey was for the other day.

[5.] Q. Mr. President, you told me last week, sir, that I put some words in your mouth about this question about General Eisenhower——

THE PRESIDENT. That's right.

Q. ——in which I said that you had told us once about taking Ike at his word, that he wouldn't ever run. Well, what I had in mind, Mr. President, was at a press conference on December 22, 1949,[6] you were asked this question: Do you feel sure that he—Ike, that is—is not a candidate for 1952 as he was not in 1948? You said yes, that Ike had said so, that his word was good with you.

THE PRESIDENT. That was—I probably quoted a conversation I had with Ike when we were discussing his appointment as commander in chief of the NATO setup. I haven't talked politics with Ike since 1949, so I don't know what his attitude is now. I notice he answered your question as to which party he belonged. [*Laughter*]

---

[2] On April 15, 1950, the President vetoed H.R. 1758, a bill to amend the Natural Gas Act of 1938, because the bill would limit the authority of the Federal Power Commission to regulate sales of natural gas to interstate pipe line companies (see 1950 volume, this series, Item 88). In the Phillips Petroleum Co. case, the Federal Power Commission decided that Phillips was not a "natural gas company" within the meaning of the Natural Gas Act, and was therefore not subject to FPC jurisdiction.

[3] The State Department release, dated July 6, 1951, is published in the Department of State Bulletin, volume 25, p. 95. On August 1, the President signed Proclamation 2935 (3 CFR, 1949–1953 Comp., p. 121), dealing with trade restrictions on furs from the U.S.S.R. and Communist China.

[4] Duke Shoop of the Kansas City Star.

[5] On July 18 the President approved H.J. Res. 292 (Public Law 80, 82d Cong.; 65 Stat. 123), providing $25 million for disaster relief. The funds were to be used to help in the recovery of the flood-stricken Middle West.

[6] See 1949 volume, this series, Item 269 [9].

Q. What I had in mind, Mr. President, does that stand, that you—you feel sure that he will not be a candidate?

THE PRESIDENT. Well, I can't—I can't speak for him, because I haven't discussed the matter with him at all. If ever I discuss the matter with him and he tells me what he is going to do, then I will rely on it, because his word is good.

Q. Mr. President, I believe you have the last word in saying whether Ike does resign—he does decide to be a candidate for President?

THE PRESIDENT. I couldn't hear you?

Q. You have the last word—he has to get your permission, as I understand it, to resign from NATO, if he decides to run for President?

THE PRESIDENT. Well, we will cross that river when we get to it.

Q. Would you say whether you would be inclined to permit him to resign?

THE PRESIDENT. I will answer that question when Ike asks me for permission.

[6.] Q. Mr. President, there are reports from Madrid that Admiral Sherman is about to reach an agreement with Spain on our using certain bases there. Yesterday Secretary Acheson spoke very forthrightly about the military importance of Spain to us.[7] Has our policy toward Spain changed?

THE PRESIDENT. To some extent.

Q. To what extent, Mr. President?

THE PRESIDENT. Well, we haven't decided yet. These are preliminary conversations, to find out just what the situation is with regard to our necessity, and what Spain is willing to do. I think Mr. Acheson covered

[7] On July 16, Adm. Forrest P. Sherman, Chief of Naval Operations, met with Generalissimo Francisco Franco, Spanish Chief of State, to discuss Spain's possible role in the defense of Western Europe. Secretary of State Dean Acheson's statement regarding the conversation, made at his press conference on July 18, was published in the Department of State Bulletin (vol. 25, p. 170).

the thing very completely yesterday.

Q. This is not the result of any National Security Council decision?

THE PRESIDENT. It is the result of the advice from the Department of Defense.

[7.] Q. Mr. President, there is a move on foot to turn the key of the Bastille, now hanging out in Mount Vernon, to the people of France on the anniversary of Yorktown. Have you any comment?

THE PRESIDENT. The key to the Bastille belonged to George Washington. That is private property, and the Government has nothing to do with it.

[8.] Q. Mr. President, what do you think of Senator Douglas polling the Chicago Bar Association [8]——

THE PRESIDENT. I haven't been officially notified about it, and besides, the bar association doesn't make my appointments. I think I told you that once before.

Q. You didn't tell *me*. [*Laughter*]

THE PRESIDENT. Well, I told the press conference, let's put it that way. [*More laughter*] The Constitution still provides that I make the appointments.

[9.] Q. Would you say, sir, whether you expect any early decision one way or the other in the Kaesong talks?

THE PRESIDENT. No, I can make no comment on that.

[10.] Q. Mr. President, several public officials, including at least one Congressman

[8] Senator Paul Douglas of Illinois opposed two nominations by the President to district judgeships in that State, citing the constitutional theory requiring the advice and consent of the Senate for judicial appointments, and stating that his own recommendations had been ignored and that he had not been consulted about the President's nominations. Senator Douglas thereupon asked the Chicago Bar Association to conduct an advisory poll regarding his recommendations and the President's. Polls were also taken by the Illinois Bar Association and the Chicago Sun-Times. On October 9, the Senate rejected the President's nominations (Congressional Record, vol. 97, p. 12838).

in my area, have accused General Marshall [9] of conspiring to overthrow this Government, and to aid the Communists. I thought comment from you might be helpful?

THE PRESIDENT. That is one of the silliest things I ever heard. And I don't think that it helps the welfare of this Nation to have people, who are supposed to be responsible for its welfare, making silly statements like that.

[11.] Q. Mr. President, can you say what

[9] Secretary of Defense George C. Marshall.

progress, if any, has been made by Mr. Harriman [10] at Tehran?

THE PRESIDENT. No. I have not heard from Mr. Harriman direct.

Reporter: Thank you, Mr. President.

NOTE: President Truman's two hundred and seventy-first news conference was held in the Indian Treaty Room (Room 474) in the Executive Office Building at 10:30 a.m. on Thursday, July 19, 1951.

[10] W. Averell Harriman, the President's representative in Iran to discuss the Anglo-Iranian oil dispute (see Items 150, 155).

166 Remarks to a Group of Danish Boys From the International Boys Camp, Inc. *July* 19, 1951

IT IS a pleasure to have you here. I hope you are all enjoying yourselves at the camp. I am sure you are, because by the looks of you, you are getting plenty to eat.

I hope that when you go back home you will carry with you an impression of this country that will be lasting, and that will be pleasant.

It is a pleasure for me to greet you this morning, and in the name of your country; and I hope that you will continue to have

a pleasant time while you are here, and when you go back home you will all be successful in your own countries.

Thank you very much.

NOTE: The President spoke at 12:10 p.m. in the Rose Garden at the White House. In addition to the high school boys attending the camp, the group included Danish Ambassador Henrik de Kauffmann and Mrs. Ruth Bryan Rohde, who had founded the camp with her late husband, Borge Rohde. Mrs. Rohde, daughter of William Jennings Bryan, had formerly been a Congresswoman and U.S. Minister to Denmark.

167 Special Message to the Congress: The President's Midyear Economic Report. *July* 23, 1951

To the Congress of the United States:

Our economic problems in this country are now based mainly upon world problems. Our economic tasks are heavy because of the weight of our world responsibility.

To succeed in our economic job at home, we must understand fully our job in world affairs.

This job is plain. By every means within our power, we must continue the search for a just and lasting peace among all peoples.

We do not seek this peace through the

medium of war. We do not seek it through appeasement. And we do not seek it alone. We seek this peace through the international cooperation of all who want sincerely to join in the effort. On these terms, the door into a friendly association of nations is open to all.

But the door is not open to aggression and conquest. To prevent that, the combined strength of the free peoples must be made so great that no aggressor will be able to destroy freedom in the world.

The security of the free world is not a

matter of guns alone. It requires also economic, political, and moral strength. The defense program of the United States embraces all of these.

In the next days and weeks, the Congress will decide the future of this comprehensive defense program.

In its consideration of military appropriations, the Congress will decide whether we as a nation are going to achieve adequate security in the next few years.

In its consideration of the Mutual Security Program, it will decide whether we will continue to join boldly in marshalling the whole strength of the free world in a common resistance to communist aggression.

In its consideration of the Defense Production Act, it will decide whether we will channel our resources effectively to meet the demands of national security.

In its consideration of that Act and of revenue legislation, it will decide whether the line will be held against inflation.

Throughout the past year, we have been going through the transition from a normal peacetime economy to a defense economy. Military production is increasing, and schedules are now becoming firm. The expansion of the basic economy, to support the defense program, is moving forward, and additional expansion goals for specific industries are being set. The pattern of economic controls required by the defense program has been generally established.

Where we go from here depends on the decisions made by the Congress.

We can drive ahead on the course of the present defense program, or we can retreat.

The safety and welfare of our country require that we drive ahead.

This Economic Report is therefore a discussion of the kind of defense build-up which we are now undertaking, and which I propose we continue to undertake. It is

also an analysis of the measures which have been taken, or must be taken, to strengthen and stabilize the economy to support that build-up.

We are engaged in a long-term effort.

The need for military strength did not begin with the Korean war. Nor will it end when and if the fighting in Korea ceases.

The need for building strength was undergoing an urgent review before the attack of June 25 on the Republic of Korea. That event precipitated a quick and clear national decision to enlarge our military strength rapidly. This course should have—and, though no doubt in smaller measure, would have—been taken anyway.

We must be ever-mindful that the Soviet imperialists are relentlessly pursuing a long-range plan. Their tactics change, but their strategy is clear and persistent. That strategy is to probe for weak spots in the strength or morale of the free people, and, if a weak spot can be found, to strike another blow.

Whatever happens in Korea, we must take into account what is happening in Iran, on the borders of Yugoslavia, in Indo-China, and, most of all, what we know to be going on inside the Soviet Union itself. The main danger to world peace comes from the Soviet rulers, from the growing military force at their disposal, and from their proved willingness to use aggression to gain their ends. The military build-up of the Soviet Union, which has been continuing since 1945, has no other purpose than to blackmail the free world into submission to communist domination. Or, if the free world lacks strength or determination to prevent it, the purpose is to overrun its members one by one.

This is the central threat to our country, and to every free country in the world. We cannot have peace unless this threat is overcome. That is the purpose of our defense program.

This sustained effort on our part is something new in history. Free men have always been willing to take up arms, and to do their utmost, in a supreme crisis. But never before have free men in such large numbers acted together in advance, to prevent a supreme crisis. Never before on so vast a scale have free men assumed great risks voluntarily, so that even greater risks may not descend upon them involuntarily. Never before has there been so deep and widespread in the hearts of mankind the feeling that the price of peace is the willingness to fight for justice.

This is an effort of great hope and promise. It is a practical means by which we can bring to reality the great vision of world peace under law. But this effort—like any enterprise on a grand scale—will succeed only if we put into it the resources, the sweat and toil, the unremitting force of will, that it requires.

Our immediate plans must be flexible, as we constantly review our progress in the light of changing conditions. Right now, for example, we are reviewing our immediate goals for military strength, and it is quite possible that we shall have to raise them in several important respects.

But our fundamental course is unaltered. The free world must build the strength— moral, economic, and military—that is needed to deter aggression or, if aggression comes, to defeat it.

The greatest weakness we could disclose would be vacillation or lack of determination. To win in the contest between justice and aggression, the purposes of free men must be clear and persistent.

We must avoid shifting from one extreme of policy to another with every new development—either international or domestic— when such developments do not alter the fundamental situation.

Immediately after the initial Korean aggression, there were some extremists both in military and economic affairs. In military affairs, these extremists wanted immediately a 10-million-man armed force and a 100-billion-dollar-a-year military budget. In economic affairs, there were some extremists who wanted to freeze the whole economy in a strait jacket of controls more extensive than anything attempted during World War II.

Fortunately, the saving common sense of the American people avoided these extremes. We embarked upon a substantial build-up of our military strength, but without going on a total war footing. We started upon an economic mobilization program which bore a sensible relationship to the size of our defense effort and the likelihood of its long duration. This economic mobilization included measures to expand production and to control inflation. But it wisely did not attempt to mix full economic mobilization with partial military mobilization. That would have gotten our great productive economy all out of joint. It would have made us weaker, not stronger.

Today, extremists are pulling in a diametrically opposite direction. At the first signs of a let-down of the conflict in Korea, they have commenced to clamor for a reduction in our defense program. On the economic front, as soon as there is a slight softening of inflationary pressures, these extremists are ready to discard the whole structure of inflationary controls or shoot it full of holes.

If we were now to heed these extremists, it would be an even more costly mistake than to have heeded the extremists of a year ago. We have no reason to believe that the events in Korea have fundamentally changed the basic Soviet intentions. The events at home have not removed the need to expand our economic strength, or to overcome the basic inflationary danger.

We must press on to build our defenses.

We must press on to strengthen the other free nations.

We must press on to expand production and prevent inflation.

Only by pressing forward can we make the vision of peace among all men a lasting reality.

BUILDING OUR DEFENSES

Our defense program is designed to create substantial armed forces, ready for action, plus the ability to enlarge those forces very rapidly if the need arises. We have almost reached our first goal of 3½ million men and women on active duty. But in the case of many types of weapons, we have months and years of hard effort ahead, before we will have produced enough modern equipment for our active forces, for helping to equip our allies, and for the reserve stocks we need.

We have accomplished large increases in military production since the Korean invasion. Deliveries of hard goods—such as aircraft, tanks, weapons, and ammunitions—have more than tripled. Nevertheless, military output as a whole has moved up somewhat more slowly than scheduled. This has been due partly to some shortages, such as in machine tools. We have been "tooling up" thus far, but this stage is now well advanced. From this point forward, every effort must be exerted to catch up with production schedules and keep abreast of them.

In the cause of national safety, these schedules must be met.

Our total security program costs have now reached an annual rate of more than 35 billion dollars. In terms of constant prices, this is almost twice the level of a year ago, and 50 percent above the level of 6 months ago. These costs are scheduled to increase to an annual rate of more than 50 billion dollars by the end of this year, and to nearly 65 billion by the middle of 1952. The pro-portion of the Nation's total output devoted to security purposes, which was about 6 percent before Korea and is about 11 percent at present, will rise to approximately 15 percent by the end of 1951, and will approach 20 percent by a year from now.

These outlays cover pay and subsistence for our military forces, deliveries of military goods to our own forces and our allies, economic aid to other free nations, and other security expenditures. More than 85 percent of the total for the present fiscal year is allotted to building up the military strength of this country. This includes the sums to be spent on our military establishment, the atomic energy program, stockpiling, and other domestic security programs.

The major part of the scheduled increase of almost 30 billion dollars in the annual rate of security expenditures from the middle of this year to the middle of 1952 will involve procurement of aircraft, weapons, tanks, and other military end items, and some of the specialized equipment used in their production. Within the next 12 months, hard goods deliveries are scheduled to rise from a monthly rate of about 1 billion dollars to about three times that amount. During the same period, aircraft deliveries are to be tripled, and the tank-automotive program increased to four times the present rate of deliveries.

Measured by costs and by the strain on the economy, this is a large program. But it is a minimum program measured against the need, and is well within our capacity. The accompanying Review by the Council of Economic Advisers reveals in detail that, with wise policies, our economy can support this effort and yet remain sound and grow stronger. Compared with the rise of almost 30 billion dollars in security outlays scheduled for the coming 12 months, we expanded such outlays by about 75 billion dollars (in terms of present prices) in the first year of our participation in World War II. The program as now scheduled is not expected to absorb at its peak more than about one-fifth of our total output, compared with almost half in 1944. A year from now the program is expected to require about 11 million men and women directly or indirectly engaged in defense, contrasted with about 25 million at the peak of World War II.

We cannot now be sure what our production needs will be beyond that. If further aggression does not occur, we hope to be able, within two or three years, to level off our defense program, and to move on to a maintenance basis. At present, however, our principal concern is not with maintaining military strength. Our principal concern is to build up military strength in the first place.

We have been moving toward interim goals for Army, Navy, and Air Force strength. It now appears, as we review our strategic situation in the light of world events, that these goals may need to be raised, whether or not we have an armistice in Korea. The strategic and military studies needed for such decisions have not been completed; if it is indeed necessary to raise our sights, I shall later submit to the Congress requests for the additional funds required.

Regardless of the need to lift our goals for the active military forces, we must move full speed ahead toward our present goals.

STRENGTHENING THE OTHER FREE NATIONS

The defenses of the free nations are inseparable. Our defenses are bound up with the defenses of other free countries in every way—strategically, economically, morally— and their defenses are bound up with ours.

Due partly to historic events since the turn of the century, the United States has greater economic strength and potential military power than any other nation. But with only 10 percent of the free world's population, and only a fraction of its natural resources, our difficulties would be enormous if we were cut off from the rest of the free world.

Western Europe, together with Turkey, has a population 80 percent greater than ours, with a high proportion of skilled workers. It produces one-third of the steel of the free world, one-fifth of the aluminum, and nearly one-half of the coal. Moreover, areas outside the United States—in many cases the economically underdeveloped countries—produce about 43 percent of the free world's crude petroleum and about half of its iron ore. They produce about 70 to 80 percent of its lead, zinc, tungsten, and rubber supply, and virtually all of its cobalt, manganese, nickel, tin, and wool. We are vitally dependent upon imports for many of these products.

It would be a military disaster to us if these resources fell under hostile domination.

But it is not only in terms of the possibility of world conflict that we should view this problem. If we establish a secure peace, our prosperity will be linked with that of other nations. The economic upbuilding of one part of the world benefits also the other parts. As standards of production and of living rise in one area, this provides more markets for the products of other areas—and expanding production and markets are the lifeblood of economic progress.

The moral aspects of this issue are even more important than the economic. The great need of the twentieth century is to achieve a steadily improving morality to keep pace with growing technology. We must cooperate with the rest of the free world because the future progress of the free world is indivisible. Even if we could prosper in a world where others did not, we could not live at peace in that kind of world.

The people of the United States should ever bear in mind the sobering obligation to live up to the responsibility which our strength imposes. The past four decades have been marked by two world-wide wars to resist aggression. In these previous wars, many of those now allied with us poured out more blood, and more treasure relative to their resources, than we did. They emerged from those fearful struggles for survival with economic handicaps which have lasted for a generation and longer. On the other hand, the United States, because of geographic and other factors, did not suffer such destruction.

At the end of World War II, the other free nations set about to repair the ruin they had suffered. The Western European countries, mainly through their own efforts, but with vital assistance from us, made a remarkable recovery. Their industrial production has by now mounted above prewar levels by about 40 percent, and their total production by more than 15 percent. On a per capita basis, the increase in their total production has been more than 5 percent above prewar levels.

This increase in production was greatly facilitated by economic aid from the United States. In the three years after 1947, our foreign economic aid to Western Europe totaled about 11 billion dollars. Over the same period, the total annual output of these aided countries expanded by about 45 billion dollars.

Even with these increases in production, these nations could not notably advance their standards of living. This was because they had to allot so much of their resources to the rebuilding of productive capital equipment. In most instances, living standards did not begin to equal or surpass prewar levels until a year before the Korean outbreak. And just when hope was bright, the new turn in the international situation required these nations to redivert more of their resources to defense purposes. Our European North Atlantic Treaty partners are doubling their

military production in the course of one year, and many of them are committed to continuing large increases in the future. Their defense expenditures are being raised from less than 5 percent of their combined total output in 1949, and about 5¼ percent in 1950, to about 7½ percent in 1951.

This is not as large an increase in defense outlays as we are making. But the total economic situation in these other countries is very different from ours. Compared with the period just before World War II, the goods and services now available to the people in our country, for purposes other than defense, have risen about 50 percent per capita in real terms. In contrast with our situation, our European North Atlantic Treaty partners now have available goods and services, for purposes other than defense, less than 10 percent more per capita than in the period just before World War II. This problem is even more clearly revealed by another comparison. In the United States, total output per person, even after deducting output for military purposes, is estimated at nearly $2,000 for 1951. Among our European North Atlantic Treaty partners, the figure is estimated at less than one-third as high as ours. Allowing for shortcomings of international income comparisons, this difference is striking.

Under these circumstances, these countries are obviously limited in the amount of resources they can rapidly divert to defense purposes, without undermining their economic and political stability, and thus playing into the hands of communist minorities.

All of these factors have been taken into account, in the development of our program to help strengthen the other free nations.

For this purpose, I have recommended appropriations of 8.5 billion dollars for fiscal 1952. Of this amount, 6.3 billion dollars are to provide military assistance to other nations of the free world where increased military strength is needed to combat or forestall communist aggression or subversion. Such assistance will consist primarily of planes, tanks, guns, and other military weapons which must be produced in the United States because they cannot be produced abroad within the required time. While the largest portion of this aid will go toward filling the equipment needs of our partners in the North Atlantic Treaty, substantial quantities are also destined for countries in the Near East, Far East, and Latin America.

The remaining 2.2 billion dollars would consist of economic aid. Over half of this amount would go to Western Europe, in order to create the kind of economic strength which is necessary to support an increased European rearmament effort, and to do this without sacrificing the political and social stability required for security over the long run. This assistance will permit the diversion of men, materials, and facilities from civilian to military production, and aid the expansion of total production. Elsewhere in the world, where the problem is more economic than military, such assistance will help the peoples to combat the poverty, disease, and illiteracy on which communist subversion thrives. It will contribute, moreover, to a substantial expansion in the production of basic materials, particularly strategic materials, which are essential to the economic and military strength of the free world.

In addition to the materials and equipment provided under the Mutual Security Program, we are giving positive assistance, where necessary, to the export of goods which represent the essential requirements of the other free nations, and are paid for by them. And these exports will be considerably larger than non-military supplies which we finance.

The magnitude of the proposed security program, including foreign assistance, is well within the capacity of our productive resources. Proposed outlays for assistance to the other free nations over the next year comes to less than 15 percent of our total security program, and to only about 2 percent of our estimated total output during this period. We can carry forward both the domestic and the foreign aspects of our total security program, and still maintain domestic consumption and business investment at high levels.

The determination of the size and scope of the aid program which we should undertake this year has resulted from the same kind of careful preparation which has gone into the development of our scheduled expansion of United States military forces. It is in fact an integral part of our over-all security program.

For example, the military assistance I have recommended will make possible a rapid build-up in Western Europe of trained forces equipped with modern weapons. The existence of such forces is essential to the security of the United States. The cost to us of supplying equipment through our aid program is only a fraction of the cost of raising a comparable force ourselves.

The value of our aid programs, however, is far broader and more significant than simply a good investment in security. These programs will mean that free men, in many countries, will be able to stand up against the threats, the lies, the subversion of communist aggression. They will be able to defend themselves against bullets—and they will be able to combat communism's allies of poverty and hunger and sickness.

That is why our military and economic aid programs are as essential and as urgent as any part of the work we are doing to build up the defenses of freedom.

As we move forward with this program, we must continuously review and, if necessary, revise it to assure maximum results. We must be sure in the conduct of this program that other nations do their full share. We are challenged by the hard task of a new kind of cooperation, based upon a new kind of international situation. We must face these problems of the future realistically and courageously.

EXPANDING AND STABILIZING THE ECONOMY

During the past year, the growth of production in the American economy has been very large. During the second quarter of 1950, our total output was at an annual rate of about 300 billion dollars, measured in today's prices. During the second quarter of 1951, measured in the same prices, our total output rose to an annual rate of 330 billion dollars, or a real gain of 30 billion. This gain far exceeded the increased outlays for national defense. Our economy is stronger now than it was when the defense build-up started.

This growth in our productive power was not achieved without considerable inflation, partly because the measures for controlling inflation took time to enact and get into operation. But since these measures have been in full swing, we have continued to expand total output without inflation. That is a salient fact about economic developments since the early part of this year.

We are now in a position where, if the Congress enacts adequate legislation, we can continue to enlarge our defense efforts, to expand our productive capacity, and to hold inflation in check. I emphasize that our success in these matters will depend on a series of legislative measures which the Congress is now considering. If the Congress enacts sound and strong legislation, as I earnestly hope it will, we can achieve our goals.

Our production goals

The Council of Economic Advisers estimates that we have the ability to increase our total output by at least 5 percent within a year's time. This goal is practicable, and we should strive to surpass it. Expansion of output will make it possible to carry forward our security program with less strain upon our economy. It will make it easier to raise necessary tax revenues, and to restrain inflation. It will offer the prospect of reducing irksome controls in due course, if the international situation does not worsen. Increasing our basic productive capacity will place us in a stronger position to mobilize fully and quickly if that necessity should be forced upon us.

Manpower is our prime productive resource. Within a year, through various programs for the voluntary mobilization of our manpower resources, as well as through population growth, we should expand our total labor force by 1½ to 2 million persons. This expansion is entirely possible, and with it there should be no general manpower shortage, although there will be shortages in certain skilled trades, and in some industries longer hours will be needed.

A major obstacle to the further expansion of production is the shortage of capacity in a number of key industries. It is not possible to expand capacity in all directions at once. We must concentrate on assuring adequate capacity for military equipment, and on basic materials, transportation, and power. We must postpone those types of investment which add least to our productive strength. We must relate our own expansion of capacity to the capacity available in other countries, and to total potential supplies of basic materials.

A number of basic expansion programs have been prepared by the defense agencies, and are now going forward under continuing review. In steel, the program calls for an increase of capacity from 107 million ingot tons annually now to nearly 120 million tons by the end of 1952. The aluminum program is planned to more than double our 1950 rate of output by the end of 1953. The proposed electric power program looks toward a 40 percent increase of generating capacity by the end of 1953.

These are only examples. Large-scale investment in tools and equipment for factory, farm, and transport must be continued for several years, at or near the peak levels which have recently been reached. We must, for a time, limit investment in nonessentials—as we are doing. But we must be very careful in deciding what can be postponed and what cannot. The strategy of a prolonged partial mobilization requires a much broader production base than the strategy of total war.

For example, it is now more urgent than before that we begin at once certain developmental projects—like the St. Lawrence seaway and power project—which will not be completed for several years, but which are especially needed in a defense economy. Furthermore, we must resume, as soon as we can, some of the programs which can only temporarily be curtailed without ultimate sacrifice of economic power. For example, the expansion of educational and health facilities, of long-range resource development and housing, as contemplated before the emergency, must be resumed in time to avoid serious impairment of our national strength.

This is why we need a production advance on a very broad front. This means more than the expansion of capacity and the improvement of tools in a few select areas. It means the application of business acumen and labor skills in a joint effort throughout the whole economy. It means the joinder of new science and new technology with the industrial machine. It means drawing upon all the resources, material and moral, which reside within our system of enterprise and government.

Production aids

To encourage the necessary expansion of our productive capacity, the Government is allocating scarce materials, and extending special aids through direct loans, government guarantee of private loans, commitments to purchase, and rapid amortization of facilities for tax purposes. These aids are becoming increasingly effective, in connection with specific expansion programs.

The authority for these production programs, with the exception of tax amortization, is included in the Defense Production Act. Renewal of this authority is urgently needed in order to achieve our production goals. Adequate funds are also required. In addition, the defense agencies should be given certain additional production powers, such as the authority to construct defense plants where this is essential to the mobilization effort.

Our stabilization goals

After the Korean outbreak, a wave of inflation swept over most countries. It was less serious in the United States than in some other places. But even here, it raised living costs by 9 percent, and wholesale prices by 16 percent. This inflation encouraged speculation, and put heavy burdens on many of our people. Those fortunate enough to have rising incomes were able to maintain their living standards. But more than half the families of the Nation had no income gains between early 1950 and early 1951, and almost one-fifth suffered actual declines.

During the past few months, there has been relative price stability. Wholesale prices are now somewhat below the peak levels of last March. Consumer prices are no longer soaring, although they rose slightly from February to May.

The easing of the inflationary pressure since spring has been due partly to larger civilian supply. It has also reflected higher taxes, credit restraints, and the application of price and wage controls early this year. Moreover, as the military situation improved, many consumers switched from frantic buying to cautious buying, while businesses felt that some inventories were excessive, and curtailed their orders.

These recent developments have led some people to think that the inflationary trend is ended. This is a dangerous assumption. We cannot accept it as a guide to national policy.

The fundamental fact is that we must increase the annual rate of national security expenditures by about 30 billion dollars during the next year. In order to produce more airplanes, tanks, and other munitions, we must continue the cutbacks which have been made in the production of consumer and investment goods, and possibly make some further cuts.

While total consumer supplies cannot be expected to rise significantly, incomes will continue to grow, because total production and employment will and must continue to expand. It is estimated that, by a year from now, personal incomes before taxes, measured at an annual rate, may rise to a level 15 to 20 billion dollars above the current annual rate. If taxes and savings are not sufficiently increased, there would thus be a growing disparity between the incomes which people would desire to spend and the supply of consumer goods. This disparity represents the inflationary gap. If controls were to be relaxed, the inflationary gap would be greater—probably very much greater. The price-wage spiral would again be set in motion.

Inflation stimulates the production of many nonessential goods, thus pulling resources away from essential production. It favors some groups at the expense of others. It lifts the cost of national defense, and shifts the burden toward those least able to bear it. Inflation impairs the value of peoples' savings, and undermines their willingness to save.

Winning the battle against inflation is an essential element in our struggle for peace. The battle cannot be won by using only one of the weapons available to us. Stabilization depends upon a combination of measures, each of which reinforces the others.

Taxation

There is no more important single measure for combatting inflation, under present circumstances, than the maintenance of a balanced budget. The substantial increases in taxes adopted by the Congress since the Korean outbreak have helped to stabilize the economy and aided in halting the price rise. The public approval of these tax increases has demonstrated that the American people are ready to pay the price of protecting our way of life.

Government expenditures for national security have risen from an annual rate of 18 billion dollars (in present prices) before the Korean outbreak to a current rate of about 35 billion dollars. It has been pointed out that the annual rate of these outlays is scheduled to increase by about 30 billion dollars within the next 12 months. This increase, even when accompanied by economy in other expenditures, is bound to result in growing deficits under present tax legislation.

To put our security program on a pay-as-we-go basis, and to reduce the inflationary pressure which this program will generate, we need an increase in taxes of at least 10 billion dollars this year.

Such an increase in taxes, though heavy, would not interfere with needed work and production incentives. It would be consistent with maintenance of a good standard of living, and an equitable distribution of spendable income. It would aid substantially in the stabilization of prices. It would ease the problems of managing the huge national debt.

Public expenditures

We must also continue to pare down less essential or postponable public spending. This is another avenue toward a balanced budget and toward the control of inflation. The less urgent public activities of Federal, State, and local governments should be reduced or retarded, until the security build-up has passed its peak, or until our over-all productive power catches up with the increased burden imposed by the security program.

In a protracted period of partial mobilization, the distinction between defense and non-defense activities is not as clear as in a total war. The strategy of our current defense effort is not to build maximum defensive power at once. It is instead to build reasonable power, and to reinforce it with the underlying productive capacity and basic economic strength which will enable us to be ready for any problem of the future. That underlying strength, for the long pull, includes education and training, health services, development of natural resources, research, and scientific progress. We must strike a careful balance, not doing as much of all of these things as we ought to do in normal peacetime, but not doing so little as to weaken ourselves for the long pull.

The budget which I have submitted to the Congress for the current fiscal year rep-resents a minimum program consistent with this policy. Further, the spending activities of the Government are under continuous review. Those which can be reduced without weakening the defense effort are being reduced. Those which can be redirected to make a further contribution to defense are being redirected.

Credit policy

Credit expansion contributed to the inflation of the past year. We must prevent it from adding to future inflationary pressures. In the current national emergency, when some types of credit extension are necessary in order to increase production of certain essential defense and civilian requirements, while other types of credit extension defeat the purpose of the mobilization program by permitting the expansion of production in unnecessary areas, it is essential to use credit controls as selectively as possible. General credit measures reach areas not touched by selective credit measures, but they do not discriminate between activities which should be supported, and those which need to be restrained. For this reason, effective measures of selective credit control, such as regulation of consumer and real estate credit, are needed. The legislative authority to impose them should not be impaired.

One important merit in the selective credit controls is that they may be loosened or tightened by prompt administrative action, in response to shifts in the economic situation. This flexibility would be destroyed, if the Congress by excessively detailed legislation were to narrow the range of administrative discretion within which the Board of Governors of the Federal Reserve System could operate in exercising selective credit controls. I recommend that the Congress avoid unwise limitations upon the use of an instrument which has clearly proved its worth.

I have recommended several times that the Congress authorize the placing of margin requirements on speculative trading in commodity futures. I repeat this recommendation now. Similar provisions for margin requirements in stock trading have proved very useful.

Authority to impose additional reserve requirements when needed would strengthen the Federal Reserve System's influence over credit conditions with minimum effects on the needs of debt management. I recommend that the Congress give careful consideration to the plans for accomplishing this purpose outlined in the attached Midyear Economic Review.

As a phase of the Government's credit policy, all major Federal lending and loan guarantee programs have been revised, to minimize their inflationary impact and to contribute most to the defense effort.

I am also glad to note that lending institutions throughout the country, and State and local governments, are cooperating in a voluntary credit restraint program which has been initiated by private financial institutions under the sponsorship of the Board of Governors of the Federal Reserve System.

Voluntary saving

Voluntary saving is an essential part of a well-rounded anti-inflationary program. Without a large volume of voluntary saving, taxes high enough to close the inflationary gap might reduce incentive and cramp production. Also, without a large volume of voluntary saving, only the most severe direct controls could prevent prices from being swept upward by a flood of demand.

In addition, voluntary saving serves other purposes in our economy. It provides a source of funds for investment. It adds to the family's sense of security for the future. When the time comes to make the transition from a defense economy to a peacetime economy, the prudent use of accrued savings will help to maintain demand and employment during the changeover period.

The Government savings bond program is very important in the effort to promote voluntary saving. The Treasury has carried on an intensified payroll savings drive since shortly after the outbreak of hostilities in Korea. Commencing on Labor Day, the Treasury will call upon all Americans to do their part in a full-scale savings bond campaign which will reach into every community and every home in the Nation. Because it is a voluntary program, this effort must be made in the last analysis not only by the Government, but also by every voice that can be heard throughout the country.

Consideration should be given to developing voluntary savings plans in connection with productivity wage increases. Such plans would help to keep these increases out of the inflationary stream. This would be beneficial to workers, who would not be trying to spend their additional income until a time when they could spend it without driving up prices. These plans should be tied in with the Savings Bond Payroll Deduction Program.

But voluntary saving is not a substitute for adequate taxation or other inflation controls. Nothing could be more destructive of the willingness or ability to save, than constantly rising prices. After other inflation controls took hold earlier this year, and helped to stabilize prices, the rate of voluntary saving moved very sharply upward.

Price and wage stabilization

Indirect measures for controlling inflation are vitally important. But with inflationary pressures as large as those which we may face in the year ahead, indirect controls are not enough. They must be buttressed by direct price and wage controls.

The basic objective of price control now is

415

to hold the general price line. Ceiling prices should not be raised except where essential to provide adequate production incentives to business, or to correct clearly inequitable situations. As a general rule, price increases should not be approved, even where some costs have risen, if the industry is earning a fair and equitable level of profits. Just as some upward adjustments of some prices will be needed, some rollbacks will be needed in selected cases, for example, where prices or profits are excessively high. This is the practical way to maintain adequate flexibility in the price structure, while holding the general price line. This requires legislation which strengthens, not weakens, price control.

Wage stabilization requires a careful balance among three major objectives. First, it should seek to prevent an increase in total payrolls so large that, after making due allowances for taxes and voluntary saving, they would seriously inflate total demand. Second, it should provide adequate incentives for increased productive effort, and redress serious inequities in the wage structure. And third, it should minimize wage increases of a kind which would require price increases.

The achievement of these objectives is the primary task of the Wage Stabilization Board. In the January Economic Report, I expressed hearty agreement with the principle that effective wage stabilization in a democracy requires the active participation and cooperation of management and labor. This is being attained through the present Wage Stabilization Board, which contains equal representation of those two groups and of the public. In addition to its stabilization responsibilities, the Board is empowered to handle labor disputes affecting the national defense program if parties jointly submit their case for recommendation or decision. The Board is also empowered to

recommend a settlement in labor disputes certified by the President as threatening the progress of the national defense program. The labor dispute responsibilities of the Board are the minimum necessary for the mobilization effort.

Fair and practical wage policies are in process of development. This is not a simple task. The Board has recognized that wages should be adjusted to compensate for changes in the cost of living. Other wage adjustments are also desirable, if hardships and inequities are to be dealt with, as required by the Defense Production Act. The Wage Stabilization Board has taken steps to deal with the difficult problems of productivity allowances and so-called fringe benefits. Within proper limits, productivity allowances provide desirable incentives and can make a real contribution to the mobilization effort while some fringe benefits may be anti-inflationary. These and many other problems must be solved in developing integrated wage policies.

Rent control

The control of rents is important to the success of our mobilization effort. As we expand output in different industrial areas, we have to attract outside workers who would be repelled if rents were allowed to rise exorbitantly. Simple justice also requires us to protect the families of our soldiers, who move to the areas where military camps are being reopened or expanded.

Despite the great postwar building boom, vacancy rates are very low, while the expanded mobilization effort is creating new and large demands for housing in many parts of the country. We cannot control prices and wages effectively if rents are uncontrolled.

The rent control law now in effect was designed to permit orderly decontrol of all rents by this time. But it was not enacted in an environment of great defense expansion. That effort is already seriously affecting the housing supply in many areas. The new law that is being considered by the Congress should be geared to the new needs of the defense effort. It should permit effective control of rents, where an inflationary rise is threatened which would be harmful to the mobilization effort.

SUMMARY OF ECONOMIC DEVELOPMENTS IN
THE FIRST HALF OF 1951

In its second half year since the Korean outbreak, our economic mobilization for defense made heartening progress. Since the middle of 1950, the economy's over-all output has increased at a faster rate than in any previous postwar period. Price and wage inflation, rampant in the first weeks of 1951, was checked by the imposition of general price and wage controls at the end of January. Soon thereafter, and partly as a result of this action, inflationary pressure subsided temporarily as consumers moderated their abnormal rates of buying. Government spending for defense and defense production mounted at an accelerating pace, however, presaging a revival of inflationary pressures later on.

Both on the production and the stabilization sides, the record leaves room for improvement.

Employment has increased substantially during the last year, with unemployment falling sharply, the total labor force growing at about twice the normal rate, and our armed forces more than doubling. Nonagricultural employment, after expanding rapidly following the Korean outbreak, has been relatively stable in 1951, while agricultural employment has continued its long-run, year-to-year decline. In June, total civilian employment was 61.8 million—300,000 higher than in June 1950.

While there is not yet any over-all manpower shortage, we do face serious shortages in certain skilled trades and professions, some of which have been long-continuing.

Unemployment in the first 6 months of this year was 1.8 million lower than in the same period last year. In June, it reached the lowest level for any June since World War II—2.0 million. The average duration of unemployment, as well as the number of people out of work, has declined.

Working hours, which lengthened considerably during the second half of 1950, declined somewhat during the first half of this year. In June, the average workweek in manufacturing industries was 40.8 hours, compared with 40.5 hours in June 1950, with all of the increase occurring in durable goods industries.

Production of goods and services as a whole (as measured by gross national product in constant prices) was more than 5 percent higher in the first half of 1951 than in the second half of 1950, and about 10 percent above the first half of last year.

Industrial production, which soared during the last 6 months of 1950, increased from an index figure of 218 in December (1935–39=100) to 223 in April. But since then, because of raw materials shortages, cutbacks, and slackening of civilian demand, the over-all index has shown no change.

Continuing high rates of agricultural production indicate that our supply of foods in the year ahead should be at least as great as in the year just passed, and fully adequate for normal requirements. The demand for food, however, is unusually high. Fortunately, current crop prospects are encouraging. Production of cotton will be sharply expanded this year.

Prices at midyear 1951 were far above their levels a year earlier, reflecting largely the surge before the General Ceiling Price Regulation was issued at the end of January.

Wholesale prices stabilized by mid-February, and tended down slightly in the second quarter, returning by midyear to a level only slightly above that at the time of the General Ceiling Price Regulation. In June, farmers were, on the average, receiving prices equivalent to 106 percent of parity, but there were wide differences among commodities. Throughout the second quarter, wholesale industrial prices were in a very slow but steady decline, and at midyear were at about their January level.

Consumers' prices, which were climbing about 1½ percent monthly in the buying wave at the turn of the year, increased only 0.9 percent from February to May, reaching in the latter month a level of 8.9 percent above that of June 1950. Retail food prices were 2.5 percent higher than in January. They moved down 0.3 percent in June, but were 11.7 percent above June last year.

Wages continued to rise in the first half of 1951, but at a diminished rate. Average hourly earnings in manufacturing, which had increased over 8 cents an hour from July to December 1950, increased by almost 5 cents an hour from January to June of this year. Weekly earnings in durable goods manufacturing advanced almost $3.00 during the first 6 months of 1951, but rose only 10 cents for workers in nondurable goods manufacturing during the same period.

Work stoppages have not been a serious problem so far this year. While the number of stoppages was higher than in the comparable period of 1950, total man-days of idleness were at considerably lower levels.

Profits of corporations, before taxes (not adjusted for changes in inventory valuations), are estimated to have reached a new record annual rate of 50 billion dollars in the first half of 1951. The level estimated for the second quarter of 1951—48½ billion—is below the peak of nearly 52 billion reached in the first quarter. It compares with 37½

billion in the second quarter of last year. Corporate profits after taxes, reflecting higher tax rates, averaged 22½ billion for the half year, compared with 19 billion in the same period of 1950 and a peak rate of nearly 28 billion in the fourth quarter of last year.

The net income of nonagricultural unincorporated business, after dropping off in the fourth quarter of 1950, reached a new peak in the first quarter of this year, and then declined. The net income of farm proprietors moved steadily upward from mid-1950 to the spring of 1951, reaching an estimated annual rate of 17 billion dollars in the second quarter of this year. This was 5 billion higher than last year, but 1½ billion short of the record level in the second quarter of 1948.

Money and credit developments in the first half of 1951, in contrast with the general expansion occurring in the first 6 months after the Korean outbreak, were divergent.

The privately held money supply (including demand and time deposits), declined in the first quarter of the year, under the usual impact of personal income tax payments, and then expanded in the second quarter.

The total loans of all commercial banks increased about 5 percent, or nearly 3 billion dollars, between December 1950 and June 1951. During the same period a year earlier, the increase was 4 percent; in the second half of 1950, it was about 17 percent. Mortgage credit continued to rise in the first half of 1951, but at slower rates than in the last half of 1950, as credit restrictions took hold. Consumer credit outstanding, after soaring 2.4 billion dollars in the second half of 1950, declined about 900 million dollars in the first 6 months of 1951.

Personal income rose nearly 6 billion dollars (annual rate) in the first quarter of 1951 and, advancing almost 6 billion more in the second quarter, reached an annual rate of

250 billion. Despite the tax increase, personal income after taxes rose from an annual rate of 215 billion dollars in the last quarter of 1950 to 217½ billion in the first quarter of 1951 and 223 billion in the second quarter.

Consumption expenditures, following roughly the same pattern as in the last 6 months of 1950, spurted in the first quarter of 1951 to a record annual rate of 208 billion dollars, and then declined to an estimated annual rate of 203 billion in the second quarter of this year. In constant prices, consumption in the first half of 1951 was about 2 percent less than in the second half of last year.

Net personal saving, under the impact of the first quarter buying wave, is estimated, in that quarter, to have amounted to only 4 to 5 percent of disposable income. In the second quarter of 1951, saving apparently rose to between 8 and 9 percent of disposable income—the highest rate of the postwar period, but far below the rates attained during World War II.

Gross private domestic investment in the first half of this year reached a record level of 62 billion dollars at a seasonally adjusted annual rate, 40 percent higher than in the same period last year, and 15 percent above the second half of 1950.

Plant and equipment expenditures reached a new high in the second quarter of 1951, nearly one-third above the corresponding quarter of 1950, with the increases concentrated in outlays for industrial facilities directly or indirectly serving the security program.

From the Korean outbreak to May, the book value of inventories in manufacturing and trade rose at a record rate. Inventory accumulation slowed in the first quarter of 1951, but then in the second quarter rose again, as sales failed to meet expectations. In May of this year, the ratio of inventories to sales dropped slightly, but was close to postwar highs. At the retail level, the inventory-sales ratio was considerably above any previous postwar figure.

While new construction activity was at a record level of about 32 billion dollars (seasonally adjusted annual rate) in the first half of 1951, the most striking change has been the increasingly sharp fall since February in seasonally adjusted new private housing expenditures, as the credit controls have begun to take hold. But private industrial and public construction have far exceeded the levels of a year ago.

International transactions of the United States in the first half of 1951 reflected expansion of United States exports and leveling off in imports, as our very heavy post-Korean buying eased somewhat. Our export surplus increased from an annual rate of 2.5 billion dollars in the fourth quarter of 1950 to an estimated 5.8 billion in the second quarter of this year.

Largely as a result of increased military aid, total net financing of foreign transactions, including export of military equipment, by the U.S. Government rose from an annual rate of 4.5 billion dollars in the last quarter of 1950 to 5.1 billion in the second quarter of 1951. With the greater export surplus, the outflow of gold and dollar assets from the United States was greatly reduced.

In Western Europe, increasing need for imports raised the trade deficit from an annual rate of 3 billion dollars in the final quarter of last year to more than 5 billion in the first quarter of this year. Price inflation during the first half of 1951 became more and more clearly a world-wide problem, with most countries suffering greater post-Korean price increases than the United States.

Government finances in the first 6 months of the year involved a temporary surplus of Federal receipts over expenditures, as the growth of defense expenditures lagged for the time being behind the increase in taxes. The budget surplus was 4.1 billion in the first half of calendar 1951, and 3.5 billion in the fiscal year ended June 30, 1951. The Government's total cash receipts from the public, including social security and other transactions as well as those appearing in budget accounts, exceeded payments to the public in the first half of 1951 by 6.9 billion dollars, or by 3.9 billion when adjusted for the seasonal peak in receipts in the first quarter.

Estimates of changes in State and local government finance indicate that in the first half of 1951 the small deficit incurred by these governments in the last 6 months of 1950 was virtually eliminated.

HARRY S. TRUMAN

NOTE: The message and the complete report are published in "The Midyear Economic Report of the President, Transmitted to the Congress July 1951" (Government Printing Office, 1951, 278 pp.). As printed above, illustrative charts and all references to them have been omitted.

168   Remarks to Delegates to the Sixth Annual American Legion "Boys Nation." *July 25, 1951*

I UNDERSTAND that you have had a very satisfactory meeting here. The Senator from Wyoming was telling me about the time you gave him with your questions, and one thing and another, and of your interest in government. He also told me that you voted statehood for Alaska and Hawaii, and that pleased me immensely.

I hope that you do have some educational interest in your Government. I think you have, or you wouldn't be here, because the time is going to come when responsibility for the operation of your Government—national, State and local—will be in your hands.

It is to your interest to know something about the basis on which our system is founded—the greatest in the history of the world, I think—the most satisfactory government in the history of the world. It is rather cumbersome and unwieldy, on account of the fact that its functions are separate. We have the executive, who carries out and enforces the laws. We have a court that sits as an arbiter between litigants. And we have a legislative branch of the government that is supposed to—and does—make the laws under which we live. And that is all founded, as you all know, on the Constitu-

tion of the United States, the greatest document of government, I think, that has ever been written in the history of the world.

It gives me a lot of pleasure to receive you young men here this morning, and I hope you will go home with a better idea of how your Government functions, and what it really means to you as an individual.

Government is an intangible thing. Government is what you make it. Government is what the people themselves want, under our system, because they have the right to elect officials, and if officials don't behave in a local community, they have the right to recall them. They don't have any right to recall the President, but they do in some States have the right to recall their public officials.

I appreciate your being here, and hope you have enjoyed yourselves, and I hope you will go home and tell the rest of the young people in your community just what you have learned.

NOTE: The President spoke at 1 p.m. in the Rose Garden at the White House. During his remarks he referred to Senator Joseph C. O'Mahoney of Wyoming, who had addressed the delegates on July 22.

169   Letter to the Chairman, Wage Stabilization Board, Requesting Investigation of a Labor Dispute Affecting the Production of Copper. *July 26, 1951*

Dear Dr. Taylor:

On the basis of the information and advice submitted to me by the Office of Defense Mobilization and the Federal Mediation and Conciliation Service, I am of the opinion that the dispute between the American Smelting and Refining Company and the United Steelworkers of America at Garfield, Utah, is of a character which substantially threatens the progress of national defense. Thus, in accordance with the terms of E.O. 10233, I am referring the dispute to the Wage Stabilization Board and asking that the Board investigate and inquire into the issues in dispute and promptly report to me with its recommendations to the parties as to fair and equitable terms of settlement.

The Director of the Office of Defense Mobilization has reported to me on the serious effect of the strike on the production of copper and sulphuric acid, both of which are extremely critical to the defense program.

It is clear from the report of the Federal Mediation and Conciliation Service that negotiations to date have been fruitless and that, although full use has been made of mediation and conciliation facilities, the strike persists and is likely to persist. I am asking the Federal Mediation and Conciliation Service to provide the Board with a record of the issues in dispute.

As you know, this is the first occasion on which I have referred a dispute to the Board. It is my earnest hope that the men involved will comply with your request that they return to work while the matter is before the Board and that the utilization of the Board's machinery will thus serve its purpose of restoring to production the facilities necessary to the national defense. I am sure that, in that event, the Board will proceed promptly in its task of recommending to the parties fair and equitable terms of settlement of the dispute.

Very sincerely yours,

HARRY S. TRUMAN

[Honorable George Taylor, Chairman, Wage Stabilization Board, Washington 25, D.C.]

NOTE: For the President's letter to the Chairman on the settlement of the dispute, see Item 277. See also Item 204.

170   Message to the Congress Transmitting Report of U.S. Participation in the United Nations for 1950. *July 26, 1951*

To the Congress of the United States:

I transmit herewith, pursuant to the United Nations Participation Act, a report on our participation in the work of the United Nations during 1950.

It is a record of decision and action in the face of danger and, at the same time, a record of increasing efforts to promote human progress in the attainment of the basic objectives of the United Nations Charter. It is for the most part a record of solidarity among United Nations members against aggression.

The struggle of the United Nations against Communist aggression in 1950 has a deep significance that reaches beyond the momentary successes and reverses recorded. This significance lies in the simple fact that the United Nations acted promptly and resolutely, and with success, against deliberate, treacherous, and well-prepared aggression. The aggressors and their supporters undoubtedly believed that the Organization and its members would not come to the defense of Korea with timely and effective help. It is probable that one of the purposes of the attack was to break down—through such a failure—any possibility of effective United Nations action against aggression in the future.

As the world knows, the United Nations met the assault squarely and without hesitation. In so doing, it made clear that an aggressor will not be allowed to isolate and destroy his victims one by one. The United Nations elected to act now rather than to drift passively once more down the fatal trail of failure to oppose aggression which leads finally to total war. Thousands of men have therefore sacrificed their lives in Korea to the end that millions may not lose their lives in a world war.

There is much to indicate that the resolute resistance of United Nations troops has given pause to those aggressive forces which cold-bloodedly brought tragedy to Korea.

In these great events the United States has taken a worthy and responsible part. American troops fighting in Korea are a major bulwark of the international community against the barbarous forces that would debase and destroy it. American fighting men have rarely in all our history struck more important blows for human freedom and welfare. I am proud—and I know the American people are proud—of the fight which our men, together with their comrades in arms, have waged in Korea.

The army and people of the Republic of Korea have heroically and patiently endured the brunt of the Communist aggression. The story of their unwavering resistance to that aggression is an epic in the annals of the

struggle of free men to maintain their liberty and independence.

I should like to pay special tribute to the gallant fighting men of the other countries who defended the cause of the United Nations in battle during 1950—men from Australia, Belgium, Canada, France, Greece, Luxembourg, the Netherlands, New Zealand, the Philippines, Thailand, Turkey, the Union of South Africa, and the United Kingdom.

Fighting units from Ethiopia arrived in Korea in early May 1951, and units from Colombia arrived in early June 1951. Hospital units and ships from Denmark, India, Norway, and Sweden also are operating in the Korean area.

United Nations action in Korea has been truly collective action. Concrete aid in the form of combat troops, ships and planes, field hospitals and medical equipment, other equipment, supplies, and food has been made available by 39 members of the United Nations; political support, by no less than 53 members. These countries vary greatly in their abilities to contribute to a collective military operation such as that in Korea. Contributions equal in number and identical in kind are obviously impossible. Nevertheless it must be recognized that every free country, large and small, is vitally—and I should say equally—interested in world security.

Much has been said in the Congress and in public forums on all phases of our action in Korea. Discussion and honest criticism are in the best traditions of our people and are in fact essential to the working of our system of government. As on other subjects, I welcome them in connection with our record in the United Nations. Throughout the world, Communist propaganda has of course sought to represent this country's action as "imperialism" dictated by material interests. I do not believe that, wherever the channels of opinion are free, our basic purposes will be misunderstood. Our action in the Korean crisis was not dictated by any American material interest there. We neither sought nor do we seek any special position or privilege in Korea. Our action in the crisis was motivated by our deep conviction of the importance of preventing a breakdown of the international security system and of the principles of the Charter. I was convinced then, and I am convinced now, that to have ignored the appeal of Korea for aid, to have stood aside from the assault upon the Charter, would have meant the end of the United Nations as a shield against aggression. It might have meant the end of any possibility that collective security could be made to work.

Under the Charter, the United Nations must afford protection against aggression, whether committed by big countries or by small countries. Just as the United Nations branded as aggression the original assault by the North Korean Communist regime, so it has branded as aggression the later intervention by the Chinese Communist regime and its attack upon United Nations forces. There are not two laws, one for small and one for large countries. Indeed it is hard to see how the United Nations could ever operate under such a double standard. This does not of course mean that the United Nations has acted blindly, without carefully considering the effects of its measures. In fact the record shows a most careful concern by the great majority of members, including this country, to avoid extension of the conflict and to preserve unity while maintaining our objective of resisting aggression.

While our primary and immediate task has been defense against aggression and the creation of collective measures for accomplishing this more effectively, we have not lost sight of the objective of creating an international security system based upon the reduction and control of armaments. In my statement to the General Assembly on October 24, 1950, I made clear our continued determination to work toward this goal in every practicable way.

The aggression against the United Nations has brought home to all peoples the imperative need for developing more effective means to deal with aggression within the framework of the United Nations. The Korean case has demonstrated that the United Nations can act effectively against aggression through recommendations of the Security Council, or the General Assembly, if the Security Council is paralyzed by the veto. But in Korea the participating nations had to improvise their measures from the ground up.

It was to meet this need that the Secretary of State launched at the beginning of the General Assembly in September 1950 the proposals which were developed into the Uniting for Peace Resolution. Mr. Acheson said:

"The world waits to see whether we can build on the start we have made. The United Nations must move forward energetically to develop a more adequate system of collective security. If it does not move forward, it will move back.

". . . The General Assembly can and should organize itself to discharge its responsibility promptly and decisively if the Security Council is prevented from acting."

This resolution can mark the beginning of a great step forward in the development of the United Nations as an instrument for collective action to maintain peace and put down aggression. We place great hope in the program projected by this resolution, particularly the provisions relative to the maintenance by members of the United Nations of armed forces for possible service as United Nations units, and the Collective Measures Committee set up to study and report on possible methods of maintaining and strengthening international peace and security. We shall give our full support to the aims and objectives of the program and to the work of this Committee in developing them.

Despite the emphasis which the United Nations has been compelled to give during the last year to action to meet aggression, it has intensified rather than slackened its various activities to promote human progress in attainment of other basic objectives of the Charter.

One of the fundamental human aspirations is the desire to control one's own destiny or, phrased in another way, to exercise the rights of self-government or independence. The organs of the United Nations which are charged with the responsibility of fulfilling the purposes of the Charter with respect to the development of non-self-governing people made notable progress during the past year. The United States has contributed fully to these efforts.

The United Nations has intensified its efforts to combat the perennial enemies of mankind—hunger, disease, and ignorance. Through many channels and in numerous programs, the United Nations and the specialized agencies have furthered the basic goal of "the creation of conditions of stability and well being which are necessary for peaceful and friendly relations among nations." Of particular significance this past year was the inauguration of an expanded program of technical assistance for the economic development of underdeveloped countries. Some 56 countries of the free world have participated by making contributions, and 48 countries have initiated programs designed to use the facilities of the United Nations and specialized agencies in the development of their own human and material resources and in raising their standards of living. The United States has actively supported these activities and will continue to do so.

The weakness and the strength of the United Nations manifested in 1950 were those of a human endeavor which is still in its infancy. Despite centuries of effort, nations have only recently been able to cooperate effectively on a world-wide scale to achieve security and their other common purposes. In our limited experience we have met with many difficulties and reverses and will meet more in the future. But we have also achieved tangible success, and this success gives ground for hope that we are moving ahead on the right track. It is essential for all of us to understand that a stable peace can be achieved only through long, hard work and sacrifice. I am sure that the people of this country and of practically all countries realize that the goal of peace is worth this work and this sacrifice.

Under the stress of events in 1950 the members of the United Nations did not, of course, always see completely eye to eye. Nevertheless as loyal members the great majority strove to accommodate their views and action to the fullest possible extent in the interest of the major purposes of the United Nations. No nation has a monopoly of wisdom. Even among peoples sincerely devoted to United Nations principles—the overwhelming majority—there are bound to be differences concerning the best methods of putting these principles into effect. When we attempt honestly and frankly to work out these differences in the common interest, no one nation can expect to have its way completely. But decisions that are the result of discussions by many countries have a moral and political force in the international community which unilateral decisions seldom have.

Two years ago I said that the first point of our four-point foreign-policy program would be "to give unfaltering support to the United Nations and related agencies" and "to continue to search for ways to strengthen their authority and increase their effectiveness."

The record of our participation in 1950, set forth in the following pages, shows that we have not faltered in our support. I know the American people are determined to persevere in this course.

HARRY S. TRUMAN

NOTE: The message and the complete report are published in "United States Participation in the United Nations; Report by the President to the Congress for the Year 1950" (Department of State Publication 4178; Government Printing Office, 1951, 429 pp.), and in House Document 196 (82d Cong., 1st sess.).

171   The President's News Conference of July 26, 1951

THE PRESIDENT. Please be seated.

I have no particular announcements to make to you. I will try to answer questions.

[1.] Q. Mr. President, General MacArthur made a speech last night,[1] and he said these things: in Korea the result has been indecisive—said that there has been appeasement on the battlefield—he said a great nation which enters upon war and fails to see it through to victory must accept the full moral consequence of defeat——

THE PRESIDENT. No comment.

[2.] Q. Mr. President, I wonder if you have gone into this charge that the St. Louis Post-Dispatch has made on Bill Boyle?

THE PRESIDENT. No, I haven't. All I know about it is what I have seen in the paper. I am looking into it.

Q. Mr. President, do you think it was proper for Mr. Boyle to take money from the American Litho—when he was paid $3,000 a year.

THE PRESIDENT. I know nothing about it, only what I have seen in the paper. I can't comment until I know the facts, and I don't believe it until I know them myself.[2]

[3.] Q. Mr. President, what is your reaction to this action of the House Public Works Committee in tabling the St. Lawrence Seaway——

THE PRESIDENT. I am still hopeful that the St. Lawrence Seaway will come out on the floor of the House.

[4.] Q. Mr. President, in that same speech last night, General MacArthur hinted that some kind of reprisal had been threatened against him——

THE PRESIDENT. Still no comment.

[*Laughter*]

Q. May I finish the question, sir?

THE PRESIDENT. Yes—I know what you are going to say. Go ahead and finish it so that it will be for the record.

Q. Has any additional disciplinary action against General MacArthur been considered?

THE PRESIDENT. No. No. I will say no to that.

Q. Mr. President, I will take it one step

---

[1] General MacArthur addressed the Massachusetts Legislature in Boston on July 25. The text of his speech appears in the Congressional Record, vol. 97, p. A4721.

[2] For a statement by the President on Democratic National Chairman William M. Boyle, Jr., and certain RFC loans to the American Lithofold Corporation, see Item 188 [3].

further, sir—has any military man ever in any way undergone any reprisal for any testimony that he has given on the Hill?

THE PRESIDENT. Never. Never.

Q. Has any ever been in your mind, sir?

THE PRESIDENT. Never. I wouldn't let them testify in the first place, if I felt that way about it.

Q. [*Inaudible*]

THE PRESIDENT. Well, they can't testify unless I let them.

[5.] Q. Mr. President, does the agreement on the agenda in Kaesong make you more hopeful now that we may get a cease-fire and armistice? [3]

THE PRESIDENT. Yes, it does.

[6.] Q. Mr. President, I write for a paper in the northwest part of Indiana, a heavy industrial steel area. We have had a chronic housing shortage since Pearl Harbor. The war veterans that came in since the World War did not go home but stayed there. Under present building regulations, they don't have the $4500 or $3500 to pay down for a house. They would be able to pay 10 percent. In the Defense Production Act there are provisions for a return of the 10 percent down payment. Twelve percent of the conferees seem to be in agreement on the bill which may be on your desk within a few days. I wonder if you would care to make any statement on that bill? [*The White House Official Reporter noted that this was condensed from a barely audible question*]

THE PRESIDENT. Well, I can't comment on that bill until it is on my desk, but the housing situation is being torn all to pieces in the

House—the public housing proposition—and they might endeavor to knock it out again in the bill that was passed in the Senate, but I don't know what will happen when it comes up to me. I will comment on it when it does. [4]

[7.] Q. Mr. President, a day or two ago you got a letter from Phil Murray, asking the administration to throw its weight behind the MVA proposal. Can you say whether——

THE PRESIDENT. I will answer that letter in due course, then I will give them both out. I don't answer letters that are published in the paper. I always am courteous when I receive a letter. I will answer it, and when Murray has had a chance to get my views, then I will give it to you. [5]

Q. Independent of his letter——

THE PRESIDENT. No comment—no comment. You know how I stand on MVA, so there is no comment on that.

[8.] Q. Mr. President, there are a lot of suggestions from Democratic leaders here and there for candidates in 1952, in case you shouldn't run. Jake Arvey out in Chicago said he had a couple, Eisenhower, and the other Douglas, if you shouldn't run——

THE PRESIDENT. No, there is no comment, only I think Jake went off half-cocked once before in the history of the country. [*Laughter*]

Q. In 1948, sir?

THE PRESIDENT. Yes.

[9.] Q. Mr. President, on the decision of the Municipal Court of Appeals on the validity of the 1873 act prohibiting discrimination in restaurants, according to most attorneys that act is now law, but just this week the District Commissioners announced that they

---

[3] On July 26 delegations representing the United Nations Command and the Communist forces, meeting at Kaesong, Korea, agreed upon a five-point agenda for the regulation of the military armistice conference. U.N. commander Matthew B. Ridgway's announcement of the agreement, including the outlined agenda, appears in the Department of State Bulletin (vol. 25, p. 231).

[4] For the President's statement upon signing the Defense Production Act Amendments of 1951, see Item 176.

[5] For the President's letter to CIO President Philip Murray on the flood control problem in the Missouri River Basin, see Item 183.

would not enforce that law until it had been decided upon by the United States Supreme Court. I wonder if you wish to comment on the stand taken by the Commissioners?

THE PRESIDENT. The matter is pending in the courts, and I never comment on things that are pending in the courts.

[10.] Q. Mr. President, have you found a successor for James Pope on the TVA Board?

THE PRESIDENT. No, I haven't. I will announce it just as soon as I do find one.

[11.] Q. Mr. President, would you care to clarify the functions of the newly formed Gordon Gray board? There seems to be a great deal of misunderstanding as to it.

THE PRESIDENT. The Psychological Warfare Board is just what it says. That board is for the purpose of coordinating things that will psychologically help win the peace. I think Gordon Gray can give you a detailed statement on the subject that will cover every phase of it. I would have to talk all afternoon to do that.

Q. May I ask one more question, sir?

THE PRESIDENT. Go ahead.

Q. Do you intend for it to be a permanent board?

THE PRESIDENT. Yes. It is a part of the Central Intelligence Agency.

[12.] Q. Mr. President, would you be able to clarify my thinking on when you will decide whether or not you will seek election in 1952?

THE PRESIDENT. You know, I am afraid that I just can't do anything for your thought factory on that! [*Laughter*]

Q. Thank you, sir. I was trying to think of a new way to phrase it. Have you decided whether or not you will do any stumping this year?

THE PRESIDENT. Can't answer that one either.

[13.] Q. Mr. President, there is a report that Ralph Bunche will be the next Ambassador to Moscow?

THE PRESIDENT. I haven't heard about it.

Q. Can you comment——

THE PRESIDENT. I say I haven't heard about it.

[14.] Q. Mr. President, can you give us any idea when you will name a new Chief of Naval Operations?

THE PRESIDENT. No, I cannot. I don't like to discuss things like that when the great man is lying in his coffin.[6]

Q. Mr. President, can't hear—we can't hear.

THE PRESIDENT. I said I don't like to discuss things like that when the man who held the place before is lying in his coffin.

Q. Do you have anything that you want to add?

THE PRESIDENT. No, I can't think of a thing, thank you very much.

Reporter: Well, thank you, sir.

NOTE: President Truman's two hundred and seventy-second news conference was held in the Indian Treaty Room (Room 474) in the Executive Office Building at 4 p.m. on Thursday, July 26, 1951.

———
[6] Admiral Forrest P. Sherman, Chief of Naval Operations, died in Naples, Italy, on July 22. He had just completed a mission to Spain where he discussed European defense measures with Generalissimo Francisco Franco.

172 Letter to Committee Chairmen on Financing the United Nations Palestine Refugee Program. *July 27, 1951*

My dear ————:

I wish to call to your attention a critical situation which now exists with respect to the financing of the Palestine Refugee Program of the United Nations. This program of relief to Arab refugees displaced from

Palestine was carried on during the fiscal year 1951 through contributions from participating countries, including a contribution from the United States of $25,450,000. The Mutual Security Program now before the Congress includes a request of $50,000,000 for the United States contribution to this program in the fiscal year 1952.

In the July Joint Resolution making temporary appropriations, no provision was made for the Palestine Refugee Program. The program was carried forward during July, however, through the use of existing stocks and funds from other sources. Available resources are now nearly exhausted.

One of the principal causes of tension in the Near East is the miserable state of the hundreds of thousands of Arab refugees from Palestine. A major step forward was recently made when the Arab League went on record in favor of a massive program of resettlement of Palestinian refugees in the Arab States. Grave damage to this program is likely to result if the present aid program

collapses because of a temporary shortage of funds.

I therefore urgently request that the pending continuing resolution provide $2,000,000 for the month of August and $3,000,000 for the month of September. Such a contribution is essential to prevent the starvation of many refugees and to avoid a deterioration in the present critical situation in the Near East.

Respectfully yours,

HARRY S. TRUMAN

NOTE: This is the text of identical letters sent to the Honorable Kenneth McKellar, Chairman of the Senate Committee on Appropriations, and to the Honorable Clarence Cannon, Chairman of the House Committee on Appropriations.

On July 31 the President approved H.J. Res. 302 (65 Stat. 149), which provided $2 million for the aid of Palestine refugees for the month of August. On August 29 he approved H.J. Res. 320 (65 Stat. 208), which provided an equal sum for September. On October 10, 1951, the President signed the Mutual Security Act of 1951 (65 Stat. 373), which provided $50 million to be "contributed to the United Nations during the fiscal year 1952, for the purposes, and under the provisions of the United Nations Palestine Refugee Aid Act of 1950 (22 U.S.C. 1556)."

173   Statement by the President on the Mass Deportations in Hungary.   *July 27, 1951*

MANY Americans have expressed concern about the mass deportations from Hungary which are being carried out by the Communist government of that country. Their condemnation of these brutal acts against the people of Hungary is in the best American tradition of concern for liberty and justice. I am deeply moved by the tragic plight of the Hungarian people, who bear a heavy burden of oppression, and I share the abhorrence which has been expressed with regard to these measures which the Hungarian Government has instituted in wanton disregard of every principle of right and decency.

The Government of the United States is

giving the closest attention to the deportations in Hungary with a view to taking such steps as may appropriately expose this situation to public view and judgment and render the Hungarian Government accountable before the world for its infamous conduct.

The forced removal of thousands of persons from their homes by the Hungarian Government under the conditions which have been reported must be regarded as a flagrant violation of the human rights provisions of the Treaty of Peace. The United States Government has already formally charged the Government of Hungary with willfully and systematically contravening these provisions, which obligate that Government to secure to all persons under its jurisdiction the enjoyment of human rights and freedoms, and has exposed these violations before the United Nations.

In accordance with the terms of a resolution passed by the General Assembly on November 3, 1950, this Government will submit to the Secretary General of the United Nations, and through him to all member governments of the United Nations, detailed evidence which the Department of State has in its possession regarding many such violations. In view of the significant bearing which the present deportations have on the general question of the Hungarian Government's suppression of human rights and freedoms, the United States Government will also submit to the Secretary General all evidence which may be available from reliable sources regarding the conditions under which such expulsions are being conducted.

174 Address in Detroit at the Celebration of the City's 250th Anniversary. *July 28, 1951*

Mr. Mayor, Governor, distinguished guests, ladies and gentlemen:

I am happy to come to this great city of Detroit and to join with you in celebrating its 250th birthday. I do not suppose that Cadillac and his little band of French pioneers would believe their eyes if they could see what has happened on the spot where they built their fort back in 1701.

To them the word Detroit meant a narrow place in the river. In George Washington's time it meant a place of danger, a source of Indian raids and scalping parties. Today the word Detroit is a synonym throughout the world for the industrial greatness of America. Today the word Detroit symbolizes for free men everywhere the productive power which is a foundation stone in world peace.

In the last war, Detroit proved itself as one of the great production centers of the arsenal of democracy. Its tanks and trucks rumbled ashore on every beachhead from Normandy to Okinawa. From Detroit and other great American cities came such an outpouring of the weapons and equipment of war as had never been seen before in all history.

That miracle of production was made possible by American industry in action. It was made possible by the expert management and skilled workers of America. Free men working together here in Detroit made it possible for free men around the world to win the war.

Today, once again, the productive power of Detroit is bringing hope and courage to brave people throughout the world who are determined to defend themselves against aggression. Today, again, the success or failure of the cause of freedom depends on what is done here in your great factories and assembly plants.

The free world is counting on you to build airplanes and tanks, army trucks and weapons. Billions of dollars worth of defense orders have been placed in the Detroit area. Production on some of these orders has already begun, and on others it will soon be starting. Military equipment will flow from Detroit factories in a growing stream.

I know that this means changes for many of you. Thousands of workers in Detroit have already shifted from nondefense to defense jobs, and thousands of others will have to shift to defense jobs. Still others are

429

affected by the cutbacks in civilian production which are necessary to make steel and other scarce materials available for military use.

But employment in Detroit is higher now than it was even at the peak of World War II. Think of that! Employment in Detroit is higher now than it was even at the peak of World War II. But these cutbacks have resulted in some temporary unemployment. Military needs have forced a reduction in metals available for making passenger cars. This means that men have been laid off, and some of them have not yet found other work.

This is a temporary situation. It is the kind of thing that has always happened in the early part of a big conversion operation. But it is important to keep unemployment and other conversion difficulties to a minimum.

I have directed the defense agencies to review the situation here thoroughly. I told them to be sure that everything possible is done to make the conversion process work smoothly. I don't propose to let the workingmen of Detroit suffer any unemployment that can be avoided. I don't propose to let their know-how, which is one of our greatest national assets, be wasted by unemployment in the middle of this immense defense program.

In working on this problem the defense agencies have been getting a lot of help from some of your able union leaders, who have been making very constructive suggestions. Detroit manufacturers have also offered some first-class ideas. And I want to assure you that Charlie Wilson, and the Department of Defense, and the other defense agencies are just as concerned about this problem as you are, and are doing their best to solve it.

One reason I am sure they are going to keep on doing their best is because of your new Senator, Blair Moody. That fellow is a go-getter, and he bothers nearly everybody in Washington to death, trying to get things for Detroit.

This problem of conversion unemployment will be with us for some months. But we will do all we can to keep it down, while defense production is taking up the slack. Our defense program is going to roll ahead bigger and bigger as we move toward our goals of national security and world peace.

This past year has been a period of challenge. It has tested all we have done since the end of World War II to bring about peace in the world. Aggression in Korea was aimed at the whole idea of the United Nations. It was the purpose of the aggressors to pick off one free nation after another. They intended to create fear in the hearts of the free peoples, and to force them to submit to Communist domination and control.

We could have given up in face of that attack. We could have abandoned the United Nations and torn up the charter. We could have retreated into a hopeless and fearful isolationism, just as we did after the First World War. But this time we didn't do that.

This time we went forward. With our allies, we met the challenge. And today the United Nations is a going concern—stronger than ever. Today the charter means more than it ever did. It has been tested by fire and sword. Today it offers real protection to the free nations of the world. The free nations have made their determination clear. We will not give in to aggression. Our plans for world peace still stand.

We will never quit in the fight for world peace.

The Communists have asked for talks looking toward a settlement of the Korean conflict. Those talks are in progress. We do not yet know whether the Communists really desire peace in Korea or whether they are simply trying to gain by negotiations what they have not been able to gain by conquest. We intend to find that out. The talks can be successful if the Communists are in fact ready to give up aggression in Korea.

But whatever happens in Korea, we must not make the mistake of jumping to the conclusion that the Soviet rulers have given up their ideas of world conquest. They may talk about peace, but it is action that counts.

What they have been doing is quite clear. They are putting themselves in a position where they can commit new acts of aggression at any time. Why right now, for example, the armed forces of the Soviet satellites are rapidly being brought to a peak of military readiness.

In the last several months the satellite countries in Eastern Europe have been forced by the Kremlin to reorganize their armies. The size of these armies has been increased, and modern Russian equipment is being furnished to them in large quantities.

We know that Bulgaria, Rumania, and Hungary now have armed forces far greater than those allowed under the peace treaties they signed in 1947. That is one of our difficulties in dealing with Soviets of any kind, they have no respect for signed treaties or their given word.

We know also that Rumania recently ordered the inhabitants moved out of a stretch of land 30 miles wide, along the Yugoslav border. Bulgaria and Hungary have done the same thing. Military preparations have been going on in those zones along the border. Actions like these are certainly no indication of peaceful intentions.

In the Far East the situation is much the same. The North Koreans and the Chinese Communists—so-called volunteers—are getting a steady flow of new equipment from the Soviet Union for ground and air use.

The Russians themselves have more than 4 million men under arms in Europe and the Far East. There are heavy concentrations of Soviet air, land, and sea forces in the Russian provinces along the Manchurian border, across from Japan, and across from Alaska.

As your President, I am telling you that the dangers in other parts of the world are just as great as they are in Korea. Every day reports come to my desk about Soviet military preparations around the world. If every one of you could see these reports and receive this same information, you would give up any thought that danger is over. You would be just as anxious as I am to see that this country builds up its armed forces, equips them with the most modern weapons, and helps to arm our allies.

Don't let anyone confuse you about this. We cannot let down our guard, no matter what happens in Korea.

The free world must have armed strength—the free world must have it now—not in reserve, not later, but now. We must have men, ships, planes, tanks, and bombs—on hand—ready for any emergency. And if we have them, we won't have to use them.

We hope and believe that we will not have to use the armed strength we are building up. Our aim is to put an end to war. But we know that unless we have armed strength we cannot put out the fires of aggression that threaten the peace of the world at this time.

The aim of this administration is world peace. My term in office is dedicated to bringing us closer to that goal. Our great chance lies in building up such strength and unity among the free nations that the Kremlin will have to drop its plans of aggression and subversion. When we reach that point, there can be peace between the Soviet Union and the rest of the world. They can have peace any time they want it.

I know of only two alternatives to this policy, and the American people have rejected both of them. One is to start a world war now, with all its horrible and unforesee-able consequences. Some people would like to do that. The other is to withdraw and isolate ourselves. That means surrendering the rest of the world to Soviet communism. Neither of these alternatives could possibly lead to peace.

Peace is the purpose of our defense program. Peace is what this great production job is all about.

We have the resources, the morale, the economic strength, to do this job. And we are going to do it!

We have this great strength because the people and the Government have been working together for the welfare of all Americans. We have this strength because we have been working for equality of opportunity and economic security for all our citizens. We have helped our farmers and our workers to reach higher and higher living standards; we have developed our natural resources for everybody's benefit. And because the welfare of the people has been our first concern, our business and industry have grown and expanded tremendously.

That is our record. That is why we stand before the world as the strongest of the free nations. That is why we have the opportunity to lead mankind to peace.

There are a lot of people in this country, however, who are trying to shake our confidence in ourselves. They want us to see ourselves not as we really are, but as they see us through their own dark glasses of fear and lack of faith. They say we cannot do the job we have set out to do.

Those people tell us we can't afford to build up our defenses because it will cost too much. They say we will go bankrupt if we carry out our program. They say we will ruin our economy.

Of course, all these howls about bankruptcy are old stuff. We have heard them time and time again. Those who are saying we cannot afford our peace program and aid to our allies abroad, are the very same ones who have been saying all along that we couldn't afford to do anything for the American people here at home.

They said we couldn't afford social security and unemployment compensation. They said we couldn't afford aid to agriculture. They said we couldn't afford TVA, and the Grand Coulee Dam, and rural electrification.

They say, today, that we can't afford housing for low-income families and veterans and defense workers.

They say we can't afford dams and reservoirs to produce electric power for defense and to prevent flood disasters. They say we can't afford the St. Lawrence Seaway to open the Great Lakes to the ocean shipping and to bring new iron ore to the steel mills in the Middle West. There never was a project in the history of the country more badly needed than the St. Lawrence Seaway.

You all know what this sort of false economizing means. It means economic stagnation and depression and ruin. It means suffering and loss for thousands of families.

Those people who are forever saying that we can't do anything because it will bankrupt us, are looking at the future through the wrong end of the telescope. If we had listened to them in the past we would never have developed the strong America we have today.

If we listen to them now, and cramp our defense program, we will not be able to defend our country, or have peace in the world.

Strong defenses are not going to bankrupt us, any more than domestic progress has bankrupted us. We can well afford to pay the price of peace.

The only alternative is to pay the terrible cost of war.

The doubters and defeatists have now taken up another battle cry. They are now saying that Americans cannot trust each other. They are trying to stir up trouble and suspicion between the people and their Government.

They are using the smear and the big lie for personal publicity and partisan advantage, heedless of the damage they do to the country. Never, not even in the bitterest political campaigns—and I have been through many a one—have I seen such a flood of lies and slander as is now pouring forth over the country.

Now, listen to this one: this malicious propaganda has gone so far that on the Fourth of July, over in Madison, Wis., people were afraid to say they believed in the Declaration of Independence. A hundred and twelve people were asked to sign a petition that contained nothing except quotations from the Declaration of Independence and the Bill of Rights. One hundred and eleven of these people refused to sign that paper—many of them because they were afraid it was some kind of subversive document and that they would lose their jobs or be called Communists.

Can you imagine!—finding a hundred and eleven people in the capital of Wisconsin that didn't know what the Declaration of Independence and the Bill of Rights provided? I can't imagine it.

Think of it, in the capital of the State of Wisconsin, on the Fourth of July this year 1951, good Americans were afraid to sign their names to the language of the Declaration of Independence. Think of that, in the home State of two of America's greatest liberal and progressive Senators, Robert M. LaFollette, and Robert, Junior.

Now that's what comes of all these lies, and smears and fear campaigns. That's what comes when people are told they can't trust their own government.

But I say to you that people can trust their Government. This Government is working for the people in foreign affairs just as it has always worked for the people in domestic affairs. Our foreign policy and our defense effort are guided by one great purpose—to protect the welfare of the American people, now and in the future. That's what your Government has been doing here at home. That's what we are doing now in every move we make, not only at home, but all over the world.

Don't let yourselves be confused by the smearers and the slanderers. There are three things I want you to remember:

First, this country is on the right track in foreign affairs. We have a goal—and that is peace in the world. We have a way to reach that goal—and that is the middle way between world war on one side and surrender to communism on the other.

Second, we are making progress toward that goal. The growing defenses of this country, the increasing strength and unity of the free nations, the set-back to aggression in Korea—all these show the progress we are making.

Third, we cannot reach that goal of peace if we falter now. We must not let up because we have made some progress. We must not be turned back by cries of bankruptcy, or by efforts to create fear and suspicion among American citizens. We are going right ahead and do what we set out to do. The people of the United States are going forward to peace.

Now, I wish some of these doubters and defeatists would come out here to Detroit and take a look around. I would like them to look at these great factories, and this industrial power, and see here the answer of a free people to tyranny in any shape or form. And I would like to ask them to look beyond the machines of Detroit—to the people who make up this great city.

Here are the men and women from every part of our country, and from dozens of nations throughout the world, working together as only free people can work together. In this great American city, the ultimate power lies with the people. The political power lies with the people and the economic power lies with the people.

This is America, and in America working men and women have a voice in their destinies—in their conditions of work and in the course their country shall follow.

There are many of you who trace your origins to Poland or Hungary or other countries now behind the Iron Curtain. You know how the people of those countries are suffering today. You know what has happened to their churches, their schools, their trade unions, and to their homes and their farms.

You can be sure that you are remembered in those countries now under the yoke of slavery. You can be sure that the people there look to you—and to all of us—as examples of what freedom means, and as a source of hope for better lives for themselves.

Here in this city, throughout America, we have a great task to perform. It is up to us, acting together as free men, to build up our defenses against aggression, to inspire and help other free men to defend themselves against tyranny, to give hope and courage to those who are now oppressed, to open the way to a better day for the world—a day of peace and security and freedom.

On this anniversary of the beginning of one of the greatest American cities, let us all pledge ourselves anew to carry out this task, with determination, with faith in God who alone can give us the will and courage to see it through.

NOTE: The President spoke at 12 noon from the steps of the City Hall in Detroit, Mich. His opening words referred to Mayor Albert E. Cobo of Detroit, and Governor G. Mennen Williams of Michigan. Later he referred to Charles E. Wilson, Director of the Office of Defense Mobilization.

The President's address was broadcast over radio and television.

175 Letter to the Chairman, Senate Committee on Expenditures in the Executive Branch, on Pending Reorganization Legislation. *July 31, 1951*

Dear Senator:

I have read with considerable interest your letter of July tenth with respect to S. 1134. As for the provisions of the bill dealing with the organization of the Executive Office of the President, I agree thoroughly with your Committee that the measure is not consistent with the recommendation of the Hoover Commission that the President "should be given complete freedom to adjust the internal relationships of the President's Office" and that he "should not be prevented by statute from reorganizing the President's Office." My experience convinces me of the wisdom of this recommendation and the

soundness of the Committee's judgment in applying it.

I also agree with your view that the adoption of a standard nomenclature for the various types of organizational units of the executive branch can best be left to administrative action.

In your letter you referred to the reorganization plans rejected by the last Congress relating to the Interstate Commerce Commission, the Federal Communications Commission, the National Labor Relations Board and the Department of Agriculture, and implied that revised plans might be presented to carry out the recommendations of the Hoover Commission on those agencies. Since the plans rejected by the 81st Congress were substantially identical with other plans which became effective for most of the other executive departments and regulatory commissions, I should be much interested in any suggestions you may be able to offer on the modifications, consistent with the recommendations of the Hoover Commission, which are needed to obtain acceptance of these remaining plans by the present Congress.

In dealing with the pending bill relating to the Department of Agriculture, I hope that your Committee will succeed in developing a bill which will carry out for that Department the basic recommendations of the Hoover Commission on departmental organization and management already applied to the other civil departments by the plans and legislation of the last two years.

Sincerely yours,

HARRY S. TRUMAN

[Honorable John L. McClellan, Chairman, Committee on Expenditures in the Executive Departments, The United States Senate, Washington 25, D.C.]

NOTE: S. 1134, a bill to establish principles and policies to govern generally the management of the executive branch of the Government in accordance with recommendations of the Commission on Organization of the Executive Branch of the Government, was introduced in the Senate on March 15, 1951, by Senator McClellan and 13 other Senators, and was referred to the Committee on Expenditures in the Executive Departments, chaired by Senator McClellan. It was not reported by the Committee.

In his letter of July 10 to the President, Chairman McClellan stated that the Committee contemplated no further action on the bill, since many of the recommendations had been accomplished by reorganization plans, and that remaining provisions could be implemented in the same way. The letter further suggested that new plans to be submitted for the Interstate Commerce Commission, Federal Communications Commission, National Labor Relations Board, and Department of Agriculture take into consideration points of objection to earlier plans which had been rejected by the 81st Congress.

Other provisions of the bill, dealing with organizational changes in the Executive Office of the President, were described by Chairman McClellan as essentially a presidential rather than a legislative matter. The Committee therefore merely called to the President's attention Hoover Commission recommendations for the creation of an Office of Personnel, an Office of Staff Secretary, and the substitution of a single Economic Adviser to the President in lieu of the existing three-member Council of Economic Advisers.

The pending bill relating to the Department of Agriculture, to which the President referred in the last paragraph of his letter, was S. 1149, "A bill to reorganize the Department of Agriculture in accordance with the recommendations of the Commission on Organization of the Executive Branch of the Government."

---

176   Statement by the President Upon Signing the Defense Production Act Amendments. *July* 31, 1951

I HAVE reluctantly signed S. 1717, the Defense Production Act Amendments of 1951, which was passed by the Congress yesterday.

Unless this measure had become law, the powers necessary for carrying out our defense program would have expired tonight.

This new act continues, with little change, the Government's authority to control production, channel materials, and aid business in the interest of national defense. To some extent the new act strengthens these powers, particularly with respect to aids for small business. The act also continues rent control, and permits recontrol of rents in certain critical areas. The production and rent provisions of the act are thus relatively adequate, though they do not meet all our needs.

But the inflation control provisions of the act are gravely deficient. If these had been the only provisions of the act, I would have vetoed it. We will not be able to hold down rising prices under this act, and I am going to ask the Congress to amend it to give us adequate controls.

435

This act will do great harm to our price and wage controls. The full extent of the damage cannot be determined until the executive agencies have had sufficient time to study the legislation in detail. Many of the new provisions are complicated and vague, and it has not been possible, in the brief time since Congress passed the law, to estimate fully all of its effects on present price ceilings and on the administration of price control.

But it is already clear that the principal effect of the new amendments will be to raise ceiling prices for the manufacturer, the wholesaler, and the retailer. Moreover, the act prohibits further rollbacks in the price of beef, and makes effective rollbacks on other vital cost-of-living commodities practically impossible. In general, the act will roll price ceilings forward from their present levels, pushing them up to heights that we cannot yet foresee. Furthermore, the act greatly increases and complicates the administrative difficulties of price control. As a result, even after prices have reached the new and higher levels which the law requires, we may not be able to keep them from going still higher.

One of the worst provisions of the act, the Butler-Hope amendment, wipes out slaughter quotas on beef, thus encouraging the return of black markets.

Another provision of the act which will operate against the interest of the American people is the Capehart amendment. This complicated amendment will force price ceilings up on thousands of commodities, clear across the board. It is like a bulldozer, crashing aimlessly through existing pricing formulas, leaving havoc in its wake.

If we are to prevent the weakening of our economy, we must change these provisions and others just as bad. As soon as the executive agencies can complete their study, I intend to urge the Congress to revise and strengthen this law, point by point, to give

us the tools we need to fight inflation.

I understand that several members of the Congress, recognizing the deficiencies of this act, have already introduced legislation to restore authority for slaughtering quotas. This is certainly a step in the right direction. But it is only one of the respects in which this law needs immediate improvement.

In future months, as our defense production takes a larger and larger share of our output, we have to expect that pressure on prices will increase. Only a tremendous drop in private investment or consumer spending could keep rising expenditures for defense from bringing on new pressures toward higher prices. And these pressures could be aggravated, at any time, by a change for the worse in the international situation.

To the extent that this act permits prices and the cost of living to rise, it will be necessary to allow reasonable adjustments in wages. We cannot ask the working people of this country to reduce their standard of living just to pay for the higher profits this act provides for business. And then we would be caught in another price-wage spiral.

If we are to prevent a serious drop in the purchasing power of the dollar, we must have a good, strong price control law to help us through the period ahead. Without that kind of law we cannot protect ourselves from the frightful damage of renewed inflation.

S. 1717 is not that kind of law. It is a law that will push prices up. It is a law that will increase the costs of business and the cost of our defense program to the taxpayer. It is a law that threatens the stability of our economy in the future. Moreover, it prevents us from giving any further price relief to the millions of consumers already penalized by the price rises in the fall of 1950.

We should never forget that more than half the families in this country had no increases in income during 1950; some of them actually had their incomes reduced last year. To all these people, inflation is not a theoretical problem for the future, but a real problem and a terrible deprivation right now.

These families, and all our other families, need real protection against inflation. The Government will not be able to give them such protection unless and until the Congress repairs the damage done by this new act.

NOTE: As enacted, S. 1717 is Public Law 96, 82d Congress (65 Stat. 131).
See also Item 199.

177   Statement by the President Announcing His Intention To Establish the Defense Materials Procurement Agency.
August 1, 1951

THE FEDERAL Government's programs for purchasing and increasing the supply of critical and strategic materials are vital to the security of this Nation. It is essential that we have ample supplies of basic and rare materials if we are to fulfill our mobilization goals during the coming months and if we are to maintain the expanding national economy which gives us one of the necessary elements of strength in international affairs.

I have decided, therefore, that we must give special attention to our organization for assuring the continued supply of critical and strategic materials. Accordingly, I am creating, under the authority of the newly extended Defense Production Act, a new independent agency whose sole job will be to procure and to increase the supply of critical and strategic materials at home and abroad.

These new organizational arrangements are being made upon the recommendation of the Director of Defense Mobilization, the Secretary of the Interior, and the Director of the Budget, with the concurrence of the Administrator of General Services, the Economic Cooperation Administrator, and other interested officials of the Government. I am confident that they will provide the Government with better machinery for continuing the vital functions of maintaining an ample supply of critical and strategic materials for our economy.

This new agency will be called the Defense Materials Procurement Agency. It will be headed by an Administrator to be appointed by me with the advice and consent of the Senate. I expect to nominate Mr. Jess Larson, who will be relieved of his present duties as General Services Administrator, to be the Administrator of the new agency. He will administer the Defense Materials Procurement Agency under the direction, control, and coordination of the Director of Defense Mobilization. The reorganization will be effected as soon as the necessary orders can be arranged by the Director of the Bureau of the Budget.

The various procurement and development functions presently vested in the General Services Administration, the Department of the Interior, the Economic Cooperation Administration, and the Defense Production Administration will be transferred to the Defense Materials Procurement Agency. Specifically, the following functions will be transferred and consolidated in the Defense Materials Procurement Agency:

From the Defense Minerals Administration in the Department of the Interior:

Responsibility for materials supply expansion, including development of supply expansion programs;

437

Responsibility for recommending tax amortization for materials expansion actions;

Responsibility for certifying Defense Production Administration loans to the Reconstruction Finance Corporation for materials expansion actions.

From the General Services Administration:

Responsibility for materials procurement under the Defense Production Act.

By delegation from the Economic Cooperation Administration:

Responsibility for serving as the agency to perform Economic Cooperation Administration materials procurement actions.

Under the planned arrangements, the Defense Materials Procurement Agency will become the operating agency for procuring and increasing the supply of critical and strategic materials both domestically and abroad. The Defense Production Administrator will continue to exercise his responsibilities concerning the development of materials requirements and will certify to the Defense Materials Procurement Agency the materials needed in the economy. The new agency will undertake both the necessary spot procurement and the development and execution of materials expansion programs.

Under the new arrangements there will be retained in the Department of the Interior—in the metals and minerals field— the regular statutory responsibilities of the Bureau of Mines and the Geological Survey, expanded to provide additional services required by the emergency programs. Also, the Department of the Interior will continue to administer the domestic exploration loans program authorized by the Defense Production Act and will carry on the priorities and allocations functions with respect to metals and minerals under that act.

The General Services Administration will continue its present responsibilities for stockpile procurement. As a rule, however, the General Services Administration will purchase stockpile materials from the Defense Materials Procurement Agency, which will act as the sole Government procuring authority for nonagricultural materials. The present arrangements for developing stockpile requirements will remain unchanged, and the General Services Administration will continue as the financial and custodial agency for the stockpile.

In providing a new agency for administering a more unified program for procuring and increasing the supply of critical and strategic materials, I shall expect that it will utilize to the maximum extent the resources of all agencies in the conduct of scheduled procurement and development projects.

NOTE: See also Item 205.

178 Remarks to Delegates of Girls Nation.
August 1, 1951

I SINCERELY hope that no hats or dresses will be spoiled by this sprinkle. I didn't bring it on. In fact, I asked for good weather, because I hope that you have a pleasant time while you are here in Washington.

I understand what you are doing: studying Government, learning how it works, and preparing yourselves to make it work when your turn comes to run it, and it will come very soon—much before you anticipate that it will be here.

Your business will be to carry on this great Republic of the United States, I think the greatest Government in the history of the world.

It is a wonderful thing to have you young ladies interested in government and how it works. The most important thing that we have in our country is freedom of action and freedom of the individual. The fundamental part of the Constitution, in my opinion, is the Bill of Rights, the first Ten Amendments to it. I hope all of you will study those first Ten Amendments to the Constitution; and when you become responsible for the operation of the Government, see that those Ten Amendments are always enforced.

That is what we mean by freedom of the individual. That is the difference between us and a dictatorship or a totalitarian state. The very fact that you can come here and face your Chief Executive and listen to him

discuss with you the Government under which we live is something not done in a great many countries. It is most difficult to see the heads of most states. You have to go through much formality—you probably couldn't even get to the front door. But you can come to the White House, you can interview the President, and he is glad to have you.

I hope you enjoy yourselves, and I sincerely hope that this sprinkle hasn't given anybody any colds.

Thank you very much.

NOTE: The President spoke at 12:45 p.m. in the Rose Garden at the White House. The delegates were in Washington attending the Fourth Girls Nation of the American Legion Auxiliary.

179   The President's News Conference of
      August 2, 1951

THE PRESIDENT. I have no announcements to make. If you have questions, I will answer them.

[1.]   Q. I'll start it, Mr. President—last week you said you were looking into Chairman Boyle's connection with the RFC loan to American Lithofold. What have you found out about it?

THE PRESIDENT. I'm still looking.

Q. Still looking?

THE PRESIDENT. I'll answer it when I get the information.[1]

Q. Do you favor a Senate investigation of that loan?

THE PRESIDENT. That's up to the Senate.

[2.]   Q. Mr. President, Senator Mundt has been advocating an alliance between Dixiecrats and northern Republicans to support a presidential ticket in 1952. Do you believe that that has any chance of success?

THE PRESIDENT. I have no comment on that. That is a little bit outside my sphere.

That is between Mundt and the Dixiecrats.

[3.]   Q. Mr. President, in view of your statement that prices would probably rise under this new bill—in view of the fact that they already are—do you believe that it is possible to hold wages in line?

THE PRESIDENT. I think I made that perfectly clear in the statement that I released. If you will read that carefully, you will find that that ground is fully covered.[2]

Q. Mr. President, you indicated in that statement that you believed wage controls might have to be increased. Would you expand on that? Do you believe the 10 percent limit on wage increases should be removed?

THE PRESIDENT. The statement speaks for itself, and if you read it carefully you wouldn't have to ask me questions like that, because it's answered in the statement.

[4.]   Q. Mr. President, in setting up the Small Defense Plants Administration, how

---

[1] See Item 188 [3].

[2] See Item 176.

soon do you intend to do that, sir?

THE PRESIDENT. Just as quickly as I can get it done.

Q. Do you have any candidates in mind?

THE PRESIDENT. No, I haven't, but there will be plenty of them.

[5.] Q. Mr. President, last week, an old friend, the Reverend Dr. Daniel Poling was nominated for mayor on the Republican ticket in Philadelphia. I wonder if you have any comment about it?

THE PRESIDENT. I am very fond of the good Baptist preacher. Of course, when it comes to electing Democrats and Republicans, I always have to be for the Democrat.

[6.] Q. May I ask another question, sir? Today Mr. Hoover urged Republicans that their campaign next year should be "Expose—Oppose—Propose." Do you think that is a good slogan?

THE PRESIDENT. I like the last word, they have never done that yet. [*Laughter*]

[7.] Q. I have a couple more——

THE PRESIDENT. Go ahead—go ahead—ask them.

Q. ——Mr. Baruch,[3] on coming back from Europe, said that he thought the people who are trying to get General Eisenhower away from—interested in politics instead of his present job, are doing the country a disservice; and he said that Eisenhower was on the greatest crusade since Peter the Hermit. Do you have any comment on that?

THE PRESIDENT. I think General Eisenhower is doing a magnificent job in Europe, and I hope he continues to do that job. And I think he will.

Q. As long as he is—necessary for him to do it?

THE PRESIDENT. What's that?

Q. As long as it is necessary for him to do it, sir?

THE PRESIDENT. Yes.

Q. I wonder whether, Mr. President—if

we could get Mr. Romagna[4] to repeat that——

Q. Can't hear.

THE PRESIDENT. I can repeat it for you. I think the question that he asked me was if I had any comment on what Mr. Baruch said when he returned from Europe, which was that General Eisenhower was doing a most magnificent job since Peter the Hermit; and he asked me if I thought General Eisenhower would continue to do that job, and I said I thought he would, as long as it was necessary.

Q. I also said that those who were trying to distract him away from his job were doing the country a disservice?

THE PRESIDENT. I have no comment on that.

[8.] Q. May I get in my last question, sir?

THE PRESIDENT. Yes—go ahead.

Q. Mr. President, there have been some suggestions that—the controversy over the Illinois judgeships—in your controversy with Senator Douglas, that your political intentions in 1952 might be involved?

THE PRESIDENT. I have appointed judges for Illinois, and that is as far as I intend to go on it.[5]

[9.] Q. Mr. President, have you given any more thought recently to your trip across the country?

THE PRESIDENT. Well, I expect to go to San Francisco on the 4th of September, to address the United Nations Japanese Peace Conference.

Q. Do you expect to make any side trips?

THE PRESIDENT. I expect to fly—I expect to fly.

Q. Mr. President, my understanding is that we might fly out one day and come back the next?

THE PRESIDENT. That's probably right.

Q. Mr. President, you said you expect to

---

[3] Bernard M. Baruch of New York.

[4] Jack Romagna, White House Official Reporter.
[5] See Item 165 [8].

go out September 4th. Do you mean the 4th to open the conference——

THE PRESIDENT. I am going out there for the purpose of opening the conference.

Q. You are not going out to sign, you will open——

THE PRESIDENT. I am going out to open the conference. We have a delegation there that will do the signing.

Q. Mr. President, does that preclude any likelihood of a whistlestop tour this fall?

THE PRESIDENT. It does, at this particular time.

[10.] Q. Mr. President, I just wonder if, without laboring the point too much—if you could say what type of inquiry you are making into Mr. Boyle's case?

THE PRESIDENT. I am trying to find the facts, just as I do in every case.

Q. You couldn't tell us the physical——

THE PRESIDENT. No. I will answer the question when I know the facts.

[11.] Q. Mr. President, what do you think of Senator Connally's position, that the ECA shouldn't be active in the Far East? [6]

THE PRESIDENT. I am very sorry that Senator Connally took that position.

[12.] Q. Mr. President, did you talk to John Nangle about that St. Louis——

THE PRESIDENT. No, I did not.

Q. Or Jim McGranery?

THE PRESIDENT. No, I did not. [7]

Q. Mr. President, this question——

THE PRESIDENT. This young man has been on his feet for a long time, Eddie. [8] Let's

give him a chance and then I will recognize you.

[13.] Q. Mr. President, sources from Geneva this morning—United States sources—say that the foreign policy of the United States is going to include land reforms for Asia, Africa, and Latin America?

THE PRESIDENT. The United States delegation at Geneva has instructions to discuss land reforms in those areas.

Eddie, what was your question?

[14.] Q. Mr. President, the question is bound to arise—how long do you think it would be necessary for General Eisenhower to remain in Europe?

THE PRESIDENT. Well now, Eddie, your guess is as good as mine. If you are referring to possibilities in 1952, I don't think those duties will interfere with that, if the General is in that frame of mind.

Q. Yes, sir.

Q. Mr. President, can we quote that?

THE PRESIDENT. I beg your pardon?

Q. Can we quote that?

THE PRESIDENT. No, you can't quote it. Use it just like you would every other question.

Q. Would you repeat it again?

THE PRESIDENT. Well, Eddie asked me if I thought Eisenhower's duties would be prolonged, and I said that I didn't think it would interfere with things that might happen in 1952, if General Eisenhower happened to be in that frame of mind.

Q. Thank you.

THE PRESIDENT. But I think General Eisenhower, under any conditions, would put duty to the country first.

[*Pause*]

THE PRESIDENT. Well, gentlemen? [*Laughter*]

[15.] Q. Mr. President, this is merely intended to be a historical question, not a leading question. Earlier in this century,

---

[6] On July 30 Senator Tom Connally of Texas, Chairman of the Foreign Relations Committee, opposed plans of the Economic Cooperation Administration to extend U.S. economic aid to Asia.

[7] John J. Nangle, Democratic national committeeman from Missouri, and Judge James P. McGranery, United States District Court, Eastern District of Pennsylvania.

[8] Edward T. Folliard of the Washington Post.

there was quite a public movement on be-half of a presidential primary system—presidential preferential primary—in some States. Apparently it didn't extend to much more than about a third of the States. Did you ever have a general view or thought as to the desirability of a presidential preferential primary system?

THE PRESIDENT. No. I think one presidential election is enough.

Reporter: Thank you, Mr. President.

THE PRESIDENT. That's all right.

NOTE: President Truman's two hundred and seventy-third news conference was held in the Indian Treaty Room (Room 474) in the Executive Office Building at 10:30 a.m. on Thursday, August 2, 1951.

180   Remarks to the Members of the United Defense Fund.
August 2, 1951

Mr. Ambassador—yesterday I would have said Mr. Secretary:

I appreciate your coming here so I can tell you that I am more than pleased that you are willing to take the time, the trouble, and the effort to do what you are doing.

You know, the Armed Forces of the country depend entirely on the morale which is given to them from back home. I know, because I was on the frontline when I was much younger than I am now, and I know how it feels to have somebody at home who was interested in what I was trying to do at that time on the front in France.

These young men are just like we were, they appreciate more than you will ever know what you people are doing.

All during World War II, Mrs. Truman was an active participant in all the work that went on here in Washington, and when she was at home the same conditions prevailed.

I just want to say to you that I am very appreciative, and I thank you sincerely from the bottom of my heart in the name of the people of the United States, and officially as President of the United States I am extending my thanks to you.

NOTE: The President spoke at 3:50 p.m. in the Rose Garden at the White House. His opening words "Mr. Ambassador" referred to Francis P. Matthews, former Secretary of the Navy who had been sworn in as Ambassador to Ireland on August 1.

For a statement by the President on the establishment of the United Defense Fund on January 5, see Item 3.

181   Veto of Bill Modifying Eligibility Requirements for Pension Payments to Certain Widows of Veterans.   *August 6, 1951*

To the House of Representatives:

I return herewith, without my approval, H.R. 3549, 82nd Congress, a bill "To modify eligibility requirements for payment of pension to certain widows of veterans of the Civil War, Indian Wars, and Spanish-American War, including the Boxer Rebellion and the Philippine Insurrection."

This bill would remove dependency as an eligibility requirement for payment of non-

service-connected death pensions to certain widows of veterans of the Civil War, Indian Wars, and Spanish-American War who married the veterans some 20 to 40 years after the respective termination dates of these wars.

The immediate effect of this bill would be to add a comparatively small number of widows of veterans of the Civil, Indian, and Spanish-American Wars to the list of those receiving nonservice-connected death pensions, and the first year's cost would be relatively small. Even in its entirety the cost would not be very great. Nevertheless, the fact remains that the bill would completely abolish the dependency requirement for the particular group to which it applies, and would not substitute any minimum income requirement in its place. This would establish a dangerous precedent and one which the legislative history clearly indicates was not intended. I believe that such action would represent a serious departure from sound financial and social policy, both from the standpoint of immediate effect and of long-range consequences. While relatively few individuals would be affected by this particular bill, acceptance of the principle underlying it would inevitably bring a demand for its extension to thousands of widows of veterans of World War I and World War II. Clearly such an extension would have serious budgetary consequences.

Existing laws require that widows of the veterans in question must be dependent in order to obtain pensions. Under present laws and regulations, the basic test of dependency is whether such a widow has income sufficient to provide for her reasonable support. In making this test, the Veterans' Administration does not limit the widow to bare necessities; its administrative determinations are guided by the facts and circumstances of the individual case. The obligations of the widow to provide maintenance for those members of her family whom she is under a moral or legal obligation to support are taken into consideration. Medical and hospital expenditures are likewise considered. In determining dependency, certain items of income are disregarded, including charitable assistance and pension or compensation under laws administered by the Veterans' Administration. I believe the existing statutory requirement of dependency is not only reasonable but entirely equitable. I also believe that the Veterans' Administration in administering the present law has fairly applied appropriate tests of dependency, and will continue to do so.

However, I would not object to legislation to provide that these widows shall not be denied pensions because of the dependency requirement in any case where the widow's income does not exceed the income limitations provided in subsection 1(c) of the Act of June 28, 1934, for nonservice-connected death pensions to widows of veterans of World Wars I and II. This would mean that a widow would not be denied a pension because of the dependency requirement if her income did not exceed $1,000 a year for a widow without a child or $2,500 a year for a widow with a child or children; and that, if her income exceeded those specified amounts, she might or might not receive a pension depending on whether or not there is a showing of dependency in the particular case.

HARRY S. TRUMAN

182   Veto of Bill To Increase the Pensions of Certain Disabled Veterans. *August 6, 1951*

To the House of Representatives:

I am returning herewith, without my approval, H.R. 3193, 82nd Congress, "An Act to establish a rate of pension for aid and attendance under Part 3 of Veterans Regulation No. 1(A), as amended."

At the outset, I want to make clear that this bill does not affect compensation to veterans who were disabled as a result of military service. It is concerned solely with pensions paid to disabled veterans whose disabilities have no connection with their military service.

Under H.R. 3193 certain veterans now receiving nonservice-connected pensions would have their pensions substantially increased. Those veterans needing the aid and attendance of another person would have their pensions increased from the present rates of $60 or $72 a month to $120 a month. The bill would apply to a few veterans of the Spanish American War, and to veterans of World War I, World War II, and the present conflict.

Enactment of the bill would cost the Government, in the first year of operation, approximately $16,700,000. This, however, is not the full story. As the veterans of the two world wars and the present conflict advance in age through the years, the cost would increase very substantially. A projection of the cost on the basis of experience under pension legislation for Spanish American War veterans indicates that toward the end of this century the cost of this bill would approach $400,000,000 a year, including only the eligible veterans of World War I and World War II.

Enactment of H.R. 3193 would aggravate an already existing disparity in the Government's treatment of non veterans and veterans whose disabilities are in no way connected with military service. Under present law a veteran and a non veteran permanently disabled, for example in the same automobile accident, would not be treated alike even if they are equally deserving and are in equal need. The veteran would be eligible for a disability pension, subject to certain income limitations. The non veteran would have no eligibility for disability benefits.

I do not believe that aggravation of this disparity is sound and I am convinced that it is contrary to the fundamental philosophy that should guide our provision of benefits to veterans. On several occasions I have said that new legislation dealing with veterans problems should be limited to meeting those special and unique needs which arise directly from military service. The other needs of veterans—those which do not arise directly from military service—should be met through comprehensive programs for veterans and non veterans alike.

Those veterans who would be affected by H.R. 3193 will continue to receive their present pensions. Hospital and medical care and other benefits will also be available to those who can qualify for them under existing law.

In view of the foregoing considerations, I feel obliged to withhold my approval from H.R. 3193.

HARRY S. TRUMAN

NOTE: On September 18 the Congress passed the bill over the President's veto. As enacted, H.R. 3193 is Public Law 149, 82d Congress (65 Stat. 324).

183 Letter to the President, CIO, on the Flood Control Problem in the Missouri River Basin. *August 6, 1951*

[Released August 6, 1951. Dated August 3, 1951]

Dear Phil:

I read with a lot of interest your letter of July twenty-third regarding the Missouri River basin. Your organization is to be congratulated for raising special funds from CIO union treasuries to help out the victims of the recent flood. I also agree with you thoroughly that such emergency relief, while necessary now that the flood has occurred, is no substitute for the real job that needs to be done—to prevent such floods from happening in the first place.

You know there are a lot of people who take little interest in flood control until a disastrous flood occurs. I am sorry to say that a majority in Congress has cut my budget requests for flood control each of the last four years, and just a few weeks ago the House of Representatives cut this year's budget requests by nearly 20 percent. We can spend little enough on flood control in emergency times like these, and I have had to hold my budget requests for flood control far below what I would have liked to recommend. I believe that cuts even below the budget requests would be the most dangerous kind of false economy. I hope very much the Senate will restore the House cuts.

I know your organization has always appreciated the need for long-term, comprehensive planning in this field. You have worked steadily, year in and year out, for sensible, effective control and use of our great rivers to prevent floods, to produce power, to irrigate lands, and to yield the other benefits that can come from wise river basin development. I appreciate your constructive attitude on these problems very much.

But you know the right kind of river basin development cannot be accomplished unless the people elect public officials who will support it. A good while ago when I was in the Senate I joined in suggesting that a Missouri Valley Authority be organized and set up. Most of the Governors and Senators in the Missouri basin opposed it bitterly, and it was clear it could not be passed at that time.

Then we went to work on a flood control-navigation-irrigation-power plan for the Missouri basin, knowing it was incomplete and would have to be improved later, but hoping we could at least get started. That was in 1944, and the plan was called the Pick-Sloan plan. There was still a lot of opposition from people who said it was wasteful to spend public funds for river development work, that it was socialism for the Government to build multiple-purpose dams, and so on. But we did manage to get a number of important projects authorized by the Congress and I think that was a step in the right direction. A lot of projects are now authorized—and some of them are under construction right now—which are sound and valuable and would be built no matter who was put in charge of Missouri basin development. In that sense, the work under the Pick-Sloan plan has been a help in getting started with much needed projects, and I think your criticism of it is far too sweeping.

But I do agree with you that we need something that is an improvement on the Pick-Sloan plan.

I am thoroughly aware of the inadequacies of the present situation. We don't have a comprehensive plan for the Missouri basin, we only have pieces of such a plan—and some of the pieces (such as the program of the Department of Agriculture) have not even been authorized by the Congress as yet. We don't have in the Missouri basin—as we do have in the Tennessee—proper arrangements by which the people of the area can participate directly in making decisions and taking actions on their flood control and other resources problems. We don't have a systematic means for arriving at wise decisions from the standpoint of the basin as a whole; too often the right action has been blocked by shortsighted people who can't see beyond their purely local interests. For example, of three key flood-control dams which have been proposed on the Kansas River and its tributaries—right where this flood hit— two have not been authorized by Congress and the third one, while authorized, has not been started, all because of opposition by the officials and Congressional representatives of the State of Kansas.

I suppose now that we've had a disastrous flood, the people who have been blocking action will now support these projects. But that is certainly the hard way to make progress—to wait until a flood forces you to do what should have been done long before.

The best way to handle this problem is the way I have advocated all along—and that you and your organization have supported me on. We ought to have a single agency, with its headquarters in the basin where it is accessible to the people who are most directly affected, and where those people can have a direct part in working out the program. That agency should be given the responsibility for making a sensible over-all plan for coordinating upstream and downstream flood control, navigation, irrigation, power and other programs in the Missouri basin, and for seeing that that plan is put into effect efficiently, and with things being done in the proper sequence. Then we'd get somewhere. It wouldn't have to be modeled after the TVA; I made a series of recommendations for a new agency to handle these problems in the Columbia River valley, and those recommendations were quite different from the way the TVA is set up. The important thing is to have an agency that will get the job done, and that is responsive to what the people of the basin as a whole need and want.

This is what we ought to have, just as you say in your letter. But it seems perfectly plain to me that we won't get efficient river basin development, such as we have had in the Tennessee Valley, in other parts of the country unless the people elect public officials who will work for it. My position on a Missouri Valley Authority has not changed, but it seems to me that there have

to be more forward-looking, liberal-minded Members of Congress from these States before you can expect any action to be taken.

In the meantime, we've got to get ahead with the work the best way we can. We should proceed with flood control and navigation, with irrigation and power, with soil conservation and better use of land. We have to take whatever forward steps we can, even though they are not as big as we would like.

I hope the people of the Missouri basin will take to heart the lesson of this terrible flood. But memory is short, and all too often people forget the floods almost as soon as the sun starts shining again. I hope it won't take any more disastrous floods to wake the people of the Missouri basin up to a proper solution.

Sincerely yours,

HARRY S. TRUMAN

[Honorable Philip Murray, President, Congress of Industrial Organizations, 718 Jackson Place, N.W., Washington 6, D.C.]

NOTE: In his letter to the President, dated July 23, Mr. Murray outlined four points on which he urged the President to provide the necessary personal leadership for their implementation. The four points were as follows:

1. Set up immediately by presidential order a President's Emergency Commission on the Missouri Valley to draw up a sound river management program for submission to Congress not later than January 15, 1952.

2. Urge Congress to take action immediately on the water storage features of the Missouri River Basin program of the Department of Agriculture.

3. Throw the weight of the administration behind the establishment of a Missouri Valley Authority with a mandate to take over from the Corps of Engineers and the Bureau of Reclamation and to "get ahead with sound engineering" on the Kansas and Missouri Rivers along lines to be marked out by the proposed President's Emergency Commission.

4. Set up, or get authority from Congress to set up, a Watershed Review Board in the White House with final authority to pass upon all surveys, programs, and decisions of the Corps of Engineers, the Bureau of Reclamation, the Federal Power Commission, and all the other Federal agencies engaged in river engineering work.

184   Letter to the Chairman, Senate Committee on Appropriations, on U.S. Contributions to the U.N. and Other International Organizations. *August 7*, 1951

Dear Kenneth:

I am gravely concerned about an item of very special significance in H.R. 4740, the State, Justice, Commerce, and Judiciary appropriation bill. This item is the appropriation to cover the contributions which we owe this year to the United Nations, the Pan-American Union, and a number of other international organizations in which we hold membership.

Our obligations to these organizations amount to slightly more than thirty million dollars this year. This is a charge, of course, which we are bound to pay as members in good standing.

Yet the House of Representatives, in passing H.R. 4740 cut ten per cent from the funds required for this purpose. In addition, the House inserted a proviso—which has the effect of a further cut in funds—requiring that the United States contribution to each organization be no more than precisely one-third of the organization's total budget. These actions by the House, if allowed to stand, would force this Government to default on its obligations to these international agencies.

I want to urge as strongly as I can that the Senate restore the needed funds and eliminate the restrictive proviso added by the House. It is my earnest hope that these vitally important changes will be made in the bill as passed by the Senate and in the final version of the measure which is sent down to me.

We are pledged in this country to support the United Nations and help make it work. This is a pledge which our Government— through the Congress and the Executive Branch alike—has given in the most solemn

and binding fashion, with the full support of both major political parties. It is a pledge which the overwhelming majority of our people endorse wholeheartedly—a pledge on which we all depend in great measure for our hopes of peace and security and a decent future for the world.

This is a pledge we have now reaffirmed by the blood and sacrifice and heroic effort of our forces fighting under the United Nations' banner in Korea.

Yet we would violate this pledge—just as surely as if we repudiated it outright—by a failure to pay what we owe for the upkeep of the United Nations and these other organizations.

The General Assembly of the United Nations and the conferences of the other agencies decide their own budgets and assess their membership for contributions to supply the needed funds. We, as a leading member, have a major voice in all decisions both as to total budgets and amounts of individual assessments. Members of the Congress from both parties, and the executive officials who serve on our delegations, have joined in determining and presenting the United States position regarding the budgets of these organizations. And once our position has been considered and a final decision reached within the organizations themselves, we have so far always honored those decisions and paid our full share.

In the United Nations, our assessment is now running a fraction over 38 per cent of total costs. This represents a reduction of about one per cent below our share two years ago—a reduction in line with the United Nations' own policy of gradually cutting down our share to a maximum of 33⅓ per cent. While the charge upon us is still higher than that, we are paying less, on a per capita basis, than several other members.

Our proportion of total expenses for the United Nations will continue to be reduced as time goes on, through cooperative agreement between us and the other members—agreement reached in the proceedings of the organization itself. That is the only way this can be done without breaking the pledges we have given. This is true not only of the United Nations, but also of the other organizations we have joined. We cannot compel reductions in our assessments by imposing arbitrary limits on the payments we can make, or by cutting the funds available to meet our obligations.

What we would accomplish by actions of that sort is a crippling effect on the work of the organizations we have promised to support—work of the greatest importance and value to us. We should keep in mind the vital things these organizations are doing, some of them little known to the general public. Take for example the work of the World Health Organization and the Pan-American Sanitary Bureau in locating and stamping out epidemics where they occur, before they can spread to the United States or our territories. Surely we must keep this work going. If we do not pay our full share of the expenses of these agencies, so they can continue to do the job, we may eventually be left to do it all ourselves, at far greater cost.

If we fail to pay the United Nations and these other agencies the full amounts we owe, we will jeopardize our leadership, our moral standing, our right to a strong voice in the conduct of their affairs. And that kind of failure on our part will jeopardize the very existence of these organizations and all their work for peace and progress in the world.

In the United Nations and its specialized

agencies, no major power has yet failed to pay its full contribution as assessed, save only China, beset as we all know by very special problems. No other member of the Security Council has failed to make its contribution, year by year. I cannot conceive that the Members of the House of Representatives meant us to fail. I cannot conceive that they wanted to take the risk of ruining these organizations and defeating their objectives merely in order to save three million dollars.

If by some chance, that is what any Member of the Congress does intend, it would be far better—and far more direct and honest—if he were to offer legislation which would withdraw this country from its membership in the United Nations, the Pan-American Union, the World Health Organization, and the rest.

But I am quite sure this was not the intention of the Members of the House who voted for these amendments. I am sure we all want the United States to continue to work actively in these organizations. After all, this country has a tremendous stake in their success and continued growth. The sum of thirty million dollars for this year is not a heavy charge upon us. It is only one-twentieth of one per cent of the appropriations for our armed forces. And no amount of military strength, no matter how much we build up our armed forces, can give us the hope for the future that is wrapped up in our work for peaceful cooperation among the nations of this hemisphere and all the world.

When the facts in this case are fully appreciated and understood, I am confident that the Congress will provide the full amount we owe these organizations and will steer clear of any rigid limitation on our share of their expenses. If your Committee desires any further information on this subject, I am sure that Secretary Acheson and

Ambassador Austin will be glad to supply it right away.

Sincerely yours,

HARRY S. TRUMAN

[Honorable Kenneth McKellar, Chairman, Committee on Appropriations, United States Senate, Washington, D.C.]

NOTE: As enacted, H.R. 4740 is Public Law 188, 82d Congress (65 Stat. 575). The final bill appropriated $30,297,861, the amount requested, for contributions to international organizations. The bill provided that in exceptional circumstances, necessitating a contribution by the United States of more than one-third of the budget of an international organization, the State Department would be required to obtain the approval of the House and Senate Appropriations Committees before it committed the Federal Government to such a contribution.

185   Letter to the Chairman, Senate Committee on Appropriations, on the Budget Requests for Flood Control Purposes. *August 8,* 1951

Dear Kenneth:

I am transmitting today supplemental estimates of appropriations for flood control work for the fiscal year 1952. At the same time, I wish to urge the Congress to restore the funds eliminated by the House of Representatives from the original budget requests for fiscal year 1952 for flood control and river and harbor development. The House cut my budget requests for this important work by nearly 20 per cent in passing H.R. 4386, the Army civil functions appropriations bill for the fiscal year 1952, which is now before your committee.

I believe this cut was false economy. The budget requests included funds for only the minimum necessary work on flood control and river and harbor work that has already been started, plus funds to start four new projects which in addition to their flood control and navigation benefits will produce hydroelectric power urgently needed as part of our defense mobilization effort. The House action would prevent any of the new projects from being started, would force the suspension of work on some projects now underway, and would seriously delay work on a whole range of projects in many parts of the country.

We can spend little enough on this kind of work in emergency times like the present. For the last several years I have not been able to include in the budget as much money for flood control and river and harbor work as I would have liked, because of the urgent need for large expenditures for national security. In the 1952 budget especially, the requests for funds for civil public works were limited very sharply in view of the increased need to devote Government funds and scarce materials and manpower to national security purposes. The 1952 budget requests for this work were at a bare minimum when I transmitted them to the Congress. I do not believe they can safely be cut further.

The recent flood disaster in Kansas, Oklahoma, Missouri, and Illinois has shown the immense damage that can result from a single flood situation. The only way to prevent such damage is to move ahead steadily on a program to control flood waters; the work of the Army Corps of Engineers which is financed by this bill is a vital part of that program. The cuts made by the House will simply increase the risk that other floods, like the one that culminated in the disaster in the Kansas River basin three weeks ago, will catch us unprepared.

As a result of the recent floods, the agencies of the Executive Branch have reviewed

449

the situation to see whether any parts of our flood control work should be accelerated.

The major conclusion of this review is that the program provided for in the fiscal year 1952 budget should go ahead. This program was carefully planned as part of our long-range effort to use and control our water resources to prevent floods, provide navigation, produce power, and bring other benefits. We know the work that has been budgeted will be good, sound work. It should be approved.

It is now clear that we should go further than the 1952 budget program. The recent floods in the Kansas area were greater than the estimated peak flood on which our previous planning had been based. Furthermore, if the heavy rain had fallen a few miles north of where it did, the flood in the Kansas River basin would have been even worse than it was. This requires us to re-examine our plans.

In the meantime, as a step toward meeting the problem, I am now recommending that an additional $21,800,000 be appropriated to carry forward certain work that we know will be necessary. These funds will provide for work on the Tuttle Creek and Toronto Dams in Kansas and the Oologah Dam in Oklahoma, for local flood protection work at Hutchinson and Wichita, Kansas, for bank stabilization work on the Arkansas River, and for levee work on the Mississippi River between Wood River, Illinois, and East Cape Girardeau, Illinois.

I believe that these funds should be added to the total appropriation, and not substituted for something that was already recommended in the budget. I cannot over-emphasize the importance of steady, well-planned progress in this field—as contrasted with hasty, stop-and-go action, prompted by temporary incidents. The task of controlling our great rivers to benefit our people is a long-range task, which must be tackled

with long-range plans. This is a lesson that has been taught us over and over again, but too many people have not yet learned it.

We have, indeed, made progress. Since the end of World War II, in spite of the pressing demand for defense and foreign aid outlays—both essential to our national security—Government expenditures for river and harbor, flood control, and navigation projects have been large. In the four fiscal years 1948 through 1951, Federal expenditures for these essential improvements totaled 2.2 billion dollars. This amount is about equal to the entire Federal investment for river and harbor, flood control, and navigation work during the previous century and a half.

Even these large sums, however, have only given us a start toward our long-range needs in many areas. For example, the Corps of Engineers has only two major reservoirs—Kanopolis and Harlan County—completed or near completion in the Kansas River basin, where most of the flood damage occurred in July. Several more reservoirs will have to be built—plus a lot of other work necessary for effective flood control—before we can be reasonably sure of controlling a major flood in that area.

In the face of this sort of need, cuts in the present budget requests would patently be false economy, just as previous cuts have been. Shortsighted opponents of orderly development of our water resources who have labeled river and harbor and flood control improvements as "pork," "fat," or "extravagance" have left their mark in the failure to do enough to develop our rivers. It is a pity that this has had to be underlined time and again by the devastation wrought by floods.

The budget requests now before the Congress are part of an orderly program for the development of our great rivers—a program founded on the principle that continued steady improvement in the harnessing of our water resources is essential to the economic growth and development of the nation. The budget requests take account of the economic and financial demands of our national security programs.

The demands of our national security reinforce the urgency of many of the projects included in the budget—projects in the planning stage, under construction, and proposed for starting construction. In particular, this is true of six projects: the redevelopment of Niagara Falls, for which additional planning funds are needed; Albeni Falls Dam in Idaho, which is under construction; and Old Hickory Lock and Dam in the Cumberland River basin, Gavins Point Dam in the Missouri River basin, and Ice Harbor and the Dalles Dams in the Pacific Northwest, on all of which construction should be started immediately. All of these projects will yield substantial amounts of hydroelectric power, in addition to other benefits. Yet all of them would be stopped cold by the House cuts.

An expanded capacity to produce power

is one of the most urgent needs of our defense mobilization program, and it is especially urgent in the areas where these projects are to be built. These projects are all sound investments of public funds. They represent precisely the kind of sensible enlargement of our basic economic strength which we must have—not only in the next year or two, but as long ahead as we can foresee—if we are to counter successfully the long-range Soviet threat to our national security.

The Corps of Engineers should go rapidly ahead on these and the other projects for which I have recommended funds in the budget or in the present supplemental estimates. I strongly recommend that those funds be approved in full by the Congress.

Sincerely yours,

HARRY S. TRUMAN

[Honorable Kenneth McKellar, Chairman, Appropriations Committee, United States Senate, Washington, D.C.]

NOTE: On October 24, 1951, the President signed H.R. 4386, the Civil Functions Appropriation Act, 1952 (65 Stat. 616).

---

186 Address at the Dedication of the Presidential Lounge at Union Station for the Use of Service Men and Women. *August 8,* 1951

Mr. Chairman, distinguished guests:

When the Union Station was built many years ago, this room was supposed to be used by the President for the reception of Kings and Queens and Presidents and Prime Ministers of various foreign governments when they visited our Nation's Capital. I have been President for a little over 6 years, and I have used it once.

This room was supposed to be used exclusively by Very Important People or VIP's. As a result it was hardly used at all. But now we are planning to make really good use of this room. We are planning to turn

it over for use, 7 days a week and 24 hours a day, by the people who are in fact "Very Important People"—just about the most important people of all—the men and women of every rank and in every branch of our armed services.

During the last war this room was turned over to the USO as a Travelers Aid Lounge, and it was used by some 6 million young men and women in our armed services. They came here to find welcome hospitality, and helpful advice on their way through Washington. That is what we want this room to be used for again. I am sure that the men and women who are going to run it and keep it open around the clock are going to do the same fine job of giving help and assistance to the boys and girls in our armed services just as they did here during World War II.

I have said this time and again that no one is more important than the young men and women of our armed services. I mean that. These young people are the basic defense of this Nation. They stand between our free country and the terrible dangers that threaten it from abroad.

They are the fundamental defense of human freedom all over the world. Free nations look to them for hope and encouragement. Our Communist foes know that the training, the equipment, the character and the discipline, and the morale of these young people constitute the greatest obstacle to their plans for world domination.

We are building up our Armed Forces because we want peace—peace in all the world. We must maintain large armed forces for a long time to come, if we are to protect our freedom and prevent world war three.

This means that all of us have to make sacrifices. We have to give up profits and wage increases—and do without things we would like to have. But the greatest sacrifices are made by our young men and women who have the job of manning defenses in the cause of world peace. All of us ought to do as much as we possibly can to back up our young people in the armed services.

We ought to see to it that they have proper recreation, decent housing for their families, and the kind of treatment they deserve in the towns and cities of this country. They have not been getting the right sort of treatment in some of our towns and cities. Now, let us give it to them.

The Armed Forces of the country depend entirely upon the morale which is given to

them from back home. I know that because I was on the frontline when I was much younger than I am now and I know what it means to have the people at home interested in supporting the men and women in the service. The young people in the service today are just the same sort of people as those back in 1918. They appreciate more than we will ever know what we do to help them. They appreciate our interest in their welfare more than we realize.

But if we are to do the job we must have an organization to represent us and through which we can work. That organization is the USO—the United Services Organizations.

At my request, the USO was reorganized on January 31st of this year, bringing together the seven voluntary agencies which have had such long experience in meeting the needs of the Armed Forces.

The old team is back together again doing the work which made the letters USO synonymous with hospitality and help for our fighting forces in World War II. Its job today is just as important as it was then.

Today its clubs and lounges offer friendship and help to our service men and women here in America and in lonely outposts around the world. Its Camp Shows are once again bringing a message from home and relief from monotony for our boys and girls in far off places.

Throughout the country, in city after city, the unions are donating their labor, contractors are donating materials, voluntary organizations are donating their services to create USO clubs, lounges, and information centers.

This is a program all of us ought to share. We cannot let our sons and daughters leave home and go into the service feeling that we don't have enough interest and concern for them to make their lives a little easier through such programs as the USO furnishes.

This USO Travelers Aid Lounge here in the Nation's Capital is one example of the way we can stand behind our men and women in uniform. About 2 months ago Harry Vaughan came to me and said that this room wasn't being used, and that it could be used to very good effect by our young men and young women who were passing through our Capital City. Now, I dedicate this lounge today to the service of men and women of this great Republic—the United States of America—this Republic which stands for freedom and liberty for the individual.

I have here the keys to this room, and I am turning them over to two of our young people, one of whom is a member of the WAVES, WAVE Seaman Shirley Burns, and the other, a sergeant in the Army, Sergeant Irving D. Wait. We have here a group of specially invited guests represent-

ing all members of the armed services—the men and women from the Army, Navy, the Air Force, and the Marines. I want these young people to accept these keys on behalf of this great country. They represent the most important people in the Nation.

The keys symbolize the gratitude and hospitality of our Nation, as expressed through the USO.

May you return to your homes safe and sound, and be as proud of your service to your Nation as we are proud of you.

Thank you very much.

NOTE: The President spoke at 4:10 p.m. In his opening words he referred to A. Marvin Braverman, local board member of the National Travelers Aid Association, and General of the Army Omar N. Bradley, Chairman of the Joint Chiefs of Staff. Later he referred to Maj. Gen. Harry H. Vaughan, Military Aide to the President, and Sgt. Irving D. Wait of Chicago, Ill., and WAVE Seaman Shirley Burns of Wyandotte, Mich., the service man and woman who accepted the keys from the President.

187   Letter to the President of the Senate and to the Speaker of the House on the International Children's Emergency Fund. *August 9, 1951*

Dear ————:

I am writing to ask that the Congress authorize a contribution of twelve million dollars by the United States to the International Children's Emergency Fund. This sum would be authorized for the current fiscal year.

The General Assembly of the United Nations, on December 1, 1950, extended the operations of the Children's Fund for a period of three years. Since the authorization to make financial contributions to the Fund expired last June 30, we can now make no further contribution without this new authority from the Congress.

The United States has a long tradition of participation in, and financial support for,

international children's w e l f a r e work. Nothing is more consistent with our basic interests or more representative of our humanitarian ideals.

The Children's Fund has done a most constructive job over the last four years. In Europe, it has helped more than fifteen million children. The main work of the Fund has now shifted from Europe to the underdeveloped areas of Asia and Latin America. Here the Fund will bring supplies and services to help meet urgent needs of children and to strengthen the permanent child welfare programs of the countries themselves.

I know that the Congress is aware of the many past accomplishments of the Children's

Fund. I am confident that the people of this country want to continue to support the great work the Fund is doing. There is real need to carry on this work. Millions of children will be helped.

I have asked the Secretary of State to prepare draft legislation to carry out this recommendation. It is my hope that the Congress will find it possible to give early consideration to this measure.

Sincerely yours,

HARRY S. TRUMAN

NOTE: This is the text of identical letters addressed to the Honorable Alben W. Barkley, President of the Senate, and to the Honorable Sam Rayburn, Speaker of the House of Representatives.

188   The President's News Conference of *August 9, 1951*

THE PRESIDENT. Please be seated.

[1.] I have a communication here from one of your members that is right interesting. It says:

"From day to day I show up neat,
Even in the worst of heat.
I'm not the one to shed my coat,
And open my shirt, or bare my throat.
I yield to none in my scorn of pain,
Smiling at sun and laughing at rain.
I appeal for other sons of toil
Who pant, perspire, and even boil.
A coatless conference would do a lot
To ease the distress of those who get hot."

[*Laughter*]

Now, I think I told you once before that anybody who wants to take his coat off could do it.

[*The White House Official Reporter noted that some newsmen took off their coats*]

Q. Who is the author of this masterpiece, Mr. President?

THE PRESIDENT. The boy with the pink tie.[1]

Q. Oh—I don't know him!

Q. Now we can stay a long time!

THE PRESIDENT. I may make you put them back on, if you do.

[2.] I understand that in the conference today there are 13 correspondents from 7 NATO countries. We are happy to have you with us, and hope you will have a chance to see the things that interest you in this country, and that you will leave here with a good impression.

[3.] Also, I have a statement that you are interested in, Pete.[2]

Q. Save me a lot of questions. [*Laughter*]

THE PRESIDENT. You will get a mimeographed copy of it after this is over.

[*Reading*] "I have examined into the facts concerning William Boyle's alleged relationship to RFC loans to the American Lithofold Corporation of St. Louis, Mo. The facts I have obtained indicate that Mr. Boyle had nothing to do with the approval of those loans by the RFC.

"I think it would be highly improper for the chairman of a national political committee to use his contacts with Government officials for his own private gain. I would not condone such conduct for a moment.

"So far as Mr. Boyle is concerned, I understand that he gave up his private law practice in order to make sure that there would be no improper mingling of his private interests and his responsibilities as Chairman of the Democratic National Committee. That was the proper thing for him to do."

I have the utmost confidence in Mr. Boyle. And I believe the statements that he made

[1] Ernest B. Vaccaro of the Associated Press.

[2] Raymond P. Brandt of the St. Louis Post-Dispatch.

to me. And I believe also that the investigations which I made in the RFC cover the matter fully.

Q. Mr. President, while you are on it, I assume just from your reading of it, that you made an independent inquiry——

THE PRESIDENT. Yes.

Q. ——of your own?

THE PRESIDENT. Yes, I'm satisfied.

Q. And you support his decision not to resign?

THE PRESIDENT. Oh sure.

[4.] Q. Mr. President, Senator Byrd introduced a bill today which would prohibit any national committeeman, any employee of the national committee, from practicing law before any Government agency or department. Vandenberg [3] introduced the same bill way back in 1934. What do you think about a bill of that sort?

THE PRESIDENT. It hasn't reached me yet. When it comes to me—time for me to comment on it, I will.

I have another statement I want to read you.

[5.] Q. Mr. President, may I ask a question?

THE PRESIDENT. Go ahead and ask it.

Q. I didn't hear Tony Vaccaro's question, but was your answer to the effect that Mr. Boyle will remain, as far as you are concerned?

THE PRESIDENT. Yes—yes.

Q. Thank you, sir.

[6.] THE PRESIDENT. [*Reading*] "The Government of the Soviet Union"—we have copies of this for you outside, too—"has replied to the resolution of the United States Congress declaring the friendship of our people for the Soviet peoples and our deep desire to achieve world peace. The Soviet Government withheld this resolution from the people of the Soviet Union for more than

a month—although of course some of them heard it over the Voice of America. Now the Soviet Government has finally released the resolution through the Soviet newspapers and over the Soviet radio.

"I am glad they did this, as millions of Soviet citizens can now hear and read for themselves the resolution of friendship enacted by the representatives of the American people.

"Mr. Shvernik's reply, naturally, was released in our country as soon as it was received, since in a free country there is no reason or desire to withhold such information from the people. I noted with special interest the statement in Mr. Shvernik's letter that the Soviet Government places no barriers in the path of the intercourse of the Soviet people with the people of other countries.

"This has not been true in the past—witness the rigid prohibitions laid down by the Soviet Government against people from the Soviet Union traveling abroad and people from other countries traveling in the Soviet Union, the rigid restrictions imposed by the Soviet Government on the reading of books and magazines and newspapers from outside of the Soviet Union by the Soviet people, the large-scale and costly effort by the Soviet Government to 'jam' the radio broadcasts of the Voice of America and other free radios, the prevention by the Soviet Government of Russian wives of citizens of other countries from leaving the Soviet Union, and many other barriers preventing travel and communication between the Soviet Union and other countries.

"I will be particularly interested to see whether the Soviet Government means what it says, and now intends to change these policies." [4]

Now I will try to answer questions.

Q. Do you intend to answer his letter, sir?

---

[3] Arthur H. Vandenberg, former Senator from Michigan.

[4] See Items 147, 197.

THE PRESIDENT. Yes.

Q. You are going to answer it?

THE PRESIDENT. Yes. Yes, I intend to answer it. I hope the correspondence may bring forth some concrete results. At least, that is what I am hoping for.

Q. Might contain some of those thoughts, Mr. President?

THE PRESIDENT. Well, you had better wait until I get it prepared, then you won't have to guess at it. [*Laughter*]

Q. The results, sir, you would like to see would be a relaxation of the tension——

THE PRESIDENT. Yes.

Q. ——developing toward peace?

THE PRESIDENT. I would like very much to have that tension relaxed. I would like very much to have complete and permanent world peace. It is not unattainable.

[7.] Q. Mr. President, there were reports last week of a compromise between the White House and Senator Douglas over the Illinois judicial appointments. Would you comment on that?

THE PRESIDENT. I know nothing about it. I have sent my appointments to the Senate. It is not customary for me to back up when I have decided to put somebody in office.[5]

[8.] Q. Mr. President, you said you were encouraged—I believe you said that peace was not unattainable. Could you say are you encouraged that the tension is relaxing by this letter from Mr. Shvernik?

THE PRESIDENT. I am not.

[9.] Q. Mr. President, Myron C. Taylor called on you last week to give you a report on that survey that he undertook for you of the European countries. I wonder if you could give us any report, after going over his report, as to whether it was encouraging or discouraging?

THE PRESIDENT. Purely verbal report, in regard to organizing the moral forces of the world. It was encouraging.

[5] See Item 165[8].

Q. It was encouraging?

THE PRESIDENT. Yes.

[10.] Q. Mr. President, do you expect to confer with Governor Dewey when he returns from the Far East?

THE PRESIDENT. Yes, I do.

Q. What would be the purpose?

THE PRESIDENT. To find out what he saw. [*Laughter*]

Q. By any chance, do you have in mind any special assignment for him?

THE PRESIDENT. No. I think he has the assignment he wants. He is Governor of New York. [*Laughter*]

[11.] Q. Mr. President, a couple of press conferences ago there was some talk about General Eisenhower's 1948 statement, that he wouldn't run for political office, and we wondered what it was in 1952. I think you said you didn't know and suggested we ask the General?

THE PRESIDENT. That's right.

Q. I would like to ask you about another statement. In the General's book "Crusade in Europe," he quotes you as having told him, when you were in Europe one time, that there was no position he wanted that you wouldn't help him get, and that specifically included the Presidency in 1948. [*Laughter*] I would like to know if that applies to 1952 as well as 1948? [*More laughter*]

THE PRESIDENT. It certainly does.

Q. It certainly does?

THE PRESIDENT. Yes. I am just as fond of General Eisenhower as I can be. I think he is one of the great men produced by World War II, and I think I have shown that, by giving him the most important job that is available for his ability.

Q. Mr. President, would that mean that if General Eisenhower wants to be President, you would help him get that job? [*Laughter*]

THE PRESIDENT. I didn't say that.

Q. Well, Mr. President, I would like to know what—not to cross examine you, but what were you referring to when you said "it certainly does" to Bill Lawrence's [6] statement? That is what we were——

THE PRESIDENT. Well, you will have to translate that any way you can. I am glad— as I say, I am very fond of General Eisenhower. I don't think he is a candidate for President on the Democratic ticket, and I couldn't very well help him to be a candidate on the Republican ticket, because I don't think that would do him any good. [*Laughter*] Anyway, I have another candidate on the Republican ticket. [*More laughter*]

Q. Who is that?

Q. Would that be Senator Taft, sir?

THE PRESIDENT. It would be.

Q. You said *would,* or *could* be?

THE PRESIDENT. I said it would be.

Q. Do you have a candidate on the Democratic ticket, sir? [*Laughter*]

THE PRESIDENT. I will tell you that later. I am not ready to make an announcement on that yet. Anyway, you fellows wouldn't have any fun.

Q. No sir.

THE PRESIDENT. If I were to tell you exactly what I was going to do, it would ruin the press conferences. [*Laughter*]

[12.] Q. Mr. President, there are reports that Mr. Averell Harriman [7] may go from Iran to Cairo, to talk with the Egyptians about the lifting of the Suez Canal blockade, to permit passage of oil tankers to the refineries in Israel?

THE PRESIDENT. I hadn't heard anything about that. Mr. Harriman has a right important job where he is. If he can be of any help in Egypt, I wouldn't mind his going

there, but I have no information on the subject.

[13.] Q. Mr. President, do you—have you asked Governor Dewey to see you when he gets back, or did you——

THE PRESIDENT. I will see him when he gets back, of course.

[14.] Q. Mr. President, away from politics for a minute, on the West Point incident, do you think that as a result of it a general program of mass information for its de-emphasis in American colleges and universities could be justified? [8]

THE PRESIDENT. I am making a survey of the situation now. I am trying to find the remedy for this situation at West Point without killing the patient, and as soon as I have something definite to talk about, why I will tell you what I am trying to do.

[15.] Q. Mr. President, you stand on the formal statement you read on Mr. Boyle, or could I ask a question?

THE PRESIDENT. Sure.

Q. Would you care to say what you found the facts to be?

THE PRESIDENT. I found the facts to be just what Boyle stated them, that he had no connection whatever with the loan or with any other loan in RFC, so far as his position with them as an attorney is concerned.

Q. Did he receive fees from the company?

THE PRESIDENT. Yes, he received fees from the company. He had a retainer fee for his firm. Perfectly legitimate. Quit it immediately, as soon as he became vice chairman of the national committee.

Q. Could you say what those fees were for?

THE PRESIDENT. What is a retainer fee usually for?

---

[6] William H. Lawrence of the New York Times.
[7] Special Assistant to the President. See Item 155.

[8] On August 3 Frank Pace, Jr., Secretary of the Army, announced that 90 cadets of the United States Military Academy at West Point were to be expelled for cheating during examinations. Many of them were on the football team.

Q. Yes.

THE PRESIDENT. A retainer fee is one that takes the fellow—puts the fellow on the payroll of a company, and then he gets extra pay for the legal business that he actually does for them, that is my understanding. Every law firm in the country has that sort of setup.

Q. There were—you found no payment other than the $1250——

THE PRESIDENT. That is correct.

Q. ——which he said that he had received?

THE PRESIDENT. That's right.

Q. Were you investigating payments through Max Siskind [9]——

THE PRESIDENT. No, I was not. He severed his partnership with Siskind. They wound up their affairs just like judges do when they go on the bench.

Q. No money or anything that Siskind is getting which might go to Boyle——

THE PRESIDENT. I don't know whether Siskind is getting anything. I am not interested in that. None of my business.

[16.] Q. Mr. President, there have been general reports that the West Point incident is not at all exclusive, that it is quite a general thing in American colleges. Would you consider forming some sort of presidential commission on scholastic honesty——

THE PRESIDENT. I told you awhile ago what I am trying to do.

Q. All right, sir.

THE PRESIDENT. I will answer you when I get that done.

[17.] Q. Mr. President, the ICC has approved rate increases—freight rate increases—from 6 to 9 percent, which will bring extra revenue to the railroads of over $500 million. Do you have any idea about

[9] Former law partner of William M. Boyle, Jr.

what that might do to the general inflation picture?

THE PRESIDENT. Well, I think that was answered by Mr. Johnston, wasn't it? [10]

Q. Yes, sir.

THE PRESIDENT. I think——

Q. I wondered if—what you thought of it?

THE PRESIDENT. I think he made a statement on the subject, and I am in agreement with the subject. That was cleared with me.

[18.] Q. Mr. President, have you chosen a successor yet to Jess Larson as head of GSA?

THE PRESIDENT. No. No. The second in command over there is acting.

[19.] Q. Would you care to comment on the propriety of General—Senator MacArthur making public today the names of the State Department employees who are under loyalty investigation——

THE PRESIDENT. I don't know any MacArthur who is in the Senate. [*Laughter*]

Q. McCarthy.

THE PRESIDENT. I have no comment to make on it at all.

Reporter: Thank you, Mr. President.

THE PRESIDENT. That's all right.

NOTE: President Truman's two hundred and seventy-fourth news conference was held in the Indian Treaty Room (Room 474) in the Executive Office Building at 4 p.m. on Thursday, August 9, 1951.

[10] On August 8 at a meeting of the Defense Mobilization Board, Eric Johnston, Administrator of the Economic Stabilization Agency, told the group that living costs were likely to advance 5 to 8 percent in the coming year.

On the same day the Interstate Commerce Commission had authorized a 9 percent freight price rise in the eastern portion of the United States and 6 percent in the other sections.

The Economic Stabilization Agency had opposed the increases as inflationary, contending that they would result in higher retail prices for goods shipped by rail.

189   Memorandum and Statement of Policy on the Need for
      Industrial Dispersion.   *August* 10, 1951

To the Heads of Executive Departments and Agencies:

There is hereby promulgated, effective immediately, the attached Industrial Dispersion Policy which I have approved on the recommendation of the Chairman of the National Security Resources Board, the Director of the Office of Defense Mobilization, and the Chairman of the Munitions Board.

This policy shall be adhered to by all Departments and Agencies with respect to programs under their control.

The Director of the Office of Defense Mobilization, in carrying out his task of directing, controlling, and coordinating all mobilization activities of the Executive Branch of the Government, shall establish general standards with respect to dispersal, which shall be followed in the granting of certificates of necessity, in the allocation of critical materials for construction purposes, and in the making of emergency loans growing out of defense production.

I shall look to the Chairman of the National Security Resources Board to keep me advised on the progress of this program.

                    HARRY S. TRUMAN

STATEMENT OF POLICY ON INDUSTRIAL
DISPERSION

The strength of our national defense and in fact our continued existence as a free nation depend largely upon our industrial capacity. The core of this capacity, so essential to our survival, lies within a relatively few densely built up centers.

Since 1945 we have experienced a period of unprecedented industrial expansion, but, except for a few examples, there has been no pronounced trend away from these concentrations. Some eighteen billions in new plants and equipment were spent annually during the past 4 years, largely in areas already highly industrialized.

Although we are increasing our defense efforts, the danger of atomic attack grows and demands that new and more positive policies be put into effect to obtain added security for our industrial establishment without jeopardizing its productive efficiency.

In September 1948 the Government, through the National Security Resources Board, issued a report, "National Security Factors in Industrial Location." The report stressed the fact that dense agglomerations of industrial plants were inviting targets for the enemy and that plants separated in space would better survive an atomic attack.

These general conclusions are as sound today as they were 3 years ago. On these first principles of security our basic policy still must rest.

Since publication of this report, several factors have added to the urgency of the problem:

1. The evidence that Russia had a successful atomic explosion.

2. The probability that a strong enemy air attack could penetrate any defenses.

3. The outbreak of hostilities in Asia as an indication of the semi-peace conditions under which we are living.

Obviously, in the light of the above, what was, in 1948, a set of desirable objectives, is today a subject of major concern and one vital to our national security.

It is recognized that the major centers of industrial production have become highly integrated and that a part of their efficiency is due to their concentration. A dispersion

459

policy to be effective and realistic must not be allowed to cripple the efficiency and productivity of our established industries, lest the remedy become worse than the ill. Our policy, therefore, must be directed mainly toward the dispersal of new and expanding industries.

Sites which meet dispersion security standards can be found in local marketing areas adjacent to industrial or metropolitan districts in all sections of the country.

Thus, this policy can be made to fit the economic and social pattern of any part of the country.

The fullest cooperation of industry, labor, and local and State governments, together with all of the measures which the Federal Government can take, will be needed to alleviate the present situation. With the necessary technical guidance as well as the positive inducements which we will give, much can be accomplished.

All departments and agencies of the Government concerned with this problem will be called upon in carrying out a coordinated policy leading to effective industrial dispersal within the concepts described above.

To this effect, the following measures will be taken:

1. To the greatest extent practicable, certificates of necessity, allocations of critical materials for construction purposes, and emergency loans growing out of defense production will be confined to facilities which meet satisfactory standards of dispersal.

2. Primary consideration to dispersal factors will be given in locating facilities built by the Federal Government.

3. Defense contracts will be awarded, and planning under Department of Defense production allocation programs will be conducted in such a manner as to make maximum use of facilities located in dispersed sites.

NOTE: See also Item 200 [3].

190 Statement by the President on the Death of Stephen T. Early. *August 11, 1951*

STEPHEN EARLY gave the best years of his life to the public service. He had been an outstanding newspaperman in Washington before he came upon the White House scene in 1933 with the advent of my predecessor, whom he served faithfully and well through all the changes and vicissitudes of the next 12 years.

Through that long and eventful period, whether the crisis was due to domestic depression, national preparedness, or the prosecution of the most devastating war in human annals, he was always at the side of President Roosevelt as secretary, friend, and sagacious adviser.

When the responsibilities of the Presidency suddenly and without warning came to me with awesome impact, Steve Early, from an impulse of selfless patriotism, consented to stand by as confidant and counselor. Because of all that he did to lighten the burden of the Executive during those momentous days I shall hold his memory in lasting gratitude and appreciation.

Not less valued was his tenure as Deputy Secretary of Defense in an interlude of public service after he had once returned to private business.

Honest, honorable, forthright—irascible sometimes but never vindictive and always just—he had vision as well as courage and a rare faculty of seeing all things in due proportion and through to their logical sequence.

In his untimely passing we mourn a true patriot who no matter what the odds always hewed straight to the line and followed the course where duty lay.

191   Address at the Dedication of the New Washington Headquarters of the American Legion.   *August* 14, 1951

Mr. Commander, distinguished guests, and ladies and gentlemen:

I am happy to be here this afternoon to dedicate the new Washington headquarters of the American Legion. I wish the Legion every success in its new home.

I have been thinking back to the early days of the American Legion, right after World War I. You know, I was very active in Legion affairs in those days. I helped to establish four different Legion posts in Missouri, and I am still a member of all four of them.

We didn't start this organization just to look out for our own interests as veterans or to give us an excuse for reminiscing about what heroes we had been. We started this organization so we could work together as patriotic citizens for the good of all Americans.

That is what we have been trying to do for the last 30 years.

Not everything we have done has been perfect, but the record is one to make us proud. The American Legion has been a powerful and constructive force in American life.

The Legion has been in the forefront of the fight to establish the best system of help and care for veterans that any country ever had in the history of the world.

The Legion has done wonderful work for the welfare of children. It established a National Child Welfare Division in 1925, and since then it has carried on a full-fledged program helping to provide home care for needy children.

Another of the Legion's principal objectives has been to help in achieving a sound national defense. At the first national convention in 1919, the Legion adopted a resolution urging a policy of universal military training. It has consistently supported that policy from that day until this. I appreciate that support very much because I have recommended universal training to the Congress at least seven times.

I am glad to be able to say that we have finally made some real progress on this issue. On June 13 I signed into law the Universal Military Training and Service bill. This is a great step toward a sensible, long-range military manpower program for this country. And, do you know, that effort was started in 1790 by George Washington himself, and we just now got it done. Think of that. We work with expedition in matters of that kind!

The Legion's interest in national defense has extended far beyond universal training—it has extended to all the measures needed for the protection of our country. In recent years the organization has supported unification of the armed services. It has supported the North Atlantic Treaty and military aid for Europe and our own rearmament program.

This participation by the Legion in our national defense activities is a very healthy thing. The members of the Legion who have served their country as citizen-soldiers know how important it is to defend our country from its enemies. And they know that citizens must take an active part in these matters if we are to maintain our tradition of civilian control over the military.

It is natural for the Legion to be especially concerned with veterans' affairs and national defense. But I am glad to say that the American Legion has never considered its responsibilities to be limited to these fields. It has recognized from the beginning that its members are not only veterans; but, more important, they are also citizens of a great Republic with all of a citizen's duties and responsibilities.

In the preamble to the Legion's constitution, its members pledged themselves—among other things—to "uphold and defend the Constitution of the United States . . . to foster and perpetuate a one hundred percent Americanism . . . to safeguard and transmit to posterity the principles of justice, freedom and democracy."

At the present time it is especially important for us to understand what these words mean and to live up to them.

The keystone of our form of government is the liberty of the individual. The Bill of Rights, which protects our individual liberties, is a fundamental part of our Constitution.

When the Legion pledged itself to uphold the Constitution, and to foster 100 percent Americanism, it pledged itself to protect the rights and liberties of all our citizens.

Real Americanism means that we will protect freedom of speech—we will defend the right of people to say what they think, regardless of how much we may disagree with them.

Real Americanism means freedom of religion. It means that we will not discriminate against a man because of his religious faith.

Real Americanism means fair opportunities for all our citizens. It means that none of our citizens should be held back by unfair discrimination and prejudice.

Real Americanism means fair play. It means that a man who is accused of a crime shall be considered innocent until he has been proved guilty. It means that people are not to be penalized and persecuted for exercising their constitutional liberties.

Real Americanism means also that liberty is not license. There is no freedom to injure others. The Constitution does not protect free speech to the extent of permitting conspiracies to overthrow the Government. Neither does the right of free speech authorize slander or character assassination. These limitations are essential to keep us working together in one great community.

Real Americanism includes all these things. And it takes all of them together to make 100 percent Americanism—the kind the Legion is pledged to support.

I'm glad the Legion has made that pledge. For true Americanism is under terrible attack today. True Americanism needs defending—here and now. It needs defending by every decent human being in this country.

Americanism is under attack by communism, at home and abroad. We are defending it against that attack. And we are protecting our country from spies and saboteurs. We are breaking up the Communist conspiracy in the United States. We are building our defenses, and making our country strong, and helping our allies to help themselves.

If we keep on doing these things—if we put our best into the job—we can protect ourselves from the attack of communism.

But Americanism is also under another kind of attack. It is being undermined by some people in this country who are loudly proclaiming that they are its chief defenders. These people claim to be against communism. But they are chipping away at our basic freedoms just as insidiously and far more effectively than the Communists have ever been able to do.

These people have attacked our basic principle of fair play that underlies our Constitution. They are trying to create fear and suspicion among us by the use of slander, unproved accusations, and just plain lies.

They are filling the air with the most irresponsible kinds of accusations against other people. They are trying to get us to believe that our Government is riddled with communism and corruption—when the fact is that we have the finest and the most loyal body of civil servants in the whole world. These slandermongers are trying to get us so hysterical that no one will stand up to them for fear of being called a Communist.

Now, this is an old Communist trick in reverse. Everybody in Russia lives in terror of being called an *anti*-Communist. For once that charge is made against anybody in Russia—no matter what the facts are—he is on the way out. And what I mean is, he is on the way out!

In a dictatorship everybody lives in fear and terror of being denounced and slandered. Nobody dares stand up for his rights.

We must never let such a condition come to pass in this great country of ours.

Yet this is exactly what the scaremongers and the hatemongers are trying to bring about. Character assassination is their stock in trade. Guilt by association is their motto. They have created such a wave of fear and uncertainty that their attacks upon our liberties go almost unchallenged. Many people are growing frightened—and frightened people don't protest.

Stop and think. Stop and think where this is leading us.

The growing practice of character assassination is already curbing free speech and it is threatening all our other freedoms. I daresay there are people here today who have reached the point where they are afraid to explore a new idea. How many of you are afraid to come right out in public and say what you think about a controversial issue? How many of you feel that you must "play it safe" in all things—and on all occasions?

I hope there are not many, but from all that I have seen and heard, I am afraid of what your answers might be.

For I know you have no way of telling when some unfounded accusation may be hurled at you, perhaps straight from the Halls of Congress.

Some of you have friends or neighbors who have been singled out for the pitiless publicity that follows accusations of this kind—accusations that are made without any regard for the actual guilt or innocence of the victim.

That is not fair play. That is not Americanism. It is not the American way to slur the loyalty and besmirch the character of the innocent and the guilty alike. We have always considered it just as important to protect the innocent as it is to punish the guilty.

We want to protect the country against disloyalty—of course we do. We have been punishing people for disloyal acts, and we are going to keep on punishing the guilty whenever we have a case against them. But we don't want to destroy our whole system of justice in the process. We don't want to injure innocent people. And yet the scurrilous work of the scandalmongers gravely threatens the whole idea of protection for the innocent in our country today.

Perhaps the Americans who live outside of Washington are less aware of this than you and I. If that is so, I want to warn them all. Slander, lies, character assassination—these things are a threat to every single citizen everywhere in this country. And when even one American—who has done nothing wrong—is forced by fear to shut his mind and close his mouth, then all Americans are in peril.

It is the job of all of us—of every American who loves his country and his freedom—to rise up and put a stop to this terrible business. This is one of the greatest challenges we face today. We have got to make a fight for a real 100 percent Americanism.

You legionnaires, living up to your constitution as I know you want to do, can help lead the way. You can set an example of fair play. You can raise your voices against hysteria. You can expose the rotten motives of those people who are trying to divide us and confuse us and tear up the Bill of Rights.

No organization ever had the opportunity to do a greater service for America. No organization was ever better suited or better equipped to do the job.

I know the Legion. I know what a tremendous force for good it can be—and what a tremendous force for good it has been.

Now go to it. The job is up to you.

God bless you.

NOTE: The President spoke at 6:15 p.m. from a stand erected in front of the new American Legion building in Washington. In his opening words he referred to Erle Cocke, Jr., National Commander of the American Legion. The address was carried on a nationwide broadcast.

192   Statement by the President Upon Signing Bill Relating to the Employment of Mexican Agricultural Workers. *August 16, 1951*

I HAVE today approved House Joint Resolution 311, making interim appropriations to the Department of Labor to begin the task of bringing Mexican farmworkers into this country under the terms of Public Law 78, approved July 12, and in conformity with the recently concluded agreement between this Government and the Republic of Mexico.

I am glad that in passing this joint resolution the Congress has begun action on those measures which will aid in the development of a well-rounded program dealing with the immigration of Mexican farmworkers. I am most hopeful that the Congress will now give expeditious consideration also to the appropriations and the substantive legislative proposals needed to complete action on the recommendations in my message to the Congress of July 13, 1951.

Our present agreement with Mexico will terminate in less than 6 months, and it is vital that the Congress complete action on these recommendations before that time runs out, if we are to negotiate with the Mexican Government for a new agreement to meet our needs for workers in the next crop year.

NOTE: As enacted, H.J. Res. 311 is Public Law 113, 82d Congress (65 Stat. 190).

See also Item 154.

193   The President's News Conference of *August 16, 1951*

THE PRESIDENT. Please be seated.

I have no particular announcements to make this morning, but I will try to answer questions, if you have any.

[1.] Q. Mr. President, you said last week you did not think General MacArthur was a candidate for the Democratic nomination——

Voices: MacArthur? Eisenhower. Eisenhower.

Q. I mean—[*laughter*]—General Eisenhower. Senator Douglas said this week that he is not a candidate. I was just wondering who is left besides you? [*More laughter*]

THE PRESIDENT. Well now, I can't answer that question. I am sure there are plenty of people who are ambitious for the job. They don't know what they are getting into, though.

Q. Could you name them?

THE PRESIDENT. No. Wouldn't be seemly for me to name them.

Q. Mr. President, could I ask—while we are on that question—when you said that General Eisenhower is not a candidate for the Democratic ticket, did you say it from first-hand information?

THE PRESIDENT. I don't think I made any such statement as that. I said I didn't think he would be a candidate on the Democratic ticket. I didn't say he wouldn't be.

Q. I see.

THE PRESIDENT. But I rather think, my friends, that we have worked that vein pretty nearly to the vanishing point, and I think there are more important things to talk about than who is going to be a candidate for the Presidency next year.

Q. Mr. President, before we seal that off, I have one question. Speaking of Senator Douglas, the other night he said that he would support you, despite the little controversy that you have been at [1]—despite that, he said he would support you for President in 1952. I wonder if you would welcome that support?

THE PRESIDENT. Certainly. If I were a candidate I would.

Q. Another question is, Mr. President, he said that—asked if you were—thought that you were a candidate—said he thought you were standing under the mistletoe to be kissed. [*Laughter*]

THE PRESIDENT. No comment.

---

[1] See Item 165[8].

Q. We didn't get that.

THE PRESIDENT. What was that?

Q. We didn't get the answer?

THE PRESIDENT. I said no comment.

[2.] Q. Mr. President, these military defense arrangements that we are working on with the Philippines and Australia, New Zealand and Japan in the past week, will they have the same effect in the Pacific area as the North Atlantic Treaty Organization?

THE PRESIDENT. That is the intention.

[3.] Q. Mr. President, there is a published report this morning that General MacArthur will address the Japanese Peace Conference in San Francisco next month. Has he been invited to speak——

THE PRESIDENT. I don't know. It will be all right, if he wants to address the Conference. I would have no objection to it whatever. And if the State Department invites him, he undoubtedly will. I think Mr. Dulles covered the situation pretty well.[2]

[4.] Q. Mr. President, I have two questions, one regional and one more or less inane—[*laughter*]—the regional question is, in your dispersal policy that you announced last Friday,[3] the work was done in Seattle by a labor industrial group. Would you comment on the work of that group?

THE PRESIDENT. The program that was announced was done by the National Security Resources Board, and they have been at it for the last year and a half.

[5.] Q. Now for the inane question. I have been asked by several women's organizations to ask you in what way or ways the average American woman can help the defense effort?

THE PRESIDENT. To support the program

---

[2] On August 15 John Foster Dulles, Consultant to the Secretary of State, released a statement on the forthcoming San Francisco Conference on the proposed Japanese Peace Treaty. Excerpts are published in the Department of State Bulletin (vol. 25, p. 346).

[3] See Item 189.

that we are trying to put across with everything they have.

Q. Can you suggest any concrete way?

THE PRESIDENT. No. That is up to them.

Q. Thank you.

THE PRESIDENT. They are citizens the same as I am.

[6.] Q. Mr. President, can you give us any further information on this overemphasis of athletics in military academies? [4]

THE PRESIDENT. I am still in the middle of the investigation, and I can't comment on it.

Q. Would you tell us, sir, who is conducting the investigation?

THE PRESIDENT. I am.

Q. [*The White House Official Reporter noted that this question was inaudible. He thought it was to this effect: "Could you tell us if anybody is helping you with the investigation?"*]

THE PRESIDENT. I am conducting it myself.

[7.] Q. Mr. President, have you anything further to say at this moment about the plans for the visit of Princess Elizabeth and her husband?

THE PRESIDENT. No, only that we are very happy that they are coming and we will try to give them as warm a welcome as we possibly can.

[8.] Q. Do you have any information that the President of the Philippines will go to San Francisco to sign that Mutual Security Pact?

THE PRESIDENT. They will.

Q. I beg your pardon?

THE PRESIDENT. They will. They are going to sign the Japanese treaty.

Q. Well, I was referring to a report from Manila that President Quirino himself would go to sign it. I was just wondering if——

THE PRESIDENT. I have no further information on that. I know they are going to sign it—both the treaty and the security pact.

[9.] Q. Mr. President, are you going to see the Russian Vice Foreign Minister Gromyko when he starts off from——

THE PRESIDENT. If he wants to see me, I will be most happy to talk with him.

[10.] Q. Do you know definitely when you will go to San Francisco?

THE PRESIDENT. Well, I am supposed to be there on the 4th.

Q. On the 4th?

THE PRESIDENT. Yes.

[11.] Q. Mr. President, do you think that the Russians will be able to succeed in doing any real damage in San Francisco, in upsetting the arrangements?

THE PRESIDENT. No. I don't think the treaty arrangements can be upset by anybody.

[12.] Q. Mr. President, after your Legion speech,[5] Senator McCarthy commented that he thought your administration was governed by Communists. Have you any comment?

THE PRESIDENT. No comment.

Q. Mr. President, do you think McCarthyism will be an issue in the 1952 election?

THE PRESIDENT. No comment.

Q. I'm not doing so well today.

[13.] Q. Mr. President, I have just come back from a trip to Haiti, and those folks down there are very much upset because they haven't seen an American Ambassador for 8 months. I wonder whether you have any such intention——

THE PRESIDENT. I appointed one yesterday.[6]

Q. Mr. President, I didn't see it. It didn't come through in the usual announcements from the Press Secretary's office?

THE PRESIDENT. I haven't signed his commission yet, but as soon as the commission is signed, why it will be announced in the regular way. But I appointed one yesterday.

---

[4] See Item 188 [14].

[5] See Item 191.

[6] Howard K. Travers of Central Valley, N.Y. Mr. Travers' nomination was confirmed by the Senate on October 2, 1951.

Q. Do you feel free to disclose his name now?

THE PRESIDENT. No. I can't remember it.

[14.] Q. Mr. President, one other thing, have you read a copy of Look magazine? A professor had an article about you.[7]

THE PRESIDENT. Yes, I saw it. I thought it was a very good article, and was written in a manner that was very truthful, and written by a man who knows what he is talking about, and I am not acquainted with him.

Q. What was that last?

THE PRESIDENT. I am not acquainted with him. Never talked to him in my life. He has worked out that article from the facts.

[15.] Q. Mr. President, as a former Senator, do you care to comment on the poll that was taken of correspondents at the Capitol, that Senator Douglas was the best Senator, and Senator McCarthy the worst?

THE PRESIDENT. Well, when I was in the Senate a similar poll was taken, and I happened to be in the position of Senator Douglas. I compliment him on being in that position.

Q. Yes sir.

THE PRESIDENT. No further comment. [*Laughter*]

[16.] Q. Mr. President, you haven't been asked yet about the situation in Korea. The peace talks—cease-fire talks, rather— have been going along for quite a while now, and not apparently getting very far. Is there any observation that you could make at this time about that general situation?

THE PRESIDENT. No. I think—there is no comment I can make at the present time.

[17.] Q. Mr. President, I would like— I am not trying to involve you in any personality controversy with Senator McCarthy, but would you care to give us an idea of your

definition of McCarthyism, which apparently will be an issue in 1952?

THE PRESIDENT. No comment.

[18.] Q. Mr. President, I just happen to have a copy of that Look magazine article with me. [*Laughter*]

THE PRESIDENT. Just happen to have!

Q. Would you—it says here: "By all normal standards his administration has been one of almost uninterrupted and unparalleled success." In another place, however, he states that he feels your domestic policy has not been as successful as your foreign policy. Would you care to comment on that?

THE PRESIDENT. I will comment on that at a later time, when it will do the most good, and tell you exactly the why and the wherefore for that statement.

[19.] Q. Mr. President, Senator Humphrey said this week, after he talked with you, that he urged you to make a whistlestop tour this fall. Would you tell us anything about your plans?

THE PRESIDENT. I have been urged to do that by a great many people. I haven't made up my mind yet, but when I do, I will let you know in plenty of time so that you can pack your grips—*if* I decide to go. [*Laughter*]

[20.] Q. Mr. President, might the answer to your—[*inaudible*]—domestic thing come at that time?

THE PRESIDENT. We will have to let that take care of itself. We will see what the conditions are.

What is it you wanted, Tony?[8]

[21.] Q. The only thing I wanted to know, when you come back from San Francisco, are we coming back direct here, or stopping——

THE PRESIDENT. I am supposed to stop at home on the way back, and stay a day or two, if something doesn't come up to force me to come back immediately.

---

[7] The article, "A Few Kind Words for Harry Truman," by Henry Steele Commager, was printed in Look magazine of August 28, 1951. The article was reprinted in the Congressional Record (vol. 97, pp. A5146 and A6214).

[8] Ernest B. Vaccaro of the Associated Press.

Reporter: Well, sir—thank you, Mr. President.

THE PRESIDENT. You're welcome.

NOTE: President Truman's two hundred and seventy-fifth news conference was held in the Indian Treaty Room (Room 474) in the Executive Office Building at 10:30 a.m. on Thursday, August 16, 1951.

194 Remarks to a Group of Exchange Teachers From Great Britain, France, and Canada. *August 16, 1951*

Mr. Ewing, and ladies and gentlemen:

It is a very great pleasure to welcome you to the United States. I hope you will enjoy your stay here, and that you will take back an impression that will make our relations with France, Britain, and Canada more cordial. And I hope our teachers who are returning your visit will come back to us with information that will improve our understanding and relations with your countries.

I hope you will enjoy yourselves while you are here. I hope you will give us something that we ought to have: more information about your own country, and how you do things, and see if we can't coordinate it so that we can travel along together on the road to freedom.

We represent, as you know, the freedom of the world—the freedom of the individual. And there is another concept which does not represent the freedom of the individual, which is totalitarianist in its approach. We can't stand for totalitarianism. Britain began coming from under totalitarianism back in the 12th century. The French began coming from under totalitarianism about the same time we did—in the 1770's–1790's. We want to continue the programs for the welfare of the world as a free place in which to live so the individual can do as he pleases, as long as he does not injure his neighbor.

I hope you will have a grand time. I want to say to you that it is not always this way in Washington, so far as sunshine and heat is concerned. It is sometimes very pleasant here. I say sometimes. But in other parts of the country—I know you are going all over the country—you will find, maybe, locations and weather conditions exactly as you have them back home. You will find some that are a little warmer than this, and some that are not quite so warm.

I appreciate your coming. I hope you will enjoy it. And I hope we will get some good out of it.

Thank you very much.

NOTE: The President spoke at 12:05 p.m. in the Rose Garden at the White House. His opening words referred to Oscar R. Ewing, Federal Security Administrator.

The teachers were in the United States under the provisions of the United States Information and Educational Exchange Act of 1948 (62 Stat. 6).

195 Remarks at the Annual Meeting of the President's Committee on National Employ the Physically Handicapped Week. *August 17, 1951*

Mr. Chairman, distinguished guests, and ladies and gentlemen:

I am glad to welcome you this morning to this annual meeting. It's good to be with you again.

This year of 1951 will be the 7th year that we have observed National Employ the Physically Handicapped Week. In those 7 years, we have made a lot of progress. The needs of the physically handicapped are much better understood throughout the country than they have ever been before. Many of the old prejudices against employing handicapped workers are disappearing. It is now well recognized that employment of the physically handicapped is a natural and very valuable part of our economic life.

The figures show that this is true. Secretary Tobin and Administrator Ewing will give you all the details. But it's very impressive to me that during this past year the public employment services were able to find 100,000 more jobs for the handicapped people than during the year before. That's a gain of more than 50 percent.

This kind of progress shows the value of the work of this committee—which has brought private citizens and private organizations and State and Federal agencies together in one great effort.

Much good has been done in these last years, but there is a great deal more that we must do. Our goal should be to see that every physically handicapped person that wants to work and who is able to work gets a chance at a job he can do.

I say this not only because we ought to do it as a matter of decency, but also because there is so much our handicapped citizens can do for us, if we help them to gain employment.

We need these people in our labor force. We need them badly. We need to use their skills and energies in our great program of defense production, to help us win the struggle for a just and lasting peace.

The production job ahead of us calls for the fullest and wisest use of all our resources—and especially of our manpower.

We are now employing more than 62½ million people in this country. As defense production expands, there are going to be more and more jobs and it will be harder and harder to find enough people to fill them. A great proportion of the able-bodied

young people who in earlier years would have been starting work for the first time, are being drawn instead into the armed services. These conditions are bound to continue for some time.

This means that in our national interest it is urgent for us to make full use of the skills and abilities of all our handicapped citizens. Those who have been trained should be employed at their highest level of skill. Those who have not yet been trained should be given rehabilitation and vocational training. Your 1951 poster puts the problem very clearly when it says—"America needs all of us."

I think that you should hammer this point over and over again. Giving the physically handicapped a job is not a charity. It is not just a gratuitous kindness. These people need jobs, it's true. But the more important fact is that the country needs their help. If they are given the right job—jobs fitted to their capabilities—they can do just as much as anyone else to increase the production of this great Nation.

The polio victim, the spastic, the blind, the deaf, and the amputee, as well as those suffering from heart disease and other disabilities can all do their part. All they need is a reasonable chance and good old American fair play. Once on the right job they ask no favors of anyone.

I hope that this committee will make every employer in the country aware of the fact that hiring the physically handicapped is not simply a humanitarian obligation, but a real business opportunity. These people include some of the best workers we have. They are people who have suffered the shock of being disabled, and have gone through the physical and mental suffering of being crippled or blinded or otherwise injured. And, in spite of all that, they have picked themselves up again, mastered their handicap and fitted themselves, sometimes through years of rigorous training, for jobs which they can do. It takes a lot of character to go through an experience like that, and in any kind of employment—I don't care what it is—it's character that counts.

I am going to have the pleasure this morning of presenting a trophy on behalf of this committee. This award is to be given annually to a handicapped individual selected by the committee for the best performance of the year on behalf of the physically handicapped.

The trophy was designed and made by four severely handicapped persons. The young man who has been selected to receive it this year is also a severely handicapped person. He is an employer in Chicago. He is in business for himself. He is successful in that business. Today, he employs 80 persons and 60 of them—three-fourths of them—are handicapped. Some of them are blind, some are deaf, some have lost an arm or leg. But that plant of his, during World War II, outproduced larger concerns that employed more workers. It did such fine work that it received the Army and Navy "E" award.

I am very proud of that young man— George Barr is his name. He has made this country a better place to live in—and he has shown what men can do if they have the courage and the will to do it.

There is a lesson for all of us in this story. That lesson is that you never know what you can do until the going gets rough. The true measure of a man's ability—the true measure of the character and ability of a Nation—comes out only in a struggle against difficulties.

A lot of people are saying these days that the people of our country are soft. They are saying that we have had things too easy for too long, and that we do not have the strength of character to impose restrictions on ourselves and to undergo hardships in this time of crisis.

I simply don't believe it. I just don't think it's true. When I look at the record of our physically handicapped, and what they have done and are doing in American industry, I know it is not true. And if any further proof is needed, we can find it in the record of our soldiers, sailors, marines, and airmen in Korea. There's nothing soft about the job our fighting men have been doing over there, and there's nothing soft about the way our physically handicapped workers have been doing their jobs here at home.

If those among us who have been disabled can pick up their lives again, and fit themselves for jobs in spite of their handicaps, I am sure that the rest of us can do what we are called upon to do in this period of national defense.

This Nation is not soft. I believe we have the same kind of character we have always had. I believe we have the strength and the know-how to carry on through these difficulties. And I am here to tell you that I think this Nation can do anything it wants to, and I think it does those things when it is on the right track, and at no other time.

I know we can face up to any problems that lie ahead, both at home and abroad.

And I am confident that with the help of God, we can reach our goal of a just and lasting peace.

NOTE: The President spoke at 9:45 p.m. in the Departmental Auditorium in Washington at the opening of the fall meeting of the Committee. His opening words "Mr. Chairman" referred to Vice Adm. Ross T. McIntire, Chairman of the President's Committee on National Employ the Physically Handicapped Week.

On the same day the President signed Proclamation 2939 "National Employ the Physically Handicapped Week, 1951" (3 CFR, 1949–1953 Comp., p. 126). The Proclamation designated the week beginning October 7, 1951 for the observance.

The President's address was broadcast.

196 Special Message to the Congress Requesting Additional
Funds for the Rehabilitation of the Flood Stricken
Areas of the Midwest. *August 20, 1951*

To the Congress of the United States:

I request your urgent consideration of a matter of grave emergency.

A great flood disaster—one of the most terrible in the history of the United States—has struck a vast area of the Middle West. The center of its devastation is the valley of the Kansas River, but destruction is spread through other Kansas valleys and parts of Missouri and Oklahoma, and has touched several of the adjacent States.

From May 15 to early July, rain fell almost constantly over an area of thousands of square miles, with the heaviest downpours concentrated in south-central Kansas. By early July, the streams and rivers of Kansas had risen to unprecedented heights. Reservoirs, where they existed, overflowed. Millions of tons of water plunged downstream, crumbling dikes and levees all along the course and sweeping away homes, farms, businesses, roads, bridges, and communication lines. The crest of the flood hit the concentrated industrial area along the river banks at Kansas City, Kansas, and Kansas City, Missouri, on July 13, and swept a path of destruction across the entire width of Missouri before its force was spent.

The velocity of the waters, as well as their depth and volume, was without parallel in the recorded history of the region. For the month of July, stream flow in central Kansas was seventy times normal.

The loss to the Nation along 1,000 miles of river valleys is now being measured. Already more than one billion dollars in physical damage and at least that much more in loss of income has been counted in preliminary estimates. When the final estimate is in, the toll will be greater.

I wish that every Member of the Congress could have flown, as I did, over these valleys at the height of the flood. I wish that every Member of the Congress could now tramp through the desolated cities of Kansas and drive through the wasteland where lie what were some of the richest farm acres in the world, their crops now obliterated.

It is estimated that 30,000 to 40,000 homes were flooded. Of these, some 10,000 or 15,000 are destroyed or have suffered major damage—many beyond repair.

At the peak of the flood, some two or three hundred thousand persons were driven from their homes. At least 20,000 of these are still displaced—living in schoolhouses, churches, auditoriums, trailer camps, temporary housing, or with relatives, friends or strangers who took them in when the disaster struck.

At least 5 million acres of farm land, including some of the richest and most productive agricultural land in the Nation, has been badly damaged. Land in the path of the floods was gouged and eroded, its topsoil carried away. At least 30,000 farms were wholly or partially under water—many standing under 25 feet or more at the peak and remaining flooded for many days. When the water left, thousands of acres were buried under sand and gravel. Thousands of acres are still covered by "trapped water" and must be drained. A year's crops were destroyed, hundreds of thousands of dollars worth of livestock killed, several million dollars worth of critical farm machinery and equipment destroyed or seriously damaged.

At least 10,000 miles of fences were destroyed—enough to skirt the perimeter of the United States. Farm buildings were damaged on 17,000 farms.

471

At least 5,000 small businesses were completely or partially destroyed. Store and factory buildings were swept away, merchandise and equipment ruined.

More than one billion dollars of loss—in property damage, and loss of production and employment—has already been suffered by the industries that are tightly concentrated along the Kansas and Missouri rivers at Kansas City, Kansas, and Kansas City, Missouri.

In many cases, particularly upstream, time was too short and trucks too few to allow families to save their furniture and other household possessions. As the crisis struck, organized effort had to be devoted to saving life. Few lives were lost, but many families today have virtually nothing beyond the clothes they wore when they fled—or were rescued from—the path of the waters.

In the American tradition, neighbors have taken care of neighbors. Every refugee is being sheltered; everyone is fed. Cities not flooded have "adopted" stricken cities. States and communities with emergency Federal aid, are restoring and repairing roads, utilities, and public buildings. A great national organization, the American Red Cross, has done and is doing the heroic emergency job that people stricken with disaster can always count upon. During the crisis, Federal agencies, particularly the units of the Armed Forces in the area, threw all available men and resources into the fight to minimize the destruction.

In the tremendous task of putting families and communities back on their feet, the Federal Government now can do two things. First, under the Disaster Relief Act of 1950, regular activities of several Federal agencies can be specially directed to emergency aid, and 25 million dollars have been appropriated to assist communities in clearing debris, in health protection, in the emergency repair of public property, and to provide temporary

housing and for other emergency relief. Mr. Raymond M. Foley, Administrator of the Housing and Home Finance Agency, is responsible for these funds, and for coordinating Federal Agency emergency relief activities.

Thus far, nearly 11 million dollars have been allocated to Federal agencies and to State governments for re-allocation to local governmental units. Temporary housing needs, remaining clean-up costs, and estimates now being completed by States and communities to cover emergency repairs to waterworks, sewer systems, streets, roads, bridges and other community facilities will probably exhaust the remaining 14 million dollars, even with the fullest contributions the local governments can themselves make.

Second, a number of lending agencies—including the Department of Agriculture, the Housing and Home Finance Agency, the Veterans Administration, and the Reconstruction Finance Corporation—can to a limited extent make or insure loans for the rehabilitation of farms, homes, and businesses.

But in a disaster of this magnitude, the combined resources now available to the Federal Government, the States and the local communities, and private organizations such as the American Red Cross, are far from enough to accomplish the tremendous task of restoring for the Nation the productivity and economic vitality of one of its major regions.

There are two reasons why the Nation must act—and at once—to restore the stricken regions to economic health.

The first is humanitarian. The victims of the flood must be given opportunity to renew their farming, to reopen their businesses, to build new homes, to find employment—and without a crushing burden of new debt for every individual. In this land, we do not take the view that a man's misfortune, suffered through no fault of his own, is his own affair, or that a stricken community shall be left to shift for itself. Normally the aid comes from local resources or from those of private relief agencies. But when the disaster spreads beyond the capacity of those resources, then the Nation itself must act to share the loss.

The second reason is that we are now engaged as a Nation in a struggle for survival, and we cannot afford to dispense for long with the industrial and agricultural production that came but is not now coming from the flooded areas. The industries in those valleys turned out hundreds of products that are critical in the building of military and economic strength. Our meat supply will be seriously affected by the loss of corn and livestock, and the food supplies of not only this Nation but the whole free world may suffer from the loss of wheat.

Because of the effect of the disaster on the defense effort, I assigned to the Director of Defense Mobilization, Mr. Charles E. Wilson, the task of coordinating long-range Federal rehabilitation activities as distinguished from the emergency relief aid previously described. Mr. Alfred E. Howse, of Mr. Wilson's staff, has been directing this work in the flood area. They have seen to it that priorities have been granted for repair work in the area, and that all types of aid have been extended within the limits of existing laws and funds. The recommendations contained in this message are based upon their estimates, after a month of close observation.

We urgently need to take steps to relieve human suffering and restore economic life in this flood area, and to protect against future losses from disasters of this type.

In the long run, of course, the greatest need is for the prevention of floods—through carefully planned and coordinated programs of conservation and water control. Until flood prevention can be assured, however, other measures are urgently required to meet the needs of the present and of the immediate future.

I recommend, therefore, that the Congress at once approve an appropriation of 400 million dollars for the following purposes:

1. To indemnify the flood victims for a portion of their loss of real and personal property.

2. To make and guarantee loans on liberal terms for the building of homes and businesses to replace those destroyed.

3. To help farmers drain and rehabilitate their land, replace buildings, and restore the productive capacity of their farms, through on-farm assistance and disaster loans.

4. To permit loans where necessary to enable State and local government participation in the rehabilitation activities.

5. To provide funds to establish a national system of flood disaster insurance, similar to the war damage insurance system of World War II.

To administer the program, I expect to establish a Flood Disaster Administration as a small policy and control body, with operating functions placed in existing Federal and State departments and agencies.

Under the circumstances, a broad degree of discretion in administering the rehabilitation funds is necessary. In this emergency, speed of action is all-important. Winter is approaching, and Congressional authorization for Federal aid cannot be delayed to await the development of fully detailed plans for the administration of aid in the variety of individual circumstances that will arise. A broad legislative directive will let the stricken region know in general what can be counted on, so that individuals and communities can make plans for going ahead with rehabilitation activities.

The loan programs represent no new departure in Government policy. My recommendations will simply increase the available funds and remove certain normal limitations

473

which are inappropriate in a disaster of this magnitude.

But loans—even on liberal terms—are not enough to meet this situation. People who lost their homes, farms, and businesses now have little or no security to offer a lender. Very few, if any, individuals or businesses had any insurance protection against their flood losses. Generally speaking, private insurance companies have not offered such protection, because of the uncertain nature of the risk. Consequently, many people were left after the flood with nothing—or with nothing but their debts. If they could borrow more, new loans added to the old ones would create a debt burden that for an indefinite time to come would be a drag on the economic vitality of the region and would impair its ability to contribute to building our national security.

For these reasons, I consider it essential to provide some rehabilitation grants, directed particularly to assist wage earners and small farmers and businessmen, whose losses in this flood represented personal financial tragedy. To accomplish the most in rehabilitation with the money available, the indemnity program should provide a sliding scale. For example, on the first $10,000 of loss (after deducting a standard amount of perhaps $200), the payment might be 80 percent, on the next $10,000, 60 percent, and so on, with a maximum payment of perhaps $20,000 for any one claimant. The ceiling would exclude the bulk of the industrial losses, but it would enable individuals and small businesses to make a prompt new start. Fortunately, most of the large industrial concerns affected have other resources; and many are, in fact, already proceeding with reconstruction of their plants.

As part of the rehabilitation program, local redevelopment plans should be required in some cases to assure that rebuilding does not take place in areas subject to recurrent flood-ing. For example, some of the devastated urban areas could best be converted to parks, recreation areas, or other public uses to minimize the amount of investment in construction on flood plains.

The whole aid program must be carried out on a basis of joint participation by Federal, State, and local governments. The States and cities that are affected have already spent much in restoring their own public services. Nevertheless, the States, and where possible the cities, should share the cost of the whole program on some equitable basis.

The lack of a national system of flood disaster insurance is now a major gap in the means by which a man can make his home, his farm, or his business secure against events beyond his control. It is a basic requisite to the rapid re-opening of plants in the flood region, where dikes cannot be re-built for some months, and companies are unwilling, in some cases, to undertake the risk of being inundated in the meantime.

The system of flood insurance should be based, if possible, upon private insurance with re-insurance by the Government. This was the principle of the war risk insurance in effect in World War II. It depends, of course, upon the demonstration by private insurers that they can meet the needs of those seeking insurance at reasonable rates.

Once the system of flood insurance is in effect, there should be no need in the future for a program of partial indemnities such as is now proposed for the Midwest flood victims. As a permanent national policy, insurance is far superior to direct Federal payments.

Suggested appropriation language to carry out these recommendations is attached to this message.

The major features of the indemnification proposals I am making are similar to those already introduced in the Congress by Senator Hennings and Representative Bolling of

Missouri. The principles incorporated in all my recommendations have the support of the Governors of Kansas and Missouri and the Governors' advisory committees which represent major groups within the two States. They will revive a region of the Nation now badly hurt—a region of such importance to the security and welfare of the whole country that its revival must be the immediate concern of all our citizens.

I urge the adoption of this program as an emergency measure. Whatever is done must be started with the greatest speed.

Homeless families must be re-housed quickly. Industrial production and trans-

portation must be restored. To avert the loss of next year's farm production from much of the flooded land, drainage ditches must be opened, debris cleared away, and silted soil seeded to cover crops in the remaining 60 to 90 days before winter sets in. Tax resources of States and communities must be re-established.

In all of these things, we must move quickly. Every day counts.

HARRY S. TRUMAN

NOTE: For the statement by the President upon signing the Flood Rehabilitation Act on October 24, see Item 269.

197   Special Message to the Congress Transmitting Soviet Reply
       to the Resolution of Friendship Adopted by the
       U.S. Congress. *August 20, 1951*

To the Congress of the United States:

On June 26, 1951, the Congress passed Senate Concurrent Resolution 11, reaffirming the friendship of the American people for all other peoples, including the peoples of the Soviet Union. On July 7, in accordance with the request of the Congress, I transmitted the resolution to His Excellency Nikolai Mikhailovitch Shvernik, President of the Presidium of the Supreme Soviet of the Union of Soviet Socialist Republics, together with a request that the Soviet Government make the contents of this resolution known to the Soviet peoples.

For a month there was no reply to my letter, nor was the resolution made public in the Soviet Union. Then on August 6, I received a letter from President Shvernik, responding to mine and transmitting a resolution adopted by the Presidium of the Supreme Soviet in the nature of a reply to the concurrent resolution of the Congress. Both communications, of course, were immediately made public in the United States and

were widely publicized by newspapers, magazines, and radio not only in this country but throughout the free world. On August 7, the congressional resolution, together with my letter of transmittal, the reply from Mr. Shvernik, and the resolution of the Presidium of the Supreme Soviet were all printed in the Soviet Government's newspapers and read over the Soviet Government's radio. This belated publication, by the Soviet Government, of the congressional resolution and my letter of transmittal was undoubtedly influenced by the fact that the Voice of America was continuously broadcasting the text of these documents, and their existence could no longer be concealed from the peoples of the Soviet Union.

I am transmitting to the Congress herewith the resolution of the Presidium of the Supreme Soviet, together with the accompanying letter from Mr. Shvernik.

The publication of Senate Concurrent Resolution 11 in the Soviet Union, even though it was accompanied by the simulta-

475

neous publication of the official Soviet reply, marks a significant step forward in the struggle to penetrate the iron curtain with words of truth. Ordinarily, it is the policy of the Soviet Government not to permit its citizens to read anything that is contrary to the official propaganda line. In this case, the adoption of a resolution of friendship by the Congress of the United States, and the efforts of the Voice of America, compelled the Soviet Government to modify its customary practices. Although the resolution adopted by the Presidium of the Supreme Soviet was obviously intended to offset and counteract the effect of the congressional resolution, it is probable that the publication of the actual text of the latter had real effect on the minds of the Russian people.

It is clear, however, that the Soviet Government has not altered the character of its own propaganda and public statements concerning the United States. In the recent youth meeting in East Berlin, we have seen a new intensification of the theme of hate for the United States and other members of the United Nations.

The arguments being made by the Soviet Government to justify its present policies are set forth in the text of the resolution of the Presidium of the Supreme Soviet and in Mr. Shvernik's letter to me. The Congress can readily recognize the errors and misrepresentations in these two documents.

I wish that I could report that these documents give substantial evidence that the Soviet Union is prepared to modify its present policies and to take steps which will relieve present world tensions. Unfortunately, this is not the case. These documents give no assurance that there will be any changes in the hostile and expansionist policies of the Soviet Union, which now threaten world peace.

If the Government of the Soviet Union wants to make progress toward peace, it can stop flouting the authority of the United Nations; it can cease supporting armed aggression in defiance of the verdict of the United Nations; it can make constructive contributions toward establishing conditions of peace with Germany, Austria, and Japan; it can refrain from employing force to maintain in other countries regimes which do not command the support of their people; it can cease supporting subversive movements in other countries; it can cease its distortion of the motives and actions of other peoples and governments; it can stop violating fundamental human rights and liberties; and it can join in good faith in the earnest effort to find means for reducing armaments and controlling atomic energy in the interests of peace.

Such acts would do far more than any words to show that the Soviet Union really wants peace.

Until we have concrete evidence that the Soviet Union has in fact changed its policies, I cannot advise the Congress to change the policies of the United States. I believe that the policies on which we are now embarked—to give every support to the constructive actions of the United Nations for peace, in Korea and elsewhere, to build our defenses and to join in building the defenses of the free world, and to contribute in every way we can to the growth and strengthening of free institutions around the world—I believe these are the policies most likely to bring about a change in the aggressive policies of the Soviet Government. Consequently, I urge that the Congress move ahead with the great program for national security and world peace that is now before it.

In particular, I urge the Congress to take all possible steps to open up channels of communications between this country and the peoples of the Soviet Union, and other peoples behind the iron curtain.

Senate Concurrent Resolution 11 has

opened at least a crack in the iron curtain and the Congress deserves the thanks of free people everywhere for this action. We should now make every possible constructive use of this small opening in the barrier which the Soviet Government has raised up against all free communication between its peoples and the outside world. If we do so, we may be able to show the Soviet peoples our real desire for peace and our genuine efforts in that direction. We may be able to dispel, at least in part, the distorted image of ourselves which is conveyed to them by Soviet propaganda.

For my part, I shall answer President Shvernik's letter in the near future. I shall ask that my reply, like the congressional resolution, be made public in the Soviet Union.

It is of immense importance to communicate the truth about the purposes and intentions of the United States to the peoples of the Soviet Union, as well as to all other peoples under the domination or the threat of domination of Soviet imperialism. Therefore, in addition to my letter I intend to explore all other means that will help to make such communication possible.

I urge the Congress to do all it can to contribute to this vital endeavor. Adequate appropriations for the Campaign of Truth,

including the Voice of America, are essential. I have requested an appropriation of $115,000,000 for this purpose in this fiscal year. The House of Representatives has reduced this to $85,000,000. Such action as this is obviously inconsistent with the purposes of Senate Concurrent Resolution 11. If the Congress expects to be successful in the battle for men's minds, it must support a sustained and consistent campaign for that purpose.

A slash in funds for the Voice of America, coming at this time, would have the effect of severely damaging our efforts to reach the hearts and minds of other peoples. It would mean retreat in the face of the mounting world-wide pressures of Communist propaganda. In the light of our present situation, I hope the Congress will restore the full amount needed for our Campaign of Truth.

I trust the Congress will also consider in what other ways it can assist in correcting Soviet distortions of the facts and in furthering our campaign to reach other peoples with true and accurate information.

HARRY S. TRUMAN

NOTE: The message from Nikolai Shvernik, President of the Presidium of the Supreme Soviet of the Union of Soviet Socialist Republics, and the text of the resolution of the Presidium are printed in House Document 229 (82d Cong., 1st sess.).

See also Items 147, 188 [6].

---

198   Statement by the President Upon Signing Bill Relating to the Tribal Funds of the Ute Indian Tribe. *August* 21, 1951

I HAVE approved H.R. 3795, "to provide for the use of the tribal funds of the Ute Indian Tribe of the Uintah and Ouray Reservation, to authorize a per capita payment out of such funds, to provide for the division of certain tribal funds with the Southern Utes, and for other purposes."

This legislation marks the fact that a sig-

nificant turn of events has been reached in the relations between the United States and the Ute Indians.

Grievances which the Ute Indians had against our Nation, for treatment accorded them long ago, have been adjudicated through orderly court procedures. The Government has paid the compensation which the court said was due these Ute Indian citizens. The legislation to which my approval has just been given makes provision for dividing this fund among the three organized tribes of Ute Indians. In addition, it sets forth a program for use of the share awarded to the Ute Indian Tribe of the Uintah and Ouray Reservation. Under this program, some part of the compensation will be used by individual Ute Indians, some of it will be soundly invested in land and capital goods, and the remainder will be held in reserve to finance future needs of the Indians. I consider this Ute tribal program eminently sound and I am especially pleased to learn that the planning was carried out by the Indians themselves.

One point of significance in this event is that the United States, by settling its score

with this group of Indians, has made it possible for the Indians to put their own affairs in order and to prepare themselves for the fullest participation in the affairs of our Nation. Another, and perhaps more important, point is that native peoples of the United States have again demonstrated that once they are given the opportunity and tools to work with, they can contribute to the stability and betterment of our civilization.

I congratulate the Indians of the Uintah and Ouray Reservation upon their sound planning. I am hopeful that the other two tribes of Ute Indians will soon complete plans for the use of their shares of the compensation that has been awarded to them.

NOTE: As enacted, H.R. 3795 is Public Law 120, 82d Congress (65 Stat. 193).

---

199 Special Message to the Congress After Further Review of the Defense Production Act Amendments. *August 23, 1951*

To the Congress of the United States:

On July 31, when I signed S. 1717, the Defense Production Act Amendments of 1951, I stated that after the Executive agencies had studied this law carefully, I would submit to the Congress recommendations to revise and strengthen it.

S. 1717 was passed by the Congress on July 30. This gave me only one day in which to act. Had I disapproved the measure, all production controls, as well as price, wage, rent and credit controls, would have expired at midnight, July 31.

The dangers in the international situation made it unsafe to permit any interruption in our mobilization program. It would be gambling with the security of the Nation to delay rearmament for any reason. These imperative considerations left me no choice but to sign the Act, despite the grave weaknesses in some of its provisions, particularly those relating to price control.

As I pointed out at that time, these weaknesses may well have most serious consequences for the people of this country and for all free peoples everywhere.

Economic preparedness is just as vital as military preparedness to the security of the Nation and the defense of freedom. The dangers of economic unpreparedness should be just as clear to us as are the dangers of military unpreparedness.

We cannot have military strength without economic strength. We cannot rearm if our economy is ravaged by inflation.

The price of a pound of meat, the buying power of the wages of our workers, the stability of agriculture, the soundness of our currency—these things can decide the success or failure of the whole mobilization program.

If we can hold down the prices of the things we have to buy, and maintain the purchasing power of the American dollar, we can carry out this vast defense effort and make our country secure.

But if we encourage prices to rise, if we allow the value of our dollar to be eaten away by inflation, then we will jeopardize our whole program of defense.

If we did that, our tax dollars would not buy enough guns and armament. The wages of our workers and the incomes of our farmers would not enable them to keep up with the rising cost of living. How then could we expect them to work harder and longer to produce the things we need?

They would see our defense program made into a spectacle of unequal burdens and unfair rewards—enrichment and profiteering for the few, economic hardship and misery for the many. Such unfairness would breed resentment, distrust, and lack of faith among our people, sapping the strength of our democracy.

We must not let that happen.

Throughout the world, free nations look to us for strength and leadership in the united effort for security and peace. The joining of our strength with theirs has provided the rallying point for freedom everywhere. This unity of effort is the only hope for stopping communist expansionism and aggression. Its effectiveness has already been proved.

But inflation threatens this whole effort. Inflation would hurt our own defense program which is the keystone of the defense of the free world. Furthermore, it would injure the efforts of our allies to build up their strength for our common defense. In the end, it could bring on the kind of economic collapse that would give the communists a cheap and easy victory over the free nations.

With the stakes so high we cannot gamble with legislation that raises prices and invites inflation.

The Congress recognized this last year in passing the original Defense Production Act. The need to be fully prepared, economically as well as militarily, prompted the 81st Congress a year ago to include price controls in the Act.

The powers granted in that Act were generally sufficient to do the job. After the Chinese communist aggression occurred in November and brought on a new wave of panic buying, it was these powers which enabled us to meet and check the price spiral that followed. As soon as a skeleton staff had been organized by the stabilization agencies, the Government used these powers to impose a general price-wage freeze.

This was successful. Following the price-wage freeze of January 26, prices generally levelled off and some even turned downward.

Since the imposition of controls, the rise in the cost of living has been held to less than one percent. Wholesale prices today are below the level of last January.

But this does not mean that the inflationary danger is past. Quite the contrary. The greatest danger of high prices is ahead—and we need stronger, not weaker, laws to control it.

Our spending for national security is now at an annual rate of about $40 billion. A year from now it will be at an annual rate of more than $60 billion. This will mean that 20 percent of our national production will be devoted to security purposes. As this process continues, present inventories of consumer goods will dwindle, and defense demands will keep them from being fully replenished. Incomes will be increased by defense work. There will be more money and less goods. Unless our controls are strong, prices will rise sharply.

Furthermore, depending upon international events, we face the possibility, at any time, of other waves of panic buying—like those last summer and fall—which would create new pressures on prices.

It was with these prospects in mind that I submitted to the Congress on April 26, a series of recommendations to strengthen the law. However, instead of strengthening the law, the Congress turned in the opposite direction and impaired the Government's ability to prevent inflation. It amended the Defense Production Act to require higher price ceilings.

The stabilization agencies cannot at this time estimate the total cost of the price boosts which the new law may require—the total ransom consumers will have to pay to this induced inflation. The cost may well be huge—billions and billions of dollars. The tragedy is that it is so unnecessary.

Action should be taken now to change the new law to prevent needless price increases. I urge the Congress not to wait until irreparable damage has been done to our economy. It should act promptly to take out of the Act the new amendments that unnecessarily raise price ceilings.

There are three amendments which are the worst provisions of the new law. If allowed to stand, they will do the greatest damage to our price controls and create the most hardship for our people. I urge the Congress to reconsider and repeal them.

The first of these is the Capehart amendment.

This amendment permits individual sellers to pass on to consumers all cost increases in the thirteen months since Korea, whether or not there is any justification for the higher prices.

The Capehart amendment saddles the consumers of America with a promissory note of higher prices payable to business on demand. And business can choose its own time to present this demand note to a helpless public.

The amendment is unnecessary. Under the previous law, there was ample provision for price relief to sellers who legitimately needed it. The fact that this amendment was not needed is amply demonstrated by the remarkable level of business profits during the last few months.

The Capehart amendment is an economic booby trap. If it had simply and openly provided a straight across-the-board increase in ceiling prices, the damage to price control would have been clear and clean. But the delayed action fuses in this amendment make it all the more insidious and all the more dangerous because these fuses are set to explode at the very moment when they will do the most damage—when inflationary pressures become most acute.

The amendment will make price control regulations more complicated and endanger the development of dollars-and-cents ceilings which are so helpful both to business and to the consumer—and so important to effective enforcement of controls. The Office of Price Stabilization had been planning to speed up the issuance of dollars-and-cents ceilings posted for everyone to see. This program will now be greatly hampered, and in many cases probably made impossible.

It is also clear that the Capehart amendment will shift more of the burden of our defense program to the shoulders of those least able to bear it. All along the line, under the Capehart amendment, business is protected. Business is told that it need not absorb rising costs. But no such assurance is extended to the consumer, the wage earner, and the people living on pensions and other fixed incomes. They stand at the end of the line, and the effect of the Capehart amendment is to take all rising costs—the cost of materials, of labor, overhead, advertising, corporate salaries—everything—out of their pockets. Some of these people may be able to get belated increases in their incomes, but others have no hope of this, and all of them will suffer.

The direct price-raising effects of this amendment are by no means the whole story. Equally serious are the enormous administrative and accounting burdens which this amendment imposes on both Government and business. The amendment may create a tremendous burden of individual price adjustments for the stabilization agencies to handle. The making of these adjustments will be particularly complex because it will require cost data which most business concerns are not equipped to supply, except on the basis of arbitrary guesses. The result will be to discriminate against small businesses which do not have the accounting staffs to compile the complex cost figures required by the amendment.

I cannot believe that the Congress was aware of the difficulties it was imposing on the whole business community—not to speak of the consumer or the Government—by its approval of this provision.

The second of the three amendments which do the most damage is the Herlong amendment, guaranteeing pre-Korean percentage mark-ups for distributors.

Under the guise of giving wholesalers and retailers their customary percentage mark-ups on the things they sell, this amendment invites America's two million distributors to become commission salesmen for inflation. It offers them a percentage stake in every price increase.

The Congress knows full well the bad effects of the cost-plus-a-percentage-of-cost principle in procurement contracts, and that is why it has limited such types of contracts to very exceptional circumstances. But here in the Herlong amendment we have a full-blown cost-plus system applied to everything that the consumer buys.

The maintenance of percentage margins in this fashion is not needed to assure the distributor a fair deal under price control. What is needed—and what the stabilization agencies were providing—is a proper recognition of increases in distributors' operating costs. But there is no reason why distributors should be allowed to make windfall commissions to cover increased operating costs that do not actually occur. There is no justification for compulsory universal application of customary percentage margins, which is what the new law requires.

Compulsory use of percentage mark-ups simply means that price increases at the manufacturing and processing levels are pyramided before they get to the consumer level. And since the new law, through the Capehart amendment, assures price increases at the producer level, the consumer has been caught between the hammer of the Capehart increases and the anvil of the Herlong increases.

It is not only the consumers in the cities who will be hurt by this. Farmers will feel this squeeze, too.

In the initial stages of inflation, the farmer appears to be helped by rising prices. But this is largely an illusion.

Industrial prices tend to rise right along with farm prices and to keep on rising after farm prices level off. Because of the sharp increases in prices paid by farmers for goods used on the farm, the current purchasing power of farmers' net incomes is actually 14 percent less than it was in 1947. Processors' and handlers' margins on food products have been rising. Although consumers' prices were fairly steady during the months from February to June, the farmer's share of the consumer's food dollar fell by 4 percent while the share going to processors and handlers rose by 4 percent. This trend is certain to be magnified by the operation of the Capehart and Herlong amendments.

The third provision of the new law which will do great damage to our price controls is the Butler-Hope amendment, prohibiting slaughter quotas.

Regardless of the reasons which prompted its enactment, this amendment does what Congress certainly had no intention of doing—it puts the black marketeer back in the meat business. And it makes him harder to catch.

This amendment knocked out the quota system which had previously been in effect on livestock slaughtering. Under the previous system, every legitimate slaughterer—large or small—was assured his fair share of all the livestock sent to market by the farmers and ranchers of America.

Quotas are a form of allocation, similar to our present system for allocating minerals, metals, and other scarce commodities during the emergency.

Imagine the chaos in our economy if those materials were not under allocation right now. Yet, that is exactly what will happen in the meat industry without a quota system.

Without quotas, the scramble for scarce supplies increases the pressures to violate ceiling prices. The black marketeer, who cares nothing about ceiling prices, finds it much easier to muscle in on the business of his legitimate competitor. This unrestricted competition for limited supplies inevitably boosts prices, and is likely to make it impossible to have any successful control of meat prices for consumers.

These three amendments, taken together, spell a real and unnecessary increase in the cost of living. Our people have demonstrated that they are ready to make every sacrifice necessary to defend our freedom and our way of life. But no one has a right to force them to make sacrifices that are unnecessary. Higher prices for food and clothing, and for many other day-to-day needs of the family, are unnecessary sacrifices which may be imposed on the American people by this law.

I am well aware that the Congress has recently completed long and intensive study of these price control issues. I appreciate the hard work that was done in committee and on the floor in trying to meet these issues seriously and sincerely. I know that many other weakening amendments were rejected by the Congress. But even so, we cannot afford to overlook the urgent problems that these three amendments have created for the economic stability of the country.

Bills have already been introduced in the Congress to restore the power to fix slaughter quotas which was taken away by the Butler-Hope amendment. I urge the Congress to act quickly on these bills and also to repeal the Capehart and Herlong amendments as promptly as possible.

Pending corrective action by the Congress, the stabilization agencies will, of course, administer the law as fairly and effectively as possible, despite the difficulties created by these amendments. I have instructed the agencies to do the best they can to minimize the many operating problems these amendments create and to preserve the structure of price control from administrative collapse.

I must point out in this connection the importance of adequate appropriations for the administration of our stabilization program. The House of Representatives has recently slashed appropriations for the stabilization agencies—as well as for the defense production agencies. These cuts are a serious blow to our economic controls and our whole defense effort.

If they remain in effect, they will be every bit as damaging to defense production and to stabilization as the amendments weakening the Defense Production Act.

I ask the Congress to restore these appropriation requests.

The steps I have requested are the most important actions which the Congress can now take in support of our stabilization program. In addition, as soon as time permits, it is my hope that the Congress will review and reconsider those other amendments to the new law which weaken our price and credit and production controls. At the same time, I hope the Congress will take up once again those of my recommendations for strengthening the Defense Production Act, which were not incorporated in the law just passed. Among other things, the lack of authority for the Government to build defense plants where necessary is becoming an increasingly pressing problem.

I also ask the Congress to repeal promptly the provision of the Act which places new restrictions on our imports of fats and oils and dairy products. These restrictions are unnecessary for the protection of domestic producers, who are amply safeguarded under other laws, and they run counter to our national policy of reciprocal trade agreements.

I ask the Congress to approach the task of revising our stabilization laws with the basic intent of bringing those laws into line with the spirit of our democracy. Too often the price control law is discussed as though its purpose were just to protect businessmen or farmers or labor unions from any harm. That is not the case.

The essential purpose of the price control law is to protect all our people from the disaster of higher and higher prices. It is consumers—housewives, old people, children, pensioned veterans—that we should keep uppermost in our minds when we write price control laws. We can and should be fair to those who produce—but they are naturally in a strong position in a period of inflation. It is the millions and millions of families living on fixed and limited incomes who need protection most. They are the ones who suffer most when prices go up and up and up.

I hope the Congress will act decisively, and with these considerations in mind, to meet the inflationary danger that faces our Nation.

HARRY S. TRUMAN

NOTE: Three bills further amending the Defense Production Act (S. 2104, S. 2170, and S. 2180) were introduced on September 7, 24, and 26, respectively. They were not enacted.
See also Item 176.

200 The President's News Conference of *August 23, 1951*

THE PRESIDENT. Please be seated.

[1.] I have a statement or two here for you, which I think may clear up some questions you might be inclined to ask, so I will read them to you.

Q. Would you mind——

THE PRESIDENT. They will be in mimeographed form outside, Tony,[1] and yes, I'll go slow. [*Laughter*]

Q. Thank you, sir.

THE PRESIDENT [*Reading*]. "General Ridgway has reported to me, and has made

[1] Ernest B. Vaccaro of the Associated Press.

public, the story of last night's episode in Kaesong. There is, of course, no truth in the Communist claim that a United Nations plane had bombed the Kaesong area. No United Nations aircraft were even in the vicinity at the time the alleged bombing took place. Whether any enemy aircraft were present is not clear, but the flimsy nature of the so-called evidence shown to the United Nations liaison officers makes it extremely doubtful that any bombing took place at all.

"We do not know the purpose of this new Communist masquerade in Kaesong. The

Communist liaison officer last night made certain statements about calling off further meetings in the armistice negotiations, but it is not clear whether he was referring to the meetings planned for today, to meetings for the next several days—or whether it is the Communist intention to back out of the armistice negotiations altogether.

"Until this is clarified, we cannot appraise the events of last night—except that they obviously were not calculated to move the negotiations forward toward an armistice."

[2.] Now, the next one is on Iran.

[*Reading*] "I have been most disappointed to learn of the suspension of the negotiations in Tehran between the British delegation and the Iranian Government, which we had hoped would lead to a settlement of the Iranian oil question.

"Since these conversations have been suspended rather than completely broken off, it remains my hope that a solution will eventually be found agreeable to both parties. It has been clear during the course of negotiations that both Iran and Great Britain sincerely desire a settlement, and in view of this fact I am confident that an arrangement can ultimately be worked out.

"Mr. Harriman has worked long and tirelessly in an effort to bring the parties together, and to set the stage for a settlement, and his activities have had my complete support. His letter to Prime Minister Mosadeq of August 21 summarizes very clearly the American point of view on the steps which led to the suspension of the conversations and the views that Mr. Harriman put forward reflect my own and the State Department's."

[3.] Now, I want to make a certain other matter clear, about which there has been a great many statements, due to misunderstanding, in the House and the Senate.

[*Reading*] "I would like to clear up a lot of misinformation about the Government's

very important industry dispersal program.

"The program has been misrepresented by critics who have mistaken it for something else. The opponents are criticizing supposed efforts to move industry and labor from one part of the country to another. That is not the Government's plan. Our program has no relationship to the Rains amendment, which intended widespread dispersal of plants.

"Our program, which was carefully described by the National Security Resources Board recently, does not tell any industry or individual where to locate. It does not propose moving of existing plants, wherever they may be. It merely encourages the spacing of *new* defense and defense-supporting industries *a few miles apart*.

"Under this program, defense plants and basic industries can, if they wish, find dispersed sites around the existing industrial centers as Detroit or New York, Pittsburgh or San Francisco. The program merely suggests that in building a *new* plant in such areas, the site of the new plant should be located a few miles away from other defense plants in the same locality. On the other hand, the program does nothing to interfere with the normal effects of nonindustrial areas to attract businesses.

"This is a commonsense program which serves the national security in the atomic age and is consistent with the American system of competitive free enterprise. I urge every Member of Congress, every industrialist, and every labor representative to take the time to read this program. They will find it economically sound and adaptable to any State or industrial area." [2]

Had the report been carefully read, there would have been no argument about it.

Now, ask any questions, I will be glad to try to answer them.

[4.] Q. Mr. President, I would like to

[2] See Item 189.

ask if you are still hopeful for the nomination of your candidate for the Republican Presidential nomination? [3]

THE PRESIDENT. I have no further comment to make on that.

[5.] Q. Mr. President, Quartermaster General—General Feldman reaches the retirement age of 62 on September 10, and he reportedly would like to stay on for 2 years, but to do so he would have to be lieutenant general. Do you have any intention of promoting him to that rank?

THE PRESIDENT. I never heard of it before. It hasn't been put up to me.

[6.] Q. Mr. President, last week you said there was no indication that the Japanese peace treaty would fail to be signed in San Francisco due to Russian attendance at the Conference. Is that situation still the same?

THE PRESIDENT. That's the way I feel about it.

[*Pause*]

Those statements must have taken all the wind out of your sails. [*Laughter*]

Q. We're writing, sir.

[7.] Q. Mr. President, will Mr. Harriman [4] stay in Tehran, or will he now return?

THE PRESIDENT. Mr. Harriman is coming home.

Q. Immediately?

THE PRESIDENT. Yes. He will be home in about a week.

[8.] Q. Mr. President, what happens if the Communists really break off the ceasefire talks?

THE PRESIDENT. Well, we will meet that situation when it comes about.

[9.] Q. Mr. President, have you had an opportunity to formulate your report on the West Point-Annapolis——

THE PRESIDENT. I don't intend to formulate any report. I am making an investigation

of conditions, with the idea of curing the patient, not killing him. [5]

[10.] Q. Mr. President, Mr. Leander Perez, head of the States rights movement, said the other day that he is confident that you will be defeated if you run next year. Do you believe he should be so confident?

THE PRESIDENT. Everybody has a right to his guess. They made a lot of guesses in 1948. [*Laughter*]

Q. Mr. President——

[11.] Q. Is there any plan to send Mr. Harriman back to Iran or——

THE PRESIDENT. Well, we hope that the negotiations will be resumed. If they want the services of Mr. Harriman, undoubtedly he would be able to go.

Did you want to ask a question, Duke? [6]

[12.] Q. Do you arrive in Kansas City the 4th or the 5th—we fly out——

THE PRESIDENT. If conditions are favorable, I hope to arrive there on the 5th, Duke—be there the rest of the week.

[13.] Q. Mr. President, have you heard anything recently about the condition of Secretary Hull? [7]

THE PRESIDENT. No, I haven't—not right recently. I heard from him about 2 weeks ago. He was getting along all right then.

[14.] Q. Mr. President, there are some rumors that Mr. Harriman might go to Egypt for some negotiations there. Is there anything you can say about them?

THE PRESIDENT. I haven't heard about that. He seems to be in great demand now. [*Laughter*] Very capable person.

Reporter: Thank you, Mr. President.

THE PRESIDENT. That's all right.

NOTE: President Truman's two hundred and seventy-sixth news conference was held in the Indian Treaty Room (Room 474) in the Executive Office Building at 4 p.m. on Thursday, August 23, 1951.

---

[3] See Item 188 [1].

[4] W. Averell Harriman, Special Assistant to the President.

[5] See Item 188 [14].

[6] Duke Shoop of the Kansas City Star.

[7] Cordell Hull, former Secretary of State.

201 Letter to the Chairman, Senate Committee on Finance, in Support of a Narcotics Control Bill. *August 24, 1951*

Dear Mr. Chairman:

From the time of the establishment of the Bureau of Narcotics in 1930 until two or three years ago, the narcotic menace in the United States was on a steady decline. Organized traffic in narcotics had been nearly wiped out and the number of drug addicts had been reduced by more than half.

However, we have recently been faced with a different and dangerous situation. The narcotics traffic has increased sharply, mostly as a result of narcotic drugs brought in illegally from abroad. The number of addicts has also increased sharply, mainly among young people under twenty-one. Two years ago, there were only a handful of young men and women under twenty-one in the Federal Narcotics Hospital at Lexington, Kentucky. Today, there are several hundred. This increase is dangerous, not only because of the tragic effect of drug addiction on the individuals concerned, but also because it is a direct cause of much crime. A confirmed addict spends as much as $15 a day on narcotic drugs alone. Since many addicts are unable to work at regular jobs, they must obtain this money through criminal activities.

I am deeply disturbed by this situation. I know that you share my concern as indeed do all citizens who are interested in the welfare of the Nation. The investigations of the Senate Crime Investigating Committee have pointed up the fact that the prevention and punishment of crime is essentially the responsibility of states and communities. However, in the narcotics field there are specific steps which the Federal Government can take to stamp out the illicit traffic in dangerous drugs.

Federal officials who have studied the problem have reported to me that severe prison sentences for the men and women who peddle narcotics are of primary importance in drying up this foul traffic. I am informed that H.R. 3490, which passed the House of Representatives a short time ago and is pending before the Senate Committee on Finance, would go far toward suppressing the abuse of narcotic drugs. I most sincerely hope that your Committee will consider this or a similar bill at the earliest possible time, so that it may be enacted into law during the present Session of the Congress. I am exceedingly anxious, as I know the Congress is, that the Federal Government take every step which is properly within its authority to eliminate organized criminal activity in the United States.

Very sincerely yours,

HARRY S. TRUMAN

[Honorable Walter F. George, Chairman, Committee on Finance, United States Senate, Washington 25, D.C.]

NOTE: For the President's statement upon signing the bill relating to narcotics laws violations, see Item 287.

202 Statement by the President Commending the Operations of the Federal Farm Mortgage Corporation. *August 24, 1951*

THE CHECK for a million dollars which has just been handed to the Secretary of the Treasury by the Governor of the Farm Credit Administration has a special significance for our farmers, and for all Americans. It brings to a total of $100 million dividends earned on a sum twice this amount advanced to meet a crying need for farm mortgage credit.

Back in the dark depression days of 1934, which many of us have now forgotten, Congress provided $200 million to capitalize the Federal Farm Mortgage Corporation and gave it authority to borrow up to $2 billion for use in making emergency farm mortgage loans. This was the period, you will recall, when farmers were engaged in a desperate struggle to hold their farms. Incomes were extremely low and group farm income was only $8½ billion in 1934, compared with $32 billion in 1950. Thousands of farmers were then losing their farms by foreclosure.

Over the years the Corporation made 679,000 loans to farmers for over one and two-tenths billion dollars. A large portion of these loans were used to refinance farmers who were overloaded with debts. These loans helped save the homes and farms for hundreds of thousands of farmers. This refinancing also helped to unfreeze the assets of many local banks and insurance companies and made a distinct contribution to putting our economy back on its feet.

This Government Corporation has paid all its operating expenses, it has paid interest on all money it borrowed and met all losses on loans from its earnings. It has been of no cost to the Government. It has also returned to the Treasury the original Government capital investment of $200 million except for $10,000. This nominal amount remains outstanding in order for the Corporation to hold its charter long enough to wind up its outstanding loans.

In addition, the check that has just been handed to the Secretary of the Treasury, John W. Snyder, by Governor I. W. Duggan of the Farm Credit Administration, brings the dividend payments made by the Corporation to the Treasury to a total of $100 million. Secretary of Agriculture Brannan tells me the Corporation still has assets, most in the form of loans to farmers that are not yet due, that will probably result in additional dividends of as much as $30 million.

We take pride in this Government institution's success in helping farmers weather an economic storm. We take pride in the way farmers and ranchers have lived up to our faith in their integrity and ability to rise above difficulties when given the opportunity.

The lending operations of the Federal Farm Mortgage Corporation were conducted by the cooperative land bank system, which at the same time was quietly and effectively going about the business of making much needed low-rate land bank loans to farmers. I might add that every dollar of Government capital that has been put in any of the farm credit banks or corporations has either been repaid or is intact and unimpaired and each of the banks and corporations has substantial reserves and surpluses.

The land bank system is deserving of our warm commendation. On behalf of all Americans I wish to thank the Secretary of Agriculture, the officers and employees of the land bank system, its farmer members, and the officials of the Farm Credit Administration under whose supervision the loan program was so successfully administered. It is heartening to know that long-term, low-cost farm mortgage credit to meet farmers' needs continues to be supplied on a sound basis by the farmer-owned Federal land bank system.

203 Remarks to a Group of High School Students From Kansas. *August 24, 1951*

IT IS a pleasure to greet you. Such trips as this do much for international goodwill. It is also great for educational purposes, because you had to inform yourselves thoroughly and completely on the country you were going to visit, and when you got there you found out that those people have the same ideals and are trying to do just exactly what we are: that is, to make their country a good place in which to live.

I am glad you took the trip. I hope these

trips will be continued, and I hope that every State in the Union will have a chance to have representatives visit some of our neighbors, and find out just what goes on across the line.

It has been a pleasure to have you here.

NOTE: The President spoke at 3:05 p.m. in the Rose Garden at the White House.

The group consisted of 31 Kansas high school students who had just finished a 10-day study tour of Canada, which they had won in a contest for the best essays on U.S.-Canadian relations. The contest and trip were under the auspices of the Veterans of Foreign Wars of Kansas.

204 Letter to the Chairman, Wage Stabilization Board, Requesting Investigation of a Strike in the Copper and Nonferrous Metals Industry. *August 27, 1951*

Dear Dr. Taylor:

The Director of the Federal Mediation and Conciliation Service has reported to me that collective bargaining and mediation have been exhausted and that a strike is in progress, effective August 27, 1951, involving the mining, milling, smelting and refining of copper and certain other non-ferrous metals.

The strike is a consequence of labor disputes between Kennecott Copper Corporation, Phelps Dodge Corporation, American Smelting and Refining Company, Anaconda Copper and Mining Company (including International Smelting and Refining Company), and other employers who are similarly engaged in mining, milling, smelting or refining copper or other non-ferrous metals and certain of their employees represented by certain labor organizations, including the International Union of Mine, Mill and Smelter Workers, several railroad brotherhoods, and unions affiliated with the American Federation of Labor.

On the basis of information and advice submitted to me by the Office of Defense Mobilization and the Federal Mediation and Conciliation Service, I am of the opinion that the disputes are of a character which substantially threaten the progress of national defense. Thus, in accordance with the terms of E.O. 10233, I am referring the disputes to the Wage Stabilization Board and asking that the Board investigate and inquire into the issues in dispute and promptly report to me with its recommendations to the parties as to fair and equitable terms of settlement. I am asking the Federal Mediation and Conciliation Service to provide the Board with a record of the issues in dispute.

The Director of the Office of Defense Mobilization has reported to me on the serious effect of the strike on the production of copper and other non-ferrous metals. The present critical shortage of copper has inhibited fulfillment of essential production schedules. Thus, the strike has an immediate and very serious impact on the defense program.

It is my earnest hope that the men involved will comply with your request that they return to work while the matter is before the Board and that the utilization of the Board's machinery will thus serve its purpose of restoring to production the facilities necessary to the national defense. I am sure that, in that event, the Board will proceed promptly in its task of recommending to the parties fair and equitable terms of settlement of the disputes.

Very sincerely yours,

HARRY S. TRUMAN

[Honorable George Taylor, Chairman, Wage Stabilization Board, Washington 25, D.C.]

NOTE: Executive Order 10233 "Amending Executive Order 10161 with Respect to Wage Stabilization and Settlement of Labor Disputes" was signed by the President on April 21, 1951 (3 CFR, 1949–1953 Comp., p. 743).

On August 29 the Wage Stabilization Board reported that (1) the International Union of Mine, Mill and Smelter Workers would give no assurance that its members would return to work until a satisfactory agreement was reached, and (2) that

it would not be appropriate for the Board to consider the merits of the dispute prior to the resumption of work. The text of the letter was released by the White House on August 30.

On August 30 the President signed Executive Order 10283 "Creating a Board of Inquiry to Report on Certain Labor Disputes Affecting the Copper and Non-Ferrous Metals Industry" (3 CFR, 1949–1953 Comp., p. 785).

The initial report of the Board of Inquiry was submitted to the President on September 4, 1951 (46 pp., mimeographed). The Board found that the strike was causing or aggravating critical shortages of vital materials and that its continuation posed a threat to the domestic economy and the national defense program.

On September 4 the President ordered the Justice Department to seek an injunction calling for a temporary cessation of the shutdown. On the following day an 80-day restraining order was issued by the United States District Court in Denver, Colo., the headquarters of the striking mineworkers.

On November 5 the Board reported that agreements had been reached with all firms that had been involved in the dispute. The Board issued a supplemental final report on November 15, 1951. On February 14, 1952, the President reported on the strike and the settlement in a message to Congress. The message, together with copies of the Board's reports, is printed in House Document 354 (82d Cong., 2d sess.).

See also Items 169, 214, 277.

---

205 Statement by the President Upon Establishing the Defense Materials Procurement Agency. *August 28, 1951*

I HAVE today signed an Executive order establishing the Defense Materials Procurement Agency and making further arrangements for the handling of loans to stimulate defense production.

The Defense Materials Procurement Agency is being established pursuant to the policy announced in my statement of August 1, 1951. This new agency will have centralized responsibility for procuring strategic and critical materials at home and abroad. The agency will also have responsibility for the Government's efforts to stimulate increased production of these ma-

terials, using the powers available under Title III of the Defense Production Act of 1950, as amended.

Under the Executive order signed today, the Defense Materials Procurement Agency will be responsible for the following specific tasks:

(1) Purchase and make commitments to purchase metals, minerals, and other materials for Government use or resale under section 303 of the Defense Production Act of 1950, as amended. This involves no change in the Department of Agriculture's present authority to purchase food.

(2) Encourage the exploration, development, and mining of critical and strategic minerals and metals under section 303 of the act. It is expected that the DMPA will redelegate to the Department of the Interior responsibility for the domestic phase of exploration for metals and minerals.

(3) Make any subsidy payments under section 303(c) of the act which may be necessary to maintain essential production.

(4) Serve as a guaranteeing agency in connection with the financing of production and deliveries or services under Government contracts in accordance with section 301 of the act.

(5) Install additional equipment, facilities, processes, and improvements in Government-owned and private plants, factories, and facilities.

Assignment of these tasks to the new agency represents a consolidation of certain functions previously performed by a number of other agencies, particularly the General Services Administration and the Defense Minerals Administration in the Department of Interior. Arrangements are now being completed for delegation to the new agency of certain other functions not transferred by this order, including the minerals and metals procurement program of the Economic Cooperation Administration.

The new agency will be subject to direction, control, and coordination by the Director of Defense Mobilization. It will operate within the framework of program objectives approved by the Defense Production Administrator.

The Defense Materials Procurement Agency will be headed by Mr. Jess Larson, now Administrator of General Services.

The Executive order signed today also redefines arrangements for loans of Government funds under section 302 of the Defense Production Act of 1950. These are loans to private business enterprises for the expansion of capacity, the development of technological processes, and the production of essential materials, including the exploration, development, and mining of strategic and critical metals and minerals.

The order provides that such loans will be handled through the Export-Import Bank of Washington, when the funds are to be used for expansion, development, or production in foreign countries. This includes loans to domestic borrowers for use abroad. These loans will be made by the Bank only upon a certificate of essentiality made by the Secretary of Agriculture in the case of food and by the Defense Production Administrator in all other cases, and will be made only in the event that private funds and the regular funds of the Export-Import Bank are unavailable for the loan involved. The terms and conditions of the loans will be determined by the Bank.

All loans for domestic use under section 302 will continue to be handled by the Reconstruction Finance Corporation. The order provides that the Reconstruction Finance Corporation will determine the terms and conditions of these loans, instead of having the determination made by the various production agencies as has occurred in the past. Certificates of essentiality from the Defense Production Administrator or the Secretary of Agriculture, as appropriate, will be required in cases where these loans are for the expansion of capacity. These certificates will no longer be necessary for loans involving working capital only, but the Reconstruction Finance Corporation will be required to check in advance with the procurement agencies concerned, as to the need for any working capital loan.

Loans by the Reconstruction Finance Corporation under section 302 of the Defense Production Act will continue to be restricted to those instances where neither private funds nor the regular funds of the RFC are available for the purpose.

NOTE: The President referred to Executive Order 10281 "Defense Materials Procurement and Supply" (3 CFR, 1949–1953 Comp., p. 781).

For the President's statement of August 1, see Item 177.

206   Letter to the President, National Farmers Union, on the Taxation of Cooperatives.   *August 28, 1951*

Dear Jim:

I fully understand the importance to members of cooperatives of the tax questions now under consideration in Congress, and I appreciate this opportunity to reiterate the Administration's long-standing support of cooperatives.

The Democratic Party has consistently encouraged the efforts of farmers and consumers to improve their economic status through cooperatives. In 1948 the Democratic Party reaffirmed this principle and I campaigned on it. The following paragraph from that platform is as good today as it was then:

"We will encourage farm cooperatives and oppose any revision of Federal law designed to curtail their most effective functioning as a means of achieving economy, stability and security for American agriculture."

I sincerely hope that this principle will be the guiding one when the current tax legislation is finally written.

Sincerely yours,

HARRY S. TRUMAN

[Mr. James G. Patton, President, National Farmers Union, 300 Independence Avenue, S.E., Washington, D.C.]

NOTE: The White House press release making public the President's letter stated that it was written in response to an inquiry from Mr. Patton about the President's views on taxation of cooperatives.

207   Letter Greeting the President of the Philippines Upon His Arrival at Washington National Airport.   *August 30, 1951*

My dear Mr. President:

It always gives me the greatest pleasure to welcome you to Washington and to have an opportunity of seeing you again. It is particularly so this time in view of the circumstances which I consider to be one of the most historic events in Philippine-American relations and a vital milestone in our mutual quest for peace and security.

I am looking forward to seeing you this noon and to having lunch with you after the signing of the Mutual Defense Treaty, as well as to the opportunity of discussing problems of common interest. Permit me again to extend to you a most cordial welcome and to express the hope that this visit in the United States will be both pleasant and profitable.

Very sincerely yours,

HARRY S. TRUMAN

[His Excellency Elpidio Quirino, President of the Republic of the Philippines.]

NOTE: Secretary of State Dean Acheson presented the letter to President Quirino upon his arrival at the airport.

208   Exchange of Remarks With the President of the Philippines at the Signing of the Treaty of Mutual Defense.   *August* 30, 1951

Mr. President, distinguished guests:

I am very glad that it was possible for you to join us here today. Mr. President, we have witnessed the signing of a mutual defense treaty between our two great countries. The signing of this treaty symbolizes the close ties that bind the people of the Philippines and the people of the United States.

Our community of interest was put to the bitter test when our two peoples stood shoulder to shoulder on the battlefield, a few short years ago, to resist aggression. In that struggle our countries went together through the agony of temporary defeat, and together rose to the heights of victory. In defeat and victory we were not divided. We showed to all the world that aggressors can defeat free men only temporarily, and divide them never, so long as the fire of freedom burns in their hearts.

In peace as well as in war our countries have worked together. The half century of peaceful and fruitful cooperation between the Philippines and the United States is proof that both our countries are guided by the same ideals and striving for the same objectives. We have demonstrated that two peoples, however different they may be in background and experience, can work together for their common welfare if they have the same belief in democracy and the same faith in freedom.

The treaty that we are signing here today, therefore, rests on firm foundations. It gives formal expression to something that already exists—to the firm relationship of brotherhood that binds our countries together.

We have already expressed in other agreements our common interest in matters of defense and in economic matters. We have shown our common devotion to the cause of peace in our support of the Charter of the United Nations. Our soldiers are fighting side by side today in Korea just as they fought at Bataan and Corregidor—and for the same purpose—to check aggression and defend the rights of free peoples.

This treaty, therefore, is a natural development springing from the long association of our countries and our common sacrifices for freedom. It is a strong step toward security and peace in the Pacific. It demonstrates to all nations that we intend to continue our common course and to work together in the future, as we have in the past, for peace for all mankind.

Mr. President, the people of the United States are happy to join with the people of the Philippines in this mutual expression of our united will to go forward in the cause of peace and freedom. And I pledge to you, Mr. President, the same pledge which you made to the United States: We shall always be your friend.

NOTE: The President spoke at 12:28 p.m. at the Departmental Auditorium in Washington. The text of President Quirino's remarks follow:

"We have witnessed today an act that may be described as the end of the beginning. Here we have set the first milestone on the road towards the enduring security of the Pacific area.

"I have special reason to rejoice at this moment because it was not so long ago, in this same capital, that I took the liberty of proposing the conclusion of a Pacific Security Pact under the initiative of the United States. This is the first fruit of that vision.

"This is a treaty of mutual defense with unavoidable connotations of military action. Yet it is, in fact, wholly dedicated to peace and to the methods of peace. It means so much to the economic development and happiness of the Filipino people. Here our two countries pledge themselves anew to the principle of the pacific settlement of disputes enshrined in the Charter of the United Nations. Here we have assumed a formal undertaking to assist each other and to stand together in the face of aggression, in the hope that hereafter we may be able to follow undistracted the fruitful pursuits of peace.

"We have no aggressive aims against anyone. Our purpose is rather to give notice that a potential aggressor must henceforth take due account of our common purpose and united will to act in self-defense. From the history of the Filipino people and of our relations with the United States during the past 50 years, nobody can have the slightest doubt about our devotion to freedom and our readiness to share in its defense.

"On this solemn occasion, Mr. President, may I convey to you, and through you to the American people, the deepest sentiments of good will and friendship from the people of the Philippines. This treaty proclaims the sense of unity of our two peoples, and this is a declaration of historic importance

especially to us. For we have established our unity of purpose, not on any considerations of race, creed, or equality of power, but solely on the ground of our common faith in freedom. Though humbled by the great significance of this alliance, the Filipino people are nevertheless proud that our young Republic has merited this recognition of its faith and its courage. I bring to witness at this signing, Mr. President, the undying faith in democracy of the Filipino people and the courage to defend it with all our strength."

Gen. Carlos P. Romulo, Secretary of Foreign Affairs of the Philippines, and Dean Acheson, Secretary of State, also spoke. The text of their remarks was released by the White House. The proceedings were broadcast.

---

209 The President's News Conference of *August* 30, 1951

THE PRESIDENT. Please be seated.

I have no special announcements for you this morning. I will try to answer questions, however, if I can.

[1.] Q. Mr. President, have you received a report from the Wage Stabilization Board yet on the copper situation?

THE PRESIDENT. No.

Q. Could you tell us what the next step in that is, sir?

THE PRESIDENT. I haven't received the report. I can't make any comment until I know what is in the report.[1]

[2.] Q. Mr. President, I have been asked to ask you this question for comment, in the case of two "engine hustlers" out in Toledo, who have been ordered discharged for refusal to join a union on religious grounds. Do you—the union has just signed a union shop contract with New York Central——

THE PRESIDENT. I don't know anything about it.

[3.] Q. Mr. President, a Senate committee—District of Columbia committee—has reported out a bill to give the people here home rule. The people would elect a city

council, and the President would appoint a mayor. Do you favor action——

THE PRESIDENT. I have been fighting for home rule for 17 years. I hope they will get it this time.

[4.] Q. Mr. President, you told us that you were going to continue correspondence with the President of the Soviet Presidium. Could you tell us anything about it—something coming up on that?

THE PRESIDENT. No, there is no hurry. Those things have to be done very deliberately. I meant what I said when I said I would pursue the correspondence.[2]

[5.] Q. Mr. President, are you going to participate in some kind of ceremony out in Kansas City next Thursday in the National Guard Armory——

THE PRESIDENT. Well, it's a Reserve Armory, not National Guard.

Q. Yes.

THE PRESIDENT. It's a dedication of the Organized Reserve Armory. Yes, I am.

Q. Will you make a speech?

THE PRESIDENT. Well, I expect so. I will make a few remarks off the cuff.[3]

---

[1] See note to Item 204.

[2] See Item 147.
[3] See Item 218.

Q. Are you going to spend your time at home, or will you be in the city——

THE PRESIDENT. At home. I'll stay at home.

Q. Thank you.

THE PRESIDENT. I'll be back and forth from the city all the time, just like I always am. I want to take a look at that flood area again, to see how it looks after they started to clean it up.

Q. Will you do that, sir, by plane or car?

THE PRESIDENT. Walk!

Q. Oh! [*Laughter*]

Q. How far is that walk going to take you?

THE PRESIDENT. Oh, it won't be very long—three or four miles. [*Laughter*]

Q. How far?

THE PRESIDENT. Three or four miles.

Q. Mr. President, will you walk slow enough so we can follow you? [*More laughter*]

THE PRESIDENT. Oh, I think I'll compromise with you and ride most of the way, but there will be some of it on foot, of course. I want to see what it looks like.

[6.] Q. Mr. President, I wonder if I could get your reaction—you are acquainted with the case of the seven newspaper people in Louisiana who were indicted——

THE PRESIDENT. All I know is what I have seen in the papers. I don't know anything about the facts. I understand the matter is now pending in the courts, and I don't usually comment on those things.

[7.] Q. Mr. President, a recent opinion poll in the Middle West shows a sharp rise in your popularity. Have you any comment?

THE PRESIDENT. No. No comment. You know how those things go up and down, and a lot of people are disappointed in the results when they finally count them. [*Laughter*]

[8.] Q. Mr. President, to get back to this business of the Russians and the Shvernik

letter, the morning papers are carrying stories from Moscow, quoting the Moscow press as accusing the United States of starting world war III. Do you have any comment on that?

THE PRESIDENT. That is nothing new for them. It isn't true, of course. Like all the rest of their propaganda, not founded on fact at all.

[9.] Q. Mr. President, did you by any chance look at that other piece by Jonathan Daniels about 1952? [4]

THE PRESIDENT. No, I haven't seen it.

Q. Well, Jonathan says that—without any qualification at all—that on the basis of recent conversations with you, he thinks your attitude to the race indicates you will run and be reelected, and by about 419 electoral votes now.

THE PRESIDENT. Well, any American citizen is entitled to his opinion. I am not expressing mine. [*Laughter*]

Q. Well, Mr. President, would you say Mr. Daniels' was an informed opinion?

THE PRESIDENT. He did not consult me about it. His guess is as good as anybody's. [*Laughter*]

Q. Before, Mr. President, we asked when that thing came up, when Jonathan—when he came out from seeing you a few weeks ago, we asked you if he was acting on anything more than reportorial instinct, and you said that was what the case was. Is that what this case is?

THE PRESIDENT. That's the same kind of a case exactly.

[10.] Q. Mr. President, do you plan to take any steps to try and restore that ECA cut in the foreign aid appropriation in the Senate?

THE PRESIDENT. I have done everything I possibly can on that part of that legislation.

---

[4] The article by Jonathan Daniels, entitled "Truman Can't Lose," is printed in the September 1951 issue of the American Magazine.

I am going to keep working at it. Looks rather hopeless now, however. It is a very serious situation.

[11.] Q. Mr. President, are we in a stronger position in Korea, if fighting has to be renewed, than we were when the talks began?

THE PRESIDENT. Yes. Certainly we are.

Q. Then, would you comment on the talks themselves—evaluate the situation?

THE PRESIDENT. General Ridgway has expressed the opinion of the American Government, and I am behind him 100 percent.

Q. We will be stronger than we were?

THE PRESIDENT. Yes.

[12.] Q. Mr. President, have you looked into that Cowart [5] case, the man who was dismissed by the Department of Agriculture and there has been some complaint about it?

THE PRESIDENT. I only know what I saw in the paper. I haven't talked to the Secretary of Agriculture about it.

Q. You haven't talked with him. Has Mr. Rayburn talked to you about it, by any chance?

THE PRESIDENT. No. I haven't talked to anybody about it.

[13.] Q. Mr. President, would you like to enlarge at this time on the possible results of the cut in the foreign aid funds?

THE PRESIDENT. Well, I can make a remark or two that I think apropos.

Back in 1947 it was decided, after Mr. Acheson stated the case at Cleveland, Miss., and General Marshall stated it at Harvard University, that economic recovery is what Europe needed in order to stave off the Red aggression.

A plan was worked out, presented to the Congress, and they were informed that we hoped over a 4-year period European re-

covery could be accomplished for less than $17 billion. The last request brought the total up to about 14½ billion, 2½ less than the original estimate, with success in sight.

Now, it is a pity to overturn the whole applecart in the interests of misplaced economy. It isn't economy, and will not be economy, if the European recovery program is ruined at its conclusion when we are just on the verge of success. And the economic improvement of Europe will be of immense assistance in the rearming of the Atlantic Treaty countries. It all fits in the same pattern. And it isn't economy to do what they are trying to do now to the economic recovery program.

Q. Mr. President, present indications are that the Congress may change the authority for administering this foreign aid and take it out of the hands of the Secretary of State. Do you think that such a plan is workable?

THE PRESIDENT. I wonder who the Chief Executive of the United States is? It is the business of the President of the United States to carry out the mandates of Congress and that is the way this will be handled.

Q. In other words, does that mean you think it will be workable under that present plan, where it explicitly leaves it up to you for all final decisions?

THE PRESIDENT. That would be absolutely necessary, anyway. It will be workable.

[14.] Q. Mr. President, the Czechoslovakian Ambassador last night said that he regards the Oatis case as closed. What do you think of that?

THE PRESIDENT. I don't think the Oatis case will ever be closed until he gets out of jail, at least not in this country. [6]

[15.] Q. Mr. President, in view of the— [*inaudible*]—control vacancy, are you planning any reshuffling of the agencies, including the abolition of ESA?

---

[5] Jack Cowart, former official of the Department of Agriculture. The reasons for his dismissal were not made public.

[6] See Item 145 [7].

THE PRESIDENT. I can't answer that question until I know just what the bills provide. It is being analyzed now by the Budget.

Q. Mr. President, I didn't get his question?

THE PRESIDENT. They wanted to know if there was going to be any reshuffling of the agencies that have to do with the price control and defense production, things of that kind, on account of the tremendous cuts which were made by this Congress. I told him I can't answer the question until the bills are analyzed and we found out just what has been accomplished—or not accomplished, whichever way you want to put it.

[16.]   Q. Mr. President, would you care to make any comment on India's refusal to attend the Japanese peace treaty conference in San Francisco?

THE PRESIDENT. No comment. We sent a message which covered the whole situation.[7]

Reporter: Thank you, Mr. President.

THE PRESIDENT. You are entirely welcome.

NOTE: President Truman's two hundred and seventy-seventh news conference was held in the Indian Treaty Room (Room 474) in the Executive Office Building at 10:30 a.m. on Thursday, August 30, 1951.

[7] The Indian note of August 23, released to the press on August 25, gave the following reasons for India's refusal to attend the Japanese peace treaty conference: "(I) The terms of the Treaty should concede to Japan a position of honour, equality, and contentment among the community of free nations; (II) They should be so framed as to enable all countries specially interested in the maintenance of a stable peace in the Far East to subscribe to the Treaty sooner or later. The Government of India have after most careful thought come to the conclusion that the Treaty does not in material respects satisfy either of these two criteria."

The Indian message and the U.S. reply of August 25 are printed in the Department of State Bulletin (vol. 25, p. 385).

210   Remarks at the Presentation of a Floral Replica of a Defense Bond. *August* 31, 1951

THANK YOU, Mr. Secretary. I am sure that this bond drive will be as successful as all the others have been, for the simple reason that it is right, that it is the safest investment in the world, that it is something that gives people with surplus funds a place to save them. Then, when the time comes that they need things in an emergency, they have got it. And they know it is just the same as money. In fact, better than money, because it is drawing interest.

I want to thank these gentlemen who are responsible for this beautiful floral piece. I hope they will take it and multiply it by a thousand times and put it into bonds.

NOTE: The President spoke at 3 p.m. in the Rose Garden at the White House. In his opening words he referred to John W. Snyder, Secretary of the Treasury.

The floral display was presented to the President by representatives of the Florists Telegraph Delivery Association. The Association was holding its annual convention in Washington.

211   Statement by the President Upon Issuing Order Delaying the Disposal of World War II Housing. *September* 1, 1951

I HAVE today issued an Executive order extending the time within which steps may be taken to dispose of World War II housing built by the Federal Government. Over 200,000 units still under the jurisdiction of the Housing and Home Finance Agency are affected. This action is one part of the program authorized by the Congress in the

Defense Housing and Community Facilities and Services Act of 1951. With the other measures which that act enables us to take, this will help to relieve the housing shortages created or intensified by the mobilization effort.

In one sense, it is too bad that we must continue to try to use our temporary housing. The present tenants, the defense workers, and the military personnel who will use these quarters on a preferred basis deserve better accommodations. I am going to do everything I can to speed the building of better, permanent housing for them. But for the time being, because of the defense emergency, we must use every decent home near military and production centers.

The housing covered by this Executive order was built to meet World War II needs. Originally the Federal Government put up 400,000 units of temporary housing and about 180,000 units of permanent housing. The 81st Congress, in the Housing Act of 1950, provided a timetable for disposition of temporary housing by transfer to local communities. Another timetable was set up for the disposal of World War II housing not so transferred. The Executive order is-

sued today revises these timetables and extends the various deadlines involved.

Immediately after the outbreak of hostilities in Korea last summer, disposition of World War II housing was suspended. We had to make sure that federally-held housing, previously scheduled for demolition, would be available for new defense needs. This Executive order will allow additional time to determine which of the projects may still be needed.

Under this order the date for notice of eviction to the present tenants is postponed from July 1, 1952, to July 1, 1953. New tenants will now be admitted as vacancies occur until July 1, 1952. Where housing is transferred to local communities, provision will be made where necessary to insure that the housing will continue to be made available to defense workers and military personnel. Any municipality which wants to apply for transfer of temporary housing may now do so until December 31, 1951, and will have until June 30, 1952, to comply with the legal requirements prior to transfer.

NOTE: The President referred to Executive Order 10284 "Extensions of Time Relating to the Disposition of Certain Housing" (3 CFR, 1949–1953 Comp., p. 785).

---

212 Statement by the President: Labor Day.
September 2, 1951

IN EXTENDING Labor Day greetings to the workers of the United States and in offering my congratulations to the great labor movement of which they are rightfully proud to be members, I prayerfully hope that all our people may recapture the spirit of social justice and human brotherhood which was originally associated with Labor Day. We have made great progress since 1894 in establishing the rights of labor and in promoting the general welfare of the American economy. But we still have a long way to go.

Our domestic responsibility at this critical period in the Nation's history is threefold. First, we must develop our productive and military resources to such a peak that the totalitarian enemies of freedom will eventually see the madness of their monstrous program of world domination. Secondly, it is important to guarantee equality of sacrifice in the defense mobilization program. And last, it is our purpose to achieve these two objectives democratically and cooperatively.

The American labor movement is second

to no other group in its determination to pursue these three objectives simultaneously. American labor is wholeheartedly in favor of all-out economic mobilization and equality of sacrifice. Even more important, it is in favor of carrying out these objectives democratically and in a spirit of voluntary cooperation between organized labor, management, and the Government.

We believe in democratic cooperation between organized labor and management and between labor, management, and Government. We believe in industrial democracy, as opposed to unregulated competition on the one hand and excessive governmentalism on the other. We believe in freedom, not the unregulated license of laissez-faire, but freedom religiously dedicated and consciously ordered to the general welfare.

We believe in these things not only for workers in our own country, but throughout the world. We recognize the dangers that face the freedom of millions of workers in many other countries. We know, moreover, that lasting peace and security can be achieved only when workers everywhere are vouchsafed the privileges and the rights that are legally recognized and protected in the United States.

As President of the United States, I congratulate the American labor movement on the soundness of its traditions and policies and pledge my continued support of its ideals. Working together—labor, management, and Government—we can safeguard our material standard of living. Even more important than that, we can hand down to our children a glorious heritage of freedom, without which even a life of material abundance and prosperity is hardly worth the living. With the help of God we can achieve the goals we have set for ourselves and help to bring peace to the world.

213   Radio Address Opening the Defense Bond Drive.
September 3, 1951
[Broadcast from San Francisco at 7:55 p.m.]

Fellow Americans:

Six years ago, here in San Francisco, the United Nations was formed. It was our purpose then to prevent another world war. That is still our purpose.

The United Nations was established to unite the moral forces of the world for peace, and to organize the strength of many nations to keep the peace.

In these last 6 years there have been many difficulties and obstructions. But today the United Nations is doing exactly what it was set up to do.

When aggression came in Korea, the United Nations took action. It labeled the aggression for what it was, it branded the North Korean and the Chinese Communists as the aggressors. It called upon peace-loving countries to unite and put down aggression.

That is what we have been doing. Young men from the United States have been fighting heroically, alongside young men from many other countries, to stop aggression in Korea. For they know, and we know, that if aggression were not checked in Korea, it would only be a matter of time until a new world war brought destruction and misery to all of us.

For the past several weeks there have been negotiations in Korea, at the suggestion of the Communist aggressors, for an armistice there as the first step to a peaceful settlement. Recently the Communists have broken off these negotiations. We do not know whether they intend to resume them or not. We are ready at any time to reach an honorable settlement in Korea, but we will not give in to aggression.

Whether negotiations in Korea are successful or not, we must continue to drive ahead to build defensive strength for our country and the free world. The plain fact is that the Communists may try to resume the offensive in Korea at any time. Moreover, they are capable of launching new attacks in Europe, in the Middle East, or elsewhere in Asia, wherever it suits them.

That is what makes it so vital that we build our defenses—and build them fast.

Right now our defense effort is beginning to roll. We have been tooling up for large-scale production of new airplanes, tanks, and weapons of all types. We have a lot of new developments that we are putting into production—ranging from faster jet planes to lighter equipment for our foot soldiers.

These things take materials and manpower. And they cost money.

That is where this savings bond campaign comes in. All of you, I know, want to help in the defense of our country.

People sometimes say to me, "I want to help in the defense effort, but I don't know what I can do. Can you tell me?"

Tonight, I am telling you about something everybody can do. This is a personal matter with every one of you.

You can help to defend your country by buying United States savings bonds.

At the same time you will be putting aside money, at a time when goods are becoming scarcer, which will be available later on when goods are more plentiful. It will be a backlog to meet emergencies, to finance the education of your children or to purchase a home, and to provide for a more comfortable old age.

The savings bonds you buy will be bonds for freedom. And they will be bonds for your personal future. I ask each of you to back the defense drive to the limit by buying extra bonds and helping to sell bonds to others.

Buying defense bonds is a way in which each of us can play a part in the defense of our country and in bringing peace to the world.

214   Telegram to the Attorney General Authorizing Him To Issue an Injunction in the Copper Industry Strike. *September 4, 1951*

My dear Mr. Attorney General:

On August 30, 1951, by virtue of the authority vested in me by Section 206 of the Labor Management Relations Act, 1947 (Public Law 101, 80th Congress), I issued Executive Order No. 10283, creating a Board of Inquiry to inquire into the issues involved in labor disputes between Kennecott Copper Corporation, Phelps Dodge Corporation, American Smelting and Refining Company, Anaconda Copper Mining Company, including International Smelting and Refining Company, and other employers who are

similarly engaged in mining, milling, smelting, or refining copper or other non-ferrous metals and certain of their employees represented by certain labor organizations, including the International Union of Mine, Mill and Smelter Workers, several railroad brotherhoods, and unions affiliated with the American Federation of Labor.

On September 4, 1951, I received the Board's written report in the matter. A copy of that report is attached hereto. The report indicates that certain of the disputes have been settled, but that others covering a substantial part of the industry are still unresolved.

In my opinion, these unresolved labor disputes have resulted in strikes or lock-outs affecting a substantial part of an industry engaged in trade and commerce among the several States and with foreign nations, and in the production of goods for commerce, which strikes or lock-outs, if permitted to continue, will imperil the national health and safety.

I therefore direct you, pursuant to the provisions of Section 208 of the Labor Management Relations Act, 1947, to petition in the name of the United States any District Court of the United States having jurisdiction of the parties to enjoin the continuance of such strikes or lock-outs where such action is necessary to secure a resumption of production in the industry, and for such relief as may in your judgment be necessary or appropriate.

Very sincerely yours,

HARRY S. TRUMAN

[Honorable J. Howard McGrath, The Attorney General, Washington, D.C.]

NOTE: For the background of the strike in the copper and other nonferrous metals industry, together with citations to the reports and other documents relating to the settlement, see Item 204.

The text of the President's telegram of September 4 was released in San Francisco.

215 Remarks in San Francisco at a Luncheon for Democrats From Western States. *September 4, 1951*

Madam Chairman, fellow Democrats, distinguished guests:

I am most happy to be here today. I was here some time ago when the United Nations was organized, and opened its first regular meeting. It was a great privilege. That organization, I am sure, will eventually cause us to have world peace.

I came here for the purpose of opening the conference for the signing of the treaty of peace with Japan. I can only be here for the day, but I couldn't possibly turn down the opportunity to talk to some of my Democratic brethren and sisters.

You know, it is good to get together with a group of Democrats, especially an enthusiastic group like this.

I had some experience here in this town in 1948—had a wonderful meeting down in front of City Hall in San Francisco. And the result was very satisfactory.

You in this city witnessed the first great step toward lasting peace back in 1945 when the United Nations Charter was signed here.

During the 6 years since then, we have been working constantly for world peace. Step by step we will keep on working for peace. We are building up our armed strength here at home just to keep the peace, and we are helping our friends to build up their strength, for the simple purpose to keep the peace.

We are trying to accomplish the purposes for which the United Nations was established—negotiation of differences between nations, instead of shooting at each other to settle their differences.

It is terrible to think of what would happen if we should have another world war. No one can imagine the destruction, the loss of life.

New weapons mean that an all-out war would wipe out civilization. It is the job of every American—be he Democrat or Republican—to do all he can to prevent all-out war.

There are a lot of people who do not seem to understand this. There are a lot of people who will not or cannot understand the world situation and the problems we face. There are a lot of people who are not willing to pay the taxes and appropriate the necesary money it takes to arm ourselves and our allies.

And you know, we must have friends and allies, and we must help to arm them to keep the peace in the world.

I say to you that these people are flirting with national suicide—flirting with the end of civilization and the return to the darkest of the Dark Ages.

It is fantastic what can happen with the use of new weapons that are now under construction in this country, not only the one which we all fear the most, but there are some weapons which are fantastic in their operation.

I hope we will never have to use them.

Now, the people who oppose our preparations are gambling with our future in a way that I am not willing to approve. Under the oath which I took to support and defend the Constitution of the United States, I must do all I can to protect this great Republic from destruction.

These antidefense, anticontrol, antieverything people are the same ones who have been against everything we have been doing in this country for the last 20 years to improve the conditions for the farmer, for labor, and for the average family.

These reactionaries and isolationists, these "antis" and false economizers are as blind about what it takes to keep our country strong here at home as they are about what it takes to keep peace in the world. In fact, those things go together. We cannot do what is necessary for peace, unless we are strong here at home.

Well, we are strong here at home—we are strong here at home. And I am very thankful for that, and the Democratic Party can be very proud of that fact. Since 1933 we

have made the United States strong and prosperous beyond anything the people ever dreamed of.

National income has gone up from $40 billion a year to $278 billion a year.

Corporate profits have gone from minus 3 billion—they were $3 billion in the red in 1932—to plus $46 billion.

And yet, according to some people, we have taken the country down the road to ruin.

It's a wonderful ruin, and I'm glad to be a part of it.

The income per person in terms of today's prices has gone up from $383 a year to $1,447 a year—more than three and a half times.

These pullbacks and "antis" talk about how the dollar has shrunk—well, let's take the figures they come with: The purchasing power of the average man—he is the one I am working for—his purchasing power, the per capita purchasing power has gone up 40 percent since 1939, using the 1939 dollar or the dollar we have today. And they can't go behind it, for figures don't lie—although liars can sometimes figure.

More people are at work right now on good jobs and good wages than ever before in the history of the country, or the history of the world by any country. Our economy is stronger than it has ever been. Farmers, businessmen, wage earners, white collar workers, professionals—all of these are better off than they have ever been before. There was never a time like this in the history of any country in the world, ancient or modern.

All this has been made possible by our system of free enterprise. The policies of the Democratic Party made it possible. The Democratic Party has saved this country from socialism and communism.

Now, why is it that one country after another all over the world has turned to socialism? I will tell you why: It is because

501

those who rule those countries did not know how to make free enterprise work for the benefit of their people.

The same thing was about to happen in this country once, and for the same reason.

Oh, we had some capable businessmen running things—they were very smart. But there was one thing they did not understand.

If Government is going to be successful, it has to be run for the benefit of all the people. We have operated the Government for the benefit of all the people since 1933, and that's the reason we are in the condition we are.

We succeeded in making farmers, laboring men, and industry prosperous. The test of the New Deal and the Fair Deal and all that the Democratic Party has done for the country since March 4, 1933, lies in the answer to a simple question: Are you better off today than you were in the last year of the Old Deal? I wonder if there is anybody here who can say no to that—I don't believe there is.

It hasn't been easy to make the New Deal and the Fair Deal a success. We have had a lot of opposition. Sometimes representatives of special privilege have been able to hold us back. They are still trying to gain control of the Government—local, State, and national.

Most of the special privilege boys are better off than they have ever been in their lives, but they still say that the New Deal and the Fair Deal are taking the country to the dogs and to ruin. As I said awhile ago, it's a wonderful ruin, and I'm glad to be a part of it.

That's what they have been saying for 18 years, and all the time they have been getting better off—been getting more prosperous all the time.

We have economic fossils today who want the profits of 1951 with the wages and hours of McKinley's first term.

These antipeople have been wrong so constantly for so long that it makes you wonder how they can keep it up. But they do.

Just let me, as the Democratic President of the United States—the maker of the Fair Deal—propose some progressive measure to improve housing, or the health or the welfare of the people, or the education of our own children, or a plan to protect the people with no lobby in Washington, or no inside pull, by keeping prices down, and you watch, the special interest representatives and the professional "antis" will be against it. They never miss. Anything I suggest for the public welfare is wrong, according to these professional "antis." Thank God there are not too many of them.

There is one thing they have been most consistent about—that is their opposition to the Democratic administration and the things it stands for.

Personally, I have no confidence in their judgment. I intend to keep right on fighting for what I think is right. I intend to keep on fighting for a strong armed force—army, navy, air force—for a military policy for the United States that will keep the peace. And that is what we have got to have, if we expect to keep the peace.

I intend to keep right on fighting for the means to join with our allies in proper arrangements for our own common defense against all aggressors.

I intend to keep right on fighting to build an economically strong country at home— one in which the people will get the benefit.

I don't believe in Government for special privilege. Our resources should be used for the benefit of all the people, not just a few.

When we produce electric power at Shasta Dam, when we develop the Roanoke Basin in Virginia, it ought to be for the benefit of the people and not for the benefit of the private power companies.

The Democratic Party stands for the

502

people and for the public interest, and we are going to keep the Democratic Party for the people and for the public interest as long as I have anything to do with it.

This opposition of ours has plenty of money, and powerful connections in Washington, ready to take over the country's great resources for special privilege.

We must not let them get away with it.

We must keep the spotlight focused where it belongs—on the representatives of special privilege who are swarming around Washington, trying to use the machinery of this great Government of ours for their own selfish interests.

The main problems in Washington today are created by the men who are trying to profiteer during a defense emergency, by people who are trying to sabotage conservation and public power projects.

I want to tell you something about that: Conservation and irrigation developments, and public power projects were started in 1902 in the administration of Teddy Roosevelt. Eighty-five percent of that development has been carried out since March 4, 1933, and 55 percent of that 85 percent has been carried out since April 12, 1945.

These are the things that are really dangerous in public life today, the people who are trying to take those projects away from the people and give them to special privilege. Those are the facts that men and women like you in this room have got to make clear. Those are the facts you must get across to the people, to let them know what is going on.

The special interests and isolationists never give up. There are a lot of people who make their living by being against whatever the Government is trying to do. They don't

care what kind of tactics they use. They are going to keep right on attacking us.

We have got to go right on doing what is right, in spite of them.

The Democratic Party has a duty to the country, and if I am not badly mistaken, the Democratic Party is going to keep right on carrying out that duty.

Next year, 1952—[*here the President was given a tremendous ovation*]—you interrupted me—[*laughter*]—that is an election year. We are going to elect a President next year, and that means that we are going to have the opportunity to see that this country stays in the right path.

That is a great responsibility. I know I can count on everyone in this crowd to do his part in meeting that responsibility.

You won't be working for the Democratic Party alone, you will be working for the people of the United States, and you will be working for world peace.

I don't know who the Democratic candidates will be next year, but I do know this: They will be fighters for peace, they will understand what it takes to make America strong, they will fight for all the people—not just a few.

I know you people here today appreciate these things. I know you understand how important it is to keep America on the right road.

I know you will give your best to see that this great Republic travels down the road to world peace.

Thank you very much.

NOTE: The President spoke at 2:05 p.m. at the Fairmont Hotel in San Francisco. His opening words "Madam Chairman" referred to Mrs. Eleanor Heller, Democratic national committeewoman from California.

216 Address in San Francisco at the Opening of the Conference on the Japanese Peace Treaty. *September 4, 1951*

Mr. Secretary, Governor Warren, Mr. Mayor, Your Excellencies, distinguished guests:

I am glad to welcome you to this conference for the signing of the treaty of peace with Japan. The people of the United States are honored to serve as hosts for this meeting.

Six years ago the nations represented at this Conference were engaged in a bitter and costly war. Nevertheless, these nations and others came together here, in this very hall, to set up the United Nations as the first essential step toward a firm and lasting peace.

Today we meet here again to take another step along the road to peace. On this occasion it is our purpose to conclude a treaty of peace with a country we were fighting in 1945. We meet to restore our former enemy to the community of peaceful nations.

The treaty we are gathered here to sign has not been drawn in a spirit of revenge. The treaty reflects the spirit in which we carried on the war. The principles for which we fought were clearly set forth by President Franklin D. Roosevelt right after Pearl Harbor. On December 9, 1941, in a broadcast to the American people, he said:

"When we resort to force, as now we must, we are determined that this force shall be directed toward ultimate good as well as against immediate evil. . . . We are now in the midst of a war, not for conquest, not for vengeance, but for a world in which this nation, and all that this nation represents, will be safe for our children."

That is our purpose here today as we gather to sign the peace treaty. We are trying to build a world in which the children of all nations can live together in peace. We hope we are attaining the ultimate good to which President Roosevelt referred.

Unfortunately, today, the world is faced with new threats of aggression. Many of the countries represented here are now engaged in a hard fight to uphold the United Nations against international lawbreaking. There are thugs among nations, just as among individuals. But we have not forgotten that our goal is peace. We will not let the present conflict deter us from taking every step we can toward peace. We will not let that happen now, any more than we let the existence of war in 1945 hold up our efforts for the creation of the United Nations.

The people of all our countries long for one thing above all else, and they are determined to have it. What they want is a world at peace—a world where there is justice and freedom for all men and all nations. Our people demand of us that we take every possible measure to reach that goal.

We who stand ready to sign this treaty with Japan believe in peace. We believe in peace based on freedom and international justice. We know that a free and independent people have more vigor and staying power, and can do more to help secure the peace, than a people held under alien control. We believe that the whole great effort for peace will be strengthened if Japan is now restored to independence and linked to other free nations by ties of mutual friendship and responsibility.

Since the fighting ended in 1945, Japan has been an occupied country. The occupation was designed by the wartime Allies to prevent future Japanese aggression, and to establish Japan as a peaceful and democratic country, prepared to return to the family of nations.

The United States, as the principal occupying power, was given a special responsibility to carry out these objectives. It is our judgment that they have been achieved.

I wish on this occasion to express the pride

that my countrymen and I feel in the way in which the Allied occupation has been carried out. Its success has been due to the devoted efforts of many thousands of people serving under the outstanding leadership of General of the Army Douglas MacArthur and his able successor, General Matthew Ridgway.

I would also like to pay tribute to the impressive effort put forward by the people of Japan in this period. They have fully complied with the surrender terms. They have cooperated fully in carrying out the purposes of the occupation.

The result has been a remarkable and unprecedented period of progress in Japanese history. Japan today is a very different country from what it was 6 years ago.

The old militarism has been swept away. This has been done not just by occupation edict, but by the overwhelming will of the Japanese people themselves.

The secret police and the police-state methods used by the former government have been abolished.

The new Japanese constitution provides a bill of rights for all citizens and establishes a government truly representative of the people.

The Japanese people now have universal suffrage, and they are taking a vigorous part in their government. In recent local elections more than 90 percent of those eligible have voted. I wish that same percentage would obtain in the United States.

Japanese women now vote and take part in the government, and enjoy full democratic rights for the first time.

Free and independent labor unions have been established, and farm cooperatives have been greatly expanded.

The monopolies that used to have such a stranglehold on the Japanese economy have been substantially broken up.

Remarkable progress has been made in land reform. Over 5 million acres of land have been purchased from the old landlords and sold to working farmers. Today about 90 percent of all the cultivated land belongs to those who work on it—and that means freedom and liberty. That compares with less than 50 percent in 1945. This is a great achievement, full of meaning for all Asia.

Through these and other reforms the Japanese people have been developing a stable economy and a democratic society. They still have a long way to go, but they are well on the road to building a new Japan—dedicated to the arts of peace and the well-being of the people.

Because of these accomplishments, it is possible at this time to restore full sovereignty to the Japanese people.

This does not mean that the slate has been wiped clean. The United States has not forgotten Pearl Harbor and Bataan, and many of the other nations represented here have similar memories that will not be easily erased. The new Japan will not find the world entirely friendly and trusting. It will have to keep on working to win the friendship and trust of other peoples over the years to come.

But the foundations for a peaceful future have been laid. It is now time to move ahead with the restoration of normal relations between Japan and the rest of the world.

This conference is the result of a year of cooperative effort toward that end.

A year ago this month, at my request, Mr. John Foster Dulles began to consult with other governments about a treaty of peace with Japan. Mr. Dulles has performed this task faithfully and well, guided by the highest traditions of statesmanship.

There were, of course, differences of opinion among the nations concerned as to many of the matters covered by this treaty. The text of the treaty now before us is the product of long and patient negotiations, among the nations, which were undertaken to reconcile these differences.

I think it is fair to say that it is a good treaty. It takes account of the principal desires and ultimate interests of all the participants. It is fair to both victor and vanquished.

But more than that, it is a treaty that will work. It does not contain the seeds of another war. It is a treaty of reconciliation, which looks to the future, and not to the past.

The treaty reestablishes Japan as a sovereign, independent nation. It provides for the restoration of Japanese trade with other nations, and it imposes no restrictions upon Japan's access to raw materials.

The treaty recognizes the principle that Japan should make reparations to the countries which suffered from its aggression. But it does not saddle the Japanese people with a hopeless burden of reparations which would crush their economy in the years to come.

In all these respects the treaty takes account of the peaceful advances the Japanese people have made in recent years, and seeks to establish the conditions for further progress. However, there is one thing we must all recognize. There can be no progress unless the Japanese people and their neighbors in the Pacific are made secure against the threat of aggression.

At the present time the Pacific area is gravely affected by outright aggression and by the threat of further armed attack. One of our primary concerns in making peace with Japan, therefore, is to make Japan secure against aggression and to provide that Japan, in its turn, will so conduct itself as not to endanger the security of other nations. To accomplish this it is important to bring Japan under the principles of the United Nations, and within the protection of the

mutual obligation of the United Nations members.

The treaty expresses Japan's intention to apply for membership in the United Nations. The other countries who sign the treaty can be counted on to work for the admission of Japan to membership. But even so, there may be delays before Japan can be admitted.

Under the treaty, therefore, the Japanese people bind themselves to accept immediately the basic obligations of a United Nations member—namely, to refrain from aggression, to settle disputes peacefully, and to support the efforts of the United Nations to maintain peace. At the same time the other nations who sign the treaty specifically recognize that Japan is entitled to the protection of the United Nations Charter.

In a sense these provisions are the heart of the treaty. Under them Japan becomes a part of the community of nations pledged to outlaw aggression and to support a world order based on justice.

This tying together of the Japanese peace treaty and the United Nations Charter is a long step toward building security in the Pacific. But more than this is needed.

In the present world situation it has been necessary to buttress the peaceful principles of the United Nations Charter with regional arrangements for the common defense against aggression. If real security is to be attained in the Pacific, the free nations in that area must find means to work together for the common defense.

The United States recognizes that fact. Our people have suffered from past aggression in the Pacific and are determined that this country shall do its part for peace in that locality. In recent days we have joined with other Pacific nations in important mutual security agreements.

Last Thursday the Philippines and the United States signed a treaty of mutual defense. Under this treaty each country recognizes that an armed attack on the other in the Pacific area would be dangerous to its own peace and safety, and declares that it would act to meet the common danger.

Last Saturday a similar security treaty was signed by Australia, New Zealand, and the United States.

These treaties are initial steps toward the consolidation of peace in the Pacific.

It is vital that Japan be included, as soon as possible, in appropriate security arrangements for keeping the peace in the Pacific. This is necessary for her own protection, and the protection of other countries.

The peace treaty, therefore, recognizes that Japan, as a sovereign nation, must possess the right of self-defense and the right to join in defense arrangements with other countries under the United Nations Charter.

The development of regional arrangements for defense in the Pacific will mean that such Japanese defense forces as may be created would be associated with the defense forces of other nations in that area. Japan's security would not depend exclusively on Japanese forces but on interrelated security arrangements with other countries. The Japanese contribution, by itself, would not constitute an offensive threat. But Japanese forces, together with the forces of other nations, would provide mutual security against threats to the independence of the nations of the Pacific, including Japan.

At present, of course, Japan is totally unarmed. In view of the open aggression taking place near Japan, the Japanese Government has requested the United States to enter into a bilateral treaty for Japan's immediate security. Under such a treaty, the United States would maintain armed forces in Japan for the time being as a contribution to international peace and to Japan's defense against attack.

Security arrangements are essential in a world in danger. In the Pacific as in other parts of the world, social and economic progress is impossible unless there is a shield which protects men from the paralysis of fear.

But our great goal, our major purpose, is not just to build bigger and stronger shields. What we want to do is to advance, as rapidly as we can, the great constructive tasks of human progress.

We in the United States respect and support the many new free and independent nations in the Pacific area and in Asia.

We want to see them grow and prosper as equal partners in the community of independent nations of both East and West. We want to cooperate with them, to help them in their agricultural and industrial development. We wish to see these nations attain in dignity and freedom a better life for their peoples—for that is the road to world peace.

These countries have a rich historical and cultural heritage. Today their people are experiencing great economic and social changes. They are stirred by a new zeal for progress and independence. Already we have seen some of the progress that can be made—progress in stamping out malaria, in building schools and training teachers, in growing more food and creating new industries. Immense opportunities lie ahead if these countries can pursue their national destinies in a partnership of peace, free from the fear of aggression.

Under this peace treaty, we believe that Japan can and will join in this partnership of peace.

We look forward to the contribution which the new Japan, with its rich culture and its dedication to peace, can bring to the community of nations. We expect this contribution to grow over the years, for the signing of a peace treaty is but one part of the process of making peace. When aggression and war have severed relations between nations, many ties which bind one nation to the others are cut. Making peace is like repairing the many strands of an intercontinental cable; each strand must be spliced separately and patiently, until the full flow of communication has been restored.

There is no other way to bring about lasting peace than this slow and patient process, step by step, of mending and strengthening the cables of communication and of understanding between nations.

In this San Francisco Conference, we have the opportunity to take one vital step toward lasting peace. Our specific task here is to conclude the treaty of peace with Japan. This will be a great step toward general peace in the Pacific.

There are other steps which need to be taken. The most important of these is the restoration of peace and security in Korea. With Japan returned to its place in the family of nations, and with the people of Korea secure, free, and united, it should be possible to find ways to settle other problems in the Pacific which now threaten the peace.

The United States has made clear on many occasions its desire to explore with other governments at the proper time and in the proper forum how this might be accomplished.

There are many well established ways in which next steps can be explored, if there is a genuine desire for peace in all quarters.

But these are not matters which can be dealt with in this present conference. We have come here to take a single step—but a step of utmost importance.

The treaty now before us offers more than talk of peace; it offers action for peace. This conference will show, therefore, who seeks to make peace, and who seeks to prevent it; who wishes to put an end to war, and who wishes to continue it.

We believe this treaty will have the support of all those nations that honestly desire to reduce the tensions which now grip the world.

I pray that we shall all be united in taking this step to advance us toward greater harmony and understanding.

As we approach the peace table, let us be free of malice and hate, to the end that from here on there shall be neither victors nor vanquished among us, but only equals in the partnership of peace.

NOTE: The President spoke at 7:30 p.m. at the War Memorial Opera House in San Francisco. His opening words referred to Secretary of State Dean Acheson, Governor Earl Warren of California, and Mayor E. E. Robinson of San Francisco. The address was broadcast and televised.

The Multilateral Treaty of Peace with Japan was signed at San Francisco on September 8, 1951. It was favorably considered by the Senate on March 20, 1952, and after ratification entered into force on April 28, 1952. It was proclaimed by the President on April 28, 1952.

The text of the treaty is printed in United States Treaties and Other International Agreements (3 UST 3169).

217 Remarks in San Francisco to the Delegates to the Japanese Peace Conference. *September 4, 1951*

THANK YOU very much. It is a pleasure to be with you tonight. I want to welcome all of you to this conference.

I am very sure that when we have finished this conference we will have made a step forward for peace in the world.

I wish it were possible for me to meet every

one of you personally and shake your hand, but that isn't possible, much to my regret, but just the same I am going to welcome you here with a handshake.

NOTE: The President spoke at 9:30 p.m. at the Palace Hotel in San Francisco. See also Item 216.

218   Remarks in Kansas City at the Dedication of the Organized
      Reserve Corps Armory.   *September 6, 1951*

General Groves, Monsignor Tiernan, privates, sergeants, and colonels and generals:

It is a pleasure indeed for me to be here this afternoon for this occasion. I have had some interest in the military since 1905—that is before most of you can remember. But, you know, in a country such as ours, the civilian background for the military is absolutely essential.

I was a lieutenant in the National Guard of Missouri when the First World War started, after having been a private and a corporal and a sergeant. I never was a second lieutenant, much to my regret. When I was promoted from the rear rank to the front rank, and when I got my warrant as a corporal, I think that was the proudest day I ever spent in the military. I can't very well appreciate this high honor that has come to me as President of the United States and the Commander in Chief of the Armed Forces. I try to exercise it as I would ideally hope a civilian would.

You know, the original greatness of Rome depended upon her citizen soldiery. When Rome's support became mercenary, and when the emperors controlled the military as military organizations to keep the Republic from functioning, then Rome was on the road to ruin and its downfall.

In this day of ours we believe in the citizen as the support of the Government, and it is the duty of every citizen in times of emergency to support his Government in any place that the Government feels that is necessary.

In the military we believe that there should be a trained civilian force to back up the regular army, the regular navy, and the regular air force, and to fill in those organizations at the proper time for the salvation of the Republic. That is the way we have handled it ever since the Republic was born.

In 1792 General Washington asked for a military training program and it looks as if in 1951, we may get it. That is really moving along! But it is a step in the right direction, and I know that it will be a great contributor in the salvation of this Republic.

I want to see this Republic continue for all time, for this reason, that we are founded on a principle that no other country in the history of the world has been founded on. We are founded on the ideal that the Government is the servant of the individual, and that it is not the master of the individual.

That is what we are fighting for now. That is what the cold war is for. That is what I was talking about in San Francisco on Monday night.

I hope you will take that to heart; and I hope you young men, who are willing to spend some time studying the military in your off hours from your regular jobs, will continue to do just that.

After the First World War, in 1920, I called together 75 Army, Navy, Air Force, and Marine former officers in World War I, at an eating place on Baltimore Avenue known as Morton's. You couldn't even find the place where it was now, unless you knew at that time where it was. We organized the first Reserve Officers Association of the United States. And from that Reserve association grew associations all over the country, and the organization of regiments, and companies, and battalion reserves.

Now, the National Guard serves one purpose in the civilian army, and the Reserves another, but they are coordinated and they work together, as I hope all the military will from this time on.

That was the first unification program, in the year 1920. It was my privilege to implement the real unification program years and years after that, when I became President of the United States.

It is a pleasure for me to be here this afternoon, to take part in the dedication of this training center for citizen soldiers. I am happy to have been invited to do it.

Thank you very much.

NOTE: The President spoke at 5 p.m. at the Armory in Kansas City, Mo. In his opening words he referred to Brig. Gen. R. Dinwiddie Groves and Monsignor L. Curtis Tiernan, both of Kansas City, Mo. At one time General Groves served as executive officer to the President in the 379th Field Artillery Regiment when Mr. Truman was both commander of that Army Reserve unit and a United States Senator. Monsignor Tiernan was the chaplain of the 129th Field Artillery Regiment, 35th Division, during World War I, at the time the President was captain of Battery D.

The President's remarks were broadcast locally.

---

219 Address at the Joint Meeting of the International Bank for Reconstruction and Development and the International Monetary Fund. *September 10, 1951*

Mr. Chairman, members of the Boards of Governors, ladies and gentlemen:

I am very happy to welcome you to Washington again. A great deal has happened since your last meeting here in 1949. The free nations of the world have joined together in a great cooperative effort to protect themselves against aggression. I am sorry to say, much of our energy must now be given to the task of building up military defenses for the free world.

Nevertheless, the tasks of the International Bank and the International Monetary Fund are as important as they ever were.

World peace and security are not merely matters of military defense. It is just as necessary and just as important to have a firm economic foundation on which the structure of peace can rest.

The two institutions that are meeting here today were created in recognition of that fact. They were started even before the end of World War II, and in fact before the United Nations was organized in San Francisco.

But these financial institutions are part and parcel of the same great effort as the United Nations: the effort to attain peace in the world. They are responsible for an es-

sential part of the work that many countries must do to secure the peace, and to make the world a better place in which to live.

The major purpose of the International Monetary Fund is to help the growth of a vigorous system of world trade. In carrying out this purpose, the Fund tries to reduce restrictions on foreign exchange that stifle world trade.

This job obviously will be more difficult because of the special economic problems created by the defense programs of the free nations. But all of us now recognize the principle that each member country has a legitimate and vital interest in the exchange rates and policies of every other member country.

I am sure, therefore, that none of the countries which are members of the Fund will use the present difficulties to justify restrictions on trade and exchange which are not actually needed to further the program of mutual defense.

The International Bank has now been in existence for more than 5 years. Last year, in spite of international tension and uncertainty, it loaned almost twice as much money as it had the year before. Virtually all these loans were made to economically underdeveloped countries. They are loans which will help to make these countries stronger and more prosperous.

I am glad to see that nearly half the money loaned by the Bank for developmental purposes has been loaned for the expansion of electric power production. Cheap electric power is one of the greatest needs of many of the underdeveloped countries. It will do wonders in opening up new opportunities for their people.

The Bank has also made major loans for such basic improvements as new roads, railroads, the construction of port facilities, increasing agricultural production, and the expansion of telephone and telegraph lines. Such projects as these are the foundation stones of a long-range program of economic development.

I hope that the Bank will continue to go ahead with projects of this kind.

The defense program of the free nations will create some difficulties. There will be shortages of certain capital goods. But we must not slacken our efforts to create new sources of wealth, and thereby to bring about higher standards of living in the economically underdeveloped areas.

The cause of freedom to which we are dedicated will not permit us to fall behind in this effort.

The economic resources of the free nations, taken together, are sufficient to provide both military security and economic progress.

As we move forward with our defense effort, we should also do everything possible to increase the prosperity and raise the living standards of the free nations. We should remember that this is one of the greatest positive goals of the United Nations.

We have not joined together for purely defense purposes. We are not an association for preserving things as they are. Our great objectives are to secure peace and to create better lives for all of the peoples of the world.

Our faith is that free men, working together, can attain these objectives.

I sincerely hope that you will have a successful meeting, and make great advances in the year ahead.

NOTE: The President spoke at 12:05 p.m. at the Shoreham Hotel in Washington. His opening words "Mr. Chairman" referred to Douglas C. Abbott, Minister of Finance of Canada and chairman of the meeting.

The sixth annual meeting of the Boards of Governors of the International Bank for Reconstruction and Development and the International Monetary Fund was held in Washington, September 10–14.

For the President's remarks at the 1949 meeting, see 1949 volume, this series, Item 210.

---

220   Remarks to Members of the International Council of the Independent Order of Odd Fellows.   *September* 10, 1951

IT IS a pleasure on my part to have you here. I think you are making a contribution to the peace of the world. When an international organization of this sort can meet in the various countries where it is represented, it creates better understanding and better feeling between the peoples of those countries.

Your great organization is founded on the fraternal program, which means the brotherhood of man. I have never had the honor or the privilege of being a member of your organization, but I know what you stand for, I know what you can do for the communities where you have lodges, and I know that you are always helpful to those communities to make them better places in which to live.

I am glad you are having your meeting here, and I hope you will have a successful and pleasant one, and I am sure you will.

And I hope you will continue to grow and prosper. You know, there are a great many countries where it is not possible for organizations such as yours to grow and prosper. The United States is not one of those countries. We welcome you, and I am glad that you can be here with us.

Thank you very much.

NOTE: The President spoke at 3:05 p.m. in the Rose Garden at the White House.

221   Address at the Cornerstone Laying of the New General Accounting Office Building. *September 11, 1951*

Mr. Comptroller General, distinguished guests, ladies and gentlemen:

We are meeting here today to lay the cornerstone of a fine new building for the General Accounting Office. This building is of special significance, because it emphasizes the fact that our Government is constantly striving for better management of its financial affairs.

Many people in the Government have wrongly considered the General Accounting Office a sort of a bugaboo that keeps them from doing what they want to do. Many people outside the Government, when they think of the General Accounting Office at all, consider it a dry and boring subject. But the General Accounting Office is neither a bugaboo nor a bore. It is a vital part of our Government. Its work is of great benefit to all of us. The people who run the General Accounting Office certainly deserve these new and better quarters. I wish we could get some like it for the President of the United States.

Under Lindsay Warren, the General Accounting Office has handled the biggest auditing job in the history of mankind and has done it well. It has continuously improved its operations so it could serve the people of this country better and more efficiently.

The General Accounting Office is an agency responsible to the Congress. But this does not mean that it works at cross purposes with the executive agencies of the Government. On the contrary, the General Accounting Office cooperates with the executive agencies, for they are working for the same great purpose, to give good government to the American people at the lowest possible cost.

One of the outstanding achievements has been the joint accounting program which the Comptroller General worked out in 1947 with the Secretary of the Treasury and the Director of the Bureau of the Budget.

As a result of this joint program, accounting improvements have been made in agency after agency of the Federal Government. These improvements have given us new machinery for tighter and more efficient control of public funds.

The success of this accounting program can be attributed largely to teamwork—cooperation of the highest degree among those responsible for fiscal affairs. On this team the Comptroller General has played a leading role.

It is especially important in this day and time for the financial affairs of the Government to be prudently managed. Taxes are high, and the people who pay the taxes are entitled to see that they get a dollar's worth of value for every dollar they pay.

Nobody likes to pay taxes. That's just human nature. A man will go to a nightclub and throw away $30 or $40 and think nothing of it. But let him get a tax bill for $30 and hear him scream! But we have to pay taxes—and for very good reasons. Since this is true, we are all entitled to know what those reasons are and what is done with our money.

I wish everybody in the country could read the Budget Message of the Federal Government. I don't mean the whole big book. That's full of tables and as thick as a Sears Roebuck catalog. But in the front of the book is a message to Congress, about 60 or 70 pages long, that explains what the budget is all about—where the money goes and what the citizen gets for his tax dollar.

I am proud of the budgets that have been prepared since I've been President. And I want to say to you that I know every figure in every one of them. I want people to understand them. I would not want anyone to give up his time-honored right to complain about paying taxes. If people couldn't blow off steam that way sometimes, they might explode. Half of the fun of being a citizen in this country comes from complaining about the way we run our governments— Federal, State, and local.

But I don't think anyone ought to take his complaints about the Government spending too seriously until he has gone to the trouble of finding out what it is all about. Most people talk about the budget and they don't know a figure in it.

I suppose it is impossible for everybody to get a copy of the regular budget message and read that. But it is possible for you to get a copy of a little book called the "Budget in Brief." This little book gives the highlights of the budget story. Every citizen who pays taxes ought to read it. You can get a copy by sending 20 cents to the Government Printing Office in Washington and asking them to send you a copy of the "Federal Budget in Brief." There it is [*demonstrat-*

ing]. It has got about 34 to 38 pages in it, and it will tell you all about what the expenditures of the Government are for, and why it is necessary to have them.

Now, I don't get any commission for selling this little book! I will be amply repaid just by having people read them. I am proud of the way the financial affairs of the Government are handled and I want just as many people as possible to know the whole story—the facts as they actually are.

I can't tell you the whole story here today. We don't have time. But I would like to mention a part of it.

The most obvious fact about the Federal budget is that it is big. Everybody knows that, but there are many people who do not know why it has to be big and what the money is used for.

I am going to tell you something about that.

In the first place, most of the money is used to provide for the national security. In the current fiscal year, national security programs will require nearly $50 billion, or 70 percent of all Federal expenditures. That is a very large sum of money. The question is: "Is it worth it?" I think the answer will come back from most of us that it is worth it. I think most of us will say that our national independence and our freedom are important enough for us to spend whatever is required to preserve them. At least, that is my answer. And I am humbly thankful that this Nation is strong and powerful enough to bear this mighty program for security.

Now, what else is included in the budget?

It includes $6 billion to pay interest on the public debt. I suppose that is noncontroversial. Surely there is no one who objects to paying this interest. We can't repudiate the signed obligations of the Government of the United States, and we don't intend to.

There is nearly $5 billion in the budget

for services and benefits to veterans. I hope this is noncontroversial, too. I don't believe in economizing at the expense of the man who bares his breast to serve his country.

The budget includes more than a billion dollars for grants-in-aid to States for assistance to the aged and the blind and other needy persons. Well, some people don't approve of this. I will say frankly that I welcome their criticism. I never saw any money spent for a better purpose. And I know we can afford it.

Then the budget has close to $500 million for grants to the States to help them build highways. I'm in favor of that, too. Highways cost money. But let me tell you something else: They also help to make money. I have no doubt that the money we spend on highways more than repays itself in greater prosperity for the country. Indeed, the same thing is true of many of the expenditures of the Government.

The things I have mentioned add up to more than $60 billion out of the total estimated expenditures of $68 billion. And yet some people are saying you can cut $6 billion from the budget. If you did that, there wouldn't be anything left to maintain the ordinary operations of the Government, like the Coast Guard, the Federal Bureau of Investigation, the Public Health Service, and the General Accounting Office.

I could go on down through every item in the budget and show you that there is a vital reason for its being there.

I don't mean to claim that there is not a single dollar wasted. In an operation as big as the Federal Government there are bound to be some cases of waste and extravagance. One of the reasons we have the General Accounting Office is to help us find those cases and to put a stop to them.

But the main point I want to make is that, although the Federal expenditures are very large, they are all made for purposes that are necessary to our national welfare; and our budget is as tight and solid as we can make it. There is a great deal of misinformation circulated on this subject. Some of it is done in ignorance and some of it is done with just malice aforethought. But it won't stand up under an honest analysis.

Let me give you an example.

In a recent issue of a magazine which is circulated widely in this country and abroad, there appeared an article purporting to show that "waste" and "extravagance" were running wild in the Federal Government. Accompanying that article was a table of figures supposedly showing that nondefense expenditures of the Government had increased anywhere from 100 percent to 1,000 percent between 1940 and 1950. It was just a pack of lies. This table was a typical example of what I once heard described as "butterfly statistics"—statistics so meaningless that they seem to have been picked right out of the air with a butterfly net. And that is where these came from.

The fact is that the expenditures of the Government, other than those arising out of past wars or out of our efforts to prevent another world war, increased 68 percent in dollar terms from 1940 to 1950. Adjusting for changes in the price level they actually declined. During the same time the country was growing, of course, and the Government had a bigger job to do. The total national output of goods and services rose about 50 percent in real terms. In 1940 the cost of these civilian Government services not connected with our national security took about 6 percent of our national output; in 1950 this had been reduced to about 4 percent. And this year it is going to be an even smaller percentage than it was in 1950. If people want to be fair about this, it seems to me that is the way to look at it.

Now, I would like to say a word to comfort and console those who fear that we are spending our way into national bankruptcy. This alarming thought has some currency in certain circles, and it is used to frighten voters—particularly as visions of elections dance through the heads of gentlemen who are politically inclined.

I want to say to these gentlemen who are spreading this story "don't be afraid—don't be afraid." This is something that has been worrying you for a number of years now. It's something you've been saying over and over again. It wasn't true when you began to say it, it has not been true as you have repeated it over and over ever since, and it's further from the truth than it ever was.

The country is stronger economically than it has ever been before. Its people are more prosperous. After paying their taxes the people have an average per capita income that will buy 40 percent more than it did in 1939, in spite of increases in prices. Corporations are making more money than they ever did and, even after paying taxes at the new high rates, their profits are running at a higher rate than in any year except the recordbreaking 1950.

I know taxes are high and I know they are burdensome, but we ought to keep this thing in the proper perspective.

The world has some great problems before it today. The United States has great responsibilities in helping to meet those problems. We must face up to these problems and do whatever is required to meet them— and it is going to cost a lot of money.

If we want to keep the country on a sound financial basis and hold down inflation, we must pay this money as we go.

One of the benefits of using the pay-as-you-go approach is that it results in a tighter check on expenditures. It is so unpleasant to increase taxes that before doing it we try to hold down on expenditures wherever we can. And that is the way it ought to be. All I ask is that we do not cut our expenditures to the point where we lose more than we gain. We must not be penny wise and pound foolish. I don't want to lose a horse by being too stingy to buy a strong enough rope to hold him, or have him starve to death because I am too stingy to buy the oats and corn to feed him.

I believe in operating the Government's finances on a sound basis. I think the record shows that. Now listen to this very carefully. Over the last 5 years we have operated the Government with a surplus—a surplus of nearly $8 billion altogether. That may be a surprise to most people, but it's true. That's something for us to be proud of.

It is difficult to overstate how much the whole future of the world depends upon the financial condition of the United States Government. We must keep it solvent. We've got to keep it sound. We've got to be sure that the Government's financial affairs are well managed. And they are, thanks to the Secretary of the Treasury.

I am sure that the General Accounting Office will be in the forefront of this effort. The Comptroller General and his staff, working in cooperation with the executive agencies, have made many notable contributions to efficiency and economy in Government.

I am confident that this splendid teamwork will continue, and that in this building we dedicate today the General Accounting Office will render even greater service in the years to come than it has in those gone by.

NOTE: The President spoke at 10:15 a.m. His opening words referred to Lindsay C. Warren, Comptroller General of the United States.

222 Letter Accepting Resignation of General George C. Marshall
     as Secretary of Defense. *September* 12, 1951

[Released September 12, 1951.   Dated September 11, 1951]

Dear General Marshall:

It is with very great reluctance that I accept your resignation as Secretary of Defense effective, in accordance with your wishes, on September twelfth.

I have stated many times, both publicly and privately, my high regard for your many services to the country throughout your long and distinguished career as a government servant. At this time I wish particularly to mention the tremendous strides that have been made, under your direct leadership, in establishing a sound basis for our military manpower and production program which already has tremendously increased our defensive strength.

I understand fully and am sympathetic with the reasons for your resignation at this time, and I am most appreciative of your willingness to remain two months beyond our agreement in order to complete your activities concerning the Universal Military Training Act.

In again accepting your resignation from a position of high responsibility I realize how many times previously you have sought to retire to private life. But one time after another you have responded to the call to public service.

To all of these offices you have brought great talent and wisdom. In fact, no man ever has given his country more distinguished and patriotic service than have you.

On behalf of our country I want to thank you for all you have done. On my own behalf, I want to tell you of my deep personal appreciation for the wise counsel and the unwavering support you have given me in these trying days.

You have earned your retirement many fold and I wish you many good years at Leesburg.

With every good wish,

Gratefully and sincerely,

HARRY S. TRUMAN

[Honorable George C. Marshall, The Secretary of Defense, Washington, D.C.]

NOTE: General Marshall served as Secretary of Defense from September 21, 1950, until September 12, 1951. His letter of resignation, dated September 1, was released with the President's reply.

223 Remarks to the National Citizens' Committee for
     United Nations Day. *September* 12, 1951

THIS IS a wonderful celebration. Most people who come to see the President come to get something. It seems that this organization has come to bring the President something that he appreciates very much.

This organization is doing a wonderful work for the peace of the world. You know, if people could understand the fundamentals on which the United Nations is founded, and could appreciate the fact that in order to maintain the peace of the world we must have an organization where we can negotiate our differences and work them out, instead of shooting them out as has been the case since the world began to today.

We still, unfortunately, are having to shoot out some of our differences. I hope that time will come to an end. That is what I have been working for since I have been President of the United States, to attain peace in the world. Nothing else matters, if we can make this world a good place to live in.

There is room enough for everybody. If the proper developments were pushed for the undeveloped sections of the world, we could maintain five times its present population in luxury.

And what you are doing is to get our country to understand what we are trying to do. I hope you keep up the good work. The very fact that in the old isolationist State of Nebraska you have got so many organizations interested in the United Nations shows that you are doing something worthwhile.

I hope you can sell it all over the country in exactly the same manner, because when people understand what it means, you don't have to do any talking to them; they will step right in and help you put it over.

Keep on.

Thank you very much for the cookbook. I have long ago quit talking about mama's cooking, because I have a good cook at home. And she also has made a good cook out of the musician who is our daughter. She can cook, too. I can't say that she likes to cook as well as she does to sing, but then she is able to do it.

And on my advice, I hope every young lady in the United States will learn to make cakes like this.

Thank you very much.

NOTE: The President spoke at 12:10 p.m. in the Rose Garden at the White House. He was presented with the first copy of a United Nations cookbook sponsored by the Committee ("The World's Favorite Recipes," Harper & Brothers, New York, 1951) and with a pound cake made from a recipe which Mrs. Truman had contributed for the book.

On the same day, the President signed Proclamation 2944 "United Nations Day, 1951" (3 CFR, 1949–1953 Comp., p. 129).

224 The President's News Conference of *September* 13, 1951

THE PRESIDENT. Please be seated.

I haven't any special announcements to make, but I will try to answer questions as best I can.

[1.] Q. Mr. President, Governor Dewey, out of courtesy to you, refused to tell us what he said to you. However, he did make this statement: Now that we have succeeded in launching the great program for the defense of Europe, our own defenses require that we develop a similar program in southeast Asia.

THE PRESIDENT. I had a very pleasant conversation with the Governor, and he came to make a report to me on his trip. We discussed everything that had to do with his trip. A most interesting meeting, and a very satisfactory one.[1]

---

[1] Governor Thomas E. Dewey of New York conferred with the President at 12 noon on September 13, at which time they discussed the Governor's recent trip to the Far East.

Q. Was there any comment——

Q. Mr. President——

Q. ——pardon me, sir—I wonder if you could comment on what he said?

THE PRESIDENT. We of course have always endeavored to have a defense in the East, just as we have created a defense in the West.

What was your question?

[2.] Q. Mr. President, several years ago, when Congress voted extra funds for the Air Force, you ordered $615 million impounded for the Air Force program, and held it down to 48 groups. Are you going to impound any of the $5 billion in extra funds which Congress hopes will be used to build up a 95-wing Air Force, and expand naval aviation?

THE PRESIDENT. I haven't seen the bill yet. It hasn't reached my desk. I will let you know about it when it comes to me for operation.

[3.] Q. Mr. President, can you tell us what you talked about this morning with the President of the Philippines? [2]

THE PRESIDENT. Discussed the welfare of the Philippine Islands and the Philippine Republic. Had a very pleasant visit with the President. He brought me a beautiful ivory cane with a silver handle on it.

[4.] Q. Mr. President, what progress has been made in breaking off trade relations with Czechoslovakia?

THE PRESIDENT. I can't answer your question.

Q. Could you say whether any steps have been taken in that direction?

THE PRESIDENT. I can't answer the question.

[5.] Q. Mr. President, could you throw any light on whether you fired Llewellyn Williams as the Secretary of Alaska—or *did* you fire him?

THE PRESIDENT. Yes, I fired him. You saw the message I sent to him, I suppose?

Q. No I didn't.

THE PRESIDENT. He was relieved of duty because he was incompetent.

Q. Because he was incompetent?

THE PRESIDENT. Yes.

Q. Were there any political differences?

THE PRESIDENT. None whatever. I think he's a Democrat.

Q. There are two kinds of Democrats— *all* kinds of Democrats.

THE PRESIDENT. Well, yes, but that had nothing whatever to do with it. He was just incompetent. We relieved him.

[6.] Q. Mr. President, the Air Force announced today something new, an Air Force squadron to use a pilotless plane to handle a new type of weapon. I was just wondering if that would be the type of weapon you referred to in San Francisco? [3]

THE PRESIDENT. That is one of them.

[7.] Q. Mr. President, quite a few folks out your way are concerned that no action has been taken by any committee, or anything else, on this request for flood relief funds for Missouri, Oklahoma, and Kansas. Do you have any hopes that Congress will do anything?

THE PRESIDENT. I have been trying my best to get them to act. I don't know what they are going to do. We are putting all the pressure possible to get some action. I want action.

Q. Have you given any consideration to another message calling it to their attention?

THE PRESIDENT. No, but I have had a conversation with the chairmen of the sponsors of the bill, and we will continue those conversations. [4]

[8.] Q. Mr. President, do you want the Japanese treaty signed as soon as possible, or are you willing to let it go over until next session?

THE PRESIDENT. The Japanese treaty has been signed, and as soon as it is ready——

Q. I mean ratified.

THE PRESIDENT. ——to send up to the Congress, I shall send it to the Senate asking them for prompt action. It is up to the Senate to follow the procedure they set forth.

Q. You want prompt action?

THE PRESIDENT. Certainly do. That is the reason we signed the treaty. [5]

Q. There has been some thought that it might be better to let it go over until next session, that is why I sought your viewpoint on it.

THE PRESIDENT. When I send the treaty to the Senate, I shall ask for prompt action, and the Senate will take its own deliberate time, as it always does. Prompt action with the Senate is within a year, sometimes. [*Laughter*]

[9.] Q. Mr. President, would you give

---

[2] President Elpidio Quirino. See Items 207, 208.
[3] The new weapon was the B–61 Matador. See Item 215.

[4] See Items 196, 269.
[5] See Item 216.

us some lead as to whether we should anticipate the resignation of Secretary Acheson
in the coming weeks or months?

THE PRESIDENT. You needn't anticipate it
at all. That is the lead I will give you. As
long as I am President of the United States,
he is going to be Secretary of State. That
may be a good while.

Q. What was that?

Q. Is that the answer to the question we
have all been asking, sir?

THE PRESIDENT. No, that is not the answer. [*Laughter*]

[10.] Q. Mr. President, is there a possibility that you may make the Cabinet slightly bipartisan before 1952?

THE PRESIDENT. The Cabinet is as bipartisan as it is likely to be.

[11.] What did you start to say,
Smitty? [6]

Q. I just wondered if we could quote that,
"As long as I am President of the United
States he is going to be Secretary of State"?
May we quote that part?

THE PRESIDENT. You can quote it, as I have
said it time and again.

Q. How about the rest of it, Mr. President?

THE PRESIDENT. No. I think I wouldn't—
no, I won't—I don't make any announcements here today.

Q. When you say "long while," you mean
4 or 5 years? [*Laughter*]

THE PRESIDENT. You know, Tony [7] gets up
here with that innocent face of his and asks
me a shotgun question like that. You will
have to do your own speculating, Tony.
[*More laughter*]

Mr. Vaccaro. Thank you, sir.

THE PRESIDENT. I can't speculate.

Q. Mr. President, could you relate "long
while" as you did "prompt"?

THE PRESIDENT. Well, you can say this for
sure, that Dean Acheson is going to be Secretary of State until January 20, 1953, and
until his successor is appointed and confirmed. You can be sure of that.
[*Pause*]

What are you laughing at, Tony?

Q. I don't know what that last question
means, Mr. President.

THE PRESIDENT. I don't want to tangle you
up.

Q. Is there any significance to the fact
when I said could we quote that—that it will
be a long time—you said you did not want
to make any announcement today? Is there
any significance in that?

THE PRESIDENT. None whatever.

Q. You said we can quote "as long as I am
President of the United States he is going to
be Secretary of State," but not the part about
that lasting a long while, is that correct?

THE PRESIDENT. That is right—that's right.
[*Pause*]

Well, what's the matter with you?

Q. I'll ask one.

Q. We're catching up.

Q. Was there anything cryptic about this
"successor appointed and confirmed"?

THE PRESIDENT. No, that's just the rule.

Q. Is that a rule for Secretaries of State?

THE PRESIDENT. Yes. Of course you never
leave the Office of Secretary of State vacant
for any length of time unless they have to.

[12.] I want to call your attention to a
fact that may interest some of you. You
may want to engage my services. I understand that "The Budget in Brief" is the best
seller of the Government Printing Office
now.

Q. In that—pardon me, sir—in that connection, Mr. President, after you made your
General Accounting Office speech, [8] there was
pretty violent reaction down on the Hill, and

---

[6] Merriman Smith of the United Press Associations.
[7] Ernest B. Vaccaro of the Associated Press.

[8] See Item 221.

some Republicans, and at least one Democrat, characterized your speech as "nonsense." Do you have any comment?

THE PRESIDENT. You know, a stuck hog always squeals. [*Laughter*] But I hope you will read "The Budget in Brief." You will have your answer.

Q. What was that?

Q. I didn't hear that beginning.

THE PRESIDENT. You have to be raised on a farm to understand that!

Reporter: Thank you, Mr. President.

THE PRESIDENT. That's all right.

NOTE: President Truman's two hundred and seventy-eighth news conference was held in the Indian Treaty Room (Room 474) in the Executive Office Building at 4 p.m. on Thursday, September 13, 1951.

225   Address at the Constitution Day Ceremonies at the Library of Congress.   *September 17, 1951*

Mr. Chief Justice of the United States, Senator Green, Doctor Evans, distinguished guests, ladies and gentlemen:

We have met here this morning to put some pieces of parchment away in specially sealed cases, in order to preserve them from physical and chemical change. And I can't help but be impressed with this magnificent collection of all the ancient, medieval, and modern documents that are in this library.

I think always of the terrible destruction of the Alexandrian Library in the Middle Ages. And this library, the British Museum, and the Louvre, are our modern replicas of that great Alexandrian Library.

The documents which we are putting away today are written in a style of handwriting which are no longer familiar to us. If they were only historical relics, it might seem strange that we should make a ceremony out of this occasion of sealing them up.

But the Declaration of Independence and the Constitution of the United States are more than historical relics. They are a living force in our life today.

We may have some difficulty in preserving the parchment on which these two documents have been written, but the ideas they set forth will never perish. These documents express the highest principles of political

life: That all men have certain unalienable rights, that governments are set up to provide for the welfare of the people, and that the rule of law stands above government and citizen alike.

These ideas have a life of their own. They have been a dynamic force in the history of our Nation. They have inspired men, all around the world, to create new and independent governments, and to improve the conditions under which they live.

These are very explosive documents, Dr. Evans. We may think we have them safely bottled up, but the ideas they express will go on forever. They will continue to give energy and hope to new generations of men, here and in other countries, in the long struggle to create a better society on earth.

The Declaration of Independence and the Constitution of the United States, when they were written, were revolutionary documents. But they were revolutionary in a very unusual sense.

Many—I might say most—revolutions are simply a resort to force and violence to impose a new despotism upon the people. But these documents were for a very different purpose; their aim was to make despotism impossible. Both the Declaration of Independence and the Constitution seek to make the rule of law and the concepts of justice the dominating factors in government. To a large extent they have succeeded.

The struggle against the use of naked force as an instrument of government was an old one even before these two documents were written. Our forefathers created a new nation, but they based it upon the long experience of the English people in maintaining human freedom.

The right to trial by jury, the right to be free from unreasonable search and seizure, the right of habeas corpus, the prohibition against cruel and unusual punishment, the guarantees of freedom of the press, freedom of assembly, and freedom of religion—all these were basic concepts in the days of our Revolution. They were concepts for which men had worked and even given up their lives for centuries.

But they never had been made the foundation stones of a government until they were put in the Declaration of Independence and in the Constitution of the United States and its first 10 amendments—the Bill of Rights—which are just as fundamental a part of our basic law as the original version of the Constitution that we are sealing up here today.

I hope that these first 10 amendments will be put on parchment and sealed up and placed alongside the original document. In my opinion they are the most important parts of the Constitution.

These rights have become so well established in this country that we take them for granted. They are so much a part of our lives that they may seem dry and uninteresting. But the history of other countries in recent years has shown us how vital and important they are. Recent history has demonstrated that the unrestrained use of force by government is just as great a danger to human progress now as it was in ages gone by. It has demonstrated that un-

less citizens have rights against the government, no one can be safe or secure.

In our own lifetime we have learned anew the human misery that an absolute, power-mad government can create. We have seen it in the brief history of the Fascist and Nazi tyrannies. We are witnessing it today in the tyranny of Soviet communism.

A constitution is not just a matter of words. There are other constitutions which may read as well as ours. Just take, for example, the constitution of the Soviet Union. That constitution has a lot of fine language in it—a lot of beautiful and meaningful words. That constitution of the Soviet Union says that Soviet citizens are guaranteed freedom of speech, freedom of the press, and freedom of assembly. I wonder what would happen to a citizen of the Soviet Union if he tried to exercise any of those freedoms? It professes to guarantee that citizens of the Soviet Union shall be secure in their persons and in their homes. And in addition, it purports to guarantee equality, the right to work, the right to an education, the right to rest and leisure, freedom of religion, and a lot of other fine things.

But these good words in the Soviet constitution mean less than nothing. They are empty promises, because the citizens of the Soviet Union have no way of enforcing their rights against the state.

In the Soviet Union the power of the state is above all rights. The government does not have to obey the law. As a result the citizens of the Soviet Union enjoy none of the freedoms which are guaranteed in their constitution. They do not have freedom of speech or freedom of the press. They may be arrested without cause; their homes may be invaded without a search warrant; they may be executed or exiled without a fair trial and without appeal.

Their constitutional guarantees are just as

false as their treaty agreements. A Bolshevik agreement is not worth the paper it's written on. It is only a scrap of paper.

The Soviet citizen lives in fear. His society is a jungle through which the naked power of the government prowls like a beast of prey, making all men afraid.

The Communists claim that they have to use the weapons of tyranny in order to improve the conditions of the people. That just isn't true. That is a rejection of the long experience of mankind. By resorting to the worst evils of ancient tyranny, the Soviet rulers have held their citizens in terror and bondage, while freedom is growing in the rest of the world.

The evils which the Communists brought back into the world—the evils of political persecution and unrestrained state power—have grown and flourished and become much more terrible than they ever were before. Modern inventions, modern means of communication, modern methods of propaganda make the power of the state more formidable than it was in the days of the stage coach and the muzzle-loading rifle. The power of the Kremlin is more effective, more violent, more far reaching than the power of the bloodiest of the czars, or the power of Genghis Khan, Tamerlane, Louis XIV, Charles V of Spain, or the power of any other of the tyrants of the past.

Today, the tyrant can uproot and liquidate whole classes of people and entire nations. The death camps of Hitler Germany or of modern Siberia demonstrate that the unrestrained power of the government can be a greater evil in our modern civilization than it ever was in ancient times.

The only guarantee against such a society of fear and cruelty is the principle that the government is not above the law. Our Declaration of Independence and our Constitution proclaim that the Government is subject to the fundamental law.

The Constitution sets up a system of internal checks and balances which may seem cumbersome to us at times, but which succeeds in preventing any part of the Government from having absolute power. Under our Constitution it is not only the citizens who are made to conform to the principles of justice, but the Government itself has to conform. And the citizen has the power to enforce his rights against the Government. The rule of law is made supreme.

Our Constitution protects us from the evils of tyranny. But this is not all our Constitution does. If it were, it would not be enough.

A constitution must do more than provide restraints against the illegal use of power. It must give the people a means of dealing with their day-to-day problems of continually correcting the injustices that spring up in human society. A constitution that is not adaptable—that prevents the government from acting for the general welfare of the people—will not survive. It will become a mere historical curiosity, as has the Soviet constitution.

Ours is not such a constitution. We have discovered, over the years, that it offers the means for correcting present evils without throwing away past gains.

There are always those who oppose necessary reforms. Such people often turn to the Constitution to justify their position. But our Constitution has seldom proved to be a barrier to changes which were needed for the welfare of all the people. Our Constitution has not set up an aristocracy of wealth or privilege. It does not serve the privileged few at the expense of the great majority of the people.

The great advances we have made in recent years in legislation to improve the condition of labor, to bring economic security to the farmer, to provide aid for the needy, to develop the resources of the country for the benefit of all, to improve the health, the education, and the housing of the average family—all these advances have been opposed in the name of the Constitution of the United States. But it never was the purpose of the Constitution to bar such advances. On the contrary, the Constitution provides the means for carrying into effect the fundamental ideas of justice and liberty and human progress on which our Government is founded.

Acting under our Constitution we have been able to solve the problems which have driven other countries into revolution. We have been able to make necessary reforms without overthrowing the ancient guarantees of our liberty. Building on the experience of the past we have opened the way to a brighter future.

On this occasion we ought to pray to Almighty God that the American people will remain faithful to the spirit of the Declaration of Independence and the Constitution. We should ask that they be ever mindful of the great wisdom and truth that are embodied in these two documents, and through them, in our form of government.

The wisdom of our form of government is that no men, no matter how good they may appear to be, may be entrusted with absolute power. The great achievement of our form of government is that it has enabled us to meet the changing needs of the people while providing a rule of law that restrains all men, even the most powerful. The glory of our form of government lies in the fact that it has held us faithful to the concept that the aims of government are human betterment and human freedom.

If the American people remember these things and understand them well, this Nation will move forward in the future as it has in the past. And these documents, which we are today sealing against physical decay, will always be remembered and cherished, finding new life in each new generation of Americans.

NOTE: The President spoke at 10:32 a.m. at the Library of Congress. His opening words referred to Fred M. Vinson, Chief Justice of the United States, Senator Theodore Francis Green of Rhode Island, and Luther H. Evans, Librarian of Congress.

The address was broadcast.

226   Address Before the National Association of Postmasters.
September 17, 1951

Mr. Postmaster of the great city of St. Louis, Mr. Postmaster General, and postmasters and ladies and gentlemen:

I am glad to welcome you to Washington this morning.

I don't believe there is a finer group of public servants anywhere than the members of the postal service.

There are some people who would call this just a meeting of bureaucrats. Well, if you are bureaucrats, so am I, and I am proud of it.

It seems to be open season, these days, on Government employees. There are a lot of people who are trying to make political capital by slurring the loyalty and efficiency of Government employees, and trying to bring the public service into disrepute.

I think that is a contemptible way to try to get votes.

We have the greatest Government in the world, and the most loyal and efficient Government servants. And I am proud to be a part of that organization. And I am sure you are proud to be a part of it, too.

It is time we made it perfectly plain that we feel it is an honor to work for our fellow citizens through public service.

The postal service is one of the key activities of the Federal Government. It employs over half a million people, one-fourth of all the civilian employees of the whole Government. It is one of the biggest businesses in the country. And without it, the rest of the country would not be able to do business at all. Without the postal service all our activities would come to a standstill—business, national defense, family life, everything.

Last year the postal service carried over 27 billion letters and 1 billion parcels. It carried over 6 billion copies of newspapers and magazines and nearly 40 million packages of books.

The postal service is not only big business, it is public business. We all ought to be concerned about the way the postal service is run. We ought to be sure that it is run on a businesslike basis—that it pays for itself.

Today it does not pay for itself. Postal rates are not set by the Post Office Department, the postal rates are set by the Congress. And these rates are not high enough to cover the cost of carrying the mail.

Right now the postal service is being run at a deficit of more than $500 million a year. The biggest part of this deficit is caused by the low rates on second- and third-class mail—that is, on newspapers, magazines, and circulars and advertising matter. Now, first-class letter mail pays its own way. There are lobbyists who are trying to raise the rate on it. But the publishers and advertisers who use second- and third-class mail to reach the public are not paying fully for the services they get.

To put it bluntly, the taxpayers of the country are subsidizing these business interests to the tune of several hundred million dollars a year. That is not right, and I have asked the Congress to raise these rates. The Congress has been considering this matter very diligently, and I hope that they will soon pass legislation to raise these second- and third-class rates substantially.

However, there is a lot of opposition to raising these rates, and I am sorry to say that most of it comes from the "slick" magazine publishers—I mean that word in two ways— who are getting the benefit of millions of dollars of the taxpayers' money each year. About $200 million a year of the taxpayers' money is going to carry second-class mail— that is, newspapers and magazines. I am glad to say that a large number of newspaper publishers know this is not right, and are entirely willing to pay their own way. It's the "slick" magazine people who don't want to pay their way. We are subsidizing them for all that bunch of advertising that we have to read in order to find something to look at in those "slick" magazines.

There is some justification for using public money to subsidize the mailing of certain publications—such as small weekly papers in rural areas. But I see no excuse whatever for subsidizing the huge publishing concerns which make millions of dollars in profits every year. Some of these concerns have come down here and lobbied Members of Congress from breakfast to bedtime, trying to prevent them from raising second-class postal rates. Some of the biggest magazine publishers in the country are fighting tooth and toenail to keep their juicy subsidies, and then write editorials about somebody else getting a subsidy.

They are strongly against subsidies—for everybody but themselves. Here they are, costing the taxpayers millions of dollars every year, and they have the nerve to complain about the high cost of government. The next time any of you see an article or editorial in one of those "slick" magazines attacking Government subsidies, I just wish you would write them a very polite—*very polite*—little letter asking them when they will be ready to pay the full cost of sending their own publications through the mail.

In addition to fair rates for postal service, I believe in fair salaries for postal workers and other Government employees. A while back I sent a recommendation to the Congress on this subject, too, asking them to raise the salaries of Government employees, including the postal workers.

In addition, I asked the Congress to remove the inequities they have allowed to creep into the postal pay scales. This is something that affects postmasters as well as employees. I hope the Congress will straighten out this situation the way it ought to be done. And there are some postmasters who are not getting as much money as the people who are working for them. And that is not fair.

Fair rates and fair salaries are the responsibility of Congress. But there is something equally as important which is the responsibility of you who work in the postal service. This is the responsibility of constantly using new ideas and new techniques to increase the efficiency of postal operations. And I want to tell you that in this field I am proud of you.

Since 1945 the output of postal employees per man-hour worked has increased by more than 10 percent. And that is a record that you all ought to be proud of.

A lot of new equipment has been put into service, and more new equipment is being tested. The postal service has new mail sorting machines, for example. It is using helicopters for short air hauls. Postal engineers have developed a new kind of light motor vehicle for mailmen who work in suburban districts where houses are far apart. And if ever I get retired from the Presidency, I am going to get me one of those machines to ride around in.

All these and many more mechanical improvements are being tried out in the effort to find more efficient ways to handle and transport the mails.

Another way in which we are improving the postal service is through administrative reorganization. Ever since I have been President I have been working for greater efficiency through the reorganization of Government departments. The Commission on Government Organization, headed by former President Hoover, studied this field thoroughly—and Mr. Acheson was the vice chairman of that organization—and made some very valuable recommendations for improving the efficiency of the Government.

The other day—just the other day, now—a Member of Congress said that we had not carried out any of the recommendations of the Hoover Commission regarding the Post Office. That man was just as wrong as he could be, and he knew it. He should talk to some of the other Members of Congress, who have been putting some of these reorganization measures through, and who know what the situation really is.

The fact is that we either have put into effect or have submitted to the Congress virtually every recommendation the Hoover Commission made concerning the Post Office—and some of them have been in effect for more than 2 years.

One of the first recommendations of that Hoover-Acheson Commission was that the Postmaster General should continue to be a member of the Cabinet, but that he should not be an official of a political party. Well now, I had accomplished that long before the Commission made any recommendation. I put the first career man in as the Postmaster General, and he has been there ever since. He came up from the ranks in the postal service. He is a fine public servant—Jesse Donaldson.

The Hoover-Acheson Commission recommended that the top level of the Post Office Department be reorganized. We've done that too. I sent up to the Congress a reorganization plan to give the Postmaster General more authority over the Department, along with a Deputy Postmaster General and four Assistant Postmasters General to help him, and a National Advisory Board to consider methods and policies for improving the postal service. Well, the Congress approved that plan and it has been in effect for 2 years, and it is working fine. I am calling the attention of this Congressman to that statement—who made the statement that we had never made any reports.

The Hoover-Acheson Commission also recommended that the fiscal affairs of the Post Office be reorganized. And that has been done, largely as a result of the Financial Control Act of 1950, which gave the Post Office Department, for the first time, the authority to establish and maintain its own accounting setup.

We have been making a lot of reorganizations like this in other departments of the Government too.

There has been a great deal of misinformation—I am kindly when I use the word "misinformation"—put out around the country lately to the effect that nothing much has been done about the Hoover-Acheson Commission's recommendations for any part of the Federal Government. Well, that is just poppycock, to put it mildly. I've been surprised to see that a lot of people have been taken in by it—including some newspapers that should have known better.

Anyone who looks at the record will see that our achievements in Government reorganization and management improvement have been outstanding. Out of the 36 reorganization plans I have submitted to the Congress, 27 have been approved. The other 9 were voted down—and some of the Members of Congress who talk the loudest about efficiency and economy voted against those 9 reorganization plans.

As a result of these reorganization plans, and other actions, I can report that we already have in effect a majority—a majority of the recommendations of the Hoover-Acheson Commission for the whole Government. The Department of Defense has been brought under more unified direction. The Department of State has been substantially strengthened. Reorganization plans have gone into effect for the Department of Commerce, the Department of the Interior, the Department of Justice, and many other departments, and agencies and regulatory commissions. The supply and property management activities of the Government have been consolidated into the General Services Administration.

Those and many other changes have stepped up the efficiency of the Federal Government. They have saved the taxpayers money. And they are standing us in good stead as we face the large, new problems brought on by the defense emergency.

Now, don't let anybody tell you that the President of the United States is not for economy and efficiency. Whenever there is any economy and efficiency in the Government, the President of the United States has been responsible for it, and don't let anybody tell you different.

But that job is not finished, of course. In fact, the job of making the Federal Government more efficient will never be finished. There are other recommendations of the Hoover-Acheson Commission to consider. I also have an advisory commission of experts on administrative management who are constantly finding new ways to improve the operations of the whole Government. One of the members of that commission is the Deputy Postmaster General, Vincent Burke.

There will always be new ideas to be tried out, better ways of doing things to be found. There will always be new challenges to be met as the Government is called on to serve the people of our country under new conditions.

Now, they are always talking about going back to something. You can't turn the clock back. You have got to go forward. And these people who talk about going back are thinking about a government for 70 or 80 million. We have got 156 millions of people now, and you have to have a government in proportion to the size of its population, and it has to expand, if we are going to run.

All of us who work for Uncle Sam should continue to strive for good government at the lowest possible cost. That is the spirit, I am sure, in which you postmasters are doing your work.

Let us continue, in everything we do, to encourage every postal employee, and every other Federal worker, to give his energy, his imagination, and his talents to continually improving the service he renders to the people of this great country of ours. And then we will be marching toward efficiency in government, toward economy in government, and toward the general welfare of all the people.

Thank you very much.

NOTE: The President spoke at 11:10 a.m. in Constitution Hall. In his opening words he referred to Bernard F. Dickmann, postmaster of St. Louis, Mo., and president of the National Association of Postmasters of the United States, and to Postmaster General Jesse M. Donaldson.

227 The President's News Conference of September 20, 1951

THE PRESIDENT. Please be seated.

[1.] I have a letter to the Vice President on the tax bill for release. It is ready and will be handed out to you after the conference. It will explain a great many questions that you may ask me here much better than I can do it off-the-cuff.[1]

Any questions? I am ready.

[2.] Q. Mr. President, on Monday, at the Library of Congress, you said that a Russian agreement wasn't worth the paper it was written on.[2] If that is the case, will this country continue to seek agreements with Russia?

THE PRESIDENT. Yes. When you are in the position to enforce those agreements, they will be kept. That is the reason for the defense program.

I wish I had the time to tell you all the things that have happened since the Germans folded up.

Q. Mr. President, along that line, in view

of the Russian diplomatic defeat at San Francisco, and the measures which were taken at Ottawa, and Senator McMahon's speech the other day, and your own statements, do you think that Russia has lost the initiative in the cold war?[3]

THE PRESIDENT. That's a question I can't answer. We will have to wait for results to find out whether that is true or not.

Q. I was wondering if you think, in view of all those things, that the prospects are a little bit more hopeful for peace?

THE PRESIDENT. There is a possibility, a stronger possibility than ever, I think, if we

---

[1] See Item 228.
[2] See Item 225.

[3] The reporter was referring to the conference for the conclusion of the Treaty of Peace with Japan, held at San Francisco September 4–8, 1951; the seventh session of the Council of the North Atlantic Treaty Organization, held at Ottawa, Canada, September 15–20, 1951, at which Greece and Turkey were admitted to membership; and a speech by Senator Brien McMahon of Connecticut, Chairman of the Joint Committee on Atomic Energy, on the floor of the Senate on September 18, in which he called for increased allocations of funds for atomic development and production.

stick to our knitting and go ahead with the defense program.

Q. Possibility of what, sir? I didn't catch——

THE PRESIDENT. Peace.

Q. If we stick to our what?

THE PRESIDENT. Our knitting.

Q. What was that last——

THE PRESIDENT. That's an old Missouri phrase. And go ahead with the defense program.

What did you want to ask me? You got up just as he did.

[3.] Q. I was just working—I tell you—I do have a question. Would you mind saying if you are considering Mayor Fletcher Bowron of Los Angeles for a Federal judgeship?

THE PRESIDENT. His name hasn't come up to me.

[4.] Q. Mr. President, would it be correct to infer from what you have just said about Russia, that in the future we will place our reliance on force rather than diplomacy in dealing with Russia?

THE PRESIDENT. Under the circumstances it is necessary. And I dislike it very much. That is what we organized the United Nations for—was to argue these things out without the use of force—but it has become impossible. Korea is the example.

Q. Could we have that answer repeated, Mr. President?

[*The President's answer was read by the White House Official Reporter*]

THE PRESIDENT. I can name you several examples if you want them: Greece, Turkey, Korea, and Berlin. Trieste in the beginning.

Q. Mr. President, when you speak of the use of force, you are referring in a general way to all the areas of disagreement?

THE PRESIDENT. To our ability to meet force with force. That is all we are aiming at. We don't want to misuse that force. Our

idea is a free and happy world. That is what we are going to continue to fight for.

Q. The other fellow has to use the force first?

THE PRESIDENT. I didn't say that. That is what brought on the Korean thing.

[5.] Q. Mr. President, do you consider the proposals made by Senator McMahon either practical or desirable?

THE PRESIDENT. I can't comment on that.

[6.] Q. Mr. President, where do all the truce negotiations in Korea fit into this picture?

THE PRESIDENT. They were requested by the opposition, and we are willing to put forth every effort possible to get a peaceful solution without killing any more people. That's the why and wherefore for it.

[7.] Q. Mr. President, Senator Lehman of New York made a statement to the Senate last Friday, pointing out that there are apparent conflicts in the testimony of Louis Budenz [4] before the McCarran committee, and his testimony last year to the Tydings committee. And Senator Lehman suggests there should be a further investigation of this apparent conflict, and I was wondering if you agree with the Senator that there should be a further investigation?

THE PRESIDENT. I am always in favor of getting the truth in these investigations, and I hope that they will go ahead and try to get the truth.

[8.] Q. Mr. President, Ed Flynn [5] said yesterday you can beat anybody next year. Do you agree with him?

THE PRESIDENT. Well now, I am happy to have Mr. Flynn's opinion, because I think

---

[4] Newspaperman and former member of the Communist Party who testified before several congressional committees on the Communist attempt to infiltrate the United States Government.

[5] Edward J. Flynn, chairman of the Democratic County Committee of Bronx County, New York City.

he is a very able political prognosticator—
[*laughter*]—but I have no comment to make
on your question. [*More laughter*]

Q. The last part was drowned out.

THE PRESIDENT. I have no comment to
make on the question.

[9.] Q. Mr. President, I read in the afternoon newspaper yesterday in Washington,
that Ambassador O'Dwyer is doing a great
job in Mexico, and he wished more than
anything else to have a picture of you. I
wonder if he can get it?

THE PRESIDENT. He has one. [*Laughter*]
Gave it to him on his first appointment, as I
do all the ambassadors.

[10.] Q. Mr. President, sir, has the testimony on the American Lithofold hearings
on the Hill changed your opinion as to the
propriety of Mr. Boyle [6] remaining chairman?

THE PRESIDENT. Now, I don't feel like commenting on the operations of the committee
until they get through. Then I will give you
all the comments you want.

[11.] Q. Mr. President, do you have any
comment on the Senate committee's action
on the Illinois judgeships?

THE PRESIDENT. No. I have no comment.
I appointed those judges, and I am the
appointive power.

Q. You are what?

THE PRESIDENT. I appointed the judges, and
I have the appointive power. The Senate
has a right to confirm or reject the appointments. They have not rejected them. They
have just refused to report them out.[7]

[12.] Q. Mr. President, in 1947 the
United States sponsored a United Nations
resolution for the extradition of war
criminals. Recently there was discovered in
California a Nazi war criminal named

Artukovic, and Jewish organizations maintained that he was responsible for the death
of many thousands of people in the death
camps in Yugoslavia, and the Yugoslavs
have asked for his extradition. Could you
tell us what you might think about this
thing? Also, sir, whether you believe we
should act in accordance with the United
Nations resolution? [8]

THE PRESIDENT. I don't know anything
about the proposition, therefore I can't
comment on it.

[13.] Q. Mr. President, reverting to the
Illinois judges, isn't refusal by a judiciary
committee to report either favorably or unfavorably—in other words, no report at all—
isn't that about equal to no action at all in
the Senate?

THE PRESIDENT. That is not a rejection.

Q. Well, are you expecting further action
by the committee?

THE PRESIDENT. Well, no. I don't expect
further action by that committee.

Q. I beg your pardon, sir?

THE PRESIDENT. I don't expect further action by the committee.

Q. Well, do you intend to send other
nominations?

THE PRESIDENT. No, I do not. I am satisfied with the ones I sent.

[14.] Q. Mr. President, do you intend
to run for the Presidency again next year?
[*Laughter*]

THE PRESIDENT. No comment. You will
be informed in plenty of time what my program will be for next year. But I am not
ready to tell you now. I told you once before: I know what I am going to do, but I

---

[6] William M. Boyle, Jr., chairman of the Democratic National Committee.

[7] See Item 165 [8].

[8] Dr. Andrija Artukovic, government official in
Croatia during World War II, was arrested in California and held until September 19, 1951, when he
was released on $50,000 bail. On July 14, 1952, he
was freed by a Federal court which denied the
Yugoslav request for extradition, stating that there
was no treaty covering the case.

am not going to tell you. [*Laughter*]

Q. Mr. President, what is "plenty of time"?

THE PRESIDENT. Oh, some time before the convention meets.

Q. Before the Democratic?

THE PRESIDENT. Yes. That's the one I am interested in. [*Laughter*]

Q. Mr. President, why are you interested?

THE PRESIDENT. Every good Democrat ought to be interested in the platform of his committee.

[15.] Q. Mr. President, do you think it is significant that Senator Sparkman said today that the only one who was asked to testify at the hearings on Ambassador Jessup's position as a delegate to the United Nations was Senator McCarthy?

THE PRESIDENT. I didn't understand it. What are you trying to get at?

Q. Senator Sparkman, who heads the Senate committee on the hearings on Ambassador Jessup's position as a delegate to the United Nations, said today that the only one who was asked to testify was Senator McCarthy.

THE PRESIDENT. Well, that is for the committee to decide.

[16.] Q. Mr. President, I don't know whether this is outside your idea or not, but do you think it is all right for the national chairman to contact Government agencies in behalf of——

THE PRESIDENT. What's a chairman of the national committee for?

Q. To run a campaign.

THE PRESIDENT. What does the chairman of the National Democratic Committee do but be kind to people who come to town, or want introductions? That's a part of the job of the Democratic national chairman. It has been carried out by every one that has ever been there. It is not right for him, though, to take fees for operations of

that kind. There is a distinction and a difference.

Q. Would that apply to all employees and officials of the national committee?

THE PRESIDENT. Yes, it would.

Q. Even volunteer workers?

THE PRESIDENT. Even these volunteer workers.

Q. They shouldn't take fees?

THE PRESIDENT. No sir.

[17.] Q. Mr. President, I am still puzzled about this judge situation.

THE PRESIDENT. I don't see how you can be puzzled.

Q. Well, it seems that there is an impasse created here that——

THE PRESIDENT. I have done my part. I didn't create the impasse.

Q. Well, the Senate has.

THE PRESIDENT. Well, all right. Let the Senate take the responsibility, or at least the Senate committee, that is. The Senate has not acted—as I told you.

Q. Well, do you expect the Senate to act?

THE PRESIDENT. Not unless the committee makes a report. You see, it takes two-thirds to discharge a committee in the Senate.

Q. That's true.

[18.] Q. Mr. President, I don't want to do any wrong to a fellow Missourian, so I would like to ask on Mr. Brandt's [9] question on those volunteer workers, Mr. Young [10] testified that at no time had he ever attempted to help anyone except to inquire the status of things, other than the two companies—Lustron and Jacobs—that he represented on a salary basis. Now, do you approve of a volunteer worker taking a regular employment from companies doing business in Washington?

---

[9] Raymond P. Brandt of the St. Louis Post-Dispatch.

[10] E. Merl Young, former examiner for the Reconstruction Finance Corporation.

THE PRESIDENT. I don't think any person who is connected with the Democratic National Committee, be he a volunteer or otherwise, has any business taking fees from anybody for what he does for them as a member of the national committee.

Q. Mr. President, is it your impression that Mr. Boyle *did* take a fee?

THE PRESIDENT. No. My impression is that he did *not*. And I have got his word for it. And I believe it.

[19.] Q. Mr. President, the politicoes have been saying lately that irrespective of all these investigations that might impair the Democratic chances in 1952, that they never throw a party out of power when the country is prosperous. Do you agree with that?

THE PRESIDENT. Yes, I agree with that.

Q. Very hopeful?

THE PRESIDENT. Here is what the difficulty is. I can give you a little lecture on politics.

There are no issues on which these people can attack the administration. The country is prosperous. We are carrying out a foreign policy which we think will be successful. We are doing everything we possibly can to keep the country on an even keel.

Now, when the opposition has no issues on which to fight, their next step is misrepresentation and smear. And that is what is going on.

Q. Well, Mr. President, do you think that this is an authentic prosperity when it is based partly on war production, partly on deficit financing?

THE PRESIDENT. It is based on neither one. It is based on neither one. That is one of your own impressions that you are putting out.

Q. I am asking you.

THE PRESIDENT. Well, I am answering you.

Q. Yes sir.

THE PRESIDENT. For the 5 years that I have been President, there has been a net surplus of $8 billion. That is not deficit financing. And this defense program has not yet made its impact on the economy.

[20.] Q. Mr. President, could you define the attitude of the two parties towards deficit financing?

THE PRESIDENT. Well, they are about the same, if I remember my history. And when it is necessary to meet a situation, it has to be met. The tail end of an administration which ended in 1932, I think, ran in the red pretty regularly. Then, when the emergency had to be met, the means to meet it were in the hands of the President of the United States, and he took advantage of them and took the country out of the hole.

Q. I meant at the present time, sir.

THE PRESIDENT. Well, I have never been for deficit financing, and I haven't had deficit financing. Read the record.

Q. Mr. President, you will have, in the next couple of years.

THE PRESIDENT. Yes, I will, if they don't give me the tax bill to meet it.

Q. Tax bills—[*Inaudible*]——

THE PRESIDENT. Yes. Yes, I can't. That's the reason I asked for it.

[21.] Q. Mr. President, when you say the opposition resorts to smears in place of issues, would you include in the smears the work of the Fulbright committee and the Hoey committee?

THE PRESIDENT. Whenever there is misrepresentation, there's a smear.

[22.] Q. Mr. President, you said the country being prosperous, and so forth, is there any occasion to revive the New Deal legislation such as the Brannan plan, and Government aid to various projects——

THE PRESIDENT. I will give you that in the Democratic platform, when we go to write it.

Q. Are you going to direct the writing of the platform?

THE PRESIDENT. I am going to help. [*Laughter*] I always help. I have been helping ever since I was—oh—it has been 30 years that I have been helping to give the Democrats the right issues to win with the people. And I have been pretty successful at it.

[23.] Q. Mr. President, any more ideas about a whistlestop tour?

THE PRESIDENT. No. Not ready yet.

Reporter: Thank you, Mr. President.

NOTE: President Truman's two hundred and seventy-ninth news conference was held in the Indian Treaty Room (Room 474) in the Executive Office Building at 10:30 a.m. on Thursday, September 20, 1951.

228 Letter to the President of the Senate on the Need for Additional Tax Revenue. *September 20, 1951*

My dear Mr. Vice President:

As the Senate begins debate on the 1951 tax legislation, I wish to emphasize the urgency of keeping the Government's finances on a sound basis. In particular, I wish to urge that the tax increases be large enough to meet the need for higher revenues, and that they be distributed fairly among the taxpayers.

Although the Congress has not yet completed action on all appropriation bills, it is already apparent that the costs associated with the defense program will exceed our expectations at the time the budget was prepared for the fiscal year ending June 30, 1952. Only last week, the Senate raised total appropriations for the military functions of the Defense Department by nearly 2 billion dollars over the budget requests. Since the beginning of this fiscal year, the Government's receipts have not kept pace with expenditures. Without new revenue legislation, the deficit for the year will be in the neighborhood of 10 billion dollars.

The prospect of a sizeable deficit under present conditions is cause for grave concern. As I have indicated on several occasions, adequate taxes are necessary to preserve confidence in the integrity of the Government's finances, to distribute the heavy defense costs fairly among our people, and to restrain inflationary pressures.

In the face of an indicated 10 billion dollar deficit, the bill which the Senate is about to consider would produce only 5.2 billion dollars in a full year and only about 2.5 billion dollars in the current fiscal year. It would yield about 1.5 billion dollars less in a full year than the bill passed by the House of Representatives.

I earnestly believe that these amounts are not sufficient. The Government's revenues should be increased by an amount that approaches as nearly as possible the 10 billion dollars I recommended. Toward this end, I suggest that the legislation now before the Senate be strengthened in several respects.

First, the tax yields under the bill from individual income and corporate profits taxes should be increased. Personal incomes and corporate profits are at record levels. The interest of those who receive this income will be best served by paying taxes at this time sufficient to maintain the stability of our economy.

Furthermore, corporation tax increases should be made applicable to all profits for the current year. Postponement of the effective date until April 1, 1951, as provided in the bill before the Senate, would result in the loss of $500 million in revenue.

In addition, the bill now before the Senate contains many changes which would impair the effectiveness of the income and profits taxes. For example, the bill would enlarge the special classes of taxpayers benefiting from the overly generous capital gains tax provisions. It would further widen the tax loopholes benefiting various mining enterprises. It would give certain corporations unwarranted relief from excess profits taxes. At a time of great national need, when everyone's tax load must be increased substantially, I feel strongly that we should not adopt provisions which weaken our tax structure for the benefit of special groups.

The revenue bill which the Committees of Congress have developed after many months of arduous work provides the basis for leg-

islation appropriate to our present requirements. I urge the Congress to build on this foundation by strengthening its revenue yield and bringing it more in accord with the principles of fairness which must underlie our tax laws. A strong revenue system is as vital to the defense of this country as strong military forces.

Very sincerely yours,

HARRY S. TRUMAN

[Honorable Alben W. Barkley, The Vice President of the United States, Washington, D.C.]

NOTE: For the statement by the President upon signing the Revenue Act of 1951, see Item 264.

229   Remarks to the Delegates to the First National Conference on Israel. *September 21, 1951*

THIS IS a very fine tribute. I appreciate it, and I hope I deserve it—and I hope I will continue to deserve it.

I have just received a book from a friend of mine awhile ago, on his tour of duty in Israel, and he passes around an immense amount of credit in my direction, which is not customary for publications in this present day and time.

I am very appreciative of your thoughtfulness in giving me this plaque. I will treasure it as long as I live.

Thank you very much.

NOTE: The President spoke at 3:40 p.m. in the Rose Garden at the White House.

The plaque, presented to the President in recognition of his assistance to the State of Israel, was presented by Henry Morgenthau, Jr., former Secretary of the Treasury and chairman of the Board of Governors of the American Financial and Development Corporation for Israel.

The book referred to by the President was presented to him earlier in the day by its author, James G. McDonald, former U.S. Ambassador to Israel. It is entitled "My Mission in Israel 1948–1951" (Simon and Schuster, New York, 1951, 303 pp.).

The First National Conference on Israel was held in Washington to formulate plans for the mobilization of capital resources to aid the economic development of Israel.

230   Letter to the Vice President Transmitting Correspondence From Henry A. Wallace Relating to His Trip to the Far East in 1944. *September 23, 1951*

[Released September 23, 1951. Dated September 22, 1951]

Dear Mr. Vice President:

I am sending you a copy of a letter, together with certain documents, which I recently received from Mr. Henry A. Wallace. These papers deal with the facts of Mr.

Wallace's trip to the Far East in 1944, and the part played by his advisers on that trip. These papers deal with certain matters which may be of interest to the Senate and its Committees. I am therefore making Mr.

Wallace's letter available to you for use in such ways as you deem appropriate.

  Very sincerely yours,

    HARRY S. TRUMAN

[The Honorable, The Vice President of the United States, Washington, D.C.]

NOTE: Mr. Wallace's letter to the President of September 19, 1951, was released by the White House on September 23 together with the related documents referred to. His report to President Roosevelt on his visit to the Far East, dated July 10, 1944, is summarized in the Congressional Record (vol. 96, p. 598).

---

231 Remarks of Welcome at Union Station Plaza to Prime Minister De Gasperi of Italy. *September 24, 1951*

Mr. Prime Minister:

  It is a very great pleasure to welcome you to the United States of America. I hope you will have a most pleasant visit while you are here, and I know there are a great many things of importance about which we want to talk. You have plenty of opportunity to do that.

NOTE: The President spoke at 9:15 a.m. Prime Minister Alcide De Gasperi responded as follows:

  "I thank you, Mr. President, for your cordial welcome. I am certain we will discuss matters for common defense, for peace, and regarding the interests of both our countries—America and Italy."

  See also Items 232, 235.

---

232 Joint Statement Following Discussions With the Prime Minister of Italy. *September 25, 1951*

PRESIDENT TRUMAN and Prime Minister De Gasperi met at the White House on Tuesday, September 25. The meeting was devoted to an exchange of views on the present international situation and on matters of mutual concern to Italy and the United States.

  The President and the Prime Minister agreed on the importance of continuing the joint effort of the free nations united in the North Atlantic Treaty Organization to the preservation of world peace. Each reaffirmed the conviction of his Government that the free nations must be strong in order to make the world safe from aggression. Prime Minister De Gasperi reaffirmed that the Italian people are fully determined to continue their efforts for the common cause. He described Italy's particular need to strengthen its economic position as part of its general defense effort. President Truman assured the Prime Minister that the

United States, as in the past, will continue to assist Italy and the other Allies in achieving economic and social stability and in increasing their capacity for defense. He agreed with Mr. De Gasperi that the defense of Europe is vital to the preservation of the free world.

  Mr. De Gasperi referred to the contradictions between the spirit of the Italian Peace Treaty and Italy's present position as an equal member of the community of free nations. He informed the President of the legitimate desire of the Italian people that these contradictions be removed. The Prime Minister also expressed satisfaction at the opportunity he has had to exchange views on the question with the Secretary of State, as well as with the British and French Foreign Ministers. The President assured the Prime Minister that the United States Government is determined that the situation he had described be corrected in a spirit of equity and friendship. He expressed confidence that the consideration now being given to this matter would be satisfactorily concluded.

The Prime Minister stressed and the President recognized the importance to the Italian people of the Trieste question, in regard to which the policies of both governments are well known. The question was fully taken into consideration.

Mr. De Gasperi emphasized to the President the seriousness of the problem of over-population in Italy and informed him of the Italian Government's efforts toward finding international solutions to the related problem of resettlement. The President assured

the Prime Minister that the United States fully recognizes the urgency of reaching international agreements which will help alleviate distress in over-populated countries such as Italy and contribute to the development of other areas.

The President and the Prime Minister each expressed gratification at the opportunity given by the latter's visit to reaffirm the friendship and identity of views of the two nations. They stated the determination of their respective governments to continue to work for a peace based on the principles of the United Nations Charter, to which each is dedicated.

NOTE: See also Items 231, 235.

233 Statement by the President Upon Signing Executive Order Prescribing Regulations for Classifying and Protecting Security Information. *September 25, 1951*

I HAVE today signed an Executive order to strengthen our safeguards against divulging to potential enemies information harmful to the security of the United States.

This order provides, for the first time, uniform standards for classifying and protecting security information throughout the executive branch of the Government. At the same time, the order prohibits the classification of any information by any agency unless it can show affirmatively that disclosure of the information would harm the national security. Therefore, some agencies will never have occasion to institute classification and many of the others will have only infrequent need to do so.

The necessity for this order arises from the fact that security information occasionally involves, and must be handled by, agencies which normally do not handle security matters. The order requires them to protect security matters in the same manner as they would be protected in one of the key

defense agencies which have traditional classification systems. On the other hand, the order prohibits any agency from classifying nonsecurity matters.

The American people have a fundamental right to information about their Government, and there is no element of censorship, either direct or implied, in this order. The order applies only to officials and employees of the executive branch of the Government. The public is requested to cooperate, but is under no compulsion or threat of penalty to do so as a result of this order. Furthermore, I have directed every agency to keep constant watch over its classification activities for the purpose of reducing or eliminating classifications wherever and whenever conditions permit. I expect each department head or his designated subordinate to investigate promptly and carefully any alleged instance of unjustified use of security classifications. As the result of these policies, and as the result of the clear segregation of security

535

from nonsecurity information, I hope that the American people will receive more, rather than less, information about their Government as a result of this Executive order.

Under the order, any agency which originates an item of security information is directed to mark it with the words "security information" plus one of the four following classifications: "top secret," "secret," "confidential," or "restricted." The Order specifies the precautions then to be taken in accordance with these classifications, ranging from the most stringent precautions for "top secret" to the minimum precautions for "restricted." The four classifications are the standard marking used by the Departments of Defense and State and no new security classifications are authorized.

To assure that this order is carried out in the spirit in which it was issued I have also directed the National Security Council, through its Interdepartmental Committee on Internal Security, to maintain a continuing review of classification activities in all agencies with a view to achieving uniform compliance with this order, both as to safeguarding security information and to prevent the classification procedure from being used to withhold information which can be divulged without harm to the national security.

NOTE: The President referred to Executive Order 10290, dated September 24, 1951, and entitled "Prescribing Regulations Establishing Minimum Standards for the Classification, Transmission, and Handling by Departments and Agencies of the Executive Branch, of Official Information Which Requires Safeguarding in the Interest of the Security of the United States" (3 CFR, 1949–1953 Comp., p. 789).

See also Items 234, 247 [1], 248, 302.

234   Memorandum on the Executive Order Prescribing Regulations for Classifying and Protecting Security Information. *September 25, 1951*

To Heads of Executive Departments and Agencies:

I have today signed an Executive Order prescribing minimum standards for the classification, transmission and handling of official information relating to the security of the Nation.

This order will apply to all Departments and agencies in the Executive Branch of the Government and, therefore, it is of the highest importance that the responsible officials of all agencies familiarize themselves with its requirements and understand its purposes. In this connection I want to emphasize particularly several aspects of this Executive Order.

In the past relatively few agencies, such as the Departments of State and Defense, have had a need to classify information for

security purposes. Now, however, with the broad ramifications of our national security effort, many additional agencies are required to handle classified security information. This, in turn, has made it necessary to prescribe these minimum standards for application throughout the Executive Branch of the Government.

However, I want it clearly understood in all agencies, defense and non-defense, that these regulations are to be used exclusively to safeguard the security of the Nation and are not to be used, under any circumstances, for any other purpose. It is my hope that the practical effect of these regulations will be to make more, rather than less, information about the Government available to the people. This should result from the segregation of security information from non-security information. To put the matter bluntly, these regulations are designed to keep security information away from potential enemies and must not be used to withhold non-security information or to cover up mistakes made by any official or employee of the Government. In order to prevent any misunderstanding about this, these regulations prohibit the use of security classifications on non-security information even when the disclosure of such non-security information is forbidden by law (as in the case of census and income tax information). This policy is spelled out in paragraph 3 of Part I of the Regulation.

Your attention is directed specifically to the fact that paragraph 25(b) of Part IV requires that security information "shall be assigned the lowest security classification consistent with its proper protection" and that paragraph 28(c) of Part IV directs that "It shall be the responsibility and obligation of every Government official to keep classified security information in his custody constantly under review, and to initiate action toward downgrading or declassification as soon as conditions warrant." Strict adherence to these provisions is absolutely essential for, otherwise, overclassification or failure to downgrade or declassify in timely fashion will defeat the very purpose of these regulations.

In order to further the above objectives of protecting that information upon which the security of the Nation depends, of limiting classification to purely security matters, of using the lowest appropriate classification, and of downgrading or declassifying information as rapidly as conditions permit, I have directed the National Security Council through its Interdepartmental Committee on Internal Security to furnish advice and assistance to the Departments and agencies in connection with these regulations and to maintain a continuing review of the classification activities in every department or agency to insure uniform and proper application of these regulations, including declassification whenever possible.

I wish to urge upon every Department and agency head conscientious adherence to the spirit and letter of these regulations in the interest of safeguarding the national security on the one hand, and the protection of the public's right to information on the other hand. In the latter connection, I expect each Department head or his designated subordinate to investigate promptly and carefully any alleged instance of unjustified use of security classifications. In considering such instances and indeed in original determinations on classification, it should be borne in mind that improper application of the classification powers is repulsive to our democratic form of Government and burdens Government procedures with unnecessary and expensive restrictions.

HARRY S. TRUMAN

NOTE: See also Items 233, 247 [1], 248, 302.

---

235 Address at the Dedication of Equestrian Statues, a Gift of the People of Italy. *September 26, 1951*

Mr. Secretary of the Interior, Mr. Prime Minister, Mr. Secretary of State, ladies and gentlemen:

On behalf of the American people, I am happy to accept the gift of these four beautiful statues from the people of Italy. These statues were designed by American artists and made by Italian craftsmen. Italian foundries and Italian workmen, using the secrets of their craft that go back to the days

537

of Michelangelo, cast these heroic figures in bronze and covered them with gold.

These statues bear witness to the artistic traditions and the fine workmanship of the Italian people.

Four of the craftsmen who made these bronze groups have come to this country for the ceremony, and we are delighted to have them with us. We are also fortunate to have with us a representative of the trade union leaders of Italy who are striving for a free, democratic labor movement in Italy. These leaders are fighting in the cause of free trade unions and free people everywhere. The presence here of these Italian citizens testifies to the friendship and trust between the people of Italy and the people of the United States in the struggle for human freedom.

Ever since the war our two countries have been working together to preserve world peace. We have been seeking to create economic conditions that will make it possible for all men to do useful work and live their lives in freedom at the same time. The Italian people have made great progress, Mr. Prime Minister, since your last visit to Washington in 1947.

Your people have made progress in agriculture and industry. Industrial production in Italy is now 45 percent higher than it was in 1947. Electric power production is almost double what it was before the war. You have been moving forward in land reclamation and flood control.

But this is not all. Italy is engaged in a program of economic and social reforms. Low-cost housing developments have been created. Land reform is giving thousands of farmers a new stake in the land they work. The whole island of Sardinia has been freed from the scourge of malaria and as a result offers new and greater opportunities for economic development.

We in the United States regard steps like these as vitally important. We earnestly believe that the benefits of economic progress and increased production should be made available to all the people.

That is why we are so glad to see the new developments that are taking place in Italy today. Italy is making progress by evolution and not by revolution. And it is progress that benefits the ordinary citizen. We are confident that the firm devotion to freedom and democratic principles that has guided you, Mr. Prime Minister, and your colleagues in office, will result in further advances for the Italian people.

Through these difficult years since the war, the Italian people have proved their right to participate fully—and as equal partners—in the great constructive tasks of the free world.

During your conferences here, Mr. Prime Minister, we have discovered ways in which our two countries can continue to work together in the effort of the free nations for peace and human advancement.

It is clear that Italy cannot do its full share in this effort under the existing restrictions of the Italian peace treaty. As it stands, the treaty does not give Italy the position of equality among the free nations to which it is entitled. Among other things, the treaty places unnecessary shackles on Italian efforts for the common defense of the community of free nations. We intend to do everything we can to see that these unfair restrictions and discriminations are removed.

We also intend to keep on working for the admission of Italy into the United Nations. If the Soviet Union keeps on vetoing Italy's membership, other ways must be found to enable Italy to play a full and equal part in upholding the principles of the United Nations.

In the economic field, we realize that one

of Italy's biggest problems is surplus man-power—and that jobs and homes must be found in other lands for many of those who cannot be employed in Italy. The history of the United States shows that a nation is most fortunate if it can obtain the energies and skills of Italian immigrants. I hope we can set up an effective international program to help solve Italy's problem of surplus man-power. There are many places in the world where people from Italy are needed and where they can lay the foundations for a prosperous future for themselves and their children.

In addition to idle manpower, Italy has factories which could be used for defense production if they were not hampered by shortages of materials and lack of foreign exchange. When factories and workers in Italy stand idle, that is a needless loss to the strength of the free world. Acting together, our governments must take steps to use the resources of Italy's manpower and industrial production as fully as possible in the great mobilization effort of the free nations for peace.

The future of Italy lies not only in domestic progress but also in closer ties and greater unity with the free nations that are its neighbors. We have followed with great interest the efforts of Italian statesmen to bring about

a greater sense of European unity, based on moral and cultural values. We expect Italy, with its great religious and cultural heritage, to take a leading part in that effort.

Greater unity in defense, greater unity in economic effort, the removal of obsolete national barriers from the North Sea to the Mediterranean—these are the things that are needed to provide not only security but social and economic advancement for the peoples of Europe.

Only by such changes can we preserve the fundamental values of the past. Only by such combined efforts can we counter the menace of Soviet aggression. Only through such cooperation by all can we raise the living standards and increase the opportunities of any single nation.

In these great tasks, Mr. Prime Minister, we wish the Italian people good fortune and speedy success. Rest assured that we are with you, and will do all we can to help you.

NOTE: The President spoke at 1:22 p.m. at the Memorial Bridge in Washington. His opening words referred to Secretary of the Interior Oscar L. Chapman, Prime Minister Alcide De Gasperi of Italy, and Secretary of State Dean Acheson.

The four statues were a gift from the people of Italy to the people of the United States in recognition of the economic assistance given by the United States to Italy following World War II. The designs and plaster models were created by two American sculptors, Leo Friedlander and James E. Fraser. See also Items 231, 232.

236 Remarks to a Group of Korean Soldiers.
September 26, 1951

WE ARE glad to welcome you. I hope you have an enjoyable visit, and that you will go back with information that will be helpful to you and to your country, to make a contribution to the victory that we expect to win in Korea.

It is a pleasure to have you here.

NOTE: The President spoke at 3:05 p.m. in the Rose Garden at the White House. The six officers of the Korean army were part of a group of 250 Korean soldiers who were brought to the United States to attend U.S. Army training schools.

237 Special Message to the Congress Recommending Conflict-of-Interest Legislation. *September 27, 1951*

To the Congress of the United States:

I recommend that the Congress enact legislation requiring officials in all branches of the Government to place on the public record each year full information concerning their incomes from all sources, public and private. I believe this will be an important step in assuring the integrity of the public service and in protecting government officials against false and unfounded charges of improper conduct.

The overwhelming majority of the people who are working for the Federal Government in the Legislative, Judicial, and Executive branches are decent, honest, and upright citizens who are doing their very best in the public interest. I believe that the standards of conduct now prevailing in the Government service compare favorably with those of the past and with the standards now prevailing in business and the professions. Nevertheless, it should be our constant aim to improve these standards. As the burdens of the Government increase during this defense period, and more and more citizens enter into business or financial dealings with the Government, it is particularly necessary to tighten up on our regulatory procedures, and to be sure that uniformly high legal and moral standards apply to all phases of the relationship between the citizen and his Government.

In operations as large as those of our Government today, with so much depending on official action in the Congress and in the executive agencies, there are bound to be attempts by private citizens or special interest groups to gain their ends by illegal or improper means. Unfortunately, there are sometimes cases where members of the Executive and Legislative branches yield to the temptation to let their public acts be swayed by private interest. We must therefore be constantly on the alert to prevent illegal or improper conduct, and to discover and punish any instances of it that may occur.

We must also guard against the danger that the misconduct of a few will result in unwarranted suspicion and distrust of the honesty of all government officials.

In recent months, there has been something amounting to a deliberate effort to discredit the government service. Attempts have been made through implication and innuendo, and by exaggeration and distortion of the facts in a few cases, to create the impression that graft and corruption are running rampant through the whole Government.

To my mind the most disturbing feature of the charges and rumors stirred up by these attempts is their effect on the confidence of the American people in their Government and in all the individuals who make up the Government. I am told that people all around the country are getting a mistaken and a distorted impression that the Government is full of evil-doers, full of men and women with low standards of morality, full of people who are lining their own pockets and disregarding the public interest.

This is a terrible distortion of the true facts about our Government. It would be tragic if our citizens came to believe it. It would be tragic for the American people themselves to have such an idea about their Government, and it would be a terrible tragedy for all those who serve within the Government. None of us can afford to let the whole body of public officials be given a bad name by accusations, rumors, and sensational publicity tending to smear everybody.

I believe the best thing we can do to spike this effort to discredit Government officials is to place all the facts right on the record. The facts themselves are the best cure for public doubts and uncertainty.

I recommend, therefore, that the Congress promptly enact a statute which will require all full-time civilian Presidential appointees, including members of the Federal bench; all elected officers of the Federal Government, including Members of the Congress; and all other top officials and employees of the three branches of the Government—say those receiving salaries of 10,000 dollars or more, plus flag and general officers of the Armed Services—to file annually a statement of their total incomes, including amounts over and above their Government salaries, and the sources of this outside income. Consideration should also be given to requiring other Government employees to file such statements if their outside income exceeds a specified amount—perhaps $1,000 a year. Some items which are not ordinarily counted as income, such as gifts and loans, should be included in the statements filed under this statute. Penalties for willful violation of this statute should be equivalent to those for violation of the laws relating to the filing of income tax returns.

These statements when filed should be made accessible to the public.

Such public disclosure will, in my opinion, help to prevent illegal or improper conduct and at the same time protect Government officers from unfounded suspicions.

The majority of Federal employees have no income of consequence other than their official salaries. Some of our best public servants, on the other hand, do have sizeable amounts of outside income. The great public service that is being rendered today by many men who have been successful in business or other forms of endeavor demonstrates that no distinction can be drawn between these two groups in terms of public good. The disclosure of current outside income, however, will strike at the danger of gifts or other inducements made for the purpose of influencing official action, and at the danger of outside interests affecting public decisions.

A disclosure of all sources of outside income will be of obvious help in tracking down any case of wrongdoing. Furthermore, the mere existence of a requirement that such disclosure be made will act as a deterrent to improper conduct.

If an official of an executive agency knew that he would have to disclose the fact that he accepted a gift or loan from a private company with which he has public business, or if a Member of Congress who is on a committee concerned with a certain industry knew that he would have to disclose the fact that he accepted a fee from a company in that industry, I believe the chances are that such gifts or fees would not be accepted.

Such a disclosure procedure will also serve to protect officials and legislators from widespread misunderstanding on the part of the public. Our citizens will be able to see for themselves that the talk about corruption and enrichment in public office is grossly exaggerated.

As a general rule, I do not like to see public officials, or any other particular group, subjected to rules and requirements which do not apply to the rest of the population. But at the same time, public office is a privilege, not a right. And people who accept the privilege of holding office in the Government, must of necessity expect that their entire conduct should be open to inspection by the people they are serving. With all the questions that are being raised today about the probity and honesty of public officials, I think all of us should be prepared to place the facts about our income on the public record. We should be willing to do this in the public interest, if the requirement is applied equally and fairly to the officials of all three branches of our Government. This is the best protection we can give ourselves and all of our co-workers against the charge of widespread graft and favoritism in the public service.

I know of no other single step that will do so much good so quickly in protecting the reputations of our public servants and—at the same time—in producing concrete indications of any really questionable practices.

Much the same considerations apply also, I believe, to those people who hold the principal positions of responsibility in our great political parties. Of course, these offices are not Government positions. But those who hold them are necessarily brought into very close contact with the Government. And our major political parties have traditionally been so much a part of our whole system of government, that those responsible for the conduct of party business are in fact, if not in law, charged with a real public responsibility. For that reason, I would favor in-

cluding the principal national party officials and employees among those persons required to file annual income statements along the lines I have described.

The legislation I have here recommended should be passed as soon as possible. If action cannot be completed before adjournment of the present session, then I earnestly hope that the Congress will finish the task as soon as it reconvenes. We should lose no time in placing all the facts before the country, and in clearing up those false impressions that are injurious to the proper functioning of our Government.

I believe also that both the Congress and the Executive should continue to search for other means, legislative and administrative alike, to reassure the American people about the high standards of their Government and to make sure that those high standards continue to be maintained by every individual who holds public office.

HARRY S. TRUMAN

238 Remarks Recorded for Broadcast on Democratic Women's Day. *September 27, 1951*

My fellow citizens:

I am speaking today especially to the women of America.

Today is Democratic Women's Day. It is the anniversary of the date, 32 years ago, when women were admitted to the highest councils of the Democratic Party.

That was a great day for the Democratic Party—and a great day for the country.

Ever since then women have helped the Democratic Party work for the things the people of this country want and need, and are entitled to have.

The women of America are working for world peace. They hate war and the de-

struction that it brings about.

The women of America are working for a prosperous nation here at home.

They want to see their Government promote higher living standards, and hold down prices.

They want better schools for our children, greater security for our older citizens, and better housing and medical care for everybody.

These are the things that the Democratic Party is working for and has worked for through most of its long existence. It has gone a long way toward achieving these goals since 1932, and it is still making progress.

The enemies of progress try to confuse the issues, but they cannot obscure the plain facts.

The Government of the United States, under a Democratic administration, is working in the interests of all of the people—of every man, woman, and child in the country. Your Government is trying to bring about peace in the world and steadily increasing prosperity here at home.

With the support of the women of America, we will continue to advance toward those goals.

World peace and human welfare are too precious to be made the footballs of partisan politics. They must not be jeopardized by men who are careless with the truth. When we face such solemn decisions as those which now confront our country, we must act on the basis of facts, not fables.

In many parts of the country, at this moment, Democratic women are gathered to observe this anniversary and to prepare for the political campaign that lies ahead.

To these women particularly, I am addressing this message.

You know what the Democratic Party stands for and what it has done for the good of the country. Make it your job to see that your neighbors know, too. Make it your job to confront the confusers with the facts.

The truth is the best weapon the Democratic Party has.

The Democratic Party is proud of its record and its program. I want you to arm yourselves with the facts and the truth about that record and program. I want you to see that they become known to everyone in your community. There's nothing more important you can do.

When the people know the truth and the facts, no one has to tell them how to vote.

NOTE: The remarks were prerecorded for release at 3 p.m. on Thursday, September 27.

239   The President's News Conference of *September 27, 1951*

THE PRESIDENT. Please be seated.

I have no statements for release, but I will try my best to answer questions—if you have any.

[1.]   Q. Mr. President, can you give us any background on the mission of General Bradley and "Chip" Bohlen [1] out to the Far East? They left last night, that much has been announced, so it is not a trick question.

THE PRESIDENT. They are going out for an interview with General Ridgway. It is a customary procedure which has been followed right along. That is about all I can say about it.

[2.]   Q. Mr. President, awhile ago in the House, Mr. Leo Allen of Illinois gave as one of the principal reasons for opposition to the Fogarty resolution on the unification of Ireland,[2] that he and other Members of the House had not been told what your views were in the matter, and he said they did not think they should pass a resolution like that unless they knew what your views were. I wonder if you would care to say——

---

[1] General of the Army Omar N. Bradley, Chairman of the Joint Chiefs of Staff, and Charles E. Bohlen, Counselor of the Department of State.

[2] On January 19, 1951, Representative John E. Fogarty of Rhode Island had introduced a resolution "to provide for the unity of Ireland."

THE PRESIDENT. I have no views on it. [*Laughter*]

[3.] Q. Mr. President, when you sent up your message this morning about the public statement on outside income of Federal employees,[3] it produced a rather varied reaction in the Senate. Senator Capehart said he would support it, but Senator Millikin said it was too degrading to even be before the Senate. What do you think of Senator Millikin's position on that?

THE PRESIDENT. Well, now, that is his opinion, and he is entitled to his opinion, the same as I am entitled to mine. And my opinion is expressed in the message.

[4.] Q. Mr. President, there is a report from Belgrade today that Britain, the United States, and France have agreed with Yugoslavia for the partition of Trieste between Italy and Yugoslavia. Can you tell us whether that is correct or not?

THE PRESIDENT. I have no comment on it.

[5.] Q. Mr. President, have you decided to appoint Telford Taylor to head up the Small Defense Plants Administration? And also, are you ready to fill that remaining vacancy on the Renegotiation Board?

THE PRESIDENT. I have no comment on either question.

[6.] Q. Mr. President, are you hopeful of a peaceful solution to the Iranian difficulties?[4]

THE PRESIDENT. Yes, I am. I am always hoping for peace everywhere in the world. Sometimes that hope never comes to fruition, but I still hope for it.

[7.] Q. Mr. President, are you going to name Joe Duke, the Senate Sergeant at Arms, to the International Boundary and Water Commission?

THE PRESIDENT. Not that I know of.

[8.] Q. Mr. President, could you tell us the purpose of Mr. Potofsky's[5] visit this morning?

THE PRESIDENT. He comes to see me whenever he feels like it. I think he is one of the ablest of the labor leaders. He came in to discuss various things with me, particularly the unemployment that now exists among the garment workers.

[9.] Q. Mr. President, in view of the power shortage in the Northeast, due to drought, are you going to try to hurry along Government action on the Quoddy tidal power project?

THE PRESIDENT. I have been trying to hurry that along for 6 years, May,[6] but your Senators and Representatives are not very enthusiastic about it. That's one of the reasons I haven't been able to get it. Mrs. Smith[7] is for it, but I don't know of anybody else who is in that neck of the woods that is for it.

Q. I understood, sir, that they had asked you in June whether they should try to get the money, and you asked them to refrain until you had got the results of a Government survey being made this summer?

THE PRESIDENT. That is correct. That survey is now finished, and that has some connection with the St. Lawrence Seaway. The power pool in that part of the country will be made up, if we get it, of the St. Lawrence Seaway and the Bay of Fundy project.

[10.] Q. Mr. President, are there any plans for Mr. Harriman[8] to return to Tehran in the near future?

THE PRESIDENT. No.

[11.] Q. Mr. President, there have been several collectors of Internal Revenue now under investigation, and I have been asked

---

[3] See Item 237.

[4] British-Iranian dispute on the nationalization of the oil industry in Iran. See Item 140 [4].

[5] Jacob Potofsky, General President, Amalgamated Clothing Workers of America.

[6] Mrs. May Craig of the Portland (Maine) Press Herald.

[7] Senator Margaret Chase Smith of Maine.

[8] W. Averell Harriman, Special Assistant to the President.

to ask you whether you are considering suggesting that these jobs be taken out of the appointive field and put under civil service?

THE PRESIDENT. I hadn't that under consideration at all.

Q. You have, or hadn't?

THE PRESIDENT. Hadn't.

[12.]   Q. Mr. President, the conference committees of the two Houses completed work today on the foreign aid military economic bill,[9] calling for a new director to handle the new agency, appointed by you. Have you decided on whether Mr. Harriman will be the man for that?

THE PRESIDENT. The bill hasn't reached me. Until I make a survey of it, I can't give you, any answer on its administration.

Q. As I remember, you told a previous conference you weren't concerned so much with operations as you were with the money that was needed?

THE PRESIDENT. That's right.

Q. But you haven't decided who will fill the job?

THE PRESIDENT. No, I haven't decided yet.

[13.]   Q. Mr. President, on the Internal Revenue collectors, I think it has been the practice for a long time to make the appointments more or less political, such as the postmaster appointments have been in many cases. I wonder if you were tending a little bit toward a career man in that field, such as Mr. Dunlap?[10]

THE PRESIDENT. The best answer to that is that I have appointed more career men in all the fields than any other President. There are two career men in my Cabinet.

Q. Yes sir. I wondered if you planned to make any particular point of that with the collectors?

THE PRESIDENT. No, not at all. If a man is able to fill the bill and has had experience in those positions, it is always best to appoint him.

Q. Mr. President, do you regard yourself as a career man?

THE PRESIDENT. Yes. I have been in elective office for 30 years. I think that's a pretty good career. Will be 30 years, at the end of my present term.

Q. That wasn't what he meant. [*Laughter*]

THE PRESIDENT. I know that's not what he meant. But he got his answer. [*More laughter*]

[14.]   Q. Mr. President, have you changed your opinion in any way on Mr. Boyle,[11] as a result of his testimony today?

THE PRESIDENT. No, I haven't.

[15.]   Q. Mr. President, would you say anything about your exchanges between the British Prime Minister on the Iranian situation?

THE PRESIDENT. No, I can't.

Q. I didn't catch the question.

THE PRESIDENT. He wanted to know if I can say anything about the exchanges between the British Prime Minister and myself on Iran, and I said I couldn't make any comment on it.

[16.]   Q. Mr. President, on your message to Congress this morning, you mentioned in one of the paragraphs that although the overwhelming majority of the people in Government administration were composed of honest, decent men, that there were some who put private interests before the public. Now, in most of the cases on which you have been questioned at these conferences you have expressed confidence in the men who have been under attack. Does that mean that you feel there have been some cases that have not been made public?

---

[9] See Item 250.

[10] John B. Dunlap, Commissioner of Internal Revenue.

[11] William M. Boyle, Jr., chairman of the Democratic National Committee.

THE PRESIDENT. None that I knew of.
[*Pause*]

What's the matter with you? Are you out of "soap"? [*Laughter*]

[17.] Q. Are you seeing the Canadian Prime Minister tomorrow, as I understand it? [12]

THE PRESIDENT. Yes. On the St. Lawrence Seaway project.

[18.] Q. The other, sir, I want to ask about—the Atomic Energy Commission has complained today, to some of the labor unions, about strikes at a couple of atomic energy plants that they are afraid may hurt the defense effort. I wonder if that had been brought to your attention?

THE PRESIDENT. No, it hasn't. Probably will be, though, before it is finished.

[19.] Q. Do you care to summarize your questions following the visit of the Italian Prime Minister?

THE PRESIDENT. Well, I think they were very well summarized in the communique which was issued by the two of us.[13] I think

[12] See Item 240.
[13] See Item 232.

that answers your question.
[*Pause*]

What's the matter?

Q. Not a thing! [*Laughter*]

Q. I will volunteer.

THE PRESIDENT. All right.

[20.] Q. Is there any reason why the St. Lawrence and Niagara power projects should be linked together?

THE PRESIDENT. Yes, there is a very good reason—because we want to get them both constructed.

Q. But the Niagara power is ready to go now—as an independent proposition.

THE PRESIDENT. Yes, but I am not for it. I never have been in favor of taking them apart, for the very simple reason that I don't want to see one constructed without the other. I would like to see them both constructed.

Reporter: Thank you, Mr. President.

THE PRESIDENT. That's all right.

NOTE: President Truman's two hundred and eightieth news conference was held in the Indian Treaty Room (Room 474) in the Executive Office Building at 4 p.m. on Thursday, September 27, 1951.

240 Joint Statement Following Discussions With Prime Minister St. Laurent of Canada. *September 28, 1951*

THE PRESIDENT and the Prime Minister discussed the St. Lawrence project. They agreed on the vital importance to the security and the economies of both countries of proceeding as rapidly as possible with both the seaway and the power phases of the project. They explored the matter of the next steps to be taken in achieving the early construction of the project. They both agreed that it would be most desirable to proceed along the lines of the 1941 Agreement between the United States and Canada.

The Prime Minister informed the Presi-

dent of the needs of Ontario for power and of the arrangement the Canadian Government could make with the government of that Province for its participation with the appropriate Federal or State authority in the United States for the power development. In these circumstances, the Prime Minister indicated the Canadian Government would be willing to construct the seaway as a Canadian project if it is not possible to have the joint development undertaken on the basis of the 1941 Agreement.

The President expressed his strong preference for joint action on the Seaway and his hope that the Congress would soon authorize such action, but stated he would support Canadian action as second best if an early commencement on the joint development does not prove possible.

241   Address to the Washington Pilgrimage of American Churchmen. *September* 28, 1951

Mr. Chairman, Dr. Pruden, my friends:

I am happy to have the privilege of speaking to this meeting of the Washington Pilgrimage of American Churchmen. You have come to the Nation's Capital to visit its monuments and to look at the basic documents on which our Government was founded. Many people come to Washington to do these things, but you have come here for a special purpose. You have come here to emphasize the fact that this Nation was founded on religious principles.

You will see, as you make your rounds, that this Nation was established by men who believed in God. You will see that our Founding Fathers believed that God created this Nation. And I believe it, too. They believed that God was our strength in time of peril and the source of all our blessings.

You will see the evidence of this deep religious faith on every hand.

If we go back to the Declaration of Independence, we notice that it was drawn up by men who believed that God the Creator had made all men equal and had given them certain rights which no man could take away from them. In beginning their great enterprise, the signers of the Declaration of Independence entrusted themselves to the protection of divine providence.

To our forefathers it seemed something of a miracle that this Nation was able to go through the agonies of the American Revolution and emerge triumphant. They saw, in our successful struggle for independence, the working of God's hand. In his first inaugural address, George Washington said,

"No people can be bound to acknowledge and adore the invisible hand, which conducts the affairs of men, more than the people of the United States."

Another fact which you will notice in the course of your pilgrimage is that the makers of our Constitution believed in religious toleration. Theirs was the highest type of religion, forbidding the use of coercion or force in matters of mind and spirit. Religious freedom was a part of their religious faith. And they received that from Roger Williams, a Baptist, from William Penn, a Quaker, and from Lord Baltimore, a Catholic. That's the reason for our constitutional approach to religious freedom.

It is said that when Benjamin Franklin left the Constitutional Convention he was asked, "What have you given us?" He answered, "A republic, if you can keep it." Millions of Americans since then have believed that the keeping of our Republic depends upon keeping the deep religious convictions on which it was founded. From the worship and teachings of the synagogues and churches of our land, have come a moral integrity, a concern for justice and human welfare, a sense of human equality, a love of human freedom, and a practice of brotherhood which are necessary to the life of our national institutions.

It is fitting and proper that at this time of international peril and uncertainty we should look back to those beginnings and rededicate ourselves to those ideals.

It is not enough, however, simply to look back. It is not enough to congratulate our selves upon the religious spirit of our forebears. We must ask ourselves if we truly believe the things which they believed. We must examine our conduct to see whether we are carrying out in our daily lives the ideals we profess.

This is not easy. Our religious heritage imposes great obligations upon us. It does not permit us to be self-satisfied and complacent. Indeed, if we accept the faith which has been handed down to us, our task as a Nation is much more difficult. We cannot be satisfied with things as they are. We must always be striving to live up to our beliefs and to make things better in accordance with the divine commandments.

The people of Israel, you will remember, did not, because of their covenant with God, have an easier time than other nations. Their standards were higher than those of other nations and the judgment upon them and their shortcomings was more terrible. A religious heritage, such as ours, is not a comfortable thing to live with. It does not mean that we are more virtuous than other people. Instead, it means that we have less excuse for doing the wrong thing—because we are taught right from wrong.

Our religious heritage, in my opinion, imposes great responsibilities upon us as we face the problems of today.

It means first of all that we must constantly strive for social justice in the life of this Republic. It means that we must fight against special privilege, against injustice to those of low income, and against the denial of opportunity, against discrimination based upon race, creed, or national origin.

Our religious heritage also means that we must struggle to maintain our civil liberties. No nation which hopes to live by the law of God can afford to suppress dissent and criticism. You may remember that Israel persecuted the prophets. The prophets had unpleasant things to say about what was

going on in ancient Israel. They criticized social injustices and the wasteful luxury of the privileged few. They criticized the way in which the ancient Hebrews had turned away from true religious principles. They said that Israel would be punished for its misdeeds. The prophets were not popular, and the kings and the priests of Israel tried to deny them freedom of speech. But the prophets were right, and Israel was punished as the prophets had said it would be.

We must always keep the way open for self-criticism. We must not stop up the mouths of those who are saying unpopular things. We must preserve the Bill of Rights—which, in my opinion, is the most important part of the Constitution—so that the voice of protest and dissent may always be heard. We must not try to destroy people by fear and slander, because if we do, we shall weaken the moral fiber of our own country.

Another great lesson which our religious heritage has for us today is that we must not be led astray by self-righteousness. We must remember that the test of our religious principles lies not just in what we say, not only in our prayers, or even in living blameless personal lives—but in what we do for others.

I am going to repeat that, because I think it is of vital importance to this meeting. We must remember that the test of our religious principles lies not just in what we say, not only in our prayers, not even in living blameless personal lives—but in what we do for others.

It is all too easy for churchgoing people to be satisfied with a superficial standard of morals. It is all too easy to sit in judgment on the shortcomings of others. It is all too easy to feel morally superior because we go to church and profess to follow the faith of our fathers.

We must remember that in his ministry on earth, Jesus delivered His strongest con-

demnation against those who were super-
ficially and publicly good. The scribes and
the Pharisees He attacked were the respect-
able people of his day. They were the leaders of the community who set the standards
for others. To them He said "Thou hypocrite, first cast out the beam out of thine own
eye, and then shalt thou see clearly to cast
out the mote out of thy brother's eye."

"Thou hypocrite, first cast out the beam
out of thine own eye, and then shalt thou see
clearly to cast out the mote out of thy
brother's eye." Ah, would that we could
live by that!

Self-interest can blind us today, just as it
blinded the scribes and Pharisees of biblical
times. We must always be on our guard
against this danger.

If we are to respond to our religious heritage, we must be guided by the principle of
charity—charity in the biblical sense of love
for one's fellow man. This is the greatest
virtue, without which other virtues are of
little worth.

We must work for morality in public life
and in private life. You can't make an
honest man by law. He has to be raised by
the rules of the 20th chapter of Exodus, and
the Sermon on the Mount, if he has the right
moral fiber to become an ethical public or
private citizen.

We must have high standards of personal
conduct. But even if we do all these things,
it is still not enough. The final question
that will be asked of us, as individuals and
as a society, is "What have we done for our
fellow man?" What have we done to ease
his burdens, to give him greater opportunity,
to help him in time of trouble, and to make
the world a better place for him to live in?
For unless we can answer those questions,
we will not have carried out in our lives the
religious heritage which has come to us from
our forebears.

Today, our problem is not just to preserve

our religious heritage in our own lives and
our own country. Our problem is a greater
one. It is to preserve a world civilization in
which man's belief in God can survive. Only
in such a world can our own Nation follow
its basic traditions, and realize the promise
of a better life for all our citizens.

Today, the whole human enterprise is in
danger—and serious danger. On the one
hand, we have to resist the expansion of a
power that is hostile to all we believe in. It
is a power that denies the rule of law, the
value of the individual, and belief in God.
It is a power which has become militant and
aggressive, using the weapons of deceit and
subversion as well as military might.

On the other hand, we must do all we can
to prevent the outbreak of another world
war. Such a war, using modern instruments
of destruction, would be more terrible than
anything the world has ever experienced.
It would make a battleground of the
crowded and complex cities of the modern
world. It might well shatter the whole
economic and social system, and plunge mankind back into barbarism.

This is the great problem we must meet.
We cannot yield to Soviet communism, without betraying the ideals we live for. We
cannot have another world war without
jeopardizing our civilization.

In this perilous strait, our greatest source
of strength, our greatest hope of victory, lies
in the God we acknowledge as the ruler of
us all. We turn to faith in Him to give us
the strength and the wisdom to carry out
His will. We ask Him to lead us out of the
dangers of this present time into the paths
of peace.

In this crisis of human affairs, all men who
profess to believe in God should unite in
asking His help and His guidance. We
should lay aside our differences and come
together now—for never have our differences seemed so petty and so insignificant as

they do in the face of the peril we confront today.

It is not just this church or that church which is in danger. It is not just this creed or that creed that is threatened. All churches, all creeds, are menaced. The very future of the Word of God—the teaching that has come down to us from the days of the prophets and the life of Jesus—is at stake.

For some time I have been trying to bring a number of the great religious leaders of the world together in a common affirmation of faith. And that common affirmation, as I said awhile ago, is in the 20th chapter of Exodus, and in the 5th, 6th, and 7th chapters of the Gospel according to St. Matthew—the Sermon on the Mount. And I have been trying to make a common supplication to the one God that all creeds and all religions profess. I have asked them to join in one common act that will affirm these religious and moral principles on which we all agree.

Such an affirmation would testify to the strength of our common faith and our confidence in its ultimate victory over the forces of Satan that oppose it.

I am sorry to say that it has not yet been possible to bring the religious faiths together for this purpose of bearing witness in one united affirmation that God is the way of truth and peace. Even the Christian churches have not yet found themselves able to join together in a common statement of their faith that Christ is their Master and

Redeemer and the source of their strength against the hosts of irreligion and danger in the world, and that will be the cause of world catastrophe. They haven't been able to agree on as simple a statement as that. I have been working at it for years.

Despite the barriers that divide the different churches, there is a common bond of brotherhood that underlies them all. We must continue our effort to find those common ties, and to bring the churches together in greater unity in a crusade for peace. In this way, we shall come closer to the one God who is the Father of us all. In this way, we shall find greater power to meet the troubles of our time.

The way to such unity is long and hard. But we must continue to strive for it. And we must ask God's help. If we really have faith, God will give us what we are not able to attain by our own efforts.

May God grant that we may speak together, as brothers, of His power and His mercy, and bear witness of Him against those who deny Him.

And may God unite the churches and the free world, to bring us peace in our time.

NOTE: The President spoke at 8 p.m. at the National City Christian Church in Washington. In his opening words he referred to Dr. J. Warren Hastings, pastor of the National City Christian Church and chairman of the meeting, and Dr. Edward H. Pruden, pastor of the First Baptist Church in Washington, which the President attended.

The pilgrimage was held in Washington, September 28–30, 1951.

242 Radio Remarks Opening the Nation's Community Chest Campaign. *September 30, 1951*

My fellow Americans:

In 1500 communities throughout the United States, we are beginning a campaign to raise funds for the Community Chest. This is an event of critical importance to this country of ours. It stands for our devo-

tion to the real, human values that make our Nation great.

The ultimate greatness of a nation can never be measured by its material riches or the strength of its armies. Instead, what really counts in the long run is how much that nation contributes to the moral and spiritual welfare of mankind.

Our own country has grown great for just that reason—because it is based on moral values. We have been taught that it is the highest duty of man to live by the Golden Rule—we acknowledge that each of us is his brother's keeper.

That is a good rule for the Government to follow, and the Government can and does do many things to help people meet the problems of their daily lives. But there are many other things that the Government does not attempt to do, things that friends and neighbors have always done for one another and will always keep on doing. Nothing can ever take the place of the good old-fashioned rule that neighbors should always help each other.

That is the heart of the American ideal—people working together, sharing their joys and their sorrows, trying to make the world a better place to live in. That is what the Community Chest means to me. It is, I think, one of the finest developments of our time.

The Community Chest gives us a chance to make sure our help will really count. As our towns and cities have grown larger, community problems have become more and more complex. It is often hard for us as individuals to know what kind of contribution will do the most good toward meeting our community needs. That's where the Community Chest comes in. When we give to the Chest, we can make sure we are helping our neighbors and our neighborhood in

the right way. And when we do that we are making our neighborhood and our country a better place to live in for ourselves and our children.

So, I say to you: Give to the Community Chest. Help to build up the things that are finest in the American way of life.

How much should you give? I can't tell you that. But I can tell you that the need is very great and most of us in this country are better able to give than we have ever been before in our lives.

The needs are greater this year, because the Community Chest has a double job to do. This year a United Defense Fund has been set up as a part of the Red Feather campaign. Through the USO and other agencies, this fund will provide special help and services for the men and women in our armed forces, for their families, and for our defense workers.

This defense job is vital and deserves the support of all of us. But at the same time, the Community Chest must keep right on with its regular job in our home towns—helping families in trouble, caring for homeless or neglected children, nursing the sick, and providing guidance and recreation for young people.

To do these two great jobs we should give all we can.

For such a cause as this, I am confident that the American people will do their utmost.

NOTE: The President's remarks were prerecorded for release at 10:55 p.m. on September 30, 1951.

---

243   Remarks to the Members of the Directing Council of the Pan American Sanitary Organization. *October* 1, 1951

IT IS a pleasure to have you come in, because I am, as Mr. Ewing says, very much interested in the public health and welfare of the whole world. And we are making some progress. We have improved the health conditions in nearly every place where we have been responsible—for instance, in Panama, Puerto Rico, and the Virgin Islands. And we have tried to contribute to the improvement of the health of the Western Hemisphere, and I think we have made some successful progress in doing just that.

We have yet a long way to go, and when we have arrived at the condition which we all hope to arrive at, we must find a way, then, to ease the pressure of population.

For instance, in Puerto Rico the population has increased at an enormous rate since we have eliminated the diseases that held that population down. Now we have got to find a way to employ those people and see that they have a living. And that will be the same situation in all the countries of the Western Hemisphere, unless we work

out a plan that will meet that very situation.

I was reading this morning in one of the releases—I think, Oscar, from your "shop"—that the number of people over 50 in the United States of America is nearly four times what it was in 1900.

We have got to meet that situation. We can do it, if we make up our minds that we want to do it.

I hope you will have a successful meeting here, and that you will consider all these questions and their end results, and then we can get somewhere in public health.

Thank you very much.

NOTE: The President spoke at 12:20 p.m. in the Rose Garden at the White House. In his opening words he referred to Oscar R. Ewing, Administrator, Federal Security Agency.

---

244 Message to the Congress Transmitting 32d Report on Lend-Lease Operations. *October 3, 1951*

To the Congress of the United States:

I am transmitting herewith the Thirty-second Report to Congress on Lend-Lease Operations, for the period from April 1, 1950, to March 31, 1951, inclusive.

During the period covered by this report, a supplement to the Lend-Lease Settlement Arrangement of April 15, 1948, was signed with Brazil and final settlement commitments were signed with Colombia, Costa Rica, and Mexico, while Bolivia, Ecuador, and El Salvador liquidated the amounts which were outstanding on their lend-lease accounts incurred within the terms of their respective lend-lease agreements.

The major development in lend-lease activities during this period was the resumption on January 15, 1951, of formal across-the-table negotiations with representatives of the U.S.S.R. In preparation for these negotiations, the Secretary of State discussed with me the major points involved and I approved

his recommendations, the objectives of which are: just and reasonable compensation to the United States for the civilian-type lend-lease supplies remaining on hand in the Soviet Union at the end of the war; the return to the United States, pursuant to a request submitted in accordance with the provisions of the master lend-lease agreement, of those defense articles transferred to the U.S.S.R. under lend-lease procedures which I have determined to be useful to our Government; and the payment by the U.S.S.R. of satisfactory compensation to United States owners of patented processes which are being used in the U.S.S.R. in oil refineries supplied under the lend-lease program. Despite the continued efforts of the United States negotiators to reach a satisfactory settlement, no substantial agreement on several of the major issues has yet been achieved. These negotiations are described more fully in the report itself.

Other lend-lease activities during the period covered by this report include negotiations for settlements with other countries and, also, the management of fiscal, administrative, and policy matters arising from and related to the lend-lease settlements which already have been concluded with certain of our Allies of World War II.

HARRY S. TRUMAN

NOTE: The 32d report to Congress on lend-lease operations is printed in House Document 227 (82d Cong., 1st sess.).

---

245 Remarks to Members of the Foreign Relations Committee of the Syrian and Lebanese American Federation.   *October* 3, 1951

YOU CAN be exceedingly helpful. I am very much interested in peace in the Near East, as I am in every other section of the world. There isn't any good reason at all why there shouldn't be peace there, and everywhere else, for that matter. And you can make a contribution to attainment of that peaceful settlement by just what you are doing now.

I am anxious to see developments in that part of the world that will relieve the pressures of the populations. In nearly every instance in the history of the world, population pressures have caused the difficulties between countries.

There are developments that can be made in the Near East that can care for a population of three or four times the amount of people that are there now. I have had surveys made in the Euphrates Valley, and along the Mediterranean coast, in Arabia, in Ethiopia, and it is fantastic the things that can be done there to make living more pleasant for the people who already live there.

That will bring about peace—that will bring about peace. And you can be very helpful in that.

NOTE: The President spoke at 12:10 p.m. in the Rose Garden at the White House.

The Federation is composed of Americans of Arabic-speaking origin, mainly of Lebanese, Syrian, and Palestinian descent. The purpose of the organization is to preserve the cultural heritage of its members and to promote better American-Arab understanding.

---

246 Statement by Direction of the President Announcing an Atomic Explosion in the U.S.S.R.   *October* 3, 1951

ANOTHER atomic bomb has recently been exploded within the Soviet Union. In spite of Soviet pretensions that their atomic energy program is being directed exclusively toward peaceful purposes, this event confirms again that the Soviet Union is continuing to make atomic weapons.

In accordance with the policy of the President to keep the American people informed to the fullest extent consistent with our national security, the President has directed me to make this statement and to stress again the necessity for that effective enforceable international control of atomic energy which the United States and the large majority of the members of the United Nations support.

Further details cannot be given without adversely affecting our national security interests.

NOTE: The statement was made public by Joseph Short, Secretary to the President.

For the statement by the President on announcing the first atomic explosion in the Soviet Union, see 1949 volume, this series, Item 216.

247 The President's News Conference of October 4, 1951

THE PRESIDENT. Please sit down.

I haven't been late for a long time, but I thought I would keep you waiting a little while.

[1.] I know what you are interested in. You are interested in censorship. And I don't believe in it. So just to keep you busy, I am going to read you a statement.

Q. Is that prepared for us?

THE PRESIDENT. Yes.

[*Reading, not literally*] "There has been considerable misrepresentation and misunderstanding of the Executive order issued on September 24, 1951, relating to the handling of information which has been classified, in order to protect the national security."

And right here I want to stop and tell you that Central Intelligence had Yale University make a survey, and that survey found—and they had no connection with the Government—that 95 percent of all our information was public property.

"This Executive order represented an honest effort to find the best approach to a problem that is important to the survival of the United States of America. I issued the order with great reluctance, and only when I was convinced, after lengthy consideration, that it was necessary to protect the United States against its potential enemies. I think my record in defending civil liberties in this country demonstrates that I have no desire to suppress freedom of speech, or freedom of the press.

"I would like for the public to understand what this order undertakes to do, and why it was necessary to issue it.

"In its simplest terms, the problem is what we should do to keep military and related secrets from falling into the hands of the enemies of the United States. I do not believe that anyone could seriously contend

that military secrets should be published in the newspapers, or that anyone has a right or a duty to see that military secrets are published. I believe that everyone, including Members of Congress and newspaper editors, should think twice before advocating a theory that would lead to that result.

"Whether it be treason or not, it does the United States just as much harm for military secrets to be made known to potential enemies through open publication, as it does for military secrets to be given to an enemy through the clandestine operations of spies."

There isn't any difference at all.

"On the other hand, I do not believe that protection of military secrets should be made a cloak or a cover for withholding from the people information about their Government which should be made known to them. I believe that everyone, including Government officials, should try to prevent this from happening.

"It is easy to agree on these two objectives, but it was difficult to establish the means for accomplishing both of them.

"In those agencies of the Government primarily concerned with national security matters, such as the Department of State and the Department of Defense, we have had for a number of years a system of classifying information to prevent its disclosure to unauthorized persons when it would be dangerous to the national security. This system has worked reasonably well, although it has not in all instances prevented the publication of information which aided our enemies against the United States, and in other cases it has been used to classify information which actually has no particular relationship to national security."

Those are the two things that we are faced with, how to prevent our military secrets from becoming the possessions of our enemies, and how to be sure that, in doing that, we don't cover up information that ought to be made public.

[*Continuing reading*] "In the present defense mobilization period, it has become necessary in an increasing number of cases to make military secrets available to executive agencies other than the military departments, in order that these other agencies might effectively perform their functions that are necessary in supporting the defense effort. It is also necessary for some of these civilian agencies—such as the Central Intelligence Agency, the Federal Bureau of Investigation, for example—to originate and protect some information vital to our defense.

"It should be readily apparent that military secrets in the hands of these other agencies should be protected just as much as when they are in the hands of the military departments. It would also seem to be sensible to provide that different agencies take the same kind of precautions to protect this information. It would not make any sense to have a paper containing military secrets carefully locked up in a safe in the Pentagon, with a copy of the same paper left lying around on the desk of a lawyer in the Justice Department.

"Now, the purpose of this Executive order is to provide a commonsense answer to these problems. It is to provide that information affecting the national security shall continue to be protected when it gets out of the hands of the military departments and into the hands of other agencies. The purpose is to provide that these other agencies shall provide the same kind of protection that is provided in the military departments.

"Another purpose of the order—and it is a most important purpose—is to provide that information shall not be classified and withheld from the public on the ground that

it affects the national security, unless it is in fact actually necessary to protect such information in the interest of national security.

"In other words, one of the purposes of this Executive order is to correct abuses which may have grown up by use of overclassification of information in the name of national security.

"I think this Executive order represents a reasonable approach to a very difficult problem. I think it will work in the public interest, and I expect to watch it closely, to see that it is not used as an excuse for withholding information to which the public is entitled.

"It may well be that experience under the order will indicate that it should be changed. In that case, I will be glad to change it— and I will be glad to give consideration to reasonable suggestions for changes that are advanced in good faith.

"I would like to suggest to those who are seriously and honestly concerned about this matter, that they consider it objectively and with the interests of the United States uppermost in their minds. I would like to suggest that they consider how we can best accomplish objectives which all of us should be able to agree upon. I do not believe that the best solution can be reached by adopting an approach based on the theory that everyone has a right to know our military secrets and related information affecting the national security." [1]

Now, I am going to hand you this in mimeographed form, and I hope every one of you will take a good look at it, and that you will give it to your editors and your publishers. And remember that 95 percent of our secret information has been revealed by newspapers and slick magazines, and that is what I am trying to stop.

Q. Mr. President, can you give us some examples of what caused this order?

---

[1] See Items 233, 234, 248, 302.

THE PRESIDENT. Yes. The most out-standing example was the publication in Fortune magazine of all the locations and the maps of our atomic energy plants. And then, in this very town—in every town in the country—were published air maps of Washington, New York, Chicago, San Francisco, Seattle, and other of our great cities, with arrows pointing to the key points in those towns.

Q. I think that information was given out by the departments——

THE PRESIDENT. Well, I don't care who gave it out. The publishers had no business to use it, if they had the welfare of the United States at heart.

Q. I don't know if the military or atomic energy——

THE PRESIDENT. I don't care who gave it out. The publisher should be just as patriotic as I am, and I wouldn't give it out.

Q. The story was over the wire——

THE PRESIDENT. Well, I don't care about that——

Q. ——attributed to a military agency——

THE PRESIDENT. Yes, and if the military agency gives you that, and an atomic bomb falls on you on account of that, at the right place, who is to blame?

Q. Well, my experience has been that the editors did not make up these maps——

THE PRESIDENT. They did, in Fortune magazine.

Q. I mean, the civil defense map——

THE PRESIDENT. Well, they were air pictures of the great cities. And it's terrible. I wish I had them of Russia and their manufacturing plants. I could use them.

Q. Mr. President, when was that Yale survey made, sir?

THE PRESIDENT. Oh, just a short time ago—just a short time ago.

Q. May I ask, Mr. President, right along the line of your effort to safeguard military and security information, what safeguards are there that the security officer will not be overzealous? As I recall, the first action taken under your Executive order was the statement by the security officer of the OPS, who said that security information is anything which is embarrassing to OPS?

THE PRESIDENT. And he had the carpet pulled out from under him, if you remember!

Q. You are the one man to watch everything, except no one human being can watch everything.

THE PRESIDENT. No—that is correct—that is correct. And I hate censorship just as badly as you do, and I will protect you against that as far as I can. But the safety and welfare of the United States of America comes first with me.

Q. As a corollary question, there was a suggestion on Capitol Hill, I believe by Senator Benton—although I am not sure—that each department which has a security officer also have a man who fights for release of information?

THE PRESIDENT. Well, I don't know about that. I don't know about that.

What is it, May? [2]

Q. Mr. President, have you weighed the importance of the free press in relation to military security——

THE PRESIDENT. Yes——

Q. ——as both important to this country?

THE PRESIDENT. Yes, yes. A free press is just as important as the Bill of Rights, and that is what is contained in the Bill of Rights.

Q. Yes sir. But do you not think you are giving dangerous power to civilian agencies to say what shall be given to the people?

THE PRESIDENT. I am not so sure. We will have to wait and find out. If that is the case, why we will change it, as I said

---

[2] Mrs. May Craig of the Portland (Maine) Press Herald.

right here—[*indicating the statement*].

Q. Do you not think that censorship is always abused to a degree?

THE PRESIDENT. I don't know. I have had no experience.

Q. I have, sir, and I find that it always is, even by the military.

THE PRESIDENT. Well, where is Elmer Davis?[3] He can tell us about that.

Mr. Davis: Is there any program giving training in uniform standards for the security officers?

THE PRESIDENT. I hope there will—I hope there will be.

Joseph H. Short (Secretary to the President): Mr. President, that was provided, sir. There is training in uniform standards by the ICIS, and ICIS is going to review all of these classifications.

Q. Didn't hear what Joe said, Mr. President?

THE PRESIDENT. He said that there was provided in the order a training program for these men, and for uniform standards, and that that training would be carefully supervised.

Q. Did I understand you to say, sir, that 95 percent of our secret information has been revealed?

THE PRESIDENT. Yes.

Q. Secret?

THE PRESIDENT. Yes. Ninety-five percent of all our information has been revealed in the press in one way or another.

Q. Mr. President, I think what's in Macon's[4] mind, you said, we got it: "Remember that 95 percent of our secret information has been revealed by newspapers and slick magazines, and that is what I am trying to stop." Is that correct—is that correct, sir?

THE PRESIDENT. That's right. That's correct. That's the answer.

Q. Mr. President, on this question of the maps, I wonder if we could recapitulate that just a little? Do we understand correctly that in event that a newspaper or magazine gets some information from, say, the Defense Department, do you think, sir, that the primary responsibility on whether that is published is on the publisher and not on the originating agency?

THE PRESIDENT. There is no question about that, because they are very careful not to publish a lot of things that I say. [*Laughter*]

Q. Mr. President, just a technical question. What maps are we having reference to here?

THE PRESIDENT. Air maps of the cities of the United States.

Q. Are you referring to any one in particular, or just some that have been published?

THE PRESIDENT. If you will look back through the magazines, you will find—or the daily papers—the News here in Washington published an air map of the city of Washington and pointed out the key places in it.

Q. Thank you very much.

THE PRESIDENT. That is what I am worried about now. I am not trying to suppress information. I am trying to prevent us from being wiped out.

Q. Mr. President, to get the record clear, those maps indicating the vital points in cities, weren't they issued by the Civil Defense Administration?

THE PRESIDENT. I don't know where they came from. I only know what I saw in the paper.

Q. Mr. President, I would like to clear up this 95 percent. You say secret information has been disclosed. You would not have had that 95 percent disclosed that has already been disclosed?

---

[3] Elmer Davis of the American Broadcasting Company, former Director of the Office of War Information.

[4] Macon Reed, Jr., of the Transradio Press Service.

THE PRESIDENT. No. There's a lot of it I wouldn't disclose, but 95 percent of it has been made public.

Q. Well, I know that the Central Intelligence and the others say that 95 percent of their information comes from magazines.

THE PRESIDENT. That is correct.

Q. Yes.

THE PRESIDENT. That is absolutely correct.

Q. As I understood the statement, that——

THE PRESIDENT. Ninety-five percent of our secret information has been disclosed.

Q. I think we are talking about two different things.

THE PRESIDENT. Well, maybe——

Q. But is that——

THE PRESIDENT. The Post-Dispatch and I are usually talking about two different things, Pete.[5] [*Laughter*]

Q. Not on military affairs. Not on military affairs. But this 95 percent of our secret information which you want to keep secret has been disclosed?

THE PRESIDENT. That is the information I have from Central Intelligence.

Q. Well, Mr. President, who classified that 95 percent as secret?

THE PRESIDENT. The military.

Q. The military? Thank you.

THE PRESIDENT. Military and State.

Q. Mr. President, could you say what is the unit of information? Is it 95 percent of the facts, or 95 percent of the documents or maps? How is the 95 percent figure arrived at?

THE PRESIDENT. It takes into consideration all the things you mentioned.

Q. Mr. President, I am a little confused. Was that the Yale survey——

THE PRESIDENT. That's right.

Q. ——that you are thinking about, that

said that 95 percent of the secret information has been revealed?

THE PRESIDENT. That's correct.

Q. Mr. President, I would like to raise a case in point and get your reaction to it. Yesterday, Mr. Short announced on your behalf, another atomic bomb had been exploded [6]——

THE PRESIDENT. That's right.

Q. ——and said that further details would not be given, because it would adversely affect our national security. Right after that, the Associated Press came through with a story quoting an unidentified, authoritative source as saying that there had been two explosions, one of them a fizzle, and then quoting still later a Congressman—also unidentified—as saying that the explosions had taken place in the last 3 or 4 days. Now, would you give me some reaction to that, as a specific example of information over and above that which was released by the White House?

THE PRESIDENT. I think that is an example.

Q. What was that, Mr. President?

THE PRESIDENT. I said I think that is an example.

Q. Of what, sir?

THE PRESIDENT. Of disclosing information that should not be disclosed.

Q. Well, Mr. President, don't you think the Russians knew it? I mean——

THE PRESIDENT. They exploded it. Of course they knew it! [*Laughter*]

Q. Yes, sir, so why would it hurt our national defense?

THE PRESIDENT. Because we have got to find out what they are doing, so we will know what to do.

Q. I didn't get the last part? Disclosure of our means of detecting——

THE PRESIDENT. That's right—that's right.

[5] Raymond P. Brandt of the St. Louis Post-Dispatch.

[6] See Item 246.

That's right—that is exactly right.

Q. Mr. President, how far did this Yale survey figure in the decision to put out this order?

THE PRESIDENT. I didn't sign the order until I got it.

Q. Mr. President, some of this information comes out from Congress. Now the Executive order doesn't apply to that. What about the responsibility of the publisher on information released by Congressmen?

THE PRESIDENT. I can't answer that.

Q. Mr. President, this may be—I may be simple-minded about this——

THE PRESIDENT. No, you're not, Smitty.[7]

Q. ——but how did Yale know? [*Laughter*]

THE PRESIDENT. They made the survey.

Q. Instead of Princeton and Harvard?

Q. How did they get all this secret information?

THE PRESIDENT. They made a survey and supplied it to Central Intelligence. That is how it came about.

Q. I just wonder what Yale was doing with that information?

THE PRESIDENT. They got it out of the newspapers and magazines and sent it down here, and Central Intelligence came to the conclusion that they knew that 95 percent of it was disclosed.

Q. Mr. President, did the CIA recognize and agree with the Yale survey that 95 percent——

THE PRESIDENT. Yes. Yes.

Q. They agreed with it?

THE PRESIDENT. Yes. They made the report to me.

Q. The CIA reported to you?

THE PRESIDENT. Yes.

Q. Mr. President, recently the Defense Department gave out certain information about the Matador, also on these guided

missiles, and so forth. That was published probably in every paper in the land. Was that the publishers' responsibility not to publish that?

THE PRESIDENT. I think so, if they want to protect the country.

Q. Wouldn't it be better to tighten up over at Defense?

THE PRESIDENT. That is what we are doing. I say, that is what we are doing, and that is what you are fussing about.

Q. Do you think publishers—if the publishers wanted to protect the country, they shouldn't have printed the pictures——

THE PRESIDENT. They ought to think about the welfare of the country, just the same as I do, and I think most of them would, if they would stop and think about it.

Q. Mr. President, I don't want to defend editors, but——

THE PRESIDENT. It's all right with me.

Q. ——these maps were used as part of the civilian defense program, to make the people alert to the dangers of atomic bombs.

THE PRESIDENT. I agree, but then I don't think that it should have been made available to the Russians.

Q. Mr. President, do I understand that you are inferring that there was no A-bomb explosion in Russia that fizzled?

THE PRESIDENT. I am making no inferences at all. I made the announcement yesterday, the only one that I can make.

Q. Mr. President, I would like to ask a question that I think maybe my editors are going to ask me if I don't ask you.

THE PRESIDENT. All right.

Q. Are you suggesting that perhaps—that the editors and publishers that we supply our news stories to, should ask some agency in the Government——

THE PRESIDENT. No, I am not.

Q. ——whether a thing should be published or not?

THE PRESIDENT. No, I am not. I am asking the editors and the publishers to take the same viewpoint of the safety of the United States that I take, and I am not asking them to ask anybody to help them do it. They ought to know.

Q. I know that many times we receive statements from Members of Congress, for instance, and we go ahead and write stories about those statements. Perhaps many times a reporter feels that that information might be of a security nature, but if it is on the record up there on the Hill, there is nothing we can really do except to go ahead and put it out.

THE PRESIDENT. That is up to you. The safety of the country is in your hands just the same as it is in mine.

Q. Mr. President, do you think everyone in Washington talks too much?

THE PRESIDENT. I wouldn't say that.

[2.] Q. Mr. President, I have a—if I may inject a political question which—we were down in the Governors' Conference, and Jimmy Byrnes [8] seems to have had some information that you were not going to run again, the burden of the office is too much, and that the two-term constitutional amendment really shows that the people apply it to you, and in case you do run—I mean, he will oppose you; and his own candidates are Senator Russell of Georgia and Senator Byrd of Virginia?

THE PRESIDENT. Jim didn't get his information from me.

Q. What's that?

THE PRESIDENT. I said Jim didn't get his information from me.

Q. Do you think he is on the—do you think he has made a fair appraisal——

THE PRESIDENT. I have no comment on that.

Q. What's your comment on his candidates, sir?

[8] James F. Byrnes, Governor of South Carolina.

THE PRESIDENT. No comment.

Q. Do you think they would be good men for the Presidency, sir?

THE PRESIDENT. No comment.

[3.] Q. Mr. President, in your reading of the—of your written statement, parenthetically you said, as I got it, that the Yale survey found that 95 percent of military information had been made public?

THE PRESIDENT. Of our secret information. That covers everything.

Q. Had been made public?

THE PRESIDENT. Not just military, but State and everything—that's right.

[4.] Q. Mr. President, there has been a controversy recently about the removal of crosses from 13,000 graves in Hawaii, and Mrs. Rogers of Massachusetts has introduced a bill to force the Army to restore those crosses to the graves. I wonder if you have been consulted, or what you think about it?

THE PRESIDENT. No, I haven't. I haven't. I know nothing about it. [9]

[5.] Q. Mr. President, could I ask one practical question? What will happen to a reporter who prints something the Government doesn't want printed?

THE PRESIDENT. Nothing. We have had him print things that would cause our men to be shot in the back, and nothing was done to them, right in the middle of the war.

[6.] Q. Mr. President, could you give us some information about this White House conference, concerning which Mr. Stassen testified on the Hill, dealing with aid to China? [10] There seems to be a little confusion——

[9] See Item 251[8].

[10] On October 1 Harold E. Stassen, president of the University of Pennsylvania, stated before the Subcommittee on Internal Security of the Senate Judiciary Committee that a White House conference had been held in October 1949 during which the proposal had been made to withdraw all aid from Chiang Kai-shek's government in China. See also Item 251 [25].

THE PRESIDENT. I have no recollection of any such conference.

Q. You have no such recollection?

THE PRESIDENT. No such recollection of any such conference.

[7.] Q. I would like to ask two questions that have been suggested by journalists visiting the conference this morning. The first question is, does the question of what line the Western allies hold in Germany— that is, in case of attack—the Elbe or the Rhine or the French quarter—does that depend on whether or not the German people agree to contribute to their own defense?

THE PRESIDENT. That is a military question, and I can't answer it.

[8.] Q. The second question, do you favor a free election over all Germany on the subject of being united, as suggested by the Adenauer government?

THE PRESIDENT. I can't answer that question, either.

[9.] Q. Mr. President, do you think that the continuing Russian A-bomb tests have made the danger of world war III more imminent?

THE PRESIDENT. I am not sure. I hope it hasn't.

[10.] Q. Mr. President, do the security rules apply to broadcasters and telecasters as distinguished from publishers?

THE PRESIDENT. Oh yes, it should.

Q. You didn't mention it.

Q. I have heard broadcasters, and I listen to a lot of them talk about visits they have had to Korea, and reveal what our strategy is going to be. And you can't fight battles on that basis.

Mr. Short: Mr. President, so far as the order itself is concerned, it applies only to officials and employees of the United States Government.

THE PRESIDENT. Joe wants me to make it perfectly clear that this order only applies to the officials of the United States Govern-

ment. My comments, though, apply to everybody who gives away our state secrets.

[11.] Q. Mr. President, I want to ask you, so there won't be any confusion, is the Government going to decontrol meat?

THE PRESIDENT. No. Period! We are going to enforce the rules against people who are disobeying the law under meat control.

Q. Well, is the OPS going to be aided by any other Government agencies?

THE PRESIDENT. Every agency of the Government will cooperate with them.

Q. In the enforcement?

THE PRESIDENT. Yes.

[12.] Q. Mr. President, as you must have known about this bomb for quite a time, is there any relationship between the fear of the new explosion in Russia and this Executive order?

THE PRESIDENT. No relation whatever. The order was signed before we knew the bomb had gone off.

Q. As I remember it, that was released at the Pentagon—on the Matador—with photographs at the same time. The question was asked the White House later, was that one of the secret weapons that you have referred to?

THE PRESIDENT. Which one was that? I don't know what you are talking about?

Q. Matador. As I understood your report——

THE PRESIDENT. Yes.

Q. ——there should have been no news printed on that?

THE PRESIDENT. Yes.

Q. Well now, when the Department of Defense hands us photographs and stories, are we supposed to censor that ourselves?

THE PRESIDENT. Well, do you believe in saving the United States from becoming attacked?

Q. I don't think it should have been given out at the Pentagon.

THE PRESIDENT. Well, that is your opinion, and you are entitled to it.

Q. Well, Mr. President, is the effect of what you are asking now, the—that the editors of the country impose a voluntary censorship?

THE PRESIDENT. I am asking them to use good judgment for the safety of the United States. I am not asking for any censorship at all.

Q. Regardless of what is put out from the Pentagon?

THE PRESIDENT. That's right—or anybody else.

Q. Mr. President, wouldn't that practically require the establishment of a security officer in every newsroom in helping to standardize their principles?

THE PRESIDENT. Well, I don't know how you can, when I read some of the papers. But I am just telling you what I think, that patriotism is universal, and the welfare of the United States is the first thing we ought to think about.

Q. Well, Mr. President, you told us at the news conference that this pilotless plane was one of the new weapons about which you had spoken at San Francisco.[11]

THE PRESIDENT. Did I? I don't remember it.

Q. I was just wondering——

THE PRESIDENT. I don't remember.

[13.] Q. Mr. President, recently Senator McMahon made a speech in Congress, in which he said among other things that a few billion dollars more spent on atomic weapons production can put such weapons on a mass-produced basis. That would make each weapon cost less than one tank now costs. Through that, the country could save a great deal of money in its defense efforts, and in effect could do away with our present conventional weapons, reduce our Armed Forces and make a great deal of saving in

that way. Is there any shortcut to national defense?

THE PRESIDENT. No, there is not.

[14.] Q. Mr. President, getting back once more to this 95 percent figure, may we have permission to quote this line: "Remember that 95 percent of our secret information has been revealed by the newspapers and slick magazines, and that is what I am trying to stop"?

THE PRESIDENT. Yes.

[15.] Q. Mr. President, when Mr. Dulles[12] left your office yesterday—when Dulles left your office yesterday, he indicated you might have some comment on his visit?

THE PRESIDENT. Well, I sent for him to offer to make him Ambassador to Japan, and he didn't think he should take the job because he thought he ought to try to save the Republican Party from going isolationist. [*Laughter*]

Q. Do you think that is a worthy objective?

THE PRESIDENT. I certainly do. [*More laughter*]

Q. What was the question?

THE PRESIDENT. They wanted to know what Mr. Dulles came to see me about. I sent for him—sent for Mr. Dulles—and told him that I would make him Ambassador to Japan if he wanted to be, and he said he couldn't take the job because he wanted to stay in civil life and try to save the Republican Party from isolationism!

Reporter: Thank you, Mr. President.

THE PRESIDENT. That's all right.

NOTE: President Truman's two hundred and eighty-first news conference was held in the Indian Treaty Room (Room 474) in the Executive Office Building at 10:40 a.m. on Thursday, October 4, 1951.

[11] See Items 215, 224 [6].

[12] On October 4, the White House released the text of a letter from John Foster Dulles reporting on the conclusion of his mission as Special Representative to the President regarding the Japanese peace settlement.

248   Statement by Direction of the President Clarifying His News Conference Remarks on Security Information. *October 4, 1951*

THE PRESIDENT has directed me to clarify his views on security information as follows:

1. Every citizen—including officials and publishers—has a duty to protect our country.

2. Citizens who receive military information for publication from responsible officials qualified to judge the relationship of such information to the national security may rightfully assume that it is safe to publish the information.

3. Citizens who receive military information from sources not having the necessary responsibilities and qualifications to evaluate such information should, as loyal Americans, exercise the most careful judgment in determining the safety of publishing such information.

4. The recent Executive order on classified information does not in any way alter the right of citizens to publish anything.

NOTE: The statement was issued by Joseph Short, Secretary to the President. See also Items 233, 234, 247 [1], 302.

249   Remarks on the Golden Jubilee of the American Motion Picture Theater. *October 8, 1951*

I AM happy today to take a part in the 50th anniversary celebration of the motion picture theater. I have some very vivid recollections of the first ones I saw. In those days, admission was 5 cents and you could stay as long as you wanted to.

The great stars of that time, I judge, were—maybe I had better not name them, because some of them wouldn't like to have their ages stated. They had great comedians in those days, as well as we have today.

The show has grown to be one of our greatest assets in the dissemination of information and entertainment.

I just wonder what will be the situation 50 years from now? I hardly believe that I'll see it, but I hope I may. I know some of these young ladies will.

So I congratulate you on the 50th anniversary. I hope you will have 50 more prosperous years.

NOTE: The President spoke at 3:30 p.m. in the Rose Garden at the White House.

250   Statement by the President Upon Signing the Mutual Security Act. *October 10, 1951*

I HAVE today signed H.R. 5113, the Mutual Security Act of 1951. Under this legislation, the United States will continue to participate in the great collective defense effort of the free nations and to assist free peoples around the world who want to develop and safeguard their freedom and maintain the peace.

This is constructive legislation—hopeful legislation. The amounts authorized are less than I requested but this act will bring substantial help to those who are eager to help themselves. It will enable our free nation partners to continue to increase their contributions to the common defense effort. Their contributions are as important as our own. We must never forget that we are just as dependent upon the efforts of other nations as they are on ours.

This act will mean military equipment for troops who want to be able to defend their homelands if attacked. It will mean raw materials and production equipment for factories that can turn out guns and tanks and planes for the common defense of freedom. It will mean technicians and books, fertilizer and seeds, irrigation pumps and medical supplies, and many other things for people in underdeveloped areas who want to grow in strength and independence. In these and many other ways, this act will mean life and energy for the great collective effort of the free nations to build a better world.

The peoples of the underdeveloped areas of the world want desperately to take fuller advantage of their human and natural resources. We are now supplying material and technical assistance to help them realize these aspirations, and I believe that we should continue to do so. I am thinking particularly of the necessity of supporting the free nations of Asia in their efforts to strengthen the economic foundations of their independence.

There is some misapprehension that the free world is embarked on nothing but an armaments race with the Soviet Empire. This is not the case. What the free world is actually doing is to unleash the constructive forces of human freedom. We are building armaments, of course—we would be fools if we did not. But we are doing far more than that. We are joining with and helping the free nations organize into stronger international associations than ever before. We are helping to restore the productive power of war-shattered countries. We are helping to build up the health, the education, and the welfare of free men all around the world.

In short, we are joining with other peoples to prove by deeds that the way to freedom is the way of peace and human progress.

NOTE: As enacted, H.R. 5113 is Public Law 165, 82d Congress (65 Stat. 373).

251   The President's News Conference of *October 11, 1951*

THE PRESIDENT. Please be seated.

I have no special announcements to make. I will try to answer questions, if I can.

[1.] Q. Mr. President, I assume that you have not seen this list of awards made by Oscar Ewing[1] this week, and announced——

THE PRESIDENT. No, I haven't. No, I haven't.

Q. May I just read one of them to you? It is very short—about four lines long. Doctor Robert F. Winch, Northwestern University, has been awarded a grant to study unconscious factors governing courtship and mate selection, and the various mutual needs entering into the choice of married partners will be surveyed in the light of his findings in the field of mental health. [*Laughter*]

I wonder if you would tell us anything about what this means?

THE PRESIDENT. No sir, I can't.

Q. When you find out "what is this thing called love," what are we going to do about it?

THE PRESIDENT. Well, sir, that has been a

---

[1] Administrator, Federal Security Agency.

question ever since Adam and Eve, and I guess it always will be. [*More laughter*]

Q. Mr. President——

THE PRESIDENT. Tony [2] wants to ask me a question.

[2.] Q. I wanted to know, Mr. President, what you will do about appointing new judges in Illinois, in view of the Senate's action rejecting the others? [3]

THE PRESIDENT. Well, we will have to have judges out there sometime, but it will take some deliberation to find good ones, I fear.

What was your question now?

[3.] Q. Mr. President, Jim Forrestal's diary [4] reports that you had a letter after the 1948 election, in which Bob Taft said that he and Mrs. Taft were not too unhappy about the outcome. One, did he write it; and two, do you expect a like letter from him next year? [*Laughter*]

THE PRESIDENT. You put a "cracker" on your question. If I told Jim Forrestal that, I certainly must have had the letter. I haven't had a chance to look it up, but I think it was a letter of congratulations on being elected as President, just as I had bushels of them at the time.

[4.] Q. Mr. President, do you expect to make any more recommendations to Congress this session on the Hoover Commission reports?

THE PRESIDENT. We are working on that situation now.

[5.] Q. Mr. President, I wonder if I could pin down that question a little more? In that letter Senator Taft actually did say that he was not——

THE PRESIDENT. I do not recall what was in the letter. I will look it up and read it, and I will tell you what he said.

[6.] Q. Mr. President, do you have any plans to withdraw the nomination of this Beck for Recorder? [5]

THE PRESIDENT. No, I do not.

Q. Has there been a suggestion by the Senate District Committee, sir, in regard to that?

THE PRESIDENT. No, they have further consideration to give it.

[7.] Q. Mr. President, have you any comment on the House Public Works Committee action in putting off any further consideration on the St. Lawrence Seaway until after January 1?

THE PRESIDENT. No comment. I am sorry they did it, is about all I could say.

[8.] Q. Mr. President, last week you were asked about the Army's order for the removal of crosses from 13,000 graves in Hawaii, and you said you didn't know anything about it. I wonder if you had looked into it, and if you knew anything new about it?

THE PRESIDENT. Yes, I have looked into it, and they are treating all the soldiers exactly alike. They have arranged to meet the Korean situation just like they have in other places, and the markers are being placed as fast as they can be obtained. [6]

[9.] Q. Mr. President, did you ever ask James Finnegan [7] not to resign his collectorship in St. Louis?

THE PRESIDENT. My recollection is rather hazy on that. They said that I did once.

Q. When did you first learn that he had extracurricular activities?

THE PRESIDENT. Just a short time ago.

[10.] Q. Mr. President, you are going to give a speech at Winston-Salem, I believe,

---

[2] Ernest B. Vaccaro of the Associated Press.

[3] See Item 165 [8].

[4] "The Forrestal Diaries," edited by Walter Millis with collaboration of E. S. Duffield, New York, Viking Press, 1951.

[5] The nomination of Earl W. Beck of Kansas City, Mo., to be Recorder of Deeds for the District of Columbia was sent to the Senate on September 26, 1951.

[6] See Item 247 [4].

[7] James P. Finnegan, former collector, first district of Missouri, Bureau of Internal Revenue.

next week. I wonder if you are going to answer any points raised by Governor Byrnes,[8] or if you will have anything to say there about the Southern political situation?

THE PRESIDENT. No, I will not. That is an educational meeting.

[11.] Q. Mr. President, one more question, do I understand correctly that you approve of the way the Army is handling this cross situation in Hawaii?

THE PRESIDENT. Yes. They are straightening everything out. I think you will find, if you will inquire down in the Department of Defense, that everything has been worked out to the satisfaction of everybody.

[12.] Q. Mr. President, Senator Lodge today suggested use of atomic weapons in Korea. Do you have any views on that?

THE PRESIDENT. No comment.

Q. Mr. President——

[13.] Q. Mr. President, do you have any general observation on the matter of Mr. Finnegan's extracurricular activities?

THE PRESIDENT. I did not approve of them—do not approve of them and never have.

What was the question over here?

[14.] Q. I was going to ask, sir—I believe I am up to date on this—I think the nomination of Miss Frieda Hennock for the judgeship is still before the committee. If it shouldn't come out before they recess, will you give her an interim appointment?

THE PRESIDENT. I will take that under consideration when the time comes.[9]

[15.] Q. Mr. President, what do you think generally of the idea of collectors of Internal Revenue having outside employment?

THE PRESIDENT. I don't think they should have, and never have thought so. I am still of that same opinion.

Q. Mr. President, are you going to do anything to stop it? As I understand it, it is permissible for collectors to have an outside——

THE PRESIDENT. Well, you will find that the vast majority of them do not have. Those that get in trouble are those that have.

Q. Sir, would you be in favor of a regulation forbidding their outside employment?

THE PRESIDENT. We will have to look at that. I don't believe that Government employees should have any extracurricular activities at all. I never have thought so, but they are making it so difficult to get good men in public service that I don't know whether that is the right thing to do or not. We will have to look into it. I have expressed my opinion on it.

Q. Mr. President, you said they are making it so difficult. Who are *they,* sir?

THE PRESIDENT. You ought to know.

Q. Well, I am asking you, sir?

THE PRESIDENT. You ought to know. If you can't answer that question, you don't know what is going on. [*Laughter*] [*Pause*]

Are you out of "soap" today, or what?

Q. Well, we're writing now.

Q. It's all so fast.

[16.] Q. Mr. President, do you plan to nominate a new man, sir, for the TVA to replace Waring?[10]

THE PRESIDENT. Yes. Yes. When I am ready to announce it, I will let you know.

[17.] Q. Mr. President, in the matter of the Illinois judgeships, the next time you said there would be some deliberations. On the next time, will you consult Senator Douglas?

THE PRESIDENT. I will take that under consideration.

---

[8] Governor James F. Byrnes of South Carolina.

[9] See Item 283.

[10] The nomination of Frank A. Waring as a member of the Board of Directors of the Tennessee Valley Authority was sent to the Senate on August 22, 1951, and withdrawn October 1, 1951.

[18.] Q. Mr. President, have you any-one in mind as a successor to Mon Wallgren as Chairman of the Federal Power Commission?

THE PRESIDENT. Not ready yet. As soon as I am ready, why I will let you know.

[19.] Q. Mr. President, what do you think of the plan the former Treasury Secretary Morgenthau came up with today, of having the United Nations create an authority to buy the British interests in the Anglo-Iranian oil——

THE PRESIDENT. I haven't given it any consideration, and I can't comment on it.

[20.] Q. Mr. President, I was just wondering—we had to come over here to beat you to the elevator, and we didn't see former Senator Stewart[11]—I just wonder if you could tell us what he talked to you about?

THE PRESIDENT. He just came in to pay his respects. He and I were good friends in the Senate, and he was in town and he just wanted to see me. We discussed old times, principally.

[21.] Q. Mr. President, would you favor taking the collectors of Internal Revenue out of politics, as the postmasterships were, and make them civil service?

THE PRESIDENT. Well, I am not so sure of that. I am not so sure of that.

Q. I wonder why?

THE PRESIDENT. Because sometimes it is very difficult to handle civil service employees when they get in places of responsibility. There are so many regulations, it would be exceedingly difficult to fire one when he went wrong. And I like to retain the idea that when a man is not right, he can be immediately fired.

Q. There have been accusations by the committees investigating this, that they haven't been fired fast enough in the present situation?

[11] Former Senator Arthur Thomas (Tom) Stewart of Tennessee.

THE PRESIDENT. Well, I think they are wrong about that. They have been fired every time one of them has been found to be wrong.

[22.] Q. Mr. President, on the Illinois judges, do you intend to withdraw the nominations of the persons you sent up to the Senate?

THE PRESIDENT. I understand the Senate rejected them. There is nothing—no further action is necessary.

Q. I see, sir.

THE PRESIDENT. You see, the Senate, having rejected them, that finishes it.

Q. I thought perhaps some move was—further on your part?

THE PRESIDENT. Nothing more to do about those two judges.

Q. Mr. President, just to clear that question, the difference between now and what you said at a previous press conference, the Senate had not actually rejected them then?

THE PRESIDENT. That's right.

Q. It hadn't been brought to the floor?

THE PRESIDENT. It hadn't been brought to the floor.

If you remember a bit of history, Andrew Jackson appointed Martin Van Buren Ambassador to Great Britain. He was 3 months in London and then was rejected by the Senate. It didn't injure his reputation, for he afterwards became President of the United States. [*Laughter*]

[23.] Q. Mr. President, Bernard Baruch said yesterday that the Russians had invited him to come to Moscow a couple of times to discuss his A-bomb control program, in 1948 and 1949, and he did not accept the invitations. Then, when he was asked why, he said that answer would have to come from officials of the Government. I wonder were you in any way involved in his not going? Do you know why——

THE PRESIDENT. I knew nothing about it. I knew nothing about it whatever. All

I know is what I see in the papers.

[24.] Q. Mr. President, do you think it would be useful, say after the British elections, to have another Big Four meeting, and if so would you be willing to go to Europe or the Middle East for such meetings?

THE PRESIDENT. I have no comment on that question.

[25.] Q. Mr. President, have you found any new records in connection with the dispute over the conference with Senator Vandenberg and others on the China policy——

THE PRESIDENT. I think that Secretary Acheson answered that completely and thoroughly yesterday in the statement.[12]

[26.] Q. Mr. President, I understand the AMVET group which you saw today asked you to get rid of Carl Gray?[13]

THE PRESIDENT. I haven't seen the letter. I understand they left a letter, but they didn't talk to me about it.

Q. Would you be likely to get rid of him, under the circumstances?

THE PRESIDENT. Well, you know how I am about the people I put in places, and I am rather contrary about having other people tell me what to do with them. [*Laughter*]

[27.] Q. Mr. President, I sort of hate to ask you this—but a lot of people want to know—have you had any contributions to your library recently?

THE PRESIDENT. I don't know. I don't know, and I don't like to refer to that as a

library of mine. It is an archives building that will belong to the United States Government, and that will contain the official papers and gifts that have been received by the President from all over the world for public use. And the land and everything will be deeded to the United States Government just as it was at Hyde Park, and there is a law authorizing such a procedure. But there is no law authorizing appropriations for its construction, and I understand that there has been an effort made to raise the funds for the construction of the building, which will then become the property of the Government of the United States.

Q. Mr. President, you are now talking about the proposed Truman Memorial Library?

THE PRESIDENT. I don't want any memorial to me! We are talking about the proposed building which will contain the archives of my administration. That is what it is, Eddie.[14]

Mr. Folliard: I don't want any memorial either, Mr. President.

THE PRESIDENT. I know you don't, Eddie. [*Laughter*]

Q. Could you elaborate on what you authorized Secretary Short to say the other day in connection with that?

THE PRESIDENT. Secretary Short said just what I authorized him to say.[15] [*Laughter*]

Q. Well, Mr. President, I am not quite clear—do you think there should be such a building?

THE PRESIDENT. Yes, I do.

Q. But you did not know about the manner in which Senator Anderson and his——

---

[12] On October 10 Secretary of State Dean Acheson commented on the testimony given by Harold E. Stassen on October 1 before the Subcommittee on Internal Security of the Senate Judiciary Committee (see Item 247 [6]).

Secretary Acheson denied Mr. Stassen's allegations that withdrawal of aid to Nationalist China had been proposed as a "dramatic peace move" at a White House conference in October 1949. The text of Secretary Acheson's statement is printed in the Department of State Bulletin (vol. 25, p. 656).

[13] Carl R. Gray, Jr., Administrator of Veterans Affairs.

[14] Edward T. Folliard of the Washington Post.

[15] At a press conference on October 10, Joseph H. Short, Secretary to the President, stated that the President favored the establishment of an archives or library to house his papers but opposed letters requesting contributions for the project. Such a letter had been sent out over the signature of Senator Clinton P. Anderson of New Mexico. The name of George E. Allen appeared on the letterhead.

THE PRESIDENT. No, I didn't know.

Q. ——colleagues were proposing to do it?

THE PRESIDENT. Mr. Short answered that. Mr. Short answered that. I didn't know anything about that procedure.

Q. Do you have any method by which you think it could possibly be financed?

THE PRESIDENT. No, I have not. I have no method at all. All I hope is that there will be a place where these papers can be stored without being scattered all over the country.

You know, the papers of nearly all the Presidents have been misplaced, and it has been very difficult to get the facts of their administrative acts. And this new archives building bill which I asked the Congress to pass is proposing to take care of that situation, not only for the President, but for all the top administrators of every administration. And then the historians will have access to the papers whenever they want to see them, and they will be all put in one place.

Q. Do you think that it is better to have them concentrated in Washington?

THE PRESIDENT. Yes, I think because it gives access to people who would not otherwise have the opportunity to see what they contain. It will be under the control of Archives. The Archives Building is fast becoming too small to hold what we have there now.

Q. When President Roosevelt decided to have his at Hyde Park, the argument was made that it would be better for scholars if it were all concentrated here, because then they could get——

THE PRESIDENT. I don't agree with that.

Q. You don't agree?

THE PRESIDENT. No, I don't agree. And I think President Roosevelt was right in what he did.

[28.] Q. Mr. President, in Forrestal's diary there is a report that you told him that you hoped General Eisenhower would take the hint and resign, so that you could put General Bradley in as Chief of Staff?

THE PRESIDENT. No indeed. No indeed. General Eisenhower came to see me and asked me to appoint General Bradley. And I never asked General Eisenhower to quit at all. Whenever I have been able to use him, I have always used him ever since.

Q. You didn't say to Mr. Forrestal that you hoped he would take the hint?

THE PRESIDENT. I never had any such conversation that I recollect. I feel—I am sure I didn't say that, because I am very fond of Eisenhower. He was an excellent Chief of Staff, and General Bradley was, too, and so was General Marshall. I haven't had a bad one.

[29.] Q. Mr. President, you said that you would like to see the archives of the President handled in a library. Would—and I say this very respectfully—would it include carbon copies of letters that you have written?

THE PRESIDENT. Oh, yes. It will contain everything. I have got a stack of files over there that is larger than any other President ever had, and it will fill two rooms like this.

Q. Mr. President, Mr. Anderson and Mr. Allen will continue in charge of this collection?

THE PRESIDENT. I suppose that Mr. Allen will. I didn't know that Anderson had any connection with it.

Q. He wrote the letter.

Q. Clint Anderson?

THE PRESIDENT. I know he did, but I say that is the first I knew about it. They are excellent and very dear friends, but sometimes your friends get overzealous.

Q. What was that last, sir?

THE PRESIDENT. I said those two gentlemen are very good friends of mine, and sometimes your good friends get overzealous without any intention of doing any harm, and I am sure that is what happened in this case.

Reporter: Thank you, Mr. President.

THE PRESIDENT. You're welcome.

NOTE: President Truman's two hundred and eighty-second news conference was held in the Indian Treaty Room (Room 474) in the Executive Office Building at 4:05 p.m. on Thursday, October 11, 1951.

252 Letters to the Chairman of the Wage Stabilization Board Authorizing Investigations of Labor Disputes Affecting Aircraft Production. *October* 12, 1951

Dear Mr. Feinsinger:

On the basis of the information and advice submitted to me by the Office of Defense Mobilization and the Federal Mediation and Conciliation Service, I am of the opinion that the dispute between the Douglas Aircraft Company, Long Beach, California, and the United Automobile, Aircraft and Agricultural Implement Workers of America (C.I.O.), is of a character which substantially threatens the progress of national defense. Thus, in accordance with the terms of E.O. 10233, I am referring the dispute to the Wage Stabilization Board and asking that the Board investigate and inquire into the issues in dispute and promptly report to me with its recommendations to the parties as to fair and equitable terms of settlement.

The Director of the Office of Defense Mobilization has reported to me on the serious effect of the strike on the production of C-124 transports. The Douglas Company is the sole producer of the C-124 transport and the Air Force has no other type which is capable of performing the mission of this aircraft. It was the C-124 which recently accomplished the evacuation from Korea of 127 wounded in a single flight. Air Force operations are already being seriously impaired by the loss of production. Continuance of the stoppage would mean loss of more planes and impose an even more serious disadvantage on the Air Force.

The report of the Federal Mediation and Conciliation Service indicates that negotiations to date have been unsuccessful and that, although full use has been made of mediation and conciliation facilities, the strike persists and is likely to persist.

I am asking the Federal Mediation and Conciliation Service to provide the Board with a record of the issues in dispute.

It is my earnest hope that the men involved will comply with your request that they return to work while the matter is before the Board and that the utilization of the Board's machinery will thus serve its purpose of restoring to production the facilities necessary to the national defense. I am sure that, in that event, the Board will proceed promptly in its task of recommending to the parties fair and equitable terms of settlement of the dispute.

Very sincerely yours,

HARRY S. TRUMAN

Dear Mr. Feinsinger:

On the basis of the information and advice submitted to me by the Office of Defense Mobilization and the Federal Mediation and Conciliation Service, I am of the opinion that the dispute between the Wright Aeronautical Corporation, Woodridge, New Jersey, and the United Automobile, Aircraft and Agricultural Implement Workers of America (C.I.O.), is of a character which substantially threatens the progress of national defense. Thus, in accordance with the terms of E.O. 10233, I am referring the dispute to the Wage Stabilization Board and asking that the Board investigate and inquire into the issues in dispute and promptly report to me with its recommendations to the parties as to fair and equitable terms of settlement.

The Director of the Office of Defense Mobilization has reported to me on the serious effect of the strike on the production of jet and reciprocating engines. Even before the strike, engine deliveries from the plant were behind schedule. Since the Wright Aeronautical Corporation is the sole source of supply for the type of engines it produces, the stoppage is having a serious impact on the progress of the defense program.

The report of the Federal Mediation and Conciliation Service indicates that negotiations to date have been unsuccessful and that, although full use has been made of mediation and conciliation facilities, the strike persists and is likely to persist.

I am asking the Federal Mediation and Conciliation Service to provide the Board with a record of the issues in dispute.

It is my earnest hope that the men in-

volved will comply with your request that they return to work while the matter is before the Board and that the utilization of the Board's machinery will thus serve its purpose of restoring to production the facilities necessary to the national defense. I am sure that, in that event, the Board will proceed promptly in its task of recommending to the parties fair and equitable terms of settlement of the dispute.

Very sincerely yours,

HARRY S. TRUMAN

[Honorable Nathan P. Feinsinger, Chairman, Wage Stabilization Board, Washington, D.C.]

NOTE: Executive Order 10233, dated April 21, 1951, is entitled "Amending Executive Order 10161 With Respect to Wage Stabilization and Settlement of Labor Disputes" (3 CFR, 1949–1953 Comp., p. 743).

On February 16, 1952, a panel appointed by the Wage Stabilization Board recommended a general wage increase in the Douglas Aircraft Company dispute of 10 to 20 cents an hour. On May 22, 1952, Mr. Feinsinger informed the President that the parties in the interval between February 9 and April 17 had reached agreement pursuant to Board recommendations on all issues except union security.

Shortly after the President referred the dispute to the Wage Stabilization Board, the employees of the Wright Aeronautical Corporation voluntarily returned to work. On February 8, 1952, the Wage Stabilization Board recommended a wage increase of 12 cents an hour. In an agreement reached on March 29, this proposal was adopted. The increase was made retroactive to October 15, 1951.

---

253   Remarks to a Delegation From the American Hungarian Federation.   *October* 12, 1951

THANK YOU very much. I appreciate that. I appreciate what you have said very much.

Our only effort in the world is for world peace. We want all the peoples of the world to enjoy the same individual liberties which we enjoy. We had hoped, after our conversations at Yalta and Potsdam, that that would be the case with Romania, Bulgaria, Hungary, Poland, and Czechoslovakia, but it is not, I am sorry to say.

We are going to continue our efforts to see if we can't get freedom in those countries as we enjoy it here.

You people know that you don't have to be afraid here. You are not going to be arrested because you don't think like I do. You are not going to be arrested because somebody says you are wrong in your political beliefs.

And that is what I would like to see in the whole world. And as long as I am President, I shall keep working for that sort of arrangement.

I can't tell you how much I appreciate this scroll.

NOTE: The President spoke at 12:55 p.m. in the Rose Garden at the White House.

Leaders of the Federation, which is composed of religious, fraternal, and other organizations whose members are of Hungarian ancestry, presented a scroll to the President, thanking him for his statement of July 27 denouncing the Communist Government of Hungary for mass internments and deportations of citizens (see Item 173).

254 Letter to the President of the Senate Requesting Appropriations for the Enforcement of Antimonopoly Legislation. *October* 13, 1951

[Released October 13, 1951. Dated October 12, 1951]

Sir:

I have the honor to transmit herewith for the consideration of the Congress, a proposed supplemental appropriation for Fiscal Year 1952 in the amount of $300,000.

This sum is urgently needed so that the Federal Trade Commission can begin a full-scale effort to enforce Public Law 899, the anti-merger statute passed last year by the 81st Congress. Approval of this appropriation request would restore funds eliminated by the Congress in passing the Independent Offices Appropriation Act for this fiscal year.

This anti-merger statute which I signed on December 29, 1950, is one of the most important anti-monopoly measures enacted by the Congress since 1914. But without funds for enforcement, its constructive purpose will be nullified.

The purpose of Public Law 899 is to arrest the continuing rise in the concentration of economic power by prohibiting business mergers which seriously injure competition and promote monopoly. This statute closes a gaping hole in the Clayton Act of 1914. Under that Act, the Federal Trade Commission had been empowered, among other things, to prevent one concern from obtaining control over a competitor through the purchase of stock, if the result would be to promote monopoly and injure competition in the industry.

However, the Act left a loophole for firms to consolidate their control over an industry by bringing about actual mergers with competitors, buying up their assets rather than their stock.

In the years since the Clayton Act was passed, this practice of acquiring assets had made the restrictions on stock acquisition virtually meaningless. In the last three decades, more than 12,000 mergers have taken place through the purchase of assets, entirely outside the control of the Federal Trade Commission. Undoubtedly, the effect has been to overcome in many industries the restraints on monopoly which the Clayton Act intended.

For years I joined with many others in urging that this loophole be closed. These efforts ended in success when the 81st Congress amended the Clayton Act by Public Law 899, to make acquisition of assets as well as stock subject to review by the Federal Trade Commission.

Yet, it is obvious that the purpose of this new law will be served only to the extent that the Federal Trade Commission can undertake vigorous enforcement. To begin effective enforcement, the Commission must have more funds.

Early this year, shortly after enactment of Public Law 899, I transmitted to the Congress an amendment to the Budget, providing a $500,000 increase in the Commission's appropriation for Fiscal 1952. Unfortunately, while the House Appropriations Committee approved two-thirds of this additional amount, that increase was cut out by an amendment adopted on the House floor. And although $250,000 was at first restored by the Senate Appropriations Committee, that sum, too, was drastically reduced by application of a general cut of 10 percent in the appropriations for most of the agencies under the Independent Offices Appropriation Act.

As a result, the funds which have now been appropriated to the Federal Trade Commission for this fiscal year will not permit anything approaching general enforcement of Public Law 899. The Commission is going to do all it can out of its present appropriation. But at best that will only make possible examination of a small portion of the many mergers now taking place.

This is a very serious prospect which may have really harmful effects on our whole antimonopoly program. The seriousness of the situation is dramatized by what has been happening to corporate mergers since the passage of Public Law 899.

Before that law was enacted, these mergers were taking place at the rate of about 200 a year. But in the months since the law was passed, the rate has shot up to about 750 a year. In the second quarter of 1951, the merger rate reached the highest level in twenty years. Of course, all mergers are not necessarily harmful to competition and do not necessarily increase monopoly. But some of the current mergers undoubtedly are hav-

ing that effect. And all this is happening *after* the Congress has passed legislation which is supposed to regulate these mergers and screen out the dangerous ones.

So long as the Federal Trade Commission is denied adequate funds to begin an effective enforcement job, we can only assume that mergers will continue at an increasing rate. If this is allowed to go on, we may well find ourselves in worse circumstances than before Public Law 899 was ever passed.

That would be a tragic reversal of the fine, progressive action taken by the 81st Congress when it passed this law. I cannot believe that the present Congress would wish to let that happen.

Therefore, it is my earnest hope that the Congress will complete action on this supplemental appropriation in the time remaining before adjournment of the present session. The amount involved is the minimum required by the Federal Trade Commission to begin adequate enforcement of Public Law 899 during the balance of this fiscal year.

Details of this appropriation estimate are set forth in the attached letter from the Director of the Bureau of the Budget.

Respectfully,

HARRY S. TRUMAN

NOTE: In the Second Supplemental Appropriation Act, 1952, signed by the President on November 1, 1951 (65 Stat. 760), the Federal Trade Commission was given an additional appropriation of $100,000 for salaries and expenses. For a statement by the President upon signing the act, see Item 285.

For the statement by the President upon signing bill amending the Clayton Act on December 29, 1950, see 1950 volume, this series, Item 319.

255   Remarks at a Luncheon in Winston-Salem, North Carolina.
October 15, 1951

THANK YOU very much, Mr. Mayor. I shall treasure it all my life. It is very kind and thoughtful of your great city to think

of making this presentation. I shall entrust it to the Secret Service to be sure that I get it home with me.

You remarked that General Washington was here in 1791, 160 years ago, and that he had come by stage coach. The most remarkable thing in our transportation system today is that I came from the capital of the United States in about an hour and a quarter. I imagine that George took at least 24 hours to come from Alexandria, Va., if that is where he started from.

And that is one of the situations that we have to meet. We have progressed so fast in things of that sort, transportation, and the know-how of other things, that we are not yet completely adjusted to them.

I hope we can make that adjustment, and I am sure that this institution we are setting up here today—or starting here today—will help us make that adjustment.

Thank you very much.

NOTE: The President spoke at 12:55 p.m. at "Reynolda," the home of Charles E. Babcock, in Winston-Salem. He was presented with a silver bowl by Mayor Marshall C. Kurfees of Winston-Salem.

256 Address in Winston-Salem at Groundbreaking Ceremonies, Wake Forest College. *October 15, 1951*

Mr. President of Wake Forest, Your Excellency the Governor of North Carolina, distinguished guests, ladies and gentlemen:

It is a privilege for me to be here today.

It is a privilege to join my fellow-Baptists in rejoicing at the enlargement and rebuilding of one of our great institutions.

It is a privilege to join the people of North Carolina in celebrating their devotion to freedom of the mind and spirit.

Freedom of the mind and the spirit are very, very important to us and to the whole world today. I believe the history of Wake Forest College has some significant lessons for us in this regard.

Wake Forest College has given 117 years of distinguished service to education and religion in this great State. Over the years this college has sent thousands of graduates throughout the land to positions of leadership and trust.

This college, like others in every part of our country, has remained loyal to the principle that the purpose of education is to seek the truth.

This is an article of faith that underlies our whole educational system: "Know the truth, and the truth shall make you free."

Students and teachers in American schools, seeking the truth without hindrance of censorship, have been largely responsible for the amazing progress of our country. We believe, in America, that the pursuit of the truth is open to all comers. No group that seeks the truth is a dangerous group, or a subversive group—not in the United States of America, at any rate. We know that any attempt to control the mind of man defeats itself. We know that as long as our schools enjoy freedom, our political liberties are safe.

For this reason, Americans of all parties and creeds can join together in their support of education—public and private.

Here in North Carolina you have built a fine public school system, crowned with a State university respected throughout the academic world. And right here I want to pay a tribute to Gordon Gray. He is one great patriot, and I am very fond of him. At the same time, you have made progress in private education, culminating in the endowment, in one generation, of two such institutions of higher learning as Duke and Wake Forest.

Right here I want to pay a tribute to the people who made this situation possible. It

574

is a wonderful thing when men of great wealth do the patriotic things that are being done here today for this great school.

The history of this college shows how all Americans can unite in support of education. It is a Baptist college; yet the magnificent gift that stimulated its rebuilding came from donors who are not themselves Baptists, and the funds that are to go into these buildings were supplied by all kinds of Protestants without regard to race or creed—and by Catholics and Jews, as well.

A college is an institution that is dedicated to the future. It is based on faith and hope—faith in the basic decency of our fellow men, and hope that the increase of knowledge will promote the general welfare.

This faith and this hope are a very important part of the American way of life, so important that if they are lost, that way of life will be destroyed. Faith that the average American is honest and trustworthy; hope that when he knows the truth, that the truth will make him free. This faith and this hope are the strong foundations on which Wake Forest College was built. They are the foundations on which this Republic has stood, unshaken by all the storms that have beaten upon it.

Yet, there are always some who do not share this faith and hope. These people go up and down the land, wailing that we must not do anything, because it might turn out wrong. For faith and hope, they have substituted suspicion and fear.

This is deplorable, but we should not let it alarm us too much, for after all it is nothing new. It is as old as this college, and a lot older.

Indeed, this college was almost strangled at its birth by this sort of reactionary attitude.

On December 21, 1833, the bill granting a charter to Wake Forest came up for final passage in the North Carolina State Senate.

Without this bill, the college could not have been founded. Yet, the vote was a tie, 29 to 29, and the bill passed only by the deciding vote of the presiding officer. And he certainly made a great name for himself when he cast that vote.

Think what this means. If there had been one more negative vote, there might never have been a Wake Forest College— with all that it has meant to North Carolina and the Nation. You might never have had such great leaders as the presidents of this college—men like W. L. Poteat, who did so much to defend freedom of thought, or Thurman Kitchin, who built undiscouraged through depression and through war. There might have been no opportunity for men like Harold Tribble to lead this institution into an era of greater service to humanity.

How was it possible for 29 men, back in 1833, to vote against such a constructive step as the founding of Wake Forest?

We have no proof whatever that they were unpatriotic men, or selfish men, or evil men. They claimed they were not. Indeed, the facts seem to show that they were simply afraid. They allowed their suspicion and fear to overcome their hope and faith.

They argued that to incorporate Wake Forest was to lead to "a proud and pompous ministry." Can you imagine a Baptist preacher being proud and pompous? They said that this sort of school was bound to become "a curse to the Church of God, and to the nations of the earth."

Their objection, in modern terms, was that the college might turn into a subversive organization which would destroy the American way of life. You hear that all the time now. Of course, Wake Forest had not done anything wrong yet, because it did not even exist. But those men argued that if it were given the right to exist, it might do wrong. Therefore, it ought to be killed in the cradle.

575

Friends of the college argued that it would do good, that it would develop character and intelligence among the people, which is the greatest good that can be done for a nation. But no, in the minds of those 29 men, the hope that it might do good was nothing. The fear that it might do harm was everything. In their minds it was more virtuous—it was safer—to try to avoid doing harm than it was to try to do good. There are a lot of people like that who are with us today by the bushel.

The fear of moving ahead, the unwillingness to try anything new, almost stifled Wake Forest at birth. But let us remember that the forces that nearly prevented the creation of Wake Forest were not peculiar to that time and place. They are deeply embedded in human nature and are alive and powerful today. There are many men of this generation who, like the 29 members of the North Carolina State Senate of 1833, allow their fears to stifle their hopes.

When the fears of such frightened men prevail, whether in a college or in a country, no progress is made, and little is accomplished for the betterment of the world. No institution and no nation can stand before the bar of history and justify itself on the ground that it never did any harm. The question that has to be answered before all mankind is "What good did you do?"

Our country is standing before the bar of history today in a very conspicuous place. All the world is watching us, because all the world knows that the fate of civilization depends, to a very large extent, upon what we do.

At the present time this Nation of ours is engaged in a great series of positive actions to secure the peace in the world. This effort is costing us a great deal—in taxes, in energy, in unwelcome changes in our daily living. It is even costing us the lives of some of our bravest and best young people who are fighting in the frontlines against aggression.

Like every positive effort, this one is being questioned and criticized. There are people who ask whether it is worth doing. There are people who point to the sacrifices, the inconvenience, the cost, and who say it would be better to do nothing—or as close to nothing as possible.

But it is clear, to most of us at least, that the effort is worth making—indeed, we have to make it.

Our great effort for peace is a national effort. It is not the decision of one group or one person. It is the result of our entire national experience, over the last few decades.

By the end of World War II we had learned, as a nation, that we could not have peace by keeping out of the affairs of the world. We were determined to act, positively and vigorously, with other nations, to preserve peace. That is why we embraced the United Nations, and pledged to support it.

Everything that we have done since has been the result of this decision. All we have done, all our treaties with other nations, our defense program, our aid to other countries, has been the result of our determination to uphold the principles of the United Nations.

It has been harder and more dangerous than we expected, because of the refusal of one of the great powers to carry out the spirit of the United Nations, and to live peacefully and cooperatively with its neighbors.

But, if I understand this country correctly, there is no desire to backtrack on the path we have taken toward peace. There is no intention of running out on the obligation we undertook to support the principles of the United Nations Charter. We made our decision, it was the right decision, we are going to follow it out—and that's that.

It is important to remember, as our defense program begins to turn out more and more weapons, and our alliances for defense begin to take effect, that our basic objective—our only objective—is peace—peace for all the world.

I am afraid that some people, here and abroad, believe that the creation of armed defenses must inevitably lead to war. That is not the case. We do not think that war is inevitable.

We believe that the creation of defenses will make war less likely. So long as one country has the power and the forces to overwhelm others, and so long as that country has aggressive intentions, real peace is unattainable. The stronger we become, the more possible it will be to work out solid and lasting arrangements that will prevent war. Our strength will make for peace.

We saw the folly of weakness in the days of Hitler. We know now that we must have defenses when there is an aggressor abroad in the world.

But once we have defenses strong enough to prevent the sneaking, creeping kind of aggression that Hitler practiced—what is the next step? Must we then have a showdown, and a war until one side or the other is completely victorious?

I think not. Our policy is based on the hope that it will be possible to live, without a war, in the same world as the Soviet Union—if the free nations have adequate defenses. As our defenses improve, the chances of negotiating successfully with the Soviet Union will increase. The growth of our defenses will help to convince the leaders of the Soviet Union that peaceful arrangements are in their own self-interest. And as our strength increases, we should be able to negotiate settlements that the Soviet Union will respect and live up to. And the only way they will respect and live up to their agreements is because they know that somebody is able to carry it out.

For example, the Kremlin may then be willing to discuss the possibility of genuine, enforceable arrangements to reduce and control armaments. Since the end of World War II, we have been trying to work out a plan for the balanced reduction and control of armaments.

Long before the Soviet Union got the atomic bomb, we developed a plan to control atomic weapons. Other nations endorsed this plan. It was a good plan. It would work. It would free the world from the scourge of atomic warfare. But the Soviet Union rejected it. We had over 260 meetings with the Soviet negotiators, trying to reach an agreement, and they wouldn't agree. And we had a monopoly on atomic weapons. We were willing to forgo that monopoly, the first time in the history of the world that a powerful nation has been willing to do anything of that sort.

Working with other nations, we also developed initial plans looking toward the balanced reduction and control of other types of weapons. The Soviet Union rejected these plans, too.

Last year, before the United Nations, I proposed further work on the problem of disarmament, and a new approach. I proposed a merger of the two United Nations commissions working in this field, the one on atomic energy, and the one on other types of weapons. Work on this proposal has gone forward and good progress has been made. We are ready now, as we have always been, to sit down with the Soviet Union, and all the nations concerned, in the United Nations, and work together for lifting the burden of armaments and securing the peace.

We are determined to leave no stone unturned in this search not only for relief from the horror of another world war, but also for the basis of a durable peace.

I hope that the growing strength of the free world will convince the leaders of the Soviet Union that it is to their best interest to lay aside their aggressive plans, and their phoney peace propaganda, and join with us and the other free nations to work out practical arrangements for achieving peace.

This is the goal we are working for. It is for this great goal of peace that we have a defense program, and higher taxes, and a program of aid to other nations. It is for this purpose that our men, and the soldiers of other free nations, are striving and fighting in the hills of Korea.

I cannot guarantee that we will reach our goal. The result does not depend entirely on our own efforts. The rulers of the Kremlin can plunge the world into carnage if they desire to do so. But that is something that this country will never do.

This I can say. Peace comes high in these troubled days, and we have shown that we are willing to pay the price for it. We have shown by positive acts that we are willing to work and sacrifice for peace.

Twice within one generation we have spent our blood and our treasure in defense of human freedom. For 6 long years now we have contended, with all the weapons of the mind and spirit, against the adherents of the false god of tyranny. When the nations of Europe, our neighbors, were left, like the man in the Scripture who fell among thieves, robbed and wounded and half dead, we have offered them our oil and our wine, without stint and without price. When one of the newest and smallest nations of Asia was invaded, we led the free world to its defense.

These positive acts have not been easy to do. They have brought upon us hatred and threats and curses of the enemies of freedom—and may bring upon us even worse troubles. Nevertheless, if this Nation is justified by history, it is these things that will justify it, and not the negative virtue of meaning no harm.

God forbid that I should claim for our country the mantle of perfect righteousness. We have committed sins of omission and sins of commission, for which we stand in need of the mercy of the good Lord. But I dare maintain before the world that we have done much that was right.

To the sowers of suspicion, and the peddlers of fear, to all these who seem bent on persuading us that our country is on the wrong track and that there is no honor or loyalty left in the land, and that woe and ruin lie ahead, I would say one thing: "Take off your blinders, and look to the future. The worst danger we face is the danger of being paralyzed by doubts and fears. This danger is brought on by those who abandon faith and sneer at hope. It is brought on by those who spread cynicism and distrust and try to blind us to our great chance to do good for all mankind."

Yet, at heart, I do not greatly fear such men, for they have always been with us, and in the long run they have always failed. To be sure, they alarm us at times. In 1833 they came within one vote of preventing Wake Forest from being born. But they didn't succeed, and that's the whole point. They have never succeeded permanently in holding back the United States—and they never will succeed in holding it back.

This college has suffered from such people and no doubt will again. This country is suffering from them, and will no doubt continue to so suffer. But college and country alike must keep on disregarding them. We have business in the world that must be attended to, and history will accept no excuses if it is neglected.

My last word to this college, therefore, is an injunction to remember the words the Lord said to Moses on the shores of the Red Sea: "Why criest thou unto me? Speak to the children of Israel, that they go forward." For when the accounts of history are rendered, it is the going forward that will constitute the record—not the hesitation and the mistakes—not how you refrained from wrong, but how you did right.

Armed with the faith and hope that made this college and this country great, you may declare in the words of King David, "Through God we shall do valiantly."

NOTE: The President spoke at 2:32 p.m. at Wake Forest College in Winston-Salem. In his opening words he referred to Dr. Harold Tribble, President of Wake Forest College, and W. Kerr Scott, Governor of North Carolina.

257   Messages on the Death of Liaquat Ali Khan, Prime Minister of Pakistan.   *October 16, 1951*

Begum Liaquat Ali Khan, Karachi, Pakistan.

I send you sincere condolences, in which Mrs. Truman and our daughter join me, in your great sorrow which has come so suddenly and under such tragic circumstances. Pakistan which under the Prime Minister's wise leadership has met and overcome so many obstacles in taking its place in the world family of nations, has suffered a grievous blow. I know the people of Pakistan, whose qualities have been so clearly reflected in the progress of your country, will carry on with calm steadfastness and wisdom.

To you I wish to convey my sorrow and that of your many American friends in the loss of your husband.

HARRY S. TRUMAN

His Excellency Khwaja Nazimuddin, Governor General of Pakistan, Karachi.

I send to Your Excellency my condolences and deep personal sympathy on the tragic death of His Excellency Mr. Liaquat Ali Khan, Prime Minister of Pakistan. The American Government and people will share with me the sorrow which has come to the Pakistan nation with such sudden impact. I know that the memory of Mr. Liaquat Ali Khan's wise leadership and statesmanship will long remain a guide and inspiration to the Government and people of Pakistan.

HARRY S. TRUMAN

NOTE: Liaquat Ali Khan, Prime Minister of Pakistan, was assassinated on October 16 in Rawalpindi, Pakistan.

258   Remarks to the Officers and Members of the Board of Trustees, American Dental Association.   *October 16, 1951*

I AM PLEASED to have you here. I have had quite a long and painful experience with your profession—and it has been very helpful. I still have, I guess, more teeth than most any other 67-year-old man, thanks to the treatment that I have received from good dentists.

I will never forget the first experience I had with a grand old man in Independence, Mo. His name was Gaines, and he had a curly goatee of the southern Confederacy. And while he worked on me, he explained various mementoes that he had, showing me a tooth about that long, a cow's tooth, which he explained to me he had taken out of a man's jaw one time, and it was very painful for him but he didn't think he was going to have to take any of mine out—which he didn't.

But I hope that you are as interested as

I am in the general health of the United States of America. I was startled when I read the figures on the rejections for draftees in the Second World War. They ran over 34 percent for various reasons, mental and physical.

Since that time I have been trying to do something about it. I have had all sorts of accusations made against me, about my intending to turn the country into a socialistic state, and all that sort of business. But all I am trying to do is to try to get the proper medical and dental care for people in a manner so they can pay for it.

And if you will study the various statements and messages that have been made on the subject, you will find that there never has been a program more widely and completely misrepresented.

I wish you gentlemen would do that just for me: Find out for yourselves just what the facts and the truth are, and I don't think you will disagree with me in the objective that I have in view. Because a nation that is in the position that ours is in, ought not to be disgraced by having more than one-third of its young men unfit for service for one reason or another.

And we have made, I think, the greatest strides in the history of the world in the medical profession, all the way down the line, and I would like for the vast majority of the people to have the benefit of that progress that we have made.

They are not getting it, and principally because they can't afford it. But I think there is a way that they can get it.

Now, if somebody has got a better way than the one I propose, I am perfectly willing to accept it; and I hope you will take a look at the situation and see what you can do to improve the physical condition of the people of this country.

It is a great challenge. You can be very helpful at it.

And all I want you to do is get the facts, and don't believe what you see in certain magazines and papers.

NOTE: The President spoke at 3:10 p.m. in the Rose Garden at the White House.

259   Remarks to the Members of the Supreme Council, Ancient and Accepted Scottish Rite.   *October 17, 1951*

I AM most happy, as always, to receive you here. I am more than pleased to see so many visitors from our neighboring countries.

I just had a report this morning from Mr. Dodd, who is the head of the United Nations branch that is implementing the operation of what they call my point 4 program. And it is remarkable what is being done in numerous countries to inform these people on the technique of how to help themselves. And it is not a costly program, it is not a relief program.

For instance, we have a team in Ethiopia that is made up of a man from Iran, and one from Great Britain, one from here, and one from one or two other foreign countries. They were anxious to get information in Brazil on how to raise dates, and Mr. Dodd went to Iraq—to Damascus—and got two date experts and sent them down to Brazil for the information of the people down there on the best way to produce dates.

In Iran, for instance, they had a pest of insects that was eating up all their crops. We sent a couple of little hedge-hopping planes over there and ended that destruction. Very simple—very easy—cost practically nothing.

And that, I think, eventually is the real foundation of peace in the world. I think that is the way we will attain peace in the world.

If we could spend over a 10-year period just one-fourth what we will have to spend for rearming ourselves and our allies, we would accomplish the very purpose that it is necessary for us to arm for.

I thought you would probably be interested in that situation, which shows that there are a lot of other things in the world that will bring people together—just as this organization does here.

When people understand each other, they don't want to shoot each other. The human animal has about the same loves and difficulties in Guatemala as he does in the United States or in Canada.

There is one thing that I think is a shining example of how we feel toward

neighbors: I don't think any of our neighbors are afraid of us. I don't think there is any fear in any of our Central American neighbors, or in Mexico, or Cuba or Canada, that we are going to do them any harm.

That is not exactly true of the neighbors of another great power in this world. And I hope maybe the time will come when that will be true, and then our troubles will be over.

I appreciate very much your coming here, and hope you have had a successful meeting, as you always have.

NOTE: The President spoke at 3:15 p.m. in the Rose Garden at the White House. In the course of his remarks he referred to Norris E. Dodd, Director General, Food and Agriculture Organization of the United Nations.

The Supreme Council, Ancient and Accepted Scottish Rite, was holding its biennial session in Washington, October 15–19, 1951.

---

260   Veto of Bill To Authorize Payments for the Purchase of Automobiles by Certain Disabled Veterans.   *October 18, 1951*

To the Senate of the United States:

I am returning herewith, without my approval, S. 1864, 82d Congress, "An Act to authorize payments by the Administrator of Veterans' Affairs on the purchase of automobiles or other conveyances by certain disabled veterans, and for other purposes."

The purpose of the enactment is to authorize payment of not to exceed $1,600 on the purchase price of an automobile or other conveyance for any veteran of World War II, or of service on or after June 27, 1950, and prior to a date to be determined by the President or the Congress, who is entitled to compensation under laws administered by the Veterans' Administration for the loss, or loss of use, of one or both hands or feet, or for defective vision to a prescribed degree.

Previous laws accorded a similar benefit to each World War II veteran entitled to

compensation for loss, or loss of use, of one or both legs, at or above the ankle, with the requirement that the veteran be qualified to operate the vehicle. Although the authority for that program expired on June 30, 1951, nearly all of the eligible World War II veterans with leg disabilities have already qualified for and received a conveyance. The principal effect of the present proposal on World War II veterans would be to grant assistance in obtaining a vehicle to those with service-connected disabilities of the upper extremities and to those with seriously impaired vision. It would also qualify veterans of the emergency period beginning June 27, 1950 for this benefit for the first time.

This proposal is very similar in essential respects to S. 2115, 81st Congress, which was passed by the Congress in the fall of 1949, and on which I withheld my approval for reasons set forth at length in a Memorandum of Disapproval of October 31, 1949.

It is significant that the considerations set forth in that Memorandum of Disapproval were accepted as sound by the Senate Committee on Labor and Public Welfare when it reported favorably on the original version of S. 1864, 82d Congress, on July 25, 1951. At that time the bill would have simply extended the previous World War II program of assistance in obtaining automobiles for veterans with compensable leg disabilities to include those suffering the same types of disabilities in the active service since June 27, 1950. Apparently recognizing the necessity for restricting this benefit to those having a definite need, in addition to compensation and other existing benefits, for assistance to overcome the handicap of decreased mobility, the Committee stated that it had "confined this bill to the same sound standards of rehabilitation which have governed this program since its inception for the benefit of World War II veterans." The Senate accepted and passed the original bill embodying this principle.

However, the bill as finally adopted by both Houses of the Congress is subject to most of the basic objections raised against S. 2115, 81st Congress. While, unlike the previous bill, this one does not include World War I veterans, it does depart materially from the principle upon which the original World War II program was founded, by extending the program to include veterans with disabilities of the upper extremities and blind veterans. As indicated with reference to S. 2115, the factor of materially diminished mobility, which was an underlying basis of the original program of automobiles for disabled World War II veterans with injury or loss of lower limbs, would be largely disregarded in the cases of the relatively large

group of veterans with disabilities of the upper extremities who would be brought in by this bill. In addition, this proposal would dispense with the requirement of the original program that the veteran must be able to drive the vehicle, at least in those instances where someone else is available to drive for him. S. 1864 would, with respect to a considerable proportion of the beneficiaries, abandon the principle upon which the original program was based.

The question of policy arising from this legislation should certainly be determined on a more solid basis than the theory that the proposed benefit is a desirable convenience. The proper test is whether it would be a necessary, sound and substantial part of the program of rehabilitation and readjustment which the Government is obligated to provide for veterans seriously disabled in the service.

The broad program which has already been placed into effect is based upon the concept that the best help which can be given the disabled veteran is that which directly assists him to the maximum extent possible in overcoming his service disability. Sound measures to this end include medical and hospital care, prosthetic appliances, vocational rehabilitation training, and liberal rates of monthly compensation, including additional amounts for dependents in severe cases. Blind veterans may be provided with guide dogs and electrical or mechanical equipment to aid them in overcoming their physical handicap. Special increased rates of compensation are granted to those with specific disabilities such as the loss of one or both hands or feet, or blindness. Veterans who would benefit by S. 1864 receive monthly compensation payments ranging from $102 to $360, with extra amounts in most cases for those with dependents. To these benefits the bill would add a payment on one automobile, which would necessarily afford but a temporary type of assistance.

It is difficult to perceive how this bill would fit into the existing benefit structure, for the reason that in a great many instances the benefit provided would not be geared to a peculiar and urgent need for rehabilitative assistance of this nature and would not be in keeping with the underlying objective of assisting these disabled veterans to be as nearly as possible self-reliant and self-sustaining members of society.

As I pointed out in the statement on the 81st Congress bill any proposal to make gifts of specific non-monetary benefits to a selected group of disabled veterans easily leads to serious inequalities. The previous World War II automobile program sought to avoid these inequalities by restricting the benefit to those with leg injuries constituting a material handicap to their mobility. The present bill would include more than 9,400 World War II veterans and an unknown but substantial number of veterans of the present emergency, with disability of the upper extremities. About 9,200 of these World War II veterans would have loss, or loss of use, of only one hand or arm. Many of these would have a disability rating of only 60 or 70 percent, with only slight impairment of mobility, if any, while at the same time a much greater number of veterans rated as 100 percent disabled, but without the specific disability covered by this proposal, will not receive automobiles. It would be easy to find wholesale discriminations as the result of enactment of this legislation. For example, of the estimated 11,700 World War II veterans who would become eligible for assistance in obtaining automobiles under this legislation, approximately

41 percent or 4,800 would be cases rated for compensation purposes as disabled 70 percent or less, while only some 3,000 would be rated as 100 percent disabled. At the same time, at least 70,000 World War II veterans receiving compensation for 100 percent disability from the Veterans' Administration will have been unable to qualify for automobiles under either this or the prior law.

What was stated by way of conclusion in the Memorandum of Disapproval on S. 2115, 81st Congress, is just as applicable in testing the merits of this legislation.

"When we move beyond the provision of individually fitted prosthetic appliances for disabled veterans into the field of compensation, the sound and equitable method of meeting the needs of disabled veterans is through the provision of a carefully considered scale of compensation rates paid in cash on a monthly basis. This is our long-tested practice from which I believe we should not depart."

Although I am impelled for the foregoing reasons to withhold my approval from S. 1864, I would be glad to approve legislation which would limit eligibility to veterans of World War II and to each person who, after June 27, 1950 and until termination of the present emergency, has served in the military forces of the United States, and who is entitled to compensation for the loss, or loss of use of, one or both legs at or above the ankle.

HARRY S. TRUMAN

NOTE: On October 20 the Congress passed the bill over the President's veto. As enacted, S. 1864 is Public Law 187, 82d Congress (65 Stat. 574).

For the President's Memorandum of Disapproval of bill to authorize payments for the purchase of automobiles by certain disabled veterans, dated October 31, 1949, see 1949 volume, this series, Item 247.

261 The President's News Conference of
       October 18, 1951

THE PRESIDENT. Please be seated.

I have no announcements, so you are free to ask questions.

[1.] Q. Mr. President, I suppose you have read that General MacArthur told the American Legion in Miami that his opposition had wrecked a secret plan to get Formosa to fall to the Chinese Reds, and give Red China a seat in the United Nations?

THE PRESIDENT. Not based on fact. The General knew it.

[2.] Q. Mr. President, Senator Taft, not to be outdone in courtesy, said he would like to see you as the Democratic nominee in 1952. Will you oblige him? [*Laughter*]

THE PRESIDENT. I can't answer that. I am not ready yet. I told you when the time came I would let you know exactly what I was going to do.

Q. Mr. President, do you think you could beat Taft if you ran against him?

THE PRESIDENT. No, I can't answer that question, either, until I decide what I am going to do.

Q. Mr. President, I thought you said that you had decided before, that you had made up your mind——

THE PRESIDENT. I have made up my mind, but I am not going to tell you what I am going to do until I get ready.

Q. Mr. President, may I ask another question on the Taft thing?

THE PRESIDENT. Yes.

Q. Senator Taft also said that he thought that the three issues would be: progress within the principles of liberty instead of socialism, the honesty and integrity of government, and also the fatal mistakes of this administration in foreign policy, which built up Russia and led to the Korean war. I wonder if you think that those will be the issues in 1952?

THE PRESIDENT. I am against—I say I am against sin, too! [*Laughter*]

Q. The Senator also said that other candidates, he thought, should announce within a reasonable time. How far in advance would you go——

THE PRESIDENT. Well, that is the judgment of every candidate, and I wouldn't try to inform any other candidates when or how they ought to announce.

Q. Mr. President, in the event that you don't run, would you like to see Justice Vinson run?

THE PRESIDENT. I will answer that question when I make my announcement.

Q. Mr. President, you spoke of other candidates, sir?

THE PRESIDENT. Well, there are always plenty of candidates. There will be no dearth of candidates. And of course, I am sorry to say, they don't understand what they are getting into or they wouldn't be candidates. [*Laughter*]

Q. Mr. President, since you do understand what you will be getting into, does that mean you won't——

THE PRESIDENT. Well, I told you I would answer that question when——

[3.] Q. Mr. President, how would you feel about Governor Sid McMath of Arkansas as the successor to Mr. Boyle?

THE PRESIDENT. I have no comment on that situation, because I have not been able to consider successors to Mr. Boyle. You see, the national committee will not meet until October 31st, and we will have plenty of time to think about that.[1]

Q. But you are bound to have some favor-

---

[1] William M. Boyle, Jr., chairman of the Democratic National Committee, informed the President of his wish to resign in a letter submitted to President Truman on October 9, 1951.

ites?

THE PRESIDENT. Well, that is what *you* think. I didn't say that. [*Laughter*]

[4.] Q. Mr. President, have you looked up the letter of congratulations that Senator Taft sent you after [2]——

THE PRESIDENT. Yes, I looked it up. Not only looked it up but I sent him a copy of it, at his request.

Q. Could you tell us, sir, what it did say?

THE PRESIDENT. I wish I had brought it over so I could read it to you. I thought he read it yesterday?

Q. Senator Taft read it.

THE PRESIDENT. Senator Taft read it to you at the Press Club, and I hope he read my reply.

I told him that I appreciated it then, I appreciated it now, and I understood that he had thrown his hat in the ring and he was going to have a lot of fun from now on. [*Laughter*]

[5.] Q. Mr. President, a committee of the American Political Science Association has recommended midterm conventions. They want the 1952 party conventions to decide now to meet again in 1954. Does that strike you as something that would help keep public interest alive in politics between the 4-year elections?

THE PRESIDENT. I have had it under consideration. Had a meeting and a discussion on it, and I think it has merit; but I haven't made up my mind on what the action ought to be.

[6.] Q. Mr. President, since the Midwest flood relief bill passed by the House and the Senate eliminated some provisions for directing grants-in-aid, don't you think there should be further provisions for that made to Congress in the next session?

THE PRESIDENT. I will attend to that in the Message on the State of the Union.

[7.] Q. Mr. President, have you made

up your mind as to when you might make your announcement?

THE PRESIDENT. No, I have not, Bob,[3] I will make it when it's politically expedient.

Q. Well—Mr. President, the other day——

THE PRESIDENT. I will be the sole judge.

Q. ——on that, let me tell you something else. The other day two or three callers, union people, came out and they seemed to have gotten the idea that you might make your announcement sooner than, say, next spring or summer.

THE PRESIDENT. Well——

Q. Are they warm?

THE PRESIDENT. ——everybody's entitled to his own thoughts on the subject, but I will reserve the right to do as I please on the subject, Robert.

Q. They also said that they got the idea that you had one or two things that you wanted to get done before you made your announcement. Could you give us any hint as to what they are?

THE PRESIDENT. No.

Q. Mr. President, that was the Bartenders' Union. [*Laughter*]

THE PRESIDENT. It was?

Q. Yes sir.

THE PRESIDENT. Oh yes. I remember when they were in.

[8.] Q. Mr. President, there has been considerable discussion down on Capitol Hill as to whether you have or might ask the CIO to call off opposition to your tax bill. Is that—have you done so, or will you do so?

THE PRESIDENT. I haven't asked anybody to interfere with the tax bill. I asked for a $10 billion tax assessment. I am trying my best to get a tax bill that will meet the situation with which we are faced. I am not talking to anybody but Members of Congress about it.

[9.] Q. Mr. President, last week you said

---

[2] See Item 251 [3].

[3] Robert G. Nixon of International News Service.

that—I mean, in former Secretary Forrestal's diary [4] he said that you had hinted to General Eisenhower that General Bradley be made Chief of Staff. Also in Forrestal's diary, he says that Mr. Wallace wanted to give the A-bomb to Russia. Is that your recollection?

THE PRESIDENT. Mr. Wallace is speaking for himself before a Senate committee this morning. He will answer that, and he will tell the truth.

[10.] Q. Mr. President, will you acknowledge Mr. Boyle's letter of resignation?

THE PRESIDENT. Yes, when I get around to it. He didn't write *me* the letter of resignation.

Q. Well, the notice——

THE PRESIDENT. He didn't write me the letter of resignation, because he has to resign to the committee.

Q. Yes.

THE PRESIDENT. And I have talked to Boyle three or four times since the letter came, and after the committee acts, I will probably write him a letter.

Q. After the committee acts?

THE PRESIDENT. Yes.

[11.] Q. Mr. President, I would like to clear up one thing. Did you say that when you sent Mr. Taft over a copy of his letter you sent him a little note saying you noticed he had thrown his hat in the ring——

THE PRESIDENT. That's right, and I was sure he was going to have a lot of fun as a result. [*Laughter*]

[12.] Q. Mr. President, have you talked to John Sullivan [5] since Boyle resigned?

THE PRESIDENT. No, I have not.

[13.] Q. Mr. President, do you have any

---

[4] "The Forrestal Diaries," edited by Walter Millis with collaboration of E. S. Duffield, New York, Viking Press, 1951.

[5] John L. Sullivan of New Hampshire, former Secretary of the Navy. Mr. Sullivan had been mentioned in the press as a possible successor to Mr. Boyle.

comment to make on the Russian statement by Mr. Vishinsky, to the effect that Russian-American relations are at an alltime low?

THE PRESIDENT. I haven't seen the statement, and therefore I can't comment on it.

Q. Mr. President, he said in that—at least as we got it—that one of the reasons they were low was that you had said that agreements with Russia weren't worth the paper they were written on?

THE PRESIDENT. I stand by that.

[14.] Q. Do you intend to try to do anything about—the Rules Committee has bottled up and approved—the so-called Capehart amendment to the Controls Act, the amendment you called terrible, I believe.

THE PRESIDENT. I hope they will pass that amendment so that the controls bill can be operative.

[15.] Q. Mr. President, may I get something clear? Did you say that you would write to Mr. Boyle after the committee meets?

THE PRESIDENT. After the committee acts on his resignation.

Q. Not before?

THE PRESIDENT. No. I have talked to Boyle every day, nearly—on various things—not necessary for me to write him a letter.

[16.] Q. Mr. President, as Congress seems to be about coming to a close in the next few days, what about the whistlestop tour? Have you made a decision on whether you are going out this year?

THE PRESIDENT. Well, I can't make a whistlestop tour until I make the announcement of what I am going to do.

[17.] Q. Mr. President, does this delay in sending the Japanese treaty to the Senate mean that you did not expect or want action at this session?

THE PRESIDENT. No. It wasn't ready to be sent. Whenever it is ready, why I will send it down. There is nothing behind the curtain on that at all.

[18.] Q. Sir, you said you can't make a whistlestop tour until you make the announcement of what you are going to do. Is that the same announcement we have been talking about——

THE PRESIDENT. That is the same announcement.

Q. ——with respect to next year?

THE PRESIDENT. That's right——

Q. Mr. President, we are——

THE PRESIDENT. ——that's right.

Q. ——we are talking about—[*laughter*]—Mr. President, did you—would you not go out on a whistlestop campaign, even if you were going to support someone else's candidacy?

THE PRESIDENT. I will answer that in a negative way: I will not say that I would not. [*Much laughter*]

Q. Mr. President, I just want to get this clear. When you say announcement, you don't necessarily refer to an affirmative announcement?

THE PRESIDENT. Or any other kind.

Q. Mr. President, this is semantic, but you said *until* you make an announcement——

THE PRESIDENT. ——there would be no decision on a whistlestop tour, that is what I said.

Q. Suggesting that it would be in the affirmative?

THE PRESIDENT. No, I told Bob that I would not say I would not.

Q. Well, Mr. President, if we are going to get semantic, would you think of calling it something else besides whistlestop?

THE PRESIDENT. That might be done.

Q. Mr. President, it is—is it *this* way? [*Much laughter*] Is it true that you have no plans for any transcontinental speaking tour until after you decide whether or not you will run in 1952?

THE PRESIDENT. The situation is this. Between now and the middle of January it is necessary for me to prepare three terrific messages, one on the State of the Union, one the Budget, and one the Economic Message. And that is going to take every minute of my time from now until I get them delivered. And after that is done, why we will be in a position to talk about other things.

[19.] Q. Mr. President, are you asking Mr. Boyle to stay or reconsider his resignation, provided the committee votes that way?

THE PRESIDENT. I asked him to do that before he decided to resign. No matter what is being said about Mr. Boyle, it is his health that caused him to quit.

[20.] Q. Mr. President, have you picked a TVA Director yet?

THE PRESIDENT. No, I haven't. I will announce it whenever I do.

[21.] Q. Mr. President, are you concerned over the tax bill situation in Congress——

THE PRESIDENT. Of course I am concerned over it——

Q. I know that—I mean——

THE PRESIDENT. ——because that has a tremendous effect on the budget.

Q. Are you confident, sir, that they will pass the bill before adjournment?

THE PRESIDENT. I am not confident of anything that the Congress will do. I hope they will pass a tax bill.

Q. Thank you.

[*Pause*]

Q. Smitty.[6] Hey, Smitty!

Q. Wait till I finish writing the answer.

THE PRESIDENT. Somebody might ask a question before you get through, Smitty. [*Laughter*]

[22.] Q. I will ask one, Mr. President. Are you going to withdraw the nomination of Frieda Hennock?[7]

---

[6] Merriman Smith of the United Press Associations.
[7] See Item 283.

THE PRESIDENT. No.

Reporter: Thank you, Mr. President.

THE PRESIDENT. That's all right, Smitty.

NOTE: President Truman's two hundred and eighty-third news conference was held in the Indian Treaty Room (Room 474) in the Executive Office Building at 10:35 a.m. on Thursday, October 18, 1951.

262 Remarks to a Group of Point 4 Agricultural Trainees. *October* 18, 1951

WELL, what I am principally interested in is development of those areas of the world that are not developed as they can be. If some of the areas of the world were in a position to produce on the basis of the efficiency that we are now acquainted with, and that you have been studying since you have been here, I am sure the world could support five times its present population in luxury.

With your indulgence, I would like to point out some of the things in which I myself am personally interested.

Dr. Bennett of Oklahoma A. & M. spent a year in Ethiopia. He made a complete survey of the situation in Ethiopia and came back and made a report to me that intrigued me immensely.

He told me that there was a plateau here— [*indicating on map*]—here in Ethiopia, between six and eight thousand feet high, that has a black soil of unknown depth, and a climate almost like the temperate climate that we are used to here, and that there are 65,000 square miles of that territory with soil just like Illinois and northern Iowa that would produce anything that will grow in a temperate zone, and that enough products could be produced there to feed 100 million people. Well, you see what a pressure that would take off.

I had an interview yesterday with Dr. Dodd, former Under Secretary of Agriculture, and who is now in the United Nations and works on the implementation of point 4—about which there has been so much conversation. And the idea, of course, on point 4, is to help people to help themselves,

to give them the know-how to produce more food, to overcome insect pests, and to make the standard of living better in the countries that are interested. And I find that nearly every country is interested.

Dr. Dodd told me that he had a United Nations team in nearly every country in the Western Hemisphere and also in the Eastern Hemisphere. We eliminated an insect pest for Iran, here last spring. All we needed to do was to take two little hedge-hopping planes over there and sprinkle a lot of bug-killing dust on the space that was covered with insects—and they all left—they saved the crops, and they got acquainted with the people who do the work in the United States.

When they find out that our interest is their interest, and not our own, eventually if the whole world gets prosperous, that is going to help keep us prosperous; that is the only selfish interest we have in the thing.

Down here, in this part of the world (Central America), there are wonderful resources that can be developed. I understand that we have a team now working on a plan to create food in this part of the world that will support hogs and cattle, and things of that sort, that up to now I understand there has been no way to raise hogs, because the feed is so expensive, it has to be transported from the north, or from Argentina, that it has not been possible to raise them. But they have discovered a way to make the food down there available, so eventually you will have exactly the same sort of program down there that we have here.

And I hope that you will go back with a

kindly and friendly feeling toward what we are trying to do.

I don't believe that there is a single country here (Mexico), or up here (Canada), or in this part of the world (Central America) or in this part of the world (South America) that feels any fear that the United States of America is going to try to cause them any difficulties. We are simply trying to be a good neighbor.

I wish that same thing could be said for this part of the world over here (Russia and Asia). It can't be, because they are afraid over there.

We want to eliminate that fear from the world, if we can. And I think such things as you have been doing will help eliminate that fear.

These United Nations teams are not made up of, and confined to, the experts from this country. For instance, some country in this part of the world (Brazil) wanted to find out the best way to raise dates. And Dr. Dodd went over to Iraq, to Damascus, and found two experts who are now on the team that is working on that very thing. We have people from The Netherlands, and from each one of your countries that you represent here, on these teams working all over the world,

in South America, and Africa, and even in Alaska, trying to find out the best way to make use of the resources of all those countries.

I just want to be perfectly plain that this is a United Nations effort, that we are making every contribution we can, and that we have experts and information and everything that we have that will be useful to make the world a better place in which to live.

I think what you are doing here, and our efforts in this improvement of the living conditions of people all over the world, is much more likely to create a peaceful world than all the armaments that we can produce.

We are certainly pleased to have you. We are mighty glad to receive you here at the White House. I hope you will go home with a pleasant and friendly feeling toward the United States of America.

Thank you very much.

NOTE: The President spoke at 12:10 p.m. in the Rose Garden at the White House. In the course of his remarks he referred to Henry G. Bennett, Administrator of the Technical Cooperation Administration, Department of State, and former president of Oklahoma A. and M. College, and to Norris E. Dodd, Director General, Food and Agriculture Organization of the United Nations.

263 Remarks Upon Presenting to General Marshall the Chair He Had Used as Secretary of State and Secretary of Defense. *October* 19, 1951

GENERAL, it gives me a lot of pleasure, on behalf of the Cabinet, to present you with the seat that you have occupied as Secretary of State and Secretary of Defense with such great honor and credit to the Government of the United States, and as a great help to the President of the United States.

We all join in wishing you a happy continuation of your retirement, and I cannot

guarantee that you will continue to be in retirement, as I have already robbed you of your time three or four times.

NOTE: The presentation was made at 11:25 a.m. in the Cabinet Room at the White House during a regularly scheduled Cabinet meeting. General of the Army George C. Marshall responded as follows:

"Thank you very much, Mr. President. I am deeply grateful. This chair will carry with it memories of what you have just said.

"This chair will also be a great reminder of my recollections and associations here with you gentlemen. And the cooperative manner in which everything was done, particularly in matters of leadership, is something I will never forget."

For the President's letter accepting the resignation of General Marshall as Secretary of Defense, see Item 222.

264   Statement by the President Upon Signing the Revenue Act of 1951.   *October* 20, 1951

I HAVE today signed H.R. 4473, the Revenue Act of 1951. This act will raise about $5.5 billion in additional revenues in a full year—the bulk of it from taxes on individual and corporate incomes. It will raise about $2.5 billion in the remaining months of the current fiscal year.

I have signed this act because we badly need these revenues to help pay for the strong defenses we are building. At the same time, there are certain features of this legislation which are unfortunate from the standpoint of a sound, fair tax system.

I know there are many Members of the Congress who feel as I do about these features of the act. I appreciate the fact that they voted for the bill, in its present form, for the same reasons that I have signed it, namely, because of the immediate need for revenue and because there was no possibility at this late point in the congressional session of making major improvements.

I do not believe, however, that we should be satisfied with the unfortunate features of this act.

This legislation will not raise enough revenue to enable us to keep on paying as we go for our defenses in this emergency period; this is a serious departure from the standards of sound government finance.

Furthermore, this legislation does little to close the loopholes in present tax laws, and in some respects provides additional means by which wealthy individuals can escape paying their proper share of the national tax load through such devices as excessively liberal capital gains provisions, family partnerships, and excessive depletion allowances on oil and gas and certain minerals properties.

In addition, the act contains a rider—the so-called Jenner amendment—which is quite unrelated to the purpose of raising revenue, and which may well result in unwarranted publicity, and personal indignity and unhappiness, for aged people and others receiving public assistance.

If we did not need the revenue from this act so badly, I would not have approved provisions such as these. As it is, I feel that I must sign this legislation, but I shall urge the Congress at its next session to give major attention to legislation improving our tax laws.

NOTE: As enacted, H.R. 4473 is Public Law 183, 82d Congress (65 Stat. 452). See also Item 228.

265   Statement by the President Upon Signing Bill Amending the Taft-Hartley Act.   *October* 22, 1951

I HAVE today signed S. 1959, a bill which makes certain revisions in the Taft-Hartley Act. This legislation eliminates the present requirement that a special election be conducted by the National Labor Relations Board before a union shop provision may be included in a collective bargaining contract. In addition, the measure preserves several thousand representation elections and collective bargaining contracts which are threatened by a recent Supreme Court decision.

These are desirable changes in the act. Union shop elections have involved expenditures in excess of $3,000,000 of public funds. Experience has proved them to be not only costly and burdensome, but unnecessary as well. In practically every election the employees have confirmed their desire for the union shop agreement. Indeed, even in those cases where both the employer and the union were in complete agreement on the desirability of the union shop, the Government nevertheless was compelled to conduct the needless election. The elimination of this requirement as to future cases is clearly a move in the right direction.

In addition, by affirming various actions of the National Labor Relations Board in past cases, this measure will avoid the costs involved in both the repetition of elections and the invitation to wasteful controversy. Of even greater importance is the fact that the protection accorded by this bill to outstanding certifications will prevent the disruption of stable labor-management relations during this crucial period in our mobilization effort.

While the sensible economies and the protection of stable industrial relations effected by this bill are salutary, I welcome its enactment for an even more fundamental reason. On numerous occasions, I have stated that the major objection to many of the provisions of the Taft-Hartley Act is their basic hostility to collective bargaining. Instead of creating an atmosphere within which management and labor may come to an agreement on the basis of mutual respect and common interest, the act imposes artificial restraints upon parties engaged in collective bargaining. Although S. 1959 eliminates only one of the act's defects, it nevertheless constitutes recognition by the Congress of the necessity to move in the direction of a new statutory framework—one which will enable both management and labor to conduct their affairs without arbitrary Government intervention in the collective bargaining process. It is my hope that this step toward improvement of our labor relations laws is the forerunner of the future development of sound legislation behind which labor, management, Government, and the public may unite to achieve industrial peace and economic progress in the national interest.

NOTE: As enacted, S. 1959 is Public Law 189, 82d Congress (65 Stat. 601).

For the text of the President's message upon vetoing the Taft-Hartley Act, see 1947 volume, this series, Item 120.

266 Statement by the President on the Recess Appointment of Philip C. Jessup to the U.S. Delegation to the United Nations. *October 22, 1951*

ON September 13, 1951, I nominated 10 persons to represent this Nation in the sixth General Assembly of the United Nations which will convene in Paris on November 6 of this year.

A subcommittee of the Senate Committee on Foreign Relations reviewed the qualifications of all 10 nominees and held extensive hearings on one of them, Ambassador at Large Philip C. Jessup. The subcommittee reported favorably to the full committee on nine of the nominees, but reported unfavorably, by a 3 to 2 vote, on Ambassador Jessup. The full committee took no action on any of the nominees. However, on October 19, 1951, by a motion made on the Senate floor, the committee was discharged from further considering the appointments of nine of the nominees (all except Mr. Jessup), and the Senate gave its advice and consent to their appointment.

This leaves the nomination of Ambassador Jessup still before the Committee on Foreign Relations. Neither the full committee nor the Senate has taken action on it. When the Senate confirmed the other nine nominees, the chairman of the subcommittee pointed out that there had not been adequate opportunity for the full committee to study the record of the hearings on the qualifications of Ambassador Jessup; consequently, the Senate agreed by unanimous consent that the name of Ambassador Jessup be left "without prejudice" before the Committee on Foreign Relations.

Thus there are now nine members of the United States delegation to the United Nations General Assembly, and one vacancy. Under the Constitution, the President is empowered to fill vacancies in appointive offices during a recess of the Senate.

I regard appointments to the United States delegation to the United Nations General Assembly as among the most important that the President has to make. In the United Nations General Assembly, our representatives must deal, on behalf of the United States, with issues which affect the peace of the world, and the security and happiness of every person in our country.

I am appointing Ambassador Jessup to fill this vacancy because he has demonstrated by actual experience on numerous occasions that he is outstandingly well qualified for this position.

Ambassador Jessup has distinguished himself as a scholar, as a lawyer, and as a public servant. The Senate has confirmed Ambassador Jessup five times for positions of great trust; three confirmations were for the identical position to which I am now appointing him.

He has a remarkable record as a representative of this country in the United Nations. This Nation's chief delegate to the United Nations, former Senator Warren R. Austin, has observed at first-hand the skill and persuasiveness with which Mr. Jessup has dealt with complex problems as an American representative. He has stated emphatically that Ambassador Jessup is needed on the United Nations delegation this fall.

Leading members of the American Bar, of which the Ambassador is a member, have given him their unqualified endorsement. Prominent educators from all over the Nation have made known their support. Officials who have worked with him in the service of this Government have attested to his devotion to the interests and the welfare of this Nation.

The reasons for this support can be found in the record of Mr. Jessup's achievements. He played a vital role in the lifting of the Berlin blockade. He represented the United States with great skill at the meeting of deputy foreign ministers at Paris last spring. In the debates in the Security Council, he has spoken for freedom in ringing tones that have made themselves heard on both sides of the Iron Curtain. His service to this country has been faithful, conscientious, and highly effective.

Against this impressive record of achievement and of support, the objections to Mr. Jessup's appointment made during the hearings of the Senate subcommittee seem to me to be erroneous, and in some cases, simply the result of partisan politics.

The record of the hearings shows that charges to the effect that he was sympathetic to Communist causes were utterly without foundation, and some of the so-called documentation introduced in support of those charges bordered on fraud. And even two of the three members of the subcommittee who voted against his confirmation went to great pains to make it clear that they had no doubt of his loyalty and integrity.

Then, Ambassador Jessup was attacked for being at a meeting which he did not attend and for policy recommendations which he never made.

Despite his record of public service and despite the patent falseness of the charges made against him, it is alleged that the American people do not have confidence in Ambassador Jessup to do a job at which he has been conspicuously successful three times before. This I find unbelievable. The American people make their judgments on the basis of fact and on the basis of performance.

I find no reason in the record of the hearings to change my high opinion of Mr. Jessup's qualifications for this post. I consider him particularly qualified to serve as a representative of the United States to the General Assembly of the United Nations. Accordingly, I am giving him a recess appointment.

NOTE: On September 13 the White House announced the nomination as Representatives to the United Nations of Warren R. Austin, Mrs. Franklin D. Roosevelt, Michael J. Mansfield, John M. Vorys, and Philip C. Jessup. The following were nominated Alternate Representatives: John Sherman Cooper, Ernest A. Gross, Benjamin V. Cohen, Anna Lord Strauss, and Channing H. Tobias.

The White House press release announcing the nominations stated that Secretary of State Dean Acheson would serve as Chairman of the Delegation, and in his absence Ambassador Austin, as Senior Representative of the United States, would serve as Chairman of the Delegation.

The press release also stated that in continuation of the practice that had been reestablished in 1950 of having Members of Congress participate in the Delegation to the General Assembly, Representatives Mansfield and Vorys had been selected after consultation with the leaders of the House Foreign Affairs Committee.

All of those nominated except Mr. Jessup were confirmed by the Senate on October 19.

Mr. Jessup served as a Representative under the recess appointment granted on October 22, and was not renominated before the session closed on February 5, 1952.

267 Remarks to a Group of Industrialists From Colombia.
October 22, 1951

IT IS a pleasure to welcome you here this morning. I hope you have had and will have a successful visit here, and get all the information you are anxious to have.

We are more than happy over the relationship between your great Republic and ours. In fact, I think our relations with our neighbors were never better. I think we have made a reputation of being really friendly neighbors.

I don't think there are any of our sister republics, or the Dominion of Canada, that are afraid of us. They know we have no ulterior motives, and what we do with them and what we want is just what you are doing: a distribution of goods and services on the basis that will be right for everybody.

And I hope that you will get that impression, and take it back home with you.

NOTE: The President spoke at 12:10 p.m. in the Rose Garden at the White House.

268 Remarks Upon Presenting the Harmon International Trophy to Col. David C. Schilling. *October 23, 1951*

IT GIVES ME a great deal of pleasure to make this presentation this morning to Colonel Schilling.

I have the honor to hand you the certificate and the medal. The trophy is a little too big to carry, but we will go around and uncover it.

I congratulate you. I congratulate the Air Force, and I congratulate you on the success you have had in getting a jet across the Atlantic for the first time without a stop—

something very fine for the welfare of the country and the world, I think.

I hope you will continue to work on these things.

NOTE: The President spoke at 12:15 p.m. in the Rose Garden at the White House. He presented the Harmon International Trophy to Col. David C. Schilling, USAF, who had been selected as the outstanding aviator for 1950. On September 22, 1950, Colonel Schilling successfully flew a Republic F-84E Thunderjet from Manston, England, to Limestone Air Force Base in Maine, accomplishing by means of inflight refueling the first nonstop transatlantic jet aircraft flight.

269 Statement by the President Upon Signing the Flood Rehabilitation Act. *October 24, 1951*

I HAVE today signed H.J. Res. 341, the Flood Rehabilitation Act, 1952. This act provides $113 million for the purpose of providing further Federal assistance in rehabilitating disaster and flood-stricken areas—particularly the flood-devastated area centering in Kansas and Missouri.

This money has been badly needed to help restore farms, homes, and businesses hard hit by the floods in the Midwest last July. I believe the Federal agencies concerned with relief and with rehabilitation in the flood area have done a good job with the limited funds at their disposal. This act will allow them to care for some of the needs they have so far been unable to meet, and I am glad to be able to approve it.

At the same time, I regret very much that the Congress did not provide more help for the people of the flood-devastated area. This act falls far short of my recommendations for a realistic rehabilitation program—recommendations which were based on the on-the-spot surveys and judgments of Federal, State, and local officials.

The bulk of the funds provided by this bill—$90 million—may be used only for loans. I expect the Federal agencies to whom these loan funds are made available—the Department of Agriculture and the Reconstruction Finance Corporation—to make loans on liberal terms to those who need it most, in keeping with the emergency situation that prevails in the flood area. But I fear that there will be thousands of wage earners, small farmers, and the owners of small businesses, whose losses in the flood represented personal financial tragedy and who cannot qualify for loans. I recommended a program of limited rehabilitation grants which would have assisted such persons; this bill unfortunately will give them little or no help.

I am particularly disappointed that this bill includes no provision for making a start toward a satisfactory system of flood insurance. Because insurance protection against flood losses is now virtually unobtainable from private insurance companies, I recommended a system whereby the Government would establish a reinsurance fund, which should make it possible for private companies to write flood insurance at reasonable rates. While the risks of floods in any one area may require prohibitive insurance rates, it is quite possible to reduce the risks and the rates by a nationwide pooling system. Until such a system is developed and put into effect, we shall continue to face the danger that floods may wipe out overnight the savings that homeowners, farmers, and businessmen have slowly accumulated over a period of years.

NOTE: As enacted, H.J. Res. 341 is Public Law 202, 82d Congress (65 Stat. 615).

270   Remarks to the 73d General Conference of the National Guard Association.   *October* 24, 1951

FIRST, I would be happy to have that applause go on indefinitely, but you know, my schedule runs every 15 minutes, and as I told some people at a briefing the other day, the President spends most of his time trying to get people to do what they ought to do without being persuaded. That is my business.

You know, there is a great deal of talk about what a powerful and wonderful office the Presidency is. There is a book just out called "The Presidency," and if you will take a look at that, you will find that most of the powers of the President are troubles. And it is his business to see that they are straightened out.

Now, I am most happy to be over here again with you today. I was here last year, and I think I told you that my first military experience was in the National Guard of the United States, in 1905 in June—the 14th day of June, on Flag Day. I had been 21 since the 8th of May of that year, and I joined the National Guard. My father and mother wouldn't give me permission to join before I was 21, and in those days you had to have permission if you were under 21, because they were afraid I would have to wear a blue uniform.

Well, I had to wear one, and it was a beautiful thing. It had a red aiguillette over the shoulder. It had red stripes down the breeches leg, and it had gold buttons on it.

I wore it out to see my old red-haired grandmother, who had gone through the War Between the States, and she looked me over very carefully, and she said, "Harry, that's the first time since 1865 that a blue uniform has been in this house. Don't bring it here any more."

And you couldn't blame the old lady for feeling like that, because she had had to cook for a regiment of Federal soldiers all day until she wore blisters on her fingers, and they weren't satisfied with that, they went down to her barnyard—my grandfather was in Salt Lake City, Utah, with a wagon team—and killed 400 of her fat hogs and just cut out the hams and left all the rest. So you couldn't blame her for being a little bit disgruntled.

But in my generation, and the ones to come, those things are all forgotten. We are now the greatest republic in the history of the world, because we are united. When it comes to doing our duty as it is set out in the Charter of the United Nations, there is no south, no north, no east, no west—we are all together.

And it is gentlemen in positions such as you are in, who are willing to give of their time, and to work for the military welfare of the country, that gives us a chance to meet the necessities with which we are now faced.

It took us more than 30 years to find out that we have a place in the world that we have to fill. We were forced into it by two world wars. I am doing my best to prevent a third one. And the job that you gentlemen are doing is contributing to the prevention of that third world war.

I can't tell you how very much I appreciate your willingness to do what you are doing. You are working for 153 million people. Just keep it up!—and one of these days we are going to reach a position and a condition in the world where the Charter of the United Nations will be implemented just as the Constitution of the United States was.

You know, it took us 80 years to make that Constitution work, and as I said awhile ago, we spent 4 years whipping ourselves before we made it work completely.

We can, I think, implement that charter without another conflagration, because another conflagration, I think, would be practically the end of civilization. And I think everybody around the world appreciates that.

Gentlemen, I thank you for this invitation. I appreciate being here. I always feel like I am coming back to my first military education when I come here to the National Guard.

I hope that you have a successful conference here, and that you will continue to do just what you are doing to make the country safe.

Thank you very much.

NOTE: The President spoke at 10:30 a.m. at the Mayflower Hotel in Washington.

The 73d General Conference of the National Guard Association of the United States was held in Washington October 22–24, 1951.

---

271 Address at the Cornerstone Laying of the District of Columbia Red Cross Building. *October* 24, 1951

Mr. Chairman, General Marshall, distinguished guests, and ladies and gentlemen:

General Marshall remarked to me, when he arose to receive that flourish, that we were breaking a precedent. General Marshall has broken many a precedent, and I am sure he will break many more before he leaves this world.

General Marshall is my ideal of a great public servant. We have a great many great public servants in the service of the Government of the United States, and when I single out General Marshall to pay that compliment, I am paying that compliment to every one of them.

I am glad to take part in laying the cornerstone of this District of Columbia chapter house of the American Red Cross. This chapter is one of the best and most active Red Cross chapters in the whole United

States. The people of this city have a splendid record of contributing to the Red Cross and in giving to the blood bank.

This proves something that I have known for a long time—the people of this city, so many of whom are Government workers, are among the finest and the most patriotic citizens we have anywhere in the United States.

It is most appropriate, therefore, that the District of Columbia chapter of the Red Cross should have a beautiful modern building like the one which is being erected on this site.

The Chairman said he was sure it was going to be finished in a year. I tried to make that prophecy about another most important building in this town, but it didn't work out. I hope he has better luck than I did.

This building will be a permanent addition to the beauty of the Nation's capital. It will be a workshop for the volunteers of the District, and a model of everything a Red Cross chapter house ought to be.

It is most fitting that the cornerstone of this building should be laid today, October 24, which is United Nations Day—the day on which we commemorate the coming into effect of the United Nations charter.

This afternoon at the White House, I expect to welcome 48 soldiers from the fighting front of Korea. These soldiers come from each of the 19 nations which now have forces serving the United Nations command in Korea. It is inspiring to call the roll of these men, because it shows how the free nations in every part of the world have joined together under the banner of the United Nations to put down aggression and to achieve peace.

Men from these nations are out there in the hills of Korea risking their lives in the service of a great ideal. They are evidence, far more powerful than any speeches ever can be, that the idea of international justice under law—the idea of international cooperation to preserve peace and freedom—has taken root and is growing and spreading throughout the world, bringing men together in new and greater bonds of brotherhood.

This is a glorious thing. Great ideas like these have to be fought for. Human progress has always cost effort and suffering and sacrifice. It has cost us much to set up a government of justice and freedom in this country and to maintain it. It has cost human lives and painful effort for those in other countries to win their independence and to advance along the road of freedom. But these advances have been worth all the sacrifices.

And I believe with all my heart that the great advances which we are making today in setting up a system of international peace and justice will prove to be worth all the sacrifice and effort which they are costing us and other nations.

I hope the time will not be far distant when the leaders of the Soviet Union and their satellites will come to see that it is utterly foolish to oppose the united will of all the other peoples of the world for peace and justice. But so long as the forces of aggression are attacking the United Nations, there must be no weakening—there must be no slackening of our effort to check aggression and to build up the defenses of the free world.

It is up to us here at home to back up these men of many nations who are fighting for us and for the freedom of the world in Korea.

One of the best things we can do is to give blood through the Red Cross for the use of our soldiers. The use of whole blood has revolutionized the treatment of battle casualties and saved the lives of thousands. I read the other day about the case of a soldier wounded in Korea whose life was saved by 75 pints of blood. A few years ago that man would have died. The blood which is being given by our people here at home is saving cases which would have been considered hopeless not long ago.

But the demand for blood is tremendous. More is needed than is being given. I urge the people of the District of Columbia—and the people all over the country—to give blood through the Red Cross so the great work of saving human life can go forward.

This building, when it is completed, will have the best possible equipment for giving blood. This building will also serve all other lifegiving and lifesaving activities of the Red Cross in this area. It will be a symbol of our faith—faith in voluntary action by free men everywhere. It will be a means for advancing our ideals of human welfare and human brotherhood.

NOTE: The President spoke at 12:50 p.m. at 21st and E Streets NW., in Washington. In his opening words he referred to John C. Folger, chairman, District of Columbia chapter, American Red Cross, and to General of the Army George C. Marshall, former president of the American Red Cross.

272   Remarks to a Group of United Nations Veterans From the Fighting Front in Korea.   *October 24, 1951*

THANK YOU, Mr. Secretary. I don't know when I have had a more pleasurable occasion. I made a speech about these young men this morning, and I hope they will be able to read it, because what I said then will be much better than what I can say now, and will completely cover the situation.

I congratulate them on their service to freedom and against aggression in the world.

This is a cross section of what the United Nations is trying to do. We all are highly pleased that you could come to see us. I hope you have an enjoyable trip around the United States of America, and carry back home a good impression of us.

I am sorry that the weather prevented us from holding the meeting where we usually

do, out here in the Rose Garden, but it is just a little damp, and I don't think it would look well for all of us to be wearing raincoats.

Enjoy yourselves all you can now. You are highly welcome to this country, and as I said, I hope you will go back feeling kindly towards us.

Have a good time now, and if there's anybody around the country that doesn't treat you right, why you tell me!

NOTE: The President received the group on the portico outside his office at the White House at 3:05 p.m. as part of the observance of United Nations Day.

The group was composed of 48 veterans of the Korean conflict from each of the 19 nations having forces serving in the United Nations command in Korea. They had been brought to the United States by the Department of Defense and were scheduled to tour the country.

273   Proclamation 2950: Termination of the State of War With Germany.   *October 24, 1951*

By the President of the United States of America a Proclamation:

WHEREAS, by a joint resolution, approved by the President on December 11, 1941, the Congress of the United States formally declared a state of war to exist between the United States and the Government of Germany (55 Stat. 796); and

WHEREAS on December 31, 1946, the President proclaimed the cessation of hostilities of World War II; and

WHEREAS it has been and continues to be the policy of the United States to bring about the conclusion of a treaty of peace with the government of a united and free Germany, but efforts to this end have been frustrated and made impossible for the time being by the policy of the Soviet Government; and

WHEREAS it has nevertheless been considered desirable to bring the existing state of war with Germany to a close and to remove Germany from its present enemy status, thus eliminating certain disabilities affecting German nationals; and

WHEREAS the rights, privileges, and status of the United States and the other occupation powers in Germany, and the rights and privileges of the United States and its nationals to which it or they have become entitled as a result of the war, as well as the right to exercise or enforce the same, derive from the conquest of Germany and the assumption of supreme authority by the Allies and are not affected by the termination of the state of war; and

WHEREAS the Congress of the United States by a joint resolution, approved October 19, 1951 (Public Law 181, 82d Congress), has resolved that the state of war declared to exist between the United States and the Government of Germany is terminated and that such termination shall take effect on the date of enactment of such resolution:

Now, THEREFORE, I, HARRY S. TRUMAN, President of the United States of America, pursuant to such joint resolution, do proclaim that the state of war between the United States and the Government of Germany declared by the joint resolution of Congress approved December 11, 1941 was terminated on October 19, 1951.

IN WITNESS WHEREOF, I have hereunto set my hand and caused the Seal of the United States of America to be affixed.

DONE at the City of Washington this twenty-fourth day of October, in [SEAL] the year of our Lord nineteen hundred and fifty-one, and of the Independence of the United States of America the one hundred and seventy-sixth.

HARRY S. TRUMAN

By the President:
DEAN ACHESON
  Secretary of State

NOTE: See also Item 149.

274 Remarks on Receiving the 1951 Histadrut Humanitarian Award. *October 25, 1951*

I HIGHLY appreciate this award. It is a wonderful thing. This is one of the things that makes it possible for a man to carry on in this job. You see, I receive more bricks than plaques, and when I receive a thing of this kind, it always touches me to the quick. I hope I deserve it.

The President, you know, has a job where he can't do anything outside of the line of duty. Most medals are presented because a man has done something that is outside his regular line of duty. It is very difficult for the President to find anything that is outside his line of duty, but I do appreciate this recognition, and it is highly thoughtful of you to come and present it to me. I hope I will always deserve it.

NOTE: The President spoke at 12:15 p.m. in the Rose Garden at the White House. The plaque was presented to the President by the National Committee for Labor Israel "in grateful appreciation of his outstanding efforts in fostering maximum understanding between the Peoples of the United States and the State of Israel and for his warmhearted recognition of the cause of the Histadrut, the General Federation of Jewish Workers in Israel."

275   The President's News Conference of
      October 25, 1951

THE PRESIDENT. I apologize for being late. I hardly ever am.

I have no announcements to make, but I will try to answer questions.

[1.] Q. Mr. President, may I ask one? I understand Senator Douglas has submitted to the Chicago Bar Association eight additional names for screening on those two judgeship vacancies.[1] Have you had any contact with him or discussion on the new judges——

THE PRESIDENT. No, I haven't, but the bar association doesn't make Presidential appointments.

Q. I am aware of it, sir.

[2.] Q. Mr. President, have the accusations of the government of Governor Luis Muñoz Marín of Puerto Rico as a dictatorship come to your attention, and if so——

THE PRESIDENT. I have heard nothing about it.

[3.] Q. Mr. President, referring to the Chicago judgeships, have you any names— can you say whether you will resubmit the names that you have submitted to the Senate——

THE PRESIDENT. They can't be resubmitted because they have been rejected. I have others under consideration.

Q. Can you tell us who they are, sir?

THE PRESIDENT. No sir. I will let you know when the time comes.

Q. There are actually other lawyers you have in mind that are under consideration?

THE PRESIDENT. I have a great many names under consideration, yes.

Q. Will you make recess appointments of those, sir?

THE PRESIDENT. I haven't made up my mind yet.

[4.] Q. Mr. President, aboard the bat-

tleship *Roosevelt* October 17th, General Eisenhower in an interview referred to the fact that with sufficient strength in Europe any proposal made for general disarmament would be given added weight. Do you agree with General Eisenhower?

THE PRESIDENT. I will answer that question at a little later date.

[5.] Q. Mr. President, possibly looking forward to that date, the Herald-Tribune this morning came out for General Eisenhower, and among the people who commented favorably on this fact is Jake Arvey of Chicago.[2] I wonder if you had any comment on that?

THE PRESIDENT. Jake was of the same frame of mind in 1948, if I remember correctly. [*Laughter*]

Q. Mr. President, pushing that one step forward, do you suppose Jake will change his mind like he did in 1948?

THE PRESIDENT. I think—I think Jake's a Democrat.

[6.] Q. Mr. President, do you have any suggestions for the chairman of the Democratic National Committee?

THE PRESIDENT. I have plenty of suggestions, but——

Q. I said have you made——

THE PRESIDENT. No, because the committee will not meet until October 31st. I am not ready to make any suggestions. It may not be necessary for me to make them.

Q. Mr. President, in that connection, would you be willing to say what—whether you would favor a chairman coming from the South, or West, or from the outpost States?

THE PRESIDENT. When I get ready to

---

[1] See Item 165 [8].

[2] Jacob M. Arvey of Chicago, chairman of the Cook County Central Committee of the Democratic Party.

make the announcement on that, I will tell you about it.

Q. Mr. President, I was a little unclear on the—you said it may not be necessary for you to make any recommendations——

THE PRESIDENT. The committee may come up with somebody that I will approve.

Q. Oh, I see. [*Laughter*]

[7.] Q. Mr. President, in view of the unusual historical interest in this Clark nomination, would you care to give us any chronology of how you arrived at the decision, any more than [3]——

THE PRESIDENT. I have been studying the matter for a long time ever since Mr. Taylor resigned, and I find that nearly all the great nations are represented at the State of Vatican City, and I finally came to the conclusion that the cause of peace would be served by our having a representative at the Vatican City.

Q. Mr. President, there has been some criticism of the fact that the appointment was put in at the very last day of the session.

Would you be able to say——

THE PRESIDENT. The only reason why that was done was because I wasn't ready to put it in before.

Q. Mr. President, could you tell us why you chose to make it an Ambassador rather than a Personal Representative?

THE PRESIDENT. Because I wanted an Ambassador there. That is my choice.

Q. There are quite a few differences——

THE PRESIDENT. That is my choice.

Q. ——which follow from an Ambassadorship, such as the concordat——

THE PRESIDENT. I say, that is my choice—nobody else's.

Q. Mr. President, you are quite a life-long Baptist and familiar with the church, I was just wondering if—do you think this appointment in any way would conflict in time with our own doctrine of separation of church and state?

THE PRESIDENT. Certainly would not.

Q. That is the principal criticism I have heard, that's the reason——

THE PRESIDENT. You hear all kinds of criticisms. I want to get it off—all off their chests, then we will argue it out.

[8.] Q. Mr. President, I believe this will be slightly noncontroversial. Would you approve, sir, of the creation of a national Rochambeau road commission to stake out the line of march of Rochambeau in the Revolution?

THE PRESIDENT. What in the world is the interest of your paper in Rochambeau? I don't know anything about it. Haven't given it any thought or any study. Don't even know where he went! [*Laughter*]

[9.] Q. Mr. President, on this Democratic chairman affair, I want to get it clear. Did you mean that you will not make any suggestions until after the committee had had a try at coming up with——

THE PRESIDENT. I didn't say that. I said

---

[3] On October 20 the White House released the following statement by Joseph H. Short, Secretary to the President:

The President has decided that it is in the national interest for the United States to maintain diplomatic representation at the Vatican.

He has therefore nominated Gen. Mark W. Clark to be Ambassador to the State of Vatican City.

During the war, the late President Roosevelt appointed Mr. Myron Taylor as the Personal Representative of the President to His Holiness the Pope.

During and after the war the Taylor mission performed an extremely useful service not only in the field of diplomacy but in the amelioration of human suffering. That service is set forth in official correspondence published from time to time.

The President feels that the purposes of diplomacy and humanitarianism will be served by this appointment.

It is well known that the Vatican is vigorously engaged in the struggle against communism. Direct diplomatic relations will assist in coordinating the effort to combat the Communist menace.

Thirty-seven other nations have for a great many years maintained at the Vatican diplomatic representatives.

the committee would not meet until October 31st, and I have the matter under consideration.

Q. But you said the committee might not come up——

THE PRESIDENT. That is possible. That is entirely possible.

[10.] Q. Mr. President, there seem to be a number of trial balloons being floated for India Edwards for chairman.[4]

THE PRESIDENT. India Edwards is perfectly capable of being chairman. She came over and told me, day before yesterday, that she did not want to be chairman.

Q. Mr. President, has anyone else said they didn't want to be chairman? [*Laughter*]

THE PRESIDENT. No one else yet has had an opportunity.

Q. Mr. President, have you talked to John Sullivan[5] about the Democratic——

THE PRESIDENT. Yes. A long time ago. I told him that if there might be a change, I would like to consider him. And he would not under any consideration want it.

Q. Well, Mr. Chairman—[*Laughter*]— what do you mean by India's opportunity——

THE PRESIDENT. What's that?

Q. What do you mean by India Edwards' opportunity? Did she have an opportunity——

THE PRESIDENT. She came in and told me that she did not want to be chairman, and that a lot of people were pushing her for chairman, and she did not want the job. Does that make it clear?

Q. No sir. I understood you to say that no one else had had an opportunity to say they didn't want it?

THE PRESIDENT. That is correct, except——

Q. I wonder what her opportunity was?

THE PRESIDENT. ——she came in for the purpose of telling me that, except the long time ago conversation I have referred to.

Q. Was that John L. Sullivan that he had asked about?

THE PRESIDENT. Yes.

Q. Well, Mr. President, could you say——

THE PRESIDENT. I had forgotten that.

Q. ——how long ago that might have been?

THE PRESIDENT. Oh, when this conversation first started.

Q. Mr. President, there have also been some trial balloons on behalf of Mike DiSalle.[6] Any comment on that?

THE PRESIDENT. I can name you about 30 on which there have been trial balloons. I have no comment to make on any of them.

Q. We're just trying.

THE PRESIDENT. That's all right. You are perfectly at liberty to try.

Q. Could you tell us anything about the talks with Paul Fitzpatrick[7] the other day? Was that just something——

THE PRESIDENT. He just came in to pay a personal call and to pay his respects.

[11.] Q. Mr. President, are you feeling hopeful, or is there any reason to feel hopeful about the progress of the Iranian talks now?

THE PRESIDENT. Yes, I am hopeful. They are making some progress.

Q. Is there anything further you could tell us about that?

THE PRESIDENT. I can't tell you anything further.

[12.] Q. Mr. President, the other day a national committeeman from Wisconsin came in, and when he came out he said that

---

[4] Mrs. India Edwards, vice chairman, Democratic National Committee and director of the Women's Division.

[5] John L. Sullivan of New Hampshire, former Secretary of the Navy.

[6] Michael V. DiSalle, Director of Price Stabilization, and former Governor of Ohio.

[7] Paul Fitzpatrick, chairman of the New York Democratic State Committee.

you had expressed yourself in favor of the elimination of Mr. McCarthy from the Senate.

THE PRESIDENT. I have no comment to make on that.

[13.] Q. I wondered, aside from that, whether you as a Democrat would feel that it would be a mistake for a Democrat to enter and vote in the Republican primary?

THE PRESIDENT. I would, surely. I am never in favor of that. I believe in a two-party system.

[14.] Q. Mr. President, would this Government be willing to mediate the Egyptian-British dispute——

THE PRESIDENT. I have no comment to make on that.

[15.] Q. Mr. President, General Vandenberg said that—yesterday, I believe it was—that the pilots flying these MIG planes in Korea spoke Russian. Would you care to enlarge on that?

THE PRESIDENT. I have no comment on that.

[16.] Q. Mr. President, was Frank McKinney of Indiana [8] one of those mentioned?

THE PRESIDENT. He has been suggested. He is in the 30 I was telling you about.

[17.] Q. Mr. President, would you care to comment directly upon the Herald-Tribune's espousal of General Eisenhower?

THE PRESIDENT. Oh, no. That newspaper has a right to do whatever it pleases, just as every other newspaper has. And they certainly picked a fine man for their candidate.

[18.] Q. Mr. President, has the General Clark appointment stirred up more hullabaloo than you expected?

THE PRESIDENT. No. Not as much. [*Laughter*]

Q. Mr. President, your Foreign Relations chairman of the Senate said he is going to

have to oppose him not on religious grounds, but because of Texas—he is opposed to the General because of the 36th Division disaster? [9]

THE PRESIDENT. That is his privilege. I hope you saw Crockett's cartoon today.[10]

[19.] Q. Mr. President, I assume from what you said that Paul Fitzpatrick did not call on you to say he did not want to be chairman?

THE PRESIDENT. It was not discussed.

Q. Is he on the list of 30 people, sir?

THE PRESIDENT. I can't comment on that. I told you about McKinney, but I think Paul is, yes, but he did not discuss it with me. Great long list, I can't remember them all. I did remember McKinney because so many people brought him up.

[20.] Q. Mr. President, about Gen. Mark Clark. As a soldier also under command, how is it that he can elect to say, I don't want to take this job unless I can have it my way?

THE PRESIDENT. He didn't say that.

Q. I see.

THE PRESIDENT. He is having it my way. He never made any such statement as that at all. Mark Clark is a good soldier.

What's the matter, May? [11]

Mrs. Craig. Well, sir—excuse me, but I understood that Clark said that he would not give up his military position?

THE PRESIDENT. When I talked to General

---

[8] Frank E. McKinney of Indianapolis became the chairman of the Democratic National Committee on October 31, 1951.

[9] General Mark Clark was in command of the 36th Division which suffered heavy casualties in Italy in World War II.

[10] The cartoon by Gib Crockett, which appeared in the Washington Evening Star on October 25, 1951, depicted Senator Tom Connally of Texas pondering a gift-wrapped package which was marked "Clark appointment, To Tom, From Harry, Do not open 'til after Christmas." Senator Connally was Chairman of the Senate Foreign Relations Committee which was considering the President's nomination of General Clark to be U.S. Ambassador to the Vatican.

[11] Mrs. May Craig of the Portland (Maine) Press Herald.

Clark about the matter, I told him he would not have to give up his military status.

Q. That was not his condition?

THE PRESIDENT. That was not his condition at all. He had nothing whatever to do with the situation. I would treat him exactly as I treat General Bradley and General Marshall and two or three others who have gone on missions for me

Q. Mr. President, to go back to another point. Do you—you said a moment ago that you thought it was fine that there was bound to be talk about this Clark appointment, and you thought it would be good to go ahead and get it off our chests——

THE PRESIDENT. Well now, Smitty,[12] I think I have commented on that quite

_____
[12] Merriman Smith of the United Press Associations.

enough, and made it perfectly plain and clear. I don't care to say anything more about it.

[21.] Q. Mr. President, I am still very much interested in that disarmament proposal. In your Wake Forest speech [13] you referred to a proposal of that type——

THE PRESIDENT. I told you that I would answer that at a later date. I appreciate your persistence, and it's all right. [*Laughter*]

Q. Mr. President, have we overlooked anything?

THE PRESIDENT. I don't believe you have. Reporter: Thank you.

NOTE: President Truman's two hundred and eighty-fourth news conference was held in the Indian Treaty Room (Room 474) in the Executive Office Building at 4:05 p.m. on Thursday, October 25, 1951.

_____
[13] See Item 256.

276 Statement by the President on the Longshoremen's Strike. *October 26, 1951*

I HAVE been informed by Mr. Charles E. Wilson, Director of the Office of Defense Mobilization, that because of the work stoppages by the longshoremen, the ports of New York and Boston have been virtually paralyzed and that equipment and material vitally needed for national defense is not moving. It has already been necessary to impose an embargo on railroad shipments to these ports.

The Director of the Federal Mediation

and Conciliation Service has reported to me that the Service has been unable to bring about a resumption of work and that all mediation efforts have been exhausted.

This work stoppage has a direct and immediate effect on our defense effort. In the national interest, the employees involved in this critical work stoppage should return to work at once.

NOTE: The 25-day strike by insurgent members of International Longshoremen's Association ended November 9, 1951.

277 Letter to the Chairman, Wage Stabilization Board, on the Settlement of a Labor Dispute Affecting the Production of Copper. *October 26, 1951*

Dear Mr. Feinsinger:

I have your letter of October 23 informing me of the action of the Wage Stabilization

Board in making its recommendation for the final settlement of the labor dispute at the American Smelting and Refining Com-

pany at Garfield, Utah. You also state that
the company and the union—The United
Steelworkers of America (CIO)—have decided to accept and act upon this recommendation of the Board. This successfully
disposes of the dispute and assures us the
uninterrupted production needed to support our national defense program.

I am very pleased that the Board has been
instrumental in settling this dispute, the first
certified to it by me under the terms of
Executive Order 10233. The Board has fully
justified the expectation that it could be
useful in the settlement of disputes affecting
the defense program. Your Board has performed a real public service in assisting the
parties to reach a peaceful settlement.

In times such as these, the parties to labor
disputes owe it to the American people to
make every effort to reach a settlement
through collective bargaining and, that fail-
ing, to cooperate with their Government in
maintaining or restoring production while
their dispute is before the Board.

Very sincerely yours,

HARRY S. TRUMAN

[Mr. Nathan Feinsinger, Chairman, Wage Stabilization Board, Washington 25, D.C.]

NOTE: Mr. Feinsinger's letter of October 23 was released with the President's reply.

Executive Order 10233, dated April 21, 1951, is
entitled "Amending Executive Order 10161 with
Respect to Wage Stabilization and Settlement of
Labor Disputes" (3 CFR, 1949–1953 Comp., p. 743).
See also Items 169, 204, 214.

278 Letter to the Chairman, Commission on Internal Security and Individual Rights. *October* 27, 1951

[Released October 27, 1951. Dated October 26, 1951]

Dear Admiral Nimitz:

Now that the Congress has adjourned
without completing action on the legislation
which was necessary if the Commission on
Internal Security and Individual Rights
was to operate effectively, I have concluded
reluctantly to accept the resignations of the
members of the Commission which were
submitted to me on May 8, 1951. Failure
of the Senate to pass H.R. 2829, a bill which
would have exempted members and employees of the Commission from certain
conflict-of-interest statutes, has not only led
to the resignation of the present members
of the Commission, it also makes it virtually
impossible to appoint new Commission
members or staff members. In the absence
of an act such as H.R. 2829, the conflict-of-
interest statutes sharply limit the field from
which members of the Commission and its
staff might be chosen. It would be extremely difficult to select a Commission of

the kind which should be chosen for this
task without including members whose private business or professional activities might
result in a technical violation of those
statutes.

For these reasons, I have decided, therefore, not to appoint new members of the
Commission to replace those whose resignations I am accepting.

Under the Executive Order establishing
the Commission, its job was to make a thorough examination of the laws, practices, and
procedures which protect our Nation against
treason, espionage, sabotage, and other subversive activities. The Commission was to
consider these matters from the standpoint
of protecting the rights of our individual
citizens as well as security of the United
States. As you know, the members of the
Commission were men and women of the
highest caliber. Their recommendations on
these matters would have been of the utmost

605

value to the Congress as well as to officers of the Executive branch of the Government. I regard it as most unfortunate that Congressional failure to waive legal technicalities will deprive the Nation of the kind of objective study which would have helped all of us in our task of keeping our democratic standards high at home while we are engaged in resisting the thrust of Soviet communism.

I had hoped that the Congress would be as anxious as I am to make sure that our procedures for maintaining the security of the Government service are working effectively. I had hoped that the Congress would be as anxious as I am to make sure that the Bill of Rights is not undermined in our eagerness to stamp out subversive activities. These were not the only purposes for which the Commission on Internal Security and Individual Rights was established, but they were among the most important.

I should like to express to you my gratitude and warm appreciation for the diligent manner in which you devoted so much of your time to studying the complex issues which the Commission was expected to analyze. I am hopeful that the knowledge that you and

the other members of the Commission have gained through your own personal studies can be drawn upon in the coming months as the National Security Council, the Civil Service Commission, and other agencies continue their scrutiny of the Federal Employee Loyalty and Security Programs.

Very sincerely yours,

HARRY S. TRUMAN

[Fleet Admiral Chester W. Nimitz, U.S.N., 728 Santa Barbara Road, Berkeley, California]

NOTE: Copies of the letter to Admiral Nimitz were sent to the other members of the Commission along with a letter of thanks for their services from the President. The members of the Commission were: Fleet Adm. Chester W. Nimitz, Chairman; the Most Reverend Emmet M. Walsh, D.D., Coadjutor Bishop of Youngstown, Ohio; the Right Reverend Karl Morgan Block, D.D., Bishop of California, San Francisco; Anna Lord Strauss, Washington, D.C.; Russell C. Leffingwell, New York, N.Y.; Charles H. Silver, vice president, American Woolen Company, New York, N.Y.; John A. Danaher, Washington, D.C.; Harvey S. Firestone, Jr., chairman, Firestone Tire and Rubber Company, Akron, Ohio; and William E. Leahy, Washington, D.C.

On November 14, 1951, the President issued Executive Order 10305, entitled "Revoking Executive Order 10207 of January 23, 1951, Establishing the President's Commission on Internal Security and Individual Rights" (3 CFR, 1949–1953 Comp., p. 833).

See also Items 20, 35, 104.

---

279 Address at the Dedication of a Square in Washington to the Memory of Samuel Gompers. *October 27, 1951*

Mr. Chairman, Mr. Secretary, distinguished guests:

I am going to open my remarks by reading you a letter:

"My dear Mr. President. I regret very much not being able to be present when you dedicate the Gompers Square, owing to my physical disability. I consider it a great tribute to my late husband. I send my heartiest greetings to those who will participate in this event. Very sincerely yours, Mrs. Samuel Gompers."

I am happy to take part in the dedication of this square to the memory of Samuel Gompers.

Many of the squares and streets in this city are named for famous men. But very few of them did as much for their fellow men as Samuel Gompers did.

In his long life of effort for the working people of this country, he was bitterly abused and vilified by the forces of special privilege. But he found out, in the end, that this country will always honor a man who dedicates his life to helping others.

Samuel Gompers was a workingman himself, and he fought to better the condition of the wage earner. But he never regarded organized labor as a pressure group concerned only with its own private and selfish gains. On the contrary, he thought of the cause of organized labor as the cause of human justice. He strove to correct the inequities of our industrial system because that was the right thing to do—the right thing not only for labor but for all parts of our society.

In his autobiography, he summed up his beliefs in these words:

". . . I have been jealous that the American labor movement should retain the character of a crusade for human justice. I know men and I love them and I also know that the effort to secure justice for the under-man must be a fight."

That is pretty good philosophy for a trade union movement to have.

And it is also good philosophy for a political movement, too. I have always believed that the American people would prefer the political party that proved it was crusading for human justice. I have seen the truth of that proposition in my own experience.

Samuel Gompers was right when he said that the effort to secure justice for the workingman means a fight. It does. It means a long, unending fight. I have seen the truth of that in my own experience, too.

It is an unending fight because the forces of reaction never give up. They have money and they have power, and they never really believe that the people ought to govern themselves. They are always trying to turn the control of the country over to a privileged few.

We have come a long way in our fight for human justice since the days of Samuel Gompers, but the gains we have made are always under attack. The forces of reaction are always trying to undo the progress we have made.

One of the greatest struggles Samuel Gompers had was to prevent our courts and legal institutions from being perverted into instruments of oppression against the workingman. That was a real danger in his day. When he started his great work, labor union activities were considered to be illegal conspiracies in the restraint of trade. Courts were constantly issuing injunctions against unions for the benefit of employers. The labor injunction was used indiscriminately to keep labor in the prison of low wages and poor working conditions.

Gompers fought this kind of thing with all the energies of his great soul and his mind.

He fought the labor injunction because it was used to undermine and destroy free trade unions.

Above all, he fought the labor injunction because it was used to violate the constitutional rights to free speech and freedom of assembly.

The fight he led resulted in great victories—the Clayton Act, the Norris-LaGuardia Act, the Wagner Act. Those laws recognized the constitutional rights of labor and made them the basis of our national labor policy.

In recent years there have been attempts to bring back the old ideas that Gompers fought against. There has been a campaign to rewrite our labor relations laws so that they would favor employers against employees. There has been a plot to devise legal machinery to cut the strength of organized labor into little pieces, and to entangle each piece in a snare of legal restrictions and red tape.

This entire effort is harmful not just to labor, but to the welfare of the country. It is a backward step, legally and economically.

We have been fighting against it, and we

must continue to fight against it.

Our objective is to have what Samuel Gompers wanted: fairness and justice in the law of labor-management relations. We do not want a law that is stacked in favor of either labor or management. We want a law that will insure free unions and free collective bargaining, and be fair to both employers and employees. And I believe we will have that kind of law, in the long run, in spite of all these efforts to turn back the clock of progress.

There is another respect in which we have been moving forward against stiff opposition since the days of Samuel Gompers. That is in creating a stable economy. One of the things that Gompers fought, all his life long, was unemployment. He knew this was not a problem that could be solved by labor alone. He knew that industry and government must work with labor and the farmers to prevent depressions and to maintain high levels of employment.

It is remarkable, when you look back on it, to realize what terrible stupidity and selfishness Gompers had to face in this part of his struggle for human justice. Economists told him that starving, unemployed workers were the result of "natural laws" that nothing could change. Business opposed his suggestion that Government agencies should take such a simple step as collecting statistics on unemployment.

We have come a long way since those days. We have adopted the principle that working people shall have insurance to give them some protection against unemployment. We believe in good wages, and we have legal wage floors to prevent sweatshops. We have set up a system of social security. We have written into our laws the principle that all groups—business, labor, and agriculture—should work together to maintain employment and expand the economy. We

have learned to use the great resources of our economy, through government, to prevent economic suffering and to protect against sharp declines in the business cycle.

It is quite clear that since Gompers' time we have made great advances in our economic theories and our economic policies. We no longer believe that "natural laws" make the poor poorer and the rich richer. We no longer subscribe to the nonsensical idea that economic well-being trickles down the scale from the well-to-do to the wage earner.

In fact, we have proved that just the opposite is true. We have proved that if the wage earner and the farmer are prosperous and secure the rest of the people will be prosperous and secure, too. Today, the working people of the United States are better off than any workers in history, and the annual income per person in this country is 40 percent higher than it was in 1939. This is a real gain of 40 percent—after taxes, and taking price increases into account. This gain is a real gain—a real gain of 40 percent. Don't let anybody tell you anything different from that. That's the truth, if it was ever told.

But we have had to fight for these advances, and we will have to keep on fighting in order to hold them. There are still people who cling to the old trickle-down theory, who think that our sole concern ought to be profits, and that wages ought to come after profits have been taken care of. This is the same blind attitude that brought on the great depression, but it is still with us.

Let me give you an example. Our defense program has brought with it the threat of inflation—and of runaway prices. Adequate price controls are essential not only for the wage earner, but for business as well. They are essential to the defense of the Nation and to world peace. In this emergency you would think that all citizens would want good, strong price controls to protect themselves and the whole economy.

But this has not proved to be the case. Scores of special interests have ganged up together for the purpose of securing special short-run advantages for themselves at the expense of all the rest of us. These special interests have adopted the principle that price control is all right if it does not require them to absorb one more penny in costs, or forego a penny of profits, no matter how high their profits may be. This is the main idea behind that terrible Capehart amendment, which I tried to have removed from the price control law. It is also the old trickle-down idea, in a new setting—take care of the profits first, and the general welfare last.

This administration will do its best, with the tools the Congress has given us, to curb inflation. But the tools are not good enough to do this job as it should be done.

Here is part of the fight for human justice which I hope the working people—and all other patriotic Americans—will carry on with increasing vigor in the months to come. We can win this fight for a strong anti-inflation program. We must not lose heart. Think of the difficulties that confronted Samuel Gompers 50 years ago.

We have far less reason to be discouraged than he had. We have seen the crusade for human justice bring about tremendous improvements in our living standards and in the stability of our economy.

These gains have brought new responsibilities to organized labor. Today labor unions are a major element in our economy. Their policies affect the whole Nation and help to shape our national destiny.

In this present time of crisis, the defense of the free world depends on the production of American mines, farms, and factories.

Labor—organized labor—has the great responsibility of using its strength to increase defense production. It has the responsibility for helping to make wage stabilization work. It has the responsibility, along with management, of preventing the interruption of defense production.

I am confident that the American labor movement will measure up to these responsibilities. For labor understands what is at stake in this struggle against aggression and the threat of war.

Labor knows that communism is the mortal enemy of free trade unions. Labor knows that free trade unionism—the international unity of free workingmen—forms one of the greatest bulwarks against communism. Labor knows that we cannot have peace for ourselves if we turn our backs on the needs and desires and hopes for progress of other free people.

That is why the American labor movement has given such firm support to the foreign policy of this country. That is why American labor is working so vigorously with free trade unions throughout the world for peace and human progress.

In all this, the labor movement has been following the principles established by Samuel Gompers. All these principles have been carried forward by great labor leaders such as my friend here, William Green. There was never anyone who worked harder than Samuel Gompers for international collaboration among free nations and free working men. There was never anyone who believed more deeply in the cause of peace and justice for all the people of the world.

That was his goal—and it is ours. It is the goal of all progressive, forward-looking Americans.

Let us go on working, as Samuel Gompers worked, for peace, freedom, and justice for all mankind.

NOTE: The President spoke at 11:45 a.m. from a platform erected in Gompers' Square at Tenth Street and Massachusetts Avenue NW., in Washington. In his opening words he referred to Secretary of the Interior Oscar L. Chapman, who served as master of ceremonies, and to Secretary of Labor Maurice J. Tobin. In the course of his remarks the President referred to William Green, president of the American Federation of Labor.

The address was broadcast.

280 Statement by the President Upon Signing Bill Increasing Benefits Under the Railroad Retirement System.
October 30, 1951

I HAVE today signed H.R. 3669, "An Act to amend the Railroad Retirement Act and the Railroad Unemployment Insurance Act, and for other purposes."

This act will provide badly-needed increases in benefit payments for more than 400,000 persons who are now receiving benefits under the Railroad Retirement Act. It will provide substantially higher benefits for railroad workers who have retired because of age or permanent disability, and for the widows and orphans of railroad workers.

I am glad to be able to approve these increases. I have been interested in the railroad retirement system for a long time, helped to work out previous amendments when I was in the Senate, and I know how much these higher amounts will mean to the retired persons, widows, and orphans who are beneficiaries.

In addition, I am glad to see that this act will provide benefits, for the first time, for the wife or husband of a retired railroad employee, and for dependent aged widowers of railroad employees. Under the new law the payment to a retired man and wife, age 65 or over, will average about $135 a month.

Heretofore the railroad retirement system has been completely separate from the general system of old-age insurance. Now, under the amended law, persons with less than 10 years of service in the railroad industry will be credited for this service under the old-age and survivors insurance system rather than the railroad retirement system, and there will be periodic financial adjustments between the two trust funds. Benefits under the new law will in all cases be at least as high as under old-age and survivors insurance, and in many cases will be somewhat higher.

In addition to the legislation I am signing today, the Congress has also adopted a resolution providing for a complete factfinding study of the railroad retirement system, including possible changes in benefits and financing, and in the relationship between the railroad retirement system and the old-age and survivors insurance system. This is a very desirable step. There are real and serious questions to be settled before we can feel confident that we are giving adequate and fair protection, on a sound financial basis, to retired workers and survivors. I hope the committee will be able to report in time for legislative action next year.

NOTE: As enacted, H.R. 3669 is Public Law 234, 82d Congress (65 Stat. 683).

281 Remarks at a Luncheon for Vice Admiral Ross T. McIntire. *October 30, 1951*

Mr. Chairman, Admiral:

I came over here unexpectedly today, after I heard that the Admiral was having a tribute paid to him, to add my nickel's worth to the performance.

I want to say to you that Admiral McIntire is in that category of people that were in the military service when I came to the White House who has been willing to do anything that is necessary for the welfare of the country, and anything that the President has ever asked him to do.

He is now in the midst of a program that is of vital importance to the Nation, the rehabilitation of the handicapped—doing a wonderful job at it. I have been in cooperation with him, and I hope that he receives the best of treatment by you here today; and I hope that when he takes his departure for the Far West, that he will still keep his connections here and come back when it is necessary in order to efficiently perform his mission.

I have a large number of people in the class of Admiral McIntire who are all willing to do whatever is necessary for the welfare of the country. It is one of the great satisfactions of being in the office that I occupy that there are people who put the welfare of the Nation above their own personal interests. And you would be surprised how many of our public servants are in that category.

I appreciate the privilege you gave me, to come over and pay tribute to the Admiral. And I hope that you will have a most successful meeting.

Thank you very much.

NOTE: The President spoke at 1:05 p.m. at the Carlton Hotel in Washington.

Admiral McIntire, former Surgeon General of the Navy and White House physician from 1933 to 1945, had resigned as chairman for medical policies and procedures of the Red Cross national blood program. He retired from the Navy in 1947.

282 Remarks of Welcome to Princess Elizabeth and the Duke of Edinburgh at the Washington National Airport. *October 31, 1951*

IT CERTAINLY is a very great pleasure for me as President of the United States to welcome you to the Capital of our country.

On behalf of the Government and the people of the United States, I bid you a most hearty welcome.

I think your visit will improve—if that is possible—the cordial relations that exist between our two great countries, and I hope that while you are here you will have a very enjoyable time.

I was most happy to hear that the King had recovered so promptly, so that you could make this trip. I remember with a great deal of pleasure the visit of the King and Queen while I was in the United States Senate. It happened to be my privilege to be presented to them when they held a reception at the British Embassy here.

I also had another very pleasant visit with the King on the *Renown* in Plymouth harbor, when I was on the way home from Potsdam. He had me on the *Renown* for luncheon, then he returned the call on the *Augusta,* and we had a most pleasant visit and conversation on world affairs as it affected Great Britain and the United States.

I hope while you are here that you will get

a chance to see a great many of our people. I am sincerely sorry that you can't go from one end of the country to the other as you did in Canada, and let everybody in the country have a chance to get acquainted with you, because Margaret tells me that whenever anyone becomes acquainted with you, they immediately fall in love with you.

She had a most pleasant visit in England, and I hope that we will be able to make you feel as happy as she was when she came back home from there.

NOTE: The President greeted Princess Elizabeth and the Duke of Edinburgh at 4:07 p.m. at the Washington National Airport. Princess Elizabeth responded as follows:

"It is a very great pleasure, Mr. President, for my husband and me to be visiting you here in Wash-

ington. During our trip through Canada, I heard much of the warm goodwill felt by the people of the United States towards the people of Canada, and I am glad that before sailing for England we are to have this chance of seeing at least some of the country with which the whole British Commonwealth has so many friendly ties.

"I know it is never possible to understand a country as great as this by visiting only its capital, even such a splendid one as Washington. But so much of the history of the United States has been enacted here, so many memorials of your national achievement stand here, that I hope before I leave to see a little deeper into the sources of your great strength.

"Free men everywhere look towards the United States with affection and with hope. The message that has gone out from this great capital city has brought hope and courage to a troubled world.

"In that other proud capital where I live, and in Canada from where I have just come, we also are determined to work with all our strength for freedom and for peace."

283   Letter to Frieda B. Hennock on Her Decision To Decline a Recess Appointment as a Federal Judge.   *November 1, 1951*

[Released November 1, 1951.   Dated October 31, 1951]

Dear Miss Hennock:

I regret that the Senate Judiciary Committee has not taken action on the confirmation of your appointment as a United States District Judge for the Southern District of New York, as I think you are highly qualified and would have served with distinction. I am mindful of the reason which you have advanced for declining a recess appointment, and I reluctantly defer to your wishes in the matter.

Your outstanding record as a member of the Federal Communications Commission has earned wide public recognition, and I am confident your continued service on the Commission will advance the public interest in the vital field of communications.

Your service has provided an outstanding example of the contributions which the women of America have to offer the people of this country, particularly in these critical times.

With assurance of my continued confidence I am,

Very sincerely yours,

HARRY S. TRUMAN

[Honorable Frieda B. Hennock, Commissioner, Federal Communications Commission, Washington, D.C.]

NOTE: Miss Hennock's letter, dated October 30, was released with the President's reply. The letter stated that the sound development of television had been her major concern during her service on the Commission, and that she thought it best for her to follow pending issues to a conclusion.

284   Memorandum of Disapproval of Bill Relating to the Bank of
       America National Trust and Savings Association.
       November 2, 1951

I HAVE withheld my approval from H.R. 1672, "An Act For the Relief of Bank of America National Trust and Savings Association."

The purpose of this bill is to pay to the Bank of America National Trust and Savings Association the sum of $20,403.65, representing the net loss sustained by that bank in connection with loans it granted under regulation V to finance the operations of San Jose Manufacturers, Incorporated, under a certain contract which that company had with the War Department during World War II.

It appears that early in 1941 the San Jose Manufacturers, Incorporated, was organized by certain citizens of San Jose, California, in order to effect a consolidation of the machinery and equipment of a number of small machine shops in that city so as to be able to assist the United States in the defense work program during World War II. The operations of San Jose were financed entirely by the claimant. The United States, in turn, through a regulation V loan, assumed 80 percent of any losses which might be sustained by the bank.

In January 1942, the San Francisco Ordnance District placed a letter order, later superseded by a formal contract, with San Jose for 98 105-mm howitzer carriages at a unit price of not to exceed $6,000. Delivery of the 98 gun carriages was required to be completed in November 1942. But up to February 1943, when San Jose was completely reorganized, none of the gun carriages had been delivered to the Government, although an amount equal to the entire contract price for the carriages had been expended. However, all of the gun carriages

ordered from San Jose were completed and delivered to the Government in January 1944.

It appears that upon the liquidation of San Jose, and after applying to its indebtedness to the bank all of the funds received from the sale of the assets of the corporation, as well as all of the funds received from the War Department in payment for said 98 gun carriages, there remained a balance due the bank of $348,676.98. Since 80 percent of this amount was covered by the V loan guarantee, the net loss to the bank, after certain other minor adjustments had been made, amounted to $69,735.40. The award contained in the present bill was computed by diminishing this latter figure by $55,000, the amount of interest paid by San Jose to the bank, and then adding to the resulting figure the sum of $5,668.65, representing the cost to the bank of maintaining one of its officials in the San Jose office for the purpose of observing the manner in which the loaned funds were expended.

Ordinary business prudence requires that a financial institution, before making a large loan to a manufacturer to finance its production of goods under a contract, ascertain full details concerning the purpose of the loan, the manner in which the money is to be applied, the ability of the borrower not only to fulfill its obligations under its production contract but also to make repayment of the loan. In the present case it appears that the bank fully informed itself concerning all such matters, and that it, in fact, had one of its officers spend a large portion of his time in supervising the operations of San Jose.

On May 22, 1945, Under Secretary of

War Robert P. Patterson, in a statement concerning the refusal of the War Department to grant relief to the bank under the broad authority contained in the First War Powers Act, said:

"Almost from the outset the company [San Jose] had difficulty in organizing properly for the performance of the contract, and over a considerable period the Ordnance Department found it necessary to give it assistance of various types.

"When the concern had not been able to make delivery of any of the carriages contracted for even after the original completion date, the Ordnance Department felt that it would be impossible for it to fulfill its obligation. However, a change of management was effectuated, and thereafter the Bank of America advanced additional funds to finance the completion of the contract.

"It is the Bank's representation that because the Ordnance Department knew of its furnishing these additional funds, it tacitly agreed to increase the price under the contract. So far as I can ascertain no responsible Ordnance Department officer or employee who had knowledge of the facts at any time stated or implied that such was the case. The willingness of the Ordnance Department to see the Bank advance additional funds was based on a hope that with the additional funds and under the new management, San Jose Manufacturers would be able to complete the contract, deliver the gun carriages, and reduce the amount of the loss both to the Bank of America and to the War Department which, as you know, guaranteed the V-Loan to the degree of 80%. The carriages were completed and the net loss to the Bank was thereby very substantially decreased.

"The initial mistake in the entire transaction appears to have been a belief on the part of San Jose Manufacturers that it could manufacture these carriages for $6,000, the maximum that Ordnance felt warranted in allocating to the project.

"The War Department was purchasing the same carriage from other manufacturers even then for less than $6,000. It is doubtful if it would have been justified in contracting originally at a higher price. There appears no basis on which it would now be proper for the War Department to increase the amount paid for these carriages over that originally contracted for. In reaching this conclusion, consideration has been given to the fact that the entire operation was carried out in an attempt to implement the desires generally expressed by Congress that small plants should be used as much as possible in the war effort."

The above-indicated facts make it clear that there is no equitable basis for payment of the proposed award, the effect of which would be to make the United States an insurer of all the losses which the bank sustained on its loans to San Jose.

If this bill were to be approved it could establish a precedent which would be extremely undesirable from the standpoint of the Government. Even though the War Department losses on V-loans during World War II were relatively small, the fact remains that the success of essential loan guarantee programs would be seriously jeopardized if, after meeting its obligation on the guaranteed portion of a loan, the Government were later compelled to pay a claim for the unguaranteed portion. I believe it would be most unwise to do anything which might tend to lessen the effectiveness of the guaranteed loan programs which have contributed so much to past and present mobilization efforts.

In my opinion, the instant bill is illustrative of a growing trend toward a philosophy which I find most disturbing. This is the disposition on the part of many individuals and organizations to assume in dealings with the Government that, no matter what contractual or other arrangements have been entered into, the United States should bear all the risk arising out of such dealings while they should receive all the profits. Such an attitude is manifestly inimical to the vitality of our free enterprise system, the maintenance of which becomes a matter of increasing concern in view of its importance to the continued strength of the free nations.

For the foregoing reasons, I feel obliged to withhold my approval from H.R. 1672.

HARRY S. TRUMAN

285　Statement by the President Upon Signing the First and Second Supplemental Appropriation Acts, 1952. *November 2, 1951*

I HAVE signed H.R. 5215 and H.R. 5650, the First and Second Supplemental Appropriation Acts of 1952, providing additional funds for carrying on activities of the Government.

These appropriations were requested for essential mobilization activities and for important programs contributing to our national security. I regret, however, that these bills fall seriously short of providing adequate funds for a number of vital activities.

The amount appropriated for civil defense is tragically insufficient. Out of a total of $535,000,000 originally requested the Congress has seen fit to grant only $74,945,000. The program for protective shelters was completely eliminated, and serious reductions were made in funds for the stockpiling of emergency supplies and equipment. Other important functions such as procurement, research, public information, and technical guidance will have to be greatly reduced. Civil defense is a vital part of our mobilization effort. It is reckless to evade, under the pretense of economy, the national responsibility for initiating a balanced Federal-State civil defense program.

I do not believe anyone can rightfully challenge the overwhelming importance of our defense production and economic stabilization programs during this emergency period. Nevertheless, the Budget estimates for these activities were reduced 37 percent.

This action comes at a time when controls over scarce materials require complicated regulation and when, as the result of the recent amendments to the Defense Production Act, the stabilization program has been made much more difficult to administer. There is no economy in shortchanging these programs. Without adequate appropriations for these activities we cannot maintain our production schedules, and all of us will pay for this lack of foresight through a higher cost of living.

Community facilities such as schools, sewerage lines, and water purification systems are basic to the development of housing for defense workers. Out of $25,000,000 requested for these purposes the Congress appropriated only $4,000,000. We just cannot meet defense production goals without funds for facilities and services which in many cases only the Federal Government is able to finance.

The inadequacy of the funds made available by these bills threatens other programs of major importance to our national security objectives. For example, plans for strengthened enforcement of our immigration laws cannot be carried out. The proposed monitoring program of the Federal Communications Commission in connection with the air defense of the United States and Alaska will have to be discarded. The initial programs of the National Science Foundation for training additional scientists and encouraging research must be drastically reduced.

I am greatly concerned by this indirect nullification of our laws which results from the action taken by the Congress on these and a number of other appropriation bills. It avails us little to enact legislation if its purposes are to be frustrated by lack of adequate appropriations. We, of course, will do our best to operate as effectively as possible within the limitations of presently available funds. However, I will continue to ask Congress for the balanced appropriations which are necessary for our national security and well-being. There are no bargain basements where we can pick up America's security at cutrate prices.

NOTE: As enacted, H.R. 5215 is Public Law 253, 82d Congress (65 Stat. 736), and H.R. 5650 is Public Law 254, 82d Congress (65 Stat. 760).

286   Memorandum of Disapproval of Bill Requiring Segregation in Certain Schools on Federal Property.   *November 2, 1951*

I AM withholding my approval of H.R. 5411, a bill to amend Public Laws No. 815 and 874 of the 81st Congress with respect to schools in critical defense housing areas and for other purposes.

The basic purpose of this bill is meritorious. It would provide for the construction, maintenance, and operation of elementary and secondary schools in those localities where defense activities of the Federal Government have created unusual burdens. Thus, this bill would complete the plan of Federal assistance now operating under the Defense Housing and Community Facilities and Services Act of September 1951. In addition, it contains perfecting amendments which would improve the administration of an established program supporting the operation of local school facilities, where they are inadequate to meet the impact of expanded defense activities.

Unfortunately, however, the Congress has included one provision in this bill which I cannot approve. This provision would require a group of schools on Federal property which are now operating successfully on an integrated basis to be segregated. It would do so by requiring Federal schools on military bases and other Federal property to conform to the laws of the States in which such installations are located. This is a departure from the provisions of Public Laws 815 and 874, which required only that the education provided under these circumstances should be comparable to the available to other children in the State. The purpose of the proposed change is clearly to require that schools operated solely by the Federal Government on Federally-owned land, if located in any of seventeen States, shall be operated on a segregated basis "to the maximum extent practicable."

This proposal, if enacted into law, would constitute a backward step in the efforts of the Federal Government to extend equal rights and opportunities to all our people. During the past few years, we have made rapid progress toward equal treatment and opportunity in those activities of the Federal Government where we have a direct responsibility to follow national rather than local interpretations of non-discrimination. Two outstanding examples are the Federal civil service and our armed forces, where important advances have been made toward equalizing treatment and opportunity.

Not every school operated on a Federal reservation has been integrated. It is never our purpose to insist on integration without considering pertinent local factors; but it is the duty of the Federal Government to move forward in such locations and in such fields of activity as seem best and appropriate under individual conditions and circumstances.

We have assumed a role of world leadership in seeking to unite people of great cultural and racial diversity for the purpose of resisting aggression, protecting their mutual security and advancing their own economic and political development. We should not impair our moral position by enacting a law that requires a discrimination based on race. Step by step we are discarding old discriminations; we must not adopt new ones.

I believe the way is open for an effective

administration of Public Laws 815 and 874 of the 81st Congress, while the present Congress reconsiders the full implications of the amendments proposed in H.R. 5411. The objectionable provision was added during the closing days of the first session without the careful consideration necessary for such an important departure from national policy. I hope the Congress early in the next session will reconsider this matter carefully and will re-enact legislation to provide the school aid urgently required in critical defense housing areas without the objectionable provision of H.R. 5411.

HARRY S. TRUMAN

---

287 Statement by the President Upon Signing Bill Relating to Narcotics Laws Violations. *November 2, 1951*

I HAVE today signed H.R. 3490, a bill which amends the penalty provisions applicable to persons convicted of violating certain narcotics laws. I have also today signed an Executive order to establish an Interdepartmental Committee on Narcotics. This Committee will be composed of representatives of the Treasury, State, Defense, Justice, and Agriculture Departments and the Federal Security Agency.

The situation existing with respect to illegal traffic in narcotic drugs and their use is one of grave concern to me. Illicit narcotic peddling has recently risen sharply in volume. Moreover, drug addiction has reached serious proportions, particularly among some of the youth of our Nation. The tragic effects of drug addiction upon the individual, the family, and the community as a whole are only too self-evident.

While the prevention of smuggling and illicit interstate traffic in narcotic drugs and the control of the major sources of supply is primarily the responsibility of the Federal

Government, the States and local communities have important enforcement responsibilities in their local spheres with respect to the suppression of illegal narcotic activity. In the latter field, I believe an area exists in which the Federal Government can be of valuable assistance to local enforcement authorities. At the present time, there is no single Federal instrumentality to which an interested local agency can turn for comprehensive information regarding control of narcotic traffic and treatment of drug addiction. In addition, no central group exists for making coordinated studies of new developments relating to narcotic law enforcement.

I believe that the Interdepartmental Committee can do much toward alleviating this situation. By maintaining and disseminating information with respect to illegal traffic in and use of narcotic drugs, the Committee will serve as a clearinghouse of information for enforcement agencies at all levels. Further, the Committee will per-

617

form a useful function in keeping under continuous review the problems arising in the administration and enforcement of the narcotics laws. The Committee will also study the problems of prevention and control of drug addiction and of the treatment and rehabilitation of drug addicts.

H.R. 3490 will make the efforts of the Federal Government to curb illicit traffic in drugs far more effective. It will strengthen the enforcement of the narcotics laws by making it impossible for hardened offenders to avoid serving their time in jail.

I am aware of the fact that some objection has been expressed to this act because of the limitations which it imposes on Federal courts in sentencing offenders. Fear has been expressed that this may result in prison sentences for unfortunates who are merely addicts and not engaged in the traffic for their own profit. The Interdepartmental Committee on Narcotics will keep this matter under review and, should it appear that these provisions of the law require amendment, appropriate recommendations to the Congress can be made.

NOTE: As enacted, H.R. 3490 is Public Law 255, 82d Congress (65 Stat. 767).

On the same day the President issued Executive Order 10302 establishing the Interdepartmental Committee on Narcotics (3 CFR, 1949–1953 Comp., p. 831).

288 Remarks in Response to the Presentation by Princess Elizabeth of an Overmantel for the White House. *November* 2, 1951

Your Royal Highness, Princess Elizabeth; Your Royal Highness, the Duke of Edinburgh:

It has been a very great pleasure to have you as our guests.

I am sure I speak for all the people of the United States, and especially for the people of Washington. We have many distinguished visitors here in this city, but never before have we had such a wonderful young couple that so completely captured the hearts of all of us. You will leave many happy memories among the people who have greeted you here.

It is very thoughtful and generous of the King, your father, to send this gift. It is magnificent. I am especially glad that he sent us something for this building, which means so much to the people of the United States.

This overmantel will be placed in the White House, and it will be greatly cherished as a mark of the close ties that bind our two countries together. This country is built upon principles which we have inherited from the British people—our love of liberty, our system of justice which is based upon the English common law, our language— these and many other things give us a strong feeling of kinship.

Over the years, we have built these ties into a remarkable international friendship. We have had our differences in the past, but today it would be just as hard to imagine a war between our two countries as it would to imagine another war between the States of this country. It just couldn't happen.

I hope the day will soon come when the same thing will be true among all the nations of the world, when war will be impossible in the world. That depends in great measure upon how well our two countries stick together and work for world peace. I am sure that we will do a better job for world peace because your visit here has tightened the bonds between us.

We want you to come back again. It has been reported to me that you would like to come back again and bring your lovely children.

When you do that, we hope that the restoration of the White House will be finished and you can see this gift installed in its place in the Blue Room. I don't know who the temporary occupants of the White House may be at that time. But you can be sure of this: No matter who they are, you and your family will always be welcome.

As you return to your home, I ask you to take our warmest greetings to the King and Queen. And I would like you to express to the King our gratitude for this beautiful gift and for the sentiment which inspired it.

NOTE: The President spoke at 12:30 p.m. in the Rose Garden at the White House.

The remarks of Princess Elizabeth in making the presentation follow:

Mr. President:

"We have spent 2 very happy days as your guests. Before we leave, I am, therefore, very glad to present to you a gift from my father, the King. I feel that this ceremony makes a fitting climax to what has been a delightful and memorable occasion for both of us.

"The renovation of the White House has attracted interest all over the world. Everyone knows how closely it has been bound up with the history of your country and how important it is to your people as a symbol of national pride.

"If it had been impossible to preserve this beautiful building many people in Britain would have shared your disappointment. As it is we are glad to join with you in celebrating its restoration; and my father, who has many happy memories of his own stay in the house, has wished to mark the event with a personal gift.

"It gave the King great pleasure when he found the overmantel which is before you now. The work of 18th century artists, and embodying the finest British craftsmanship, it seems perfectly suited for the place which it will occupy.

"It gives me great pleasure on behalf of my father, to present this overmantel to you. It is his hope, and mine, that it will be a welcome ornament to one of your proudest national possessions and that it will remain here, as a mark of our friendship, so long as the White House shall stand."

The overmantel consisted of a rare pair of English candelabra and a three-part mirror with an oil painting of flowers set above it in a carved gilt frame.

---

289 Remarks to Members of the Defense Advisory Committee on Women in the Services. *November 5, 1951*

IT IS a very great pleasure to meet all of you this morning. I want to express my appreciation for the time and effort you are putting in, to help us with the defense program. And it needs your help. There never was a time in the history of the country when the good women of the country could make a greater contribution than they can at this time.

We need you. We also want you as a committee to make it perfectly plain to the people of this country just exactly what we are up against. I don't think a large number of the people really appreciate that we are in the midst of one of the greatest crises we have ever faced, and that we must meet it, and that we must not, under any circumstances, let down. Because this great country of ours is the hope of the free world, and we must make good on that hope.

In the history of our country the women have always been a help in its settlement, in civilizing it, and in keeping it a republic. If you remember, in Puritan times, in Virginia, when the first settlers came in, the women manned the forts just as the men did. In the late 1840's and early 1850's, my grandmothers were first settlers in western Missouri, and they had trouble with Indians at that time. My grandfathers were in the trading business across the plains, and my red-haired grandmother, on one occasion, routed a whole band of Indians by herself and two great big shepherd dogs, and they didn't come back and bother her any more. But she maintained the home and did it just as my grandfather would have done, had he been there.

The women of this day and age have that same spirit, and I want you to arouse them and see if you can't get them to come help us.

It has been a privilege to see you.

NOTE: The President spoke in the Rose Garden at the White House at 12:10 p.m.

The Committee met in Washington on November 4 and 5. The Committee had recently announced plans for a recruiting drive to focus the Nation's attention on the urgency of the defense effort and to increase the percentage of women in the services.

290   Remarks at a Breakfast of the National Cartoonists Association. *November 6, 1951*

I CAN'T tell you how much I appreciate this book. I have, I think, as large a collection of cartoons on myself as any other President ever had, and I am very proud of them. There isn't wall space enough in my present cramped quarters in the White House Office to hang them all up, so I hang as many as I can for awhile then take them down and hang some others. And these will go with that collection. I shall probably take them out of the book and have each one of them framed, and when I get my archives building constructed, I will put these in a special room.

About that silver dollar in the Potomac. It was a Spanish piece of eight, and it was thrown across the Rappahannock. If you go down there and take a look at the place where Washington lived, any 10-year-old boy could throw a dime across at that place. But I am doubtful that Washington, with his acquisitive habits, would ever let loose of a Spanish piece of eight. That is where we got that "bit" proposition. They took a Spanish piece of eight and cut it into eight parts. One "bit" was 12½ cents, you see—two bits, four bits. Our present generation of kids doesn't know what "two bits" means, because they never heard of it. My grandmother didn't call it any other figure but "bits."

Rube, you are an artist, and should there be—I say, *should* there be, now; this is a question—a whistlestop proposition, I would like to have you for the principal introducer.

Talking about that gentleman whom the storyteller mentioned, there are a great many stories on that subject, none of which I know. But if you will look up the history on that subject, you will find that it is most interesting.

I am here to tell you how very much I appreciate your willingness to take a hand in this anti-inflation move. You know, beginning in December of last year, we had managed to get on top of the price and wage situation, and we needed a few more powers to carry the thing to its logical conclusion. Well, on account of the fact that the situation had leveled off, our friends decided that the emergency was over and we didn't need any more powers. So the spiral has begun again. And this drive that is on now for savings is the best break that we possibly can have to prevent that spiral from going to disaster.

We had the same situation with regard to the economic recovery program. The countries that we had been helping had arrived at a position where they were just on the verge of being self-supporting, and then the key and fundamental proposition in the economic recovery program was taken away from us, and we are going to have much trouble.

That is the reason—all the speculation to

the contrary—that is the reason General Eisenhower came to see me. We had matters that affected the welfare of the whole world to discuss.

And the fundamental basis of the world stabilization proposition is the Treasury of the United States of America. It is the only fundamental currency that is sound and solvent.

And what you are doing is to keep that fundamental basis of trade in a position and in a condition where the finances of the world can be eventually stabilized.

I am no economist, and don't pretend to be, but it is my business to find out what remedies are necessary to meet not only our domestic situations, but the world situation.

What you are doing is a contribution, not only to the stabilization of our domestic economy, but it is a stabilization program that affects the world around.

Whether we like it or not, we have been forced into a position of world leadership. We shirked it in 1920. We kept our backs turned on it all through that period from 1920 until 1939. And it became perfectly apparent that difficulties were going to affect the whole world. A meeting was held on the cruiser *Augusta,* on which the Atlantic Charter was signed. That was the beginning of the present foreign policy of the United States, and there hasn't been any change in it from then until now.

We are trying to assume the responsibility which God Almighty has given us, and you are helping us to assume that responsibility in a way that will be effective by what you are doing for this savings bond and stamp drive.

I can't express to you the appreciation that I feel for what you are doing. It is a patriotic gesture that is practical. Patriotism is a practical thing. It means that you are trying to make your country arrive at a position where it can meet the responsibilities which it now has in the world.

Ham, I appreciate that statement you made about your loyalty to the President. I think most every person—I don't care what his politics is—appreciates that the Office of the President—not the man that is in it—is due a certain respect.

I don't understand, sometimes, the kudos that I get, unless I think back to the time when I was 18 years old, when I saw the President of the United States for the first time. I ran three blocks, and almost couldn't breathe when I got to the point where he was making a speech on a street corner in Kansas City, Mo.

I will never forget the thrill I got at seeing the man who represented the Government of the United States, in person. I always have to think back to that, when somebody like Ham comes in and gives me a lot of kudos, and bows, and things—because I am not used to that sort of thing, and don't like it, personally.

But, there are a lot of things in the Office of the Presidency that I don't like, but that doesn't make a bit of difference, I have to take them anyway.

Keep up the good work that you are doing. You are really helping save the financial structure of the world in the program that you are carrying out.

I hope that the next time you have a breakfast, you will invite me, whether I have the title or not, and that you will have it a little earlier. I was terribly hungry when I got here!

NOTE: The President spoke at 9:05 a.m. at the Carlton Hotel in Washington. In the course of his remarks he referred to cartoonists Rube Goldberg and Ham Fisher.

291 Remarks to Members of the Executive Committee of the Polish Legion of American Veterans. *November 6, 1951*

Mr. Commander:

I appreciate this statement of yours very much. I have always, all my life, been interested in Poland, because Poland has been through, I guess, as much suffering as any other one country in the world.

But Poland has always survived the bad years and has come to life again. And Poland will come to life again, I am sure, because the Polish people are liberty-loving people, and always have been liberty-loving people.

I have another very good reason for admiring Poland, because of your Prime Minister, Paderewski and his music, which I love very much. One of the few themes I can still play is Paderewski's Minuet.

I hope that Poland will continue the struggle, and that the time will come when Poland will again be a free country among the free nations of the world.

I am sure that time will come.

NOTE: The President spoke in the Rose Garden at the White House at 12:15 p.m. His opening words "Mr. Commander" referred to George L. Mark of Cleveland, Ohio, commander of the Polish Legion of American Veterans.

The organization presented President Truman with a portrait of himself painted in Warsaw in 1946 by Bernard Frydrysiak.

292 Letter to Committee Chairmen on the Decision To Furnish Military and Economic Assistance to Yugoslavia. *November 7, 1951*

My dear Mr. Chairman:

As you know, the United States has for some time been supplying economic assistance to Yugoslavia in order to strengthen the defense capabilities of that country. Part of this assistance has come from funds appropriated for the Mutual Defense Assistance Act of 1949, as amended, and on each occasion when such funds were to be used, your Committee has been notified in accordance with the requirements of that Act.

Yugoslavia is being subjected to continued and increasing pressure by the Soviet Union and its satellites. Particularly during the past year, steps have been taken by the Soviet Union to augment the size and effectiveness of the armed forces of the Soviet satellites bordering on Yugoslavia. To meet this situation, there is an urgent need to strengthen the Yugoslav armed forces which, as you know, both from the point of view of num-

bers and training, constitute a significant obstacle to aggression in Southeastern Europe. Yugoslavia has been unable to manufacture locally, or to fill from outside sources, many of its requirements for military equipment. The situation has become so acute as to jeopardize the combat effectiveness of the Yugoslav armed forces. As a result, the security interests of the United States and also of the free world now require that we undertake to provide military assistance to Yugoslavia.

Our security interests also require that we continue to provide economic assistance to Yugoslavia in order to enable that country to sustain and increase its defense capabilities. The extent of the Yugoslav defense effort has made very heavy demands upon the country's resources. In addition, the Cominform economic blockade and last year's serious drought have added to the strain. Without such economic assistance, essential production in Yugoslavia will be curtailed and the ability of Yugoslavia to defend itself will be dangerously impaired.

In view of the foregoing and in accordance with Section 101(a)(1) of the Mutual Security Act of 1951, I have determined that Yugoslavia is a country which is of direct importance to the defense of the North Atlantic area and that the increased ability of Yugoslavia to defend itself is important to the preservation of the peace and security of the North Atlantic area and to the security of the United States. Military and economic assistance will be furnished to Yugoslavia as a result of this determination in accordance with concrete programs developed in terms of materially increasing the ability of that country to defend itself.

This letter constitutes the notification required by Section 101(a) of the Mutual Security Act of 1951.

Sincerely yours,

HARRY S. TRUMAN

NOTE: This is the text of identical letters addressed to the Honorable Richard B. Russell, Chairman of the Senate Committee on Armed Services, the Honorable James P. Richards, Chairman of the House Committee on Foreign Affairs, the Honorable Tom Connally, Chairman of the Senate Committee on Foreign Relations, and the Honorable Carl Vinson, Chairman of the House Committee on Armed Services.

For the statement by the President upon signing the Mutual Security Act of 1951, see Item 250.

---

293   Radio and Television Report to the American People on International Arms Reduction. *November 7*, 1951

[Broadcast from the White House at 10:30 p.m.]

My fellow Americans, and free peoples all around the world:

The General Assembly of the United Nations is now meeting in Paris. This great town meeting of the world has assembled for its annual session. What is done there will be of vital importance to us in the United States and to all the people of the earth.

A few hours ago the United States, Great Britain, and France announced that they would present to the General Assembly a joint proposal of great significance. This is a proposal for lessening the burden of armaments which now bears so heavily upon the world. It is a commonsense way of getting started toward the regulation and balanced reduction of all armed forces and all implements of war, including atomic weapons. We hope the General Assembly will consider this proposal as an urgent and important matter.

Tonight, I want to tell you something about this proposal, and why we are making it.

Let's begin by talking about the nature of the disarmament problem.

All of us know how difficult the world situation is today. Fighting is going on in Korea, and the threat of Communist aggression hangs over many other parts of the world. To meet this situation the United States is now rapidly building up its armed forces. So are other free countries.

We are doing this because we must. The Soviet Union and its satellites have very large military forces ready for action. The Soviet Union has a growing stock of atomic bombs. The aggression in Korea has shown that Communist imperialism will resort to open warfare to gain its ends.

In these circumstances, we must have strong military defenses and we are building them.

623

General Eisenhower has just given me an encouraging report of the progress that is being made under his command in Europe. Serious difficulties still remain, and they will require vigorous effort from us and from our allies. But the free nations of Europe are creating effective defenses. As a result of General Eisenhower's visit, arrangements are being made to speed up the training and equipment of the combined defense forces in Europe.

We shall continue to build strong defenses in Europe and in other parts of the world—just as long as that is necessary.

Our own armed forces and those of our allies are essential to the protection of freedom. They are an essential part of our efforts to prevent another world war. As they increase in size and effectiveness, they make it plain to an aggressor that he can have no hope of quick and easy conquest. As the Kremlin comes to see that its aggressive policies cannot pay off, it may abandon them and join in reasonable settlements of world problems.

This buildup of the defenses of the free world is one way to security and peace. As things now stand, it is the only way open to us.

But there is another way to security and peace—a way which we would much prefer to take. We would prefer to see the nations cut down their armed forces on a balanced basis that would be fair to all. This is the way we hoped the world would follow 6 years ago, when we helped to set up the United Nations. And it is what we are still working for—an international order without the burden of tremendous armaments.

It may seem strange to talk about reducing armed forces and armaments when we are working so hard to build up our military strength. But there is nothing inconsistent about these two things. Both have the same aim—the aim of security and peace. If we can't get security and peace one way, we must get it the other way.

The way of reducing armaments—the way we prefer—can be undertaken only if there is a workable international system which makes reduction possible without endangering the security of any nation. No country can afford to reduce its defenses unless it is sure the other fellow is reducing his at the same time. To reduce armaments, therefore, we must have, first of all, a safe and a fair procedure.

Three weeks ago, in a speech in North Carolina, I said that we are willing, as we have always been, to sit down in the United Nations with the Soviet Union, and all the other countries concerned, and work together for lessening the burden of armaments. The proposal we have announced today, along with France and Great Britain, offers a practical way to do just that.

This proposal is in the nature of a fresh approach. It has been very carefully prepared, and we believe it is an improvement over the previous approaches. If it is accepted it will open a way to reduce armaments and lessen the risk of war.

The basic principles for a real, workable system for reducing armaments are well known. I outlined them in my speech before the General Assembly of the United Nations a little more than a year ago. The General Assembly has endorsed them. They are simple, and here they are. First, such a system must include all types of weapons—such a system must include all types of weapons; second, it must be accepted by all nations having substantial armed forces; and third, it must be based on safeguards that will insure the compliance of all nations—in other words, it must be foolproof.

I also suggested to the General Assembly that the two United Nations commissions working on the control of armaments be consolidated into one. One of these commissions has been working on atomic energy, and the other commission on all other types of weapons and armed forces. It is clear, however, that all types of weapons and armed forces must be covered by one overall plan, and should therefore be under the jurisdiction of the same United Nations commission.

As a result of work during the past year, the General Assembly is now in a position to merge the two commissions and to direct the new body to get to work on concrete steps for reducing and controlling all kinds of armaments.

We hope the proposal we are now making will be the first order of business of this new commission.

Let me tell you just what it is that we are proposing.

First, we propose that a continuing inventory of all armed forces and armaments be undertaken. This inventory would take place in every country having substantial military power, and it would be checked and verified in each of those countries by inspectors who are nationals of other countries, working under the United Nations. These inspectors would have authority to find out what the real facts are.

Second, we propose that, while this process of inventory and inspection is taking place, the nations work out specific arrangements for the actual reduction of armed strength.

Third, we propose, on the basis of these two steps, that the reductions which are the goal of the program be made as soon as that can be done with full knowledge and fairness to all.

Such a program would have to be agreed upon by all the countries having substantial military power and ratified according to their own constitutional practices.

The key to this plan is the proposal to find out exactly and precisely what arms and armed forces each country has. This is

the first essential, on which all else depends. Unless this step is taken, no real progress can be made toward regulating and reducing armaments.

Any nation which is not willing to agree to this step, and to carry it out, is not really interested in disarmament. The Soviet Government has at various times talked about reducing armaments, but they never have proposed an effective system for finding out the facts. No responsible government can agree to cut its own defenses unless it knows where such a cut will leave it in relation to the armed forces of other countries. That is why we propose the first step of an honest, continuing inventory of all armed forces and armaments, including atomic weapons.

Such an inventory would proceed by stages, disclosing the least vital information first, and then proceeding to more sensitive areas. Each stage would be completed before the next began, until all armed forces and armaments of every kind had been included.

There is another important point. Any program for reducing armaments will necessarily be complex and even with the fullest cooperation of all the parties, will take quite a while to work out and put into effect. Even after it is put into effect, there will have to be safeguards against its violation. The factfinding, therefore, must be continuous. It cannot be a one-shot affair. The factfinders must know not only what the state of armament is on any given date, but how it is proceeding—whether the armed forces of the country concerned are increasing or diminishing.

As the facts are revealed, progress can be made toward working out, by mutual agreement, the exact amounts and kinds of armaments and armed forces which each country will finally be permitted to have. It might be possible, for example, to agree that each country would have armed forces proportionate to its population, with a ceiling beyond which no country could go. Furthermore, each country might be limited to using no more than a fixed portion of its national production for military purposes. That is most important. That is the key to armament reduction.

With respect to atomic weapons, the plan already approved by a majority of the United Nations fits right into this present proposal of ours for the control and reduction of armaments. Atomic weapons would be revealed at the appropriate stage in the process of disclosure. Such weapons would ultimately be prohibited, and atomic energy would be controlled under the provisions of the United Nations plan. We continue to support this plan as it now stands, but we are, of course, always ready to consider any better plan.

Let me stress that each stage of this program for reducing armaments would be entered upon only after the previous one had been completed. And each stage would be continuously policed by inspectors, who would report any breach of faith.

If the Soviet Union and its satellites are really afraid of the intentions of any of the free countries, as they say they are, here is a plan they can adopt with safety. It would give them the same protection, every step of the way, that it gives every other country. And on the other hand, we can afford to go into such a plan as this because we would have safeguards against bad faith.

All nations would have to lay their cards on the table and keep them there at all times—face up.

Here, then, is a real, down-to-earth approach, fair to all concerned. It would move forward step by step. Each step, when completed, would build up mutual confidence for the next step. If at any stage there were a breach of trust, or an act of bad faith, all participating nations would

have immediate notice, and could act in time to protect themselves.

In the face of the long and gloomy history of our negotiations with the Soviet Union, there are, no doubt, many people who think that any further attempts to control and reduce armaments are a waste of time. It is true that we have experienced much bad faith, deceit, and broken promises on the part of the Soviet Union over the last 6 years. It is true that we have met rebuffs and refusals from the Soviet Government, ever since the day we offered to give up our monopoly of atomic weapons and to prohibit them under a system of international control.

Nevertheless, as responsible men and women, we must try for disarmament in spite of all difficulties. We cannot permit the history of our times to record that we failed by default.

We make this proposal because it is the right thing to do. We are not making it in any sudden spirit of optimism. We are not making it as a last gesture of despair. We are making it because we share, with all the members of the United Nations, the responsibility of trying to bring about conditions which will assure international peace and security in the world.

The people of the world want peace. To work in every possible way for peace is a duty which we owe not only to ourselves, but to the whole human race.

In making our proposal for reducing armaments, we are not suggesting that the crisis in world affairs has passed, or even that it has lessened. I am sorry to say it has not lessened. We cannot afford, for one minute, to let down our guard, or to falter in our defense program. We must not weaken in our firm stand to resist aggression in Korea.

While aggression and fighting continue— as in Korea—and while the major political issues that divide the nations remain unsettled, real progress toward reducing armaments may not be possible.

But we cannot fail to bring before the world the problem of growing armaments, which presses so heavily on all mankind. We believe deeply that discussions of this question in the United Nations can and should begin now, even though tensions are high. Indeed, one way to reduce these tensions is to start work on such proposals as the one we are now making.

I urge the Kremlin to accept this proposal. I urge them to make it known to the people of the Soviet Union. The men in the Kremlin are responsible for the lives and the future of a great nation—of a great and creative people—a people who long for peace, even as all people long for peace. The men in the Kremlin must know how the people behind the Iron Curtain are crushed down by the burden of armaments and production for war—how they hope for release and for enjoyment of the better things of life.

And there can be a release from the burden of increasing armaments and the fear of war. The nations are not helpless chips in the tide of events. They can control their destiny, if they will. The burden of armaments can be lifted. It can be done. And if it is done, think what a prospect would open up for the future of mankind.

The United States and other countries are now helping the people of the free nations to fight against the ancient enemies of man—hunger, disease, and injustice. But what we can do now is sharply limited by the cost of maintaining defenses to prevent aggression and war. If that cost could be reduced—if the burden of armaments could be lessened, new energies and resources would be liberated for greatly enlarged programs of reconstruction and development.

New hope and opportunities would be given everywhere for better conditions of life. There would be greater freedom—greater production—greater enjoyment of the fruits of peaceful industry. Through the United Nations we could wage the only kind of war we seek—the war against want and human misery.

In the lifetime of our own generation, we could bring about the greatest period of progress for the world in all recorded history.

This is our vision. This is our hope. This is what all free people have been striving for. We are determined to gain these tremendous opportunities for human progress. We are determined to win real peace—peace based on freedom and justice.

We will do it the hard way if we must—by going forward as we are doing now, to make the free world so strong that no would-be aggressor will dare to break the peace.

But we will never give up trying for another way to peace—the way of reducing the armaments that make aggression possible.

That is why we are making these new proposals to the United Nations. We offer them in good faith and we ask that they be considered in good faith.

We hope all other nations will accept them—and will join with us in this great enterprise for peace.

294 Radio Address to the American People on Armistice Day. *November 11, 1951*

THIS Sunday is Armistice Day, the anniversary of the day the fighting ended in World War I.

On that first Armistice Day, we hoped that we had won a real and lasting peace for all the world.

We were disappointed in that hope. We were disappointed because, having won the peace, we failed to measure up to our responsibilities for keeping the peace. And because we failed to do this after World War I, we had to fight a second terrible world war.

We have learned a lesson out of that experience. Today, we face new threats of aggression in the world, new dangers of world war. But this time we have accepted our responsibility to meet those threats and dangers.

Peace—real lasting peace—remains our greatest goal. But this time we are not just going to hope for peace; we are determined to work for it, hard and actively, with all our resources.

Now we are engaged in a great national effort to build up enough strength and economic power so we and all the peaceful nations can be secure against the threats of new aggression in the world today.

This way we hope to prove to the aggressors that they cannot afford the cost of war. This way we hope to keep the peace.

In building up this great strength, there is work for all of us to do. It will take all of us to do the jobs that must be done in our Armed Forces, in our civil defense organizations, on our farms, and in our mines and factories. This is not just a man's job. It is a woman's job too. There is great work to be done by the women of this country in every part of our national effort.

Take our military forces, for example.

There are now 40,000 women on active duty in the Army, Navy, Air Force, and Marines. In the next 7 months, we hope at least 72,000 more will volunteer for service.

Our Armed Forces need these women. They need them badly. They need them to undertake every type of work except duty in actual combat formations.

Women are now serving in every branch of the Armed Forces. They serve in communications centers and supply organizations, and medical installations, and many, many other vital activities. They are continuing to do fine jobs as nurses and medical specialists. They have won for themselves a full place as regular members of our Armed Forces.

This is a tribute to the young women of our country. But it is more than a tribute—it is a great opportunity, too. For the armed services have much to offer the young women who join our active forces. These women have an opportunity to make a vital contribution to our national security. They have an opportunity to learn new skills that will help them advance in their chosen fields of work.

There is nothing more constructive that young women in the United States can do for themselves and for their country than answer the call to service with our Armed Forces.

This is a way—a real, direct, and positive way—that they can help secure the peace and safeguard freedom in the world.

NOTE: The President's address was prerecorded for release at 11 a.m.

295 The President's News Conference at Key West. *November 15, 1951*

THE PRESIDENT. Go ahead, what's on your mind?

Q. First, Mr. President, have you anything you want to tell us before we start?

THE PRESIDENT. No. I have nothing.

[1.] Q. Mr. President, since we last saw you, Mr. Auriol of France has proposed a Big Four meeting. We know what your views on that have been in the past. I wonder what you think of this proposal of his?

THE PRESIDENT. My views haven't changed. The United Nations is the conference we should attend and work with.

[2.] Q. Do you have anything to add to your meeting with Mr. Churchill in January?

THE PRESIDENT. No.

[3.] Q. Mr. President, do you care to comment on the killing of the 2,500 American prisoners of war by the North Koreans and Chinese?

THE PRESIDENT. I think it is a horrible thing. I have no official facts on the subject as yet, but I suppose they will come up to me eventually. But I think it is a horrible thing. It's the most uncivilized thing that has happened in the last century, if it's true.

Q. Mr. President, does the killing of these Americans bring any closer the day when tactical atom bombs may be used in Korea?

THE PRESIDENT. No comment.

[4.] Q. Mr. President, did you at any time in your conversations with General Eisenhower discuss domestic politics?

THE PRESIDENT. Did not.

Q. You did not?

THE PRESIDENT. He has made that statement, and so have I, and I think we both have reputations for telling the truth. And so they end right there.

Q. Mr. President, the Krock story, though, does beg one question, sir. Do you have any intentions of supporting General Eisenhower for the Democratic nomination? [1]

THE PRESIDENT. No comment.

[5.] Q. Mr. President, what was your reaction to Vishinsky's response to your proposal,[2] that he laughed all night and couldn't sleep?

THE PRESIDENT. Well, if Vishinsky laughed all night, that's the first time in his life that he has ever had a hearty laugh that I know of.

Q. Do you have hopes, Mr. President, despite Vishinsky's laughing all night, that perhaps the Russians might come around to the peace proposal?

THE PRESIDENT. We of course have no official communication from the Russian Government itself on its attitude toward the proposal that was made by the three powers. We hope that that reaction will be favorable. I think the Russian people want peace just as all the rest of the world wants peace.

Q. You say you think it will be favorable, Mr. President?

THE PRESIDENT. I hope it will be favorable.

Q. That is, the response of the Russian people themselves, I take it?

THE PRESIDENT. The response of the Russian Government to the proposal.

Q. You haven't heard anything officially from them?

THE PRESIDENT. Nothing official at all.

[6.] Q. Mr. President, what do you think of Governor Warren's announcement? [3]

THE PRESIDENT. Governor Warren is a fine man. I once said that he is a Democrat and didn't know it. [*Laughter*]

Q. Does that still go, Mr. President?

THE PRESIDENT. Still goes.

[7.] Q. Mr. President, Senator Taft says that the Korean war is a Truman war and hasn't done any good. Do you think that thing is in politics, or that it should be an

---

[1] An article by Arthur Krock, published in the New York Times on November 8, stated that "this correspondent was assured today by a person whom he believes to be thoroughly reliable and informed" that during the recent visit of Gen. Dwight D. Eisenhower to Washington, President Truman had offered to support him as a Presidential candidate in 1952.

[2] See Item 293.

[3] On November 14 Governor Earl Warren of California declared himself a candidate for the Republican presidential nomination.

issue in the campaign?

THE PRESIDENT. It should not.

[8.]   Q. Mr. President, I have been asked to ask you about your best recollection again of a conversation you had with Chief Justice Hughes, when you were filling the vacancy of Chief Justice. There seems to be some conflict in the new book that has just come out, an authorized biography of Hughes,[4] as to whether he recommended Mr. Vinson to you, or whether he recommended Mr. Jackson?

THE PRESIDENT. Well, the facts are these. I don't mind telling you what the facts were.

I telephoned to Justice Hughes—Chief Justice Hughes was retired at that time—and told him that I would like to come out and see him; he was up in the eighties at that time—and discuss the then vacancy of the Chief Justice, on account of the death of Chief Justice Stone.

He said that he would immediately come down to the office—which he did, and we had a most pleasant conversation, I imagine it lasted an hour or more.

And we went over all the judges of the Circuit Courts of Appeals of the United States—discussed various individuals all around the country, and some State supreme court judges. And at the end of the conversation, the Chief Justice said that there was a man in my Cabinet who was eminently fitted for the position—he hadn't been mentioned up to that time—and it was the Secretary of the Treasury, Mr. Vinson.

I had the same sort of conversation with Mr. Justice Roberts, along exactly the same lines, and he wound up with exactly the same recommendation.

Those are the facts.

Q. Mr. President, Justice Roberts had left the Court by that time?

THE PRESIDENT. Yes, he was living in Philadelphia, and he came down to see me, at my invitation, on the same subject.

Q. Came down from Philadelphia?

THE PRESIDENT. Philadelphia, yes.

Q. What year was that, sir?

Q. 1946.

THE PRESIDENT. 1946, yes—that's right.

Q. I believe so.

THE PRESIDENT. I think that is correct—1946. I was down the Chesapeake Bay on the *Williamsburg* when we got word that the Chief Justice had passed away.

[9.]   Q. Mr. President, when are you going to, or are you going to, issue the order that Representative King[5] requested?   He said yesterday that you told him you would issue that——

THE PRESIDENT. I suggested to Representative King that he call me and discuss the situation that has been developing before his committee.   Then I suggested to him to send me a memorandum on the subject, which he agreed to do.   That memorandum has not arrived, and I don't want to comment on what took place until we see the memorandum.

Q. But you have made no promise to issue the order?

THE PRESIDENT. I made no promise of any kind to anybody.   But I want to see that we get to the bottom of the inquiry, with justice to all concerned, and if anybody's at fault, they will have to take the consequences.

[10.]   Q. Mr. President, in your State of the Union Message, do you expect that you will recommend again your Fair Deal program?

---

[4] "Charles Evans Hughes," by Merlo J. Pusey, 2 volumes, The Macmillan Company, New York, 1951.

[5] Representative Cecil R. King of California, Chairman of the House Ways and Means subcommittee which was investigating the Bureau of Internal Revenue.

THE PRESIDENT. Oh, of course. The Fair Deal will be a part of the Democratic platform, too, I can guarantee you that. [*Laughter*]

Q. Regardless of who runs, sir?

THE PRESIDENT. Regardless of who runs. [*More laughter*]

[11.] Q. Mr. President, there has been another Washington report that while you were down here—that some intimates of Washington said you might announce your own plans for 1952?

THE PRESIDENT. I didn't get that. Say it again a little louder.

Q. Well, Paul Leach [6] is saying that intimates in Washington said that while you were here that you expected to announce your plans for 1952 perhaps?

THE PRESIDENT. No. I have no intention of doing that.

Q. You will let us know if you change your mind?

THE PRESIDENT. Oh, yes, I will—probably see you a time or two before I leave. You can still ask the same question and I'll give you the same answer!

Q. The last word was that you wouldn't disclose it, anyway, until after you had presented the three messages?

THE PRESIDENT. That's right.

Q. That still stands?

THE PRESIDENT. That still stands. It may be a little later than that before I make any announcement.

[12.] I want to say something further about these investigations that have been going on, and the discoveries of some malfeasance in office.

Whenever that is discovered, immediate action has always been taken to part the men who have done the wrong from the service, and if they have committed any criminal acts, they have been put before a grand jury.

---

[6] Paul R. Leach of the Chicago Daily News.

It is my opinion that the average of Government employees is above the average of employees of big business, and newspapers, and every other line of business. But whenever a Government employee goes wrong, it is my—always been my attitude to immediately take the necessary steps to part him from the service, and take whatever legal procedures are necessary to see that he is punished if he has committed a crime.

I still think that the average Government employee is an honorable man, or an honorable woman, and I think that the vast majority of them, I would say more than 95 percent, try to deliver to the Government what they are paid for. And some of them—a great many of them—deliver a great deal more than they are paid for.

I think you ought to make that perfectly clear.

Some effort on the part of some columnist to whom you referred—not the one you referred to specifically—but some columnists have been trying to imply that the President of the United States condoned misconduct in public office. That is not true at all. The record will speak for itself.

[13.] Q. You are looking well, Mr. President. You are obviously enjoying yourself down here.

THE PRESIDENT. Yes, I am feeling well, and getting an immense amount of work done—you would be surprised. I get to work in the daytime now, instead of all night. I get to sleep at night, that's the reason I feel better.

[14.] Q. Mr. President, in connection with my question about the Fair Deal program, do you anticipate that the Taft-Hartley Act will again be an issue in the campaign?

THE PRESIDENT. We will have to analyze any amendments that are made by the next session of Congress before I can answer that question.

Q. I see. I was going to ask this question: Do you favor a change in the law as it now stands?

THE PRESIDENT. Yes.

Q. Would you be able to say——

THE PRESIDENT. No, I don't want to elucidate on it, because it is a very complicated proposition.

Reporter: Thank you, Mr. President.

Q. Thank you. I hope you have a nice swim.

THE PRESIDENT. That was easy this morning.

NOTE: President Truman's two hundred and eighty-fifth news conference was held on the lawn of the Little White House at Key West, Fla., at 9:40 a.m. on Thursday, November 15, 1951.

296 Remarks to Delegates and Trainees From the World Land Tenure Conference. *November* 20, 1951

THANK YOU very much, Doctor. It is a very great pleasure and privilege to meet you this afternoon.

I am highly interested in what you are doing. I am highly interested in the exchange of ideas which take place and how little difference they find there is between them.

It has taken us a long time to discover that agriculture is the fundamental basis on which we all live. We must have things to eat and things to wear and they must come from but one place and that is the land.

It took us a long time to discover that farm credit and farm management are the two most important things of the foundation of a republic. I think we have made some progress in this country in the past hundred years. We don't say we made all the progress.

Ideas come from all around the world. The world is full of ideas, it is whirling with ideas and it is a good thing. The very fact that you are here shows that in the long run we will have a friendly world and I hope

our young people, and we have some in the same sort of errands that you have here, will come back with information for us that will give us a chance to progress and do better than we are now.

I thank you all for coming. I hope during the year you will become imbued with such close friendships to us that we can never have a falling out.

Thank you very much.

NOTE: The President spoke in the Rose Garden at the White House at 3:30 p.m. In his opening words he referred to Dr. Henry G. Bennett, Administrator of the Technical Cooperation Administration, Department of State.

The World Land Tenure Conference was sponsored jointly by the University of Wisconsin, the Technical Cooperation Administration, and the Economic Cooperation Administration. The Department of Agriculture and the Food and Drug Organization of the United Nations assisted in its operation.

The conference opened on October 8, 1951, at the University of Wisconsin and lasted 6 weeks, after which the members made a brief tour, ending in Washington on November 16. There were 51 delegates and 20 trainees from 38 countries in attendance at the conference.

297 Address Before the Woman's National Democratic Club. *November* 20, 1951

Madam President, the Woman's National Democratic Club, ladies and gentlemen:

I am glad to be here tonight.

You know, I just flew up here from Key West, and I'm going to fly back down there tomorrow. I have left Washington a good many times for a one-night stand somewhere else, but this is the first time I have ever come to Washington for a one-night stand.

I want you to know how happy I am to be here. I am delighted to speak to this crowd of Democrats—especially at a dinner given by such a fine group of Democratic women. Besides, Mrs. Truman—under pressure from Mrs. Edwards—made this engagement for the two of us; and when I have a date with Mrs. Truman, I usually keep it.

I've been having an interesting time at Key West—and I have been doing some things that I don't have time to do here in Washington. For one thing, I have been getting some extra sleep. You know, the President usually has so much work to do that it keeps him busy all day and most of the night.

Down at Key West, I have also had more time than usual to think about some of the things that lie ahead of us.

One of the things I have been thinking about is next year's election. I am sure that is a matter of considerable interest to all of you people here tonight. It's a matter of considerable interest to me, too, and that's what I want to talk to you about.

I'm not going to make any announcement about who the candidate will be, although I do have some ideas on that subject. What I want to talk about tonight is the broad picture of what this election means. I want to talk about where this Nation stands in the world and about what the future holds in store for us. I want to impress upon you, if I can, just how important that election next year will be.

In a presidential election, we do more than choose between candidates—we also choose a course of action for our country to follow for the next 4 years. That is a matter for every one of us to consider very seriously and, I am sure, prayerfully. A wise choice can do much to insure the prosperity and security of our Nation. A mistake in a presidential election can cause the country untold harm.

You remember what happened in 1920. When the people voted for Harding, that meant a tremendous change in the course the United States was following. It meant that we turned our backs on the newborn League of Nations. It meant that we tried to isolate ourselves—we simply shut our eyes to the international facts of life.

Well, it didn't work. The United States was a major world power in 1920, even if it did not like to act as one. I think most people now recognize that the country chose the wrong course in 1920—and that choosing the wrong course then had a lot to do with the eventual necessity of fighting a Second World War.

Now, this is an example of why a presidential election in this country is so vitally important. It affects the future of every citizen, and our national position in the world. I hope that we will never repeat the mistake of 1920.

The course America chooses in 1952 will be even more important than the choice in 1920. This is because of the great change which has taken place in our position among the nations of the world.

We have now achieved a position of leadership in the world that gives us opportunities and responsibilities never before equaled in human history.

I think we should all understand that. There is so much carping criticism nowadays about what's wrong with the country that people don't seem to think much about what's right with the country. You hear it on every hand: "The trouble with the country today is this" and "The trouble with the country is that." We ought to stop once in a while and spend a little time counting our blessings.

So far as the United States is concerned, we can all be proud of where it stands and the condition it is in today. Some people, of course, have political reasons why they can't admit that to be true. But it is a fact, nevertheless. We have the strongest and most productive economic system the world has ever seen. We have come out of the most devastating war of all time with our free institutions intact. This country today stands at the highest point in its history.

One of the things that gives me the greatest pride is our moral position before the world.

We are taking the lead in a great crusade for peace.

We are giving our unfaltering support to the United Nations because it is the world's best hope for peace.

We are striving mightily to build a firm structure of international law and order, so that wars shall be no more.

We are using our strength, not to take advantage of the rest of mankind, but to help them—to help them to help themselves. We are doing that because we know the welfare of all men will contribute to world peace. We know that helping others is the best way—probably the only way—to achieve a better future for ourselves.

In this endeavor we have already had results. We have halted the economic and social decline which so gravely threatened the civilization of Western Europe. We have thrown back lawless aggression in Korea. We have curbed the creeping menace of Communist subversion that was attacking one country after another around the world.

It is still too early to say exactly what the outcome of this great effort will be. But we can be sure that if we had not acted as we did, many of the countries that are free today would have long since vanished behind the Iron Curtain to become slaves to dictatorship.

If we had followed this kind of a course back in the years after the First World War—if we had accepted our international responsibilities at that time—the Second World War could have been prevented.

This time, I believe deeply that we are following the right course, and that we can and will be successful in preventing another world conflict.

If we are successful, a great age—an age of great achievements for mankind—lies ahead of us. It is a wonderful picture. When I think about it, I wish I were beginning my life all over again.

Science and invention are opening up new possibilities that are simply fantastic. Atomic energy, which is such a danger to the world now, can bring marvelous benefits when it is turned to peaceful uses. Medical science is discovering new ways to improve health and cure disease. Scientists are constantly finding means to get more and better production from our farms and industries.

These advances in technology will help to make possible great social advances. More and more of our people can have better educations, better homes, better health, and greater security. A happier life can be brought within the reach of all our citizens and, I hope, of all the people in the world.

These new discoveries should make it possible to liberate millions of men and women in other lands from the terrible burdens of disease and poverty that now hold them down.

These are some of the things that are within our reach.

When we think about next year's election, we ought to place it in this perspective. We ought not to think about that election just as a matter of parties or candidates. We ought to think about it in terms of what it would mean to our national prosperity, to our efforts for peace, to our chance of realizing all our opportunities in the years ahead.

When you think about it like that, I believe you will understand why I say we ought to pray over it.

As Democrats, we naturally want to win the election, but in making our fight we must put the national interest ahead of everything else.

I sincerely hope that the foreign policy of the United States will not become a partisan political issue in the campaign. I believe in a bipartisan approach to foreign policy. I don't want to give foreign interests, of any kind, the opportunity to enter into our domestic politics, and try to set Americans against one another. Partisan politics ought to stop at the water's edge.

Since I have been President, I have sought to steer a straight course of handling foreign policy matters on the sole basis of the national interest. The people I have chosen to fill the major government positions concerned with foreign policy have been picked solely on merit, without regard to party label. In making important decisions on foreign policy, I have consulted regularly with leaders of both parties—Democrats and Republicans alike.

For my part, I want to keep it that way— I want to keep our foreign policy out of domestic politics. I am happy to say that there are many patriotic Republicans who have the same view of this question. They have gladly given of their wisdom and their help because they put the country first, too. I might add that these are the Republicans— in Congress and out—who know most about foreign affairs.

But I am sorry to say that there is another group of Republicans—a group who want to put foreign policy into domestic politics. They want to play with dynamite, and they may have their way. I don't know how the Republican convention will decide the matter, next July.

But we can meet this issue if it comes. This is a warning. If the Republicans do make foreign policy an issue in the campaign, it will be the best issue the Democratic Party has. We can stand on our record on foreign policy, and our achievements in the struggle for peace. If the Republican Party takes the fatal step, and decides to throw our program for world peace into the midst of a political fight, I am sure that the Republican Party will be overwhelmingly repudiated by the people.

This is no time to play petty politics with the Nation's safety, and the people of this country will surely rise up against the political party that attempts to do it.

But whether or not foreign policy is made an issue, the campaign next year will be a hard fight. There will be loud Republican voices trying to destroy our faith in ourselves and in our present course of action as a nation. There will be a deliberate attempt to misrepresent the basic facts. The bitter, partisan, backward-looking "old guard" will try to belittle our progress and prosperity at home. They will try to discredit the effort we are making to bring about peace. They will try to destroy our hope in the vision of the future that leads us on.

The attack will be well organized—and well financed. We've had a sample in the congressional elections of last year. We saw how the special interests poured money into Ohio last year to elect a Republican senator. Now they will be thinking that if money can win an election in Ohio, maybe money can win a national election. I venture to predict that there is going to be more money spent in trying to defeat the Democratic

Party next year than has ever before been spent in any election in the history of this Republic.

And that is not all. The opposition is sure to be fully equipped with slick public relations counselors and gigantic national advertising campaigns. The art of misrepresentation can be expected to reach new heights—if that is possible.

We saw some samples of that last year, too. Do you remember what happened in Maryland? It was all described in sworn testimony before a Senate committee. Use the "big doubt" technique, they said. First, tell a lie to create the doubt, and then use all the tricks of propaganda to exploit it. Create the doubt, and then exploit it. Isn't that a comedown for the party of Abraham Lincoln?

They tried it—and they managed to fool the people. So they are sure to try it again— lies and smears. Maryland is not the only place they tried it. Look at what they did to Senator Elbert Thomas of Utah. There never was a better man nor a more able Senator than Elbert Thomas. But did that keep the Republicans from conducting a dirty smear campaign to defeat him? No, it did not.

Now, because they got away with it once, they think they can do it again. Now they are going to try it on a national scale.

I do not expect the Democratic Party to take that kind of attack lying down. I do not expect my party to run away from a fight. It never did, and it never will.

We can't stoop to character assassination as the Republicans practiced it in 1950. And we won't have the enormous slush funds they will have.

But we will have some things the Republicans won't have. We will have the record and the issues. The truth and the facts will be on our side. If we get the truth and the facts before the people—if we make sure they know what the real issues are—then, the people will be on our side, too. We proved that conclusively in 1948.

The American people have a lot of commonsense. They know what they want, and they will not be fooled for long by any political confidence men or sleight-of-hand artists.

The way to meet the Republican campaign is to stand firm, and to fight for what we believe is right. I believe the Democratic Party can win and I believe it will win—because it is following the course which corresponds most truly to what the American people deeply feel and believe.

The Democratic Party stands for the people and for progressive policies. It is the party that recognizes the needs of the people, and works to meet those needs.

I have seen the Democratic Party do more for this country in recent years than any party ever did in all our history. I have seen prosperity restored, liberty strengthened, incomes increased, and opportunities enlarged. I have seen all this done because of the progressive ideals of the Democratic Party—and because the Democratic Party has put those ideals into action.

I believe in those ideals.

I believe in them because I know the purpose of Government is to serve the people— all the people, and not just those who have money and power.

And I believe the Democratic Party has what it takes to lead the American people in the great struggle we are making for peace and human progress.

If we stand firm and fight for our ideals with courage and with faith in the future, I have no doubt that the American people will choose the Democratic Party to lead this Republic toward prosperity at home and peace in the world.

NOTE: The President spoke at 10 p.m. at the May-flower Hotel in Washington. His opening words "Madam President" referred to Mrs. Fred W. Morrison, president of the Woman's National Democratic Club. In the course of his remarks the

President referred to Mrs. India Edwards, vice chairman of the Democratic National Committee and director of the Woman's Division, and to former Senator Elbert D. Thomas of Utah.

The address was broadcast.

298   The President's News Conference at Key West.
November 29, 1951

THE PRESIDENT. [1.] I am going to read you a statement on a matter about which you are very much interested.

[*Reading*] "I hope everyone understands now that there has been no cease-fire in Korea, and that there can be none until an armistice has been signed.

"It is our duty to continue our efforts until the United Nations objectives have been achieved."

Get that now.

[*Continuing reading*] "It is our duty to continue our efforts until the United Nations objectives are achieved. Only then will the future safety of the United Nations forces, including those who are prisoners in the hands of the enemy, only then can their safety be assured. We cannot allow our men to be caught off balance by the enemy, in case we cannot reach a satisfactory armistice agreement. The continued pressure of our forces on the enemy constitutes the strongest incentive for the latter to agree to a just armistice.

"Any premature slackening of our effort would cost us more casualties in the long run than need be lost."

I want to give you a lecture on fake stories about cease-fires and armistices, and things of that kind.

I was marching down the road in France on October 27, 1918, with a battery—my battery. The other batteries in the regiment were strung out along the road, one behind the other, and here came a French paper with block headlines as big as the French can make them, saying that an armistice

had been signed. And just as I read that headline, a 150 mm. shell burst about a hundred yards away from me on that side, and another one on this side. And that story was put out by Roy Howard. It was a fake.[1]

This A.P. story that has been put out on a cease-fire is parallel with it. It doesn't do the peace of the world one bit of good for things like that to be put out, and they should not be. You have the responsibility for the welfare of this country just the same as I have, and I'm talking to the press associations and the independent newspaper representatives who are here, not you gentlemen individually because I get along with you all right, but you must be careful in this very dangerous time to stick to the truth.

Now, I understand that this story came out because of intense competition. Well, it seems to me that the welfare of the United States and of the United Nations and of the world is much more important than any competitive situation which may exist among newshounds.

Now, go ahead with your questions.

---

[1] According to the New York Times of November 30, 1951, the White House Press Office issued a clarifying statement 90 minutes after the close of the President's news conference, as follows:

"After refreshing his memory about his experience of reading a false armistice report in a French newspaper on October 27, 1918, the President is not sure that this report originated with Mr. Roy Howard. However, it is well known that Mr. Howard was responsible for a false armistice report which reached the United States on November 7, 1918, and the President wanted it known how much harm such false reports created."

Q. Mr. President, would it be possible for you to release what you just said for quotation, so that we can use the recorded tape that has been made on it?

THE PRESIDENT. Well, wait until it is transcribed and then I will give you the answer. I want to see what it looks like.

Q. Mr. President, one question—what was that date, 18?

THE PRESIDENT. October 27th, 1918.

Q. What kind of shell was that?

THE PRESIDENT. A 150 mm. German shell on each side of me.

Q. That means what?

THE PRESIDENT. Well, that is about a six-inch shell.

Q. October 17th, sir?

THE PRESIDENT. October 27th. It created a riot over here, and the people had a terrible letdown when they found out it wasn't so.

Q. As I understand it, the direct quotation stops just before you start what you called your lecture on the story?

THE PRESIDENT. It stops with the sentence, "Any premature slackening of our effort would cost us more casualties in the long run than need be." That will be mimeographed, so you will have a copy, Joe [2] tells me. We'll look this other tape over, and if it's in proper shape, why we'll let you have it.

Q. We would sure like to have it.

THE PRESIDENT. All right, I think we will be able to release it.

[2.] Q. Mr. President, would you care to comment on the assertions by Senator Taft before the Senate committee on Monday, that the campaign to defeat him in Ohio was a sinister conspiracy blueprinted by a Communist and directed from the White House?

THE PRESIDENT. There was no conspiracy that I know anything about. Of course, all the Democrats wanted a Democratic Sena-

---

[2] Joseph H. Short, Secretary to the President.

tor from Ohio, and I'll admit that I was very anxious to see a Democratic Senator from Ohio, but we didn't succeed in getting one. I think the conspiracy was probably in the slush fund on the Republican side of the campaign.

[3.] Q. Mr. President, have you been informed that Senator Kefauver has given the people permission to enter his name in the presidential primary in California?

THE PRESIDENT. I didn't know about that, but I saw where he was perfectly willing to let the lightning strike him if it felt that way. Everybody has a right to run for President if he wants to.

[4.] Q. Mr. President, are you planning to do anything about the Chief Counsel of the Internal Revenue Bureau, Mr. Oliphant, who has been brought into the Caudle case because he took some free plane rides? [3]

THE PRESIDENT. I have no facts to justify any action as yet.

Q. Mr. President, Senator Nixon made a suggestion today, that you guarantee the employees of the Internal Revenue Bureau freedom from any reprisal, if they will report cases of wrongdoing which he says they know about and haven't reported?

THE PRESIDENT. That isn't true. They have always had immunity on that subject. Whenever a man knows of any malfeasance in office and doesn't report it, he is *particeps criminis* in connection with it.

Q. Would you give us that again, please sir? [*Laughter*]

THE PRESIDENT. He is a party to the crime, if that will suit you better.

Q. When he doesn't report it?

THE PRESIDENT. That's right.

---

[3] Charles Oliphant, Assistant General Counsel, Bureau of Internal Revenue, and T. Lamar Caudle, former Assistant Attorney General, Tax Division, Department of Justice, whose names figured prominently in the congressional investigation of the Bureau of Internal Revenue. See also Item 300.

[5.] Q. Mr. President, what do you think of the Russians shooting down one of our planes off Vladivostok?

THE PRESIDENT. Of course I don't like it. I don't know whether it is true or not. I haven't had the official report as yet.

[6.] Q. Mr. President, do you agree with the Senate Preparedness Subcommittee, that military production is dangerously behind schedule because guns are not getting priority over——

THE PRESIDENT. I think that question is rather loaded. I think the very best effort is being put forth to meet the different requirements. If it isn't, I'll soon find out about it, and we will do something about it. I have had experience along that line, as you know.

Q. Is there a plan, sir, to revise our production schedule somewhat, to bring along some small arms faster ahead of the long lead items, so to speak, to speed up the——

THE PRESIDENT. Whatever is necessary in that line will be done. It is being surveyed all the time. It is in constant condition of being looked into by the National Security Council, by Mr. Wilson,[4] and by the Cabinet.

[7.] Q. Mr. President, were you advised of the death of Senator Wherry?[5]

THE PRESIDENT. Yes, and I was very sorry to hear it. Senator Wherry and I were very good personal friends. We had a lot of political dogfights, but personally he and I were always very friendly. I sent a telegram of sympathy to his wife today, immediately, as soon as I heard it.

[8.] Q. Mr. President, if the CIO breaks through wage ceilings in the negotiations about to start, do you think that that will affect the fight against inflation in any great degree?

THE PRESIDENT. That's a hypothetical question—starts with if and ends with the prospective something that hasn't happened yet. When the time comes, I will answer it. I don't mean to step on you, but then you can't answer questions like that.

[9.] Q. In regard to Mr. Oliphant, you said you have no facts to justify any action as yet. Do you——

THE PRESIDENT. Whenever the facts come to me to justify action, I'll take the action, as I always do; but you can't convict a man until you have the evidence. That has been the policy of some of our committees in Congress, and I don't want to follow that policy.

Q. Mr. President, do you expect any other dismissals and firings in this inquiry?

THE PRESIDENT. I'm making no anticipatory remarks on that. It's like this other question down here, it is hypothetical.

[10.] Q. Mr. President, the question in which we all have quite a personal interest—when are we going home?

THE PRESIDENT. Well, sir, I don't care. The longer we stay the better I'll be pleased. As soon as I know the answer, I'll give it to you. I'll have a lot of trouble when I get back to Washington. I do an immense amount of work around here without interruption. That's not possible in the White House.

Q. Do you expect to spend Christmas somewhere besides Key West?

THE PRESIDENT. That's another hypothetical question. I expect to spend it in Independence, Mo.

[11.] Q. Mr. President, have you ever received a letter from this mayor of Ithaca, N.Y., who wanted a million-dollar Government loan to raise city employee's salaries up there?

THE PRESIDENT. Never heard of it. Didn't

---

[4] Charles E. Wilson, Director, Office of Defense Mobilization.

[5] Senator Kenneth S. Wherry of Nebraska died at the George Washington University Hospital in Washington on November 29.

reach me. Joe says it was just a publicity stunt. I guess that's right.

Q. Well, Mr. President, have we overlooked anything?

THE PRESIDENT. I can't remember anything you have overlooked. Seems to me you

have covered the waterfront pretty thoroughly.

Reporter: Thank you, Mr. President.

NOTE: President Truman's two hundred and eighty-sixth news conference was held in the lobby of Bachelor Officers Quarters No. 128 at the United States Naval Base, Key West, Fla., at 4 p.m. on Thursday, November 29, 1951.

299   Statement by the President on Establishing the Committee on Government Contract Compliance.   *December 3, 1951*

I HAVE today signed an Executive order creating the Committee on Government Contract Compliance.

The purpose of this order is to secure better compliance by contractors and subcontractors with certain provisions now required in their contracts with the U.S. Government. For nearly 10 years it has been mandatory to include in such contracts a clause obligating the contractor to practice nondiscrimination in the performance of his contract. The clause specifically forbids discrimination because of race, creed, color, or national origin; relates to the various aspects of employment; and extends to subcontracts as well as to original contracts.

The inclusion of this nondiscrimination clause in Government contracts has been helpful in reducing the practice of discrimination. In the past, however, compliance has not been secured by any system of uniform regulation, or inspection, common to all the contracting agencies of the Federal Government, and widely understood by contractors and their employees.

The present order is designed to correct this deficiency. It places the primary responsibility for securing compliance with the nondiscrimination clause with the head of each contracting agency of the Federal Government. This is as it should be, for this is where the primary responsibility rests for securing compliance with contractual

provisions generally. The same means used to obtain compliance generally can be used by the contracting agencies to obtain compliance with the nondiscrimination clause. The Committee will be expected to examine and study the compliance procedures now in use and to recommend to the department and agency heads changes that will strengthen them. As part of its functions, the Committee may confer with interested persons. Recommendations of this Committee are subject to review under certain conditions by the Director of Defense Mobilization, so that our efforts towards eliminating discrimination in employment will at all times aid in increasing defense production.   •

The creation of this Committee on Government Contract Compliance is one more step in the program I have undertaken to use the powers conferred on the Executive by the Constitution and the statutes to eliminate the practice of discrimination in connection with activities of the Federal Government. The Fair Employment Board of the Civil Service Commission carries this responsibility with respect to the Federal Government as an employer. The President's Committee on Equality of Treatment and Opportunity in the Armed Services pointed the way toward ending discrimination in our fighting forces. In fulfilling a contract with the Federal Government a contractor should follow the national policy of equal treatment and opportunity. It is my hope and my belief that the Committee on Government Contract Compliance will show us the way.

NOTE: The President referred to Executive Order 10308 "Improving the Means for Obtaining Compliance with the Nondiscrimination Provisions of Federal Contracts" (3 CFR, 1949–1953 Comp., p. 837).

The statement was released at Key West, Fla.

300   The President's News Conference of December 13, 1951

THE PRESIDENT. Please be seated.

I have no special announcements to make, but I understand that there are quite a number of questions that you would like to ask, and I will listen. I am ready.

[*Pause*]

Q. Mr. President—[*laughter*]——

THE PRESIDENT. Well! Yes, Eddie? [1]

[1.]   Q. Chairman McKinney told us the other day that you were planning to take drastic action, looking to a Government housecleaning.[2]

THE PRESIDENT. Well, Eddie, let's use a different verb on that. Let's say *continue* drastic action. Whenever it has been necessary to take drastic action, it has been taken by the President whenever it is necessary, and I will continue to do just that.

If you will study the history of the situa-

tion, you will find that there has never been one of those things that you refer to that has come to the President on which he has not taken drastic action. That is what he proposes to continue to do.

What are you looking at me like that for? Do you want to write a sob sister piece about it? I don't need any sob sister pieces!

Q. Mr. President, are you going to implement it this time?

THE PRESIDENT. What do you mean?

Q. Are you going to set up any special organization to take action, or are you going to do it through regular channels?

THE PRESIDENT. If I make up my mind on that, I will let you know, Pete.[3]

Q. The general idea is to have a special committee like the Roberts-Pomerene [3a]——

THE PRESIDENT. It's not a committee like anybody's. If there is one, it is going to be mine. It's going to be an original one.

Q. It is going to be like the previous one, called the Truman committee?

THE PRESIDENT. Yes sir, I had a Truman committee once that worked very well.

Q. Did you consult with J. Edgar Hoover[4] on that subject?

THE PRESIDENT. I have consulted with everybody in the Government.

Q. That includes Mr. Hoover?

---

[1] Edward T. Folliard of the Washington Post.

[2] Frank E. McKinney, chairman of the Democratic National Committee. On November 1, the day after Mr. McKinney became chairman, the White House released the following letter from Mr. McKinney to the President:

"When you asked me to become chairman of the Democratic National Committee, you told me of your firm purpose that the Federal service be maintained at the highest standards of integrity and ability and with spotless honor. My every effort will be directed toward that goal. I will seek its accomplishment in every way possible.

"Toward that end I recommend that Collectors of Internal Revenue be brought under Civil Service and subjected to the selection standards of that Service. It is your objective, I know, that the public have every confidence in the integrity and ability of our Federal tax administration. I believe the adoption of this recommendation will further that objective."

[3] Raymond P. Brandt of the St. Louis Post-Dispatch.

[3a] Owen Josephus Roberts and Atlee Pomerene were appointed by President Coolidge in February 1924 as special counsels for the United States to prosecute the Teapot Dome oil fraud case.

[4] Director, Federal Bureau of Investigation.

THE PRESIDENT. That includes Mr. Hoover.

Q. Are you going to draw on whatever special agents he may——

THE PRESIDENT. Mr. Hoover always does his duty as he has always done it as the chief investigator for the Government.

Q. There has been some speculation he may replace Mr. McGrath.[5] Is that unfounded?

THE PRESIDENT. You mean that he would be Attorney General?

Q. Yes sir.

THE PRESIDENT. No. That is unfounded.

[2.] Q. Mr. President, some young Congressman—I have forgotten his name, I think he is from Wisconsin—Republican from Wisconsin—has demanded that you fire Attorney General McGrath.

THE PRESIDENT. Well, I don't think there's a single member of the Cabinet that some Congressman hasn't demanded to be fired. They haven't been very successful at that sort of an approach.

Q. Could I put it more pointedly?

THE PRESIDENT. Sure.

Q. There were reports—there are reports that you are going to drop Mr. McGrath from the Cabinet?

THE PRESIDENT. I hadn't heard any of those reports. They haven't reached the White House yet.

Q. Is there any—[*laughter*]. Are you considering any change, Mr. President, in the post of Attorney General?

THE PRESIDENT. No.

Q. Thank you.

THE PRESIDENT. If you had asked it that way in the first place, I would have answered it that way.

Q. I'm sorry—I'm sorry.

THE PRESIDENT. It's all right, we have a little fun as we go along.

[*Pause*]

---

[5] Attorney General J. Howard McGrath.

THE PRESIDENT. Well, well, well!—are you stymied?

[3.] Q. Mr. President, Mr. McKinney said in Chicago this morning that he thought you were going to set up a special agency?

THE PRESIDENT. Mr. McKinney made the statement in the White House, and he has to be consistent. [*Laughter*]

Q. Mr. President, is he correct?

THE PRESIDENT. I cannot answer that question.

[4.] Q. Mr. President, do you have any intention of asking Mr. McKinney to leave the national committee?

THE PRESIDENT. I certainly don't. Mr. McKinney suits me down to the ground. I don't put people in places or ask them to serve in places and then pull the rug from under them the first time anything happens that the newspapers don't like. It pleases me when they don't like it, because I think it's right.

[5.] Q. Mr. President, would you care to indicate some of the instances in the past where you have taken action—drastic action?

THE PRESIDENT. Oh yes, there are plenty of them. I have dispensed with several Cabinet officers in times past. The collector in Boston was fired before anybody began to look into his situation, except the Treasury Department. The collector of revenue in St. Louis was dispensed with long before anything was looked into by any committee. The collector in San Francisco was fired before any committee went into it, and a grand jury right now in California has just indicted him. The necessary action in all these things has been taken by the executive branch of the Government whenever it was necessary.

You remember all the ballyhoo about Communists in Government. The Loyalty Board which I set up took care of that situation before anybody outside the executive branch of the Government took any action. The Communists who have been tried and convicted, were tried and convicted by the Attorney General, not by any outside agency.

The Government has been carried on just as it should be, by the President of the United States who is the Chief Executive of the Nation, and that is the way it will continue to be carried on.

[6.] Q. Mr. President, can we get the record clear on the collector in St. Louis?

THE PRESIDENT. Yes.

Q. As I understand it, he was investigated in May 1950, and it wasn't until March or April that he resigned, and at that time a grand jury was looking into his activities?

THE PRESIDENT. He was asked to resign long before that. It was very difficult to get his resignation.

Q. Did you ask for it?

THE PRESIDENT. I didn't want to fire him— yes, long before.

Q. Secretary Snyder said he asked them for it in October and again in January——

THE PRESIDENT. That's right.

Q. ——and was told—no, wait a minute—Finnegan [6] testified that you had asked that he remain——

THE PRESIDENT. No, no, that's a mistake.

Q. He said the White House had——

THE PRESIDENT. I backed Mr. Snyder up in his request in the first place.

Q. But he was allowed to resign.

THE PRESIDENT. Well, what would you do under the circumstances?

Q. In the case of Finnegan? [*Laughter*]

THE PRESIDENT. Of course, I know what the Post-Dispatch would do to any Democrat, they would cut his head off every time they had a chance.

Q. We would do the same for a Republican.

THE PRESIDENT. I am not so sure. I remember a certain mayor of St. Louis which you loved very much.

[7.] Q. Mr. President, there was one thing you said in there, the answer to the previous question, which I would like to ask a further question about. I believe you said, after talking about the investigations, that that is the way it will continue to be done by the President. Does that indicate then, sir, that in handling this situation which has arisen, that you will go ahead through your regular investigative channels——

THE PRESIDENT. I didn't say that, and you can't put words in my mouth.

Q. No sir—I'm not trying to.

THE PRESIDENT. I didn't say that at all. I said that the executive branch of the Government would continue to do its duty, and whatever is necessary to be done will be done. And if you gentlemen will just have a little patience, you will find out something a little later that will be for your welfare and benefit.

Q. How much later, sir?

THE PRESIDENT. Well, I will have to take time on these things. You know I can't be pushed into doing anything——

Q. Can you give us an estimate?

THE PRESIDENT. ——by anybody.

[8.] Q. Mr. President, did Mr. McKinney quote you correctly as saying that he said that you were very angry because you felt that some people had sold you down the river?

THE PRESIDENT. Well, who wouldn't feel that way? A man who has taken an oath to support and defend the Constitution of the United States, and who doesn't do it would make any executive angry. Even your paper ought to get angry at something like that. [*Laughter*]

Q. Mr. President, does that specifically apply to Mr. Caudle? [7]

[6] James P. Finnegan, former collector, 1st District of Missouri, Bureau of Internal Revenue.

[7] See Item 298 [4].

THE PRESIDENT. What?

Q. Does that specifically apply to Mr. Caudle?

THE PRESIDENT. It applies to all these people who have been fired.

Q. Mr. President, what was your attitude about Mr. McGrath's testimony on the Hill, that he saw nothing wrong with Mr. Caudle?

THE PRESIDENT. I haven't read Mr. McGrath's testimony.

[9.] Q. Do you expect to have Mr. McGrath as Attorney General as long as you are President?

THE PRESIDENT. Mr. McGrath has made no motion to me that he expects to resign, and I haven't asked him to resign.

[10.] Q. Mr. President, I would like to pursue that, if I may. That has been one thing that puzzled so many of us.

THE PRESIDENT. Well, you are easily puzzled.

Q. What?

THE PRESIDENT. I say you are easily puzzled. Always speculating about something that you don't know anything about, but go ahead.

Q. This is speculation, but Mr. Short [8] said in Key West that Mr. Caudle was put out because of outside activities incompatible with his public duties. Then Mr. McGrath's testimony went right down the line for Mr. Caudle, saying he saw nothing wrong in Caudle's actions.

THE PRESIDENT. I don't think it is right for any Government employee in a responsible position to have outside interests. And I expect to do something about that before we get through with this situation. I think it's unethical for people in key positions to be outside practicing law, or taking fees that have nothing to do with their position as a Government employee. If they want to do

that, they ought to quit and open a law office and go at it.

[11.] Q. Do these measures you have in mind require any legislation?

THE PRESIDENT. Some of them may, yes.

Q. Well, would you care to discuss them at all?

THE PRESIDENT. No, I will discuss that in the Message on the State of the Union.

[12.] Q. Mr. President, there was an O'Mahoney [9] amendment to the armed services appropriation which provided that any company representative, or anyone dealing with the Government, who gave so much as a cigar—as the thing may be interpreted—to a Government employee in the handling of contracts, that the contract would be canceled and the company prosecuted for failure to meet the contract. But there is nothing said in that act about prosecuting an employee who accepts gratuities. Do you think that should be made stronger?

THE PRESIDENT. I think it—it's a two-way street.

Q. Awhile ago, somebody was pressing you about what action you would take, and it sounded over here as if you said you would find out something later in the week. Can we hear this week?

THE PRESIDENT. What was that?

Q. It sounded over here as if you would find out something later in the week?

THE PRESIDENT. That's right.

[13.] Q. Mr. President, may we wrap up all the rumors about resignations in the Cabinet, offered or to be asked for? Are there any resignations to be asked for, or to be accepted, from the Cabinet or top bureaus in the Government?

THE PRESIDENT. Whenever that situation comes about, I always inform you in plenty of time so you can get it in the next day's paper, or that afternoon's paper. I have

---

[8] Joseph H. Short, Secretary to the President.

[9] Senator Joseph C. O'Mahoney of Wyoming.

nothing to say on the subject.

[14.] Mr. Short: Mr. President, I think you misunderstood Mr. Riggs [10] over there. He said "later this week," and you just said "later."

THE PRESIDENT. Joe says I didn't say later in the week, I said later. But then you can leave it at later in the week. [*Laughter*]

Q. Mr. President, could we file that down to a little later in the day, maybe?

THE PRESIDENT. No sir, don't get too specific. [*More laughter*]

[15.] Q. Mr. President, do you expect a truce in Korea by Christmas?

THE PRESIDENT. No.

Q. Do you expect one by the 27th?

THE PRESIDENT. I don't expect anything until it happens. I do not want to be quoted on anything in regard to Korea. Now, this situation is exceedingly delicate and dangerous, and it is your situation as well as mine, and anything that is done over here that embarrasses General Ridgway injures our bargaining position and may get some boys shot that otherwise wouldn't be shot. So keep still about Korea and the truce.

Q. Mr. President, is that off the record, all this you have said about Korea?

THE PRESIDENT. Yes, it's off the record—it's off the record. I just want you to use the same judgment that I have to use as a citizen of the United States for the protection of our forces in Korea. It is up to you just as well as it is to me, to see that those boys don't get shot in the back. And the Korean truce matter is not a public document to be discussed. And I am emphatic about that, because it is a dangerous situation—a very dangerous situation. And this is all off the record.

Q. Well, just for the record, may we get where that off the record starts, please?

THE PRESIDENT. Starting with Miss Montgomery's [11] question.

Q. That question was whether or not you expected a truce by Christmas?

THE PRESIDENT. Yes.

You don't know what an injury it can be to those people who are trying to negotiate something, and to have people back here stab them in the back.

What is it?

[16.] Q. Senator Connally has indicated that your appointment of General Clark to the Vatican is going to stay pigeonholed. Do you anticipate taking any action to further that appointment?

THE PRESIDENT. I expect to send that appointment down as soon as the Congress meets. Then it is up to the Congress to take whatever action is necessary.[12]

Q. What was that?

THE PRESIDENT. General Clark as Ambassador to the Vatican.

[17.] Q. Mr. President, you said a moment ago—you were discussing whether Government employees should have outside interests—you said you are expecting to do something about it soon, and then you said that it would be in your State of the Union Message.

THE PRESIDENT. No, no. No, I didn't say that. He asked me would any legislation be necessary on some of these things, and I said they would be taken up in the State of the Union Message. That had no connection.

Q. Not specifically different?

THE PRESIDENT. No. No.

Q. Mr. President, could you say whether you have yet decided what action you may take, or is it still in the formulation stage?

THE PRESIDENT. It is in the formulation

---

[10] Robert L. Riggs of the Louisville Courier-Journal.

[11] Ruth S. Montgomery of the New York Daily News.

[12] See Item 275 [7, 18].

stage, and as soon as I have it ready I will inform you.

Q. That is in connection with this thing we were talking about at the outset?

THE PRESIDENT. That's right?

Q. About housecleaning?

THE PRESIDENT. That's right.

Q. That's what you meant in your answer about the need for legislation?

THE PRESIDENT. That's right.

Q. That's what will come later this week?

THE PRESIDENT. Not necessarily. I don't want to confuse you, but they are two different things. We are talking about two different things.

Q. The two different things are, one——

THE PRESIDENT. One is where it may be necessary to have legislation to meet the situation, and one is the direct action that the Executive himself may take. That will come sooner, of course, than the legislative action.

Q. Mr. President, I may not have made myself clear. My question did concern the action which you may take this week?

THE PRESIDENT. I expect to take action as promptly as possible and get the situation cleaned up, and whatever action is necessary for the Chief Executive to take, why he will take; because there is nobody believes more than I do in clean government. That has been my record and my theory ever since I became a public officeholder. You can go all the way back to 1922 when I was first elected to public office, and you will find that has been the policy I have pursued until this date, and I expect to continue to pursue it. And wrongdoers have no house with me, no matter who they are or how big they are.

Q. Mr. President, could we quote that last little bit there directly? Could Jack [13] read it to us?

THE PRESIDENT. Yes, if you like. I don't

know whether he can or not, that was pretty fast. [*Laughter*] Go ahead, Jack, and I'll correct you.

[*The President's remark was read back.*]

Q. Is that a direct quote?

THE PRESIDENT. That is a direct quote.

[18.] Q. There have been some indications lately that there might be Members of Congress who would not quite be in the position of being able to cast the first stone. Would your recommendations to Congress follow along anything in that line?

THE PRESIDENT. It is not customary for one of the three great branches of the Government to—in any way to reflect on either one of the other two, so I have no comment to make on that question.

[19.] Q. Mr. President, looking over my notes, I think there may be a little confusion. I therefore would like to repeat a question not quite so broad as Mr. Leach's: [14] Do you anticipate in the near future the voluntary or requested resignation of any member of your Cabinet?

THE PRESIDENT. I do not.

[20.] Q. Mr. President, Mr. McKinney says he did not think that this situation would be an issue in the 1952 campaign; that is, the matter of these so-called scandals. Do you agree with Mr. McKinney?

THE PRESIDENT. Yes, because it will all be cleaned up long before the campaign takes place. It will be past history, just like the Communists in Government and all the rest of these things have been. I have cleaned every one of them up, and this will be cleaned up just the same way. It's lack of issues that caused these things, because this would have been cleaned up, anyway, without all this ballyhoo.

[21.] Q. Would you give us your analysis of how it came about that you had to take this drastic action with people like

---

[13] Jack Romagna, White House Official Reporter.

[14] Paul R. Leach of the Chicago Daily News.

Caudle and these collectors?

THE PRESIDENT. Such action has been taken ever since I have been President, wherever it has been necessary. It is nothing unusual, or nothing new. Whenever it is necessary to make the Government clean by firing somebody that is doing wrong, I haven't hesitated to do it, no matter what his position is.

Q. Well, Mr. President, there seems to be a little bit more of it now, though, than there has been?

THE PRESIDENT. Well, I don't think so. If you will look over the records, you will find the average number of people in the Internal Revenue Department who have been fired every year has been about the same right along. It hasn't been any greater now than it was then. It has been a little higher up in some places now than it has been in the past, but there isn't any more of it than there always has been. You have to be constantly on the watch for just such things all the time.

Q. Why? Why?

THE PRESIDENT. Because every time one of these fellows goes wrong, he has the complete and hearty cooperation by some fellow on the outside who wants to profit by it, and he is just as guilty as the man.

Q. Why is it, sir, that if there is nothing new, or no greater numbers, that you are even considering some extraordinary action such as this?

THE PRESIDENT. I want to have the situation completely developed, and show that the vast majority of the Government employees are honest people, trying to do their duty, and I want to see that they do not get smeared by the actions of a few people who are not the right sort in the first place. That's what I am trying to do, and I think the Government employees are entitled to just such treatment.

Q. Mr. President, to get this clear, you said that this had been going on, and there have been the firings, etc. How does it come that the present situation arises from congressional investigation rather than Executive——

THE PRESIDENT. It did not arise from congressional investigations, Pete.[15] That is just what I am telling you. Every one of those things was ferreted out and taken care of, and the congressional investigation came in after the fact and made the headline.

Q. The Caudle thing?

THE PRESIDENT. Yes. Yes. We were on him quite awhile ago. I knew all about the situation, and was ready to fire him sometime back.

Q. Before the Congress started in?

THE PRESIDENT. Yes, before the Congress started in on the thing. That's the case all the way down the line.

Of course the Post-Dispatch won't believe it, but it's true! [*Laughter*]

Q. Mr. President, Attorney General McGrath says he never knew anything about the Caudle thing?

THE PRESIDENT. Maybe so. I don't keep books for the Attorney General when he is Attorney General. I keep books for myself.

[22.] Q. Mr. President, as to the right sort of people, how did they get in the Government in the first place?

THE PRESIDENT. I don't know. How do you get people in banks that rob them sometimes? [*Laughter*]

[23.] Q. Mr. President, is there anything you would like to say about McKinney's dealings with Mr. Cohen, with whom I believe you have had some past investigatory experience?

THE PRESIDENT. I have no comment. Mr.

[15] Raymond P. Brandt of the St. Louis Post-Dispatch.

McKinney has made that perfectly clear himself.

Reporter: Thank you, Mr. President.

THE PRESIDENT. You're welcome.

NOTE: President Truman's two hundred and eighty-seventh news conference was held in the Indian Treaty Room (Room 474) in the Executive Office Building at 10:30 a.m. on Thursday, December 13, 1951.

301 Remarks Upon Presenting the Collier Award Trophy for 1950. *December* 17, 1951

IT IS a pleasure to me to present this trophy, which I do every year, to the winners. Particularly am I interested in the presentation this year because in 1942 or 1943 I held a hearing with a certain Senate committee with which I was connected, and Dr. Sikorsky was there and told me all about helicopters and what they could do. I went up to the Bell air plant in New York, and had a visual demonstration of what they could do, and it is due to the Doctor and the Defense Department and the Coast Guard that the machine is now being used for rescue work and lifesaving. It is one of the great contributions to the air development of this country.

I noticed this morning where some transcontinental airline pilot had re-created the Wright pusher machine, and that he was going to drive it across the country. If you look at that Wright pusher machine, and then look at the transport that he is using from New York to Seattle, and then see the improvement on the Doctor's first helicopter, you can see how progress comes. It never comes all at once. We want to keep trying, because I really think we have barely scratched the surface.

It is a great pleasure to me to present this trophy to you three gentlemen.

NOTE: The President spoke at 11:55 a.m. in his office at the White House. The Trophy was presented jointly to the helicopter industry, the military services, and the United States Coast Guard for their respective parts in the development and use of rotary-wing aircraft for air rescue operations. Dr. Igor I. Sikorsky represented the helicopter industry; Secretary of Defense Robert A. Lovett, the military services; and Vice Adm. Merlin O'Neill, Coast Guard Commandant, the Coast Guard.

302 Letter to the President of the Associated Press Managing Editors Association on the Executive Order Safeguarding Security Information. *December* 18, 1951

[Released December 18, 1951. Dated December 17, 1951]

Dear Mr. Corn:

I am unable to reconcile your letter of December fourth with statements made to me by members of the special committee of the Associated Press Managing Editors Association on October seventeenth.

That committee, which included you, made the following statements to me:

(1) The Associated Press Managing Editors were as interested as I am in protecting secrets from the enemy.

(2) That you were sure I had acted in good faith in signing the order and that I was sincere in the letter of transmittal to Departments and Agencies in admonishing all officials of the Executive Branch to guard

648

against abuse of the order.

(3) You (the committee) told me that the order was imperfectly drawn and, at the conclusion of our conversation, you as a group informed me that you would suggest changes therein.

You may recall that, as we sat down together, Mr. Wiggins, Chairman of the Committee, assured me that the committee had constructive criticisms to make and I replied that I wished to hear them. The burden of your criticism, as I recall it, was against "definitions" and you went out of my office promising to write better ones.

Your concern over definitions seemed to arise from a fear that some agencies, particularly civilian agencies, might classify non-security information, something I had explicitly prohibited in my memorandum to all Department and Agency heads. I said, "To put the matter bluntly, these regulations are designed to keep security information away from potential enemies and must not be used to cover up mistakes made by any official or employee of the Government." Although I thought your fears were groundless, nevertheless I was glad to have you offer suggestions so that every effort could be made to reinforce my policy of confining the order to matters genuinely involving the safety of our country.

I hope I was not naive in accepting in good faith the statements made by Mr. Wiggins and other members of the committee. The atmosphere of our meeting was one in which all agreed that working together we could bring forth changes that would be satisfactory to all.

My attitude has not changed. I still feel that way. But your letter would indicate that the Associated Press Managing Editors, after indicating otherwise, intend to stand on the outside and carp and criticise without being at all helpful.

I would like to remind you that I received your committee at the request of Mr. Wiggins. I did not single out your Association for the role of re-drafting the order. At their meeting with me, members of the committee suggested that improvements could be made in the order. Then when I countered that I would be glad to improve the order, you said that your committee would make a try.

I thought that, because your group espouses freedom of information, it might be willing to join me in reinforcing that principle. I still cannot understand why you editors reversed yourselves and passed up this opportunity to serve the cause of freedom of information in the dangerous days ahead when the safety of our country and the freedoms for which it stands are in peril.

I also want to refer again to the matter of protecting secrets from the enemy and to say: This is your country as well as mine. We can only win in the present world struggle if we all work together.

> Very sincerely yours,
>
> HARRY S. TRUMAN

[The following postscript was handwritten by the President.]

I have not given up the idea of advice from *practical* newsmen.

[Mr. Herbert F. Corn, President, Associated Press Managing Editors Association, The Evening Star, Washington 4, D.C.]

NOTE: Mr. Corn's letter to the President, dated December 4, follows:

Dear Mr. President:

The committee of the Associated Press Managing Editors Association, which was given a courteous hearing by you and Mr. Joseph Short on October 17, has reported that conversation to the executive committee of APME. As you know, the APME is an association of newspaper editors from the 1700 American newspapers which are members of the Associated Press. It was these editors, in convention in San Francisco, who unanimously condemned the executive order extending the right of government departments to classify information.

The committee delivered your suggestion that APME try to write better definitions as to which government records shall be classified as top secret, secret, confidential and restricted.

The executive committee of the APME cannot accept this invitation because it feels that the order, itself, erects dangerous barriers between the people and their government.

Sincerely yours,

HERBERT F. CORN
*President, Associated Press
Managing Editors Association.*

See also Items 233, 234, 247 [1], 248.

---

303   Letter to the Administrator, Housing and Home Finance
Agency, on the Problem of Employee Integrity.
December 18, 1951

Dear Ray:

I have examined with much interest the material you sent me with your letter of December 12, 1951, concerning the policies and procedures of the Housing Agency with respect to the integrity of its operations. You are to be commended for the attention you have given to this matter.

Because of the general public interest in this subject at the present time, I believe your letter should be made public as an example of the manner in which this problem has been dealt with in the past, and is now being dealt with, by the Government.

I think the policy you have set out with respect to the acceptance of gifts by employees is a wise one, and I believe that this is the correct policy for all of the Government.

Sincerely yours,

HARRY S. TRUMAN

[Honorable Raymond M. Foley, Administrator, Housing and Home Finance Agency, Washington, D.C.]

NOTE: Mr. Foley's letter, dated December 12, was released with the President's reply.

The letter stated, in part:

"With the full cooperation of the heads of our constituent agencies, we have thought it wise to strengthen our protective measures and to inten-

sify and reiterate our instructions. It is not a new policy—but a further effort to be sure it is effective. This is for three purposes:

"(1) To make as certain as we can that our prescribed standards of conduct are being observed;

"(2) That we do not unnecessarily permit our people to be exposed to temptation;

"(3) That our reputation for integrity does not suffer through ill-advised, though honest, actions that give rise to suspicion. Our policy on this has been a progressive one as our experience has developed.

"The present intensified program covers these points:

"(1) A review of all our operations on an Agency-wide basis to identify points of vulnerability and make sure we have adequate safeguards erected;

"(2) Re-issue of our warnings about gifts, gratuities, etc., usually put out at the holiday season and this year even more specific than in the past;

"(3) A complete summary of previous instructions on conflicting interests;

"(4) An 'outside interest' statement from all employees, to be taken this month. In the past we required this only in the Federal Housing Administration at entry upon duty and occasionally renewed, as in 1946 and 1949;

"(5) Strengthening of our 'compliance staffs' who do our investigatory work, in connection with our fixed policy of investigating every charge or substantial rumor, and our system of reporting status to the Administrator.

"None of this is new with us, and all of it supplements a system of reporting, documentation, supervision and cross-checking of operations that of course has always been fundamental."

304 Statement by the President on the Labor Dispute in the Steel Industry. *December 22, 1951*

I HAVE today referred to the Wage Stabilization Board the labor dispute between the United Steelworkers of America, CIO, and various companies in the steel industry. This dispute has now arrived at a stage where it gravely threatens the progress of national defense.

According to the report of the Director of the Federal Mediation and Conciliation Service, the union presented a list of 22 proposals covering both economic and noneconomic matters. No counterproposals were made by the leading companies on any of the economic items. The companies asserted that any wage increases in the steel industry would necessarily require an equivalent increase in steel prices. The union declined to modify its position on any of the major issues in the absence of counterproposals from the companies.

Negotiations between the union and the steel companies are at an impasse, and there appears to be no hope of settlement through mediation. Unless some means is found for breaking this impasse, a shutdown of the steel industry at the end of this month is in prospect.

It is of the utmost importance to prevent an interruption in the production of steel. Steel is a key material in our entire defense effort. Each day of steel production lost is a day lost forever in the achievement of our production schedules. Continuous production of this industry is essential in order to meet urgent demands for steel—steel for weapons, for factories, for highways and hospitals and schools.

It is for this reason that I have certified this matter to the Wage Stabilization Board. This will provide the parties with a forum where their differences may be resolved, and

a fair settlement reached, without resort to a costly shutdown.

Steel is of such basic importance to the defense effort, and wages and prices in the steel industry have such a profound effect throughout our economy, that the public has a very vital interest in the outcome of this dispute. In order to have a proper understanding of what is involved, there are certain essential facts that should be kept clearly in mind.

Over the past 18 months, we have developed an anti-inflation program as an integral part of our mobilization effort. In this program, we have established machinery for the equitable handling of such situations as that which now confronts us. We have the Wage Stabilization Board to consider the question of what wage increases should be allowed the steelworkers and how the other issues in dispute between the parties should be settled. We have the Office of Price Stabilization to consider whether or not the steel companies are entitled to a price increase on account of any wage increase or other cost increases which might result from the settlement of the dispute.

The Wage Stabilization Board is made up of representatives of labor, management, and the public. This Board will give both sides an opportunity to present the facts and arguments they think the Board should consider. Then the Board will consider the case, trying to find the best solution from the standpoint of labor, industry, and the public—balancing the equities and the interest of all three. The Board will consider the case promptly on its merits and make recommendations for a fair settlement, consistent with sound stabilization policies.

No one is in a position as yet to say how

much of an increase in wages or other benefits would be permissible under wage stabilization policies. The Wage Stabilization Board is the only body qualified to make such a determination, and the matter has not been before the Board. The "dope stories" that have been appearing in the press stating the amount of the wage increases that could be allowed without "piercing existing ceilings" have no official basis and are not to be relied upon.

We must wait for the Wage Stabilization Board's report before any sound judgment is possible as to what wage increases are proper in this case.

After the decision is reached as to wages, the Office of Price Stabilization will be responsible for determining whether or not any wage increase justifies a price increase. The law and regulations assure that the steel companies will get price increases if they are entitled to them. No other advance assurances are necessary.

Thus, the machinery we have provides a reasonable and practicable method for doing justice to the parties, for preventing an inflationary price-wage spiral, and for meeting the overriding necessity for keeping steel production going. This machinery should

be given an opportunity to meet the present crisis. The national interest demands it.

This means that the steel companies and the steelworkers must continue production in the industry while the matter is before the Board, and cooperate fully with the Board's proceedings.

The immediate obligation on the steel companies is to maintain normal work and production schedules, and to be prepared to lay the full facts in the case before the Board.

The immediate obligation on the steelworkers is to decide to remain at work while the Board considers the case. This is a decision that should be made before a strike begins—not afterward. The United Steelworkers of America is a responsible union. Its members are good citizens. Its leaders are distinguished Americans.

The union members and their leaders, and the managers of the steel companies, have a responsibility to defend the United States against its enemies just as I do. In my judgment, they will not be living up to that responsibility by permitting a needless stoppage in steel production for even a single day.

NOTE: See also Item 305.

305 Letter to the Chairman, Wage Stabilization Board, Requesting an Investigation of the Labor Dispute in the Steel Industry. *December 22, 1951*

Dear Mr. Feinsinger:

On the basis of the information and advice submitted to me by the Office of Defense Mobilization and the Federal Mediation and Conciliation Service, I am of the opinion that the labor disputes between the United Steelworkers of America, CIO, and various companies in the steel industry are of a character which substantially threaten the progress of national defense. Thus, in accord-

ance with the terms of Executive Order 10233, I am referring the disputes to the Wage Stabilization Board and asking that the Board investigate and inquire into the issues in dispute and promptly report to me with its recommendations to the parties as to fair and equitable terms of settlement.

The report of the Federal Mediation and Conciliation Service indicates that the union and the leading steel producers have made no progress in resolving their differences. It appears entirely unlikely, on the basis of practical experience, that the present stalemate could be broken by further bargaining or mediation and conciliation in time to avoid early and serious production losses in this vital industry. Because of the historical processes of negotiation in the steel industry, this observation applies also to companies other than leading steel producers.

The United Steelworkers of America, CIO, has contracts throughout the entire steel industry—with ore mining companies, producers of steel, and with steel fabricators. I am sending under separate cover a list of the ore mining companies and steel producing companies whose contracts with the Union expire beginning December 31, 1951. The work stoppage which is threatened by these expirations, without new agreements, would paralyze the entire steel industry. Key agreements in basic steel customarily pave the way for agreements throughout the rest of the industry. I am therefore suggesting that the Board, in its proceedings, direct its attention in the first instance to the disputes involving the following companies along with any others which in the judgment of the Board should be added.

Armco Steel Corporation
Bethlehem Steel Corporation
Inland Steel Corporation
Jones & Laughlin Steel Corporation
Great Lakes Steel Corporation
Republic Steel Corporation
Sharon Steel Corporation
United States Steel Corporation
Wheeling Steel Corporation

Youngstown Sheet & Tube Company

Any curtailment of operations in the steel industry will have an immediate and serious impact on the defense program. The Director of the Office of Defense Mobilization has advised me on the extent to which the mobilization program would be affected by an interruption of steel production. The entire steel industry is straining to meet pressing demands for steel and hence a stoppage would cost us vitally needed steel—steel for weapons, for new factories, for highways, schools, hospitals and for a variety of products supporting the civilian economy as well as the defense effort.

In these perilous times, the parties to disputes in the steel industry owe it to the American people to cooperate with their government in maintaining normal work and production schedules while this matter is before the Board.

Very sincerely yours,

HARRY S. TRUMAN

[Honorable Nathan P. Feinsinger, Chairman, Wage Stabilization Board, Washington 25, D.C.]

NOTE: Executive Order 10233 is entitled "Amending Executive Order 10161 with Respect to Wage Stabilization and Settlement of Labor Disputes (Apr. 21, 1951; 3 CFR, 1949–1953 Comp., p. 743).

On March 22, 1952, the Wage Stabilization Board recommended a wage increase and a modified union shop for steel workers, but the steel companies would not accept these terms. On April 8 the President ordered Federal seizure of the steel plants in order to avert the threatened strike. This was ruled unconstitutional by the United States Supreme Court on June 2.

On July 24, 1952, the union and the steel companies agreed on contract terms at a meeting at the White House, and the union issued back-to-work orders.

306   Address in Connection With the Lighting of the National Community Christmas Tree on the White House Grounds.   *December* 24, 1951

[Broadcast nationally from Independence, Mo., at 5 p.m.]

CHRISTMAS is the great home festival. It is the day in all the year which turns our thoughts toward home.

And so I am spending Christmas in my old home in Independence with my family and friends. As the Christmas tree is lighted on the White House grounds in Washington, I am glad to send this greeting to all of my countrymen.

Tonight we think of the birth of a Little Child in the City of David nineteen and a half centuries ago. In that humble birth God gave his message of love to the world. At this Christmas time the world is distracted by doubt and despair, torn by anger, envy and ill will. But our lesson should still be that same message of love, symbolized by the birth of the Redeemer of the World in a manger "because there was no room for them in the inn."

Our hearts are saddened on this Christmas Eve by the suffering and the sacrifice of our brave men and women in Korea. We miss our boys and girls who are out there. They are protecting us, and all free men, from aggression. They are trying to prevent another world war. We honor them for the great job they are doing. We pray to the Prince of Peace for their success and safety.

As we think about Korea, we should also think of another Christmas, 10 years ago, in 1941. That was just after Pearl Harbor, and the whole world was at war. Then almost every country, almost every home, was overshadowed by fear and sorrow.

The world is still in danger tonight, but a great change has come about. A new spirit has been born, and has grown up in the world, although perhaps we do not fully realize it. The struggle we are making today has a new and hopeful meaning.

Ten years ago total war was no longer a threat but a tragic reality. In those grim days, our Nation was straining all its efforts in a war of survival. It was not peace—not the prevention of war—but the stark reality of total war itself that filled our minds and overwhelmed our hearts and souls at Christmas, 1941.

Tonight we have a different goal, and a higher hope. Despite difficulties, the free nations of the world have drawn together solidly for a great purpose: not solely to defend themselves; not merely to win a bloody war if it should come; but for the purpose of creating a real peace—a peace that shall be a positive reality and not an empty hope; a just and lasting peace.

When we look toward the battlefields of Korea, we see a conflict like no other in history. There the forces of the United Nations are fighting—not for territory, not for plunder, not to rule the lives of captive people. In Korea the free nations are proving, by deeds, that man is free and must remain free, that aggression must end, that nations must obey the law.

We still have a long struggle ahead of us before we can reach our goal of peace. In the words of the Bible, the day is not yet here when the bow shall be broken, and the lance cut off, and the chariot burned. But we have faith that that day will come.

We will be strong so long as we keep that faith—the faith that can move mountains, the faith which, as St. Paul says, is the substance of things hoped for, the evidence of things not seen.

654

Let us ask God to bless our efforts and redeem our faults. Let us resolve to follow his commandments—to carry the gospel to the poor; heal the brokenhearted; preach deliverance to the captive; give freedom to the slave. Let us try to do all things in that spirit of brotherly love that was revealed to mankind at Bethlehem on the first Christmas day.

The victory we seek is the victory of peace. That victory is promised to us. It was promised to us long ago, in the words of the angel choir that sang over Bethlehem: "Glory to God in the highest, and on earth peace, good will toward men."

To all my countrymen: Merry Christmas.

307 Statement by the President on Establishing the Commission on the Health Needs of the Nation. *December* 29, 1951

I HAVE today signed an Executive order creating the President's Commission on the Health Needs of the Nation.

The Commission has one major objective. During this crucial period in our country's history it will make a critical study of our total health requirements, both immediate and long-term, and will recommend courses of action to meet these needs.

I have long been interested in safeguarding and improving the health of our people. The provision of adequate health care for all of our population must be a matter of national, as well as local, concern. It is particularly important that in this day of world crisis we should seek to limit the drain upon our strength through illness and death.

We have made progress in our attack upon health problems through such measures as aid for hospital construction, medical research, and maternal, child health, and crippled children's services. And we are making every effort for the most effective utilization of available health resources during this emergency. The Health Resources Advisory Committee in the Office of Defense Mobilization, the Interagency Health Council, and the Armed Forces Medical Policy Council, in cooperation with other Federal, State, and local agencies and our civilian health professions, are doing a good job in coordinating programs so that mobilization needs may be met without endangering the health services which are vital to our civilian population.

We still have a long way to go, however, before we can hope to provide for the health needs of our people on both an immediate and longtime basis. Many vital problems remain unanswered, such as insuring an adequate supply of physicians, dentists, nurses and allied personnel; developing local public health units throughout the Nation; making more hospitals and hospital beds available where needed; stepping up the tempo of fundamental medical research; meeting the needs of the chronically ill and aged; and providing adequate diagnostic, rehabilitative, and other health services to all income groups.

I have repeatedly endorsed programs to solve these problems. Our attempts to take constructive action on these issues have met enthusiastic support from some quarters and bitter opposition from others. As a result, our people are confused about the proper course of action on subjects so vitally important to their welfare. On a number of occasions I have stated that I would be happy to consider suggestions which were better than the measures I have endorsed to bring the continuing achievements of medical progress to all our people. But such counterproposals have not been forthcoming.

I have, therefore, established the President's Commission on the Health Needs of the Nation to study the facts and to present its recommendations for safeguarding and improving the health of the Nation. Since we need the advice of all viewpoints, the Commission contains both professional and lay members. It will make a searching inquiry into the facts and give us the benefit of objective and constructive thinking on these problems which are of vital concern to every American.

The Commission is authorized to present interim reports on its findings, so that we shall have the benefit of its timely studies within the next 12 months. To aid in its deliberations within this period, the Commission will have available a number of studies in the health field of governmental agencies, congressional committees, and other public and private groups. Moreover, I have asked the Commission to give its immediate attention to an evaluation of the most recent information on subjects currently pending before the Congress and requiring consideration in the next session, such as aid to medical education and aid to local public health units.

We must dedicate ourselves to the continuing search for what is best for the Nation in solving our health problems. I am certain that the President's Commission on the

Health Needs of the Nation will make an invaluable contribution toward preserving one of our most precious assets, the health of all of our people.

NOTE: The President referred to Executive Order 10317 "Establishing the President's Commission on the Health Needs of the Nation" (3 CFR, 1949–1953 Comp., p. 845).

The Commission was composed of the following members: Paul B. Magnuson, M.D., orthopedic surgeon, formerly medical director of Veterans Administration, Chicago, Ill., Chairman; Dean A. Clark, M.D., general director of Massachusetts General Hospital, Boston, Mass.; Joseph C. Hinsey, Ph. D., dean of the Cornell University Medical College, New York, N.Y.; Russel V. Lee, M.D., associate clinical professor of medicine, Stanford University School of Medicine, San Francisco, Calif.; Evarts A. Graham, M.D., surgeon, St. Louis, Mo.; Marion W. Sheahan, R.N., director of the National Committee for the Improvement of Nursing Services, New York, N.Y.; Ernest G. Sloman, D.D.S., president elect of the American Association of Dental Schools, San Francisco, Calif.; Walter P. Reuther, president of the United Automobile Workers, CIO, Detroit, Mich.; A. J. Hayes, president of International Association of Machinists, Washington, D.C.; Clarence Poe, president and editor of "The Progressive Farmer," Raleigh, N.C.; Charles S. Johnson, president of Fisk University, Nashville, Tenn.; Lowell J. Reed, Ph. D., vice president of Johns Hopkins University and Hospital, Baltimore, Md.; Chester I. Barnard, president of the Rockefeller Foundation, New York, N.Y.; Elizabeth S. Magee, general secretary of National Consumers' League, Cleveland, Ohio; and Gunnar Gundersen, M.D., member of the Board of Trustees of the American Medical Association, LaCrosse, Wis.

On December 30, 1951, Dr. Gundersen requested that his name be removed from the list of appointees.

Appendix A—White House Press Releases

NOTE: Includes releases covering matters with which the President was closely concerned, except announcements of Presidential personnel appointments and approvals of legislation with which there was no accompanying statement.

Releases relating to Proclamations and Executive orders have not been included. These documents are separately listed in Appendix B.

For list of Press and Radio Conferences, see subject index under "News conferences."

January

2 Special message to the Senate transmitting cultural convention with Brazil

3 Statement by the President upon signing the Excess Profits Tax Act of 1950

3 Statement by the Director of Defense Mobilization on the establishment of a new Defense Production Administration and a Defense Mobilization Board

5 Statement by the President on the establishment of the United Defense Fund

6 Memorandum of disapproval of bill for the relief of Bernard F. Elmers

8 Annual message to the Congress on the State of the Union

9 Special message to the Congress on the need for more equal apportionment of congressional districts

10 Remarks at the Woodrow Wilson Foundation award ceremonies

10 Statement by the President on the award conferred upon him by the Woodrow Wilson Foundation

11 Special message to the Congress transmitting report on Foreign Service retirement and disability system, fiscal year 1950

11 Statement by the President clarifying his State of the Union Message regarding the Fair Deal program and the Democratic platform

11 Remarks at a buffet supper for Democratic members of Congress

12 Remarks to members of the National Advisory Committee on the Selection of Physicians, Dentists, and Allied Specialists

12 Statement by the President upon signing the Federal Civil Defense Act of 1950

12 Annual message to the Congress: The President's Economic Report

January

13 White House release on the disposition of surplus memento material created by the renovation of the White House

15 Annual Budget Message to the Congress: Fiscal Year 1952

15 Special message to the Congress on the transfer or sale of surplus military property

15 Letter accepting resignation of James G. McDonald as Ambassador to Israel

17 Memorandum establishing a national manpower mobilization policy

19 Letter to the Chairman, Committee on Religion and Welfare in the Armed Forces, on the conclusion of the Committee's work

19 Letter accepting resignation of Alan Valentine as Administrator, Economic Stabilization Agency

19 Remarks at a dinner of the Society of Business Magazine Editors

22 Message to the Congress transmitting 36th annual report of the National Advisory Committee for Aeronautics, fiscal year 1950

22 Letter to William S. Paley on the creation of the President's Materials Policy Commission

23 Statement upon issuing order establishing the President's Commission on Internal Security and Individual Rights

24 Remarks at a dinner in honor of Joshua Evans

25 Statement by the President on Ambassador Austin's resolution declaring the Chinese Communists aggressors in Korea

27 Memorandum urging agency cooperation in enforcing price and wage stabilization orders

29 Message to the Congress transmitting 67th annual report of Civil Service Commission

29 Letter accepting resignation of Robert Butler as Ambassador to Cuba

657

Appendix A

658

Appendix A

660

June

21 Letter to the Speaker proposing an accelerated civil defense program

21 White House announcement of appropriations requests for administrative expenses for defense production activities

21 Letter accepting resignation of Marriner S. Eccles as member, Board of Governors, Federal Reserve System

21 Remarks to a group of newsboy bond salesmen

22 Joint statement following discussions with the President of Ecuador

22 Address at the dedication of the National Institutes of Health Clinical Center

22 Toasts of the President and the President of Ecuador

22 Report to the President by the National Advisory Board on Mobilization Policy

23 Letter to the President of the Senate and to the Speaker of the House transmitting report of the National Advisory Board on Mobilization Policy

25 Address in Tullahoma, Tenn., at the dedication of the Arnold Engineering Development Center

25 Message to the Congress transmitting third semiannual report on the mutual defense assistance program

27 Letter accepting resignation of William E. DeCourcy as Ambassador to Haiti

27 Letter accepting resignation of George J. Schoeneman as Commissioner of Internal Revenue

27 White House announcement of suspension of Denis W. Delaney, Collector of Internal Revenue, Massachusetts District

27 Remarks to members of the Student Citizenship Seminar

28 Statement by the President on extension of the Defense Production Act

28 Letter accepting resignation of Nathaniel P. Davis as Minister to Hungary

28 Letter accepting resignation of Milton Katz as U.S. Special Representative in Europe and U.S. Delegate to the Economic Committee for Europe

28 Letter to the President from the Prime Minister of Iran on the nationalization of the oil industry

29 Statement by the President on transferring the Trust Territory of the Pacific Islands and American Samoa to civilian administration

July

2 Letter to the Chairman, Council of Economic Advisers, in response to report "The New England Economy"

2 Report to the President entitled "The New England Economy" transmitted by the Council of Economic Advisers

3 White House release on report to the President by the Commission for the Commemoration of the 175th Anniversary of the Signing of the Declaration of Independence

4 Letter to the President of the Senate on the continued need for effective price, wage, and production controls

4 Second quarterly report to the President by the Director of Defense Mobilization, entitled "Meeting Defense Goals"

4 Address at the ceremonies commemorating the 175th anniversary of the Declaration of Independence

5 Remarks upon presenting Congressional Medals of Honor to Capt. Raymond Harvey, Capt. Lewis L. Millett, M. Sgt. Stanley T. Adams, and Corp. Einar H. Ingman, USA

7 Message to the President of the Presidium of the Supreme Soviet, U.S.S.R., transmitting a resolution expressing American friendship

7 Remarks to members of the 25th Infantry Division Association

9 Letter to the President of the Senate recommending legislation to terminate the state of war with Germany

9 Message to the Prime Minister of Iran following the breakdown of oil discussions with Great Britain

9 Letter accepting resignation of Katharine F. Lenroot as Chief of the Children's Bureau, Federal Security Agency

10 Remarks upon accepting a piece of the Rock of Corregidor as a gift from the people of the Philippines

11 Message from the Prime Minister of Iran thanking the President for his interest in the oil dispute

11 White House release making public a report by the Public Advisory Board of the Economic Cooperation Administration

12 Letter to committee chairmen on the need for a pay increase for Federal employees

13 Special message to the Congress on the employment of agricultural workers from Mexico

July

13 Remarks to W. Averell Harriman before his departure on a mission to Iran

14 Letter to the Executive Secretary, National Security Council, requesting a study of the employee security program

14 Message to the President of France on Bastille Day

.16 White House release announcing the removal from office of the collector of internal revenue for the Massachusetts District

17 Remarks in Grandview, Mo., after viewing the flood disaster area

18 Letter to the President of the Senate on a pending bill to increase public assistance payments

18 White House announcement of a gift to the American people of 10 Audubon paintings

18 Remarks to a group representing the French provincial press

18 White House release of an amendment to National Security Council Determination No. 1 deleting Canada from list of countries receiving U.S. economic and financial aid

18 Report by the National Security Council on trade between India and the Soviet bloc in the light of section 1302 of Third Supplemental Appropriation Act, 1951; NSC Determination No. 4

19 Message to the Congress transmitting the first annual report of the Civil Service Commission under the Classification Act of 1949

19 Letter to the President, American National Red Cross, on the flood disaster areas in the Middle West

19 Letter to the Director, Office of Defense Mobilization, on Federal activities in the flood disaster areas

19 Letter to Mrs. C. Irving Guyer on the need for controlling inflation

19 Remarks to a group of Danish boys from the International Boys Camp, Inc.

20 White House announcement of U.S. delegations to conclude the peace treaty with Japan, and related security treaties

23 Special message to the Congress: The President's Midyear Economic Report

25 Remarks to delegates to the Sixth Annual American Legion "Boys Nation"

26 Letter to the Chairman, Wage Stabilization Board, requesting investigation of a labor dispute affecting the production of copper

July

26 Letter accepting resignation of Francis P. Matthews as Secretary of the Navy

26 Message to the Congress transmitting report of U.S. participation in the United Nations for 1950

27 Letter to committee chairmen on financing the United Nations Palestine Refugee Program

27 Statement by the President on the mass deportations in Hungary

28 Address in Detroit at the celebration of the city's 250th anniversary

31 Letter to the Chairman, Senate Committee on Expenditures in the Executive Branch, on pending reorganization legislation

31 Statement by the President upon signing the Defense Production Act Amendments

August

1 Statement by the President announcing his intention to establish the Defense Materials Procurement Agency

1 Remarks to the delegates of Girls Nation

1 Remarks to the members of the United Defense Fund

1 Message to the Congress transmitting 12th report of the Economic Cooperation Administration

3 Report by the National Security Council on trade between Turkey and the Soviet bloc in the light of section 1302 of the Third Supplemental Appropriation Act, 1951; NSC Determination No. 5

6 Veto of bill modifying eligibility requirements for pension payments to certain widows of veterans

6 Veto of bill to increase the pensions of certain disabled veterans

6 Letter to the president, CIO, on the flood control problem in the Missouri River Basin

6 Veto of bill for the relief of George H. Whike Construction Company (Congressional Record, vol. 97, p. 9505)

7 Letter to the Chairman, Senate Committee on Appropriations, on U.S. contributions to the United Nations and other international organizations

7 White House release on the extension of the date for applying for White House mementos

Appendix A

Appendix A

Appendix A

Appendix A

Appendix B—Presidental Documents Published in the Federal Register

PROCLAMATIONS

Appendix B

EXECUTIVE ORDERS

Appendix B

Appendix B

Appendix B

674

Appendix B

Appendix B

PRESIDENTIAL DOCUMENTS OTHER THAN PROCLAMATIONS AND EXECUTIVE ORDERS

Appendix C—Presidential Reports to the Congress

Subject	Published	Sent to the Congress	Date of White House release
Foreign Service Retirement and Disability System	. . . . .	Jan. 11 (S) Jan. 12 (H)	Jan. 11 . . . .
Economic Report	H. Doc. 30	Jan. 12 (H) Jan. 15 (S)	Jan. 12 . . . .
Midyear	H. Doc. 190	July 23	July 23
National Advisory Committee for Aeronautics, 36th annual report. .	H. Doc. 48	Jan. 22	Jan. 22
Civil Service Commission	H. Doc. 13	Jan. 29	Jan. 29
National Capital Housing Authority		Feb. 2 (H) Feb. 5 (S)	Feb. 2 . . . .
Economic Cooperation Administration 10th report.	H. Doc. 52	Feb. 6 (H) Feb. 8 (S)	Feb. 6 . . . .
11th report.	H. Doc. 115	May 14	May 14
12th report.	H. Doc. 198	Aug. 2	Aug. 2
13th report.	H. Doc. 249	Nov. 6	Nov. 6
Air Coordinating Committee.	H. Doc. 55	Feb. 8	Feb. 8
Commodity Credit Corporation	H. Doc. 64	Feb. 26	Feb. 26
National Advisory Council on International Monetary and Financial Problems.		Mar. 1	. . . .
Railroad Retirement Board	H. Doc. 50	Mar. 12	Mar. 12
Department of State, operations under section 2 of Public Law 584. .	H. Doc. 86	Mar. 19	. . . .
Panama Railroad Company, Report of the Board of Directors	. . . . . .	Mar. 27 (S) Apr. 2 (H)	Mar. 27
Mutual Defense Assistance Program	H. Doc. 119	Apr. 26	Apr. 26
United States Participation in the United Nations	H. Doc. 196	July 26	July 26
Office of Alien Property	H. Doc. 168	Sept. 24	Sept. 24
Lend-Lease Operations, 32d report	H. Doc. 227	Oct. 3	Oct. 3

Appendix D—Rules Governing This Publication

[Reprinted from the Federal Register, vol. 29, p. 11792, dated August 18, 1964]

TITLE I—GENERAL PROVISIONS

Chapter I—Administrative Committee of the Federal Register

PART 32—PUBLIC PAPERS OF THE PRESIDENTS OF THE UNITED STATES

PUBLICATION AND FORMAT

Sec.
32.1 Publication required.
32.2 Coverage of prior years.
32.3 Format, indexes, ancillaries.

SCOPE

32.10 Basic criteria.
32.11 Sources.

OFFICIAL DISTRIBUTION

32.15 The Congress.
32.16 The Supreme Court.
32.17 Executive agencies.
32.18 Governmental requisitions.
32.19 Extra copies.

PUBLIC SALE

32.22 Sale of annual volumes.
AUTHORITY: The provisions of this Part 32 issued under sec. 6, 49 Stat. 501, as amended; 44 U.S.C. 306. Sec. 6, E.O. 10530, 19 F.R. 2709; 3 CFR 1954–1958 Comp.

PUBLICATION AND FORMAT

§ 32.1 *Publication required.* There shall be published forthwith at the end of each calendar year, a special edition of the FEDERAL REGISTER designated "Public Papers of the Presidents of the United States." Ordinarily each volume shall cover one calendar year and shall be identified further by the name of the President and the period covered.
NOTE: This program started with the year 1957.
§ 32.2 *Coverage of prior years.* After conferring with the National Historical Publications Commis-

sion with respect to the need therefor, the Administrative Committee may from time to time authorize the publication of similar volumes covering specified calendar years prior to 1957.
NOTE: The committee has approved the publication of volumes starting with the year 1945.
§ 32.3 *Format, indexes, ancillaries.* Each annual volume, divided into books whenever appropriate, shall be separately published in the binding and style deemed by the Administrative Committee to be suitable to the dignity of the office of President of the United States. Each volume shall be appropriately indexed and shall contain appropriate ancillary information respecting significant Presidential documents not published in full text.

SCOPE

§ 32.10 *Basic criteria.* The basic text of the volumes shall consist of oral utterances by the President or of writings subscribed by him.
§ 32.11 *Sources.* (a) The basic text of the volumes shall be selected from: (1) Communications to the Congress, (2) public addresses, (3) transcripts of press conferences, (4) public letters, (5) messages to heads of state, (6) statements released on miscellaneous subjects, and (7) formal executive documents promulgated in accordance with law.
(b) In general, ancillary text, notes, and tables shall be derived from official sources.

OFFICIAL DISTRIBUTION

§ 32.15 *The Congress.* Each Member of the Congress, during his term of office, shall be entitled to one copy of each annual volume published during such term. Authorization for furnishing such copies shall be submitted in writing to the Director and signed by the authorizing Member.

§ 32.16 *The Supreme Court.* The Supreme ·Court of the United States shall be entitled to 12 copies of the annual volumes.

§ 32.17 *Executive agencies.* The head of each department and the head of each independent agency in the executive branch of the Government shall be entitled to one copy of each annual volume upon application therefor in writing to the Director.

§ 32.18 *Governmental requisitions.* Legislative, judicial, and executive agencies of the Federal Government may obtain, at cost, copies of the annual volumes for official use upon the timely submission to the Government Printing Office of a printing and binding requisition (Standard Form 1).

§ 32.19 *Extra copies.* All requests for extra copies of the annual volumes must be addressed to the Superintendent of Documents, Government Printing Office, Washington, D.C. 20402. Extra copies must be paid for by the agency or official requesting them.

PUBLIC SALE

§ 32.22 *Sale of annual volumes.* The annual volumes shall be placed on sale to the public by the Superintendent of Documents, Government Printing Office, Washington, D.C. 20402, at prices determined by him under the general direction of the Administrative Committee.

*   *   *   *   *

ADMINISTRATIVE COMMITTEE OF
THE FEDERAL REGISTER,
WAYNE C. GROVER,
Archivist of the United States,
Chairman.
JAMES L. HARRISON,
The Public Printer,
Member.
CHARLES F. SIMMS,
Representative of the
Attorney General, Member.

APPROVED:
ROBERT F. KENNEDY,
Attorney General.
BERNARD L. BOUTIN,
Administrator of General Services.

[F.R. Doc. 64–8366; Filed, Aug. 17, 1964; 8:49 a.m.]

INDEX

[Main references are to items except as otherwise indicated]

681

Index

Index

Index

Index

Index

Index

Index

Index

Index

Index

Index

[Main references are to items except as otherwise indicated]

Index

[Main references are to items except as otherwise indicated]

[Main references are to items except as otherwise indicated]

Index

Index

Index

Index

Index

Index

Index

[Main references are to items except as otherwise indicated]

[Main references are to items except as otherwise indicated]

[Main references are to items except as otherwise indicated]

Index

Index

Index

Index

Index

[Main references are to items except as otherwise indicated]

Index

Index

Index

Index

Index

Index

[Main references are to items except as otherwise indicated]

Index

Index

Index

Index

Index

Index

Index

Index

Index

Index

Index

Index

Index

[Main references are to items except as otherwise indicated]

Index

Index

Index

[Main references are to items except as otherwise indicated]

Tribble, Harold, 256

Trieste
Economic assistance, 114
Territorial settlement with Italy, 232, 239 [4]

Trowel, silver, presentation to New York Avenue Presbyterian Church, 68

Truman, Harry S., personal reminiscences
Aberdeen Proving Ground, visits to, 38
American Legion activities, 191
Bevin, Ernest, recollections of, 88
British sovereigns, visits with, 282
Congressional Medal of Honor presentations, 115
Democratic National Convention (1912), 6
Employment in bank, 21
Family dentist in Independence, Mo., 258
Farming experiences, 122
First sight of a President, 290
Ford, Henry, wartime interview with, 38
Forebears, defense against Indians, 289
Military service
National Guard, 218, 270
Reserve Officers Association, role in founding, 218
World War I, 38, 298 [1]
Musical interests, 21, 99
Senate, service in, 18, 27, 32, 33 [2], 51, 56 [24], 98
Truman Committee, chairmanship of, 7 [13], 33 [2], 46
Wooton, Paul, recollections of, 18

Truman, Mrs. Harry S., 70 [11], 113 [3, 5], 136, 180, 223, 257, 297

Truman, Margaret, 18, 21, 76, 99, 136, 223, 257, 282
News conference remarks on, 63 [4], 70 [11]
Travel abroad, 145 [5], 160

Truman Committee, 7 [13], 33 [2], 46

Truman Memorial Library, proposed, 251 [27]

Trust funds, 13 (pp. 98, 99)
Old-age and survivors insurance, 13 (p. 99)
Railroad retirement, 13 (p. 98)
Unemployment insurance, 13 (pp. 80, 81)
Veterans insurance, 13 (p. 103)

Tuberculosis, 135

Tullahoma, Tenn., 138

Turkey
Assistance
Economic, 114, 138
Military, 114
Communist aggression in, 138
Korean war, participation, 170
NATO membership, 227 ftn. (p. 527)

Turner, Gov. Roy J., 118 [2], 145 [8]

Tydings, Sen. Millard E.
Loyalty investigating subcommittee, 22 [14], 35
1950 election campaign, 49 [19]

Typhus, prevention, 135

Uintah Indian Reservation, 198

Unemployment, 11, 174
Decrease, 167
Garment industry, 239 [8]
Veterans, allowances, 13 (pp. 99-102)

Unemployment compensation, 13 (pp. 79-81)
Defense workers, 11
Extension of benefits, 4, 12 [33]
Trust funds, 13 (p. 80)

UNICEF. See United Nations Children's Emergency Fund

Union Station, Washington, dedication of Presidential Lounge as servicemen's center, 186

United Airlines, labor dispute, 132 [1], 140 [10]

United Automobile, Aircraft and Agricultural Implement Workers of America, 252

743

Index

Index

Index

Index

Index

☆ U. S. GOVERNMENT PRINTING OFFICE : 1971 O - 411-925